AN ARCHAEOLOGICAL HISTORY OF RELIGIONS OF INDIAN ASIA

AN ARCHAEOLOGICAL HISTORY OF RELIGIONS OF INDIAN ASIA

Jack Finegan

PARAGON HOUSE
NEW YORK

First edition, 1989

Published in the United States by

Paragon House
90 Fifth Avenue
New York, NY 10011

Copyright © 1989 by Jack Finegan

All rights reserved. No part of this book may be reproduced, in any form, without written permission from the publishers, unless by a reviewer who wishes to quote brief passages.

Manufactured in the United States of America

Library of Congress Cataloging-in-Publication Data

Finegan, Jack, 1908–
    An archaeological history of religions of Indian Asia / Jack Finegan.
      p. cm.
    Bibliography: p.
    Includes index.
    ISBN 0-913729-43-4
      1. India—Religion—to 1200. 2. Asia—Religion. 3. Hindu antiquities. 4. Buddhist antiquities. 5. Jaina antiquities.
I. Title.
BL2005.F56   1989
294'.09—dc19   88-25244
                                                             CIP

DESIGN: Stanley S. Drate/Folio Graphics Co. Inc.

CONTENTS

Tables	ix
Maps	xi
Illustrations	xiii
Abbreviations	xxiii
Preface	xxvii
Acknowledgments	xxix

1
HARAPPAN CIVILIZATION   1
EARLY HARAPPAN SITES / 2
MATURE HARAPPAN SITES / 2
END OF HARAPPAN CIVILIZATION / 6
HARAPPAN MONUMENTS AND ARTIFACTS / 7

2
LITERATURE OF HINDUISM AND THE VEDIC AND EPIC PERIODS   12
LANGUAGES / 12
CLASSES OF LITERATURE / 13
VEDIC GEOGRAPHY / 15
VEDIC ARYANS / 16
MOUNT MERU / 17
PERIODS OF TIME / 18
SOLAR DYNASTY / 21
LUNAR DYNASTY / 24

3
VEDIC AND UPANISHADIC RELIGION AND PHILOSOPHY   30
DEITIES OF THE RIG VEDA / 30
PHILOSOPHY IN THE BRAHMANAS AND THE UPANISHADS / 49

4
CHRONOLOGY OF THE KALI AGE   54
BEGINNING OF THE KALI AGE / 54
PURANIC DYNASTIC LISTS / 55
PURANIC DATES / 63
MAHABHARATA WAR CHRONOLOGY / 64

JAINA DATES / 65
MAHAVIRA CHRONOLOGY / 69
BUDDHA CHRONOLOGY / 70

5
GEOGRAPHY, CLANS, KINGDOMS, CITIES   79
CLANS / 79
KINGDOMS / 84

6
ALEXANDER THE GREAT AND EMPIRES SUBSEQUENT TO HIS COMING   102
ASSYRIANS / 102
ACHAEMENID PERSIANS / 103
ALEXANDER THE GREAT / 104
MAURYA EMPIRE (322–185 B.C.E.) / 109
KUSHANA EMPIRE / 116
GUPTA EMPIRE (320–600 C.E.) / 118
EMPIRE OF HARSHA (606–647 C.E.) / 125
KINGDOMS OF THE MEDIEVAL PERIOD (650–1200 C.E.) / 130
DECLINE AND RENEWAL OF JAINISM AND BUDDHISM AND CONTINUANCE OF HINDUISM / 130

7
LATER HINDUISM   133
THREE PATHS / 133
FOUR AIMS / 134
FOUR STAGES / 135
SIX SCHOOLS / 136
THREE INTERPRETERS OF VEDANTA / 138
TRIMURTI / 140

8
MONUMENTS OF HINDUISM IN INDIA   160
SYMBOLS AND IMAGES OF THE GODS / 160
TEMPLES / 176

9
LITERATURE AND EARLY HISTORY OF JAINISM   209
LITERATURE / 210
JAINA COSMOGRAPHY AND CHRONOGRAPHY / 223
ILLUSTRIOUS PERSONS / 226

10
MONUMENTS OF JAINISM IN INDIA   242
SYMBOLS / 242

IMAGES / 245
STUPAS / 261
TEMPLES / 264

11
EARLY HISTORY AND LITERATURE OF THERAVADA BUDKHISM   291

TRADITION / 291
FOUR COUNCILS IN INDIA / 293
FOUR COUNCILS IN SRI LANKA / 300
THREE BASKETS / 330
THREE JEWELS / 345

12
EARLY HISTORY AND LITERATURE OF MAHAYANA AND VAJRAYANA BUDDHISM   358

RISE OF SCHOOLS / 358
MAHAYANA / 362
TEACHERS AND TEXTS OF THE MAHAYANA / 367
VAJRAYANA / 390
TEACHERS, TANTRAS, AND YOGAS OF THE VAJRAYANA / 392

13
MONUMENTS OF BUDDHISM IN INDIA, PAKISTAN, AND SRI LANKA   419

INDIA AND PAKISTAN / 419
ARCHITECTURAL FORMS / 426
CAVES / 427
CONSTRUCTIONS / 437
SITES AND MONUMENTS OF SRI LANKA / 457

14
MONUMENTS OF HINDUISM AND BUDDHISM IN SOUTHEAST ASIA   473

EXPANSION OF INDIAN INFLUENCE / 473
INDONESIA / 475
JAVA / 476
BALI / 508
MALAYSIA / 529
KAMPUCHEA / 531
BURMA / 546
LATER HISTORY / 550
MONUMENTS / 552
THAILAND / 562
MONUMENTS / 569

15

MONUMENTS OF HINDUISM AND BUDDHISM BY THE HIGH HIMALAYA AND AT THE GATES OF INNER ASIA   585

NEPAL / 585
MONUMENTS / 598
KASHMIR / 616
MONUMENTS / 619
BUDDHISM IN SWAT / 621
AFGHANISTAN / 623
BUDDHISM ON THE ROUTES TO CENTRAL ASIA / 624
XINJIANG / 633
TURPAN / 633
TIBET / 636
LADAKH / 653
BHUTAN / 659

Notes   665

Index   719

TABLES

2.1	The Ages of the World	19
4.1	Pradyotas of Avanti	58
4.2	Śaiśunagas of Magadha	58
4.3	Mauryas	62
4.4	Śungas	62
4.5	Kanvas	63
4.6	From Palaka to Vikramaditya in Avanti	66
4.7	From Vikramaditya to the Śakas in Ujjayini	68
4.8	Chronology of Mahavira	70
4.9	Chronology of Buddha, Bimbisara, and Ajataśatru according to the *Mahavamsa*	71
4.10	Chronology of Buddha according to Burma Tradition (astronomically revised)	72
4.11	Chronology of Pradyota and Palaka, and of Mahavira and Buddha, according to a Tibet Tradition	73
4.12	Chronology of Mahavira, Buddha, Pradyota, Palaka, Bimbisara, and Ajataśatru	77
4.13	Official Indian Eras	78
4.14	Historically Probable Dates	78
5.1	Clans in Ancient India	80
5.2	Mahajanapadas	85
6.1	Earlier and Later Imperial Guptas	119
9.1	Relationships and Status of Early Jaina Leaders	211
9.2	Jaina Sacred Literature (Siddhanta, Agama)	212
9.3	Jaina Cycles of Time	225
9.4	Units of Measurement	226
9.5	The Twenty-four Tirthankaras of Bharatavarsha in the Present Utsarpini Age	228
11.1	Kings of Lanka from Vijaya to Devanampiyatissa	301
11.2	Kings of Lanka from Uttiya to Dutthagamani	307
11.3	Kings of Lanka from Saddhatissa to Vattagamani	312
11.4	Lunar Months in the Indian Calendar	355
12.1	Tathagatas, Bodhisattvas, and Manushi Buddhas	366
14.1	Śiva and the Guardians of the Regions	511
14.2	Goddesses of the Regions	511
14.3	Demons of the Regions	512
14.4	Śaivite and Buddhist Figures in the Regions	512

MAPS

1.1	Hindu India	xxx
9.1	Jaina India	208
11.1	Buddhist India	290
14.1	Southeast Asia	474
15.1	Lands of the Himalaya and Central Asia	584

ILLUSTRATIONS

1.1	General View of Moenjo-daro, with the Buddhist Stupa crowning the Citadel Mound	4
1.2	Great Bath on the Citadel (SD Area) at Moenjo-daro	5
1.3	Excavated House Walls and Well, standing high above ground and exhibiting progressive deterioration of brickwork, at Moenjo-daro (DK Area)	6
1.4	Moenjo-daro Seal Impression (replica), portraying a Humpless Bull	8
1.5	Moenjo-daro Seal Impression (large replica on the wall of the Moenjo-daro Museum), portraying a Humped Bull	9
1.6	Moenjo-daro Seal Impression (replica), portraying a Seated Deity	10
1.7	Squatting Monkey-like Figure, in the Moenjo-daro Museum	10
6.1	Excavated Bhir Mound at Taxila	106
6.2	Statue of Kanishka, in the Archaeological Museum, Mathura	117
6.3	Statue of Kanishka, in the Kabul Museum	118
6.4	Big Wild Goose Pagoda, Xian	129
8.1	Yaksha from Parkham, in the Archaeological Museum, Mathura	164
8.2	Brahma from Aihole, in the Prince of Wales Museum of Western India, Bombay	165
8.3	Vishnu from Mathura, in the Archaeological Museum, Mathura	167
8.4	Vishnu on Śesha, from Aihole, in the Prince of Wales Museum of Western India, Bombay	168
8.5	Vishnu and His Man-lion and Boar Incarnations, in the Prince of Wales Museum of Western India, Bombay	169
8.6	Śiva as Nataraja, in the National Museum of India, New Delhi	171
8.7	Śiva with Parvati, from Aihole, in the Prince of Wales Museum of Western India, Bombay	171
8.8	Bhairava from Karnataka, in the Prince of Wales Museum of Western India, Bombay	172
8.9	Lakshmi from Mathura, in the National Museum of India, New Delhi. Photograph from C. Sivaramamurti, *Masterpieces of Indian Sculpture in the National Museum* (New Delhi: National Museum, 1971), Pl. Va.	173
8.10	Sarasvati from Karnataka, in the Prince of Wales Museum of Western India, Bombay	174
8.11	Vidyadharas from Gwalior, in the National Museum of India, New Delhi	175
8.12	Śiva Linga in Cave 4 at Udaigiri	178
8.13	Vishnu as the Boar Varaha rescues the Earth Goddess, Sculptured Panel at Cave 6 at Udaigiri	178
8.14	Vishnu raises the Earth Goddess on His Shoulder, Detail of the Sculptured Panel at Cave 6, Udaigiri	179
8.15	Durga battles Mahisha in the Mahishamardini Cave Temple at Mahabalipuram	180

8.16	Milking Scene in the Krishna Cave Temple at Mahabalipuram	180
8.17	Śiva Maheśvara in the Elephanta Cave Temple, Central Face and Face at the Left (as seen by the viewer)	182
8.18	Pandava Rathas at Mahabalipuram	183
8.19	Kailasa Rock-Cut Temple at Ellora	185
8.20	In the Forecourt of the Kailasa Temple	186
8.21	Cennakeśava Temple and Gopura at Belur	189
8.22	Dancing Lady, Bracket Figure in the Cennakeśava Temple, Belur	189
8.23	Lady with Mirror, Bracket Figure in the Cennakeśava Temple, Belur	190
8.24	Frieze of Śardulas, Hoyśaleśvara Temple at Halebid	191
8.25	Frieze of Musicians, Hoyśaleśvara Temple, Halebid	192
8.26	Frieze of Makaras, Hoyśaleśvara Temple, Halebid	192
8.27	Frieze of Hamsas, Hoyśaleśvara Temple, Halebid	193
8.28	Rama shooting His Arrow through Seven Palm Trees, Hoyśaleśvara Temple, Halebid	193
8.29	Rama in Battle with Ravana, Hoyśaleśvara Temple, Halebid	194
8.30	Vishakanya, Hoyśaleśvara Temple Outdoor Museum, Halebid	194
8.31	Keśava Temple at Somnathpur	195
8.32	Camunda, Victor over Mahishasura, Keśava Temple, Somnathpur	196
8.33	Nandi Bull above Mysore City	197
8.34	Camunda Temple Gopura, above Mysore City	197
8.35	Matangeśvara and Lakshmana Temples at Khajuraho	199
8.36	Śikhara of the Lakshmana Temple, Khajuraho	200
8.37	Group Erotic Scene, Lakshmana Temple, Khajuraho	201
8.38	Erotic Scene, Lakshmana Temple, Khajuraho	202
8.39	Maithuna Scene, Lakshmana Temple, Khajuraho	202
8.40	Three Bands of Sculptures, Devi Jagadambi Temple, Khajuraho	203
8.41	Maithuna Scene, Devi Jagadambi Temple, Khajuraho	203
8.42	Citragupta Temple, Khajuraho	204
8.43	Kandariya Mahadeva Temple, Khajuraho	205
8.44	Ritual Scene, Kandariya Mahadeva Temple, Khajuraho	205
8.45	Tower of the Jagdish Temple, Udaipur	206
8.46	Belur Math Temple	207
10.1	Tablet of Homage from Kankali Tila, Mathura, with the Symbol of the Wheel, in the State Museum, Lucknow. Photograph from Vincent A. Smith, *The Jain Stûpa and Other Antiquities of Mathurâ* (ASI 20) (Allahabad: Government Press, 1901), p. 15, Pl. VIII.	224
10.2	Tablet of Homage from Kankali Tila, Mathura, with the Figure of a Jina, in the State Museum, Lucknow. Photograph from Smith, *The Jain Stûpa and Other Antiquities of Mathurâ*, p. 14, Pl. VII.	246
10.3	Standing Image of Rishabha, in the Archaeological Museum, Khajuraho	249
10.4	Seated Image of Neminatha, in the Archaeological Museum, Mathura	250
10.5	Seated Image of Parśvanatha, in the Victoria and Albert Museum, London. Photograph from the Victoria and Albert Museum.	252
10.6	Standing Image of Mahavira, in the Prince of Wales Museum of Western India, Bombay	253
10.7	Seated Image of the Yakshini Padmavati, in the Prince of Wales Museum of Western India, Bombay	256
10.8	Seated Image of the Yakshini Kali in the Prince of Wales Museum of Western India, Bombay	258
10.9	Standing Image of Sarasvati, in the National Museum, New Delhi	260

10.10	Jaina Stupa on a Tablet of Homage, in the Archaeological Museum, Mathura	263
10.11	Attempted Abduction of Radanika, Sculpture from Mathura, in the National Museum, New Delhi	265
10.12	Colossal Statue of Adinatha in the Śantinatha Temple, Khajuraho	268
10.13	Two Digambara Saints in the Śantinatha Temple, Khajuraho	269
10.14	Gomedha and Ambika in the Śantinatha Temple, Khajuraho	269
10.15	Doorway of the Central Shrine in the Adinatha Temple, Khajuraho	270
10.16	Parśvanatha Temple, Khajuraho	270
10.17	Vishnu and Lakshmi, Parśvanatha Temple, Khajuraho	273
10.18	Lady applying Eye Paint, Parśvanatha Temple, Kharjuraho	274
10.19	Lady applying Lac Dye to Foot, Parśvanatha Temple, Khajuraho	274
10.20	Dancer affixing Bell Anklets, Parśvanatha Temple, Khajuraho	275
10.21	Colossal Statue of Gommateśvara in the Indrabetta, Śravanabelgola	277
10.22	Anthills at the Feet of Gommateśvara, Śravanabelgola	278
10.23	Tendrils wrapping the Thighs and Arms of Gommateśvara, Śravanabelgola	278
10.24	Back and Head of Gommateśvara, Śravanabelgola	279
10.25	Rishabhanatha in Side Chapel of the Vimala-vasahi, Mount Abu	280
10.26	Hall of Music and Dance, looking forward to the Central Shrine, Vimala-vasahi, Mount Abu	281
10.27	Sarasvati in Corridor Ceiling, Vimala-vasahi, Mount Abu	282
10.28	Śitala in Corridor Ceiling, Vimala-vasahi, Mount Abu	282
10.29	Ceiling in the Luna-vasahi, Mount Abu	283
10.30	Parśvanatha in Small Shrine in the Luna-vasahi, Mount Abu	283
10.31	Adinatha Temple at Ranakpur	284
10.32	Śikhara over the Central Shrine, Adinatha Temple, Ranakpur	285
10.33	Worshipers before the Central Shrine, Adinatha Temple, Ranakpur	286
10.34	Dome Pendant, Adinatha Temple, Ranakpur	286
10.35	Celestial Musician, Adinatha Temple, Ranakpur	287
10.36	Thousand-hooded Parśvanatha, Adinatha Temple, Ranakpur	287
10.37	Naked Woman, Parśvanatha Temple, Ranakpur	288
10.38	Badridas Temple, Calcutta	288
13.1	Seated Bodhisattva/Buddha Image, Gift of Amohasi, from Katra, in the Archaeological Museum, Mathura	421
13.2	Standing Buddha with Alms Bowl, from Takht-i-Bahi, in the Archaeological Museum, Peshawar	422
13.3	Head of Buddha, from Shahr-i-Bahlol, in the Archaeological Museum, Peshawar	423
13.4	Śakyamuni in Extreme Emaciation, Replica in the Taxila Museum	423
13.5	Standing Statue of the Buddha, Gift of the Monk Yaśadinna, from Jamalpur, in the Archaeological Museum, Mathura	425
13.6	Buddha Head from Camunda Tila, in the Archaeological Museum, Mathura	425
13.7	Valley of the Ajanta Caves	428
13.8	Façade of Cave No. 19, Ajanta	429
13.9	Vidhurapandita in the Palace of the Naga King, Cave No. 2, Ajanta	433
13.10	The King and the Princess in the Story of Kalyanakarin, Cave No. 1, Ajanta	434
13.11	Bodhisattva Padmapani, Cave No. 1, Ajanta	434
13.12	Couple of Lovers, Cave No. 1, Ajanta	434
13.13	Buddha in Cave No. 10, Ellora	436

13.14	Stupa No. 1 at Sanci, General View from the East	437
13.15	Lion Capital of Aśoka Pillar, in the Archaeological Museum, Sanci	438
13.16	Vrikshaka Bracket Figure, East Gate, Stupa No. 1, Sanci	440
13.17	Inner Side of Architraves, East Gate, Stupa No. 1, Sanci	441
13.18	Buddha Walking on the Flooded River, Southern Pillar, East Gate, Stupa No. 1, Sanci	441
13.19	Return of Buddha to Kapilavastu, Northern Pillar, East Gate, Stupa No. 1, Sanci	442
13.20	South Gate and Stump of the Aśoka Pillar, Stupa No. 1, Sanci	442
13.21	West Gate, Stupa No. 1, Sanci	444
13.22	North Gate, Stupa No. 1, Sanci	444
13.23	Vrikshaka and Lion, North Gate, Stupa No. 1, Sanci	445
13.24	Seated Buddha, Stupa No. 1, Sanci	445
13.25	Western Monastery, Sanci	447
13.26	Dharmarajika Stupa, Taxila	448
13.27	Two Seated Buddhas on Small Stupa, Jaulian Main Stupa Court, Taxila	450
13.28	Dhamekh Stupa, Sarnath	454
13.29	Mahabodhi Temple, Bodhgaya. Photograph from Heinrich Zimmer, *The Art of Indian Asia* (Bollingen Series XXXIX) (Princeton: Princeton University Press, 2 vols., 3d printing with revisions 1968), 2, Pl. 99, by permission of Princeton University Press.	456
13.30	Maha Seya Dagoba at the Summit of the Mihintale Hill	458
13.31	Lower Courses of the Kantaka Cetiya, Mihintale	458
13.32	Thuparama Dagoba, Anuradhapura	460
13.33	Elephant Head at the Isurumuniya Rock Temple, Anuradhapura	461
13.34	Isurumuniya Lovers, Anuradhapura	461
13.35	Moonstone at Anuradhapura	463
13.36	Lion's Paw on the Sigiriya Rock	464
13.37	Apsaras, Fresco on the Sigiriya Rock	465
13.38	Apsarases, Fresco on the Sigiriya Rock	465
13.39	Statue of Parakramabahu I at Polonnaruwa	468
13.40	Vatadage, Polonnaruwa	469
13.41	Kiri Vehera, Polonnaruwa	470
13.42	Large Seated Buddha at the Gal Vihara, Polonnaruwa	471
14.1	Niche and Kala-Makara at Candi Kalasan	478
14.2	Taras on the Wall of Candi Sari	479
14.3	Candi Mendut	480
14.4	Kacchapa Jataka Scene on the South Wing of the Stairway, Candi Mendut	481
14.5	The Yaksha Atavaka and Children on the South Wall of the Antechamber, Candi Mendut	481
14.6	The Buddha in Candi Mendut	482
14.7	Borobudur, the North Side with Central Staircase	484
14.8	Makara Spout in the Main Wall of the Processional Path, Borobudur	485
14.9	Kala Spout on the Fourth Terrace, Borobudur	485
14.10	Relief Panel of the Covered Base, Borobudur	486
14.11	Double Relief Panel in the First Gallery, Borobudur, showing above (Ia 95) the Temptation of Śakyamuni by the Daughters of Mara, and below (Ib 95) a scene from the *Bhallatiya Jataka*, with a band of spiral ornament between the upper and lower panels	487
14.12	Relief Panel (Ib 91) in the First Gallery, Borobudur, showing a scene from the *Bhallatiya Jataka*	489

14.13	Relief Panel (IIa 108) in the Second Gallery, Borobudur, showing Sudhana and a Goddess of Night	490
14.14	Relief Panel (IVb 54) in the Fourth Gallery, Borobudur, showing Samantabhadra and Many Buddhas	491
14.15	Tathāgata (Dhyani Buddha) in Niche, Borobudur	492
14.16	Buddha Image in Dismantled Stupa, Borobudur	493
14.17	Crowning Stupa, Borobudur	493
14.18	Tower of the Śiva Temple, Candi Lara Jonggrang, Prambanam	496
14.19	Image of Śiva in the Central Chamber of the Śiva Temple, Candi Lara Jonggrang, Prambanam	496
14.20	Image of Durga in the North Cell of the Śiva Temple, Candi Lara Jonggrang, Prambanam	497
14.21	Characteristic Prambanam Motif with Lion and Trees of Heaven on the Terrace of the Brahma Temple, Candi Lara Jonggrang, Prambanam	498
14.22	Rama shoots the Bow of Śiva and wins the Hand of Sita, Śiva Temple Relief, Candi Lara Jonggrang, Prambanam	499
14.23	Sita in Lanka, Śiva Temple Relief, Candi Lara Jonggrang, Prambanam	499
14.24	Hanuman reports to Rama on His Mission in Lanka, Śiva Temple Relief, Candi Lara Jonggrang, Prambanam	500
14.25	The Monkey Army builds the Bridge to Lanka, Śiva Temple Relief, Candi Lara Jonggrang, Prambanam	500
14.26	Arrival of Rama, Lakshmana, Sugriva, and the Monkey Army on Lanka, Śiva Temple Relief, Candi Lara Jonggrang, Prambanam	501
14.27	Portrait Statue of Airlanga as Vishnu on Garuda, from Belahan, in the Municipal Museum, Modjokerto, Java. Photograph from A. J. Bernet Kempers, *Ancient Indonesian Art* (Amsterdam: C. P. J. van der Peet, 1959), Pl. 202, by permission of C. P. J. van der Peet.	503
14.28	Statue of Cakracakra (Śiva in the form of Bhairava), from a Temple at Singhasari. Photograph from the Rijksmuseum voor Volkenkunde, Leiden.	505
14.29	Statue of Prajnaparamita from Singhasari. Photograph from the Rijksmuseum voor Volkenkunde, Leiden.	505
14.30	Portrait Statue of King Kritarajasa of Majapahit, in the Museum of Indonesian Culture, Jakarta. Photograph from A. J. Bernet Kempers, *Ancient Indonesian Art* (Amsterdam: C. P. J. van der Peet, 1959), Pl. 247, by permission of C. P. J. van der Peet.	507
14.31	Portrait Statue of Queen Regent Tribhuvana of Majapahit, in the Museum of Indonesian Culture, Jakarta. Photograph from A. J. Bernet Kempers, *Ancient Indonesian Art* (Amsterdam: C. P. J. van der Peet, 1959), Pl. 248, by permission of C. P. J. van der Peet.	507
14.32	Façade of Goa Gajah, the Elephant Cave near Bedulu Village	518
14.33	Vidyadharis in the Sanctuary and Watering Place by the Elephant Cave near Bedulu	519
14.34.	Conflict of Sutasoma and the ten-faced demon Daśamukha, Painting in the Royal Pavilion, Klungkung	520
14.35	Stairway and Split Gate leading to the Central Sanctuary at Pura Besakih	522
14.36	A Sarad or Symbolic Representation of the Cosmos and Its Gods, at Pura Besakih	523
14.37	Main Meru in Pura Kehen, Bangli	523
14.38	Padmasana in Pura Kehen, Bangli	524
14.39	Roofed Gate, Bali Museum, Denpasar	525

14.40	Drummer, Bali Museum, Denpasar	526
14.41	Vishnu on Garuda, Bali Museum, Denpasar	526
14.42	Ravana on Wilmana, Bali Museum, Denpasar	526
14.43	Barong, Bali Museum, Denpasar	527
14.44	Rangda, Bali Museum, Denpasar	527
14.45	Priest conducting Wedding Ceremony in Singapadu	528
14.46	Cremation Procession at Besan	528
14.47	Girl Dancers in the Barong-Rangda Dance Drama at Batubukan	529
14.48	Reclining Buddha in Penang	530
14.49	Buddha flanked by Taoist Deities, Penang Buddhist Association	531
14.50	Pre Rup at Angkor	537
14.51	Phimeanakas at Angkor	538
14.52	Śiva and Parvati on Mount Kailasa, at Banteay Srei	539
14.53	Tevoda at Banteay Srei	540
14.54	General View of Banteay Samre	541
14.55	View from the Air of Angkor Wat and Its Surrounding Moat	541
14.56	Battle Scene from the *Mahabharata* at Angkor Wat	542
14.57	Hanuman and the Gods in the Scene of the Churning of the Sea of Milk, Angkor Wat	543
14.58	Apsarases at Angkor Wat	543
14.59	Approach to the South Gate, Angkor Thom	545
14.60	Foot Soldiers and Elephants, Bayon Bas-Relief, Angkor Thom	545
14.61	Bayon Face, Angkor Thom	546
14.62	General View of a Portion of Pagan from the Thatbyinnyu Temple, looking southeast toward the Dhammayangyi Temple (left) and the Shwe Sandaw Pagoda (right)	553
14.63	Shwezigon Pagoda, Pagan	553
14.64	Buddha and His Disciples, Shwezigon Pagoda, Pagan	554
14.65	Wall Paintings in the Kubyauk Kyi Pagoda, Pagan	555
14.66	Colossal Standing Statue of the Buddha in the Ananda Temple, Pagan. Photograph by Arthur S. Merrow, Jr.	556
14.67	Mingalazedi Pagoda, Pagan	557
14.68	Kuthodaw Pagoda, Mandalay	559
14.69	Shwe Dagon Pagoda from Its Main Platform, Rangoon	560
14.70	Monks at a Small Shrine, Shwe Dagon Pagoda, Rangoon	560
14.71	Golden Buddha in Side Chapel, Sule Pagoda, Rangoon	561
14.72	Dome and Spire of the Botataung Pagoda, Rangoon	561
14.73	Head of Reclining Image of the Buddha, Chauk Htat Kyi Temple, Rangoon	562
14.74	Approach to Phra Pathom Chedi at Nakhon Pathom	570
14.75	Golden Buddha in the Phra Pathom Chedi, Nakhon Pathom	571
14.76	Buddha on Naga, from Lopburi, in the National Museum, Bangkok	572
14.77	Buddha Head from Sukhothai, in the National Museum, Bangkok	572
14.78	Row of Seated Buddhas, Wat Yai Chaya Mongkol, Ayutthaya	574
14.79	Head of Colossal Reclining Buddha, at Ayutthaya	574
14.80	Wat Arun, Thonburi	575
14.81	Roofs and Towers of the Grand Palace, Bangkok, seen from the Chao Phraya River	576
14.82	Roofs and Tower of Dusit Mahaprasad, Grand Palace, Bangkok	577
14.83	Demon guarding an Entrance to Wat Phra Keo, Grand Palace, Bangkok	578
14.84	Golden Chedi, Wat Phra Keo, Grand Palace, Bangkok	578

14.85	In the Grounds of Wat Po, Bangkok	579
14.86	Buddha of Solid Gold in Wat Traimitr, Bangkok	581
14.87	Buddha in Wat Bovornives, Bangkok	581
14.88	Wat Benchamaborpit, Bangkok	582
14.89	Phra Buddha Jinaraj Replica in Wat Benchamaborpit, Bangkok	283
15.1	Svayambhunath Hill, near Kathmandu	599
15.2	Dome and Tower of the Large Stupa at Svayambhunath	599
15.3	Gilt Buddha in the Svayambhunath Monastery	600
15.4	Monks Playing Musical Instruments and Chanting in the Svayambhunath Monastery	600
15.5	Bodhnath Stupa near Kathmandu	601
15.6	Tibetan Monks in the Bodhnath Monastery	602
15.7	Tenzing Ghelek Rimpoche in the Bodhnath Monastery	602
15.8	Śiva Shrines at Paśupatinath	603
15.9	Interior of Śiva Shrine, Paśupatinath	604
15.10	Burning Ghats and Hostels at Paśupatinath	604
15.11	Paśupatinath Devi	605
15.12	Jalaśayana Narayana at Budhanilakantha	605
15.13	Aśoka Stupa at Patan	606
15.14	Kalabhairava in Durbar Square, Kathmandu	608
15.15	Lion and Hanuman at the Lion Gate, Royal Palace, Bhadgaon	609
15.16	Golden Gate, Royal Palace, Bhadgaon	610
15.17	Bhairava Temple and Festival Wagon, Bhadgaon	610
15.18	Nyatapola Temple, Bhadgaon	611
15.19	Stairs and Pairs of Guardian Figures, Nyatapola Temple, Bhadgaon	611
15.20	Many-armed Deity, Nyatapola Temple, Bhadgaon	612
15.21	Tanka showing Viśvarupa, National Museum of Nepal, Kathmandu	613
15.22	Bronze Tara, National Museum of Nepal, Kathmandu	614
15.23	Yab Yum Bronze, National Museum of Nepal, Kathmandu	614
15.24	Agni and His śakti, National Museum of Nepal, Kathmandu	615
15.25	Nativity of the Buddha, National Museum of Nepal, Kathmandu	615
15.26	Vishnu and Two Consorts, Relief Sculpture on Pilaster of Gateway Stair, Avantisvami Temple at Avantipur	621
15.27	Ruins of the Butkara Stupa and Surrounding Structures, near Mingora	622
15.28	Statues of the Buddha at the Butkara Stupa, near Mingora	623
15.29	Buddha from Hadda, in the Kabul Museum	625
15.30	Aphrodite from Begram, in the Kabul Museum	626
15.31	Women under a Torana, Ivory Plaque from Begram, in the Kabul Museum	627
15.32	Ivory Statuette of a Yakshi, from Begram, in the Kabul Museum	527
15.33	Carved Cover of Ivory Jewel Chest, from Begram in the Kabul Museum	628
15.34	Bamiyan Valley and the Cliff with the Smaller Buddha, with the Snows of the Hindu Kush beyond	629
15.35	Smaller Buddha and Adjacent Caves, Bamiyan	630
15.36	Larger Buddha, Bamiyan	631
15.37	Two Persons standing in front of the Right Foot of the Larger Buddha, Bamiyan	631
15.38	Looking across the Bamiyan River to Shahr-i-Zohak	632
15.39	Shahr-i-Gholghola, Bamiyan	632
15.40	Ruins of the Ancient City of Kaochang, looking toward the Flaming Mountains	634
15.41	Caves of the Thousand Buddhas at Bezeklik in the Flaming Mountains	634

15.42	Painting from Bezeklik in the Museum of the Xinjiang Uygur Autonomous Region in Urumqi	635
15.43	The Yumbulagang Palace	639
15.44	Statue of Nyathir Tsenpo in the Yumbulagang Palace	640
15.45	Statue of Trhisong Detsen in the Yumbulagang Palace	641
15.46	Tanka depicting the Samye Monastery, Collection of the Newark Museum	641
15.47	Façade of the Samye Monastery	642
15.48	Wall Painting of the Buddha in the Samye Monastery	642
15.49	Statue of Padmasambhava in the Samye Monastery	643
15.50	Statue of Atiśa in the Samye Monastery	643
15.51	Statue of Drom in the Samye Monastery	644
15.52	The Dolma Lhakhang at Nethang	644
15.53	Chorten of Atiśa in the Dolma Lhakhang at Nethang	645
15.54	The Potala from the Two Glasses Lake in Lhasa	646
15.55	Empty Throne of the Dalai Lama in the Potala	646
15.56	Chorten of the Fifth Dalai Lama in the Potala	647
15.57	The Jokhang seen from the Hospital of Tibetan Medicine	648
15.58	The *Jo bo* Śakyamuni in the Jokhang	649
15.59	The Ramoche in Lhasa	649
15.60	Statue of Tsongkhapa in the Drepung Monastery	650
15.61	Statues of Jamyang and Śakyamuni Buddha in the Drepung Monastery	651
15.62	Filming an Enactment of the Engagement of Princess Wencheng and King Songtsen Gampo at the Drepung Monastery, Lhasa	651
15.63	The Wheel of Existence, Wall Painting at the Sera Monastery, Lhasa	652
15.64	The Leh Khar on the Slope of Namgyal Peak in Leh	655
15.65	Colossal Head of Śakyamuni Buddha in the Monastery Temple at Shey	656
15.66	The Protective Goddess Pelden Lhamo in the Monastery Temple at Shey	656
15.67	The White Tara in the Form of Ushnisha Sitatapatra in the Leh Khar Temple	657
15.68	Padmasambhava and Shelves of Books in the Leh Khar Temple	658
15.69	The Protective Deity Padma Heruka and Padma Dakini in the Leh Khar Temple	658
15.70	Taktshang or Tiger's Den Monastery above the Paro Valley	660
15.71	Tantric Wall Painting in the Taktshang Monastery	660
15.72	The Tashicho Dzong in Thimphu	661
15.73	The Chorten of Jigme Dorje Wangchuck in Thimphu	664
15.74	The Cosmic Mandala in the Rimpong Dzong in Paro	664
15.75	Statues of the Buddha and Avalokiteśvara in the Tshongdi Lhakhang in Paro	663

ABBREVIATIONS

AA	*Artibus Asiae*
AAA	*Archives of Asian Art*
ABIA	*Annual Bibliography of Indian Archaeology* (Kern Institute, Leiden)
AF	*Asiatische Forschungen, Monographienreihe zur Geschichte, Kultur und Sprache der Völker Ost- und Zentralasiens, herausgegeben für das Seminar für Sprach- und Kulturwissenschaft Zentralasiens der Universität Bonn*
Afghanistan	*Afghanistan, Historical and Cultural Quarterly*
AMAN	*American Anthropologist*
AMG	*Annales du Musée Guimet*
AMGBE	*Annales du Musée Guimet, Bibliothèque d'Études*
AMN	*American Museum Novitates* (American Museum of Natural History, New York)
ANET	*Ancient Near Eastern Texts relating to the Old Testament*, ed. James B. Pritchard (Princeton: Princeton University Press, 1954, Supplement 1969)
Antiquity	*Antiquity, A periodical Review of Archaeology*, ed. Glyn Daniel
AONI	*Archaeologisch Onderzoek in Nederlandsch-Indië*
AOS	*American Oriental Series*
ARAS	*Ars Asiatica*
Archaeology	*Archaeology* (Archaeological Institute of America)
ASB	*Archaeological Survey of Burma*
ASC	*Archaeological Survey of Ceylon* (Sri Lanka)
ASCAS	*Archaeological Survey of Ceylon* (Sri Lanka), *Art Series*
ASI	*Archaeological Survey of India*
ASWI	*Archaeological Survey of Western India*
BB	*Bibliotheca Buddhica*
BBU	*Bhavan's Book University*
BCE	Before the Common Era
BEFEO	*Bulletin de l'École Française d'Extrême-Orient*
BH	*Bibliotheca Himalayica*
BI	*Bibliotheca Indica*
BIIN	*Bibliotheca Indonesica*
BJ	*Bibliotheca Jainica*
BSOAS	*Bulletin of the School of Oriental and African Studies*
CE	*Common Era*
CHI	*The Cambridge History of India*, ed. E. J. Rapson (Cambridge: University Press, 6 vols. plus supplementary volume, 1922–60)
CII	*Corpus Inscriptionum Indicarum*
CLS	*The Clear Light Series*
COS	*Calcutta Oriental Series*
CSHA	*California Studies in the History of Art*
CSHI	*The Cambridge Shorter History of India*, ed. H. H. Dodwell (Cambridge: University Press, 1934)

CSS	*The Chowkhamba Sanskrit Series*
CSSA	*Cambridge Studies in Social Anthropology*
EAW	*East and West* (Istituto Italiano per il Medio ed Estremo Oriente, Rome)
EB	*Encyclopaedia of Buddhism*, ed. G. P. Malalasekera and (in 1979–) Jotiya Dhirasekera (Published by the Government of Sri Lanka, 1961ff.)
EIAR	*Encyclopedia of Indo-Aryan Research*
ERCEW	*Ethical and Religious Classics of East and West*
GIAPA	*Grundriss der indo-arischen Philologie und Altertumskunde*
GJ	*The Geographical Journal* (The Royal Geographical Society, London)
GOS	*Gaekwad's Oriental Series* (Oriental Institute, Baroda)
HBO	*Handbuch der Orientalistik*
HCDA	*Historical and Cultural Dictionaries of Asia*
HJAS	*Harvard Journal of Asiatic Studies*
HOS	*Harvard Oriental Series* (Cambridge: Harvard University Press)
IAC	*The Indo-Asian Culture* (Indian Council for Cultural Relations, New Delhi)
IHQ	*The Indian Historical Quarterly*
IIM	*Indo-Iranian Monographs*
IIMEO, SOR	*Istituto Italiano per il Medio ed Estremo Oriente, Serie Orientale Roma*
IIS	*Institute of Indology Series*
IKE	*Der indische Kulturkreis in Einzeldarstellungen*
IR	*Iconography of Religions* (Institute of Religious Iconography, State University, Groningen)
IRIFA	Indian Research Institute Publications, Fine Arts Series
ISS	Indian Sculpture Series
ITS	Indian Texts Series
JAOS	*Journal of the American Oriental Society*
JAP	*The Jaina Academy Publications*
JBORS	*The Journal of the Bihar and Orissa Research Society*
JCBRAS	*Journal of the Ceylon Branch of the Royal Asiatic Society*
JJG	*Jivaraja Jaina Granthamālā*
JJMS	*Jagmandarlal Jaini Memorial Series* (Lucknow: The Central Jaina Publishing House)
JLCR	*Jordan Lectures in Comparative Religion* (School of Oriental and African Studies, University of London)
JMG	*Jñānapīṭha Mūrtīdevī Granthamālā*
JPTS	*Journal of the Pali Text Society*
JRAS	*The Journal of the Royal Asiatic Society of Great Britain and Ireland*
JSS	*Journal of the Siam Society*
JUHRI	*Journal of Urusvati Himalayan Research Institute* (Urusvati Himalayan Research Institute of Roerich Museum, New York City)
KITLV	*Koninklijk Instituut voor Taal-, Land-, en Volkenkunde, Translation Series*
LOS	*London Oriental Series*
MAEFEO	*Mémoires archéologiques, École Française d'Extrême-Orient*
MAES	*Monographs of the American Ethnological Society*
MAS	*Mysore Archaeological Series*
MASC	*Memoirs of the Archaeological Survey of Ceylon*

MASI	*Memoirs of the Archaeological Survey of India*
MBRAS	*The Malaysian Branch of the Royal Asiatic Society*
MDAFA	*Mémoires de la Délégation Archéologique Française en Afghanistan*
MK	*The Making of the Past Series* (Lausanne: Elsevier Publishing Projects)
MKB	*Materialien zur Kunde des Buddhismus*
MUHS	*Madras University Historical Series*
NCA	*Nations of Contemporary Asia*
NGM	*National Geographic Magazine*
NISABA	*Religious Texts Translation Series*
NMW	*Nations of the Modern World*
NT	*News Tibet* (The Office of Tibet, New York)
OR	*Orientations* (Hong Kong: Pacific Communications Ltd.)
OTF	Oriental Translation Fund
PCP	Praeger Country Profiles
PEFEO	*Publications de l'École Française d'Extrême Orient*
PJIRP	*Prakrit Jain Institute Research Publications Series*
PMGRDAA	*Publications du Musée Guimet, Recherches et Documents d'Art et d'Archéologie*
POS	*Poona Oriental Series*
PSS	*The Punjab Sanskrit Series*
PTS	*Pali Text Society*
PVS	*Parshvanath Vidyashram Series*
RGFLW	*Rijksuniversiteit te Gent, Werken uitgegeven door de Faculteit van de Letteren en Wijsbegeerte*
RM	*Die Religionen der Menschheit*
RTTS	*Religious Texts Translation Series*
SBB	*Sacred Books of the Buddhists* (London: Humphrey Milford)
SBE	F. Max Müller, ed., *The Sacred Books of the East translated by Various Oriental Scholars* (Oxford: Clarendon Press, 50 vols., 1885–1910)
SBH	*The Sacred Books of the Hindus*
SBJ	*The Sacred Books of the Jainas*
SIS	*Soviet Indology Series*
SJKSS	*Sri Jaina Kala Sahitya Samsodhak Series*
SOR	*Serie Orientale Roma*
SPS	*Śata-Piṭaka Series* (International Academy of Indian Culture, New Delhi)
SSI	*Selected Studies on Indonesia by Dutch Scholars*
Sumer	*Sumer, A Journal of Archaeology in Iraq*
Syria	*Syria, Revue d'art oriental et d'archéologie*
TAPS	*Transactions of the American Philosophical Society*
TCNS	*Thai Culture New Series*
TOS	*Trübner's Oriental Series*
TTS	*Tibetan Translation Series*
UBSSPP	*University of Bombay Studies, Sanskrit, Prakrit and Pali*
VKNAW, AL, NR	*Verhandelingen der Koninklijke Nederlandse Akademie van Wetenschappen, Afdeling Letterkunde, Nieuwe Reeks*
WES	*The Wisdom of the East Series*
WS	*Wheel Series*
WTS	*The Wisdom of Tibet Series*

PREFACE

In Western terminology it may be said that three main religions—more accurately stated, religio-philosophical systems—originated in India, namely, Hinduism, Jainism, and Buddhism, and it is the archaeological history of these three in India and in the wider sphere of Indian influence from Sri Lanka, Indonesia, Malaysia, Kampuchea, Thailand, and Burma in the South and East, to Nepal, Pakistan, Kashmir, Swat, Afghanistan, Xinjiang, Bhutan, Ladakh, and Tibet in the North and West, that is the subject of this book.

In common with Judaism, Christianity, and Islam—Hinduism, Jainism, and Buddhism all recognize sites, as well as monuments said to mark those sites, which serve the purpose of commemoration and devotion. These monuments are important in both their history and their contemporary life. But in contrast with the *aniconic cultus* in Judaism (where the prohibition of the making of any likeness of anything in heaven, earth, or water did not, however, exclude, for example, the paintings in the Dura-Europos synagogue), the limited use of icons in Christianity (restricted by iconoclastic protest in various times and places), and the rigorous iconoclasm of Islam (where the chief decoration of mosques may be only the calligraphic rendition of Quranic texts), there is no hesitation in the three Indian religions in the use of images (although supreme reality and supreme experience are beyond representation). Therefore the monuments of Hinduism, Jainism, and Buddhism—both structures and images—are very numerous.

Whether the sites and structures are visited by pilgrims and used by worshipers as places of devotion, with the images seen by devout individuals as helps on the path to illumination, or whether the sites, structures, and images are the objects of study by archaeologists and historians seeking all available documentation of the happenings of the past, by philosophers and sociologists who include such tangible materials as part of the data for a phenomenological analysis of religion, or by students of the history of art (including architecture) who are alert to effective representation of human conceptions in concrete media—in other words, whether the monuments are viewed in terms of personal response, historical research, comparative study, or aesthetic appreciation—they are significant expressions of the human spirit and, religiously speaking, significant expressions of the human response to the sense of the ultimate.

Since the approach in the present book is primarily archaeological and historical, the effort is made to locate the monuments geographically and chronologically, to describe them accurately, and to see their place in the developing history and thought of the religions involved. The understanding of the developing history and thought, of course, also requires acquaintance with and use of the literatures of the religions. This approach in terms of archaeological history should, however, bring into view materials which are basic and hardly dispensable in approaches along other lines. Further, in the area dealt with, history in general and the history of religions in particular are hardly separable, so the book might just as well be called an archaeological history as an archaeological history of religions.

The writer has lived in India (Fulbright research scholar at the Indian Museum, Calcutta, 1952–1953) and through many years has traveled, in most cases repeatedly, in all the lands dealt with, from Bali to Afghanistan, from Sri Lanka to Swat, and to Xinjiang in 1980, Xizang (Tibet) in 1981 and 1985, and Ladakh (Western Tibet) in 1982, and Bhutan in 1987, and most of the illustrations are the writer's own personal photographs. It will also be observed that in the notes the works of Asian scholars have a very large place, while literary sources are cited in standard translations.

JACK FINEGAN

ACKNOWLEDGMENTS

Except where otherwise indicated in the List of Illustrations, all photographs are by Jack Finegan. For the photographs made by permission in museums, acknowledgment is made to the respective institutions as noted in the List of Illustrations, and additional acknowledgment is made to:

Putu Budiastra, Director, Museum Bali, Denpasar
Mrs. Chira Chongkol, Director, The National Museum, Bangkok
The Trustees of the Prince of Wales Museum, Bombay
J. K. Shrestha, Director, National Museum of Nepal, Kathmandu
Prof. Fidaullah Sehrai, Director, Peshawar Museum, Peshawar
Han Guang-fu, Director, Museum of the Xinjiang Uygur Autonomous Region, Urumqi

Of the maps, the first four are reproduced from the writer's *Archeology of World Religions* by permission of Princeton University Press, while the fifth map was drawn by Adrienne Morgan, Cartographer, the University of California, Berkeley.

Quotations from published books made by permission of the publishers are acknowledged at the relevant points in the notes.

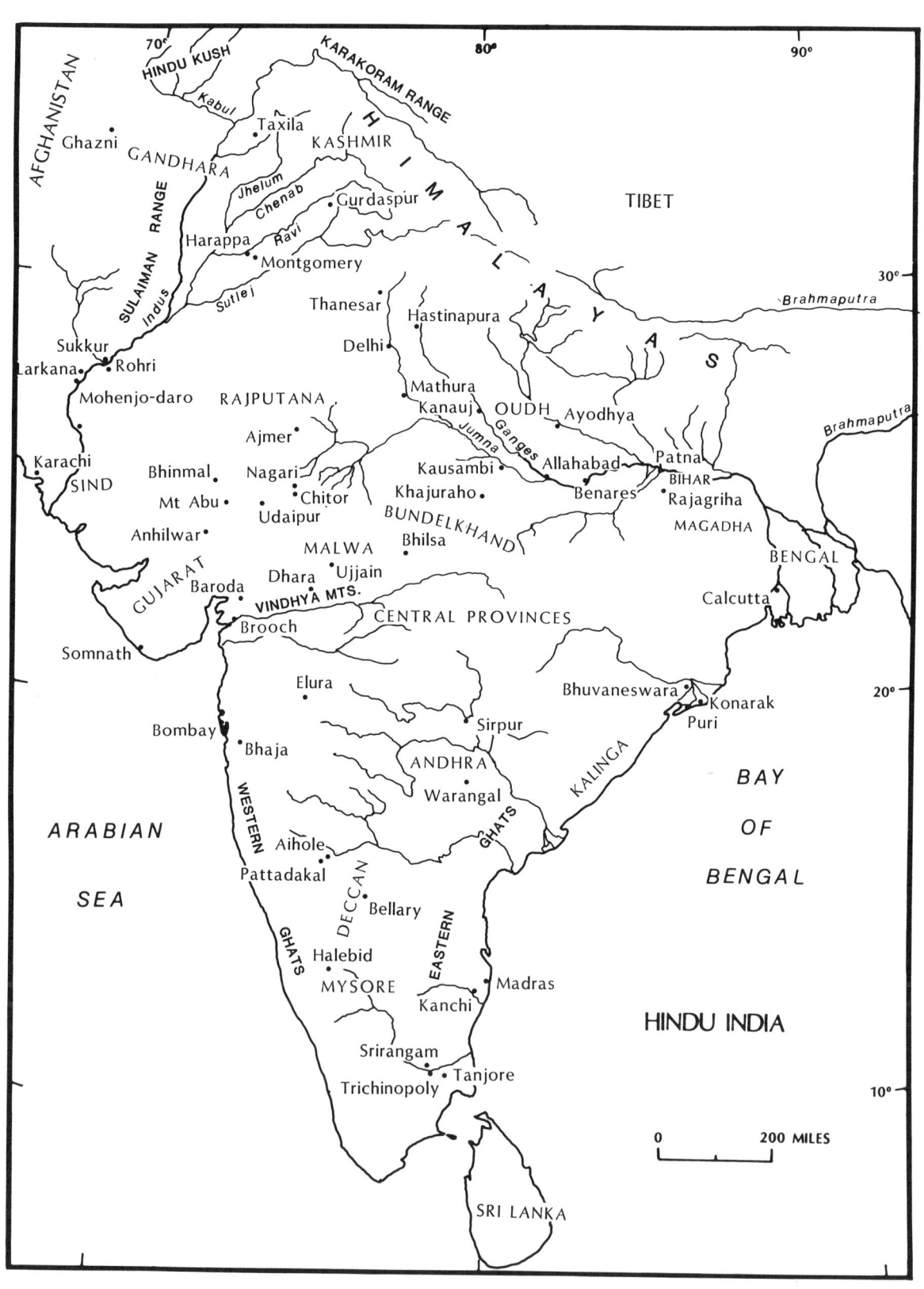

1

HARAPPAN CIVILIZATION

Various factors must have contributed to the rise of the first cities in the world, not only the invention of farming and the domestication of animals which made permanent settlement possible, but also such other developments as the pressure of increasing population, the need for security, and the relationships of trade. At the present stage of discovery, the earliest relatively large cities have been found at Jericho in Palestine (seventh millennium B.C.E.), Çatal Hüyük in Anatolia (sixth millennium B.C.E.), and Tepe Yahya in Iran (fourth millennium B.C.E.), all apparently favorably located with respect to trade. But only in major river valleys did irrigation agriculture sustain at an early time the largest and longest continuing agglomerations of urban centers. Of these valleys, the chief in the ancient world were the valley of the Tigris and Euphrates where the Sumerian civilization emerged in the fourth millennium B.C.E.; the valley of the Nile where Egyptian civilization was probably largely independent and almost as early; the valley of the Indus where the Harappan civilization had its beginnings not much later, reaching its height in the third millennium; and the valley of the Huang (Yellow) River where the civilization of the Shang Dynasty was at its height in the second millennium.[1]

In the subcontinent now occupied by the nations of India, Pakistan, and Bangladesh, the first agriculturalists are thought to have come in from Iran, probably around the middle of the fifth millennium, and farming communities were subsequently established which formed the basis of civilization in the Indus Valley. This civilization is more specifically known as Harappan, from Harappa where it was first discovered, and is now recognized at nearly 270 sites, chiefly in Pakistan and India. These sites extend from Sutkagen Dor on the Makran Coast of the Arabian Sea in Baluchistan 325 miles (500 km.) west of Karachi, to Alamgirpur northeast of Delhi, and from Sarai Khola and Jhang, northwest of Rawalpindi, to Malvan near Surat on the Gulf of Cambay north of Bombay—a distance of 1,000 miles (1,500 km.) from west to east, and nearly as much from north to south. Archaeological stratification at various of these sites and corrected Carbon 14 dates indicate a cultural phase called Early Harappan, which began by circa 3500 B.C.E., and a full urban civilization known as Mature Harappan, which emerged by circa 2600 B.C.E. and endured until it reached its end circa 1900 B.C.E.[2]

EARLY HARAPPAN SITES

Jalilpur, a site in the Punjab in Pakistan 64 miles (74 km.) southwest of Harappa, provides an example of the Early Harappan culture. Excavation shows six levels and two main occupational periods (Jalilpur I and Jalilpur II). In the first period are found mud floors, stone tools, and plain red handmade pottery; in the second period are rooms made of mud brick, pottery made on the wheel and painted with black or brown designs on red, animal figurines especially of humped bulls, terra cotta toy carts, shell bangles, and female figurines. At other sites, for example, Kot Diji and Amri, there are early levels comparable to these at Jalilpur, almost immediately above which are levels with materials characteristic of the Mature Harappan period. While some of these early levels (such as the Kot Dijian and Amrian) have long been called pre-Harappan, it appears rather, from the sequence of the strata and the continuity of the cultural traits, that they should be seen as Early Harappan and that the Mature Harappan civilization should be recognized as the result of a long development, a process of urbanization which probably began, as already stated, as early as the middle of the fourth millennium B.C.E.[3]

Kot Diji is a site in Upper Sind in Pakistan, 25 miles (40 km.) east of Moenjo-daro. Excavation shows sixteen strata, of which all the lowest are called Kot Dijian, while the uppermost three, above a burned layer, are Mature Harappan. In the earlier time Kot Diji was a small town with a fortified citadel, the walls of which were built of mud brick on stone foundations. The houses were also of mud brick built on foundations of stone. Good stone implements and thin wheel-turned pottery were in use. The pottery was usually pink to red in color and decorated in black with straight horizontal lines, or with waves and loops, and sometimes with a pattern or scales. The women wore beads and bangles of shell and terra cotta, and the children played with such toys as stone or baked-clay balls and marbles, miniature clay pots, and cowrie shells. For this Kot Dijian period corrected Carbon 14 dates fall between circa 3155 and 2590 B.C.E.. As represented in its uppermost three strata, Kot Diji was an open settlement, with pottery of the Mature Harappan type and with copper and bronze occurring for the first time in these layers.[4]

Amri is in Lower Sind, 100 miles (170 km.) south of Moenjo-daro. In the lowest levels, dating probably around the beginning of the third millennium B.C.E., four phases of Amrian culture are distinguished and labeled as Period I A–D. Pottery is found in all four of these levels, and structural remains of mud brick in the upper three. In the two uppermost layers there are rectangular houses with mud floors and outdoor fireplaces, and also small enclosures without doors, which probably served as basements. The pottery was made on a wheel and covered with a thin slip which, after firing, turned to a buff or pink color. The decoration is in black and reddish brown and shows straight and wavy lines, loops, scales, chevrons, lozenges, and checkerboard patterns. In addition to geometrical patterns, at the end of the period, animal forms appear. Above Period I, Period II is intermediate, and Period III corresponds with Mature Harappan.[5]

MATURE HARAPPAN SITES

In the entire large area already described in which the Harappan culture prevailed, many of the sites are Early Harappan (such as Jalilpur), many have levels belonging to both Early and Mature Harappan (such as Kot Diji and Amri), and yet many more represent Mature Harappan and possibly also Late Harappan at the end of the period. Some of the Mature Harappan sites (such as Sutkagen Dor and Malvan) are farther afield than any of the Early Harappan sites, and show a considerable enlargement of the Harappan sphere in the Mature period. While Mature Harappan is essentially a full urban civilization, only half a dozen or so of the sites represent real cities or large towns—Moenjo-daro, Harappa, Chanhu-daro, Pathiani Kot, Judeirjo-daro, and Lothal, the first two being the largest—while the great majority of the sites represent villages.

Referring first to the farther out sites of the Mature Harappan period, some of these are especially interesting because they suggest widespread trade relationships. On the Makran Coast of the Arabian Sea there is, in addition to Sutkagen Dor, another site about 85 miles (140 km.) to the east called Sotka Koh. Although both of these sites are now inland (respectively 30 miles [48 km.] and 8 miles [13 km.] from the shore), there is reason to think that the coastal area has risen and that these two places were originally ports that also guarded the approaches to the only two practical routes from the sea to the interior. It is probable, therefore, that the sites were associated both with maritime trade which went by way of the Gulf of Oman and the Persian Gulf to Mesopotamia, and with overland trade to the West by way of such trading centers as Tepe Yahya in Iran (where an impression of an Indus Valley seal has been found). Likewise the city of Lothal (250 miles [400 km.] north of Bombay and now 100 miles [160 km.] inland from the Arabian Sea) may once have been a port at the head of the Gulf of Cambay, and the location suggests seafaring trade by the Harappans along that route as well.[6]

In Mesopotamia in archaeological levels chiefly of the time of Sargon of Akkad (2371–2316 B.C.E.) objects have been found, notably seals, which show evidence of Harappan contacts or influence. These confirm that the Mature Harappan culture was flourishing around the middle of the third millennium. Also, from the time of Sargon of Akkad, a cuneiform text states that ships from Meluhha, Magan, and Tilmun moored at the wharf of Agade. Tilmun (Dilmun) is with little doubt the island of Bahrain in the Persian Gulf, and Magan and Meluhha appear to be places farther east; thus, Meluhha was at this time very probably the Mesopotamian name for the region of the Harappan civilization.[7]

Referring now to the central sites of the Mature Harappan period, the largest known cities are Harappa and Moenjo-daro. Harappa was on the Ravi River (which is now distant from the site 6 miles [10 km.] to the north) in the Punjab, and Moenjo-daro was on the Indus River (which is now distant from the site nearly 3 miles [5 km.] to the east) in Sind, 400 miles (640 km.) southwest of Harappa. At their height, both cities were major metropolitan centers, each more than 3 miles (5 km.) in circuit, and each surrounded by additional small settlements as well. Each city had defensive walls of mud brick and buildings of fired brick. Public buildings occupied a citadel, streets were laid out on a gridiron plan, and there was an excellent main drainage system.

At Harappa modern archaeological excavation was preceded by exploitation of the ruins as a quarry for fired bricks for the roadbed of the Lahore-Multan link of the Indian Railroad; therefore, even what was left was found in great disarray.[8]

At Moenjo-daro a number of mounds represent the ruins of the ancient city, and in the reports of the excavations the main areas are referred to by abbreviations of the names of the principal archaeologists who were originally in charge of these areas respectively: SD for A. D. Siddiqi, HR for H. Hargreaves, VS for M. S. Vats, and DK for K. N. Dikshit.

The highest or citadel mound including the SD archaeological area is on the

1.1 General View of Moenjo-daro, with the Buddhist Stupa crowning the Citadel Mound

west, and is crowned by a ruined Buddhist *stupa* of the Kushan period, dating in the second century C.E. (Fig. 1.1). The somewhat lower HR, VS, and DK mounds lie to the east. Of these, the HR mound rises to a height of about 35 feet (11 m.) above the present level of the plain, and test borings at its base have shown occupation down to about 39 feet (12 m.) below the surface, so the total depth of occupation is here about 74 feet (23 m.). At the time of the test borings (1965), the level of the groundwater was 15 feet (4.5 m.) below the surface, so the lowest 24 feet (7 m.) of the occupation levels were inaccessible to any large-scale excavation. By 1973, due to the continuing effects of irrigation water from the Sukkur Barrage 50 miles (80 km.) upstream, the groundwater was reported as only 12 feet (3.5 m.) below the plain level in the winter and 5 feet (1.5 m.) in the summer, and even the excavated ruins were being threatened with destruction.[9]

On the citadel in the SD area is a great bath or tank, built of brick and waterproofed with bitumen (39 × 24 feet [12 × 7 m.] in area and 8 feet [2.4 m.] in depth), which is entered by steps at the north and south ends, and was presumably intended for ritual purposes (Fig. 1.2) like the later lotus pond (*pushkara*) so often adjoining an Indian temple. Adjacent to the bath to the northeast is a large, long building, surmised to have been the residence of a very high official, possibly of a high priest, or perhaps the residence of a whole college of priests. West of the bath, on the edge of the citadel mound, another large building is identified as a great granary, complete with a loading platform and intersecting ventilation channels, and it is supposed that this was a storage place for grain belonging to the government, thus being an important economic center. In the southern part of the citadel mound are also two large halls, one with pillars and one with rectangular piers, probably assembly halls of some sort, something like the later audience hall (*apadana*) of Persepolis. In all, the citadel may reflect some kind of combination of kingly and priestly rule.

In the lower city, explored in the mounds of the HR, VS, and DK areas, main

1.2   Great Bath on the Citadel (SD Area) at Moenjo-daro

streets (e.g., "First Street" in the HR and VS areas, 30 feet [9 m.] wide) run north and south and are crossed by other streets at right angles, forming blocks, each some 600 feet (180 m.) by 1,200 feet (360 m.) in size. Within these blocks, lanes, which are relatively narrow—5 feet (1.5 m.) to 10 feet (3 m.) wide—and sometimes crooked, perhaps to break the impact of the prevailing winds, gave access to the houses. A typical house was built around a courtyard, had stairs leading to a flat roof or an upper story, was provided with a bathroom and perhaps a well, and was connected with a drain to a covered drain channel in the street. In the lower city there were also shops and public buildings. An estimate of the population of the city is 40,000 inhabitants.

As now excavated, the walls of the houses and the linings of the wells often show successive rebuildings through many centuries, and thus stand high above the lowest level, the wells looking much like silos (Fig. 1.3). In the upper levels a great deterioration in the character of the brickwork is observable, evidently indicating increasingly difficult conditions of existence in the later phases of life in Moenjo-daro.

In the final decline of Moenjo-daro in the Late Harappan period, the excellent residential areas of the earlier period, and even the citadel itself, were covered with poor huts and the streets were gradually choked with refuse. At some other sites, notably at the city of Chanhu-daro (about 80 miles [130 km.] south of Moenjo-daro), in the Late Harappan period or after its end, there was occupation successively by two peoples of inferior cultures, who are known respectively by the names of two places in Sind where their pottery was first discovered, namely, Jhukar (6 miles [10 km.] west of Larkana) and Jhangar (about 43 miles [70 km.] northwest of Chanhu-daro). The pottery found at Jhukar and Jhangar is relatively coarse, and at Chanhu-daro the Jhukar people seem to have lived in some deserted Harappan houses and to have made huts of matting paved with broken brick, while the habitations of the Jhangar people have entirely disappeared and were probably

1.3 Excavated House Walls and Well, standing high above ground and exhibiting progressive deterioration of brickwork, at Moenjo-daro (DK Area)

simple huts of grass or reeds. The Jhukar people are thought to have occupied Chanhu-daro around 1700 B.C.E., and the Jhangar people came after them for a brief time.[10]

END OF HARAPPAN CIVILIZATION

As to the causes of the decline and fall of Moenjo-daro and of the Harappan civilization of which it was the greatest center, it does not appear that any radical change in the climate was a factor, for the ancient climate of the region seems to have been much the same as it is today.[11] In the ruins of Moenjo-daro, however, there are deposits of silty clay which must have come from flooding, and it is theorized that there may have been tectonic changes in the earth and a disastrous change in the course of the Indus which were destructive of the agricultural and economic bases of the life of the city.[12]

There is also some evidence of human violence in the end of the Harappan civilization. At Harappa there are traces of a final conflagration, and at Moenjo-daro in the uppermost levels were found a number of skeletons of persons who were not buried in any normal way, having apparently perished in some disaster. In the DK area two skeletons lay across the steps leading down to a well, two others were in the neighboring lane, and in another place nine skeletons including five children were crowded together. In the VS area six skeletons, one of a child, lay in a street between two houses. In the JR area one room contained fourteen skeletons of men, women, and a child, two having cuts on the head, and in a lane between high walls there were five skeletons under an accumulation of collapsed brick, ashes, and broken pottery.[13]

As to the significance of this evident violence at the end of the Harappan civilization, several theories have been expressed. One is that the economic and cultural decline of the cities in their later years simply laid them increasingly open to attack, and that the Moenjo-daro skeletons may attest to raids, possibly from Baluchistan, long the home of turbulent and warlike tribes.[14] Again it has been held that the Harappan civilization was non-Aryan (probably Dravidian) in character,[15] and that its final destruction was at the hands of invading Aryans, the people who in the *Rig Veda* call themselves Aryas (Sanskrit *arya*, noble) and their opponents Dasas (Sanskrit *dasa*, later meaning slave).[16] But the Harappan civilization has also been held to exhibit so many similarities with Vedic civilization that the former may be considered a part of the latter. In this view the Aryans and the Dravidians were closely related, and the references to the struggle between the *aryas* and the *dasas* only mean political civil wars. Along with the *dasas* the *Rig Veda* mentions the *panis*, who appear as malevolent, unbelievers, and stingy with money and possessions, so it could be that both of these groups constituted the rich and greedy in the cities, against whom the poor of the cities and of the far more numerous villages rose up in revolt, thereby bringing the Harappan civilization to an end in social commotion. In fact, as deduced from its monuments and artifacts, it is held by some that the religious outlook and philosophical conceptions of the Harappan civilization are so similar to those of the *Rig Veda* that the Harappan may well be seen as the expression of the presumably even older Vedic culture.[17]

HARAPPAN MONUMENTS AND ARTIFACTS

In spite of the present lack of sufficient evidence to resolve the foregoing questions conclusively, the monuments and artifacts of the Harappan civilization show not a little of the life and ideas of the people. Although the buildings on the citadel at Moenjo-daro (bath, granary, and halls) suggest religious, economic, and political functions, there are no structures that can properly be called actual palaces or temples. There is also a scarcity of offensive weapons, and the civilization would appear to have been essentially unwarlike. It has also been thought that Moenjo-daro was primarily a religious and ceremonial center, and such an inference can be supported not only by the supposition that the great bath on the most prominent place in the city was intended for ritual purposes, but also by the evident religious nature of many of the artifacts described below.[18]

Pottery

The pottery of Moenjo-daro and of the Mature Harappan civilization is relatively uniform throughout the area and the period. The ware is usually wheel-turned, coarser than the fine thin wares of Kot Diji and Amri (perhaps because of mass production for the increased population), and painted usually in black on a red slip. Many of the geometrical patterns of the Kot Diji and Amri pottery are continued, but there is also a preference now for floral and animal motifs rather than geometrical alone. Along with loops and wavy lines, scales, lozenges, chevrons, and the like, there are also to be seen the leaf of the pipal tree (*Ficus religiosa*) and the frond of the palm, the ram and the ibex, birds, snakes, and fishes. Rarely, too, there is a human figure. Many of the decorative patterns and animal figures, e.g., the chevron and the lozenge, the ram and the ibex, have parallels in Iran and Mesopotamia and probably reflect relationship with the West; on the other hand items such as the pipal tree leaf are distinctively Indian. On the whole, however, the Harappan painted pottery has its own individuality. At the same time many items which will be mentioned below as appearing on the seals are not found on the pottery (e.g., the rhinoceros, tiger, water buffalo, crocodile, and elephant), or appear only infrequently (e.g., the humped bull). Thus different traditions are evidently represented in the painted pottery and in the seals respectively, although both are contemporary and both are authentic expressions of the Mature Harappan civilization.[19]

Seals

The seals are the most distinctive artifacts of the Harappan civilization, and more than 1,200 have been found at Moenjo-daro alone. Unlike Mesopotamia, where the cylinder seal is characteristic, here only a few cylinders are found and most of the seals are stamp seals. The material is usually steatite; some of the seals are round, most are square or rectangular. Most have a small ring on the back, presumably so that they could be carried on a cord. On the front is usually a scene carved in intaglio, and at the top an inscription in pictographic script.

One supposition is that the seal was used, stamped on clay, as the equivalent of the signature of the owner and, if this is so, the inscription may often contain the name of the ower. Other uses may have been intended, however, and it is notable that many of the scenes are of an apparently ritual character.

The script itself has not as yet been positively deciphered, and still hides its secrets. It seems evident that it is not connected with Sumerian or any other script so far understood. One attempt at decipherment, assisted by computer technology, tends to show that the language of the Harappan civilization was Proto-Dravidian, but the result is not yet fully established.[20]

Religion

On the seals the most common representation is of a single animal standing before an object of some sort. The most frequent portrayal is of the sort seen in Fig. 1.4, in which a humpless bull *(Bos primigenius)* is seen in apparent profile with only

1.4 Moenjo-daro Seal Impression (replica), portraying a Humpless Bull

one horn visible, pointing forward. The figure is sometimes called a unicorn, a legendary creature ascribed to India by Ktesias and Aristotle, but it is probable that the animal actually has two horns which are shown superimposed on each other, and this manner of representation might even have given rise to the idea of the "unicorn" in India. In front of the animal is an object variously interpreted as a standard, a decorative manger, or an incense burner, and any of these interpretations at least agrees with the understanding of the bull as playing a role in a religious cult. Prominent also, although less frequently found, is the humped bull *Bos indicus)*, carefully depicted with hump, two horns, and neck folds (Fig. 1.5).

1.5 Moenjo-daro Seal Impression (large replica on the wall of the Moenjo-daro Museum), portraying a Humped Bull

This is the animal that is so familiar in India today as the Brahmany bull, and the fact that it is still held sacred may well reflect a position which it had already in the Harappan civilization. Other animals on the seals, which also stand before a standard, manger, or incense burner, are the rhinoceros, tiger, water buffalo, and elephant. On other seals there are only symbols, among which the swastika is prominent.

A remarkable seal found in a house in the lower city at Moenjo-daro shows what appears to be a deity, seated in a *yoga* position on a low platform (Fig. 1.6). He is portrayed with three faces, and wears a headdress consisting of a central part and two horns. His arms and chest are covered with bracelets and necklaces, and he wears a waistband and appears to be ithyphallic. On one side are a rhinoceros and a buffalo, on the other an elephant and a tiger with a human figure between them, the last possibly a pictograph for which there was no room in the inscription line at the top. Beneath the platform two animals, probably deer, look up. The main figure

10 | An Archaeological History of Religions of Indian Asia

1.6 Moenjo-daro Seal Impression (replica), portraying a Seated Deity

1.7 Squatting Monkey-like Figure, in the Moenjo-daro Museum

is usually regarded as a prototype of Śiva, because this god is later shown with three or more faces, is considered the typical ascetic, is the herdsman or lord of animals *(paśupati),* and has the trident *(triśula)* as a symbol.[21] Perhaps supporting this identification, many stones identical in form with the *linga,* the phallic emblem of Śiva, have also been found at Harappan sites, as well as ringstones which are like the *yoni* of the *śakti,* the spouse of Śiva.[22]

Rather than a proto-Śiva the figure has also been identified as that of a bull-man,[23] or has been thought to agree with the portrayal of Tvashtri (the fashioner), who appears in the *Rig Veda* as the creator of the universe and the one to whom all beasts belong. Tvashtri (who is also synonymous with the creator Prajapati) incarnates himself in his own son Viśvarupa (having all forms), and the latter has three heads which are mind, life, and matter, the effective elements of creation. In the *Rig Veda* (2.11.19; 10.8.7–9; 10.99.6) Viśvarupa is described as a *dasa* with three heads and six eyes, and is said to have been destroyed by Indra, or by Trita, a deity similar to Indra.[24] A figure similar to that on the seal in question also appears on two other seals, in one case seated alone, in the other with a kneeling person on either side, and each of these persons is overshadowed by a great cobra.[25]

Many figurines have also been found at the Harappan sites, and prominent among these are terra-cotta figures of women, usually represented as wearing a wide girdle, a necklace, and an elaborate fan-shaped headdress or hairdo. These figures are apparently of the mother goddess type, widely familiar throughout the ancient Middle East, and here they may well be the prototype representation of the *śakti,* the female creative energy, mentioned already in the Vedas by this name.[26] Yet another small figure is one which exhibits both human and monkey traits (Fig. 1.7), and is perhaps related to the later monkey god Hanuman. Still other figurines are of various animals, and of these many were doubtless children's toys.

Of large stone sculpture relatively little has been found, but there is one impressive example of such work in the upper part of the figure of a man, executed in steatite. He wears over the left shoulder a robe decorated in a trefoil pattern, has a beard and close-cut moustache, prominent nose, narrow eyes, and low forehead, and his hair is parted in the middle and bound with a hairband. The appearance is formal and austere, and he is usually thought to have been a priest or priest king; indeed the wearing of the robe with the right shoulder bare was the style of the later Buddhist monks.[27]

2

LITERATURE OF HINDUISM AND THE VEDIC AND EPIC PERIODS

LANGUAGES

In later India there are two main families of languages, the Dravidian and the Aryan. The Dravidian linguistic group is the smaller of the two, with about 100 million speakers, chiefly in the South, and it includes the Tamil, Telugu, Kanarese, and Malayali languages. It is believed that Dravidian is distantly related to the Ural-Altaic languages of Central Asia, and the line of connection would be down through Turkmenia, Afghanistan, and Baluchistan to the Indus Valley where, according to a theory noted in the preceding chapter the language was Proto-Dravidian.

The Aryan languages and the peoples who spoke them are also supposed to have come out of Central Asia and to have spread into Europe, the Middle East, and India, since unmistakable linguistic relationships connect all of these areas. In Europe, Greek and Latin were the classical Aryan (Indo-European) languages, and from these developed the Romance (e.g., Italian, Spanish, French), Teutonic (e.g., German, English), and Slavic (e.g., Russian, Polish) languages. In the Middle East the language of the Hittites had an Aryan base. Records of a king of Mitanni found at Boghazköy (circa 1400 B.C.E.) show the worship of Aryan gods (Mitra, Varuna, Indra, and the twin Nasatyas), who were also worshiped by the Persians prior to the reformation of Zarathustra, while the Medes and the Persians had an Aryan speech, and Xerxes (485–465 B.C.E.), for example, explicitly calls himself "the son of King Darius, the Achaemenian, a Persian, son of a Persian, an Aryan of Aryan descent."[1] So Gathic, Avestic, Old Persian, Middle Persian (e.g., Pahlavi, Parsi), and Modern Persian are all a part of the Indo-Iranian group.

As for the Indo-Aryan group, the classical language is Sanskrit, and it is found in an early form as Vedic—the language of the Vedas. Sanskrit also developed into various dialects which are collectively called Prakrits. Among these are Pali, also called Magadhi because it was spoken in Magadha, which is the language of the oldest Buddhist scriptures; and Ardha-Magadhi (half-Magadhi), which is the mixed language of the oldest scriptures of Jainism. From the Prakrits come the modern Hindi, Bengali, Panjabi, Kashmiri, Marathi, and other languages.

Although the Dravidian and the Aryan are separate linguistic families, there was interaction between them, and already in the Sanskrit of the *Rig Veda*—the oldest of the Vedas—there are unmistakable loanwords from the Dravidian. This can support the belief that Dravidian was the language of the Harappans, and that it exerted substratum influence on the Old Indo-Aryan already in the time of the Harappan civilization.[2] As for the modern Aryan languages in India, they, too, often contain words derived from local Dravidian dialects.

CLASSES OF LITERATURE

In the accepted order of their authority the main works of Hindu literature are divided into four classes: (1) *śruti*, or revealed literature, including the *Vedas, Brahmanas, Aranyakas,* and *Upanishads;* the last, namely, the Upanishads, are also called the Vedanta, i.e., the end or concluding portion of the Veda; (2) *smriti*, or traditional literature, including the Epics (the *Ramayana* and the *Mahabharata*, the latter containing the *Bhagavad Gita*), the *Laws of Manu*, the *Sutras*, and the *Sastras;* (3) *purana*, encyclopedic collections of ancient lore; and (4) *tantra*, mystical or esoteric books.[3]

Of all this literature the Vedas are the oldest part. Essentially the Vedas comprise materials which were recited or chanted by the priests in sacrificial rites. The works are organized in four collections *(samhitas)*. The *Rig Veda Samhita* consists of 1,028 hymns *(suktas)* addressed to the gods, arranged in ten books or "circles" *(mandalas)*, of which the tenth book appears to be later than the first nine. The *Yajur Veda* is a collection of ritual formulas. The *Sama Veda* is a collection of hymns, repeating many that are in the *Rig Veda*. The *Atharva Veda* is an assemblage of hymns and incantations.

Rishis

The Vedic texts often contain the names of those who composed them, and these personages are known by the title *rishi*. The Sanskrit word is of uncertain derivation, but refers to the person of inner spiritual vision *(dhi)*, the sage or seer who "sees" into and enters into contact with transcendent reality. The *rishi* may also be called a *muni*, which name designates a silent and contemplative one, and suggests that the vision of the truth arises out of such contemplation. It is the "knowledge" of the truth which is received which is *veda* (the word is akin to Greek oida, Latin *videre*, German *wissen*, and archaic English *wit*, meaning to know). The metrical verses of the Veda are also called by the term *mantra*, which literally denotes an instrument of thought and comes to mean any sacred text with power inherent in its very sounds. In fact the Rig-Vedic verses were articulated by the seers in a way intended to make the very sound of the words a symbol of their meaning. Often associated with the *rishi* in the *Rig Veda* is also the word *brahman*, usually translated as prayer (1.88.4), spell (2.2.7), or sacred word (2.5.3), but explainable more fully as the power immanent in the words and formulas of the Veda, these being the expression of the profound intuitions achieved by the mental energy and visionary insight of the holy seers.[4]

Of the ancient *rishis* seven *(saptarishi)* were the most famous, and are usually named as Kaśyapa, Atri, Vasishtha, Viśvamitra, Gotama, Jamadagni, and Bharadvaja. They were often identified with the seven stars of the Ursa Major (the Great Bear).

Vyasa

The Vedic texts were handed down in a long line of oral transmission, and eventually put in writing, but are still preferably recited from memory. The arrangement of the several collections was supposedly made by a great *rishi* known as Vyasa (arranger). This title is given to the compilers of various sacred works, and the *Bhagavata Purana* (2.7.36) says: "Appearing age after age . . . Vyasa divides the Tree of Knowledge into parts."[5] The famous Vyasa, who is supposed to have not only arranged the Vedas but also to have compiled the *Mahabharata,* was the son of the *rishi* Paraśara (author of several hymns in the *Rig Veda*) and a *dasa* princess named Satyavati. He was born on an island *(dvipa)* in the Yamuna River, not far from the modern town of Kalpi, and was also known as Krishna-Dvaipayana (dark-skinned island born) as well as Vedavyasa (Veda arranger). He is supposed to have lived in the closing years of the preceding world age (Dvaparayuga) and at the beginning of the present world age (Kaliyuga, traditionally beginning in 3101 B.C.E.).

The *Brahmanas* (priestly manuals) are commentaries on the Vedas; the *Aranyakas* (forest treatises for hermits and saints) are appended to the *Brahmanas;* and the *Upanishads* (sessions of pupils with their teacher) form the last part of the series and represent the philosophical climax of Vedic thought.

Even if the oldest Vedic manuscripts only date back to the fourteenth century C.E., these are no doubt copies of earlier written texts, while back of any written texts there was certainly a very long period of oral transmission. In modern study the composition of the *Rig Veda* is often placed circa 1500–1000 B.C.E., and such a date allows on the one hand for some connection between the incoming of the Vedic Aryans and the end of the Harappan civilization, and on the other hand for the priority of the Vedic Aryans to the introduction of iron in the area (not mentioned in the *Rig Veda*), which was probably circa 1050 B.C.E.[6] At least some portions of the Rigvedic materials must, however, be much earlier. On astronomical grounds some items have been shown to come from circa 4500 B.C.E. while on geological grounds some are even put back to circa 7000 B.C.E. In modern study the *Brahmanas, Aranyakas, Upanishads,* and *Mahabharata* are often placed in the period 1200–900 B.C.E., some of the *Sutras* and *Śastras,* the *Bhagavad Gita,* the *Ramayana* of the sage Valmiki, and the *Laws* of Manu are put in the period 900–300 B.C.E., while the *Puranas* are believed to have taken their present form in 300–400 C.E., and the *Tantras* in the next several centuries after that.[7]

Of this literature the *śruti* (e.g., *Vedas*) and the *smriti* (e.g., *Mahabharata, Ramayana*) will be drawn upon primarily in the present chapter and the next, the *purana* in the present chapter and in Chapter 4, and the *tantra* in Chapter 7.

While the Vedic texts are primarily communications of the truths envisioned by the ancient seers and, as such, have been the inspiration of much of Indian philosophy and religious experience for thousands of years, it is also in them that the earliest traditions may be sought as well about historical events in the Indian past, even if the history appears in a mythical or legendary guise. Likewise the Epics and the Puranas contain much which is mythical and legendary, yet also surely preserve many traditions of actual early history.

VEDIC GEOGRAPHY

Geographically the area chiefly in view in the *Rig Veda* is called *sapta sindhava*, the land of the seven rivers (8.24.27). A hymn addressed to the streams (*Rig Veda* 10.75) is dedicated primarily to the Indus and its tributaries, and therefore it is the northwestern part of the Indo-Pakistani subcontinent that is mainly in view, but to the east the Ganga (Ganges) and the Yamuna (Jumna) are also mentioned.

In Sanskrit the word *sindhu* means river (sometimes sea), and it is used in particular to designate the Indus River, and also the territory of the Lower Indus Valley, which is modern Sind. In the hymn just cited (*Rig Veda* 10.75.1) the Sindhu (Indus) is praised as surpassing in might all the streams that flow. In Iran the word in Avestan and Old Persian corresponding to the Sanskrit *sindhu* was *hindu*, and the Greeks, omitting the *h*, called the river o 'Ivdós, the country n 'Ivdikń, and the people oı 'Ivdoí—hence Indus, India, and Indians. Thus Strabo (15.1.1–13) uses these names for India and the Indus, describes India as "the first and largest country that lies out towards the East," and identifies the Indus as the boundary between India and Ariana. Finally, in English from the same etymological background the word Hindu designates a person of India who adheres to the system of religion and social practice which is most widely and from very ancient times established in the land, a religion and its concomitant practices which are also most simply (from the outside) designated as Hinduism, although the adherents thereof would hardly use the term and would, as mentioned above in the preface, preferably use such a term as *dharma* as descriptive of their whole way of life.

Along with the Indus River, its several main tributaries are also mentioned in the hymn to the rivers (10.75) and elsewhere in the *Rig Veda*, namely, the Kubha or modern Kabul (10.75.6) which comes in from the west after receiving its own tributary the Suvastu or Swat (8.19.37), and the "five waters" of the modern Punjab which come in from the east, the Vitasta or Jhelum, Asikni or Chenab, Parushni or Ravi, Vipas or Beas, and Sutudri or Sutlej (3.33.1; 10.75.5). Together the Indus, Kabul, and five Punjab streams could be considered those of the seven-rivers land (*sapta sindhava*). The seven-reckoning was apparently variable, however, for in one verse of the hymn (10.75.5) there is an enumeration which proceeds from the east to the west and lists Ganga, Yamuna, Sarasvati, Sutudri, Parushni, Marudvrdha with the Asikni and the Vitasta, and Arjikiya with the Sushoma, making seven chief streams and three tributaries. The Arjikiya and the Sushoma may be the present Haro and Sohan which now flow into the Indus northwest of the Jhelum but may have had different courses previously. The Marudvrdha may be the Maruwardwan which flows into the Chenab from the west—at any rate, it was evidently associated in some way with the Chenab and the Jhelum. The Sarasvati, and its goddess, are frequently and highly praised (e.g., 6.61). The Sarasvati flowed from the mountains to the sea (7.95.2), and was associated with the Apaya and the Drishadvati (3.23.4). Although no longer certainly identifiable, these streams were evidently to the east of the Indus system, and now lose themselves in the Great Indian Desert of Rajasthan. The Ganga and the Yamuna are, of course, the Ganges and the Jumna, flowing yet farther to the east and increasingly important in later Indian history.[8]

In the *Laws of Manu* (2.17–22)[9] the Sarasvati is described as disappearing at a place called Vinaśana, and the country between the Sarasvati and the Drishadvati is named Brahmavarta (the land of Brahma). The region between the Ganga and the Yamuna (now called the Doab, two rivers), from the neighborhood of Delhi as far as Mathura, is Kurukshetra (the plain of the Kurus, the locale of the Great Battle between the Kurus and the Pandavas in the *Mahabharata*). The region from the Himalaya in the north to the Vindhya mountains in the south, and from Vinaśana in the west to Prayaga in the east, is Madhyadeśa (the middle country). The region between the same mountain ranges and the eastern and western oceans is Aryavarta (the land of the Aryans).[10]

VEDIC ARYANS

Culturally the *Rig Veda* provides a picture of the people who call themselves *arya* (noble) as a pastoral people, who have horses, sheep, goats, and cattle, and who cultivate barley and wheat, and later rice. They make tools and weapons of a metal which is described as red and must be copper or bronze, while black metal, which must be iron, is not yet mentioned in the *Rig Veda* but only in the *Yajur* and *Atharva Vedas,* i.e., at a later time.

Politically the *aryas* are organized in tribes, each ruled by a chief or king. They are involved in conflicts with other tribes who are *anarya*, i.e., non-*arya*, which can mean ethnically different or perhaps only different in culture and customs. These opponents are named by various terms which at least later have a derogatory connotation: *dasa* (which later means slave), *dasyu* (which later means brigand), *danava* (titan), *daitya* (devil), *asura* (demigod or demon), *rakshasa* (demon or ogre); and by what have been thought to be their totemic designations: *vanara* (monkey), *naga* (serpent), and *matsya* (fish). The opponents are also described as black *(krishna),* in color *(varna,* which later means caste), godless *(adevayu),* and worshipers of the phallus *(sisna,* the linga). One other term is *anasya,* usually taken to mean flat-nosed, but possibly meaning mouthless; i.e., devoid of good speech. Occasionally named as opponents are the *panis*, and these people appear as wealthy, covetous, and treacherous. The *panis* also appear, however, in mythical form as demons who would hold back the light of dawn and are only overcome by the Vedic sacrifice and chant which evoke the power of *brahman*.[11]

Religiously many hymns of the *Rig Veda* are addressed to many deities worshiped by the Aryans, and among these at least several are recognizably the same as ones worshiped in Iran prior to the reformation of Zarathustra. These include Mitra, Varuna, Indra, and the twin Nasatyas (mentioned above as known in the West in the kingdom of Mitanni). Also the worship of fire (called Agni) is prominent here in India as well as in Iran; and in both regions a sacred drink was used, called *soma (haoma* in Iran).

On the other hand there is differentiation too. In the oldest parts of the *Rig Veda* the term *asura* is applied in the sense of lord or god to several of the chief deities—to Indra, Agni, and Varuna—and is the equivalent of *ahura* in Iran, where Ahura Mazda becomes the great and only god of Zarathustra. But in India *asura* comes to have the opposite meaning, and to signify a demigod or even an enemy of the gods, an antigod *(a-sura* as opposed to a god, *sura).* Contrariwise, in the *Rig Veda* the term *deva* (from the root *div,* meaning to shine, cf. Latin *deus)* designates the major deities, but in Zoroastrian Iran the corresponding term (also *daiva)* applies to the evil beings who oppose Ahura Mazda, and the *deva* is a demon.

In the *Rig Veda,* therefore, the *devas* are found fighting on the side of the *aryas,* while the enemies are the *anarya* people, the *asuras, dasas, dasyus, panis, rakshasas,* and others. This intermingling of Aryans and their deities on the one side, and of supposedly inferior peoples and demons on the other side, makes it possible to suppose that the mythology actually incorporates reminiscences of actual struggles of some of the Aryan tribes against other inhabitants of India, whether the latter were another branch of the Aryans or were a different people, presumably the Dravidians. If, however, the enemies who are so described were people of the Harappan civilization they were surely of higher culture than the derogatory terms here applied to them would suggest.

Of the deities in the *Rig Veda* the greatest and most often invoked god is Indra, who appears as a warrior charioteer, championing the cause of the Vedic Aryans and brandishing his thunderbolt against their enemies. It is possible, therefore, to think of Indra as a personification of these Aryan people or even to suppose that he was originally an Aryan chieftain or that Indra was the title of a series of such chieftains. At any rate Indra is many times invited to drink the sacred *soma*, and to lead his Aryan followers to victory. His names are Purandara, the destroyer of cities, and Vritra-han, the slayer of Vritra, the latter being an especially prominent demon leader of the *asuras*. Thus a prayer in the *Rig Veda* (1.51.8–9) calls upon Indra to "distinguish between the *aryas* and the *dasyus;* by punishment make the disobedient subject to the performers of sacrifice! In all your exploits I rejoice at the *soma* feast. Indra is he who makes the disobedient subject to the obedient, who with his adherents casts down the opponents." In later Hinduism Indra is also known as Devendra (Indra the deity), Mahendra (great Indra), Śakra (mighty), Vajrapani (thunderbolt holder); and he is characteristically pictured as riding upon his cloud elephant, Airavata, and brandishing the thunderbolt *(vajra)* as his mighty weapon.

MOUNT MERU

In view of this apparent intermingling of the human and the divine actors in the mythology, it is possible to look also in the Vedic, Epic, and Puranic traditions for other reminiscences of early Indian history. As to the earlier homeland of the Aryans, linguistic considerations have already been mentioned as pointing to Central Asia, and this appears to be confirmed and made more precise in the Vedic-Puranic tradition. The *Vayu Purana,* perhaps the earliest of the Puranas, describes a great mountain called Meru, locates the various gods on its various peaks, and concludes: "This is the abode of the holy gods. . . . All the four Vedas also place the Devaloka on this mountain" (24.86).[12] The Sanskrit *devaloka* is literally the place *(loka)* of the gods *(devas),* and it is not unlikely that in the course of a long time the Aryans would have come to look back upon their earlier homeland as the very abode of the deities.

As for the location of the mountain named Meru, in the Puranas generally the world is divided into seven concentric rings of island continents *(dvipa,* land with water on both sides) of which the central one is Jambudvipa, and it is in the center of Jambudvipa that Mount Meru stands. The mountain rises also, however, into the heavens (the area of which is called Ilavrita (divine enclosure), and is at the center of the whole universe, so that the peak is the "circle" of all the astronomical bodies and the sun goes about its summit *(Vayu Purana* 52.98–99). On the mountain grows a very large rose-apple tree *(jambu),* and this overshadows the continent below, hence the name Jambudvipa.

From the focal point of Mount Meru four great rivers flow in the four directions and may be identified as follows: the Vakshu (Oxus or Amu Darya) flows to the west; the Śita (Yarkand-Tarim) flows to the east; the Bhadrasoma (Syr Darya) flows to the north; and the Alakananda (Ganges) flows to the south.

Likewise there are four regions *(varshas)* of Jambudvipa on the four sides of Mount Meru (and later six or nine are enumerated), and their approximate areas in terms of modern geography are: on the west, Ketumala-varsha, Bactria and associated territories, south of the Oxus; on the east, Bhadraśva-varsha, Xinjiang south of the Yarkand, and northern China; on the north, Uttarakuru-varsha, from the Oxus to the Arctic, including Samarkand, Bukhara, and Siberia; and on the south, Bharata-varsha, India. In another picture the earth is a lotus with Mount Meru as its central part, and the four countries, Ketumala, Bhadraśva, Uttarakuru, and Bharata, extend outward like its petals (*Vishnu Purana* 2.2.)[13]

Geographically the most central spot toward which these indications would seem to point is the Pamirs, the plateau and mountains where the Himalaya, Karakorum, and Hindu Kush ranges converge, a region now largely in the Badakhshan area and the Tadzhik S.S.R. of Central Asia, 11,000 feet (3,355 m.) to 25,000 feet (7,620 m.) high, called by the Iranians Bam-i-Dunia (roof of the world). Etymologically the name Pamir itself may be derived from the Persian *pae-meer* and Sanskrit *meru-pada,* meaning at the "foot of Meru."[14]

This identification of Mount Meru with the region of the Pamirs is further supported in the record of the Chinese Buddhist pilgrim Xuan Zang (629–645 C.E.) who passed this way on his return journey from India to China (probably in the summer of 642 C.E.). He tells of advancing along a dangerous and precipitous road and coming to the valley of Po-mi-lo, i.e., the Pamir Valley. In the middle of this valley, says Xuan Zang, is a great Naga lake *(nagahrada),* which may be identified with the Sarik-kul, the Lake of the Yellow Valley, also known as Kul-i-Pamir-kulan, the Lake of the Great Pamir (latitude 37°27' north, longitude 73°40' east, elevation 13,950 feet (4,250 m.). This lake is the source of the Oxus River (Sanskrit Vakshu, Chinese Fo-tsu) which flows to the west, while the Yarkand River (Sanskrit Sita, Chinese Si-to) passes the lake to the east, and Xuan Zang mentions both rivers as on the two sides of the lake respectively. Of this lake in the middle of the Pamir Valley Xuan Zang also says that it is in the midst of the great Tsung-ling mountains, and that it is "the central point of Jambudvipa."[15]

Interestingly enough, to the north of the Pamirs there is a region bounded on the north by Lake Balkhash, which is still called "the land of the seven streams" (in Russian, Semiretchenski-krai, referring to the Lepsa, Baskan, Aksu, Sarkau, Biyen, Kartal, and Koksu rivers, all of which flow into the lake), and it is possible that the Aryans brought with them from this region the name which they applied to the land to which they came in northwest India, which seemed to them similar in the number of its rivers *(sapta sindhava,* the land of seven rivers).[16]

PERIODS OF TIME

As to early history reflected in the Indian tradition, in the Puranas events are set within the framework of various divisions of time called by various terms, *yuga, mahayuga, kalpa,* and *manvantara.* While there are some differences of interpretation in the coordination of the several designations, suggesting that they may have come originally from separate chronological systems, they are most usually explained in the following way *(Vishnu Purana* 1.3; 3.1–2).[17]

Yugas

A *yuga* is a world age, i.e., an age of humankind in Bharata-varsha. Of these ages there are four, each one-fourth shorter, darker, and less good than the preceding. The durations of these ages are stated in "divine" years or years of celestial time, which are converted into solar years or years of human time by multiplying them by 360, on the basis that a year of human time equals one day and one night of the gods. Also each *yuga* is preceded by a dawn *(sandhya)* and followed by a dusk *(sandhyansa)*, each of which has as many hundred years as there are thousands in the *yuga*. The resultant time scheme is shown in Table 2.1.

TABLE 2.1.
THE AGES OF THE WORLD

Ages of the World	Years of Celestial Time	Years of Human Time
Kritayuga	4,000	
dawn	400	
dusk	400	
	4,800	1,728,000
Tretayuga	3,000	
dawn	300	
dusk	300	
	3,600	1,296,000
Dvaparayuga	2,000	
dawn	200	
dusk	200	
	2,400	864,000
Kaliyuga	1,000	
dawn	100	
dusk	100	
	1,200	432,000
Total	12,000	4,320,000

The total of the four ages (4,320,000 years, equaling two and one-half equinoctial precessions), constitutes a *mahayuga* (great *yuga*). At the end of each *mahayuga* the world is destroyed in flood and fire.

Kalpas

One thousand *mahayugas* make one *ardha-kalpa* (half-*kalpa*), which is a "day" of Brahma. At the end of this "day" the material universe and the lesser gods are dissolved, and Brahma sleeps during his "night," which is another half-*kalpa*, then awakens to renew the cycle of the ages *(yugas)* in his next "day." Together the "day" and the "night" constitute a full Day of Brahma, and this full Day is a full *kalpa* or an aeon. In a lifetime measured in such Days, Brahma lives for 100 years (or 864,000 million years in human time), then himself perishes in a universal cataclysm. After a further period, itself as long as the preceding lifetime of Brahma, another Brahma is born and the cycle begins again. In terms of this scheme, the present Brahma is now in his fifty-first year.

Manvantaras

In a thousand great ages, i.e., in a "day" of Brahma, there are some fourteen *manvantaras*. A *manvantara* is a Manu-period *(Manu-antara)*, i.e., a period presided over by a Manu (Sanskrit *manu,* man), who is a patriarch, a progenitor of humankind, a ruler of the earth, and a lawgiver. The duration of the *manvantaras* is variously given, but at any rate from the point of view of the *Vishnu Purana* the first six *manus* who are named belong to the past, the seventh is the *manu* of the present *manu*-period, and seven more are yet to come.

Each *manu* is distinguished by a particular surname, and of the first seven the *Vishnu Purana* gives the names as follows: "The first Manu was Svayambhuva (i.e., the son of Svayambhu, the 'self-existent' Brahma), then came Svarochisha, then Auttami, then Tamasa, then Raivata, then Cakshusha: these six Manus have passed away. The Manu who presides over the seventh Manvantara, which is the present period, is Vaivasvata (from Vivasvat, the 'resplendent' or 'brilliant' sun god Surya) the son of the sun."

Manu Vaivasvata. Manu Vaivasvata, also known as Satyavarta, was the sole survivor of a great flood which immediately preceded the ensuing *manu*-period, over which he continues to rule. As the story is related in the *Satapatha Brahmana* (1.8.1–6) and the *Mahabharata* (3.185),[18] there was an occasion when Manu Vaivasvata was instrumental in saving the life of a small fish. The fish, in turn, advised Manu to prepare a ship in view of a flood which was to come, and promised to return to help him at that time. In the flood the towing line of Manu's ship was tied to the horn of the fish, which was then grown large (and was actually Vishnu in his Matsya or fish incarnation), and the fish pulled the ship to the highest peak of the Himalaya. This mountain was thereafter named "Manu's descent" *(manoravasarpanam)* and the "mooring" *(naubandhana).* "The flood then swept away all these creatures, and Manu alone remained there."

After the flood, Manu Vaivasvata became the progenitor of the human race and the ancestor of the ruling families of ancient India. Accordingly the *Rig Veda* calls him "father" and "our father" (e.g., 1.80.16; 2.33.13), and represents him as the first of men and the first of sacrificers (10.63.7). It is also stated that Indra, after overcoming the *dasyus,* gave territory to Manu (2.20.7). "Indra, the slayer of Vritra and the destroyer of cities, overthrew the army of the black *dasyus.* He created land and water for Manu." Similarly in another statement (6.21.11) Agni gives Manu rule over the *dasas.* So if historical circumstances are reflected in the reported conquest of the *dasas* by Indra and Agni, the same may be true of these references to the subsequent rule of Manu, and he may appear as the first Aryan king of India as well as the ancestor of the Indo-Aryans.

The genealogies of the dynasties descended from Manu Vaivasvata are preserved in the Epics and the Puranas, and are arranged in two main lines of descent, the Solar dynasty coming down from Manu's son Ikshvaku, and the Lunar dynasty coming down from Manu's daughter Ila (e.g., *Vishnu Purana* 4.1ff.).[19]

In the texts the dynastic families are called by the term *vamśa,* and the different aggregates of people or tribes by the terms *jana* (an ethnic tribe), *janapada* (a tribe settled in a particular territory, a territorial state, or community), and *mahajanapada* (a larger state or kingdom, a great community). In the Puranas the *janapadas* are most often listed in seven major divisions, Madhyadeśa (central region), Udichya or Uttarapatha (northern region), Prachya (eastern region), Dakshinapatha (southern region), Aparanta (western region), Vindhyavasins (Vindhya mountain region), and Parvataśrayins (Himalayan region).[20]

Ikshvaku and Ila. In all, as the details of the tradition are set forth in the Puranas, Manu Vaivasvata was the father of nine sons, and Ikshvaku was the first of these. Since Manu was himself the son of Vivasvat (Surya, the sun), Ikshvaku was the grandson of the sun, and as such he was the founder of the Solar dynasty *(Surya vamśa)*, while his descendants were also called the *manavas* (sons of Manu).

Even before the birth of the nine sons, Manu was the father of a daughter named Ila, but in the course of events she was changed into a man named Sudyumna, was changed back into a woman, and again into the man. As a woman Ila married Budha, who was the son of the moon god named Candra or Soma. The son of Ila and Budha was Pururavas Aila (the son of Ila), so he was the grandson of the moon, and as such he was the founder of the Lunar dynasty *(Candra vamśa* or *Soma vamśa)*, also known as the Aila dynasty *(Aila vamśa)*.

In all, the Solar race, which began with Ikshvaku, had three kingdoms, those of Kośala with Ayodhya as its capital, of Videha with Mithila as its capital, and of Vajji with Vaiśali as its capital. The line which was centered at Ayodhya was the greatest, and was especially known as the Solar dynasty. The Lunar race, which began with Pururavas Aila, soon branched out into the families of the Pauravas, Yadavas, Turvaśus, Druhyus, and Anavas. Of these the Paurava line was the greatest, and its main branch, which reigned at Hastinapura, constituted the kingdom of Kuru, and was especially known as the Lunar dynasty.

SOLAR DYNASTY

Kośala and Ayodhya

Ayodhya, capital of Ikshvaku and his successors in the main Solar line in the kingdom of Kośala, was supposedly founded by Manu Vaivasvata himself. The city was situated on the south bank of the Śarayu (now the Ghaghara River), about 4 miles (6 km.) from modern Faizabad, in the present state of Uttar Pradesh, and has given its name to the modern district of Oudh. In terms of the major groupings of the *janapadas,* the kingdom of Kośala was in Madhyadeśa (the middle country). More specifically, as centered at Ayodhya, this was the kingdom of North Kośala, in distinction from South Kośala, which southern kingdom had its capital at Kuśasthali in Vindhyavasins.

In the *Mahabharata* and the *Ramayana* there are glowing descriptions of Ayodhya and other towns of the Epic period, but at the same time plain statement of the social stratification which prevailed. In summary from these sources Ayodhya is pictured thus:

> Of unequalled splendor is the sacred city, embellished with marble palaces, whose domes resemble the tops of mountains, adorned with banners and high arched porticoes, beautified with stone temples and sacred tanks, graced with charming buildings and spacious gardens. It is guarded by brave heroes who ride on elephants, chariots, and horses. The halls are filled with dancing girls and musicians who intoxicate the air with their notes. The bazaars are crowded with merchants from all corners of the kingdom. The city is laid out in several quarters, the large houses with gardens for the three castes, small squalid huts for the Śudras in keeping with their servile birth, while outside the town, like the dens of unclean animals, are the dwellings of the outcastes.
>
> The precious city is sanctified by the presence of thousands of Brahmans and sages, in power equal to the gods, whom it is an honor to feed with rice, whose presence is perfumed with natural incense, and around whose sacred necks are garlands of scented flowers. Thus the holy city of Kośala echoes to the twang of the bow, the thunder of war-chariots, the music of the flute, tabor, and harp, and the songs of the moon-bosomed dancers, while from the *agraharas*

(the quarters reserved for the Brahmans) proceed the sounds of the holy ones reading and teaching the Vedas, Śastras, logic, poetry, stories, rules for sacrifice, precepts for kings, and the holy science of *yoga* which makes them immortal.[21]

Videha and Mithila

The oldest son and successor of Ikshvaku in rule at Ayodhya was Vikukshi, while the second son was Nimi. Nimi founded a separate dynasty in which he was succeeded by a king known variously as Mithi, Videha, and Janaka. From the latter king his capital was called Mithila and his kingdom and ensuing dynasty were called Videha. The territory of Videha was in what is now North Bihar and in the adjacent southern part of the present Nepal. The capital city of Mithila is identified with the present Janakpur, a small town within the Nepal border. Some twenty generations after the first Janaka there ruled at Mithila another Janaka—Siradhvaja Janaka—who was a famous philosopher-king and the father of Sita the heroine of the *Ramayana*. In the *Mahabharata* (3.198.6-9) Mithila is described as a "lovely town . . . defended by gates and watch towers . . . adorned with houses and walls . . . surrounded by many palaces, filled with many wares, with the main streets well laid out, crowded with many horses, chariots, elephants, and wagons, teeming with happy, well-fed people, and bristling with constant festivals."[22]

After Kośala and Videha the third of the Solar dynasty kingdoms was that of Vajji, with its capital at Vaiśali. The founder of this city and the head of this dynasty was Veśali, who was said to be either another son of Ikshvaku (*Ramayana* 1.47.11-12) or a descendant of Nabhaga, who was one of the nine sons of Manu Vaivasvata and a brother of Ikshvaku (*Vishnu Purana* 4.1). The site of the city of Vaiśali is identified with the present village of Besarh, 20 miles (35 km.) north of Hajipur in the Muzaffarpur district of North Bihar, where there are numerous ancient ruins. The adjacent village of Vasukunda is believed to be the ancient Kundagrama, the suburb of Vaiśali which was the place of birth of Vardhamana Mahavira, the twenty-fourth Jaina *tirthankara*.

Returning to Ayodhya and Ikshvaku's first son Vikukshi, Vikukshi in turn had a son whose name was Puranjaya (city conqueror). In a violent war which broke out in the Tretayuga or second age of the world between the *devas* and the *asuras*, Puranjaya fought for the gods and, when Indra assumed the form of a bull and carried Puranjaya into battle on his hump, Puranjaya became also known as Kakutstha or "hump stationed" (*Vishnu Purana* 4.2).

Sixth in descent from Puranjaya was Śravasta, and he founded the city of Śravasti, which became the most important later capital of the kingdom of Kośala. The grandson of Śravasta was Kuvalaśva and his grandson in turn was Haryaśva. Haryaśva had five (*panca*) sons after whom the country of Pancala in the Punjab was named.

Later descendants of Puranjaya, ruling at Ayodhya, include Mandhatri, Harischandra, Sagara, Raghu, and Daśaratha, and Daśaratha was the father of Rama, the hero of the *Ramayana* and as such the most famous of the Solar kings.

Ramayana

In the *Ramayana* we learn that at Mithila King Janaka had promised his lovely daughter Sita to the man who could lift and string a powerful bow of Śiva which belonged to the king, and this Rama accomplished and thus received Sita as his wife. At Ayodhya Daśaratha, growing old, appointed Rama, as his oldest son and the offspring of his chief queen Kausalya, to be his successor. A second wife Kaikeyi, however, seeking the place for her own son Bharata (not Bharata Dauhshanti, who will be named below), managed to have Rama banished from Ayodhya for fourteen years. Upon this occurrence Daśaratha died of grief, and Bharata took the throne, but honorably ruled only in the name of Rama.

In the long exile Rama was accompanied by Sita and also by his half-brother Lakshmana, son of Daśaratha and the king's third wife Sumitra, whose other son was Śatrughna. In the course of their wandering the exiles came more than once to the hermitage of the sage Valmiki at Citrakuta, on the river Piśuni (or Mandakini) in the modern district of Banda in Bundelkhand, and later when Sita was banished by the suspicious Rama she came back to this place and there gave birth to her two sons, Lava and Kuśa. Upon the advice of the *rishi* Narada, Valmiki became a poet and it was he who, learning from Rama and Sita of their many adventures, wrote the story of these in the *Ramayana*.

In the vicinity of Citrakuta, Rama and Sita also visited the forest hermitage of Atri, author of many Vedic hymns, and his wife Anasuya, celebrated for her loyalty to her husband, and Anasuya treated Sita with great kindness and gave her an ointment to keep her beautiful forever.

Eventually the exiles settled in the forest of Dandaka near the source of the Godavari River, and from there Sita was abducted by the *rakshasa* king Ravana and carried off to his realm on the island of Lanka. In the ensuing attempt to recover Sita, Rama and Lakshmana were assisted by the Vanara or monkey people *(vanara,* an animal belonging to the *vana* or forest, specifically the monkey). The Vanara king was Sugriva and his army was commanded by the famous monkey chieftain Hanuman. A Vanara artisan named Nala built a bridge of stepping stones across the strait to Lanka *(Rama-setu,* Rama's bridge, a series of small islands now also known as Adam's Bridge), and made invasion of the island possible. In a terrific battle Ravana was slain and Sita was brought back, having in fact been treated chivalrously by Ravana throughout her ordeal.

Rama and Sita then returned to Ayodhya, and Rama ascended the throne that was rightfully his. Under his just rule there ensued an age of peace and prosperity. This was marred, however, by Rama's unjustified suspicion of Sita, and her second banishment, a suspicion of Rama which was only overcome shortly before the death of Sita, a death to which she went saying:

> If unstained in thought and action I have lived from day of birth,
> Spare a daughter's shame and anguish and receive her, Mother Earth!
>
> If in duty and devotion I have labored undefiled,
> Mother Earth! who bore this woman, once again receive thy child!
>
> If in truth unto my husband I have proved a faithful wife,
> Mother Earth! relieve thy Sita from the burden of this life![23]

So the *Ramayana* presents its picture of the ideal man whose life involves trial and endurance, and of the ideal woman whose life manifests devotion and faithfulness to the end.

In the conclusion of the epic and also in the Puranic tradition *(Vishnu Purana* 4.4)[24] we are told that Rama and his brothers each had two sons, and that the sons were the founders and rulers of great cities and kingdoms. The sons of Rama were Kuśa and Lava: Kuśa reigned at Kusavati (Kuśasthali) at the foot of the Vindhya mountains in South Kośala; Lava ruled at Śravasti in North Kośala. The sons of Lakshmana were Angada and Candraketu: both ruled kingdoms near the Himalaya. The sons of Bharata were Taksha and Pushkara: Bharata himself conquered the country of the Gandharas, and Taksha founded Takshaśila (Taxila) east of the Indus, while Pushkara founded Pushkaravati (Pushkalavati) west of the Indus. The sons of Śatrughna were Subahu and Surasena: Śatrughna himself took possession of the city of Mathura (on the right bank of the Yamuna River, 50 miles [80 km.] southeast of Delhi), which had belonged to Lavana, a nephew of Ravana, and both Subahu and Surasena reigned at Mathura.

LUNAR DYNASTY

The place of rule of Pururavas Aila, with whom the Lunar dynasty began, was at Pratishthana. This city (not to be confused with the other Pratishthana, the modern Paithan, on the north bank of the Godavari River in the Aurangabad district of Maharashtra) was on the left bank of the Ganges opposite modern Allahabad (which is at the confluence of the Ganges and Yamuna and supposedly of the subterranean Sarasvati was well). At Pratishthana Pururavas was followed in succession by his son, grandson, and great-grandson, who were named Ayu, Nahusha, and Yayati.

In turn, Yayati and his wife Devayani were the parents of Yadu and Turvaśu, and Yayati and his wife's handmaiden Śarmishtha were the parents of Druhyu, Anu, and Puru. These five children were the ancestors respectively of the five main branches of the Lunar family, namely, the Yadavas, Turvaśus, Druhyus, Anavas, and Pauravas, and through these of a further proliferation of descendants. Thus Yadu was the ancestor not only of the Yadava line, but also the Haihaya, Vidarbha, Bhoja, Cedi (in part), Avanti, Andhaka and Vrishni families. Turvaśu was the founder of the Turvaśus, and Druhyu of the Druhyus of Gandhara. Anu was the ancestor of the Anava line, and also of the Uśinara, Yaudheya, Ambashtha, Sauvira, Kekeya, and Madra families of northwest India, and of the Anga, Vanga, Kalinga, Pundra, and Suhma families of eastern India. Puru was the progenitor of the Paurava line, and also of the Bharata, Pancala, Kaurava, Pandava, and Cedi (in part) families. Of these several lines of the Lunar race the most important was that of the Pauravas. They seem to have inherited the main kingdom of Yayati, and almost the whole of Madhyadeśa, except for Kośala, came into their possession. The Bharatas of the great epic, the *Mahabharata,* belong to this line.

Yadava Line

In the Yadava line *(Matsya Purana* 45–46)[25] in the Andhaka family there was a certain Ahuka, and he was the father of two sons named Ugrasena and Devaka, and of seven daughters. In the time now in question Ugrasena was king at Mathura, and was himself the father of a son named Kamsa, while Devaka was the father of a daughter named Devaki. In the Vrishni family of the Yadava line there was a certain Śura, and he was the father of many children, among them most importantly two sons Vasudeva and Samudravijaya, and two daughters Kunti and Śrutadeva. Vasudeva married many wives, and had many children. Among the wives were all seven daughters of Ahuka, and of these the youngest, named Rohini, became the mother of Balarama. Another wife of Vasudeva was Devaki, daughter of Devaka, and she became the mother of the famous Krishna. Thus Krishna was the younger half-brother of Balarama *(Vishnu Purana* 4.14–15).[26]

In his old age Ugrasena was dethroned and his place usurped by his son Kamsa (said to have actually been the offspring of a demon who impersonated Ugrasena), while the usurper also attempted to kill all of the sons of Devaki because of a prophet's warning that he himself would be slain by one of those sons. Under this threat Vasudeva secretly carried the child Krishna across the Yamuna and entrusted him to the care of Yaśoda, wife of the cowherd Nanda, and this couple became the foster-parents of Krishna. When Kamsa learned of the escape of Krishna he ordered a general massacre of little children, and Nanda and Yaśoda fled with Krishna to the village of Gokula (7 miles [11 km.] southeast of Mathura, on the left bank of the Yamuna). From Gokula Krishna removed to Brindaban (Vrindavana, herd-forest, on the right bank of the Yamuna, 6 miles [10 km.] north of Mathura) in the Braj country, where he spent his youth in the company of cowherds (*gopas*) and milkmaids (*gopis*). The *gopis* were irresistibly attracted to Krishna by his playing of his wonderful flute, and he was amorously associated with many of them, most of all with his favorite Radha, wife of the cowherd Ayanaghosha, from whom Krishna took Radha for himself.

Not far from Brindaban was a hill called Govardhana (cow prosperity, because it was made of cowdung; now the low narrow range on which is the town of Gobardhan, 16 miles (26 km.) west of Mathura). Because the god Indra was his rival, Krishna taught the cowherds to pay homage to this hill instead of to Indra. Indra, infuriated, sent a flood to wash away the hill and destroy the people of Braj, but Krishna lifted up the hill and held it on his finger for seven days and nights to provide a shelter for his friends, until Indra desisted and went away.

Reflecting these experiences, among the names by which Krishna is known are Gopala (cowherd), Venugopala (cowherd with the *venu* or flute), Madanagopala (passionate cowherd), Rajagopala (king of cowherds), Govardhanadhara (upholder of the hill Govardhana), and Govinda (cow keeper).

Finally Krishna was able to slay Kamsa, and Ugrasena was reinstated on the throne of Mathura, while Krishna and Balarama lived on there for some time. Kamsa, however, had been married to two daughters of Jarasandha, the king of Magadha with capital at Rajagriha, and when Krishna killed Kamsa, Jarasandha became the implacable foe of Krishna and besieged Mathura no less than eighteen times. Although Jarasandha was killed in the struggle, Krishna thought it well to transfer the Yadava capital from Mathura to a more secure site near the western ocean. This site was the ancient city of Kuśasthali, founded by Raivata (whose daughter Revati married Balarama), after whom was named the adjacent Mount Raivata (Raivataka).[27]

Under Krishna, Kuśasthali was enlarged and fortified, and thereafter was known as Dvaraka (Dvaravati) from its many *dvaras* or gateways, while Krishna himself was called Dvarakanath (lord of Dvaraka). After the death of Krishna (often considered to coincide in time with the beginning of the present Kaliyuga), Dvaraka was engulfed by the sea, but the present Dvaraka (Dwarka) on the extreme west coast of Kathiawar is named after it (*Vishnu Purana* 4.1; 5.23, 38). In the waters near the shore at Dwarka the marine archaeological unit of the Indian National Institute of Oceanography has discovered the remains of temples and a town, and the radiocarbon technique has indicated the approximate date of submergence as around the fifteenth to fourteenth century B.C.E. Also onshore excavation has revealed the remains of three temples built one over another, which subsequently were destroyed by the sea.[28]

Samudravijaya, the second of Śura's sons named above, is said by the Jainas to have been the father of Arishtanemi, the twenty-second Jaina *tirthankara*. Arishtanemi was therefore the cousin of Krishna.

Kunti (also known as Pritha), the first of Śura's daughters named above, was given by Śura to his childless friend Kuntibhoja, king of the little-known Kunti people, and she grew up at the court of Kuntibhoja. As a result of a union with the sun god Surya, Kunti bore a son whom, as illegitimate, she felt compelled to set adrift in a basket on the rivers. In this manner the infant came down the Ganges to the city of Campa, and was there found by a charioteer from Anga, named Nandana (or Adhiratha), who with his wife Radha raised the child and named him Karna (also Vasusena). Eventually Karna became a warrior of great strength and prowess. Although a half-brother of the Pandavas (immediately below), he took the side of the Kauravas in the battle of Kurukshetra, and lost his life in the Great War.

Later Kunti was married to Pandu at Hastinapura, and became the mother of Yudhishthira, Bhima, and Arjuna, three of the Pandava brothers, while the other two, Nakula and Sahadeva, were borne by Pandu's other wife Madri.

Śrutadeva, the second of Śura's daughters named above, married Damaghosha, king of Cedi, and became the mother of Śiśupala, who also took the throne of Cedi. Although Śiśupala and Krishna were cousins, Śiśupala became a fierce enemy of Krishna and the Pandavas, especially after Krishna carried off Śiśupala's betrothed, Rukmini. In the end Krishna killed Śiśupala, and Rukmini remained Krishna's principal wife, although Krishna's mistress, the *gopi* Radha, was the more prominent.

Paurava Line

In the Paurava line, in approximately the fifteenth generation down from Puru *(Matsya Purana* 49–50, with variations in other forms of the genealogies)[29] a king named Dushyanta ruled at a capital called Gajasahvaya, and assisted Indra in a war against the *asuras*. The beautiful wife and queen of Dushyanta was Śakuntala, and she is the heroine of a masterpiece by the famous Indian poet Kalidasa (circa 400 C.E.).

Dushyanta and Śakuntala were the parents of Bharata Daushanti (son of Dushyanta), and he was an even more famous warrior than his father, and won victories in the region of the Yamuna and Ganges which are celebrated in the *Śatapatha Brahmana* (13.5.4.11),[30] where it is said of him that he "attained that wide sway which now belongs to the Bharatas." A reference in the *Rig Veda* (3.23.1–4)[31] also associates certain Bharatas (Devaśravas and Devavata) with the rivers Drishadvati, Apaya, and Sarasvati. It was from Bharata Daushanti, therefore, that the Indo-Gangetic plain became known as Bharata, a name which was later that of the entire subcontinent, Bharata-varsha, and is the official name of India today. Likewise it is with the struggle for the succession in the kingdom of the Bharatas that the great Bharata epic, the *Mahabharata,* deals, and in particular with the Great Battle which was fought between the Kauravas and the Pandavas on the plain of Kurukshetra in the heart of the Bharata realm and in the climax of that struggle. Two capital cities were ultimately involved, Hastinapura and Indraprastha, and the development of events was as follows.

Bharata Daushanti was the ancestor of many tribes. Fourth in the main line of descent (according to the *Matsya Purana)* after him was Hastin, who was called after the "elephant" *(hastin)* lake where he was born. Hastin founded a capital on what was the course of the Ganges at that time, and it was called Nagasahvaya after the Naga people who inhabited the region. This city was later called Hastinapura (city of the elephant) after its founder, and the ruins are on the banks of the former bed of the Ganges, 22 miles (35 km.) northeast of Meerut (which is 41 miles [66 km.] northeast of Delhi).

Seventh in descent from Bharata was Samvarana, who was driven from Hastinapura by the Pancalas. Samvarana's son was Kuru, after whom was named the tribe of the Kurus (or Kauravas). The Kurus retook Hastinapura, and made it the capital of their kingdom of Kuru, and Kurukshetra was named after them as the "plain of the Kurus" (*Vishnu Purana* 4.20).[32] One of the sons of Kuru was Parikshit (I), and after fourteen generations in this line of descent was Śantanu, who in legend was married to Ganga. Ganga was the daughter of Himavat (the personification of the Himalaya) and the sister of Parvati (the wife of Śiva), and was herself the goddess of the Ganges River.

Śantanu was the last king of Hastinapura whose claim to succession as the ruler of the entire Bharata kingdom was undisputed. With his offspring the complications began which led directly to the Great Battle which is the climax of the *Mahabharata*. Śantanu and the river goddess Ganga were the parents of Bhishma (awe inspiring), and he was called Śantanava after his father, and Gangeya and Nadi-ja (river born) after his mother. In his old age, however, Śantanu desired also to marry Satyavati, daughter of King Uparichara of Cedi. This king was only willing to give Satyavati to Śantanu if it were promised that Satyavati's sons should be in first place as Śantanu's heirs, and that Bhishma should not have sons that could be rivals of the sons of Satyavati. Bhishma agrees to all of this in the "awe inspiring" way that his name connotes. Śantanu and Satyavati have two sons. They are Citrangada and Vichitravirya and, with Bhishma's consent, they have the throne in turn after the death of Śantanu. When these two also pass off the scene, Bhishma still acts only as regent, while he brings up Vichitravirya's two sons, Dhritarashtra and Pandu, and then sees to it that they also have the throne. Because Dhritarashtra was blind, it was Pandu who came to rule first.

Pandu (pale) had two wives, Kunti, daughter of King Śura of Mathura, and Madri, who came from Madra, a Śaka state with capital at Sakala in the northwest (perhaps modern Sialkot in Pakistan). As already noted, Kunti became the mother of Yudhishthira, Bhima, and Arjuna, while Madri became the mother of Nakula and Sahadeva. These five sons of the two mothers were the famed Pandavas, and it will be seen below that all five were married to a single wife, Draupadi.

When Pandu died Dhritarashtra (holding the realm) took the throne of Hastinapura. He himself had one hundred sons, of whom the oldest was Duryodhana (tough fighter). While the name Kaurava belongs properly to all the descendants of Kuru, it is applied in particular to these one hundred sons of Dhritarashtra and distinguishes them from the Pandavas, the sons of Pandu.

At this juncture Dhritarashtra took the Pandava princes under his own care and, with the continuing assistance of Bhishma, had them educated there at Hastinapura along with his own sons. The teacher of the young men in arms was a *brahmana* and famous archer named Drona. As their warlike education progressed, of all the young men, Duryodhana came to excel in fighting with the club, Yudhishthira in chariot-fighting, Bhima in club-fighting, Arjuna in archery, and Nakula and Sahadeva in fencing.

Between the Pandavas and the Kauravas there was, however, growing rivalry, and this came to an open break when Dhritarashtra selected to be the heir apparent to the throne of Hastinapura not his own oldest son Duryodhana representing the Kauravas, but his nephew Yudhishthira, the oldest of the Pandavas, a man known for his honesty, integrity, and justice. Under these circumstances the Pandavas went twice into exile, and the kingdom was divided, with Yudhishthira ruling for a time in a new capital called Indraprastha (the modern Indarpat on the banks of the Yamuna near Delhi).

While the Pandavas were living in their first exile in the forest in the disguise of *brahmanas,* Drupada king of Pancala held a contest *(svayamvara,* bride's choice) to select a husband for his beautiful daughter Draupadi, and the Pandavas came. The contest involved stringing a powerful bow and shooting five arrows through a whirling disk held on high. Celebrated heroes, including the famous archer Drona, failed the test, while the mighty Karna, being the supposed son of a lowly chariot driver, was refused a chance. Then Arjuna stepped forward and easily performed the feat. Draupada recognized Arjuna beneath his ascetic's garb, and was pleased that he had won Draupadi. When the brothers returned home they cried out to their mother, Kunti, that they had obtained a great gift that day, and she, unwittingly, bade them share the gift between themselves like brothers, so Draupadi became the common wife of all five Pandavas.

During the second exile of the Pandavas, Arjuna in particular experienced many adventures. For one thing, he went off for a time to the Himalaya to propitiate the gods and, in view of the increasing probability of war with the Kauravas, to ask for divine weapons for battle. On the way he had a fight with a Kirata mountaineer, as his opponent appeared to be, but when he discovered that this was actually Śiva in disguise Arjuna fell down and worshiped him. Thereupon, Śiva, being pleased with this devotion, presented Arjuna with the *paśupata* (herdsman's staff), this being Śiva's own favorite weapon, with which he kills the *daityas* in battle and with which, at the end of the ages, he destroys the universe *(Mahabharata* 3.41.1–24).[33]

Ultimately came the almost inevitable war between the Pandavas and the Kauravas, and along with them many other individuals and tribes were involved. Karna, although he had now learned from Kunti that he was her son and the half-brother of the Pandavas, joined with their opponents so that he might have the chance of fighting his long-time rival Arjuna. So also Bhishma and Drona took the side of the Kauravas, and other peoples allied with them included those of Anga, Gandhara, Kalinga, Kośala, Magadha (east), Sindhu, Vanga, Videha, and Yadava (in part), these being in the east, northwest, and west. On the side of the Pandavas Krishna, son of the Yadava king Vasudeva, acted as charioteer for Arjuna, and the peoples allied with the Pandavas included those of Cedi, Kaśi (Varanasi, where the ruling dynasty was founded by Kshatra-vriddha, a grandson of Pururavas), Magadha (west), and Pancala, these being in Madhyadeśa and Gujarat.[34]

The terrible conflict was fought on the plain of Kurukshetra, between the Yamuna and the Ganges (probably near Panipat, not far from modern Delhi), and was afterward remembered as the Great Battle *(mahayuddha)* or the Battle of the Eighteen Days. In the fierce fighting the one hundred Kaurava sons of Dhritarashtra, and many other heroes, fell, and the Pandavas emerged as the victors.

Afterward, accordingly, the oldest Pandava, Yudhishthira, was recognized as king in Hastinapura. But in the aftermath of the battle the Pandavas themselves were increasingly burdened with grief and remorse at the folly of the war and the slaughter of kinsmen by kinsmen. So finally Yudhishthira gave away his kingdom, dividing it into two parts. Of the two capitals, Hastinapura went to Parikshit II, who was the son of Abhimanyu and the grandson of Arjuna, and Indraprastha went to Yuyutsu, a son of Dhritarashtra by a handmaid, Dhritarashtra himself having left the Kauravas and gone over to the side of the Pandavas in the war. Then, in the garb of beggars, Yudhishthira and his brothers, together with Draupadi their wife, departed for the Himalaya on their way to Mount Meru, and finally, in heaven, the Pandavas and the Kauravas were reunited. So, the *Mahabharata* concludes:

> These and other mighty warriors in the earthly battle slain,
> By their valor and their virtue walk the bright ethereal plain,
>
> They have cast their mortal bodies, crossed the radiant gate of heaven,
> For to win celestial mansions unto mortals it is given,
>
> Let them strive by kindly action, gentle speech, endurance long,—
> Brighter life and holier future unto sons of men belong![35]

3

VEDIC AND UPANISHADIC RELIGION AND PHILOSOPHY

DEITIES OF THE RIG VEDA

Harappan Heritage

Of the deities in the *Rig Veda* some undoubtedly have connection with the Harappan civilization. An example has been noted already in the case of the three-faced figure on the seal from Moenjo-daro (Fig. 1.6), who may be plausibly identified as the prototype of Rudra/Śiva or possibly of Tvashtri/Viśvarupa. Likewise, female figurines, apparently representing a mother goddess, are prominent in the Indus Valley, and in the Vedas and thereafter in India the mother goddess concept is very important.

In the *Rig Veda,* for example, we meet Aditi, who is mentioned very frequently. Her name connotes immeasurableness, vastness, or infinity, and she is the mother of all, i.e., the feminine principle of creation. She is described as intact, widely expanded and extensive, bright and luminous, and the Dawn is her visage. She is the earth (1.72.9), the sky, the air, the mother and also the father and the son; she is all the gods, the five tribes, what has been and what shall be (1.89.10). Although identified with earth and sky, she is also differentiated from both (10.63.10). She is the mother of the Adityas, who take their name from her, and for them she provides sweet milk (10.63.2–3). Along this line of thought she is called the cow and the milk cow (1.153.3; 8.101.15), the bull is her son (10.11.1), and the *soma* drink is her milk (9.96.15). As for the Adityas, the name sometimes describes all the gods, sometimes designates in particular a group of eight (10.72.8), or seven (9.14.3), or six (2.27) deities. In the last enumeration the six are usually identified as Mitra (friendship), Aryaman (chivalry), Bhaga (inherited share), Varuna (fate), Daksha (ritual skill), and Amśa (the gods' share), and most or all of these are probably of Indo-Iranian origin.

Of the Adityas here named, Daksha is especially important, and apparently stands as the masculine principle of creation alongside Aditi as the feminine principle of creation. At any rate the two evidently shared in each other's nature, for it is said in the *Rig Veda* (10.72.4–5) that Daksha was born of Aditi, and Aditi was born of Daksha, and after that the gods were born. Daksha also appears as a primordial *rishi* with many daughters (usually said to be fifty in number), one of whom, in this view, was Aditi herself. These daughters were themselves married to various gods and *rishis*. Sati was married to the god Śiva, Anasuya was married to the *rishi* Atri, twenty-seven of the young women were married to the god Soma and became the mothers of the twenty-seven *nakshatras* (constellations), and thirteen of them were married to the *rishi* Kaśyapa, including Aditi the mother of the Adityas, Arishta mother of the *gandharvas*, Danu mother of the *danavas*, Diti mother of the *daityas*, Kadru mother of the *nagas*, Khaśa mother of the *yakshas* and *rakshasas*, Somati the mother of Sumati who married Sagara, and Vinata mother of Garuda.

Among the other Adityas in the same enumeration, Mitra and Varuna are especially important, and they are grouped with Aditi, and also associated with Indra, in a supplication in the *Rig Veda* (2.27.14): "Aditi, Mitra, and Varuna, be gracious, if we have committed any sin against you. O Indra, I would attain to the wide unimperiled light; let not the long darkness come over us."[1]

In the *Atharva Veda* (7.6.3–4) Aditi is called the mistress of Rita (which is the cosmic order, the fundamental moral and physical law of the universe), and is saluted in the words:

> The well-preserving earth, the unenvious sky, the well-sheltering, well-conducting Aditi, the well-oared ship of the gods, unleaking, may we, guiltless, embark on in order to have well-being.
> Now, in the impulse of might, will we commemorate with utterance the great mother, Aditi by name, whose lap is the broad atmosphere; may she confirm to us thrice-defending protection.[2]

On the other hand, over against the adoption of beliefs from Harappan sources, such a feature as phallic worship, which appears to be prominent in the Indus Valley, is viewed with abhorrence in the *Rig Veda*, where it is hoped that those who venerate the phallus will not intrude into the right practice of worship (7.21.5), and where it is said that Indra struck dead the adorers of the phallus (10.99.3). Nevertheless this aspect of religion also persisted and came to the fore again strongly in Later Hinduism.

Aryan Heritage

That Mitra, Varuna, and Indra (just named along with Aditi) probably belong to an Indo-Iranian or Indo-European background has already been noted, as indicated by the appearance of their names in a Mitannian text at Boghazköy (circa 1400 B.C.E.), and it has also been considered possible that Indra was originally a personification of the Aryan people or even the deification of an Aryan leader or series of leaders. Similar explanations may apply to other of the Vedic deities.

For example, the Nasatyas are also named in the Mitannian text at Boghazköy, and the Nasatyas or Aśvins are invoked in many hymns of the *Rig Veda* (4.4–45; 5.73–78; 7.67–74; 10.39–41, 106, 143). The word *aśva* means horse, and the Aśvins are twin horsemen (Aśvinau as the dual form). They ride through space in a golden car in the early morning, and are closely associated with the Dawn. The name of one of the pair is Nasatya (inseparable) and of the other Dasra (miraculous), and as twins they are often called by the one name as the Nasatyas, the Inseparables. They are also noted as healers and helpers of the sick. In view of these characteristics it has been theorized that they were originally a tribe of horsemen or warriors, also skilled in healing, who later became identified with dual kings who ruled over them, and so eventually were transformed into deities of the earliest dawn and destroyers of darkness and disease.

At any rate, the deities who are met with in the Vedas—both those whose antecedents can be traced or surmised in the Indus Valley or in Indo-Iranian background or Indo-Aryan experience, and those who are now encountered for the first time in the *Rig Veda*—are for the most part connected with aspects of nature but are not limited thereto, and may be active in more than the single sphere with which they are primarily associated. They are anthropomorphically pictured, and it is said (*Rig Veda* 1.27.13) that some are great, some small, some young, and some old. They are called in Sanskrit by the word *deva* (e.g., 1.114.10), feminine *devi*, translatable as deity, god, goddess; while the word *devata* also occurs, usually with an adverbial sense, meaning "among the gods" (e.g., 1.165.9) and later this is the term for a lesser or local god, a godling.

The total number of the deities is usually said to be thirty-three (e.g., *Rig Veda* 1.45.2), but more than this many are actually named, so the number must be symbolic. The *Satapatha Brahmana* (11.6.3.4),[3] in fact, also mentions the numbers of 303 and 3,003. As for the thirty-three, the *Satapatha Brahmana* (4.5.7.2; 11.6.3.5–9) explains that this number is made up of eight Vasus, eleven Rudras, twelve Adityas, and two more deities who are named in the first passage cited as Dyaus (sky, heaven) and Prithivi (earth), and in the second passage as Indra and Prajapati (early a title of Indra, later a deity in his own right, the supreme creator).

Statistically, in the *Rig Veda* the individual deities most frequently mentioned are Indra, Agni, Soma, the Asvins, the Maruts, and Varuna. In the character of their work, two are of the most importance, namely, Indra as the great ruler, and Varuna as the lord of the physical and moral order, while Agni and Soma are of especial importance in connection with Vedic sacrificial ritual.

Adityas. Of the three main groups of deities outlined in the *Satapatha Brahmana*, the Adityas have already been met as the children of Aditi where, in the *Rig Veda*, they number from six to eight. In the *Satapatha Brahmana* they are twelve, and the names added to the six listed above are usually given as Tvashtri (fashioner), Savitri (power of words), Pushan (nourisher), Sakra (mighty), Vivasvat (social law), and Vishnu (cosmic law). All together, the Adityas may be considered as personifications of the laws which control the universe and human society, and the *Satapatha Brahmana* (11.6.3.8) also identifies them with the twelve months of the year.

Rudras. The Rudras are usually seen as the manifestations or associates of Rudra/Siva and, like Rudar/Siva, belong to the sphere of aerial space. They are sometimes considered to be the same as the Maruts, who are especially known as the associates of Indra. The *Satapatha Brahmana* (11.6.3.7) identifies the eleven Rudras with the vital energies or vital breaths (*prana*) of a human being, of which there are ten, with the self (*atman*) as the eleventh entity. The same text explains that when these energies depart from the mortal body they cause weeping (*rud*), and this is why they are called Rudras.

Vasus. The word *vasu* means "dwelling" or "dweller," and refers to what we may call the spheres of existence toegther with the powers or principles which rule or are active in them. The *Satapatha Brahmana* (11.6.3.6) identifies the eight Vasus as the earth (*Prithivi*) in which fire (Agni) is active, aerial space (*Antariksha*) in which there is wind (Vayu), the sky or heaven (*Dyaus*) in which is the sun (Surya), and the constellations (*Nakshatras*) in whose realm is the moon (Candra, later identifed with Soma).

Deities of the Sphere of Earth

Prithivi. The earth (*kshama* or *prithivi,* the latter word meaning broad or widely extended) is personified as the goddess Prithivi. As the source of abundance Prithivi is a great mother and, in that respect, may be identified with Aditi, the primordial mother of all, as in the apposition (*Rig Veda* 1.72.9): "The Earth has spread herself far and wide . . . the mother Aditi, for the nourishment of the bird (probably meaning Agni, to whom the hymn is addressed)."

As the earth, Prithivi is very frequently joined with the sky or heaven (*Dyaus*), and the compound form *dyavakshama* or *dyavaprithivi* is used for the two together. A prayer in the *Rig Veda* (3.8.8) reads: "May the Adityas, the Rudras, the Vasus, the good leaders, Heaven and Earth, the Earth and the Air—may the gods unanimously bless this sacrifice"—and here the earth is mentioned twice, first in the compound Dyava-Kshama, and then separately as Prithivi, along with the Air.

In the same conjunction the earth is the Mother and the sky is the Father (*Rig Veda* 1.160.1–2): "These two, indeed, Heaven and Earth (Dyava-Prithivi), are beneficial to all, observing order, supporting the sage of the air: between the two divine bowls that produce fair creations the divine bright Surya (the sun) moves according to fixed law. As Father and Mother, far-extending, great, inexhaustible, the two protect [all] beings."

Likewise a prayer in the *Atharva Veda* (6.120.2) reads: "The earth is our mother, Aditi our kin, the air our protector from hostile schemes. May father sky bring prosperity to us from the world of the fathers; may I come to my [departed] kin, and not lose heaven!"[4]

It is also the case that Heaven and Earth are designated by the name Rodasi (e.g., *Rig Veda* 10.11.9; 10.12.4). This is a feminine dual form, as if the two were called the two mothers, and suggests the predominance of the feminine in the combination of Prithivi and Dyaus.

At the same time Prithivi is also called the wife of Parjanya (rain giver), the god of the rain cloud, who is often associated with Indra, the storm god. Thus a long hymn to the Earth goddess in the *Atharva Veda* includes the stanza (12.1.42): "To the earth upon whom are food, and rice, and barley, upon whom live these five races of men, to the earth, the wife of Parjanya, that is fattened by rain, be reverence!"[5]

Later names of Prithivi, of appropriate etymology, are Urvi (wide), Bhumi (earth), and Bhudevi (earth goddess).

Agni. The earth is the dwelling place of fire, called Agni (Latin *ignis*), known in the *Rig Veda* (e.g., 1.146.1) as the son of Heaven and Earth, and one of the most important of the deities. Agni is fire in all of its natural forms (in burning fuel, in the sun's rays, in lightning) and its ritual forms (the fire kindled daily in the home from the two kindling sticks called *arani,* the morning and evening fire-offering called the *agnihotra,* and the fire of the funeral pyre).

In relation to people and their households, Agni is a friend and guardian. In the home he is the master of the house (*grihapati*) and a guest (*atithi*) who is gladly received (*Rig Veda* 1.12.6; 5.4.5): "Welcome, as our household god and the guest in our dwelling, come to this our sacrifice as the knowing one."

In relation to sacrifice Agni is called priest (*ritvig, vipra*), and is seen as concentrating in himself the functions of the traditional "seven priests" (*Rig Veda* 2.1.2; 10.91.10), namely, the *hotri* (invoking priest), *potri* (cleanser), *neshtri* (leader), *agnidh* (kindler), *praśastri* (director), *adhvaryu* (minister), and *brahmana* (praying priest). As the sacrificial fire itself, Agni is "a carrier of offerings," and "the unwearied messenger, the bearer of oblations" (1.67.2; 1.72.7).

At the sacrifice Agni looks in all directions to protect the man who has no quiver and cannot, therefore, protect himself; he accepts the offering of the poor (1.31.13); "Thou, O Agni, art kindled four-eyed, as the closest guardian for the sacrificer who is without (even) a quiver. Thou acceptest in thy mind the hymn even of the poor who has made offerings, that he may prosper without danger."

Prayer is made to Agni (1.27.11): "May he, the great, the immeasurable, the smoke-bannered, rich in splendor, incite us to [pious] thoughts and to strength."

Agni is known by many epithets, some of which have already appeared in the preceding quotations, e.g., Vahni (carrier, i.e., of offerings), and Dhumaketu (smoke-bannered), while other names are Jataveda (former of the Vedas), Pavaka (purifier), Saptajihva (seven tongued), and Vaiśvanara (all pervading). It is with his flames that Agni purifies (e.g., 3.9.8), and his seven tongues are these flames (3.6.2). As Agni Vaiśvanara, he fills both halves of the world (earth and heaven), and it is from him that the rising sun is born in the morning (10.88.3, 6).

Of Agni as pervading all, in its hymn to the goddess Earth, the *Atharva Veda* says (12.1.19–21): "Agni (fire) is in the earth, in the plants, the waters hold Agni, Agni is in the stones; Agni is within men, Agnis (fires, plural) are within cattle, within horses. Agni glows from the sky, to Agni the god belongs the broad air. . . . The earth (is) clothed in Agni. . . ."[6]

The wives of Agni are Agnayi (a feminine name derived from the masculine Agni) and Svaha (a name which is the same as the sacred syllable that is pronounced over a sacrifice). According to the Puranas the sons of Agni and Svaha are Suchi, Pavaka, and Pavamana, and they are the fires in heaven, in aerial space, and on earth respectively. Pavamana is also called Nirmathya, because this fire is produced by the rubbing together of two kindling sticks (*arani-manthana*), and is graphically described as the child of the two Aranis. In turn Suchi, Pavaka, and Pavamana have forty-five sons and, counting Agni himself, there are thus forty-nine members of the Agni family, identified with forty-nine fires (*Matsya Purana* 51; *Markandeya Purana* 52.27–29).[7]

So fire continues to be of primary importance in Hinduism until today, and most sacred rites from birth to death (cremation) are performed with fire.

Soma. Although later identified with the moon, Soma is in the first instance a deity of the sphere of earth, being the "pressed juice" (from the root *su*, to press) of the *soma* plant. The preparation and offering of this juice was the central feature of Vedic sacrificial ritual and, because of the connection of Agni with sacrifice, Soma is often associated with Agni. In the *Rig Veda* the entire ninth book and other hymns as well are in praise of Soma, and the whole of the *Sama Veda* is also dedicated to Soma.[8]

The *soma* juice is frequently called the "bright drop" (*indu*), and the "sweet draught" (*madhu*) and, as filtered and purified, is termed *pavamana*. In its exhilarating power it is considered to have imparted strength to Indra in his conflict with hostile powers, regarded as capable of bestowing immortal life, and called the "draught of immortality" (*amrita*).

We have drunk Soma; we have become immortal; we have gone to the light; we have found the gods. What can hostility now do to us, and what the malice of mortal man, O immortal one? Do good to our heart when quaffed, O Indu; kindly like a father, O Soma, to his son, thoughtful like a friend to his friend, O far-famed one, prolong our years that we may live, O Soma (*Rig Veda* 8.48.3–4).

O Pavamana, place me in the world where the eternal light is, in the deathless, undecaying world. Make me immortal in that realm where Vivasvat's son (Yama) is king, where the hidden place of heaven is, where are those waters young and fresh. Make me immortal in that realm where one may walk as one wishes, in the threefold firmament, in the threefold room of heaven, where the worlds are full of light. Make me immortal in that realm of eager wish and strong desire, the region of the zenith of the sun, where food and full delight are found. Make me immortal in that realm where happiness and pleasures, joys and delights dwell, and longing wishes are fulfilled (*Rig Veda* 9.113.7–11).

The *soma* plant has been variously thought to be the *Ephedra intermedia* of the northwestern Himalaya and northeastern Afghanistan, or the mushroom *Amanita muscaria*, but these identifications are doubtful. In the *Satapatha Brahmana* (5.1.2.10; 5.1.5.28; cf. 12.8.1.4) the beneficial gifts of the *soma* juice are contrasted with the damaging effects of an evidently fermented and intoxicating liquor called *sura*: "The *soma* is truth, prosperity, light, and the *sura* untruth, misery, darkness."[9] While the use of *soma* ultimately did not continue, the offering of different kinds of drink and food remains an essential part of Hindu worship.

Rivers. In the sphere of the earth the rivers are also sacred, and we have already noted the several streams which are saluted in the *Rig Veda*. The rivers are feminine, and lend themselves to indentification with river goddesses, among them, very importantly, Sarasvati. Already in the *Satapatha Brahmana* (3.9.1.7) the Sarasvati River is connected with speech, and as a goddess Sarasvati is considered the consort of Brahma and is very prominent as the patroness of learning, of arts, and of music. In every form water is a purifying and life-giving agent, so water is used in almost every Hindu rite, and bathing in sacred rivers is an act of special importance. "May the motherly waters cleanse us. . . ; for the goddesses carry off all defilement, from them I come forth pure and clean" (*Rig Veda* 10.17.10).

Deities of the Sphere of Aerial Space

Antariksha. The sphere of existence which is intermediary between the earth and the sky is called *antariksha*, which we translate as space or air, i.e., aerial space, or the atmosphere. In a remarkable hymn to the unknown god (to be quoted below more fully), which concludes every stanza with the unanswered question, "Who is the god, to whom we shall offer sacrifice?" it is said of this unknown creator that it is he through whom the heaven (*dyaus*) and the earth (*prithivi*) were made fast, he through whom the sky and the firmament were established, and he who in the air (*rajas*) is the measurer of aerial space (*antariksha*) (*Rig Veda* 10.121.5).

Vayu. In the sphere of aerial space the active principle is that of the wind, named Vayu or Vata (from the root *va*, to blow). There Vayu/Vata rides in his car, drawn by 99, 100, or 1,000 steeds, and Indra his friend often rides with him (*Rig Veda* 4.47.3; 4.48.4–5).

Now for the greatness of Vata's car: its sound goes shattering, thundering. Touching the sky it goes producing ruddy hues (*arunani*, the reddish colors of lightning); and it also goes along the earth scattering dust. . . .

Going along his paths in the air he rests not any day. The friend of the waters, the first-born, the holy, where was he born, whence has he arisen?

Breath of the gods, germ (*garbha,* literally womb) of the world, this god fares according to his will. His sounds are heard, [but] his form is not [seen]. To that Vata we would pay worship with sacrifice" (*Rig Veda* 10.168.1, 3–4).

May Vata waft medicine, healthful, delightful to our heart; may he prolong our lives!
Thou, O Vata, art our father, and our brother, and our friend; do thou grant us to live!"
(*Rig Veda* 10.186.1–2).

Matariśvan. A lesser wind deity is Matariśvan. In the *Rig Veda* his closest association is with Agni whom, in many passages (e.g., 1.60.1; 3.9.5; 6.8.4) Matariśvan is said to have brought down from heaven. In one passage (3.29.11) several stages in the life of Agni are indicated, and it is said that at one point he himself was called Matariśvan.

Indra. Indra, the friend of Vayu, is a very prominent god in the sphere of aerial space, and more hymns are addressed to him in the *Rig Veda* than to any other single deity. We have already seen him as the warrior charioteer, brandishing his thunderbolt on behalf of the *aryas* and slaying the *asura* demon Vritra. In the myth of the slaying of Vritra, to which there are numerous allusions in the *Rig Veda* (e.g., 1.32; 2.12.3; 2.14.2; 2.19.2–4; 4.18.7), it seems that Indra slew a dragon (either Vritra or Vritra's mother Danu), which was lying on the mountains and keeping back the waters, whereupon the seven streams flowed to the sea, and the light shone forth, thus inaugurating creation and establishing cosmic order (*rita*), and this is done over and over, and Indra is besought to do it again in the future as in the past. So Indra is the "bearer of the bolt" (*vajrin*), and the mountains on which the dragon lies are the clouds which are dark with the coming storm; when Indra's thunderbolt (*vajra*) flashes, the rain pours down, and afterward the sun shines out. Also the rain itself is the god Parjanya, who multiplies the plants and the waters (5.83; 7.101–102).[10]

In view of the exploit just described, Indra's most frequent epithet is Vritra-han (Vritra-slayer) (e.g., *Rig Veda* 1.186.6), and he is also called Śakra (mighty), Śatakratu (having a hundred powers), Somapa (*soma* drinker), and Marutyant (accompanied by the Maruts).

Maruts. As the last title of Indra suggests, the god is often associated with the Maruts, and in particular these deities assisted him in the slaying of Vritra. The Maruts are the twenty-one (*Rig Veda* 1.133.6) or sixty-three (8.96.8) sons of Rudra (2.33.1) and, on account of this relationship, are often identified with the Rudras. The name of the Maruts is probably derived from the root *mar,* to shine, and thus they are the "shining ones." Like Indra, they are storm gods. They break forth with the winds, lightning is in their hands, and they make the rain waters flow (e.g., 1.38.8–9; 8.7).

Rudra/Śiva. As for Rudra himself, he is probably also a storm god, and that with an emphasis upon the destructive aspect of the storm. In the three hymns of the *Rig Veda* which are addressed to Rudra (1.114; 2.33; 6.74) he wields the thunderbolt (*vajra*) and carries the bow and arrows (lightning); it is presumably on account of his use of the fire of lightning that he is upon occasion identified with Agni (2.1.6). With these weapons Rudra kills both cattle and people, and he is the "manslaying Rudra" (4.3.6). For this reason the most urgent prayers are offered, asking him not to do harm. Remarkably enough, at the same time he is a physician with healing medicines in his hand, and his touch is gentle and cooling (2.33.4, 7). It may be both in appreciation of the benevolent side of his nature, and also in a euphemism intended to convert the destructive side of his nature into its opposite, that the adjective *śiva* (auspicious) is applied to Rudra (*Rig Veda* 1.114.9). Thus prayer is made to him in the *Śvetasvatara Upanishad* (3.5–6): "O Rudra, thou dweller in the mountains, look upon us with that most blessed form of thine which is auspicious, not terrible, and reveals no evil! O lord of the mountains, make lucky that arrow which thou, a dweller in the mountains, holdest in thy hand to shoot. Do not hurt man or beast!"[11]

So Śiva becomes another name of Rudra (e.g., *Ashvalayana Griha Sutra* 4.8.19), and the *Yajur Veda* devotes a whole section to him as the god embodying everything.[12] In later time and until today Śiva is the object of worship in the largest section of Hinduism, known as Śivaism or Śaivism.[13]

Deities of the Sphere of the Sky

Dyaus. As a sphere of existence, *dyaus* is the bright sky, heaven, the place where the gods live, and Dyaus himself (the Greek Zeus) is the Father (*Rig Veda* 4.1.10), often linked with Prithivi as the Mother (e.g., 1.160.1–2), or again mentioned as the parent of various of the gods, e.g., of Agni (e.g., 1.146.1), of Surya (immediately below), of the Aśvins (e.g., 4.43.3).

Surya. In the sphere of the sky the active principle is that of the sun, known as the god Surya. Surya is the son of Heaven (*Rig Veda* 10.37.1) and, along with Agni and Indra, one of the three chief deities of the Vedas. The name of Surya is derived from the word *svar* (light), and from the same root comes also the term *svarga*, which denotes heaven proper. Many titles apply to Surya, and most of them refer to the brilliance of the sun, notably the name Vivasvat (resplendent). Sometimes Surya is called an Aditya, sometimes he is distinguished from the Adityas. In an enumeration of eight sons of Aditi, the sun is counted as the eighth, and is said to have come forth as what at first appeared to be a lifeless egg (*mritanda*), hence his name Martanda (*Rig Veda* 10.72.8–9; *Satapatha Brahmana* 3.1.3.2–4).

It has already been noted that Manu Vaivasvata was considered the son of the sun god and the ancestor of humankind, but another representation makes Yama and his sister Yami the children of Vivasvat and themselves the first human pair and the parents of the human race, while Yama, as the first man to die, thereupon became the king of the dead (*Rig Veda* 10.10–19).

The *Rig Veda* describes Surya as the golden ornament of the sky, a flying falcon, and the very countenance and eye of the gods, especially the eye of Mitra, Varuna, and Agni; he fills heaven and earth and air; he is the soul of all that is (1.115.1; 7.63.4–5; 7.77.3).

As a visible symbol of the year or of time, the sun is a car or a wheel, drawn across the heaven by a steed called Etaśa. As a wheel the sun has twelve spokes, which are the twelve months of the year. The sun also has 720 "sons," joined in pairs together, and these are the 720 days and nights of the year (1.164.2, 11, 48). Traversing heaven and earth in a single day, Surya observes the whole world from on high (1.115.3; 4.13.3; 7.60.2). It is his work to dispel the dark night of ignorance and to dispense the light of life and health.

> Like thieves yonder constellations stealthily depart with the nocturnal darkness before the all-beholding Surya. His signs, his beams, are widely visible in the world, shining forth in splendor like fires that burn and blaze. Punctual, seen by all, you are the maker of light, O Surya; you illuminate all the radiant realm. You traverse the sky and the wide air, you measure the days with the nights, O Surya, you behold all the creatures. Looking upon the higher light above the darkness, we have come to Surya, the god of gods, the highest light. When you rise today as an honored friend and climb higher in the heaven, O Surya, drive far away the sickness of my heart and my jaundice! With all his might this Aditya has risen, and he casts down for me the enemy; let me not be overcome (*Rig Veda* 1.50 in part).

Savitar. Surya is also known by the name Savitar, which is derived from the root *su* (to bring forth), and refers to the sun as the source of creation. At the same time, Savitar is often distinguished from Surya and spoken of as a separate deity. As such, Savitar is preeminently a golden deity, golden eyed, golden tongued, and riding in a golden car (*Rig Veda* 1.35.2, 8; 6.71.3). As the great stimulator of life and motion in the world, and the regulator of time, Savitar brings both the day, which wakens people to go to their work and priests to go to their sacrifices, and the night, which allows all beings to rest. Addressing Savitar as the god of the evening and of the morning, a hymn of the *Rig Veda* says (1.35.1–3):

> I call on Night (*nakta*) that brings the world to rest; I call on god (*deva*) Savitar for help. Rolling hither through the dark space, bringing to rest the immortal and the mortal, on his golden car god Savitar comes seeing [all] creatures. The god goes by a downward, he goes by an upward path; adorable he goes with his two bright steeds. God Savitar comes from the distance, driving away all hardships.

In the entire *Rig Veda*, the one verse which is most of all considered central is addressed to the sun (3.62.10). It is composed in a meter of twenty-four (3 X 8) syllables, a meter which is named after the goddess Gayatri (second wife of Brahma), and is therefore known as the Gayatri Mantra. Gayatri is often identified with another goddess named Savitri and, both with reference to this goddess and also to the sun as Savitar, the verse is also called the Savitri Mantra. As containing within its syllables the substance of the four Vedas, yet another name for the verse is Vedamatri (mother of the Vedas). The composition is attributed to the *rishi* Viśvamitra. As the most sacred verse in the Hindu scriptures, it is recited to this day three times daily by countless Indians. In a modern paraphrase in English it reads:

> Let us adore the supremacy of that divine sun, the godhead, who illuminates all, from whom all proceed, to whom all must return, whom we invoke to direct our understandings aright in our progress towards his holy seat.[14]

Ushas. The sun is preceded in the sky by the Dawn (*Rig Veda* 1.115.2), who is named Ushas (from the root *vas*, to shine). Ushas is a beautiful young woman, daughter of heaven (e.g., 1.48.1), consort of the sun (7.75.5), and sister of the night (4.52.1). Ushas wakens the Aśvins (8.9.17), the twin gods of the early morning, and she wakens the whole world.

> She has shone brightly forth like a youthful maiden, stirring to motion every living creature. She has made light and driven away the darkness. Facing all, far-spreading, she has risen and shone in brightness with white robes about her. Shine upon us with the most beautiful beams, O goddess Ushas, and give us lengthened life (*Rig Veda* 7.77 in part).

Mitra and Varuna. Surya the sun is also often associated with Mitra and Varuna (*Rig Veda* 7.60–66), two deities who are most frequently referred to together, and who are the equivalents of Mithra and Ahura Mazda in Iran. Surya is the eye of Mitra and Varuna (10.37.1), so Mitra and Varuna are also solar deities. They are sons of Aditi (5.67.1), they have a golden throne on high (1.139.2), they mount a chariot in the highest heaven (5.63.1), they cause the sun to rise (4.13.2). They possess magic power (*maya*, the same word which later means cosmic illusion), and through it they send rain and guard their law (1.151.9; 5.63.3, 7).

The name of Mitra is the same as the word "friend," and the god Mitra is in fact outstanding for his friendliness (1.156.1). He brings men together, and watches over people with unwinking eye (3.59.1, 4): "This Mitra, adorable, most propitious, a king wielding fair sway, has been born as a disposer: may we remain in the goodwill of him the holy, in his auspicious good graces."

The name of Varuna may be derived from the root *var*, meaning to restrain, and may be connected with his character as the giver of justice, whose duty it is to punish the guilty. At any rate he is the omniscient creator and sustainer of the world, who has established and maintains the natural and moral laws which are expressions of the cosmic order (*rita*), and it is he above all to whom the sinner looks for forgiveness.

> He has encompassed the nights and established the mornings through his magic art; he is visible over all the earth. . . . He is like a watchful shepherd (8.41.3–4).

> He knows the path of the birds which fly in the air, as sovereign of the seas he knows the ships that are thereon. True to his holy law, he knows the twelve months with their offspring (the days and nights); he knows the posthumous one (the intercalary month). He knows the pathway of the wind, which is broad and high and great; he knows the ones (the gods) who dwell above. Varuna, true to holy law, has established in the waters the throne of his rule; from there perceiving, he beholds all things that have been or shall be (1.25.7–11).

The Rig-Vedic poet Vasishtha has sailed with Varuna on a ship in Varuna's heaven, and Varuna has made him a *rishi* and a singer (7.88.4). Vasishtha, however, is conscious of sin, and prays for forgiveness and release.

> Release us from the sins of the fathers, release us from what we ourselves have done. Release Vasishtha, O king. . . . The failure is not of our own will, O Varuna; it is drink, anger, gambling, and folly. The older one leads the younger one astray; sleep itself does not prevent transgression. Freed from the guilt of sin, I wish to serve you as a slave serves his master. Let this song of praise be pleasing to you, O invincible lord, be laid close to your heart. May it be well with us in peace and in war. Guard us always with your blessing (7.86.5–8 in part).

Vishnu. The god Vishnu seems also to be of solar character, and thus to belong to the sphere of the sky. The name is probably derived from the root *vish*, meaning to spread in all directions, to pervade. Vishnu is most famed for his three steps (e.g., *Rig Veda* 1.22.18), in connection with which his most characteristic epithets are "wide pacing" (*urugaya*) and "wide striding" (*urukrama*) (1.154.3, 5). With his three paces he has measured out the common dwelling place of all; within his three wide strides all beings dwell (1.154.2–3). Two of his steps are visible to human beings, but the third and highest is beyond human approach, and beyond even the flight of birds (1.155.5). The two regions of earth human beings know, the highest region only Vishnu knows (7.99.1). The highest step is like an eye in heaven, whence it shines down brightly, i.e., it is the sun (1.22.20). There in the dear abode of Vishnu, pious men are happy; thither the Rig Vedic singer fain would come (1.154.5–6).

Thus the three steps of Vishnu no doubt refer to the course of the sun, and in particular to its passage through the three spheres of earth, aerial space, and highest heaven. Vishnu has also set in motion like a revolving wheel his ninety steeds (i.e., days), with their four names (i.e., seasons), an allusion to the 360 days of the year (1.155.6). In other respect, Vishnu is the friend of Indra, with whom he is associated in the latter's battles (6.69) and, on this account, Vishnu is also associated with the Maruts (5.87).

Although not one of the most prominent gods in the *Rig Veda*, in later times Vishnu became very important, and is worshiped in the various schools of Vishnuism or Vaishnavism, the second largest section of Hinduism (after Śaivism).[15]

Deities of the Sphere of the Constellations

Nakshatras. Beyond the sun, which is the center and limit of our world, is the transcendent sphere of the constellations (*nakshatras*). The constellations shine by night, but when the sun rises they pass from view (1.50.2), and the question may be asked as to where they go by day, but Varuna's holy laws control natural phenomena and are inviolable; therefore, the constellations will in proper time reappear (1.24.10).

In particular, the *nakshatras* are the lunar mansions, i.e., the asterisms or groups of stars in the apparent monthly path of the moon around the earth (as the signs of the zodiac are the constellations in the ecliptic, the apparent annual path of the sun). The *nakshatras* are usually reckoned as twenty-seven in number, and thus the moon is in each "mansion" a little in excess of one lunar day, with an interval of "balance" (*abhijit*) between the twenty-first and twenty-second asterisms making up for the daily excesses in the month.

Candra/Soma. In the realm of the *nakshatras* the active principle is that of the moon. The moon is known as Candra (luminous) and Nakshatranatha (lord of constellations), but is also identified with Soma. In the creation that took place with the sacrifice of Purusha (to be described below), the moon was produced from the mind of Purusha, as the sun was born out of the eye of Purusha (*Rig Veda* 10.90.13). The sun and moon are the two eyes of heaven (1.72.10), and they rise and run their respective courses alternately (1.102.2; 10.68.10). The moon is the month (10.89.13) and, as such, it is also the basis of the year (10.85.5). There may be said to be two moons (10.64.3), i.e., the new moon (which begins the approximately fifteen days that are the *śukla-paksha* or bright half of the month) and the full moon (which begins the approximately fifteen days that are the *krishna-paksha* or dark half of the month), and the phases of the moon are the points with respect to which the times of festivals are determined (1.94.4).

How it came about that Soma was identified with the moon is not made plain; perhaps it was due to the supposed connection of the moon with plant life. In one passage Soma is compared with the reflection of the moon in water (8.82.8); perhaps the "bright drop" (*indu*) of the *soma* juice was like the moon's rays so reflected. At any rate, in a wedding hymn in the *Rig Veda*, Soma is the husband of Surya, has a place in heaven, is in the midst of the constellations, and is surely recognizable as the moon (10.85.1, 2, 5). The *Atharva Veda* calls the moon *Candra* and *Candramas* and, in a prayer for deliverance, makes the identification with Soma unmistakable (7.6.5, 7): "Now do we speak to day and night, to Surya (sun) and to Candramas (moon), the twain. . . . Day and night, and Ushas (dawn), too, shall deliver thee from curses! Soma, the god, whom they call Candramas, shall deliver me!"[16]

In another account (*Mahabharata* 1.60.8–17) the moon is married to twenty-seven of the fifty daughters of Daksha, and these "faithful wives" are the spirits of the twenty-seven lunar mansions, "which regulate the life of the world."[17] As the story is elaborated in the Puranas (*Vishnu Purana* 1.15; 4.6; *Matsya Purana* 23–24; *Siva Purana, Kotirudrasamhita* 14),[18] Soma (here identified as the son of the ancient *rishi* Atri) shows partiality to the fourth wife, named Rohini, and for this Daksha curses him with consumption so that his body wastes away progressively for a fortnight, until he repents and his strength is restored during the next fortnight—obviously a reference to the waning and waxing of the moon. Later Soma abducts Tara (or Taraka), the wife of Brihaspati (or Brahmanaspati, the lord of prayer, the high priest of the gods), and only gives her back after a long struggle (the Tarakamaya war), in which the *daityas* (demons) and *danavas* (titans) take the side of Soma, and the gods, led by Rudra, fight against them. Afterward, Tara gives birth to a son whose father, she finally admits, was Soma. This son of the moon god is named Budha (he who knows), and it is his son, Pururavas, who was the founder of the Lunar dynasty of Indian kings.

Goddesses

It has already been noted that there are many feminine as well as masculine deities in the Vedic pantheon, e.g., Aditi the mother of all, Prithivi the mother earth, Sarasvati, and other river goddesses, and that the feminine and the masculine are often associated in pairs, e.g., Prithivi and Dyaus (Dyava-Prithivi), Agnayi and Agni. Other wives of main gods, with names derived from their husbands' names by the use of a feminine termination, are Indrani the wife of Indra (*Rig Veda* 2.32.8; 10.86), and Varunani the wife of Varuna (2.32.8; 7.34.22).

Vak. Am important goddess in her own right is Vak (speech), who personifies the power of the word and the sound of truth. Her origin is in the depth of the waters, she blows like the wind, she fills heaven and earth with her presence, and she assumes many forms. Whoever sees, whoever breathes, whoever hears the spoken word, does so only through her. Whom she loves she makes a priest, a *rishi*, a wise one. Yet she also creates strife among the people. She utters the word of truth, so let people hear! (*Rig Veda* 10.125). At least later Vak is identified with Sarasvati as herself the goddess of wisdom and science, of speech and music, and the chief wife of Brahma.

Uma. Sometimes identified with Vak, is the goddess Uma, who is first mentioned by this name in the *Kena Upanishad* (3.12),[19] where she is able to communicate knowledge of Brahman to Agni, Vayu, and Indra. At this point she is described as most beautiful, and is called Uma Haimavati, i.e., Uma the daughter of Himavat (the personification of the Himalaya). She is the wife of Rudra/Siva, is sometimes called Rudrani (*Mahabharata* 5.115.10),[20] and is often identified with Siva's other consorts, Parvati, Durga, and Kali.

Sri. In the *Rig Veda* the word *sri* means happiness, splendor, beauty, glory (e.g., 1.43.7; 1.72.10; 1.85.2; 5.61.12), and in the *Satapatha Brahmana* (11.4.3.1)[21] the same word is the name, Sri, of a resplendent and shining goddess of fortune and beauty, who springs from Prajapati the creator. Eventually, known also by the name of Lakshmi, she is the wife of Vishnu.

Other Superhuman Beings

Gandharvas. Among other superhuman beings in the *Rig Veda* are the *gandharvas* and the *apsarases.* The *gandharva,* it is said, stands upon the firmament and clothes himself in a fragrant garment, looking like the sun (10.123.7; cf. 9.83.4); and again the *gandharvas* (the plural here being used less frequently than the singular) are described as having hair like the wind (3.38.6). Dwelling thus in the sky or the atmosphere, in the later mythology the *gandharvas* become heavenly musicians and singers. According to one view, their ruler is Narada, a *rishi* to whom several hymns of the *Rig Veda* are attributed, and who was a patron of music and the inventor of the lute (*vina*).

Apsarases. The *apsarases* are the heavenly mates of the *gandharvas.* The Sanskrit name literally means "moving in the waters," so the *apsarases* are evidently water nymphs or cloud maidens, and in the later mythology they become the courtesans and dancers of heaven. Only one of them is spoken of by personal name in the *Rig Veda* (10.95), and she is Urvaśi, who is said to have been the wife of Pururavas, the ancestor of the Lunar race of kings. In the description of Urvaśi she is connected with the waters, she fills the atmosphere, and traverses space.

Referring to both of these categories of superhuman beings, in one Rig Vedic passage (10.136.4–6) the long-haired *muni,* who is an ascetic with magic powers, a friend of the wind and able to fly through the air, is said to move on the path of the *apsarases* and the *gandharvas.*

Kinnaras. In the later mythology there is also a variety of the *gandharvas* known as the *kinnaras* and, like the *gandharvas,* they are also celestial musicians. The *kinnara* (related to Greek and Latin centaur) is a being with a human body and the head of a horse, or the body of a horse and the head of a man. The *kinnaras* belong to the court of Kubera (named already in the *Atharva Veda* 8.10.28), who is the god of wealth and the chief of the *yakshas.*

Vidyadharas. In the later mythology we also meet the *vidyadharas* (bearers of wisdom), who are aerial spirits, both masculine and feminine. They fly in the space between heaven and earth, upon occasion are attendant upon Indra, Śiva, and other deities, and generally are benevolent in their relationship to human beings.

Yakshas. The *yakshas* (masculine *yaksha,* feminine *yakshi, yakshini*) are elemental spirits, referred to as *punya-jana* (propitious folk), who are mostly benevolent, although sometimes evil, and who are the special guardians of previous stones and metals hidden in the roots of trees, hence they are often called tree deities or earth spirits.

Rakshasas. Often mentioned either alone or along with some of the foregoing spirits are the *rakshasas.* They may appear variously as genii, titans, or most often as demons. In the *Rig Veda,* for example, Soma is asked to kill all the *rakshasas,* and they are called by the name *atrin,* which originally means an ogre with large teeth or jaws, a devourer (9.86.48; 9.104.6; cf. 1.21.5). In the *Atharva Veda* (e.g., 2.3.6; 4.37.1–2)[22] many incantations are directed against the *rakshasas* and some of the other evil spirits. In the *Mahabharata* the *rakshasas* are often male, in the *Ramayana* some are also female (*rakshasi*). In the *Ramayana* the mightiest of the *rakshasa* kings is Ravana, half-brother of Kubera, ruler of Lanka, and abductor of Sita.

Divine Animals

Various animals appear in the *Rig Veda,* often in association with the deities or as their symbols, and sometimes as themselves objects of worship or objects of sacrifice.

Horses. Famous warhorses and racehorses are spoken of in the *Rig Veda* as deified, and as the objects of worshipful thought and the source of hoped-for benefits (7.38.7–8; 7.40.6; 10.64.6; 10.74.1).

One famous horse is named Dadhikra. He belonged to an early king, Trasadasyu the son of Purukutsa (e.g., 1.112.14; 5.33.8), and is praised in several hymns (4.38–40). In the first of these hymns Dadhikra is celebrated for bravery in battle and speed in running. In the second and third hymns he is recognized as a gift from Mitra and Varuna, a guide for mortals, and a bringer of food, strength, and light. In the last verse of the third hymn (4.40.5) the thought of Dadhikra leads to thought of (and perhaps to the identification of Dadhikra with) the eternal law of the universe and all forms of the Supreme Being, the swan at home in the light of heaven (i.e., the sun), the Vasu in the air (i.e., the wind), and the priest at the altar and the guest in the house (i.e., Agni—for these interpretations of these figures of speech see the *Śatapatha Brahmana* 6.7.3.11).[23]

That the horse is closely connected with the sun, and probably seen as a personification of the sun, is confirmed in another Rig Vedic hymn (10.178), in which a divine horse name Tarksya is compared with the sun. The name Etaśa is certainly also that of a sun-horse or sun-horses. In the singular Etaśa is the horse that, appearing daily (1.168.5), draws the car of the sun (8.1.11; 8.6.38); in the dual the same name designates two bright-colored sun-horses (8.70.7); and in the plural it refers to more steeds, which go before the sun (10.49.7), and are described as winged (10.37.3). Yet other passages speak of seven (1.50.8–9; 1.164.2–3) or of ten (1.164.14; 9.63.9) horses of the sun, while the sun itself is also pictured as a beautiful white horse, led forth in the morning by Ushas, the dawn (7.77.3).

The original prototype of the horse (later named Uccaihśravas and associated with the churning of the ocean) was a splendid creature with the wings of an eagle, which was fashioned out of the sun by the gods (1.163.1–2). As a creature of such divine associations, the horse is a sacrificial animal, and in the horse sacrifice (*aśvamedha*) was sent back to the gods to obtain benefits for his sacrificers (1.162). In a funeral address for a "strong steed" (*vajin*), the horse is envisioned as going from one light (that of the funeral pyre) to another (in the firmament) and yet on to a third (in the highest region above the firmament), there in the presence of the gods to be united with a glorified body, which will afford blessing to earthly worshipers (10.56.1–3).

Cattle. The bull stood for virility and power, represented natural forces, and was a symbol for Soma, Indra, Agni, and other gods (10.11.1). When Agni's lightning flashes and the dark rain clouds thunder, it is the black Bull who has bellowed (1.79.2).

The case is similar with the cow. Cows are rain clouds (1.151.5; 1.164.7; 3.55.16; 5.55.5), brightly flaming cows are clouds that emit flashes of lightning before they pour down the rain (2.34.5), the black cow is night, and the red cow is the ruddy light of dawn (10.61.4). The goddess Vak is represented in the figure of a cow (8.100.10–11), Aditi, the mother of all, is a cow and a milk cow (1.153.3; 8.101.15), and the gods are born of the cow (6.50.11).

In line with the sacred character of cattle, there are instructions against their slaughter, although some of the passages at the same time reflect some use of cattle for sacrifice or for food. In a text in which the cow is equated with Aditi and identified as the source of the words of the Vedic singer (cf. 8.100.10), the cow herself speaks and says, "Kill not the blameless cow" (8.101.15–16). In the *Atharva Veda* (12.4.12; 12.5.38)[24] the cow belongs upon request to the *brahmana* priest; if eaten by someone else instead, there is punishment here and hereafter: "Whoever is not willing to give the cow of the gods to the sons of seers that ask for her, he falls under the wrath of the gods and the fury of the Brahmanas. . . . When partaken of, the Brahmana cow cuts off the Brahmana scorner from the world, from both this one and the one yonder."

In the *Satapatha Brahmana* (3.1.2.21)[25] the sage Yajnavalkya is said to have eaten beef upon occasion, but on the other hand the following instruction is given concerning an initiate who is preparing to take part in a religious ceremony:

> Let him not eat (the flesh) of either the cow or the ox; for the cow and the ox doubtless support everything here on earth. . . . Hence, were one to eat (the flesh) of an ox or a cow, there would be, as it were, an eating of everything. . . . Such a one indeed would be likely to be born (again) as a strange being . . . let him therefore not eat (the flesh) of the cow and the ox.

Birds. In one case the Vedic poets are compared to birds, singing to Indra (8.21.5), while in many cases birds are symbols of the gods. Soma is an eagle (9.85.11) or a falcon (9.67.14); Indra is an eagle (10.99.8) or a swan (10.124.9); Agni also is like an eagle (4.6.10) or a swan (1.65.9); and Brihaspati is a vulture (1.190.7) because of his sharp eyesight.

Like the horse, the bird is a symbol of the sun and, with its flight through the air, an especially appropriate figure for the sun in its course through the sky. The comparison is often with the eagle or with the *hamsa*, the latter name translated both as swan and as goose, the latter, with its high flight and loneliness above other birds, being especially appropriate to the sun. The sun-horse is a bird that flies beneath the heaven; the coursers of the sun in the heavenly causeway move in a row like geese (1.163.6, 10). Dadhikra, the horse of the sun, is the swan or goose (*hamsa*) who is at home in the light of heaven (4.40.5). The traces of the sun in its passage are as invisible and mysterious as those of a bird in its flight; the heavenly eagle, the great bird, is to be invoked for help (1.164.7, 52).

Twice in the *Rig Veda* the sun (Surya/Savitar) as a bird is called by the name Garutmant. From this arises in the later mythology the sun bird Garuda, the son of Vinata, conceived as having the body and limbs of a man and the head, beak, and talons of an eagle, and understood as the destroyer of serpents. Vishnu most characteristically rides upon Garuda as his mount (*vahana*). Other birds serving as bearers of deities are the goose or swan (*hamsa*), mount of Brahma; the owl, vehicle of Lakshmi; and the peacock, bearer of Sarasvati.

Serpents. The serpent or snake (*sarpa, naga*) is a dangerous creature, ranking along with the wolf and with the demons as a source of danger (*Rig Veda* 7.38.7). The serpent is capable of inflicting a wound which Agni is besought to heal (10.16.6), and the god Soma is described as delivering over evil speakers and slanderers into the power of the serpent (7.104.9). Yet serpents are also credited with wisdom and power such as may be attributed to the gods themselves (6.52.15; 10.63.4).

In his battles on behalf of the *aryas* against the *dasyus* and others, Indra smote various demons such as the *asura* Śambara (4.26.3; 6.18.8), and among these enemies was the serpent demon Arbuda (1.51.6; 2.11.20; 2.14.4, 6; 8.32.3, 26). In the *Mahabharata* (2.19.9)[26] Arbuda is an "enemy-burning" snake, and later tradition identifies him as the composer of the Rig Vedic hymn 10.94, as the son of the serpent queen (*sarparajni*) Kadru (herself the author of *Rig Veda* 10.189, according to the *Satapatha Brahmana* 2.1.4.29),[27] and as the father of Urdhvagravan (author of *Rig Veda* 10.175)[28] and of two more sons named Arbudi and Nyarbudi.

In spite of the hostility of Indra to Arbuda in the *Rig Veda*, in the *Atharva Veda* (11.9) the serpents Arbudi and Nyarbudi appear as friends and companions of Indra, and prayer is made to them for help in battle: Arbudi should envelop the enemy army with his coils (11.9.5); Nyarbudi should show them the seven kinds of specters (11.9.6); and Arbudi should make them see the *gandharvas* and the *apsarases*, the serpents, gods, propitious folk (*punya-jana*), and departed fathers (11.9.24). A similar prayer is made to Indra: "The Gandharvas and Apsarases, the serpents, the gods, the propitious folk, the fathers, those seen, those unseen I dispatch, that they may slay yonder army" (8.8.15).[29]

A famous early event was the Sacrifice of the Snakes, which is narrated at length in the *Mahabharata* (1.13–53).[30] Kadru the serpent queen and her sister Vinata were among the thirteen daughters of Daksha who were married to the *rishi* Kaśyapa, and Kadru became the mother of one thousand snakes, and Vinata became the mother of Aruna (dawn charioteer of the sun) and of Garuda (1.14). Between Kadru the mother of the snake people (*nagas*), and Vinata the mother of Garuda, there was great enmity, as a result of which Garuda inherited his mother's dislike for snakes, and Garuda became famous as the destroyer of serpents.

As the offspring of Kadru the serpent people are known as the Kadraveya, and their rulers are called by the title *nagaraja* (serpent king). The three main kings of the *nagas* are Śesha, Vasuki, and Takshaka. Śesha (remainder) is the serpent upon whose coils Vishnu reclines. Śesha is also often identified with Ananta (endless), the serpent whose great coils encircle and support the earth (*Mahabharata* 1.32.20–25). Vasuki is the serpent who served as the churning rope when the gods and *asuras* churned the celestial ocean of milk (*Mahabharata* 1.16). Vasuki's sister is Jaratkaru (also known as Manasa), who married a sage of the same name (Jaratkaru) and became the mother of the sage Astika (*Mahabharata* 1.44), through whom the snake sacrifice was finally stopped. Takshaka is the nine-hooded son of Kadru, whose action (narrated just below) led to the original institution of the snake sacrifice and thus to the fulfillment of a curse uttered by Khadru upon her offspring.

It seems that when Khadru and Vinata saw the wonderful horse Uccaiḣśravas, which was born out of the churning of the ocean, they made a wager about its color, which Kadru could have won if her offspring would have cooperated in a strategem which she proposed, but they refused and she accordingly cursed them that they should be burned in the fire when the snake sacrifice of Janamejaya should take place (*Mahabharata* 1.18). Because the snakes were numerous and their poison virulent, Brahma condoned the curse, but bestowed the art of healing snakebites on Kaśyapa. In due time King Parikshit II was hunting in the forest, and asked directions from a hermit, who was immersed in meditation and gave him no answer. In annoyance the king put a dead snake around the hermit's neck. For this insult to a pious man, the hermit's son cursed the king, and within a week Parikshit received a fatal bite from the snake king Takshaka (*Mahabharata* 1.45–46). Parikshit was then succeeded by his son Janamejaya and, because his father had been killed by a snake, Janamejaya performed the snake sacrifice, in which vast numbers of snakes perished in a blazing fire (*Mahabharata* 1.47). As a king of the snakes Vasuki was greatly distressed at the loss of so many of his race, and besought his sister's son Astika to intervene with Janamejaya. This Astika did, and the sacrifice was terminated, just as Takshaka was about to fall into the fire. The grateful surviving snakes asked Astika what wish they might grant him, and they gave him the boon which he asked, namely, that those who would recount his story might be free from danger from snakes (*Mahabharata* 1.48–53). But Janamejaya was always afterward remembered as *sarpasattrin* (serpent sacrificer).

The Many and the One

While the *Rig Veda* names many deities, even as there are many energies in the universe, the seer often addresses himself to a given one of them as if that one alone were thought of, or he combines or interchanges different ones as if they shared the same nature. In at least two passages it is strikingly affirmed that all of the names of the various gods are indeed only varying designations of one underlying reality or one deeper truth:

> They call (it) Indra, Mitra, Varuna, Agni, and it is the heavenly bird Garutmant (the sun). To what is only the One the wise give many names. They call it Agni, Yama, Matariśvan (1.164.46).[31]
> The bird which is only One, the wise seers divide with words into many (10.114.5).[32]

The *Śvetāśvatara Upanishad* (6.15) likewise affirms that "the one bird (*hamsa*)" alone exists in this universe; and the *Maitrayana-Brahmana Upanishad* (6.8) names various gods and powers, including the bird (*hamsa*), as identical with the supreme Self.[33]

Various Gods as Creator

When the question of the origin of all things is raised, different gods, or the gods collectively, may be named as the creator, or an unnamed and perhaps even unknowable One who is behind all else may be referred to.

Tvashtri. Tvashtri (the fashioner) has shaped all forms, has made all animals (*Rig Veda* 1.188.9); as the artisan of the gods he turned out the well-made, golden, thousand-edged thunderbolt of Indra (1.85.9); Agni is the son of Tvashtri (1.95.2; 3.7.4; in 2.1.5 Agni is Tvashtri), and Tvashtri is invoked for the birth of sons (1.142.10; 2.3.9); Tvashtri is indeed the first, and all forms belong to him (1.13.10).

Brahman and Brahmanaspati. In the *Rig Veda* the term *brahman* means a sacred word (2.5.3) in the sense of a spell (2.2.7), a hymn (1.37.4), or a prayer (e.g., 1.88.4; 1.165.2). The same term also means a priest (e.g., 4.50.8; 4.58.2), and is one of the terms applied to the god Agni as embodying in himself the functions of the human priesthood (2.1.2; 4.9.4; 10.91.10). Also in some passages the same word carries the suggestion of a holy power, so that one may speak of "the *brahman*." Thus in one hymn (10.162.1) it is desired that Agni should in conjunction with the *brahman* drive out a certain sickness.

Incorporating the word *brahman* (or the related root *brh*) we have in the *Rig*

Veda the title or name Brahmanaspati (or Brihaspati), meaning the "lord of prayer." Upon occasion this appears to be applied, appropriately enough, as a title to Agni: "Invite thou hither with this son, for praise, Agni the lord of prayer, him who is fair as Mitra is (1.38.13)"; "Agni, thou art Indra, thou art Vishnu of the mighty stride, adorable: thou, Brahmanaspati, the Brahman finding wealth.... (2.1.3)."

Usually, however, Brahmanaspati is an independent figure, plainly separate from Agni (e.g., 7.41.1). Likewise Brahmanaspati is sometimes closely allied with Indra, but is at the same time plainly a separate figure (2.23.18; 4.50.10–11; 8.96.15). As an independent deity Brahmanaspati (Brihaspati) is the subject of eleven hymns in the *Rig Veda* (1.40; 1.190; 2.23–26; 4.49–50; 10.67–68; 10.182) and is mentioned many other times.

In his own right Brahmanaspati is called the "father of all sacred prayer" (2.23.2), and "the father of the gods" (2.26.3). Most notably, in a hymn (10.72) on the origin of the gods, Brahmanaspati is said to have blown them together as a blacksmith would do (with his bellows). In the sequence of events here described, being (*sat*) was born from nonbeing (*asat*). Then the regions of the universe and the earth came into existence and Daksha (the masculine principle of creation) was born of Aditi (the feminine principle of creation), and Aditi was born of Daksha, and after that the gods were born. In a role of such importance as this, Brahmanaspati may be recognized as a prototype of the later Brahman and Brahma.

In the Upanishads, Brahman (neuter and accented on the first syllable) is the ultimate essence of the universe, and in Later Hinduism Brahma (masculine and accented on the last syllable) is the creator and is associated with Śiva and Vishnu in the major triad of Hindu deities. Likewise the priest himself is known as a *brahmana* (in English often spelled Brahmin to avoid confusion with the books called Brahmanas) and Brahmanism is often used as a name for Hinduism or at least for Early Hinduism.

Viśvakarman. Viśvakarman (all accomplishing) is also named as the creator (*Rig Veda* 10.81–82). In these hymns he is called "our father" and "the only god," and allusion is made to his offering up of all existing things, evidently a sacrifice of some kind which was involved in his creative work (10.81.1). His work is also likened to that of a carpenter, when it is asked what was the tree and what was the wood out of which earth and heaven were framed, and where did he stand as he established all things (10.81.2, 4). In a different metaphor there is mention of an original germ or embryo, out of which the universe evolved (10.82.5): "What was that then which the water received as the first germ, wherein all the gods were reckoned?"

In his role as architect and builder Viśvakarman is identified with Tvashtri (*Śiva Purana, Rudrasamhita* 2.25.1–2; 2.27.10),[34] and as creator he is identified with Prajapati. In the *Rig Veda* the name Prajapati (lord of offspring) is used as a title of the sun god Savitar (4.53.2) and of other gods, but is also the name of a distinct deity (10.184.1), and in the *Satapatha Brahmana* "Viśvakarman is Prajapati" (7.4.2.5), and Prajapati is the great creator (11.1.6).[35]

The Gods Collectively and the Sacrifice of Purusha

In the Rig-Vedic hymn to Viśvakarman (10.81.1) there is, as just noted, allusion to a sacrifice which was involved in creation, and according to the hymn known as the *Purusha-sukta* (*Rig Veda* 10.90) the creation was accomplished by the gods acting collectively in the sacrifice of Purusha.

Purusha is the cosmic Person, with a thousand heads, eyes, and feet, i.e., Purusha is the primordial and eternal principle which is immanent in all humankind. By extension this Person is also the entire world, both that which has been and that which is in process of becoming. In fact all beings comprise only one part of the Person, while three other parts are immortal in heaven. Mythologically speaking Purusha is the primeval male, and his counterpart is Viraj the primeval female, and they sprang from one another (later it was said that it was Brahma who divided himself into these two). This cosmic Person the gods then offered as a sacrifice, and this sacrifice was the prototype of all future sacrifice (*yajna*). From that cosmic sacrifice came the seasons, the beasts and birds, the hymns and *mantras* of the Vedas, the four classes of people, and the various aspects of the universe. The mouth of the Person became the *brahmana*, the arms were made into the *rajanya*, the thighs produced the *vaiśya*, and from the feet came the *śudra*. In the *Laws of Manu* (especially 1.31; 10.4)[36] these are the four castes (*varnas*) which are very strictly differentiated, the *brahmana* or priestly, the *kshatriya* (corresponding to the *rajanya*) or warrior and princely, the *vaiśya* or mercantile and agricultural, and the *śudra* or artisan and laboring. In the words of the *Purusha-sukta* (10.90.6, 11–14):

> When the gods spread out the sacrifice with the Purusha as oblation, spring was its oil, summer the fuel, autumn the oblation.
> When they divided the Purusha, into how many parts did they arrange him? What was his mouth? What his two arms? What are his thighs and feet called?
> The Brahmana was his mouth, his two arms were made the Rajanya, his two thighs the Vaisya, from his feet the Śudra was born.
> The moon was born from his spirit, from his eye was born the sun, from his mouth Indra and Agni, from his breath Vayu was born.
> From his navel arose the middle sky, from his head the heaven originated, from his feet the earth, the quarters from his ear. Thus did they fashion the worlds.[37]

The Unnamed and Unknown

The theme of a primeval germ or cosmic embryo, which occurs in a hymn to Viśvakarman (*Rig Veda* 10.82.5), is elaborated in another Rig Vedic hymn (10.121). The latter hymn opens with the statement that in the beginning there arose a golden germ (*hiranyagarbha*, literally golden womb, sometimes translated golden egg). He was born as the only lord of creation, he established this earth and heaven. He is the life and breath of all, the snowy mountains and the sea are his, he inaugurated sacrifice and promulgated good laws. Then each verse in which these characteristics are described concludes with the question as to the identity of this unnamed one: "Who is the god, to whom we should offer sacrifice?" A final verse states that Prajapati is this god, but this verse is probably a later addition, and the original hymn probably concluded with the unanswered question, "Who is the god?"[38]

Yet another hymn (*Rig Veda* 10.129), this one attributed to the *rishi* Prajapati Parameshthin, deepens the mystery to the point of unfathomability. The hymn to Brahmanaspati (10.72) expressed the opinion that being (*sat*) arose out of nonbeing (*asat*), while on the other hand the *Chandogya Upanishad* (6.2.2) asks, "how could being be produced from nonbeing?" and declares that "on the contrary . . . in the beginning this was being alone, one only, without a second."[39] The present hymn (*Rig Veda* 10.129), however, takes a middle way and affirms that in the beginning there was neither nonbeing nor being, no realm of air and no sky beyond it, neither death nor immortality, nor any distinction of night and day. There was, however, "the One," and it breathed by its own nature, although there was as yet no breath or wind; apart from it there was nothing whatsoever. This One was born by the great power of "fervor" (*tapas,* literally "heat," a word which describes the more extreme aspects of renunciation and austerity which result in the acquisition of spiritual power, a word which is used of the great ascetics; cf. 10.190.1, "from fervor kindled to its height eternal law and truth were born"). After that, in the beginning, there arose "desire" (*kama,* the longing of love), and this was the primal seed of consciousness. So it is possible to recognize that being is inherent in nonbeing, and that the two are closely related. Desire is also, we gather, the urge to creativity, for a dividing line is now recognized between below and above, which must mean that the original One has become a duality. But even if this is a correct description of the process, the ultimate riddle remains. Was there a creator of everything? The gods themselves cannot be it, because they only came into being along with the creation of the world itself. On high there must indeed be a director or overseer of the world, but is he also the one who created everything? Does even he know the ultimate answer? In the words of the hymn by Prajapati Parameshthin:

> The non-existent was not, the existent was not then; air was not, nor the firmament that is beyond. What stirred? Where? Under whose shelter? Was the deep abyss water?
> Death was not, immortality was not then; no distinction was there of night and day. That One breathed, windless, self-dependent. Other than that there was nought beyond.
> Darkness there was, plunged in darkness in the beginning; undistinguished water was all this. That which was, was covered with the void; through the power of heat was produced the One.
> Desire first stirred in it, desire that was the first seed of spirit. The connection of the existent in the non-existent the sages found, seeking in their hearts with wisdom.
> Their cord was stretched across. Was there a below? Was there an above? Impregnators there were; powers there were; will was below; endeavor was above.
> Who verily knows? Who will here declare whence this creation is born, whence it is? On this side are the gods through the creation of this universe; who then knows whence it has come into existence?
> Whence this creation has come into existence, whether he established it or did not, he who is its overseer in the highest firmament, he verily knows, or he knows not.[40]

Already in the *Rig Veda,* therefore, as seen in the foregoing quotations and references, are found many of the deities (even if some are relatively less important at this time than later), many of the practices (including sacrifice, bathing in the waters, austerities, and the differentiation of classes in society), and many of the concepts (including rebirth, and the reality of the One in the many), which are characteristic of Later Hinduism. Here also are the beginnings of the three main "paths" (*margas*) of Later Hinduism, namely, *bhakti marga* or the way of personal devotion directed toward a deity, *karma marga* or the way of action, and *jnana marga* or the way of knowledge.

PHILOSOPHY IN THE BRAHMANAS AND THE UPANISHADS

Knowledge in the Brahmanas

In the Brahmanas as commentaries on the Vedas, and in the Upanishads as the concluding portion of the Vedas, it is most of all the way of knowledge which is emphasized, and these works are thus essentially philosophical in character.

The *Śatapatha Brahmana* (10.5.3.1ff.), for example, quotes the opening statement of the Rig Vedic creation hymn of Prajapati Parameshthin (10.129) and explains substantially in line with the original but at much greater length that Mind, which was at the outset neither existent nor nonexistent, wished to become more substantial and have a self (*atman*), therefore practiced austerity and solidified itself. Then mind created speech, speech created breath, breath created ear, ear created work, and work created fire. Knowledge also built the fire altar, and the altar is the earth, air, sky, sun, stars, year, and body. So it is by knowledge that persons may ascend to the state where desires have vanished. "He who does not know this does not attain to that world either by sacrificial gifts or by devout practices, but only to those who know does that world belong" (10.5.4.16).[41]

As to the manner of the creation of the world, another passage in the *Śatapatha Brahmana* (11.1.6.1ff.) takes up the Rig Vedic conception of the *hiranyagarbha* or golden germ (*Rig Veda* 10.121.1), and explains that in the beginning there was nothing but a sea of water; the waters toiled and became heated with fervid devotion, and a golden germ was produced; from this came Prajapati and he, in turn, by the breath of his mouth created the gods and by downward breathing created the *asuras,* then made the day and the night, the year, and so on.[42]

Again, the *brahman* (neuter), which was prayer or spell or holy power in the *Rig Veda* (10.162.1), is identified as the cause and creator of the world. The *Śatapatha Brahmana* (11.2.3.1ff.) explains: "Verily, in the beginning this (universe) was the Brahman. It created the gods and, having created the gods, it made them ascend these worlds: Agni this earth, Vayu the air, and Surya the sky." The passage then goes on to say that form (which is explained as equivalent to mind) and name (which is equivalent to speech) are the two great manifestations or phantasmagoric representations of Brahman, "and verily he who knows these two great manifestations of the Brahman becomes himself a great manifestation."[43]

Doctrine in the Upanishads

In the climax of the philosophical development in the Upanishads terms already encountered are employed and it is affirmed that the essential reality underlying the world, called Brahman or Being (*sat*), and the essential reality in human persons, called the Self (*atman*), are identical; indeed, Atman is equally well the name of the Supreme Self.

About the Brahman the *Taittriya Upanishad* (3.1.1), for example, says: "That from whence these beings are born, that by which, when born, they live, that into which they enter at their death, try to know that. That is Brahman."[44]

About the Self (*atman*) the *Brihad-Aranyaka Upanishad* (3.7.16ff.) says: "He who dwells in the breath, and within the breath, whom the breath does not know, whose body the breath is, and who rules the breath within, he is thy Self, the ruler within, the immortal." Similar statements follow with respect to the tongue, eye, ear, mind, skin, understanding, and so forth and then the passage concludes: "He is ... unseen but seeing; unheard, but hearing; unperceived, but perceiving; unknown, but knowing. There is no other seer but he, there is no other hearer but he, there is no other perceiver but he, there is no other knower but he. This is thy Self, the ruler within, the immortal."

So an equation may be stated which affirms the identity of *brahman* and *atman*. The Brahman is vast, resplendent, of unthinkable form, and far beyond what is far; yet at the same time is near at hand, hidden in the cave of the heart, among those who see it.

Manifest, near, moving in the cave (of the heart) is the great Being. In it everything is centered which ye know as moving, breathing, and blinking, as being and not-being, as adorable, as the best, that is beyond the understanding of creatures. . . .

That shines forth grand, divine, inconceivable, smaller than small; it is far beyond what is far and yet near here, it is hidden in the cave (of the heart) among those who see it even here (*Mundaka Upanishad* 2.2.1; 3.1.7).

He is my self within the heart, smaller than a corn of rice, smaller than a corn of barley, smaller than a mustard seed, smaller than a canary seed or the kernal of a canary seed. He also is my self within the heart, greater than the earth, greater than the sky, greater than heaven, greater than all these worlds.

He from whom all works, all desires, all sweet colors and tastes proceed, who embraces all this, who never speaks and who is never surprised, he, my self within the heart, is that Brahman. When I shall have departed from hence, I shall obtain him. He who has this faith has no doubt (*Chandogya Upanishad* 3.14.3–4).

Among many other illustrations by which to explain the doctrine of the universal being which is diffused throughout the world and yet present within the individual, the *rishi* Uddalaka Aruni asks his son Śvetaketu to place salt in water overnight and try to find it in the morning, when it was of course completely dissolved in the water. Then, using the phrase *tat tvam asi* (that thou art), the father says to his son: "Here also, in this body, forsooth, you do not perceive the True (*sat*), my son; but there indeed it is. That which is the subtle essence, in it all that exists has its self. It is the True. It is the Self, and thou, O Śvetaketu, art it" (*Chandogya Upanishad* 6.13.1–3).

The Path

As to how to attain to realization of this underlying reality of Brahman/Atman which is in everything, the *Mundaka Upanishad* (3.1.8) states that it is not to be apprehended by sight or speech or any other of the senses, nor by austerity nor by good works. Rather, it is only when one's nature has become purified by the serene light of knowledge that one sees it.

Meditation. Therefore it is primarily concentration of the mind (*dharana*) and meditation (*dhyana*) which the Upanishads recommend as constituting the path which leads to the realization of Brahman/Atman. "All this is Brahman. Let a man meditate on that (visible world) as beginning, ending, and breathing in it (the Brahman)," says the *Chandogya Upanishad* (3.14.1).

As a specific procedure the mind may be concentrated on a *mantra* or sacred verse from the Vedas or other scriptures, and especially on a single syllable (a monosyllabic *mantra*) of mystic significance (*bijakshara,* seed syllable, or *bijamantra,* seed *mantra*). Of all such mystic syllables, the most solemn is Om (Sanskrit *aum*), and the *Chandogya Upanishad* (1.1.1) begins with the instruction that one should meditate on this syllable, while the *Mandukya Upanishad* is entirely devoted to the exposition of the significance of this syllable. Originally Om denotes assent (yes, cf. amen), and with this meaning was pronounced at the beginning of every recital of a Vedic chant, coming to stand for the whole Veda, and for the knowledge which the Veda conveys, particularly the knowledge of Brahman. So the syllable is the symbol of Brahman, and of all that is. Thus the *Mandukya Upanishad* (1) declares that all that is past, present, and future is only the syllable *aum*.[45]

As an illustration of the effect of meditation so focused, the *Śvetaśvatara*

Upanishad (1.13–14) adduces a piece of firewood. In the wood, fire is essentially present all the time, but the fire is not seen until the friction produced by the fire drill causes it to ignite. So the body may be considered the piece of firewood, and the *mantra* Om the fire drill, and by practicing the friction of meditation (*dhyana*) one may see the bright god (*deva*) who is hidden in the self like the spark in the wood.

Yoga. Along with such concentration of the mind, physical practices are also recommended, and the combination of physical and mental disciplines is called *yoga* (literally "union"). In this there is connection with the idea of the spiritual efficacy of austerities (*tapas*) already found in the Vedas. In the *Maitri Upanishad* (6.18) "the sixfold *yoga*" is described as consisting in "restraint of the breath, restraint of the senses, meditation, fixed attention, investigation, absorption." By these means "the sage, shaking off good and evil (a phrase found also in the *Mundaka Upanishad* 3.1.3), makes everything to be one in the Highest Indestructible."

The Goal

The Upanishadic goal is thus the attainment of spiritual union with the Brahman, the realization of the identity of the personal self with the holy power which is the supreme reality of the universe. Those who have followed after both meditation (*dhyana*) and proper discipline (*yoga*) have seen the power of the divine hidden in its own qualities (*Śvetāśvatara Upanishad* 1.3). Already in the present existence such persons achieve an inner detachment from subservience to all the contingencies of life. "Through the practice of *yoga* one obtains contentment, power to endure good and evil, and tranquility" (*Maitri Upanishad* 6.29).

Even now, while the person is still alive and still on this earth, this represents an experience of deliverance and liberation, which is called *jivan-mukti*, "living release." As the *Paingala Upanishad* (3.2) puts it, the knower of Brahman, the one who has a direct and immediate perception of Brahman, becomes a person who is liberated while still in life.[46] But the ultimate deliverance which is hoped for is release from the contingency that is life itself, liberation from the cycle of birth, death, and rebirth.

Already in the *Rig Veda* (7.59.12) there is an anticipation of this ultimate goal in the prayer: "May I be detached from death like a gourd from its stem, but not from the immortal."[47] Now in the Upanishads the doctrine of reincarnation is clearly enunciated, which holds that living beings are repeatedly born again in mortal forms determined by deeds in previous existences. The endless cycle of birth, death, and rebirth and the world in which this cycle operates inexorably, are *samsara*, while actions together with their inevitable consequences are *karma*, and the desired deliverance is in union with the infinite reality. Ignorance allows the illusion that persons and the world are separate from the ultimate reality; as long as the illusion persists reincarnation holds sway; but with right understanding rebirth ends and final release is attained.

Thus the *Mundaka Upanishad* (1.2.7, 10–11) says that while sacrifices and good works have their place, they are really "frail boats," and deluded persons who think that these are the highest good "are subject again and again to old age and death . . . and enter again this world or a lower one." But "those who practice austerity (*tapas*) and faith—in the forest, tranquil, wise, and living on alms—depart free from passion through the sun to where that immortal person dwells whose nature is imperishable." So also the *Śvetāśvatara Upanishad* (1.11) affirms that by knowing the one god "all fetters fall off, sufferings are destroyed, and birth and death cease."

In the *Mundaka Upanishad* (3.2.8–9) the matter is pictured by comparison with the rivers and the ocean. "As the flowing rivers disappear in the sea, losing their name and their form, thus a wise man, freed from name and form, goes to the divine Person, who is greater than the great. He who knows that highest Brahman, becomes even Brahman. . . . He overcomes grief, he overcomes evil; free from the fetters of the heart, he becomes immortal."

In the *Chandogya Upanishad* (6.14.1–2) Aruni follows the experiment with the salt in the water with a parable. A man was brought blindfolded from his home in Gandhara and abandoned in an uninhabited place. In that place he could only turn in all directions and cry for help. But if someone would remove his blindfold and tell him, "Go in that direction, it is Gandhara, go in that direction," then he would be able to find his way home again. Even so, one who gains true knowledge from a teacher will reach perfection.[48]

4

CHRONOLOGY OF THE KALI AGE

BEGINNING OF THE KALI AGE

In traditional Indian chronology, which speaks of four successive ages (*yugas*) of the world, the fourth and present age, the Kaliyuga, is reckoned as beginning shortly after the *Mahabharata* war, and more precisely as beginning at the point of the death of Krishna at Dvaraka, and the accession of Parikshit II in succession to Yudhishthira at Hastinapura.

Death of Krishna

With respect to Krishna, after serving as charioteer for Arjuna in the Great Battle on the plain of Kurukshetra, Krishna returned to Dvaraka. Many signs of coming disaster then manifested themselves, and most of the Yadava chiefs perished in quarrels with one another. Krishna himself retired to the forest, together with Balarama, his older half-brother, but there Balarama died in his sleep, while Krishna himself was mistaken by a hunter for a deer and shot in the foot with an iron arrow, from which wound he died. In grief for his two sons, Vasudeva, the aged father, also lay down and died. Arjuna performed the funeral ceremonies for all three, and Rohini, Devaki, and other wives of Vasudeva, eight queens of Krishna with Rukmini at their head, and Revati the one wife of Balarama, all immolated themselves in the flames of the funeral fire. Then the ocean rose and submerged Dvaraka, and so the end of the Yadavas came to pass. It was on the very day that Krishna departed from the earth (according to the account of these events in the *Vishnu Purana* 5.38),[1] that "the powerful dark-bodied Kali age descended."

Accession of Parikshit II

With respect to Yudhishthira and Parikshit II, it was Yudhishthira who, after the Pandavas were successful in the famous war, being himself their oldest member, took the throne at Hastinapura, only finally to abdicate, leaving a divided kingdom to Parikshit II at Hastinapura and to Yuyutsu at Indraprastha. Like Yudhishthira, Parikshit II was a member of the Pandava family in the Paurava line, being himself the son of Abhimanyu and the grandson of Arjuna. Abhimanyu, the father, lost his life in the Mahabharata war, being slain on the thirteenth day of the Great Battle. The mother was Uttara, a princess from the Virata country, and the son was born at about the time of the father's death. As king, Parikshit II is eulogized in the *Mahabharata* (1.45.5–15) as a man of great spirit who, for sixty years, was the herdsman of his people. Under his rule the four classes of society, the *brahmanas, kshatriyas, vaiśyas,* and *śudras,* did their work gladly. He was impartial and beneficent to all creatures, and gave food to the widowed, orphaned, maimed, and poor. "To all the world the famous man was friend."[2]

As to calendar dates for these events, there are various calculations, but the precise point of the beginning of the Kaliyuga is usually identified with the accession of Parikshit II and dated in the year corresponding to 3101 B.C.E. Since Yudhishthira is usually supposed to have reigned for thirty-six years prior to his abdication, the date of the Mahabharata war is thereby placed in 3137 B.C.E..[3] The Kaliyuga era remains in current use in India, and in this era the year 5088 began on April 16, 1987 C.E.[4]

PURANIC DYNASTIC LISTS

For the Kali age as it went on from shortly after the Mahabharata war and more precisely from the death of Krishna and the accession of Parikshit II, the Puranas continue to provide chronological data in the form of their genealogies and lists of the kings of various dynasties. The *Vishnu Purana* (4.20),[5] indeed, represents itself as recited originally in the reign of Parikshit II son of Abhimanyu, and most of the other Puranas profess to come from a time in the reign of Adhisimakrishna (the great-great-grandson of Parikshit II). Thus Adhisimakrishna is also a significant figure from the point of view of chronological reckoning. But the Puranic lists actually extend far beyond the times of Parikshit II and of Adhisimakrishna, and it is plain that the Puranas must have been composed at least as late as the time to which their lists extend, and in fact they may have only reached their present form circa 300–400 C.E. To accommodate this situation the Puranic authors ordinarily use three tenses, the present for the time in which the works purport to have been composed, the past for the time prior thereto, and the future for the time ahead thereof. Lists and genealogies are available, therefore, which extend far down in the Kali age.

As preserved in the several Puranas (e.g., *Vishnu Purana* 4:21ff.; *Matsya Purana* 271–273),[6] there are differences in names and years in the lists, but at least broadly speaking it is substantially the same picture which is presented, and various opportunities are provided for the establishment of synchronisms among the various rulers and with events known from other sources. Thus by following down in these lists to points, the dates of which are otherwise relatively well established in later Indian history, it is possible to obtain at least an approximate idea of the span of time thereby indicated as intervening between the Mahabharata war and/or Parikshit II and such later relatively well established points, an approximation of time which may suggest dates for the war and for Parikshit II which will be more recent and will appear historically more probable than the apparently excessively remote dates of 3137 and 3101 B.C.E.[7] Chiefly involved are, on the one hand, the Puranic dynastic lists for four kingdoms, namely, the kingdoms of Magadha, Kosála, Vatsa, and Avanti, and on the other hand the relatively well fixed points of the accessions of Candragupta, the founder of the Maurya dynasty, and of Pushyamitra, the founder of the Śunga dynasty.

The four kingdoms just mentioned were all in the central region (Madhyadeśa) of Northern India. Their locations, capitals, and kings known from Jaina and Buddhist sources as reigning in the time of Mahavira and the Buddha, were the following: Magadha, in the modern districts of Patna and Gaya, with its ancient capital at Rajagriha (Girivraja) and later at Pataliputra, ruled by King Bimbisara and afterward by his son Ajataśatru; Kośala, to the northwest in the modern district of Oudh, with its capital earlier at Ayodhya on the river Sarayu (and at Saketa, a suburb of Ayodhya), and later at Śravasti (identified with modern Saheth-Maheth on the river Rapti in the Gonda district), reigned over by King Prasenajit; Vatsa (Vamsa), to the south, on the Yamuna River before its confluence with the Ganges, with its capital at Kauśambi (identified with modern Kosam in the district of Allahabad), reigned over by King Udayana; and Avanti, still farther south and west, with its capital at Ujjayini (modern Ujjain), ruled by King Pradyota.[8]

As for the Puranic dynastic lines (*vamsas*), those here involved are: the Ikshvakus in Kośala, the Pauravas in Vatsa, the Barhadrathas and the Śaiśunagas in Magadha, and the Pradyotas in Avanti.

Ikshvakus of Kośala

The genealogy of the Solar race begins with Ikshvaku and comes down in the line of descent through the most famous Solar king, Rama, to Brihadbala (Vrihadbala) who, as king of Ayodhya, led the troops of Kośala on the side of the Kauravas in the Bharata war, and was killed in the battle by Abhimanyu son of Arjuna (*Vishnu Purana* 4.4).[9] Then the dynastic list continues (*Vishnu Purana* 4.22; *Matsya Purana* 12.271–273)[10] with twenty-seven to twenty-nine names (in the several versions of the list) inclusively from Brihadbala to Sumitra II, who is the last king of this line. The third (or in some lists, the fourth) king prior to Sumitra II is Prasenajit, who reigned in Śravasti in the time of the Buddha. At this time Kośala was the predominant kingdom in Northern India, but it would soon be outstripped by Magadha.

Pauravas of Vatsa

The genealogy of the Lunar race begins with Pururavas Aila, and its most important line is that of the Pauravas, descended from Puru, one of the five sons of Yayati. The Paurava line in turn comes down through many generations including Dushyanta and his son Bharata, Kuru and his son Parikshit I, and many others, to the Bharatas, both the Kauravas and the Pandavas, who fought each other in the great Bharata war. At this point the Pandava line which we have to follow goes on (*Vishnu Purana* 4.20–21; *Matsya Purana* 49–50)[11] from Arjuna's son Abhimanyu, who died in the war, to Parikshit II, Janamejaya, Satanika, Adhisimakrishna, and Nichakshu (Vivakshu). As already noted, Parikshit II reigned in Yudhishthira's capital of Hastinapura, and the same city was the seat of his successors down to Nichakshu. In the time of Nichakshu, however, Hastinapura was submerged by a flood of the Ganges, and Nichakshu changed his capital to the city of Kauśambi in the country of Vatsa. In the thus newly founded Kauśambi branch of the Bharata/Paurava/Pandava line, there were twenty-four kings, counting inclusively from Nichakshu to Kshemaka, who was the last king of the dynasty. In this series of twenty-four kings, the twentieth (i.e., the fourth predecessor of Kshemaka) was Udayana, who is known as the ruler of Kauśambi in the time of the Buddha.

Barhadrathas of Magadha and Avanti

In the Lunar Paurava line, Kuru had many sons in addition to Parikshit I, with whom we are already acquainted, his first being Sudhanush. The great-great-grandson of Sudhanush was Uparichara, known as the Vasu (demigod), who conquered and ruled the country of Cedi, but also spent time as a hermit. The country of Cedi was near the Yamuna River (probably corresponding roughly to modern Bundelkhand), and contiguous to the kingdom of the Kurus, and the capital city was Śuktimati (Sotthivatinagara) on the Śuktimati River. Concerning Uparichara it has already been noted that his daughter Satyavati became the wife of the Lunar king Śantanu, and the mother of Citrangada and Vichitravirya. As to the sons of Uparichara, he had them anointed kings in different kingdoms, and of them the first was Brihadratha (Vrihadratha), who became king of the Magadhas (*Mahabharata* 1.57.1–31),[12] and gave his name to the dynasty of the Barhadrathas (Varhadrathas) of Magadha (*Vishnu Purana* 4.19, 23; *Matsya Purana* 271–273).[13] The people called Magadhas are mentioned already in the *Atharva Veda* (5.22.14),[14] but only at the present point under Brihadratha and his successors was there a dynasty of kings in the country. This new kingdom of Magadha would, however, develop rapidly and would soon, under the Śaiśunagas and their successors, become the greatest of the many Indian kingdoms.

After Brihadratha, one of his sons of whom we have already heard, namely, Jarasandha, ruled Magadha and Cedi, and made his capital at Rajagriha, also called Girivraja (now Rajgir, between Patna and Gaya). It was he who gave his two daughters in marriage to Kamsa at Mathura, and finally lost his life in the ensuing long hostilities with Krishna. In turn, the son of Jarasandha was Sahadeva, who was crowned king of Magadha, became an ally of the Pandavas (one of whom was also named Sahadeva), and fought in the Mahabharata war.

From this point onward the genealogy of the Barhadrathas is especially valuable for chronological purposes, because it gives not only names but also years. Thus Sahadeva (who is contemporary with the great Bharata war) is succeeded by his son Somadhi, who is credited with either fifty-eight or fifty years (due to the variations in the Puranas). Then, counting inclusively, from Somadhi onward there are twenty-two kings (with some variations in this figure also in the several Puranas) down to Ripunjaya, who is the last king in the list and is credited with fifty years. In between, the years range from a maximum of eighty-three to a minimum of twenty-three, and the total of the individual figures in the several Puranas usually comes to slightly less than 1,000. At the end a round figure is employed, the future tense is used (as explained above), and it is stated (*Vishnu Purana* 4.23): "These are the Varhadrathas, who will reign for a thousand years."[15]

This concluding statement sounds as if the years given for the kings were years of reign, and if twenty-two kings reigned for 1,000 years, the average reign was 45.45 years, a not unreasonable figure, although some of the larger figures possibly represent life span rather than length of reign.

At this point the *Vishnu Purana* (4.24)[16] states (still using future tense) that Ripunjaya, the last of the Barhadratha dynasty, will have a minister named Sunika (Punika, Pulika), who will kill his sovereign and place his own son, Pradyota, upon the throne. Since Pradyota and Pradyota's successors are known as rulers in the city of Ujjayini in North Avanti (see immediately below), it seems indicated that, at some time prior to Punika's action, the Barhadrathas had changed their seat of rule from Magadha to Avanti, and this could be well understandable if the Barhadrathas were displaced in Magadha by the Śaiśunagas, who appear there as contemporaries of the Pradyotas. The *Matsya Purana* (271–273)[17] provides another version of the event when it states that when the Barhadrathas, Vitihotras, and Avantis (or the Vitihotras in Avanti) had passed away, Pulika killed his master and anointed his own son, Pradyota. The Vitihotras were a contemporary, less important dynasty of the Haihaya family (*Matsya Purana* 43),[18] with their capital at Mahishmati on the Narmada River in South Avanti, south of the Vindhya mountains. If it were the last of the Vitihotras whom Pulika killed (rather than the last of the Barhadrathas), it could be that the capital was thereafter moved from Mahishmati to Ujjayini, where Pradyota ruled. At any rate, the Puranic tradition represents the Pradyotas as, temporally, the immediate successors of the Barhadrathas.

Pradyotas of Avanti

In the house of Pradyota the Puranas (*Vishnu Purana* 4.24; *Matsya Purana* 271–273)[19] list five kings reigning for 138 years as shown in Table 4.1.

TABLE 4.1.
PRADYOTAS OF AVANTI

Kings	Years
1. Pradyota	23
2. Palaka	24
3. Viśakhayupa	50
4. Ajaka	21
5. Nandivardhana	20
	138

The name of the last king in the list, Nandivardhana, is the same as the name of the next to the last king in the Śaiśunaga dynasty (Table 4.2), but the Puranic texts also give the name Vartivardhana for this Pradyota king, and he is probably to be recognized as a totally separate personage. There are also several variant readings

TABLE 4.2.
ŚAIŚUNAGAS OF MAGADHA

Kings	Years
1. Śiśunaga	40
2. Kakavarna	36
3. Kshemadharman	20
4. Kshatraujas	40
5. Bimbisara (Vimbisara)	28
6. Ajataśatru	25
7. Darśaka (Dharbaka)	25
8. Udayin (Udayaśwa)	33
9. Nandivardhana	40
10. Mahanandin	43
	330

for the individual lengths of reign, and one reading makes the total length of the dynasty only fifty-two years instead of 138.[20] Of the kings of the dynasty, Pradyota appears in the Buddhist sources as ruling in Ujjayini in the time of the Buddha, and according to Jaina tradition Palaka began his reign at exactly the time that Mahavira died.

Śaiśunagas of Magadha

The Barhadrathas were the first dynasty of the kingdom of Magadha, and the Śaiśunagas were the second. Since the Śaiśunagas were thus the successors of the Barhadrathas in Magadha, and since the Pradyotas arose in Avanti after the Barhadrathas passed away, the Śaiśunagas and the Pradyotas were contemporaries. The Puranic list of the Śaiśunaga rulers (*Vishnu Purana* 4.24; *Matsya Purana* 271–273)[21] begins with Śiśunaga—from whom the dynasty takes its name—and states that Śiśunaga placed his son in Varanasi, and then made himself master of Girivraja (Rajagriha) for forty years. The entire list in direct line of descent stands in the Puranas as shown in Table 4.2.

The individual years, presumably of reign, in Table 4.2 total 330, the Puranic texts state the total as 360 or 362 years, but there is reason to think that these figures are a corruption of an original 163 years, a perhaps more likely total and one, of course, requiring reductions in the lengths of at least some of the individual reigns.[22]

There is also a problem in the fact that Buddhist sources make Bimbisara a member of a line called Haryanka, and make Śiśunaga the founder of a distinct line of rulers which followed rather than preceded that of Bimbisara.[23] If this were correct the sequence of kings would probably be: Kshatraujas, Bimbisara, Ajataśatru, Darśaka, Udayin, Nandivardhana, Mahanandin, Śiśunaga, Kakavarna, Kshemadharman. In the Puranic tradition Udayin built his capital at Kusumapur or Pataliputra (modern Patna), and this remained the great capital city under the later Śaiśunagas, the Nandas, the Mauryas, and the first of the Guptas. If, therefore, Śiśunaga were a later king, in order to accord with the statement cited just above that he made himself master of Rajagriha for forty years, it would have to be supposed that for some reason he went back to what was an earlier capital. Accordingly it would seem that the Puranic sequence of the kings is to be preferred. At any rate, both Jaina and Buddhist sources speak often of Bimbisara (also called Śrenika, Seniya) and Ajataśatru (also called Kunika, Kuniya) as ruling in the time of Mahavira and the Buddha.

All together then, except for the temporal succession of the Barhadratha and Pradyota lines, the several dynasties just outlined were more or less contemporary, for like Pradyota of Avanti and Bimbisara and Ajataśatru of Magadha, the Ikshvaku Prasenajit of Kośala and the Paurava Udayana of Vatsa were also contemporaries of the Buddha. All of these more or less contemporary dynastic lists come to an end, however, a few generations after the time of the Buddha, except that the Śaiśunagas of Magadha are succeeded by direct descendants in a new dynastic group (the Nandas). Thus the royal houses of the Pauravas and the Ikshvakus disappear at the same time, and Magadha and its rulers remain as sovereign in a much expanded empire.[24]

Nandas of Magadha

The Puranas (*Vishnu Purana* 4.24; *Matsya Purana* 271–273)[25] state (in the future tense for the Kali age) that Mahanandin (Mahanandi, Mahananda), the last king in the Śaiśunaga dynasty (Table 4.2), will have a son by a *Śudra* woman, whose name will be Nanda (probably showing his direct descent from both Mahanandin and also Nandivardhana in the Śaiśunaga line). Nanda will also be called Mahapadma. He will annihilate all the *kshatriyas,* and after him the kings will be *śudras.* He will be sole monarch, and will bring the whole earth under one umbrella, i.e., under his sole sway. He will be on the earth for eighty-eight years, and eight sons will succeed him as kings for twelve years, thus the Nandas will govern for 100 years. Some texts, however, give Mahapadma twenty-eight years instead of eighty-eight, in which case the total Nanda dominion would be only forty years.[26] Buddhist sources also give the names of all nine of the Nanda kings, calling the first one Ugrasena (Uggasena) and the last one Dhana; therefore Nanda/Mahapadma may also have been known as Ugrasena.

Nanda/Mahapadma. The affirmation that Nanda/Mahapadma (possibly also known as Ugrasena) brought the whole earth under his sole sway must mean that he accomplished a major expansion and consolidation of the Magadhan empire, and this obviously prepared the way for the even greater empire of the Mauryas which was to follow.[27]

At a later point in the Puranas (*Vishnu Purana* 4.24; *Matsya Purana* 273),[28] when the dynastic lists of the past, the present, and the future are being concluded, a cumulative chronological summary is stated in the words: "From the birth of Parikshit to the coronation of Nanda it is to be known that 1,015 years have elapsed." Because of the epoch-making work of Nanda/Mahapadma/Ugrasena it may be presumed that he is the Nanda here referred to. On the other hand, he himself came from a line in which the Nanda name first appeared with Nandivardhana (Table 4.2), and it could be supposed that Nandivardhana is the Nanda to whom reference is here made.

In the several texts the summary figure (1,015 years) is also variously given as 1,050 and 1,500 years. The largest figure (1,500 years) could be arrived at by assuming that the Barhadrathas in Magadha, the Pradyotas in Avanti, and the Śaiśunagas in Magadha were successive dynasties, and adding the maximum figures given for them respectively, namely, 1,000, 138, and 362. Reason was seen, however, to think that those several maximum figures were too large, and in the instance of the present cumulative figures it is also probably indicated to prefer the smallest figure, namely, 1,015. Thus, although all discrepancies are still not reconciled, it may be taken that the best reading of the Puranic tradition gives 1,015 years from the Mahabharata war (in which time Parikshit II was born) to the accession of Nanda/Mahapadma/Ugrasena, the founder of the Nanda dynasty, or possibly to his second predecessor, Nandivardhana, the first of the Nanda name.

Kautilya/Canakya. In his expansion of the Magadhan empire, Nanda/Mahapadma must have overthrown many of the contemporary dynasties, and it is plainly in connection with such action that it is stated that he annihilated all the *kshatriyas,* i.e., those who were the ruling classes as provided for in the system of the castes. It was obviously a contradiction of that system when rule was thereafter in the hands of Nanda/Mahapadma, who was known to be the offspring of a *śudra* mother, and in the hands of his successors, all of whom were classified as *śudras.* It is therefore not surprising that it was a *brahmana* who, as a defender of the system of the castes, put an end to the Nanda dynasty and accomplished the installation of a new king. Under the circumstances the new king must surely have belonged to one of the higher castes, presumably the *kshatriyas,* although in the Śunga, Kanva, and Andhra dynasties (which followed the Maurya) the kings were *brahmanas,* a situation for which the way may have been prepared by the political action of the *brahmana* who is on the scene at the present point. His name is Kautilya, and in Buddhist sources he is called Canakya (Canakka).

The transition in rule just described is recorded in the Puranic account (*Vishnu Purana* 4.24; *Matsya Purana* 271–273) in these words: "The *brahmana* Kautilya will root out the nine Nandas. Upon the cessation of the rule of Nanda, the Mauryas will possess the earth, for Kautilya will place Candragupta on the throne."[29]

The *Mahavamsa* (5.16–17) (a Buddhist chronicle written in Sri Lanka at the beginning of the sixth century C.E., based upon the *Dipavamsa* written in the latter part of the fourth century C.E., and upon earlier sources) recounts the same event: "Then did the *brahmana* Canakka anoint a glorious youth, known by the name Candagutta, as king over all Jambudipa, born of a noble clan, the Moriyas, when, filled with bitter hate, he had slain the ninth (Nanda) Dhanananda."[30]

With Candragupta/Candagutta on the throne, Kautilya/Canakya served as his prime minister, and is known to us directly as the author of a still extant work on statecraft, called the *Artha Sastra*. In the last verse of this work (15.430) Kautilya alludes to what he did to eliminate the Nandas and to secure the throne for a new king: "This book (*sastra*) has been made by him who from intolerance (of misrule) quickly rescued the scriptures (*sastram*) and the science of weapons (*sastram*) and the earth which had passed to the Nanda king."[31]

Mauryas

As for Candragupta and the Moriyas (or Mauryas), of which clan Candragupta was a member, the Buddhist sources explain that the Mauryas were originally Sakyan princes of Kapilavastu (Kapilavatthu) who went to the Himalaya to escape an attack by Vidudabha, king of Kosala, and established a city there. In the new region were many peacocks, and these people became known as those belonging to the place of peacocks (Sanskrit *mayura,* Pali *mora,* peacock), hence Mauryas (Moriyas). Since the *kshatriya* tribe of the Sakyas in Kapilavastu was that to which the Buddha also belonged (in the Gautama clan), the Buddha was a kinsman of Candragupta and of the latter's descendants including Asoka.[32]

According to the Puranic lists the dynasty which was founded by Candragupta consisted of nine or ten kings who reigned for a total of 137 years. At the point of this dynasty the text of the Puranas is especially corrupt, but the names and years of the first four kings are relatively well attested, while there is much more variation in the remaining names and figures. The reconstruction of the list which appears most probable is given in Table 4.3. The total of the individual reigns is in excess of the summary total which is stated as 137, a discrepancy which may be due to giving full years for each king without regard to overlaps. Of these kings, Asokavardhana (Asoka Maurya) was the great patron of Buddhism.

Sungas

After Asoka the power of the Maurya dynasty declined and the extent of the Maurya empire lessened. Finally a *brahmana* named Pushyamitra, who had the title of Senapati or commander-in-chief, murdered the last Maurya king, Brihadratha, seized power in Pataliputra, and inaugurated a new dynasty known as that of the Sungas. The Puranic tradition (*Vishnu Purana* 4.24; *Matsya Purana* 271–273)[33]

TABLE 4.3.
MAURYAS

Kings	Years
1. Candragupta	24
2. Bindusara (Vindusara)	25
3. Aśokavardhana	36
4. Kunala	8
5. Daśaratha	8
6. Samprati	9
7. Śaliśuka	13
8. Devadharman	7
9. Śatadhanvan	8
10. Brihadratha	7
	145

states that the Śunga dynasty consisted of ten kings with a total reign of 112 years. The kings and their individual lengths of reign are listed in Table 4.4. The total of the individual lengths of reign is in excess of the stated total of 112 years for the dynasty, perhaps again due to giving full years for each king without regard to overlaps.

TABLE 4.4.
ŚUNGAS

Kings	Years
1. Pushyamitra	36
2. Agnimitra	8
3. Vasujyeshtha	7
4. Vasumitra	10
5. Andhraka	2
6. Pulindaka	3
7. Ghosha	3
8. Vajramitra	9
9. Bhagavata	32
10. Devabhumi	10
	120

Kanvas

In turn Devabhumi, the last of the Śungas, was murdered by his own minister, Vasudeva, and a new dynasty was established, which the Puranas call that of the Kanvas, describing the kings as *brahmanas*. The kings are listed (*Vishnu Purana* 4.24; *Matsya Purana* 271–273)[34] as shown in Table 4.5.

Andhras/Śatavahanas

Once again the Puranas (*Vishnu Purana* 4.24; *Matsya Purana* 271–273)[35] tell us that Suśarman, the last of the Kanvas, was killed by a powerful servant named

TABLE 4.5.
KANVAS

Kings	Years
1. Vasudeva	9
2. Bhumimitra	14
3. Narayana	12
4. Suśarman	10
	45

Simuka, and a new dynasty was established. Simuka is called a member of the Andhra tribe, so the new dynasty is that of the Andhras, and it is stated that there would be thirty Andhra kings who would rule for 460 years. In inscriptions of the time the name Śatavahana also occurs and is recognized as the family name of the Andhra kings. The area of Andhra/Śatavahana rule was not in Magadha, but south of the Vindhya mountains, with centers at Amaravati on the Krishna River in the Madras district, and at Pratishthana (modern Paithan) on the Godavari River in the Aurangabad district.

Of the thirty kings in the dynasty, many bore the name Śatakarni, among them Śri Śatakarni I (the third king of the dynasty), Śri Śatakarni II (the sixth king), Gautamiputra Śatakarni (the twenty-third), and Śri Yajna Śatakarni (the twenty-seventh). Dates have been variously assessed, but Simuka may probably have begun to reign around 230 B.C.E., Śri Śatakarni I around 200 B.C.E., Śri Śatakarni II in about 172 B.C.E. (for a reign of 56 years, the longest of any of the kings), Gautamiputra Śatakarni about 80–104 C.E., and Śri Yajna Śatakarni about 170–199 C.E. Gautamiputra Śatakarni is described as the destroyer of the Śakas, Pahlavas, and Yavanas, and is said to have been the lord of both the western and eastern portions of the Vindhya range, while Śri Yajna Śatakarni appears to have been the last great Śatavahana king to rule over both the western and the eastern Deccan.[36]

Finally, when the kingdom of the Andhras has come to an end, there will be kings belonging to various races—e.g., Gardabhins (or Gardabhilas), Śakas (Scythians), Yavanas (Greeks)—and the long dynastic lists of the Puranas come to a close with brief enumeration of these (*Vishnu Purana* 4.24; *Matsya Purana* 273),[37] many of which were evidently local and contemporary with each other. Figures for lengths of reign are variant or not even given, but one series gives seven Gardabhins 72 years, eighteen Sakas 183 years, and eight Yavanas 87 years.

PURANIC DATES

Candragupta Maurya

In the long series of Puranic dynastic lists the most specific contact with exterior history is at the point of the reign of Candragupta, the founder of the Maurya dynasty, for he is almost certainly to be recognized as the Sandracottos (Androkottos) who is named by the Western historians in connection with the invasion of India by Alexander the Great. As related by Plutarch (*Life of Alexander* [62]), Androkottos (Candragupta) met Alexander while Androkottos himself was yet a youth, then "not long afterward" Androkottos took the throne of India.

Alexander died in Babylon in 323 B.C.E., and his successors met there on the day after his death to partition his empire, then toward the end of 321 B.C.E. they met again at Triparadisus in Syria for a second division of territory, and in this second partition the easternmost satrapy was that of Paropanisus, west of the Indus, and India proper was not counted as a part of the empire. Therefore Candragupta must have made himself the ruler of Magadha, and also have driven Alexander's remaining representatives out of northwestern India, between 323 and 321 B.C.E., and a date in 322 B.C.E. may be taken as most probable for the accession to sovereignty of Candragupta and for his inauguration of the Maurya dynasty.[38]

Aśoka

With the accession of Candragupta fixed with considerable probability in 322 B.C.E., his 24-year reign (Table 4.3) was 322–298, the 25-year reign of his son and successor, Bindusara, was 298–273, and the accession of Aśokavardhana (as his name is given in full in the Puranas), son and successor of Bindusara, was in 273.[39] For some reason, which may have been due to difficulties about the succession, the solemn consecration or coronation ceremony (*abhisheka*) of Aśoka only took place in Pataliputra four years after his actual accession to sovereignty (*Mahavamsa* 5.22);[40] therefore, the year of the coronation was 269 B.C.E.

It is from the coronation rather than the accession that Aśoka himself counts his regnal years in his own inscriptions. His Rock Edict 13, for example, was written in his thirteenth regnal year which, reckoning from 269 B.C.E., was 256. In this edict he mentions five western kings of the Hellenistic world, who are identifiable and dated as follows: Antiyoga (Antiochos II Theos of Syria, 261–246 B.C.E.), Tulamaya (Ptolemy II Philadelphus of Egypt, 285–247), Antekina (Antigonas Gonatas of Macedonia, 278–230), Maka (Magas of Cyrene, 300–250), and Alikasudara (Alexander of Epirus, 272–255). Since all of these kings are obviously living and ruling at the time of the writing of the edict, and since one of them died in 255, the date of 256 for the edict is well confirmed. So also (since the edict was written in Aśoka's thirteenth regnal year) is confirmed the date of 269 for the coronation of Aśoka, this being an important result in respect to a centrally important date, in which the convergence of Puranic, Buddhist, and foreign sources is remarkable.[41]

For the entire reign of Aśoka the Puranas (Table 4.3) give a total of thirty-six years, and the *Mahavamsa* (20.6), which also counts from the coronation rather than the accession,[42] gives an only slightly different total of thirty-seven years. Taking the larger figure, the death of Aśoka may have been in 232 B.C.E., and his inclusive dates of official reign in that instance would have been 269–232 B.C.E.

Pushyamitra

The Puranic tradition allows a total of 137 years for the entire Maurya dynasty, i.e., to the point where the murder of Brihadratha Maurya by Pushyamitra inaugurated the new Śunga dynasty. Reckoned from the accession of Candragupta in 322 B.C.E., this places the accession of Pushyamitra in 185 B.C.E., and dates his 36-year reign (Table 4.4) in 185–149 B.C.E.[43]

MAHABHARATA WAR CHRONOLOGY

The accession of Candragupta in 322 B.C.E. and the accession of Pushyamitra in 185 B.C.E. are, therefore, relatively well fixed dates in Indian history and, since the Puranic genealogies extend down as far as these points, further chronological calculations are possible.

Parikshit II

Taking the figures in the main Puranic tradition, the accession of Candragupta (322 B.C.E.) was preceded by 100 years of rule of the Nandas, and the coronation of Nanda, presumably meaning Mahapadma as the founder of the Nanda dynasty (or possibly meaning Nandivardhana, the first "Nanda," eighty-three years before), was 1,015 years after the birth of Parikshit II in the time of the Mahabharata war. These figures, therefore, suggest a date for the Great Battle not far from 1500 B.C.E. (322 + 100 + 1015 = 1437; 322 + 100 + 83 + 1015 = 1520).[44]

Adhisimakrishna

It is also possible to deal with the entire scope of the Puranic lists by taking the reign of Parikshit II's great-great-grandson Adhisimakrishna (whom most of the Puranas treat as the present king of the supposed time of their composition) as a zero point of reference, and by then counting back before Adhisimakrishna (B.A.) ninety-eight generations or steps to Ikshvaku, and after Adhisimakrishna (A.A.) thirty-seven generations or steps down to the accession of Pushyamitra. Then further, if one generation or step be estimated at twenty years in length on the average, with 135 generations from Ikshvaku down to the accession of Pushyamitra (185 B.C.E.), the date of Ikshavaku may be estimated at approximately 2900 B.C.E. (135 × 20 + 185 = 2885), and with the Mahabharata battle at a point forty-two generations before Pushyamitra, its date may be estimated at 1000 B.C.E. (42 × 20 + 185 = 1025).[45] Obviously the resultant dates would be pushed farther back if the Puranic generation or step were estimated as of greater length than the figure just used. At all events, broadly speaking, the Puranic materials seem to suggest a date circa 1000–1500 B.C.E. for the Great Battle of the *Mahabharata*.

JAINA DATES

In respect of chronology there are Jaina chronological works known as Pattavalis which, in recording a succession of important persons, overlap the main later Puranic dynastic lists cited above, and continue yet farther. The data relevant at the present point are summarized in the *Vicaraśreni* of the Jaina author Merutunga (circa 1306 C.E.) as follows:

> Palaka, the lord of Avanti, was anointed during that night in which the *arhat* and *tirthankara* Mahavira entered *nirvana*.
> Sixty are (the years) of King Palaka, but one hundred and fifty-five are (the years) of the Nandas; one hundred and eight those of the Mauryas, and thirty those of Pusamitra (Pushyamitra).
> Sixty (years) ruled Balamitra and Bhanumitra, forty Nabhovahana; thirteen years likewise lasted the rule of Gardabhilla, and four are the years of Śaka.[46]

It is plain that in these names and figures Merutunga intends to give the sequence of rulers in Avanti and its capital Ujjayini (modern Ujjain), a place especially important in Jaina history, from Palaka, the successor of Pradyota (Table 4.1), to the time when the Śakas or Scythians were dominant there for four years. At the end the *Vicaraśreni* sums up the figures of the entire period, and names the king who put an end to the brief Śaka rule, by saying: "After the lapse of 470 years from the *nirvana* of Mahavira, having uprooted the family of the Śakas, there will be a Malava-raja, namely, Vikramaditya."[47]

The names and figures just given are set forth in Table 4.6 alongside comparable items in the Puranic tradition. Obviously there are considerable differences, but it will be remembered that there are also many differences in the figures preserved in different texts of the Puranas.

Gardabhilla

With respect to the latter part of Table 4.6, the names of Gardabhilla, Balamitra, and Bhanumitra are known to us from a Jaina work called *Kalakacaryakatha* (The Story of the Teacher Kalaka). According to this account, the Jaina monk Kalaka (the second person of three of the same name) came to Ujjayini together with his sister, the nun Sarasvati (or Śilamati), and converted many people to Jainism. The king of Ujjayini at this time was Darpana, who was also nicknamed Gardabhilla on account of a magic art (called *gardabhi*) which he possessed. When Gardabhilla abducted Kalaka's sister, the nun Sarasvati, for his harem, Kalaka protested but without avail. Thereupon Kalaka journeyed to the "Śaka bank" and persuaded the Śakas to come and attack Ujjayini and overthrow Gardabhilla which, in spite of the king's magic art, they were successful in doing.[48]

TABLE 4.6.
FROM PALAKA TO VIKRAMADITYA IN AVANTI

Jaina Tradition	*Years*	*Puranic Tradition*
1. Palaka (presumably meaning his dynasty)	60	The Jaina total of 60 years is not far from the Puranic total (Table 4.1) for Palaka (24 years, but in some Puranic texts only 20), Ajaka (21 years), and Nandivardhana (20 years), and agrees with the supposition, for which there is some other evidence, that Viśakhayupa does not belong in the list.*
2. Nandas	155	The Nandas, beginning with Nanda/Mahapadma, are given 100 years of rule, but if the reckoning were begun with the Śaiśunaga Nandivardhana (40 years) and Mahanandin (43 years) (Table 4.2), the total would be 183 years.
3. Mauryas	108	The Mauryas are given a total of 137 years.
4. Pusamitra (Pushyamitra)	30	Pushyamitra, 36 years.
5. Balamitra and Bhanumitra	60	
6. Nabhovahana (Naravahana)	40	
7. Gardabhilla	13	Gardabhins, 72 years, close to the total of 73 years for the three rulers, Gardabhilla, Balamitra, and Bhanumitra.
8. Śaka	4	
9. Vikramaditya	470	

*Muni Shri Nagrajji, *The Contemporaneity and the Chronology of Mahāvīra and Buddha* (New Delhi: Today and Tomorrow's Book Agency, 1970), p. 100 n. 1.

Śakas

With respect to such an invasion in Western India by the Śakas, it may be remembered that the great kingdom of Magadha, which was at its height under Aśoka Maurya, was diminished in extent under his successors in the Maurya line, and in turn in the Śunga line Pushyamitra and his successors ruled over only a relatively small part of North India, while elsewhere there were other independent kingdoms, e.g., the kingdom of Andhra in the South under the Śatavahanas. Also in the northwest, Candragupta Maurya had indeed driven out the Greeks who remained after Alexander the Great, but many Greeks continued to live not far away, especially in Bactria. There, when Aśoka was reigning at Pataliputra, the Seleucid governor of the Greek colony of Bactria named Diodotus freed himself from the Seleucid yoke and became independent, founding a dynasty of Bactrian Greeks, and they soon made renewed incursions into Northwest India, where we hear of them as Yavanas in the Puranas.

The Yavanas, in turn, were displaced as rulers by further foreign conquerors in the Northwest. The new invaders belonged to three main groups, all of whom came from Central Asia. These were Scythians, known in India as Śakas, Parthians distinguished in India as Pahlavas, and the Yueh-chi, who comprised five tribes among which that of the Kushanas was the most important.[49]

In the *Kalakacaryakatha* the "Śaka bank," to which Kalaka journeyed, is the west bank of the Indus River, so the Śakas had already come that far, and then apparently readily came on to capture Ujjayini. After telling of the overthrow of Gardabhilla, the account mentions Kalaka's two nephews, Balamitra and Bhanumitra, as respectively the king and the heir apparent in Avanti, so these two were presumably installed in rule by the Śakas.[50]

All together the Śakas and also the Pahlava kings ruled relatively wide empires, and within these the smaller provinces were administered by governors known as satraps (*kshatrapas*) and great satraps (*mahakshatrapas*), several of whom are named in various inscriptions. The best known of these is Nahapana, who is called both a *kshatrapa* and a *mahakshatrapa*. He belonged to the Kshaharata race, probably a branch of the Śakas. Although he ruled a large territory in Western India, he was threatened by the Malavas from the north and the Śatavahanas from the south, and was finally overthrown by the Śatavahana king, Gautamiputra Śatakarni, whom an inscription calls the "uprooter of the Kshaharata race," and the "restorer of the glory of the Śatavahana family."[51]

With respect to the name Nabhovahana (Naravahana) which occurs prior to the name of Gardabhilla in the list in Table 4.6, it has been suggested that the name is a mistake for Nahavahana and actually refers to Nahapana, and that he was the leader of the Śakas who were brought to Ujjayini by Kalaka for the overthrow of Gardabhilla.[52] More probably, however, Nabhovahana may be recognized as a predecessor of Nahapana, and as perhaps the first Kshaharata satrap to occupy Ujjayini.[53] In this case the names of Nabhovahana, Balamitra, and Bhanumitra should follow rather than precede the name of Gardabhilla in the list.

Vikramaditya and the Vikrama Era

In what several of the texts of the *Kalakacaryakatha* call a "digression" from the main story, it is recorded that after some time Vikramaditya drove out the Śakas, became king of Malava, and established his own era. After another 135 years, however, the Śakas regained the ascendancy and, in turn, instituted their own era. The passage here cited reads:

After some time there arose Vikramaditya, who uprooted the line of the Śakas and became king of Malava . . . who made folk free of debt by the bestowal of great wealth, and established his own era in the world. Afterwards there was born a Śaka king, who destroyed his line as well, before whose lotus-feet the vassal kings bowed in the capital Ujjayini, who, when 135 years of the Vikrama era had elapsed, overthrew it (the era) and established his own era."[54]

When this text says that Vikramaditya became king of Malava, and when Merutunga calls Vikramaditya by the title of a *raja* of the Malavas, it is plain that the reference is still to the country previously called Avanti, with its capital at Ujjayini. In fact the Avantis were the tribe earlier settled in the region, and the Malavas were another tribe which came in later, and also gave their name to the country, Malava (modern Malwa). Gardabhilla, the king of Ujjayini in the time of Kalaka, was evidently a member of the Malavas and their political leader, and Vikramaditya is identified in various sources as the son of Gardabhilla, thus Vikramaditya probably restored the family dynasty when he expelled the Śakas.[55]

The era here said to have been instituted by Vikramaditya was known as the Malava Era or the Vikrama Era (*samvat*), and was reckoned from the equivalent of 57 B.C.E. (or, according to some, from 58 B.C.E.). The era is still in current use in India. The completion of the second millennium in this reckoning was celebrated in 1943 C.E., and the year 2044 of the Vikrama Samvat began on March 30, 1987, or October 23, 1987 according to different systems of reckoning.[56]

In Table 4.6 the number of years from the beginning of the rule of the Mauryas to the beginning of the rule of Vikramaditya is 255 and, if Vikramaditya began to rule and established his new era in 57 B.C.E., this would place the beginning of Maurya rule in 312 B.C.E. In apparent contrast with this date, we have seen that the accession of Candragupta, the founder of the Maurya dynasty, was probably in 322 B.C.E.; this, however, was the date of the beginning of his rule in the kingdom of Magadha, and it must be remembered that the present list is a sequence of the rulers of Avanti in Ujjayini; therefore, 312 B.C.E. may have been the date when Candragupta acquired Avanti.[57]

In the Jaina Pattavalis the names and lengths of reign of Vikramaditya and his successors are given in Table 4.7, covering a period of 135 years. At the end of this period of 135 years, as the *Kalakacaryakatha* has told us, the rule of the family of Vikramaditya was terminated by the reoccupation of Ujjayini by the Śakas, and at that point the Śaka Era (*samvat*) was inaugurated.[58]

TABLE 4.7.
FROM VIKRAMADITYA TO THE ŚAKAS IN UJJAYINI

Kings	Years
1. Vikramaditya	60
2. Vikramacharita (Dharmaditya)	40
3. Bhailla	11
4. Nailia	14
5. Nahada	10
	135

Śaka Era

Beginning 135 years after the beginning of the Vikrama Era (57 B.C.E.), the Śaka Era dates from 78 C.E., and is still very widely used in India. In this Śaka Samvat the year 1909 began on March 22, 1987 C.E.[59]

While the *Kalakacaryakatha* speaks about a Śaka king, who destroyed the line of Vikramaditya and replaced the Vikrama Era with his own era, it does not give the name of the king in question. Lacking more specific evidence, one theory supposes that the person was Kanishka, the Kushana king, whose first year of reign may have been 78 C.E. As a Kushana, Kanishka was not, strictly speaking, a Śaka, but the term may have been used in a wide sense to include all the kindred tribes of the time.[60] Another theory connects the origin of the era with the accession of a certain Castana, probably in 78 C.E. He was a Śaka *kshatrapa*, and was perhaps originally in the service of Nahapana. The line which Castana founded is credited with 242 years of rule, and was only eclipsed by the rise of the Guptas in 320 C.E.[61]

MAHAVIRA CHRONOLOGY

Reckoning back 605 years (135 years in Table 4.7, plus 470 years in Table 4.6) from the beginning of the Śaka Samvat in 78 C.E., and 470 years (in Table 4.6) from the beginning of the Vikrama Samvat in 57 B.C.E., we reach 527 B.C.E. as the date of the anointing of Palaka as the lord of Avanti, which was also the time, according to Merutunga, of the death of Mahavira. It was also seen that the same chronology places the beginning of the rule of Candragupta and the Mauryas in Avanti in 312 B.C.E., and reckoning back from that point 215 years (Nandas 155 years plus Palaka 60 years, in Table 4.6) also brings us to 527 B.C.E.

It is true that in the *Pariśishtaparvan* (8.339), which is an appendix to his *Trishashtiśalakapurushacaritra*, Hemachandra places the accession of Candragupta 155 years after the death of Mahavira, but this is probably only an error due to omitting the 60 years of Palaka in the calculation. Actually in the *Trishashtiśalakapurushacaritra* itself, Hemachandra puts the accession of his own contemporary king Kumarapala 1,669 years after the death of Mahavira and, since Kumarapala's accession took place in 1142 C.E., this also leads back to 527 B.C.E. for the death of Mahavira.[62]

Mahavira Nirvana Era

In the year 527 B.C.E. the death of Mahavira transpired, according to the precise details of the Jaina tradition (*Kalpasutra* 123),[63] in the very last rainy season experienced by the venerable ascetic, "in the fourth month of that rainy season, in the seventh fortnight, in the dark (fortnight) of Kartika, on its fifteenth day," and this exact date—reckoned as equivalent to October 31, 527 B.C.E.—provides the beginning point of the Mahavira Nirvana Era (Vira Nirvana Samvat or Vira Samvat, abbreviated VS).[64]

If the interpretation of the text by its discoverer is correct, the first known use of this era appears in a stone inscription found by G. H. Ojha in the village of Barli, near Ajmer, in which the figure 84 occurs, and if this is a date in the Vira Samvat it corresponds to 443 B.C.E.[65] In literature the earliest use known of the era is in an epic of Rama called the *Paumachariya* by the Jaina author Vimalasuri, who says that he completed this work in the year 530 of the Vira Samvat, which corresponds to the year 3 C.E.[66]

In the current usage of the era in India, the 2,500th anniversary of the *nirvana* of Mahavira was celebrated by the entire Jaina community in the year 1974 C.E.— equivalent to Vikrama Samvat 2031 and Vira Nirvana Samvat 2500[67]—and the year 2514 of the Vira Samvat began on October 23, 1987.[68]

In summary of the entire life of Mahavira, the *Kalpasutra* (147) states that he "lived thirty years as a householder, more than full twelve years in a state inferior to perfection, something less than thirty years as a *kevalin,* forty-two years as a monk, and seventy-two years on the whole."[69] With 527 B.C.E. as the year of the death of Mahavira, and with the month and day of the decease as presently calculated, the resultant chronology of the life of Mahavira is as shown in Table 4.8.[70]

TABLE 4.8.
CHRONOLOGY OF MAHAVIRA

	BCE
Birth	599
Renunciation, age 30	569
Enlightenment, age 42	557
Nirvana, age 72	October 31, 527

BUDDHA CHRONOLOGY

According to Buddhist tradition Siddhartha Gautama or Śakyamuni, who became the Buddha, renounced the world at the age of twenty-nine (*Digha Nikaya* 2.151),[71] spent six years in austerity and search before attaining enlightenment at the age of thirty-five (*Mahavastu* 2.206),[72] and, after forty-five years of teaching and gathering followers, entered the final *nirvana* at the age of eighty (*Digha Nikaya* 2.100).[73]

As to the date of the *nirvana* of the Buddha, from which the other dates in his life may be calculated in accordance with the figures just given, there are several traditions in the Buddhist world, and the available data are variously believed to indicate points within a range from 544 to 483 B.C.E.

Sri Lanka Traditions

In the tradition preserved in Sri Lanka in the *Dipavamsa* and the *Mahavamsa,*[74] the life and death of the Buddha are referenced chronologically to the reigns of Bimbisara and Ajataśatru, contemporary kings of Magadha, and to the reign of Aśoka, later king of the Maurya dynasty. As set forth earlier in the present chapter, Candragupta must have founded the Maurya dynasty between 323 and 321 B.C.E., probably in 322, and is credited with a 24-year reign (therefore 322–298), was followed by his son Bindusara who had a 25-year reign (298–273), and by his grandson Aśoka, whose accession must have been in 273, with coronation four years later in 269. With the coronation (rather than the accession) of Aśoka as their usual point of reference, the *Dipavamsa* (6.1) and the *Mahavamsa* (3.2; 5.21) state that the *nirvana* (Pali *nibbana*) of the Buddha took place on the full-moon day of the month Vesakha (Vaiśakha, April/May), and 218 years before the consecration of Aśoka, and this places the death of the Buddha in 487 (269 + 218 = 487) B.C.E.

A variation of this date has been proposed in terms of the following calculation: If the date of the accession of Candragupta be placed in 321 (the latest possible year) rather than 322, and if Bindusara be given 28 years of reign as stated in the *Mahavamsa* (5.18) rather than 25 years as in the Puranas, then the accession of Aśoka is in 269 (rather than 273) and his coronation in 265 (rather than 269), and the death of the Buddha accordingly in 483 (rather than 487). In spite of the fact, however, that this date of 483 for the *nirvana* of the Buddha is now widely quoted, it can hardly be accepted in preference to 487, because of the convergence of evidence for the date of 269 for the coronation of Aśoka.[75]

The *Mahavamsa* (2.25–32)[76] also connects the life of the Buddha chronologically with the reigns of Bimbisara and Ajataśatru, kings of Magadha, and gives all of the following figures and synchronisms. The Buddha was five years older than Bimbisara. Bimbisara was anointed king when he was fifteen years old (and thus when Gautama was twenty). The two met for the first time when Bimbisara had reigned for fifteen years, and when the king was thus thirty years old. At this point the Buddha had only shortly before experienced his enlightenment, and thus he was thirty-five years old at this time. After this time, Bimbisara continued on the throne for thirty-seven years more, and thus completed a reign which was fifty-two years in length altogether. Then Bimbisara's son, the traitor Ajataśatru, slew his father and took the throne for thirty-two years. In the eighth year of the reign of Ajataśatru the Buddha entered the final *nirvana*. Thereafter Ajataśatru reigned yet twenty-four years more. Assuming the date of 487 B.C.E. for the death of the Buddha (218 years before the consecration of Aśoka in 269 B.C.E.), the foregoing figures can be translated into the dates shown in Table 4.9.

TABLE 4.9.
CHRONOLOGY OF BUDDHA, BIMBISARA, AND AJATAŚATRU ACCORDING TO THE *MAHAVAMSA*

BUDDHA	BCE	BIMBISARA	BCE
Birth	567		
		Birth	562
Age 20	547	Accession, age 15	547
Renunciation, age 29	538		
Enlightenment, age 35	532	Meeting with Buddha, age 30	532
		Death, age 67	495
		AJATAŚATRU	
		Accession	495
Nirvana, age 80	487	Eighth year of reign	487
		Death	463

At a later time, however, probably in the middle of the eleventh century C.E., a new reckoning was made in Sri Lanka and the *nirvana* of the Buddha was dated 544 B.C.E., and the era which counts from this point is still in use in Sri Lanka.[77] This date is also accepted in several other Buddhist countries and, in spite of the existence of other systems of chronology, it was generally agreed in the Buddhist world to recognize the full-moon day of May 1956 as the 2,500th anniversary of the *nirvana* of the Buddha.[78] In India the year 2531 of this Buddha Nirvana Era began on May 13, 1987.[79]

Burma Traditions

A very long account of the life of the Buddha and of subsequent Buddhist history is found in two Burmese manuscripts, one known under the Pali name of *Tathagata-oudana* (Praise of the Tathagata (the Buddha), and the other a translation of a Pali text called *Malla-linkara-wouttoo* (History of the Most Excellent Flower).[80]

In these works three main eras are named. The first was instituted at the accession of Eetzana as king of Dewaha. This king is recognizable as Anjana king of Devadaha (as the name stands in the Pali texts), the father of Maya, who became the mother of the Buddha. Maya (Maia in the Burmese accounts) was born in the twelfth year of the new era,[81] the Buddha was born in Year 68 of the Eetzana era, made his great renunciation in Year 96, experienced enlightenment in Year 103, and died in Year 148.[82]

At the conclusion of the First Buddhist Council, which was held very shortly after the death of the Buddha, King Adzatathat of Pataliputra substituted a new "era of religion," and this dated from the Buddha's death in the Year 148 of the preceding era.[83]

Yet again, in Year 1182 of the "era of religion," a king of Pagan named Pouppadzau instituted a new era, and this is known as the Pouppadzau or the Pagan Era, and is still in common use in Burma. As so used, the Pagan Era is considered to date from 638/639 C.E., so the "era of religion" dates from 544/543 B.C.E., which is the date for the death of the Buddha now generally accepted in the entire Buddhist world.[84]

Along with some of the dates, however, and in particular along with the year dates of the main events of the Buddha's life in the Eetzana Era, there are also given the weekdays, the lunar days, and the constellations with which the moon was in combination on those days. A study of these data suggests that the Eetzana Era actually began at a point equivalent to February 17, 648 B.C.E., and that the dates in the life of the Buddha should be translated into the equivalents shown in Table 4.10.[85]

TABLE 4.10.
CHRONOLOGY OF BUDDHA ACCORDING TO BURMA TRADITION (ASTRONOMICALLY REVISED)

BUDDHA	BCE
Birth	581
Renunciation	553
Enlightenment	546
Nirvana	501

Guangzhou Tradition

Among his immediate disciples, the Buddha declared that it was Upali who was preeminent for knowing by heart the disciplinary rules (*vinaya*) of the order (*Anguttara Nikaya* 1.24),[86] and when the monks collected the Buddhist texts after the death of the Buddha it was Upali whom they asked about the *vinaya* (*Dipavamsa* 4.11; 5.11).[87] Eventually the *vinaya* collection, the *Vinayapitaka*, was brought to Guangzhou (Canton), China, by a monk from the "Western Region" named Sanghabhadra. The information he conveyed was that after the death of the Buddha and the ensuing collection of the *Vinayapitaka*, on the closing day of the summer Rainy Season Retreat (*vassa*), Upali had marked the date with a dot, then Upali and successive teachers had added a dot to the record each following summer. Finally in Guangzhou Sanghabhadra himself held the Rain Retreat *(vassa)* in the year 489/488 C.E., and at the close added a dot to the *Vinayapitaka*. At that time the total number of dots was 975. Thus this "dotted record" of Guangzhou preserves a date for the decease of the Buddha equivalent to 487/486 B.C.E., the same as the date derived from the *Mahavamsa*.[88]

Tibetan Traditions

The widely accepted date of 544 B.C.E. for the *nirvana* of the Buddha is found in Tibet, for example, in the *Blue Annals* written by the Tibetan scholar *Gos lo-tsa-ba*. In this work the author identifies what he calls "the present . . . year" (i.e., the year in which he is writing) as equivalent to 1476 C.E., and states that this year is the 2,020th year after the *nirvana* of the Buddha, thus placing the *nirvana* in 544 B.C.E.[89]

It is possible, however, to derive a different date from a Tibetan source. In the life of the Buddha as recorded in the *Dulva*, which is the Tibetan version of the *Vinayapitaka* and is found in the very voluminous Tibetan Buddhist canon, the Buddha is said to have been born at the same time that Pradyota was born, and to have attained enlightenment at the same time that Pradyota acceded to the throne of Ujjayini.[90] According to the Puranic and Jaina sources cited above (cf. Table 4.1), Pradyota reigned twenty-three years and was succeeded by Palaka (for a twenty-four year reign) at the very time that Mahavira, aged seventy-two, entered *nirvana*. As we have already seen, the probable date of the *nirvana* of Mahavira is 527 B.C.E. and, reckoned from this date, Pradyota must have begun to reign in 550, so this, according to the Tibetan source, is also the date of the enlightenment of the Buddha. The *nirvana* of the Buddha, forty-five years after his enlightenment, was therefore in 505 B.C.E., a date met not far from the astronomically revised date (501 B.C.E.) derived from the Burma tradition. The dates thus indicated for the lives of both Mahavira and the Buddha, alongside the reigns of Pradyota and Palaka, are shown in Table 4.11.

TABLE 4.11.
CHRONOLOGY OF PRADYOTA AND PALAKA, AND OF MAHAVIRA AND BUDDHA, ACCORDING TO A TIBET TRADITION

PRADYOTA	BCE	MAHAVIRA	BCE	BUDDHA	BCE
		Birth	599		
Birth	585			Birth	585
		Renunciation, age 30	569		
		Enlightenment, age 42	557		
				Renunciation, age 29	556
				Enlightenment, age 35	550
Accession	550				
End of reign	527				
PALAKA					
Accession	527	Nirvana, age 72	527		
				Nirvana, age 80	505
End of reign	503				

Buddha Nirvana Era

According to the foregoing evidence, the dates which chiefly come into consideration for the *nirvana* of the Buddha cluster at three main points: the earliest date 544/543 B.C.E. (the later traditions found in Sri Lanka, Burma, and Tibet, and the date now generally accepted in the Buddhist world); the middle date 505/501 B.C.E. (derived from interpretations of sources in Burma and Tibet); and the latest date 487/486 B.C.E. (dependent upon the *Mahavamsa* and the "dotted record" of Guangzhou, with a modern revision giving 483).

In one of the foregoing calculations the probable date of the *nirvana* of Mahavira was a factor, and in fact it is necessary to bring any acceptable chronologies of Mahavira and the Buddha into some kind of relationship, for the two teachers were certainly contemporary in at least part of their work. Since the Jaina tradition is, as we have seen, almost unanimous in placing the *nirvana* of Mahavira in the equivalent of 527 B.C.E., and since, in contrast, the Buddhist traditions exhibit many variations, it may be proper to take the Jaina date as a relatively well-fixed point of reference, and to assess the several Buddhist dates in comparison therewith.

While the earliest date for the *nirvana* of the Buddha in 544/543 B.C.E. is widely accepted in the present Buddhist world and was the basis of the celebration of the 2,500th anniversary of the *nirvana* in 1956 C.E., this date means that, in comparison with the date of 527 B.C.E. for the death of Mahavira, the Buddha died before Mahavira. The following considerations, however, make it probable that, on the contrary, Mahavira was older than the Buddha and that Mahavira predeceased the Buddha.

In the Jaina canonical sources there is no specific mention of the founder of Buddhism, while the Buddhist scriptures frequently mention the Nigantha Nataputta, who is certainly to be recognized as Mahavira, since the latter was a member of the Jnatri (Prakrit Naya or Nata) clan and thus a "son of Nata" (Nataputta), and he and his followers as possessionless ascetics were Nigranthas (Niganthas), which means "ones without any tie, unfettered."[91]

Furthermore, the Buddhist sources themselves make it plain that Mahavira was older than the Buddha, and was the first of the two to die. Thus it is related that upon one occasion King Ajataśatru (Ajatasattu) came to visit the Buddha while the latter was dwelling at Rajagriha (Rajagaha) in the Mango Grove of the physician Jivaka. Here Ajataśatru told of having gone first to six other teachers in search of understanding, all of whom were evidently older than the Buddha (since the king went to them first), and among them was "the Nigantha of the Nata clan" (*Digha Nikaya* 1.57). Likewise a wandering mendicant named Sabhiya went to the same six other teachers, including "Nigantha Nataputta," then wondered whether he should even go to the Buddha since the Buddha was "both young by birth and new in ascetic life," but did go to him at Rajagriha, because though young, he was mighty and powerful (*Sutta Nipata* 3.6).[92] Also King Prasenajit (Pasenadi) of Kośala came to the Buddha at Śravasti (Savatthi) and asked him if he claimed to be perfectly and supremely enlightened. When the Buddha answered in the affirmative, the king cited the same six other teachers as disclaiming such complete enlightenment, and asked the Buddha how he could make the claim: "For (as compared with them) master Gautama (Gotama) is young in years, and is a novice in the life of religion"—in answer to which the Buddha cited several creatures—including a prince, a snake, a fire—which would only at peril be held of no account because they were young (*Samyutta Nikaya* 1.68–69).[93]

As for the death of Mahavira being prior to the death of the Buddha, in three separate passages Buddhist references state that Mahavira died while the Buddha was still actively engaged in his own ministry. In the *Digha Nikaya* (3.117) and in the *Majjhima Nikaya* (2.243)[94] it is related that at a time when the Buddha was in the village of Samagama among the Sakyas, "at that time Nataputta the Nigantha had just died at Pava." We are told that it was Cunda (a metalworker in Pava in whose home the Buddha would later eat his last meal) who came to Samagama with the news, informed the Buddha's close disciple, Ananda, and the two of them went and told the Buddha. In the *Digha Nikaya* (3.209–210)[95] it is reported that the Buddha and his disciple Śariputra (Sariputta) came to Pava (evidently at a slightly later time), and Śariputra spoke to the brethren and referred to the recent decease of Mahavira. In each of these three passages there is also reference to division among the followers of Mahavira, which arose after his death.

It must be accepted, therefore, on the basis of the Buddhist records themselves that Mahavira predeceased the Buddha, so if the *nirvana* of Mahavira was in 527 the *nirvana* of the Buddha could not have been in 544/543.

The latest date for the *nirvana* of the Buddha in 487/486 B.C.E. certainly allows for the earlier decease of Mahavira in 527, and may also seem to be strongly supported by the close concurrence in this respect of the *Mahavamsa* and the "dotted record' of Guangzhou,[96] and the modern revision of this date to 483 is widely cited.[97]

The *Mahavamsa* of Sri Lanka and the "dotted record" of Guangzhou, however, probably only represent one and the same tradition which was carried from the one place to the other, for Sanghabhadra, who brought the "dotted record" to China was said to have come from the "Western Region"—a name often used for India, no doubt including Sri Lanka.

Furthermore, to put the life of Mahavira in 599–527 (Table 4.8) and that of the Buddha in 567–487 (Table 4.9), with a consequent interval of forty years between the deaths of the two teachers, makes it difficult to associate the events in the lives of the two as closely as they appear to be associated in the sources which refer to them both.[98]

Also, the data in the *Mahavamsa*, providing the chief basis for the 487 date of the *nirvana* of the Buddha, and which appears to be so precise, are actually themselves open to question. As noted (Table 4.9), the *Mahavamsa* places the death of the Buddha in the eighth year of the reign of Ajataśatru. It will also be remembered that upon one occasion Ajataśatru paid a visit to the Buddha, who was at that time dwelling in Rajagriha (*Digha Nikaya* 1.47–85).[99] This is the only recorded visit by Ajataśatru to the Buddha, and it must have taken place in the rainy season of the year, because it was only in the rainy season that the Buddha stayed for a longer time in any one place. In the Buddhist records all the places are noted where the Buddha spent the successive Rainy Season Retreats (*vassas*) of his entire ministry subsequent to his enlightenmnent. Shortly after the enlightenment he proceeded to Isipatana (Rishipatana), which was an open space near Varanasi and the site of a Deer Park (Migadaya), and there preached his first sermon and there also spent his first rainy season. Of the rainy seasons which followed, he spent the second, third, fourth, seventeenth, and twentieth in Rajagriha, several others in other places, and finally the twenty-first to the forty-fifth in Śravasti (Savatthi) and the forty-sixth and last in Vaiśali (Vesali). Obviously if the Buddha died in the eighth year of King Ajataśatru (Table 4.9), the king must have visited the Buddha within the last eight years of the Buddha's life, but at that time the Buddha was spending all of his rainy seasons at Śravasti (and one at Vaiśali) and not at

Rajagriha.[100] Therefore the *Mahavamsa* must be in error, and its synchronisms between the life of the Buddha and the years of reign of Ajataśatru and also of his father Bimbisara become suspect.[101]

As to both Bimbisara and Ajataśatru, there are numerous references to them in the Buddhist and also the Jaina sources, and these allow some conclusions as to the dates of their reigns.

Bimbisara (also called Śrenika and Seniya) first saw the future Buddha when the latter was leading the ascetic life but before his enlightenment, when he came to Bimbisara's capital city of Rajagriha (Rajagaha) for alms. Already at this time the king was impressed by the young man's appearance, and offered to give him wealth, which was of course declined (*Sutta Nipata* 3.1.4–20).[102] Sometime after his enlightenment the Buddha returned to Rajagriha, and Bimbisara made a donation to him of his own royal pleasure garden called Veluvana (bamboo grove) as a place for the Buddha and his monks to live (*Mahavagga* 1.22).[103] Thereafter, during the balance of his reign, Bimbisara continued to be a friend and patron of the Buddha.

Ajataśatru (also called Kunika and Kuniya), son and eventual successor of Bimbisara, however, while still the crown prince, became a friend of Devadatta. Devadatta was a cousin of the Buddha (son of the Śakyan Suppabuddha, maternal uncle of Buddha), and a member of his monastic order, but aspired to be himself the head of the order, and made several unsuccessful attempts upon the life of the Buddha, while he also instigated an unsuccessful attempt by Ajataśatru to kill his father Bimbisara with a dagger. At this juncture Bimbisara relinquished the throne to his son, but Ajataśatru killed his father anyway by starving him to death in prison (*Kullavagga* 7.2ff.).[104]

It was after this murder of his father that Ajataśatru paid the already mentioned visit to the Buddha, in the course of which Ajataśatru confessed his crime and expressed remorse for it. Since this visit took place in Rajagriha, Ajataśatru was evidently still ruling in this city, but soon after his accession Ajataśatru—probably on account of the same remorse for the death of his father—moved his capital to Campa, so the visit must have been early in the reign of Ajataśatru. At the time the Buddha was still himself evidently a relatively youthful teacher.

As related in the *Samyutta Nikaya* (1.82),[105] soon after his accession Ajataśatru was involved in a war with the aged king Prasenajit (Pasenadi) of Kosala (Kośala), whose sister was Kośaladevi. The latter was the chief queen of Bimbisara and the mother of Ajataśatru, and was said to have died of grief after the murder of her husband by her son. According to a Jaina tradition, however, the wife of Bimbisara who was the chief queen and the mother of Ajataśatru was Cellana, the daughter of the Licchavi king Cetaka of Vaiśali (Vesali), whose sister Triśala was the mother of Mahavira.[106] At a later date, after his first war with Prasenajit of Kośala, Ajataśatru was also engaged in a second war in which he fought against and conquered Vaiśali. Of these two wars the first was known to Gośala (Gosala) (once an associate and later an enemy of Mahavira) on the eve of Gośala's own death, therefore Gośala died not long after the accession of Ajataśatru. In turn Mahavira stated that he himself would die sixteen years after Gośala (Viyahapannati [Bhagavati],15),[107] and it is the Śvetambara Jaina tradition that Mahavira attained *nirvana* in the sixteenth year of the reign of Ajataśatru.[108] Therefore, reckoned back from the date of 527 B.C.E. for the *nirvana* of Mahavira, we come to 543 as the probable date of the accession of Ajataśatru,[109] and this is far different from the date (495) required by the data in the *Mahavamsa* (Table 4.9). All of these facts, then, make the 487/486 (483) date for the *nirvana* of the Buddha historically unlikely.

Because of the difficulties which thus beset the early and late dates for the *nirvana* of the Buddha, we are pointed to a date within the middle range of possibilities derived from the astronomically revised Burma tradition (501) and the date calculated from a source in Tibet (505). Although the Tibetan source offers a reasonable synchronism with the reign of Pradyota (Table 4.11), other synchronisms in the same source (e.g., with the reign of Ajataśatru) are open to question, and we may prefer the 501 date.

Dates in the Life of Buddha

Table 4.12 shows the resultant figures alongside those for Mahavira, Pradyota and Palaka, and Bimbisara and Ajataśatru. The point of transition between Bimbisara and Ajataśatru is taken as 543, as explained in the second paragraph above. Figures for the lengths of reign of Bimbisara and Ajataśatru vary (Table 4.2 and Table 4.9); so, although they are far from certain, Table 4.12 uses the lengths of reign provided by the *Mahavamsa* (Bimbisara 52 years, Ajataśatru 32 years). As required by data noted above, the scheme agrees with the temporal relationships of the Buddha with Mahavira and Pradyota/Palaka, and allows for the acquaintance of Bimbisara with the Buddha both before and after the enlightenment of the Buddha, and for the visit of Ajataśatru to the Buddha in one of the early rainy seasons (probably the fourth) spent by the Buddha at Rajagriha.[110]

TABLE 4.12.
CHRONOLOGY OF MAHAVIRA, BUDDHA, PRADYOTA, PALAKA, BIMBISARA, AND AJATAŚATRU

MAHAVIRA	BCE	BUDDHA	BCE	PRADYOTA	BCE	BIMBISARA	BCE
Birth	599						
						Accession	595
		Birth	581				
Renunciation, age 30	569						
Enlightenment, age 42	557						
		Renunciation, age 29	552				
				Accession	550		
		Enlightenment, age 35	546				
						End of reign	543
						AJATAŚATRU Accession	543
				End of reign	527		
Nirvana, age 72	527			PALAKA Accession	527		
						End of reign	511
				End of reign	503		
		Nirvana, age 80	501				

For convenient reference the chief dates dealt with in the present chapter are summarized in Tables 4.13 and 4.14.

TABLE 4.13.
OFFICIAL INDIAN ERAS

	BCE
Beginning of the Kaliyuga Era	3101
Beginning of the Buddha Nirvana Era	544
Beginning of the Mahavira Nirvana Era	527
Beginning of the Vikrama Era	57
	CE
Beginning of the Śaka Era	78

TABLE 4.14.
HISTORICALLY PROBABLE DATES

	BCE
Mahabharata war (according to Puranic data)	1500–1000
Ajataśatru accession	543
Mahavira *nirvana*	527
Buddha *nirvana*	501
Candragupta accession	322
Candragupta rule in Avanti	312
Aśoka accession	273
Aśoka coronation	269

5

GEOGRAPHY, CLANS, KINGDOMS, CITIES

In the Vedic period the geographical area chiefly in view was that of Northwestern India, around the Indus River and its tributaries. In the Epic period the chief events centered in the Upper Ganges basin, particularly in the plain of Kurukshetra between the Yamuna and the Ganges, and the most prominent cities were Indraprastha and Hastinapura in the general region of modern Delhi. After the Epic period tribes and states of course continued to exist in the Northwest and in the Upper Ganges basin, but the geographical focus of events also expanded to the East to include the Middle Ganges basin, where the Yamuna and the Ganges join (at modern Allahabad), and the Eastern Ganges basin, where (near modern Patna) the Ghaghara (ancient Sarayu) and the Gandak flow into the Ganges from the north and the Son from the South, with the largest and most important states being in these areas of the Middle and Eastern Ganges basins. It was also in these latter areas that Vardhamana Mahavira (599–527 B.C.E.) and Śakyamuni Buddha (581–501 B.C.E.) came forward and the Jaina, Buddhist, and Hindu records now provide geographical and historical information.

In respect of the chronology of the Kali age (given in Chapter 4) four of the main kingdoms (Magadha, Kosála, Vatsa, Avanti) and their dynasties have already concerned us, but in all there were many more political units than these. The Puranas,[1] Jaina, and Buddhist literature[2] name a large number of tribal groups, autonomous clans as well as larger kingdoms, ranging all across North and Central India from the Indus to the Lower Ganges, and from the Himalaya to the Vindhya mountains and below.[3] Used in the plural the names in question designate the tribes and peoples; in the singular the same names stand for the countries and kingdoms.[4]

CLANS

The various clans number at least ten and are shown, together with their capitals, in Table 5.1.

TABLE 5.1.
CLANS IN ANCIENT INDIA

1. Śakyas (Sakiyas), capital Kapilavastu
2. Koliyas, capital Ramagama
3. Mallas, capital Kuśinagara (Kusinara)
4. Mallas, capital Pava
5. Videhas, capital Mithila
6. Licchavis, capital Vaiśali (Vesali)
7. Bhaggas, capital on Sumsumara Hill
8. Bulis, capital Allakappa
9. Kalamas, capital Kesaputta
10. Moriyas, capital Pipphalivana

The territories of these clans were for the most part in the region between the Ganges and the Himalaya. Politically, most of the groups were organized in somewhat the fashion of republics (*ganas*). Public affairs were determined in an assembly (*parisha*), which met in a council hall (*santhagara*), and the elected chief of the group had the title *raja*. Some of the groups enjoyed complete or partial independence, while others such as the Śakyas, Bulis, Koliyas, and Moriyas were vassals under more powerful adjacent states.[5]

Śakyas

Of the groups, the best known is that of the Śakyas since Gautama Buddha, called Śakyamuni, the Sage of the Śakyas, was from this clan. Their territory extended from the tropical jungle of the Tarai (meaning a low plain) of northern India and southern Nepal, to the foothills of the Himalaya. To the East the Rohini River (perhaps the modern Rohwaini which joins the Rapti at Gorakhpur, India) separated the Śakyas from the Koliyas; to the West and South was the kingdom of Kośala (Kosala), ruled by descendants of the Solar dynasty, and Śakya was subservient to that kingdom. Thus the Buddha described his land and people by saying: "Flanking Himalaya, in Kosala, yonder extends a land both rich and brave. By lineage 'the Kinsmen of the Sun' are we, and Sakiyans by family" (*Sutta Nipata* 3.1.422–423).[6]

The capital of the Śakyas was the city of Kapilavastu. Kapilvastu (as it is now spelled) is still the name of an administrative district of Nepal, bounded by the Rapti River on the west and by the Indian border on the south, with the town of Taulihawa as its administrative center.[7] North of Taulihawa at a distance of 2 miles (3 km.) are the ruins which are probably to be identified with the ancient city of Kapilavastu. Later legend connected the name of the city with the sage Kapila (who figures in the story of the 60,000 sons of Sagara), but the Pali name is Kapilavatthu, which means "monkey place." According to Buddhist tradition the *raja* of Kapilavastu at the time of chief interest was Śuddhodana, a member of the Gautama clan of the Śakya tribe and a *kshatriya*, and his queen was Maya (Mahamaya, Maya Devi), a Licchavi princess, and it was their son, Siddhartha, who eventually renounced his princely heritage and went forth to seek the enlightenment which made him the Buddha.

Koliyas

The Koliyas were adjacent to the Śakyas to the east, with the Rohini River as the boundary between the two lands (*Theragatha* 10.233.529).[8] The Koliyas had two main settlements, one at Ramagama, which was considered the capital, and is identified with the present Rampur Deoriya in the district of Basti in Oudh in North India, and the other at Devadaha. Devadaha was the residence of the father of Queen Maya and, according to the *Nidanakatha* (2 Avidura Nidana),[9] Maya was on her way to Devadaha and to the home of her father when Siddhartha was born.

The place of the birth of the child who was to become the Buddha was in the Lumbinivana, the Lumbini grove. Today Lumbini is a small town in the Nepal administrative district of Rupandehi. This district has Bhairawa as its administrative center, and lies immediately to the east of the district of Kapilvastu, of which Taulihawa is the administrative center. The present town of Lumbini is between Taulihawa and Bhairawa, and about 10 miles (16 km.) east of the probable site of ancient Kapilvastu. Lumbini is now also the name of an entire Nepal administrative zone, which includes Kapilvastu, Rupandehi, and several other districts, and is situated partly in the Tarai and partly in the mountain region, bounded by India on the south, the Rapti River on the west, the Kali Gandaki River on the north, and the Narayani River on the east.[10]

Near the present town of Lumbini, at a shrine called Rummindei, there was discovered in 1896 a broken column of Aśoka, with an inscription in which the emperor says that, when he had been crowned twenty years (249 B.C.E.), he visited this site and erected the pillar "because the Buddha Śakyamuni was born here." Also he announced a tax exemption for the village Lummini, which must be the same as the place Lumbini.[11]

Although the Śakyas and Koliyas were neighbors, sharing use of a common dam on the Rohini River, they quarreled over the irrigation water, but the Buddha was able upon an occasion to accomplish a reconciliation (*Jataka* 21.536).[12]

Mallas of Kuśinagara and Mallas of Pava

The Mallas of Kuśinagara and the Mallas of Pava were located to the east and south of the Koliyas. The site of Kuśinagara (Kusinara) is quite certainly to be seen in extensive ruins near the present village of Kasia at the junction of the Rapti River and the Little Gandak River (the ancient Hiranyavati, a tributary of the Sarayu or Ghaghara), 37 miles (60 km.) east of Gorakhpur and on the border of North Bihar. Pava (Papa) was at no great distance from Kuśinagara, and has been variously located at Padrauna 12 miles (19 km.) north of Kasia, or at Sathiyamva Fazilanagara 9 miles (14 km.) southeast of Kasia in the Meveris district of North Bihar.

It was in Pava that Mahavira attained final liberation in death at the age of seventy-two years, at which time he was staying in the office of the writers in the palace of King Shashthipala (Hastipala) (*Kalpa Sutra* 123).[13] It was also in Pava that the Buddha ate his last meal in the house of a metalworker named Cunda, a meal of truffles from the jungle, from which the Buddha fell ill of dysentery.

From Pava the Buddha proceeded, sick and weary, to Kuśinagara as his chosen place of death. There, as the *Mahaparinibbana Suttanta* (*Digha Nikaya* 2.72–167) relates the great decease, he lay down upon a couch in the Sala grove of the Mallas, the Upavattana of Kusinara, on the farther side of the Hiranyavati River (2.137). When his closest disciple Ananda spoke disparagingly of Kusinara as only a small wattle-and-daub town in the midst of the jungle, and suggested that one of the great cities, Campa, Rajagaha, Savatthi, Saketa, Kosambi, or Varanasi, would be a more appropriate place for the death of the Buddha, the Buddha pointed out that Kusinara had formerly been a splendid royal city named Kuśavati, ruled over by Maha Sudassana, a great king of glory and a king of kings, and he described that city as follows (2.146–147):

> Just, Ananda, as the royal city of the gods, Alakamanda by name, is mighty, prosperous, and full of people, crowded with the gods, and provided with all kinds of food, so, Ananda, was the royal city Kusavati mighty and prosperous, full of people, crowded with men, and provided with all kinds of food.
>
> Both by day and by night, Ananda, the royal city Kusavati resounded with the ten cries: that is to say, the noise of elephants, and the noise of horses, and the noise of chariots; the sounds of the drum, of the tabor, and of the lute; the sound of singing, and the sounds of the cymbal and of the gong; and lastly, with the cry, "Eat, drink, and be merry!"

When the great decease was accomplished, Ananda went into Kusinara and made the news known to the Mallas, who were assembled in their council hall (*santhagara*). They provided the official last rites for the Buddha, bringing the body into the city through the north city gate, and taking it out by the east gate to the place of cremation.

Presumably on the basis of having had association with the Buddha during his life and work, claims for a share in the relics were made by Ajataśatru of Magadha, the Licchavis, the Śakyas, the Bulis, the Koliyas, a *brahmana* of Vethadipa, the Mallas of Pava, and the Mallas of Kuśinagara, and each of these erected a sacred cairn or memorial mound (Pali *thupa*, Sanskrit *stupa*) over the portion of the remains received. These cairns were put up in Rajagriha, Vaiśali, Kapilavastu, Allakappa, Ramagama, Vethadipa, Pava, and Kuśinagara. A *brahmana* of Kuśinagara named Drona (Dona), who had supervised the distribution, received the vessel in which the remains had been collected, and made a cairn over it. The Moriyas of Pipphalivana received and similarly commemorated the embers of the fire. "Thus there were eight cairns for the remains, and one for the vessel, and one for the embers. This was how it used to be" (2.167).[14]

The ruins at the site of ancient Kuśinagara near Kasia are in no less than six groups, and include the remains of several *stupas* and monasteries, and a temple with a colossal recumbent image of the dying Buddha, some 20 feet (6 m.) in length, with an inscription recording the erection of the temple by an abbot named Haribala in the fifth century C.E. Also in a *stupa* behind the temple a copper plate was found with an inscription with the words *nirvana caitya*. The term *caitya* (Pali *cetiya*) may be derived from a root *ci*, which means to "pile up," and usually refers to a memorial mound (*stupa*), or also to a sanctuary hall. So the shrine at this place commemorated the great decease, and the site of Kuśinagara is well established.

Videhas and Licchavis

The Videhas and the Licchavis were joined in a confederation with certain other clans including the Jnatrikas or Jnatris and the Vrijis or Vajjis, and the entire confederation was known by the name of Vriji or Vajji. The territory of these clans was to the east of the main Gandak River, which flows into the Ganges prior to Hajipur and across from Patna, and the territory probably extended as far as the

Kosi River (the ancient Kausiki), which flows into the Ganges in the district of Purnea.

The capital of the Videhas was Mithila, already mentioned as the city of Janaka, the father of Sita, the heroine of the *Ramayana,* and as probably identifiable with the town of Janakpur, just within the border of Nepal and the administrative center of the Janakpur zone.[15]

Like the *Mahabharata* (3.198.6–9), the *Jataka* (22.539) describes Mithila in glowing terms:

> By architects with rule and line laid out in order fair to see,
> With walls and gates and battlements,—traversed by streets on every side,
> With horses, cows, and chariots thronged, with tanks and gardens beautified,
> Videha's far-famed capital, gay with its knights and warrior swarms,
> Clad in their robes of tiger-skins, with banners spread and flashing arms,
> Its Brahmans dressed in Kasi cloth, perfumed with sandal, decked with gems,—
> Its palaces and all their queens with robes of state and diadems![16]

In Jaina tradition Mithila was the home of Malli and of Nami, the nineteenth and twenty-first *tirthankaras* (*Trishashtisalakapurushacaritra* 1.276–325),[17] and Mahavira spent six rainy seasons there (*Kalpa Sutra* 122).[18] The Buddha also stayed upon occasion at Mithila and taught there (*Majjhima Nikaya* 2.74).[19]

Vaisali. The capital of the Licchavis, which was also the metropolis of the entire Vajjian confederacy, was at Vaisali, known already as the seat of a Solar dynasty and a city figuring in the *Ramayana*. A suburb of Vaisali was called Kundagrama or Kundapura. This suburb was the residence of the Jnatri (or Nata) clan, and was divided into a northern part which was *kshatriya* and a southern part which was *brahmana*. Mahavira was born in Kundagrama. His embryo (it was said) was originally in the mother Devananda, wife of the *brahmana* Rishabhadatta, but by the intervention of the gods was transferred prior to birth to the mother Trisala, wife of the *kshatriya* Siddhartha of the Jnatri clan (*Acaranga Sutra* 2.3.15).[20] The personal name given to the son was Vardhamana (the increasing one), and his later title was Mahavira (great hero), but he was also known from his family background as Jnatriputra of Nataputta (son of Jnatri or Nata), and he was described as a famous citizen of Vaisali (*Sutra Kritanga* 1.2.3).[21] During his ministry Mahavira spent no less than twelve rainy seasons here in his home city of Vaisali.

The Buddha also visited Vaisali frequently, and delivered a number of his discourses to various Licchavis, who came to him both individually and in large groups (e.g., *Anguttara Nikaya* 2.190–194; 3.167–168).[22] At Vaisali he stayed upon occasion in a mango grove, which was presented to him as a gift by Ambapali, a courtesan who became a member of the order.[23] Again he stayed in a village named Beluva on a slope at the foot of a hill near Vaisali, and it was when he was staying at Beluva, in his last rainy season and turning eighty years of age, that the Buddha suffered a dire sickness which, even though recovered from, was a forewarning of his approaching death (*Mahaparinibbana Suttanta, Digha Nikaya* 2.95–99).[24] Later, Vaisali was the site of the Second Buddhist Council.[25]

Vaisali was near the modern Besarh (20 miles (35 km.) north of Hajipur), and the site of the ancient city is called Raja Visal ka garh. Excavations have brought to light pottery, terracottas, clay seals, and other objects, confirming the location of Vaisali at this place, and attesting occupation during four periods between 500 B.C.E. and 500 C.E.

Bhaggas, Bulis, Kalamas, Moriyas

The remaining clans in Table 5.1 are relatively little known but, like the foregoing clans, each had some connection with the life and work of the Buddha. Upon at least one occasion the Buddha stayed among the Bhaggas at their town named Sumsumaragiri (crocodile-haunt hill), so called it was said because when it was first being built a crocodile made a noise in a lake nearby (*Samyutta Nikaya* 3.1).[26] The Bulis of Allakappa were one of the groups which made claim to a portion of the relics of the Buddha, and evidently had close relations with Vethadipa, where a *brahmana* also claimed a portion of the relics (*Dhammapada Commentary* 1.161–162).[27] The center of the Kalamas, Kesaputta, was in the kingdom of Kośala. Before he attained the great enlightenment, Śakyamuni came to a sage of the Kalamas named Alara, and listened to his teaching, but was not satisfied (*Buddha-charita* 12.1–81).[28] Later the Buddha himself taught in Kesaputta (*Anguttara Nikaya* 1.188–192).[29] The Moriyas of Pipphalivana were a branch of the Śakyas, and they also obtained a portion of the relics of the Buddha and erected a *stupa* over these. Moriya is the Pali form of the name Maurya, so it must have been from this clan that the Maurya dynasty, the greatest dynasty in the history of Magadha, arose, and in fact the *Mahavamsa* (5.16)[30] states that Candragupta, the grandfather of Aśoka, was born a member of the Moriya clan.

KINGDOMS

The larger states were for the most part organized as kingdoms, and are called *janapadas* (communities) or *mahajanapadas* (great communities). In the several Puranas there are named in the central region (Madhyadeśa) alone no less than twenty-one *janapadas*, including the main kingdoms of Kośala, Vatsa, and Avanti, and in the other of the seven major regions of India there are many more.[31] Likewise in the Buddhist sources there are named several times in more or less identical lists no less than sixteen *mahajanapadas* (*Anguttara Nikaya* 1.213; 4.252; *Digha Nikaya* 2.200; *Mahavastu* 34),[32] also including the main kingdoms of Kośala, Vatsa, and Avanti, and Magadha as well. Even as in the case of the clans (Table 5.1), so also here in the case of the kingdoms the listing usually gives the names of the peoples, thus reflecting the original tribal basis of the organization. As it appears in the *Anguttara Nikaya* the list of the sixteen "great peoples" is reproduced in Table 5.2, where the capitals of the several kingdoms are also given. In general the order of mention is from east to west. The first fourteen communities were in the central region (Madhyadeśa), the last two, Gandhara and Kamboja, were in the northern region (Udichya or Uttarapatha). The Buddha appears to have worked in all fourteen of the states in Madhyadeśa, and the *Mahavastu* claims that he converted people and had followers of his doctrine in all of the states which it names.

Of these *mahajanapadas* the Vajjis have already been mentioned among the clans as giving their name to the confederation of the Videhas and Licchavis, with their capitals at Mithila and Vaiśali; and the Mallas have been mentioned as comprising two groups, centered at Kuśinagara and Pava respectively.

Angas

The kingdom of the Angas was the easternmost of those listed in Table 5.2. The territory of the Angas lay south of the Ganges and east of the Campa River, mainly in what is now the eastern part of South Bihar.

TABLE 5.2.
MAHAJANAPADAS

1. Angas, capital Campa
2. Magadhas, capitals Rajagriha, Campa, and Pataliputra
3. Kasis, capital Varanasi
4. Kosalas, capitals Ayodhya, Saketa, and Śravasti
5. Vajjis, capitals Mithila and Vaiśali
6. Mallas, capitals Kuśinagara and Pava
7. Cetis, capital Śuktimati
8. Vamsas, capital Kauśambi
9. Kurus, capital Hastinapura
10. Pancalas, capital of Southern Pancala, Kampilya
11. Macchas, capital Vairata
12. Surasenas, capital Mathura
13. Assakas, capital Potana
14. Avantis, capitals Ujjayini and Mahishmati
15. Gandharas, capitals Pushkalavati, Takshaśila, and Purushapura
16. Kambojas, capital Rajapura

The capital of Anga was Campa (Campapuri), a large town at the confluence of the Campa River (probably the modern Candan) and the Ganges, and is doubtless still represented by the two villages of Campanagara and Campapura, 24 miles (34 km.) east of modern Bhagalpur.

As has been noted already, Campa was the home of Karna, a hero in the Great War (*Mahabharata* 2.292ff.).[33] In Jaina tradition, Campa was the home Vasupujya, the twelfth *tirthankara*, and Mahavira spent three rainy seasons there. A Jaina book on Jaina sacred places, called the *Vividhatirtha Kalpa*, provides the information that Ajataśatru (Kunika), son of Bimbisara (Śrenika), abandoned Rajagriha upon the death of his father and made Campa his capital.[34] The Buddha also traveled through the country of the Angas and, on one occasion, came to Campa and lodged on the bank of the Gaggara Lake (named after an early queen of Anga), where a notable *brahmana* named Sonadana came to him for a lengthy conversation (*Digha Nikaya* 1.111–126).[35]

Magadhas

The kingdom of the Magadhas was separated from that of the Angas by the Campa River, and its territory extended on westward to the Son River, corresponding approximately to the present Patna and Gaya districts of South Bihar.

The early capital of Magadha was the city called both Girivraja and Rajagriha, both of which names occur in the *Mahabharata* (1.2.98; 1.196.17).[36] The name Girivraja means a "hill-girt city," and the city was in fact set in a valley surrounded by five hills, and also encircled by streams. The name Rajagriha means a "royal abode."

In the Epic period a powerful king of Rajagriha named Jarasamdha was overcome in a long duel and finally killed by the Pandava Bhima (*Mahabharata* 2.18–22), and in this connection there is a description of the city (ibid., 2.19.1–3): "This . . . is the large and beautiful capital city of Magadha, agreeable, cattle-rich, always flowing with water, healthy and wealthy with fine houses. The five beautiful mountains, the wide Vaihara, Varaha, Vrishabha, Rishigiri, and Caitya . . . with their high peaks and cool trees, massing together, their interstices walled off, seem to stand guard over Girivraja."[37]

The site of the ancient city is now marked by the town of Rajgir, about midway between Patna and Gaya. The oldest remains are prehistoric walls of large stones, running around the crest of the encircling hills, and extending for a circuit of 25 miles (40 km.) or more. There are also numerous ruins of *stupas* and shrines, and Hindu, Jaina, and Buddhist sculptures have been found here.[38]

Not far from Rajagriha was Nalanda, which figures prominently in the lives of Mahavira and the Buddha, and was afterward a very famous seat of Buddhist learning. The *Mahavastu* (3.56)[39] calls the place Nalandagramaka, and says that it was half a *yojana* (a *yojana* is usually reckoned at from 5 miles [8 km.] up to twice that much) from Rajagriha.

The ancient site is identified with the present village of Bargaon, 7 miles (11 km.) northwest of Rajgir, and 6 miles (9.5 km.) southwest of the modern town of Bihar. Excavation shows that the great university which existed here covered an area of at least 1 mile (1.6 km.) in length and one-half mile (0.8 km.) in breadth. The central college had seven halls attached to it, and there were some 300 smaller lecture rooms. Monastery buildings were arranged in a row, paralleled by a row of imposing *stupas,* with a broad avenue between the two. In addition to Buddhist structures, there were Hindu and Jaina temples, where Hindu, Jaina, and Buddhist sculptures have been found.

It was while Siddhartha Gautama was wandering and receiving alms in Magadha that he came to the place where he finally attained the great enlightenment or the wisdom (*bodhi*) which made him the Buddha. In the *Majjhima Nikaya* (1.167) he relates the event:

> Still in search of the right, and in quest of the excellent road to peace beyond compare, I came, in the course of an alms-pilgrimage through Magadha, to the Camp township at Uravela and there took up my abode. Said I to myself on surveying the place:—Truly a delightful spot, with its goodly groves and clear flowing river with ghats and amenities, hard by a village for sustenance. What more for his striving can a young man need whose heart is set on striving. Subject in myself to rebirth—decay—disease—death—sorrow—and impurity, and seeing peril in what is subject thereto, I sought after the consummate peace of *nirvana,* which knows neither rebirth nor decay, neither disease nor death, neither sorrow nor impurity;—this I pursued, and this I won; and there arose within me the conviction, the insight, that now my Deliverance was assured, that this was my last birth, nor should I ever be reborn again.[40]

The river, unnamed in the foregoing passage, is in the *Mahavagga* (1.1.1)[41] called the Neranjara, and the Buddha is described as continuing to sit there afterward, cross-legged at the foot of the Bodhi tree for seven days in the enjoyment of the bliss of emancipation. In the *Digha Nikaya* (2.7)[42] the tree is identified as the Assattha, i.e., the pipal tree or sacred fig (*Ficus religiosa*).

The site in question has long been called Bodhgaya, being 6 miles (10 km.) south of the city of Gaya.[43] Gaya itself is mentioned frequently in the *Mahabharata* and other works as an ancient holy place and place of pilgrimage, taking its name from a saintly king Gaya, who performed a religious sacrifice here.[44] On one occasion the Buddha stayed at Gaya, where he answered fearlessly a certain *yakkha* (a usually inimical being) named Suciloma, who threatened to destroy him (*Sutta Nipata* 2.5).[45]

It was in the time of the Śaiśunaga kings Bimbisara and Ajataśatru that Rajagriha reached the height of its prosperity, and this was also the time of Mahavira and the Buddha (Tables 4.2 and 4.12).

According to Jaina tradition, Rajagriha was the home of Suvrata, the twentieth *tirthankara,* and Mahavira himself spent fourteen rainy seasons there and in Nalanda. In the Jaina record Mahavira is also shown to have enjoyed family relationship with Bimbisara and Ajataśatru, inasmuch as Mahavira's mother Triśala (sister of king Cetaka of Vaiśali) was the aunt of Cellana (daughter of King Cetaka), and Cellana was the wife of Bimbisara and the mother of Ajataśatru, both of these kings being generally represented as favorable to Mahavira.

The *Uttaradhyayana* (20), for example, tells how Śrenika (Bimbisara) once came upon Mahavira, engaged in his austere life, in the Mandikukshi Caitya (here *caitya* denotes a park, in this case a pleasure garden which is compared with the Nandana, the park of Indra), and asked him how he, at a young age that was fitted for pleasure, came to be exerting himself as a monk and an ascetic *(śramana)*. To this Mahavira gave such an answer that the king was persuaded of his doctrine and praised Mahavira as having truly entered upon the path of the best *jinas* (conquerors). "When the lion of kings had thus, with the greatest devotion, praised the lion of houseless monks, he, together with his wives, servants, and relations, became a staunch believer in the Law, with a pure mind."[46]

In addition to Cellana and Kośaladevi, the two wives of Bimbisara who have already been named, the king had many other wives, and the *Antagadadasao* (7)[47] gives the personal stories of thirteen of these, all of whom renounced the world and became Jaina nuns.

Likewise the *Aupapatika* [48] is largely occupied with a meeting of Mahavira and Kunika (Ajataśatru) upon the occasion of the consecration of this king in the city of Campa. Whether this event took place upon an earlier occasion when Ajataśatru might have been installed there as a viceroy of his father, or later when he moved there for his own capital, is not made plain. At any rate both in this source and in other Jaina books we hear of how Ajataśatru used to go, at various times, with his queens and a great retinue, to pay his respects to Mahavira.

As for the Buddha, his rainy seasons spent at Rajagriha and his relationships with Bimbisara and Ajataśatru have already been noted, and in addition to the Veluvana (the "bamboo grove," which Bimbisara gave to the Buddha), other particular spots at Rajagriha where the Buddha spent time were the Banyan Grove, the Black Rock on the slope of Mount Isigili, the Deer Forest at Maddakucchi, the Mango Grove of the Physician Jivaka, the Robbers' Cliff, the Sappasondika Cave in the Sitavana Grove, the Sattapanni Cave on the slope of Mount Vabhara, the Tapoda Grove, and the Vulture's Peak (Gridhrakuta) (*Digha Nikaya* 2.116).[49] Also at nearby Nalanda a wealthy man named Pavarika presented a mango grove to the Buddha, and the Buddha often stayed there too (*Digha Nikaya* 1.211; 2.81; 3.99).[50] Later the First Buddhist Council was held at Rajagriha, and the site of the meeting was at the Sattapanni Cave at Mount Vebhara.[51]

Nalanda was the home of a young man named Upatissa, who was also called Śariputra (Sariputta) after his mother (son of Śari), and the nearby town of Kolita was the home of his friend who was named Kolita (evidently after the town), but was also known by his family name of Maudgalyayana (Moggallana). These two companions were *brahmanas,* but at this point were leading the religious life at Rajagriha as followers of a teacher named Sanjaya.

Wanderers

Sanjaya was a wandering ascetic (*paribbajaka*), and was only one of several teachers all of whose adherents were known collectively as the Paribbajakas or

Wanderers. The Wanderers included both men and women, and some of the latter were called "top-knotted girl-Wanderers," since they evidently tied up their hair in the fashion of the top-knot of *brahmana* ascetics. At Rajagriha many of the Wanderers enjoyed residence in a park where peacocks were fed. It was the doctrine of this sect, as stated for example by one of their teachers named Uggahamana, that future bliss can be won by abstaining from all evil in acts, words, thoughts, and manner of getting a living (*Majjhima Nikaya* 2.24).[52] These four standards of conduct were also to be found in the Buddha's Noble Eightfold Path, and the Wanderers often claimed that their teachings were the same as his, but the Buddha criticized them even as he also criticized the *brahmanas*, and the Buddha's followers claimed that their master alone dealt not with effects but with causes, and with how causal states could be done away with forever. So when, at Rajagriha, Śariputra as a young *brahmana* Wanderer encoutered Assaji, one of the five original disciples of the Buddha, Śariputra was converted by Assaji's simple statement: "The Buddha has explained the cause of all things, and has also explained their ceasing" (*Mahavagga* 1.23.5).[53] This enlightenment was conveyed by Śariputra to Maudgalyayana, and both came to the Buddha who was then in the Bamboo Grove (Veluvana), and became his two chief disciples.

In the time of Ajataśatru and while the Buddha was staying at Rajagriha, other religious teachers were said to have been active there, not only *brahmanas* and *paribbajakas*, but also six teachers in particular, to whom Ajataśatru himself went in his own inquiry after religious truth before he went to the Buddha (*Digha Nikaya* 1.47–59).[54] As described at this point in the *Digha Nikaya* and also in other Buddhist texts, all representing the polemic of the Buddha against them all, the six teachers and their doctrines were the following: (1) Purana Kaśyapa (Kassapa) expounded a theory of "non-action," according to which there is no guilt for murder and no merit for giving alms; in other words, it does not matter whether actions are good or bad (cf. *Majjhima Nikaya* 1.516).[55] (2) Makkhali Gośala ("of the cow-shed," since it was in such a place that he was born) taught "purification through transmigration." He characterized all living beings as "without force and power and energy of their own," and declared that "they are bent this way and that by their fate," i.e., by the necessary conditions of the class to which they belong, and by their individual nature. Therefore, utterly powerless as they all are, both fools and wise alike wander through a series of successive existences, and pain will only end when the allotted term of those existences has been finished (cf. *Samyutta Nikaya* 1.66).[56] (3) Ajita Keśakambalin ("of the garment of hair," since he was so attired) set forth a theory of "annihilation," in which it was held that a human being is composed of four elements and, upon death, the earthly returns to the earth, the watery to the water, the fiery to the fire, the windy to the air, and the faculties pass into space, so that at that point sages and fools alike perish without any future after death (cf. *Majjhima Nikaya* 1.515).[57] (4) Pakudha Kachchayana identified seven substances as constituting the immutable totality of everything, namely, earth, water, fire, air, pleasure, pain, and life, so a person is nothing other than these, and "When one with a sharp sword cleaves a head in twain, no one thereby deprives anyone of life, a sword has only penetrated into the interval between seven elementary substances" (cf. *Majjhima Nikaya* 1.517).[58] (5) Sanjaya of the Belattha clan—the Wanderer whom Śariputra and Maudgalyayana at one time followed—declined to answer either in the affirmative or the negative to questions as to whether there is another world or not, whether there is any result of good or bad actions, and whether a person who has won the truth continues or not after death, in other words Sanjaya was, according to this description, a complete agnostic (cf.

Majjhima Nikaya 1.521).⁵⁹ (6) The Nigantha of the Nata clan is to be recognized as none other than Mahavira, generally known as Nataputta and called, as were his followers, by the term Nirgrantha (Nigantha) which means one "without any ties." As described here, he taught that by "restraints" or austerities the misdeeds of past existences are expiated, and by not doing fresh misdeeds nothing accrues for the future, so as misdeeds die away "all Ill will wear out and pass away" (cf. *Majjhima Nikaya* 2.218).⁶⁰

It was after going to hear all six of these teachers and committing himself to none of them, that Ajataśatru visited the Buddha in Jivaka's Mango Grove at Rajagriha, where he was moved to confess the murder of his father and to ask to be accepted as a disciple of the Buddha, a request which was apparently granted (*Digha Nikaya* 1.60–85).⁶¹ Devadatta also, at the moment of his own death, turned to the Buddha for refuge, and was also accepted (*Milinda-panha* 111).⁶²

Other persons of whom we hear who, like Ajataśatru, went first to all the same six celebrated teachers and finally became followers of the Buddha were the Wanderers Sabhiya and Subhadda. The latter described the six teachers as well-known, renowned, founders of schools of doctrine, and esteemed by the multitude as good men, but himself accepted the teachings of the Buddha and became the last disciple converted by the Buddha before the Buddha's death. According to tradition this Subhadda, the last convert, was the younger brother of Anna Kondanya, who was the Buddha's very first convert (*Mahaparinibbana Suttanta, Digha Nikaya* 2.150–153).⁶³ In fact the fame of the six teachers was such that the *Milinda-panha* (4.420)⁶⁴ pictures King Milinda (who actually lived much later—in the second century B.C.E.) going to the six of them, before himself finally being converted to Buddhism.

Of the six teachers, three—Purana Kaśyapa, Makkhali Gośala, and Pakudha Kachchayana—are called Ajivikas, and Gośala is recognized as the chief leader if not the founder of this sect.⁶⁵ In doctrine the fundamental principle of Ajivika thought was fate, usually called *niyati,* as exemplified by the statement of Gośala cited above about the powerlessness of the individual to alter a lot already completely predetermined. In practice the Ajivika manner of life was also exemplified by Gośala, and by two other mendicants as well, namely, Nanda Vaccha and Kisa Sankicca (who were either contemporaries or predecessors of Gośala), all three of whom are called the "shining lights" of the movement, and described as going naked, flouting life's decencies, and existing on a rigid scale of rationing of food received by begging (*Majjhima Nikaya* 1.238.524).⁶⁶

Upon an occasion probably in the latter part of his life the Buddha was in a village on the south bank of the Ganges called Pataligrama (Pataligama), and there saw two of Ajataśatru's ministers named Sunidha and Vassakara engaged in building a fortress in order to repel an attack which was expected from the Vajjian confederacy (the Licchavis and others), whose territory was on the north side of the river. The Buddha prophesied that the village where the ministers were building the fortress would become a chief city and a center for the exchange of all kinds of wares, and would be called Pataliputra (Pataliputta). The two ministers thereupon proposed to call the gate by which the Buddha would depart from the place the Gautama Gate (Gotamadvara), and the ferry by which he would cross the river Gautama's Ferry (Gotamatittha). The Buddha, however, although the Ganges was in flood, vanished from the one side of the river and instantaneously stood on the other side with some of the brethren (*Digha Nikaya* 2.84–89).⁶⁷

In a genealogical listing somewhat different from that of the Puranas, the *Mahavamsa* (4.1–4)⁶⁸ names the next successors of Ajataśatru in direct line of descent as Udayabhaddaka or Udayibhadda (Udayin in the Puranas), Anuruddhaka, Munda, and Nagadasaka, and states that each of these in turn killed his own father even as Ajataśatru had killed Bimbisara. Perhaps Ajataśatru had a premonition that his son would perform such an act of violence, for when Ajataśatru paid his visit to the Buddha after the death of his father he saw the Buddha seated amidst his monks in a scene of perfect silence and calm, and he remarked, "Would that my son, Udayibhadda, might have such calm as this assembly of the brethren now has" (*Digha Nikaya* 1.50).[69]

According to the Jaina *Vividhatirtha Kalpa,* upon the death his father Ajataśatru (Kunika), this son Udayi (Udayibhadda, Udayin) became the king of Campa. Udayi was so overwhelmed with grief, however, that his ministers thought it desirable to change his capital (as Ajataśatru had moved from Rajagriha to Campa after the murder of Bimbisara), and it was for this reason that the capital was moved from Campa to Pataliputra.[70] Thereafter Pataliputra remained the capital of the other later Śaiśunagas, the Nandas, the Mauryas, the Śungas, and the earlier Guptas, and thus the prophecy of the Buddha was abundantly fulfilled.[71]

The name of Pataliputra was explained as derived from the *patali* tree (*Bignonia suaveolens*), and the city was also called Kusumapura because the tree was laden with many *kusumas* (flowers). To the Greeks the city was known as Palimbothra or Palibothra, and it was described by Megasthenes, ambassador of Seleucus I Nicator (312–281 B.C.E.) to the court of Candragupta Maurya, as the greatest city in India, located at the confluence of the Erannoboas (Son) and Ganges rivers, built in the form of an oblong eighty stadia (more than 9 miles [14.5 km.]) in length and fifteen stadia (2 miles [3 km.]) in breadth, and surrounded by a moat and a wall which was crowned with 570 towers and entered by sixty-four gates.[72]

As the later great capital of Magadha, Pataliputra was the scene of important events in the history of both Jainism and Buddhism. In or shortly after the reign of Candragupta Maurya a Jaina council was held in Pataliputra,[73] and during the reign of Aśoka the Third Buddhist Council took place there.[74]

The site of ancient Pataliputra is near the confluence of the Ganges and the Son (although the Son has now somewhat changed its course), and near modern Patna, which preserves the root of the ancient name. Because of the high water level and because of the location of the modern city over much of the ancient one, excavation at Pataliputra has been limited. Four ancient periods are distinguished, between 600 B.C.E. and 600 C.E. Remains of wooden palisades, remains of temples and monasteries, pottery, and coins have been found.[75]

Kaśis

The kingdom of the Kaśis (Kasis) was farther up the Ganges, between Magadha and Kośala, and was from time to time incorporated in either one or the other of those two larger kingdoms.

The capital of the people of Kaśi was on the banks of the river Varana (*Mahavastu* 3.401),[76] a northern tributary of the Ganges, and near another stream, the Asi, and the name of the capital was compounded of these two names, making Varanasi. This name was later corrupted to Banaras, but is now used again in its original form. The city was also known as Kaśi and as Sankaśya.

In mythology Varanasi was the site of a ten-horse sacrifice (*daśaśvamedha*) by Brahma, and of the performance of several austerities by Śiva, and the city has ever since remained a very important center of Śiva worship and place of Hindu pilgrimage. In the Epic period Bhishma abducted the three daughters of the king of the Kaśis and, having defeated those who tried to stop him, brought them to Hastinapura with the intent that they should become the wives of Vichitravirya. The oldest, named Amba, pleaded a previous betrothal and was allowed to leave. The other two were married to Vichitravirya and eventually one named Ambika became the mother (by the sage Vyasa) of Dhritarashtra, and the other named Ambalika became the mother of Pandu (*Mahabharata* 1.96–100).[77]

In Jaina tradition Varanasi was the home of Suparśva and Parśva, the seventh and twenty-third *tirthankaras*. The Buddha also spent much time in Varanasi and its environs, particularly including Isipatana.

The most ancient city of Varanasi was situated at the place now marked by the fort of Rajghat. Here the Varana River flowed on the northeast and the Ganges protected the southeast side of the area. In excavation six main levels of occupation have been distinguished between 800 B.C.E. and 1200 C.E. and later. In the earliest occupation a very large clay rampart was constructed, which rose to a height of 33 feet (10 m.) and sloped toward the river.

The modern city of Varanasi is itself on the north bank of the Ganges, and about 7 miles (11 km.) farther north is Sarnath, which represents ancient Isipatana, the place of the famous Mrigadawa (Migadaya) or Deer Park, once donated by a king of Varanasi as a sanctuary for these animals to wander unmolested. When Siddhartha Gautama abandoned the austerities in which he had been engaged at Uruvela together with five other ascetics, and proceeded on his own "middle path," the five (Kondanya, Bhaddiya, Vappa, Mahanama, and Assaji, known collectively as the Pancavaggiya) left him in disappointment and went off to Isipatana. After his attainment of enlightenment the Buddha himself came to Isipatana and preached his first sermon to the five ascetics, and they became his disciples. This was the sermon which is known as the Setting into Motion of the Wheel of the Law (*dharma, dhamma*). It outlines the Buddha's hard-won understanding of life in terms of the four "Aryan truths" of suffering, its origin, its destruction, and the way to its destruction. The way is a "middle path" between the pleasures of sense on the one hand and the painfulness of selfmortification on the other hand, and is further definable as an "Aryan eightfold way" of right understanding, thought, speech, action, livelihood, effort, mindfulness, and concentration.[78] The word *ar(i)yan* which is here applied to the basic truths enunciated and the practical way recommended, means already in the Vedas not only "of Aryan race" but also "gentle, kindly, noble." In Buddhist usage the word conveys all of these senses, and may be understood as having, in varying degrees, and in different passages, racial, ethical, and even esthetic connotation.[79]

The Buddha also spent his first rainy season at Isipatana, and on various occasions gave many of his other teachings in the same place. For example, a lay disciple named Dhammadinna came there with five hundred of his own lay disciples to say that it was difficult for them, with the responsibilities and luxuries of the life of householders, to comprehend the more abstruse teachings of the Buddha. Dhammadinna elaborated the problem in these words:

> Lord, it is no easy thing for us, living as we do in crowded houses, encumbered with children, enjoying the use of Varanasi sandalwood, decking ourselves with garlands and unguents, handling gold and silver,—it is no easy thing for us from time to time to spend our days learning these discourses uttered by the Tathagata.

To this the Buddha responded that they should maintain the four practices of loyalty to the Buddha, the Law (*dhamma*), and the Order (*sangha*), and the cultivation of the "Ariyan virtues," which conduce to concentration of mind, and when Dhammadinna affirmed that they were already so living, the Buddha expressed his satisfaction (*Samyutta Nikaya* 5.406–7).[80]

Kośalas

The kingdom of the Kośalas (Kosalas) was divided into two parts, Northern Kośala (Uttarakośala) on the banks of the Sarayu River (the modern Gaghara) and extending northward to the foothills of the Himalaya, and Southern Kośala (Dakshinakośala) extending southward to the Vindhya mountains. At one time Kośala was the most powerful kingdom in North India, but it was eventually overshadowed by Magadha.

The ancient capital of Kośala was Ayodhya, already described above as located on the Sarayu River near modern Faizabad in Uttar Pradesh. The city was the residence of Ikshvaku and the seat of rule of his descendants in the Solar dynasty, in which Rama was the most illustrious king of all. Rama's sons, it has also been noted, ruled in Kośala, Kuśa at Kuśavati in the south, and Lava at Śravasti in the north.

In Jaina tradition Ayodhya, also called Vinita, was the home of Rishabha, Ajita, Abhinandana, Sumati, and Ananta, the first, second, fourth, fifth, and fourteenth *tirthankaras*.

In the *Samyutta Nikaya* (3.140)[81] the Buddha is reported to have visited Ayodhya (Ayojjhaya), but the city is described as located on the bank of the river Ganges, whereas Ayodhya was actually on the Sarayu, but the Sarayu was a tributary of the Ganges which may justify the reference.

By the time of Mahavira and the Buddha Saketa is named along with Śravasti as a capital city of Kośala, and together they are accounted two of the great cities of India. The site of Saketa has been identified with Sujan Kot on the river Sai in the Unao district.[82]

According to Puranic tradition already cited above, Śravasti (Savatthi) was founded by and took its name from Śravasta, an early member of the Ikshvaku line. Śravasti was located on the bank of the Achiravati River (the modern Rapti), and was six leagues (about 45 miles [72 km.]) from Saketa (*Mahavagga* 5.9.1–2; 7.1.1),[83] a distance which could be covered in one day with seven relays of horses (*Majjhima Nikaya* 1.149).[84]

In Jaina tradition Śravasti was the home of Sambhava and Candraprabha, the third and eighth *tirthankaras,* and Mahavira spent one rainy season there.

In Śravasti there was a wealthy householder named Anathapindika, and on a business trip to Rajagriha he visited the Sitavana Grove and listened to the discourse of the Buddha and became his disciple. Then he invited the Buddha to come to Śravasti, and undertook to find a dwelling place for him. A garden which belonged to a certain Prince Jeta seemed desirable, and Anathapindika purchased it from the prince for as much gold as would cover the ground, and built there for the Buddha and his followers the Jetavana monastery (*Kullavagga* 6.4.1–10).[85] In all, the Buddha exercised a great deal of his ministry in Śravasti, and spent no less than twenty-five rainy seasons there, and the city with its most important establishment, the Jetavana, continued to be a great center of Buddhism down into the twelfth century C.E.[86]

The site of Śravasti is identified with Saheth Maheth, situated on the south bank of the Rapti River, about midway between Bahraich and Gonda (some 26 miles [42 km.] from either city), in the district of Oudh in Uttar Pradesh. The remains of *stupas* and other structures, and a colossal statue of the Buddha with an inscription containing the name of Śravasti, have been found there.

In the time of Mahavira and the Buddha, and contemporary with Bimbisara and Ajataśatru of Magadha, Udayana of Vatsa, and Pradyota of Avanti, the king of Kośala who was reigning at Śravasti was Prasenajit (Pasenadi). According to Puranic tradition Prasenajit was the twenty-sixth king in a list of twenty-nine or thirty solar kings of the Ikshvaku dynasty reigning in the *Kaliyuga* or present age of the world (*Matsya Purana* 271–273; *Vishnu Purana* 4.22).[87]

In the same list in the *Vishnu Purana*, the names Sakya, Śuddhodana, and Ratula (or Rahula) immediately precede the name of Prasenajit. In this sequence, Sakya must be the name of the Buddha who was called Śakyamuni (the sage of the Śakyas); Śuddhodana was the father (not the son) of the Buddha, these two names obviously being out of proper order; and Rahula was the son of the Buddha. Thus the Buddha and his father and his son are all listed as belonging to the family line of the Ikshvaku or Solar dynasty. As noted above, the Śakya clan was vassal to the Kośala kingdom at this time, and the Buddha comprehended the several relationships when he spoke of coming from Kośala and being of the lineage of the Kinsmen of the Sun and of the family of the Sakiyans.

In the Buddhist literature there are many references to Prasenajit (Pasenadi), and in particular the entire third chapter of the *Samyutta Nikaya* is devoted to the record of conversations between "the Kosalan Pasenadi" and the Buddha at Śravasti.[88] The king and the Buddha were of the same age. In youth the king was educated at Takshaśila (Taxila), already a celebrated seat of learning in the Northwest, then upon his return was placed upon the throne by his father Maha Kośala. The daughter of Maha Kośala and sister of Prasenajit, named Kośaladevi, who became one of the principal queens of King Bimbisara, has already been mentioned, and also the war in which, in spite of the family relationship, Ajataśatru was involved with Prasenajit.

The war involved two separate battles (*Samyutta Nikaya* 1.82).[89] In the first Ajataśatru won the victory, in the second Prasenajit defeated Ajataśatru and captured him alive. Prasenajit thought to himself: "'Although this king injures me who was not injuring him, yet is he my nephew. What if I were now to confiscate his entire army—elephants, horses, chariots, and infantry—and leave him only his life?' And he did so."

When the Buddha heard about the matter he uttered the saying:

> A man may spoil another, just so far
> As it may serve his ends, but when he's spoiled
> By others he, despoiled, spoils yet again. . . .
> The slayer gets a slayer in his turn;
> The conqueror gets one who conquers him. . . .
> Thus by the evolution of the deed,
> A man who spoils is spoiled in his turn.

A Prasenajit came back, defeated, from the first battle, he saw Mallika, daughter of the chief of the garland makers in Śravasti, a good and beautiful young woman who had just given bowls of gruel to the Buddha, and the king took her to be his chief queen (*Jataka* 7.415; 16.519).[90] At a later time when Prasenajit and Mallika were engaged in a dispute, the Buddha became aware of it and went and reconciled them with a word (*Jataka* 4.306; 15.504).[91] On another occasion, when Prasenajit was disturbed, Mallika advised him to go and consult with the Buddha

(*Jataka* 4.314).[92] At Śravasti there was a park which bore the queen's name, and in this Mallika Park there was a hall which was simply called "the Hall," in which various teachers, *brahmanas,* Niganthas, and Wanderers, as well as the Buddha, came together to expound and discuss their views (*Digha Nikaya* 9.1).[93]

At one conversation of Prasenajit with the Buddha, the king's sister, Sumana, was present and decided to enter the Buddhist order, but delayed in order to care for an elderly relative. The latter was the grandmother of the king, and she died at the age of 120 years, and left a legacy of furniture to the Buddhist monks, the use of which the Buddha allowed but only under severe restrictions (*Kullavagga* 6.14.1).[94] When Prasenajit came, with sorrow, to tell the Buddha of the decease of his grandmother, the Buddha remarked that all pottery, whether baked or unbaked, is breakable, and went on to say (*Samyutta Nikaya* 1.96):[95]

> All creatures have to die. Life is but death.
> And they shall fare according to their deeds,
> Finding the fruit of merit and misdeeds:—
> Infernal realms because of evil works;
> Blissful rebirth for meritorious acts.

As for Sumana, relieved of her care but then herself elderly too, she carried out her resolve and entered the Buddhist order, to become one of the seventy-three nuns whose poems are preserved in the *Therigatha* (16).[96]

As for Prasenajit, his last visit with the Buddha was at Medatalumpa in the Śakyan country, when each of the two was eighty years of age. At that time the king expressed his conclusion that the Buddha was indeed the all-enlightened one, that he had preached his doctrine well and truly, and that his confraternity was walking aright (*Majjhima Nikaya* 2.4.89).[97] During his absence on this very trip, Prasenajit was displaced on the throne in Śravasti by his son, Vidudabha, and Prasenajit himself died soon afterward.[98]

Cedis

The Vajjis and the Mallas have already been noted above, and they are followed in the list of the *mahajanapadas* by the kingdom of the Cedis or Cetis. The Cedi country probably lay between the Yamuna and the Narmada rivers. A river called the Śuktimati flowed past a city also named Śuktimati (*Mahabharata* 1.57.32),[99] and this city was probably the capital of the kingdom. The site of the city may have been in the vicinity of the present town of Banda (90 miles [145 km.] west of Allahabad).

In the Epic period, it will be remembered, a great Cedi monarch named Śiśupala wished to slay Krishna and all of the Pandavas, but was killed by Krishna (*Mahabharata* 2.37–42).[100]

In his time the Buddha won converts in Cedi as elsewhere, and we hear of his monks and especially of Maha Cunda, the younger brother of Śariputra, as living among the Cedis (*Samyutta Nikaya* 5.436; *Anguttara Nikaya* 3.355).[101]

Vamśas

The kingdom of the Vamśas (Vamsas) or Vatsas occupied territory south of the Ganges, and the capital of the country was Kauśambi (Kosambi) on the Yamuna, near the confluence of this river with the Ganges, the site being near the modern Kosam, about 30 miles (48 km.) southwest of Allahabad. Several of the kings of the Vamśa/Vatsa dynasty ruling at Kauśambi bore the name of Udayana, and in the time of the Buddha one Udayana was famous as the king of the Vatsa *mahajanapada*. In Tibetan tradition a son of this last Udayana became the first king of Tibet.

In the Puranic tradition it will be remembered that the present age (Kaliyuga) began with the accession to the throne at Hastinapura of Parikshit II son of Abhimanyu, in the Paurava family (descended from Puru) of the Lunar dynasty. As the Puranas continue the record from that point, the great great grandson of Parikshit II was Adhisimakrishna, and his son was Nichakra (also called Nichakshu and Vivakshu). In the time of Nichakra, Hastinapura was ruined by the floods of the Ganges, and Nichakra founded the city of Kauśambi and inaugurated the Kauśambi branch of the dynasty (*Vishnu Purana* 4.21).[102]

Sixteen and seventeen steps down from Nichakra in the same Puranic genealogy (the sequence in the *Matsya Purana* 50.78–87[103] differs slightly from that in the *Vishnu Purana*) are Śatanika and his son Udayana, then four more kings bring the dynasty to a close. While there were several kings by the name of Udayana, this one was presumably the Udayana (Udena in the Pali texts) who is named in Buddhist literature as a contemporary of the Buddha (*Mahavastu* 2),[104] thus was also a contemporary of Mahavira and of Bimbisara, Ajataśatru, Prasenajit, and Pradyota.[105]

In Jaina tradition Kauśambi was the home of Padmaprabha, the sixth *tirthankara*.

The Buddha visited Kauśambi on several occasions, and spent his ninth rainy season there. Alrady in his time there were four establishments for his order in Kauśambi. These were the Kukkutarama, the Ghositarama, the Pavarika-ambavana (donated respectively by Kukkuta, Ghosita, and Pavarika, three eminent citizens of the city), and the Badarikarama. It was at Kauśambi that the Buddha set forth the rule that monks should not drink fermented liquors (*Kullavagga* 12.2.8).[106]

Near Kauśambi was "King Udena's park," called the Udakavana, where the king enjoyed himself with the ladies of the palace. On one occasion Ananda so pleased the ladies with his preaching that they contributed five hundred robes for the monks. The king was indignant at the gift, but when Ananda explained that the new robes would replace worn-out ones, and that the old robes would provide material for the replacement of other items, and that in each case the old would be used for something lesser, down to carpets, towels, and the like, the king was pleased to learn that nothing would be wasted, and himself made a gift of five hundred more pieces of cloth (*Kullavagga* 11.1, 13–14).[107]

Among the monks at Kauśambi there was once a great schism over the proper treatment of an offender among them, and the dispute became so bitter that it even led to blows. The Buddha endeavored to reconcile the antagonists, but without success, and finally went away to the forest at Parileyyaka where, although alone and without a companion, he found that he could live for a time "pleasantly and at ease, remote from those litigious, contentious, quarrelsome, disputatious *bhikkus* (monks) of Kosambi, the constant raisers of questions before the *sangha*" (*Mahavagga* 10.4.6).[108]

The site of ancient Kauśambi (modern Kosam) was marked by an Aśokan pillar. Modern excavation has identified four main periods of building, from the twelfth century B.C.E. to the sixth century C.E. An excavated monastery structure is identified as the Ghositarama, one of the monastic establishments where the Buddha stayed on his visits to Kauśambi.

Kurus

During the time here dealt with, the kingdom of the Kurus was still a realm in the plain of Kurukshetra between the Yamuna and the Ganges, where its capital cities of Hastinapura (northeast of Meerut) and Indraprastha (near Delhi) had played such large roles in Epic times, but in this later time the Kurus were of relatively little political importance.

Hastinapura was often visited by Mahavira, and the site is an important place of Jaina pilgrimage.[109] The Buddha also stayed at times among the Kurus and taught there (*Samyutta Nikaya* 2.91, 106).[110]

The site of Hastinapura is on an old bed of the Ganges in the Meerut district, and excavation indicates five occupational periods, from before 1200 B.C.E. down to the early fifteenth century C.E. Toward the end of the second period (1100–800 B.C.E.) there is evidence of a destructive flood, but while this confirms that Hastinapura was then washed by the Ganges, there is no certainty that this particular inundation was the flood which, according to Puranic tradition, caused Nichakra to move away to Kauśambi.

Pancalas

The kingdom of the Pancalas, named after descendants of Puranjaya, was the territory east of the country of the Kurus. In the Epic period Pancala was divided by the Ganges into two parts: Northern Pancala with its capital at Ahicchatra, now a ruined site of the same name near the village of Ramnagar in the Bareilly district; and Southern Pancala with its capital at Kampilya, now represented by ruins at the village of Kampil in the Farrukhabad district; and both capitals are named in the *Mahabharata* (1.128.14–17).[111] In this time the king of Southern Pancala was Drupada, and it was his beautiful daughter Draupadi who was won by Arjuna in a feat with the king's great bow, and who became the wife of the five Pandavas and the heroine of the *Mahabharata* (1.174ff. for the famous contest).[112]

In Jaina tradition Kampilya, capital of Southern Pancala, was the home of Vimala, the thirteenth *tirthankara*.

Matsyas

The kingdom of the Matsyas or Macchas was an extensive territory to the south of Kuru and the west of the Yamuna, which river separated this country from Southern Pancala. Matsya was reputed to have had one hundred kings (*Mahabharata* 2.8.21),[113] and in the time of the Pandavas its king was Virata and his capital city was Vairata, identified with modern Bairat near Jaipur. In the thirteenth year of their exile from Hastinapura the Pandava brothers and their wife Draupadi, living in disguise, came to Matsya and entered the service of Virata. When enemies attacked Vairata and captured Virata, the Pandavas fought against the attackers and rescued the king. In gratitude Virata offered his daughter Uttara to Arjuna for a bride, but Arjuna asked that she be given instead to his son Abhimanyu.

Śurasenas

The kingdom of the Śurasenas (Surasenas) occupied the territory immediately west of the Yamuna, and its capital was Madhura or Mathura on the Yamuna, usually identified with Maholi, 5 miles (8 km.) southwest of the present city of Mathura.

At the spot just mentioned, on the bank of the Yamuna, there was originally a holy place said to have been called Madhu or Madhuvana (grove of Madhu) after an *asura* of that name who dwelt there. The son of Madhu was the *rakshasa* chieftain Lavana, who was himself a nephew of Ravana, who abducted Sita. Lavana was killed by Śatrughna (foe destroyer), who was the twin brother of Lakshmana and the half-brother of Rama. With the death of Lavana, Śatrughna took possession of Lavana's stronghold, and thus Śatrughna was considered the founder of the city of Madhura or Mathura. Likewise one of the sons of Śatrughna was Śurasena, and it was after him that the country of Śurasena was named (*Vishnu Purana* 1.12; 4.4).[114] In the time of Krishna the rulers of Madhura claimed descent from the Yadava line, and it has already been seen that Krishna was born there at Madhura/Mathura, and grew up to slay the tyrant Kamsa and allow the rightful king, Ugrasena, to have the throne again.

In his time the Buddha visited Madhura/Mathura (*Anguttara Nikaya* 2.57),[115] but he spoke unflatteringly of the city when he told his monks that there were five disadvantages in the place (*Anguttara Nikaya* 3.256): "(The ground) is uneven; there is much dust; there are fierce dogs; bestial genii (*yakkhas*); and alms are got with difficulty."[116]

Madhura/Mathura was, however, the residence upon occasion of Maha Kaccana, who was one of the Buddha's most eminent disciples, and considered the best among the disciples at giving a full and detailed explanation of the brief sayings of the Buddha (*Anguttara Nikaya* 1.24).[117] At a time after the death of the Buddha, when Maha Kaccana was staying in a grove outside Madhura, the king of Madhura, named Avantiputta, came to converse with Maha Kaccana and professed belief in the doctrine which he heard (*Majjhima Nikaya* 2.83–90).[118]

Later, too, Madhura/Mathura was an important center of Buddhism, notably under the Kushanas. Like many other of the conquering invaders of India, the Kushanas found Mathura to be an important place on the main route from the northwest to the great centers farther east, and they made Mathura one of their capitals. From the second century B.C.E., also, Mathura was an important center of Jainism, and many Jaina monuments and inscriptions, as well as Buddhist, have been found there.

Aśmakas

The kingdom of the Aśmakas or Assakas was in the southeast on the banks of the Godavari River. Its capital was named Potana, possibly to be identified with the present Bodhan northwest of Hyderabad. According to the *Mahabharata* (1.168.26).[119] Potana was settled by a royal seer named Aśmaka, after whom the kingdom took its name.

Avantis

The kingdom of the Avantis was in the southwest, and was divided into two parts by the Vindhya mountains. The northern part had its capital at Ujjayini (Ujjeni, modern Ujjain), north of Indore, on the Sipra River (which rises in the Vindhyas and flows into the Cambal, a tributary of the Yamuna). The southern part lay along the Narmada River, and its capital was at Mahishmati (Mahissati), possibly identifiable with the present Maheshwar on the Narmada River south of Indore (*Mahabharata* 2.26.10–11; 3.87.1).[120]

The first dynasty at Mahishmati is supposed to have been the Haihaya, descended from Yadu (*Matsya Purana* 43).[121] At Ujjayini King Pradyota (Pajjota) was on the throne in the time of the Buddha, and the king's daughter Vasavadatta was married as chief queen to King Udayana of Vatsa. Shortly after the death of the Buddha, Ajataśatru of Magadha was repairing the defenses of Rajagriha because of suspicion of an impending attack by Pradyota (*Majjhima Nikaya* 3.7),[122] and Pradyota also made war, unsuccessfully, on Pushkarasarin, the king of Takshaśila (Taxila). According to the *Matsya Purana* (271–273),[123] Pradyota had five descendants who ruled after him for 138 years (Table 4.1), and of these the first was Palaka, whose consecration coincided with the *nirvana* of Mahavira.

Gandharas

While the foregoing fourteen *mahajanapadas* were in Madhyadeśa (the central region of India), the last two of the sixteen in the early Buddhist texts were in Udichya or Uttarapatha (the northern region), namely, the countries of the Gandharas and the Kambojas. The Gandharas are located in the modern Rawalpindi-Peshawar region on either side of the Indus River in Pakistan, since their two chief cities were Takshaśila in the Rawalpindi district and Pushkalavati in the Peshawar district.

According to the epic of Rama, after Rama returned to his rightful throne at Ayodhya, his brother Bharata (who had ruled in his name, but then gave back the sovereignty to him) went on to make himself master of the country of the Gandharas, and the two cities of Takshaśila and Pushkalavati were founded by the two sons of Bharata, namely, Taksha and Pushkara.

In the Mahabharata war the Gandharas were strong allies of the Kauravas against the Pandavas, and many years later Janamejaya, son of Parikshit II and grandson of Arjuna, marched against Takshaśila and put the country in his own power (*Mahabharata* 1.3.20).[124]

Probably already in the reign of Cyrus II the Great (559–530 B.C.E.) and certainly under Darius I the Great (521–486) Gandhara was incorporated in the Achaemenid Persian empire. Then Alexander the Great marched through Gandhara and beyond, and took both Pushkalavati and Takshaśila. Afterward Candragupta drove out the governors whom Alexander left behind, and Gandhara and neighboring areas became a part of the Maurya empire.

According to the Rock Edict 5 of Aśoka (of his regnal Year 13, 256 B.C.E.), there were three important peoples then living in the northwestern regions, for he speaks of the activities of his officers for the welfare "of the Yonas, the Kambojas, the Gandharas, and of (my) other western Borderers."[125]

The Yonas (or Yonakas or Yavanas), as they were called in India, were the Greeks. Many Greeks evidently remained in the Northwest after Alexander the Great, and others were settled in Bactria. Bactria (called Bactrian by the Greeks and Bahlika by the Indians), bounded by the Hindu Kush on the south and east and by the Oxus (Amu Darya) on the north and east, with its capital at Balkh in Northern Afghanistan, was a province of the Seleucid empire until the middle of the third century B.C.E. when it became an independent kingdom under Diodotus I, thus was not a part of the Maurya empire. But in the second century B.C.E., the Bactrian Greeks began a further series of foreign invasions of northwestern India, and these incursions were continued in the first century B.C.E. and the first century C.E. and afterward by the Śakas (Scythians), Pahlavas (Parthians), and Kushanas.

Of the Bactrian Greeks the most famous king in India was Menander or Milinda, who ruled around 161–145 B.C.E. Strabo (11.11.1) says that Menander extended his power even farther east than Alexander the Great had done, and the Buddhist *Milinda Panha* (Questions of Milinda) describes Milinda (who must be the same as Menander) as ruling in a city called Sakala (Sagala), which is identifiable with modern Sialkot in the Punjab. Thus at this time the Yavana country evidently extended all the way from Afghanistan to the Punjab.

In the *Milinda Panha* (1.1–2)[126] the city of Sagala (Śakala) is described as laid out by wise architects. It was defended "with many and various strong towers and ramparts, with superb gates and entrance archways." The royal citadel was in its midst, with white walls and a deep moat.

> Well laid out are its streets, squares, crossroads, and market places. . . . Its streets are filled with elephants, horses, carriages, and pedestrians, frequented by groups of handsome men and beautiful women, and crowded by men of all sorts and conditions, *brahmanas,* nobles, artificers, and servants. They resound with cries of welcome to the teachers of every creed, and the city is the resort of the leading men of each of the differing sects.

In short, Sagala was comparable in glory (as was also ancient Kuśavati) to Alakamanda, the city of the gods.

Milinda himself, according to the same source, was very learned, and was accustomed to engage in conversation with the most learned men he could find. He was satisfied, however, by neither recluse nor *brahmana,* but was finally converted to the Buddhist belief by the very scholarly elder (*thera*) Nagasena, whose discourses with the king are recounted at length.

Pushkalavati, called Peukelaotis by the Greeks, was west of the Indus, and is identified with the modern Charsadda, a little above the junction of the Swat River with the Kabul River, 17 miles (27 km.) northeast of Peshawar. The excavated mounds called Bala Hisar and Shaikhan show extensive settlement from the sixth century B.C.E., i.e., from the Achaemenid occupation, onward. In the Shaikhan mound there is evidenced a rebuilding of the city on a regular Greek plan, much in agreement with the description above of Sagala under Milinda.

Takshaśila (Takkasila), called Taxila by the Greeks, was east of the Indus and between that river and the Jhelum (Hydaspes), in a valley bounded on the east by the Murree hills. The site, still called Taxila, is some 20 miles (32 km.) northwest of the modern city of Rawalpindi. The location was on three major routes of ancient travel and trade: one came from Western Asia by way of Bactra, Kapiśi, and Pushkalavati; another came from Central Asia through Kashmir and the Śrinagar valley; and yet another continued to Pataliputra and the heart of India.

At the site, the most southerly Bhir mound represents the oldest city (from the sixth or fifth, to the second century B.C.E.). In approximately the fourth century B.C.E. the distinguished Hindu grammarian Panini taught here, and in the Buddhist *jatakas* there are many stories (e.g., Nos. 50, 55, 61, 71, 80),[127] which reflect the fact that Takshaśila was a notable educational center, to which students used to come from all over North India for their higher studies. After earlier subjection under the Persians, the city gained independence and, when Alexander the Great came, it was the Indian king Taxiles (as the Greeks called him) who surrendered the city to the new invader. In the Maurya period there was an uprising in Taxila against Bindusara, and the king sent his son Aśoka (the future emperor) to put down the revolt and serve as governor. Later, Aśoka's own son, Kunala, also served as viceroy in Taxila.

In the excavation of the Bhir mound it appears that the city was destroyed three times and three times rebuilt before. In the early years of the second century

B.C.E. the Bactrian Greeks transferred the city to a new site to the northeast now known as Sirkap, moving from the one location to the other much as they did at Pushkalavati when they abandoned the old city at Bala Hisar and founded a new one at Shaikhan. At Sirkap as at Shaikhan the new city was laid out on a typical Greek plan with the streets running at right angles to one another, and with regularly aligned blocks of buildings. This city remained in occupation for three centuries under successive rule by the Bactrian Greeks, the Śakas (Scythians), and the Pahlavas (Parthians). Of the Śaka rulers at Taxila the most important (with very tentative dates of accession) are Azes I (circa 45 B.C.E.), his son Azilises (circa 10 B.C.E.), and his grandson Azes II (circa 5 C.E.). Of the Parthians the most famous king was Gondopharnes or Gondophares, who succeeded Azes II and ruled at Taxila probably 19–45 C.E.

Soon after Gondophares, in the middle of the first century C.E., came the Yueh-chi, known in India as the Kushanas. Under them, Taxila remained at first centered in Sirkap but, by around 80 C.E., this location was also abandoned and the city was transferred again to the northeast to the site now called Sirsukh. Of the Kushana kings the most important was Kanishka (probably 78–103 C.E.), but his actual capital was at Purushapura (Peshawar) rather than Taxila. At Taxila in this time Buddhism was very prominent, and there are many Buddhist *stupas* and monasteries in the area. These and the other monuments of Taxila suffered wholesale destruction from the invasion of the Ephtalites or White Huns around 460–470 C.E., and Taxila never again recovered from this calamity.

The Chinese Buddhist pilgrims Fa Xian (Fa Hien) (399–414 C.E.) and Xuan Zang (Hiuen Tsang) (629–645 C.E.) traveled through Gandhara and provide information concerning the area in the time of Kanishka and later.[128] At his capital city of Purushapura, Kanishka built a great *stupa* and a monastery. The alms bowl of the Buddha was supposedly preserved in Gandhara, and was still there in the time of Fa Xian.[129] Under Kanishka the Buddhist assembly was held which is recognized in India as the Fourth Buddhist Council.[130]

Kambojas

In the Aśoka edict cited above (Rock Edict 5), the Kambojas are closely associated with the Gandharas and the Yavanas, and in the *Mahabharata* (5.19.21–22)[131] we hear of a king of Kamboja named Sudakshina, who joined the Kauravas with a large army, along with Yavanas (Greeks) and Śakas (Scythians), therefore the country of the Kambojas must also have been somewhere in the same northwestern region. On the basis of the similarity (but not identity) of name, it is held by some that it was these Indian Kambojas who founded the overseas Kamboja, which was the Khmer Kambuja, i.e., the present Kampuchea (Cambodia).[132]

A passage in the *Mahabharata* (7.4.5) states that the formidable warrior Karna defeated the Kambojas at Rajapura, which was presumably their capital city. This Rajapura may possibly be identified with a place south of Kashmir, which is mentioned by Xuan Zang,[133] but on the other hand *rajapura* may only mean the "royal city" of the Kambojas, and be presently unidentifiable.[134]

Of the sixteen *mahajanapadas*, then, which existed in the time of Mahavira and the Buddha the four greatest were Magadha under Kings Bimbisara and Ajataśatru, Kośala under King Prasenajit, Vamsa under King Udayana, and Avanti under King Pradyota. The six greatest cities were recognized as Campa in Anga, Rajagriha in Magadha, Śravasti and Saketa in Kośala, Kauśambi in Vatsa, and Varanasi in Kaśi (*Digha Nikaya* 2.146).[135] Except for the two states in the far Northwest (Gandhara and Kamboja), the other fourteen *mahajanapadas* were in the "middle country," and Mahavira and the Buddha worked in most of them, while the Buddha is specifically said to have converted people and to have had followers of his doctrine in all fourteen (*Digha Nikaya* 2.200; *Mahavastu* 34).[136] As to individual places connected with the life of the Buddha, there were four in particular of which it was said that the believer could always visit them with feelings of reverence, namely, the place where the Buddha was born (Lumbini), the place where he attained enlightenment (Bodhgaya), the place where he began to turn the Wheel of the Law (Isipatana), and the place where he entered into the final *nirvana* (Kuśinagara) (*Digha Nikaya* 2.140).[137]

6

ALEXANDER THE GREAT AND EMPIRES SUBSEQUENT TO HIS COMING

As distinct from the tribal migrations, e.g., of the Aryans, seen in the earlier history of India, there was at least now in the time of the kingdoms just dealt with, and as mentioned in the preceding chapter, actual intervention by foreign powers.

ASSYRIANS

It is possible that such incursion had begun already in the time of the Assyrians. According to Diodorus (2.6; 16–19), who cites the history of Assyria by Ktesias (fifth century B.C.E.), the famous Assyrian Queen Semiramis (probably to be identified with Sammuramat, wife of Shamshi-Adad V, 823–811 B.C.E., and mother of Adad-nirari III, 810–783), captured Bactra, the capital of Bactria, and from there invaded northwestern India and crossed the Indus River, but was driven back and retreated to Bactra with a fragment of her forces. Bactria (also called Bactriana by the Greeks) was the country between the Oxus River (now the Amu Darya) and the Hindu Kush, and Bactra is now Balkh near Wazirabad 12 miles (19 km.) west of Mazar-i-Sharif in Northern Afghanistan. The Hindu Kush is the great water divide between the basins of the Oxus and the Kabul rivers, and the Kabul River flows on to join the Indus; thus, the route from Bactra over the Hindu Kush and down the Kabul River was a major way into India.

ACHAEMENID PERSIANS

Cyrus II the Great

According to Herodotus (1.153) it was the purpose of Cyrus (559–530 B.C.E.), the founder of the Persian empire, to incorporate Bactria in his empire, and Xenophon (*Cyropaedia* 1.1.4) says that, among many other places, Cyrus ruled over Bactria and also India. Likewise Arrian (*Indica* 1.3) speaks of the Indian tribes which dwell in the territory between the Kophen River (the ancient Kubha, the modern Kabul) and the Indus River, and says that these people were long ago subject to the Assyrians, then to the Medes, and so they became subject to the Persians; and they paid tribute to Cyrus son of Cambyses from their territory, as Cyrus commanded.

It is true that Arrian (*Anabasis of Alexander* 6.24.2–3; *Indica* 9.10) and Strabo (15.1.5–6) quote Nearchus, the admiral of Alexander the Great, to the effect that when Alexander was planning his return march from India through Gedrosia (Baluchistan) he learned that Semiramis had also fled this way with the remnant of her army, and that Cyrus had lost the greater part of his army here when he intended to invade India; and Arrian and Strabo cite Megasthenes, the ambassador of Seleucus I to the court of Candragupta, to the effect that neither Semiramis nor Cyrus invaded India. The Indus River, however, was considered the boundary between India and Ariana (the land of the Iranians), as Strabo (15.1.10) explicitly says, so the statements just cited probably only mean that Semiramis and Cyrus did not go east of the Indus, and this negative emphasis was probably intended to heighten, by way of contrast, the accomplishment of Alexander who did go beyond the Indus.

It remains probable, therefore, that at least Cyrus—if not the legendary Semiramis—not only subjugated Bactria but also established his authority over the territory between the Kabul and the Indus, as the statement of Arrian in *Indica* 1.3 surely means.

Darius I the Great

This conclusion concerning Cyrus is substantiated by the fact that under Darius I (521–486 B.C.E.) the Persian empire certainly included the territory just described, and Herodotus (3.88) says that the whole of Asia which was made subject to Darius was subdued first by Cyrus and by Cambyses (529–522) after him. Since the chief accomplishment of the short reign of Cambyses was the conquest of Egypt, the conquest of the eastern regions must have been accomplished by Cyrus.

How far these regions extended is shown unambiguously in the lists of the provinces (satrapies) of the Persian empire in the inscriptions of Darius I at Bisitun and Naqsh-i Rustam.[1] The twenty-three provinces named at Bisitun include Bactria (Old Persian Baxtri) and Gandhara (Old Persian Gandara). The thirty provinces named at Naqsh-i Rustam include Bactria, Gandhara, and Sind (Old Persian Hindu).

In the Elamite and Akkadian versions of the Bisitun text, in place of the Old Persian Gandara is the name Paruparaesanna, which means "beyond (the mountain called) Uparaesanna." The name Uparaesanna, in turn, is recognizable as the Avestan Upairisaena, which means "higher than the eagle," and was evidently the Iranian name of the Hindu Kush. From Paruparaesanna the Greeks made the name Paropanisus (with several variants in the spelling), and called the province which lay beyond the Hindu Kush the province of the Paropamisadae, i.e., "the land beyond the mountain that is higher than the eagle." So the province called either Gandhara or Paropanisus was beyond the Hindu Kush, i.e., in the basin of the Kabul and Indus rivers, the territory which paid tribute already to Cyrus (Arrian, *Indica* 1.3) and was a satrapy in the empire of Darius I.

In Paropanisus were several important cities. Kapiśa or Kapiśi (Latin Capisa), which Pliny (6.25.92) says was destroyed by Cyrus, was probably in the plain northeast of Charikar, where the Panjshir and Ghorband rivers come together, on the east bank of the united stream, opposite Begram on the west bank (about 28 miles [45 km.] north of Kabul). The Ghorband flows on to the southeast and joins the Kabul River, which in turn flows eastward and receives the Swat River (the ancient Suvastu, Greek Soastos) before it finally joins the Indus. Near the junction of the Swat and the Kabul, on the east side of the Swat, was the large city of Pukhala or Pushkalavati (Greek Peukela, Peukelaotis, e.g., Arrian, *Anabasis of Alexander* 4.22.7; *Indica* 1.8), which is represented by the modern Charsadda 17 miles (27 km.) northeast of Peshawar. Beyond the Indus, in the district between this river and the Jhelum (the ancient Vitasta, Greek Hydaspes), was Takshaśila (Greek Taxila). Under Darius I and his first successors the district of Taxila was probably incorporated in the satrapy of Gandhara Parapamisadae, but in the later decline of the Persian empire it evidently became independent, for it had a king who was acting in his own authority when Alexander came (Arrian, *Anabasis of Alexander* 5.3.6). Nevertheless the Jhelum (Hydaspes) was evidently always considered the easternmost boundary of the Persian empire, for Alexander and his army went that far in their conquest of the entire empire, and even proceeded somewhat beyond.

Since the inscription of Darius I at Naqsh-i Rustam includes not only Bactria and Gandhara but also Sind (Old Persian Hindu), this territory, which was in the Lower Indus valley, was also evidently incorporated as a satrapy of the empire. Herodotus (4.44) relates that Darius sent a Greek sea captain named Skylax to explore the course of the Indus, and Skylax set out from a city called Kaspatyros, which was probably somewhere on the Lower Kabul, sailed down the Indus and along the coast of Baluchistan and Arabia, reached Egypt thirty months later, and eventually wrote a book on his journey called the *Periplus* (circumnavigation). Herodotus says that "after this circumnavigation" Darius subdued the Indians and made use of the sea which Skylax had traversed, which suggests that the voyage down the Indus was preparatory to the conquest of Sind; yet it might seem more likely that the voyage could only have been made after the territory had been conquered. At any rate Herodotus (3.94) is probably referring to the satrapy of Sind when, in a list of twenty satrapies of the Persian empire under Darius, he says that the Indians made up the twentieth and paid a larger tribute than any other province, no less than three hundred and sixty talents of gold dust.

ALEXANDER THE GREAT

When Alexander the Great conquered the Persian empire he came all the way to the easternmost limits (as described just above) of that empire, and even slightly beyond. His campaign is reconstructed chiefly on the basis of the times and places indicated or implied in the detailed account by Arrian (*Anabasis of Alexander* 4.22ff.).[2] In the spring of 327 B.C.E., he came across the Hindu Kush from Bactria and down into the Kabul valley. From there he sent a large part of his army ahead to prepare for the crossing of the Indus, and they presumably went by the most direct route which would have been somewhere on the south side of the Kabul River and perhaps through what is now the Khyber Pass. With a smaller and more mobile force Alexander himself went into the northern hill country to secure those regions, which were on the left flank of his main advance. By a rough and mountainous route he marched up the Khoes River (probably the Kunar, which joins the Kabul near Jalalabad) and, after various engagements, crossed with difficulty the Guraios River (the ancient Gauri, modern Panjkora).

At this point Alexander was in the territory of the Assakenoi, which extended eastward to the Indus, and is recognizable as modern Swat. Here he marched first against Massaga, which (although it has not been located) was evidently the capital, since in the siege of the city the chief named Assakenos was killed. After that Alexander took Ora, which is almost certainly to be identified with Udegram in the Central Swat valley, where there are excavated ruins of a city (fifth century B.C.E. to fourth century C.E.) at the foot of a very steep 2,000-foot (600 m.) high ridge, on which are ancient fortifications.

The Swat River (Suvastu, Soastos) is joined by the Panjkora west of the Malakand Pass in Lower Swat, and then flows down to its junction with the Kabul River not far from modern Peshawar. Here, near this junction, Alexander received the surrender of the great city of Peukelaotis (Pushkalavati).

Aornos

Many of the Indian tribesmen, however, withdrew to a very strong position on the rock called Aornos, which is described by Arrian as 200 stadia (23 miles [37 km.] in circuit), and 11 stadia (6,670 feet [2,035 km.] in height), and was clearly a massive mountain summit, but Alexander managed to conquer this too.

In a great bend of the Indus, north of the present Gunangar, there is a bare rocky peak (8,720 feet [2,660 m.] above sea level) called Una-sar or Mount Una, the name of which may be derived from the name rendered in Greek as Aornos. A long ridge that extends from the mountain in a north-south direction is 7,100 feet (2,165 m.) above sea level and more than 5,000 feet (1,500 m.) above the Indus, and is now known as Pir-sar, "the holy man's height." This ridge occupies a dominating position and its sides fall off for the most part in steep rocky slopes and sheer cliffs, but there is an almost level plateau on top, so Pir-sar is a natural mountain fastness. The character of the ridge and the correspondence of its topography with details in the narrative by Arrian make it probable that this was the rock of Aornos taken by Alexander.[3]

Taxila

Meanwhile the other part of Alexander's army had come down to the junction of the Kabul River with the Indus, and had prepared a bridge (presumably of boats) across the Indus. In the spring of 326 B.C.E. Alexander and his contingent arrived from the northern hills and the entire force, reunited, crossed the great river. The junction of the Kabul and the Indus is at the present town of Attock (where the modern railroad from Peshawar to Rawalpindi crosses the Indus), and an appropriate place for Alexander's crossing is probably to be seen at modern Und (ancient Undabhanda), 16 miles (25 km.) up the river.

Beyond, between the Indus and the Hydaspes (Jhelum), was Taxila, where the excavated Bhir mound (Fig. 6.1) in the southern part of the area dates from the sixth to the second centuries B.C.E. and was thus the city of the time of Alexander.

When Alexander first came down into the Kabul valley the ruler of Taxila, whose name (according to the Greek sources) was Taxiles, urged to the action by his own son Ambhi, came to Alexander and offered his submission and cooperation. By the time Alexander arrived at Taxila, Taxiles was dead and Ambhi was on the throne. Ambhi now himself welcomed Alexander to the city and offered his kingdom to him. Alexander, pleased, gave the kingdom back to Ambhi, and thereafter held him as a friend and ally. Alexander also changed Ambhi's name to

6.1 Excavated Bhir Mound at Taxila

Taxiles (Diodorus 17.86.7), so the Taxiles who appears in the narrative from this point onward is none other than Ambhi, the son of the preceding Taxiles.

In Taxila the invaders found much that interested and amazed them. Aristobulus of Cassandreia, a Greek historian in Alexander's company, heard of tribes in which wives were glad to be burned along with their deceased husbands. Onesicritus, formerly a pupil of the Cynic philosopher Diogenes, was sent out of the city by Alexander to visit a group of naked ascetics, and found them exhibiting great endurance, standing, sitting, or lying motionless all day long in the burning sun. Both Aristobulus and Onesicritus were later quoted in these and other observations by Strabo (15.1.62–65).

Poros

But another and rival principality lay yet farther to the east, occupying the territory from the Hydaspes (Jhelum) to the Akesines River (the ancient Asikni, the modern Chenab). Here the tribe was that of the Purus, and their chief had the title Paurava. Arrian apparently considers this the name of the ruler, and calls the ruler Poros. Poros, as the narrative continues, was bravely determined to resist the invaders. Alexander pitched his camp on the west bank of the Hydaspes, probably near the present village of Haranpur, while Poros guarded the crossing from the other side with all his forces, including a squadron of elephants. Alexander, however, crossed the river about 150 stadia 17.5 miles (28 km.) farther upstream where an island provided some protection (probably near modern Jalalpur), and defeated Poros in a major battle on the far side. At the end of the battle Alexander was so impressed by the courage and kingly bearing of Poros that he restored to Poros his sovereignty and thereafter found him a faithful friend.[4]

It was by then the summer of 326 B.C.E., and Alexander moved eastward across the Akesines (Chenab) and the Hydraotes (the ancient Parushni, the modern Ravi) rivers. The military engagements were now of lesser magnitude than the great battle with Poros, but snakes were a peril, some reportedly 16 cubits (24 feet [7 m.]) in length (presumably pythons), and some whose bites brought sudden death (presumably cobras and others). Trees were an amazement too, some (presumably the banyan) casting a shadow of three plethra (perhaps three-quarters of an acre).

Retreat

So the invaders came to the Hyphasis (the ancient Vipaśa, the modern Beas). Save only for the Zaradros (the ancient Śutudri, the modern Sutlej) this was the easternmost and last of the five streams of the Punjab, and it was the easternmost point to which Alexander was to advance. The king of the last kingdom through which they had passed was Phegeus, and he not only welcomed Alexander but also gave him information about what lay beyond. There was a desert to traverse for twelve days, and then the river would be reached which was called the Ganges, 32 stadia (more than 3.5 miles [5.5 km.]) in width, and the deepest of all the Indian rivers. In the Ganges region dwelt the peoples of the Tabraesians and the Gandaridae, whose king was Xandrames. Xandrames had 20,000 cavalry, 200,000 infantry, 2,000 chariots, and 4,000 elephants equipped for war (Diodorus 17.90, 93). Xandrames is identifiable with Dhana Nanda, the last king of the Nanda dynasty in the kingdom of Magadha. According to Plutarch (*Life of Alexander* 62), Candragupta (called Sandracottos in Greek)—who was at this time a commander under Dhana Nanda and was later to slay the king and take the throne of Magadha for himself as the founder of the Maurya dynasty (Table 4.3)—met Alexander here in the Punjab and perhaps even suggested to him that Alexander might do well to attack Dhana Nanda.

In spite of the formidable opposition that would lie ahead, it was Alexander's strong desire to press on, but his soldiers now refused to go farther and, with extreme reluctance, Alexander gave the order to turn back and began the long return to the West where, in Babylon in June 323 B.C.E., he died.[5]

The Hellenization of the Northwest

In spite of Alexander's retreat, the way was now open more than ever before between the West and the East, and both Persian and Greek influences continued to be felt in India, especially in the Northwest, during the next several centuries. As he had done already in more westerly regions, when he came over the Hindu Kush and down into Gandhara and the Punjab Alexander founded cities and settled in them some of his own Greek and Macedonian followers along with indigenous people, thus intending to promote the intermingling of cultures in which he was interested, and these cities remained as centers of such Hellenism (a trace of which is to be seen even today in the Greek hat still worn in Swat). For example, when Alexander came over the Hindu Kush he founded Alexandria of the Caucasus (Arrian, *Anabasis of Alexander* 3.28.4; 4.22.4; 5.1.5). This city was at the gateway to India (Diodorus 17.83.1, assuming that "Media" in the present text is a scribal error for "India"), and at the meeting place of the three routes which crossed the Hindu Kush from Bactra (Strabo 15.2.8), one of which was down the valley of the Ghorband River, and another down that of the Panjshir. The site of Alexandria of the Caucasus was, therefore, probably near the confluence of these two rivers, and perhaps on the west bank of the united stream near Begram, and opposite the former Achaemenid capital of Kapiśa on the east side; thus, the new Alexandria formed a double city, which Alexander intended to be a new capital.[6] Another city was somewhere between Alexandria of the Caucasus and the Kabul River, and was named Nicaea in honor of Alexander's victory (Arrian, *Anabasis of Alexander* 4.22.6). Yet again at the Hydaspes where he won the victory over Poros, Alexander founded a second Nicaea, and also a city called Bucephala in memory of his horse Bucephalas which died there, worn out by age and exhaustion (Arrian, *Anabasis of Alexander* 5.19.4).

It was of course the intention of Alexander that the Indian territories that he had conquered, like all the other portions of his conquests, should remain as parts of his unified world empire. The two large rival states, the one at Taxila ruled by Taxiles (Ambhi) who had assisted Alexander's entrance into India, and the other beyond the Hydaspes under Poros whom Alexander had defeated and befriended, were reconciled with each other and recognized as continuing entities. In his own principality between the Hydaspes and the Hyphasis Poros was allowed to act as both prince and satrap (Plutarch, *Life of Alexander* 60). At Taxila in the realm of Taxiles, along with that ruler, Alexander appointed the Macedonian Philip, son of Machatas, as satrap, and gave him authority extending westward as far as the passes over the Hindu Kush to Bactria, and southward down the Indus to its confluence with the Akesines (Chenab). He also gave Philip troops sufficient to garrison the country, especially including a considerable body of Thracians under the command of the Macedonian Eudamus, son of Crateas. On the Lower Indus, from its confluence with the Akesines down to the sea and along the coast of India, Alexander made the Macedonian Pithon, son of Agenor, satrap (Arrian, *Anabasis of Alexander* 5.8.3; 6.2.3; 6.15.4).

The End of Macedonian Authority in India

As soon as Alexander left, however, the situation as he had arranged it began to deteriorate. Increasingly, conflict developed among the Greeks, the Macedonians, and the Indians. Alexander was still marching westward when he received word that the satrap Philip had been treacherously killed, and Alexander sent word that the commander Eudamus should take charge of the district along with Taxiles until a new satrap should be appointed (Arrian, *Anabasis of Alexander* 6.27.2).

It was not long, however, until Alexander himself died (as earlier mentioned, 323 B.C.E.), and after his death the satrapies of the empire were twice reorganized by his generals, by Perdiccas at Babylon in 323, and by Antipater at Triparadisus in 321. As far as India is concerned the end result was that the district of the Paropamisadae (with its capital at Alexandria of the Caucasus north of Kabul) was added to the domain of the Bactrian Oxyartes, father of Alexander's wife Roxane; the district between the Paropamisadae and the Indus was under Pithon son of Agenor; the kingdom of Taxila between the Indus and the Hydaspes remained under Taxiles; and the kingdom of Poros beyond the Hydaspes was enlarged with additional territory down along the Indus, it being recognized that both Taxiles and Poros were too strong to be removed (Diodorus 18.3.2–3; 18.39.6).

Even this arrangement did not last. Eudamus, who was evidently still in a position of power, was able to have Poros treacherously slain, and Taxiles also disappeared from the scene at some point. By about 317 B.C.E. both Eudamus and Pithon went away to die in other conflicts within the empire, and therewith Macedonian authority vanished from India (Diodorus 19.14.8; 19.44.1; 19.85.2).

MAURYA EMPIRE (322–185 B.C.E.)

Candragupta Maurya

In the meantime on the Ganges, where Alexander had not come, Candragupta (322–298 B.C.E.) defeated Dhana Nanda, occupied Pataliputra, and instituted the rule of the Maurya dynasty (so called from the surname of Candragupta) in the kingdom of Magadha. This kingdom Candragupta soon expanded into the first great Indian empire (Table 4.3).[7]

Within a few years after his own accession to rule in the West, Seleucus I Nicator (312–281 B.C.E) undertook to recover Alexander's provinces in India and marched across the Indus, but Candragupta confronted him with very large forces. The result was an agreement, probably made in 305 B.C.E., in which Seleucus, upon terms of intermarriage and of receiving in exchange 500 elephants, retained Bactria but "gave" Candragupta the provinces of the Paropamisadae (around Kabul), of Arachosia (around Kandahar), of Aria (around Herat), and of Gedrosia (Baluchistan); thus the boundaries of Candragupta's empire were the Hindu Kush in the north and the Afghan highlands above Herat in the west, and so he held much of Ariana, as Strabo calls the country west of the Indus River (15.1.10; 15.2.9). To the east the sway of Candragupta probably extended to the Bay of Bengal; thus, in all, his empire comprised substantially all of India north of the Narmada River, as well as most of Afghanistan.

In line with the good relations between the Seleucid and the Maurya empires, in probably about 302 B.C.E. Seleucus I sent as ambassador to the court of Candragupta a Greek named Megasthenes, who had already been with the satrap of Arachosia, and who now visited Pataliputra a number of times (Arrian, *Anabasis of Alexander* 5.6.2). On the basis of his observations Megasthenes wrote an account of India which, although lost in its original, is quoted in extensive fragments by Strabo, Arrian, and other ancient writers.[8]

As described by Megasthenes (Fragments 25–26; Strabo 15.1.36; Arrian, *Indica* 10.2–7), the Indian cities of the time that were beside rivers or seas were built of wood, because sun-dried mud brick would not hold out against the rains and the floods, but cities on elevated locations were made of brick and clay. Of all the cities Pataliputra was the greatest.

The Indian people, Megasthenes says, live a simple life, but nevertheless they like to adorn themselves, for they wear gold-embroidered apparel, use ornaments set with precious stones, wear gay-colored linen garments, and are accompanied with sun-shades (Fragment 27; Strabo 15.1.53–54). The population generally is divided into seven classes: philosophers, farmers, shepherds, and hunters, artisans and tradesmen, warriors, government inspectors, and royal councilors. This enumeration presumably reflects the activities which Megasthenes observed about him, but hardly equates with the four regular castes of Hinduism, yet Megasthenes evidently reports some of the requirements of the caste system when he goes on to say that it is not legal for a man to marry a wife from another class or to change his work from one kind to another (Fragment 33; Strabo 15.1.39–41, 46–49).

Of the philosophers Megasthenes says that those who live in the mountains worship Dionysus (presumably meaning Śiva) and those who live in the plains worship Herakles (presumably Krishna). The philosophers are also divided into Brachmanes (i.e., *brahmanas*) and Garmanes (i.e., *śramanas*). The *brahmanas* "converse more about death than anything else, for they believe . . . that death, to those who have devoted themselves to philosophy, is birth into the true life, that is, the happy life; and they therefore discipline themselves most of all to be ready for death." It is also their opinion "that the universe was created and is destructible . . . and that it is spherical in shape, and that the god who made it and regulates it pervades the whole of it . . . and that the earth is situated in the center of the universe." The *śramaṇas* are ascetics who live in the forest or go about begging, and they are accustomed to "practice such endurance, both in toils and in perseverance, that they stay in one posture all day long without moving" (Fragment 41; Strabo 15.1.58–60).

According to the Puranas Candragupta had a relatively brief reign of twenty-four years (322–298 B.C.E.) and, according to unanimous Jaina tradition represented in a number of different works, Candragupta was a convert to Jainism and actually abdicated the throne in favor of his son (here named Simhasena) and followed the Jaina saint Bhadrabahu to South India, where both lived at Śravanabelgola. After the death of Bhadrabahu, whom Candragupta had attended as his chief disciple, Candragupta himself lived on as an ascetic until he died of self-imposed starvation according to Jaina practice.[9]

At Śravanabelgola one of the two main hills is called Candragiri because Candragupta lived there, and there is a cave on the hill which is named after Bhadrabahu, and a temple which is called Candragupta *basti* (temple) and said to have been built originally by Candragupta. On the same hill are relatively early inscriptions which refer to the connection of both Bhadrabahu and Candragupta with the place, and speak of the king as the disciple of the great saint. Inscription No. 1, dating from around 600 C.E., speaks of the migration to the South led by Bhadrabahu:

> Bhadrabahuswami . . . having learned from an omen and foretold in Ujjayini a calamity lasting for a period of twelve years, the entire community (*sangha*) set out from the North to the South and reached by degrees a country counting many hundreds of villages and filled with happy people, wealth, gold, grain, and herds of cows, buffaloes, goats, and sheep.

Inscription No. 67, also on the Candragiri hill and dated in 1129 C.E., contains the sentence:

> Say, how can the greatness be described of Bhadrabahu whose arms have grown stout by subduing the pride of the great wrestler delusion, and through the merit of being whose disciple Candragupta was served for a very long time by the forest deities.

On the higher Vindhyagiri hill at Śravanabelgola, Inscription No. 258 mentions "the lord of ascetics, Bhadrabahu," "who arose on the earth . . . as the full moon in the milk ocean," and continues:

> Pre-eminent for the wealth of perfect intelligence, of brilliant perfection of conduct, breaker of the bond of *karma*, of a fame increased by the growth of penance, Bhadrabahu of supernatural powers lifted up here the pure doctrine of the *siddhas* (perfected beings) beautifully composed with faultless words. Though the last of the lords of sages, the *śrutakevalins* (ones having full knowledge of the sacred Jaina texts), on earth, Bhadrabahu became the foremost leader of the learned by his exposition of the meaning of all the scriptures. His disciple was Candragupta, who was bowed to by the chief gods on account of his perfect conduct and the fame caused by the greatness of whose severe penance spread into other worlds.[10]

It seems probable that Bhadrabahu would have chosen to go to a place where he could be confident of a favorable reception, and this suggests that Jainism was already known prior to that time in the region of Śravanabelgola. This supposition is supported by the fact that Niganthas (Jainas) are mentioned already in Sri Lanka in the reign of King Pandukabhaya (377–307 B.C.E.), and the faith would presumably have moved through South India to reach Lanka (*Mahavamsa* 10.97–99).[11] Thus a date prior to the fourth century B.C.E. is suggested for the spread of Jainism in the South. With the coming of Bhadrabahu and Candragupta, that spread was presumably further accelerated. Since Bhadrabahu was the leader of the stricter unclothed Jainas (at least later known as Digambaras, "sky clad") these events were probably of the most significance for that branch of Jainism.[12]

Bindusara

Bindusara, son and successor of Candragupta for a reign of twenty-five years (298–273 B.C.E.) according to the Puranas, was apparently not, like his father, an adherent of Jainism, but rather an adherent of the Vedic religion, for the *Mahavamsa* (5.34)[13] says that he showed hospitality to 60,000 *brahmanas*. The Greek writers refer to a king of India whom they name Amitrochates or Amitraghata, who is almost certainly to be recognized as Bindusara, and Athenaeus (*Deipnosophists* 14.652–653) states that Amitrochates wrote to Antiochus I of Syria (281–261 B.C.E.) begging him "to purchase and send him grape-syrup, figs, and a sophist." Antiochus wrote back: "Figs, to be sure, and grape-syrup we will dispatch to you, but it is against the law in Greece to sell a sophist." So, although Bindusara was unsuccessful in the effort to obtain such a teacher for his court, it is evident that his interests extended to the world of Greek philosophy.

Aśoka

The son and successor of Bindusara is called Aśoka (free of sorrow) in the Buddhist sources (Aśokavardhana in full in the Puranas), which is probably his personal name, and Priyadarśin or Piyadasi (one who is of pleasant looks, or one who looks [on others] with kindness) in his own inscriptions, which from the frequency of its usage was probably his formal name, perhaps assumed at his coronation. With this formal name the king also regularly uses the title *devanampriya* or *devanampiya*, meaning "beloved of the gods."[14]

According to tradition, Aśoka served already under his father as governor of Taxila in Gandhara and also as governor of Ujjayini in Avanti,[15] and these appointments are not at all unlikely, for Aśoka's own Separate Kalinga Rock Edict I shows that at that time princes of the royal family were in charge both at Ujjayini and at Taxila.[16] On the way to Ujjayini Aśoka stopped in Vidiśa (Vedisa, Vedisagiri, a place now represented by ruins called Besnagar, in the fork of the Bes or Vedisa River and the Betwa River, about 2 miles (3 km.) from modern Bhilsa. Here at Vidiśa Aśoka met a lovely young woman named Devi, the daughter of a merchant, and took her as his wife. Afterward she bore in Ujjayini a son Mahinda and a daughter Sanghamitta, and it was they who later accomplished the conversion of Sri Lanka to Buddhism (*Dipavamsa* 6.15–17; *Mahavamsa* 13.8–11).[17] Other queens of Aśoka named in the various records were Asandhamitta, Tissarakkha, Karuvaki, and Padmavati.

When Bindusara fell sick and was near his end, Aśoka came back from Ujjayini to Pataliputra (Pupphapura) and made himself master of the city, then after his father's death caused his oldest brother, Sumana, to be killed, and in 273 B.C.E. assumed the sovereignty of the empire (*Mahavamsa* 5.39–40).[18] Another statement (*Mahavamsa* 5.20)[19] to the effect that Aśoka slew his ninety-nine brothers is surely a great exaggeration; nevertheless, the difficulties connected with the succession may have been responsible for the fact that Aśoka's formal coronation only took place four years (in 269 B.C.E.) after the actual accession to sovereignty. Reckoned from the coronation, his reign was of thirty-six or thirty-seven years duration (269–232 B.C.E.).

The empire which thus came into the hands of Aśoka had already been extended by Candragupta to borders as far apart as Afghanistan and the Bay of Bengal, and Aśoka himself engaged in only one war of conquest, that of Kalinga in southeast India (corresponding roughly to modern Orissa). This took place when Aśoka had been crowned eight years (261 B.C.E.) and was recorded in Rock Edict 13 of his 13th regnal year (256).[20] The war evidently fell heavily upon the civil population of Kalinga as well as upon the combatants, and affected the religious communities as well as others, for Aśoka states that 150,000 men were taken captive, 100,000 were slain, and nearly as many (evidently non-combatants) died, and he stresses the suffering which came to *brahmanas,* ascetics, and other sects, as well as householders. Afterward Aśoka experienced remorse for what he had done, considered that such slaughter and deportation were very evil, and felt a strong inclination for *dharma (dhamma)* and for instruction in *dharma.*

According to the *Dipavamsa* (6.25–99) and the *Mahavamsa* (5.34–38, 62–72),[21] Aśoka must have been an adherent of the Vedic religion at the commencement of his reign, for he continued to follow the precedent of his father Bindusara and for three years provided the *brahmanas* with food. But after three years, noting their lack of self-control at the distribution of the food, he had the followers of the different schools brought into his presence and tested them in an assembly before he gave them food. In all there were active at the time not only the *brahmanas* but also Niganthas (Jainas), Wanderers, "and other upholders of heretical views," and many of these Aśoka invited into his abode and questioned. Then one day the king saw "a peaceful ascetic," the Buddhist monk Nigrodha, passing along the street in his collection of alms, and was attracted to him. This Nigrodha was the son of Aśoka's own older brother, Sumana, whom Aśoka had slain in order to secure the throne for himself, and Nigrodha was born after the death of his father. At the king's invitation Nigrodha came into the palace and gave religious instruction to Aśoka, Nigrodha himself being very well versed in Buddhist doctrine and discipline (in *dharma* and *vinaya*). "Earnestness," said Nigrodha, "is the path of immortality; indolence is the path of death. Those who are earnest do not die. Those who are indolent are as if dead." Aśoka was persuaded, and declared that he was taking refuge forthwith in the Buddha, his doctrine (*dhamma*), and his community (*sangha*). "With wife, and children, and relatives I announce (my) discipleship," he said. Then he put aside the 60,000 false teachers who had been supported by his father and for a time by himself, and substituted a like number of Buddhist monks. He also built many monasteries, including the Aśokarama at Pataliputra.

Since the accounts here cited make Aśoka spend three years "in mastering the idea of the heretics," before his conversion to Buddhism, they apparently place that conversion in the fourth year after his coronation, i.e., in 265 B.C.E. In his own Minor Rock Edict 1 Aśoka says that he was a lay disciple (*upasaka*) and not very zealous for more than two and one-half years, probably during 264–261, but by the time of issuing this edict he had joined the *sangha* (literally, "I went to the *sangha*," perhaps meaning that he actually entered monastic life for a limited period, as Buddhism allows), and had been very zealous for more than a year, probably 261–260. This understanding of these dates allows it to be thought that Aśoka was a follower of Buddhism, but only an indifferent one, prior to the

Kalinga war (261), by which experience he was led to devote himself to strenuous exertions in Buddhism and in behalf of the order.[22]

In the next year when he had been crowned ten years (i.e., in 259), Aśoka went on a "*dharma* tour" to Sambodhi, probably meaning to the present Bodhgaya, where the Buddha had attained enlightenment (Rock Edict 8).[23] This was only the first such "tour of religion," by which Aśoka replaced the pleasure tours on which kings formerly went with hunting and other amusements. Instead of those pleasure tours there were now visits and gifts to *brahmanas* and ascetics, visits to and provision of gold for the aged, and visits to the rural population with such *dharma* instruction as was suitable for them, and it was in these things that Aśoka found pleasure.

According to northern tradition, Aśoka was guided on his tours by the Buddhist elder Upagupta (sometimes identified with Moggaliputta-Tissa, who presided over the Third Buddhist Council in the seventeenth year of Aśoka, but more likely a different person), and was encouraged by Upagupta in the building of *stupas* for the relics of the Buddha in many places. As related by Xuan Zang (629–645 C.E.), Aśoka opened the *stupas* of the eight countries in which the bodily remains of the Buddha were originally placed, divided the relics, and distributed them in *stupas* which he himself built throughout the whole of Jambudvipa. According to the *Fo-sho-hing-tsan-king* (the Chinese translation of Aśvaghosha's *Buddhacarita*), 2297, and the *Sang-kia-lo-c'ha-sho-tsih-fo-hing-king* (the Chinese translation of a work by Sangharaksha, a priest also contemporary with Kanishka), no less than 84,000 such *stupas* were built all together, so that the benefits of the relics might be diffused everywhere.[24] In fact Aśoka did evidently make visits and/or erect monuments not only at the main pilgrimage places that were associated with chief events in the life of the Buddha—Lumbini where the Buddha was born, Bodhgaya where he attained enlightenment, Isipatana where he first preached, and Kuśinagara where he died—but also at Kapilavastu where he renounced the world, Śravasti where he mostly lived and taught, and at yet other places which had Buddhist associations of other sorts, such as Sanci and Nigalisagar.[25]

Sanci is near Vidiśa (close to Bhilsa), which was the home of Aśoka's queen Devi, and probably already had a Buddhist establishment. Devi, also called Vediśa-Mahadevi, was descended from a Śakya family which had migrated to Vidiśa to escape the attacks of Vidudabha (son of Prasenajit) on the Śakyans, thus was herself related to the Buddha's own clan and was probably already a Buddhist before her marriage to Aśoka. Devi is also credited with the construction of the monastery known as Vediśagiri, and this was probably the first of the monuments at or near Sanci. These facts, therefore, may explain why Aśoka also built at Sanci.[26]

When Aśoka went to Pataliputra as sovereign, Devi seems to have stayed on in Vidiśa, for in Pataliputra Asandhamitta (*Mahavamsa* 5.85)[27] and later Tissarakkha (who killed the Bodhi tree at Bodhgaya by means of poisonous thorns, but only after Devi's daughter Sanghamitta had carried a branch to Lanka, *Mahavamsa* 18.1ff., 20.1–5)[28] appear in the position of chief queen. Also Devi was in Vidiśa when her son, "the great *thera* (elder) Mahinda," was preparing to go to Lanka, and came to visit his mother on the way. The *Mahavamsa* (13.6–7) relates: "When he (Mahinda) came in time to Vedisagiri the city of his mother Devi, he visited his mother and when Devi saw her dear son she made him welcome, and his companions likewise, with foods prepared by herself, and she led the *thera* up to the lovely *vihara* (monastery) Vedisagiri."[29]

Nigalisagar (Nigliva) is in the Terai of Nepal (13 miles [21 km.] northwest of Rummindei), and was a site associated with the Buddha Kanakamuni

(Konagamana). Kanakamuni is the second of the three supposed predecessors in the present world age of the historical Śakyamuni Gautama Buddha, and the cult of the worship of the previous Buddhas was evidently already in existence in the time of Aśoka. The Nigalisagar Pillar Inscription of Aśoka states that Aśoka, when crowned fourteen years (255 B.C.E.), enlarged the *stupa* of Buddha Kanakamuni (which was obviously already there) to double its former size, and when crowned twenty years (249), came here to worship and erected the stone pillar.[30] Probably, therefore, Aśoka visited this spot on the same trip on which he went to Lumbini (Rummindei) and erected his pillar at that place too.

In his pillar and rock inscriptions which were carved at these and many other places over almost all of India, Aśoka is mainly concerned for the promotion of *dharma*, which is for him not primarily a theological doctrine but a practical way of life. This concern was surely inspired by his conversion to Buddhism, but the ethical principles he advocates, such as truthfulness, gentleness, moderation, and mutual help are common to all Indian religions, and his special emphasis on non-killing of all life was taught not only by Buddhism but also to an even greater extent by Jainism. Furthermore Aśoka called for toleration and harmony among the different religious sects, and he mentions specifically not only the *sangha* (of the Buddhists), but also the *brahmanas*, the Ajivikas, the Nirgranthas, and "all the other sects" (e.g., Pillar Edict 7),[31] and his benefactions were extended to others besides the Buddhists, e.g., to the Ajivikas, to whom he donated several caves in the Barabar Hills (15 miles [24 km.] north of Gaya), so that these naked ascetics might have shelter from "the approach of the roar of waters," i.e., from the monsoon rains (Barabar Cave Inscriptions 1–3).[32]

As to ethical conduct, Aśoka asked, "What constitutes the *dharma*?" and answered: "Little sin, many good deeds, mercifulness, charity, truthfulness, purity" (Pillar Edict 2).[33]

On kindness to animals as well as human beings, Aśoka said: "Here (in my dominion) no living beings are to be killed and offered in sacrifice" (Rock Edict 1).[34]

As to religious toleration, he affirmed that he honored all sects and that all sects ought to be honored: "By doing so, one promotes one's own sect and also benefits other sects; by doing otherwise, one hurts one's own sect and also harms other sects" (Rock Edict 12).[35]

And as to the fruit of the practice of *dharma*, he exhorted both the small and the great to be zealous in such practice, and declared: "Even by the small (person), if he is greatly zealous, is heaven capable of being attained" (Minor Rock Edict).[36]

Certainly Aśoka also exemplified in his own life and undertakings the virtues he commended. He was himself "very zealous in the way of *dharma*" (Minor Rock Edict).[37] In his own royal kitchens, where formerly hundreds of thousands of animals had been killed "for the sake of curry," he ordered that in the future none should be killed (Rock Edict 1).[38] Within his empire and even among peoples bordering upon his own dominions, he instituted provision for medical treatment for human beings and medical treatment for animals (Rock Edict 2).[39] On the roads he planted banyan trees to provide shade, and at intervals dug wells and built rest houses, all for the benefit of animals as well as of people (Pillar Edict 7).[40] Not unjustly the *Dipavamsa* (1.26; 6.23) and the *Mahavamsa* (11.18–19) call the great emperor Asokadhamma or Dhammasoka, i.e., Aśoka the righteous.[41]

Successors of Aśoka

In the Puranic listing (as reconstructed from corrupt texts, above Table 4.3) of the members of the Maurya dynasty, Aśoka is followed in turn by Kunala, Daśaratha, and Samprati.

Kunala, also known by the name of Dharmavivardhana, was the son of Aśoka and his queen Padvamati. According to an account preserved by Xuan Zang[42] and also alluded to by Fa Xian (399–414 C.E.),[43] Kunala was unjustly accused by his stepmother, Aśoka's last queen Tissarakkha (Tishyarakshita), and by her intrigue was sent to Taxila to deal with a revolt (as Aśoka had been sent by Bindusara), and was there eventually blinded, a *stupa* being later built to commemorate the tragic event. Being thus incapacitated, Kunala was presumably unable to rule in succession to his father, except perhaps in name, and it is probable that Daśaratha and Samprati were his sons and did have the rule, although the succession is not very clear.

Like his grandfather, Daśaratha bestowed caves in the Nagarjuni Hills (near the Barabar Hills) upon the Ajivikas, and is known from his three dedicatory inscriptions in these caves, so his existence is confirmed and he may have indeed succeeded Aśoka in rule at Pataliputra, although little is known of him otherwise.[44]

According to some sources, Samprati was nominated by Aśoka to be his successor at Pataliputra, but joined with disloyal officers of the king in conspiring against him and stopping Aśoka's benefactions to the Buddhist community.[45] Other sources, however, make Ujjayini the place of rule of Samprati and, if Daśaratha held Pataliputra, this may be the more likely, although Jaina sources represent Samprati as ruling over both Pataliputra and Ujjayini.[46] If the reign of Aśoka terminated around 232 B.C.E., and if Kunala be allowed the eight years attributed to him in the Puranic listing, Daśaratha and Samprati (credited with eight and nine years respectively in the Puranas) would presumably have begun to reign around 224 B.C.E.

At any rate the Jaina sources consider Samprati to have been very important in the history of Jainism. It will be remembered that Candragupta Maurya (322–298 B.C.E.) was converted to Jainism and in the end followed the Jaina saint Bhadrabahu to Śravanabelgola, these events being of much importance for the spread of Jainism in the South in the form at least later known as the Digambara. In the North, Bhadrabahu's disciple Sthulabhadra remained as the head of the Jaina community, in which the more lax practice of wearing clothing developed and led to what was at least later called the Śvetambara (white clad) form of Jainism. In turn it was a disciple of Sthulabhadra named Suhastin who was associated with Samprati, and under the influence of Suhastin Samprati became a great patron of Śvetambara Jainism and did much for its spread in West and also South India and elsewhere. Thus Samprati is often considered the Aśoka of Jainism.[47]

An account of these matters is given by the Jaina author Hemacandra (1088–1172 C.E.), who writes concerning Samprati and Suhastin as follows:

> He (Samprati) showed his zeal by causing Jaina temples to be erected over the whole of Jambudvipa. During Suhastin's stay at Ujjaini, and under his guidance, splendid religious festivals and processions in honor of the *arhat* (worthy one) were celebrated, and great was the devotion manifested by the king and his subjects on this occasion. The example and advice of Samprati induced his vassals to embrace and patronize his creed, so that not only in his kingdom but also in adjacent countries the monks could practice their religion.

Hemacandra also explains that Samprati sent Jaina missionaries to South India, and that these were Śvetambaras. "Thus," Hemacandra concludes, "the uncivilized nations were brought under the influence of Jainism."[48]

The last of the imperial Maurya line was Brihadratha (Table 4.3), and when he was assassinated (185 B.C.E.) by his commander-in-chief Pushyamitra the Mauryas were succeeded in Pataliputra by the Śungas (184–72, Table 4.4) and they in turn by the briefly ruling (forty-five years) and little known Kanvas (Table 4.5). Meanwhile the disintegration of the great Maurya empire allowed the rise of other kingdoms, notably the Andhras or Śatavahanas in the South, and the incoming of foreign invaders in the Northwest, notably the Yavanas (Greeks), Śakas (Scythians), Pahlavas (Parthians), and Kushanas.

KUSHANA EMPIRE

The five principal Kushana kings were Kulala Kadphises I, Vima Kadphises II, Kanishka, Huvishka, and Vasudeva I. About 40 C.E., Kadphises I united the five Yueh-chi tribes, came down over the Hindu Kush, and soon mastered Eastern Afghanistan and the Punjab; Kadphises II extended these dominions eastward to the Ganges and Yamuna; and Kanishka, the most important of the Kushana kings, ruled over a large empire, the centers of which were Purushapura, his capital in the Northwest, and Mathura in the Southeast. The accession of Kanishka is usually placed in 78 C.E. (or some fifty years or more later), and the length of his reign was probably around twenty-five years; thus, the dates of his reign are 78–103 C.E. if the early beginning point is taken. Inscriptions attest a total of ninety-eight years for Kanishka and his two successors, which would terminate the reign of Vasudeva I in 176 C.E., if the ninety-eight years are reckoned from 78 C.E.

After Vasudeva I and in the course of the third century C.E. the Indian empire of the Kushanas disintegrated, probably due in part to the rise of the Sassanid power in Persia (229–651 C.E.), and the Andhra/Śatavahana kingdom also came to its end at more or less the same time, leaving something like a century of relative darkness in Indian history until the rise of the next great empire, that of the Guptas. In Kabul and neighboring regions, however, strong Kushana dynasties continued to exist until nearly the end of the fifth century, when the invasion of the Ephtalite Huns (White Huns) laid waste most of Gandhara.[49]

In Bactria there is some illumination of the period from excavations at Yemshi-tepe (west of Balkh) and in the adjacent Tillya-tepe. Tillya-tepe was an occupied site from the end of the second millennium B.C.E. to the middle of the first millennium B.C.E., when it was abandoned; then, as shown by coins, from the first century B.C.E. to the first century C.E.—the little-known time when the Bactrian Greek state was no longer in existence and the Kushana state not yet established—it was the site of a necropolis in which remarkable objects of gold were preserved. Furthermore, Yemshi-tepe itself represents an important capital city which existed during Kushana times, dating from the first to the fourth centuries C.E.[50]

In Buddhist history the Kushana king Kanishka is considered a great patron of Buddhism, comparable to Aśoka, and it was in the Kushana period that the first known images of the Buddha were made in Mathura and Gandhara.

Kanishka himself is represented in a headless standing statue in buff sandstone, which was found in the ruins of a shrine near the village of Mat (9 miles [14 km.] from Mathura on the opposite, i.e., east side of the Yamuna River), and is now in the Archaeological Museum in Mathura (Fig. 6.2). The statue is 5 feet 4 inches (1.63 m.) tall. The king wears a tunic which reaches below the knees and is held by

6.2 Statue of Kanishka, in the Archaeological Museum, Mathura

a belt at the waist, ornamented with metal plaques. Over the tunic and extending below it, is a long coat, which is open at the front and turned back on the sides. Pajama-type trousers (Persian *shalwar*) are tucked into heavy boots, which appear to be made of felt and are characteristic of Central Asian nomads. With his right hand the king holds a long, heavy mace, and with his left hand a sword, the pommel of which is shaped like the head of a bird. An inscription is written on the front of the king's tunic and coat, and reads: "The great king, the king of kings, the son of god, Kanishka." Since the Kushana kings thus claimed to be the descendants of god, the shrine in which the statue was found may have been a sacred house (*devakula*), dedicated to the kings.[51]

A similarly headless statue from the ruins of a Kushana temple at Surkh Kotal (in the southern part of the Bactrian plain), now in the Kabul Museum (Fig. 6.3), is posed in a way so nearly identical with that of the Mathura figure that the two statues are surely related and this one—which is probably the earlier of the two—is probably also of Kanishka, although it carries no inscription to provide positive identification.[52] In both cases the figure is clothed in what is evidently Central

6.3   Statue of Kanishka, in the Kabul Museum

Asian garb, and the swirl of the trousers in particular may be compared with similar representations in an imposing, more than life-size (6 feet 4.4 inches [1.94 m.]) statue of a Parthian from Shami in Susiana, dating perhaps circa 250 B.C.E., now in the Archaeological Museum in Teheran;[53] and in a marble statue of the princess Washfari, daughter of the Parthian king Sanatrouq of Hatra, dated by its inscription in the year 449 of the Seleucid Era (137 C.E.), now in the Iraq Museum in Baghdad.[54]

GUPTA EMPIRE (320–600 C.E.)

The Guptas find bare mention at almost the end of the Puranic tradition—e.g., in the *Vishnu Purana* (4.24),[55] "the Guptas of Magadha (will reign) along the Ganges to Prayaga"—but other source materials are relatively abundant. Prayaga (place of sacrifice) is the ancient name of the modern Allahabad, at the confluence of the Ganges, the Yamuna, and the fabled subterranean Sarasvati, and Pratisthana, legendary capital of the Lunar kings, was in the vicinity. Pataliputra, however, the seat of the Mauryas, was the first capital of the Guptas, and after that Ayodhya.

Already with Candragupta Maurya, *Gupta* appears as part of a king's name, but there is apparently no relationship between the founder of the Maurya dynasty and the kings of the Gupta empire. By way of distinction, therefore, it is customary to write the word Gupta separately in the names of the members of the Gupta dynasty, e.g., Candra Gupta.

Early Imperial Guptas

In the period prior to the foundation of the Gupta empire there are some occurrences of the name Gupta standing alone. Then finally there appears in the inscriptions a *Maharaja* Gupta, who is succeeded by his son *Maharaja* Ghatotkacha, and he by his son Candra Gupta I, and the last named becomes the founder of the Gupta empire and the Gupta dynasty.

Candra Gupta I comes forward first in a subordinate role at Pataliputra. Pataliputra was originally built and fortified as a defense of Magadha against the Licchavis and their confederates on the north side of the Ganges, and it appears that in the course of the long rivalry between the two regions and perhaps in the disturbed times which came after the reign of Pushyamitra, the Licchavis were able to take possession of the city. At any rate the rise of Candra Gupta I to rule in Pataliputra seems to have been associated with his marriage to a Licchavi princess named Kumara Devi. Thereafter, as king, he struck coins in the names of himself, his queen, and the Licchavis, and his son and successor Samudra Gupta designated himself as the son of the daughter of the Licchavis. The coronation of Candra Gupta I probably took place in 320 C.E., and this date was taken as the beginning of the Gupta era which was in use for several centuries. As known from various lines of evidence, including coins and inscriptions, the rulers of the Gupta line in the earlier and later parts of their imperial period are shown in Table 6.1, with dates, and identifications (in parentheses), which are often conjectural.

Samudra Gupta (330–375 C.E.), son of Candra Gupta I and Kumara Devi,

TABLE 6.1.
EARLIER AND LATER IMPERIAL GUPTAS

	CE
Earlier Imperial Guptas	
Candra Gupta I	320–330
Samudra Gupta	330–375
Candra Gupta II (Deva Gupta I)	375–413
Kumara Gupta I	413–455
Skanda Gupta	455–467
Later Imperial Guptas	
Puru Gupta	467–472
Narasimha Gupta	473
Kumara Gupta II	473–476
Budha Gupta	476–495
Tathagata Gupta (Vainya Gupta)	c. 507
Baladitya (Bhanu Gupta)	c. 510
Vajra	after c. 510

extended the Gupta sway by wide conquests. A record of his work is preserved in a contemporary Sanskrit composition (a *praśasti* or poetic eulogy) by a poet named Harishena. The text was inscribed on a stone pillar which was set up long before by Aśoka, probably in Kauśambi, and is now in Allahabad. In the text the campaigns of Samudra Gupta are classified geographically in four sections: as those against eleven kings in the South (in the Eastern Deccan), against nine kings in the North (in Aryavarta, the Gangetic plain), against the chiefs of wild forest tribes, and against the rulers of frontier kingdoms and republics. In all, North India was evidently brought under the direct rule of Samudra Gupta from the Lower Ganges on the east to the Yamuna and Cambal rivers on the west, and from the foothills of the Himalaya on the north to the Narmada River on the south, while frontier kingdoms and free tribes were subordinated and the Eastern Deccan was at least temporarily overrun.

The Allahabad text of Harishena also praises Samudra Gupta for his intellectual ability, his musical accomplishments, and his poetical compositions. Like most of the Gupta sovereigns, Samudra Gupta was a Brahmanical Hindu, but he was not unfriendly to the Buddhists. In his time the king of Lanka, named Siri Meghavanna or Meghavarna (352–379 C.E.), sent two Buddhist monks, one of them his own brother, to visit sacred places in India, but they found that even in the Buddhist monasteries they were treated with disdain as foreigners. King Maghavanna thereupon sent a gift of rich gems to Samudra Gupta, and asked permission to build in India a monastery where monks from his own country might have a place of rest. "Thus," Meghavanna said, "the two countries will be bound together and travelers be refreshed." This request was granted by Samudra Gupta, and accordingly a large and splendid monastery (the Mahabodhi *sangharama*) was erected at Bodhgaya north of the Bodhi Tree. This monastery was seen in the 7th century C.E. by the Chinese Buddhist pilgrim Xuan Zang, and described as an edifice of six halls, with three-storied observation towers, and a defence wall 30–40 feet (9–12 m.) in height. Inside was a statue of the Buddha, cast of gold and silver, and decorated with gems and precious stones. Relics of the Buddha were also kept there, and "every year on the day of the full moon of (the month when) Tathagata displayed great spiritual changes (in India the thirtieth day of the twelfth month), these relics are taken out for public exhibition."[56]

The son and successor of Samudra Gupta was Candra Gupta II (375–413 C.E.), who was also known as Deva Gupta I, and who also took the name Vikramaditya as a title (sun of power). He continued the conquests of his father in the West, and added Malwa and the peninsula of Surashtra (Kathiawar) to the Gupta empire. While Pataliputra may have continued to be regarded as the official capital, both Samudra Gupta and Candra Gupta II made their center at times at Ayodhya, the ancient capital of Rama, while Candra Gupta II, with his western conquests, also resided in Malwa, possibly first at Vidiśa and later at Ujjayini.

It was in the reign of Candra Gupta II that the Chinese Buddhist monk and pilgrim Fa Xian (Fa Hien) (illustrious master of the Law) traveled in India and Sri Lanka (399–414 C.E.). Afterward Fa Xian wrote a record of his travels, from which we learn of a truly remarkable journey.[57]

The record begins with the statement that Fa Xian had been living in Chang'an. This city was at or near modern Xian (Sian), which is located in the center of the Guanzhong (Kuanchung) Plain, and is now the capital of Shaanxi (Shensi) Province. This city and other towns in the plain nearby served intermittently as the capitals of the most famous dynasties in ancient Chinese history— Western Zhou (Chou) (1066–771 B.C.E.), Qin (Chin) (221–206 B.C.E.), Han

(206 B.C.E.–220 C.E.), Tang (618–907 C.E.)—and of many shorter-lived dynasties, there being here some eleven capitals in all, of which Chang'an was the greatest.

In Chinese history the period of Fa Xian was that known as the Six Dynasties (220–581 C.E.), when there was a multiplicity of kingdoms in the land. Of these the kingdom of the Eastern Jin (Tsin) (317–420), with capital at Nanjing (Nanking), was at the immediate time the most important, but Chang'an was the capital of a lesser kingdom, which was at least semi-independent.

The famous route of travel and trade, which we know as the Silk Road, which connected China with the West from at least the Han Dynasty (206 B.C.E.–220 C.E.) onward, began at Chang'an, and Fa Xian set forth on his journey on this route, even as Buddhist missionaries had come to China on the same route long before. The route led from Chang'an to the northwest through what is now Gansu (Kansu) Province, reached the end of the Great Wall at the Jade Gate, and went on to Dunhuang (Tunhuang). Beyond Dunhuang, in what is now the Xinjiang (Sinkiang) Uygur Autonomous Region of China, are the vast Tarim Basin and the Taklimakan Desert, which are enclosed by the Tian Shan (Heavenly Mountains) in the north, the Kunlun Shan in the south, the Altun Shan in the east, and the Pamirs in the west. Here the Silk Road proceeded by two branches to go around the desert on the north by the oases of Turpan (Turfan), Qarashahr, and Kucha, and on the south by Lake Lob-nor and the oases of Khotan and Yarkand, the branches coming together again at Kashgar in the west. Beyond, the route led on across the Pamirs, along the Oxus (Amu Darya) River, and to Bactra (Balkh), where a southern way went south across the Hindu Kush to India, and the western way went on across Iran and Iraq to the Mediterranean.[58]

At Dunhuang a start had already been made on the famous Buddhist caves. Here the governor provided Fa Xian and the friends who were journeying with him with all the necessities for crossing the desert ahead of them. This desert is designated by the term *gobi*, which is understood in geology as a basin structure scoured out by wind, and is used in general for a sandy or rocky waste and is often applied to all the desert lands east of the Pamirs and north of Tibet. As confronted by Fa Xian and his small party, the desert was truly fearsome:

> In this desert there are a great many evil spirits and also hot winds; those who encounter them perish to a man. There are neither birds above nor beasts below. Gazing on all sides as far as the eye can reach in order to mark the track, no guidance is to be obtained save from the rotting bones of dead men, which point the way.[59]

Seventeen days of travel took the party to the country of Shan-shan (probably near Lake Lob-nor), where they found a Buddhist king and a monastery with 4,000 monks of the Hinayana or Lesser Vehicle, and where they stayed for a month. Fifteen days of travel to the northwest took them to Qarashahr where there was a like number of Hinayana monks. The people did not treat the strangers well, and several of the party went back to Kaochang (near Turpan) to obtain funds for the further journey. This return to Kaochang suggests that the party had probably come by that way. Thereafter, a difficult advance of thirty-five days through uninhabited country brought the travelers to Khotan. Here all the inhabitants were Buddhists, and the monks numbered several tens of thousands, most of them belonging to the Mahayana or Greater Vehicle. The ruler of the country lodged Fa Xian and his companions in the Gomati Monastery, where there were 3,000 monks. The monks were called to their meals by the sound of a bell, and Fa Xian describes their behavior as follows: "When they enter the refectory, their demeanor is grave and ceremonious; they sit down in regular order; they all keep silence; they make no clatter with their bowls and other utensils; and for the attendants to serve more food, they do not call out to them, but only make signs with their hands."

From Khotan some of Fa Xian's companions went on toward Kashgar, but he himself and the others stayed longer to witness an impressive procession in which were carried images of the Buddha, *bodhisattvas,* and *devas,* a procession attended by the king and queen of the kingdom. Seven or eight *li* (one *li* perhaps equivalent to 1,890 feet [576 m.]) to the west of the city they also saw what was called the King's New Monastery, the construction of which took eighty years and extended over three reigns. The pagoda was about 250 feet (75 m.) in height, and ornamentally carved and overlaid with gold and silver, while a Hall of Buddha was behind the pagoda and also splendidly decorated.

Beyond Xinjiang, Fa Xian and his party crossed mountains where "there is snow in winter and summer alike," and where "there are also venomous dragons, which, if provoked, spit forth poisonous winds, rain, snow, sand, and stones. Of those who encounter these dangers not one in ten thousand escapes." Finally they followed "a difficult, precipitous, and dangerous road, the side of the mountain being like a stone wall 10,000 feet (3,000 m.) in height. On nearing the edge, the eye becomes confused; and wishing to advance, the foot finds no resting place." Below, at last, they saw the Indus River, descended to it by rock-cut steps and ladders arranged by men of former times, and crossed the river by a suspension bridge of ropes. Having crossed the river, the pilgrims arrived at the country of Udayana (Swat), and proceeded to Gandhara and their further destinations in India.[60]

At Pataliputra Fa Xian stayed for three years, engaged in Sanskrit studies and the copying of Buddhist texts. Proceeding to Tamralipti (Tamalipti), he spent another two years in similar pursuits. Tamralipti was a seaport, and is the modern Tamluk on the Hooghly River, now inland 60 miles (97 km.) from the Bay of Bengal. From that port Fa Xian sailed to Singhala (the kingdom of the lion), i.e., Sri Lanka, and there he also stayed for two years, and copied Buddhist texts. Finally he continued by sea to Javadvipa (the island of Java) and further by sea home to China.[61]

As far as the kingdom of Candra Gupta II is concerned, Fa Xian found that under his rule the land was prosperous and peaceful. Of all the regions of the Middle Kingdom (Central India), Magadha had the largest cities and towns. The people were rich and prosperous, and vied with one another in practicing charity of heart and duty to one's neighbor. Free hospitals were established in the cities, to which poor and helpless patients, orphans, widowers, and cripples came for treatment.

As for Buddhism in India, as in Xinjiang, Fa Xian speaks of both the Mahayana or Greater Vehicle and of the Hinayana or Lesser Vehicle (evidently his name for the Theravada and other earlier Buddhist sects). At Pataliputra, for example, he found a Mahayana monastery which was very imposing in appearance, and also a Hinayana monastery, the two together containing six to seven hundred monks. In one of the monasteries a famous *brahmana* teacher was also in residence, and to both monasteries many students and scholars came from many quarters. On the other hand, many famous Buddhist sites in North India were nearly deserted. Śravasti was sparsely inhabited by two hundred families, and Kapilavastu, Kuśinagara, and Gaya were almost empty and desolate, although there were three monasteries with some resident monks at Bodhgaya.[62]

The son and successor of Candra Gupta II was Kumara Gupta I (413–455 C.E.). Near the end of his reign there was apparently a serious but unsuccessful attack upon his rule by a tribe or nation called Pushyamitra (Pushpamitra), which is mentioned in the *Vishnu Purana* (4.24)[63] along with Patumitra, as ruling over Mekala, a country on the Narbada River, at the southern foot of the Vindhya mountains.

Kumara Gupta I was succeeded by his son, Skanda Gupta (455–467 C.E.), who followed the example of his grandfather and assumed the title Vikramaditya (sun of power). In his time there was further threat to the empire in the form of an invasion by the Ephtalites or White Huns, who were nomads out of Central Asia, with headquarters at Bamyin (near Herat) and Balkh. For the time being Skanda Gupta was able to repel the invaders, and an inscription (on the Bhitari Pillar) compares his victory with that of Krishna over his enemies. The inscription also states that afterward Skanda Gupta reported his success to his mother, who was obviously still living and who evidently had the same name, Devaki, as that of the mother of Krishna:

> Who, when [his] father had attained heaven (died), vanquished [his] enemies by the strength of [his] arm, and steadied once more the drifting fortunes of [his] family; and then exclaiming "the victory has been won" betook himself, like Krishna, when his enemies had been slain, to his weeping mother, Devaki.[64]

Later Imperial Guptas

In spite of the success of Skanda Gupta in saving the empire for the time being, after his death the White Huns renewed their attacks and established themselves in the northwestern regions, with a capital at Śakala (Sialkot), where their rulers Toramana (died circa 510 C.E.) and his son Mihirakula gained a reputation for the greatest cruelty.

Although the Gupta empire was at this point in decline, it did not perish but continued as an entity in Central and Eastern India. The known later Gupta rulers in this period were Puru Gupta (brother of Skanda Gupta), Narasimha Gupta (son of Puru Gupta), Kumara Gupta II (son of Narasimha Gupta), Budha Gupta (son of Puru Gupta), Tathagata Gupta (son of Budha Gupta), Baladitya (son of Tathagata Gupta), and Vajra (son of Baladitya).[65]

According to Xuan Zang (Hiuen Tsang), Baladitya took Mihirakula prisoner, but set him free. Mihirakula then obtained a small territory for himself from the king of Kashmir, but soon rebelled, killed the king of Kashmir, and placed himself on the throne of Kashmir. From there he invaded Gandhara, slaughtered myriads of people on the banks of the Indus, and overthrew many *stupas* and monasteries. Taking the wealth of the country, he returned to his own realm, but before the year was out he withered away like a falling leaf—as Xuan Zang puts it—and died. The Buddhists said: "For having killed countless victims and overthrown the law of Buddha, he has now fallen into the lowest hell, where he shall pass endless ages of revolution."[66]

A contemporary king of Malwa named Yaśodharman may also have had a part in the final overthrow of Mihirakula, for in an inscription (Mandaśor Stone Pillar) Yaśodharman is called the one "to whose feet respect was paid . . . by even that [famous] king Mihirakula, whose head had never previously been brought into the humility of obeisance to any other save [the god] Sthanu (a name of Śiva)."[67]

While most of the imperial Guptas were Brahmanical Hindus and showed a preference for the worship of Vishnu and Krishna (both known by the title of Bhagavat), they were tolerant of other forms of faith, and allowed full freedom of worship to others, including the Jainas and the Buddhists. Among the later imperial Guptas, the *Life* of Xuan Zang provides the information that Budha Gupta, Tathagata Gupta, Baladitya, and Vajra all built monasteries at Nalanda.[68]

Latest Guptas

In the provinces in the heart of what had once been the vast Gupta empire there continued yet for some time to be rulers most of whose named included the Gupta name, although their relationship to the imperial Guptas of the earlier periods is not known. These form a line in which inscriptions provide the names of Krishna Gupta, Harsha Gupta, Jivita Gupta I, Kumara Gupta III, Damodara Gupta, Mahasena Gupta, Deva Gupta II, Madhava Gupta, Adityasena, Deva Gupta III, Vishnu Gupta, and Jivita Gupta II.

Of these latest Guptas, Madhava Gupta was a contemporary and subordinate ally of the more powerful and more famous Harsha of Thanesar and Kanauj, but after the death of Harsha (647 C.E.) Adityasena asserted his independence and he and his several successors again claimed and evidently to some extent exercised imperial sovereignty. Other rival kingdoms existed, however, and of these a kingdom of Gauda (in Central Bengal) appears as especially hostile and finally put an end to the Gupta empire when, in the first half of the eighth century C.E., a king of Gauda occupied the throne of Magadha.[69]

EMPIRE OF HARSHA (606–647 C.E.)

Harsha

Harshavardhana, best known as Harsha for short, and associated with the cities of Thanesar and Kanauj, is dated 606–647 C.E., and is considered along with Candragupta Maurya and Aśoka Maurya as one of the greatest kings of ancient India. Relatively full information is provided concerning him and his time by Bana and Xuan Zang.

Thanesar (in the eastern Punjab) was the ancient Sthanviśvara (from Sthanu, a name of Śiva, and *iśvara*, "lord") or Sthaneśvara (from *sthana*, "shrine," and *iśvara*), and a holy town from early times. Here there was a dynasty which claimed descent from a certain Pushyabhuti (Pushpabhuti), who was remembered as a devout worshiper of Śiva. In this line in the latter part of the sixth century C.E. the *raja* was Prabhakaravardhana (also called Pratapaśila), whose wife, Yaśomati, was a princess of the Gupta line. Their children were an older son Rajyavardhana, a younger son Harshavardhana, and a slightly younger daughter Rajyaśri.

Prabhakaravardhana engaged in successful wars against his neighbors, including the Malavas, the White Huns, and others. The daughter Rajyaśri was married to the *raja* Grahavarman of the Maukhari people, which provided an alliance with this people, also located in the Upper Ganges valley and also engaged in fighting the Huns. As crown prince, Rajyavardhana participated in the war against the Huns, and then upon the death of his father returned to ascend the throne. Almost immediately, however, he went into the field again, this time to defeat the king of the Malavas, who had just killed Grahavarman and imprisoned Rajyaśri. But again very shortly thereafter Rajyavardhana himself was assassinated by the treacherous king Śaśanka of Gauda (in central Bengal).

With Rajyavardhana thus eliminated from the succession, a major statesman at Thanesar and Kanauj named Bhandi urged the acceptance of the younger brother, Harshavardhana, as king, and the latter took the rule, but at first with only the modest title of *rajaputra* (prince) Śiladitya. The date of his accession was 606 C.E., and an era was begun from this point, an era which was called after the name of Harsha. With the assistance of Madhava Gupta, Harsha first recovered his sister Rajyaśri, who had escaped into the Vindhya jungles. Then for nearly six years Harsha fought continuous wars which extended his empire over most of North India, and only then (in 612 C.E.) enjoyed his formal coronation. For his capital he selected the ancient town of Kanauj (Kanyakubja) on the east bank of the Ganges. Here he reigned for thirty-five years longer, still engaged in occasional wars, but largely occupied with the administration of a very large realm, and finally in his very last years living as a devotee of Buddhist teachings. His death was probably in 647 C.E.

Bana

Bana and Xuan Zang, who give most of the facts about the life of Harsha which have just been outlined, also provide much information about the general conditions and the social and religious life of the time. Bana (Banabhatta) was a *brahmana* and a Sanskrit poet, who paid a visit of some length to the court of Harsha and afterward wrote a romantic narrative, the *Harshacarita,* of the career of Harsha up through the point of Harsha's recovery of his sister.[70]

As reflected in this work, Brahmanism, Jainism, and Buddhism, as well as other sects, were all existing side by side and without great mutual antagonisms.

As a *brahmana* and a devotee of Śiva, Bana himself performed many rites before starting on his journey to the king's court (62–63):

> Having risen and bathed betimes, and put on a dress of white silk and seized his rosary and repeatedly recited the hymns and sacred texts fit for one starting on a journey,—after washing the image (of Śiva) with milk, he offered worship to Śiva, with lighted lamps, ointments, oblations, banners, perfumes, incense, and sweet flowers. Then, having offered a libation with profound reverence to the holy fire . . . he distributed wealth according to his means to the *brahmanas,* and walked solemnly around a sacred cow which faced the east, himself decked with white unguents, and wearing white garlands and white garments. . . .[71]

Harsha was also a devotee of Śiva, as was his ancestor Pushpabhuti, and Harsha is likewise pictured as offering worship to Śiva before setting out on a campaign (226).[72] Later, however, Harsha inclined more toward Buddhism, and after the recovery of his sister both of them are said to be intending to assume the red robes of the Buddhist order (288).[73]

The Jaina asetic of the time is described as carrying peacock feathers, to sweep insects out of his path for fear of taking life. The sight of a naked Jaina, "a fellow all lampblack as it seemed with the collected filth of many days besmirching his body," is taken as a bad omen (168);[74] therefore, the Digambara sect at least may not have been popular in North India. On the other hand, however, it is also said that, even as "the Buddhists are skilled in the self-devotion of relieving every sorrow," so also "the Jaina saintship is ever ready to help everybody" (274).[75]

In the Vindhya jungle was a holy man, a venerable mendicant, who had been a leading *brahmana* teacher but had abandoned the three Vedas and turned his studies to the Buddhist doctrine, and assumed the red robe. Around him was gathered a remarkable assemblage of members of many sects—Buddhists, Jainas in white robes (i.e., Śvetambaras), white mendicants (i.e., Hindu ascetics in white robes), followers of Krishna, religious students, ascetics who pulled out their hair—and all were "diligently following their own tenets, pondering, urging objections, raising doubts, resolving them, giving etymologies, disputing, studying, and explaining" (265).[76]

Xuan Zang (Hiuen Tsang)

The entire visit to India of the Chinese Buddhist pilgrim Xuan Zang (Hiuen Tsang) (629–645 C.E.) fell within the reign of Harshavardhana (606–647 C.E.), and we have the record of the travels of Xuan Zang from his own pen and also in his *Life*, written by his friend Hwui-li.[77] In these works Harsha is called by his name Siladitya, and in the biography of Xuan Zang the latter is designated as the Master of the (Buddhist) Law.

In Chinese history the period was that of the illustrious Tang dynasty (618–907 C.E.), and the greatest emperor of the dynasty, Tai Tsung (627–649), was ruling in the capital cities of Chang'an, modern Xian (Sian), and Luoyang (Loyang). Xuan Zang made request three times of the emperor for permission to leave the country on his proposed journey but, when no reply was received, he was unable to restrain his desire and, accordingly, left without permission.

Like Fa Xian before him, Xuan Zang departed from Chang'an and followed the Silk Road northwestward. At Lanzhou (Lanchow) in West Gansu (Kansu) he found the city filled with merchants from Central Asia and beyond. At Kaochang (near Turpan) there were several thousand Buddhist monks, and the king endeavored to keep Xuan Zang there to teach the Buddhist doctrine in his kingdom. In desperation, Xuan Zang undertook a fast to show his determination to press on, and the king relented and provided him with an escort for the further way and with letters of recommendation to the princes of twenty and more kingdoms of the West, that they might also help the pilgrim on his way.

At Qarashahr Xuan Zang found 2,000 monks belonging to the Hinayana of the school of the Sarvastivadas; at Kucha there were 5,000 and more disciples of the same persuasion. Farther on, Xuan Zang turned to the northwest to cross the Tian Shan by a very difficult pass, and in it he lost a dozen or more of his companions and many animals. Coming down out of the mountains, he reached the great Tsing Lake (now Issyk Kul, 5,200 feet [1,585 m.] above sea level), and proceeded to Samarkand, Balkh, and Bamiyan, coming on at last to Gandhara and India.[78]

Concerning Harsha, Xuan Zang credits the king with a fighting force of 5,000 elephants, 2,000 cavalry, and 50,000 foot soldiers, and describes the king's work in both years of war and years of peace as follows:

> He went from east to west subduing all who were not obedient; the elephants were not unharnessed nor the soldiers unbelted. After six years he had subdued the Five Indies. Having thus enlarged his territory, he increased his forces; he had 60,000 war elephants and 100,000 cavalry. After thirty years his arms reposed, and he governed everywhere in peace. He then practiced to the utmost the rules of temperance, and sought to plant the tree of religious merit to such an extent that he forgot to sleep or to eat. He forbade the slaughter of any living thing or flesh as food throughout the Five Indies on pain of death without pardon. He built on the banks of the river Ganges several thousand *stupas*, each about 100 feet (30 m.) high; in all the highways of the towns and villages throughout India he erected hospices, provided with food and drink, and stationed there physicians, with medicines for travelers and poor persons round about, to be given without any stint. On all spots where there were holy traces [of the Buddha] he raised monasteries (*sangharamas*).[79]

As Xuan Zang describes Harsha's capital city of Kanauj (Kanyakubja), its citadel was fortified with a dry ditch and strong and lofty towers, and it was a great mercantile emporium. Its people were well off and contented. For clothing they wore brightly ornamented fabrics. They applied themselves very much to learning, and were much given to discussion of religious subjects. The believers in the Buddha and the "heretics" were about equal in number. "There are," Xuan Zang reports of the city, "some hundred *sangharamas* with 10,000 priests. They study both the Great and Little Vehicle (*mahayana* and *hinayana*). There are 200 *deva* temples with several thousand followers."[80]

As seen both in Xuan Zang and in Bana, the followers of the various religions lived together, for the most part, peaceably. The royal family, and probably much of the population, were eclectic in faith. The remote ancestor Pushpabhuti worshiped Śiva. Harsha's father Prabhakaravardhana worshiped the Sun. The older brother Rajyavardhana and the sister Rajyaśri were Buddhists. Harsha himself recognized all three, Śiva, the Sun, and the Buddha, and by this time the Buddha probably had virtually the place of a deity along with the others.

In the latter part of his reign Harsha was increasingly attracted to Buddhism. With Xuan Zang at his court, Harsha instituted at Kanauj in the spring of 643 C.E. an assembly for the prolonged discussion of religious topics. As a meeting place for the assembly the king constructed on the west bank of the Ganges a great *sangharama* with pavilions and rest houses. In the midst was a golden statue of the Buddha of the same height as the king himself, and another golden statue of the Buddha 3 feet (1 m.) in height was carried in procession on a gorgeously caparisoned elephant. In attendance at the assembly, along with Harsha, were Kumara the *raja* of Kamarupa (Assam), the *raja* of Valabhi in Western India, who was connected with Harsha by marriage, and eighteen other tributary *rajas;* as well as 4,000 Buddhist monks including 1,000 from the Nalanda monastery, and about 3,000 *brahmanas* and Nirgranthas (Jainas).

In the discussions Xuan Zang presented the doctrines of Mahayana Buddhism so effectively that "the followers of error withdrew and disappeared," and a vast number of persons "were converted from error and entered on the right path; forsaking the Little Vehicle, they found refuge in the Great Vehicle," while the king declared: "The Master of the Law from the kingdom of China has established the principles of the Great Vehicle and overthrown all opposing doctrines. . . . Let this be known everywhere, as it ought to be!"[81]

Following the disputation at Kanauj, Xuan Zang was constrained (although by then desirous of being on his way home to China) to accompany Harsha to Prayaga (Allahabad). There, in accordance with the custom of his ancestors, on a plain between the Yamuna and the Ganges called the "arena of charitable offerings," Harsha was accustomed to hold a great assembly every five years, at which to distribute his accumulated treasures to the poor and destitute, as well as to the religious of the various sects. At this event, on the occasion witnessed by Xuan Zang, there were present not only the vassal kings and the members of the religious bodies but some half a million of the common people, which must have made a gathering not unlike that of the crowded fair still held annually on the same ground at Allahabad.

In the ceremonies, on the first day an image of the Buddha was set up, and gifts given; on the second and third days images of the Sun and of Śiva were installed, and gifts given, but only in half the amount of the first day. On the fourth day 10,000 religious persons of the Buddhist order received coins, a pearl, a cotton garment, food and drink, flowers and perfumes. For twenty days similar gifts were bestowed on the *brahmanas*. For ten days gifts were given to the "heretics," here evidently the Jainas and members of lesser sects. For the same length of time there were distributions to mendicants from distant regions. Then for a month the distribution was to the poor, the orphans, and the destitute. With everything given away, the king begged from his sister a second-hand garment, paid worship to the "Buddhas of the ten regions," and rejoiced that his wealth, for the safety of which he had previously feared, was well bestowed in the field of religious merit.[82]

Then, although both Kumara and Harsha desired him to stay in their respective kingdoms, Xuan Zang departed to return to China. He did not, like Fa Xian, go to Lanka, nor take the southern sea route home, which Harsha suggested to him, but went back by the same northern route by which he had come.

For the journey, Harsha provided Xuan Zang with an elephant to ride, and gold and silver to defray his expenses. In his luggage Xuan Zang carried relics and images of the Buddha and many volumes of Buddhist manuscripts. In an accident in the crossing of the Indus River fifty of the manuscripts were lost, and in the mountains the elephant fell to its death. In a Dunhuang painting reflecting the journey an Indian elephant and a Chinese monk are shown, and at the bottom of the fresco a man emerges from a mountain pass and kneels to give thanks before a waterfall.

After surmounting the many difficulties en route Xuan Zang came back again to the borders of China. Nearly seventeen years before, he had left without imperial permission; now he had gained fame by his travels, and the emperor Tai Tsung forgave his illegal departure and sent orders to Khotan and other oases in Xinjiang to provide him with fresh transport and escorts. So Xuan Zang returned to Chang'an and, for the eighteen years which remained until his death in 664 C.E., devoted himself to the translation of the books he had brought with him. Under the emperor Kao Tsung, who succeeded Tai Tsung in 650 C.E., a tall pagoda was constructed in the capital city in which Xuan Zang deposited his sacred books and images.[83] Built of shaped bricks, held together by lime and glutinous rice, and restored many times over the centuries, the pagoda still stands (240 feet [73 m.] in height) at the edge of modern Xian (Sian), where it is known as the Tayen or Big Wild Goose Pagoda (Fig. 6.4).

Yi Jing (I-tsing)

It was not long afterward that the third famous Chinese Buddhist pilgrim of antiquity came to India. This was Yi Jing (I-tsing), who was an admirer of both Fa Xian and Xuan Zang, and his own travels occupied the years 671–695 C.E. Unlike his famous predecessors, however, Yi Jing came by sea, by way of the Malay peninsula, and arrived at Tamralipti, and finally returned by sea too. In India he proceeded from Tamralipti in a westward direction, survived an attack by robbers, reached the monastery at Nalanda, and made pilgrimages to the Vulture's Peak at Rajagriha, Bodhgaya, Vaiśali, Kuśinagara, Kapilavastu, Sravasti, and Isipatana. He then lived for ten years in the Nalanda monastery, and collected a large number of texts of the Buddhist scriptures (the Tripitaka). Finally he returned to China, again traveling by sea and bringing the manuscripts home with him, to the translation of which he devoted many later years.

From Yi Jing we have both a brief biography and a relatively long and detailed account of the customs which he observed, especially in the Buddhist community, in India and in the adjacent regions which he visited.[84]

Concerning the *brahmanas* Yi Jing says that they are regarded throughout India as the most honorable caste. Their scriptures are the four Vedas, which

6.4 Big Wild Goose Pagoda, Xian

contain about 100,000 verses, and in every generation there are some intelligent *brahmanas* who can recite the whole 100,000 verses. By training, there are those who become able to commit to memory whatever they have heard only one time, and Yi Jing himself met persons of this ability.[85]

Concerning the Nalanda monastery, where he lived so long, Yi Jing describes it as having eight halls and three hundred apartments, with more than 3,000 monks in residence. Lands in the possession of the monastery contain more than two hundred villages, bestowed upon the monastery by kings of many generations. Along with Nalanda there was also a great educational center at Valabhi in Western India, and at these two places "eminent and accomplished men assemble in crowds, discuss possible and impossible doctrines, and after having been assured of the excellence of their opinions by wise men, become far famed for their wisdom. . . . When they are refuting heretic doctrines all their opponents become tongue-tied and acknowledge themselves undone."[86]

KINGDOMS OF THE MEDIEVAL PERIOD (650–1200 C.E.)

With the death of Harsha (647 C.E.) the last time when ancient India was at least largely united over a relatively large area under one imperial rule came to an end, and a similar situation was not restored in any considerable measure until the invasions of the Arabs and the Turks brought the most important provinces under the rule of the Muslim Sultans of Delhi (1206 C.E.). Thus from the middle of the seventh century to the end of the twelfth there were for the most part many different kingdoms in many different parts of the country, and this span of time is commonly known as the medieval period of Hindu India.[87]

Toward the end of the period there was indeed an attempt by several of the kings to revive the traditions associated with the empire of Harsha, and the *rajas* of the Gaharwar (Gahadavala) clan, in particular, actually succeeded in restoring the power of the kingdom of Kanauj to a considerable extent. The founder of this Gahadavala dynasty was a certain Candradeva, and his grandson, Govinda Candra, ruled most of Madhyadeśa (the Upper Ganges valley) for half a century (as crown prince 1104–1114, as king 1114–1154 C.E.). His grandson, Jayachcandra (Jaicand), in turn, was accounted by Muslim writers as the greatest king in India, and was known by them as the king of Varanasi, which was evidently his principal residence. In the Muslim conquest of India the defeat of Jayachcandra at Candwar on the Yamuna River in 1194 C.E. by Muhammad of Ghur (Mu'iz-ud-din) and his officer, the one-time slave, Qutb-ud-din Aibak, was one of the decisive events, being followed before long by the death of Muhammad of Ghur (1206 C.E.) and the accession of Qutb-ud-din Aibak as the first Sultan of Delhi and the founder of the so-called "slave dynasty."[88]

DECLINE AND RENEWAL OF JAINISM AND BUDDHISM AND CONTINUANCE OF HINDUISM

In their own time both Mahavira and the Buddha enjoyed family relationships with, and favorable support from, some of the contemporary rulers and, later, Jainism was notably furthered by Candragupta Maurya and Samprati, and Buddhism by Aśoka Maurya.

By the time Fa Xian and Xuan Zang came to India in the fifth and seventh centuries C.E. respectively, and even though both pilgrims came to India because it was the holy land of Buddhism, it seems evident that both Jainism and Buddhism were in relative decline. As for Jainism, the only mention which Fa Xian makes of it is when he reports the legend that at Rajagriha "the Nirgrantha made a pit of fire and poisoned the rice, and then invited Buddha (to eat with him)."[89] Also, as we have seen, Bana seems to reflect a popular aversion to the Jaina ascetic, and Xuan Zang apparently classifies the Jainas as just one of the lesser "heretical" sects.

As for Buddhism, Fa Xian found many places especially associated with the life of the Buddha and the history of Buddhism in a state of almost complete emptiness and desolation. Xuan Zang, although able to convert many people to the Mahayana doctrines in which he believed, tells about violent attacks which had been made upon Buddhism, notably the slaughter of Buddhists and the destruction of *stupas* and monasteries in Northwest India by Mihirakula in the time of the later Gupta empire.

Xuan Zang also tells about the attacks upon Buddhism by Śaśanka, the king of Gauda in Central Bengal, who murdered Harsha's older brother Rajyavardhana. Śaśanka, Xuan Zang says, destroyed monasteries and scattered monks, carrying his persecutions up to the hills of Nepal. While he was thus overthrowing and destroying the law of Buddha, Śaśanka broke into pieces and cast into the Ganges a stone at Pataliputra, which was supposed to be marked with the footprints of the Buddha, a stone that was near the royal precinct and to which Aśoka had paid devotion. At Bodhgaya the Bodhi tree had evidently been reestablished or restored after it was poisoned by Aśoka's jealous queen Tissarakkha, and Śaśanka now cut it down and tried to dig it up, but did not get to the bottom of the roots. A few months later, a king of Magadha named Purnavarman, the last of the race of Aśoka, revived the tree with milk upon its roots, and then surrounded it with a protective wall which, when Xuan Zang saw it, was still 20 feet (6 m.) high. Śaśanka also desired to replace a statue of the Buddha at Bodhgaya with a figure of Maheśvara (Śiva), of whom he himself was evidently a worshiper, but the project was only partially carried out (the statue of the Buddha was hidden by a wall, and the figure of Maheśvara was drawn on the wall), and Śaśanka himself died soon thereafter.[90]

In the cases just cited the attacks on Buddhism were after all by a foreign ruler (Mihirakula) and by a king of only local sovereignty (Śaśanka), and against such events it may be remembered that Gupta kings, although not themselves Buddhists, were nevertheless friendly to Buddhism and gave it their encouragement (e.g., Samudra Gupta), and the same was also true of the Śatavahana kings in Southern India, while Harsha was himself increasingly attracted to Buddhism in the latter part of his reign. A similar instance was still to be found, for example, at the very end of the medieval period when the Muslim invasions were already beginning, and when Govinda Candra (1114–1154 C.E.) was ruling in Madhyadeśa. Against the invaders Govinda Candra defended not only Hindu but also Buddhist holy places. Also he himself built a monastery at the site of the Jetavana at ancient Sravasti, and his queen Kumaradevi built another monastery at Sarnath.[91]

Both Jainism and Buddhism were, of course, weakened by their own internal divisions, in Jainism notably that between the Digambaras and the Śvetambaras, and in Buddhism that between the Hinayana and the Mahayana, as observed by Xuan Zang. Furthermore, Hinduism itself was greatly furthered in the medieval period by the work of such eminent Hindu philosophers as Śankara and Ramanuja.

In general, then, by the end of the medieval period, both Jainism and Buddhism were in decline, and with the incoming of Islam they, and Hinduism too, suffered heavy blows. As a result of the many factors which were involved, Buddhism for the time being virtually disappeared from the land of its birth (although long since widely spread in many other lands), while Jainism (in reduced proportion) and Hinduism lived on.

The situation in the ensuing time is reflected in the account (called the *Akbarnama*) of the reign of the Mughal emperor Akbar (1556–1605 C.E.), written by his Persian secretary of state, Abu-l Fazl. In the process of evolving a composite religion of his own, Akbar invited to participate in religious discussions at Fatehpur Sikri not only Muslims but also Hindus, Jainas, Parsis, and Christians. Akbar does not seem, however, to have known any Buddhist scholars. Abu-l Fazl met a few Buddhists in Kashmir, but "saw none among the learned," and he remarks that "for a long time past scarce any trace of them has existed in Hindustan." The relative and renewed prominence of Jainism, on the other hand, is seen in the occurrence in Abu-l Fazl's lists of the learned men of the time of the names of three eminent Jaina teachers, Hiravijaya Suri, Vijayasena Suri, and Bhanucandra Upadhyaya. These were members of the Śvetambara branch of Jainism, and Abu-l Fazl studied the Śvetambara doctrine carefully, but was unable to obtain equally satisfactory information about the Digambaras. Concerning Hiravijaya we learn that, upon Akbar's invitation (in 1582 C.E.), he walked (as was requisite according to his beliefs) all the way from Gujarat to Fatehpur Sikri, and was so influential in conversation with Akbar that the emperor was persuaded to release prisoners including caged birds, and to prohibit the killing of animals at least on certain days. Afterward, under the influence of Jaina teaching, the emperor restricted the destruction of animal life yet further, and himself gave up hunting and abstained almost wholly from eating meat.[92]

Thus, Jainism has always lived on in India, even if relatively restricted in numbers. Today the Jainas constitute a minority of about four million members in modern India, but the influence of Jaina philosophy and ethics upon Indian thought and life far surpasses what the numbers would suggest. As for Buddhism, it experienced renewal in India in the nineteenth and twentieth centuries, and there are now many millions of adherents of this "Neo-Buddhism," while a so-called "Crypto-Buddhism" is discernible underneath Hindu forms in some areas of Hindu social life, and the pervasive influence of Buddhism is evidenced in the use of Buddhist symbols in the national flag and the state insignia of modern India. From the oldest times until now, however, Hinduism is the main religion of India.[93]

7

LATER HINDUISM

THREE PATHS

Already in the *Rig Veda* the beginnings were seen of the three paths—knowledge, action, and devotion *(jnana, karma, bhakti)*, of which the path of knowledge was thereafter especially emphasized in the Brahmanas and Upanishads. After that, in Later Hinduism, all three paths have their place, and all three are set forth in the *Bhagavad Gita*.

Bhagavad Gita

The *Bhagavad Gita* is found in the *Mahabharata* at the point where the armies of the Kurus (Kauravas) and the Pandavas face each other at Kurukshetra, the battlefield of Kuru (near modern Delhi). The prospect of the imminent Great Battle between those who, after all, are cousins occasions grave doubts in the mind of Arjuna, third prince of the five Pandu brothers, and he converses with his charioteer, who is the god Krishna, an incarnation of Vishnu and at the same time himself the supreme deity.

Jnana Marga

In the Upanishads it is seen that progress on the path of knowledge *(jnana marga)* involves grasping the truth that the *atman* in one's self is identical with the *brahman* in the universe, and is facilitated by the methods of meditation *(dhyana)* and discipline *(yoga)*. Here now in the Bhagavad Gita (4.34–36, cf. 6.29), in the same respect, Krishna, speaking as the supreme lord, advises Arjuna to learn from the wise, for then he will know that all living beings, including himself, are but part of God. So, even if Arjuna were the worst sinner of all sinners, in the boat of knowledge he would be able to cross over the waters of evil and rebirth.

Karma Marga

The path of action *(karma marga)* calls for doing one's own work (whether it be that of the priest, the warrior, the artisan, or the servant) even poorly, rather than doing another's work well, but above all it calls for doing this work without attachment, i.e., without anxiety about results (4.19–23; 18.42–47).

Bhakti Marga

The path of devotion *(bhakti marga)* is that of love and trust directed toward a personal deity, whether it be Krishna, Vishnu, Indra, Śiva, or some other, for all are one (10.21ff.). This way of love is open to all classes of people, even those of lower birth—women, artisans, servants—and even they may go by this path to the supreme goal; indeed even a very evildoer, who loves the lord with all his might, is to be reckoned as righteous, because he has the right resolution (9.30, 32). Krishna says: "If one offers Me with love and devotion a leaf, a flower, fruit or water, I will accept it. . . . Always think of Me and become My devotee *(bhakta)*. Worship Me and offer your homage unto Me. Thus you will come to Me without fail. I promise you this because you are My very dear friend" (9.26; 18.65).[1]

Whether one is proceeding on the path of knowledge, of action, or of devotion, the practices of meditation *(dhyana)* and discipline *(yoga)* are important helps. One passage in particular in the *Bhagavad Gita* (6.10–15)[2] describes the yogic practice of meditation in some detail. The *yogi* (Sanskrit *yogin*, feminine *yogini*) or "mystic transcendentalist," as the practitioner of *yoga* may be called, should sit in a secluded place and concentrate the mind on one single point. One should hold body, head, and neck erect and motionless, and gaze steadily at the tip of the nose (or perhaps at the root of the nose, between the eyebrows, above which is the "third" spiritual eye, cf. 8.10).[3] One should be calm and unworried, and put one's thoughts upon the lord. Thus constantly practicing control of oneself, one may attain to that peace which culminates in final emancipation.

FOUR AIMS

As seen thus far the goal envisaged at the end of any of the paths of knowledge, action, or devotion is that of the spiritual salvation or deliverance called *moksha*, or the entry into *nirvana*. In Later Hinduism, however, no less than four aims all together are considered as belonging properly to human existence, namely, *artha*, *kama*, and *dharma*, as well as *moksha*.

Artha

The term *artha* connotes material welfare, and involves matters of economics and politics. In this area the *Artha Sastra* is a famous work on statecraft (of a very harsh sort), attributed to Kautilya Chanakhya, prime minister of the emperor Candragupta Maurya of Pataliputra (fourth century B.C.E.).[4]

Kama

The word *kama* means love and is the name of the god of love, so this area involves all aspects of love including the realm of the erotic. In this area the *Kama Sutra* of Vatsyayana is an encyclopedic work complied in perhaps more or less the same period as that of the *Artha Sastra*.[5]

Dharma

The word *dharma* is of manifold meaning, but basically signifies that state of affairs which is real and true, and therefore that which is to be held fast or kept; in other words *dharma* is the order of the world and the way which is in harmony with that order. Translatable simply as law, *dharma* as an aim in life has to do with right conduct and the virtues of justice and duty. The term also serves as the usual designation of what the outside world commonly calls Hinduism, i.e., the religion, social customs, and way of life of the Hindus, and it is also called *sanatana dharma* (eternal law), with the connotation of divine authority and permanence. In this area the *Laws of Manu* are representative,[6] and probably date in about the same period as the *Artha Sastra* and the *Kama Sutra*, while additional *Dharma Sastras* were probably composed around 200 B.C.E. In the *dharma* texts the pattern of social life is codified in terms of the four classes *(varnas)* of people, *brahmanas, kshatriyas, vaisyas,* and *sudras,* and of the four stages of life *(asramas),* and the scheme of the four aims of human life is outlined.[7]

Moksha

Of the four aims of human life, *moksha* is the supreme and ultimate, and as such it is called *paramartha* or "highest wealth." Etymologically *moksha* means to be freed, released, liberated, and is synonymous with *nirvana* which means to be extinguished, emptied. As described in the *Bhagavad Gita*, however, the entry into *nirvana* or the attainment of *moksha*, although it means the cessation of all material existence, does not mean passing into a void, but rather means entering into the spiritual kingdom which is the immaterial realm of Krishna or of Brahman. "Those who are free from anger and all material desires, who are self-realized, self-disciplined, and constantly endeavoring for perfection, are assured of liberation in the Supreme in the very near future *(abhito brahma-nirvanam)*. . . . Thus practicing control of the body, mind and activities, the mystic transcendentalist attains to the kingdom of God by cessation of material existence *(nirvana-paramam)*" (5.26; 6.15).[8]

FOUR STAGES

On the way to *moksha* there are, at least in theory, four stages *(asramas)*.

The first stage, called *brahmacarya* (religious living), is that of the celibate religious student, who is known as a *brahmacari*. In this period the student generally lives with his teacher, the *guru,* from whom he is receiving instruction.

The second stage is that of the *grihastha* or married householder *(grihya,* household). In this period the man marries, has children, performs the daily sacrifices in the home, and discharges his responsibilities in the community.

The third stage calls for "forest departure" *(vanaprasthana)*, when the householder leaves his home and family and lives in the forest as a *vanaprastha,* either alone or in a group of others like himself. The term *asrama* is often used to designate the forest retreat of this period. In this period the person devotes himself to meditation, and practices various austerities and penances, making preparation for the final renunciation.

The fourth stage is called *sannyasa* (renunciation), and the person is now a *sannyasi* or ascetic mendicant, having given up all his possessions except minimal clothing, begging bowl, and water pot. In this period he obtains food by begging, but otherwise reduces human contacts to the minimum, and seeks to attain complete equanimity as he approaches his final release.

SIX SCHOOLS

As to systems of philosophy in Later Hinduism, the commonly accepted word for philosophy is *darśana,* which is derived from *dṛś,* "to see," and thus means an act of perception and a viewpoint. Of such systems some are described as *nastika* (denier) and some as *astika* (asserter).

The *nastika* systems commonly deny the validity of the Vedas and the existence of God, and are materialistic and fatalistic. As such they are called *avaidika* (non-Vedist), *lokayata* (world directed), and *dishtika* (determined). Historical founders and exponents of this position include teachers named Brihaspati (600 B.C.E.), Carvaka (date unknown), and Jayarśi (650 C.E.).[9] With a negative reference to the term *iśvara* (a generic title meaning "who is able," often used for a personal deity and translated as "lord," and often compounded with other titles, e.g., *maheśvara,* "great lord"), the *nastikas* are also spoken of as *niriśvara* (godless), a designation which is also sometimes used loosely to include the Buddhists and the Jainas, and also the Samkhya, Yoga, and Vaiśeshika schools, insofar as all of these do not necessarily or at least originally posit a divine Being.

As for the *astika* schools, there are six of these which are commonly recognized as the orthodox systems of Hindu philosophy and, as such, are known as the *shad-darśana* or "six views." All claim to rest upon Vedic and Upanishadic foundations, and all aim for the attainment of deliverance *(moksha).* Some were originally atheistic but, at least in their later formulation, all affirm the existence of a Supreme Being.

Samkhya

The Samkhya school is associated with a sage named Kapila, who is supposed to have lived around 500 B.C.E. The system is dualistic, and considers the two ultimate realities to be Purusha or cosmic spirit, infinite in number, and Prakriti or cosmic matter, which is only one. Spirit stimulates activity in matter, and so the universe evolves. Since no personal creator *(iśvara)* is recognized the system is sometimes called godless *(niriśvara).*[10]

Yoga

The word *yoga* literally means "union," the derivation being from the Sanskrit root *yuj,* "to join" (closely related to the English verb "to yoke"). The union in view is that of the human consciousness with the object to which attention is directed, this direction of attention ordinarily involving a combination of physical and mental disciplines. Although the object of attention is not necessarily the deity, the most usual implication is of the yoking or joining of the lower human nature to the higher divine nature.

As a school of philosophy, Yoga was presented systematically by Patanjali in his treatise called *Yoga Sutras,* as well as in his commentaries. Whether this Patanjali is the same as the grammarian Patanjali, who probably lived circa 200 B.C.E., is debatable, but at any rate the practices of asceticism and meditation which the *Yoga Sutras* present are very old (cf. the yogic posture of the figure at Moenjodaro, Fig. 1.6).

In the *Yoga Sutras* Patanjali analyzes the human personality and finds that the mind or mind-stuff *(citta)* is constantly filled with fluctuating ideas *(vritti)*, and that there are thus constantly changing states of consciousness *(cittavritti)* (1.2). These are produced by five "hindrances" *(kleśas)*, namely, ignorance *(avidya)*, egoism *(asmita)*, passion *(raga)*, aversion *(dveśa)*, and possessiveness *(abhiniveśa)* (2.3). These are all painful and sources of trouble, therefore human existence is essentially pained and troubled, but salvation can be attained by *yoga*.

The practices of *yoga*, as Patanjali proceeds to outline them, are eight in number, and they are at the same time stages of the *yogi* on the way to liberation (2.29): (1) Restraint *(yama)* consists in the five abstentions, from killing *(ahimsa)*, lying *(satya)*, stealing *(asteya)*, impurity *(brahmacariya)*, and covetousness *(aparigraha)* (2.30). (2) Discipline *(niyama)* consists in the five items of cleanliness, serenity, asceticism *(tapas)*, study, and devotion to the lord *(iśvara)* (2.32). (3) Posture *(asana)* is defined as stable and easy (2.46), and refers to the various yogic positions such as the lotus posture *(padmasana)*, in which the legs are crossed with the right foot on the left thigh with the sole uppermost, and left foot on the right thigh also with the sole uppermost, and the hands are on the lap or the knees with palms upturned. (4) Regulation of the vital force *(pranayama)* is accomplished by control of breathing to establish a rhythm and prolong the periods of inhalation, retention, and exhalation of the air. (5) Sense withdrawal *(pratyahara)* means that sensory activity is no longer dominated by external objects (2.54). (6) Concentration *(dharana)* is fixed attention of thought on a single point (3.1), leading to a centralization of consciousness called "onepointedness" *(ekagrata)* (3.12). (7) Meditation *(dhyana)* is such a prolongation of fixed attention as seems to penetrate into the essence of objects (3.2). (8) Contemplation or ecstasy *(samadhi)* is an indescribable state of superconscious awareness, sometimes (inadequately) called trance, ecstasy, or rapture, in which there is a shining forth of insight (3.3, 5). These last three levels *(dharana, dhyana, samadhi)* are so closely related that they are also grouped together under the name of *samyama* (mind poise).

With the foregoing practices the *yogi* is able not only to develop himself but also to influence others. When he becomes grounded in non-injury *(ahimsa)*, for example, his very presence causes a suspension of all enmity around him (2.35). On the levels of *samyama* the *yogi* spontaneously acquires various miraculous powers, which are called *siddhis* (accomplishments). Of these Patanjali mentions knowledge of past and future, knowledge of previous births, knowledge of the thoughts of others, power to make oneself invisible, knowledge of the time of one's death, knowledge of the structure of the universe and of the constitution of the body, and power to travel in the ether *(akaśa)* (3.16, 18, 19, 21, 22, 26–29, 42). But of some of these powers Patanjali remarks that they are indeed "accomplishments" in the waking state, but that they constitute obstacles in the state of *samadhi*, i.e., they are not themselves the supreme goal and must themselves finally be left behind for the sake of that goal of emancipation. Patanjali also notices that these powers may come from birth (i.e., heredity or natural endowment), or may be gained by the use of drugs or incantations *(mantras)* or austerities, but he places concentration and meditation *(samyama)* at the climax of the list of means (4.1).[11]

Vaiśeshika

The Vaiśeshika system is set forth in the *Vaiśeshika Sutras* of Kanada (eater of atoms), who is possibly identifiable with the sage Kaśyapa, associated in legend with Rama. The system analyzes the universe in terms of various substances and of atoms, each with its own distinctive characteristic *(viśesha)*. These elements existed from all time, and it seems probable that the Vaiśeshika system was originally atheistic, although a creator *(paramatman)* is introduced later who fashions the world out of what was already there.[12]

Nyaya

The Nyaya system was formulated by the philosopher Gautama Akshapada (eye-footed, from his habit of walking with eyes cast down in deep thought). His *Nyaya Sutras* may be of more or less the same date as the *Vaiśeshika Sutras* of Kanada, and the two schools were similar and eventually merged. The word *nyaya* signifies "going into" a subject, and there is strong emphasis upon logical thought in order to distinguish true knowledge from false. The original doctrine may have been atheistic, but at a later time logical argument was employed to prove the existence of a creator. In both Vaiśeshika and Nyaya, ignorance is the cause of suffering and rebirth, and only complete knowledge *(jnana)* of the true nature of things will lead to deliverance, here called *apavarga*.[13]

Purva Mimamsa

The Purva Mimamsa or Early Mimamsa system of philosophy is based on the *Mimamsa Sutras* of Jaimini (circa 200 B.C.E.). The word *mimamsa* means "inquiries" (from the root for "man" and "to think"), and the system is concerned with the correct interpretation of the Vedic tradition, particularly of the Brahmanas. The philosophical tenets of the other orthodox schools are accepted, but it is held that knowledge alone cannot give salvation. Right action is also required, and this especially includes the correct performance of Vedic ritual, although belief in a creator of the world is not required. Because of the emphasis on action the system is also called Karma Mimamsa.[14]

Uttara Mimamsa

The Uttara Mimamsa or Later Mimamsa system was set forth in the *Vedanta Sutras,* also called the *Brahma Sutras,* which were formulated by Badarayana. This philosopher is sometimes identified with Vyasa, the compiler of the Vedas and the *Mahabharata,* and at any rate Badarayana's work may have been done in the period 500–300 B.C.E.

The emphasis of Badarayana was upon the teachings concerning knowledge in the Vedas, particularly in the Upanishads, and the system became known by the name of Vedanta, which was originally a name applied to the Upanishads as the "end of the Veda." In Vedanta the basic texts are the ten major *Upanishads*, the *Bhagavad Gita,* and the *Brahma Sutras,* also known as the *Vedanta Sutras*.[15]

THREE INTERPRETERS OF VEDANTA

Śankara

Śankara (or Śankara *acarya*, Śankara the teacher, 788–838 C.E.) wrote commentaries *(bhashyas)* on all of the just mentioned works, and largely through his influence and wide travels from his home in South India to the Himalaya and from Assam to Kashmir, Vedanta became the prevailing philosophy of India. As expounded by Śankara this philosophy is an uncompromising monism, and is called Advaita Vedanta, or nondualistic Vedanta.[16] The ultimate, impersonal, transcendent principle called Brahman is alone real; all phenomena are illusion *(maya)*, caused by ignorance *(avidya)*; knowledge alone is the means to liberation, and liberation consists in the realization of the absolute unity of the individual soul and Brahman. Quoting the saying, "That art thou" (e.g., *Chandogya Upanishad* 6.8.7) and other Upanishadic texts of similar import, Śankara declares that "the attainment of the highest human goal [of liberation] becomes an accomplished fact only when the total eradication of all sorrows comes about as a result of the realization of the Self as Brahman beyond acceptance and rejection"; and he describes the state of liberation in the words: "But *moksha* is eternal in the true sense of the word; it does not undergo any transformation, and it is immovable. All-pervading like *akaśa* (ether, space), existing by itself, content with itself, without body, parts or modifications, it is self-illuminating, timeless and unaffected by merit or demerit. Therefore *moksha* or the disembodied condition is the same as *Brahman*" (*Commentary on the Brahma Sutra* 1.1.4).[17]

At the same time there is a distinction, according to Śankara, between higher knowledge *(paravidya)* and lower knowledge *(aparavidya)*. On the higher level the Brahman is realized as absolute and unqualified, while on the lower level it may be regarded as possessing the attributes of a personal deity *(iśvara)*, the contemplation of which may prepare the mind for higher knowledge. Likewise there is no need for the performance of any acts, since knowledge alone leads to liberation; yet at the same time religious actions can serve a disciplinary function and lead the mind in the direction of knowledge. Accordingly Śankara himself visited the shrines of various deities, and composed hymns in honor of Vishnu, Surya, Śiva, Śakti, Parvati, and Durga.[18] He was usually considered a Śaivite, but he actually taught that the worship of the divine in any name and form can lead to the same goal.

Furthermore, according to Vedanta, liberation may be experienced as *jivan-mukti* (living release), i.e., salvation while yet in this life and still here on earth, and in this state one may properly work for the welfare of humanity. So Śankara, who was born in Kaladi in Kerala in Southwest India and died in Kedarnath in the Himalaya, during his lifetime traveled all across India to spread his teachings, and founded monasteries at Badrinath in the Himalaya, Puri in the east, Dvaraka in the west, and Śringeri in the south in Mysore.

Ramanuja

A second major interpretation of Vedanta was given by Ramanuja (1017–1137 C.E.). He was born at Śriperumbudur near Madras, journeyed to places of pilgrimage as far away as Kashmir and Badrinath, and did his life work at Śrirangam in South India. Like Śankara, he also wrote commentaries on the *Vedanta Sutras* and the *Bhagavad Gita*. To him the supreme deity, referred to variously as Brahman, Iśvara, or Vishnu (with Lakshmi as mediator of the divine grace), is the creator and ruler of the world, but the world also has reality as the "body" of Brahman rather than being an illusion, and the individual human soul *(jiva)* has a separate identity and will retain individuality and consciousness even when finally reunited with the supreme reality. In distinction from the *advaita* (nonduality) doctrine of Śankara, this is therefore called *viśishtadvaita* (qualified monism).

For Ramanuja the fundamental obstacle on the way to deliverance *(moksha)* is not ignorance but unbelief, and he emphasizes devotion *(bhakti)* rather than knowledge *(jnana)* as the means of salvation. In his commentary on the *Vedanta*

Sutras, which is known as the *Sribhashya* and is still the major Vaishnavite text, he quotes, for example, the saying, "Manifest, near, moving in the cave (of the heart) is the great Being" (*Mundaka Upanishad* 2.2.1), and goes on to say that the remainder of the Upanishad "teaches how this highest Brahman, which is imperishable and higher than the soul, which itself is higher than the unevolved; which dwells in the highest heaven; and which is of the nature of supreme bliss, is to be meditated upon as within the hollow of the heart; how this meditation has the character of devout faith *(bhakti);* and how the devotee, freeing himself from nescience, obtains for his reward intuition of Brahman, which renders him like Brahman" *(Śribhashya* 1.2.23).[19]

Madhva

A third interpretation of Vedanta was set forth by Madhva (1197–1280 c.e.), who was born and taught at Udipi on the southwest coast of India. He too wrote commentaries on the *Vedanta Sutras, Upanishads,* and *Bhagavad Gita,* and other works, and in all these works he set forth a system of dualism *(dvaita),* according to which *Brahman* and *jiva* (the human soul) are separate and distinct and always will be, even when the soul finds final deliverance. In worship Madhva directed his devotion to Vishnu, with special emphasis upon Vayu as the son of Vishnu and the mediator. Madva's followers, the Madhvas, still worship Vishnu, and some acknowledge Śiva too.[20]

TRIMURTI

It has been seen that Indian systems of philosophy include schools which deny the existence of a supreme Being as well as schools which affirm the existence of a supreme Being. Insofar as the existence of a supreme Reality is affirmed, it has also just been noted that even an interpreter of Vedanta such as Śankara, who holds that the ultimate Reality is absolute and unqualified, may also teach that the worship of the divine under any name can lead to deliverance, and may even give himself to the worship of various personal deities.

The supreme Reality may therefore be conceived as without attributes *(nirguna),* or as possessing attributes *(saguna).* In the former case the proper manner of reference is to say It; in the latter case, to say He or She. Of the deities considered as masculine, the chief are the three, Brahma, Vishnu, and Śiva, and for the most part worship is directed either to Vishnu (by the Vaishnavas) or to Śiva (by the Śaivas). As for the supreme deity conceived as a female principle, her title is usually Śakti or Devi, and her worshipers are Śaktas. Although such classification is useful for clarity, the categories are not necessarily mutually exclusive, and Vaishnavas and Śaivas may also, for example, worship the Devi.

The grouping of leading deities in threes is found already in the *Rig Veda,* where the triad of Agni (fire), Vayu (wind), and Surya (sun) is, for example, familiar. Now in Later Hinduism it is Brahma, Vishnu, and Śiva who constitute the trinity that is known as the *trimurti* or the "three forms" of the ultimate Brahman.[21] As the *Vishnu Purana* (1.22) explains the matter, the blaze of a fire burning on one spot diffuses light and heat around, and as the light and heat are stronger or feebler according as we are nearer the fire or farther from it, so also the energy of the supreme Reality is more or less intense in the beings which are less or more remote from him. "Brahma, Vishnu, anmd Śiva are the most powerful energies of god; next to them are the inferior deities, then the attendant spirits, then men, then animals, birds, insects, vegetables; each becoming more and more feeble as they are farther from their primitive source."[22]

Brahma

Brahma (masculine and accented on the last syllable) is the personified form of the indescribable Brahman (neuter and accented on the first syllable), and is himself the creator, and thus is identifiable with Hiranyagarbha (the golden germ, womb, or egg) and with Prajapati (the lord of offspring). Since Brahma was the first individual entity to be manifested, he is also called Svayambhu, meaning self-born or self-existent. Using this name, the *Laws of Manu* (1.5ff.) relate the creation in this way:

> This universe existed in the shape of darkness, unperceived, destitute of distinctive marks, unattainable by reasoning, unknowable, wholly immersed as it were in deep sleep. Then the divine self-existent *(svayambhu)*, indiscernible, but making all this, the great elements and the rest, discernible, appeared with irresistible power, dispelling the darkness. . . . He, desiring to produce beings of many kinds from his own body, first with a thought created the waters and placed his seed in them. That became a golden egg, in brilliancy equal to the sun; in that he himself was born as Brahma, the progenitor of the whole world. . . . The divine one resided in that egg during a whole year, then he himself by his thought divided it into two halves; and out of those two halves he formed heaven and earth. . . . From himself he also drew forth the mind . . . and with particles of himself he created all beings. . . . To all created beings he assigned their several names, actions, and conditions. . . . He created the class of the gods. . . . From fire, wind, and the sun he drew forth the threefold eternal Veda. . . . Time and the divisions of time, the lunar mansions and the planets, the rivers, the oceans, the mountains, plains, and uneven ground, austerity, speech, pleasure, desire, and anger, he likewise produced. Moreover, in order to distinguish actions, he separated merit from demerit, and he caused the creatures to be affected by the pairs of opposites, such as pain and pleasure. . . . But for the sake of the prosperity of the worlds, he caused the *brahmanas,* the *kshatriyas,* the *vaiśyas,* and the *śudras* to proceed from his mouth, his arms, his thighs, and his feet.[23]

The abode of Brahma is the *Brahma-loka* (Brahma region), and he dwells there in its highest part, *Satya-loka,* the realm of infinite wisdom and truth, himself alone and lost in eternal contemplation (*Vishnu Purana* 1.6; 2.7).[24] Brahma is also known by other names, e.g., Abjabhu (lotus born), Caturmukha (four faced), Dhatri (originator), Lokeśa (world lord), Pitamaha (great patriarch), Sanat (ancient), Vidhatri (creator).

Vishnu

Vishnu bears a name which is explainable as derived from a Sanskrit root *(vishir)* which means "to spread in all directions," "to pervade." Thus he can be understood as representing the cohesive tendency in the universe, the force which holds all things together, corresponding to the quality (*guna*) of matter (or of anything) which is called *sattva,* meaning that which makes for orderliness and harmoniousness. So in the *Mahabharata* (2.192.10–19) Vishnu is praised (in the words of a famous seer named Utanka), as the one who pervades all creatures: heaven is his head, the sun and moon his eyes, the wind his breath, the four regions his arms, the earth his feet, and so on. "When thou (Vishnu) art contented, all the world is breathing; but in great danger, when thou art angered: thou alone art the remover of dangers, supreme Person."[25]

Likewise the *Vishnu Purana* (1.2)²⁶ says that Vishnu "consists of the world," i.e., the world is not an emanation or an illusion but is consubstantial with Vishnu. Considering him as the All, the same text says that he "is Hiranygarbha, Hari, and Śankara, the creator, the preserver, and destroyer of the world," i.e., he is the supreme Being in the three deities of the trinity, for Hiranyagarbha is a name of Brahma, Hari (remover [of ignorance and sorrow]) is a title of Vishnu, and Śankara (beneficent) is a designation of Śiva. So, as individual divinities, Brahma is creator, Vishnu is preserver, and Śiva is destroyer.

It is when Vishnu sleeps that the universe is dissolved into a formless state, represented as the cosmic ocean. What is left of manifestation amounts to the serpent Śeshsa (remainder), also known as Ananta (endless), and the serpent floats upon the waters while Vishnu reclines upon his coils. Then when creation begins again, Brahma appears on a lotus which arises from the navel of Vishnu, and Brahma himself is therefore known as Navel-born *(nabhi-ja)*, Lotus-born *(abja-ja, kanja-ja)*, and Lotus-like *(sarojin)*. In the *Mahabharata* (3.194.9–12) this sequence of events is described in these words:

> When there was but a single, dreadful ocean, and the moving and standing creation had perished, and all the creatures had come to an end . . . the blessed Vishnu, the everlasting source of all creatures, the eternal Person, slept solitarily on his ocean bed in the vast coil of the boundlessly puissant snake Śesha. The maker of the world . . . slept . . . while encompassing the girth of this earth with the vast coil of the snake. While the god was sleeping a lotus of the luster of the sun sprouted from his navel; and there, in that sun-like and moon-like lotus . . . was born Brahma. . . .²⁷

In all, Vishnu has a thousand names, a number which represents totality ("for a thousand is everything," *Śatapatha Brahmana* 4.6.1.15), and even more than this many names are given in a passage in the *Mahabharata* (Anusasana Parva 13.149).²⁸ Of these many names, twenty-four are considered the most important: (1) Keśava, the long-haired one; (2) Narayana, moving on the waters; (3) Madhava, lord of knowledge; (4) Govinda, rescuer of the earth; (5) Vishnu, the pervader; (6) Madhusudana, destroyer of the *asura* Madhu; (7) Trivikrama, three striding; (8) Vamana, the dwarf, deserving of praise; (9) Sridhara, bearer of fortune; (10) Hrishikesha, lord of the senses; (11) Padmanabha, lotus naveled; (12) Damodara, self-restrained; (13) Sankarshana, having a ploughshare; (14) Vasudeva, beneficent lord; (15) Pradyumna, wealthiest; (16) Aniruddha, unopposed; (17) Purushottama, best of persons; (18) Adhokshaja, sphere of the universe; (19) Narasimha, man-lion; (10) Achyuta, never failing; (21) Janardana, giver of rewards; (22) Upendra, Indra's brother; (23) Hari, remover, also green, greenish-yellow, tawny; (24) Kirshna, black. Yet other familiar names (to mention only a few) are: Anantaśayana, reposing on Ananta (the serpent often identified with Śesha); Pundarikaksha, lotus eyed; Urugaya, wide going; Urukrama, wide strider; Varadaraja, boon-granting king; Viśvarupa, of many forms.

Śiva

In the *Rig Veda* (1.114.9) śiva (auspicious) is an adjective applied to Rudra, while already in the *Śvetaśvatara Upanishad* (1.3.2–11)²⁹ Rudra-Śiva is identified as the one Supreme Being, the person *(purusha)* who fills the whole universe, who exists in the faces and dwells in the heart of all beings, who is all-pervading—the omnipresent Śiva. In this passage it is Rudra-Śiva who, having created all the world, also "rolls it up at the end of time," and in the *trimurti*, where Brahma appears as the creator and Vishnu as the preserver, Śiva is the destroyer. In these terms, if Vishnu represents the cohesive tendency in the universe and the quality which makes for orderliness *(sattva)*, Śiva stands for the disintegrative tendency and the quality called *tamas,* which makes for inertia and darkness.

The very extensive *Śiva Purana* is largely occupied with materials concerning Śiva and his worship, and in this source (*Śatarudrasamhita* 1.39–49)[30] Śiva is said to have five famous forms, namely, Iśana (ruler), Tatpurusha (supreme person), Aghora (non-fearful), Vamadeva (left-hand deity), and Sadyojata (suddenly born). These correspond respectively with the five elements (ether, wind, fire, water, earth), the five senses (hearing, touch, sight, taste, smell), and with the five aspects of a person (soul, nature, intellect, ego, mind), and indicate that Śiva is the ruler of all of these realms.

In his character as destroyer, Śiva is identified with time, which brings all things to an end. Accordingy he is called Kala (time), Mahakala (great time), Kalahani (destroyer of time), and Kalasamhara (slayer of time). In all Śiva, like Vishnu, is said to have a thousand names, and a single chapter (*Kotirudrasamhita* 35)[31] in the *Śiva Purana* lists, with some repetitions, more than that many. As found here and elsewhere the names of Śiva include Ardhanariśvara (androgynous lord), Candraśekhara (moon crested), Devadeva (god of gods), Gangadhara (Ganges bearer), Giriśa (mountain lord), Hara (seizer), Iśana (ruler of the northeast direction), Iśvara (lord), Jatadhara (wearing matted hair), Jatin (having matted hair), Kailasaśikharavasin (resident on the top of Mount Kailasa), Kala (time), Kalahani (destroyer of time), Kalasamhara (slayer of time), Kamadeva (god of love), Kapalamalin (wearing a garland of skulls), Kapaleśvara (skull lord), Kedarnath (mountain lord), Lingadhyaksha (presiding lord of *lingas*), Lokapala (protector of the worlds), Mahadeva (great god), Mahakala (great time), Mahayogi (great *yogi*), Maheśvara (great lord), Matanga (elephant), Nandiśvara (lord of the bull Nandi, the bull also being called Nandiśvara, lord Nandi), Nataraja (dance king), Nilakantha (blue throated), Nityanritya (ever dancing), Panchanana (five faced), Paśupati (herdsman, lord of beasts), Samavarta (whirling the wheel of wordly existence), Śramana (ascetic), Trilocana (three eyed), Tripurantaka (triple world ender, i.e., destroyer of earth, heaven, and hell), Tryambaka (three eyed), Vajreśvara (thunderbolt lord), Vamadeva (lovely lord), Virupaksha (having ill-formed eyes), Viśvanatha (universal lord), Viśveśvara (universal deity), and Yogeśvara (lord of *yoga*).

Insofar as Śiva and Rudra are distinguished, Śiva represents the more peaceful aspect of the deity, and Rudra the more fierce, Rudra being described as "the lord of the zone of fire" (*Vayaviyasamhita* 2,31,118).[32] Rudra in turn is also manifest in the form of Bhairava (wrathful), who is the most fearsome of destroyers. Upon one occasion Śiva said to Bhairava (Śatarudrasamhita 8.47–51):

> You are called Bhairava because you are of terrifying features and you are capable of supporting the universe. Since even Kala (time) is afraid of you, you are called Kalabhairava. When you are angry you will be suppressing the wicked souls. Hence you will be known everywhere as the suppressor of the wicked. Since you will be devouring the sins of devotees in a trice your name will be famous as sin-eater. O Kalaraja, you will have forever the suzerainty over my city Kaśi, the city of liberation, which is greater than all other cities. You alone will be the chastiser of those who commit sins there.[33]

Avatars

It is believed that for special purposes certain of the gods have at various times become incarnate in various forms on earth. Such an incarnation is known by the term *avatara* (descent).

Avatars of Śiva. In the time when the Pandavas were in their second exile and prior to their battle with the Kauravas, Arjuna went for a while to the Himalaya to do penance and to ask the gods for divine weapons for the coming struggle. On this journey Arjuna was involved in a fight with a stranger who appeared to be a mountaineer of the Kirata tribe, but afterward Arjuna discovered that the stranger was actually Śiva in disguise, and Arjuna then fell down and worshiped him. Śiva thereupon explained that he had only taken this form in order to test Arjuna and, being pleased with Arjuna's devotion, bade him terminate his penance and presented him with the *paśupata*, Śiva's own wonderful herdsman's weapon (*Śiva Purana, Śatarudrasamhita* 41.25, 55).[34]

Further, the *Śiva Purana (Śatarudrasamhita* 42)[35] enumerates twelve incarnations of Śiva in the form of *jyotirlingas*. The *linga* (discussed also in the *Linga Purana*)[36] is the phallic emblem of Śiva, and the *jyotirlingas* are "effulgent phalluses." Thus upon one occasion, for example, Śiva incarnated himself as Mahakala in the city of Ujjayini for the protection of his devotees, because a certain demon named Dushana, who was a defiler of Vedic rites, a hater of *brahmanas*, and a destroyer of everyone, had come there. So Mahakala killed the demon and afterward, as requested by the gods, Mahakala stayed in Ujjayini in the form of a *linga*. In 1231 C.E. in the reign of Iltutmish this *linga* image was taken off to Delhi and broken up.

The other of the twelve famous *linga* shrines of Śiva, deriving from his phallic incarnations, are Somnath in Saurashtra, Mallikarjuna on the mountain Śriśaila overlooking the Krishna River, Amareśvara in the Nimar district in Madhya Pradesh, Kedara at Kedarnath in the Himalaya, Bhimaśankara on the Bhima River northwest of Poona, Viśveśvara in Varanasi, Tryambaka on the Godavari River, Vaidyanatha at Deogarh in Bengal, Nageśa near Kedara, Rameśvara on the island of this name between India and Sri Lanka, and Ghuśmeśvara at Ellora.

Avatars of Vishnu. The *Bhagavata Purana* (1.3.6–26) names twenty-two incarnations of Vishnu, and concludes the list with the statement that "the incarnations of the lord are innumerable, like rivulets flowing from inexhaustible sources of water."[37] The twenty-two *avatars* are: (1) the Kumaras, who were sons of Brahma; (2) Varaha, the boar; (3) Narada, the *rishi* who inspired Valmiki to become a poet, who was himself the author of several hymns of the *Rig Veda,* and who was also a notorious mischief-maker, especially causing great trouble for Anasuya, wife of Atri; (4) Nara and Narayana, two saints, who were the sons of Dharma; (5) Kapila, the sage who destroyed the 60,000 sons of Sagara; (6) Kattatreya, son of Atri and Anasuya, who became a great *yogi,* and is credited with restoration of Vedic rites and origination of the Tantras and Tantric rites; (7) Yajna, the personification of sacrifice, with Dakshina (the personification of the gift to the priests) as his wife; (8) Rishabha, the king who became the first *tirthankara* and first lord (Adinatha) of Jainism; (9) Prithu, a form of Vena (who was sixth in descent from Manu Svayambhuva), and himself considered to have been the first man to be installed as a king, and the inventor of agriculture; (10) Matsya, the fish; (11) Kurma, the tortoise; (12) Dhanvantari, the physician of the gods, who appeared during the Churning of the Ocean, bearing the chalice of the nectar of immortality *(amrita),* and was the author of the science of health and medicine known as Ayurveda (life knowledge); (13) Mohini, an enchantress who gave the first drink of *amrita* to the gods, and who in union with Śiva became the mother of the androgynous deity Harihara; (14) Narasimha, the man-lion; (15) Vamana, the dwarf; (16) Paraśurama, Rama with the ax; (17) Vyasadeva, the Vyasa who supposedly arranged the Vedas and compiled the *Mahabharata;* (18) Rama, the hero of the *Ramayana;* (19) Balarama, the older brother of Krishna; (20) Krishna; (21) Buddha, Siddhartha Gautama Sakyamuni, the founder of Buddhism; (22) Kalki, the future *avatar,* yet to come.

Other sources sometimes list even more *avatars,* or sometimes fewer, while it is often held that there are ten main incarnations, distributed in the several ages *(yugas)* of the world as follows:

In the long Kritayuga, or best age, were Matsya, Kurma, Varaha, and Narasimha.

Matsya. In the dawn of time there was a long-continued conflict between the gods and the demons (e.g., *asuras, daityas*). At the end of one of the *kalpas* or "days" of Brahma the demon Hayagriva (horse neck) stole the Veda as it slipped out of the mouth of Brahma, who was then asleep. Vishnu wished to recover the scripture, and also to deliver Manu Vaivasvata—the seventh Manu, who presides over the present Manu-period *(manvantara)*—from a great flood which was to come, and to give him the Veda for the guidance of humanity during the present cycle of four world-ages *(yugas),* and in order to accomplish these ends Vishnu determined to assume the form of a fish *(matsya).* As is related in the *Matsya Purana* (1)[38] and other sources, and has already been noted above (in Chapter 2), the fish was first saved by Manu Vaivasvata, and then Manu was saved by the fish.

Kurma. In the deluge, from which Manu Vaivasvata was saved by the fish, certain precious things were lost, including a chalice containing the nectar of immortality *(amrita).* Vishnu suggested to the gods that they churn the celestial ocean of milk to recover the lost objects, and the demons *(asuras)* agreed to help, but with the secret intention of stealing the chalice of nectar. Vishnu assumed the form of the tortoise Kurma, and positioned himself at the bottom of the ocean. The mountain Mandara (a spur of Mount Meru) was placed on his back as the dasher of the churn, the serpent Vasuki was wound around it as a rope, and the gods pulled on one end of the rope, and the *asuras* on the other. The first result of the churning was the appearance on the surface of the ocean of a scum of poison, caused either by the sweat of the demons in their labor or by the suffering of Kurma as the mountain was turned on his back. Siva swallowed much of the poison, and from the stain it left he was known as Nilakantha (blue throated). Vasuki the serpent drank the remainder of the scum, and bequeathed its venom as an inheritance to other serpents. Then fourteen valuable things came forth from the ocean. These "fourteen jewels" *(caturdaśa-ratnam)* are usually listed as: (1) Candra, the moon; (2) Parijata, a celestial tree which was taken by Indra and planted in his paradise; (3) Airavata (named from *iravat,* "moisture possessing," and also called Abhramatanga, cloud elephant), a four-tusked elephant also taken by Indra; (4) Kamadhenu (wish cow), a miraculous cow of plenty; (5) Mada, goddess of wine, taken by Varuna as his wife; (6) Kalpavriksha, a wish-fulfilling tree; (7) Rambha, an *apsaras,* the prototype of the nymphs of Indra's heaven; (8) Uccaihśravas, a wonderful white horse taken by Indra; (9) Lakshmi, the goddess of fortune and beauty, who was taken by Vishnu as his wife; (10) Sankha, the conch of victory, given to Vishnu; (11) Gada the mace of sovereignty, and Dhanus a magic bow, both given to Vishnu; (12) Ratna, gems of many kinds; (13) Dhanvantari, the physician of the gods, who appeared bearing the most precious gift of all, namely, (14) the nectar of immortality *(amrita)* in a golden chalice. The demons seized the chalice and tried to flee, but Vishnu took the form of the beautiful woman Mohini, obtained the nectar by a stratagem, and gave it to the gods to drink.

In the *Markandeya Purana* (58),[39] the entire Indian continent is described as resting permanently upon Vishnu in this form of the tortoise, with the various countries and peoples distributed over the several parts of his body, together with the corresponding constellations.

Varaha. In the continuing conflict between the gods and the demons, the *daitya* king Hiranyaksha (golden eye) was one of the most formidable opponents of the gods. Upon one occasion he seized the earth and dragged it to the bottom of the ocean, and then threatened to invade heaven. When the gods were terrified, they appealed to Vishnu to act, and Vishnu assumed the form of a boar named Varaha, plunged into the waters, and struggled with Hiranyaksha for a thousand years. In the end Vishnu was victorious, and raised the earth up again out of the abyss.

Recounting the event, and calling Vishnu Narayana, Hari, and Vasudeva, the *Vishnu Purana* (1.4) says that, "as in preceding *kalpas* he had assumed the shape of a fish or a tortoise, so in this he took the figure of a boar." Seeing him thus descending into the subterranean regions, the goddess Earth, called Prithivi or Bhudevi, uttered a salutation:

> Hail to thee, who art all creatures; to thee, the holder of the mace and shell: elevate me now from this place, as thou hast upraised me in days of old. . . . Thou art the creator of all things, their preserver, and their destroyer, in the forms of Brahma, Vishnu, and Rudra, at the seasons of creation, duration, and dissolution. When thou hast devoured all things, thou reposest on the ocean. . . . They who are desirous of final liberation, worship thee as the supreme Brahma; and who that adores not Vasudeva, shall obtain emancipation?

Then, the account continues, " . . . the mighty boar, whose eyes were like the lotus, and whose body, vast as the Nila mountain, was of the dark color of the lotus leaves, uplifted upon his ample tusks the earth from the lowest regions." He "raised it quickly, and placed it on the summit of the ocean, where it floats like a mighty vessel." Then, having leveled the earth, he divided it into portions, by mountains, and made seven continents. "Thus Hari, the four-faced god, invested with the quality of activity and taking the form of Brahma, accomplished the creation."[40]

Narasimha. The demon king Hiranyaksha was succeeded on the throne by his twin brother Hiranyakaśipu (golden vesture), and then by the latter's son Prahlada. Prahlada became a devotee of Vishnu, to the great displeasure of Hiranyakaśipu, who persecuted and tried unsuccessfully to kill his son. As for himself, Hiranyakaśipu believed that he was invulnerable, because Brahma had stated that he could not be killed by man or beast, neither in a house nor outside, neither by day nor by night. Depending upon this supposed invulnerability, Hiranyakaśipu told his son that Vishnu was obviously not omnipotent, because Vishnu could not kill him, Hiranyakaśipu. Nor was Vishnu omnipresent, Hiranyakaśipu declared, since Vishnu was obviously not in a pillar on the porch of the palace, which the king struck vigorously to illustrate his point. Thereupon, to save Prahlada and to destroy the evil king, Vishnu appeared out of the pillar (on the threshold of the palace and therefore neither in a house nor outside), at twilight (neither day nor night), and in a form half man and half lion (neither man nor beast). So, "after his father had been put to death by Vishnu in the form of the man-lion, Prahlada became the sovereign of the *daityas;* and possessing the splendors of royalty consequent upon his piety, exercised extensive sway, and was blessed with numerous progeny" (*Vishnu Purana* 1.17–20).[41]

In the Tretayuga or second world-age, the major incarnations of Vishnu were Vamana, Paraśurama, and Rama.

Vamana. The son and successor of Prahlada on the throne of the *daityas* was Virocana, and his son in turn was Bali, also known as Mahabali (great Bali). Bali married the beautiful princess Vindhyavali, and ruled from a capital at Mahabalipuram. Through austerities and valor, Bali gained sovereignty over the three worlds of heaven, earth, and the nether world. The gods, who were thus deprived of their own dwelling place, and of the sacrifices which were made to them on earth, again appealed to Vishnu for help. Vishnu was now born as Vamana, the "dwarf" son of the famous *rishi* Kaśyapa and Aditi, the daughter of Daksha. In this dwarf form Vishnu came to Bali and asked of him as much land as he could cover in three steps. When Bali acceded to the apparently modest request, the dwarf became a giant who strode over the whole earth in a single step, over heaven in a second step, and would have traversed the nether region in a third, but out of consideration for Bali's generosity refrained from doing so, and left the underworld under the sway of the *daitya* king. Thus Vamana, the dwarf, was Trivikrama, the "three-striding" deity (*Vamana Purana* 23–31, 89–94).[42]

Paraśurama. At the time of this incarnation the Haihaya king Kartavirya (or Arjuna Kartavirya) had been given by the great *yogi* Dattatreya a thousand arms and the power to conquer the earth, and was usurping the power of the priests and oppressing the people and the gods, whereupon Vishnu descended to earth to overcome Kartavirya and rectify the lamentable situation. Vishnu was born as Rama, the fifth and youngest son of the pious sage Jamadagni and his beautiful wife Renuka. Rama was a worshiper of Śiva, and Śiva gave him the *paraśu*, a wonderful battle-ax, on account of which the young man was called Paraśurama, i.e., Rama with the Ax. On an occasion when Jamadagni and his sons were absent from their Himalayan hermitage, Kartavirya came there and received a courteous welcome from Renuka. In spite of that, Kartavirya devastated the hermitage and carried off a sacred cow which belonged to Jamadagni, a cow which was the calf of the wonderful wish-cow Kamadhenu. When Paraśurama returned and learned of the happening, he pursued the evil king, cut off his thousand arms, and killed him. In turn, when Paraśurama was again absent, Kartavirya's heirs came to the hermitage and slew Jamadagni while the sage sat in deep meditation. Paraśurama then vowed to exterminate the entire ruling class. All by himself, he slew the sons of Kartavirya and, after them, whatever *kshatriyas* he encountered. "Thrice seven times did he clear the earth of the *kshatriya* caste" (*Mahabharata* 3.116–117; *Vishnu Purana* 4.7).[43]

Rama. This Rama, the seventh of the major incarnations of Vishnu, is the Rama whose story is told in the *Ramayana* and other works, including several of the Puranas.

In the Dvaparayuga or third age of the world, the incarnations of Vishnu were Krishna and Balarama, the latter of less importance.

Krishna. Krishna, considered either as an independent god or as the eighth major incarnation of Vishnu, is doubtless the most celebrated deity of the later Hindu pantheon. His story is the main subject of the *Bhagavata Purana* and is included in other Puranas (e.g., *Vishnu Purana* 5.1–33)[44] and in the *Mahabharata*, where Krishna himself is the main speaker in the *Bhagavad Gita*. In the *Bhagavad*

Gita Krishna explains to Arjuna the manner and significance of his own *avatars* in this passage (4.5–9):

> Many, many births both you and I have passed. I can remember all of them, but you cannot, O subduer of the enemy! Although I am unborn and my transcendental body never deteriorates, and although I am the lord of all sentient beings, I still appear *(sambhavami,* I do incarnate) in every millennium *(yuga)* in My original transcendental form. Whenever and wherever there is a decline in religious practice, O descendant of Bharata, and a predominant rise of irreligion—at that time I descend *(srjami,* manifest) Myself. In order to deliver the pious and to annihilate the miscreants, as well as to reestablish the principles of religion, I advent Myself *(sambhavami,* I do appear) millennium *(yuga)* after millennium *(yuga).* One who knows the trancendental nature of My appearance and activities does not, upon leaving the body, take his birth again in this material world, but attains My eternal abode, O Arjuna.[45]

As for Balarama (Rama the strong), he was the older half-brother of Krishna, and is sometimes considered a partial incarnation of Vishnu; otherwise he is also described as an incarnation of the serpent Śesha (remainder), which was seen issuing from his mouth when Balarama died (*Vishnu Purana* 5.37).[46]

In the present world-age, the Kaliyuga, which began with the death of Krishna and the accession of Parikshit II (in 3101 B.C.E.), the major incarnations of Vishnu are Buddha and Kalki.

Buddha. In the list of ten incarnations of Vishnu in the *Matsya Purana* (in which list there are some variations in individual names as compared with what has been set forth above) there is this statement concerning Buddha, presumably meaning Siddartha Gautama Śakyamuni (47.247): "For the establishment of righteousness and the destruction of *asuras,* through asceticism, there was the ninth incarnation, in the form of Buddha of divine splendor, with his eyes as beautiful as lotus, and with the sage Dvaipayana Vyasa as the officiating priest."[47]

The *Bhagavata Purana* is no doubt also referring to Śakyamuni Buddha when it states in the form of a prophecy (1.3.25): "Then, in the beginning of Kaliyuga, the Lord will appear as Lord Buddha, the son of Anjana, in the province of Gaya, just for the purpose of deluding those who are envious of the faithful theist."[48] This apparent disapprobation of the Buddha's "atheism" over against Hindu theism, combined nevertheless with recognition of the Buddha as an *avatar* of Vishnu, may perhaps be intended to say that Vishnu acted in this way in order deliberately to accelerate the decline of religion which must necessarily mark the present dark age as it goes toward its end.

Kalki. Along with the other Puranas, the *Bhagavata Purana* also looks forward to the time when, in the ceaseless cycle of the ages of the world, the present worst Kali age will give way to the new best Krita age. At that juncture, as the old age ends in great degeneration and the new age dawns, the tenth and last of the major incarnations of Vishnu will appear, namely, Kalki. The *Bhagavata Purana* states the expectation and describes the situation of that time (1.3.24): "Thereafter, at the conjunction of two *yugas,* the Lord of the creation will take his birth as the Kalki incarnation and become the son of Vishnu Yaśas. At this time the rulers of the earth will have degenerated into plunderers."[49]

In the *Mahabharata* (3.37),[50] while the Pandavas and Draupadi were living in the forest in banishment, they were visited by the *rishi* Markandeya. This sage (after whom the *Markandeya Purana* is named) was famed for longevity, reputedly having lived through all the *yugas,* therefore was besought by Yudhishthira to tell the exiles about the ages and the end of the world. After outlining the four ages and their durations in the usual way, Markandeya described the world in its time of troubles at the end of the present Kali age.

Markandeya said that at that time barbarian kings will rule the earth with false policies. People will be short-lived and weak-bodied, and will rarely speak the truth. The *brahmanas* will plunder the land for alms. Because of the burden of taxes householders will become thieves. The law will lose strength, and lawlessness will gain strength. Finally a storm of fire will devastate the land, and then rain will flood the earth until all is one ocean. But after the old age ends in the midst of such terrifying destruction, the new age will begin, and once again there will be safety, abundance of food, and health without sickness. It is at this point that the future incarnation of Vishnu will take place. He will be born as Kalki, in the family of Vishnu Yaśas, a *brahmana* priest in a village named Śambhala. Kalki will be of great prowess, wisdom, and might. He will destroy the robbers, and bring this turbulent world to tranquility.

Assuming the duration of the Kaliyuga as 432,000 human years, and its beginning at a point corresponding to 3101 B.C.E. the year 1988 C.E. is somewhat more than 5,000 years into the age, and the end of the age and the coming of Kalki are slightly less than 427,000 years in the future.

Śakti and Śaktis

Among the artifacts of the Harappan civilization there are many figurines evidently representing a mother goddess, in the Vedic pantheon there are many goddesses and divine couples (e.g., Daksha and Aditi, Dyaus and Prithivi, Agni and Agnayi), and in the Vedic philosophy the concept of duality in unity is intimated in the hymn (*Rig Veda* 10.129) which states that in the beginning, in the One, desire arose and became the "primeval seed." The underlying idea in this hymn is developed more fully in later works. The *Brihad Aranyaka Upanishad* 1.4.1–3)[51] explains that in the beginning there was only the Self, in the form of a person. When he looked around he saw nothing else than himself, and therefore experienced a feeling of loneliness and a desire for companionship. Thereupon he caused the self to divide into two parts. The two parts are called husband and wife and, from the union of the two, the race of human beings was produced. In the *Laws of Manu* (1.5, 9, 11, 32–33),[52] it is explained that in the beginning all was unconditioned, unknowable darkness, then the "self-existent" One, Svayambhuva, placed a golden egg *(hiranyagarbha)* in the waters, issued from it in the form of Brahma, and divided his own body into two so that it became half male (Purusha) and half female (Viraj), and from their union came Manu Svayambhuva. In the *Vishnu Purana* (1.7),[53] the two into whom Brahma divides himself are Manu Svayambhuva the male, and Śatarupa a "hundred-aspected" female, and from them are born sons and daughters.

Thus from early time these concepts of the feminine and of the combination of the feminine and the masculine are very important in Indian religious thought. In particular, in Vedic symbolism, the power of a god is represented by his consort, and she is known by the term *śakti* (strength, power, energy). This word is found already in the *Rig Veda* (1.31.18), where the favor of Agni is praised as "strength-bestowing." Then in the *Kena Upanishad* (3.11–12; 4.1)[54] we find that the gods Agni, Vayu, and Indra themselves do not know who Brahman is, but Uma, who is the *śakti* or power of Śiva and thus also of Brahman, makes the Brahman known. So the *śakti* may be an individual goddess, or the wife or consort of one of the gods, or the feminine aspect of the ultimate reality itself. It is of course well understood that the ultimate reality is not finally describable as masculine, feminine, or even neuter, but in the manner of human speech and using a term of admittedly limited significance, the *śakti* is the feminine aspect of deity. In Later Hinduism the cults which are devoted to the worship of the *śakti* are known collectively as the Śakta cults.[55]

Devi. As a goddess in her own right, the female deity may simply be named Śakti (e.g., *Mahabharata* 3.215.10), or she may be called Devi (goddess, e.g., *Mahabharata* 2.11.29).[56] With a view to her maternal nature, Devi is the Mother (Amba, Ambalika, Ambika, Amma, Mata, Matri, Matrika), the Great Mother (Maha-amma, corrupted to Mahamba, Momba, or Bimba, after whom Bombay gets its name), and the Mother of the World (Jagadmata, Jagadmatri), and there are also very many lesser *matri* (mothers). With a view to her nature as a devoted wife or consort, Devi is known under many different names, and is associated with many different gods. In the conjunction of goddess and god it is, in Hindu thought, usually but not always the female who is considered to be active, and the male to be passive.

Śaktis of Brahma

Brahma, the creator, is associated with two wives.

Sarasvati. The chief wife of Brahma is Sarasvati, originally the personification and goddess of the river Sarasvati, and later the patroness of learning, knowledge, science, art, and music. In accordance with her character, Sarasvati is also known as Vagdevi or Vagiśvari (goddess of learning) and Śrutadevi or Śrutadevata (goddess of *śruti,* i.e., the Vedas and other revealed literature), and she is also identified with and named Vak, the goddess of speech. In accordance with this identification the Rig-Vedic hymn to Vak (10.125), called the *Devi-sukta,* is used in the worship of Sarasvati. In this hymn the goddess is speech in many places and many forms, and in particular she is the voice of the hymn which is the communication between heaven and earth at the sacrifice (10:125.5): "I myself proclaim the word which gods and men alike shall welcome. I make the one I love a mighty one, a priest, a *rishi,* a sage."

The son of Sarasvati is the *rishi* Sarasvata. During a great drought and famine the *brahmanas* neglected their studies in order to search for food and, by this neglect, the Vedas were lost. Sarasvata, however, was nourished with fish by his mother (the personified river), kept up his studies, and thus became one of the Vyasas who preserved and reconstituted the Vedas (*Vishnu Purana* 3.3).[57]

Gayatri/Savitri. Upon one occasion Sarasvati was late for an important sacrifice, and Brahma hastily married Gayatri as a substitute and as his second wife. Gayatri is also called Savitri, although the two are sometimes distinguished. It is Gayatri/Savitri after whom the Gayatri meter and the Gayatri or Savitri Mantra are named.

Śaktis of Vishnu and of His Avatars

Vishnu, the preserver, and his numerous *avatars* have many wives and consorts.

Śrī/Lakshmi. The chief wife of Vishnu is Lakshmi (auspicious), also known as Śrī (beautiful). As her names indicate, she is a goddess of beauty and good fortune, and she is also equated with the four branches of knowledge, *yajnavidya* (knowledge of devotion, i.e., knowledge of religious rites), *mahavidya* (great knowledge, i.e., knowledge of Tantric worship), *guhyavidya* (mystical knowledge, i.e., knowledge of *mantras* and prayers), and *atmavidya* (spiritual knowledge, i.e., knowledge of self or soul).

In respect of her origin, Śrī is said in one account to have sprung from the creator Prajapati, but in another account she was the daughter of an early *rishi* named Bhrigu, suffered his displeasure and took refuge in the primeval waters, and reappeared at the churning of the ocean. The *Vishnu Purana* (1.8–9) describes the latter event: "Then, seated on a full-blown lotus, and holding a water lily in her hand, the goddess Śrī, radiant with beauty, rose from the waves. . . . Ganga and other holy streams attended for her ablutions; and the elephants of the skies, taking up their pure waters in vases of gold, poured them over the goddess."

Immediately thereupon, Śrī gave herself to Vishnu, and so the "daughter of ocean" became the "beloved of Vishnu." In their union they complement each other. As Vishnu is all-pervading so also is Śrī/Lakshmi omnipresent. He is meaning, she is speech; he is understanding, she is intellect; he is righteousness, she is devotion; he is creator, she is creation; he is all that is called male, she is all that is termed female; he is the father of all beings, she is their mother. "I bow down to Śrī, the mother of all beings, seated on her lotus throne, with eyes like full-blown lotuses, reclining on the breast of Vishnu. . . . Thou, beautiful goddess, art power, faith, intellect. . . . Health and strength, power, victory, happiness, are easy of attainment to those upon whom thou smilest."

As the eternal spouse of Vishnu, Lakshmi is also incarnate in the wives and consorts of the *avatars* of Vishnu. When Vishnu was born as the dwarf Vamana, Lakshmi appeared from a lotus and was known as Padma or Kamala. When Vishnu was born as Paraśurama, Lakshmi was Dharani (the Earth). When Vishnu came as Rama, she was Sita. When he was Krishna, she became Rukmini, his principal and lawful wife, and also Radha, his favorite among the *gopis* of Brindaban. "In the other descents of Vishnu, she is his associate. If he takes a celestial form, she appears as divine; if a mortal, she becomes a mortal too, transforming her own person agreeably to whatever character it pleases Vishnu to put on."[58]

Bhudevi. The earth goddess, called Dharani, was just mentioned in association with Vishnu's *avatar,* Paraśurama. Otherwise also the Earth, called Bhudevi (also Bhumidevi), appears as the second wife of Vishnu. The union of the two may also be called that of Prithivi and Narayana.[59] When Vishnu was incarnate as the boar named Varaha which brought up Prithivi from the ocean depths, the earth goddess said to him: "I am of thee, upheld by thee; thou art my creator, and to thee I fly for refuge; hence, in this universe, Madhavi (feminine, from Madhava, a name of Vishnu as lord of knowledge) is my designation (*Vishnu Purana* 1.4).[60]

Śaktis of Śiva

The *Vishnu Purana* (1.8), the *Śiva Purana* (*Rudrasamhita,* 2, *Satikhanda,* 3, *Parvatikhanda*), and other sources tell much about the wives and consorts of Śiva.[61]

Sati. The first wife of Śiva was Sati (true), a daughter of the primordial *rishi* Daksha. On one occasion there was a quarrel between Daksha and Śiva, and

Daksha conducted a sacrificial offering without providing a part for Śiva. Sati was so distressed by this slight to her husband that she destroyed herself in fire, and it was from her that the custom of *sati* (anglicized as *suttee*), in which a widow immolated herself on the funeral pyre of her husband, derived its name. Śiva recovered the body of Sati, and the pieces of the body, dismembered by the disk *(cakra)* of Vishnu, fell in many places throughout India, all of which became famous *pithas,* or places of pilgrimage, in honor of the goddess. Afterward, Sati was born again, and again became the wife of Śiva. In this new incarnation the goddess is sometimes herself called Śiva (auspicious lady, a feminine form of the name of Śiva), and is also designated by many others names and epithets, of which the best known are the following.

Uma. The goddess was born at this time as the daughter of Himavat (the personification of the snowy mountains, the Himalaya) and his wife Mena. According to the *Śiva Purana (Rudrasamhita, 3, Parvatikhanda* 7.11–17),[62] the daughter was called Kali, Parvati, and other "pleasing names," but received the name Uma when, upon one occasion, she wanted to perform a penance but was forbidden by her mother, who said, "O, no *(u ma)*." Other interpretations, however, explain the name Uma as meaning "light" or "the peace of the night."

Parvati. The name Parvati also designates the goddess as the daughter of the mountain *(parvata),* and other names call her Annapurna (giver of food and plenty), Bhavani (giver of existence), Girija (mountain born), Haimavati (daughter of the snowy mountains), Kumari (the maid), Maheśvari (great goddess), Vijaya (victorious), and others as well.

In the continuation of the account just cited in the *Śiva Purana,* Parvati is described as both beautiful and learned, but it was only the arrow of Kama, the god of love, which attracted the attention of Śiva to her, and led to their eventual marriage. At this time the demon *(asura)* Taraka was oppressing the three worlds, and it was said that only a son of Śiva would be able to overcome him. So it came to pass that a son was born to Śiva and Parvati, and this was the six-headed Karttikeya, who eventually destroyed Taraka and many other *asuras.*

The second son of Parvati and Śiva was Ganeśa, the elephant-headed god. Ganeśa is the lord of the Ganas, lesser deities who are attendants of Śiva, and he is therefore also known as Ganeśvara and as Ganapati (Gana lord). Another of his names is Vinayaka (remover of obstacles), and he is considered to be the bringer of good fortune. His vehicle is the rat. In the *Ganeśa Gita,* a work more or less modeled after the *Bhagavad Gita,* he is the supreme god and the all-pervading world-soul, mystical union with whom through worship leads to deliverance.[63]

The union of Śiva and Parvati is also seen in the androgynous form of Śiva as Ardhanariśvara, the lord who is *ardha-nari* (half female).[64] Likewise the union of the god and the goddess is represented in the combined images of the *linga* and the *yoni,* which are almost universally found in Śiva sanctuaries.

Kali. The name of Kali is the feminine of the word *kala* (time), and in this form (also Mahakali, great time) the goddess is the power of time, which destroys all things. In Hindi *kālā* means black and, as the destroyer, Kali is black and terrible in appearance.

Kali has ten manifestations (*Śiva Purana, Umasamhita* 50.28–29),[65] and these are ten aspects of the inexorable, all-destroying cycle of time. As such they are ten *mahavidyas* or objects of higher knowledge, because only knowledge of the power of time, which is the power of death, leads to the desire for liberation. Of the ten, some of the best known are Tara (just below), Chinnamasta (beheaded, also known in Buddhism as Vajra-yogini, the thunderbolt goddess), Bhuvaneśvari (lady lord of the world), Bhairavi (terror inspiring, the feminine of Bhairava, a name of Śiva), Bagala (crane-headed killer, the crane being considered gentle in appearance but the most deceitful of creatures), Dhumra (smoke colored, as the Universe is to go up in smoke), and Matangi (elephant, the feminine of Matanga, a name of Śiva). Kali is also attended by many *dakinis* (fiendesses), who are female evil spirits and feed on human flesh.

In the *Mahabharata* (*Bhishma Parva* 6.23), just prior to the *Bhagavad Gita,* Arjuna invokes Kali in the words:

> O thou that art identical with Brahman . . . O thou that art freed from decrepitude and decay, O Kali . . . O thou that art of a black and tawny hue! I bow to thee, O bringer of benefits to thy devotees, I bow to thee, O Mahakali. O wife of the universal destroyer, I bow to thee, O proud one, O thou that rescuest from dangers, O thou that art endued with every auspicious attribute. . . . With inner soul cleansed, I praise thee, O great goddess. Let victory always attend me through thy grace on the field of battle.[66]

Durga. Durga is usually identified as another form of Kali, and is said to have received the name Durga (inaccessible, fort) to commemorate her victory over a demon *(asura)* of that name, while another of her names is Candika (fury). It is as a slayer of *asuras* that Durga is especially known. In this respect her most notable exploit was the conquest of the buffalo demon Mahisha, on account of which she is also called Mahishasuramardini, the destroyer of the demon Mahisha. In the long war of the gods, led by Indra, against the *asuras,* Mahisha (powerful) won a victory and seized heaven. Thereupon the gods concentrated their respective energies in Durga (Candika) and equipped her with their own weapons, and she undertook the battle against the demon. It was said of Mahisha that he could not be killed by either man or beast, but as a woman and a divinity Durga was not in either of these categories. In the struggle Mahisha assumed many shapes, and finally that of a buffalo as the symbol of death, but Durga, riding upon a lion, was able to slay him and to return heaven to the control of the gods (*Markandeya Purana, Devi-Mahatmya,* 82–83).[67]

Another exploit of Durga (Kali) was the defeat of the *asura* twins Śumbha and Niśumbha and their generals Canda and Munda (bald headed), on account of which she received the names of Camunda and Mundamardini. In connection with this battle the *Markandeya Purana* (87.5–7) describes Durga/Kali/Camunda as " . . . of terrible countenance, armed with a sword and noose, bearing a many-colored skull-topped staff, decorated with a garland of skulls, clad in a tiger's skin, very appalling because of her emaciated flesh, exceedingly wide of mouth, lolling out her tongue terribly, having deep-sunk reddish eyes, and filling the regions of the sky with her roars."[68]

Including Camunda and Mundamardini, the *Śiva Purana* (*Rudrasamhita,* 2, *Satikhanda* 33.11–12, 15)[69] gives a list of nine Durgas, and also speaks of sixty-four groups of *yoginis,* who are demonesses and attendants of Durga.

In the *Mahabharata* (*Virata Parva* 4.6), Yudhishthira, having lost his kingdom and being on his way in exile to the city of Virata, sings a hymn to Durga, whose name he connects with rescue from difficulty. He describes the goddess as a beautiful virgin, the slayer of Mahisha, and one who dwells always on the Vindhya mountains, and he prays to her for protection:

Because thou rescuest people from difficulties whether when they are afflicted in the wilderness or sinking in the great ocean, it is for this that thou art called Durga by all. Thou art the sole refuge of men when attacked by robbers or while afflicted in crossing streams and seas or in wilderness and forests. Those who remember thee are never lost, O Mahadevi. . . . I, who have been deprived of my kingdom, seek thy protection.[70]

Tara. The goddess Tara (star) is a manifestation of Kali too, and is also recognized in Jainism (where she is called Sutara, good star), and is very prominent in Vajrayana Buddhism. Tara has different forms and names. She is Nilasarasvati (*nila,* blue, therefore the Blue Sarasvati) as the goddess of wisdom, who endows with the power of good speech. She is Ugratara (the terrible Tara) as the one who liberates from the most grave calamity, i.e., from the fetters of existence. She is Ekajata (having one chignon) as the one who gives the realization *(kaivalya)* of identity with the highest.

In addition to the feminine deities already named there are yet many more mother goddesses. On one occasion the *asura* Andhaka (blind) sought to snatch away Parvati from Śiva, and a terrible battle was fought in which thousands of Andhaka demons were killed, and a large number of divine mothers was created to drink their blood; at the same time we hear of thirty-two divine mothers created by Vishnu alongside those created by Śiva (*Matsya Purana* 179).[71] Even as Śiva has more than a thousand names, so also for each of these names there is a counterpart feminine name. Included are Annapurna (giver of nourishment), Bhadrakali (prosperity making), and Bhairavi (terror inspiring).

Among the many a special place is accorded to the Seven Mothers *(sapta matrikas),* and these are usually listed as Brahmani (consort of Brahma), Maheśvari (consort of Śiva), Vaishnavi (consort of Vishnu), Kaumari (consort of Skanda, a name of Karttikeya), Varahi (consort of Varaha), Indrani (consort of Indra), and Camunda (Durga as destroyer of demons).

Further there are almost innumerable village goddesses, many with features common to the mother goddess, some associated with animals (e.g., Manasadevi, serpent goddess; Dakshinirai, tiger goddess), some associated with disease (e.g., Sitala, goddess of smallpox).

In the worship *(puja,* adoration) and festivals *(utsava)* of the Hindu religious year, the goddesses play an important part; e.g., Durga is celebrated in the Durga-*puja* (September/October); Lakshmi and Parvati are honored at the beginning of the five-day festival (October/November) called Divali (Sanskrit *dipavali,* a row of lights).[72]

Tantras

As noted above, the fourth class of books in the literature of Hinduism is designated by the term *tantra.* The word *tantra* is usually explained as originally meaning "web" (from *tantu,* thread), and then "a system of doctrines," so a Tantra is a book in which a system of doctrines is woven together, somewhat as *sutra* originally means "thread" and then "a short precept," and so a Sutra is a book in which such precepts are strung together. In line with this general meaning, the name Tantra is used for various types of books, e.g., the *Panca Tantra,* which is a collection of animal fables.[73] Another etymology, however, derives *tantra* from the root *tan,* meaning "to expand," and so a Tantra is a book intended to expand human consciousness and faculties through the knowledge it communicates and the methods it teaches. In line with this more particular meaning the name Tantra is most distinctively applied to books of a mystical and esoteric sort and especially to those which direct meditation and practice toward the divine feminine energy or energies (*śakti* or *śaktis*).

Although there is much overlapping of material and terminology, it is usual to recognize three groups of these books, namely, (1) those of the Vaishnavas, usually called by the term *samhita* (collection of sacred texts), which feature Vishnu and his *avatars* and their *śaktis*, e.g., Krishna and Radha; (2) those of the Śaivas, called either *agama* (tradition) or *samhita*, in which Śiva is the chief deity and usually appears together with his *śakti*; and (3) those of the Śaktas, usually called *agamas* or *tantras*, in which the *śakti* herself is most prominent, usually in conjunction with Śiva. In addition there are also many Buddhist Tantras.

In form a great many of the Śaiva and Śakta Tantras consist of a dialogue between Śiva and Parvati, and here a distinction is made: when the goddess asks the questions and Śiva gives the answers the texts are called Agamas; when Śiva is the questioner and the goddess is the teacher, they are called Nigamas. If complete, a Tantra is thought of as properly treating of four main themes, namely, *jnana* (knowledge), *yoga* (union), *kriya* (ritual action), and *carya* (social conduct). In the Tantric terminology, the spiritual discipline which the Tantras teach is called *sadhana*, and the adept is a *sadhaka* (male) or *sadhika* (female). A single ritual act may employ a symbolical diagram called a *mandala* (circle) or *yantra* (instrument), and include *mantra* (sacred formula), *mudra* (yogic gesture), *asana* (yogic posture), *pranayama* (control of *prana*, vital force, by regulation of breathing), and *dhyana* (concentration, meditation).[74]

Śiva Samhita. In the *Śiva Samhita* Śiva sets forth the doctrine, and Parvati appears as questioner.[75] Ultimate reality, it is explained, consists in one universal, eternal, self-luminous Spirit, which is all-pervading and is "entirely itself" (1.54).[76] Within this one reality, or Brahman, there is a "self-combination" of Śiva and Śakti, i.e., of the male principle of *purusha* (cosmic consciousness), and the female principle of *prakriti* (cosmic energy or nature), and it is through the "inherent interaction" of these two on each other that all creatures are born (1.92).

In its totality the whole universe is the Brahmanda, i.e., the "egg" (*anda*) of Brahman, and the entire macrocosm also exists as a microcosm in the body of the individual human being, which is itself therefore also called Brahmanda (1.91; 2.6). The human body consists not only of a gross physical body but also, substantially parallel therewith, of a subtle or psychic body.

In the subtle body there are various channels (called *nadi*, tube) and centers (called *cakra*, wheel or vortex) of psychic energy, and the structure of these is analogous to the cosmological spheres (2.1ff.). The spinal column is equated with the axial cosmic Mount Meru, and is called the Meru or the Merudanda or Brahmadanda (rod of Meru or of Brahma). At the bottom of the Meru (in the Muladhara *cakra*, 2.10; 5.106) is the sun; at the top (in the Sahasrara *cakra*, 2.6; 5.103, 147) is the moon. Enclosed within the spinal column is the principal channel of the psychic body. It is called the *sushumna*, and is equated with the Sarasvati River. Within the *sushumna* is an innermost hollow called the Brahmarandhra (the hole of Brahma), and it is up this that the *kundalini* (described below), when awakened, proceeds. On the left side of the Meru is the channel named *ida*. It is equated with the Ganges River, and it corresponds to the lunar principle. On the right side is the *pingala* channel. It is equated with the Yamuna River, and it corresponds to the solar principle. These are the three chief *nadis* or psychic channels, but there are also very many more, and all together they extend to all parts of the body (2.29–30).

Shatcakranirupana. There are also very many *cakras* or psychic centers which are associated with the body. Of these the chief are seven in number, six of them (*shatcakra*) in the body and one just above the head. These too are enumerated in the *Śiva Samhita* (5.56ff.), and they are also the chief subject of the *Shatcakranirupana* or Description of the Six Centers. The latter text is the sixth chapter of a much longer work on Tantric ritual called the *Śritattvachintamani*, written by Swami Purnanda in the period 1499–1577 C.E.[77]

As related in both the *Śiva Samhita* and the *Shatcakranirupana*, the *cakras* lie, one above the other, below, in, and above the *sushumna*, and each is pictured as a lotus, with its own number of petals, distinctive color, and presiding deity. From the bottom upwards, the seven are the following:

(1) The Muladhara (root foundation) Cakra is located at the bottom mouth of the *sushumna* channel (at the base of the spine, in the region of the sacral plexus), and is a red lotus of four petals. Brahma is here in the form of a *linga*—the Svayambhu (self-existent) *linga*—and with the *linga* is a *yoni* where the goddess Kundalini dwells. Kundalini (coiled) is the *śakti* or feminine energy, and she is visualized as a serpent wrapped around the *linga* in three and one half coils, sleeping with its tail in its own mouth (*Śiva Samhita* 5.57; *Shatcakranirupana* 10–11).

(2) The Svadishthana (pleasant) Cakra is at the base of the sexual organ (in the region of the prostatic plexus), and is a vermillion lotus with six petals. The presiding deity is Vishnu.

(3) The Manipura (gem site) Cakra is situated near the navel (in the lumbar plexus), and it has ten cloud-colored petals. The presiding deity is Rudra.

(4) The Anahata (new) Cakra is in the heart (in the cardiac plexus), and has twelve golden petals. The presiding deity is Pinaki, a form of Rudra.

(5) The Viśuddha (pure) Cakra is in the throat (in the laryngeal plexus), and it has sixteen petals of smoky purple hue. The presiding deity is Sadaśiva (the everlasting Śiva).

(6) The Ajna (understanding) Cakra is situated between the two eyebrows, and it has two white petals resembling the shape of a third eye. The presiding deity is Śiva in his form as Mahakala (great time) or as Maheśvara (great lord). At this point, in the upper course of the channels, the *ida* is also equated with the Varana River, and the *pingala* also with the Asi River, and the space between them is equated with Varanasi, the sacred city of Śiva (*Śiva Samhita* 5.100, 104–105). Just above, at the upper mouth of the Brahmarandhra, all three "rivers" (*ida, pingala,* and *sushumna,* i.e., Ganges, Yamuna, and Sarasvati) meet in a triple confluence called the *triveni* (triple braid). Whoever bathes (mentally) at this sacred junction certainly obtains salvation (*Śiva Samhita* 5.131–134).

(7) The Sahasrara (*sahasra*, thousand) Cakra is above the upper end of the *sushumna* channel and outside the body (apparently just above the crown of the head, something like a halo or emanation), and is a white lotus of a thousand petals, with its head turned downwards (*Shatcakranirupana* 40). The Sahasrara is also named Mount Kailasa, and that is where the great lord Śiva dwells (*Śiva Samhita* 5.151–152).

As to the method by which to gain emancipation, the *Śiva Samhita* teaches *yoga,* with special emphasis on *pranayama.* The *prana* is the vital energy of the cosmos and is manifest in the human body in the breath of life; therefore, regulation of breathing is a way by which to control the flow of this energy. As a beginning (3.20ff.) the practitioner sits in the lotus posture (*padmasana*, cross-legged with right foot on left thigh and left foot on right thigh, 3.88), closes the right nostril and breathes in through the left (the *ida* channel), holds the breath as long as possible, afterward breathes out through the right nostril, then reverses the procedure. This rhythmical respiration with longer and longer periods of breath-retention (called *kumbhaka*) concentrates the pranic energy more and more and sends it down the channels, where at last it awakens the sleeping Kundalini. The hitherto coiled and dormant energy of the goddess, now aroused, ascends in fiery power through the several psychic centers (a process which is called *cakrabheda*, piercing the *cakras*), releases on its way various wonderful manifestations, and at last reaches the highest level (*Siva Samhita* 4.13, 53). There in the Sahasrara Cakra the mystic union of the cosmic energy which is Kundalini with the cosmic consciousness which is Śiva takes place and precious nectar pours down; thus the individual person within whom this transpires has a direct experience of transcendent reality (*Shatcakranirupana* 51): "In her subtle state, lustrous like lightning and fine like the lotus fiber, she [the Devi Kundalini] goes to the gleaming flame-like Śiva, the supreme bliss, and of a sudden produces the bliss of liberation."[78]

Kularnava Tantra. The *Kularnava Tantra,* a work of probably the twelfth century C.E., opens (Chap. 1) with a question by Devi, the Mother, to Śiva, her eternal spouse, as to how all the creatures involved in the ceaseless round of birth, suffering, and death, can find release.[79] To this Śiva replies that liberation cannot be obtained by ritualism or asceticism, but only by knowledge of the divine truth which is within oneself.

This truth is called Kuladharma (Chap. 2), or the doctrine of *kaula (kula)*, and its adherents are Kaulas or Kaulikas (words and names of uncertain derivation). Śiva has extracted this truth by churning the ocean of the Vedas and Agamas, and it must be communicated by a qualified *guru*. Of all the paths which are available, e.g., the Vedic path of ritual and works *(karma)*, the Vaishnava path of devotion to a deity *(bhakti)*—the Kulamarga or Kaula path is the highest, the most secret, and the most preeminent. It is most preeminent because it is based upon the truth of both Śiva (cosmic consciousness) and Śakti (cosmic energy). In it there is a place for both *yoga* (union with the divine) and *bhoga* (enjoyment of the manifestations of the divine), and it gives both *sukha* (pleasure) and *moksha* or *mukti* (liberation). In it even what is called sin and evil is turned into a force for good, and the very means of fall become the means of rising. Other paths call for travail, struggle, and strenuous study, but it is not so here where the result is direct and swift.

On the other hand, the Kaula path is more difficult and dangerous than to walk on the sharp edge of a sword, and it is only for the mature person whose mind is pure and who has controlled his senses. In this respect there are three classes of persons, namely, (1) the *paśu*, who is still bound by the bonds of existence *(paśa)*, (2) the *vira* (hero), who has the inner strength to participate properly in Tantric rites, and (3) the *divya* (godly), who best understands the inner meanings of Tantric experience.

Because the Kuladharma is based on the truth of both Śiva and Śakti, it naturally involves the worship of the Devi. In this worship *(puja)* five ingredients are employed (Chap. 4), and these are called the five Ms *(panchamakaras)* because their names all begin with the letter M, namely, *madya* (wine), *mamsa* (meat), *matsya* (fish), *mudra* (seal or mark, here represented by a cereal cake), *maithuna* (sexual union, cf. *mithuna,* paired). The different classes of persons may use these "ingredients" differently. For the *pasu* substitutions are suggested, e.g., coconut water instead of wine, garlic instead of meat, and joining of particular flowers in dedication instead of *maithuna*. For the *vira*, engaged in the *cakrapuja* (circle worship) with his *śakti* on his left side (thus probably giving rise to the designation of the "left-hand" path or *vamamarga*, in which the woman *[vama]* is included), the meaning is literal, but what is important is the spirit in which things are used, and it is when the ingredients are consecrated and offered with devotion that inner bliss is experienced. For the *divya* in the "right-hand" path *(dakshinamarga)*, the meaning may be entirely symbolic, and the "woman," for example, "is none other than the inner Śakti that is lying asleep in the ordinary animal man and is awake in the Kaulika and in him will rise to union with the lord who waits above—anything other is only animal behavior."[80]

Since this transcendent union is an inward experience within the microcosm of the body, it is not necessary to repair to external temples or make pilgrimage to distant sacred places, and Śiva says (Chap. 9): "I dwell not in Kailas nor in Meru nor in Mandara; I dwell where dwell the knowers of Kula."[81]

Tantrasara. The *Tantrasara* or Essence of Tantra is a compendium of Tantric doctrine by an author of unknown date named Krishnananda, who quotes from various earlier works including the *Kularnava Tantra*. The characteristics of a good *guru* and of a good disciple are described. Only Tantric rites, it is said, are effective in the present age, and the use of *mantras, yantras, mandalas,* and *mudras* is explained. Especially notable are hymns to the Devi, under her names, e.g., Bhairavi, Bhubanesvari, Kali, Lakshmi, Mahishamardini, Annapurna, and Sarasvati.[82]

A hymn to Bhairavi (the feminine form of a name of Śiva) reflects the ascent of the goddess through the psychic centers to the union with Śiva:

> I worship in my heart the Devi whose body is moist with nectar,
> Beauteous as the splendor of lightning,
> Who, going from her abode to that of Śiva,
> Opens the lotuses on the beautiful way. . . .[83]

A hymn to Bhubaneśvari (lady lord of the world) sees ascent to the point of human incarnation as the time of greatest opportunity for liberation, but notes that the opportunity is wasted if one fails to worship the goddess and thus falls again:

> O Mother of the worlds!
> Those who have reached that birth amongst men
> Which is so difficult to attain,
> And in that birth their full faculties,
> Yet nevertheless do not worship thee,
> Such, though having ascended to the top of the stairs,
> Nevertheless fall down again.[84]

Nila Tantra. The goddess Tara is an object of devotion in the *Tantrasara* and likewise in the *Nila Tantra*. In the latter source a hymn to Tara begins:

> O Mother, Devi Nilasarasvati Tara,
> Refuge with thee I crave.
> Giver of prosperity and wealth art thou
> To those who worship thee. . . .

Then, in accordance with the view of the male as passive and the female as active, Tara is pictured as standing on the prostrate Śaiva.

> ... Standing on Śiva,
> Thy right foot upon his breast and left upon his thigh,
> Ever art thou, with smiling, lotus-like face.
> Thy three eyes are, as it were, full-blown lotuses.
> In thy hands thou holdest a knife, a skull, a lotus, and a sword.

Further, the goddess is described as the giver of all *siddhis* (accomplishments) and in particular, as "the presiding Devi of speech," she bestows the power to write both verse and prose. She is also the giver of both pleasure *(sukha)* and liberation *(moksha),* and she is both saluted and supplicated:

> Ocean of kindness and compassion art thou.
> I pray thee of thy mercy shower upon me the nectar of prosperity.[85]

Mahanirvana Tantra. The *Mahanirvana Tantra* is a relatively late work (probably eighteenth century C.E.), but recapitulates many far earlier materials such as have been noticed in the Tantric works already cited.[86] The book opens with a description of Mount Kailasa as a most beautiful mountain, its breezes laden with the fragrances of every season. This idyllic place is the abode of Śiva, who is the lord of the universe and the lord of *yogis*. He is described as seated there in meditation, naked, garnished with ashes, his hair matted, wearing a wreath of serpents and bearing human skulls, with three eyes, and with the trident as his symbol. Parvati is there with Śiva, and the balance of the book is occupied with the questions which Parvati asks and the teachings which Śiva, in reply, enunciates. These teachings have to do, at the outset, with the nature of the supreme Brahman, and then with many matters of duty, ritual, and worship.

In the course of the book there is a hymn to Devi as Kali (Chap. 7),[87] in which the goddess is praised under one hundred of her names, all beginning with the letter "K," Kali, e.g., Kalyani (she who bestows peace and happiness), Kalamata (mother of time), Kripapara (whose mercy is without limit), Kaulikapriyakarini (benefactress of the Kaulikas), Kanchanachalakaumudi (she who is like a moonbeam on the mountain of gold), Kalakantakaghatini (destructress of the fear of death).

Finally Śiva declares to Parvati that this Tantra which he has set forth is the quintessence of all Agamas and Tantras, and is the way to full liberation *(mahanirvana).* The person who has understood it does not need to visit sacred shrines, nor read the Vedas, Puranas, and other scriptures. "As thou art the energy of Brahma and most beloved unto me," Śiva says to Parvati, "so is this Tantra."

> This Tantra is identical with all religions and the secondless expedient for acquiring the knowledge of Brahma. . . . He, who is blinded with ignorance, stupid, and fettered with actions, will be released from it by reading this *Mahanirvana Tantra*. O great goddess, by reading, hearing, adoring, and worshiping this great Tantra one attains to emancipation.[88]

8

MONUMENTS OF HINDUISM IN INDIA

SYMBOLS AND IMAGES OF THE GODS

The deities of Later Hinduism are some whose images and symbols are probably identifiable already in the Harappan civilization (above, Chap. 1), others who are named and often vividly described in the Vedas (above, Chap. 3), and others who appear for the first time in the post-Vedic period (above, Chap. 7).

As to images and symbols of the deities, an image of a god may be a mental concept or a visible representation, i.e., an icon, while a symbol is a sign, either conceptualized or visible, associated in some way with the reality in question.

In the language of the *Rig Veda* there are picturesque, anthropomorphic descriptions of many of the deities (e.g., Ushas the dawn is "like a youthful maiden," 7.77.1; Surya the sun drives across the sky in his chariot, 1.50.8), and in at least one passage (3.4.5) there may be allusion to concrete images of the gods. The hymn at the point just indicated has to do with the ancient *soma* sacrifice, and at the outset Agni is invoked as personified in each log of fuel which is placed on the sacrificial fire; then the seven priests of the sacrifice are described as coming to the offering through "the divine doors," the ornamentation of which is with figures "having the form of men *(nripesas),*" probably therefore anthropomorphic images of the gods.[1]

Colorful descriptions of spiritual realities also appear in the Upanishads. The *Iśa Upanishad* (16) speaks of the "fairest form" of the Supreme Being; the *Mundaka Upanishad* (3.1.3) describes the Creator as being of the color of gold; and the *Chandogya Upanishad* (1.6.6–7) says that the golden Person who is seen within the sun has a golden beard and golden hair; all is golden to the very tips of his nails, and his eyes are like a blue lotus flower. In his commentary on the *Brahma Sutra* (1.1.21) Ramanuja cites the foregoing passage from the *Chandogya Upanishad* and then goes on to explain:

> The highest Brahman, whose nature is fundamentally antagonistic to all evil and essentially composed of infinite knowledge and bliss—whereby it differs from all other souls—possesses an infinite number of qualities of unimaginable excellence, and, analogously, a divine form suitable to its nature and intentions, i.e., adorned with infinite, supremely excellent and wonderful qualities—splendor, beauty, fragrance, tenderness, loveliness, youthfulness, and so on. And in order to gratify his devotees he individualizes that form so as to render it suitable to their apprehension—he who is a boundless ocean as it were of compassion, kindness, and lordly power, whom no shadow of evil may touch—he who is the highest Self, the highest Brahman, the supreme Soul.[2]

According to analysis in Later Hinduism, therefore, meditation may be directed toward the supreme, attributeless, formless Being (*nirguna* Brahman), or toward the manifested Brahman (*saguna* Brahman) who has properties and qualities, or toward any of the many and various gods *(devas)* or their incarnations *(avatars)* or consorts *(saktis)*, or toward *pratikas*, which are symbols or images, and thus *pratikopasana* or the worship of symbols and images may be an aid in moving toward the higher levels of meditation.

Symbols

On the level of symbols, since the ultimate Reality dwells in everything, anything and everything may be seen as a symbol of divinity and therefore worthy of worshipful attention. On this account, the *Yajnavalkya Upanishad* (7) says, a wise man bows before a man of low birth or a horse or a cow. The *Vishnu Purana* (3.17.14–34) names Vishnu as the supreme spirit, the cause of causes, who has neither color, nor extension, nor bulk, nor any describable qualities, whose essence is only appreciable by holy sages, but at the same time says that the substance of Vishnu is the whole of this universe, and his primeval form is the object of perception, heaven, animals, men, and gods. "You are earth, water, fire, air, and space. . . . All, from Brahma to a blade of grass, is your body, visible and invisible, diversified by place and time. . . . You are Indra, the Sun, Rudra . . . and even ourselves. You are the *yakshas* . . . brute animals . . . the spirit which is diversified in the vegetable world. . . . We bow to you."[3] Accordingly an aphorism of Patanjali in his *Yoga Sutras* (1.39) authorizes "meditation as per liking," and the commentary of Vyasa explains that this means "meditation on anything that appeals to one as good."[4]

Specific and widely used symbols of the divine include *mandalas* and *mantras*. A *mandala* (circle), or in Tantrism a *yantra* (instrument), is a symbolical diagram, usually geometrical, floral, or figured in design, with each god or goddess having its own such diagram, which its worshiper may build up mentally or look at in objective form.[5] Each god or goddess also has its own *mantra*, which here amounts to a "body of sound" of the deity, and may be heard internally or uttered aloud.

Images

As for images of the deities, these are considered to be of eight kinds, purely mental, painted, or made of stone, wood, metal, clay, sand, or precious stones (*Bhagavata Purana* 11.27.12).[6]

As an example of a purely mental image, the *Bhagavata Purana* (2.2.8) tells of people who fix their minds through meditation on the Supreme Being, who resides within the body in the region of the heart in a form only as large as a thumb (a comparison also found in *Katha Upanishad* 6.17; *Śvetāśvatara Upanishad* 3.13), and who is seen with four hands carrying respectively a lotus *(padma)*, a discus *(cakra)*, a conchshell *(śankha)*, and a mace *(gada)*, with garments yellowish like saffron, ornaments made of gold set with jewels, and a glowing headdress and earrings.[7] This description corresponds, of course, with actual idols of Vishnu, as will be noted below.

As rendered in gross matter the image of a deity is a "materialization" *(murti)*. As well as in a mental image, so also in an actual icon the attributes and powers of the deity may be represented by the number of heads or hands, the auspicious marks on the body, the dress and ornaments, the objects held in the hands, the mount or vehicle *(vahana)*, usually a bird or animal, the bodily position *(angika* and *bhanga)*, the stance or seat *(asana)*, the hand pose *(hasta)* or gesture *(mudra)*, and the companion or companions, especially the consort *(śakti)*. Such iconographical details are of course found also in Jainism and Buddhism as well as in Hinduism.[8]

The actual image of a deity provides a concrete form on which the mind may be concentrated in the endeavor to grasp the principle which is beyond form. In more advanced stages meditation may be directed toward the *yantra* or *mantra* expressing the nature of the deity more abstractly, and finally it may be possible to reflect in entire abstraction on the attributeless Brahman—but along the way images are helps. Thus the *Jabala-darśana Upanishad* (4.59) says of the disciplined man: "The *yogi* perceives the Giver-of-Peace (i.e., Śiva) in his own heart, not in images. Images are meant to meet the need of the unrealized."[9] In the *Bhagavad Gita* (7.21, 23), where Krishna is the supreme deity, Krishna says to Arjuna that whatever form of the divine a worshiper wishes to worship with faith, he himself (Krishna) will approve and will make the worshiper's faith steadfast; however, the one who worships a lesser god will go to that god, whereas the one who worships Krishna will come to him.[10] The *Brahma Sutra* teaches that "image worship is the first; doing *japa* [chanting *mantras*] is the middle; meditation or mental worship is superior; reflection on one's own true nature is the highest of all";[11] and Śankara in his *Commentary on the Brahma Sutra* (1.1.24) explains that Brahman may be connected with a multiplicity of limited abodes and worshiped in these, but with results of only limited benefit, whereas it is the worship of the highest Brahman, "free from all connection with distinguishing attributes," which leads to final release.[12]

Early Literary References. A possible reference in the *Rig Veda* to actual images of the gods has been noted above, and at least in the Epics, the *Laws of Manu,* and some of the Sutras (circa 500–300 B.C.E.), the existence of such images is taken for granted. In the *Mahabharata* there is a long section (3.80–153)[13] on pilgrimage to various sacred spots *(tirtha,* a ford across a stream, a bathing place) and it is said that at Dharmaprastha, for example, *dharma* is always present and by approaching it one may obtain a reward (3.82.87); while at the highly esteemed ford Iyeshthila, for another example, one may set eyes on the resplendent Viśveśvara (universal deity, a title of Śiva) and Devi (goddess, the *śakti* of Śiva), and thus may attain to the world of Mitra and Varuna (3.82.115–116); accordingly at both *tirthas* the references are probably to actual images of the deities.

In the *Laws of Manu* in the rules for a *snataka* (a *brahmana* who has completed his studentship), he is directed to pass an idol keeping it on his right hand (4.39), not to step on the shadow of images of the gods (4.130), and to go to visit the images on Parvan, i.e., the new and full moon days (4.153); and in the description of legal procedures it is stipulated that evidence shall be given in the presence of images of the gods (8.87).[14]

In the *Shankhayana-Grihya Sutra* (4.19.5) there is possible mention of the images of the *nakshatras* (the constellations). In the *Paraskara-Grihya Sutra* in the formulas for the blessing of a new house there is mention of the seats and shrines for the images of the gods (3.49); in regulations for animal sacrifices there is reference to the sending of a messenger to carry an offering to a god installed at a distant sacred place (3.11.10); and in instructions with respect to driving in a chariot it is said that if one is going toward images of gods one should descend from the chariot before reaching them (3.14.8). In the *Grihya Sutra of Apastamba* (7.20.1ff) we hear of offerings of water and boiled rice to the images of Iśana (a name of Śiva as "ruler" of the northeast direction), Midhushi (bountiful goddess), and Jayanta (victorious, a son of Indra).[15]

When we come to the encyclopedic work of Varahamihira (505–587 C.E.) called the *Brihat Samhita* we find sections on both temples (56.1–31) and images (58.1–58), in which their proportions and details are described; and the same is true in the *Manasara* (building summary), a work of unknown authorship on architecture and related subjects, probably dating around 500–700 C.E., in which again there are sections on temples and houses (11–34) and on images (51–70, including 55 on Jaina images, and 56 on Buddhist images). Finally the medieval *Silpa-Sastras* give the most authoritative specifications on these matters. The rules that are thus set forth must represent the artistic canons which were developed over a long period of time, but they may be understood as only providing the framework within which the artist was to operate, and thus they bear somewhat the same relation to the finished works of art that the rules of grammar may have to a completed literary composition; thus the character and the vision of the artist are considered of the utmost importance. Speaking of the artist as a *silpin*, one of the *Silpa-Sastras* says: "The *silpin* should understand the *Atharva Veda*, the thirty-two *Silpa-Sastras*, and the Vedic *mantras* by which the deities are invoked. He should be one who wears a sacred thread, a necklace of holy beads, and a ring of Kusa grass on his finger; delighting in the worship of God, faithful to his wife, avoiding strange women, piously acquiring a knowledge of the various sciences, such a one is, indeed, a craftsman."[16]

Yakshas. As for actual extant images of supernatural beings, the earliest which have been found are probably to be recognized as statues of *yakshas* and (feminine) *yakshis* or *yakshinis*. While these beings are only among the demigods, in the *Bhagavad Gita* (10.23) the supreme lord who is identifiable with everything is, among other identifications, equated with Kubera, the king of the *yakshas*, therefore these elemental spirits are also possible objects of worship *(bhakti)*. As visualized, they were evidently often thought of as impressive and attractive in appearance, for in the *Mahabharata* (3.40.30; 3.52.16; 3.249.1–2),[17] for example, an unusually strong or handsome man is said to look like a *yaksha*, and an unknown woman of exquisite loveliness is asked if she is a *yakshi*. Also at some of the sacred pilgrimage fords *(tirthas)* there were evidently images of these beings, for example, an image of a world-famous *yakshi* at the Gate of Kurukshetra near Munjavata, where a pilgrim, by attending on her, might attain to blissful worlds, and an image of a *yakshini* at Rajagriha, where a pure man, by tasting of the daily offering to her, might by her favor be absolved from sin (3.81.19; 3.82.90).[18]

The oldest known Indian stone sculpture in the round is (according to the most probable interpretation) a *yaksha* figure found at Parkham (14 miles [23 km.] south of Mathura) and now in the Archaeological Museum at Mathura (Fig. 8.1). The statue is 8 feet 8 inches (2.6 m.) high including the pedestal. The figure is standing, with the left knee slightly bent; the arms are missing. A *dhoti* is secured by

8.1 Yaksha from Parkham, in the Archaeological Museum, Mathura

a flat girdle, with a knot in front, another girdle is around the chest, which is also decorated with a large necklace, and large earrings are worn. When found the image was worshiped by the Parkham villagers, who called it *devata* (deity). An inscription on the base states that it was "made by Bhadapugarin . . . Gomitaka the pupil of Kunika." On the grounds of the inscription an alternate identification supposes that the figure represents Kunika Ajataśatru of the Śaiśunaga dynasty, but there is no proof that this is the Kunika mentioned, and it remains probable that this is a *yaksha* and, in view of the corpulence of the figure, possibly even Kubera, the god of wealth and the king of the *yakshas*. A date in the Maurya period in the third or early second century B.C.E. is considered probable. Artistically the statue is of archaic, massive, and forceful appearance.[19]

Akin to the *yakshi (yakshini)* in later art are other beautiful feminine figures, the *apsaras* (nymph), *madanikai* (divine damsel), *salabhanjika* (tree spirit), *surasundari* (beautiful divinity), *vrikshaka* (dryad), and other female dancers and musicians.

Brahma. The image of Brahma is usually that of a man with four heads facing the four quarters, and these are considered symbolic of the four Vedas, the four *yugas* (world ages), and the four *varnas* (castes). Brahma also usually has four arms, and may hold in his hands the four Vedas or other accessories such as a scepter, a drinking vessel, or his bow called Parivita. He is shown either standing or seated, perhaps on the lotus that springs from the navel of Vishnu, or on his own vehicle *(vahana),* which is the milk-white Hamsa, a mythical bird usually identified as either a swan or a goose. When seated, Brahma is often in the *yogasana* or the *lalitasana* posture and, since these are positions of meditation or of royal ease, it is often considered correct that his eyes should be closed.

In a pink sandstone ceiling slab from the hall *(mandapa)* of the Huchchappayya Gudi temple at Aihole (second quarter of the seventh century C.E.), now in the Prince of Wales Museum of Western India, Bombay, Brahma is shown with three faces and four hands (Fig. 8.2). He sits in the *lalitasana* on a lotus seat *(padma pitha),* and wears a collar and an antelope skin across his chest. Starting in the usual way of enumeration from the lower right and going upward around the image, the hands hold a rosary *(akshamala),* a sacrificial ladle *(śruva),* and a water flask *(kamandalu),* while the lower left hand is in the attitude of giving boons *(varadamudra).* The vehicle *(vahana)* and bird symbol of Brahma, the swan or goose *(hamsa),* is at his right knee. Three male figures with offerings are in the foreground, and above on either side two celestial *rishis* emerge from the clouds to pay homage.[20]

8.2 Brahma from Aihole, in the Prince of Wales Museum of Western India, Bombay

Vishnu. Vishnu is represented variously as standing, sitting, or reclining. He usually has four arms and hands, although sometimes only two, or again even as many as eight. With four hands, he usually holds (1) a spiral conch shell *(śankha),* which can symbolize the evolution of the universe and, with its sound, suggest the primeval sound from which creation developed; (2) a discus or wheel *(cakra),* which can stand for the revolution of the universe and of the seasons; (3) a lotus *(padma),* which can represent the unfolding of the universe from the ocean of creation, as the flower unfolds from the water out of which it grows; and (4) a mace *(gada),* which can indicate power, including the power of knowledge and the power of time; or otherwise one hand may be held in the *abhaya mudra,* expressive of reassurance. In the full iconography of Vishnu, his twenty-four main forms are distinguished by the different arrangements of his attributes, i.e., the conch, discus, lotus, and mace, in his several hands. For example, in his form as Keśava (the long-haired one), Vishnu holds the lotus in his front right hand, the conch in his back right hand, the discus in his back left hand, and the mace in his front left hand. When Vishnu is awake and the universe is in process, the vehicle upon which he often stands, sits, or rides is the mythical half bird, half man, named Garuda. When Vishnu is asleep and the next round of creation is awaited, he reclines upon the serpent Śesha (remainder), also called Ananta (endless), who floats upon the waters.[21]

In an image from the Gatashrama Temple, Mathura (tenth century C.E.), in the Archaeological Museum at Mathura (Fig. 8.3), Vishnu is seated as a *yogi* on a lotus throne *(in padmasana)* and in the position of meditation *(dhyana mudra),* with the two lower hands folded upon his lap, while the two upper hands hold the mace and the discus. In this position the image is much like that of the Buddha in meditation, but is clearly distinguished as Vishnu by the four arms and the distinctive attributes of the mace and discus. In this form the figure is called Yogeśvara Vishnu or Yoganarayana. In the present sculpture there is a group of miniature figures beneath the lotus seat of Vishnu: in the center a seated cross-legged female figure with hands joined in adoration; on either side of this figure two *nagas;* and at either end a kneeling figure, probably the two donors of the work. On either side of the lotus throne are two larger standing figures, one female, the other male, and they also hold attributes of Vishnu, the lotus, conch, and wheel, while one holds a cobra. Above these figures, on either side, are rampant *śardulas* standing on elephants, above which are *makara* heads on which female musicians are standing. The *śardula,* often translated as tiger, is a mythological animal, a sort of lion-griffin (leogryph), resembling a beaked or horned lion. The *makara* is also a mythological creature, a sea monster, usually with a crocodilian or serpentine body, an elephantine or other head, and perhaps yet another animal, bird, or fish features, apparently symbolizing both the fearsome and the creative aspects of the waters. At the top of the present sculpture are also three chapels in which are seated figures of the *trimurti,* Vishnu in the center, Brahma at his right, and Śiva at his left. On either side of the highest and central chapel are flying and garland-carrying celestials.[22]

In a ceiling slab from the Huchchappayya Gudi temple at Aihole (second quarter of the seventh century C.E.), in the Bombay Museum (Fig. 8.4), Vishnu reclines with crossed legs upon the serpent Śesha or Ananta, the coils of the serpent providing a bed, and the serpent's seven heads forming a halo behind the crowned head of the god. Vishnu has four arms, and the hands are without attributes. The front right hand supports his head; the other hands rest upon or reach toward his body or the serpent. In the foreground to the left are the discus and the mace, while

8.3 Vishnu from Mathura, in the Archaeological Museum, Mathura

beneath the serpent bed are two goddesses (Bhudevi and Sridevi) and the winged Garuda is in the right corner with hands folded. At the top are the conch shell and two broken figures of the *asuras* Madhu and Kaitabha holding clubs. So Vishnu rests upon the world serpent (remainder or endless) in the period between the dissolution of the universe and its new creation. In this form the figure is known as Vishnu Anantaśayana or Śeshaśayi.[23]

Another example of the same theme is an image from Dohad (eleventh century C.E.), also in the Bombay Museum, in which Vishnu rests upon his back on the coils of Śesha, and supports his head with his upper right hand, while the seven hoods of the serpent rise behind his head. Vishnu's upper left hand holds the discus, but the lower hands and the right foot are damaged. In this case Brahma is seated on a lotus which springs from Vishnu's navel, and Lakshmi, the consort of Vishnu, is seated at the feet of Vishnu, but her head is broken away. Beneath the

8.4   Vishnu on Śesha, from Aihole, in the Prince of Wales Museum of Western India, Bombay

serpent bed are nine seated *nagas*, with folded hands. At the top is a longer row of female figures with garlands and musicians. Below them, at the viewer's right, are some warriors engaged in battle, signifying the fight of Vishnu with the *asuras* Madhu and Kaitabha. The story to which allusion is here made is that these two demons concealed themselves in the ear of Vishnu, intending to destroy Brahma as he reclined on the lotus from Vishnu's navel, but Vishnu slew them and from their fat fashioned the earth.[24]

In a marble Vishnu sculpture from Gujarat (eleventh century C.E.), in the Bombay Museum (Fig. 8.5), three heads are combined. The middle is the human head of Vishnu. The face is expressive of peace; a richly decorated crown *(kirita)* is worn, and earrings, and the ear lobes are elongated. The head to his right is that of Vishnu in his incarnation as a man-lion (Narasimha); the head to the left is that of Vishnu in his incarnation as a boar (Varaha). The name of this threefold figure is Vaikuntha Caturmurti.[25]

Śiva. Although the more common representation of Śiva is the *linga* (or *lingam*, literally "sign," the stylized emblem of the phallus, signifying creative power, and often placed in the *yoni*, the female emblem signifying universal energy), the god is also represented in a number of anthropomorphic forms. In the form of Dakshinamurti, Śiva is the teacher of *yoga*, and he sits in the pose of a *yogi*; the name is explained from the fact that he was seated facing south *(dakshina)* when he taught the *rishis*. As Nataraja (lord of the dance) Śiva is the great master of the art of dancing, and the image of his dance signifies his rhythmic activity as the source of all movement within the cosmos. As Gangadharamurti Śiva received the Ganges in his matted hair and let it descend gently to earth when, as a result of the tremendous austerities of the sage Bhagiratha, the heavenly river was first brought

8.5 Vishnu and His Man-lion and Boar Incarnations, in the Prince of Wales Museum of Western India, Bombay

down to earth and washed the ashes of the 60,000 sons of King Sagar, so that they might be purified and go to heaven. In a number of terrific aspects Śiva is known for having destroyed particularly malevolent beings, e.g., he is Gajahamurti because he killed an *asura* in the form of an elephant; Kalarimurti because he destroyed Kala (time), the god of death; and Kamantakamurti because he burned to death Kama, the god of love, who came to interrupt his austerities. Especially fearsome is the form of Śiva as Bhairava, who is so called because he protects the universe *(bharana)* and because he is terrifying *(bhishana)*. Śiva is also known as Kalabhairava for even Kala, the god of death, is afraid of him; Amarddaka because he destroys evil persons *(marddana)*; and Papabhakshana because he swallows up the sins of his devotees *(bhaktas)*. In other aspects Śiva is also recognized as pacific and, as such, he is often shown together with his *śakti* (Uma, Parvati, or another), because the presence of the *devi* is conducive to such a turn of his mind. The pair with the goddess on the left side of the god is known as the Umasahitamurti. Finally, as Maheśamurti Śiva is the fully manifested supreme deity, who is the cause of the creation, protection, and destruction of the universe. In a full representation of this form Śiva should have five heads, corresponding to his fivefold nature but, of these, the faces of only four should be visible. The face of Śiva is usually shown with three eyes, the central one in the forehead being the eye of higher perception, and his hair is ordinarily matted. He usually has four arms, he may wear a garland of skulls, and snakes may surround his body. The trident *(triśula)* is his symbol, and can stand for his three functions as creator, preserver, and destroyer. The vehicle of Śiva is the bull, symbolic of creative power, and Śiva's bull is named Nandi (glad) or Nandikeśvara (lord of gladness).

Nataraja. As Nataraja, the lord of the dance, Śiva is said in the *Śaivagamas* to have danced in 108 different modes, and all 108 poses are carved in high relief in small size, with accompanying Sanskrit inscriptions, on the panels of the eastern gateway of the Nataraja temple at Chidambaram (150 miles [240 km.] south of Madras). Of the dances of Śiva one of the most famous, called the Nadanta dance, is described as follows in the *Suprabhedagama*. In the forest of Taragam on the slopes of Mount Meru Śiva was attacked by heretical *rishis* who, by means of incantations, directed against him a tiger, a snake, and a dwarf demon called Apasmarapurusha or Muyalaka. Śiva killed the tiger and used its skin for a shawl, wrapped the serpent around his neck like a garland, and trod the demon underfoot. Then in the golden hall of Chidambaram or Tillai, the center of the universe, he danced his dance in the presence of the gods and the *rishis,* the latter thereupon becoming his devotees. Accordingly, the *Suprabhedagama* indicates, the figure of Śiva should have three eyes, four arms, snakes on the crown of matted hair *(jatamukuta),* a tiger-skin garment, a necklace *(hara),* an ornament on the arm *(keyura),* a sacred thread *(yajnopavita),* and other items. The *Amśumadabhedagama* gives similar details and also specifies that the front left hand of the image should be held across the front of the body in the *dandahasta* or the *gajahasta* pose, and the back left hand should carry fire *(agni).* The front right hand should be held in the *abhaya* pose of reassurance, and the back right hand should carry a drum *(damaru).* The right leg should be slightly bent, and the foot should be placed upon the back of the dwarf demon Apasmarapurusha, while the left leg should be lifted up and turned toward and across the right leg. Other texts explain the cosmic significance of the dance, and elucidate the symbolisms of the image. As the dancer, Śiva is like the heat latent in firewood, for he diffuses his power in mind and matter and makes them dance in their turn. His dance represents his five activities of creation, preservation, destruction, veiling, and giving release. Creation arises from the drum, protection proceeds from the hand of hope, destruction proceeds from the fire, the foot held aloft gives release, and the fourth hand points to this lifted foot as the refuge of the soul. So the purpose of the dance is to release all beings from the snare of illusion, and the place of the dance—Chidambaram, the center of the universe—is within the heart.[26]

As seen in many typical representations, e.g., a Chola bronze of the twelfth century C.E. in the National Museum of India, New Delhi (Fig. 8.6), the image is supported on a lotus pedestal and surrounded by an encircling arch of glory *(tiruvaśi),* fringed with flame, which is the fiery circle of the cosmos. So vigorous is the dance itself that five locks *(jatas)* of the god's matted hair are whirling out on either side, and among them are flowers and the figure of Ganga.[27]

In a ceiling slab from the Huchchappayya Gudi temple at Aihole (second quarter of the seventh century C.E.), in the Bombay Museum (Fig. 8.7), Śiva is shown in pacific aspect together with his consort, Uma or Parvati, and the scene is known as Umamaheśvaramurti. Śiva is four-armed, and seated in the *lalitasana* pose of royal ease. Uma/Parvati is seated at his left, and Śiva holds her with his lower left hand. With his raised upper left hand he touches a *linga* in the background; in his raised upper right hand he holds a trident *(triśula),* and in his lower right hand he holds a serpent. Śiva wears a high coil of matted hair *(jatamukuta),* necklaces, armbands, bracelets, a sacred thread *(yajnopavita)* of three strands, an abdominal belt *(udarabandha),* and a tiger skin. At his right, behind, is the bull Nandi in crouching position. Three lesser attendant deities *(ganas)* are at the bottom. The standing figures at either side are identified as Ganeśa (left) and Kumara (right), both sons of Śiva and Parvati. Above on either side are a flying *gandharva* and a *siddha* ("accomplished" ascetic).[28]

8.6 Śiva as Nataraja, in the National Museum of India, New Delhi

8.7 Śiva with Parvati, from Aihole, in the Prince of Wales Museum of Western India, Bombay

Bhairava. In his most terrifying aspect Śiva is known as Bhairava, and he is represented in this form in a black stone statue from Karnataka (twelfth century C.E.), in the Bombay Museum (Fig. 8.8). The figure is nude, save for a garland of skulls, necklaces, earrings, armlets, bracelets, and anklets, and a cobra is coiled around the head. The deity stands in the *tribhanga* pose, with the body bent one way from feet to hips, a second way from hips to shoulders, and yet a third way from shoulders to head. In his lower right hand he holds a sword, in his upper right hand a trident *(triśula)*, in his upper left hand a drum *(damaru)*, and in his lower left hand a bowl made of a human skull *(kapala)*. In the foreground at the bottom are minor attendant deities *(ganas)* and a dog. Surrounding the figure is a gateway *torana)*, decorated with seated figures and with a grotesque *makara* head at the top *(kirtimukha)*.29

Devi. Devi, the supreme goddess, who is the all-pervading energy *(śakti)* of the universe, is manifest in many forms, and three of the chief of these are Sarasvati consort of Brahma, Lakshmi consort of Vishnu, and Parvati consort of Śiva.

8.8 Bhairava from Karnataka, in the Prince of Wales Museum of Western India, Bombay

Parvati. Parvati, the lovely daughter of the snowy mountain, has already been seen with Śiva (Fig. 8.7), where she is represented as a normal (i.e., two-armed) beautiful woman. When she stands alone she may be a two-armed figure, holding a trident and mirror in her two hands; or, as a four-armed figure, she may exhibit the gestures of reassurance *(abhaya)* and boon bestowing *(varada)* with two hands and with two hold a trident and a chisel *(tanka)*, or may hold a rosary *(akshamala)*, images of Śiva and Gaṇeśa, and a water vessel *(kamandalu)*.[30]

Lakshmi. Lakshmi or Śri, the daughter of ocean and goddess of beauty, good fortune, and knowledge, may be represented as a normal beautiful woman both when she is by the side of Vishnu and also when she stands alone. If she has two hands she holds a conch shell *(śankha)* and a lotus *(padma)*. She may also have more hands, and if four-handed she may hold lotus, *bilwa*-fruit (wood apple), conch, and vessel of ambrosia *(amritaghata)*; while if eight-handed she may hold bow, mace, arrow, lotus, wheel, conch, wooden pestle, and goad. In reminiscence of the way in which she was washed when she first emerged from the primeval waters she is also shown with elephants emptying water on her head from pots brought by attendant celestial maidens.[31]

In a partly damaged standing stone statue from Mathura, attributed to the first century C.E., in the National Museum of India, New Delhi (Fig. 8.9), Lakshmi is

8.9 Lakshmi from Mathura, in the National Museum of India, New Delhi. Photograph from C. Sivaramamurti, *Masterpieces of Indian Sculpture in the National Museum* (New Delhi: National Museum, 1971), Pl. Va.

two-armed and wears a necklace, bracelets, and an ornamental belt below the waist. On her upper arm there is a flat ornament *(keyura)* with a peacock motif, which suggests joy and prosperity, as does the smile upon her face.[32]

Sarasvati. Sarasvati, the personification of the famous river and the goddess of learning, knowledge, science, art, and music, is often represented as a beautiful woman sitting on a lotus seat in the relaxed *lalitasana* posture with one leg hanging down, and playing on a lute-like stringed instrument *(vina)*. Her usual vehicle *(vahana)* is the swan *(hamsa)*, although according to some the vehicle should be the peacock. Riding upon the swan or the peacock, Sarasvati often holds a lute *(vina)* in her hands. As a seated or a standing figure, if she has two hands she may hold the lute and a water vessel *(kamandalu)*; if she is four-handed she may hold a rosary *(akshamala)*, a lotus, a book, and a lute, or rosary, book, lute, and water vessel; or may show yet other combinations of objects and hand poses. If she has eight hands she may hold bow, mace, noose, lute, wheel, conch, wooden pestle, and goad; if she

8.10 Sarasvati from Karnataka, in the Prince of Wales Museum of Western India, Bombay

is ten-handed she may carry wheel, conch, skull-cap, noose, battle-axe, vessel of ambrosia, Veda, rosary, *vidya* (emblem of knowledge), and lotus.[33]

In a damaged stone sculpture from Gadag in the Deccan, attributed to the eleventh century C.E., in the Bombay Museum, Sarasvati is a four-armed figure, seated in a simple cross-legged position *(ardhapadmasana)*, and wearing a conical crown *(kiritamukuta)*, necklaces, armlets, and bracelets. While the upper hands and the objects they held are lost in the damage the figure has suffered, the lower right hand still holds a rosary *(akshamala)* and the lower left hand holds a manuscript. In another stone sculpture from Karnataka, of the twelfth century C.E., in the Bombay Museum (Fig. 8.10), Sarasvati is seated in the same cross-legged position on a lotus pedestal. She wears an ornamented conical crown *(kirita)*, earrings, jeweled necklaces, armlets, bracelets, and anklets. Her lower right hand holds a rosary of beads *(akshamala)*, her upper hands hold a goad and a stringed instrument *(vina)*, but her lower left hand is broken off. On either side of her lotus pedestal is a small standing female attendant. The main figure is framed in an ornamental gateway *(torana)*, with a *makara* head at the top, and blowing out on each side a floral scroll.[34]

Vidyadharas. In addition to the greater gods and goddesses there are many lesser deities and attendant figures, and of these there are also many images. On a slab from Gwalior (fifth century C.E.), for example, in the National Museum of India, New Delhi (Fig. 8.11), there are two *vidyadharas*. These are "knowledge-holding" flying celestials, and they sweep splendidly across the sky, the female carried upon the legs of the male.[35]

8.11 Vidyadharas from Gwalior, in the National Museum of India, New Delhi

TEMPLES

Characteristics of the Temple

Although the presence of the divine and the experience of release *(moksha)* are finally to be realized within the heart, external places both natural and artificial are recognizable as special dwelling places of the divine, and therefore as places in which it is helpful to be present on the way to salvation.

A sacred center of pilgrimage may be a river, a mountain, a city, or any spot with some special connection with religious belief, e.g., the sites of the *jyotirlingas* of Śiva, or the locations where the fragments of the body of Sati fell. The terms by which a pilgrimage place are designated are *pitha* or *pitha-sthana* (seat place) and *tirtha*, the latter work signifying a bathing place or a ford across a stream and, by extension, a place of crossing over into release.[36] As for a temple, it is called variously a *prasada* (seat or platform of god), a *devagriham* (house of god), a *devalaya* (residence of god), and also a *vimana* (well measured, well proportioned), and a *mandira* (gladdening).[37]

The ancient residences of the gods were typically in caves and on mountains, and even as a structure the temple may be understood on its horizontal level as like a cave which the worshiper penetrates in order to approach the most holy place, and in its vertical dimension as like a mountain which suggests the ascent to enlightenment and deliverance.[38]

In its elaborated form the Hindu temple may include some or all of the following elements. The central shrine is a small, square, usually dark chamber, and it is known as the *garbhagriha* (womb chamber). The stone statue or emblem of the main deity of the temple is in this innermost cell, and behind or beside this chamber there may be a second chamber to house the consort of the deity. Above the central shrine rises the main tower of the temple, and it is called the *śikhara* (summit) and has a *stupi* (finial) on top. The word *vimana* (well measured, well proportioned) is also applied to the tower, but is used too to designate both the central shrine and the tower above it, or even the entire temple. The door of the *garbhagriha* opens almost always to the east, and into another rectangular chamber, which is called the *antarala* or vestibule. This in turn opens into a pillared hall called the *mandapa*, which is where worshipers gather. Entrance to this hall is through a smaller pillared porch known as the *ardha-mandapa* or half-*mandapa*. If there is a transept on either side of the central hall the whole is called a *maha-mandapa*. An ambulatory passageway around the sanctuary is the *pradakshina-patha* (processional path). Subsidiary buildings are the *nat mandir* or hall of dancing, for the female temple dancers; the *bhog mandir* or hall of offerings; and shrines for associated lesser deities. Large temples may be surrounded by an enclosing wall, and here there may be additional cells facing the temple. Furthermore the temple is ordinarily provided both within and without with such a wealth of carvings, showing the life of the gods and perhaps of people as well, that the whole structure becomes in effect one vast sculpture.

While the foregoing description is generally applicable to temples throughout India, there are differentiations of architectural style in different regions. It has already been noted that the literature which includes the *Śilpa-Śastras* gives specifications for temples as well as images, and the part which deals with the science of building *(vastu)* is known more particularly as the *Vastu-Śastras*. In these texts the terms *nagara*, *vesara*, and *dravida* distinguish three styles of architecture which are respectively quadrangular, round, and hexagonal or octagonal in shape.[39] The three terms are also usually understood as being descriptive of the styles found in different geographical regions. The *nagara* style is found largely in the North (between the Himalaya and the Vindhya mountains), and is characterized not only by its usually rectangular shape but also especially by its lofty *śikhara* (here the name of the entire tower) over the shrine, constructed with a convex curve as it rises. The *vesara* style is found in the Central region (between the Vindhya mountains and the Kistna River), and is a mixed style, combining with a nearly circular or many-pointed star-shaped plan elements from both the North and the South. The *dravida* style is found chiefly in the South (from the Kistna River on down to Cape Cormorin). Here the entire structure from base to finial is called by the term *vimana*, and the word *śikhara* is used for only the usually octagonal dome at the summit of the temple tower, and not for the entire tower. The South India temple is also often distinguished by its *gopura* or *gopuras*. The *gopura* is a very elaborate gateway or gate tower in the enclosing wall or walls of the temple, and usually rises in many richly decorated stories to a barrel vaulted roof at the top.[40] By way of distinction from the *vimana* as the entire characteristic temple of South India, the temple of North and Central India is sometimes designated by the term *prasada*.

Hindu temples are of course also distinguishable by the main deity to which they are dedicated, Vishnu or Śiva or another, and this is evident from the main image or symbol in the central sanctuary. In the case of a Śiva temple there is ordinarily a pavilion in front of the porch for Śiva's bull Nandi. If a banner flies over the temple, its color is red for Vishnu, white for Śiva.

Temples are also classifiable as cave temples, carved temples, and constructed temples, and examples of all are found throughout India.

Cave temples

Many temples in India are caves, whether natural or modified or fully excavated.[41]

Udaigiri. At Udaigiri (near Vidiśa) there is a group of some twenty Hindu caves, both Vaishnavite and Śaivite, dating from the time of the Gupta rulers (320–600 C.E.). Not far away there is a bathing and pilgrimage spot on the Betwa River (the ancient Vetravati, a tributary of the Yamuna), and Rama in exile is supposed to have bathed here and then to have visited the caves in question. In Cave 7 there is a historical inscription which mentions a visit by Candra Gupta II (circa 400 C.E.). The caves are cut into a low range of sandstone cliffs, and adorned with various sculptures inside and out.

In Cave 3 (circa fifth century C.E.), for example, there is a large standing relief figure of Vishnu. In Cave 4 (fourth century C.E.) there is a *linga* carved with the face of Śiva (Fig. 8.12), a symbolism which suggests the divine energy radiating outwards. On the outside of Cave 6 there is a large sculptured panel (circa 400 C.E.) which shows the boar incarnation (Varaha) of Vishnu (Fig. 8.13), in which he brought up from the depths of the ocean the earth goddess Prithivi or Bhudevi. Vishnu appears here as a man with the head of a boar. He stands upon the coils of the serpent Śesha, and holds up a lotus to support the feet of the earth goddess, who leans against his shoulder (Fig. 8.14).[42]

Mandapas at Mahabalipuram. Mahabalipuram (also Mamallapuram), on the coast 36 miles (58 km.) south of Madras, was an important port city of the Pallava

8.12 Śiva Linga in Cave 4 at Udaigiri

8.13 Vishnu as the Boar Varaha rescues the Earth Goddess, Sculptured Panel at Cave 6 at Udaigiri

8.14 Vishnu raises the Earth Goddess on His Shoulder, Detail of the Sculptured Panel at Cave 6, Udaigiri

kings. Here a large hill of granite about 0.6 mile (1 km.) long, 0.3 mile (0.5 km.) wide, and 98 feet (30 m.) high rises from the sand of the seashore and, together with other outcrops of rock provided place for excavations and sculptures which were initiated by the Pallava king Narasimhavarman I Mamalla "the hero" (630–668 C.E.), and continued and completed by his immediate successors Mahendravarman II (668–672) and Parameśvaravarman I (672–700).[43]

In all there are ten *mandapas,* i.e., cave-temple halls, cut back into the rock of the granite hill, about 15–20 feet (5–6 m.) in height, with pillars on their façades and panels of sculptures in their interiors. Of these the Mahishamardini Mandapa, for example, is notable for a large sculptured relief which shows the goddess Durga in her battle against the demon Mahisha, the battle from which she derived the name of Mahishasuramardini, the destroyer of the demon Mahisha. Here (Fig. 8.15) the youthful goddess rides forward upon her lion, brandishing sword, bow, and arrows in her several hands, while the buffalo-headed demon leans away, but still has a king's parasol over his head, and obviously only waits the opportunity to hurl his heavy iron club against his antagonist. Numerous lesser attendants of Durga press forward with her with their own weapons, while Mahisha's warriors, armed with swords and shields, fall back behind Mahisha. Although the battle is still fierce, it is plain that Durga will in the end be victorious. The Krishna Mandapa, for another example, is notable for a large sculptured relief of Krishna holding up the hill of Gobardhan. In line with the pastoral life of Krishna at Gobardhan and Brindaban, the central figure in the scene is that of a cow being milked, and turning her head to her calf by her side (Fig. 8.16).

8.15 Durga battles Mahisha in the Mahishamardini Cave Temple at Mahabalipuram

8.16 Milking Scene in the Krishna Cave Temple at Mahabalipuram

Ellora. Ellora (Elura) is a village in the western Deccan, 12 miles (19 km.) northwest of Aurangabad. The village is now the site of the shrine of Ghuśmeśvara, one of the twelve sacred *tirthas* or *jyotirlingas* of the Hindus, but it is probable that the original Ghuśmeśvara pilgrimage place was at the caves which are about to be described, in particular probably at the carved Śiva temple called the Kailasa.

The caves of Ellora are about 0.5 miles (0.8 km.) east of the village, and are cut into the steep west face of a rocky hill. In all there are thirty-four excavations, and they are referred to by number from south to north.[44] First, coming from the south, are twelve Buddhist caves, dating probably from the fifth to the eighth century C.E.; then seventeen Hindu excavations (including the carved-out Kailasa temple), dating probably from the sixth to the eighth century; and at the north five Jaina caves, dating probably from the eighth to the thirteenth century.

Of the principal Hindu caves, Cave 15 is called Das Avatara (Ten Avatars). It consists of an open courtyard with a small Śiva shrine in the middle; and then a two-storied cave, with sculptures relating to both Śiva and Vishnu. A major relief, for example, shows Vishnu in his man-lion (Narasimha) incarnation, in which he destroyed the demonic tyrant Hiranyaksha.[45]

Cave 21 is the Rameśvara. Here in the forecourt a platform is carved out of the rock, and Nandi rests upon it. A veranda gives access to the cave, and the massive pillars of the façade are adorned with figures of the river goddesses Ganga at the north end and Sarasvati at the south end. Inside, the main hall is 69 feet (21 m.) wide and 251 feet (76 m.) deep, and contains many sculptures. In the north chapel there is a large relief of Durga slaying the buffalo demon. In the south chapel there is a long panel with the Seven Mothers seated in a row between Ganeśa at the right end of the row (as seen by the viewer) and Śiva at the left end. On the wall to the right of this panel is a ghastly but much damaged relief of Kali and Kala, the goddess of destruction and her partner.[46] On the wall to the left of the Seven Mothers panel is a large relief of Śiva performing his dance as Nataraja in the presence of male and female spectators.

Cave 29 is the Dhumar Lena, also called Sita-ki-Nahani (Sita's Bath). The entrance is by a flight of steps, guarded by lions. The great interior hall is 148 feet (45 m.) wide and 149 feet (45.4 m.) deep, with four wings giving it the form of a cross, and its ceiling, nearly 18 feet (5.5 m.) high, is supported by twenty-six massive pillars. Among the many sculptures, the Marriage of Śiva and Parvati (Uma) is represented on the east wall of the south portico.[47] The two stand side by side, Parvati at Śiva's right, holding right hands and each with a flower in the left hand. Below, beside Śiva, is Brahma with three heads, acting as priest and kneeling at a sacrificial fire; and beside Parvati are Mena and Himalaya, the mother and father of the bride. Above are gods and goddesses, Vishnu mounted on Garuda, and others. In the west aisle of the cave the panel at the right end shows Ravana under Kailasa, a frequently represented scene, a superior example of which is in the Kailasa temple. In the back wing or recess of the Dhumar Lena, at the main focal point of the cave, is the main shrine, containing the *linga* of Śiva. Like the main shrine in the somewhat later Great Cave at Elephanta, this is a quadrangular chamber with four doors, each guarded by two gigantic gate keepers *(dvarapalas)*, each holding a flower in the right hand and attended by a female figure also holding a flower.[48]

Elephanta. The island of Gharpuri in the harbor at Bombay was called Elephanta by the Portuguese on account of an elephant-shaped rock which once stood on it but is now broken. On the island are a number of Śaivite caves and temples, dating from the time of the Rashtrakuta kings about 750 C.E., and of these the chief is the so-called Great Cave.⁴⁹ This is a subterranean hall, about 130 feet (40 m.) square, with a wide entrance from the north. In the interior are rows of colonnades and, on the right, the main *linga* shrine. Like the main shrine in the Dhumar Lena cave at Ellora, this is a square structure with doorways on each side, guarded by very large gate keepers *(dvarapalas)*. Inside are the emblems of the *yoni* and *linga*, the latter about 3 feet (1 m.) in height. Against the south wall, at the focal point of the temple, is the colossal three-faced bust of Śiva Maheśvara (great lord), an image 23 feet (7 m.) high and 19.5 feet (6 m.) across. As seen by the viewer the face at the left is masculine and the hand on that side holds a serpent; the face on the right is feminine and the hand holds a lotus; and the face in the center is again masculine (Fig. 8.17). These presumably represent three of the five forms of

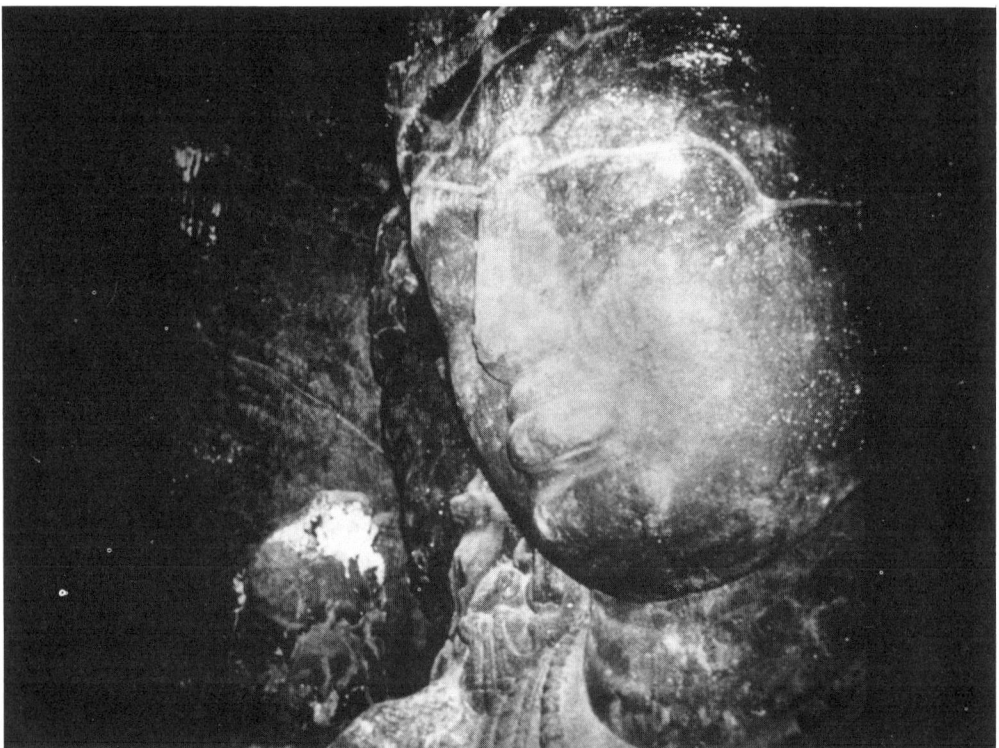

8.17 Śiva Maheśvara in the Elephanta Cave Temple, Central Face and Face at the Left (as seen by the viewer)

Siva, the left face Aghora, understood as wrathful and standing for the destructive principle in Śiva, the right face Vamadeva, seen as blissful and standing for the generative principle, and the central face Tatpurusha, seen as the supreme transcendent person. On either side of Śiva Maheśvara is also a large sculptured panel, to the left Śiva Ardhanariśvara, the androgynous lord, shown as a figure half male and half female, and to the right Śiva together with Parvati in their marriage.

Carved Temples

In some cases a monolithic mass of rock is available or is isolated by excavation, and then is carved into a whole temple.

Monuments of Hinduism in India | 183

Rathas at Mahabalipuram. At Mahabalipuram there are isolated masses of rock and great boulders which were carved into monolithic temples, work that was contemporary with the *mandapas* cut into the hillside. These monolithic shrines are known as *rathas,* using the word *ratha,* which means a chariot, especially a chariot of the gods.[50] The carving was evidently done working from the top down, and of course from the outside in, except that, in accordance with ritual requirements, the finial *(stupi)* was completed at the consecration of the temple and after the ceremonial installation of the image of worship in the interior.

There are nine of these *rathas* at Mahabalipuram, and they are locally associated with the heroes of the *Mahabharata,* and known as the Pandava Rathas, some being specifically named for some of the individuals, for example, for Arjuna, and for Draupadi the wife of all five Pandavas. Although among themselves the *rathas* exhibit many differences of plan, in general they all represent the so-called *vimana* style of South Indian temples, with the word *vimana* denoting the entire temple from base to finial.[51] The main portion encloses the image chamber *(garbhagriha),* there may be an entrance porch *(ardha-mandapa),* and the upper portion may culminate in a curved roof or may rise in successive stories in pyramidal form to an octagonal dome at the top, and here in the South it is this dome which is called the *śikhara.*

In Fig. 8.18, looking northeast, from right to left, the Bhima Ratha (20 feet [6 m.] long, 12 feet [3.7 m.] wide, 30 feet [9 m.] high) has an entrance in the middle of the western-facing long side, and is crowned with a heavy barrel-vault or wagon-top roof *(sala-śikhara),* making it on a small scale a prototype of the barrel-roofed *gopuras* so characteristic of later South Indian temples; the Arjuna Ratha rises in two upper stories to an octagonal dome; the Draupadi Ratha is a small hut-like temple (11 feet [3.4 m.] square, 20 feet [6 m.] high), dedicated to Durga whose

8.18   Pandava Rathas at Mahabalipuram

image is in a small inner rectangular cell; and the Nakula-Sahadeva Ratha (in front on the west of the Arjuna and Draupadi Rathas) has a so-called elephant back (*gaja-pristha*), while the adjoining sculpture of an elephant was carved out of the same rock as the temple. On to the south, in line with the Draupadi, Arjuna, and Bhima Rathas, the large Dharmaraja Ratha is of the same plan as the smaller Arjuna Ratha and rises in an upper tower of three stories to an octagonal dome, while inside a *linga* is the main emblem.

Not far from the *rathas* at Mahabalipuram and south of the hill in which are the *mandapas,* is another granite hill about 245 feet (75 m.) long and 50 feet (15 m.) high, and one whole side of this is covered with a very large sculptured panel (30 feet [9 m.] high and 88 feet [27 m.] long) known as the Descent of the Ganges, and probably of the same seventh century date as the *rathas* and *mandapas.* According to the underlying story, the sage Bhagiratha undertook fearful austerities in order to obtain the descent of the heavenly Ganges (the goddess Ganga) to earth to wash and purify the ashes of his ancestors, the 60,000 sons of King Sagar, to make it possible for them to go to heaven, and it was Śiva who received the descending torrent in his matted hair and modified its otherwise destructive force so that it came down from the Himalaya as a beneficent stream. In the present sculpture a vertical cleft in the center of the rock represents the course of the river, and in it are *naga* figures. On the left (as seen by the viewer) a bearded man sits in meditation beside a small temple in which is a four-armed image of Vishnu, and this is presumably Bhagiratha beginning his austerities. Above and slightly to the left a similar bearded man stands in a *yoga* posture on one foot and with uplifted arms, while at his right is the four-armed Śiva with his attendants (*ganas*), and the god extends one of his left hands in the gift-bestowing gesture (*varada mudra*), so here Bhagiratha is evidently receiving his boon. Elsewhere on the vast panel is a host of deities, human beings, and animals. Of the animals far the largest are the elephants at the viewer's right at the bottom of the composition.

Kailasa at Ellora. Of all the Indian temples which were carved directly out of the rock the largest and greatest is the Kailasa temple at Ellora, which stands as No. 16 in the numerical sequence by which the Ellora monuments are designated. Here the temple as a mountain is identified with Mount Kailasa, the peak of Mount Meru which is the sacred abode of Śiva, himself among many other titles named Kailasaśikharavasin, the resident on the top (*śikhara*) of Kailasa.

The carving of this temple is attributed to the Rashtrakuta king Krishna I (756–775 C.E.), among whose achievements is said to have been the making of a wonderful Śiva temple in "the hill Elapura." The work was done by cutting trenches into the hillside to isolate a mass of rock about 270 feet (84 m.) long, 154 feet (47 m.) wide, and from 50 feet (15 m.) to 100 feet (30 m.) high, and this mass was then carved into a complete, richly sculptured monolithic temple (Fig. 8.19).

The entrance on the west is a two-storied *gopura*. The lower level gives access to the forecourt and the passage by which it is possible to circumambulate the main temple complex. The upper level of the entrance connects by a rock bridge to the upper level of the two-storied hall of Nandi, where the lower level is only a support, and the image of the bull is in the upper level. On either side of the Nandi shrine are two square pillars (*dhwajastambhas,* literally banner staves), nearly 50 feet (15 m.) high, bearing the three-pronged emblem (*triśula*) of Śiva. A further bridge leads to the porch (*ardha-mandapa*) and to the main hall (*maha-mandapa*) of the temple. The roof of the main hall is approximately flat, and a large lotus is carved on top of it, with a finial in the center. Beyond the main hall is the *vimana* proper, which is a massive square with a pyramidal superstructure rising in four suc-

8.19 Kailasa Rock-Cut Temple at Ellora

cessively smaller stories. On the level of the first of these four stories there is a gable-like projection to the west, which is called a *sukanasika* or *sukanasa*. On the very top there is an octagonal dome *(śikhara)*, and this was also once surmounted by a separate finial. The total height of the *vimana* to the top of the dome is 96 feet (29 m.).

With its *gopura* entrance and main pyramidal tower, the Kailasa may to that extent be classified as a temple of the South Indian type (cf. the Arjuna and Dharmaraja Rathas at Mahabalipuram), yet some features such as the free-standing pillars *(dhwajastambhas)* are characteristic of the North Indian style, and the Kailasa is in fact of mixed type.[52]

Sculptures adorn not only the main temple complex but also the walls of the forecourt (Fig. 8.20) and the circumambulatory passage. Throughout there are many animals, e.g., a large freestanding elephant in the forecourt north of the Nandi shrine, eight pairs of elephants who serve as caryatids to support the main platform of the temple, lions on the roof of the *mandapa*, and bulls at the base of the octagonal *śikhara*. Behind the free-standing elephant in the northwest corner of the forecourt is the so-called Lankeśvara Cave, which is a shrine of the river goddesses. Here in three panels are three standing figures, on the left (as seen by the viewer) the river goddess Sarasvati, the one on the right the river goddess Yamuna (both leaning slightly toward the central figure), and the one in the center the river goddess Ganga. Other sculptured panels, for example, are the Abduction of Sita by Ravana, where the demon king carries Sita (her figure now damaged) away in his aerial car, while a huge bird named Jatayu (king of the vultures), being a friend of Rama, tries in vain to halt the abduction; the Battle of Durga with the Buffalo

8.20 In the Forecourt of the Kailasa Temple

Demon; and Ravana under Kailasa.[53] In the last scene Śiva and Parvati are on Mount Kailasa, while the demon king Ravana has been imprisoned within the mountain beneath, because of an impious attempt to remove it to Lanka. Now Ravana, with several heads and twenty arms, is trying to break free. The mountain shakes, and Parvati seizes Śiva's arm in fright, while her maid flees. Śiva, however, with undisturbed calm, holds everything in control beneath his foot.

The first structural temples, presumably built of wood, brick, or similar perishable materials, have disappeared, but it may also be presumed that at least to some extent they provided models for what was later executed and further developed in stone. Of stone-built and still existent temples there are many in all parts of India.

South Indian Temples

Shore Temple at Mahabalipuram. As its usual designation indicates, this temple is on the edge of the sea at Mahabalipuram. The oldest item in the complex is an image of the sleeping Vishnu, which was cut out of a natural outcrop of rock, probably in the seventh century, contemporary with the *mandapas* and *rathas* which are not far away. On the structure itself are the titles of the Pallava king Rajasimhavarman (700–728 C.E.), third successor of Narasimhavarman I, so the temple may be dated in the first quarter of the eighth century. The material of the construction is a blackish variety of leptinite, a stone so hard that the temple has survived relatively intact, in spite of its exposed seashore location, for more than twelve centuries, although its sculptures are much eroded.

The entire complex consists of three sanctuaries, all rectangular in base. The largest is at the east, facing the sea, and it encloses the main shrine, above which rises the temple's main tower. Adjacent to this to the west is a rectangular hall *(mandapa)* without a superstructure, built over the previously existing recumbent Vishnu. Joining this hall in turn and facing to the west is the third sanctuary, also crowned by a pyramidal tower, but one much smaller than the main tower. Each of the towers rises in its stories to an octagonal dome *(sikhara)* and pot-shaped finial *(stupi)*. In all, the architecture and seaside setting of this building make it one of the most notable as well as one of the earliest of the structural Indian temples.[54]

Kancipuram. The continuation and development of the South Indian tradition is seen, for example, at Kancipuram (golden city, also Conjeeveram). Kancipuram is 60 miles (96 km.) south-southwest of Madras, and was the capital of the Pallava kings. Here Rajasimha and his son Mahendra III built the Kailasanatha temple, and in general appearance this is much like the Shore Temple at Mahabalipuram.[55] In all there are said to be a thousand temples in and around Kancipuram, and among these the Varadarajaswami is notable. This temple dates from the time of the Vijayanagar kings, who halted the Muslim inroads and dominated South India from 1336 to 1565 C.E., making their capital at Vijayanagar (city of victory), modern Hampi.

In the temples of the Vijayanagar type it is usual to have, besides the shrine of the main deity in the center, separate shrines for other deities, chief among these a shrine for the goddess who is the consort of the main deity. Pavilions and halls are also provided for special rituals, of which the chief is the symbolic celebration of the wedding of the deity with his consort, observed annually in South Indian temples. The hall for this ritual is the *kalyana mandapa,* with a throne seat on a low platform in the center for the images of the deities, which are also carried in procession in great cars with massive wooden wheels. Particularly characteristic of the Vijayanagar temples are also the veritable forests of piers and pillars utilized in their construction, and carved so fully and elaborately with animal, human, and divine figures that they amount to highly complicated statuary. Varadarajaswami, the name of the temple already mentioned, is a designation of Vishnu as the "boon-granting king *swami.*" The temple is marked by high *gopuras* at the east and west entrances. The main hall is one of the finest examples of a "marriage hall" *(kalyana mandapa)* of the deities, and contains ninety-six pillars, carved mainly with illustrations of the *avatars* of Vishnu and of incidents in the *Mahabharata* and *Ramayana.* In procession, the temple car of the deities from the Varadarajaswami temple is pulled by 600 people.[56]

Belur, Halebid, and Somnathpur. In the twelfth and thirteenth centuries C.E. under the Hoyśala kings, a notable series of three temples was constructed at Belur, Halebid, and Somnathpur in Mysore. In accordance with their geographical location, and in their basic scheme, with pyramidal towers and, at least at Belur, a high *gopura,* these edifices exhibit major features of the South Indian style of temple architecture. The stories of the towers are relatively low, however, so that the total height of the towers is not great; the roofs are of inverted bell-like shape; and the horizontal lines tend to lose their emphasis on account of the many sculptural details worked out on all the levels. In these and other respects the temples therefore represent a mixed architectural type and probably reflect traditions from Central India as well as those of South India.

The typical plan is polygonal, like a many-sided star, and the temple stands on a platform (called *jagati*) of the same shape, which provides an ambulatory. Both within and without, the temple is characteristically filled with sculptures. On the exterior walls, around which the ambulatory runs, the sculptures are arranged in parallel horizontal bands. The subjects of these are usually arranged in a specific order: in the first and lowest band, elephants, presumably for stability; in the second, the mythical lions called *śardulas;* above that, horsemen, floral patterns, musicians, *makaras* (here shown as composite monsters with crocodile head, elephant body, peacock tail, and lion feet), *hamsas* (swans or geese), and so forth, while usually placed at eye level are scenes from the Epics. Figures of the deities and their attendants are, of course, also prominent. Likewise the capitals of the pillars both outside and inside the temples are often decorated with bracket figures (*madanikas*), female figures in the *tribhanga* pose.

This great elaboration of sculptural work in the temples was facilitated by the use in construction of a kind of steatite, a stone, abundant in the Mysore country, which is soft when quarried and suitable for the execution of fine work, but is hard after exposure for some time to sun and air. Many of the temple sculptures are signed by their artists, among them, Dasoja, Jakanacarya, Kannara, and Malitamma.

The traditional founder of the Hoyśala dynasty was Śala, a Jaina who, according to legend, in spite of his Jaina beliefs killed a tiger to save the life of an ascetic, and was blessed by the sage and commissioned to found a line of kings. Śala made his capital at Dorasamudra, the site of which is now marked by the village of Halebid (old capital), and he also established two religious centers, one at Belur (10 miles [16 km.] west of Halebid) on the right bank of the Yagachi River in the Hassan district of Mysore, and the other at Somnathpur (25 miles [40 km.] east-northeast of Mysore City).

Cennakeśava Temple at Belur. It was under King Vishnuvardhana, who came to the throne around 1050 C.E., that the Hoyśalas attained great prominence, and it was he who founded the Cennakeśava temple at Belur. An inscription in the temple says that Vishnuvardhana built the temple in the year corresponding to 1117 C.E. to commemorate his important victory over the rival Colas. Another tradition connects the foundation of the temple with the conversion of the king from Jainism to Vaishnavism.

The Belur temple is dedicated to Vishnu as Cennakeśava, Keśava (the long-haired one) being the first of the twenty-four main forms in which the god is worshiped. The temple (Fig. 8.21) is enclosed within a walled courtyard (440 × 360 feet [134 × 110 m.]), which is entered on the east side through a *gopura*. The central building is of star-shaped plan, is 178 feet (54 m.) long and 156 feet (47.5 m.) wide, and is raised on a platform about 3 feet (1 m.) high. The main hall (*mandapa,* here called *navaranga*) has entrances from the east, north, and south, and is filled with many intricately carved pillars. The central ceiling of the hall is a sort of octagonal hollow dome, with its ascending rings of stone becoming smaller as they go upward, all intricately carved. In the central shrine is an elegant image of Keśava, about 6 feet (1.8 m.) high, standing on a pedestal of half that height. Any tower or superstructure which may once have risen above is now lost, so the main temple remains a single, low, flat-roofed *vimana*.

Both within and without there are abundant sculptures. Unique to this temple are thirty-eight (out of an original forty) bracket figures (*madanikas*) positioned slantwise on the exterior pillars of the main hall and under the overhanging eave,

8.21 Cennakeśava Temple and Gopura at Belur

while four more similar figures adorn the four central pillars within the main hall. These are presumably *apsarases,* celestial nymphs or divine damsels of the gods. Some are musicians, some are dancers (Fig. 8.22); one looks at herself in a convex metal mirror (Fig. 8.23).[57]

8.22 Dancing Lady, Bracket Figure in the Cennakeśava Temple, Belur

8.23 Lady with Mirror, Bracket Figure in the Cennakeśava Temple, Belur

Hoyśaleśvara Temple at Halebid. At Halebid the Hoyśaleśvara (lord of the Hoyśalas) temple was begun by King Viranarasimhadeva in 1235 C.E. In 1310 and again in 1326 the city was plundered by Muslim invaders, and the temple may have been damaged and not completed. Some of the upper sculptural friezes remain unfinished and, like the Cennakeśava temple at Belur, the temple is low, flat-roofed, and lacks any superstructure.

In plan the Hoyśaleśvara is a double temple, with two almost identical *vimanas,* both dedicated to Śiva.[58] Each structure is about 112×100 feet (34×30.4 m.) in size, and the two are joined by their adjacent transepts, while each half has a Nandi pavilion in front for the bull of Śiva. Like the other Hoyśala temples, this one is also built on a low platform, and this provides a broad circumambulatory. The exterior exhibits numerous projections in accordance with the star-shaped plan of the structure.

To be viewed during circumambulation of the temple are continuous parallel

8.24   Frieze of Śardulas, Hoyśaleśvara Temple at Halebid

horizontal bands of sculptures. In their successive levels, these show elephants (1,465 of them in the first frieze), *śardulas* (Fig. 8.24), horsemen, floral patterns, musicians (Fig. 8.25, with an artist's uncompleted sketch), *makaras* (Fig. 8.26), *hamsas* (Fig. 8.27), and the like. Included also are scenes from the *Mahabharata* and the *Ramayana*, e.g., Rama in an exploit of shooting an arrow through seven palm trees, with some of his monkey-people friends present (Fig. 8.28); and Rama (in the horse-drawn chariot at the right, assisted by Hanuman who goes in front) in battle with Ravana (in the donkey-drawn chariot at the left) (Fig. 8.29). Higher above are many panels of figure sculptures, in which are seen Indra on his elephant, the dancing Sarasvati, and a veritable pantheon of deities. The four doorways of the temple are also intricately carved, with lace-like *makara-torana* lintels at the top. Inside, there are many closely spaced, highly polished pillars, only a few of which still retain their original bracket figures *(madanikas)* at their capitals. Other pieces of sculpture are preserved in an adjacent outdoor collection, e.g., a panel with six of the Seven Mothers *(saptamatrikas)*, and a figure of Vishakanya, the poison lady, with a lizard and a scorpion beside her, and presumably herself adept in the science of venoms *(vishavidya)* (Fig. 8.30).

Keśava Temple at Somnathpur. At Somnathpur the Keśava temple (Fig. 8.31) was built in 1268 C.E. by Somanatha, an officer of the Hoyśala king Narasimha III. Like the other Hoyśala temples, it is constructed on a star-shaped plan and raised on a low platform (about 3 feet [1 m.] high), which provides an ambulatory. The temple occupies the middle of a large rectangular enclosure (215 × 177 feet [65.5 × 54 m.]), in the walls of which are sixty-four niches containing statues. The

8.25 Frieze of Musicians, Hoyśaleśvara Temple, Halebid

8.26 Frieze of Makaras, Hoyśaleśvara Temple, Halebid

8.27 Frieze of Hamsas, Hoyśaleśvara Temple, Halebid

8.28 Rama shooting His Arrow through Seven Palm Trees, Hoyśaleśvara Temple, Halebid

8.29 Rama in Battle with Ravana, Hoyśaleśvara Temple, Halebid

8.30 Vishakanya, Hoyśaleśvara Temple Outdoor Museum, Halebid

8.31   Keśava Temple at Somnathpur

main structure is a triple temple, with three *vimanas* of equal size, facing north, east, and south, respectively, and all opening into a common main pillared hall *(mandapa)* in the center. In this case the three identical pyramidal towers of the three shrines were completed and are intact, making a total height of the temple of 30 feet (9 m.), including the base. All three shrines are dedicated to Vishnu in different forms, the central shrine to him as Keśava (long haired), that on the north to him as Janardhana (reward giver), and that on the south to him as Gopala (cowherd, i.e., Krishna).

As in the other Hoyśala temples, the indented exterior of the walls is filled with friezes and panels of sculptures. Shown are elephants and horsemen, mythical lions and swans (*śardulas* and *hamsas*), a dancing lion which was the symbolic animal of the Hoyśala kings, and figures of gods and goddesses, e.g., Camunda (Mahishamardini) as killer of the buffalo demon Mahishasura, a sculpture signed by the artist Kannara (Fig. 8.32).[59] In the interior the main hall is filled with pillars and ceiled with domes of concentric diminishing circles, with pendants like banana flowers hanging from the center, while the shrines contain images of Vishnu, and other deities.

Camunda Temple at Mysore City. Mahisha, the fierce *asura* who was finally overcome by Durga/Camunda as the destroyer of demons, is supposed to have had his kingdom in South India, and is honored as the founder of Mysore State and Mysore City, the name being derived from his name, Mahishasura—Mahisur—Maisur—Mysore. Above Mysore City 2 miles (3 km.) to the southeast is an isolated peak (3,489 feet [1,063 m.]) called the Camunda Hill, ascended both by a road and by a path of 1,000 steps. Two thirds of the way up the hill is a colossal image of Nandi, the bull of Śiva. The figure, dating from the twelfth century C.E., is 16 feet (5 m.) in height, sculptured from one piece of white granite and heavily ornamented in the Hoyśala style, now black from the oil which has been poured over it

8.32 Camunda, Victor over Mahishasura, Keśava Temple, Somnathpur

in homage (Fig. 8.33).⁶⁰ On the top of the hill is the temple of Camunda, Śiva's consort (also Parvati, Durga, Mahishasuramardini). The temple dates from the fourteenth century, and its compound is entered through a lofty South Indian *gopura* of the seventeenth century (Fig. 8.34).

North India

Khajuraho. Of the structural temples of North Indian style, characterized as they are especially by a lofty convex curvilinear tower *(śikhara)* over the central shrine, there is a notable group at Khajuraho, in the Chhatarpur district in Madhya Pradesh. This entire central part of North India was ruled from around 800 to 1202 C.E. by the Candella kings. Although the dynasty claimed descent from an early progenitor, the sage Candrateya, born of the moon god, the first historical name is that of Nannuka, also called Candravarman, who around 800 established

8.33 Nandi Bull above Mysore City

8.34 Camunda Temple Gopura, above Mysore City

his capital at a supposedly very ancient site near a lake, and named the place Mahoba (a present town bears the same name, 36 miles [58 km.] north of Khajuraho). The more important successors of Candravarman include Yaśovarman (circa 950), Dhanga (954–1002), Ganda (1002–1018), Vidhyadhara (1025–1050), Kirtavarman (1070–1098), and Madanavarman (1129–1163), the last of whom did so much to beautify the lake on which the capital was situated that the lake was renamed Madana Sagar after him, as it is still called. Finally in 1202 the Muslim conqueror Qutb-ud-din Aibak plundered Mahoba, and the Candellas were reduced to little power from then on.

It was at Khajuraho that the Candellas developed their major center of religious architecture. In all, eighty-five temples were built at this site, and about twenty remain in a good state of preservation. In date the temples probably extend over a period of two and one-half centuries, from not much later than 850 to somewhat after 1100.[61] Religiously the temples divide into three groups—devoted to Vaishnavism, Śaivism, and Jainism—and the Candella kings were probably of likewise varied religious preference, Yaśovarman being a worshiper of Vishnu, Dhanga a worshiper of Śiva, and Madanavarman a Jaina in faith.[62] Geographically the main temples are found in two large groups, twelve of the Vaishnava and Śaiva temples to the northwest, and six Jaina temples to the southeast. In spite of differences in sectarian affiliation, the main temples are much the same in architecture and sculpture. Except for some of the earliest structures in which some granite was used, the construction material is normally sandstone.

Typically the temples are not enclosed within a wall, but stand upon a high terrace platform (*jagati*), which also provides an ambulatory. Arranged and connected in a line from east to west are an entrance porch (*ardha-mandapa*), an assembly hall (*mandapa*), a vestibule (*antarala*), and the central sanctuary (*garbhagriha*). In some of the larger temples are also subsidiary shrines at the four corners of the platform, making a complex of five shrines (*panchayatana*), and in a Śiva temple there is also a pavilion for Nandi. Around the central sanctuary there is usually an ambulatory passageway, and balconies on the sides of the building admit light to this passageway and to the assembly hall. The interior of the temple has tall slender pillars with bracket figures at the capitals, and there are sculptured dome-like ceilings. The exterior walls are decorated with parallel horizontal friezes in high relief. The tower (*śikhara*) above the sanctuary rises to a relatively great height, and is crowned with a ribbed-cushion-like dome (*amalasaraka*), a similar smaller dome (*amalaka,* named after the Indian gooseberry fruit), and a pot-shaped finial. Rising over other parts of the entire temple are secondary *śikharas*, each crowned with *amalaka* and finial, and all ascending progressively toward the main tower, so that the entire profile of the temple is like a mountain range (Kailasa or Meru), soaring into the heights and leading the human spirit upward.

The sculptures of the Khajuraho temples, both in the interior and on the exterior, portray Vishnu, Śiva, and Devi in various forms (and the *tirthankaras* in the Jaina temples), together with many minor and miscellaneous deities and attendants, notably including the celestial nymphs and beautiful divinities known as *apsarases* and *surasundaris*.[63] Likewise the sculptures mirror a great many aspects of the life of the times. Social life is reflected in domestic scenes which show husband and wife, mother and child, and similar tableaux, while other scenes depict the life of ascetics. Dress, ornaments, hair styles, and cosmetics are shown with great attention to detail. In the areas of hobbies and recreations persons are seen engaged in reading, writing, painting, playing on musical instruments, dancing, playing with a ball, exercising, wrestling, hunting, and also enjoying animal pets. Both wild animals and domesticated animals and beasts of burden are shown, together with carts and chariots as means of transport. In their occupations people are seen in different walks of life, women carrying water, laborers carrying loads, masons chiseling stone, physicians feeling the pulse of the sick, surgeons operating on their patients, teachers teaching their students, and soldiers on foot or horseback or elephant, and armed with sword and shield.[64]

Many of the sculptures portray amorous couples in an attitude of physical affection *(mithuna)* or in physical union *(maithuna)*. These are capable of being understood variously, e.g., as representations of the temple courtesans called *devadasis* (servants of god);[65] as portrayals of the beauty and pleasure of love *(kama)* as one of the four aims of human life, and therefore as illustrations of the *Kama Sutra*;[66] or as symbols of *moksha* and the union of the human with the divine.[67] The teaching that the union of the man and the woman both symbolizes and actualizes the transcendent union was elaborated in Tantra and in particular in the Kaula-Kaulika cults, and there is evidence of the practice of these cults at Khajuraho under the Candellas (e.g., in the time of King Kirtavarman). At least some of the large sculptured scenes in question are so evidently ritualistic that they may be understood as pictures of Tantric practices and Tantric teachings on the union of Śiva and Śakti. In this light it might also be considered that some of the smaller scenes in lower panels (below, Figs. 37, 38) picture orgiastic practices of the sort which the *Kularnava Tantra* calls animal behavior, in contrast with the exalted and ritualistic.[68]

Matangeśvara. Of the Hindu temples at Khajuraho one of the earlier is the Matangeśvara, which stands at the south side of the western group of temples (at the left in Fig. 8.35). It is a square structure, built entirely of sandstone, with a high tower and smaller towers climbing toward it. A colossal Śiva *linga* (8 feet 4 inches

8.35 Matangeśvara and Lakshmana Temples at Khajuraho

[2.5 m.] high and 3 feet 8 inches [1.1 m.] in diameter) stands in the inner sanctuary, and is still worshiped.

Lakshmana. Of the later and truly typical Khajuraho temples the first is the Lakshmana, and it is followed, among the largest and most important examples, by the Jagadambi, Chitragupta, and Kandariya Mahadeva, the last being the finest of them all.

The Lakshmana temple was built by King Yaśovarman around 950 C.E., and stands just to the north of the Matangeśvara (at the right in Fig. 8.35). It is a Vaishnava temple of the *panchayatana* (five-shrined) type, i.e., there are four subsidiary shrines at the four corners of the main temple platform; and there is also a pavilion for the boar which represents the boar incarnation (Varaha) of Vishnu. The lintel over the main entrance is intricately carved, and Vishnu appears there and in the image in the central sanctuary *(garbhagriha)*, where he is a four-armed figure with three faces, the central face that of a man, the side ones of the boar and of the man-lion (Narasimha). Above the central shrine the main tower *(śikhara)* rises to an impressive height (Fig. 8.36).

8.36 Śikhara of the Lakshmana Temple, Khajuraho

The sides of the terrace platform of the Lakshmana temple are adorned with an elephant frieze, scenes of camels and men, soldiers mounted and on foot, and so forth. Small side panels show a variety of orgiastic scenes (Figs. 8.37, 38), which may represent group rituals of a lower sort of the Kaulas.[69] On the upper exterior walls of the temple are two bands of larger sculptures, some of these including a variety of divine figures, *mithuna* and *maithuna* couples. In a *maithuna* scene, for example (Fig. 8.39), the woman is, as often, the most active partner, and has assumed the *asana* (stance, position) which is known by the term *lata* (creeper), a word used in Tantra for a woman embracing a man as a creeper enfolds a tree. That a ritual act is portrayed is suggested not only by the *lata asana* but also by the attendants on either side, who are in autoerotic poses, with the man, perhaps a priest, carrying what appears to be a ceremonial staff. Thus, from the point of view of Tantra, this is a cosmic couple, and the creeper-like embrace of the man by the woman is the union of cosmic energy with cosmic consciousness, accompanied by the supreme bliss of liberation.[70]

Devi Jagadambi. The Devi Jagadambi temple stands to the north of the Kandariya Mahadeva, the façade of which is resembled in its own structure. Like the Lakshmana the Devi Jagadambi was originally a Vishnu temple, and built on the *panchayatana* plan with five shrines. The subsidiary shrines have disappeared, however, and the temple itself was in time believed to be a shrine of Kali as the goddess mother of the world. In the central sanctuary the image of Vishnu was replaced by a black image of Kali, but in the many sculptures of the exterior walls (Fig. 8.40) Vishnu may be seen, standing with his mace and conch and with Lakshmi as his consort. In *maithuna* scenes the *lata asana* pose is again represented in various ways, in one of which the woman grasps the topknot of her partner (Fig. 8.41).[71]

8.37 Group Erotic Scene, Lakshmana Temple, Khajuraho

8.38 Erotic Scene, Lakshmana Temple, Khajuraho

8.39 Maithuna Scene, Lakshmana Temple, Khajuraho

8.40 Three Bands of Sculptures, Devi Jagadambi Temple, Khajuraho

8.41 Maithuna Scene, Devi Jagadambi Temple, Khajuraho

8.42 Citragupta Temple, Khajuraho

Citragupta. The Citragupta temple (Fig. 8.42) is situated just to the north of the Devi Jagadambi, and is a temple of the sun god Surya, with a damaged image of Surya, once shown driving his seven-horse chariot, still standing in the central sanctuary. Exterior walls show scenes of hunting, processions, dance, and *maithuna*.[72]

Kandariya Mahadeva. The Kandariya Mahadeva temple (Fig. 8.43), which stands in the midst of the western group, is the largest, loftiest, and finest of the Khajuraho temples. It is thought that it was constructed under the Candella king Vidyadhara (1025–1050 C.E.). The dimensions are 109 feet (33 m.) in length, 60 feet (18 m.) in width, and 116 feet (35.5 m.) in height. An ascending series of eighty-five smaller towers builds up to the impressive main *śikhara*. The terrace platform *(jagati)* is the highest of any of the Khajuraho temples, and is surrounded by two friezes of elephants, horses, soldiers, hunters, acrobats, musicians, dancers, and erotic couples. In the architectural plan, all the features of a fully developed Khajuraho temple are included—*ardha-mandapa, mandapa, antarala,* and *garbhagriha*—while the ambulatory has been enclosed within the building. The temple is dedicated to Śiva, and the central sanctuary contains his *linga*. The ceilings of the interior are richly carved, and the pillars have fine capitals and female bracket figures. On the exterior walls are three bands of sculptures, filled with figures of gods and goddesses, celestial nymphs, couples in various poses, and the like. In one *maithuna* scene (Fig. 8.44), placed centrally on the south wall of the temple, the pose *(cakra asana,* wheel position) of the couple is of such difficulty, with the headstand of the man, which is surely a *yogic* posture, that the two are assisted by two female attendants who are also involved by the hands of the man, and it must be supposed that this is indeed a ritual ceremony.[73]

8.43 Kandariya Mahadeva Temple, Khajuraho

8.44 Ritual Scene, Kandariya Mahadeva Temple, Khajuraho

8.45 Tower of the Jagdish Temple, Udaipur

Later Temples

Jagdish Temple at Udaipur. Another impressive temple which, although of much later date, still preserves the lofty North Indian *śikhara*, is the Jagdish temple at Udaipur, built in 1652 C.E. It is a Vishnu temple, and is also called by the name Jagannath (world lord), which is a title of Vishnu's incarnation, Krishna. The tower rises in reduplicated series of lesser towers, the exterior walls carry many bands of statuary and other sculptural decorations, and the red banner of Vishnu flies at the top (Fig. 8.45).

Viśvanath Temple at Varanasi. The Viśvanath Temple, commonly known as the Golden Temple, stands in the heart of Varanasi, not far from the Ganges waterfront, between the Mir Ghat and the Jalsain Ghat (the Burning Ghat, its name derived from Vishnu in his manifestation as Jalsai, the sleeper on the ocean).

The temple is dedicated to Śiva as Viśvanatha or Viśveśvara, the lord of the universe, and is one of the major *linga* shrines *(jyotirlingas)* of Śiva. The older temple on the site was destroyed by Qutb-ud-din Aibak and converted into a mosque. The present structure was only erected in the eighteenth century, but is famous for its gilded domes and spires, the central tower rising as a *śikhara* to a height of 51 feet (15.5 m.).

Calcutta Temples. At Calcutta three Hindu temples are noteworthy. The city derives its name from Kalighat, a burning ghat on a branch of the Hooghly River (itself a branch of the Ganges) and the site of a temple in honor of the goddess Kali, the wife of Śiva. The spot derives sanctity from the legend that this was the place where a finger of Siva's wife (Sati) fell when her body was cut in pieces by the disk of Vishnu. The present temple is said to have been built about three centuries ago. It is the scene of the blood sacrifice of goats in honor of Kali, and a center of the annual religious festival in honor of Durga, the Durga *puja*. The temple of Kali at Dakshineśvar, on the Hooghly River north of Calcutta, is where Ramakrishna (1836–1886) was in his youth a temple priest *(pujari)*, and where he meditated on the image of Kali as the mother of the universe, and received from her, as he believed, the revelation of the limitless ocean of the spirit. The Belur Math temple (4 miles [6.5 km.] north of Howrah) (Fig. 8.46) is the home of the Ramakrishna Mission, founded by Ramakrishna's greatest disciple, Vivekananda (1863–1902).

8.46 Belur Math Temple

9

LITERATURE AND EARLY HISTORY OF JAINISM

The usual classification of the sects of ancient India divides them into two large classes, namely, Brahmana (Mahana) and Śramana (Samana), i.e., Vedic and non-Vedic. In general the Śramanas are the "ascetics" (as the word may be rendered), those who are accustomed to perform rigorous penances. In particular, five sects of Śramanas are mentioned, and their members are designated by the following terms: (1) The Nirgrantha (Niggamtha, Nigantha) is etymologically the one "without any tie, unfettered," and describes the adherent of Mahavira, or Parśva, and of the other *tirthankaras* in the order of Jainism. (2) The Śakya (Sakka) is the follower of Śakya, which is another name of the Buddha, hence refers to Buddhism. (3) The Tapasa (Tavasa) used to live in the forest and perform severe penances. (4) The Gairika (Geruya) was a mendicant (Parivrajaka, Parivvayaga) who used cloths dyed in red chalk. (5) The Ajivika (Ajiviya) is a member of the sect of naked ascetics of which Gosala was the most prominent leader. Because of their practice of going stark naked the Ajivikas were also known as Acelakas (*acelaka*, unclothed), and in this they were distinguished from the Nirgranthas, not all of whom dispensed with clothing. Of the five sects it is chiefly those of Jainism and Buddhism which continue as important religious bodies, while the Ajivikas are especially of significance in their connection with Jainism in the time of Mahavira.

Both the Jainas and the Buddhists use many of the same terms, although perhaps with varying frequency and emphasis, e.g., characteristic titles for their prophets: *arhat* (deserving respect, worthy), *buddha* (awakened, enlightened), *jina* (conqueror, victor), *kevalin* (having *kevalajnana*, i.e., total knowledge), *mukta* (freed, emancipated), *siddha* (accomplished, perfected), *tathagata* (thus come, or thus gone), and *tirthankara* (ford finder, congregation founder).

In Jainism the *tirthankaras* are a long line of twenty-four great ascetics and teachers, of whom the last and most recent in the present age of the world was Vardhamana Jnatriputra (some of the Jnatri clan), in his status as prophet of the Jainas called Mahavira (great hero). These *tirthankaras* are *jinas,* because they have conquered the enemies of human existence, such as lust and anger, and the same term may also describe other great personages who have attained a *jina's* quality.

From this word the religion of the adherents of the Jinas is commonly known as Jainism.[1]

LITERATURE

The teachings of the *tirthankaras* were handed down orally for a long time, then finally reduced to writing in the sacred books known collectively as the *Siddhanta* or the *Agama*.[2]

Kevalins and Śrutakevalins

According to Jaina tradition, Vardhamana Mahavira attained enlightenment and became a *kevalin,* a supreme omniscient, in the thirteenth year of his extreme ascetic practice, and he then taught Jaina doctrine to eleven principal disciples, who were known as *ganadharas* (heads of schools). In virtue of the instruction they received from Mahavira, the eleven *ganadharas* had the status of *śrutakevalins,* which means that they had complete knowledge of the teachings (in particular of the fourteen Puvvas). In addition three of them attained omniscience, and thus they became *kevalins* as well as *śrutakevalins* within their own respective lifetimes. These three were Mahavira's first principal disciple Gautama Indrabhuti (Goyama Imdabhui), Mahavira's fifth principal disciple Arya Sudharman (Ajja Suhamma), and Sudharman's disciple Jambusvamin (Jambu).[3]

Indrabhuti attained the experience of omniscience in the same night in which Mahavira died and, as a *kevalin,* Indrabhuti was no longer expected to be active in the administration of the affairs of the movement, but he lived on until he reached his own final emancipation in *nirvana* at the age of ninety-two. Of the other *ganadharas* nine had entered *nirvana* even before this, so of the original eleven Sudharman was left to become the first head of the ongoing Jaina community. He himself finally obtained omniscience at the age of ninety-two, and reached the ultimate liberation at the age of one hundred. Sudharman was succeeded in the headship of the church by his disciple Jambusvamin, who was also a *śrutakevalin* and who attained omniscience before he died, and became the last of the *kevalins* of the present age.

After that, the next four heads of the church, although not *kevalins,* were still *śrutakevalins,* i.e., they still had full knowledge of the sacred texts both in words and in meanings. These four were Prabhava (Pabhava), Sayambhava (Sejjambhava), Yaśobhadra (Jasabhadda), and Sambhutavijaya (Sambhuya). In the time of Sambhutavijaya two more very important persons in Jaina history enter the picture, namely, Bhadrabahu (Bhaddabahu) and Sthulabhadra (Thulabhadda). Both Sambhutavijaya and Bhadrabahu were disciples of Yaśobhadra, and both were *śrutakevalins*. Sthulabhadra, in turn, was a son of Śakatala (Sagadala), who was the minister of Mahapadma (Mahapauma) the ninth and last king of the Nanda (Namda) dynasty in Pataliputra (Padaliputta) in the kingdom of Magadha, but Sthulabhadra renounced the world, became a disciple of Sambhutavijaya, and eventually succeeded Sambhutavijaya in the headship of the church. Sthulabhadra is sometimes considered a *śrutakevalin,* but if so he was the last of the *śrutakevalins* and his own knowledge of the sacred texts was in fact already less than perfect, as will appear in what follows. As just set forth the relationships and status of the foregoing personages may be seen in Table 9.1.[4]

TABLE 9.1.
RELATIONSHIPS AND STATUS OF EARLY JAINA LEADERS

Indrabhuti, first *ganadhara*, *kevalin*, *śrutakevalin*
Sudharman, fifth and last surviving *ganadhara*, first head of the church, *kevalin*, *śrutakevalin*
Jambusvamin, disciple of Sudharman, second head of the church, last *kevalin*, *śrutakevalin*
Prabhava, disciple of Sudharman, third head of the church, *śrutakevalin*
Sayambhava, disciple of Prabhava, fourth head of the church, *śrutakevalin*
Yaśobhadra, disciple of Sayambhava, fifth head of the church, *śrutakevalin*
Sambhutavijaya, disciple of Yaśobhadra, sixth head of the church, *śrutakevalin*
Bhadrabahu, disciple of Yaśobhadra, *śrutakevalin*
Sthulabhadra, disciple of Sambhutavijaya, seventh head of the church, last and imperfect *śrutakevalin*

Bhadrabahu and Sthulabhadra

It was in the year that Candragupta (Camdautta) (322–298 B.C.E.) dethroned the last Nanda king and established his own Maurya dynasty in Pataliputra, that Sambhutavijaya died. At the same time a severe famine devastated the whole kingdom of Magadha and lasted for twelve years. Under the circumstances Bhadrabahu led a large body of Jainas to Śravanabelgola in South India, where they were able to maintain the strict rules of the order as naked, possessionless ascetics, and whither Candragupta Maurya eventually followed them. In Magadha in the north, however, many other Jainas remained under the spiritual leadership of Sthulabhadra, but became increasingly lax in discipline, even adopting the wearing of clothing in the form of white garments. Thus a division, which may have existed already in the time of Mahavira, was accentuated and led eventually to the separation of the two groups under the names of the Digambaras (sky clad) and the Śvetambaras (white clad).

Council of Pataliputra

In the same period it was recognized that the sacred texts were falling into oblivion and, in the absence of Bhadrabahu, Sthulabhadra called a council at Pataliputra to collect and edit the canonical books. Because Sthulabhadra's own knowledge of the texts was not perfect, he went off to visit Bhadrabahu in Nepala (either the country in the south where Bhadrabahu stayed during the twelve-year famine, or the modern Nepal where Bhadrabahu settled afterward) and to learn from him. Bhadrabahu, however, withheld the meaning of some of the texts and forbade teaching them, therefore the council was able to reestablish only an incomplete canon.

Council of Valabhi

Under the circumstances further attempts were made at further councils to bring the canon into better order. Such an attempt was made at Mathura under a certain Skandila Suri, probably sometime between *Vira Samvat* 827 (300 C.E.) and 840 (313 C.E.), at any rate in the early fourth century C.E., and a similar effort was made at almost the same time at Valabhi in Gujarat under Nagarjuna Suri. Finally a fourth council was held at Valabhi under the famous teacher Devarddhi, called the

Kshamaśramana. The date of this council was in *Vira Samvat* 980 (453 C.E.) (according to the followers of Skandila), or 993 (466 C.E.) (according to the followers of Nagarjuna)—at any rate not far from the middle of the fifth century C.E. At this council an attempt was made to reconcile the versions of the texts already established at Mathura and Valabhi, and the texts were written out again and codified in the form thereafter considered the standard. This is the canon of the Śvetambara Jainas, but it is largely rejected by the Digambaras as inauthentic, although they too recognize the twelve *Angas* and a few other texts of the Śvetambaras, to which they add other late works of their own.

As extant the Śvetambara canonical books are in the Prakrit dialect known as Arsha (the language of the *rishis,* the holy seers) or Ardha-Magadhi (half-Magadhi). This Ardha-Magadhi is largely the Magadhi language, but with other elements mixed in, and is supposed to have been the language in which Mahavira himself taught, because he wished to be understood not only in his homeland of Magadha but also in neighboring territories. As for actual copies of the canonical books, there are palm-leaf manuscripts at least as old as the second quarter of the twelfth century of the Vikrama Era, the era which began in 58/57 B.C.E.[5]

Śvetambara Canon

In outline the chief divisions and works recognized in the Śvetambara canon are shown in Table 9.2, and may be briefly described as follows:

TABLE 9.2.
JAINA SACRED LITERATURE (SIDDHANTA, AGAMA)

I. *Puvvas (Purvas)*
   1. *Uppaya (Utpada)*
   2. *Agganiya (Agrayaniya)*
   3. *Viriyappavaya (Viryapravada)*
   4. *Atthinatthippavaya (Astinastipravada)*
   5. *Nanappavaya (Jnanapravada)*
   6. *Saccappavaya (Satyapravada)*
   7. *Ayappavaya (Atmapravada)*
   8. *Kammappavaya (Karmapravada)*
   9. *Paccakkhanappavaya (Pratyakhyanapravada)*
   10. *Vijjanuppavaya (Vidyanupravada)*
   11. *Avamjha (Avandhya)*
   12. *Panaum (Pranayuh)*
   13. *Kiriyavisala (Kriyaviśala)*
   14. *Logavindusara (Lokabindusara)*

II. *Angas*
   1. *Ayara (Acara)*
   2. *Suyagada (Sutrakrita)*
   3. *Thana (Sthana)*
   4. *Samavaya*
   5. *Viyahapannatti (Bhagavati)*
   6. *Nayadhammakahac (Jnatadharmakathah)*
   7. *Uvasagadasao (Upasakadaśah)*
   8. *Antagadadasao (Antakrddaśah)*
   9. *Anuttarovavaiyadasao (Anuttaraupapadikadaśah)*
   10. *Panhavagaranaim (Praśnavyakaranani)*

	11. *Vivagasuyam (Vipakaśrutam)*
	12. *Ditthivaya (Drshtivada)*
III.	*Uvangas (Upangas)*
	1. *Uvavaiya (Aupapatika)*
	2. *Rayapasenaijja (Rajapraśniya)*
	3. *Jivabhigama*
	4. *Pannavana (Prajnapana)*
	5. *Suriyapannatti (Suryaprajnapti)*
	6. *Jambuddivapannatti (Jambudvipaprajnapti)*
	7. *Candapannatti (Candraprajnapti)*
	8. *Niryavali*
	9. *Kappavadamsiao (Kalpavatamsikah)*
	10. *Pupphido (Pushpikah)*
	11. *Pupphaculiao (Pushpaculikah)*
	12. *Vanhidasao (Vrsnidaśah)*
IV.	*Painnas (Prakirnas)*
	1. *Causarana (Catuhśarana)*
	2. *Aurapaccakkhana (Aturapratyakhyana)*
	3. *Bhattaparinna (Bhaktaparijna)*
	4. *Samthara (Samstara)*
	5. *Tandulaveyaliya (Tandulavaitalika)*
	6. *Candavijjhaya (Candravedhyaka)*
	7. *Devindatthava (Devendrastava)*
	8. *Ganivijja (Ganitavidya)*
	9. *Mahapaccakkhana (Mahapratyakhyana)*
	10. *Viratthava (Virastava)*
V.	*Cheyasuttas (Chedasutras)*
	1. *Nisiha (Niśitha)*
	2. *Mahanisiha (Mahanisitha)*
	3. *Vavahara (Vyavahara)*
	4. *Ayaradasao (Acaradaśah)* or *Desasuyaskhandha (Dasaśrutaskhandha), Kalpasutra* of Bhadrabahu
	5. *Brihatkappa (Brihatkalpa)*
	6. *Pancakappa (Pancakalpa)*
VI.	*Mulasuttas (Mulasutras)*
	1. *Uttarajjhayana (Uttaradhyayana)*
	2. *Avassaya (Avaśyaka)*
	3. *Dasaveyaliya (Daśavaikalika)*
	4. *Pindanijjutti (Pindaniryukti)*
VII.	Two Solitary Texts
	1. *Nandisutta (Nandisutra)*
	2. *Anyuogadarasutta (Anuyogadvarasutra)*

Puvvas (Purvas). The first division consists of fourteen *Puvvas* (Sanskrit *Purvas,* old texts), usually thought to have been taught to his *ganadharas* by Mahavira himself or, in one view, considered traceable to the first *tirthankara,* Rishabha. Bhadrabahu was supposedly the last person to know the words and meanings of these texts completely, and it was the meaning of the last four *Puvvas* which he withheld from Sthulabhadra, also forbidding Sthulabhadra to teach these texts even verbally. Thus when Bhadrabahu himself died (in *Vira Samvat* 170, 357 B.C.E.) the last four *Puvvas* were lost irretrievably, and in subsequent time all the rest of the Puvvas were also lost.[6] They are mentioned, however, in other works, making possible the following listing: (1) *Uppaya (Utpada)*. Origin of substances. (2) *Agganiya (Agrayaniya)*. Basic truths. (3) *Viriyappavaya (Viryapravada)*. Powers of substances. (4) *Atthinatthippavaya (Astinastipravada)*. Nature of substances from seven logical standpoints. (5) *Nanappavaya (Jnanapravada)*. True and false perception. (6) *Saccappavaya (Satyapravada)*. True and false speech. (7) *Ayappavaya (Atmapravada)*. Characteristics of souls. (8) *Kammappavaya (Karmapravada)*. Nature of *karma*. (9) *Paccakkhanappavaya (Pratyakhyanapravada)*. Renunciation as the means to the eradication of *karma*. (10) *Vijjanuppavaya (Vidyanupravada)*. Various sciences. (11) *Avamjha (Avandhya)*. Chief points in the lives of sixty-three great men. (12) *Panaum (Pranayuh)*. Medicine. (13) *Kiriyavisala (Kriyaviśala)*. Music, poetry, and other arts. (14) *Logavindusara (Lokabindusara)*. Ceremonies and salvation.

Angas. The second division consists of twelve *Angas* ("limbs" of the body of the religion), and these contain the oldest source material on Jainism which is still available.

(1) ***Ayara (Acara)***. The way of life of a monk. The work contains two books (*śrutaskandhas*) which are very different in style, and of these the first (*Bambhaceraim, Brahmacaryani*, rules for the holy life) may be one of the most ancient parts of the entire *Siddhanta*. In the opening statement of this first book Sudharman, as one of the first principal disciples (*ganadharas*) of Mahavira, addresses his own disciple, Jambusvamin, and tells Jambusvamin what he himself has heard from Mahavira: "O long-lived one (i.e., Jambusvamin): I [Sudharman] have heard the following discourse from the venerable (i.e., Mahavira.)"[7] Also throughout the book each "lesson" closes with the words, "Thus I say," likewise characterizing the contents as oral tradition, handed down presumably from Mahavira. Included in the material is one large section (2.15) which provides biographical information concerning Mahavira, and gives the five "great vows" (*mahavratas*) which he taught, namely, not to destroy life (*ahimsa*), not to speak untruth (*sunrita*), not to steal (*asteya*), not to engage in sexual intercourse (*brahmacarya*), and not to have property (*aparigraha*).[8]

(2) ***Suyagada (Sutrakrita)***. Instructions for monks and refutation of heretical teachings. Here also Sudharman appears to be communicating to Jambusvamin the teachings of Mahavira, and the sections of the book close with the words, "Thus I say" (1.1.1; 1.2.3),[9] so the work may be of antiquity comparable to the *Ayaranga*. In fact, Jaina commentators even suppose that a portion of the book consists of teachings given by the first *tirthankara*, Rishabha, to his sons (1.2.1).[10] In the book four creeds are named (1.12): The Kriyavada affirms that the soul exists, and is the teaching of the Jainas. The Akriyavada denies that the soul exists, and is probably a name for Buddhist doctrine. The Vinayavada teaches that release is reached through discipline. The Ajnanavada professes agnosticism.[11] Stating that "a man believes himself a hero as long as he does not behold the foe," the temptations and hardships which beset the life of a monk are set forth at length (1.3.1–3; 1.4.1–2),[12] and so also are the punishments which await the sinner in the various hells which Jainism envisions (1.5).[13]

(3) ***Thana (Sthana)***. Jaina concepts arranged by categories. *Thananga* means "the *Anga* of the categories," and refers to the main subjects which are numbered from one to ten. In the eighth section, e.g., the subject is philosophers, and eight

types of philosophers are enumerated: Egavatis or monists, theists, and monotheists; Anegavatis or pluralists; Mitavadis or extensionists; Nimittavadis or cosmogonists; Sayavatis or sensualists; Samucchedavatis or annihilationists; Nitavadis or eternalists; and Nasantiparalogavatis or materialists-hedonists.

(4) **Samavaya.** Continuation of the preceding work. The title means "group" or "aggregate," and the items are enumerated in numerically increasing groups from one up to ten to the fourteenth power ($1-10^{14}$). The work gives a table of contents of the fourteen *Puvvas,* and describes the extent and contents of all twelve of the *Angas.* Among the enumerations are lists of the twenty-four *tirthankaras,* twelve *cakravartins* (world rulers), nine *vasudevas* and nine *baladevas* (heroes) of the present "descending" world age *(avasarpini).*

(5) **Viyahapannatti,** usually called *Bhagavati* (holy). Jaina teachings in dialogues and legends. The full title means "proclamation of explanations," and refers to answers given by Mahavira to individual questions asked by his disciples, most often by Gautama Indrabhuti. We also hear about followers of Mahavira's predecessor Parśva (5.9.4; 9.32; 25.7.1), and about Mahavira's rivals, Jamali (9.3) and Gośala (15).[14]

(6) **Nayadhammakahao (Jnatadharmakathah).** Stories and parables. The title probably means "examples and religious narratives." The very numerous parables are intended to inculcate such virtues as patience, kindness, caution, perseverance, and the like. The narratives include stories about Malli, the nineteenth and only female *tirthankara* (although with the Digambaras Malli is a man), whom the Śvetambaras say was the daughter of the king of Mithila; about Draupadi (Dovai) the wife of the five Pandavas; and about Kali the goddess.

(7) **Uvasagadasao (Upasakadaśah).** Legends concerning pious laymen who became adherents of Jainism. In Jainism the term *upasaka* designates a lay adherent, i.e., a person who has accepted the teachings of Mahavira, but without renouncing the world and assuming the ascetic vows (enumerated above in the *Ayaranga*), and the title of the present work means "the ten (chapters on the duties) of the lay adherent." There are also two classes of such lay adherents, the *śravaka* who only declares his belief in the principles of Jainism, and the *śramanopasaka* who takes five "lesser vows" *(anuvratas)* and seven reinforcing vows *(śilavratas).* The book narrates the lives of ten outstanding laymen *(mahaśravakas)* of the time of Mahavira. Most of them were rich men, but by virtue of their asceticism they attained miraculous powers, finally died a voluntary death by starvation as Jaina saints, and were reborn as gods in the heaven of the faithful. The first, for example, was a wealthy householder named Ananda, who lived in the city of Vaniyagama. Mahavira came to a suburb of the city called Kollaga and there, after listening to the instruction in religion which Mahavira gave, Ananda affirmed his acceptance of the doctrine, and declared to Mahavira: "I will, indeed, in your presence . . . accept the twelvefold religious discipline of the householder, which consists of five lesser vows and the seven disciplinary vows. . . . May it please you; do not cause obstruction to me (i.e., to my taking the vows)."[15] The seventh outstanding layman, likewise, was a wealthy potter named Saddalaputta, who lived in a town called Polasapura. He had been a disciple of Gosala Makkhaliputta and the Ajivikas, but was won over by Mahavira to accept the tenets of the Niganthas (Nigranthas), Mahavira's "unfettered" followers. In both of these cases the wives also joined their husbands in the

acceptance of Jainism and the taking on for themselves too of the twelvefold law of the householder.[16]

(8) *Antagadadasao (Antakrddaśah)*. Narratives of ten ascetics who attained liberation. The title means literally "the ten (chapters) on the (pious ascetics) who have put an end to existence." In many cases only parts of the stories are preserved in the extant work, and other parts have had to be pieced together from other *Angas*. The first chapter, e.g., begins the story of Prince Goyama, and when the whole account is assembled we learn that the prince was induced by the saint Aritthanemi (Arishtanemi or Nemi) who is the twenty-second *tirthankara* and a cousin of Krishna, to take the Jaina vows. So Goyama plucked out his hair with his own hands in five handfuls, and said to Aritthanemi:

> The world is aflicker, sir, the world is aflame, sir . . . with age and death. Even as a householder when his house is on fire takes thence some treasure of small mass and great worth that is therein, and goes aside with it, thinking that this which he has put away for himself will be in far or near life to his weal, pleasure, comfort, and bliss afterward; so this my one agreeable . . . treasure of righteousness which I have put away for myself will cut short my life-wanderings.

Then Goyama besought Aritthanemi to accept him in the order, and to teach him such essentials of the religious life as monastic discipline, the begging of alms, the limitation of food, and pilgrimage. After practicing intense asceticism, Goyama finally starved himself to death in the Jaina manner, was reborn as a god in the Accue (Acyuta) *kalpa*, the twelfth celestial sphere above the earth, and was destined eventually to "become beatified, enlightened, released, extinguished, and . . . reach an end of all his sorrows in Mahavideha (a region in the center of Jambudvipa in which all *karma* may expect to be consumed)."[17]

(9) *Anuttarovavaiyadasao (Anuttaraupapadikadaśah)*. Narratives of saints who attained to the highest heavens. The title means literally "the ten [chapters] on the [pious ascetics] who sprang into being (i.e., were reborn) in the Anuttara Mansions." In Jaina cosmography the Anuttara "mansions" *(vimanas)* are very lofty celestial spheres, even higher than the twelve *kalpas* mentioned in the preceding section. The narratives are comparable to those in the *Antagadadasao*, with special emphasis on the details of the self-starvation by which the saints finally attained to the highest perfection. Mahavira is characteristically called "the ascetic" *(samana, śramana)*, and out of 14,000 ascetics who were his followers Mahavira especially praises a certain Friar Dhanna who, after his final death-month of starvation, would be reborn as a god in the mansion of Savvattha- (Sarvartha)-siddha, the fifth and highest of the Anuttara-vimanas, and thereafter pass on to be purified in the land of Mahavideha.

(10) *Panhavagaranaim (Praśnavyakaranani)*. Commandments and prohibitions. The title means "questions and explanations," but the work deals with the five evils to be avoided—not to hurt any living being, not to lie, not to steal, not to be unchaste, not to be attached to possessions—and with the five positive virtues which correspond to these.

(11) *Vivagasuyam (Vipakaśrutam)*. Legends concerning recompense for good and evil deeds. The title means "the text of the ripening (of actions)." Goyama Indabhuti (Gautama Indrabhuti) observes the present state of various

persons and Mahavira explains to him what each person did in a previous human existence to lead to this result. For example, Miyaputta, a deformed child, was previously an unjust governor named Ekkai; Umbaradatta, now suffering from a severe illness, had been Dhammantari, a doctor who prescribed a meat diet for a patient and thus caused the killing of numerous living creatures; and Subahu, a layman and a prince, had been Samuha, who was once hospitable to the pious Sudatta.[18]

(12) *Ditthivaya (Drshtivada)*. This *Anga* is no longer extant, but the title means "doctrine of the various views." According to other references the work consisted of five divisions, of which one, called *Puvvagaya (Purvagatam)*, contained the fourteen *Puvvas,* named above.

Uvangas (Upangas). The third division of the canon consists of twelve *Uvangas (Upangas)*, corresponding in number with the number of the *Angas*.

(1) *Uvavaiya (Aupapatika)*. The first part records the preaching of Mahavira to King Kunika (Ajataśatru) at Campa. Good and evil deeds, it is taught, have their outworkings in the four forms of existence, as inhabitants of hell, as animals, as human beings, and as gods. In the second part Indrabhuti questions Mahavira about rebirths, and the circumstances are discussed which lead to the "attainment of existence" *(uvavaya)* in the twelve celestial spheres of the gods. Above those spheres and above everything else, at the very top of the universe, is a spotless realm called Isipabbhara (Ishatpragbhara), into which the ultimately liberated ones (the *siddhas*) enter in the form in which they left their earthly existence, only that this form is now compacted only of soul-atoms, and in this realm and state they enjoy utter omniscience and illimitable blessedness without end.[19]

(2) *Rayapasenaijja (Rajapraśniya)*. The conversion of King Paesi by Keshi, a disciple of Pasa (Parśva). The monk argues for the existence of the soul independent of the body, the king thinks a body can be cut in pieces and no soul found, but Keshi says the king is more foolish than certain people who wished to make a fire and only chopped up the sticks.

(3) *Jivabhigama.* The world and the beings that are in it. All animate objects are classified in terms of such characteristics as their number of senses, and the universe is described in the details of its continents *(divas, dvipas),* oceans *(sagaras),* and so forth.

(4) *Pannavana (Prajnapana)*. Characteristics and dwelling places of living beings. Under "human beings" the Aryans *(ariyas, aryas)* and the barbarians *(milikkhas, mlecchas)* are mentioned with their habitations. The work is attributed to Ajja Sama (Arya Śyama), who is said to have lived 376 or 386 years after the death of Mahavira (i.e., in 151 or 141 B.C.E.), and to have been the twenty-third head of the church after Mahavira. Arya Śyama is also said by some, however, to be identical with the famous teacher Kalaka (first century B.C.E.).

(5) *Suriyapannatti (Suryaprajnapti)*. Concerning the sun and moon. (6) *Jambuddivapannatti (Jambudvipaprajnapti)*. Concerning Jambuddiva, the central continent of the universe. (7) *Candapannatti (Candraprajnapti)*. Although appearing as a separate work, the text is virtually identical with the *Suriyapannatti*.

Together these works deal with astronomy, geography, cosmology, and the divisions of time.

(8) *Niryavali*. War of ten half-brothers of King Kunika (Ajataśatru) of Campa against their grandfather King Cedaga (Cetaka) of Besali (Vaiśali). After their death the ten were reborn in various hells *(niraya)*. (9) *Kappavadamsiao (Kalpavatamsikah)*. Conversion and salvation of sons of the princes mentioned in the preceding work. These were all reborn in different heavens. (10) *Pupphido (Pushpikah)*. Pre-existence of certain deities who did reverence to Mahavira. (11) *Pupphaculiao (Pushpaculikah)*. Similar to the preceding work. (12) *Vanhidasao (Vrsnidasah)*. Conversion of princes of the Vrsni dynasty by Aritthanemi (Arishtanemi, Nemi). These five *Upangas* (8–12) are sometimes considered as one work, called after its first section the *Nirayavalisuyakkhandha*.

Painnas (Prakirnas). The fourth division of the canon is made up of ten *Painnas* or *Prakirnas*. These are "scattered pieces," which deal with many different subjects.

(1) *Causarana (Catuhśarana)*. Prayers. The work begins with mention of the six essential daily duties *(avaśyakas)* of a Jaina, namely, (a) "equanimity" *(samaiam, samayikam)* gained by desisting from all evil; (b) "glorification of the twenty-four" *(cauvisaithaa, caturvimśatistava)* tirthankaras; (c) "veneration" *(vamdana)* of the *guru* or teacher; (d) "confession" *(padikkamanam, pratikramana)*; (e) penance through certain postures of the body *(kaussagga, kayotsarga)*; and (f) "refusal" *(paccakkhanam, pratyakhyana)* of sensual pleasures. The prayers which comprise the balance of the work have to do with the "fourfold refuge" to which the title of the work refers, namely, the refuge which may be found by recourse to the saints *(arhats)*, to the perfected ones *(siddhas)*, to the living pious ones *(sadhus)*, and to the religion *(dharma)*. The author of the book is named as Virabhadra, and he is supposed to have been a pupil of Mahavira.

(2) *Aurapaccakkhana (Aturapratyakhyana)*. Rites in preparation for death. The title means "the sick one's refusal," and refers to the renunciation of all that is evil in making approach to death. A formula of confession lists sixty-three items. (3) *Bhattaparinna (Bhaktaparijna)*. Similar to the preceding text. The title means "dispensing with food." (4) *Samthara (Samstara)*. Also about matters connected with death. The title means "the pallet of straw," and refers to the deathbed of the sage. In these and yet other Jaina works of similar sort, various types of death are distinguished, and the stages arrived at by these types are indicated. The "death of the fool" *(balamarana)* is the involuntary death, from various causes, of the non-Jaina, and also the suicide of such a one. The "death of the semi-sage" is that of the lay adherent who dies after making confession, but without practicing the rite of self-starvation. The "death of the sage" is the solemn passing by means of voluntary fasting of the person who also completes confession and all vows and penances.

(5) *Tandulaveyaliya (Tandulavaitalika)*. Embryology and anatomy. (6) *Candavijjhaya (Candravedhyaka)*. Concerning teachers and pupils. (7) *Devindatthava (Devendrastava)*. Enumeration of the kings of the gods (Indras). (8) *Ganivijja (Ganitavidya)*. Astrology. (9) *Mahapaccakkhana (Mahapratyakhyana)*. Formulas of confession. (10) *Viratthava (Virastava)*. Praise of Mahavira and enumeration of his names.

Cheyasuttas (Chedasutras). The fifth division comprises six *Cheyasuttas* or *Chedasutras*. In general these works are concerned with the rules of life for the Jaina monks and nuns. (1) Nisiha (Niśitha). Duties of monks and penalties for transgressions. (2) *Mahanisiha (Mahanisītha)*. Moral transgressions, confession, and penance. (3) *Vavahara (Vyavahara)*. Instruction for monks and nuns. (4) *Ayaradasao (Acaradaśah)* or *Desasuyaskhandha (Dasaśrutaskhandha)*. Various teachings concerning the monastic life. The eighth section of this work is the *Kalpasutra*, long known as the *Kalpasutra* of Bhadrabahu, thus being attributed in its original form to Bhadrabahu, the last *śrutakevalin* who had complete knowledge of all the *Puvvas*. At the same time the book itself states that it was written in the year 980 after the *nirvana* of Mahavira (i.e., in 453 C.E.), and read publicly in the year 993 reckoned from the same point (i.e., in 466 C.E.). The public reading, it is also explained, was on the occasion of the death of the son of King Dhruvasena (probably Dhruvasena I) of Gujarat, and the king was invited to the reading in order to thereby bring him consolation.[20] The reference to the writing of the work thirteen years before the public reading could mean that the earlier date was when the book was compiled in final form at the Council of Valabhi.

In its present form the *Kalpasutra* of Bhadrabahu is divided into three sections. The first is the *Jinacariya (Jinacarita)* or "biographies of the *jinas*," which gives a lengthy account of the birth and life of Mahavira, and also brief biographies of Parśva, Arishtanemi, and Rishabha. The second section is the *Theravali (Sthaviravali)*, and it enumerates the Jaina schools (*ganas*), their branches (*śakhas*), and their heads (*ganadharas*), with the dates of the latter's deaths in years after Mahavira. This list begins with Sudharman and comes to Bhadrabahu and Sthulabhadra (as in Table 9.1 above), but also continues to Devarddhi, so could have been completed at the time of his death some time after the Council of Valabhi. If there were such later insertions it still does not necessarily invalidate the supposition of original composition by Bhadrabahu. The third section of the book is the *Samayari (Samacari)*, which gives "rules for the ascetics," in particular rules for the rainy season (*pajjusan*). From this third section the whole work is also known as *Pajjosavanakappa (Paryusanakalpa)*. (5) *Brihatkappa (Brihatkalpa)*. Rules and regulations for monks and nuns. (6) *Pancakappa (Pancakalpa)*. Similar to the preceding.

Mulasuttas (Mulasutras). The four works in this sixth division of the canon are called "root *sutras*," using a term (*mula*) which is generally employed in the sense of a "fundamental text." (1) *Uttarajjhayana (Uttaradhyayana)*. Poems, parables, dialogues, and sermons. Among the dialogues in this book there is a long conversation between Gautama Indrabhuti the first principal disciple (*ganadhara*) of Mahavira, and Keśi, a learned follower of the doctrine of Parśva. Parśva had enjoined four vows on his followers, namely *ahimsa*, not to destroy life; *sunrita*, not to lie; *asteya*, not to steal; and *aparigraha*, not to have property. To these Mahavira had added as a fifth the vow of *brahmacarya*, not to have sexual intercourse, probably already thought of as implicit in the fourth vow of Parśva but here made explicit. Parśva had also allowed the wearing of an under and an upper garment, but Mahavira had forbidden the wearing of any clothes whatsoever. It is these differences between the respective teachings about which Keśi asks Indrabhuti, and Keśi also poses certain other questions in a riddle-like form. To everything Indrabhuti answers to the satisfaction of Keśi, and Keśi accepts the law as explained by Indrabhuti, while the whole assembly which has listened to the two of them is greatly pleased. This evidently means that at this point the old church of Parśva and the new church of Mahavira were united. Later, however, there was a fresh division, namely, between the Śvetambaras and the Digambaras, in which the Śvetambaras followed the rule of Parśva in that they wore clothes while the Digambaras dispensed therewith according to the practice of Mahavira.[21] (2) *Avassaya (Avaśyaka)*. Daily duties. These are the same six "essentials" *(avaśyakas)* listed in the *Causarana*. (3) *Dasaveyaliya (Daśavaikalika)*. Rules for the ascetic life. The author of the work is named as Sejjambhava (Śayyambhava), identified as a disciple of Prabhava, who himself died in *Vira Samvat* 98 (i.e., in 429 B.C.E.). The account is that after Śayyambhava became an ascetic his eight-year-old son Manaka came to him for instruction, and the father, knowing that his son had only six more months to live, taught him the entire contents of this book within that time. (4) *Pindanijjutti (Pindaniryukti)*. The food of monks. A detailed discussion of the sort of food which may be accepted as alms *(pinda)*.

Two Solitary Texts. These two works are sometimes counted among the *Painnas*, but usually stand as independent texts either before or after the *Mulasuttas*.

(1) *Nandisutta (Nandisutra)*. Modes of perception. The title means "auspicious introduction," and the main subject is the consideration of five kinds of knowledge (with their various subdivisions), climaxing in *kevalajnana* or perfect knowledge, an unaided form of knowledge which is enjoyed in one form by a human being who is far advanced in spiritual progress (a *bhavastha*), and in another form by one who has been perfected (a *siddha*). At the beginning there is a hymn of praise to Mahavira, followed by a list of the twenty-four *tirthankaras* (as in *Samavaya*), a list of the eleven *ganadharas* of Mahavira, and a list *(Theravali)* of the twenty-seven teachers from Sudharman to Dusagani, the last being the teacher of Devarddhi. Devarddhi himself is supposed to have been the writer of the entire work.

(2) *Anyuogadarasutta (Anuyogadvarasutra)*. An encyclopedia of the most varied sciences. Both this book and the preceding one mention not only other Jaina books, but also non-Jaina works including the *Mahabharata* (called *Bharaha*) and *Ramayana*, the *Arthaśastra* of Kautilya (Kodillaya), the doctrine of Buddha *(Buddhasasana)*, one or more of the *Puranas*, and the four *Vedas*. The *Anyuogadarasutta* is supposed to have been compiled by Aryarakshita Suri, a teacher who still knew nine of the *Puvvas* and part of the tenth, and died in *Vira Samvat* 584 or 597 (i.e., in 57 or 70 C.E.).

Noncanonical Writers

In addition to canonical works the Jainas also have an extensive noncanonical literature, which includes commentaries on the canonical texts, theological and scientific compositions, stories, poetry, and drama. The language of the noncanonical works is partly Prakrit—the form that is known as Jaina Maharashtri, i.e., the language spoken in Maharashtra on the west coast of India—and partly Sanskrit.

The oldest commentaries are called *Nijjuttis (Niryuktis)* and are very concise metrical explanations, written in Jaina Maharashtri. The first of these are attributed to Bhadrabahu, who was also believed to be the author of the *Kalpasutra*. At a later date the *Nijjuttis* formed the basis for more exhaustive commentaries in Prakrit, known as *Bhashyas* and *Cunnis*, and for yet other commentaries written in Sanskrit and known as *Tikas*.

Kundakunda. The oldest theological works are by Kundakunda and Umasvati. Both of these writers are recognized by Śvetambaras and Digambaras alike, probably because at their relatively early time the divergence between the two sects was not as sharp as it became later. According to the genealogical lists of the Digambaras (called *Pattavalis* and corresponding to the *Theravalis* of the śvetambaras), Kundakunda lived in the first century C.E. Kundakunda calls himself a pupil of Bhadrabahu, but at this date this cannot be the Bhadrabahu already mentioned (who died in *Vira Samvat* 170, i.e., 357 B.C.E.), and must be a second teacher of the same name, Bhadrabahu II. Kundakunda also dedicates three of his works *(Prabhrita triya)* to a royal pupil named Śivakumara Maharaja, and the latter may probably be identified with Sivaskandavarma of the Pallava dynasty in South India. The original name of Kundakunda was Padmanandi, and the name by which he is best known was apparently derived from the place where he lived, the village of Kondakunda, now Konakondla in the Anantapur district of South India. Also in South India several inscriptions relating to later Jaina teachers state that they are of the line of Kundakunda. The chief works of Kundakunda are *Panchastikayasara* (the five cosmic constituents), *Samayasara* (the soul essence), and *Niyamsara* (the perfect law), all composed in Prakrit.[22]

Umasvati. According to the Digambaras, Umasvati—whom they call Umasvami—was a disciple of Kundakunda, and this relationship is confirmed by an inscription found at Śravanabelgola. The Digambaras also make Umasvati the successor of Kundakunda as the head of the ascetics, and some put his date as corresponding to 135–219 C.E. The Śvetambaras, however, make him a pupil of Ghoshanandi Kshamana, who was a pupil of Vachakamukhya, and they sometimes call him Umasvativachakacharya. Umasvati was born in a town called Nyagrodhika, and did his major work in Kusumapur, both places perhaps in South India (although the latter place has often been thought to be Pataliputra, the modern Patna). Umasvati is credited with many writings, of which the most famous is the *Tattvarthadhigamasutra,* composed in Sanskrit, and considered in its ten relatively short chapters a veritable compendium of Jaina doctrine. As he begins the work Umasvati writes: "Right belief, (right) knowledge, (right) conduct, these (together constitute) the path to liberation *(moksha).*"[23] These are the three gems *(ratna-traya)* of Jainism.

Siddhasena. Siddhasena is also claimed by both the Digambaras and the Śvetambaras. He is called Siddhasena Divakara, and his home was in the Karnataka region in South India. According to Śvetambara tradition, however, he went north to the capital city of Ujjayini (Ujjain) in the country of Malwa and there converted King Vikramaditya. This was in the year 470 after the *nirvana* of Mahavira or 57 B.C.E. (although the Digambaras give Siddhasena's time as 714 to 798 years after Mahavira, i.e., 187–271 C.E.). The king was presumably Vikramaditya, son of Gardabhilla, who expelled Śaka (Scythian) invaders and reestablished his father's dynasty in Ujjain, where he inaugurated the Vikrama Era in 58/57 B.C.E., and this era is still in progress among the Jainas of North India. Siddhasena was both a poet and a logician, he wrote in both Prakrit and Sanskrit, and his most famous book is a metrical work on logic called *Nyayavatara,* composed in Sanskrit.

Nemicandra. Later writers of the greatest fame are Nemicandra among the Digambaras, and Haribhadra and Hemacandra among the Śvetambaras. Nemicandra lived in South India, and was the teacher of Camundaraya. Camundaraya was the minister and general of the Ganga kings, Marasimha II (died in 974 C.E.) and Rajamalla II (974–984 C.E.), but in his later life devoted himself to religious works and erected the colossal statue of Gommata at Śravanabelgola. Nemicandra was also known as Siddhanta-Cakravartin, meaning that he was like a universal monarch in his mastery of the sacred writings. Nemicandra wrote in Prakrit *Davvasamgaha* (compendium of substances), which deals with substances both living *(jiva)* and lifeless *(ajiva);* and *Gommatasara,* in which he explains the essence *(sara)* of Jaina doctrine for the benefit of Camundaraya, the latter here being called Gommataraya because he erected the Gommata statue. The very large *Gommatasara* is in two parts, *Jivakanda* which deals with the origin and nature of souls, and *Karmakanda* which has to do with *karma* and its relationship to the soul.[24]

Haribhadra. From the references which he makes to other writers it is believed that Haribhadra lived circa 750 C.E. He was born in Chitrakuta, the modern Chitor in Central India, and was the son of a *brahmana* and instructed in Brahmanical learning. He was converted, however, by a Jaina nun named Yakini, and called himself thereafter her "spiritual son" *(dharmaputra).* Haribhadra spent most of his later life in Rajputana and Gujarat, became a prolific writer, and received the title Suri, the honorific epithet of a learned Jaina monk. His compositions were in both verse and prose, and he wrote in both Prakrit and Sanskrit, being the first to write commentaries on the canonical books in Sanskrit. His fame as a poet rests mainly upon a book called *Samaraichcha Kaha,* composed in Jaina-Maharashtri verses. In the book he tells the stories of various persons who, after experiencing *karma* in many ways, finally renounce the world and enter the order. The environment of the time is reflected in many descriptions including those of journeys, voyages at sea, life at court, legal procedures; and the Jaina ideal of life is proclaimed:

> Living beings should not be injured by the activities of mind, body, and speech. Falsehood should not be spoken. What is not given, should not be taken. Sensual pleasures should not be enjoyed. Paraphernalia should not be kept through greed. Food should not be taken at night. Forbearance should be practiced. Softness should be contemplated. Deceit should be avoided. Greed should be killed. One should wander unattached; should reside in mountains, forests, and gardens; should avoid activity, and should be free from desire.[25]

Hemacandra. Hemacandra (1088–1172 C.E.) was born in the town of Dhundhuka in the vicinity of Ahmedabad in Gujarat, and spent most of his life in the capital of Gujarat at the court of the Calukya kings Jayasimha Siddharaja (1094–1143) and his successor Kumarapala. Although both rulers were originally worshipers of Śiva, Jayasimha was interested in the philosophies of different sects, and Kumarapala was converted to Jainism (in 1159 C.E.) by Hemacandra. As a result of his conversion Kumarapala prohibited the hunting and slaughter of animals and the drinking of intoxicants in his realm, erected Jaina temples, and supported Jaina literary and scientific work. Hemacandra himself was called Kalikalasarvajna (the omniscient of the Kali age). He wrote on grammar (both Sanskrit and Prakrit) and poetry as well as on Jaina doctrine. His works on religious subjects include an exposition of asceticism named *Yogaśastra,* a long epic poem entitled *Trishashtiśalakapurushacaritra* which recounts the lives of sixty-three illustrious persons *(śalakapurusha),* and a supplement thereto called *Pariśishtaparva* (appendix section) or *Sthaviravalicaritra* (lives of the series of the Elders) on the lives of the disciples of Mahavira and the earliest teachers of the Jaina religion. The *Trishashtisalakapurushacaritra* was written (in Sanskrit) at the request of King Kumarapala between 1160 and 1172 C.E., and was described by Hemacandra as a *mahakavya* (great ornate epic). The sixty-three "illustrious persons" are the twenty-four *tirthankaras*, twelve *cakravartins* (world rulers), nine *vasudevas* (or *ardhacakrins*, of whom Krishna was the ninth), nine *baladevas* (or *balaramas*, of whom Balarama, Krishna's older brother, was the ninth), and nine *prativasudevas* (or *Vishnudvishas*, who were enemies of the nine incarnations of Vishnu). Thus along with its own teachers, Jainism incorporates in its account of world history many world rulers and heroes from Hinduism as well.[26]

JAINA COSMOGRAPHY AND CHRONOGRAPHY

Description of the Universe

As in Hinduism so also in Jainism the earth is the continent Jambudvipa, with Mount Meru in the center, and is surrounded in concentric circles by a series of seas and other continents, while below are the infernal regions and above are the celestial spheres. In the detailed Jaina view, as set forth in various Jaina works and in particular in Hemacandra's *Trishashtiśalakapurashacaritra*,[27] the three divisions of the universe are the Middle, Lower, and Upper Worlds, and there is space between the Middle World and the beginning of the Lower World, and space between the Middle World and the beginning of the Upper World.

Middle World. In the Middle World (Madhyaloka), Jambudvipa (Jambuddiva in Prakrit) has a diameter of 100,000 *yojanas* (1 yojana = approximately 5 miles [8 km.]). Mount Meru (Mandara) in the center, is a truncated cone, buried 1,000 *yojanas* in the ground at its base and rising 99,000 *yojanas* in height, with a diameter of 10,000 *yojanas* at the surface of the earth, and a diameter of 1,000 *yojanas* at the top. The entire Jambu continent is divided from east to west by six great mountain ranges, and is thereby also divided into seven zones (*varshas* or *kshetras*). The breadth and height of the mountains and the size of the zones increase from the south to the middle, then from the middle to the north decrease again. The southernmost zone is Bharatavarsha (Bharahavasa). It is bounded on the north by the Himalaya (Himavanta) mountains, and it is where the present human race lives. The central zone surrounds Mount Meru, and is called Mahavideha. It contains four subdivisions, Purvavideha (Puvvavideha) to the east of Mount Meru, Aparavideha (Avaravideha) to the west, Devakuru to the south, and Uttarakuru to the north. Finally (for just one more example of the seven zones), the northernmost zone is the Airavatavarsha (Eravayavasa), and it is exactly the same in size as the Bharata zone in the southernmost part of Jambudvipa.

Jambudvipa is surrounded by a great salt sea which is called Lavanoda (Lavana). Surrounding this sea in turn is the next and larger continent called Dhatakikhananda (Dhayaisanda) and its larger sea called Kaloda (Kaloya), while after this yet more continents and seas succeed each other in countless number, each larger than the last, until finally the Svayambhuramana (Sayambhuramana) continent and the Svayambhuramana ocean enclose the whole of the Middle World.

Lower World. In the Lower World, far below the present earth, are seven more levels, each thinner but wider than the one above it. These seven subterranean levels are named Ratnaprabha, Śarkaraprabha, Valukaprabha, Pankaprabha, Dhumaprabha, Tamahprabha, and Mahatamahprabha. In them are very many hells (*narakas* or *nirayas*), ranging in number from 3,000,000 in Ratnaprabha to five in Mahatamahprabha, and these are "the places for experiencing bad *karma*." In Ratnaprabha are also the dwellings of a first class of lesser deities known collectively as Bhavanapatis (Bhavanavasis). They comprise ten groups, including the *asuras* (demon princes), the *nagas* (serpent princes), and others, each group under two kings (Indras), one of the south and the other of the north. Likewise in a portion of Ratnaprabha and in the space between the Lower World and the Middle World, as well as in mountain-caves, forests, trees, unoccupied places, and so forth, in the human world, dwell the deities of a second class called the Vyantaras or Vanamamtaras. These comprise eight groups, including the *yakshas* (custodians of treasures), the *rakshasas* (ogres), the *kinnaras* and the *gandharvas* (the latter two, musicians), and others, each group also under two lords.

In the space just above Jambudvipa is the stellar world, and this is the realm of a third class of gods, the Jyotishkas (Jyotishas or Joisas), who are the deities of the heavenly bodies. They are of five categories, namely, the sun (Surya, Sura), the moon (Candra, Camda), the planets (Grahas, Gahas), the lunar asterisms or constellations associated with the path of the moon (Nakshatras, Nakkhattas), and the fixed stars (Taras). There are, however, not just one but two suns circling over Jambudvipa, and yet larger numbers of suns over the outer seas and other continents. Associated with each sun are also one moon, eighty-eight planets, twenty-eight constellations, and 6,697,500,000,000,000,000 stars. This stellar realm extends from 790 to 900 *yojanas* above the surface of the earth.

Upper World. Still farther above is the Upper World. Here, as in the Lower World, there is also a series of levels. Of these the first twelve are heavens called *kalpas,* rising one above the other, and their names are Saudharma, Iśana, Sanatkumara, Mahendra, Brahmaloka, Lantaka, Śukra, Sahasrara, Anata, Pranata, Arana, and Acyuta. Above these are nine heavens called Graiveyakas. They are named Sudarśana, Suprabuddha, Mancrama, Sarvabhadra, Suviśala, Sumanas, Saumanasa, Pritikara, and Aditya. Yet higher are five Anuttara heavens, called Vijaya, Vaijayanta, Jayanta, Aparajita, and Sarvarthasiddha (Savvatthasiddha) in the center. In all of these levels of the Upper World are the mansions or palaces *(vimanas)* of the fourth class of gods, the Vaimanika gods. These gods, too, have their kings (Indras) and in Brahmaloka, for example, Brahma is its lord.

In respect to these successive levels of the Upper World, rebirth may be up to and including the Saudharma heaven for monks and laymen of good character, Iśana for goddesses, Brahmaloka for wandering mendicants, the highest of the Graiveyakas for monks who have wrong belief but have observed the practices, and from Brahmaloka to Sarvarthasiddha for those who have known all the fourteen *Puvvas.*

Ishatpragbhara. Finally, at a height of twelve *yojanas* above the Sarvarthasiddha heaven is the glorious ultimate realm called Ishatpragbhara (Isipabbhara). As described in the *Aupapatika* (43) and the *Uttaradhyayana* (36.58–64), this place has the form of an outspread umbrella, forty-five *lakhs* (1 lakh = 100,000) of *yojanas* in diameter, eight *yojanas* in thickness in the middle, and tapering toward the edges until it is thinner than the wing of a fly. It is all white and gold, pure and spotless, shining and radiant, and beautiful in every aspect. One *yojana* thence is the end of the world, and in the uppermost part of that *yojana* is the dwelling place of the *siddhas*. "There at the top of the world reside the blessed perfected souls, rid of all transmigration, and arrived at the excellent state of perfection."[28]

Such is the universe—lower, middle, and upper—and all is enclosed by three atmospheres, described in respect of density as thick water, thick wind, and thin wind. Beyond these is the non-world *(aloka)*, i.e., absolutely empty space. In form the universe may be pictured as a man or woman standing with legs spread apart and hands on the hips, the lower extremities representing the subterranean regions, the waist being the earth, and the upper part of the body standing for the heavens. In total dimensions the universe is seven *rajjus* wide at the bottom, one *rajju* at the middle, five at Brahmaloka, and one at the very top (one *rajju* = the distance a god can go in six months when he goes 100,000 *yojanas* in the winking of an eye). "With a well-supported appearance," the universe "was made by no one and is supported by no one. It is self-produced and, moreover, remains in space without support. The wise man should meditate on this universe...."[29]

Cycles of Time

As in Hinduism so also in Jainism there is a conception of vast and ever recurring cycles of time, and time is pictured as a great wheel, turning ceaselessly. Although the situation may be different in different parts of the universe, in the Middle World and in the two zones of Jambudvipa called Bharatavarsha and Airavatavarsha, as the *Trishashtiśalakapurushacaritra* explains, "the twelve-spoked wheel of time is the basis of the law of time."[30] Six spokes of the wheel represent six eras in a descending cycle of time, called Avasarpini (Osappini), six more spokes represent the six eras of an ascending cycle, called Utsarpini (Ussappini). At the beginning of the descending cycle everything is in the best possible state, but as the ensuing eras follow each other there is a decay of knowledge, longevity, stature, energy, and so forth, until the worst possible state of affairs is reached. In the ascending cycle all of these things improve until the best possible state is again attained. The quality of each era in each cycle is indicated by the word *sushama (susama)* meaning a good and happy state, a state of bliss, or by the word *duhshama (dusama)* meaning a bad and unhappy state, a state of sorrow, or by some combination of the two words indicating something better or worse than the average represented by one of them alone. The duration of each division is indicated in years or larger units, since at the maximum very long periods of time are involved. Table 9.3 provides an outline of the two cycles and the twelve eras, and Table 9.4 defines the units of measurement employed in this Table and also in Table 9.5.[31]

TABLE 9.3.
JAINA CYCLES OF TIME

Avasarpini

Character of the era	*Duration of the era*
1. *sushama-sushama*, pure bliss	4 *kotikotis* of *sagaras*
2. *sushama*, bliss	3 *kotikotis* of *sagaras*
3. *sushama-duhshama*, bliss-sorrow	2 *kotikotis* of *sagaras*
4. *duhshama-sushama*, sorrow-bliss	1 *kotikoti* of *sagaras* minus 42,000 years
5. *duhshama*, sorrow	21,000 years
6. *duhshama-duhshama*, pure sorrow	21,000 years
Total duration of Avasarpini, 10 *kotikotis* of *sagaras*	

Utsarpini

1. *duhshama-duhshama*, pure sorrow — 21,000 years
2. *duhshama*, sorrow — 21,000 years
3. *duhshama-sushama*, sorrow-bliss — 1 *kotikoti* of *sagaras* minus 42,000 years
4. *sushama-duhshama*, bliss-sorrow — 2 *kotikotis* of *sagaras*
5. *sushama*, bliss — 3 *kotikotis* of *sagaras*
6. *sushama-sushama*, pure bliss — 4 *kotikotis* of *sagaras*

Total duration of Utsarpini, 10 *kotikotis* of *sagaras*

TABLE 9.4.
UNITS OF MEASUREMENT

1 *lakh* (Sanskrit, *laksha*) = 100,000
1 *krore* (Sanskrit, *koti*) = 100 *lakhs* = 10,000,000
1 *kotikoti* = 10,000,000 × 10,000,000 = 100,000,000,000,000

1 *hasta* = 18 inches (0.457 m.)
1 *dhanus* = 4 *hastas* 6 feet (1.8 m.)
1 *yojana* = 5 miles (8 km.)

1 *purva* = $8,400,000^2$ years
1 *palya* (or *palyopama*) = the length of time required to empty a receptacle one *yojana* wide and deep, which is filled with new lamb's hairs grown within seven days, when one hair is taken out every hundred years.
1 *sagara* (or *sagaropama*), "ocean of years," = 10 *krores* of *palyas* = 100,000,000 *palyas*

So in Avasarpini there are ten *kotikotis* of *sagaras*, and in Utsarpini a like number, together twenty *kotikotis* of *sagaras*, all of these "oceans of years" representing just one revolution of the great wheel of time *(kalacakra)*. The wheel turns forever at constant speed, and thus descending and ascending cycles of time follow each other in ceaseless succession throughout eternity.

ILLUSTRIOUS PERSONS

In all places, whether on this continent (Jambudvipa) or elsewhere, where the descending and ascending eras succeed each other, in the *sushama-duhshama* and *duhshama-sushama* eras, sixty-three "illustrious persons" *(śalakapurushas)* appear, namely, twenty-four *tirthankaras*, twelve *cakravartins* (world rulers), and twenty-seven heroes (nine *vasudevas*, nine *baladevas*, and nine *prativasudevas*), and it is these personages of our present world age who are the subject of Hemacandra's *Trishashtiśalakapurushacaritra*.

As far as our world (Bharata) is concerned, the present cycle of time is the descending Avasarpini age, and the first *tirthankara* (Rishabha) and his accompanying *cakravartin* (Bharata) and other associates lived in the *sushama-duhshama* era, while the twenty-three succeeding *tirthankaras* (from Ajita to Mahavira) and their associates lived in the *duhshama-sushama* era. The *duhshama-sushama* era came to an end three years and eight and one half months after the *nirvana* of Mahavira, and the world is now in the *duhshama* (sorrow) era of 21,000 years, which will be followed by the *duhshamaduhshama* (pure sorrow) era of another 21,000 years. In the increasingly bad time, Jainism itself will disappear, but at last the time will come for the new ascending age of Utsarpini to begin, and when the periods of *duhshama-sushama* and *sushama-duhshama* arrive twenty-four new *tirthankaras* and their associates will appear and the true religion will be reestablished.

In other zones of Jambudvipa, however, the time situation is different. In Mahavideha, for example, the situation is static, and there is neither Avasarpini nor Utsarpini. In the subregions of Devakuru and Uttarakuru (to the south and the north of Mount Meru) it is always the era of *sushama-sushama* (pure bliss). In the subregions of Purvavideha and Aparavideha (to the east and west of Mount Meru) it is always *duhshama-sushama* (sorrow-bliss) and *tirthankaras* are always preaching there. In the *duhshama* (sorrow) era which presently prevails in Bharata it is no longer possible to obtain deliverance, but if a Jaina who is ready for salvation can be born again in Videha he may there reach emancipation.

Tirthankaras

The title *tirthankara* (Prakrit *titthamkara*) or *tirthakara* (Prakrit *titthayara*) contains the word *tirtha*, one meaning of which is "ford." A *tirthankara* is therefore one who finds the ford and leads the way to cross over the river or the ocean of birth and rebirth. The word *tirtha* can also be taken as meaning the religious congregation *(sangha)*, and on this basis the *tirthankara* may be defined as one who founds a congregation, i.e., a fourfold Jaina community, consisting of disciples and lay adherents, with both males and females in both categories.

In the life of a *tirthankara* five important occasions *(kalyanas)* are regularly emphasized in the Jaina biographies, namely, the event of the embryo *(garbha kalyanaka)*, i.e., the entering into the womb of the mother; the event of being born *(janma kalyanaka)*, normally in a family of high status; the event of renunciation of the world *(diksha kalyanaka)*; the event of enlightenment and the attaining of omniscience *(kevala jnana kalyanaka)*; and the event of reaching the final liberation *(nirvana kalyanaka)*. It is usual for a *tirthankara* to be attended by a *yaksha* and a *yakshini*, and to have a chief male disciple *(ganadhara)* and a chief female disciple *(arya)*. On the five specific occasions just enumerated the *tirthankara* is worshiped by many celestial beings, who are of course of lower status than he. In the course of his career the *tirthankara* normally preaches in many places and wins thousands of followers. Many men and women accept his teachings in general but remain in their positions as householders, others leave their homes and become monks and nuns. The first and last *tirthankaras* proclaim five vows *(pancayama)* and nakedness *(aceladharma)*, the others teach four vows *(caturyama)* and the wearing of clothes *(saceladharma)*. When the work is accomplished and the time approaches for entry into *nirvana*, the *tirthankara* desists completely for a final period from food and drink and, having destroyed all *karma*, leaves behind the hull of the earthly body and rises to the place of ultimate blessedness at the top of the universe.

The twenty-four *tirthankaras* of the present world and the present age are listed in Table 9.5, together with various items concerning them. In most cases it is customary to add to the name the word *natha* (lord), and Rishabha, as the first of the series, is often simply called the first *(adi)* lord, Adinatha. In many cases there is divergence between the Digambaras and the Śvetambaras on an item, and this is indicated in the Table by "D" for the Digambara version and "Ś" for the Śvetambara.[32]

TABLE 9.5.
THE TWENTY-FOUR TIRTHANKARAS OF BHARATAVARSHA IN THE PRESENT UTSARPINI AGE

Name	Parents (usually a king and queen)	Birthplace
1. Rishabha (Usabha), called Adinatha, "first lord"	Nabhi and Marudevi	Ayodhya (Vinita)
2. Ajita (Ajiya)	Sitaśatru and Vijaya	Ayodhya
3. Sambhava	Jitari and Sena	Śravasti (Savatthi)
4. Abhinandana	Samvara and Siddhartha	Ayodhya
5. Sumati (Sumai)	Megha and Mangala	Ayodhya
6. Padmaprabha (Paumappabha)	Dhara and Susima	Kauśambi (Kosambi)
7. Suparśva (Supasa)	Pratishtha and Prithivi	Varanasi (Vanarasi)
8. Candraprabha (Camdappabha)	Mahasena and Lakshmana	Candrapuri (Camdapura)
9. Suvidhi (or Pushpadanta, Pupphadamta)	Sugriva and Rama	Kakandi (Kagamdi)
10. Śitala (Siyala)	Dridharatha and Nanda	Bhadrilapura (Bhaddilapura)
11. Śreyamśa (Sejjamsa)	Vishnu and Vishna	Sinhapura (Sihapura)
12. Vasupujya (Vasupujja)	Vasupujya and Jaya	Campapuri (Campa)
13. Vimala	Kritavarman and Śyama	Kampilya (Kampillapura)
14. Ananta	Sinhasena and Suyaśa	Ayodhya
15. Dharma	Bhanu and Suvrata	Ratnapura (Rayanapura)
16. Śanti	Visvasena and Acira	Hastinapura (Gayapura)
17. Kunthu	Śura and Śri	Hastinapura
18. Ara	Sudarśana and Devi	Hastinapura
19. Malli	Kumbha and Prabhavati	Mithila (Mihila)
20. Munisuvrata (Munisuvvaya) or Suvrata	Sumitra and Padma	Rajagriha (Rayagiha)
21. Nami	Vijaya and Vapra	Mithila
22. Arishtanemi (Aritthanemi) or Nemi	Samudravijaya and Śiva	Śauryapura (Soriyapura)
23. Parśva (Pasa)	Aśvasena and Vama	Varanasi
24. Vardhamana (Vaddhamana) or Mahavira	Siddhartha and Triśala	Kundagrama (Kumdapura)

Bodily Color	Emblem	Height		Age	Interval reckoned from Nirvana to Nirvana
(1.) Golden	Bull	500	*dhanushas*	84 *lakhs* of *purvas*	50 *lakhs* of *krores* of *sagaras*
(2.) Golden	Elephant	450	"	72 *lakhs* of *purvas*	30 *lakhs* of *krores* of *sagaras*
(3.) Golden	Horse	400	"	60 *lakhs* of *purves*	10 *lakhs* of *krores* of *sagaras*
(4.) Golden	Ape	350	"	50 *lakhs* of *purvas*	9 *lakhs* of *krores* of *sagaras*
(5.) Golden	Heron	300	"	40 *lakhs* of *purvas*	90,000 *krores* of *sagaras*
(6.) Red	Red Lotus	250	"	30 *lakhs* of *purvas*	9,000 *krores* of *sagaras*
(7.) Golden (Ś) Green (D)	Swastika	200	"	20 *lakhs* of *purvas*	900 *krores* of *sagaras*
(8.) White	Moon	150	"	10 *lakhs* of *purvas*	90 *krores* of *sagaras*
(9.) White	Dolphin, Crab (D)	100	"	2 *lakhs* of *purvas*	9 *krores* of *sagaras*
(10.) Golden	Śrivatsa, *Ficus religiosa* (D)	90	"	1 *lakh* of *purvas*	9,999,900 *sagaras*
(11.) Golden	Rhinoceros, Garuda (D)	80	"	84 *lakhs* of years	54 *sagaras*
(12.) Red	Buffalo	70	"	72 *lakhs* of years	30 *sagaras*
(13.) Golden	Boar	60	*dhanushas*	60 *lakhs* of years	9 *sagaras*
(14.) Golden	Falcon (Ś), or Bear (D)	50	"	30 *lakhs* of years	4 *sagaras*
(15.) Golden	Thunderbolt	45	"	10 *lakhs* of years	3 *sagaras* less 3/4 *palya*
(16.) Golden	Antelope	40	"	1 *lakh* of years	1/2 *palya*
(17.) Golden	Goat	35	"	95,000 years	1/4 *palya* less 6,000 *krores* of years
(18.) Golden	Nandyavarta (Ś), or Fish (D)	30	"	84,000 years	1,000 *krores* less 6,584,000 years
(19.) Green (Ś) Golden (D)	Water-jar	25	"	55,000 years	54 *lakhs* of years
(20.) Bluish-black	Tortoise	20	"	30,000 years	9 *lakhs* of years
(21.) Golden	Blue Lotus (Ś), or Aśoka-tree (D)	15	"	10,000 years	5 *lakhs* of years
(22.) Bluish-black	Conch	10	"	1,000 years	84,000 years
(23.) Blue	Snake	9	*hastas*	100 years	250 years
(24.) Golden	Lion	7	"	72 years	

The texts also give other information concerning each *tirthankara,* including such items as the *tirthankara's* previous births, the heaven from which descent to earth was made, the constellation under which the birth took place, the tree under which omniscience was attained, and the place where *nirvana* was reached. For twenty of the twenty-four *tirthankaras* the place of *nirvana* was on Mount Sammeta (Sammeya), now known as Mount Parasnath because it was the place of the *nirvana,* among the others, of Parśva. In the cases of the other four *tirthankaras,* the *nirvana* of Rishabha was experienced on Mount Ashtapada (Atthavaya), identified with Mount Kailaśa; of Vasupujya at Campapuri, his birthplace; of Arishtanemi on Mount Ujjayanta (Ujjimta), now known as Mount Girnar in Kathiawar; and of Mahavira at Pavapuri (Majjhima-Pava, a town near Rajagriha).

Of the twenty-four *tirthankaras,* all of whom appear in the *Trishashtiśalakapurushacaritra* of Hemacandra, the lives of four are also found in the *Kalpasutra* of Bhadrabahu in the section called "biographies of the Jinas" *(Jinacaritra),* and these four may be considered the most important ones, namely, Rishabha, Arishtanemi, Parśva, and Mahavira.

Rishabha

Rishaba (Usabha), the first *tirthankara* and thus the "first lord" (Adinatha) in Bharata in the present descending world age (Utsarpini), was born in Ayodhya as the son of a law-giver and governor named Nabhi and of Nabhi's sister and wife named Marudevi.[33] In dreams presaging the birth of this son, Marudevi saw a bull *(rishabha),* white and massive-shouldered, so Rishabha was named after the bull and eventually had the bull as his emblem. In due course Rishabha himself was married to two wives, Sumangala and Sunanda. To him Sumangala bore a son Bharata, a daughter Brahmi, and no less than forty-nine pairs of twin-sons; while Sunanda bore a son Bahubali and a daughter Sundari—in all one hundred sons and two daughters.

At the request of the people and with the approval of his father Nabhi, Rishabha became ruler of Ayodhya, and was the first person to have the title of king. For the welfare of his subjects Rishabha instructed them in agriculture and cooking, and taught them the works of the potter, carpenter, painter, weaver, and barber, as well as writing and arithmetic, and many other arts and sciences as well. He also divided the people into four divisions, headed by the *kshatriyas,* and thus arranged a new order of customs and law. In this connection he "prescribed a punishment according to the crime for those deserving punishment, just as a doctor prescribes a medicine for the sick according to the disease." The result was that the people did not commit theft or any other crime. "Verily the law of punishment alone is a snake-charmer for the serpent of all crime."[34]

In time, however, Rishabha saw the emptiness of existence, and resolved to renounce the world. He anointed his hundred sons as kings, and gave each a kingdom, while he himself withdrew to a garden near Ayodhya called Siddhartha, where he abandoned all clothes and ornaments, tore out the hair of his head in four handfuls, and entered the state of homelessness. Thereafter he wandered as a mendicant in many countries, then under a banyan tree *(nyagrodha)* in a park outside a town called Purimatala, attained omniscience. As a teacher he attracted a large following of monks and nuns, and male and female lay adherents. Finally, in the company of many of these monks, on the summit of Mount Ashtapada (Kailaśa), after fasting six and one half days without drinking water, he entered into *nirvana.* So Rishabha is known as the first king, first mendicant, and first omniscient, as well as the first *tirthankara* and first lord (Adinatha).

Rishabha's son Bharata was the first *cakravartin* (world ruler) of the land of Bharata, and it is after him that the Indian continent is called Bharatavarsha. Bharata was married to his half-sister Sundari. When Bharata demanded the submission of his brothers, the forty-nine pairs of twins, his full brothers, gave up their kingdoms to him, and then joined their father Rishabha in the ascetic life. The half-brother Bahubali was married to his half-sister Brahmi, and became king of the country of Bahali, with Takshaśila (Takkhasila, Taxila) as its capital. He declined to submit to Bharata, and the two fought a great battle. In the end, however, although Bahubali appeared to be victorious in the struggle, he left the sovereignty to his brother, and himself renounced the world. Bahubali tore out the hair of his head and began the practice of asceticism in the form called *kayotsarga*, which means indifference to the body (literally, dismissing the body), the posture being either standing or sitting, with the arms hanging down. In his case Bahubali remained standing thus in one place for a full year, without taking food, while anthills arose around his feet, plants grew up and wrapped their tendrils about him, and wild animals rubbed themselves against him. The *Trishashtiśalakapurushacaritra* of Hemacandra describes the austere practice of the great saint in these words:

> The blessed *muni*, Bahubali, remained there alone, as if sprung up from the earth, as if fallen from the sky. Devoted to meditation, his eyes fixed on the end of his nose, motionless, the *muni* appeared like a signpost. Like a forest tree his body endured the wind in the hot season spreading hot grains of sand like grains of fire. Plunged in the nectar of good meditation, he was unconscious of the sun in the middle of the hot season, like a fire pit, over his head. . . . In the rainy season he was no more disturbed by streams of water than a mountain by trees shaken by wind and rain. He was not shaken from *kayotsarga* nor from meditation by the flashes of lightning nor by the mountain peaks shaken by thunderstorms. . . . In the winter season in which elephant-deep streams were frozen, he remained comfortable from the fire of meditation active in burning the fuel of *karma*. On winter nights when trees were frozen by cold, Bahubali's pious meditation bloomed especially, like jasmines (which in India bloom during the winter).
>
> Forest buffaloes scratched themselves on him just as on the trunk of a huge tree, at the same time splitting their horns. . . . He was surrounded completely by creepers with a hundred branches shooting up. . . . His feet were surrounded by serpents, like anklets, that had left the anthill near his feet. As he stood thus in meditation, a year passed without food. . . .

Even so, Bahubali was not yet free of pride, for he was unwilling to pay homage to his half-brothers, who were younger than he but had become ascetics before himself. Brahmi and Sundari, his half-sister and his sister, came to him, however, and said, "*Kevala* can not arise in those seated on an elephant's shoulder," and he realized his pride, started off to pay homage to his brothers, and immediately obtained omniscience.[35]

Bahubali is also known as Gommata and Gommateśvara, and it is he who is honored in the colossal statue erected at Śravanabelgola by Camundaraya.

Arishtanemi

Arishtanemi (Aritthanemi) or Nemi, the twenty-second *tirthankara*, was born in Śauryapura (Soriyapura, modern Sauripur, on the Yamuna River below Mathura), as the son of King Samudravijaya (Samuddavijaya) and his queen Śiva (Siva).[36] Samudravijaya was the brother of Vasudeva, the father of Balarama and Krishna. Accordingly, in the Jaina scheme of the present world age (Avasarpini), along with Arishtanemi as the twenty-second *tirthankara*, Krishna appears as the ninth and last *vasudeva*, Balarama as the ninth and last *baladeva*, and Krishna's enemy Jarasandha as the ninth and last *prativasudeva*. Thus there is lengthy narrative in the *Trishashtiśalakapurushacaritra* about Vasudeva and Krishna, as well as about Samudravijaya and Arishtanemi.[37]

Prior to the birth of Arishtanemi, Śiva saw in a dream the outer rim of a wheel *(nemi)*, which was made of a kind of black jewel called *arishta*, therefore the son was given the name which combined these two words.[38] When the time came for Arishtanemi to marry, it was arranged that he should take the hand of Rajimati (Raimai), the young and beautiful daughter of King Ugrasena (Uggasena), and Arishtanemi was proceeding in pomp to Dvaraka for the wedding ceremony. On the way he saw caged animals, which were obviously miserable and overcome by fear. "Why are all these animals, which desire to be happy, kept in cages and enclosures?" he asked his charioteer. The latter answered that the animals were to provide food at the forthcoming wedding celebration. "If for my sake many living beings are killed, I shall not obtain happiness in the next world," Arishtanemi reflected, and forthwith gave up the wedding, renounced the world, and withdrew to Mount Raivataka (Ujjayanta, now Mount Girnar), where he attained omniscience in fifty-four days and where also, after much wandering and teaching and the winning of many disciples, he finally entered *nirvana*. Meanwhile Rajimati was devastated with sorrow at the broken plans, but rejected the advances of Rathanemi, Arishtanemi's younger brother, and both she and Rathanemi entered the company of Arishtanemi's numerous disciples and eventually attained emancipation as nun and monk (*Uttaradhyayana* 22).[39]

From Rishabha to Arishtanemi the Jaina scheme (Table 9.5) uses very large figures for the stature, longevity, and antiquity of the *tirthankaras,* but in fact some such teachers may have appeared in at least relatively early times. Thus, for example, it may be possible to recognize already in the *Rig Veda* the existence of teaching and practice comparable to that later characteristic of Jainism, e.g., in the description (in 10.136.2) of the *munis* as ascetic ecstatics who are "girdled with the wind," i.e., naked.[40] Likewise Arishtanemi appears as a contemporary and relative of Krishna, and the latter of course plays a prominent role in the events narrated in the *Mahabharata*.

Parśva

With Parśva (Pasa), the twenty-third *tirthankara,* except for his height which is evidently still somewhat exaggerated (9 *hastas*), the figures set forth in the Jaina scheme (Table 9.5) are no longer too extraordinary: he lived to the age of 100 years; there were 250 years from his *nirvana* to the *nirvana* of Mahavira. According to the narrative of his life, Parśva was born in Varanasi, the son of King Aśvasena (Assasena) and his chief queen Vama.[41] Prior to the birth Vama saw a black serpent *(parśva)* crawling about, hence the name which was given to the boy, and the emblem of the snake which is associated with him.

Even from childhood Parśva was undesirous of marriage, but in due time at his father's insistence he was wed to Prabhavati, daughter of a king named Prasenajit (Pasenadi, but not the king of this name who was a contemporary of the Buddha), and he continued in this state until the age of thirty.

One day at Varanasi Parśva observed an ascetic named Katha, who was practicing the so-called penance of five fires, by sitting in the midst of four burning fires, with the sun as a fifth fire blazing down upon him from above. Parśva saw, however, that a serpent was caught in the wood of one of the fires, and that the ascetic had no compassion for it, therefore Parśva himself compassionately rescued the snake, and it later became the *naga* king Dharana. Having reached the age of thirty Parśva renounced the world and entered the state of a houseless mendicant, wandering from place to place. In one place he was standing motionless in meditation under a banyan tree when a terrible rainstorm threatened his life, but the *naga* king Dharana, remembering the kindness he had received from Parśva, came and covered Parśva with his coils and raised his seven hoods above him like a protective umbrella.

After eighty-four days in this ascetic life, Parśva returned to Varanasi and there, in a garden under a *dhataki* tree, after fasting for two and one-half days without drinking water, and being engaged in deep meditation, he reached omniscience. After that he wandered, preached, and won many disciples. Finally, when he knew that his emancipation was near, he proceeded to Mount Sammeta (Sammeya, now Mount Parasnath, preserving his name), fasted for a month, and passed into *nirvana*. He had lived for thirty years as a householder and seventy years as an ascetic *(śramana, samana),* one hundred years in all.

Parśva had eight *ganadharas* or chief disciples, namely, Śubha (Śubhadatta), Aryaghosha, Vasishta, Brahmacari, Saumya, Śridhara, Virabhadra, and Yaśas. Of these Śubha became the head of the church after the death of the master, and was followed in turn by Haridatta, Aryasamudra, Prabha, and Keśi. It is in a conversation (*Uttaradhyayana* 23)[42] between Keśi and Indrabhuti (Imdabhui, also known as Gautama or Goyama), the first principal disciple of Mahavira, that we learn that the law preached by Parśva recognized four vows (not to destroy life, speak untruth, steal, or own property), and that Parśva allowed clothes to a monk. Being free from the entanglements and bonds of passions and possessions, Parśva and his followers were Nirgranthas (Niganthas), i.e., "unfettered ones," ones "without any tie."

Vardhamana Mahavira

Vardhamana Mahavira is the twenty-fourth and last *tirthankara* in the current descending cycle (Avasarpini) in the Bharata region. His life and teachings occupy a large place in Jaina literature, especially in the *Acarangasutra,* the *Sutrakritangasutra,* the *Kalpasutra,* and the *Trishashtiśalakapurushacaritra.*[43]

According to the *Trishashtiśalakapurushacaritra,* he had experienced many previous births. Of these an early incarnation was when he was born as Marici (Marii) the son of Bharata and the grandson of Rishabha, the first *tirthankara.* At that time Marici heard that he himself was to be the last *tirthankara,* named Mahavira, and this engendered pride in him. In the final outworking of the *karma* due to that pride, he was about to be born as the son of a *brahmana* Rishabhadata and his wife Devananda, who lived in the southern brahmanical part of the town Kundagrama (Kundapura), a suburb of Vaiśali (Vesali). It was noted among the gods, however, that a future *tirthankara* would normally be born in a royal family, and therefore an embryonic exchange was ordered by Indra (Śakra), and the child was born in the northern *kshatriya* section of Kundagrama as the son of King Siddhartha (Siddhattha) of the Jnatri (Jnata or Naya) clan, and of his wife Triśala (Tisala). King Siddhartha was himself a descendant of Ikshvaku, and Triśala was the sister of King Cetaka (Cedaga) of Vaiśali (Vesali). In this case the Digambaras do not agree with the Śvetambaras as to the transfer of the embryo and, without mention of Devananda, simply state that Mahavira was born by Triśala.

In the night in which the child entered her womb, Queen Triśala experienced fourteen wonderful dreams, in which she saw (1) an elephant possessing all lucky marks, (2) a white bull, (3) a white lion, (4) the goddess of famous beauty, Śri, on a lotus in the lotus lake on top of Mount Himavat, being anointed with water from the trunks of the guardian elephants, (5) a garland of fragrant flowers, (6) the white moon, (7) the red sun, (8) a large flag, (9) a full vase, (10) a lotus pond, (11) a milk-ocean of tossing waves, (12) a celestial palace, (13) a heap of jewels, and (14) a smokeless fire (*Kalpasutra* 33–46). The Digambaras vary this list of auspicious signs slightly and expand it to a total of sixteen items.

From the time that the child was to be born in their family, King Siddartha found that the family's treasure increased, therefore he gave his son the name Vardhamana (Vaddhamana), which means the Increasing One. In addition to this personal name, Vardhamana was in the course of time known by other designations and, in all, three names were considered especially significant, namely, Vardhamana, Śramana (Samana, i.e., Ascetic), and Mahavira (Great Conqueror) (*Kalpasutra* 108; cf. *Acarangasutra* 2.15.15):

> His three names have thus been recorded: by his parents he was called Vardhamana; because he is devoid of love and hate, he is called Śramana; because he stands fast in the midst of dangers and fears, patiently bears hardships and calamities, adheres to the chosen rules of penance, is wise, indifferent to pleasure and pain, rich in control, and gifted with fortitude, the name Venerable Ascetic Mahavira has been given him by the gods.[44]

The name Mahavira also occurs in the short form Vira (conqueror, hero). As a citizen of Vaiśali (Vesali) Mahavira was called Vaiśalika (Vesalia). As a person of the Jnatri (Jnata, Naya) lineage he was known as Jnatriputra (Jnataputra, Nayaputta, Nataputta), i.e., a "son" of this clan. Like Parśva and his followers, Mahavira was an "unfettered" Nirgrantha (Nigantha), a term which he applied to his own monks too (e.g., *Uttaradhyayana* 16).[45] Therefore, and especially in Buddhist sources (e.g., *Digha Nikaya* 2.57),[46] Mahavira is called Nigantha Nataputta, i.e., the Nigantha of the Nata clan.

When Vardhamana passed the age of eight his father began his education. When he reached maturity his parents wished him to marry, and he was wed to Yaśoda (Jasoya), the daughter of a certain King Samaravira, and she bore him a daughter Anavadya (Annujja), also known as Priyadarśana (Piyadamsana), "pleasant to the sight." Anavadya married a prince named Jamali, and both became disciples of Mahavira, but Jamali differed from Mahavira on a point of philosophy, and is considered the first of seven *ninhavas (nihnavas)* who falsified the right faith.

As described in the *Acarangasutra* (2.15.16),[47] Siddartha and Triśala, the parents of Vardhamana, were worshipers of Parśva and followers of the *śramanas*, and as such they presumably brought up their son in the teachings of Parśva. When Vardhamana was twenty-eight years old, his parents died in the Jaina manner, by rejecting all food in the last days of their lives. Up to this time Vardhamana had felt it incumbent upon himself to remain at home, but now he felt free to retire from the world, and his elder brother granted him permission to do so. During a whole year he gave away his wealth. Then, at the age of thirty, he proceeded through Kundagrama to a park called Jnatakhanda (Nayasamda) and stopped under an Aśoka tree. There he took off his ornaments, plucked out his hair in five handfuls, and putting on a single robe entered the state of homelessness. He resolved that for twelve years he would neglect his body and meditate on his self, bearing with equanimity all calamities coming from divine powers, human beings, or animals. Soon he also abandoned all clothing and even the possession of an alms bowl. "For a year and a month (he) wore clothes; after that time he walked about naked, and accepted the alms in the hollow of his hand" (*Kalpasutra* 117).[48]

Mahavira was now "Nata's son the unclothed" (*Anguttara Nikaya* 1.220;

Samyutta Nikya 4.398),[49] truly a naked, houseless, world-relinquishing ascetic. Except in the rainy season, he stayed in villages only a single night, and in towns only five nights. He sometimes lodged in workshops, under a shed of straw, on a burying-ground, in abandoned houses, or at the foot of a tree. In his resting places and on the road he sustained manifold calamities: crawling or flying animals attacked him, dogs ran at him and bit him, and evil people struck him and beat him. In spite of everything he was always well controlled, and persevered in his meditations day and night, free from resentment. Whether wounded or not wounded he did not desire medical treatment. In the summer he exposed himself to the heat, and sat squatting in the sun. Wandering about, he killed no creatures, and he begged for his scanty food. Often he did not drink for weeks or months at a time. "Bearing all hardships, the Venerable One, undisturbed, proceeded (on the road to *nirvana*)" (*Acarangasutra* 1.8).[50]

Gośala. In the second rainy season of his wanderings, Mahavira stayed in a weaver's workshop at Nalanda (Nalamda), a suburb of the city of Rajagriha (Rayagiha). The *Bhagavatisutra* (15)[51] relates that at this time Gośala (Gosala) came to the same place and made the acquaintance of Mahavira. Gośala was the son of a wandering painter named Mankhali (Mamkhali) and his wife Bhadra (Bhadda), and was himself born in a cowshed *(gośala),* from which he received his name. At a place called Kollaya (Kollaa) not far from Nalanda, Gośala accepted Mahavira as his teacher, and the two were associated in the ascetic life for the next six years, doubtless for the most part, except for the rainy seasons, wandering about the country together. After these six years of association, however, the two became opponents and separated from each other. After eighteen years more, Gośala claimed to have reached the state of a *jina* (two years earlier than Mahavira), and declared himself to be the twenty-fourth and last *tirthankara.* Gośala was now established in the workshop of a female potter named Halahala in the city of Śravasti (Savatthi), and was recognized as the leader of the Ajivika (Ajiviya) sect. He taught a doctrine of fatalism, and to his numerous followers expounded six inviolable principles, namely, acquisition and nonacquisition, happiness and suffering, and life and death. In a final meeting with Mahavira at Śravasti, Gośala attempted to kill Mahavira, but (as the Jaina source tells the story) some of Gośala's followers went over at this time to Mahavira, and after seven days Gośala himself repented, recognized Mahavira as the true *jina,* and died, while Mahavira lived on for sixteen years.

Teaching of Mahavira. For the twelve years envisioned in his original resolution of renunciation Mahavira endured all afflictions and calamities with a calm mind, and performed long and hard penances, then finally in the thirteenth year (when he was forty-two years of age) attained omniscience *(kevala jnana)*:

> Outside of the town Jrimbhikagrama (Jambhiyagama) on the northern bank of the river Rijupalika (Ujuvaliya), in the field of the householder Samaga, in a northeastern direction from an old temple, not far from a *śala (sal)* tree, in a squatting position with joined hands exposing himself to the heat of the sun, with the knees high and the head low, in deep meditation, in the midst of abstract meditation, he reached *nirvana* (not the "final release" which is reached at death, but the "living release" which the Hindus call *jivanmukti*), the complete and full, the unobstructed, unimpeded, infinite and supreme, best knowledge and intuition, called *kevala.* When the Venerable One had become an arhat and *jina,* he was a *kevalin,* omniscient and comprehending all objects, he knew all conditions of the world, of gods, persons, and demons; whence they came, where they go, whether they are born as persons or animals, or become gods

or hell-beings; their . . . open and secret deeds . . . and the thoughts of their minds; he saw and knew all conditions in the whole world of all living beings" (*Acarangasutra* 2.15.25–26; cf. *Kalpasutra* 120–121).[52]

After obtaining omniscience Mahavira went to Madhyama Papa (Majjhima Pava, or just Pava), a city where he had previously suffered persecution, and stayed in a park called Mahasenavana. There he preached a sermon, and initiated disciples. As the *Trishashtisalakapurushacaritra* tells the story, the gods erected in the park a preaching hall (*samavasarana*), and Mahavira entered by the east door, circumambulated a tall *caitya*-tree, sat down on a lion-throne with a footstool, and "delivered a sermon in a speech similar to all dialects" (presumably in Ardha-Magadhi). He said:

> Look you! The ocean of existence is boundless like a cruel sea; and the cause of that is *karma* and nothing else. . . . A creature devoid of discernment attains a low state of existence like a well-digger, by means of his *karma* created by himself only. A creature with a pure heart attains a high state of existence, like the builder of a palace, by his own *karma* alone. One should not destroy life, the cause of acquiring *karma*; one should be as intent on saving the lives of others as one's own life. A person should certainly not speak falsely, but should speak what is pleasant and true, avoiding pain to others like pain to one's self. One should not take property that has not been given, for it resembles an external breath of men. Actual murder would be committed by taking their property. One should not have sexual relations which cause the destruction of many souls. The wise man should practice continence only, the cause of emancipation. One should not acquire possessions, for a man worried about his possessions falls down like an overloaded ox. If people eager to abandon fully these things, [e.g.,] destruction of life, are not able to abandon them fully, in that case they should abandon gross offenses."[53]

The *Acarangasutra* (2.15.29ff.),[54] telling how Mahavira taught the law (*dharma*), says that he set forth the five great vows, with their clauses, and the six classes of lives. Here the vows are phrased, "I renounce all killing of living beings. . . . I renounce all vices of lying speech. . . . I renounce all taking of anything not given. . . . I renounce all sexual pleasures. . . . I renounce all attachments. . . ." As an example of the clauses by which the vows are elucidated, it is explained in reference to the first vow that in order not to destroy life a Nirgrantha is careful in walk, in thought, in speech, in laying down the utensils of begging, and in inspecting food and drink before partaking of them, lest any living beings be hurt, displaced, injured, or killed.

That the vows stated by Mahavira were the four previously enunciated by Parsva, plus the added vow of chastity probably thought of as only making explicit what Parsva's renunciation of possessions and attachments implied anyway, has already been noted. Another example where Mahavira can be seen to continue the teachings of Parsva is where (in the *Bhagavatisutra* 5.9)[55] it is on the authority of Parsva that Mahavira describes the world as eternal, with neither beginning nor end, limited and surrounded by the non-world, expanded below and like a bedstead, in the middle narrow and like the flat discus of Indra's thunderbolt, and above broad and like a drum standing upright.

As to the six classes of lives which Mahavira set forth, an outline of the Jaina categories may be seen in the *Uttaradhyayana* (36).[56] This world (*loka*) is made up of beings with life or soul (*jiva*) and things without life or soul (*ajiva*), and the two categories together account for the universe, without need to speak of a creator. Things without life (*ajivas*) are of two kinds: without form (*arupi*), e.g., space and time; and with form (*rupi*), where there are various concentrations of *pudgala*, a term roughly translatable as "matter." Beings with life (*jivas*) are also of two kinds:

the perfected souls *(siddhas)* which reside on the top of the universe in Ishat-pragbhara; and the living beings which still belong to the world of rebirth *(samsara),* are under the bondage of *karma,* and are entangled with *ajiva.* The latter beings (the *samsari)* are of two kinds with six subdivisions: the immovable (earth lives, water lives, plants); and the movable (fire lives, wind lives, lives with an organic body).

The six classes of living beings which are still in the *samsara* may also be placed in five groups in terms of the number of senses they possess. (1) Ekendriya *jivas* possess only one sense, that of touch. Such *jivas* exist in stones, water, fire, wind, and plants, which consequently are capable of pain and suffering. According to the strictest interpretation of Jainism, the vow of non-injury *(ahimsa)* begins to be applicable with this very first group of *jivas;* therefore monks may refuse to touch a stone or fire, and avoid the eating of many vegetables. (2) Dviindriya *jivas* have two senses, touch and taste (e.g., worms and creatures living in shells). For the lay adherent of Jainism the vow of non-injury is held to be in effect first with regard to this class. (3) Triindriya *jivas* have three senses, touch, taste, and smell (e.g., ants, bugs, and centipedes). (4) Caturindriya *jivas* possess four senses, touch, taste, smell, and sight (e.g., flies, mosquitoes, bees, and moths). (5) Panchindriya *jivas* enjoy five senses, namely the four hitherto enumerated plus hearing, and these *jivas* include denizens of hell, higher animals (aquatic, terrestrial, and aerial, some produced from eggs, some from a womb), human beings, and gods.

All of the living beings with five senses are also characterized by six *leśyas,* which are different conditions produced in the soul by different kinds of *karma* *(Uttaradhyayana* 34).[57] The *leśyas* are named in terms of six colors—black, blue, gray, red, yellow, and white—and described in terms of taste, smell, and touch, running from bitter to pleasant, objectionable to fragrant, and rough to gentle. Thus a person who acts on the impulse of sinful inclinations, e.g., does not cease to injure the six kinds of living beings, commits cruel acts, is wicked and violent—develops the black *leśya,* which has the color of a rain cloud, a taste more bitter than a bitter fruit, an odor utterly repulsive, and a touch worse than that of a saw. The person, however, who abstains from thinking about his misery and about sinful deeds, but engages in meditation on the law and truth only, who controls himself, is calm, subdues his senses, and so forth, develops the white *leśya,* which has the color of a conch shell, a taste better than that of dates, a smell more pleasant than that of perfume, and a touch more pleasant than that of cotton.

The *jivas* of all classes which still belong to the *samsara* are thus moving through successive reincarnations toward an ultimate goal in which they will be freed from *ajiva,* liberated from *karma,* and attain final enlightenment *(bodhi)* and deliverance *(moksha).* Of them all, it is only human beings who are at the stage where it is possible to pass on into the ultimate deliverance, for even the gods will be reborn as human beings or as animals in accordance with their *karma.* But of human beings those souls who cherish heretical opinions, commit sins, kill living beings, and are enveloped in black *leśya,* will not reach deliverance when they die, but those souls who cherish orthodox opinions, do not commit sins, and are enveloped in white *leśya,* will reach *bodhi* at the time of death *(Uttaradhyayana* 36.256–258).[58] From a position now in the present age of sorrow *(duhshama)* in our part of the world, however, it is usually held that it is no longer possible for a person to pass on directly into the ultimate deliverance, but at least a new birth in the heavens above may be attained.

Since, then, all the innumerable *jivas* are in their own various stages of development toward perfection, no *jiva*—even if at a higher stage of development—should cause harm to any other *jiva*—even if it is at a lower stage—and thus interfere with its prospects for spiritual progress. Thus reverence for life is the essential basis of the Jaina doctrine of *ahimsa* and of the first vow of nonviolence to any living being, which was taught by Parśva and by Mahavira.

In his teaching Mahavira often used simile and parable to make his doctrine understandable. Speaking, e.g., about *samsara* and *karma*, he used the comparison of a net to picture the way in which life spans are interwoven but separate (*Bhagavatisutra* 5.3):

> Suppose that there is a net in which knots have been woven one after another; that these have been woven without omission of any; that these have been woven in a continuous series; and that these have been woven one tied to the other; and so on. And the said net exists in its expanse, in its entire weight, in its entire expanse and weight, and in its entirety. . . . In the same manner, many life spans connected with many births in the case of each living being are interwoven, one with the other, in proper order, as knots in the net. It is for this that a living being, at any one time, experiences one life span (only).[59]

Again Mahavira is represented as telling this parable, which also has to do with reincarnation (*Uttaradhyayana* 7.14–16):

> Three merchants set out on their travels, each with his capital; one of them gained there much, the second returned with his capital, and the third merchant came home after having lost his capital.
> The capital is human life, the gain is heaven; through the loss of that capital a person must be born as a denizen of hell or a brute animal.[60]

Similarities and Contrasts of Mahavira and Gośala. If the vows and presumably the general tenor of the teaching of Mahavira were much along the lines of his predecessor Parśva, there are also points of contact in practice and teaching between Mahavira and his one-time associate Gośala. Before Gośala became a disciple of Mahavira at Kollaya, he had given away all his possessions (*Bhagavatisutra* 15), presumably including any clothing, and one account reports a much earlier event in which an angry master caught the garment of Gośala, and Gośala fled naked, and chose to remain that way in the hope of being honored as a holy man.[61] Thus in practice both Mahavira and Gośala must have appeared before the world as identically naked ascetics, and the adoption of the custom of nakedness by Mahavira may have been due to the influence of Gośala and the Ajivikas, since it did not come from Parśva who allowed clothing for his monks, and since the Buddhist sources regularly distinguish between the followers of Mahavira simply as Niganthas (unfettered) and the followers of Gośala specifically as Acelakas (unclothed).

In teaching, the classification of lives by Mahavira appears to have been perhaps in part derived from a scheme attributed to Gośala, for in the Buddhist *Digha Nikaya* (2.53), Gosala is quoted as enumerating four classes of living beings, these categories apparently being intended to include all that has life, namely, (1) *sabbe satta*, all animals; (2) *sabbe pana*, all creatures (with one, two, or more senses); (3) *sabbe bhuta*, all beings (produced from eggs or in a womb); and (4) Sabbe *jiva*, all souls (in plants).[62] Also the Jaina doctrine of the six *leśyas* resembles a division of humankind into six classes, which was used by Gośala. Since the Jaina scheme is usually the more elaborate, as far as we can see, the borrowing, if there were such, may have been by Mahavira from the Ajivikas.[63]

On the other hand there were sharp differences between the teachings of

Mahavira and of Gośala. Since Mahavira held that "restraints" could wear out *karma* (as noted above in Chapter 5), observance of the five great vows was of great importance, and the implications of the vows were elaborated so that the Niganthas, his followers, were prohibited, for example, from the use of cold water, the eating of seeds, and the acceptance of things especially prepared for them. Since Gośala, on the other hand, maintained that everything in a person's life is already absolutely determined, conduct appeared irrelevant to destiny, and the Ajivikas, although practicing stringent asceticism in many regards, at the same time felt themselves free from many moral restrictions which prevailed among the Jainas. Thus in conversation with a prince named Ardraka, who was a disciple of Mahavira, Gośala criticized Mahavira for surrounding himself with many monks and thus abandoning the lonely and vulnerable life of a true ascetic, but Gośala also declared that "according to our law an ascetic, who lives alone and single, commits no sin if he uses cold water, eats seeds, accepts things prepared for him, and has intercourse with women" (*Sutra Kritanga* 2.6.7).[64]

The Ajivikas, then, following Gośala as their chief teacher, were nudist ascetics of a strictly deterministic philosophy and a relatively unconventional morality, while the Niganthas, as disciples of Mahavira, were also nudist ascetics, but not fatalists, believing that conduct has a bearing on destiny and that rigorous regulation of conduct is therefore necessary. As for the Buddha, in relation to both of these teachers, he was like Mahavira and unlike Gośala in that he did not teach fatalism, but he was unlike both Mahavira and Gośala in that he turned away from extreme asceticism and held it to be unprofitable. Accordingly the Buddha was involved in arguments with "disputatious" Ajivikas and Niganthas alike, as well as with *brahmanas* (*Sutta Nipata, Culavagga* 380–381).[65] But of all the six most famous contemporary teachers of his time the Buddha considered Makkhali Gośala his most formidable rival, and he pictured Gośala as an "infatuated man," and characterized his theory as the "meanest" of all the theories put forth by the various recluses (*Anguttara Nikaya* 1.286).[66]

Disciples of Mahavira. After his sermon in the Mahasenavana park, as the *Trishashtiśalakapurushacaritra* continues the account, Mahavira initiated disciples, both men and women, and also established other men and women as lay disciples. The first were the eleven principal disciples, Indrabhuti (Imdabhui), Agnibhuti (Aggibhui), Vayubhuti (Vaubhui), Vyakta (Viyatta), Sudharman (Suhamma), Mandika (Mamdiya), Mauryaputra (Moriyaputta), Akampita (Akampiya), Acalabhratr (Ayalabhaya), Metarya (Meyajja), and Prabhasa (Pabhasa), who became *ganadharas (ganaharas)* or "heads of schools," together with their own numerous disciples. "These eleven, well-born, very intelligent, desiring emancipation, honored by everyone, were the original disciples of the Teacher of the World."[67]

Ultimately, as listed in the *Kalpasutra* (134–145),[68] Mahavira had in the category of ascetics 14,000 monks *(śramanas, samanas)* with Indrabhuti at their head, and 36,000 nuns with Candana (Camdana), daughter of King Dadhivahana (Dahivahana) of Campa at their head, and in the category of lay votaries *(upasakas)* 59,000 men with Śankhaśataka (Samkha) at their head, and 318,000 women with Sulasa and Revati (Revai) at their head.

Together the male and female ascetics and the male and female lay votaries constitute the fourfold congregation (*tirtha* or *sangha*) of Jainism. The ascetics are bound by the five great vows *(mahavratas)*, *ahimsa* (nonviolence), *satya* (truth), *asteya* (nonstealing), *brahmacarya* (celibacy), and *aparigraha* (nonpossession). The lay votaries take upon themselves the five lesser vows *(anuvratas)*, which represent the spirit of the great vows but with sufficient modification (e.g., limitation rather than complete abandonment of possessions) to be possible of practice by the householder. Even as the great vows are supplemented with additional "clauses," so the lesser vows of the lay votary may also be supplemented with additional commitments, e.g., restriction of travel, practice of meditation and fasting, and perhaps at the end of life voluntary self-starvation to death *(samlekhana)*, as was the practice of Mahavira and many of the ascetics.[69]

In addition to the ascetic and lay members of his congregation, Mahavira also had many other sympathizers and supporters, and many of these were in high places. His own mother Triśala (Tisala), it has been noted above, was the sister of King Cetaka (Cedaga) of Vaiśali (Vesali), and Mahavira spent twelve rainy seasons in Vaiśali and its suburb Vanijagrama (Vaniyagama), and the king was a great devotee of his. Mahavira also spent fourteen rainy seasons in Rajagriha (Rayagiha) and its suburb Nalanda (Nalamda), and there King Bimbisara, called Śrenika (Seniya) by the Jainas, paid homage to him and sometimes held discussions with him. The principal wife of Bimbisara was Cellana, daughter of King Cetaka of Vaiśali, and she also was a devotee of Mahavira. One of the sons of Bimbisara and Cellana was Ajataśatru, called Kunika (Kunia) by the Jains, who imprisoned his father and took the kingdom for himself. Bimbisara died in prison, and Kunika moved the capital of the kingdom from Rajagriha to Campa. Mahavira spent three rainy seasons in Campa and neighboring Prishtha-Campa (Pittha-Campa), and Kunika often visited him. Yet other kings who took an interest in Mahavira were Pradyota (Pajjota, Pajjoa), king of Ujjayini, Udayana king of Kauśambi (Kosambi), and Udayana king of Titabhaya (Viyabhaya), and the last of these eventually renounced the world and became an actual disciple and monk under Mahavira.

Death of Mahavira. In all, in the forty-two years of his life as a monk Mahavira spent his first rainy season in Asthikagrama (Atthiyagama, probably Hatthigama in Pali texts), three rainy seasons in Campa and Prishtha-Campa (Pittha-Campa), twelve in Vaiśali (Vesali) and Vanijagrama (Vaniyagama), fourteen in Rajagriha (Rayagiha) and Nalanda (Nalamda), six in Mithila (Mihila), two in Bhadrika (Bhaddiya), one in Alabhika (Alabhiya), one in Panitabhumi (Paniabhumi), one in Śravasti (Savatthi), and one in Madhyama Papa (Majjhima Pava).

The last named city, best known simply as Pava, was where Mahavira had preached his first sermon after attaining omniscience, and now in his last rainy season he was staying in the same city in the office of the writers *(rajjukasabha, rajjugasabha)* of King Hastipala. Knowing that his final emancipation was at hand, and knowing also that his oldest disciple, the monk Gautama Indrabhuti, would be greatly saddened, Mahavira sent Indrabhuti away on a missionary journey. Having made a two-day fast, having proclaimed his last teachings about the good results of merit and the bad results of sin, and being seated in the *paryanka* (or *samparyanka*) posture (a seated meditative pose, in which the legs are placed one upon the other with both the soles of the feet in visible), Mahavira "died, went off, quitted the world, cut asunder the ties of birth, old age, and death; became a *siddha*, a *buddha*, a *mukta*, a maker of the end (to all misery), finally liberated, freed from all pains" (*Kalpasutra* 123).[70]

The decease transpired in the fourth month of that rainy season, on the fifteenth day of the dark fortnight of Kartika. It was 250 years since the emancipation of Parśva, and three years and eight and one-half months before the expiration of the *dushama-sushama* (sorrow-bliss) era of the present Avasarpini (descending) cycle of time. According to virtually unanimous Jaina tradition the date was equivalent to 527 B.C.E.[71]

Upon the passing away of Mahavira, King Cetaka of Vaiśali, who was his maternal uncle, and many confederate kings, together instituted a great lighting of lights to commemorate the great ascetic, for they said, "Since the light of intelligence is gone, let us make an illumination of material matter" (*Kalpasutra* 128).[72] So until now the fall festival of lights known as Divali (Sanskrit *dipavali,* "a row of lights," observed by the Hindus primarily in honor of Lakshmi) is observed by the Jainas as the commemoration of the *nirvana* of Mahavira.[73]

10

MONUMENTS OF JAINISM IN INDIA

In Jainism as in Hinduism there are many symbols and images—often indeed the same ones in both cases, and in Buddhism as well—but whereas in Hinduism these may represent deities who are the objects of worship, in Jaina philosophy (as in Buddhist) there is no creator-god and therefore properly no worship in the strict sense of the word as the expression of reverence to deity. Rather, Jaina worship—if the word worship may be used here in a broad sense—is reverential homage to one or more human beings, who have found the way across the ocean of existence, attained liberation, and reached perfection, i.e., homage to the *jinas* (conquerors) and *tirthankaras* (ford finders). Insofar as not a few gods, goddesses, and other divine beings also appear, they are of lesser status than the great personages just mentioned, and are often in positions of helpful attendance upon or respectful salutation to them. The symbols and the images are therefore properly objects of meditation, through attention to which the devotee recalls the qualities of the great saints and tries to appropriate the same in personal life; and the temples in which the symbols and images are usually found are places for such meditation.

SYMBOLS

Both symbols and anthropomorphic images of the *jinas* appear on early Jaina monuments, and it is probable that the use of the symbols preceded the making of images of the *tirthankaras* in human form, even as in Buddhist art symbols of the Buddha preceded his human figures.[1]

Ashtamangalas

Among the Jainas it is considered that there are eight auspicious symbols (*ashtamangalas*). The Digambaras enumerate these as (1) umbrella, (2) banner, (3) pot, (4) fly whisk *(cauri)*, (5) mirror, (6) seat or throne, (7) fan, and (8) vessel; while the Śvetambaras name them as (1) *svastika*/swastika (perhaps derived from the wheel as a symbol of the sun, it resembles a "Greek cross" with the ends of the arms extended at right angles and turned to the right), (2) *śrivatsa* (originally a curl of hair on the chest, represented like four petals in a rectangular background, or a diamond-shaped mark), (3) *nandyavarta* (an elaborated form of the *svastika*, (4) seat or throne, (5) pot, (6) pair of fishes, (7) mirror, and (8) powder box.

Other widely encountered symbols include the *triśula*, the *caitya* tree, the *kalpa* tree, the *mana-stambha*, the *dharmacakra*, and the *stupa*. The *triśula* or trident (*tri*, three, *śula*, point), well known in Hinduism as the favorite weapon of Śiva, is found in Jainism in various stylized forms. The tree *(vriksha)*, widely an object of worship, is of special importance in Jainism because Mahavira renounced the world under an Aśoka tree and attained enlightenment under a *śala* tree, and each of the *tirthankaras* is associated with the special tree under which enlightenment was experienced. Since the word *caitya* means something built up or piled up and hence applies to many kinds of sacred objects—a *stupa*, a chapel, a sanctuary—a *caitya* tree *(caityavriksha)* is a sacred tree. A *kalpa* tree *(kalpavriksha)* is a "wishing tree," supposed to have made it possible in early days to obtain desires by sitting under it to make a wish. A *stambha* is a column or pillar, widely used with manifold significance; a *mana-stambha* is a "pillar of glory," a free-standing commemorative column in a Jaina temple.

With respect to the *dharmacakra*, a *cakra* is a wheel or discus, and was a form of weapon, a sign of a ruler and, in particular, the mark of a world ruler, who was known as a *cakravartin*, literally "a turner of the wheel," in indication of his universal sway. In accordance with this significance, the wheel was appropriate as the symbol of a *jina* who was also, in his own way, a great conqueror. In its use in Jainism (as in Buddhism) the wheel is commonly called a *dharmacakra*, i.e., a wheel of *dharma* (doctrine or law), and thus it also stands for the doctrine of the *tirthankaras* (or of the Buddha). According to the *Trishashtiśalākāpurushacaritra* the first *dharmacakra* was installed by Bahubali, the son of the first *tirthankara*, Rishabha. At the time here involved, Rishabha came to Takshaśila, the city of Bahubali, and stood in meditation in a garden outside the city. Bahubali, then taking his ease in the palace, waited until morning to go out to see his father and was then dismayed to find that by that time Rishabha had already departed elsewhere. There were left, however, where Rishabha had stood, the prints of his feet, marked with various auspicious symbols which came from the soles of the feet, the thunderbolt, goad, disk, lotus, banner, fish, and the like. Over these Bahubali placed flat upon the ground a large jeweled *dharmacakra*, and paid homage to it with so many flowers that it looked to the townspeople like a mountain of flowers. Thus the *dharmacakra* is a symbol of the invisible presence of a *tirthankara*.[2]

Ayagapatas

The earliest monuments which show Jaina symbols and images are the *ayagapatas*. An *ayagapata* is a carved ornamental slab. Such objects, with Jaina symbols and figures, were placed by donors in Jaina cult places, and inscriptions on them often say that they are "in honor of the *arhats*," thus they may be called votive tablets or tablets of homage and veneration.

A number of *ayagapatas* have been found in the Mathura region, chiefly at a site locally called Kankali Tila (mound), near the southwestern corner of the city of Mathura. At this site there are the ruins of a Jaina *stupa*, and from the site have come, in addition to the *ayagapatas*, many Jaina images, architectural fragments, pillars of the railing of the *stupa*, etc. Some of the pieces bear inscriptions and some have dates, and all together it is indicated that the place was a main Jaina establishment already in the second century B.C.E. and continuing for many centuries afterward.[3]

As an example of the dating of the Kankali Tila *ayagapatas* in particular, one votive tablet was donated by a lady named Amohini and is essentially an *ayagapata*, even though it is not so called in its inscription and even though its sculptures only show a royal lady and her attendants. The inscription at the top of the tablet begins, "Adoration to the Arhat Vardhamana!" and contains a date under a great satrap (*mahakshatrapa*) named Śodas and in the year 42 or 72 (the reading is uncertain) of an unnamed era. If the year is ascribed to the Vikrama era, as is probable considering the king involved, and if the larger figure is taken, the date is equivalent to 15 C.E.[4]

As to Jaina symbols on the *ayagapatas*, there is an example in a tablet of homage found near the Kankali Tila and now in the State Museum, Lucknow (Fig. 10.1).[5] The incomplete inscription which belongs to the tablet begins with an

10.1 Tablet of Homage from Kankali Tila, Mathura, with the Symbol of the Wheel, in the State Museum, Lucknow. Photograph from Vincent A. Smith, *The Jain Stûpa and Other Antiquities of Mathurâ* (ASI 20) (Allahabad: Government Press, 1901), p. 15, Pl. VIII.

expression of adoration to the Arhat Mahavira, calls the tablet an *ayagapata,* and describes its donor, whose name is lost, as a lady who was an inhabitant of Mathura. No date is given but, like the dated tablet just mentioned, this one also probably belongs to the first century C.E. In the relief carvings on the tablet the central object is a large wheel with sixteen spokes. Around the wheel is a second rim and, in the space between, are figures of dancers forming a circle. In the borders of the tablet are decorative carvings and symbols such as the *śrivatsa* and *triśula.* These and many other symbols also appear on the *ayagapatas* which contain *jina* images (immediately below).

IMAGES

Jinas and Tirthankaras

Ayagapatas. The earliest known representations of the *jina* in human form are on some of the *ayagapatas* from Mathura. A tablet with such an image comes from Kankali Tila and is now in the State Museum, Lucknow (Fig. 10.2).[6] It has no date but is similar in style to the *ayagapata* with the wheel symbol (Fig. 10.1) and is probably also of the first century C.E. The inscription on the tablet gives the name of the donor, a man named Sihanadika, and refers to his parents, and reads in full: "Adoration to the *arhats*! A tablet of homage *(ayagapata)* was set up by Sihanadika, son of the Vanika (clan) Sihaka and son of a Kosiki (mother), in honor of the *arhats*."

In the center of the tablet, against a circular background and on an elevated pedestal, is a *jina* figure, seated erect and cross-legged with hands laid one upon the other in his lap, and wearing a headdress and with some sort of canopy over his head.

At the edges of the tablet to the left and right are two massive ornamental pillars (apparently prototypes of the *mana-stambhas* or pillars of glory), one surmounted by a wheel of the law *(dharmacakra)* and the other by an elephant. In the other borders of the tablet are various decorative carvings and symbols, e.g., in the upper border a pair of fishes, and at the four corners the *śrivatsa*.

Other *ayagapatas* from Kankali Tila with a *jina* figure in the center are one of probably the second century C.E. given by an unknown donor (since the inscription at the base is illegible), in which the central circle is surrounded by two fishes, a *śrivatsa,* a *śvastika,* and a *triśula,* and the outermost circle contains a second seated *jina* figure at the bottom, a *stupa* at the top, and a *caitya* tree at the right;[7] and another of similar arrangement and presumably similar date, donated (according to the partially preserved inscription at the base) by "the wife of Śivaghoshaka," in which the seated *jina* has a seven-hooded snake canopy over his head and is saluted with folded hands *(anjali)* by an attendant on either side.[8]

As to the origin of the *jina* image, found here on these tablets of homage of probably the first and second centuries C.E., the pose of the figure is that of an Indian *yogi,* seated in meditation, and it may be taken as likely that it was from such a prototype that the *jina* image was derived.[9]

As to the identification of any individual personages, it is only in the last of the three examples just noted, namely, in the tablet set up by the wife of Śivaghoshaka, that there is a clue. Here the fact that the head of the *jina* is canopied by a sevenheaded snake shows that this is Parśvanatha, the twenty-third *tirthankara,* for the snake canopy is the regular mark of Parśvanatha in Jaina iconography (Table 9.5).

10.2 Tablet of Homage from Kankali Tila, Mathura, with the Figure of a Jina, in the State Museum, Lucknow. Photograph from Smith, *The Jain Stûpa and Other Antiquities of Mathurâ*, p. 14, Pl. VII.

Characteristics of the Images. As in the examples already noted, images of the *tirthankaras*, whether seated or standing and whether in relief or free-standing, tend to be virtually identical in appearance. This is understandable because the *tirthankaras* are considered to be perfect beings, and thus their images must be intended to represent perfection, which would be the same in all cases.

The *tirthankara* image is always that of a human being. The body is smooth and firm, as that of one who has gained complete control of the physical being and is capable of protracted immobility. In these ways the statue of a *tirthankara* contrasts with that of a Hindu god or goddess, who may combine animal and human features, whose attributes may be symbolized by the multiplication of the number of heads and arms, and who may manifest violent action or voluptuous form. Many attendants of the *tirthankaras,* however, are the same as figures of the Hindu pantheon and are represented in similar opulence. The countenance of the *tirthankara* is also so undisturbed as to exhibit complete control of the emotions and imperturbable quiet; yet this is hardly the serenity, gentleness, and compassion of the typical Buddhist figure.

Since the Digambara monk is utterly possessionless and naked, the Digambara image of a *tirthankara* is entirely unclothed; since the Śvetambaras allow clothing the Śvetambara image may be clothed. Since Rishabhanatha, Neminatha, and Mahavira attained *nirvana* while they were sitting in the *padmasana* position (cross-legged with the right leg resting on the left and the left pulled through to rest on the right thigh), and in the *dhyana mudra* (hands in the middle of the lap, one upon the other, palms up, the right over the left), and all the twenty-one other *tirthankaras* made the same attainment while they were standing in meditation in the attitude known as *kayotsarga* or "dismissing the body" (upright, with the feet on the ground and arms held downwards without touching the body), the images also show the *tirthankaras* as they thus were when they left the earth, i.e., the images are either sitting (in full *padmasana* or sometimes in *ardha-padmasana,* half *padmasana,* legs simply crossed) or standing.

Whether sitting or standing, the image of the *tirthankara* may show a *śrivatsa, svastika,* or other mark on the chest; the eyes may be half-closed in meditation; the ear lobes are often elongated; there is often a protuberance *(ushnisha)* on the top of the head, perhaps covered with coiled ringlets of hair; and signs such as wheels may be marked on the palms of the hands and the soles of the feet. In some cases some event connected with the *tirthankara* is symbolized in a major additional feature connected with the figure, e.g., the snake with Parśva, but otherwise identification of individual personages is usually only possible if the name occurs in an inscription (which is rare), or if a distinctive emblem from the standard Jaina iconography (Table 9.5) is shown; in fact such a recognition symbol *(lanchana)* is often carved on the seat or pedestal of the image.

Along with the *tirthankara* it is usual to show other lesser figures, such as disciples *(ganadharas)* often with flywhisks, a *yaksha* on the right side of the main figure and a *yakshini* on his left, gods and goddesses, heavenly musicians *(gandharvas)* and nymphs (e.g., *apsarases).* Other accompaniments may be a sacred tree (such as the Aśoka tree, under which Mahavira made his great renunciation), a lion throne, or a triple umbrella.

Although there are *tirthankaras* of other ages both before and after the present world age, it is the twenty-four *tirthankaras* of this present age who are represented in images and, of them, it is Rishabha, Nemi (Arishtanemi), Parśva, and Mahavira who are the most important and who are the ones most frequently represented. Where other *tirthankaras* are shown with one or more of these, it is still usually one of these four who is the main figure. All twenty-four *tirthankaras* are men, except for the nineteenth, Malli, who according to the Śvetambaras was a woman, but this is not accepted by the Digambaras and a feminine representation is rare. In addition to the four major *tirthankaras,* the great ascetic Bahubali, also known as Gommata and Gommateśvara, the second son of Rishabha, is a very important figure, especially among the Digambara Jainas, and is frequently represented.

Literary References. Of literary references stating standards for the portrayal of a *jina,* the earliest datable is a description by Varahamihira (505–587 C.E.) in his *Brihat-samhita* (58.45): "The god of the Jainas, namely, Jina, should be represented naked, young, handsome and serene in appearance, with his arms reaching the knees [i.e, as he is standing in meditation], and his breast marked with the *śrivatsa* figure."[10]

Somewhat more fully, Chapter 55 of the *Manasara* (500–700 C.E.) says that Jaina images, including those of the twenty-four *tirthankaras,* may be (like all other images) either stationary or movable, and may be in either the erect or the sitting posture. The figure should have two arms and two eyes (i.e., be purely human), and have a clean-shaven head and a top knot. There should be no ornaments and no clothes on any part of the body, which should be beautiful in and of itself. The *śrivatsa* symbol should, however, be marked on the chest in gold. The legs (presumably when standing) should be straight, and the two long hands be in the same posture. In the sitting posture the two feet are placed on the lotus seat, and the whole image is in a stiff attitude and bears a meditative look. In either the erect or the sitting position the image may be placed on a throne decorated with a *makara-torana* and an ornamental wishing tree *(kalpavriksha)*. The main image may also be accompanied by Narada and other sages, as well as by the assembly of gods and goddesses in a praying attitude. Other attendants, which should be carved in the same attitude, may be *yakshas, vidyadharas, lokapalas* (guardians of the cardinal points), Nagendra (the serpent king), and others.[11]

Rishabhanatha. In the standard Jaina iconography (Table 9.5) Rishabhanatha or Adinatha, the first *tirthankara,* is golden in color and his emblem is the bull, reminiscent of the bull seen by his mother in premonition of his birth. In its long account of Rishabha, the *Trishashtiśalakapurushacaritra* of Hemacandra gives a detailed personal description of him.[12] His body was perfectly symmetrical. On his feet and hands were auspicious marks, the conch, the *śrivatsa,* the *svastika,* and the like. His toes were straight like the petals of a lotus; his legs were strong like the legs of a deer; his breast was broad as a slab of gold, and marked with the *śrivatsa;* his shoulders were massive like the hump of a bull; his arms were massive, and terminated by hands like serpents' hoods, hanging down to the knees; his face was like another moon; his ears, pretty with inside convolutions, hanging to the shoulders, were like pearl oysters on the bank of the river of the beauty of his face; his eyebrows were dark and curved, with the beauty of a creeper that had appeared on the shore of the lotus pond of the eye; his hair shone, black as bees, curled, soft, and glossy, like the waves of the Kalindi (the Yamuna River, taking its rise in the mythical Kalinda mountains). On his head was a round, tall headdress, indicating lordship over the three worlds. He was attended by the serpent king Dharanendra acting as door keeper, by *yakshas* holding flywhisks *(cauris)* as the insignia of royalty or divinity, by beautiful *apsarases,* and by gods saying, "Long live!"

In his great renunciation Rishabha tore out the beautiful hair of his head in four handfuls and was on the point of pulling out the rest of his hair in a fifth handful, but was told by Namucidvish (i.e., Sakra, Indra), "O Lord, this hair-creeper brought by the wind to your golden shoulders shines like an emerald. So let it remain."[13] Accordingly long locks of hair falling on his shoulders are a mark of Rishabha, along with the bull as his *lanchana,* with his *yaksha* attendants, and so forth.

In the Archaeological Museum, Khajuraho, there is a large stone plaque with a relief image of Rishabhanatha (Fig. 10.3). The monument comes from the vicinity of the Khajuraho temples and is presumably of the same date as they (850–1100 C.E.). The *tirthankara* is standing in the *kayotsarga* posture. The lower left arm is broken off; otherwise, the figure is intact, and completely unclothed. Behind the head is a halo, and above is a three-tiered umbrella. In smaller size on the right of

10.3 Standing Image of Rishabha, in the Archaeological Museum, Khajuraho

the main figure is the *yaksha* Gomukha and on the left the *yakshini* Cakreśvari, and there are other yet smaller figures on the monument. On either side of the halo are elephants, and above are flying celestials.[14]

Neminatha. Neminatha or Arishtanemi, the cousin of Krishna and the twenty-second *tirthankara,* named for the wheel *(nemi)* of black jewel *(arishta)* which his mother saw in a dream prior to his birth, is black in color and the conchshell *(śankha)* is his emblem. At least one point of connection of the conch with Neminatha lies in an event in his life narrated in the *Trishashtiśalakapurushacaritra.*[15] It seems that Krishna once slew a marine demon named Pancajana, who lived at the bottom of the sea in the form of a conchshell, and afterward Krishna used the body of the demon, the *pancajanya,* as a trumpet, wherefore conches came to be blown in temple worship and in battle. Upon the occasion here of interest, Nemi noticed the *pancajanya* in the armory of Vasudeva (i.e., Krishna), and was told by the keeper of the armory that even though he (Nemi) was the brother of Hari (Krishna), he would not be able to lift, much less to blow the conch, for no one, except Hari, was able to do this. Thereupon Nemi smiled, lifted the conch with ease, and blew it with a sound which filled heaven and earth and rivaled the sound of the ocean with high waves pounding against Dvaraka's walls. Govinda (Krishna) heard the sound and wondered who had blown his conch. When he learned that it was his brother (in fact his cousin) Nemi who had done so, there ensued a contest of strength in which Nemi easily bent the arm of Vishnu (Krishna) like a lotus stem, while Vishnu clung to Nemi's arm with all his strength, like a monkey to a tree, but was not able to bend Nemi's arm in the least.

In the Archaeological Museum, Mathura, is a seated stone image of Neminatha (Fig. 10.4), which was found in the construction of the Cantonments at Mathura, and is of approximately the twelfth century C.E. in date. Neminatha is seated cross-legged in the attitude of meditation *(dhyana mudra)*. His throne is supported on two small pillars and on a pair of lions, each seated with one paw raised. Two small figures, male and female, standing with hands folded, are half

10.4 Seated Image of Neminatha, in the Archaeological Museum, Mathura

hidden behind the pillars, and are probably the donors of the monument. On a hanging between the lions there appears to be a wheel, and there is a conch, the emblem of Neminatha, on the plain rim of the pedestal beneath. On either side of the main figure is an attendant standing with a flywhisk *(cauri)* in one hand, and these are either disciples *(ganadharas)* or perhaps Gomedha and Ambika, the *yaksha* and *yakshini* properly attendant upon Neminatha. Behind the head of the main figure is a halo, and on either side of this is a flying celestial, probably a *gandharva* and an *apsaras,* the male figure carrying a garland as an offering, and the female apparently showering down flowers. Above on each side are traces of an elephant standing on a lotus flower. The head of the *tirthankara* is surmounted by a triple parasol, on top of which a small prostrate figure is beating a hand drum.[16]

Parśvanatha. Parśvanatha, the twenty-third *tirthankara* and immediate predecessor (250 years before) of Mahavira, is blue and his emblem is a hooded snake, reminiscent of the black serpent *(parśva)* which his mother saw prior to his birth and of the *naga* king who protected him in a storm.

The *Trishashtiśalakapurushacaritra* explains that the blue color of the body of Parśva looked as if made from the essence of blue lotuses. It also describes Parśva as long armed, so that he looked like a tree with long branches; as having a broad, firm chest, so that he looked like an immovable mountain. From his hands, feet, face, and eyes, he had the beautiful appearance of a pool with a bed of blooming lotuses. He was slender and flat at the waist, and marked with the thunderbolt and other auspicious signs.[17]

The same work also provides details concerning the events when Parśva compassionately rescued the serpent which became the *naga* king Dharana (also Dharanendra) and the latter later protected him in danger. It seems that the ascetic Katha, from whose fire Parśva delivered the snake, was reborn as an *asura* called Meghamalin (whose name suggests a rain-cloud demon), and Meghamalin was intensely hostile to Parśva. So when Parśva was standing motionless in meditation under a banyan tree, it was Meghamalin who sent against him many fierce animals and then a terrible rainstorm and flood. Neither the animals nor the storm diverted Parśva from his meditation, although he was finally standing in water up to the tip of his nose. When the serpent king Dharana realized what was happening he came with his wives, with all speed:

> Dharana bowed to the Master and placed beneath his feet a tall lotus with erect stalk, resembling the seat of an omniscient. The serpent king covered the Lord's back, sides, and breast with his own coils and made an umbrella with seven hoods over his head. The Blessed One, standing comfortably on the lotus with a stalk the length of the water, absorbed in meditation, looked like a *rajahamsa* (king swan).

So Parśva was delivered from danger and, in the aftermath, Meghamalin was convinced of his crime and asked forgiveness of Parśva.[18]

In the Victoria and Albert Museum, London, is a seated stone image of Parśvanatha (Fig. 10.5), which was once in a Jaina temple at Gyaraspur in the district of Vidiśa, and is probably of the seventh century C.E. At the base of the monument two crouching lions with long curled tails support a platform *(simhasana),* and on the base there is also a dwarf figure, holding a wheel in his hands. It is the time when Meghamalin has loosed against Parśva the great storm but the *naga* king Dharanendra has come to his rescue, and Parśva is seated undisturbed, cross-legged in meditation *(dhyana mudra),* on the coils of the serpent, while the

10.5 Seated Image of Parśvanatha, in the Victoria and Albert Museum, London. Photograph from the Victoria and Albert Museum.

serpent's seven hoods are raised above his head. Also the consort of the serpent king, the *nagi* Padmavati, is standing to the rear and holding a white umbrella yet higher over the *jina*. On either side *cauri* bearers attend the main figure, and above, on either side of the cobra hoods, celestials hover in the sky, holding garlands. Finally, on either side at the top, are hands beating drums, in this case perhaps to represent the thunder of the storm from which Parśva is being protected.[19]

Mahavira. Mahavira, the twenty-fourth and last *tirthankara* of the present world age, is identified in Jaina iconography as golden in color and with the lion as his mark of recognition, the lion perhaps being chosen as the most fitting symbol of his spiritual heroism. The *Trishashtiśalakapurushacaritra* states that the beauty of Mahavira was the greatest in the three worlds. It describes him as walking with a beautiful gait like an elephant of the forest, but in his ascetic life most often tells of his standing motionless, utterly absorbed in meditation, as on this occasion when he was observing a fast: "Standing on a stone slab that was devoid of injury to living creatures, his arms hanging down to his knees, his body slightly bent, his mind firm, unwinking, his gaze fixed on one gross object, the Lord stood there in statuesque posture for one night long."[20]

A great many identifiable statues of Mahavira have been found in both North and South India, and it is also traditionally held that all images without any symbol represent Mahavira. In the Prince of Wales Museum of Western India, Bombay, is a standing stone image of Mahavira (Fig. 10.6), which comes from Karnataka and is attributed to the twelfth century C.E. The naked figure is standing in the *kayotsarga* pose and under a triple sunshade. As is usually the case the ears are elongated, and the hair is done in curls. On the pedestal is the lion symbol of Mahavira. At his right stands the *yaksha* Matanga, and at his left the *yakshini* Siddhaika. On either side are pilasters which support a *makara-torana*.[21]

10.6 Standing Image of Mahavira, in the Prince of Wales Museum of Western India, Bombay

Attendants of the Tirthankaras

Yakshas and Yakshinis. As already noted, it is usual to consider that a *tirthankara* may be attended by *ganadharas* (disciples), *yakshas* (feminine *yakshis* or *yakshinis*), celestial beings, and so forth. Of these the most prominent are usually the *yakshas*. According to Jaina belief, Indra appoints one *yaksha* and one *yakshini* to serve as attendants of each *tirthankara,* and these personages are therefore also known as *śasana-devatas* or attendant deities. They are all known by their personal names, and their king is Kubera (also called Vaiśravana, being the son of Viśravas and thus the half-brother of Ravana), who serves as well as the attendant *yaksha* of Mallinatha, the nineteenth *tirthankara*. In art the *yaksha* is normally shown on the *tirthankara's* right side, the *yakshini* on the left. Each has distinctive attributes, such as a particular vehicle *(vahana)*. On the details of the attributes, and even on the names of the personages, there are, however, differences between the Digambaras and Śvetambaras, and also idiosyncrasies in individual works of art, and the same is true not only for *yakshas* and *yakshinis* but also for other attendant figures.

Of all the *yakshas* and *yakshinis,* those who are attendant upon the four most prominent tirthankaras are naturally themselves treated with special respect on account of the high position of their masters. With their most familiar names, these are Gomukha and Cakreśvari who attend Rishabhanatha (Adinatha), Gomedha and Ambika who are with Neminatha, Dharanendra and Padmavati who assist Parśvanatha, and Matanga and Siddhayika who are attached to Mahavira.[22]

Gomukha and Cakreśvari. Both the Digambaras and Śvetambaras give these names for the *yaksha* and *yakshini* of the first *tirthankara*. In respect to the attributes of Gomukha, both sects are in general agreement, although some of their texts vary as to whether he rides upon a bull or an elephant. In the case of Cakreśvari, however, the Digambaras give her either four or twelve hands, while the Śvetambaras think of eight hands, and the number of objects held vary as well, but both sects agree that she rides upon a *garuda*.

The *Trishashtiśalakapurushacaritra* of the Śvetambara author Hemacandra tells how Rishabhanatha founded the first Jaina congregation, and how Gomukha and Cakreśvari (whom it calls Apraticakra) came forward to become his chief attendants, and it will be noted that the two are described in terms of the Śvetambara conception:

> A Guhyaka *(yaksha)* named Gomukha, who appeared in the congregation, adorned with two right arms—one in *varada* (boon bestowing) position and one holding a rosary, and with two left arms—one holding a citron and one a noose, gold color, having an elephant vehicle, became the Lord's attendant.
>
> Apraticakra (Cakreśvari), gold color, with a *garuda* seat, with one right arm in *varada* position and the others holding an arrow, disk, and noose, her left arms holding a bow, thunderbolt, disk, and goad, originated in that congregation and became the Lord's messenger deity.
>
> Then the Blessed One went elsewhere to wander, surrounded by great *rishis* like the moon by constellations. . . . Wherever the Master went, there was no hostility, pestilence, drought, famine, excessive rain, no fear of one's own ruler nor of another. . . .[23]

Gomedha and Ambika. Both the Digambaras and the Śvetambaras name the *yaksha* of Neminatha, the twenty-second *tirthankara*, Gomedha and describe him as having three faces, six hands, and the vehicle of a man. As for the *yakshini*, the Digambaras call her Amra and picture her with two hands holding a bunch of mangoes and a child, while the Śvetambaras name her Ambika and describe her as having four hands and holding a bunch of mangoes, a noose, a child, and a goad. Both sects agree, however, that the *yakshini* rides upon a lion.

Corresponding with the Śvetambara conception, the *Trishashtiśalakapurushacaritra* tells of the rise of Gomedha and Ambika in the congregation of Neminatha and enumerates their distinctive attributes:

> Gomedha, originating in that congregation, three-faced, dark, with a man for a vehicle, carrying a citron, an axe, a *cakra* in three right hands, an ichneumon, a trident, and a spear in his three left hands, became Nemi's messenger deity.
>
> His vicinity always superintended by them, Nemi passed the rainy season and autumn. Then he set forth to wander elsewhere, moving like a *bhadra*-elephant, seeking the good (*bhadra*) of the people.[24]

Dharanendra and Padmavati. The *yaksha* of Parśvanatha, the twenty-third *tirthankara*, is called both Parśva and Dharanendra by both the Digambaras and the Śvetambaras, and we have already seen him coming from the serpent world, with his consort Padmavati, to rescue Parśvanatha from the great flood. Both the Digambaras and the Śvetambaras make a tortoise the vehicle of Parśva/Dharanendra, and describe him as having four hands, but they vary slightly as to the attributes in the several hands. Both sects also agree in naming the *yakshini* of Parśvanatha Padmavati. The Digambaras, however, see her in different forms with anything from four to twenty-four hands, while the Śvetambaras picture her with four hands holding a lotus, noose, fruit, and goad. Some Digambara texts give her a snake and cock as her vehicle, others give her a lotus seat, while the Śvetambaras regularly represent her as riding on a snake and cock.

The *Trishashtiśalakapurushacaritra* describes the two in their association with Parśvanatha:

> Originating in that congregation, the *yaksha* Parśva, with a tortoise for a vehicle, dark, elephant-faced, splendid with an umbrella of serpent hoods, four-armed, holding an ichneumon and a serpent in his left hands, a citron and a serpent in his right hands, became the Lord's messenger deity.
>
> Likewise the goddess Padmavati, with a *kurkuta* serpent for a vehicle, gold colored, carrying a lotus and a noose in her right hands, a fruit and a goad in her left hands, became the second messenger deity of Lord Śri Parśva.
>
> The Lord, his vicinity unceasingly presided over by the messenger deities, wandered over the earth, attended by reverent gods and others.[25]

In the Prince of Wales Museum of Western India, Bombay, is a stone image of the *yakshini* Padmavati (Fig. 10.7), which comes from Karnataka and is attributed to the twelfth century C.E. The *yakshini* has four arms and is seated on a cushion in the *lalitasana* posture, with the right leg crossed and the left foot lowered. In this case the lower right hand holds a lotus, the upper right hand holds a goad, the upper left hand a noose resembling a snake (*nagapaśa*), and the lower left hand is broken off. She wears a richly decorated tiered crown (*karandamukuta*), a long chain (*mala*), necklaces, earrings, armlets, bracelets, and anklets. Above her head is the single hood of a cobra, and this indicates her association with serpents and the nether world. Pilasters on either side support a *makara-torana*, with the *makara* at the top blowing scroll patterns.[26]

Matanga and Siddhayika. Matanga and Siddhayika who attend on Mahavira are not named in the *Trisashtiśalakapurushacaritra* but are described in other Jaina

10.7 Seated Image of the Yakshini Padmavati, in the Prince of Wales Museum of Western India, Bombay

sources and, as the attendants of the last *tirthankara,* are the last and most important of the *yakshas* and *yakshinis.*[27] The name of Matanga means "elephant," and the elephant is appropriately his vehicle and symbol. In the iconography he appears with two hands. According to the Digambaras the left hand holds a citron and the right a mongoose, while according to the Śvetambaras the left hand holds a citron but the right is in the *varada* (boon bestowing) position. Siddhayika, consort of Matanga and *yakshini* of Mahavira, rides upon a lion, appropriately enough, inasmuch as this is the emblem of Mahavira too. She has four hands, and the two on the left hold a citron and a lute, while one on the right holds a book and the other is in the *varada* position of boon bestowing (according to the Digambaras) or the *abhaya* position of reassurance (according to the Śvetambaras).

Yakshesvara and Kali. Of the *tirthankaras* of lesser prominence the fourth in the entire series, for example, is Abhinandanatha. Both the Digambaras and the Śvetambaras name the *yaksha* of Abhinandanatha Yakshesvara (king of *yakshas*), sometimes shortened to Iśvara. They agree in making his vehicle the elephant and in describing him as having four hands, but they vary as to the objects held in the hands. The *yakshini* of Abhinandanatha is named Vajrasrimkhala by the Digambaras, and is described as riding on a swan and as holding in her four hands a snake, noose, rosary, and fruit. The same *yakshini* is named Kali by the Śvetambaras, and is described as seated on a lotus and as having four hands, one in the *varada* (boon bestowing) position, and the others holding a noose, snake, and goad. In the case of the Digambaras the name Kali is that of the *yakshini* of Suparśvanatha, the seventh *tirthankara*, whose *yakshini* the Śvetambaras call Śanta. This later Kali, *yakshini* of Suparśvanatha, is described by the Digambaras as riding on a bull and as having four hands, one in the *varada* position, and the others carrying a trident, fruit, and bell. The name Kali is also that of the consort of Śiva in Hinduism, so the Jaina *yakshini* and the Hindu *śakti* are evidently related, and similar relationships are observable in the case of not a few of the other attendants of the *tirthankaras*.

The *Trishashtiśalakapurushacaritra* tells of the foundation of the congregation of Abhinandanatha, and describes Yakshesvara and Kali, the latter here called Kalika:

> In this congregation arose Yakshesvara, dark, with an elephant for a vehicle, his two right hands holding a citron and a rosary, his two left hands carrying an ichneumon and a goad, a messenger deity always near the Lord.
>
> Likewise Kalika appeared, dark colored, seated on a lotus, one right hand in *varada* position and one holding a noose, her two left hands holding a snake and a goad, a messenger deity always in attendance on the Lord.[28]

In the Prince of Wales Museum of Western India, Bombay, is a stone image of the *yakshini* Kali (Fig. 10.8), which comes from Karnataka and is attributed to the twelfth century C.E. Kali is seated on a pedestal in the *lalitasana* position, and on her head is a conical crown *(kirita)* with a seated *jina*, and above it is a cobra with a single hood. The *yakshini* has four hands, with attributes corresponding to the Śvetambara conception, but in different order from the description in the *Trishashtiśalakapurushacaritra* just given. The lower left hand is in the *varada mudra*, the upper right hand carries an elephant goad *(ankuśa)*, the upper left hand holds a noose, and the lower left holds a *naga*. On the pedestal, however, we do not have a lotus which is the seat and recognition symbol *(lanchana)* of Kali according to the Śvetambaras, but rather the swan which is the vehicle of the same *yakshini*, called Vajrasrimkhala by the Digambaras. This recognition symbol also clearly distinguishes this Kali from Kali the *yakshini*, according to the Digambaras, of Suparśvanatha, the seventh *tirthankara*, the *yakshini* whose vehicle is the bull. Likewise the attributes of the hands correspond with those proper to Kali the *yakshini* of Abhinandanatha, and not with those belonging to the later Kali.[29]

In the immediately foregoing quotations from the *Trishashtiśalakapurushacaritra* it has been seen that in the entourage of the *tirthankaras* were not only a *yaksha* and a *yakshini* but also many more figures, e.g., "great *rishis*" and "reverent gods and others." In particular, Jaina iconography often represents, along with the *tirthankaras*, such figures as *dikpalas*, *navagrahas*, *vidyadevis*, and miscellaneous other divinities, and many of these are the equivalents of the same figures in Hinduism.[30]

Dikpalas. The *dikpalas* (region guards), also called *lokapalas* (place guards), are the guardian deities of the directions. Starting from the east (the direction of the sunrise and the direction usually faced by the worshiper), they are Indra (east), Agni (southeast), Yama (south), Nrutti (southwest), Varuna (west), Vayu (north-

10.8 Seated Image of the Yakshini Kali in the Prince of Wales Museum of Western India, Bombay

west), Kubera (north), Iśana (northeast), Brahma (upper regions), and Naga (nether regions).

Indra. In the Jaina view there are no less than sixty-four Indras in the twelve heavens *(kalpas)* of the Upper World, and of these the chief Indra, here dealt with, is the Indra of the first heaven, the heaven called Saudharma. As the king of this heaven the Digambaras call this Indra the Saudharma-Indra. The Śvetambaras use for him the various epithets commonly belonging to Indra, such as Mahendra (great Indra), Purandara (destroyer of cities), and Śakra (mighty).

According to the *Trishashtiśalakapurushacaritra,* Śakra played a special part in the five important events in the lives of the twenty-four *tirthankaras*. With respect to Rishabhanatha, for example, it was Śakra who gave him his birth-bath, arranged his wedding, crowned him king, held his initiation festival, and conducted his funeral rites, while all sixty-four Indras were present at his death. With respect to Mahavira, it was Śakra who arranged for the embryonic transfer at his birth, saved him from danger in his wandering life, and at the end conducted his funeral rites.[31]

As in Hinduism, the wife of Indra is Sachi (Indrani), and his chief characteristics, iconographically, are his elephant called Airavata and his *vajra* or thunderbolt.

As in Hinduism, Agni is the sacrificial priest and his wife is Svaha. Agni rides a ram, holds a spear *(śakti)*, and carries seven flames, or bow and arrow. Yama, the god of the dead, rides a buffalo and holds a staff. Nrutti (also Nairta, Nirrta) carries club, sword, and bow, and rides upon a bear according to the Digambaras, or upon a corpse or goblin according to the Śvetambaras. Varuna rides a dolphin or a fish, and carries a noose. Vayu rides a deer, and carries a wooden weapon (Digambara), or a *vajra* or a banner (Śvetambara). Kubera, treasurer of Śakra (Indra), carries gems and a club, and rides in a chariot called Pushpaka (Digambara), or upon a man (Śvetambara). Iśana (a name of Śiva) rides characteristically upon a bull, carrying bow and trident (Śvetambara) and also a skull (Digambara). Brahma and Naga appear only in Śvetambara lists of the *dikpalas*, not in Digambara lists. As in Hinduism, Brahma has four heads, rides upon a swan *(hamsa)*, and carries a book and a lotus. Naga sits upon a lotus, and holds a snake in his hand.

Navagrahas. The *navagrahas* are the nine planets, considered to be Surya (sun), Candra (moon), Mangala (Mars), Budha (Mercury), Brihaspati (Jupiter), Sukra (Venus), Sani (Saturn), Rahu and Ketu (the waxing and waning phases of the moon). Digambara and Śvetambara representations are generally similar, but the Digambara is sometimes simpler. According to the Śvetambaras, Surya carries two lotuses and rides in a chariot drawn by seven steeds; Candra holds an urn of nectar and rides in a chariot drawn by ten white horses; Mangala has one hand in the *varada* (boon bestowing) position and holds spear, trident, club, or shovel; Budha rides swan or lion and holds book or sword, shield, and club, and has one hand in the *varada* pose; Brihaspati has a swan as vehicle (lotus according to the Digambaras), and carries rosary and staff (rosary, vase, book, according to the Digambaras); Sukra rides a snake and carries an urn or threefold thread, snake, noose, and rosary; Sani rides a tortoise and carries an axe; Rahu rides a lion and carries an axe (flag according to the Digambaras); Ketu rides on a cobra and carries a cobra.

Vidyadevis. The *vidyadevis* are goddesses of learning (*vidya*, learning, knowledge, science). In the Jaina view there are sixteen of these, and most of their names are the same as the names of *yakshinis*, especially *yakshinis* of the Digambaras. They are the following: Rohini (*yakshini* of Ajitanatha); Prajnapati (*yakshini* of Sambhavanatha); Vajrasrimkhala (*yakshini* of Abhinandanatha); Vajramkuśa (*yakshini* of Anantanatha); Apraticakra or Jambunada (*yakshini* of Rishabhanatha); Purushadatta (*yakshini* of Sumatinatha); Kali (*yakshinis* of Abhinandanatha and Suparśvanatha); Mahakali (*yakshinis* of Sumatinatha and Suvidhinatha); Gandhari (*yakshini* of Naminatha); Gauri (*yakshini* of Śreyamśanatha); Mahajvala or Jvalamalini (*yakshini* of Candraprabha); Manavi (*yakshinis* of Sitalanatha and Śreyamśanatha); Vairoti (*yakshini* of Vimalanatha); Achyupta (cf. Achyuta, *yakshini* of Padmaprabha); Manasi (*yakshini* of Dharmanatha); Mahamanasi (*yakshini* of Śantinatha).

Sarasvati. At the head of the sixteen *vidyadevis* is Sarasvati, well known also in Hinduism as the goddess of learning, speech, and music, and the consort of Brahma. Her other names include Vagdevi (goddess of learning) and Śrutadevi (goddess of *śruti*). In Hinduism *śruti* refers to the Vedas and other revealed literature; here in Jainism, in her role as Śrutadevi, Sarasvati presides over the *śruti* in the sense of the preaching of the *tirthankaras*. In general, her attributes are the same in Jainism as in Hinduism, and include book and lute. As for her vehicle *(vahana)*, in most of the Digambara images she is mounted on a peacock, and in those of the Śvetambaras, on a swan.

A very delicate and graceful sculpture in marble of Sarasvati/Vagdevi in the National Museum, New Delhi (Fig. 10.9), comes from Bikaner in Rajasthan from the time of the Gahadavala dynasty (1085–1194 C.E.), and the style of its execution is judged to be Jaina. The goddess stands upon a lotus, her head backgrounded by an elaborated halo. On her head is a crown, surmounted by a small seated figure. Her rich ornaments include necklace, arm- and wrist-bands, waistband, and anklets. Her lower right hand holds a rosary, the upper right hand a lotus, the upper left hand a book, and the lower left hand a water vessel. On the two sides of the main figure are attendant female musicians. On either side at the feet of the main figure is also a kneeling figure, with hands folded in the attitude of adoration or prayer *(anjali)*, and these are presumably disciples or donors.[32]

10.9 Standing Image of Sarasvati, in the National Museum, New Delhi

In association with the *tirthankaras* are yet other figures who, at least in several cases, are the counterparts of deities of Hinduism, and are represented in much the same way.

Naigamesha. According to the narrative in the *Trishashtiśalakapurushacaritra*, when Śakra (Indra) commanded the embryonic transfer at the birth of Mahavira, it was the general of his army, named Naigamesha, who carried out the order.[33] Images of Naigamesha show him with the head of a ram, antelope, or goat.

Śri/Lakshmi. Śri or Lakshmi, known in Hinduism as the goddess of beauty and good fortune, has a similar and important place in Jainism. In the Hindu account of the goddess it is told how she emerged from the primeval waters, seated on a lotus, and was washed by the elephants of the skies, and this event was likewise the subject of the fourth dream of Queen Triśala prior to the birth of Mahavira, an event referred to in a concise list of the fourteen dreams of the queen in the *Trishashtiśalakapurushacaritra* as "Sri being sprinkled."[34]

Ganeśa. Ganeśa or Ganapati, the elephant-headed son of Śiva and Parvati, who is shown in a great many different forms in Hindu iconography, is also variously represented in Jaina images. He may have two, four, six, nine, eighteen, or one hundred and eight hands, and they may be in *varada* (boon bestowing) and *abhaya* (reassurance) positions, and hold axe *(paraśu)*, sweetmeat ball *(modaka)* and other items. As in Hinduism, his vehicle is the rat or mouse.[35]

Kshetrapala. This deity is installed as a guardian at the entrance of Jaina temples. He has six or twenty hands; with six hand he may hold mace, noose, drum *(damaru)*, dog, goad, and stick; with twenty hands he holds many weapons. Although he does not appear to be recognizable as the counterpart of any Hindu deity, Kshetrapala is known as the leader of sixty-four *yoginis,* and demonesses of this designation are otherwise associated with Durga.

STUPAS

Jainism shares with Hinduism the making of cave, carved, and constructed temples, and with Buddhism the making of *stupas*.

Characteristics of the Stupa

The *stupa* was originally a burial mound or tumulus, and became a memorial monument which served to enshrine relics or to mark some place or to recall some event of sacred history. The form of the *stupa* is essentially that of a hemisphere, perhaps resting on a terrace base, and surmounted by a square or circular enclosure *(harmika)* from the center of which an umbrella *(chhatra)* rises as a symbol of royalty. The *stupa* proper is usually surrounded by a processional path *(pradakshina patha)*, enclosed by a railing *(vriti)* built of upright posts *(stambhas)* and horizontal crossbeams *(suchis)*, and with four ornamental gateways *(toranas)* in the four directions.

In contrast with Buddhism where relics are of great importance, Jaina *stupas* apparently did not serve for the preservation of such objects—since relic worship does not seem to belong to the Jaina faith; and also in contrast with Buddhism, where the *stupa* always continued to be a most important monument and symbol, *stupas* belong, as far as the evidence goes, only to the earlier history of Jainism, but at least in that period the *stupa* was a significant Jaina cult center.

Remains at Mathura

The first and most important evidence for the use of the *stupa* in Jainism comes from Kankali Tila at Mathura, already mentioned above in connection with Jaina *ayagapatas*. The excavation of this mound brought to light the actual ruins of a Jaina *stupa* as well as the evidence of two Jaina temples, one in the western part of the mound apparently belonging to the Digambaras, and the other nearer the center apparently belonging to the Śvetambaras. After the site fell into disuse the mound was long used as a quarry for bricks, and therefore not much of the ancient structures remains. The *stupa* is represented, however, by masses of brick, and its ground plan is discernible in the form of a large eight-spoked wheel. This was presumably a construction device to save expensive masonry, and the spaces between the radii were presumably filled in with clay. Above that, the structure was built in brick.[36]

Among other remains at Mathura which relate to Jaina *stupas* and, at least in some instances, probably to the very *stupa* just described, is a portion of the base of a statue, found in the Kankali mound.[37] In the sculptures on the front side of this base, in what was probably the center of the complete panel, is a wheel resting on a *triśula* which is supported by a lotus blossom. To the side are three women wearing long robes and holding long-stalked lotus flowers, and a small girl holding her hands in the gesture of adoration *(anjali)*. At the end of the scene is a large crouching lion. The accompanying inscription is dated in the Year 79 which, if the date is ascribed to the Śaka era, is equivalent to 157 C.E. The inscription further gives the information that the image which the base once supported was "of the Arhat Nandyavarta" (which presumably means Aranatha, the eighteenth *tirthankara*, whose recognition symbol is the *nandyavarta* sign), and "was set up at the Vodva *stupa*, built by the gods." In view of the find place of the statue base, the *stupa* to which reference is made was very probably the *stupa* the ruins of which are still at Kankali Tila, and the statement that the *stupa* was "built by the gods" probably means that it was already, at the time this inscription was composed, very ancient.[38]

A sculptured beam, found near one of the Jaina temples at Kankali Tila, was the central portion of the lowest architrave of an ornamental gateway *(torana)* in the railing around a *stupa*, and again, in view of the place of discovery of this object, the *stupa* to which it belonged was very possibly the same Kankali *stupa*. On the reverse side of the beam a procession is pictured, with persons on foot, on horseback, on elephant-back, and in a covered horse-drawn cart, a procession which is apparently moving to visit some sacred place. On the obverse side of the beam there is the representation of a *stupa* in the center, to which homage is paid by *kinnaras* and centaurs, and this *stupa* may well be the place to which the procession is moving and, if the beam belonged to the Kankali Tila *stupa*, that may be the very *stupa* which is here pictured.[39]

The lower preserved portion of a tablet of homage from Kankali Tila shows the lower part of a *stupa*, surrounded by a processional path enclosed within a railing, in which is an ornamental gateway with three architraves, from the lowest of which hangs a heavy wreath. At either side is a female dancer or *yakshini*, wearing jewelry and sash, and beside each of them is a massive pillar. Above, a portion of an upper circumambulatory can be seen. The inscription reads: "Adora-

10.10 Jaina Stupa on a Tablet of Homage, in the Archaeological Museum, Mathura

tion to the *arhats!* By Śivyaśa, wife of the dancer Phaguyaśa . . . a tablet of homage *(ayagapata)* was caused to be made in honor of the *arhats*."[40]

A tablet of homage, dating probably from the first century C.E., which was at one time let into the wall of a small shrine outside the Holi Gate (the main gate of Mathura) and is now in the Archaeological Museum at Mathura, shows a complete *stupa* (Fig. 10.10).[41] The structure is of a high cylindrical type, is surrounded by a railing and approached by a flight of steps and an ornamental gateway *(torana)* with three architraves. The projecting ends of the lowest architrave are supported by lion brackets. The *stupa* is flanked by two pillars, the one at the viewer's left surmounted by a wheel *(dharmacakra)*, and the one at the right surmounted by a sitting lion. Immediately beside the drum of the *stupa* are two female dancers or *yakshinis,* standing in the *śalabhanjika* posture. Above them are two *kinnaras* with birds' tails and claws, the one on the left holding a bunch of flowers, the one on the right holding a garland. Yet above them are two flying figures, possibly *munis* who have the power of transporting themselves through the air. Each holds a pot or bowl in the left hand, and touches the right hand to the forehead in a gesture of respectful salutation. At the base of the *stupa*, on each side of the staircase, is a niche containing a standing figure, the one on the left a male accompanied by a child, the one on the right a female.

The inscription of the tablet is written on the dome of the *stupa*. It begins, "Adoration to the Arhat Vardhamana!" and goes on to say that the slab was erected by the courtesan Vasu, the daughter of the courtesan Lonaśobhika, the disciple of the ascetics.

In this inscription the word *araye* (Sanskrit *aryayah*) occurs with the name of Lonaśobhika, and the word *nadaye* (Sanskrit *nandayah*) with the name of Vasu, and it is surmised that these may designate certain ranks (matron? junior?) among the courtesans. An example of the place of a courtesan in the society of the time is provided in a play called *Mrichchhakatika* (the little clay cart) by Śudraka (low-caste-ling), a Sanskrit dramatist who may possibly be identified with the servant, Simuka, who founded the Andhra dynasty, and who may then be dated around 200 B.C.E. This play is also quite evidently an expansion and refinement of a play called *Carudatta* by a yet earlier Sanskrit dramatist named Bhasa.

The play is set in the city of Ujjayini, and the heroine is a young, rich, and beautiful courtesan of noble character, named Vasantasena, who loves a once wealthy *brahmana* youth named Carudatta (he who gives nobly), who is now impoverished by his great generosity in response to every private and public need. The generosity of Vasantasena herself is shown when Carudatta's small son is crying because he is given a little clay cart (hence the title of the play) instead of the golden one he wanted, and she gives him her own ornaments from which to get a cart made.

In the course of the play Vasantasena is courted and pursued by an evil and foolish prince named Sakara, who is the brother-in-law of Palaka, the king of Ujjayini. When Vasantasena, ever faithful to Carudatta, rejects Sakara, he strangles her and leaves her for dead, managing at the same time to make it appear that Carudatta was the murderer and to bring him under sentence of death. Vasantasena is found in time, however, and revived by a Buddhist mendicant, Carudatta is eventually cleared of suspicion, released, and raised to high office, and he takes Vasantasena as his wife.

At an early point in the play, when Sakara, assisted by his two followers, Vita and Ceta, is pursuing Vasantasena and she has taken refuge in Carudatta's mansion, they enter the house and, in the dark of the night, mistake Radanika, herself the daughter of a courtesan and a maid in the employ of Carudatta, for Vasantasena, and endeavor to make off with her, even though Vita observes that her voice is different from that of the woman they are after. Radanika resists Sakara's attempt to pull her away with him, and the episode is ended by the opportune entrance of Maitreya, the constant companion and confidant *(vidushaka)* of Carudatta.

A stone sculpture from Mahuli near Mathura, probably dating in the first or second century C.E. and now in the National Museum, New Delhi, may almost certainly be recognized as a depiction of the scene just described (Fig. 10.11). Radanika—if this is the correct identification—has fallen upon one knee as she resists the abduction, and is assisted by a girl cup-bearer at her side; Sakara pulls with both hands on her right arm, and Vita (who upon occasion does not hesitate to call his master a fool) looks on quizzically.[42]

TEMPLES

Structurally there is no essential difference between Jaina and Hindu temples, except that the arrangement of space in a Jaina temple is focused upon the images of

MONUMENTS OF JAINISM IN INDIA | 265

10.11 Attempted Abduction of Radanika, Sculpture from Mathura, in the National Museum, New Delhi

the various *tirthankaras* housed there, often together with various of their attendants. Also it is often characteristic of Jainism to group a number of shrines on high hills or other relatively secluded places, and to treat these as places of pilgrimage without allowing permanent settled habitation in the immediate vicinity. As in Hinduism so also in Jainism there are cave, carved, and constructed temples.

Cave and Carved Temples

Ellora. At Ellora, already described in connection with Hinduism, there is at the north end of the entire series of excavations and separated from the most northerly of the Hindu caves by about 1,200 feet (365 m.), a group of five Jaina excavations (Nos. 30–34 in the sequential numbering from the south). The date of the Jaina work is probably from the eighth to the thirteenth century. There are many sculptures and some paintings, and the iconography is that of the Digambaras.[43]

Chhota Kailasa. The first excavation (No. 30) is an entire temple carved out of the rock, like the Hindu Kailasa temple, and popularly called the Chhota Kailasa or Little Kailasa. The area of the temple with its side corridors is 130 × 80 feet (40 × 25 m.), much smaller than the larger Kailasa. Only one story in height, the temple has a *gopura* entrance, a portico supported by two pillars and two pilasters, a main hall 36 feet (11 m.) square, supported by sixteen pillars, and a relatively low tower.

The many sculptures include the following. On the inside right side wall of the *gopura* are three *tirthankaras* with attendants; on the left side wall is Cakreśvari, *yakshini* of Rishabhanatha, the first *tirthankara,* her figure now partly damaged but shown originally, in accordance with Digambara iconography, with twelve hands, holding her characteristic attributes. On the portico are a *yaksha, gandharvas,* and other figures, and vestiges of painting on the ceiling. In the main hall are many *tirthankaras,* including Parśvanatha on the front wall. The small central shrine at the back has Gommateśvara at the left and Parśvanatha at the right, while inside, Mahavira is seated on a lion throne in the *padmasana* position and the *dhyana mudra* of meditation.

Of the Jaina caves, Nos. 31 and 34 are relatively small, while Nos. 32 and 33 are very extensive and are the principal Jaina works.

Indra Sabha. Cave No. 32 is known locally as the Indra Sabha. It is in fact a group of caves, consisting of a central two-storied cave with a court in front and smaller caves forming wings on either side. From the south an entrance gateway with a barrel roof gives access to the front court. As in the large Kailasa temple, there are in the court a great elephant and two massive pillars *(stambhas),* one intact, one with only its base preserved. At the farther side of the court is a small hall *(mandapa)* with a tiered roof surmounted by an octagonal dome. Behind this is the two-storied cave, the lower hall preceded by an unfinished veranda, the upper hall approached by a staircase and preceded by a veranda. The upper hall is the main chamber of the entire excavation. It is 78 feet (24 m.) wide and 55 feet (17 m.) deep; its veranda is 54 feet (16 m.) long and 10 feet (3 m.) wide. The ceiling of the main hall was once painted, and it is supported by twelve highly decorated pillars.

In the front veranda of the ground floor there is a chamber at the left on an elevated platform, and on two side pillars are figures of *tirthankaras* standing in the *kayotsarga* pose. Below the figure on the right is an inscription which reads, "This image has been carved by Nagavarma." Below the corresponding figure on the left an inscription reads, "Śri Sohila, a *brahmacari,* has carved this image of the *tirthankara* Śantinatha." The script is recognized as of the tenth century C.E., and provides a date for the Indra Sabha.[44]

At each end of the upper level veranda there is a colossal image, each identifiable by its vehicle, at the left the *yaksha* Matanga seated on his elephant, at the right the *yakshini* Siddhayika seated on her lion. Over the head of each is the foliage of a tree, and in the foliage over the head of Siddhayika are parrots, other birds, and monkeys. Because the elephant is also the symbol of Indra, it was previously thought that the figure at the left was Indra, and the figure at the right his wife Indrani,[45] and it was for this reason that the temple became popularly known as the Indra Sabha. Matanga and Siddhayika are appropriately found here at the approach to the main hall, for they are the chief attendants of the *tirthankara* Mahavira, and the temple is evidently dedicated to him, for in the main hall there are many figures of Mahavira, including his image seated cross-legged in the main shrine on the back wall.

On pilasters at each side of the main shrine door are nude Jaina door keepers *(dvarapalas),* and beside each is a deep recess containing a colossal standing figure, with attendants. The figure on the left is Parśvanatha, standing unclothed in the *kayotsarga* position, and identified by the cobra which raises its seven hoods over his head. The figure on the right is Gommateśvara. In accordance with his history, he stands unclothed in the *kayotsarga* pose, his body entwined by creepers, and surrounded by all kinds of animals, such as deer, serpents, and scorpions. On either side is a female figure, and these may be his half-sister and sister, Brahmi and Sundari, who came to request him to give up his pride.

Jagannath Sabha. Cave No. 33, immediately adjacent to the Indra Sabha, is known as the Jagannath Sabha. This is also a two-storied cave with a court in front, but it is smaller than the Indra Sabha, the main hall of the upper level here being 57 feet (17 m.) by 44 feet (13 m.) in dimension. At the entrance to the hall on the ground level are figures of Matanga and Siddhayika, and in the shrine in the back wall is Mahavira, seated in *padmasana* and in the *dhyana mudra*. On the upper level, the ceiling of the main hall was once painted in concentric circles, and is supported by twelve huge pillars, while the walls are sculptured with many figures of Mahavira.

Constructed Temples

Khajuraho. Along with the Vaishnava and Śaiva temples at Khajuraho, and falling in the same general period under the Candella kings (circa 800–1202 C.E.), there are also Jaina temples at the site, and they are found in the southeastern area. In architectural style they are essentially the same as the Hindu temples, with porch *(ardha-mandapa),* hall *(mandapa),* vestibule *(antarala),* and sanctuary *(garbhagriha),* while the superstructures rise in pyramidal shape over the first parts of the building and the tallest peak *(śikhara)* rises in curvilinear outline over the sanctuary. Like the Hindu temples also, the Jaina edifices exhibit a wealth of sculpture both on the exterior and the interior, and in general the themes are the same, except that it is of course the *tirthankaras* and their attendants upon whom central attention is focused.

Of the Jaina temples four are the most important, the Ghantai, Śantinatha, Adinatha, and Parśvanatha.

Ghantai. The Ghantai temple stands a little apart from the other Jaina temples. It was apparently similar in plan and design to the Parśvanatha, and even somewhat larger, but now all that remains is a flat-roofed cluster of twelve fine pillars, surviving from the porch and main hall of the original building. On the pillars are prominent chain and bell *(ghanta)* carvings, and it is from these that the temple is called the Ghantai.

Like all the Jaina temples here, the Ghantai represents the Digambara sect. For example, on the lintel of the doorway of the main hall is a frieze of the sixteen auspicious symbols (as against the fourteen of the Śvetambara tradition) seen in a dream by the mother of Mahavira prior to his birth. As shown here these are (1) Airavata elephant, (2) bull, (3) lion, (4) Śri-devi, (5) garland enclosing a *kirttimukha,* (6) full moon with hare in the middle, (7) rising sun with the sun god in the middle, (8) a pair of fishes, (9) a pair of jars, (10) a tank with a tortoise, (11) stormy sea, (12) lion throne, (13) palace, (14) *naga* couple seated in a pavilion, (15) heaps of jewels, and (16) Agni seated with flames issuing from his shoulders. Also numerous nude images of *jinas,* after the Digambara tradition, were excavated in and around the Ghantai.

On the structure itself was found an inscription datable to the end of the tenth century C.E., and this is the probable date of the original temple. On a fragmentary sculpture of Adinatha found in the vicinity is a date corresponding to 1085 C.E.[46]

Śantinatha. The Śantinatha, Adinatha, and Parśvanatha temples all stand inside a modern compound wall. The Śantinatha, situated to the south of the

10.12   Colossal Statue of Adinatha in the Śantinatha Temple, Khajuraho

Parśvanatha, has been entirely renovated and is the principal place of contemporary Jaina worship. Although it is known by the name of the sixteenth *tirthankara*, the figure in the central shrine is that of Adinatha (Fig. 10.12). This is a colossal statue (15 feet [4.5 m]) which, while modern, stands on a pedestal on which is a dedicatory inscription with a date corresponding to 1027/1028 C.E. The temple also preserves many ancient sculptures, e.g., the figures of two Digambara saints standing side by side in the *kayotsarga* position (Fig. 10.13), and a male and female couple (Fig. 10.14). In the latter sculpture, of which there is also a duplicate in the Khajuraho Museum, the man holds a fruit in his right hand and there is a disk above his left shoulder, and the woman holds a fruit in her right hand and the figure of a very small child in her left hand. These personages have been called the parents of a *jina*,[47] but are more probably to be recognized as the *yaksha* Gomedha and the *yakshini* Ambika, the attendants of Neminatha, the twenty-second

10.13 Two Digambara Saints in the Śantinatha Temple, Khajuraho

10.14 Gomedha and Ambika in the Śantinatha Temple, Khajuraho

270 | An Archaeological History of Religions of Indian Asia

tirthankara, for fruit and disk are among the usual attributes of Gomedha, and Ambika also regularly holds fruit and a child.⁴⁸

Adinatha. This temple, bearing the name of the first *tirthankara,* and situated to the north of the Parśvanatha, has completely lost its original *ardha-mandapa* and *mandapa* (which are replaced by a modern structure), but preserves its original *antarala* and *garbhagriha* with their roofs, and the original *śikhara* over the sanctuary still soars to an impressive height and is surmounted by a large ribbed *amalaka.* In general appearance the Adinatha is similar to the Hindu Vamana temple (named for an incarnation of Vishnu), which is also one of the southeastern group of Khajuraho temples, and both the Vamana and the Adinatha are generally attributed to the tenth or eleventh century C.E.

The exterior walls of the Adinatha are adorned with three rows of sculptures, the top row smaller than the other two. On the doorway to the central shrine there are various goddesses on the side panels, river goddesses on the base, and five goddesses in niches on the lintel (Fig. 10.15). On the lintel the central and end

10.15 Doorway of the Central Shrine in the Adinatha Temple, Khajuraho

10.16 Parśvanatha Temple, Khajuraho

niches represent seated goddesses, while the niches on either side of the central one show standing goddesses. As seen by the viewer, the figure on the left is the *yakshini* Ambika, the figure on the right is the *yakshini* Padmavati, and the figure in the center is the *yakshini* Cakreśvari. Within the shrine is a modern image of Adinatha, in place of the old one of which only the pedestal survives. The central figure of Cakreśvari, *yakshini* of Adinatha, on the lintel of the doorway of the shrine attests, however, that the temple was in fact originally dedicated to Adinatha.[49]

Parśvanatha. The Parśvanatha, named for the twenty-third *tirthankara,* is the largest, best preserved, and most excellently carved of the Jaina structures, and is one of the finest of all the Khajuraho temples (Fig. 10.16). An inscription records the construction of the temple by a certain Pahila, who was honored by King Dhanga (954–1002 C.E.), thus it is of more or less the same date as the Ghantai which, as far as the remains of the latter indicate, was of much the same plan.[50]

Like the other Khajuraho temples, the Parśvanatha faces to the east. It is 68 feet (21 m.) in length and 35 feet (11 m.) in width. It stands upon a terrace platform *(jagati)* 3.9 feet (1.2 m.) high, has an entrance porch, a main pillared hall, and a central shrine. A unique feature is another shrine at the back of the sanctuary, projecting to the west. The superstructures of the first parts of the building are either original or restored after the normal Khajuraho type; the original *śikhara* over the sanctuary still soars to a lofty height and is surmounted by a large ribbed *amalaka*.

In accordance with the common name of the temple, there is in the inner sanctuary a black marble image of Parśvanatha, but this is modern, having been installed in 1860 C.E. The statue stands on a pedestal made of sandstone, which is the same material of which the temple and its sculptures are made, and this pedestal is carved with a bull, which is the recognition symbol of Adinatha, therefore the temple must originally have given its central place of honor to the first *tirthankara*.

The interior of the temple is richly sculptured, and the elaborately carved ceiling of the entrance hall is particularly notable, with a pendant terminating in a pair of intertwined flying *vidyadharas*. Appropriately, Sarasvati, the head of the *vidyadharas,* and Cakreśvari, the *yakshini* of Adinatha, are seen in niches at either end of the lintel of the doorway of this hall.

On the exterior there are three bands of sculptures, diminishing in size as they go up. In all there are figures of gods and goddesses, *apsarases* and other feminine figures, and *mithuna* and a few *maithuna* couples.

In one panel of sculptures we see the image of a four-armed god standing side by side with his consort (Fig. 10.17). In his lower right hand the god holds an object which is now broken, in his upper right hand a conchshell, in his upper left hand a discus, and with his lower left hand he embraces the woman in one of the gestures of affection known by the term *alingana mudra,* while she returns the embrace with her right arm, meanwhile holding a convex metal mirror in her left hand. From the four arms and the attributes of conch and discus the male figure may probably be identified as Vishnu, and the female figure will therefore probably be Lakshmi. A different proposed identification is with Śiva and Parvati,[51] which can be supported by the mirror in the left hand of the woman, since this is a characteristic attribute of Parvati, but as a woman Lakshmi might also well carry a mirror, and has perhaps only just finished adorning herself for the meeting. In another panel of sculptures we recognize the same god and goddess in almost identical pose, except that the god's right hand hangs down and the positions of the discus and conch are reversed, and the woman does not hold a mirror. In this case the two figures are flanked by elephants beside the woman and another female figure beside the god. Assuming that the two main figures are Vishnu and Lakshmi, the second female figure may be taken to be Bhudevi, the earth goddess, the second wife of Vishnu.[52]

Many other feminine figures which appear on the walls of the Parśvanatha temple are presumably *apsarases* or other heavenly damsels, yet they also certainly reflect the life and customs of the ladies of Khajuraho of the time. One lady, who may be a *surasundari* or damsel of the gods, is using an eye-pencil *(śalaka)* to apply antimony or collyrium *(anjana)* for the beautification of her eyelids (Fig. 10.18). At the same time a boy attendant stands by with a toilet kit in his hands. In dress and ornament the lady wears headdress, necklaces, waistband, armlets, and anklets.[53] Another lady, probably also a *surasundari,* is standing on one leg and bending the other sharply upward in order to apply lac dye *(altaka)* to the sole of her foot, while a small boy assists her with a bowl or mirror in his hand (Fig.

10.17 Vishnu and Lakshmi, Parśvanatha Temple, Khajuraho

10.19).[54] This scene has sometimes been interpreted as the removal of a thorn from the foot, which is here incorrect, although such an action could well be necessary upon walking in the fields of Khajuraho. Yet another lady or *surasundari* is a dancer, preparing for her performance (Fig. 10.20). She has already put on breast band and patterned *sari* as well as headdress, necklaces, and armlets, and now with raised right foot is tying on an anklet with tiny bells *(payala)*, while a small attendant holds another anklet for her use.[55]

Temple Cities and Places of Pilgrimage

In distinction from the situation at Khajuraho, where the Jaina temples are in close proximity to the Vaishnava and Śaiva temples of the same site, it was more characteristic of Jainism to establish temple centers in separate and often relatively

10.18 Lady applying Eye Paint, Parśvanatha Temple, Khajuraho

10.19 Lady applying Lac Dye to Foot, Parśvanatha Temple, Khajuraho

10.20 Dancer affixing Bell Anklets, Parśvanatha Temple, Khajuraho

isolated places, which then became places of pilgrimage. With sufficient accommodations for those who came, and with monasteries *(viharas)* for pilgrim monks and nuns, these places amount to temple cities, but are not for the permanent habitation of a settled population. As centers of pilgrimage they are called by the term *tirtha,* which means "ford," and is here thought of as a crossing-over place through the ocean of rebirth. As such, the *tirtha* is a place especially appropriate for the person who wishes to end life by the Jaina custom of fasting to death. The Jaina temples at these places usually form complexes or clusters, which are known as *bastis,* and the places themselves are almost always of scenic beauty, most often on a hilltop. Among the most important *tirthas* are Śravanabelgola in Karnataka, and Mount Abu and Ranakpur in Rajasthan.[56]

Śravanabelgola. Śravanabelgola is the later name of the place in South India to which, toward the end of the fourth century B.C.E., the Śrutakevalin Bhadrabahu led a migration of strict Jainas, to be followed by the Maurya emperor Candragupta, and the place where both Bhadrabahu and Candragupta died. The grandson of Candragupta is said to have visited the spot with an army, and from his camp arose the town of Śravanabelgola or Belgola of the Śravanas, i.e., of the Jainas.

Near the town are two rocky hills, the higher Indragiri to the south, and the lower Candragiri to the north. On the Candragiri hill, named for Candragupta, are fifteen Jaina temples. Of these, two complexes are the most important, the Candragupta-basti and the Camundaraya-basti.[57]

Candragupta-basti. The Candragupta-basti is a complex of three shrines (*trikuta*). Traditionally associated with Candragupta himself, it is the earliest extant monument at Śravanabelgola, and is presently attributed to about 850 C.E. In the twelfth century the façade of the main hall of the *basti* was covered with an intricately carved soapstone trellis, with a doorway at the center on which is a frieze of sculptures including the story of the association of Candragupta with Bhadrabahu. The sculptor's name is given here and is Dasoja, the same person who also wrought many of the sculptures in the Hoyśala temple at Belur.

Camundaraya-basti. On the same Candragiri hill, at some distance to the north of the Candragupta-basti, is the Camundaraya-basti. As the name indicates, this was built by Camundaraya, who was a student of the Digambara teacher Nemicandra and the minister of the Ganga kings Marasimha II and Rajamalla II in the last quarter of the tenth century C.E. Inside the southern entrance to the enclosure which surrounds the many temples on the hill, is a lofty pillar, called Brahmadeva from the figure on its top, and the pillar carries an inscription commemorating the death of Marasimha II in 974 C.E. and was evidently erected soon after.

The Camundaraya-basti is the finest of the Śravanabelgola temple complexes. The main temple is built in two large stories, with a smaller square third story surmounted by an octagonal dome. There are many sculptures of *tirthankaras*, *yakshas*, *yakshinis*, men and women devotees. In the central shrine in the first story is a seated image of Neminatha, the *tirthankara* to whom the temple is dedicated, but it is a later replacement of the original image. A foundation inscription gives the date of the beginning of the temple, and this corresponds to 982 C.E. In the central shrine in the upper story is a later image of Parśvanatha, and here an inscription on the pedestal indicates that the consecration of the original image was under the son of Camundaraya in the year 995 C.E. Work on the temple, under both father and son, therefore continued for some thirteen years.

Indrabetta. The Indragiri hill is a great rounded mass of rock which rises 460 feet (140 m.) above the surrounding countryside. On the summit is a Jaina shrine of the type called a *betta*, which consists of cloisters around an open courtyard in which stands a statue of an illustrious person of the Jaina faith. Here the *betta* is known from the hill as the Indrabetta, and it honors the great ascetic Bahubali or Gommateśvara, who was the son of Rishabha, the first *tirthankara*.[58]

The approach to the Indrabetta on the Indragiri is by a steep, narrow stairway which goes straight up the slope of the rock. At the point of 200 steps up, there is an arch over the stairs; 300 more steps go up to the first entrance to the shrine; and 120 more steps lead to the uppermost court. In a preliminary shrine is a black image of Śantinatha, the sixteenth *tirthankara*. On the rock face at the entrance to the top level is a relief of a cow and calf. On the top of the cloister at the north side are the images of five goddesses in small niches, and around the entire cloister are many more small Jaina figures.

The central figure of the *betta* is the colossal statue of Gommateśvara, standing in the midst of the courtyard and facing to the north (Fig. 10.21). Inscriptions at the side of the statue state that Camundaraya caused the image to be made, and the date is placed at about 983 C.E. There was already on the crest of the hill a vertical projection of grayish-white granite, and this was carved directly into the shape of the figure. Gommata stands erect on a full-blown lotus, in the *kayotsarga* position, hands hanging at his side. The feet measure 9 feet (2.75 m.), the hips are 10 feet (3

10.21   Colossal Statue of Gommateśvara in the Indrabetta, Śravanabelgola

m.) wide in front, the broad shoulders are 26 feet (8 m.) across, the head is 7.5 feet (2.3 m.) high, and the total height of the image is 58 feet 8 inches (17.9 m.).

Masses of the original rock behind and on the sides support the figure up to the thighs; above that, the image stands free in the round. The rock behind is supposed to have been that upon which Bahubali stood in his long penance. The rock on the sides is carved to represent the anthills which grew up beside the saint (Fig. 10.22); from the anthills cockatrices *(kukkutasarpas)* emerge, and plants grow up to wrap their creepers around his legs and arms (Fig. 10.23). The hair of the head is in tight curls, the fingers and their nails are carefully delineated. Standing unclothed and motionless, absorbed in profound meditation, the great ascetic looks upon the world in utter serenity (Fig. 10.24).

The entire statue of Gommateśvara was originally given a smooth and shining polish and the stone still, a thousand years later, looks as fresh as if newly quarried.

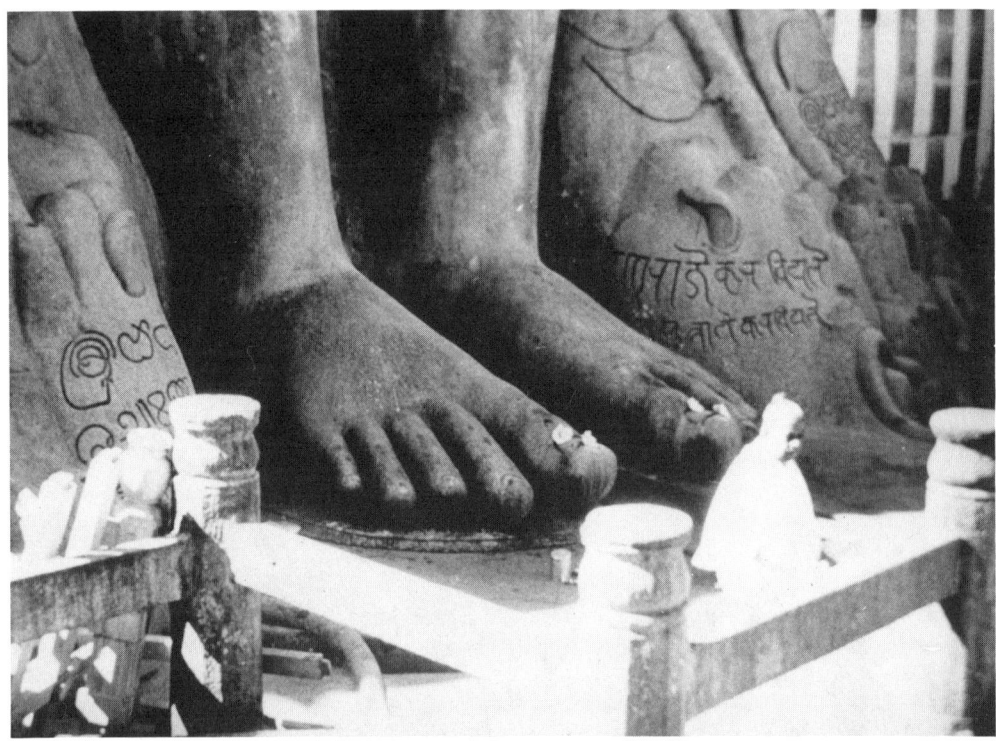

10.22 Anthills at the Feet of Gommateśvara, Śravanabelgola

10.23 Tendrils wrapping the Thighs and Arms of Gommateśvara, Śravanabelgola

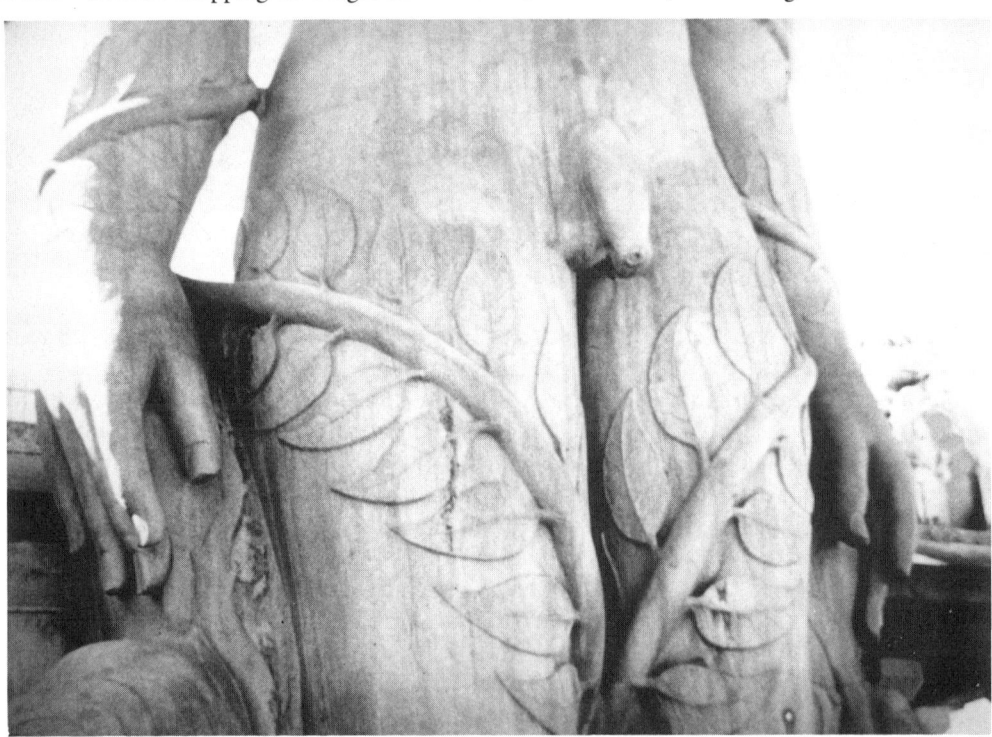

10.24 Back and Head of Gommateśvara, Śravanabelgola

Offerings are constantly placed at the feet; in a great ceremony performed every twelve to fourteen years (most recently in 1981) the head is profusely anointed in a "great head bathing."

Mount Abu. Mount Abu is an isolated and impressive mountain ridge which rises out of the desert of southern Rajasthan to a maximum elevation of 5,650 feet (1,722 m.) above sea level, and has long been a sacred mountain to both Hindus and Jainas. On the mountain, at a height of about 4,000 feet (1,220 m.), near the village of Dilwara (from *deul,* temple, and *vara,* place or precinct) and not far from the Nakhi Tal lake and the Sunset Point on the west side of the ridge, is a cluster of four Jaina temples, of which the principal ones are the Vimala-vasahi and the Luna-vasahi.[59]

Involved in the history of the temples are the kings of several Rajput clans, the Solankis, the Paramaras, and the Vaghelas (or Bathelas), and several wealthy Jainas who were involved both in financial dealings and in government service.

The temples are built entirely of white marble, which must have been transported from the quarries of Makrana some 25 to 30 miles (40 to 50 km.) away. The exterior of the temples is relatively plain; in the interior the marble is carved in the most delicate and intricate detail.

Vimala-vasahi. The Vimala-vasahi (Vimala's residence) was built by Vimala Shah, who was a wealthy banker and the minister of Bhimadeva I (1022–1064 C.E.), the first Solanki king of Gujarat. The ground is said to have been purchased from the Paramara king of Dhara by covering it completely with pieces of silver. The consecration of the temple was in 1031 C.E., by the Śvetambara teacher Vardhamana Suri.

The temple proper is 98 feet (30 m.) long and 42 feet (13 m.) wide at its widest point, and consists of a pillared hall open on all sides *(ranga-mandapa),* used as a hall of dance and music, a vestibule three steps higher up, and the yet slightly higher central shrine *(garbhagriha)* containing the main image, that of Rishabhanatha, the first *tirthankara,* to whom the temple is dedicated. In the twelfth century other features were added. At the east is the *hastiśala* or elephant hall, a rectangular pavilion containing ten free-standing figures of elephants, on which were formerly statues of Vimala and members of his family, but most of these are now missing. Surrounding the entire courtyard of the temple is a high wall which contains fifty-two cells, and an arcade of carved pillars in front of them, and in each cell is the seated image of a *tirthankara* (now mostly replacements of earlier figures). The most important figure is Rishabhanatha (Fig. 10.25), but here he is in smaller size than in the central shrine.

10.25   Rishabhanatha in Side Chapel of the Vimala-vasahi, Mount Abu

10.26 Hall of Music and Dance, looking forward to the Central Shrine, Vimala-vasahi, Mount Abu

From the open hall of music and dance *(ranga-mandapa)* in the temple proper there is a view outward to the surrounding arcade and forward to the central shrine (Fig. 10.26). The pillars of the hall are connected with arches and architraves, and all are richly carved, e.g, with decorative patterns and figures of goddesses. Overhead, the ceiling of the hall is a dome of eleven concentric rings, supported by sixteen brackets bearing the standing figures of the sixteen *vidyadevis* or goddesses of learning, the group over which Sarasvati presides. In ceiling panels of a side corridor, accompanied by lesser deities, are Sarasvati (Fig. 10.27), Śitala (cool) goddess of smallpox (Fig. 10.28), and others.[60]

Luna-vasahi. The temple known as the Luna-vasahi was built in 1231, two hundred years after the Vimala-vasahi, by two brothers, Tejahpala and Vastupala, who were wealthy ministers of the Vaghela king Viradhavala of Dholka. The temple is dedicated to Neminatha, the twenty-second *tirthankara*. In architectural style it is much like the Vimala-vasahi.

In the *hastiśala* (elephant hall) are portraits of Vastupala and his wives, and ten marble elephants which once carried members of the Vastupala family.[61]

As in the Vimala-vasahi, the pillars and arches of the halls are intricately carved, and the ceiling of the *ranga-mandapa* is much like that in the Vimala-vasahi, and is especially notable for its fine lotus-like pendant (Fig. 10.29).

The central shrine *(garbhagriha)* contains a colossal image of Neminatha, with his conchshell symbol on the seat. In all there are thirty-nine cells in the temple, each containing one or more images. The image of Parśvanatha seen in Fig. 10.30, for example, exhibits the prominent eyeballs characteristic of the Śvetambara tradition.[62] Overhead, some of the ceilings of the porticoes are elaborately carved with scenes from the life of Neminatha.[63]

10.27 Sarasvati in Corridor Ceiling, Vimala-vasahi, Mount Abu

10.28 Śitala in Corridor Ceiling, Vimala-vasahi, Mount Abu

10.29 Ceiling in the Luna-vasahi, Mount Abu

10.30 Parśvanatha in Small Shrine in the Luna-vasahi, Mount Abu

10.31 Adinatha Temple at Ranakpur

The site of Ranakpur (or Ranpur) is in a beautiful valley on the western slope of the Aravalli mountain range, near Sadari in Mewar.

Adinatha. Of the several Jaina shrines at Ranakpur, the principal one is the Adinatha, also known as the Adiśvara or Yugadiśvara temple (Fig. 10.31). An inscription beside the entrance of the main hall states that the temple was built by an architect named Depaka at the request of Dharanaka, "a devout worshiper of the *arhats*," and gives a date corresponding to 1439 C.E. The entire work of construction is supposed to have taken sixty-five years. As the name of the temple indicates, it is dedicated to the first *tirthankara*.

The architectural type of the temple is designated by the terms *caumukha* or *caturmukha*. The terms mean four-faced or quadruple, and a *caumukha* image is one with four faces, or one where four images are placed back to back, facing the four directions. The original thought is that a *tirthankara* so represented is preaching in all four directions; sometimes the four figures represent four different *tirthankaras*. A shrine which contains a *caumukha* image is therefore usually square, with openings in each of its four sides, and a temple which is oriented to such a shrine as its central sanctuary is a temple of *caumukha* or *caturmukha* type.

In the Adinatha temple at Ranakpur the central shrine contains a four-faced image of Adinatha, and opens on each side into a *ranga-mandapa* (hall of music and dance). This in turn connects with a two-storied *mandapa* and, beyond this, with a two-storied portal. Around these architectural elements are grouped other pillared halls and corridors, until the whole constitutes an almost square rectangle, 203 × 197 feet (62 × 60 m.) in size. In the four corners of the entire rectangle are four additional shrines. Surrounding the whole is a wall in which, facing the inner rectangle, are eighty-six chapels for minor deities. In the middle of three sides, west, north, and east, there are entrances in the wall and, of these, the one on the west is the largest and main entrance to the temple.

In the superstructure, eighty-six small spires rise over the chapels in the enclosure wall, twenty domes cover the pillared halls below, four *śikharas* surmount the four corner shrines, and a *śikhara* of the greatest height and prominence rises over the central shrine (Fig. 10.32). In the interior are lavishly decorated pillars—426 in number and no two alike—as well as carved arches, ceilings, and so forth, and worshipers have a place to sit on the floor in the hall before the central shrine (Fig. 10.33). Overhead are elaborate dome pendants (Fig. 10.34), celestial musicians playing the flute (Fig. 10.35), and so forth. In an intricately carved wall panel (Fig. 10.36) we see the thousand-hooded *(sahasra-phana)* Parśvanatha, standing in a Śvetambara representation under very numerous cobra hoods. He is flanked by his *yaksha* and *yakshini,* Dharanendra and Padmavati, and they by two *naginis,*

10.32 Śikhara over the Central Shrine, Adinatha Temple, Ranakpur

10.33 Worshipers before the Central Shrine, Adinatha Temple, Ranakpur

10.34 Dome Pendant, Adinatha Temple, Ranakpur

10.35 Celestial Musician, Adinatha Temple, Ranakpur

10.36 Thousand-hooded Parśvanatha, Adinatha Temple, Ranakpur

10.37 Naked Woman, Parśvanatha Temple, Ranakpur

10.38 Badridas Temple, Calcutta

shown as half human and half serpent, each with a large flywhisk *(cauri)* in hand. Overhead two elephants are purifying Parśvanatha.[64]

Parśvanatha. A somewhat smaller temple dedicated to Parśvanatha is not far to the west of the temple dedicated to Adinatha, and is said to have been built with surplus materials left over from the building of the former temple. Here in the Parśvanatha temple the exterior walls are covered with many panels of sculptures in much the style of the Khajuraho temples (Fig. 10.37).[65]

Of later Jaina temples there are four built in the late nineteenth century in the Badridas Temple Street in Calcutta.

Badridas. Of these the most important is the Badridas temple, which was erected by Rao Bahadur Badridasji Babu, and dedicated to Sitalanatha, the tenth *tirthankara* (Fig. 10.38).[66]

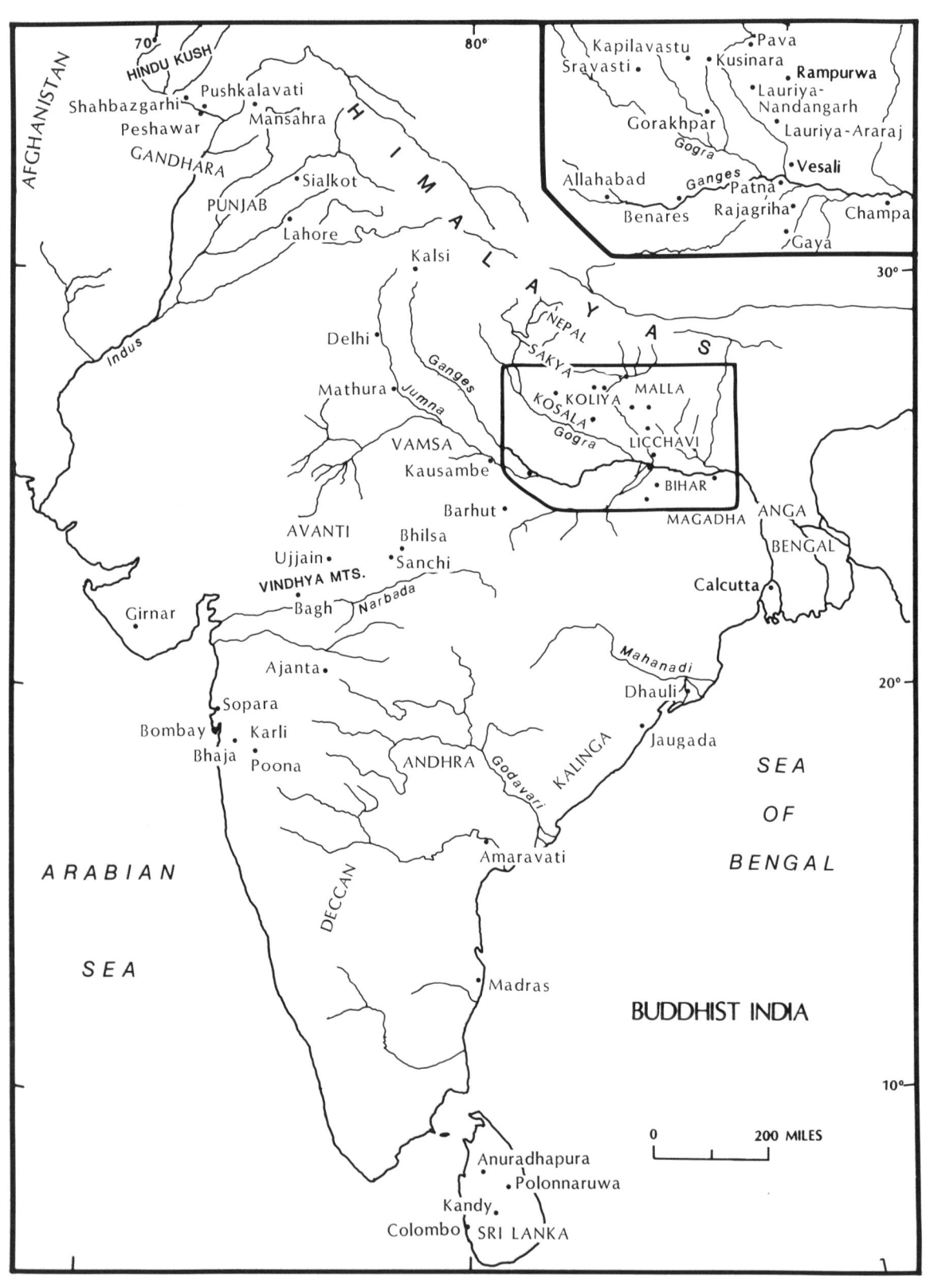

11

EARLY HISTORY AND LITERATURE OF THERAVADA BUDDHISM

TRADITION

When Śakyamuni Buddha was about to enter into the final *nirvana* he remarked to his disciple Ananda that his death might lead some to think, "The word of the Master is ended, we have no teacher more!" but the Buddha declared: "O Ananda, the Doctrine *(dhamma)* and the Discipline *(vinaya)* I have declared to you and laid down before you [respectively], that itself will be your Teacher after my demise" (*Digha Nikaya* 2.154).[1]

Dhamma and Vinaya

The Pali word *dhamma* corresponds to the Sanskrit *dharma,* and is a term of such wide connotation that it can stand for the sum total of Buddhism (as *dharma* for the sum total of Hinduism) and be rendered as "religion" or "truth." In a more restricted sense, however, and particularly over against *vinaya,* it means "doctrine" or "law," and is the name for the specific teachings of Buddhism. As for *vinaya,* it is the name for the rules of the Buddhist order, both the prescriptions for the daily life of the monks *(bhikkhus)* and nuns *(bhikkhunis)* and the regulations for the conduct of the whole community *(sangha)*. Since Śakyamuni Buddha lived through a long ministry and had a large body of followers, surely requiring organization, he no doubt did lay down rules and regulations for his order as well as declare doctrinal truths.

After the death of the Buddha, therefore, the *dhamma* and the *vinaya* were handed on down (and no doubt amplified and explicated) as the authoritative texts of Buddhism. In accordance with ancient Indian custom, seen also in the transmission of the sacred texts of both Hinduism and Jainism, these materials of Buddhism were for a long time communicated orally and then finally put into writing.

The word "elder" (*thera,* feminine *theri,* Sanskrit *sthavira*) was applied as a term of respect to prominent monks and nuns, especially to those of venerable age, and it was such personages who were most of all depended upon for the preservation and transmission of the tradition and for decision on questions which might arise, so the form of Buddhism which developed under their leadership—the form of Buddhism which its adherents believed to be most directly in the true line of descent from the teaching and practice of the Buddha himself—became known as the Theravada, the "way of the elders."

Canonical Texts

In Theravada Buddhism the canonical texts are in Pali and constitute the Tipitaka (Tripitaka), in addition to which there are also many commentaries and other noncanonical books.[2] The word *pitaka* is understood to mean a basket containing manuscripts, with the further meaning of a traditional handing on of materials. The *ti-pitaka (tri-pitaka)* are the three such baskets of the canonical texts.

The first of these is the Vinayapitaka, the "basket of the discipline of the order." The fact that the Vinayapitaka stands in the first place is no doubt a reflection of the fact that in the Theravada *vinaya* (discipline) was considered as of first importance even over *dhamma* (doctrine).

The second basket is the Suttapitaka. The word *sutta* (also *suttanta*) corresponds to the Sanskrit *sutra* (also *sutranta*) which means a "thread" and is used for a string of concise statements, but here in Buddhist usage a *sutta* is a "discourse," so this is the "basket of discourses," for the most part sermons, dialogues, and the like, of the Buddha. In the restricted sense of the word, as against *vinaya*, *dhamma* is also a designation of this second division of the canon.

The third basket is the Abhidhammapitaka. This is also *dhamma,* and the added word *abhi* (higher) designates this as the "basket of higher doctrine."

Councils

The collection, recital, and establishment of the canonical texts, and also of the commentaries which came to be appended to them, was above all the work of a series of early Buddhist councils. The term for such a council is *dhammasangiti,* the original meaning of which is a recitation of the canonical texts, while the related word *dhammasangaha* denotes the settling or redaction of the texts carried out by such recitation. In typical procedure an eminent *thera* presides, and another *thera* of eminence and special qualification recites the texts sentence by sentence, and the assembly repeats them after him in unison.

Information concerning the early Buddhist councils is provided chiefly in the *Cullavagga,* the *Dipavamsa,* the *Mahavamsa* and *Culavamsa,* and in the *Samantapasadika* of Buddhaghosa.

Cullavagga. In the Vinayapitaka the second part is called the *Khandhakas* (sections), and of the *Khandhakas* the first part is the *Mahavagga* (greater division) and the second the *Cullavagga* (lesser division).[3] In the *Cullavagga* the first ten sections are occupied with the duties of monks and nuns, and the last two sections (11–12) give an account of the first two Buddhist councils, those of Rajagriha and Vaiśali.

Dipavamsa. The *Dipavamsa* (island chronicle)[4] is the oldest extant Pali chronicle of the island of Lanka (now Sri Lanka, formerly Ceylon). The work is based upon the commentary *(atthakatha)* handed down in the Mahavihara, the great monastery at Anuradhapura, which was the center of the orthodox tradition. The chronicle conveys an impression of many fragments taken from that tradition and strung together rather loosely. In its present form it dates about the fourth century C.E., and the *Culavamsa* (38.59)[5] states that King Dhatusena (460–478 C.E.) made an endowment for the recital of the *Dipavamsa*.

***Mahavamsa* and *Culavamsa*.** The *Mahavamsa*[6] is the "great chronicle" of Lanka. Like the *Dipavamsa* it is based upon the *atthakatha* of the Mahavihara, and probably upon the *Dipavamsa* itself. The first part of the work, the *Mahavamsa* proper, extends to the reign of King Mahasena (334–361 C.E.), and is attributed to a Buddhist elder, Mahanama Thera, generally identified as an uncle of King Dhatusena (460–478) (*Culavamsa* 38.16; 39.42).[7] The continuation of the work is called the *Culavamsa*. The first part of the *Culavamsa*, extending from King Mahasena to King Parakkamabahu II (1236–1271 C.E.), is traditionally ascribed to Dhammarakkhita Thera, an elder of the time of Parakkamabahu II (*Culavamsa* 84.11–16).[8] The second part continues to the time of King Kittisirirajasiha (1747–1782 C.E.), who himself ordered the book as it existed in Lanka compared with a copy brought from Siam (Thailand), and the work of comparison and of completion of the Lanka version was done by Tibbatuvava Thera, an elder of the Puppharama (now the Malvatu-vihara), a monastery in Sirivaddhanapura (modern Kandy) (*Culavamsa* 99.78–80).[9] Finally a brief supplement by Hikkaduve Sumangala Thera covers the reigns of two more kings, until the time of the British occupation (1815 C.E.).

***Samantapasadika*.** The *Samantapasadika* is a commentary on the Vinayapitaka written by Buddhaghosa. According to the author's own statement in the colophon of the book, the work was undertaken in the twentieth and completed in the twenty-first regnal year of King Sirinivasa (also known as Sirikudda and as Mahanama), who reigned in Lanka from 409 to 431 C.E.; therefore, the commentary was written in 429–430 C.E. In the introduction to the *Samantapasadika,* called the *Bahiranidana,*[10] in order to show the authencity of the *vinaya* upon which he is about to comment, Buddhaghosa gives an account of the four councils through which the canonical texts were handed down, namely, the first gathering of 500 monks in Rajagriha, the second assembly of 700 monks in Vaiśali, the third meeting of 1,000 monks in Pataliputra, and the fourth council of 68,000 monks at the Thuparama in Anuradhapura.

FOUR COUNCILS IN INDIA

First Council in Rajagriha under Ajataśatru

The First Council is described in the *Cullavagga* (11), the *Dipavamsa* (4.1–31), the *Mahavamsa* (3), and the *Samantapasadika* (4–30).[11]

The meeting place of the Council was in Rajagriha (Rajagaha), and the immediate occasion was the fact that no sooner had Śakyamuni Buddha passed into the final *nirvana* than disharmony came to the surface within his order. How this came about was as follows.

The Buddha, on one occasion, had gone on pilgrimage with 250 monks to Atuma, a town between Kuśinagara and Śravasti. In Atuma was a monk who had entered the Order in his old age and had previously been a barber. Knowing that the Buddha was coming, the monk sent his two sons to beg food and prepared a large repast. This the Buddha refused to accept, for he said that it was not allowable for one monk to beg for another. The Buddha also ruled that it was not allowable for a monk who had formerly been a barber to carry about with him a barber's equipment (*Mahavagga* 6.37).[12]

The monk who figures in this incident is not named in the *Mahavagga*, but is almost certainly to be recognized as the monk Subhadda (not the monk Subhadda, who was the Buddha's own last convert), of whom we hear in the *Digha Nikaya* and the *Cullavagga* that he had renounced the world in his old age, that he was irked by the regulations of the Buddha, and that he took the occasion of the death of the Buddha to express his resentment. Upon that occasion Subhadda spoke of the Buddha as the great *samana* (*śramana*, ascetic), and said (*Digha Nikaya* 2.162; *Cullavagga* 11.1.1):

> We are well rid of the great *samana*. We used to be annoyed by being told, "This beseems you, this beseems you not." But now we shall be able to do whatever we like; and what we do not like, that we shall not have to do.[13]

Mahakassapa. In the face of this insubordination in the ranks, one of the oldest and most distinguished followers of the Buddha, named Mahakassapa, proposed that a gathering should be held in which to rehearse and settle the doctrinal teachings *(dhamma)* and the disciplinary instructions *(vinaya)* as received from the Buddha, and thus have authoritative guidance for the Order. Mahakassapa said (*Cullavagga* 11.1.1):

> Come, Sirs, let us chant together the *dhamma* and the *vinaya* before what is not *dhamma* is spread abroad, and what is *dhamma* is put aside; before what is not *vinaya* is spread abroad, and what is *vinaya* is put aside; before those who argue against the *dhamma* become powerful, and those who hold to the *dhamma* become weak; before those who argue against the *vinaya* become powerful, and those who hold to the *vinaya* become weak![14]

The assembly which came together in response to this call consisted of 499 chosen *thera bhikkhus* (elder monks) plus Mahakassapa as the presiding officer, 500 in all, and met at Rajagriha (Rajagaha). According to the *Mahavamsa* the death of the Buddha took place in the eighth year of King Ajataśatru (Table 4.9, a chronology which may not be correct), and according to the same source (3.17–22)[15] it was Ajataśatru who built for the assembly a splendid hall by the side of the Vebhara Rock at the entrance to the Sattapanni grotto at Rajagriha. In the hall, mats were placed for the monks, a seat *(therasana)* was provided for the presiding elder, and another seat *(dhammasana)* for the preacher, i.e., for the elder who would recite the texts.

Upali and Ananda. On one occasion the Buddha himself said that among his disciples Ananda was supreme in retentive memory (and thus best able to remember all that the Buddha had said), and that Upali was outstanding in knowing the disciplinary rules by heart (*Anguttara Nikaya*).[16] On another occasion the Buddha spoke especially of the importance of the disciplinary rules and again singled out Upali for commendation for his mastery of the rules, and accordingly Upali taught the rules to many of the other monks (*Cullavagga* 6.13.1):

> Now at that time the Blessed One spoke in many a figure concerning the *vinaya*, speaking in praise of the *vinaya*, in praise of learning the *vinaya*, and again and again in reference thereto in praise of the venerable Upali. Then said the *bhikkhus*: ". . . Come, let us learn the *vinaya*

under the venerable Upali." And many *bhikkhus,* senior and junior, and of medium standing, went to learn the *vinaya* under the venerable Upali.[17]

As the Council came together at Rajagriha, therefore, the *theras* chose Upali to speak for the *vinaya,* and for the rest of the *dhamma* they chose Ananda (*Mahavamsa* 3.30).[18] As to which to take up first, *vinaya* or *dhamma,* the monks said: "The *vinaya* is the very life of the Dispensation *(sasana)* of the Enlightened One: so long as the *vinaya* endures, the Dispensation endures, therefore let us rehearse the *vinaya* first" (*Samantapasadika* 1.13).[19]

So Mahakassapa sat in the president's seat and questioned Upali concerning the *vinaya,* and then he questioned Ananda concerning the *dhamma.* When everything had in this manner been determined, the council accepted a resolution phrased by Mahakassapa (*Cullavagga* 11.1.10): "If the time seems meet to the *sangha,* not ordaining what has not been ordained, and not revoking what has been ordained, let it take upon itself and ever direct itself in the precepts according as they have been laid down."[20]

In summary of the entire undertaking, the *Dipavamsa* (5.7–14) says:

> Kassapa was the foremost among those who inculcate ascetic practices in the religion of the Conqueror, Ananda among the learned (in the *suttas*), Upali in the *vinaya.* . . . There were many other great Elders who were the original repositories of the faith.
>
> By these and other Elders numbering five hundred who performed their duties properly, the collection of the *dhamma* and *vinaya* was made. It is called the doctrine of the Elders because the collection was made by the Elders.
>
> The *thera* Upali and Ananda, who obtained perfection in the true Norm, both of them learned *dhamma* and *vinaya* from the Conqueror. . . . Learning the excellent word of the Tathagata from the first, the Elders, who were the original repositories of the faith, made the first collection; therefore the doctrine of the Elders is called the first doctrine.[21]

Likewise the *Mahavamsa* (3.37, 40) concludes the account of the Council, saying: "Thus in seven months was that compiling of the *dhamma* to save the whole world completed by those *(theras)* bent on the whole world's salvation. . . . Now since the canon was compiled by the *theras* it was called the *thera* tradition."[22]

Second Council in Vaiśali under Kalasoka

The Second Council is described in the *Cullavagga* (12), the *Dipavamsa* (4.52–58; 5.16–29), the *Mahavamsa* (4), and the *Samantapasadika* (30–37).[23]

The meeting place of the Council was in Vaiśali (Vesali) in the Vajjian confederacy, and the meeting was occasioned in response to actions of the Vajjian monks. According to the *Mahavamsa* (4.7–8),[24] the time was in the tenth year of King Kalasoka, the son and successor of Susunaga, at the end of which year a century had gone by since the *nirvana* of the Buddha. This Kalasoka son of Susunaga must be identical with Kakavarna son and successor of Śiśunaga in the Puranas where, however, these two kings and some others precede Bimbisara and Ajataśatru (the contemporaries of the Buddha), rather than coming at some considerable distance in the succession after them (Table 4.2). Therefore the chronology of the *Mahavamsa* may again be open to question, although the placement of the Second Council a century after the First Council is also attested in the *Cullavagga* (12.1.1), the *Dipavamsa* (4.52; 5.16), and the *Samantapasadika* (33),[25] and may probably be accepted at least as a round number.

The monks of the Vajji clan at Vaiśali drew up a list of "ten points," which provided for an equal number of practices in respect to eating and other matters, which they considered permissible for themselves. The tenth of these points affirmed that it was allowable to receive gold and silver, and the monks proceeded to ask publicly for their lay disciples to give them money.

The monk Yasa Kakandakaputta (the son of a *brahmana* named Kakandaka), and himself a pupil of Ananda, was wandering through the Vajjian country at the time, and witnessed this behavior. When Yasa protested what he saw, the Vajjian monks offered him a share of the money they had collected, hoping to win him over, but Yasa refused it. He strongly declared that the rules laid down by the Buddha would not permit the taking of money, and to prove this Yasa quoted several discourses of the Buddha.

In one of these discourses (*Cullavagga* 12.1.3),[26] for example, the Buddha compared four obstructions of the sun and moon (by clouds, fog, smoke, and eclipse) with four "stains" by which, when *samanas* and *brahmanas* are affected, they also give forth "neither heat nor light nor sheen." These four stains are drinking strong drink, practicing sexual intercourse, accepting silver and gold, and gaining livelihood by low arts (according to the so-called "long paragraphs on conduct" in the Maha Sila,[27] "low arts" are such as divination or predicting rainfall).

Afterward Yasa took the problem of the "ten points" of the Vajjian monks to Revata (also called Soreyya-Revata, because he lived in a town named Soreyya), a monk who was also a pupil of Ananda, knew by heart the *dhamma*, the *vinaya*, and other texts, and was reputed to be capable, if asked a puzzling question, of spending a whole night on that one question (*Cullavagga* 12.1.10).[28] The Vajjian monks also tried to win over Revata with gifts, but without success, and Revata suggested that the dispute should be settled by the Order *(sangha)* in a meeting in the place where the matter arose, namely, in Vaiśali.

In this meeting, after the legal question had been debated for some time, Revata declared that "there has been much pointless talk among us, and in no single utterance is the sense clear" (*Cullavagga* 12.2.7).[29] Therefore (in accordance with a procedure for which the authority of the Buddha is cited in *Cullavagga* 4.14.19),[30] Revata proposed the appointment of a jury or commission, composed in this case of eight monks, four from the East and four from the West, to whom to refer the problem. Both Revata and Yasa were members of the jury from the West, and from the East one of the members was Sabbakami, who was also a pupil of Ananda and was at that time the oldest living Buddhist monk. The commission met in the Valikarama monastery at Vaiśali. Revata acted as questioner, and Sabbakami answered his questions. The outcome of the matter was that the "ten points" were found to be "false *dhamma* and false *vinaya*, and not contained in the teaching of the Master" (*Cullavagga* 12.2.8).[31]

This decision was conveyed to the assembly, and then a recital of the *vinaya* was held. Out of the entire number of monks, 112,000 in all, Revata chose 700, and the recital which they conducted was therefore called the *sattasati* (seven hundred). Likewise the twelfth chapter of the *Cullavagga*, which gives the oldest account of this Second Council, is called the *Sattasatikakhandhaka*. Because of the prominence of Yasa in the proceedings, the assembly was also called the Yasatherasangiti.

In conclusion of its record of the event, the *Mahavamsa* (4.63–64; cf. *Dipavamsa* 5.29) says: "All these (*theras* met) in the Valikarama protected by Kalasoka, under the leadership of the *thera* Revata, (and) compiled the *dhamma*. Since they accepted the *dhamma* already established in time past and proclaimed afterward, they completed their work in eight months."[32]

Although there was a threat of division among his followers at the death of the Buddha, the redaction of the *dhamma* and *vinaya* accomplished by Mahakassapa and the others at the First Council provided a basis of unity, and it was considered that the Buddhist community remained "one and united" for the first hundred years, i.e., up to the time of the Second Council. At that point, however, the Vajjian monks, whose "ten points" were repudiated at the Second Council, and many others too, who from the standpoint of the Second Council were heretical, assembled and made a collection of *dhamma* to suit themselves. There were 10,000 of these, and their congregation was called the Mahasanghika (great community). The Mahasanghika itself divided into two sects, however, and subsequently many more sects arose.

As they describe this development, the *Dipavamsa* (5.39–54)[33] and the *Mahavamsa* (5.1–13)[34] state that after the first hundred years (i.e., after the Second Council), along with the doctrine of the Elders (Pali *theravada*, Sanskrit *sthaviravada*), there arose no less than seventeen other schools of doctrine (*acariyavada*, the way of the teachers), making a total of eighteen sects in all. "Seventeen were the schismatics; one doctrine remained unbroken [the Theravada]; all of them were eighteen together with the unbroken doctrine. The best of the doctrines of the elders is like a big banyan tree; it is without deficiency, not redundant, and forms the complete religion of the Conqueror; the remaining doctrines have come into existence like thorns in a tree" (*Dipavamsa* 5.51–52).

It was this situation of the multiplication of divisions regarded as heretical, which led to the calling of the next council under Aśoka.

Third Council in Pataliputra under Aśoka

The Third Council is described in the *Dipavamsa* (7.39–59), the *Mahavamsa* (5.231–281), and the *Samantapasadika* (37–61).[35]

In the time of Aśoka (269–232 B.C.E.) the capital city of Pataliputra was at its greatest glory, and the king built many buildings there for the Buddhists, among them a large monastery known as the Aśokarama (*arama*, "park," "garden," and the designation of a Buddhist convent, the same as *vihara*).

Moggaliputta-Tissa. In Pataliputra at this time the leading Buddhist elder was Tissa, the son of a *brahmana* of the city named Mogalli, and therefore himself known as Moggaliputta-Tissa (Tissa the son of Moggali). As for Aśoka, not only was he himself a convert to the teachings of the Buddha, but several members of his family were ordained in the Order. The king's brother and vice-regent, Tissakumara, became a monk under the teaching of Yonaka Mahadhammarakkhita, and lived in the Aśokarama, and the king's nephew, Aggibrahma, the husband of the king's daughter Sanghamitta, entered the Order on the same day as Tissakumara. At the festival of dedication of the Aśokarama and other *viharas* built by Aśoka, in answer to a question by the king Moggaliputta-Tissa told him that one becomes "a kinsman of the religion" of the Buddha by letting one's son or daughter enter the Order, and Aśoka acted on the suggestion and had both of his children ordained. These were the son Mahinda, at that time twenty years old, and the daughter Sanghamitta, then eighteen years old. Upon entrance into the Order a novice is under a master (*upajjhaya*) and a teacher (*acariya*), and Mahinda's "master" was Moggaliputta-Tissa himself, while the directress of Sanghamitta was Dhammapala Theri and her teacher was Ayupala Theri. In three years with his master, Mahinda learned all three of the Pitakas (*Mahavamsa* 5.194–211).[36]

Under the patronage of Aśoka the revenues of the main body of the Buddhists increased, and this attracted into their group heretics, who brought with them their own practices. As the acknowledged leader of the Order in Pataliputra, Moggaliputta-Tissa was so distressed that he turned over the direction of the Order to Mahinda, and himself went away for seven years in a solitary retreat farther up the Ganges on the Ahoganga mountain.

Finally Aśoka asked Moggaliputta-Tissa to return, in order "to befriend religion." With Moggaliputta-Tissa present, the king called the monks together and questioned them on their various doctrines, then expelled from the Order all those (60,000 in number) who held heretical views, Moggaliputta-Tissa declaring that the Vibhajjavada (religion of reason, apparently more or less identical with the Theravada) alone contained the true teaching of the Buddha (*Mahavamsa* 5.272).[37]

After that, Moggaliputta-Tissa chose one thousand learned monks and brought them together in the Aśokarama, where they made "a compilation of the true *dhamma*." In the midst of this gathering Moggaliputta-Tissa also set forth the *Kathavatthu*, a work which he composed in refutation of false doctrines, and a work which appears as one of the seven books of the Abhidhammapitaka.[38]

Thus, "even as the *thera* Mahakassapa and the *thera* Yasa had held a Council so did the *thera* Tissa" (*Mahavamsa* 5.277).[39] In all the assembly lasted for nine months, and it was brought to a close in the seventeenth year of Aśoka (252 B.C.E.). At the time of the Council Moggaliputta-Tissa was himself seventy-two years old, and finally "Tissa, the son of Moggali, making his pupil Mahinda the chief of *vinaya*, obtained *nirvana* at his eightieth year" (*Dipavamsa* 5.107).[40]

Since, according to the above sources, Aśoka participated personally in the proceedings of the Third Buddhist Council and in the expulsion of schismatics from the Order, it is of interest in confirmation of his activity in these regards that one of his own edicts deals with punishment for schism in the *sangha*. This Schism Pillar Edict is preserved in copies on pillars at Allahabad, Sanci, and Sarnath. In the text Aśoka says that the *sangha* is "(now) made united," therefore the edict was probably issued upon the conclusion of the Council, which was considered to have accomplished such unity. Then the emperor decrees that whoever splits the *sangha* is not to be admitted into it, and whatever monk or nun breaks the *sangha* is to be divested of monastic garb ("made to put on white clothes") and expelled from the monastery ("made to reside in a non-residence").[41]

The work of the same Council and the texts recited in it are also almost surely reflected in another edict of Aśoka. A copy of this edict is on a rock, which was found on a hill about 1 mile (1.6 km.) southwest of the town of Bairat (about 42 miles [68 km.] northeast of Jaipur in Rajasthan) and placed with the Asiatic Society of Calcutta. In the text the emperor salutes the Buddhist *sangha* and expresses his faith in the Buddha, the *dharma*, and the *sangha*. He then declares, "Whatever, Sirs, has been spoken by the blessed Buddha, all that is well spoken indeed," and goes on to state the wish that the monks and nuns and also the laymen and laywomen should listen to and remember a number of "*dharma* texts," the names of which he cites in the Magadhi language.[42] The declaration in the edict that "whatever . . . has been spoken by the blessed Buddha . . . is well spoken," is practically a quotation from the *Anguttara Nikaya* (4.164),[43] which reads, "Whatsoever be well spoken, all that is the word of the Exalted One." Likewise some or all of the "*dharma* texts" named by Aśoka are probably identifiable with other passages found in the Theravada canon, e.g., the *Anagata-bhayani* (fears to come) with the passage in the *Anguttara Nikaya* (3.100–109),[44] which begins, "Monks, there are these five fears in the way. . . ."

Missions. At the conclusion of the Third Council Moggaliputta-Tissa made arrangements for monks to go for the propagation of the religion to many countries, to Kashmir and Gandhara, to provinces in South India (Mahishamandala, Vanavasa, Aparantaka, Maharashtra), to the country of the Yona or Yavana (i.e., the Greeks, probably in Bactria), to the Himalaya country, to Suvarnabhumi (Suvannabhumi, land of gold), probably some part or parts of Southeast Asia, and to "the lovely island of Lanka" (Ceylon, Sri Lanka). To the last destination was sent "the great *thera*," Mahinda the son of Aśoka and disciple of Moggaliputta-Tissa, together with four of the disciples of Mahinda, the *theras* Itthiya, Uttiya, Sambala, and Bhaddasala.[45]

Fourth Council in Kashmir under Kanishka

The Kushana king Kanishka, who probably began to reign in 78 C.E., held sway over a large territory extending from Kabul to Mathura (in both of which places his statues have been found) and including Gandhara, Sindh, and Kashmir, with his capital at Purushapura (Peshawar). On his coins are representations of Zoroastrian, Hellenistic, and Hindu deities, as well as of the Buddha, therefore he was probably at the outset an adherent of some form of Iranian religion and was afterward converted to Buddhism.

According to the Chinese Buddhist pilgrim Xuan Zang (Hiuen Tsang) (629–645 C.E.),[46] Kanishka was a student of the sacred books of the Buddha, but was perplexed by the contradictory views of the different Buddhist schools. Of these we have already learned that there were no less than eighteen and, although the Third Council under Aśoka was intended to overcome heresy, it is plain that the sectarian divisions continued to exist. As Xuan Zang tells the story, an honored Buddhist elder named Parśva explained to Kanishka:

> "Since Tathagata left the world many years and months have elapsed. The different schools hold to the treatises of their several masters. Each keeps to his own views, and so the whole body is torn by divisions."
>
> Kanishka thereupon resolved:
>
> "I will dare to forget my own low degree, and hand down in succession the teaching of the law unimpaired. I will therefore arrange the teaching of the three Pitakas of Buddha according to the various schools."

To this end the king summoned from far and near an assembly of holy teachers. A multitude of those distinguished for talents and holiness of life came together and, from among them, 499 men were chosen, who were the most advanced in their knowledge of the Buddhist scriptures. They then proceeded to another place, where Kanishka built a monastery to serve as a meeting place. Since Xuan Zang tells of these events as a part of his account concerning Kashmir, it may be supposed that the Council was held in Kashmir, and tradition names the *vihara* at Kundalavana in Kashmir as the site. Another tradition places the Council at the Tamasavana monastery at Jalandhara in the Punjab, but Xuan Zang says nothing of the Council as he tells of Jalandhara,[47] so Kashmir may be regarded as the probable place.

To serve as the president of the Council the venerable Vasumitra was selected, and this made an assembly of 500 persons in all. The actual work done, according to Xuan Zang, was the composition of three commentaries, each 100,000 verses in length, one on each of the three Pitakas, the *Upadeśa Śastra* to explain the Sutra

Pitaka (Suttapitaka), the *Vinaya Vibhasha Śastra* to explain the Vinayapitaka, and the *Abhidharma Vibhasha Śastra* to explain the Abhidharma Pitaka (Abhidhammapitaka).

At the end Kanishka had the discourses engraved on sheets of copper and enclosed in a stone receptacle, and over this he erected a *stupa*. Then, "having finished this pious labor, he returned with his army to his own capital [i.e., presumably to Purushapura]."

As the names given for the commentaries suggest, it is probable that the language of the Council was Sanskrit. Concerning the accomplishment of the Council Xuan Zang says: "There was no work of antiquity to be compared with their productions; from the deepest to the smallest question, they examined all, explaining all minute expressions, so that their work has become universally known and is the resource of all students who have followed them."

The statement of Xuan Zang suggests that a basis of common understanding among the many different Buddhist sects was reached, but sectarian divisions were hardly eliminated. Presumably most or all of the then known eighteen sects of Buddhism were represented in the Council, and this would presumably have included the Sthaviravada, for this "way of the Elders" surely still existed in India. The corresponding Theravada in Sri Lanka, however, appears to have kept aloof from this assembly; at any rate the Southern Buddhists do not recognize this Council and there is no record concerning it in the Sinhalese Chronicles.

On the other side, the tendencies which resulted in Mahayana Buddhism were probably already felt, and the Mahayanists and all the Northern Buddhists recognize the authority of this Council. Furthermore, Aśvaghosha, the poetic author of the *Buddha-carita* and other works claimed by the Mahayanists as belonging to their party, is said to have lived and worked at the court of Kanishka; and Nagarjuna, recognized as the first great philosophical systematizer of Mahayana doctrines, is supposed to have been born at the very time of the Council convoked by Kanishka. Thus it is probably correct to recognize as already in existence at this time the two large divisions of Buddhism known as the Hinayana or Little Vehicle (a term which Xuan Zang apparently uses for the Sthaviravada and the other old sects collectively) and the Mahayana or Great Vehicle.[48]

FOUR COUNCILS IN SRI LANKA

As told in the *Dipavamsa* (9ff.) and the *Mahavamsa* (6ff.) the island of Lanka (also Lankadipa, Lankatala) (later Ceylon and now Sri Lanka) was originally inhabited by *yakkhas* (Sanskrit *yakshas*), while the island was later colonized by Vijaya and his companions, and Vijaya became the first Aryan king of the island and he and the others the ancestors of the Sinhalese race.[49] It is probable, however, that even as the Vedic Aryans disparaged their enemies as *dasas, dasyus,* and the like—at least in later usage derogatory terms which would not be properly applicable at any rate to the people of the Harappan civilization—so here too the description of the indigenous inhabitants of Lanka as *yakkhas,* and also as *nagas* and *rakshasas*—also at least in later usage derogatory terms suggesting genii, demons, and the like—represents the viewpoint of the Aryan conquerors and does not do justice to the probably already advanced civilization of these peoples and their rulers (e.g., Ravana the *rakshasa* king, later considered as the demon king of Lanka). In fact in the *Mahavamsa* itself we learn, for example, that the *yakkhas* had cities named Lankapura and Sirisavatthu, that Vijaya married a *yakkha* princess

TABLE 11.1.
KINGS OF LANKA FROM VIJAYA TO DEVANAMPIYATISSA

Name	Length of Reign in Years	Buddha Nirvana Era (reckoned from 483 BCE)	BCE
1. Vijaya	38	1–38	483–445
Interregnum	1	38–39	445–444
2. Panduvasudeva	30	39–69	444–414
3. Abhaya	20	69–89	414–394
Interregnum	17	89–106	394–377
4. Pandukabhaya	70	106–176	377–307
5. Mutasiva	60	176–236	307–247
6. Devanampiyatissa	40	236–276	247–207

(whom he later abandoned), that later Aryan kings also married *yakkha* princesses, and so on, so that we must conclude that the historic civilization of Sri Lanka actually developed as an amalgamation of Yakkha and Aryan cultures.[50]

As given in the chronicles just cited, the line of the kings from Vijaya to Devanampiyatissa is shown in Table 11.1. The dates in this table and the tables which follow it in sequence are based upon the chronology of the *Mahavamsa* and the *Culavamsa,* and upon the modern calculation of the date of the *nirvana* of the Buddha as falling in 483 B.C.E. but as discussed above in Chapter 4 this date is open to question, and the dates of the ancient kings of Lanka are, at best, approximate.[51]

From Vijaya to Devanampiyatissa

Vijaya. Vijaya himself was the son of a king named Singha (Siha), the Lion. This king, also called Singhabahu (Sihabahu), was said to be the son of a lion and a princess of Vanga (Bengal) named Susima, and he ruled in a city called Sihapura (city of the lion) in the country of Lala (probably in modern Gujarat). As for Vijaya, because of his evil conduct he and seven hundred others, both men and women, were deported, and they sailed by way of Suppara (modern Sopara, 37 miles [60 km.] north of Bombay) to Lanka, arriving at the island on the day of the death of the Buddha.

When they disembarked from the ship in Lanka, Vijaya's followers sat down, wearied, resting their hands upon the ground, and found their hands made red by touching the red dust which is characteristic of the soil of the island. From this feature the region was named Tambapanni (from *tambapani,* red hand), and later Vijaya founded his capital there, with the same name, so after that the entire island was called Tambapanni (Tamraparni in Sanskrit) too (*Mahavamsa* 7.40–42).[52] The same name, probably also referring to the whole island, appears in the Rock Edicts 2 and 13 of Aśoka, where Aśoka mentions his "borderers."[53]

Since, it was said, the king Singhabahu (Sihabahu) had slain the lion, he was called Singhala (Sihala), and by reason of the ties between him and Vijaya and his followers, all of them were also called by the same name. Therefore the kingdom which Vijaya founded in Lanka was known as Singhala (Sihala), the Singha (Siha) kingdom, "the kingdom of the Lion," and Vijaya and his associates were the ancestors of the Singhalese (Sinhalese) race in Sri Lanka.

There in Lanka, Vijaya married the *yakkhini* Kuvanna and, with her assistance, killed the *yakkhas* of Lankapura and Sirisavatthu. Then not only did Vijaya found his own capital of Tambapanni, but his chief ministers, Anuradha, Upatissa, Ujjena, Uruvela, and Vijita, also founded separate settlements, named after themselves, Anuradhagama, Upatissagama, and so forth.

When Vijaya was to be consecrated as king he desired a maiden of a noble house to be consecrated as queen at the same time, so he sent away the *yakkhini* Kuvanna and their two children, a son and a daughter, and obtained as his new wife a daughter of the Pandu king of Madhura. The Pandu nation, or the Pandyas, were located in South India, and their capital of Madhura is the modern Madura, south of Madras. The Pandyan kings claimed descent from the Lunar race, and their kingdom was in constant relationship with Lanka, but frequently in war rather than in peace.

Panduvasudeva. Vijaya reigned in Tambapanni for thirty-eight years (483–445 B.C.E.) but at the end, since there was no son of himself and his Pandyan queen to succeed him, he sent for his brother Sumitta to come and take over the government. Sumitta was reigning in Sihapura after the death of the father Sihabahu, but was then himself elderly, and chose rather to send his youngest son, Panduvasudeva. Panduvasudeva only arrived after a year, and in the interval the ministers of Vijaya governed from Upatissagama.

Panduvasudeva landed with his retinue at the mouth of the Mahakandara River (probably one of the rivers entering the sea north of Manaar on the northwest coast), and assumed rule, like the ministers before him, at Upatissagama, where he reigned for thirty years (444–414 B.C.E.).

The wife of Panduvasudeva was Bhaddakaccana, the youngest daughter of a Sakyan king, who had moved his kingdom to the farther side of the Ganges. There, seven kings had sought the hand of Bhaddakaccana, for she "was (even as) a woman made of gold" (*Mahavamsa* 8.20),[54] i.e., her skin was of golden color, always, in Sinhalese literature, considered a mark of special beauty. Her father, however, sent her away by ship on the Ganges, and she landed in Lanka at Gonagamaka, a place at the mouth of the Mahakandara River, where Panduvasudeva had also arrived. From there she and her companions proceeded to Upatissagama where, ere long, she was consecrated as Panduvasudeva's queen. Later, six of the brothers of Bhaddakaccana also came to Lanka and settled in different parts of the island. Some of the brothers bear the same names as some of the ministers of Vijaya, and one of these was Anuradha, to whom tradition also assigns the foundation of the Anuradha settlement. Another brother was named Rohana, and he settled in the southeastern part of the island, where the province and kingdom of Rohana afterward bore his name.

Abhaya. Panduvasudeva and Bhaddakaccana had ten sons and one daughter, the oldest the son Abhaya (fearless), the youngest the daughter Citta. Abhaya was made vice-regent by his father, then after the ruler's death was consecrated as king, and reigned in Upatissagama for twenty years (414–394 B.C.E.).

Citta was so beautiful that the sight of her was said to drive men mad, therefore she was called Ummadacitta (from *ummadeti*, makes mad). After various vicissitudes Ummadacitta was married to a cousin named Dighagamani and became the mother of a son named Pandukabhaya. Because it was foretold that Ummadacitta's son would slay his uncles in order to obtain possession of the kingdom, all of Ummadacitta's brothers except Abhaya tried repeatedly to kill

Pandukabhaya. Finally Pandukabhaya made war upon the uncles and slew nine of them, sparing Abhaya who had befriended both his mother and himself.

Pandukabhaya. Thus Pandukabhaya obtained the rule, and when he did so he removed the capital from Upatissagama to Anuradhagama, the site of the settlements started originally by the two Anuradhas. Thereafter the new city was known as Anuradhapura, and it remained the capital or at least the religious center of Lanka for more than fifteen centuries, only being finally deserted in the thirteenth century C.E.

To govern Anuradhapura Pandukabhaya appointed two Guardians of the city (*nagaraguttika*), one for the day and the other for the night, and gave the latter position to his oldest and surviving uncle, Abhaya. In the *Mahavamsa* (10.105–106)[55] it is considered that there were seventeen years without a king between Abhaya and Pandukabhaya, and Pandukabhaya himself is said to have reigned for seventy years (377–307 B.C.E.), and to have died at the age of 107.

Anuradhapura is in the northern relatively dry part of Sri Lanka, but there was an important natural pond there which Pandukabhaya deepened, and it was called Jayavapi (tank of victory) because, being victorious, Pandukabhaya had used water from it for the consecration of himself as king and of his wife, Suvannapali, as queen. Pandukabhaya also constructed a second artificial lake, and it was called the Abhayavapi. The city itself was laid out with four suburbs, residential sections for laborers and for huntsmen, a place of execution, a common cemetery, and temples to various deities. Among the buildings which Pandukabhaya erected were hermitages for the Niganthas (Jainas) Jotiya, Giri, and Kumbhanda, and abodes for the Ajivikas, the *brahmanas,* and various wandering mendicant monks. The king also built "a lying-in shelter and a hall for those recovering from sickness" (*Mahavamsa* 10.83–102).[56]

Mutasiva. Pandukabhaya was succeeded by his son Mutasiva, who ruled "in splendid Anuradhapura" for sixty years (307–247 B.C.E.). At Anuradhapura, to the south of the city, Mutasiva laid out a beautiful garden called the Mahameghavana (grove of the great cloud), full of fruit trees and flowering trees, and between this and the southern wall of the city there was also another park called Nandanavana (*Mahavamsa* 11.2; 15.2, 11).[57]

Even if not as long as that of his father, the reign of Mutasiva was long, and it began in the time of Candragupta Maurya (322–298), and continued into the reign of Asoka (269–232) (cf. *Dipavamsa* 11.12–13)[58] and through the time of the Third Buddhist Council (252) in India. At the close of the Third Council Asoka's son Mahinda was commissioned to go to Lanka, but evidently felt that conditions were not favorable under the then elderly Mutasiva, and did not proceed to Lanka until Mutasiva was deceased and Mutasiva's son Devanampiyatissa had become king (*Mahavamsa* 13.2).[59]

Devanampiyatissa. Mutasiva had ten sons (Abhaya, Tissa, Mahanaga, Uttiya, Mattabhaya, Mitta, Mahasiva, Asela, Suratissa, Kira) and two daughters (Anula, Sivali). Abhaya renounced the throne in favor of his next brother, so the succession came to Tissa and he ruled for forty years (247–207 B.C.E.). Since Tissa had Sakyan blood he could claim family connection with Asoka, who was a Moriyan, a branch of the Sakyans, and, like Asoka, Tissa enjoyed the title *devanampiya* and was regularly known by this title alone, or by his name compounded with the title, Devanampiyatissa, Tissa the beloved of the gods.

According to the *Mahavamsa* (11.19),[60] Devanampiyatissa and Dhammasoka (Aśoka the righteous) had already been friends for a long time, although they had never seen each other. Accordingly, after his own coronation, Devanampiyatissa sent tokens of esteem to Aśoka in the form of priceless jewels and pearls. These gifts were carried by an embassy of ministers, led by the king's nephew and chief minister, Maha-Arittha. The embassy embarked at the Jambukola harbor on the northern coast of Lanka, sailed to Tamalitti (Tamralipti, the port near the mouth of the Ganges from which Fa Xian later sailed for Lanka), and proceeded to Pataliputra. Aśoka received them with honor and, in due time sent them back, accompanied by his own envoys, bearing return gifts. These gifts included materials for the ceremony of consecrating a king, and the envoys were instructed to carry out such a ceremony for Devanampiyatissa, so upon their arrival in Lanka Devanampiyatissa was honored with a second coronation, evidently confirming his sovereignty and strengthening the family connections between Aśoka and himself.

Aśoka also sent a message to Devanampiyatissa inviting Devanampiyatissa to accept Buddhism. Aśoka said (*Mahavamsa* 11.34–35): "I have taken refuge in the Buddha, his Doctrine *(dhamma),* and his Order *(sangha).* I have declared myself a lay disciple in the religion of the Sakya son; seek then even you, O best of men, converting your mind with believing heart, refuge in these best of jewels!"[61]

Mahinda. As the *Dipavamsa* (12ff.)[62] and the *Mahavamsa* (13ff.)[63] continue the narrative at this point, it was in the year of Devanampiyatissa's second coronation that Mahinda arrived in Lanka. Commissioned for this mission by Moggaliputta-Tissa after the Third Council in Pataliputra, Mahinda had at this time been an ordained monk for twelve years. On the mission he was now accompanied not only by his four disciples, Itthiya, Uttiya, Sambala, and Bhaddasala (also commissioned by Moggaliputta-Tissa), but also by the novice Sumana (the son of Sanghamitta and Aggibrahma) and the lay disciple Bhanduka. In Lanka the group came to Missakapabbata, the Missaka mountain (now called Mihintale, possibly "plain of Mahinda," 8 miles [13 km.] east of Anuradhapura), and stopped on the northern peak of the mountain called Silakuta (*Dipavamsa* 12.25–43; *Mahavamsa* 13).[64]

In the last month of summer Devanampiyatissa was hunting at the mountain, and on the small tableland below the peak, called Ambatthala, met Mahinda. Mahinda recited to him the *Culahatthipadopama Sutta* or "lesser discourse on the simile of the elephant's foot," an allegory once propounded by the Buddha and now found in the *Majjhima Nikaya* (1.175–184). The attention of the king had already been directed to the new religion by Aśoka, and at the end of Mahinda's discourse Devanampiyatissa and the large number of men with him "came unto the (three) refuges," i.e., *buddha, dhamma, sangha,* the Buddha, his Doctrine, and his Order (*Mahavamsa* 14.23).[65]

On the next day at the invitation of the king Mahinda and his companions came on into Anuradhapura. There Devanampiyatissa invited his sister Anula (daughter of Mutasiva and wife of Mahanaga, who was younger brother and viceroy of Devanampiyatissa) also to listen to Mahinda. Mahinda now preached the *Petavatthu,* the *Vimanavatthu,* and the *Sacca Samyutta,* the first two works describing the abodes of blessedness and of punishment in the world beyond, and the third quoting the sermon by the Buddha at Isipatana in which he set the wheel of the doctrine rolling (*Dipavamsa* 12.83–86; *Mahavamsa* 14.57–58).[66] Upon hearing, Anula and the women with her attained to the first stage of sanctification in the Buddhist faith (*sotapatti,* the stage of a *sotapanna,* "who has entered the stream").

Later in the day Mahinda preached further texts to many more people in the stable of the royal elephant and in the Nandana park. In the evening Mahinda and his companions proposed to return to the Missaka mountain, but the king suggested that they take their rest in the Nandana garden. When they declared that this was too near the city, the king offered them a place in the Mahameghavana and, on the next day, donated the entire garden to the brotherhood.

Anula and her companions now attained to the second stage of salvation (*sakadagamiphala*, a *sakadagami* being one who will be reborn in the human world only once more before attaining *nirvana*), and wished to be ordained as nuns. Since it was not allowed for men to ordain women, Mahinda proposed to send for his younger sister, the nun Sanghamitta, that she might come and perform this function.

In the following days Mahinda delivered many more discourses, and converted large numbers of people. The Mahamegha park remained the center of the Order, and became known as the Mahameghavanarama. One day Devanampiyatissa came there to see Mahinda, and proceeded to plough a furrow in a great circle, beginning near the Gangalatittha ford on the Kadambaka (the river that flows past the east side of Anuradhapura, now called the Malvatu Oya) and ending again at the river. This boundary went around the hermitages of the Niganthas Jotiya, Giri, and Kumbhanda, and hermitages of Wanderers, and even included the shrine of the guardian deity of Anuradhapura (*Mahavamsa* 25.87),[67] but it was intended to mark out a very large area to be used primarily for a very large *vihara* for the Buddhists. The name of the *vihara* was simply the Mahavihara, the "great monastery," and this was thenceforward also the name for the entire Mahameghavanarama. As thus founded by Devanampiyatissa, the Mahavihara was for many centuries the chief seat of Theravada Buddhism in Lanka.

For the rainy season retreat (*vassa*) Mahinda went to the Missakapabbata, and Devanampiyatissa erected there a *vihara*—the second *vihara* built in Lanka—and cut out sixty-eight rock cells for the monks. This was in the place where the *stupa* called the Kantaka Cetiya afterwards stood.[68]

After the retreat was ended with the usual *pavarana* ceremony, Mahinda sent Sumana to Pataliputra (Pupphapura) to obtain relics of the Buddha, saying, "If we behold the relics we behold the Conqueror" (*Mahavamsa* 17.3).[69] The relics which were thus obtained included a tooth and a collarbone of the Buddha, and the alms bowl which he had used. When the relics were brought they were placed for the time being on the Missaka mountain and, for this reason, and perhaps also for reason of the many shrines (*cetiyas*) which were built there, the mountain was called the Cetiya mountain (Cetiyapabbata, also Cetiyagiri), and the monastery on the mountain was called the Cetiyapabbata-*vihara*.

From the Missaka mountain the collarbone relic of the Buddha was brought into Anuradhapura and deposited in a *stupa* (*thupa*) which Devanampiyatissa erected for the purpose in the Nandana garden just outside the southern wall of the city. Since this was the first and only such monument in the country at the time it was known as the thupa, and the monastery connected with it was called the Thuparama.

In the meantime the queen Anula and her women companions were still waiting for ordination as nuns, and were living as lay sisters and observing the "ten precepts" (not to kill any living being; not to take the property of others; not to commit adultery; not to lie; not to drink intoxicating drink; to take food only at prescribed hours; to avoid worldly amusements; to use neither unguents nor ornaments; not to sleep on a high or decorated bed; not to accept any gold or silver). Accordingly Devanampiyatissa built a nunnery in Anuradhapura for their use, and it became known as the Upasika-*vihara* (*vihara* of the lay sisters) (*Mahavamsa* 18.9–12).[70]

Sanghamitta. For the ordination of the women Mahinda had suggested that his sister might come, and Devanampiyatissa now again sent his nephew and minister, Prince Arittha, to ask Aśoka to send Sanghamitta to Anuradhapura, and also to send with her a branch of the Bodhi tree. Aśoka acquiesced in the request, although he expressed grief at having to part with Sanghamitta as well as already with a son (Mahinda) and a grandson (Sumana, the son of Sanghamitta and her onetime consort Aggibrahma).

Accordingly Sanghamitta and with her the south branch taken from the Bodhi tree were transported by ship from Tamalitti to Jambukola, where Devanampiyatissa met the ship in person. At Anuradhapura the Bodhi tree was planted in the Mahameghavana, where the king instituted in its honor a festival which was observed thereafter for many centuries. Bodhi saplings were also planted at a number of other places, including one in the Thuparama and one on the Cetiya mountain. As planned, Sanghamitta conducted the ordination of Anula and her following. For Sanghamitta and the nuns, Devanampiyatissa constructed, in addition to the Upasika-*vihara*, the Hatthalhaka-*vihara* (so named because it was near a post where the state elephant was tethered at night).

Likewise Mahinda conducted the ordination of Prince Arittha, and 500 nobles who were his followers received ordination too, and for them all Devanampiyatissa built the Issarasamana-*vihara* (Isurumuniya). Nearby the king also built the Vessagiri-*vihara*, a residence for 500 *vessa* people (of the third caste, Sanskrit *vaiśya*), converted by Mahinda. The last two *viharas* were adjacent to a large tank which the king constructed to the southwest of the city, which was known by his name as the Tissavapi. According to the *Culavamsa* (37.94),[71] Devanampiyatissa also built on the royal territory at Anuradhapura the building known as the Dhammacakkapasada (its name honoring the "wheel of the law"), which later under the reign of Sirimeghavana (362–409 C.E.) became the repository of the tooth relic of the Buddha.

Thus, throughout his whole life, Devanampiyatissa "heaped up works of merit," and during the forty years of his reign the island of Lanka flourished (*Mahavamsa* 20.27–28).[72]

First Council at the Thuparama under Devanampiyatissa

As Buddhaghosa relates in the *Samantapasadika* (102–104),[73] after Devanampiyatissa had seen the Bodhi tree planted at Anuradhapura, and had built many buildings for the Buddhist Order, he asked Mahinda whether the Dispensation (*sasana*) of the Buddha were then indeed established in the island. Mahinda replied that the Dispensation was established, but its roots were not yet deep. Echoing what was said at the First Council in Rajagriha about the Dispensation enduring as long as the *vinaya* endures, Mahinda declared that what was yet needed was a recital of the *vinaya,* and that by a Sinhalese monk. Accordingly, at the suggestion of Mahinda, the king erected in the precincts of the Thuparama monastery a pavilion which resembled the hall which Ajataśatru constructed for the First Council. Here sixty-eight great elders came together, each with a following of 1,000 monks, making an assembly of 68,000 in all. Following the custom begun already at the First Council, a seat was provided for the presiding officer, and this was occupied by Mahinda, and a seat for the preacher, and this was occupied by Maha-Arittha.

Maha-Arittha. When Devanampiyatissa sent gifts to Aśoka the embassy was headed by Maha-Arittha, identified as the nephew and chief minister of Devanampiyatissa, and when the king sent again to Aśoka to ask for the sending of Sanghamitta and a branch of the Bodhi tree, it was also the king's nephew and minister, named Arittha—presumably the same as Maha-Arittha—who went on the mission. In the second instance Arittha agreed to go if he would be allowed to enter the Buddhist Order when he came back and, upon his return, he was ordained as a monk, together with a retinue of 500 men (*Mahavamsa* 18.5, 66).

By the time of the great assembly at the Thuparama, it was Maha-Arittha who was thought most capable of carrying out the task of the preacher, and it was for that reason that he was given the seat of that dignitary and was called upon to proceed with the recital of the *vinaya*. Immediately around him, to receive the teaching, were 500 monks under the leadership of the *thera* Mattabhaya, a younger brother of Devanampiyatissa, and he had the role of the chief in office, literally, "he who has taken the yoke upon himself," i.e., he would have the responsibility for handing on down the *vinaya* tradition. As for the remaining monks and the people and the king himself, they sat in the places assigned to them. Thus in his recital of the *vinaya* Maha-Arittha performed the same function as Upali in the First Council, but there was not a corresponding recital of the *dhamma* such as was performed by Ananda in the First Council. Such was the first assembly held in Sri Lanka, and such was the emphasis there upon the *vinaya*. In general it is commonly said that of the three great Theravada countries even today, Sri Lanka gives precedence to the study of the *vinaya*, Thailand to that of the *suttas*, and Burma to that of the *abhidhamma*.[74]

From Uttiya to Dutthagamani

Devanampiyatissa died without a son, and after him no fewer than four of his many brothers, the sons of Mutasiva, had the throne in Anuradhapura and appear in the list in Table 11.2, namely, Uttiya, Mahasiva, Suratissa, and Asela.

Uttiya. The third son of Mutasiva, named Mahanaga, was a viceroy of Devanampiyatissa, and was married to Anula, who was ordained by Sanghamitta. A second wife of Mahanaga tried to poison Mahanaga in order to get the throne for her son, but it was her own small son who took the poison instead and died. After that Mahanaga went off to Rohana in the southeastern part of Lanka, where

TABLE 11.2.
KINGS OF LANKA FROM UTTIYA TO DUTTHAGAMANI

Name	Length of Reign in Years	Buddha Nirvana Era (reckoned from 483 BCE)	BCE
7. Uttiya	10	276–286	207–197
8. Mahasiva	10	286–296	197–187
9. Suratissa	10	296–306	187–177
10. Sena 11. Guttika	22	306–328	177–155
12. Asela	10	328–338	155–145
13. Elara	44	338–382	145–101
14. Dutthagamani	24	382–406	101–77

the Sakyan prince Rohana, one of the brothers of Bhaddakaccana, had founded the settlement which bore his name. There Mahanaga ruled in a capital named Mahagama, and there he founded many *viharas* (*Mahavamsa* 22.1–9).[75] When the northern part of Lanka was in the hands of invaders or usurpers, members of the Sinhalese court often found refuge in Rohana, and so did Buddhist monks in time of persecution in the north. Likewise, various rebellions against the ruler in Anuradhapura originated in Rohana.

Instead of Mahanaga, the third son of Mutasiva, it was therefore the fourth son, Uttiya, who succeeded Devanampiyatissa and ruled at Anuradhapura (207–197 B.C.E.). Mahinda lived on into the eighth year of the reign of Uttiya. In the last years of his life Mahinda dwelt on Cetiyagiri, and he died on the mountain in his last rainy season, being at the time sixty years from his ordination. Uttiya caused Mahinda's body to be cremated at Cetiyagiri, and his relics were preserved there in *stupas* and also distributed in *viharas* elsewhere.

Sanghamitta lived a year longer than Mahinda and died in the ninth year of Uttiya. She was cremated at a place east of the Thuparama, in sight of the Bodhi tree, and Uttiya erected a *stupa* there in her memory. So also the companions who had come to Lanka with Mahinda died, and many other monks as well, and many other nuns who were companions of Sanghamitta, and Uttiya himself died after ten years of reign. "Thus is mortality the destroyer of the whole world," comments the *Mahavamsa* (20.57–58):

> One who, although knowing this overmastering, overwhelming, irresistible mortality, yet is not discontented with the world of existence and does not feel, in this discontent, resentment at wrong or joy in virtue—that is the strength of the fetters of evil delusion!—such a one is knowingly fooled.[76]

Mahasiva and Suratissa. Mattabhaya, the fifth son of Mutasiva, was an ordained monk, and has already been seen at the Thuparama assembly, where he was charged with the duty of learning the *vinaya* from Maha-Arittha. Mitta, the sixth son, is known only from the occurrence of his name in the list of the children of Mutasiva (*Dipavamsa* 11.6–7),[77] and presumably passed off the scene at some relatively early time. It was, accordingly, the seventh son, Mahasiva, who was next on the throne at Anuradhapura (197–187 B.C.E.).

In turn, Mahasiva was succeeded by his brother Suratissa (187–177 B.C.E.). In the list of the ten sons of Mutasiva just cited in the *Dipavamsa* (11.6–7), Suratissa indeed appears in the ninth place, with Asela as the eighth and Kira as the tenth. The *Mahavamsa* (21.11–12),[78] however, explicitly calls Asela the ninth among the brothers, so Suratissa must have been in fact the eighth, as corresponds with his assumption of the throne in succession to Mahasiva. As for Kira, he does not appear further at all.

Mahasiva is said to have been devoted to the *thera* Bhaddasala, and to have built for him the *vihara* called Nagarangana in the eastern quarter of Anuradhapura. Suratissa, likewise, is said to have been "devoted to the three gems (i.e., *buddha, dhamma, sangha*)," and to have built many *viharas* at and near Anuradhapura (*Mahavamsa* 21.1–9).[79]

Sena and Guttika. In the reign of Suratissa there came the first of the many foreign invasions to which Lanka was exposed from this time on. Two Damila (Tamil) merchants from South India, named Sena and Guttika, attacked Suratissa, took possession of his territory, and ruled for twenty-two years (177–155 B.C.E.).

Presumably these invaders were Hindus, and nothing is said of any actions on their part in support of Buddhism.

Asela and Elara. Asela, the last of the sons of Mutasiva and of the brothers of Devanampiyatissa to rule at Anuradhapura, was able to overpower Sena and Guttika, and to hold the throne for ten years (155–145 B.C.E.). Like the preceding members of his line, Asela was a patron of Buddhism, and is credited with the construction of a shrine in the place called the Asokamalaka in the Mahameghavana garden at Anuradhapura.

Another Tamil, named Elara, came in, however, from South India, overpowered Asela, and himself reigned in Anuradhapura for forty-four years (145–101 B.C.E.). He, too, was presumably a Hindu, but is praised in the *Mahavamsa* (21.13–34) for his even-handed administration of justice toward friend and foe alike, and for his protection of "tradition," "albeit he knew not the peerless virtues of the most precious of the three jewels (i.e., virtues of the Buddha himself)," and did not ever "put aside false beliefs."[80]

Dutthagamani Abhaya. In spite of the evidently honorable character of Elara, the Tamils were foreign, non-Buddhist invaders, ruling over most of North Lanka from the ancient capital of Anuradhapura, and rebellion against their domination arose from the indigenous population and from the line of the ancient Sinhalese kings.

In addition to the main kingdom of which the center was Anuradhapura, there were in existence several small independent kingdoms. One of these was Rohana already mentioned, located in the southeastern part of the island and separated from the North by the Mahavalukaganga, the chief river of Lanka, the modern Mahavaliganga. In Rohana's capital city of Mahagama the king at this time was Kakavannatissa, a great grandson of Mahanaga, who had established his line here in the time of his brother Devanampiyatissa. Two other kingdoms were originally settlements of the Nagas (probably non-Aryan tribes, and associated with snakes), namely, Nagadipa (identified with the modern Jaffna peninsula and the northwestern part of Lanka) and Kalyani (at the mouth of the river of the same name, now the Kelani, near Colombo), and both of these, as well as Rohana, were already important centers of Buddhism.

In Kalyani, at this time, the king was Kalyani-Tissa, and he had a pious and beautiful daughter named Devi (later Viharadevi, Viharamahadevi). After various adventures, in which she was cast adrift in a boat on the ocean, Devi landed in Rohana and became the queen of Kakavannatissa. Their sons were Gamani and Saddhatissa.

Already as a young man Gamani wished to undertake war against Elara and the Tamils. In this he was encouraged by his mother, who was very much opposed to the foreign domination of the greater part of the country, but he was restrained by his father who, although he gathered many famous warriors at his court, referred to the Mahavalukaganga as the natural boundary of Rohana and said, "The region on this side of the river is enough" (*Mahavamsa* 24.4).[81] This made Gamani angry with his father, and Gamani withdrew to Malaya, the central mountain region in the interior of the island. Because Gamani was wroth with his father they named him Dutthagamani, which means "the angry Gamani." His full name was Dutthagamani Abhaya.

Meanwhile the younger brother, Saddhatissa, was in charge of Dighavapi, a district apparently lying between Rohana and the Tamil kingdom. When Kakavannatissa died, in the absence of Dutthagamani the older brother, Saddhatissa came and seized the throne in Mahagama. Dutthagamani thereupon made war upon his brother and, after initial defeat, was victorious, while Saddhatissa fled to a Buddhist monastery. Through the influence of the monks there was a reconciliation of the brothers, and Saddhatissa returned to Dighavapi.

Dutthagamani then proceeded with his long desired war against the Tamils. In a series of successful engagements he reached Anuradhapura, and there slew Elara in singlehanded combat near the southern gate of the city. Afterward, however, Dutthagamani built a tomb over Elara's ashes, and was considered to have acted very chivalrously toward the defeated enemy. Elara's nephew, Bhalluka, also came with reinforcements from India, but he too was defeated. So Dutthagamani united Lanka in one kingdom, and ruled in single sovereignty (101–77 B.C.E.).

Afterward, however, in somewhat the manner of Aśoka after the Kalinga war, Dutthagamani was filled with remorse for the destruction of life which his successful war had caused, but the monks of Piyangudipa (an island probably near Lanka), who enjoyed a reputation for extreme holiness, sent a delegation which absolved him from blame for the slaughter of his enemies. Thereafter, having first given gifts to his generals and soldiers, Dutthagamani inaugurated great works of piety, and many chapters of the *Mahavamsa* (26–32)[82] are occupied with descriptions of the numerous buildings which he erected at Anuradhapura for the glorification of the Buddhist faith.

Throughout his military career Dutthagamani's standard was a spear containing a relic of the Buddha, and this standard was now enshrined in the Maricavatti *cetiya*, with which the Maricavatti *vihara* was associated. The name came from the fact that the building of the *cetiya* and the *vihara* was intended by the king as an act of expiation for his once having eaten a pepper-pod (*maricavatti*) without first sharing the food with the monks, a custom of sharing which he had been taught by his mother and father and had otherwise maintained from childhood.

Another building constructed by Dutthagamani was the Lohapasada in the Mahavihara in the Mahamegha garden. This building was intended as a splendid dwelling for the residents of the monastery. It was a structure of nine stories, diminishing in size toward the top, and the successive stories were occupied by monks of successively higher attainments. The word *pasada* refers to the type of construction, and is now also used to designate the graduated galleries which form the base of *stupas*. The word *loha* refers to the copper plates, with which the building was roofed. So the Lohapasada was the "brazen palace." In particular function the Lohapasada was a *uposathagara*, i.e., a house for the ceremonies of the *uposatha* (Sanskrit *upavasatha*), the Buddhist holy day (which occurs four times in the month, on the full and new moon days and on the eighth day following each). In view of this function the Lohapasada contained a large assembly hall, with a preacher's seat. On one occasion Dutthagamani occupied this seat and attempted to preach to the assembly the text called the *Mangalasutta*,[83] but was too overcome with reverence for the Order to proceed. Realizing then how difficult was the task of preachers, he ordered gifts for them in every *vihara* (*Mahavamsa* 32.42–46).[84]

The largest undertaking of Dutthagamani in his works of building was the erection of the Mahathupa (great *stupa*), also called the Hemavaluka-*cetiya* and the Ratanavaluka-*cetiya*, and now known as the Ruwanweli Dagoba. The site was at the upper end of the Kakudhavapi, a little pond in the Mahameghavana. The location was indicated originally by Mahinda to Devanampiyatissa as a desirable place for a monument, because the spot had been visited by three former Buddhas and by Śakyamuni Buddha on his own third visit to Lanka (his first visit to drive out the *yakkhas*, the second to subdue the *nagas*, and the third at the invitation of the *naga* Maniakkhi in Kalyani). Accordingly Devanampiyatissa wished to build a *stupa (thupa)* at the spot immediately, but Mahinda told him that this would only be done by his descendant, Dutthagamani, in the future, so Devanampiyatissa only recorded Mahinda's prophecy on a pillar of stone at the place (*Mahavamsa* 15.51–173).[85] When Dutthagamani saw this pillar he resolved to carry out the prophecy and build the monument, even though its expense would be very great and he hesitated to tax the people again after having burdened them heavily at the conquering of the Tamils. Nevertheless bricks, copper, silver, gold, pearls, and gems were found, and the work went forward.

In plan the Mahathupa consisted essentially of a circular terrace as the base, then a hemispherical dome containing in its upper part a relic chamber, above that a four-sided block of brickwork, and uppermost of all a conical spire. In this case the relic chamber was of special magnificence. It contained a Bodhi tree made of jewels, a golden image of the seated Buddha, statues of Brahma, Mara, and various gods, and pictures—presumably in the form of bas-reliefs—of many events in the historical life of the Buddha, and of events in his previous existences as related in the Jatakas.

Before the construction was finished, however, Dutthagamani fell ill. He sent for his brother Saddhatissa to come from Dighavapi to complete the work, and Saddhatissa made a covering of white cloth and a spire of bamboo, so that from this temporary construction the dying king could visualize the completed structure.

In addition to the information provided by the *Mahavamsa*, there is also a Pali work named the *Thupavamsa* (chronicle of the *thupa*), composed by a Buddhist elder named Vacissara (probably between 1236 and 1270 C.E.), the main theme of which is the building of the Mahathupa by Dutthagamani.[86] To provide full background the account begins with previous Buddhas and *thupas* built in earlier times, then tells of the disposition of the relics of Śakyamuni Buddha after his death, and of the building works of Aśoka, and so comes on to Dutthagamani and the construction of the Maricavattivihara, the Lohapasada and, climactically, the Mahathupa.

In a book in which he himself put down the meritorious acts of his twenty-four year reign, Dutthagamani recorded that altogether he built ninety-nine *viharas*, held twenty-four Vesakha festivals (the traditional date of the death of the Buddha was on the full moon day of the month Vesakha, March/April), made many gifts to the Order, in twelve places kept 1,000 oil lamps burning perpetually in adoration of the Buddha, and in eighteen places constantly bestowed on the sick the foods and the remedies "ordered by the physicians" (*Mahavamsa* 32.25–38).[87] Plainly Dutthagamani is, for his many good works, the most highly regarded of all the kings in the *Mahavamsa*.

Buddhist Gatherings under Dutthagamani

Under Dutthagamani there were several gatherings in Anuradhapura of large numbers of Buddhists. On one occasion, according to the *Dipavamsa* (18.20–23), five well-known nuns, with a following of 20,000 more, came from Rohana and taught the Vinayapitaka at Anuradhapura. Likewise, according to the *Mahavamsa* (26.15), at the festival of the consecration of the Maricavatti-*vihara*, 100,000 monks and 90,000 nuns assembled in Anuradhapura.[88]

But the largest gathering of all was at the laying of the foundation stone of the Mahathupa. For that occasion delegations came not only from all over Lanka but also from many places in India, reportedly 80,000 monks from Rajagriha, 12,000 from Isipatana, 60,000 from Savatthi, 18,000 from Vesali, 30,000 from Kosambi, 40,000 from Ujjeni, 160,000 from Pataliputta, and yet others from other places. In the assembly Dutthagamani took his place near the *thera* Piyadassi, who was the head of the delegation from the Jetavana monastery at Savatthi (Śravasti), and Piyadassi "preached the true doctrine to him," with many persons being converted at the same time (*Dipavamsa* 19.5–7; *Mahavamsa* 29.29–69).[89] By one reckoning this large gathering under Dutthagamani was the Fifth Buddhist Council,[90] but the assembly is not usually counted as one of the great councils, and in fact the records do not speak of any recital at this time of *vinaya* and/or *dhamma*, usually the main feature of a full-scale council.

From Saddhatissa to Vattagamani

Saddhatissa. The son of Dutthagamani, named Salirajakumara, loved a beautiful outcaste woman (*candala*, offspring of a *brahmana* woman and a *śudra* man) named Asokamaladevi, and cared nothing for the kingship, so it was Dutthagamani's younger brother Saddhatissa who, as shown in Table 11.3, took the throne next (77–59 B.C.E.). Like his older brother and predecessor, Saddhatissa was devoted to Buddhism and, with a play on his name, it was said that he won his name by his faith (*saddha*, faith). He completed the unfinished work on the Mahathupa and, when the Lohapasada caught fire from a lamp and burned down, he built it anew, this time seven stories high. He also built many *viharas* at Anuradhapura and elsewhere, reportedly including one for every *yojana* on the road from Anuradhapura to Dighavapi, where he had lived so long (*Mahavamsa* 33.1–13).[91]

Thulathana, Lanjatissa, and Khallatanaga. Four sons of Saddhatissa were the next holders of the throne. Thulathana was the second son rather than the first but, for some reason, the ministers and monks consecrated him as king instead of

TABLE 11.3.
KINGS OF LANKA FROM SADDHATISSA TO VATTAGAMANI

Name	Length of Reign in Years	Buddha Nirvana Era (reckoned from 483 BCE)	BCE
15. Saddhatissa	18 years	406–424	77–59
16. Thulathana	1 month, 10 days	424	59
17. Lanjatissa	9 years, 15 days	424–433	59–50
18. Khallatanaga	6 years	433–439	50–44
19. Vattagamani	5 months	439	44
20. Pulahatta			
21. Bahiya	14 years, 7 months	439–454	44–29
22. Panayamara			
23. Pilayamara			
24. Dathika			
25. Vattagamani	12 years	454–466	29–17

his older brother. After a reign of only one month and ten days (59 B.C.E.) the older brother, Lanjatissa, overpowered him and seized the throne and ruled for nine years and fifteen days (59–50 B.C.E.). For three years Lanjatissa slighted the Buddhist Order because they had passed him over for the kingship, but after that he was reconciled and made atonement with many building works. He leveled the ground between the Thuparama monastery and the Mahathupa (about 1,200 feet [365 m.] away), made stone mantlings for some of the *thupas* including the *thupa* in the Thuparama and the Kantaka-*cetiya* in the Cetiya mountain, built a hall for the monks called the Lanjakasana hall, and erected yet other buildings. On one occasion he also distributed the so-called six garments to 60,000 monks (i.e., to each a pair of the three articles of clothing, the undergarment, robe, and mantle).

When Lanjatissa died his younger brother, Khallatanaga, reigned for six years (50–44 B.C.E.). Khallatanaga built a monastery called the Kurundavasoka-*vihara*, added dwellings at the Lohapasada, and constructed a "sandcourt boundary" at the Mahathupa, this being now the so-called elephant path that runs around the terrace of the Ruwanweli Dagoba (*Mahavamsa* 33.29–32).[92]

Vattagamani Abhaya. When a troop commander named Maharattaka killed Khallatanaga, the king's younger brother, the fourth son of Saddhatissa, named Vattagamani, killed the troop commander and took over the government. Vattagamani also took Khallatanaga's widow Anula as his queen, and the son of Khallatanaga and Anula, named Mahaculika, as his own son; since Vattagamani had thus taken the place of a father they called him Pitiraja (king father). Vattagamani also had a second wife, Somadevi, and a son of his own, called Coranaga. The king's own full name was Vattagamani Abhaya.

After only five months of reign by Vattagamani Abhaya, a *brahmana* in Rohana, named Tissa, raised a major rebellion against the king, but at the same time seven Tamils also invaded Lanka and defeated both Tissa and Vattagamani. The battle in which Vattagamani was defeated took place near the village Kolambalaka not far from the north gate of Anuradhapura and in the vicinity of the Tittharama, a monastery occupied by a *tittha* (sect) of non-Buddhist monks. As the king fled in his car from the field of battle, a Nigantha (Jaina) named Giri saw him and cried out loudly, "The great black lion (*mahakalasihala*, a play on the word *siha*, "lion," and the name *sihala*) is fleeing." The king, hearing, thought: "If my wish be fulfilled I will build a *vihara* here" (*Mahavamsa* 33.43–44)[93]—and this led eventually to the establishment of the Abhayagiri *vihara* and *thupa*.

At the time of his flight Vattagamani lost to the Tamils his wife Somadevi, and also the alms bowl used by the Buddha, which had been in Anuradhapura since the time of Devanampiyatissa, but he himself and his queen Anula and his two sons (Mahaculika and Coranaga) hid in the Vessagiri forest south of Anuradhapura and were rescued by the *thera* Mahatissa, who belonged to the Kupikkala *vihara*. Mahatissa then entrusted the fugitives to the care of a supporter of himself, a landowner in Malaya (the central mountain region in the interior of the island), named Tanasiva, and the king and his family lived there for the next fourteen years, while the Tamils ruled in Anuradhapura.

Coincident with the rebellion of the *brahmana* Tissa and the invasion by the Tamils, a famine of unparalleled severity began in Lanka and continued for twelve years. Thus natural catastrophe as well as non-Buddhist rule combined to bring hardship and oppression to the Buddhist Order, and many monks also withdrew to the mountainous districts of the island, where they experienced near starvation, while others of them went off, at least for the time being, to India.

Finally, as a result of a dispute between Anula and Tanasiva's wife, Vattagamani killed Tanasiva. When Vattagamani also killed one of his own ministers, named Kapisisa, for what he thought was lack of respect, the king's seven other ministers withdrew from him, but were persuaded to return by the *thera* Mahatissa, who suggested that the doctrine of the Buddha would be better furthered under the king than under the Tamils.

Meanwhile, of the seven Tamils who had invaded the island, one took Somadevi for himself and returned overseas to India, another took the alms bowl of the Buddha (which was believed to have miraculous powers) and also returned home, while it was the remaining five (Pulahattha to Dathika in Table 11.3) who reigned successively in Anuradhapura, each slaying his predecessor and taking the throne for himself. The last of these was Dathika, and Vattagamani now attacked and slew him, regained the throne in Anuradhapura, and also recovered his wife Somadevi.

In the course of his further reign (29–17 B.C.E.) Vattagamani built various buildings for the Buddhist cause. Remembering his earlier vow, he destroyed the Tittharama on the north side of Anuradhapura, where the Nigantha Giri made the insulting remark at the time of his flight, and built there the Abhayagiri, combining in its name his own name and the name of the Nigantha. The Abhayagiri comprised both a large *vihara* and a great *thupa*. When it was completed it was given to the *thera* Mahatissa of Kupikkala, who had befriended Vattagamani in his time of misfortune. The date of the foundation of the Abhayagiri was 217 years, 10 months, and 10 days after the founding of the Mahavihara, built by Devanampiyatissa in the Mahameghavana on the south side of Anuradhapura.

At the spot near the Abhayagiri where Somadevi alighted from his car prior to the great battle, Vattagamani built in her honor a convent called the Somarama, and at a spot north of the Mahathupa where he himself had taken refuge during his flight the king built a shrine *(cetiya)* called Silasobbhakandaka. Also several of the seven ministers of the king built *viharas,* and they also gave these to the *thera* Mahatissa in gratitude for his kindness.

With the cessation of the famine and with the more favorable conditions provided for them by the resumption of power by Vattagamani, the monks who had gone to India returned, and those who had taken refuge in the hills came forth again. In spite of every difficulty, each group had continued to recite the sacred texts, and when the surviving members of each group compared their respective versions as thus preserved, it was said that they still agreed word for word. Among the monks who returned from India there arose a discussion, however, as to which were the more basic to the continuation of the Dispensation (*sasana*) of the Buddha, *pariyati* (learning) or *patipatti* (living the life), and in the argument the *dhammakathikas* (preachers of the *dhamma*, the doctrine) won out over the *pamsukulikas* (observers of the ascetic practice called *pamsukulikanga,* and more broadly observers of the *vinaya* in general). Obviously this was a reversal of the opinion previously predominant that the *vinaya* was of the first importance even over the *dhamma*.[94]

There also came to be disagreement and rivalry between the Mahavihara and the Abhayagiri. When a *thera* named Mahatissa (probably a different person than the *thera* Mahatissa from the Kupikkala-*vihara,* who was the friend of Vattagamani) was expelled from the Mahavihara by reason of his too close association with lay families, this *thera's* disciple, named Bahalamassutissa, withdrew to the Abhayagiri-*vihara* and formed a separate faction. This was the first outright schism in the Order in Lanka, and the monks at the Abhayagiri-*vihara* did not come any more to the Mahavihara. "Thus did the *bhikkhus* of the Abhayagiri secede from the Theravada" (*Mahavamsa* 33.97).[95]

Second Council at Aluvihara in the Time of Vattagamani

No doubt because of the disagreements which were emerging, and also because of the difficulty which had been experienced in preserving intact the sacred texts in the days of famine and foreign invasion, a new great Council was held, and in this assembly it was judged desirable and necessary to put into writing for the first time the texts which had been for so long transmitted orally.

It was the monks at the Mahavihara who evidently considered that they were the true adherents of the Theravada, over against the faction which withdrew to the Abhayagiri-*vihara,* and it was the Mahavihara monks who seem to have instigated the new assembly. Since Vattagamani had built the Abhayagiri and given it to his friend Mahatissa of Kupikkala, the king probably favored that institution, and he does not appear to have been directly involved in the Council. In fact this Council did not even meet in Anuradhapura, for Sinhalese tradition locates it at the Aloka-*vihara,* also called Alokalena. This site, now called Aluvihara, is 2 miles (3 km.) north of Matale in Central Sri Lanka, and is marked by a great cleft in the rock which gives access to a large cave. Under King Sirivijayarajasiha (1739–1747 C.E.) the rock cave was adorned with life-size statues of the Buddha in recumbent, standing, and sitting postures (*Culavamsa* 98.65–66).[96]

It was, therefore, the great work of this Council to commit to writing in the Pali language the Buddhist scriptures, and what was put down here became the orthodox version of the scriptures of Theravada Buddhism, the Tipitaka.

The *Dipavamsa* (20.19–22)[97] dates the council under Vattagamani and describes its work in these words: "The king Vattagamani Abhaya ruled for twelve years and in the beginning five months. Formerly wise monks brought orally the text of the three Pitakas and its commentary *(atthakatha).* At that time, seeing the loss of living beings, the monks assembled. They wrote in books for the long standing of the religion."

The *Mahavamsa* (33.100–101) likewise places the council in the reign of Vattagamani and gives a similar description: "The text of the three Pitakas and the Atthakatha thereon did the most wise *bhikkhus* hand down in former times orally, but since they saw that the people were falling away (from religion) the *bhikkhus* came together, and in order that the true doctrine might endure, they wrote them down in books."[98]

That the canonical texts put into writing at this Second Council in Lanka at the Aloka-*vihara* in the time of King Vattagamani (29–17 B.C.E.) were indeed substantially those of the Tipitaka as it was known thereafter, is confirmed by the *Milinda Panha,* a work written in North India in about the first century C.E., not long after the Council at Aloka.[99] In this work the author mentions each of the three Pitakas, the Vinaya, the Sutta, and the Abhidhamma (1),[100] speaks of the three collectively as the "three baskets" (18, 21, 348),[101] and names and quotes identifiable passages from most of the individual books.[102] Thus it is quite certain that the author knew virtually the entire Pali canon of Theravada Buddhism even as it exists today, i.e., as it was handed down through several councils in India and Lanka, and put into writing at the Aloka-*vihara* (Aluvihara) in the time of Vattagamani, toward the end of the first century B.C.E.

Because of the great accomplishment of this Council in for the first time putting the *dhamma* and the *vinaya* into written form, the Sinhalese and Burmese

Buddhists consider this the Fourth Great Buddhist Council (counting the first three Councils in India, followed by this Council), while the Thai Buddhists take as the Fourth the Council under Devanampiyatissa and reckon the Council at Aluvihara as the Fifth.[103]

Theravada and Mahayana in Sri Lanka

The division between the Mahavihara (on the south side of Anuradhapura), whose monks brought the Theravada canon into written form at the Council at Aluvihara, and the Abhayagiri-*vihara* (on the north side of the city), whose monks seceded from the Theravada (as above we have seen the *Mahavamsa* stating the matter), continued and grew more acute in later years.

Voharikatissa. By the time of King Voharikatissa (269–291 C.E.) the Abhayagiri monks had evidently openly adopted the Vaitulya (Vetulya) Pitaka, also known as the Vaipulya Sutras. This name ordinarily covers a number of works including the *Prajnaparamita* texts, which are accounted as Mahayanist, so what apparently began as only a dispute over the personal behavior of the *thera* Mahatissa has at this point evidently developed into a full-scale doctrinal divergence, with the Abhayagiri monks taking the position of the Mahayana over against the Theravada of the Mahavihara. At any rate we are told that King Voharikatissa (whose name *voharika* connotes knowledge of law and tradition, and who was the first Sinhalese king to set aside bodily injury as punishment for offenders of the law) suppressed the Vetulya doctrine and kept the heretics in check with the help of his minister Kapila (*Mahavamsa* 36.41).[104]

Mahasena. When King Mahasena (334–361 C.E.) came to the throne he found two sections of monks—no doubt the two groups just described—and wondered which held the correct doctrine and which held the false doctrine. According to the *Dipavamsa* (22.66–76),[105] it was the sinful monks and other shameless people, including Dummitta (bad Mitta) and Papasona (evil Sona), who were able to get the ear of the king. These two individuals are evidently identifiable with Mahasena's teacher Sanghamitta, and his minister Sona, both of whom are named in the *Mahavamsa* (37.1ff.).[106] There we are told that the *thera* Sanghamitta came to Lanka from India with the express purpose of making the Sinhalese monks accept the Vaitulya teachings. To enforce his view, Sanghamitta told Mahasena that the dwellers in the Mahavihara did not teach the true *vinaya,* and persuaded the king to fine heavily anyone who gave food to them. The monks of the Mahavihara were therefore compelled by the threat of starvation to abandon their residence and go away to Malaya and Rohana, while their opponents despoiled the Mahavihara, destroyed the splendid Lohapasada and various other buildings, and enriched the Abhayagiri-*vihara* with the material which they carried off.

Another minister named Meghavannabhaya, however, persuaded the king that he had done wrong, so Mahasena rebuilt the Mahavihara, while one of his wives, who had grieved over the destruction of the Mahavihara, caused the death of Sanghamitta and Sona. But no sooner was this done than the easily influenced Mahasena was persuaded by yet another "evil friend," the *thera* Tissa, to build the Jetavana-*vihara* (named after the famous park in Śravasti which Anathapindika give to the Buddha and his Order) within the precincts of the Mahavihara in spite of the protests of the Mahavihara monks. From this time on, the monks of the Jetavana-*vihara* also accepted the Vaitulya Pitaka and joined with the monks of the Abhayagiri in their position (*Culavamsa* 78.21–22).[107]

Sirimeghavanna. As the *Culavamsa* (37.53ff.)[108] relates, King Sirimeghavanna (362–409 C.E.), the son and successor of Mahasena, regretted the destruction wrought by his father, and restored the monastic buildings which Mahasena had torn down, beginning with the reconstruction of the Lohapasada, the splendid dwelling of the residents of the Mahavihara. Being greatly impressed by the story of the original conversion of Lanka to Buddhism, Sirimeghavanna made a life-size gold statue of Mahinda and set it up in the Ambatthala-*cetiya,* a shrine built by King Mahadathika-Mahanaga (67–79 C.E.) on the little Ambatthala tableland on the Missaka mountain (Mihintale), where Devanampiyatissa first met the missionary monks, and in an accompanying festival decreed the freeing of all the prisoners in Anuradhapura, gave the "four necessaries" (clothing, food, dwelling, medicine) to the monks, and instituted a great almsgiving for all living beings.

Temple of the Tooth in Anuradhapura. According to the *Dathavamsa* (a work probably translated into Pali in 1200 C.E. but written much earlier),[109] when the Buddha was cremated and the distribution of his relics made, in addition to the eight main measures of the remains, a certain Khema obtained the left eye-tooth and took it to Dantapur (city of the tooth) in the kingdom of Kalinga, where he gave it to King Brahmadatta. Later, in a time of war, a king of Kalinga named Cuhasiva sent this tooth relic *(dathadhatu)* on to Lanka by his daughter the *brahmani* Hemamala and her husband (the king's nephew) the *brahmana* Danta.

As the *Culavamsa* (37.92) also states,[110] it was in the ninth year of Sirimeghavanna that the tooth relic was brought in this manner to Anuradhapura. The king received the relic with high honor and placed it in the Dhammacakkapasada, the building originally erected by Devanampiyatissa adjacent to his own palace, and this building now became the first Temple of the Tooth Relic (in Pali the Dathadhatughara or "house of the tooth relic," in Sinhalese the Daladamaligava or "palace of the tooth relic"). In honor of the relic Sirimeghavanna held a great festival and decreed that every year the relic should be brought to the Abhayuttara-*vihara* and a similar festival be held. The Abhayuttara-*vihara* is the "northern *vihara* of Abhaya," and is another name for the Abhayagiri-*vihara,* thus Sirimeghavanna was plainly well disposed toward this monastery as well as toward the Mahavihara (which he had reconstructed), in spite of the high degree of rivalry between the two.

Mahanama. The successors of Sirimeghavanna were Jetthatissa II (skilled in ivory carving), Buddhadasa (noted as a physician who cured the diseases of animals and people), Upatissa I (who swept the ground with a peacock's feather where he walked lest he harm ants and other insects, and who built hospitals and tanks for his subjects), and Mahanama (*Culavamsa* 37.100–248).[111]

Mahanama (409–431 C.E.), known also as Sirinivasa and Sirikudda, was the younger brother of Upatissa I, and was a monk for some time, but became involved with his brother's wife, and she then murdered Upatissa, whereupon Mahanama became a layman, assumed the sovereignty, and took Upatissa's wife as his queen.

Between the Abhayagiri-*vihara* and the Mahavihara, Mahanama seems to have favored the former, for he built three *viharas* and gave them to the Abhayagiri monks (perhaps having belonged to that institution himself when he was a monk), but this was not entirely to the exclusion of the Mahavihara from favor, for, at the instigation of his queen, Mahanama also built a *vihara* on the Dhumarakkha mountain (on the left bank of the Mahaveliganga River east of Polonnaruwa) and bestowed it on the monks of the Theravada school, i.e., on the monks of the

Mahavihara, which was the center of the Theravada as the Abhayagiri was the center of the Mahayana.

Fa Xian in Singhala. After his long stay in India the Chinese Buddhist pilgrim Fa Xian (Fa Hien) spent two years in Singhala (Lanka) and, according to the date of his travels (399–414 C.E.), this must have been within the reign of Mahanama (409–431 C.E.). In the record of Fa Xian's experiences in Lanka,[112] we hear of three large monasteries at Anuradhapura. Of these the Abhayagiri, north of the city, was the largest with 5,000 monks in residence. The Caitya, as it is called in Fa Xian's record, was the *vihara* on the hill east of the city (i.e., at Mihintale), and had an estimated 2,000 monks. The Mahavihara, south of the city, was the residence of 3,000 monks.

The tooth relic of the Buddha, which was brought to Anuradhapura under Sirimeghavanna, was still being carried in annual procession to the Abhayagiri-*vihara* and made the object of homage in extended ceremonies. The other most famous Buddhist relic, the alms bowl of the Buddha, which was brought to Lanka under Devanampiyatissa and carried off by the Tamils in the time of Vattagamani, Fa Xian had already seen at Purushapura (Peshawar), and here at Anuradhapura he heard an Indian devotee reciting a *sutra* and saying of the alms bowl that it was first in Vaiśali, "and now it is in Gandhara." The Indian also went on to predict that after further wanderings the bowl would come (again) to Singhala before it would return to Central India and afterward ascend to heaven, where it would be received by the Bodhisattva Maitreya. Thereafter, he said, the bowl would disappear and the Law of Buddha would gradually be extinguished, with concomitant worsening of conditions upon earth, until finally the wicked would exterminate one another; then the blessed would cultivate faith and righteousness, earthly conditions would improve, and Maitreya would come as the future Buddha to save the disciples of the Law.[113]

The manuscripts of which Fa Xian was able to obtain copies in Lanka were Sanskrit works including the Vinayapitaka of the Mahaśasakah (Mahimsasaka) school (usually reckoned as a branch of the Sarvastivada, a northern sect roughly parallel to the southern Theravada), and the *Dirghagama* (parallel to the *Digha Nikaya*) and *Samyuktagama* (parallel to the *Samyutta Nikaya*) Sutras, thus all works of the Hinayana.

Third Council at the Mahavihara under Mahanama

After telling about the Mahavihara at Anuradhapura, and about the arrival of Fa Xian just in time to witness the cremation, carried out by the king (who must have been Mahanama), of a famous *śramana* on a funeral pile to the east of the monastery, the record of Fa Xian continues:

> At that time the king, who was a sincere believer in the Law of Buddha and wished to build a new *vihara* for the monks, first convoked a great assembly. After giving the monks a meal of rice, and presenting his offerings (on the occasion), he selected a pair of first-rate oxen, the horns of which were grandly decorated with gold, silver, and the precious substances. A golden plough had been provided, and the king himself turned up a furrow on the four sides of the ground within which the building was to be. He then endowed the community of the monks with the population, fields, and houses, writing the grant on plates of metal, [to the effect] that from that time onwards, from generation to generation, no one should venture to annul or alter it.[114]

It was also in the time of King Mahanama and in conjunction with the monks of the Mahavihara that Buddhaghosa did his work in Lanka. As the *Culavamsa* (37.215–246) tells of the life of this famous scholar, Buddhaghosa was a *brahmana* born near the place where Śakyamuni Buddha attained enlightenment (Bodhgaya), who himself renounced the world, learned the whole Tipitaka, and was called Buddhaghosa (voice of the Buddha) because his speech resounded through the earth like that of the Buddha. When Buddhaghosa began to compose some commentaries a leading elder, Ravata *thera*, said to him:

> The text alone has been handed down here (in Jambudipa), there is no commentary here. . . . The commentary in the Sihala tongue is faultless. The wise Mahinda who tested the tradition laid it before the three Councils as it was preached by the perfectly Enlightened One and taught by Sariputta and the others, wrote it in the Sihala tongue and it is spread among the Sihalas. Go thither, learn it and render it into the tongue of the Magadhas. It will bring blessing to the whole world.[115]

So Buddhaghosa proceeded to Lanka and went to the Mahavihara at Anuradhapura. There he entered the Mahapadhana hall (*padhana* refers to meditative practices of the monk on the way to perfection) and studied the Sinhalese commentary (*atthakatha*) and the Theravada doctrine under a monk named Sanghapala. Being thoroughly convinced that this system was a proper interpretation of the teachings of the Buddha, Buddhaghosa asked the community of monks (the *sangha*) if he might have access to all their books for the purpose of translating the commentary. To test his qualifications the monks gave Buddhaghosa two verses of scripture and asked him to write a thesis on them. This Buddhaghosa did in a work composed in Pali and called *Visuddhimagga* (path of purity).[116]

At the outset of the *Visuddhimagga*, and again at the close, Buddhaghosa quotes a text which is presumably that which was assigned to him by the monks. It is a saying of the Buddha which is found in the *Samyutta Nikaya* (1.20)[117] and, like many of the other sayings of the Buddha (e.g., *Digha Nikaya* 1.206–208),[118] explains the noble path in terms of the three-fold training of right conduct or virtue (*sila*), self-concentration or consciousness (*samadhi*), and intellect or understanding (*panna*):

> When a wise man, established well in virtue,
> Develops consciousness and understanding,
> Then as a *bhikkhu* ardent and sagacious
> He succeeds in disentangling this tangle.[119]

The "tangle," Buddhaghosa explains, is like that of a bamboo jungle, and is the tangle of craving in which all living beings are involved, but the three-fold path of purification leads to extrication from that involvement. So Buddhaghosa divides the bulk of his book into one section each on virtue, concentration, and understanding. Within this framework he gives a summary of all three Pitakas, together with numerous quotations from the Sinhalese commentary (*atthakatha*), and the whole amounts to a veritable encyclopedia of Buddhism.

Upon his completion of the *Visuddhimagga* (as the *Culavamsa* continues the account), Buddhaghosa read his work to the Mahavihara community gathered in the vicinity of the great Bodhi tree, and the monks were so pleased that they were willing to think that Buddhaghosa was Metteyya (Maitreya, the next expected Buddha), and they handed over to him the three Pitakas together with the commentary. Thereupon Buddhaghosa took up residence in the Ganthakaraparivena, a dwelling attached to the Mahavihara, which had the advantage of being "far from all unquiet intercourse," and there he "rendered the whole of the Sihala commentaries into the tongue of the Magadhas." Thereafter, "having accomplished what he had to do, he set out for Jambudipa to adore the sacred Bodhi tree," i.e., the original tree at Bodhgaya, of which the Bodhi tree in the Mahavihara at Anuradhapura was a cutting.

The Sinhalese commentary which Buddhaghosa thus rendered into Pali is the *Samantapasadika,* the very long commentary on the Vinayapitaka, to which the *Bahiranidana* is an introduction. Thus with the putting in writing in Pali of the previously orally transmitted Tipitaka at the Aluvihara, and with the rendering into Pali of the Sinhalese *vinaya*-commentary by Buddhaghosa at the Mahavihara, the most important materials of the Theravada tradition were made widely available.

That Buddhaghosa had the highest regard for the Theravada tradition as maintained by the monks of the Mahavihara at Anuradhapura, is plain. In his introduction to the *Visuddhimagga* Buddhaghosa says that his exposition rests upon "the strict rules of the devout dwellers" at the Mahavihara, and in his conclusion he repeats the same words and gives special credit to the Mahavihara monk named Sanghapala as his teacher.[120] In the introduction *(Bahiranidana)* to the *Samantapasadika* Buddhaghosa says that he will base this commentary chiefly on three main versions of the Sinhalese commentary, namely, the *Maha-atthakatha,* the *Mahapaccariya,* and the *Kurundi,* and he declares his reliance upon "the preeminent teachers of yore who have washed away the stains of defilements with the water of their wisdom, being endowed with analytical knowledge arising from their clear wisdom and being adept in the exposition of the Good Teaching—and who are like unto the banners of the Mahavihara," and he mentions especially the Mahavihara monk named Buddhasiri (probably the same as Buddhamitta, who is named in the colophon) at whose request he writes.[121] Similar comments are also made by Buddhaghosa in other commentaries which he wrote later, e.g., in the introduction to the *Atthasalini* (his commentary on the first book of the Abhidhammapitaka), in which he emphasizes the purity of the views of the Mahavihara, where there is neither "taint nor base commixture of the heresies."[122]

In view of this importance of the work of the Mahavihara monks and of Buddhaghosa as he dwelt in their midst, it is sometimes considered that an assembly at the Mahavihara under King Mahanama and in the time of Buddhaghosa constituted the Third Buddhist Council held in Sri Lanka, and the Thai Buddhists in particular count this gathering as the Sixth Council in the entire series (three in India, and three to this point in Sri Lanka).

Sihagiri Interval

Dhatusena. After Mahanama there was a fresh Tamil invasion from Pandu in South India, which established foreign rule in Anuradhapura for some twenty-seven years. The Sinhalese nobles fled again to Rohana, until they found a leader in Dhatusena, who drove out the Tamils and reunited the island under his own rule (460–478 C.E.). Both secular and religious institutions had suffered under the foreign rule, and Dhatusena did many works of restoration and of new building. He constructed eighteen tanks, of which the greatest was the Kalavapi (now the Kalavewa, 25 miles [40 km.] southeast of Anuradhapura), damming up the Gona River. He restored and ornamented the Mahavihara, erected a splendid house for the Bodhi tree, repaired the Temple of the Tooth, and had eighteen new *viharas* built and provided with revenues for the adherents of the Theravada. With an allusion to the Third Council at Pataliputra under Aśoka, it is even said of Dhatusena that "like Dhammasoka he brought about a redaction of the three Pitakas," but whatever was done at this time is not ordinarily counted as one of the series of great Buddhist Councils.

Actually the Dhammarucikas (probably a name given to the monks of the Abhayagiri when they seceded from the Mahavihara) seem to have been favorites of Dhatusena, and they are spoken of as occupying the Mahavihara at this time. The king then bulit the Ambatthala-*vihara* on the Missaka mountain and wished to give it to the Theravadins, but the Dhammarucikas wanted it, and he made it over also to them (*Culavamsa* 38.35–79).[123] Dhatusena's uncle, the *thera* Mahanama, it has already been noted, is the probable author of the *Mahavamsa*.

Kassapa. Dhatusena had two sons, Moggallana (Mugalan) and Kassapa (Kaśyapa) (the latter by a wife of inferior caste), and a charming daughter. The daughter was married to the son of the king's sister, but was ill treated by this husband. When the king punished the husband, his nephew, for this, the nephew stirred up his brother-in-law Kassapa to rebel against Dhatusena. So Kassapa imprisoned his father and hoped to secure his treasure, but when he failed to get the treasure he had Dhatusena buried alive. After that it was the intention of Moggallana to fight against Kassapa. Kassapa therefore tried to kill Moggallana, but Moggallana escaped to India, and Kassapa (whom we know as Kassapa I) established himself at Sihagiri, where he reigned for eighteen years (478–496 C.E.).

Sihagiri. Sihagiri (Simhagiri), now known as Sigiri (Sigiriya), is in the mountainous Malaya district, about 38 miles (61 km.) southeast of Anuradhapura, and is a great granite rock, rising 600 feet (183 m.) from the surrounding plain. Of Kassapa and his move to this place the *Culavamsa* (39.5) says:

> He betook himself through fear to Sihagiri, which is difficult of ascent for human beings. He cleared (the land) round about, surrounded it with a wall and built a staircase in the form of a lion. Thence it took its name [Sihagiri, meaning "lion hill"]. He collected treasures and kept them there well protected, and for the [riches] kept by him he set guards in different places. Then he built there a fine palace, worthy to behold, like another Alakamanda (the heavenly capital of the god Kubera), and dwelt there like Kubera.[124]

Before long, however, Kassapa I began to regret the deed he had done in the murder of his father, and he lived always in fear of the other world and of his brother Moggallana. In the hope of expiating his crime and securing his safety, he undertook many deeds intended to gain merit. Near Sihagiri he built a *vihara* and gave it to the Dhammarucis, who were evidently of influence with him as they had been with his father. At Anuradhapura he restored the Issarasamanarama (built originally by Devanampiyatissa), and named it after himself and his two daughters, Bodhi and Uppalavanna. When he wanted to give this monastery to the monks of the Thera school they hesitated to take it, fearing the reproach of the people because it was the work of a parricide. Then Kassapa presented it to the image of the Supreme Buddha, and the *bhikkhus* agreed, thinking that it thus belonged to the Master.

Moggallana. In the eighteenth year of Kassapa, Moggallana returned from India with twelve friends and with some kind of assurance of support from the

Niganthas. He lived for a time at the Kuthari-*vihara* in the Ambatthakola district (near the modern Kurunegala, 55 miles [90 km.] south of Anuradhapura), and collected an army. In this district, when Kassapa came out from Sihagiri to meet him, Moggallana defeated his brother in battle, and Kassapa committed suicide. Glad that he was spared the necessity of meting out justice himself, Moggallana carried out the cremation of his brother, took the royal treasures from Sihagiri, and returned to Anuradhapura, where he reigned for eighteen years as Moggallana I (496–513 C.E.).

When he came to the Mahameghavana at Anuradhapura, Moggallana turned his army back at the elephant wall (*hathipakara,* the supporting wall of the terrace, adorned with brick and stucco elephants) of the Mahathupa, and paid his respects to the Mahavihara community of monks, then also visited the two other main *viharas,* the Jetavana and the Abhayagiri. At first he showed great cruelty to his father's enemies, but afterward under Buddhist preaching became peaceful in spirit and did many good works. Like his brother and his father, Moggallana I was specially a patron of the Dhammarucikas and also of the similar sect of the Sagalikas, and he gave them two *viharas* on Sihagiri, named Dalha and Dathakondanna, and also built a shelter for the *bhikkhunis* of the Sagalika school. In his reign a certain Silakala, who had also fled to India out of fear of Kassapa I, returned to Lanka bringing the hair relic of the Buddha, and Moggallana I housed this relic in a fine building and instituted celebrations in its honor (*Culavamsa* 39.20–58).[125]

Polonnaruwa Period

Although one of the actions of Moggallana I was to institute a guard for the seacoast of Lanka, by which the island was supposed to be secured from the danger of invasion from India (*Culavamsa* 39.57),[126] hostile attacks continued not infrequently. In this time (in the fifth and sixth centuries C.E.) there were three main states in South India, those of the Pandyas, Pallavas, and Colas, all of which were Dravidian in culture, Tamil in language, and militantly Hindu in religion, and they were the source of not a few invasions of Lanka, while the Sinhalese themselves sometimes called in some of them to assist in dynastic disputes, even as Moggallana seems to have brought help for himself from India in his own return to the island. It was largely because of the pressure of foreign invasions that the capital of Lanka was eventually moved from the ancient Anuradhapura to a more defensible site at Pulatthinagara (Polonnaruwa).

Sena I. The move was made in the reign of the Sinhalese king Sena I (831–851 C.E.). At this time the king of the Pandyas invaded Lanka with a large army, the Tamils resident in the island joined him, and he sacked Anuradhapura, "leaving the splendid town in a state as if it had been plundered by *yakkhas.*" When peace was made with the Pandyas Sena I first returned to Anuradhapura but afterward left the plundered city and established himself at Pulatthinagara, where he died (*Culavamsa* 50.36, 85).[127] From then to the thirteenth century, except for a brief interval, Pulatthinagara was the capital of Lanka.

Pulatthinagara. Pulatthinagara (Pulatthipura), now known as Polonnaruwa, is some 15 miles (25 km.) east of Sigiriya, and not far from the main crossing place on the Mahavaliganga, the main river of Sri Lanka. The region was of importance even before the capital was brought here. King Mahasena (334–361 C.E.) built a tank called Manihira (now the Minneriya tank) and a *vihara* of the same name near Polonnaruwa (*Mahavamsa* 27.40, 47).[128] Kings Aggabodhi III and Aggabodhi IV reigned between 626 and 641 C.E., and the former built the Mahapanadipa-*vihara* in the town—the account of this work providing the first mention of the name of Pulatthinagara in the *Culavamsa* (44.122)[129]—while the latter at one time took up his abode there—the account of this fact providing the first mention of Pulatthinagara as a royal residence, although only temporarily (*Culavamsa* 46.34).[130]

Even after Sena I moved the capital to Pulatthinagara, Anuradhapura remained a very important religious center, and various kings still did building work there, but the last of the Sinhalese kings actually to reign at Anuradhapura was Mahinda V, who ascended the throne in 981 C.E., and he only stayed for ten years. At that time a mutiny of his mercenaries from Kerala forced Mahinda V to flee to Rohana, then in his thirty-sixth year of reign he was captured in a Cola invasion, and the whole country was pillaged, while the Colas themselves used Pulatthinagara as a base, and renamed it Jananathapura (*Culavamsa* 55.1–22).[131] Even as late as Vijayabahu IV (1271–1273 C.E.) this king went to Anuradhapura and cut back the encroaching forest and built new buildings at the sacred places, but after that the whole Anuradhapura district was abandoned and relapsed into jungle.

At the new capital of Pulatthinagara Sena I erected several buildings, including the Senaggabodhi shrine, which was near a tank called the Thusavapi (*Culavamsa* 50.73).[132] After their capture of Mahinda V, the Colas held sway at Pulatthinagara, and they built many Hindu shrines in the city.

Vijayabahu I. After many years of Cola domination, a Sinhalese prince named Kitti made himself master of Malaya and Rohana, assumed the name of Vijayabahu, finally succeeded in expelling the Colas from Lanka, and himself reigned as Vijayabahu I (1059–1114 C.E.). Although he also regained control of Anuradhapura, Vijayabahu I continued the practice of the Colas and made his capital at Pulatthinagara, which he renamed Vijayarajapura. During his long reign the country recovered from the misrule of the foreign invaders, and Buddhism was reestablished in importance after the supremacy of Hinduism under the Colas.

Throughout the country Vijayabahu I repaired many tanks and restored many *viharas,* and at Pulatthinagara he built fortifications, restored relic shrines which the Colas had destroyed, and erected many religious buildings. In order to reinforce the depleted Buddhist community he had learned *bhikkhus* brought from the Ramanna country (Lower Burma) and, after giving them gifts, "the king had the ceremonies of world-renunciation and of admission into the Order repeatedly performed by them and the three Pitakas together with the commentary frequently recited and saw to it that the Order of the Victor which had declined in Lanka again shone brightly" (*Culavamsa* 60.7–8).[133]

Temple of the Tooth at Pulatthinagara. Of the religious buildings which Vijayabahu I constructed at Pulatthinagara the chief was a temple for the tooth relic of the Buddha, previously housed at Anuradhapura, and in honor of the relic in this place he instituted a great festival intended to be continued permanently (*Culavamsa* 60.16).[134]

By this time or soon afterward the other famous Buddhist object, the alms bowl relic *(pattadhatu)* of the Buddha, was evidently back in Lanka (as the Indian devotee, heard by Fa Xian, predicted), for in the period from after the reign of Vijayabahu I down to the reign of Parakramabahu IV (circa 1325 C.E.) the tooth relic and the alms bowl are frequently mentioned together. The son of Vijayabahu I was Vikramabahu (Vikkamabahu) II (1116–1137 C.E.), who ruled from Pulatthinagara but with sway only over part of the country, and when he oppressed the Buddhists the monks took the tooth relic and the alms bowl relic both off to

Rohana (*Culavamsa* 61.6).[135] The nephew and second successor of Vikramabahu II was Parakramabahu I (immediately below), and when he put down a revolt in Rohana he recovered the tooth and bowl relics and brought them both back to Pulatthinagara and installed them there again with great ceremony (*Culavamsa* 74.99–248).[136] As this and many other incidents show, the two famous relics were closely associated with the Sinhalese kingship, and possession of them quite evidently signified the sovereignty of Lanka (e.g., *Culavamsa* 88.65–66).[137]

Parakramabahu I. In spite of the accomplishments of Vijayabahu I his reign was followed by another period of civil war and of invasion from abroad, out of which the country was only delivered by Parakramabahu (Parakkamabahu) I, who has already (just above) been identified in his ancestry, and who reigned at Pulatthinagara (Polonnaruwa) from 1153 to 1186 C.E. This king is plainly the hero of the *Culavamsa* as Dutthagamani Abhaya is of the *Mahavamsa,* and the account of his family and of his own reign occupies much space in the *Culavamsa* (62–79).[138]

After many adventures and many wars Parakramabahu I unified the whole island of Lanka under his sole rule, and he even warred abroad against the king of Ramanna in Lower Burma and against the Colas and Pandyas in South India (*Culavamsa* 76–77).[139] Then in the latter part of his reign he was able to devote himself to more peaceful pursuits.

For the improvement of irrigation and the lessening of famine, Parakramabahu I dammed the Karaganga River with a great barrier between the hills, brought its waters down by a vast canal called the Akasaganga (the name of the Ganges as flowing in space before descending to earth), formed a great central reservoir called the Parakrama Samudra (Parakkamasamudda, "sea of Parakrama"), and constructed many other canals and tanks throughout the country. Being versed in medical lore and himself free from disease year by year, he encouraged the physicians in their work, and built a great hall in Pulatthinagara for the care of the sick. He also instituted a daily almsgiving "for many thousands of *bhikkus* from all four regions of the earth . . . for *brahmanas* belonging to a mendicant order, as well as for many other supplicants and poor travelers. . . ." (*Culavamsa* 73.23ff.; 79.1ff.).[140]

Fourth Council at Polonnaruwa under Parakramabahu I

The state of the Buddhist community was the matter of greatest concern to Parakramabahu I, and the *Culavamsa* (73.12–22; 78.2ff.)[141] says that his efforts at reform were more burdensome to himself than his efforts for the royal dignity. Due to the divisions which had persisted since the time of Vattagamani there were, as the *Culavamsa* calls them, "two Orders" and "three fraternities," i.e., the Hinayana, chiefly the Theravada, with its principal seat at the Mahavihara in Anuradhapura, and the Mahayana centered in the Abhayagiri and the Jetavana *viharas* at Anuradhapura. "From the days of King Vattagamani Abhaya the three fraternities had lost their unity, despite the vast efforts made in every way by former kings. . . . They turned away in their demeanor from one another and took delight in all kinds of strife." "Since the shamelessness had passed all bounds and the schism had lasted a long time, many *bhikkhus* would hear nothing of conciliation. Many began departing to foreign lands, others left the Order. . . ."

Mahakassapa. So, as the *Culavamsa* relates and as is confirmed in general by an inscription of Parakramabahu I at the Gal-*vihara* in Polonnaruwa, the king called together at Pulatthinagara a great assembly from the three fraternities and from the several provinces of the island. Parakramabahu I was present at the assembly in person and, even as Dhammasoka (Aśoka) entrusted the leadership of the Council at Pataliputra to Moggaliputta-Tissa, so the king now entrusted the presidency of this assembly to Mahakassapa. This *thera* (with the same name as the president of the Council at Rajagriha) was a resident of the Udumbaragiri-*vihara,* a monastery at the Dhumarakkha mountain (identified with the present Gunners' Quoin Hill on the right bank of the Mahavaliganga, not far from Polonnaruwa), and was "an experienced man, who knew the Tipitaka and was exceedingly well versed in the *vinaya,* a light of the race of *theras,* conciliatory, long since consecrated."

Under Mahakassapa as the oldest, the *bhikkhus* settled each single point in dispute as it arose, and—the "undisciplined" being expelled—harmony was established among the monks of the Mahavihara. There was greater difficulty with the *bhikkhus* of the Abhayagiri—who were a separate group since the time of Vattagamani Abhaya—and of the Jetavana—who were separate since the time of Mahasena and who taught the Vaitulya Pitaka—but here too the "undisciplined" were excluded from the community. So the Theravada of the Mahavihara was confirmed, the Vaitulya heresy disappeared, and the Order was "established again . . . as it had been in Buddha's time," so that it could last in purity for five thousand years."

After the assembly, and annually thereafter, the king brought the community of monks to the bank of the Mahavaliganga and built on ships anchored in the river a *mandapa* (here a roofed, arbor-like structure) for their rituals, even as the monks of Sri Lanka, for the sake of seclusion, still until today like to perform their rites in a pavilion built on piles out in the water. So, with the conduct of ceremonies of admission, the Order grew and increased in numbers.

Although the assembly under Parakramabahu I and Mahakassapa probably only revised the commentaries on the Tipitaka, the gathering was an event of such importance that the Thai Buddhists, at any rate, count it as the Seventh Buddhist Council (reckoning three in India, and four in Sri Lanka).

Pulatthinagara under Parakramabahu I. As a result of the troubled times which had gone before, Pulatthinagara had come to such a state by the time of Parakramabahu I that it was said (surely with some exaggeration) that nothing remained of the city but its name. The king therefore now enlarged and fortified the place, beautified it with numerous gardens and palaces, called it by his own name Parakramapura (Parakkamapura, "city of Parakrama"), and brought it to the height of its greatness as a capital comparable in splendor to the earlier Anuradhapura, although smaller in size.

As described in the *Culavamsa* (73.148–163),[142] the city "possessed a splendid wreath of walls . . . was resplendent with fair dwellings . . . contained large as well as small streets," was entered by fourteen gates [King's Gate, Lion Gate, Elephant Gate, Indra Gate, Hanuman Gate, Kubera Gate, Candi Gate (naming a Hindu goddess), Rakkhasa Gate (naming a demon), Serpent Gate, Water Gate, Garden Gate, Maya Gate (remembering the mother of the Buddha), Mahatittha Gate (from which the road departed for the Mahatittha port on the western coast of the island), and Gandhabba Gate (honoring the heavenly musicians, the *gandharvas* in Sanskrit], and was surrounded by three suburbs, Ravjavesibhujanga, Rajakulantaka, and Vijita.

Even as the benefactions of the king included the *brahmanas,* and as the gates of the city recognized Hindu deities and lesser beings, so also among the buildings erected by Parakramabahu I in the city were "thirteen temples for the gods" (*Culavamsa* 79.19),[143] and numerous temples to Vishnu and Śiva have in fact been found at Polonnaruwa.

As described in the *Culavamsa* (78.31–95),[144] however, the greatest building works of Parakramabahu I at his capital city and its suburbs were those done for the Buddhist community, and it is indeed the ruins of some of these that are the most impressive monuments of Polonnaruwa today.

In the vicinity of the royal palace Parakramabahu I built the Jetavanarama, a great monastery complex named, like the Jetavana at Anuradhapura, for the celebrated park at Śravasti which Anathapindika presented to the Buddha. The Jetavanarama of Parakramabahu I contained the Thuparama (named after the Thuparama at Anuradhapura; not mentioned in the *Culavamsa* at this point probably because it already belonged to the time before Parakramabahu I), a round stone temple for the tooth relic of the Buddha (probably the present Vatadage, which is said in the *Culavamsa* 80.19[145] and in an inscription on the monument to be a work of King Nissanka Malla [Kittinissanka, 1187–1196 C.E.] but was probably only restored by the latter), a *cetiya* (probably the present Satmahalpasada), several bath houses including the Padumanahanakottha (the present lotus bath house), and many other buildings, reportedly 520 in all in the Jetavanarama.

To the north of the Jetavanarama was a group of buildings known as the Alahana-*parivena* (a *parivena* is a residence of monks and now denotes a building intended in particular for their instruction). To mark out the boundary of the Alahana the king himself plowed a furrow, even as Devanampiyatissa did for the Mahavihara at Anuradhapura. In the Alahana group were a twelve-storied Uposatha-house named the Baddhasimapasada (the so-called "priory"), several *stupas* including the present Kiri-vehera (probably founded by a queen of Parakramabahu I named Subhadda), and the Lankatilaka-*vihara* with a five-storied "image house," which contained a standing image of the Buddha, was ornamented with figures of gods and Brahmas, and was surrounded by various halls and buildings.

Other establishments were the Pacchimarama (west monastery) and the Uttararama (north monastery). At the latter the *Culavamsa* (78.74–75)[146] states that there were three image shrines made by expert craftsmen, namely, Vijjadhara-guha lena (Cave of the Spirit of Knowledge), Nisinna-patima lena (Cave of the Seated Buddha), and Nipanna-patima lena (Cave of the Recumbent Buddha). The reference is to what is now known as the Gal Vihara. Another structure in this area of the city was the Mahathupa (great *stupa*), which took its name from the Mahathupa (Ruwanweli Dagoba) in Anuradhapura, but was also known as the Damila Thupa because it was built by Tamils who were brought here after Parakramabahu I's conquest of the Pandu kingdom in South India. With an intended circumference of 1,300 cubits (about 1,950 feet [595 m.]) this would have been the largest *thupa* in Sri Lanka, but the structure was probably left unfinished. Like many other *stupas* and *cetiyas* (e.g., *Culavamsa* 68.41)[147] the Mahathupa was compared with Mount Kailasa (Kelasa).

In the suburbs of Pulatthinagara Parakramabahu I built other *viharas*, and he also restored the shrines at Anuradhapura. Naming four great *stupas* with their heights, all of which were previously destroyed by the Tamils—the Ratanavaluka-*thupa* (Mahathupa), 120 cubits (180 feet [55 m.]), the Jetavana-*thupa*, 140 cubits (210 feet [64 m.]), the Abhayagiri-*thupa*, 160 cubits (240 feet [73 m.]), the Maricavatti-*thupa*, 80 cubits (120 feet [37 m.])—the

Culavamsa (78.96–101) describes the situation at the time and the work of Parakramabahu I: "These were (all) overgrown with great trees, bears and panthers dwelt there, and the ground of the jungle scarce offered a foothold by reason of the heaps of bricks and earth. After having the forest hewn down and (the *thupas*) built in the proper fashion, and faced with stucco, he also cleared the courtyard of the *cetiya*."[148]

The king also restored the Lohapasada at Anuradhapura "by raising again its thousand and six hundred pillars" (in fact the number of foundation pillars still standing), and on the Cetiyagiri (the Mihintale mountain) he had sixty-four *thupas* rebuilt.[149]

So the *Culavamsa* (79.85–86) concludes its account of the entire reign and many accomplishments of Parakramabahu I:

> By constructing in this way beautiful *viharas,* gardens, tanks, and the like he adorned with these numerous (works) the whole of Lanka.
> Thus Parakramabahu, the ruler of men, by whom were performed divers and numerous kinds of meritorious works, who continually found the highest satisfaction in the teaching of the Master, who was endowed with extraordinary energy and discernment, carried on the government for thirty-three years."[150]

After Parakramabahu I

After Parakramabahu I Pulatthinagara was at times still held by Sinhalese kings, at times was in the hands of invaders, and at last was completely abandoned. Of the Sinhalese kings Nissanka Malla (Kittinissanka, 1187–1196 C.E.) built the Ratanavali-*cetiya* in Pulatthinagara, "and embellished the splendid structure with a golden point" (*Culavamsa* 80.20)[151]—this being the Ruwanweli Dagoba or Rankot Dagoba (golden-point *dagoba*) at Polonnaruwa—and also claimed credit for many buildings which were actually already built by Parakramabahu I. Nissanka Malla also improved the caves of the Jambukola-*vihara* and placed seventy-three golden statues of the Buddha in them—these being the cave temples of Dambulla, southeast of Sigiriya and 47 miles (76 km.) north of Kandy on the road to Anuradhapura.

The most devastating invasion of the time was by a king named Magha, of the Kalinga race, who brought a large army of Keralas and Tamils, captured Pulatthinagara, deposed the Sinhalese king Parakrama Pandya (Parakkamapandu) II (1211–1214 C.E.), plundered the island, persecuted the Buddhists, and "forced the people to adopt a false faith [i.e., Hinduism]," and himself ruled at Pulatthinagara for twenty-one years (1214–1235 C.E.) (*Culavamsa* 80.58–79).[152] From this disaster Pulatthinagara never fully recovered, although a few more Sinhalese kings made attempts to restore the city, while others placed their seat of government elsewhere.

Alms Bowl Relic and Tooth Relic. In the time while Magha ruled at Pulatthinagara some of the Buddhist monks went abroad to the Cola and Pandu countries, and others carried away from Pulatthinagara the alms bowl relic and the tooth relic of the Buddha and took refuge on the Kotthumala mountain (Kotmale).

Vijayabahu III (1232–1236 C.E.) succeeded in defeating the Tamils, but established his seat of government on the Jambuddoni mountain (near Dambadeniya, about 18 miles [29 km.] southwest of Kurunegala). He called back and the monks from South India, and brought the two relics of the tooth and the alms bowl—the symbols so closely associated with sovereignty—to Jambuddoni, but afterward had them taken to a yet more inaccessible place on the Billasela mountain (now Beligala in the Kegalla district), and he also did many other things to restore the Buddhist order (*Culavamsa* 81.10–79).[153]

Parakramabahu II (1236–1271 C.E.), son of Vijayabahu III, also reigned at Jambuddoni, and brought the tooth relic there from the Billa mountain, then regained Pulatthinagara from the Tamils, while his nephew, Prince Virabahu, repulsed an attack by a Javanese invader named Candrabhanu (Candabhanu) (*Culavamsa* 82.6ff.).[154]

Vijayabahu IV (1271–1273 C.E.), son of Parakramabahu II, had his seat of government at Subhagiri (Subbhapabbata, Sundarapabbata, now Yapahu, an isolated rock like Sigiri, not far from Maho), and there was challenged, unsuccessfully, by the Javanese Candrabhanu, who said to him: "Yield up to me therefore together with the tooth relic of the Sage, the bowl relic, and the royal dominion" (*Culavamsa* 88.65–66).[155] Afterward Vijayabahu IV restored Pulatthinagara, thought that it then surpassed such famous Indian towns as Mithila, Kancipura, Sravasti, Mathura, Varanasi, Vaiśali, and Campa, and deposited the tooth and alms bowl relics there (*Culavamsa* 88.121; 89.41).[156]

Bhuvanaikabahu (Bhuvanekabahu) I (1273–1284 C.E.), son of Parakramabahu II and successor of Vijayabahu IV, lived for several years at Jambuddoni, but then built an extensive royal city at Subhagiri and abode there. He also evidently brought the sacred Buddhist relics back from Pulatthinagara to Subhagiri, for in or just after his reign an invading Tamil general named Aryacakravarti (Airyacakkavatti) entered Subhagiri, seized the tooth relic, and took it back to King Kulasekhara (1268–1308 C.E.) of the Pandyan kingdom (*Culavamsa* 90.34–35, 46–47).[157]

Parakramabahu III (1284–1291 C.E.), son of Vijayabahu IV, recovered the tooth relic from the Pandu king by peaceable and perhaps subservient persuasion and installed it once again in Pulatthinagara, which was where he reigned (*Culavamsa* 90.51–56).[158] Parakramabahu III was, however, the last Sinhalese king to rule from Pulatthinagara, and the long period of this city's splendor was now at an end.

Bhuvanaikabahu II (1291–1302 C.E.), son of Bhuvanaikabahu I, and Parakramabahu IV (circa 1325 C.E.) son of Bhuvanaikabahu II, both reigned in Hatthiselapura (the modern Kurunegala), named for a nearby mountain shaped like a reclining elephant. In this capital Parakramabahu IV built a temple for the tooth relic in the royal courtyard, and made a place of honor in it for both the tooth relic and the alms bowl relic. It was his thought that what the daily ceremonial had been in the lifetime of the Buddha should from this time on be directed toward the tooth relic, as taking the place of the presence of the Buddha. To that end he composed in Sinhalese a book entitled *Ceremonial of the Tooth Relic* (Pali *dathadhatucaritta*, Sinhalese *daladasirita*), a work which is still extant, and in keeping with it he performed a daily ceremony for the relic (*Culavamsa* 90.66–79).[159]

The immediately foregoing mention of the tooth relic (*dathadhatu*) and the bowl relic (*pattadhatu*) in the reign of Parakramabahu IV is the last time that we hear of the alms bowl of the Buddha, and from that time on the tooth relic remains alone the supreme object of veneration. As such, as the times demanded, the tooth relic was carried from place to place, to be where the Sinhalese capital was, or to be in a place of maximum security.

Under Parakramabahu VI (1410–1468 C.E.), who was the last Sinhalese ruler to hold the whole island under his sway, the tooth relic was in his capital, a town named Jayavaddhanakotta (later simply called Kotta, corresponding with the eastern districts of Colombo) (*Culavamsa* 91.16–17).[160]

In the course of the troubled times which ensued again later, the tooth relic was taken to the Labujagama-*vihara* in the province of Saparagamu (now the province of Sabaragamuwa, in front of the southwestern slopes of the central mountains), and then finally, learning that it was there, Vimala Dharma Surya (Vimaladhammasuriya) I (1592–1604 C.E.) had it brought to his capital, which was Sirivaddhanapura. This place (also called Senkhandasela after a hermit named Senkhanda) is the modern Kandy. It first became the capital under King Viravikrama (Viravikkama) (circa 1542 C.E.), and it remained the capital until the reign of the last Sinhalese monarch, Sri Vikrama Rajasimha (Sirivikkamarajasiha) (1798–1815 C.E.), after which the island was ceded to the British (*Culavamsa* 92.7; 101.19–29).[161]

In Sirivaddhanapura King Vimala Dharma Surya I built a temple for the tooth relic in the neighborhood of the royal palace, thus maintaining the proximity of the relic to the palace, which was established originally in Anuradhapura (*Culavamsa* 94.12–14).[162] In the time of Sri Vira Parakrama Narendra Simha (Siriviraparakkamanarindasiha) (1707–1739 C.E.) the temple was in decay, and was rebuilt by this king (*Culavamsa* 97.37–38).[163] Again (according to local tradition) the temple was rebuilt by King Kirtti Sri Raja Simha (Kittisirirajasiha) (1747–1782 C.E.), and (according to the *Culavamsa* 100.21–22)[164] the casket which Vimaladhammasuriya had made for the relic was at that time overlaid with gold. The temple was also added to by the last of the Sinhalese kings, Sri Vikrama Rajasimha, and has been repaired again in recent times, and stands thus as the present Temple of the Tooth (Dalada Maligawa) at the south end of the former king's palace on the north side of the lake at Kandy.

Later Councils and the Counting of the Councils. In the entire Buddhist world there are various reckonings of the several Buddhist assemblies which have been described in the foregoing, and of some assemblies which were held yet later, as to which of them are properly to be included in the official series of *sangitis* (recitals) or major Councils in which the Buddhist scriptures were fixed.[165]

In India four Great Councils are recognized: the First in Rajagriha under Ajatasatru, with Mahakassapa as president, just after the death of the Buddha; the Second in Vaisali under Kalasoka, with Yasa as the leading figure, one hundred years after the death of the Buddha; the Third in Pataliputra under Asoka, with Moggaliputta-Tissa as president, in 252 B.C.E.; and the Fourth at the Kundalavana monastery in Kashmir under Kanishka in the first century C.E.

In Sri Lanka, after the first three Councils in India (in Rajagriha, Vaisali, and Pataliputra), the Fourth Great Council is taken to be that of the Mahavihara monks at Aluvihara in the time of Vattagamani Abhaya in the first century B.C.E., at which the canonical texts were for the first time committed to writing in the Pali language. A Fifth Council was held at Ratnapura under the presidency of the Venerable Hiddaduve Siri Sumangala in 1865 C.E.

In Thailand the *Sangitivamsa* (history of the recitals), written in 1789 C.E., recognizes nine Councils: the first three in India (as above); the Fourth in Anuradhapura (at the Thuparama) under Devanampiyatissa, with Mahinda as president, in the third century B.C.E.; the Fifth that at Aluvihara in the time of Vattagamani in the first century B.C.E., with the writing down of the Pali texts; the Sixth in Anuradhapura (at the Mahavihara) under Mahanama, in the time of

Buddhaghosa, in the fifth century C.E.; the Seventh in Polonnaruwa under Parakramabahu I, with Mahakassapa as president, in the twelfth century C.E.; the Eighth under King Sridharmacakravarti Tilaka Rajadhiraja, the ruler of Northern Thailand, in Chiengmai, his capital, between 1457 and 1483 C.E., with a meeting lasting for a year in the Mahabodhi-arama; and the Ninth convened in Bangkok in 1788 C.E. by King Rama I.

In Burma as in Sri Lanka, after the first three Councils in India the Fourth is considered to be that at Aluvihara in Sri Lanka in the time of Vattagamani when the Pali texts were put into writing. After that the Fifth Great Council is that which was convened in Mandalay in 1871 C.E. under the patronage of King Mindon (1853–1878 C.E.). This Council brought together in the royal palace, under the king as the presiding officer, learned monks from all parts of the country, and they worked for more than three years to produce an authoritative Pali version of the Tipitaka. When the work was complete, the corrected text was inscribed on 729 marble slabs which were placed vertically within small enclosures set at regular intervals within a large precinct of the Kuthodaw Pagoda at the base of Mandalay Hill at Mandalay.

Finally the Sixth Great Council (according to this manner of reckoning) was convoked by Prime Minister U Nu of Burma in Rangoon in 1954, with the Venerable Abhidhaja Maharattha Guru Bhadanta Revanta as president, and with learned *bhikkhus* present from many lands in addition to Burma, particularly India, Sri Lanka, Thailand, Laos, Cambodia, Nepal, and Pakistan. The meeting place was in the Maha Pasana Guha, a large cave hall built especially to house this international assembly. The session, which was again devoted to the editing and codifying of the Buddhist scriptures, lasted for two full years, and reached its climax and conclusion at the full moon of May 1956, taken as the official 2,500th anniversary of the death of the Buddha, reckoned from 544 B.C.E.

THREE BASKETS

As recited and fixed in the great Buddhist Councils, the canonical texts of Theravada Buddhism are those of the Pali Tipitaka.[166]

Vinayapitaka

The Vinayapitaka or "basket of the discipline of the order" is the chief source for knowledge of the Buddhist order *(sangha)* and the life of Buddhist monks *(bhikkhus)* and nuns *(bhikkhunis)*. It contains the following three works:

(1) *Suttavibhanga*. The title means "analyses of the suttas," and in this case the *suttas* are 227 rules for monastic life, which were compiled already in an earlier work called the *Patimokkha*. The discussions in the *Suttavibhanga* cite these rules, tell how and when they were laid down, and consider many matters connected with them. It is possible, therefore, to extract the *Patimokkha* from the larger work of which it is the basis.[167] As the material is usually arranged in the entire *Suttavibhanga*, there is a story leading up to a *Patimokkha* rule, then the rule is cited together with the penalty incurred for breaking it, then old commentary on the rule is adduced, and finally more stories are told which tell of deviation from the rule. The rules fall into eight sections, classified according to the gravity of offense against them. Two major classifications are *parajika* rules, for breaking which the punishment is expulsion from the order, and *pacittiya* rules, for breaking which

some expiation is specified. The larger part of the entire *Suttavibhanga* is the *Mahavibhanga* (great analysis) which contains the rules for the monks; the smaller part is the *Bhikkhunivibhanga* (nuns' analysis) which contains the rules for the nuns.[168]

(2) **Khandhakas.** These "sections" are a continuation and supplement of the *Suttavibhanga*, and as the *Patimokkha* underlies the *Suttavibhanga* so an old collection of formulas called the *Kammavaca* (words for the acts) underlies this work. The *Khandhakas* are in two divisions. The *Mahavagga* (greater division) begins with the experience of Śakyamuni Buddha immediately after his enlightenment and gives his sermon at Isipatana, then continues with rules (illustrated from biographical episodes in the life of the Buddha) for admission to the *sangha*, for the *uposatha* or holy day, the *vassa* or rainy season retreat, and the *pavarana* or celebration at the end of the rain retreat, and also deals with clothing, medicines, and the like. The *Cullavagga* (lesser division) also contains anecdotes from the life of the Buddha, sets forth numerous rules for *bhikkhus* and (in section 10) for *bhikkhunis*, while its last two sections (11 and 12) recount the first two Buddhist Councils at Rajagriha and Vaiśali.[169]

(3) **Parivara.** Parivara is a supplementary summary and digest of the *Suttavibhanga* and the *Khandhakas*. At the end the author is named as Dipanama (probably a Sinhalese monk), who "asked this and that about the way of former teachers," and who "remembered what he had heard, attentive," and of the work it is said that "it encompasses *(parivaresi)* the Dispensation [of the Buddha] as the ocean [encompasses] India" (*Parivara* 226).[170]

Suttapitaka

The Suttapitaka or "basket of discourses" is the chief source for knowledge of the doctrine (*dhamma*, as distinguished from *vinaya* or discipline) of the Buddha. The discourses are arranged, according to their length or subject matter, in five *nikayas* or "collections." Of these the first four contain chiefly discourses or dialogues of the Buddha (or sometimes of one of his disciples), while the fifth is more miscellaneous in contents.

Digha Nikaya ("collection of long discourses") contains thirty-four discourses *(suttas* or *suttantas)* of considerable length, arranged in three books.[171]

The first book is called *Silakkhandha*, and in it the *suttas* (1–13) deal mainly with ethical questions, particularly with *sila* (conduct or virtue), and also with *samadhi* (concentration) and *panna* (insight) as leading to the state of an *arhat* (*arahat, arahant,* "worthy"), i.e., one who has attained *nirvana*, the ideal. The first of these *suttas*, for example, the *Brahmajala Sutta*, contains the Buddha's descriptions of many occupations and modes of life of *brahmanas* and ascetics, from which his followers are to remain aloof, while the second *sutta*, the *Samannaphala Sutta*, tells in the form of a dialogue with King Ajataśatru about the fruits which may be obtained in the Buddhist way of life. Some other subjects dealt with in succeeding *suttas* include caste, sacrifice, asceticism, soul, and trance, while in the thirteenth and last *sutta* of the first book, the *Tevijja Sutta*, the Buddha criticizes the *brahmanas* who, although they are "wise in the three Vedas" (*tevijja*, Sanskrit *traividya*), do not really know how to attain union (in rebirth) with Brahma—which is itself only a limited goal.

The second book is called *Mahavagga,* and most of its *suttas* (14–23) contain the word *maha* (great) in their titles. Here, for example, the *Mahapadana Sutta* (No. 14) names six Buddhas (Vipassi, Sikhi, Vessabhu, Kakusandha, Konagamana, Kassapa) who preceded Śakyamuni Buddha, and tells at some length the life story *(apadana)* of Vipassi, the first of these; the *Mahanidana Sutta* (No. 15) elucidates the doctrine of events as arising from causes; the *Mahaparinibbana Sutta* (No. 16) recounts the last year of life of the Buddha and his final decease *(parinibbana,* Sanskrit *parinirvana)* in the small town of Kuśinagara; and the *Mahasudassana Sutta* (No. 17) contains a *jataka* story, which the Buddha told while lying on his deathbed, about the time in a prevous existence when he was Sudassana, the king of kings, ruling in this very same place, Kuśinagara, which was at that time the splendid royal city of Kusavati.

The third book *(suttas* 24–34) is called *Patikavagga* after the name of its first *sutta,* the *Patika Sutta* (No. 24). In this book, for example, the *Pasadika Sutta* (No. 29) and the *Sangiti Sutta* (No. 33) are of special historical interest inasmuch as they show that the Nigantha Nataputta (Vardhamana Mahavira) predeceased Śakyamuni Buddha; while the *Lakkhana Sutta* (No. 30) lists the thirty-two marks possessed by a great man, destined to become either a world ruler or a Buddha; the *Sigalovada Sutta* (No. 31) gives a very complete discussion of the duties of the householder, the lay adherent of Buddhism *(upasaka,* feminine *upasika);* and the *Atanatiya Sutta* (No. 32) again names the six Buddhas who preceded Śakyamuni Buddha.

Majjhima Nikaya. This "collection of middle length discourses" consists of 152 *suttas,* arranged in three books.[172] The *suttas* are generally somewhat shorter than those in the *Digha Nikaya,* but contain much the same sort of materials, discourses, dialogues, and narratives.

Here, for example, the *Sabbasava Sutta* (No. 2) tells how the "cankers" of life *(asavas)* can be overcome. The *Akankheyya Sutta* (No. 6) teaches observance of right conduct *(sila)* in order to obtain many desires in the spiritual life, of which the highest is the attainment of *arahatship.* Toward this consummation the Buddha advises also the practice of solitude:

> If a *bhikkhu* should desire . . . to know and realize and attain to *arahatship,* to emancipation of heart and mind, let him then fulfill all righteousness, let him be devoted to that quietude of heart which springs from within, let him not drive back the ecstasy of contemplation, let him look through things, let him be much alone![173]

The *Cetokhila Sutta* (No. 16) enumerates various types of spiritual barrenness and mental bondage. The *Culahatthipadopama Sutta* (No. 27) is the "lesser discourse on the simile of the elephant's footprint," and uses this illustration to elucidate the teachings of the Buddha (this was the first text preached by Mahinda to Devanampiyatissa upon the missionary's arrival in Sri Lanka). The *Mahahatthipadopama Sutta* (No. 28) uses the same simile to affirm that just as the foot of every creature will go into an elephant's footprint, which is the largest of all, so all right states of mind are included in the four truths enunciated by the Buddha. The *Airyapariyesana Sutta* (No. 26) and the *Mahasaccaka Sutta* (No. 36) contain a portion of the autobiography of the Buddha. The *Upali Sutta* (No. 56), the *Mahasakuladayi Sutta* (No. 77) and others give information about the six contemporary teachers, e.g., Nataputta the Nigantha (Mahavira) and Makkhali Gośala. The *Brahmayu Sutta* (No. 91) enumerates the thirty-two marks of a great man. The *Assalayana Sutta* (No. 93) contains the Buddha's doctrine of "the purity of the four castes," in opposition to the assumption that only *brahmanas* form the best caste. In the *Anuruddha Sutta* (No. 127) the venerable Anuruddha (first cousin of the Buddha and one of his most eminent disciples) and in the *Mahakaccanabhaddekaratta Sutta* (No. 133) the venerable Mahakaccana (also one of the most eminent of the disciples of the Buddha) give extended expositions of the brief sayings of the Buddha, which seem like forerunners of the "higher" expositions in the Abhidhammapitaka.

Samyutta Nikaya. In this "collection of grouped discourses" there are five *vaggas* or "divisions," fifty-six *samyuttas* or "groups," and 2,889 short *suttas* or individual sayings.[174] The grouping is largely according to points of doctrine or according to personalities—gods, demons, human beings—which appear in the materials. There is much of myth and legend, but also much of the actual teaching of Buddha, and the materials are often in the form of aphorisms, riddles, and poetry (*gathas,* verses).

In the first or *Sagathavagga* in the *Devata* (No. 1) and *Devaputta* (No. 2) *Samyuttas* the Buddha answers questions posed by certain *devatas* (deities), *devaputtas* (sons of the *devas*), and *devadhitas* (daughters of the *devas*). The *Kosala Samyutta* (No. 3) is entirely devoted to Pasenadi, the king of Kośala, and the conversations of the Buddha with the king. The *Mara Samyutta* (No. 4) recounts many attacks by Mara, the evil one, upon the Buddha, not only when he had just won enlightenment on the banks of the Neranjara River, but also on many other occasions; and the *Bhikkhuni Samyutta* (No. 5) tells of many attempts by Mara to dissuade various nuns from following the Buddhist way. Again in the *Yakkha Samyutta* (No. 10) the Buddha has to do with *yakkhas* and *yakkhinis,* but these supernatural beings are here not yet considered demons as they were later.

In the second or *Nidanavagga,* the *Nidana Samyutta* (No. 12) contains the Buddha's explanation of the chain of causation, which begins with ignorance (*avijja*) and leads to birth, old age, and death; the *Kassapa Samyutta* (No. 16) gives the Buddha's praise of the venerable Mahakassapa for his contentment in all circumstances, no matter what robe, alms, lodging, or medicine he might have; the *Rahula Samyutta* (No. 18) quotes the lessons the Buddha gave to his son, the venerable Rahula, on the fleeting nature of all things; and the *Opamma Samyutta* (No. 20) cites some of the similes by which the Buddha illustrated the origin of all wrong states in ignorance.

The third or *Khandhavagga* opens with the long *Khandha Samyutta* (No. 22), which explains the five *khandhas* (aggregates) or constituent elements which make up a person; the *Ditthi Samyutta* (No. 24) goes on to show how false views arise through clinging to the same five *khandhas;* and the *Okkantika Samyutta* (No. 25) says that the person who recognizes that eye, ear, nose, tongue, body, and mind are all impermanent and changeable, may be called a "walker in faith" and a "stream-winner . . . bound for enlightenment." In the *Sariputta Samyutta* (No. 28) the venerable Sariputta (the chief disciple of the Buddha) describes his experience of the four stages of trance or concentrative meditation (*samadhi),* which are called by the term *jhana* (Sanskrit *dhyana*): "first *jhana,* which is born of solitude and full of zest and happiness," "second *jhana,* that inward calming, that single-mindedness of will, apart from thought applied and sustained, born of mental balance," "third *jhana,* disinterested, mindful and self-possessed," and "fourth *jhana,* a state wherein is neither pleasure nor pain, an equanimity of utter purity;" and the four yet higher stages of *arupa* (formless) *jhana,* in which Sariputta dwelt successively in the sphere of the infinity of space, the sphere of infinite consciousness, the sphere of nothingness, and the sphere neither of perception nor non-perception. In the *Jhana* (or *Samadhi*) *Samyutta* (No. 34) the Buddha deals with the same topics. In the *Naga Samyutta* (No. 29), the *Supanna Samyutta* (No. 30), and the *Gandhabbakaya Samyutta* (No. 31) there are also sayings of the Buddha about several classes of supernatural beings, familiar from the Vedas, the *nagas* (serpent deities), the *garudas* (mythical birds which make war on snakes), and the *gandharvas* (heavenly musicians).

In the fourth or *Salayatanavagga* the basic teachings of the Buddha, e.g., on impermanence, on *nibbana* and *arahatship*, and on the *jhanas*, are set forth by the Buddha himself (*Salayatana Samyutta*, No. 35), by Sariputta (*Jambukhadaka* and *Samandaka Samyuttas*, Nos. 38, 39), by Moggallana (the second of the chief disciples of the Buddha) (*Moggallana Samyutta*, No. 40), and others. In the last *Samyutta* (No. 40) just cited, psychic power *(iddhi)* is attributed to the Buddha, and in the *Gamani Samyutta* (No. 42) the Buddha does not repudiate the assertion of others that he knows magic *(maya)*, the latter idea presumably being an interpretation of his psychic powers by unfriendly outsiders. The *Matugama Samyutta* (No. 37) deals with womankind, and considers that a woman is reborn in purgatory if she is faithless, shameless, unscrupulous, wrathful, and of weak wisdom, but is reborn in the heavenly world if she is faithful, modest, scrupulous, not wrathful, nor envious, rich in wisdom, moral and so forth. The *Avyakata Samyutta* (No. 44) contains a series of sayings about the unrevealed *(avyakata)*. A woman named Khema Theri (who was the wife of King Bimbisara, but became a nun and the chief of the Buddha's women disciples for her great insight, *mahapanna*) is questioned by King Pasenadi as to whether the Tathagata exists after death, and she replies that this is unrevealed. A certain Wanderer comes to the Buddha and asks him, "Is there a self?" at which words Śakyamuni is silent. When Ananda afterward asks the reason for the silence the Buddha explains that if he had said that there is a self this would have been to side with the eternalists, but if he had said that a self does not exist this would have been to side with the annihilationists. So the teaching of the Buddha is a mean between two extremes, and this idea of such a middle way in philosophy is of great importance in later Buddhist thought. In the same passage the Buddha also suggests that it is the recognition that all things are impermanent *(anicca)* which makes it impossible to make the unqualified assertion that there is a self, for that which is impermanent is not autonomous.

The fifth or *Mahavagga* is, as its name suggests, the largest of the five divisions of the *Samyutta Nikaya*, and contains no less than 1,208 sayings, a great many of them said to have been uttered at Savatthi. In the materials are a great variety of similes and not a few picturesque tales and parables.

According to the Mahaparinibbana Sutta (*Digha Nikaya* 2.120),[175] before he left Vaiśali for the last time the Buddha delivered an address to his disciples in which he summarized the truths which he had perceived and made known to them under seven topics and in thirty-seven items; namely, four stations of mindfulness, four ways of right effort, four stages on the way to psychic power, five powers, five faculties, seven kinds of wisdom, and the eightfold way. Here in the *Mahavagga* the first seven *Samyuttas* present exactly the same seven topics and thirty-seven items, although in a different order. The "Ariyan eightfold way *(ariya-atthangika-magga)*" consists of (1) right view *(samma ditthi)*, i.e., right understanding or knowledge of ill *(dukkha)*, its arising, its ceasing, and the way to its ceasing; (2) right aim *(samma sankappa)*, i.e., the aim to renounce, to be free from malice, to be harmless; (3) right speech *(samma vaca)*, i.e., avoidance of lying, calumny, and wanton speech; (4) right action *(samma kammanta)*, i.e., avoidance of taking life, of stealing, of unchastity; (5) right living *(samma ajiva)*, i.e., getting a living by a right way of life; (6) right effort *(samma vayama),* i.e., striving to destroy unprofitable states of mind and to further profitable states of mind; (7) right mindfulness *(samma sati),* i.e., abiding in contemplation; and (8) right concentration *(samma samadhi),* i.e., the calming down of thought which leads to the four stages of trance *(Magga Samyutta,* No. 45).

The seven kinds of wisdom are mindfulness, investigation of *dhamma,* energy, zest, tranquility, concentration, and equanimity *(Bojjhanga Samyutta,* No. 46). The four stations of mindfulness are contemplation of body, of feelings, of mind, and of self—all seen as transient *(Satipatthana Samyutta* No. 47). The five faculties are faith, energy, mindfulness, concentration, and insight *(Indriya Samyutta,* No. 48). The four right efforts are the endeavors to prevent sinfulness from arising, to put away sinful states which have arisen, to produce goodness when it does not exist, and to further goodness when it does exist *(Sammappadhana Samyutta,* No. 49). The five powers are the same as the five faculties—faith, energy, mindfulness, concentration, and insight *(Bala Samyutta,* No. 50). The four stages to psychic power are desire, i.e., the will to acquire such power, united with earnest meditation and the struggle against sin; energy, i.e., the necessary exertion, united with earnest meditation and the struggle against sin; thought, i.e., the necessary preparation of the mind, united with earnest meditation and the struggle against sin; investigation, i.e., the use of the mind, united with earnest meditation and the struggle against sin (and the accomplishments of psychic power are, in part, to walk on the water, know the minds of other beings, and recall former births). *(Iddhipada Samyutta,* No. 51).

Elsewhere in the *Mahavagga* of the *Samyutta Nikaya,* the *Anuruddha Samyutta* (No. 52) tells of the attainment of great supernormal power by the venerable Anuruddha; the *Jhana Samyutta* (No. 53) deals with the four trances; the *Anapana Samyutta* (No. 54) recommends the control of in-breathing and out-breathing as conducive to the destruction of the *asavas;* the *Sotapatti Samyutta* (No. 55) commends loyalty to the Buddha, the *dhamma,* and the *sangha;* and the *Sacca Samyutta* (No. 56) contains again the sermon of the Buddha at Isipatana which set rolling the wheel of the doctrine, together with the Buddha's remark: "I would not deem the full comprehension of four Ariyan truths to be won with sorrow and woe, but with joy and gladness" *(Samyutta Nikaya* 5.441).[176] The *Sacca Samyutta* was one of the texts preached by Mahinda at the court of Devanampiyatissa early in his mission to Sri Lanka.

Anguttara Nikaya. This "collection of numerically arranged discourses" contains more than 2,300 *suttas* grouped in eleven sections *(nipatas).*[177] The numerical arrangement consists in the fact that the first section deals with things of which there is only one example, the second with things of which there are two examples, and so on up to eleven.

The *Eka* (first) *Nipata* discusses such individual items as the cultivated mind, and friendship with the lovely, and names outstanding individual monks and nuns, and lay followers, both men and women. The *Duka* (second) *Nipata* states that there are two companies of monks, one discordant and the other harmonious, one trained in bluster and the other trained in inquiry; that there are two fools, one who shoulders a burden that does not befall him, and the other who shirks a burden that befalls him. The *Tika* (third) *Nipata* explains that there are three messengers of the gods, namely, old age, disease, and death; three practices, the practice of the hardened sensualist, that of the self-tormenter, and the midway practice.

The *Catukka* (fourth) *Nipata* names four holy places to be visited by the followers of the Buddha, the places where he was born, became enlightened, set rolling the wheel of the *dhamma,* and attained the final *nibbana;* four lamps, of the moon, the sun, the fire, and wisdom, of which the lamp of wisdom is the chief. The *Pancaka* (fifth) *Nipata* recommends contemplation of five things, of old age, of disease, of death, of variableness with and separation from those near and dear, and of the fact that one is the result of one's own deeds, and then pictures the disciple reflecting thus:

> "I am not the only one subject to old age, to disease, to death, not to me only is there variableness with and separation from those near and dear, I am not the only one who is the result of his deeds." And while he often contemplates these thoughts, the Way comes into being; and that Way he follows, makes become and develops; and in so doing the fetters are got rid of, the tendencies are removed.

> "While living thus, I have come to know
> Religion. . . . never now can I become
> Addict of sense desires.
> Now I am bound to become one turning no more back;
> I shall become a Further-Farer in the life divine."[178]

The *Cakka* (sixth) *Nipata* declares that there are six ways of being considerate, six roots of contention, and the like. Also in one dialogue in this section, a visitor to the Buddha affirms the doctrine that "there is no self-agency," and the Buddha declares that, on the contrary, the indubitable fact of initiative, in which a person can, for example, step forward or backward, shows that there is "self-agency."[179]

The *Sattaka* (seventh) *Nipata* states that there are seven tendencies or leanings, lust, enmity, false opinion, doubt, conceit, desire for rebirth, and ignorance; seven ways for settling disputes; and the like.[180] The *Atthaka* (eighth) *Nipata* says there are eight marvels about the ocean, eight ways of giving alms, eight causes of earthquake, and the like. The *Navaka* (ninth) *Nipata* enumerates nine classes of persons living in the world, from the average person up to the *arahant;* describes nine bases of strife and nine ways of dispelling strife, and so forth. In the *Dasaka* (tenth) *Nipata* the Buddha lists ten fetters, five pertaining to this world (the wrong view of the individual, doubt, wrong handling of ritual, sensuality, and malevolence), and five pertaining to the higher world (desire for rebirth in the world of form, desire for rebirth in the world of no form, conceit, excitement, and ignorance),[181] and describes the disciple as properly increasing in ten growths ("by faith, by virtue, by wisdom, generosity, and lore. . . "), while Sariputta, speaking on an occasion when the Buddha rests, calls for "growth in good states," which is like the waxing of the moon in its bright period.[182] Finally, the *Ekadasaka* (eleventh) *Nipata* tells of eleven disasters for abusive monks, eleven qualities of good disciples, eleven advantages to be expected from the practice of amity, eleven doors leading to *nibbana,* and so forth.

Khuddaka Nikaya. This "collection of smaller pieces" contains sixteen miscellaneous works, many of them brief, but a few very extensive. For the most part these works are written in verse, and the most important examples of Buddhist poetry are here, including some of the oldest extant Buddhist poems. Not a few of the texts duplicate materials found elsewhere in the Pali canon.

The *Khuddakapatha* (little readings) consists of four short texts called *pathas,* and five *suttas*. It is the shortest of all the books in the Pali Tipitaka, and constitutes a handbook for the Buddhist novice. There is also a relatively short commentary on the book by Buddhaghosa called the *Paramatthajotika* (illustrator of ultimate meaning).[183]

The first text *(patha)* is the Buddhist confession of faith ("I go for refuge to the Buddha, the *dhamma,* the *sangha*"); the second text states the ten precepts for monks; the third enumerates thirty-two parts of the human body, the contemplation of which leads to recognition of the transiency of human existence; the fourth gives ten questions of the novice, the concise answers to which outline Buddhist doctrines in an ascending series, e.g., "Four is what?—the four truths. . . . Eight is what?—the eightfold path," and so forth.

The first *sutta (Mangala Sutta)* teaches good omens *(mangalas)*, e.g.,

> Aid for mother and for father,
> And support for wife and children,
> Spheres of work that bring no conflict:
> This is a supreme good omen.[184]

The second *sutta (Ratana Sutta)* praises the "three jewels" *(buddha, dhamma, sangha)*. The third *sutta (Tirokudda Sutta)* describes the departed spirits as waiting outside the walls of their erstwhile earthly homes, and says that they cannot be benefited by any kind of mourning, but can be benefited by gifts given in their honor to the community. The fourth *sutta (Nidhikanda Sutta)* teaches that a treasure of good works is the best treasure to get. The fifth *sutta (Karaniyametta Sutta)* calls for lovingkindness *(metta)* toward every living being:

> . . . Joyful and safe
> Let every creature's heart rejoice.
> Whatever breathing beings there are,
> No matter whether frail or firm,
> With none excepted, long or big
> Or middle-sized or short or small
> Or thick, or those seen or unseen,
> Or whether dwelling far or near,
> That are or that yet seek to be,
> Let every creature's heart rejoice,
> Let none another one undo
> Or slight him at all anywhere;
> Let them not wish each other ill. . . .[185]

The *Dhammapada* (path of *dhamma*) is a compilation of the Buddha's teachings in 423 verses divided into twenty-six *vaggas* or chapters, and is considered a classical work, the knowledge of which is basic to the *upasampada* ordination in Sri Lanka.[186]

The first saying of the Buddha after his attainment of enlightenment is quoted (153–154):

> Looking for the maker of this tabernacle, I shall have to run through a course of many births, so long as I do not find [him]; and painful is birth again and again. But now, maker of this tabernacle, thou hast been seen; thou shalt not make up this tabernacle again. All thy rafters are broken, the ridge-pole is sundered; the mind, approaching the eternal *(nirvana)*, has attained to the extinction of all desires.[187]

Many ethical teachings are given. On happiness, for example, it is said (197–201, 204):

> Let us live happily then, not hating those who hate us! . . . Let us live happily then, free from greed among the greedy! . . . Victory breeds hatred, for the conquered is unhappy. He who has given up both victory and defeat, he, the contented, is happy.
>
> Health is the greatest of gifts, contentedness the best riches; trust is the best of relationships, *nirvana* is the highest happiness.[188]

The *Udana* (utterances) is a collection of eighty pronouncements of the Buddha, each usually coming as the conclusion of a brief narrative, and the whole arranged in eight chapters *(vaggas).*[189]

The *Bodhivagga* or "enlightenment chapter" (No. 1) tells of how, in the days after his enlightenment, the Buddha thought out the chain of cause and effect. The *Mucalindavagga* (No. 2) tells of the great unseasonable rainstorm which came while the Buddha was still seated on the bank of the Neranjara River, and of how Mucalinda, the snake *raja,* protected the Buddha by encircling his body with his own coils and rearing his great hood above the Buddha's head. In the *Nandavagga* (No. 3) the Buddha's cousin, the venerable Nanda, is about to abandon monastic life, but is persuaded by the Buddha to persevere. In the *Meghiyavagga* (No. 4) the Buddha counsels the venerable Meghiya about his thoughts. The *Sonatherassavagga* (No. 5) tells of the ordination of the venerable Sona, previously a lay follower, and recounts other events including a visit to the Buddha by King Pasenadi. In the *Jaccandhavagga* (No. 6) the Buddha is at Vaiśali and gives Ananda a hint, not understood by Ananda, of his own approaching death. In the *Culavagga* or "little chapter" (No. 7), among other events, Sariputta instructs a dwarf named Bhaddiya. The *Pataligamiyavagga* (No. 8) takes its name from the experience of the Buddha at Pataligama, but also tells of his falling ill from food eaten in the house of Cunda in Pava, and quotes his illustration of the indescribable blessedness of *nirvana.*[190]

The *Itivuttaka* [this was said] is a collection of 112 short *suttas,* arranged in four sections called *nipatas.*[191] In many of the *suttas* an idea is expressed in prose and then repeated in verse. The four sections represent a numerical arrangement of the *suttas,* according as they deal respectively with one, two, three, and four things.

In the *Ekanipata* or "section of ones" the Buddha speaks repeatedly of "one thing," such as ill-will, which must be given up, but also of one other thing, namely, lovingkindness, friendliness, or goodwill *(metta)* toward all beings, which surpasses all other good works as the moon's radiance surpasses the light of the stars.[192] In the *Dukanipata* or "section of twos" the Buddha says that two trains of thought much occupy the *tathagata,* the *arahant* who is rightly awakened—the two thoughts, namely, of serenity and of seclusion. In the *Tikanipata* or "section of threes" the Buddha says that if a monk is possessed of an aggregate of virtues *(sila),* an aggregate of concentration *(samadhi),* and an aggregate of wisdom *(panna),* he passes beyond the realm of Mara, the evil one, and shines like the sun. In the *Catukkanipata* or "section of the fours" the four major truths of *dukkha* are enumerated, namely, ill, the arising of ill, the ending of ill, and the method of the ending of ill.

Aside from the numerical sequences there are many other passages. For example, the Buddha speaks of nearness to himself as a spiritual rather than a spatial matter (3.91):

> Monks, even if a monk should seize the hem of my garment and walk behind me step for step, yet if he be covetous in his desires . . . that monk is far from me and I am far from him. . . . Monks, even though a monk should dwell a hundred *yojanas* away, yet if he be not covetous in his desires . . . then indeed that one is nigh unto me and I am nigh unto him.[193]

Again the Buddha calls himself the "incomparable physician and surgeon," and his monks his own "true sons" and "spiritual heirs." He also describes virtuous monks as "teachers, caravan-leaders (*satthavaha*, a term elsewhere used only for Buddhas), passion-scatterers, dispellers of gloom, bringers of light, bringers of luster, radiance, torch-bearers, enlighteners," and outlines the reciprocal relationships between the monastic and the lay members of the *sangha* in these words:

> Monks, *brahmanas* and householders are most helpful to you, since they support you with robe and bowl, with lodging and seat, medicines and necessaries for sickness. You also, monks, are most helpful to *brahmanas* and householders, since you teach them *dhamma* that is lovely at the beginning, lovely in the middle, and lovely at the end (of life), both in the spirit and in letter, and you proclaim to them the Brahma-life in its completeness and utter purity. Thus, monks, this Brahma-life is lived in mutual dependence, for ferrying across the flood, for utter ending of ill.[194]

The *Sutta Nipata* (section of discourses) is a collection of poetical *suttas* in five chapters *(vaggas).*[195] For the most part the materials seem to be relatively very early, giving prominence to the hermit life rather than to life in the great monasteries, and to ethical teachings rather than to elaborated philosophical systems, although the beginnings of the latter are discernible.

In the first *Uragavagga* (chapter of the snake) two main religious sects are recognized, that of the *brahmana* who belongs to the system of caste, and that of the *samana* who is a "recluse" like the Buddha himself. The Buddha declares, however, that in reality it is not by birth that one becomes an outcaste or a *brahmana*, but only by deeds (1.142).[196] Thus in effect Buddhism is represented as true *brahmanism*. Likewise the Buddhist monk, who is content to wander lonely as the rhinoceros (1.35ff.),[197] is described as the true *muni* or "silent sage," a term primarily applied to *brahmanical* ascetics (1.207–221).[198]

In the second *Culavagga* (little chapter) the Buddha explains that the *rishis* of old were the true *brahmanas,* but were corrupted by wealth and pleasure, and wrongly instituted animal sacrifice, in which even the innocent cow is slain (2.284–315).[199] In the third *Mahavagga* (great chapter) there are poetic accounts of the birth (3.679ff.)[200] and "going forth" *(pabbajja,* 3.405–424)[201] of the Buddha, and of his temptation by Mara (3.425–449).[202] In the fourth *Atthakavagga* (chapter of eights) the Buddha describes those who are devoted to philosophy as going fruitlessly from one teacher to another, and says that the different schools of philosophy contradict one another and cause strife in the world (4.788ff., 878ff.).[203] Again in the fifth *Parayanavagga* (chapter on the way to the beyond) the Buddha says that it is not because of any philosophical view, or tradition, or knowledge, that anyone is to be called a true *muni,* but both *samanas* and *brahmanas* who are free from craving are flood-crossers" (5.1077–1083).[204]

In the *Vimanavatthu* (stories of the mansions), the venerable Moggallana and others are able to visit the heavens of the gods and ask the persons who have been reborn there as *devas* what deeds of merit they did in order to obtain such splendid dwelling places after death.[205] In general the answers emphasize individual morality and duty, and picture a happy survival of the meritorious on the levels above. With all their pleasures, however, the "mansions" *(vimanas)* are themselves only stages of progress, and occasionally there is an allusion to a more ultimate end. Thus, for example, Catta, the son of a certain *brahmana,* is slain by robbers only shortly after hearing the Buddha's word but, on the basis of only briefly carrying out this teaching, is reborn in a pure and lovely mansion, and thinks that an even higher destiny will be possible for those who have longer time in the way (53):

> See how for such brief homily
> I've won this happy bourn, this weal,
> While they who long can hear thee teach
> Methinks must win immortal goal.[206]

In the *Petavatthu* (stories of the departed), the *peta* (Sanskrit *preta*) is one who has "passed on," and the *petas* and *petis* (feminine) in these tales are hungry and unhappy ghosts who relate the sufferings they are experiencing on account of their misdeeds in earthly life, especially their lack of charity.[207] Correspondingly it is set forth that by charitable gifts on earth, benefit can be conveyed to the spirits of the deceased. Thus, for example, there was a lay disciple named Nandasena, whose wife Nanda was irreligious and avaricious. Reborn as a *peti* after death, Nanda was of ugly appearance and unhappy. Nandasena wished to give her clothes and food, but any direct gift was impossible. When he gave such gifts to the monks, however, it redounded to her credit, and she appeared and said to her former husband (2.4): "I am Nanda, Nandasena; formerly I was your wife. For having committed an evil deed, I went from here to the *peta*-world. Through the gift given by you, I rejoice, being free of fear from any quarter."[208]

As noted above, both the *Petavatthu* and the *Vimanavatthu* were texts preached at the court of Devanampiyatissa by Mahinda early in his mission to Sri Lanka.

Theragatha (verses of the elders) and *Therigatha* (verses of the [female] elders) are two collections, the first of 107 poems with 1,279 verses or stanzas *(gathas)* attributed to 264 personal male disciples of the Buddha, and the second of 73 poems with 522 verses attributed to 73 personal female disciples of the Buddha.[209]

In general, these are among the most beautiful of Indian poems. In ethical ideals they are like the *Dhammapada* and the *Sutta Nipata* in teaching kindness toward all beings *(metta)*, nonviolence *(ahimsa)*, self-control, and related virtues. In line with the Buddha's commendation of solitude (e.g., in the *Akankheyya Sutta* cited above), the writers speak often of withdrawal to the jungles and the mountains, and there are many beautiful descriptive passages expressive of the love of nature, e.g., the verse which recurs several times in the *Theragatha* (113, 601, 1070):

> Crags where clear waters lie, a rocky world,
> Haunted by black-faced apes and timid deer,
> Where 'neath bright blossoms run the silver streams:
> These are the highlands of my heart's delight.[210]

Finally, however, everything here is impermanent, as Moggallana says in respect of the passing away of Sariputta (*Theragatha* 1159):

> O transient are our life's experiences!
> Their nature 'tis to rise and pass away,
> They happen in our ken, they cease to be,
> O well for us when they are sunk to rest![211]

As for the ultimate goal, it is seen both negatively as the going out of craving and the end of ill, and positively as insight, happiness, and peace, as is stated, for example, by a former courtesan who is now the *bhikkhuni* Vimala (*Therigatha* 76):

> Now all the evil bonds that fetter gods
> And men are wholly rent and cut away.

> Purged are the *asavas* that drugged my heart,
> Calm and content I know *nibbana's* peace.212

Jataka are birth stories, their title deriving from the word *jata* (birth), specifically, the births of the Buddha in his many previous existences, concerning which more than 500 stories are related in this collection.213 In those existences, and indeed in his historical life up until the point of his enlightenment, he was, properly speaking, a *bodhisatta* (Sanskrit *bodhisattva*), i.e., a being (*satta*, Sanskrit *sattva*) who was destined to obtain enlightenment *(bodhi)* and become a *buddha* (enlightened one). Thus these tales may also be called *bodhisatta* stories. In the previous existences narrated in these stories the *bodhisatta* was variously man, animal, and god; thus in fact almost any folk tale might become a *jataka* if the character in it were identified as the *bodhisatta*.

As the *Jataka* exists in its full form, each story opens with a preface in which some circumstance is described in the life of the historical Buddha which leads him to tell about his experience in some former birth. Then the story of that previous existence is related, usually including a portion in verse. At the end the Buddha identifies the various persons in the story in their present births.

While much of the material in the *Jataka* must be considered to belong to the realm of folklore, there is also much that reflects the civilization of ancient India (e.g., descriptions of the wooden palaces of kings, and of magnificent subterranean buildings), and there may also be information of historical importance concerning the life of Śakyamuni Buddha (e.g., cf. items cited above in Chapter 5 from the introduction to the *Jataka* called the *Nidanakatha* and from the *Jataka* proper). As for the stories, they include animal fables (e.g., No. 278, where the *bodhisatta* is a patient buffalo with a mischievous monkey on his back) and anecdotes (e.g., No. 46, where monkeys are to water some trees, and they pull up each tree by its roots to see how much water it will require); narratives of men and women, both wise and foolish (e.g., No. 546, in which the *bodhisatta* is the wise Mahosadha, who is able to solve the most difficult riddles and perform the most puzzling tasks); and legends of kings and saints (e.g., No. 440 in which the *bodhisatta* is Prince Kanha, who gives away all he possesses and retires to the Himalaya as a hermit, asking only that nothing ever be harmed on his account). In many of the stories the main point is the kindly action of the *bodhisatta,* often at the cost of major self-sacrifice, for the benefit of other beings.

In addition to their circulation in the form of a literary work, the stories of the *Jataka* were also very influential in the realm of art, and provided many of the subjects of sculpture and painting at Bharhut, Sanci, Ajanta, and elsewhere.

Mahaniddesa (great explanation) and *Cullaniddesa* (short explanation) are commentaries, with detailed grammatical explanations, on portions of the *Sutta Nipata*.

Patisambhidamagga (path to analysis) is divided into three large chapters *(vaggas),* each of which contains ten treatises on important points of Buddhist doctrine. The subjects are treated in the form of questions and answers, in the manner of texts in the Abhidhammapitaka.

Buddhavamsa (Buddha chronicle) is a poetical work in which Śakyamuni Buddha gives an account of each of the twenty-four former Buddhas (Dipankara, Kondanna, Mangala, Sumana, Revata, Sobhita, Anomadassi, Paduma, Narada, Padumuttara, Sumedha, Sujata, Piyadassi, Atthadassi, Dhammadassi, Siddhattha, Tissa, Phussa, Vipassi, Sikhi, Vessabhu, Kakusandha, Konagamana, and Kassapa, of whom the last six are also named in the *Digha Nikaya*), under each of whom he had himself also lived in a former existence.[214] Under Dipankara, the first Buddha in the list, for example, he was a *brahmana* named Sumedha who became a hermit in the Himalaya, and was told that he would be a future Buddha. Under other Buddhas he was at one time Sakka the king of the gods, and at other times a lion, a king of the *nagas*, a *yaksha*, and several times an ascetic. Toward the end of the *Buddhavamsa* (25) there is a brief autobiography of Sakyamuni Buddha, and there is a bare mention of the future Buddha, Metteyya (Maitreya).

Cariyapitaka (basket of conduct) consists of accounts similar to those in the *Jataka* and often derived therefrom, in which the Buddha gives a narrative in verse of thirty-four of his former births.[215] All of the stories are directed to show how, by his conduct *(cariya)* in the previous existences, he achieved the ten *paramitas* or "perfections," which are the necessary possessions of a *bodhisatta*, namely, generosity, virtue, renunciation, wisdom, energy, patience, truthfulness, determination, kindness to all beings, and equanimity.

Apadana consists of stories of heroic deeds. The word *apadana* (Sanskrit *avadana*) means a heroic or glorious deed, and refers here to such deeds of piety and self-sacrifice. This collection contains accounts in verse of the lives and former lives of 550 *theras* and 40 *theris* of the time of the Buddha, most of whom became *arahants*. Included among the monks are the famous Sariputta, Moggallana, Kassapa, Anuruddha, Upali, Ananda, Rahula, and many others; among the nuns Mahapajapati Gotami, Khema, and others.

Abhidhammapitaka

The Abhidhammapitaka or "basket of higher doctrine" consists of seven treatises *(sattapakarana)* which amount to a supplement to the Suttapitaka, inasmuch as they deal with essentially the same subjects as the works in the "basket of discourses." The treatment of the topics is chiefly in the form of questions and answers, as is also the case already, for example, in the abovementioned *Patisambhidamagga*, and there are many definitions and classifications of Buddhist terms. The "doctrine" *(dhamma)* is therefore "higher" *(abhi)*, not in respect to its content, but only in respect to the more detailed treatment, so that the treatises amount to manuals for advanced study.

Dhammasangani (enumeration of *dhammas*) is a textbook on psychological ethics, and there is a commentary on it by Buddhaghosa called the Atthasalini (the expositor).[216] Topics dealt with include consciousness, intelligence, mental states, and objects of meditation.

Vibhanga (classification) is further analysis of matters such as those already dealt with in the *Dhammasangani*.[217]

Dhatukatha (discourse on elements) is a discussion, supplementing the *Dhammasangani*, of the mental characteristics generally associated with persons of religious faith.[218]

Puggalapannatti (description of persons) is a work, the object of which is to classify the various types of individuals according to the qualities they possess and the perfections they have achieved.[219] The listing is in numerical groupings; for example, in the grouping of human types by threes, there are the despairing, the hopeful, and the one above aspiration; in the grouping by fours, there are four types of preachers of *dhamma (dhammakathikas)*, namely, the one who speaks but little and what he says is irrelevant, the one who speaks but little and what he says is relevant, the one who speaks much and what he says is irrelevant, and the one who speaks much and what he says is relevant.

Kathavatthu (subjects of discussion) is a book of debates, affirmations, and refutations relating to controversial points of doctrine.[220] According to tradition the work was composed in refutation of false doctrines by Moggaliputta-Tissa, the president of the Third Buddhist Council held at Pataliputra under Aśoka. The points of controversy revolve around doctrines held by the Mahasanghika and many other dissenting schools. Questions taken up include the existence or not of a personal entity, whether or not an *arahant* can fall away from *arahantship*, whether or not a lay person can become an *arahant*, whether or not there is an intermediate state before a next rebirth, and whether or not all dreamconsciousness is ethically neutral.

Yamaka (pairs) is a book consisting of an arrangement of pairs of questions to provide the outline for an analysis of psychological matters.

Patthana (causes) holds that, except for *nibbana*, which is absolute, everything is relative, and the relationships of things are analyzed in twenty-four categories.[221]

Other Pali Texts

While the foregoing constitute the canonical texts as recognized in Sri Lanka, the Buddhists of Burma include in the *Khuddaka Nikaya* four additional works:

Suttasamgaha is an anthology compiled from the Suttapitaka.

Nettipakarana or *Netti* (book of guidance) is a work on exegetical methodology, and seems to be intended as a guide for commentators.[222] In the course of the work there are many quotations from the teachings of the Buddha, almost all from the Suttapitaka. The book is attributed by tradition to Mahakaccana, the disciple of the Buddha who was accounted, both by the Buddha and by his own fellows, to be the one best able to expound and elucidate the terse utterances of the Buddha (*Majjhima Nikaya* 1.110; 3.194–195, 223–224).[223]

Petakopadesa (instruction of the students of the Pitakas) is a continuation of the *Netti*, also attributed to Mahakaccana. The work begins with an introduction which affirms that there are two conditions for the arising of a hearer's right view, namely, "another's utterance sequential upon truth, and reasoned attention in oneself." Then "another's utterance" is defined as "any teaching, advice, instruction, talk about truth, in conformity with truth, from another. The Truths are four: they are Suffering, Origin, Cessation, and the Path. Any teaching, showing, divulging, analyzing, exhibiting, displaying these four Truths is called another's utterance in conformity with truth." After that, the analysis goes on in exhaustive detail.[224]

Milinda Panha (questions of Milinda) is a work that recounts the conversations of the *thera* Nagasena with the Bactrian Greek king Milinda (circa 161–145 B.C.E), called Menander by the Greeks.[225] For a single example of the dialogue, the king asks—evidently in view of the Buddhist doctrine that a person is an always changing combination of "aggregates"—whether, when a person is reborn, the person is the same or is another. Nagasena replies that the person is neither the same nor another, and gives two illustrations, the baby and the man, and the lamp and its flame (40):

> Nagasena: "Now what do you think, O king? You were once a baby, a tender thing, and small in size, lying flat on your back. Was that the same as you who are now grown up?"
> Milinda: "No. That child was one, I am another."
> Nagasena: "If you are not that child, it will follow that you have had neither mother nor father, no! nor teacher. You cannot have been taught, either learning, or behavior, or wisdom.

What, great king! . . . Is the person who goes to school one, and the same when he has finished his schooling another? . . ."

Milinda: "Certainly not. But what would you, Sir, say to that?"

Nagasena: "I should say that I am the same person, now I am grown up, as I was when I was a tender tiny baby, flat on my back. For all these states are included in one by means of this body."

Nagasena: "Suppose a man, O king, were to light a lamp, would it burn the night through?"

Milinda: "Yes, it might do so."

Nagasena: "Now, is it the same flame that burns in the first watch of the night, Sir, and in the second?"

Milinda: "No."

Nagasena: "Or the same that burns in the second watch and in the third?"

Milinda: "No."

Nagasena: "Then is there one lamp in the first watch, and another in the second, and another in the third?

Milinda: "No. The light comes from the same lamp all the night through."

Nagasena: "Just so, O king, is the continuity of a person or thing maintained. One comes into being, another passes away, but at the same time there is something which unites them. Thus neither as the same nor as another does one go on to the last phase of one's self-consciousness."

So, as Nagasena explains the matter, one is at any given moment the totality of that of which one is conscious, and this is constantly changing, but at the same time there is a continuity in the whole series, which is dependent upon the body; even so, in the second illustration, the flame is the changing self-consciousness, and the lamp is the body.[226]

Pali Compendia and Commentaries

On the basis of the canonical texts, numerous and voluminous compendia and commentaries were composed, and these constitute the bulk of the noncanonical Pali literature.

Buddhaghosa. Of all the authors in this area the most famous is Buddhaghosa, who worked in Sri Lanka in the fifth century C.E., in the time of King Mahanama and of what is sometimes counted as the Sixth Buddhist Council. References have been made above to his great compendium of Buddhist doctrine, primarily ethical and psychological in orientation, called the *Visuddhimagga,* to his commentary on the Vinayapitaka called the *Samantapasadika* and the introduction to it called the *Bahiranidana,* to his commentary on the *Khuddakapatha* in the Suttapitaka called the *Paramatthajotika,* and to his commentary on the *Dhammasangani* in the Abhidhammapitaka called the *Atthasalini.*

Anuruddha. Anuruddha, a Sinhalese *thera* believed to have lived between the eighth and twelfth centuries C.E., is credited with the composition of an Abhidhamma compendium called the *Abhidhammattha-sangaha.* The range of subjects is in general the same as in the *Visuddhimagga* of Buddhaghosa, but the treatment is briefer and the emphasis is more on the theoretical and philosophical than on the ethical and psychological. Together Buddhaghosa's *Visuddhimagga* and Anuruddha's *Abhidhammattha-sangaha* are the two major textbooks for students of Buddhism in Theravada countries.

The major Pali chronicles have also been cited already, the *Dipavamsa* (island chronicle) of the 4th century C.E., the *Mahavamsa* (great chronicle) of the 5th century, and its continuation the *Culavamsa* which, with its final supplement, comes down into the 19th century, and also the *Thupavamsa* (chronicle of the *thupa*) compiled in the 13th century.

THREE JEWELS

In the last year of his life, at the age of 80, the Buddha fell ill at Beluva (near Vaiśali) but recovered, and Ananda, aware of the possibility of the death of the Buddha, asked him about leaving instructions for the Order *(sangha)*. The Buddha replied that he had taught openly, without making any distinction between exoteric and esoteric doctrine, and therefore his disciples should not look to any other leader for guidance, but should look only to themselves and to the truth (the *dhamma*): "Therefore, O Ananda, be ye lamps unto yourselves. Be ye a refuge to yourselves. Betake yourselves to no external refuge. Hold fast to the truth as a lamp. Hold fast as a refuge to the truth. Look not for refuge to any one besides yourselves." And when the great decease finally occurred at Kuśinagara, the Buddha's last words were a concise restatement of his doctrine, and a renewed exhortation to personal responsibility: "Decay is inherent in all component things! Work out your salvation with diligence!" (*Digha Nikaya* 2.72–167).[227]

So the Buddha himself, and the teaching he gave, and the association of his disciples, who are working out their own salvation in accordance with his teachings, are the main facts which provide an outline of Buddhism, and in Buddhism these are the "three jewels" *(triratna, tiratana)* and the "three refuges" *(tisarana)*. The oldest and continuing affirmation of the adherent, whether monastic or lay, is the thrice-repeated statement: "I take my refuge in the Buddha, I take my refuge in the *dhamma*, I take my refuge in the *sangha*" (*Mahavagga* 1.12.5)[228]

In the *Tevijja Sutta* in the *Digha Nikaya* (1.234ff.), a young *brahmana* named Vasettha, who was well versed in the three Vedas (Sanskrit *traividya*, Pali *tevijja* means knowledge of the three Vedas or, as an adjective, a person possessed of that knowledge, hence the name of this *sutta*), asked Śakyamuni Buddha to explain the way to a state of union with Brahma, and the Buddha began his answer by saying:

> "Know, Vasettha, that [from time to time] a *tathagata* (the term usually employed by the Buddha when referring to himself and to the *buddhas* in general) is born into the world, an *arahat*, a fully awakened one, abounding in wisdom and goodness, happy, with knowledge of the worlds, unsurpassed as a guide to mortals willing to be led, a teacher of gods and men, a blessed one, a *buddha*. He, by himself thoroughly understands, and sees, as it were, face to face this universe—including the worlds above with the gods, the *maras* [Mara, the prince of evil was the tempter of Śakyamuni Buddha, and the *maras* are the 'evil ones'], and the *brahmas;* and the world below with its *samanas* and *brahmanas*, its princes and peoples;—and he then makes his knowledge known to others. The truth doth he proclaim both in the letter and in the spirit, lovely in its origin, lovely in its progress, lovely in its consummation: the higher life doth he make known, in all its purity and in all its perfectness."[229]

Thus it is believed, even in the Theravada, that there is in all a long series of Buddhas, in fact no less than twenty-four who preceded Śakyamuni Buddha and one, Maitreya (Metteyya), who is yet to come. Also it is believed that Śakyamuni Buddha himself went through a long series of previous existences in many different forms, while he was still a *bodhisatta* (Sanskrit *bodhisattva*) and on his way to his final attainment of enlightenment and Buddhahood. As earlier stated, the stories of these former lives are contained in the *Jataka*.

As to the historical Buddha of the present age, the texts record that he was born in Lumbini (in what is now southern Nepal), and that his father was Suddhodana, the ruler of the Sakya (Śakya) clan, subordinate to the Kosala (Kośala) kingdom, and his mother was queen Maya (the political divisions and geographical locations are described above in Chapter 5). His personal name was Siddhattha (Sanskrit Siddhartha), his family name was Gotama (Gautama), and he was commonly known as Śakyamuni, "the sage of the Śakyas."

Siddhartha's early life in his father's palace at Kapilavastu was sheltered and luxurious. At the age of sixteen he was married to princess Yasodhara (Yaśodhara), and they had a son named Rahula. When Siddhartha did go out of the palace he saw four "signs," an aged man, a sick man, a dead man, and a mendicant wandering recluse who had renounced the world and attained serenity. He thereupon determined upon his own great renunciation and, at the age of twenty-nine, left his kingdom. For six years he wandered, sought out various teachers, and associated himself with five other men in extreme ascetic practices, but did not find what he sought. Then, to the disapproval of his erstwhile associates, he went his own way. Seated beneath the *bodhi* tree (enlightenment tree, as it was afterward called) on the bank of the Neranjara River, in profound meditation, undeterred by the temptations of Mara, he attained enlightenment *(bodhi)* and thus, at the age of thirty-five, became the Buddha, the Enlightened One.

Thereafter, at Isipatana (near Varanasi), the Buddha delivered his first sermon to the five ascetics, his former associates, and thus set turning, it was said, the Wheel of the Law *(dhamma, dharma,* his teaching, doctrine). Then for forty-five more years he continued to wander, preach, and teach. He directed his message to all without distinction of race or caste, and to both men and women. He talked with kings, but did not involve himself with government or social programs, although his influence was conducive to gentleness toward all living beings, and in the long run led at least one successful conqueror (Aśoka) to give up war and devote himself to works of piety and charity. Essentially the Buddha seems to have held that self-realization is the greatest contribution that one can make to others, and that self-realization can only be attained by one's self. Thus his already quoted last word to his followers: "Work out your salvation with diligence!" (*Digha Nikaya* 2.156).[230]

Dhamma

The teaching, doctrine, or law *(dhamma, dharma)* of the Buddha was outlined in his sermon at Isipatana in four truths and an eightfold way. The first two truths constitute an analysis of the human situation, and the second two propose a way to deal with that situation, a way spelled out in eight further items.

Dukkha. The first truth is stated in terms of the word *dukkha* (Sanskrit *duhkha*), usually translated as "suffering," as opposed to *sukha* or "happiness." In its broad meaning in Buddhist usage the word refers to suffering in the various painful experiences of life, to suffering which ensues when pleasurable experiences come to an end as they inevitably do, and to suffering which is equivalent to the impermanent and conditional character of human existence itself. As a term comprehending all the unsatisfactoriness of human existence, other translations of *dukkha* are "ill," "frustration," and the like. Using the translation "suffering," the sermon says: "Birth is suffering; decay is suffering; illness is suffering; death is suffering. Presence of objects we hate is suffering. Separation from objects we love is suffering; not to obtain what we desire is suffering. Briefly, the fivefold clinging to existence is suffering" (*Mahavagga* 1.6.19).[231]

The "fivefold clinging" here mentioned refers to the five "aggregates" (literally "heaps," Pali *khandhas*, Sanskrit *skandhas*), the ever-changing combinations of physical and mental energies that are the basic elements of the universe and the elements which constitute a person, namely, (1) *rupa*, form, (2) *vedana*, sensation, (3) *sanna*, *samjna*, perception, (4) *sankhara*, *samskara*, volition, and (5) *vinnana*, *vijnana*, consciousness. The corollary of this analysis of a person as a composite bundle of elements in an impermanent series of successive states is in the basic Buddhist doctrine of *anatta (anatman)* or "no-self," a doctrine which nevertheless allows for a "self-agency" (see above in the *Cakka Nipata* of the *Anguttara Nikaya*) and for consciousness *(vinnana, vijnana)* as a connecting link between one life and the next, in which the rebirth of a new person, psychologically one with the deceased, is due to the working of *kamma, karma* (see just below).

Samudaya. The second truth is that of the arising *(samudaya)* of *dukkha*. The immediate cause of the human predicament is *tanha*, translated as craving or thirst. "[It is] thirst that leads to rebirth, accompanied by pleasure and lust, finding its delight here and there. (This thirst is threefold), namely, thirst for pleasure, thirst for existence, thirst for prosperity" *(Mahavagga* 1.6.20).[232]

In another figure of speech this thirst is described as a burning fire:

> Everything is burning. The eye is burning; visible things are burning; the mental impressions based on the eye are burning; the contact of the eye [with visible things] is burning; the sensation produced by the contact of the eye [with visible things], be it pleasant, be it painful, be it neither pleasant nor painful, that also is burning. With what fire is it burning? I declare unto you that it is burning with the fire of lust, with the fire of anger, with the fire of ignorance; it is burning with [the anxieties of] birth, decay, death, grief, lamentation, suffering, dejection, and despair" *(Mahavagga* 1.21.2).[233]

Yet again it may be said that human life is beset with four *asavas* or "cankers," namely, *kamasava* or attachment to the sensual realm; *bhavasava* or attachment to "becoming"; *ditthasava* or attachment to (false) views; and the *asava* of *avijja* or ignorance *(Majjhima Nikaya* 1.7).[234]

So the immediate fact of thirst or craving is connected with and conditioned by other things, and may appear as only one item in a long chain of causation, a chain which can be traced back at last to ignorance, and a chain which accounts for and describes the state of *dukkha*.

> Conditioned by rebirth is decay and death,
> conditioned by becoming is rebirth,
> conditioned by grasping is becoming,
> conditioned by craving is grasping,
> conditioned by feeling is craving,
> conditioned by contact is feeling,
> conditioned by sense is contact,
> conditioned by name and shape is sense,
> conditioned by consciousness is name and shape,
> conditioned by activities is consciousness,
> conditioned by ignorance are activities *(Samyutta Nikaya* 2.25).

Summing up the foregoing teaching in aphoristic brevity, it is said: "Conditioned by this, that comes to be." Since each link in the whole causal chain is conditioned by or dependent on the adjacent link, the entire system is called "conditional causation" or "dependent origination" *(paticcasamuppada/pratityasamutpada)*, and this doctrine is so basic that it is declared that the one who sees dependent origination sees the *dhamma/dharma*, and the one who sees the *dhamma/dharma* sees dependent origination *(Majjhima Nikaya* 1.190–191). Further, since each of the links in the whole chain only exists in dependence on another link, no single link has a real existence in and of itself, and in fact every composed thing is "empty" *(sunna/śunya)*—a notion of "emptiness" *(sunnata/śunyata)* which appears here *(Samyutta Nikaya* 4.54) for the first time and will become increasingly important in later Buddhist thought.[235]

Nirodha. The third truth is that of the cessation *(nirodha)* of *dukkha*. "[It ceases with] the complete cessation of this thirst—a cessation which consists in the absence of every passion—with the abandoning of this thirst, with the doing away with it, with the deliverance from it, with the destruction of desire" *(Mahavagga* 1.6.21).[236]

If the thirst or craving is comparable to a burning fire, then it is plain that the fire should not be fed.

> It is just as if there should be a blazing bonfire of ten, or twenty, or thirty, or forty loads of faggots; thereon no man should from time to time throw dry grasses, dry cow-dung, dry sticks. Verily that great bonfire, when the first laid fuel were come to an end, and it were not fed by other fuel, would without food become extinct. Even so in him who contemplates the misery that there is in all that makes for grasping, craving ceases, and hence grasping ceases, becoming, birth, decay-and-death, and sorrow cease. Such is the ceasing of this entire mass of ill *(Samyutta Nikaya* 2.85).[237]

Likewise if the chain of causal connections can be followed from its beginning in ignorance to its consequence in rebirth, the chain of causality may also be followed in another sequence in which birth is indeed causally associated with suffering, but suffering is causally associated with faith, faith with joy, joy with rapture, rapture with serenity, serenity with happiness, happiness with concentration, and concentration with the knowledge and vision of things as they really are *(Samyutta Nikaya* 2.30).[238]

Magga. The fourth truth is that of the path *(magga,* Sanskrit *marga)* which leads to the cessation of *dukkha,* and it is detailed in terms of the eight items of right understanding, thought, speech, action, livelihood, effort, mindfulness, and concentration. This is the "middle path" between hedonism and asceticism, which leads to insight and wisdom, and conduces to calm, to knowledge, to enlightenment, and to *nirvana (Mahavagga* 1.6.18).[239]

It seems evident that the foregoing teaching assumes the age-old Indian ideas of the ceaseless round of existence, of *karma,* and of ultimate release, but in Buddhist philosophy these are analyzed in a distinctive way.

Rebirth. Since, in the Buddhist analysis, a person is not a self *(atman)* but a constantly changing combination of physical and mental energies (the five aggregates), it is not strictly correct to speak of a transmigration of the self, but one should rather speak of a rebirth, in which the aforesaid energies assume another form in another existence.

Buddhaghosa *(Visuddhimagga* 17.553–554) explains:

> It is only elements of being possessing a dependence that arrive at a new existence: none transmigrated from the last existence, nor are they in the new existence without causes contained

in the old. By this is said that it is only elements of being, with form or without, but possessing a dependence, that arrive at a new existence. There is no entity, no living principle; no elements of being transmigrated from the last existence into the present one; nor, on the other hand, do they appear in the present existence without causes in that one.[240]

The *Milinda Panha* (71) provides an illustration in this conversation between King Milinda and the *thera* Nagasena:

> The king said: "Where there is no transmigration, Nagasena, can there be rebirth?"
> "Yes, there can."
> "But how can that be? Give me an illustration."
> "Suppose a man, O king, were to light a lamp from another lamp, can it be said that the one transmigrates from, or to, the other?"
> "Certainly not."
> "Just so, great king, is rebirth without transmigration."[241]

Karma. The chain of causal conditioning already noted shows that as long as there is thirst or craving the process of rebirth goes on (craving—grasping—becoming—rebirth). Similarly it may be said that as long as there is *karma* there is continued existence. The Sanskrit *karma* (Pali *kamma*) is from the root *kr* (to do) and means doing or action, specifically volitional action, and it is the "fruit" or "result" of that action *(kamma-phala* or *kamma-vipaka)* that determines the character of each new form of existence. Karma may be relatively good and meritorious *(kusala,* profitable) and thus produce relatively good results, or bad and demeritorious *(akusala,* unprofitable) and thus produce bad results, and there is also a kind of *karma* which is neutral as to result.

Buddhaghosa *(Visuddhimagga* 19.601–602) provides detailed classifications of *karma,* e.g., "*kamma* is fourfold: to be experienced here and now, to be experienced on rebirth, to be experienced in some subsequent becoming, and lapsed *karma,*" and he refers to *kamma* and to its results both in the saying:

> Kamma-result proceeds from *kamma,*
> Result has *kamma* for its source,
> Future becoming springs from *kamma,*
> And this is how the world goes round.[242]

In the *Abhidhammattha-sangaha* (5.1–11), attributed to Anuruddha, there is an outline of the divisions and subdivisions of the universe (whether these are objective places or levels of consciousness is probably open to interpretation), and *kamma* is said to work out its results through all of these worlds.

The first world is that of sense desires, the *kamaloka* or *kamadhatu*. In it are two planes, the plane of misery and punishment, and the plane of fortunate sense experience. In the plane of punishment are four subdivisions, namely, from the lowest upward, hell, the animal kingdom, the realm of the *pretas* or hungry ghosts, and the place of the *asuras* which are demigods. In the plane of fortunate sense experience there are seven subdivisions, namely, the realm of human beings and, above that, the heavens of various classes of gods.

Above the *kamaloka* is the second world, that of form, the *rupaloka* or *rupadhatu* (and if two planes are reckoned in the *kamaloka* this can be counted as the third plane). Here in the world of form there are sixteen subdivisions, and they are occupied successively by higher grades of gods, who yet have a material body.

Above the *rupaloka* is the third world, that of formlessness, the *arupaloka* or *arupadhatu* (which may also be reckoned as the fourth plane). Here there are four grades of consciousness, the first in which consciousness dwells on the infinity of space, the second in which consciousness dwells on the infinity of consciousness, the third in which consciousness dwells on nothingness, and the fourth in which there is neither consciousness nor unconsciousness. So, in the entire universe, there are three worlds, four planes, and thirty-one subdivisions.

Good and bad *karma* may also be classified according to the working out of their effects. There are twelve kinds of bad *karma*, which arise in act, speech, and thought, and have their roots in hate, greed, and erroneous opinion; and eight kinds of good *karma*, which also arise in act, speech, and thought, but consist in charity, service, correct views, to list only three; and all twenty of these kinds of *karma* work out their effects in the *kamaloka*, the bad producing rebirth on the plane of misfortune, the good producing rebirth on the plane of fortunate conditions.

In addition to such *kamaloka-karma*, there are also good *rupaloka-karma* and good *arupaloka-karma*, both of which consist in mental culture and involve the attaining of ecstasy. In their working out of the first of these results in rebirth in the *rupaloka*, the second in rebirth in the *arupaloka*.

> Even thus our merit, waxing great and for this
>   plane, or that one bound,
> Brings forth results like to itself, in rebirth
>   and the vital round.[243]

As to expectations in respect to rebirth, there are four stages of attainment as the individual proceeds on the path of the Buddha (*Abhidhammattha-sangaha* 9.10).[244] The stream-enterer *(sotapanna)* has put away erroneous views, and will at the most experience seven more rebirths, none of these below the human level, and all in the more fortunate levels of the *kamaloka*. The once-returner *(sakidagamin)* has so attenuated lust, hate, and ignorance as to be liable to come back to this world, i.e., to the seven happier levels of *kamaloka*, only one more time. The never-returner *(anagamin)* has put away utterly the lust of sense and ill-will, and does not ever come back again to things as we know them, i.e., to *kamaloka*, but is reborn in the higher planes and is capable of attaining *nirvana*. The *arahant* has completely overcome and is wholly free from the cankers *(asavas)* of sense desires, becoming, error, and ignorance, as well as all the other categories of evil (which are called floods, bonds, ties, graspings, hindrances, inherent tendencies, fetters, and defilements, *Abhidhammattha-sangaha* 7.2).[245] Therefore, as the name indicates, the *arahant* is "worthy." Living in the state of arahantship *(arahatta)*, this person has already obtained enlightenment, is free from rebirth, and has attained *nirvana*.

Nirvana. When, after his experience of enlightenment *(bodhi)*, Śakyamuni Buddha preached his first sermon to the five ascetics at Isipatana, he declared that he had obtained the highest, universal *sambodhi* (full enlightenment), and he called himself the *sambuddha* and the *tathagata* (one who has come thus, or one who has gone thus, i.e., one who has reached such a [transcendent] state), and he also affirmed that the "middle path," which he proclaimed is that "which leads to insight, which leads to wisdom, which conduces to calm, to knowledge, to the *sambodhi*, to *nirvana* (*Mahavagga* 1.6.16–29). Later, in an address to his disciples at Śravasti, the Buddha recalled his long search and attainment in the words: "I sought after the consummate peace of *nirvana*, which knows neither rebirth nor decay, neither disease nor death, neither sorrow nor impurity—this I pursued, and this I won" (*Majjhima Nikaya* 1.167).²⁴⁶ Speaking further of the absolute reality of *nirvana* as the guarantee that it can be reached, he declared:

> Monks, there is a not-born, a not-become, a not-made, a not-compounded. Monks, if that unborn, not-become, not-made, not-compounded were not, there would be apparent no escape from this here that is born, become, made, compounded.
>
> But since, monks, there is a not-born, a not-become, a not-made, a not-compounded, therefore the escape from this here that is born, become, made, compounded, is apparent (*Udana* 8.3).

Such is the transcendent, to which the Buddha points, a concept corresponding, it may be held, to the concept of God in other religions.²⁴⁷

Since rebirth and decay, disease and death, sorrow and impurity, are all component parts of the unsatisfactoriness of human existence, called *dukkha*, *nirvana* is the "cessation" (*nirodha*) of unsatisfactoriness. By the Buddha's own description in the passages just quoted, *nirvana* is also "calm" and "consummate peace," and elsewhere he speaks of it as "bliss" and "boundless peace" (*Anguttara Nikaya* 3.214, 294).²⁴⁸

In his sermon on "the burning" (quoted above under *samudaya*), the Buddha said that life is like a fire burning with the flames of desire, wrath, and confusion; since, therefore, *nirvana* is where all such flames are extinguished, he appropriately calls *nirvana* "the cool," and says that the person who experiences it is enveloped in "cool" (*Anguttara Nikaya* 3.214; 4.29).²⁴⁹

Etymologically, the term *nirvana* (Pali *nibbana*) is derived from the Sanskrit *nir* (out) and the root *va* (to blow), and this suggests the blowing out of the flame, or the flickering out of the lamp, of unsatisfactory existence. Thus the Buddha describes the monk who approaches the end of his pilgrimage (*Anguttara Nikaya* 1.236):

> Him do they call the wakened of the world,
> Brave hero faring to the way's high end.
> To him when consciousness doth near its end,
> To him from craving utterly set free,
> Nibbana of the burning flame hath come,
> And to his heart release (and liberty).²⁵⁰

In terms of such a person's pilgrimage, *nirvana* is also described as "that quarter where in this long journeying he has not been before, where there is rest for all things made, a complete pouring away of all [rebirth] substance, a destruction of craving, a release from passion, an ending" (*Anguttara Nikaya* 3.163).²⁵¹

In illustration the Buddha tells parables. In one story there are two men, one unskilled and the other skilled in wayfaring. The former asks the way, and the latter tells him that ahead he will see the road divide into two, at which point he should leave the path on the left and take the path on the right. Thereafter he will see a thick forest, then a great marshy swamp, then a steep precipice, and finally a delightful stretch of level ground. The unskilled man, the Buddha explains, represents the many people. The skilled man is an *arahant*. The divided way is the state of wavering. The left-hand path is the false eightfold path of wrong views, wrong intention, and so on; the right-hand path is the true eightfold path of right views, and so on. The thick forest is a name for ignorance. The great marshy swamp is a name for feelings and desires. The steep precipice is a name for vexation and despair. The delightful stretch of level ground is a name for *nibbana* (*Samyutta*

Nikaya 3.108).²⁵² In another parable, which pictures the cycle of birth-death-rebirth (*samsara*) as the ocean of existence, there is a man who, fleeing in terror of snakes and murderous foes, comes to a great broad water where there is no boat nor any bridge. He, however, gathers sticks, branches, and the like, makes a raft and, working with hands and feet, crosses safely to the other shore. The snakes are elemental forces, the murderous foes are factors of grasping and desire, the great broad water is the flood of *dukkha,* the raft is the Buddhist eightfold path, and "the further shore . . . secure and safe from fears—that is a name for *nibbana*" (*Samyutta Nikaya* 4.173–175). So also the Buddha's disciple Sariputta, being asked by a Wanderer for a definition of *nirvana,* replied: "The destruction of lust, the destruction of hatred, the destruction of illusion . . . is called *nibbana*" (*Samyutta Nikaya* 4.250–251).²⁵³

That the attainment of *nirvana* is possible in this present life (like *jivan-mukti,* "living release," in Hinduism), is shown by the experience not only of Śakyamuni Buddha himself but also by that of others. Thus when the Buddha preached to his five former associates at Isipatana, and they were converted, it is said of them that they

> . . . being liable to birth because of self . . . won the unborn, the uttermost security from the bonds—*nibbana;* being liable to ageing because of self . . . won the unageing . . . being liable to decay because of self . . . won the undecaying . . . being liable to dying because of self . . . won the undying . . . being liable to sorrow because of self . . . won the unsorrowing . . . being liable to stain because of self . . . won the stainless, the uttermost security from the bonds—*nibbana* (*Majjhima Nikaya* 1.173).²⁵⁴

The one who makes this attainment here and now is called a "winner of *nibbana* in this very life" (*Samyutta Nikaya* 2.18; 3.162; 4.140),²⁵⁵ and, as noted above, is named an *arahant* (worthy). In the course of the Buddha's ministry many of his followers made this attainment, until with him on one occasion at Kapilavastu, for example, was "a great band of the brethren, about five hundred of them, all being *arahants*" (*Samyutta Nikaya* 1.25).²⁵⁶

Serenity and equanimity are characteristics of the *arahant*. When the industrialist Anathapindika first visited the Buddha at Rajagriha he had himself spent a restless night, and he saluted the Buddha in the morning with the question, "Lord, has the Blessed One rested happily?" to which the Buddha, calling himself an *arahant,* replied (*Samyutta Nikaya* 1.212):

> Surely at all times happily doth rest
> The *arahant* in whom all fire's extinct.
> Who cleaveth not to sensuous desires,
> Cool all his being, rid of all the germs
> That bring new life, all cumbrances cut out,
> Subdued the pain and pining of the heart,
> Calm and serene he resteth happily
> For in his mind he hath attained to peace.²⁵⁷

Speaking to a *brahmana* at Śravasti, whom the text calls "pridestiff," the Buddha describes the *arahants* as "the saintly cool" (*Samyutta Nikaya* 1.178).²⁵⁸ In a discourse to a young man at Rajagriha named Pukkusati, the Buddha pictures the person who has reached this state as completely calmed within (*paccattam yeva parinibbayati,* literally "fully blown out within"). If such a person experiences a pleasant, unpleasant, or neutral feeling, he knows that it is impermanent and that he is not bound by it. He knows also that upon the dissolution of the body after the life-principle has come to an end, all will "become cool" (*sitibhuta,* a term often combined with *nibbuta,* gone out, extinguished), just as the flame of a lamp goes out when oil and wick are exhausted (*Majjhima Nikaya* 3.244–245).[259]

So in distinction from *nirvana* (Pali *nibbana*) experienced already in this life, when the Buddha or an *arahant* dies he enters the final *nirvana,* and the phrase "attained final *nibbana*" is used, for example, of the Buddha, of the venerable Bakkula, of the venerable Punna (*Majjhima Nikaya* 2.90, 162; 3.7, 127–128, 269). Strictly speaking, in Buddhist terminology *nirvana* is the state, and *parinirvana* (*parinibbana*) is the attaining of the state, while the distinction between *nirvana* at enlightenment and *nirvana* at death is expressed as *saupadisesa* and *anupadisesa.*[260]

Concluding its long section on the four great planes of life, on rebirth, *karma,* and death, the *Abhidhammattha-sangaha* (5.16) summarizes in memorable form the whole picture of the stream of becoming and the ultimate goal of *nirvana:*

> Birth, life-flux, processes of thought, decease,
> Both here and in existence yet to be,
> Birth, life again . . . and thus incessantly
> Doth this conscious continuum turn round.
> But the Enlightened, pondering release
> From this that passeth ever by, have found—
> Steadfast down the long years in piety,
> All bonds of cleaving severed utterly—
> The Path sublime, where death and rebirth cease;
> And they, so faring, shall attain to Peace.[261]

Sangha

The Buddhist community (*sangha,* literally, gathering) is made up in the narrower sense of the monk (*bhikkhu,* Sanskrit *bhikshu,* religious mendicant) and the nun (*bhikkhuni*); in the broader sense it includes the layman (*upasaka*) and laywoman (*upasika*). Basically applicable to all are five precepts much like those also held up in Hinduism and Jainism—as mentioned earlier—to refrain from killing, stealing, unchastity, lying, and drinking intoxicating liquors.

Monastic Order and Ordination

The ordination of monks was conducted first by the Buddha himself, then as the monks themselves went far afield he authorized them to perform ordination for others. He said (*Mahavagga* 1.12.3–4):

> I grant you, O *bhikkhus,* this permission: Confer henceforth in the different regions and in the different countries the *pabbajja* and *upasampada* ordinations yourselves [on those who desire to receive them]. And you ought, O *bhikkhus,* to confer the *pabbajja* and *upasampada* ordinations in this way: Let him [who desires to receive the ordination], first have his hair and beard cut off; let him put on yellow robes, adjust his upper robe so as to cover one shoulder, salute the feet of the *bhikkhus* [with his head], and sit down squatting; then let him raise his joined hands and tell him to say [three times]: "I take my refuge in the Buddha, I take my refuge in the *dhamma,* I take my refuge in the *sangha.*" I prescribe, O *bhikkhus,* the *pabbajja* and *upasampada* ordinations consisting in the three times repeated declaration of taking refuge.[262]

The *pabbajja* (Sanskrit *pravrajya,* leaving the world, adopting the ascetic life) is the initial act of admission to the order by which the person becomes a novice (*samanera, śramanera*); the *upasampada* is the ordination by which one becomes a monk or nun with the privileges and responsibilities of a full member of the order. Admission is open to all who wish, both men and women and without distinction of race or caste, except for some exclusions, e.g., of those with contagious diseases, soldiers, robbers, and slaves (*Mahavagga* 1.39–47).[263] Admission of young novices (*samaneras*) to the *pabbajja* requires the consent of parents and an age of at least a full seven years. Admission of monks (*bhikkhus*) to the *upasampada* ordination requires an age of twenty years or more, for reasons which the Buddha explained thus (*Mahavagga* 1.49.6): "A person under twenty years, O *bhikkhus*, cannot endure coldness and heat, hunger and thirst, vexation by gadflies and gnats, by storms and sun-heat, and by reptiles; [he cannot endure] abusive, offensive language; he is not able to bear bodily pains which are severe, sharp, grievous, disagreeable, unpleasant, and destructive to life."[264]

The novice is under the guidance of a preceptor (*upajjhaya*) in respect of personal conduct, and of a teacher (*acariya*) in respect of education. He is bound by ten precepts, which require abstinence from (1) destroying life, (2) stealing, (3) unchastity, (4) lying, (5) drinking intoxicating liquors, (6) eating at forbidden times, (7) dancing, singing, music, and seeing spectacles, (8) use of garlands, perfumes, unguents, ornaments, and finery, (9) use of high or broad beds, and (10) acceptance of gold or silver (*Mahavagga* 1.56).[265]

The monk who receives full ordination assumes responsibility not only for the foregoing requirements but for no less than 227 rules in all, and these are set forth in the work called the *Patimokkha* (Sanskrit *Pratimoksha*), which is the nucleus of the Vinayapitaka.[266]

Nuns. The reception of women into the order as nuns only came about after an initial reluctance of the Buddha was overcome by the intercession of Ananda on behalf of Mahapajapati Gotami. This lady was the younger sister of Queen Maya (Mahamaya), the mother of the Buddha, and like Mahamaya was married to King Suddhodana. When Mahamaya died seven days after the birth of Siddartha, Mahapajapati looked after the child and nursed him. When the Buddha first returned to his father's palace after his own enlightenment his son Rahula was ordained (and later became an *arahant*), and Mahapajapati herself heard the Buddha's preaching and became a stream-enterer (*sotapanna*). When King Suddhodana died Mahapajapati resolved to renounce the world. When the Buddha visited Kapilavastu to settle the dispute of the Sakyans and the Koliyans over the water of the Rohini River, five hundred young Sakyan men joined the order, and their wives, led by Mahapajapati, asked to be ordained as nuns. The Buddha refused, and went on to Vaiśali, a distance of 200 miles (322 km.). The women cut their hair, put on yellow robes, and followed on foot. When they reached the Buddha's monastery in Vaiśali, Ananda saw Mahapajapati standing outside, and appealed to the Buddha:

> "Behold, Lord, Mahapajapati Gotami is standing outside under the entrance porch, with swollen feet and covered with dust, sad and sorrowful, weeping and in tears, inasmuch as the Blessed One does not permit women to renounce their homes and enter the homeless state under the doctrine and discipline proclaimed by the Blessed One. It were well, Lord, if women were to have permission granted to them to do as she desires."

After continuing to demur, the Buddha later acknowledged that women are capable of attaining arahantship, and finally granted them admission to the order, but subject to eight strict conditions. Also he predicted that with the admission of women his discipline would only last for five hundred years, whereas otherwise it would have stood fast for a thousand years. As for Mahapajapati, it was under her that Yaśodhara (wife of the Buddha and mother of Rahula, herself also known as Rahulamata) became a nun, and all of these—Yaśodhara, Mahapajaptai, and Mahapajapati's five hundred companions—eventually became *arahants*. As binding on all the *bhikkhunis* many special rules are contained in the Vinaya (*Culavagga* 10). In the course of time, however, some limitations were again imposed and in Theravada Buddhist countries valid ordination of women as nuns is regarded as having ended in 456 C.E. and, while they may still take some of the vows and even wear the monastic robe, they are, strictly speaking, only lay members of the community.[267]

Uposatha. In the Indian calendar there are twelve lunar months in the year (Table 11.4), and the discrepancy with the solar year is solved by various calculations and intercalations. The lunar month (*masa*) begins with the new moon and consists of 30 lunar days called *tithi* (equivalent to 29 and a fraction solar days, but for practical purposes each taken as beginning at sunrise). Each month is divided into two halves, each consisting of 15 lunar days. The 15 days following the night of the new moon, when the moon is waxing, is the bright half (*sudi*) of the month and is auspicious; the corresponding period following the night of the full moon, when the moon is waning, is the dark half (*badi*) of the month and is inauspicious.

In the month, in imitation of the practice of other sects and at the specific suggestion of King Bimbisara, the Buddha adopted for his community the observance of a weekly holy day, to be observed on the eighth and fourteenth (or fifteenth) day of each lunar half-month, i.e., on the new- and full-moon day, and on the eighth day following the new- and full-moon. This day is called the *uposatha*, and is used for rest, fasting, meditation, and preaching. On two of these four days in the month the *Patimokkha* is recited, and the members of the order confess any transgressions which they have committed (*Mahavagga* 2).[268]

Vassa. In the Indian year there are three four-month seasons, summer, rainy season, and winter, and the beginning of each was anciently celebrated with a sacrificial festival on the full-moon day of the months Phalguna, Asadha, and Karttika (or, as the year dictated, a month later in Caitra, Sravana, and Margaśirsha). It was the custom of the Buddha during his ministry to wander during

TABLE 11.4.
LUNAR MONTHS IN THE INDIAN CALENDAR

Name	Approximate Equivalent in Western Months
1. Caitra	Mar.–Apr.
2. Vaiśakha	Apr.–May
3. Jyeshtha	May–June
4. Ashadha	June–July
5. Śravana	July–Aug.
6. Bhadrapada	Aug.–Sept.
7. Aśvina	Sept.–Oct.
8. Karttika	Oct.–Nov.
9. Margaśirsha	Nov.–Dec.
10. Pausha	Dec.–Jan.
11. Magha	Jan.–Feb.
12. Phalguna	Feb.–Mar.

the summer and winter, but to stay for the most part in one place in the rainy season. In the pursuit of their missions, however, his *bhikkhus* went at first on their travels alike during winter, summer, and the rainy season, and this annoyed many people, who said that they were "crushing the green herbs, hurting vegetable life, and destroying the life of many small things," whereas the ascetics of certain other sects, and even the birds, were in the habit of retiring during the rainy season and arranging places for themselves to live in during that time. In accommodation to contemporary custom, therefore, even as in the institution of the *uposatha*, the Buddha instructed his followers to observe a rainy season retreat. This is called the *vassa* (Sanskrit *varshika*), and is held for a longer (four-month) or shorter (three-month) period, beginning at the full moon of Ashada or (depending upon the year) at the full moon of Sravana, and in either case closing with the full moon of Karttika. During this rain retreat the monks cease their wandering and make their residence in their home monastery (*Mahavagga* 3).[269]

Pavarana. At the end of the rain retreat, on the fourteenth and fifteenth days of the bright half of the month, there is a ceremony called the *pavarana* (*pravarana*). In this ceremony each monk asks his companions to charge him with any offence of which they may think he is guilty, and if he is guilty he is to make atonement (*Mahavagga* 4).[270]

Laity. In the broader sense the Buddhist *sangha* includes along with the monk and nun also the layman (*upasaka*) and laywoman (*upasika*), and both the Buddha himself and also his monks won large numbers of such lay disciples (e.g., *Majjhima Nikaya* 1.490–491; 3.269).[271] When the Buddha was asked how a person becomes a lay disciple, he replied (*Anguttara Nikaya* 4.219–220): "When . . . he has found refuge in the Buddha, found refuge in *dhamma*, found refuge in the *sangha*, then he is a lay disciple."

And when the Buddha was asked further how a lay disciple would live virtuously, he said: "When . . . a lay disciple abstains from taking life; abstains from taking what is not given him; abstains from lustful and evil indulgences; abstains from lying; and abstains from spirituous intoxicants, the cause of indolence—then a lay disciple is virtuous."[272]

These requirements are identical with the first five of the ten precepts for a novice, and "if possible" all ten of the precepts are recommended even for the lay person (*Visuddhimagga* 1.15).[273] At any rate in the lay adherent's observance of the *uposatha*, for that period of time at least three more precepts are added, namely, (1) to abstain from food from after noon of one day until the morning of the next; (2) to abstain from adornment of the body or participation in inappropriate shows or sports; and (3) to abstain from the use of a comfortable bed or seat—and thus most of the remaining precepts of the novice are taken on for the *uposatha* period (*Anguttara Nikaya* 4.248–251).[274]

Living in the world, the lay adherent engages in the usual activities of the world, but there are five trades which ought not to be plied by a lay disciple: trade in weapons, in human beings, in animal flesh, in spirits, and in poison (*Anguttara Nikaya* 3.207–208).[275] With the fruit of acceptable labor, the lay adherent is then able to do meritorious works, for example, by giving to the monastic members of the order such needful things as robes, alms-food, lodging, and requisites and medicines for use in sickness. It is also meritorious in the lay adherent to be possessed of loyalty to the Buddha, the *dhamma*, and the *sangha*, and to be possessed of the virtues of the Buddhist way of life which lead to concentration of the mind. In fact, in practice in the Buddhist world it is possible for the lay adherent to engage for a time in the monastic life and then to return to the realm of the laity.

Thus there is reciprocity in the entire *sangha,* the contribution of the lay adherent making it possible for the monastic member to attain unbounded concentration and to render services of many sorts, while the attainment and activity of the monastic member bring benefit to the lay adherent and indeed to the whole world. So the monk and nun make progress on their chosen way, and the lay adherent also wins many a "flood of merit, a flood of things profitable, bringing happiness, giving the best things, whose fruit is happiness, leading to the heaven world, leading to what is dear, delightful and pleasant, to profit and happiness." The extent of the flood of merit is indeed incalculable, and the life of the person so benefited is not in vain (*Anguttara Nikaya* 2.54–57):

> To boundless mighty ocean, mighty pool,
> Fearsome, the resting-place of divers gems,
> As rivers bearing multitudes of men
> Flow broadly down and to that ocean come;
> Just so to him that giveth food, drink, clothes,
> Who bed and seat and coverlet provides,
> Torrents of merit flood that mortal wise,
> As rivers, bearing water, reach the main.
>
> Whoso hath faith in the *tathagata*
> Unwavering and firm, whose life is good,
> Praised by the Ariyans and dear to them;
> Whoso is likewise loyal to the Order
> And looks straight forth—"He is not poor" they say,
> "Not [lived] in vain the life of such a man."
> So let the wise man cultivate [these four]
> Faith, virtue, piety, and seeing *dhamma,*
> Bearing the Buddha's message in his mind.[276]

12

EARLY HISTORY AND LITERATURE OF MAHAYANA AND VAJRAYANA BUDDHISM

RISE OF SCHOOLS

In the preceding chapter it has been noted that when the Second Buddhist Council, held at Vaiśali one hundred years after the death of the Buddha, decided against the Vajjian monks, those who were adjudged heretical separated themselves and founded the school which was called the Mahasanghika (great community), and from this arose more schools until there were eighteen in all (and subsequently even more). Likewise the *Kathavatthu*, composed in refutation of false doctrines by Moggaliputta-Tissa at the time of the Third Buddhist Council at Pataliputra under Aśoka (coronation 269 B.C.E.), discusses many points which were under controversy with the Mahasanghikas and many other dissident schools.

So when the Chinese Buddhist pilgrims Fa Xian (Fa-Hien) (399–414 C.E.), Xuan Zang (Hiuen Tsiang) (629–645 C.E.), and Yi Jing (I-tsing) (671–695 C.E.) came to India, the records of their travels also speak of not a few of these and other schools. In addition to naming such individual schools, however, they also use the terms Mahayana (great vehicle) and Hinayana (little vehicle), and sometimes designate individual schools as belonging to one or the other of these two larger groupings. In this usage the term "vehicle" (*yana*) conveys the idea of a raft or ship to carry persons across the ocean of this world of suffering to the other shore of *nirvana*. The Mahayana is "great" (*maha*) in the thought of its adherents because of the universality of its intention to provide for the salvation of all beings; the Hinayana is called "little" (*hina*) because, at least in the view of the Mahayanists, it is of narrower outlook and can provide a way for only a relatively few to reach the goal soon. Yet the two names hardly have strictly fixed limits, and those who belonged to the Mahayana and those who belonged to the Hinayana, so called, were all within the general framework of Buddhism which, in the *Kathavatthu* (21.1), is called "our religion (*sasana*)," and is clearly distinguished as a whole from the doctrines of "many other teachers not belonging to the *sasana*."[1]

In his travels Fa Xian finds that in some places all the monks are students of the Hinayana, in some places most are students of the Mahayana, and in some places they are students of both the Mahayana and the Hinayana. At Pataliputra, for example, he finds both a very grand Mahayana monastery and also a Hinayana monastery; in the Mahayana institution he finds and transcribes a copy of the Vinaya, containing the Mahasanghika rules; and also (apparently in the other monastery) he gets a transcript of the Sarvastivada rules.[2]

Xuan Zang also finds that in some places the monks mostly study the Hinayana, in some places all study the Mahayana, and in some places they study equally the Mahayana and the Hinayana.[3] He names a number of the individual schools, and sometimes indicates the larger groupings to which they belong (e.g., the Sthaviras—who must here be some later development of the old school of the "elders"—belong, he says, to the Mahayana;[4] the Sarvastivadins,[5] the Mahiśasakas,[6] the Sammatiyas,[7] and others belong to the Hinayana). As for himself, Xuan Zang is an effective advocate of the Mahayana.

Yi Jing recalls the story of how King Bimbisara once saw in a dream that a piece of cloth was torn, and a gold stick broken, each into eighteen fragments. Being frightened, the king asked the Buddha to interpret what he had seen. The Buddha explained that more than a hundred years after his own attainment of *nirvana*, in the time of a king named Aśoka, the Buddha's teaching would be split into eighteen schools, yet all eighteen would agree on the goal of final liberation, therefore Bimbisara need not be afraid.

Of the individual schools (*nikayas*) Yi Jing names four, the Mahasanghikanikaya (school of the great brotherhood), the Sthaviranikaya (school of the elders), the Mulasarvastivadanikaya (fundamental school which affirms the existence of all things), and the Sammitinikaya (school of the right measure), but says that "which of the four schools should be grouped with the Mahayana or with the Hinayana is not determined."

Concerning the Mahayana and the Hinayana, Yi Jing defines the two large groups in the statement: "Those who worship the *bodhisattvas* and read the Mahayana *sutras* are called the Mahayanists, while those who do not perform these are called the Hinayanists." Probably still referring to the two large groups he says that, in spite of their differences, both conform to truth and lead to *nirvana*. "For, if we act conformably with any of these doctrines, we are enabled to attain the Other Shore, and if we turn away from them, we remain drowned, as it were, in the ocean of transmigration." As to geographical distribution of the two groups, Yi Jing says that the Buddhists in China devote themselves to the Mahayana, while those in Northern India and the islands of the Southern Sea generally belong to the Hinayana.[8]

Sarvastivadins

Of the individual schools, that of the Sarvastivada (all-is doctrine) appears to have been the most prominent. Fa Xian says that it was followed in China as well as in Pataliputra, the latter city being where he obtained Sarvastivada texts.[9] Xuan Zang encounters the Sarvastivadins on his route all the way from Central Asia (before he reaches Bamiyan) to the Punjab, and in Western and Central India, and even reports their existence in Persia; also he specifically identifies them as belonging to the Hinayana.[10] Yi Jing himself belonged to the Sarvastivada school, and is careful to state that his own record is in accordance with this school and no other; in North India, he says, all belong to the Sarvastivadanikaya, and it has been almost universally adopted in the islands of the Southern Sea, but in South India and in the Sinhala island (Sri Lanka) all belong to the Sthaviranikaya.[11]

In the *Kathavatthu* (1.2; 1.6; 11.6)[12] the Theravadin disputant directs three questions to the Sarvastivadins (Pali, Sabbatthivadins)—Can an *arahant* fall away from arahantship? Does everything exist persistently? Is simple continuity of consciousness equivalent to concentration of mind (*samadhi*)? All of these questions would be answered in the affirmative by the Sarvastivadins (and in some cases by some of the other schools), against the negative and orthodox opinions of the Theravadins. But if only such points were at issue between the two schools, their basic outlook must have been much the same, and it is probably the case that the Theravada (or Sthaviranikaya, as Yi Jing calls it) of South India and Sri Lanka was at least roughly paralleled by the Sarvastivada of North India and farther regions. Broadly speaking, both the Sarvastivadins and the Theravadins, and doubtless many other of the eighteen and more early schools, may be considered to belong to the Hinayana.

In North India and Central Asia the language of the Sarvastivada was Sanskrit, and this school had, in fact, a collection of accepted scriptures of its own, composed in Sanskrit. Unlike the well-preserved Pali canon, this canon is known only from fragments of manuscripts, quotations in other Buddhist Sanskrit works, and translations into Tibetan, Chinese, and other languages. From these remnants, however, it is possible to ascertain that the wording and arrangement of texts in the Sanskrit canon was very similar in many points to the Pali canon, but that there were also not a few differences. From this it is surmised that both canons derive from a common source, perhaps a lost Magadhi canon, from which the Pali texts branched off in one part of India and, later, the Sanskrit in another region.

An example of a Sanskrit text (with translations in Chinese, Tibetan, and other languages) which probably belonged to the Sarvastivadins is the *Catushparishat Sutra,* contained in manuscripts found in East Turkestan and in Gilgit.[13] The name of the work refers to the "fourfold order" (*catushparishat*), i.e., the Buddhist community consisting of monks and nuns, and male and female lay disciples, and the account extends from the enlightenment of the Buddha to the conversion of his two main disciples, Śariputra and Maudgalyayana, the two here called Upatishya and Kolita.

At the outset (Introduction) the *bodhisattva* (i.e., Śakyamuni before he became the Buddha) is staying on the bank of the river Nairanjana (Neranjara) at the foot of the tree of enlightenment. There he engages in methodical meditation on the factors related to enlightenment, and attains the six higher knowledges (*abhijna*), namely, the knowledge of supernatural power; the recollection of his own former existences; the divine ear to hear sounds both human and non-human, both near and far; the divine eye to see beings in various stages of existence; the knowledge of the thoughts of other beings; and the knowledge of the four noble truths. Having attained enlightenment, the Buddha then (Ch. 1–3) sits in the meditation posture for seven days, experiencing the joy and happiness of liberation, and receives alms from two merchants, Tripusa and Bhallika, who become his first lay disciples. When (Ch. 4–5) the Buddha becomes ill from the honey and milk which the merchants gave him, Mara, the evil one, tries to persuade him to enter at once into the complete extinction of *nirvana,* but the Buddha repudiates the suggestion; then Śakra, the king of the gods, brings the Buddha fruits which cure his illness. Afterward (Ch. 6), at the abode of the *naga* king Mucalinda, the Buddha is caught out in an unseasonable rain for seven days, during which time Mucalinda wraps his coils around him and makes a large hood over him for protection. Returning (Ch. 7) to the tree of enlightenment, the Buddha reflects on "origination by dependence," and decides to preach the truth (*dharma*) which he has obtained. This he does in the Deer Park at Varanasi to the five ascetics who were his former associates, and explains the four noble truths and the doctrines of no-self (*anatman*), impermanence (*anitya*), and suffering (*dukkha*). Thereafter there were many conversions, of Yasa and other sons of leading families in Varanasi (Ch. 16–21), of prominent men and women and many ascetics, including the aged and esteemed Urubilvakaśyapa, in Gaya and vicinity (Ch. 22–26), and of King Bimbisara, Upatishya, and Kolita at Rajagriha (Ch. 27–28).

Mahasanghikas

In the account of the Second Buddhist Council at Vaiśali a century after the death of the Buddha, we learn that at that time the Mahasanghika (great community) broke away and became the first schismatic school, and that from them arose the Gokulika and Ekavyoharika schools, and thereafter yet many more (*Mahavamsa* 5.1–13).[14] In his time Fa Xian obtained in the Mahayana monastery in Pataliputra a copy of the Vinaya containing the Mahasanghika rules, and in the record of Xuan Zang the Mahasanghikas are named along with the Sarvastivadins and others in a group of five "schools of the Vinaya," and are mentioned as known in Swat, Kashmir, and Afghanistan.[15]

The naming of the Mahasanghikas along with the Sarvastivadins may suggest that, like the Sarvastivadins, the Mahasanghikas were considered to belong to the Hinayana. But as they appear in the *Kathavatthu* the Mahasanghikas represent at least some views which are like those of the Mahayana. A question at issue, for example, is whether the Buddhas can persistently pervade all four quarters of the firmament, the nadir, the zenith, the realms above, and the realms below, and on this, as portrayed by their Theravadin interrogator, the Mahasanghikas answer in an affirmative but also self-contradictory way (*Kathavatthu* 21.6).[16]

Mahavastu. The Mahasanghikas are directly represented by a large work which is written in "mixed Sanskrit" (a Middle Indian dialect assimilated to Sanskrit), and named the *Mahavastu* (great subject).[17] This work states that it is based on a redaction of the Vinayapitaka, "made by the noble Mahasanghikas, the Lokottaravadins of the Middle Country" (1.2);[18] thus, the Lokottaravadins may be recognized as a subdivision (probably much like the Gokulikas) of the Mahasanghikas. The *Mahavastu* gives a biography of the Buddha, elaborated with many legends and stories of miracles. In respect of the Buddha's historical existence, the account is much like the materials in the *Mahavagga*, and in respect of his previous existences as a *bodhisattva* it is like the *Nidanakatha* and the *Jataka*.

In the Theravada literature there was already not only the idea of the many former births of the *bodhisattva*, but also the belief in a plurality of Buddhas (twenty-four in the *Buddhavamsa*, as noted above). Here now in the *Mahavastu* these aspects of belief are greatly expanded. Five hundred Buddhas are named (1.136–141),[19] and in all there are said to be "innumerable countless thousands of *kotis* (1 *koti* = 10 million) of Buddhas and their companies of disciples" (1.243).[20] Likewise ten *bhumis* are elaborated in the life of a *bodhisattva* (*bhumi* is literally "ground," and is used here for a career or stage of development of a *bodhisattva*) (1.63ff.).[21] Most distinctively—and giving rise to the name of the Lokottaravadin school—a docetic doctrine is affirmed according to which the Buddhas are transcendental (*lokottara*, exalted above the world) beings, who only seem to conform to the habits and conditions of the world. Although they appear to be born of a mother and father, to eat and drink, to assume the four postures of the body (walking, standing, sitting, lying down), to experience disease and old age, all of this is only in appearance, and in reality they are supramundane.

For example: "They take on the semblance of being old, but for them there is no old age, for the Conquerors have the gift of overcoming it. This appearance of old age is mere conformity with the world." Furthermore, such personages remain in the world of their own free will, and not because any remaining *karma* of theirs has compelled their rebirth. "Although they could suppress the working of *karma,* the Conquerors let it become manifest and conceal their sovereign power. This is mere conformity with the world" (1.169).[22]

In contrast with the *arahant* in the Theravada, who has attained *nirvana* and is beyond the mortal state, the Buddha of the *Mahavastu,* who is still present in the world (at least in appearance, even if his true reality is exalted above the world), can be the object of worship. Such is the purity of such a great personage that to worship him, e.g., with flowers, or just to walk around his *stupa* reverentially, is to gain much merit on the way to enlightenment. And since the presence of the Buddha is thus a benefit to others, those who worship him should seek their own enlightenment in order to be of help to others: "He who, having turned his thoughts to enlightenment for the sake of all living things, reverentially salutes (literally, keep to one's right in going around) the *stupa* of the Savior of the world, becomes everywhere in all his lives as he fares on the way to enlightenment, mindful, thoughtful, virtuous, and assured" (2.362).[23]

By such points of emphasis as these—the recognition and worship of so many Buddhas and *bodhisattvas,* and the ideal of seeking enlightenment and remaining in the world "for the sake of all living things"—the teachings of the Mahasanghikas and of the Lokottaravadins in the *Mahavastu* appear as forerunners of the Mahayana.

In the long run and especially after the Muslim invasions of India, of the eighteen early sects only the Theravada—from the outside called Hinayana—survived, to become the national religion of Sri Lanka, Burma and Thailand; but from the tendencies already evident in the Mahasanghikas and the *Mahavastu* the Mahayana developed to become the prevailing form of Buddhism in Nepal, Tibet, China, Korea, and Japan. Yet as the eighteen traditional schools of the early days were all embraced within one larger movement ("our religion," *sasana*), so also the Theravada and the Mahayana both belong to the inclusive Buddhist fellowship.

MAHAYANA

The Mahayana is characterized, as Yi Jing said, by the worship of the *bodhisattvas* and the reading of the Mahayana *sutras.*

Bodhisattvas

At the outset Śakyamuni Buddha may have spoken of *sambodhi* (full enlightenment) even more than of *nirvana,* and even as he himself had pity on his fellow-creatures he sent his disciples out to "wander . . . for the welfare of the many, out of compassion for the world" (*Mahavagga* 1.11.1).[24] Also the Theravada scriptures included the *Jataka* stories about the previous existences of the Buddha as a *bodhisattva,* when he did many acts, often of a self-sacrificing sort, for others.

But at least from the point of view of the Mahayana, the ultimate aim in the Hinayana appeared to be self-centered and world-abandoning, because an *arahant* is one who has destroyed his own pain and suffering, and the *nirvana* which he enters is an inconceivable sphere which can have no touch with this world of conditioned phenomena. Thus in the *Milinda Panha* (19, 31) of the Hinayana, for example, these answers are given to questions as to the reason for the renunciation practiced by the members of the Buddhist order, and as to the highest good at which the members aim:

> "Our renunciation . . . is for the sake of being able to live in righteousness, and in spiritual calm."

> "Our renunciation is to the end that this sorrow may perish away, and that no further sorrow may arise; the complete passing away, without cleaving to the world, is our highest aim."[25]

In texts of the Hinayana and texts intermediate between the Hinayana and the Mahayana we also encounter two figures in particular, namely, those of the *śravaka* and of the *pratyekabuddha*. The *śravaka* is a "hearer," i.e., a disciple of the Buddha, who may be a stream-enterer, a once-returner, a never-returner, or an *arahant*, and who upon reaching his goal causes others to hear that he has done so. The *pratyekabuddha* is a "solitary realizer," i.e., a disciple of the Buddha who is enlightened by and for himself alone. He is called a *buddha* because he has reached enlightenment; he is solitary because in the end he has made the attainment by his own effort and without a teacher; and he does not undertake to preach to others.[26]

Illustrative of these concepts we find already in the *Majjhima Nikaya* (3.68–69, 254–255),[27] for example, the names of thirteen *paccekabuddhas* (the Pali form of *pratyekabuddha*) who lived once upon a time on the Isigili mountain near Rajagriha, and in a list of offerings graded in worth and merit according to the worth and merit of the recipient, the recipient ranges from an animal to an ordinary person to a once-returner, continuing finally to a *paccekabuddha* and to a *tathagata* or full *buddha*. Likewise in the *Mahavastu* (1.301) it is explained that "whenever *buddhas* appear in the world, *pratyekabuddhas* also appear, who, splendid in their silence and of great power, live in loneliness like a rhinoceros, train each his own self, and finally pass away," and many of these personages are introduced in the course of the narrative, with a characteristic description of the demeanor of one of them as follows:

> He was courteous of manners, both in approaching and in taking his leave, in looking forwards and backwards, in extending and withdrawing his hand, and in carrying his cloak, bowl, and robe. He was like a *naga*. He had accomplished his task; his faculties were turned inwards; his mind was not turned outwards. He was unwavering as one who had achieved harmony with *dharma*. He did not look before him farther than the length of a plough.[28]

From the point of view of the Mahayana, therefore, the ideals of the *arahant*, the *śravaka*, and the *pratyekabuddha*, all tend toward individualism and withdrawal from the world, while in the Mahayana the early Buddhist ideas of helpfulness toward all beings are reemphasized, and the concept of the *bodhisattva* is greatly amplified, with the multiplication of these beings, and the teaching that they are above all characterized by compassion for all sentient beings.

The title of the *bodhisattva* (Pali *bodhisatta*) contains the term *bodhi* or "enlightenment," together with the term *sattva* (*satta*), which is capable of various interpretations, among which "a living being" is perhaps here the most likely, yielding for *bodhisattva* the meaning of an "enlightenment being" (also *mahasattva*, great being), i.e., a being whose ultimate aim is to become a *buddha* by achieving complete *bodhi* (enlightenment, *sambodhi*, full enlightenment, *anuttara* [nothing higher] *samyak* [perfect] *bodhi*), but whose present desire is not yet to enter *nirvana* but to remain in touch with the world in order to help other beings to liberation.[29]

So already in the *Mahavastu* (1.61) one who aspires to become a *bodhisattva* expresses himself thus:

> "When beings come to be without refuge, support, protection, shelter, and succour, when they become characterized by fickleness, malice, and folly, when they live in accordance with wrong standards of conduct, and generally go to crowd the worlds of woe, then may I awake to the unsurpassed perfect enlightenment. May I do so for the benefit and welfare of mankind, out of compassion for the world, for the sake of the multitude, for the good of *devas* and men."[30]

Likewise in the description (*Mahavastu* 1.136, 142) of the progress of the *bodhisattva* through the ten *bhumis* (stages of development), it is said of them that as they advance from the seventh *bhumi* to the eighth "there arises in them . . . a heart that is set on the great compassion (*maha karuna*)," and that in the tenth *bhumi* they have wonderful and marvelous attributes which are not shared by *pratyekabuddhas* or lesser personages. The *Mahavastu* (2.362) also alludes, therefore, to three *yanas* (vehicles, also translatable as ways or careers), and in this respect the three are the *śravakayana* (the way of the *śravaka*), the *pratyekabuddhayana* (the way of the *pratyekabuddha*), and the *bodhisattvayana* (the way of the *bodhisattva*). Since the *bodhisattva* seeks to become a *buddha,* with supreme and perfect omniscience, this is also called the *buddhayana,* the vehicle or way or career of the *buddha.* In the Mahayana it is plain that the last way is the supreme way, and the sign of belonging to it is that one possesses great compassion for all sentient beings.[31]

In the Mahayana work called the *Saddharmapundarika* it is represented that Śakyamuni Buddha taught all three of the foregoing ways or vehicles as an "expedient" by which he wished to attract people to his wisdom. To illustrate, he tells a parable (Ch. 3).[32] The house of a rich man was on fire, but his sons were at play and oblivious to the father's command to leave the building. Therefore, as an expedient to gain their attention and lead them to go outside, the father told the children that there were toys outside—sheep-carts, deer-carts, and bullock-carts. These were toys which the boys had long wished to have, and they went out of the burning building quickly. In the same manner the Buddha saved all living beings from the burning house of the world by the "expedient" of offering them the teaching of the "three vehicles," the *śravaka*-vehicle, the *pratyekabuddha*-vehicle, and the *buddha*-vehicle. So those who seek *nirvana* with strenuous efforts to get out of the world are called *śravakas,* and may be likened to the sons who left the burning house to get the sheep-carts. Those who seek independently-attained wisdom, and wish tranquility and seclusion, for the sake of their own complete *nirvana,* are called *pratyekabuddhas,* and may be likened to the sons who got the deer-carts. Those who seek independently-attained wisdom, and wish to give peace to all living beings out of compassion for them, for the benefit of the whole world, are called *bodhisattvas, mahasattvas,* and persons of the "great vehicle," and may be likened to the sons who left the burning house in order to get the bullock-carts. Later in the *Saddharmapundarika* (Ch. 7)[33] it is again said that the Buddhas teach the three vehicles only as an expedient, for there is only one *buddha*-vehicle, and the other two are only spoken of in order to help creatures and provide resting places along the way.

As for the individual *bodhisattvas* in the Mahayana, among their innumerable host some of the most prominent are Avalokiteśvara (the lord who looks down with compassion), also called Padmapani (lotus bearer), Maitreya (loving one), now living as a *bodhisattva* and to come as a *buddha* in the future, Manjuśri (charming splendor), Ratnapani (jewel bearer), Samantabhadar (all goodness), also called Cakrapani (wheel bearer), Vajrapani (thunderbolt bearer), and Viśvapani (double thunderbolt bearer). Most of these and many more are named in the *Saddharmapundarika*.[34] Since it is the last goal of a *bodhisattva* to become a *buddha*, the dividing line between *bodhisattva* and *buddha* is not always distinct. Since the *bodhisattvas* are marked above all by their concern for the welfare and salvation of all living beings, they are naturally looked to for help and regarded as objects of worship.

Buddhas

Already in the Theravada, in addition to Śakyamuni Buddha, a number of other Buddhas, both of the past and of the future, were recognized, and in the Mahayana the number of these is further increased until, like the *bodhisattvas,* they too are innumerable. Most important is a sequence beginning with the Adi-Buddha (first Buddha), who is the primordial ultimate omniscience. The Adi-Buddha is manifest in the *tathagatas,* popularly called the Dhyani Buddhas (meditation Buddhas), they in the *bodhisattvas,* and the *bodhisattvas* in the Manushi Buddhas (earthly Buddhas), while *buddhata* (buddhaness) is the fragment of the divine which resides in all human beings and guarantees that ultimately all will attain enlightenment and be saved. The *tathagatas* are Vairocana (brilliant light), Akshobhya (unshakable) also called Vajrapani (thunderbolt bearer), Ratnasambhava (jewel being), Amitabha (infinite light) or the closely related Amitayus (infinite life), and Amoghasiddhi (infallible power), and—like the *bodhisattvas*—most of them are named already in the *Saddharmapundarika*.[35] The Manushi Buddhas are a series of seven leading up to and including Śakyamuni Buddha (Vipaśyin/Vipassin, Śikhin/Sikhin, Viśvabhuj/Vessabhu, Krakucchanda/Kakusandha, Kanakamuni/Konagamana, Kaśyapa/Kassapa, Śakyamuni/Sakyamuni), together with the future Buddha Maitreya/Metteyya as an eighth. In a usual outline five *tathagatas* are correlated with and manifested in a like number of *bodhisattvas,* and the *bodhisattvas* with and in a like number of Manushi Buddhas (the three who immediately preceded the historical Buddha together with Śakyamuni himself and Maitreya who is yet to come), as in Table 12.1. From the correlation in the several categories it may be noted that Śakyamuni Buddha is the earthly manifestation of Avalokiteśvara, who is himself the *bodhisattva* manifestation of Amitabha.[36]

In the Theravada many items of description of the Buddhas were formulated, e.g, the thirty-two marks of a great man as already noted above (in Chapter 11) in the *Digha Nikaya* and the *Majjhima Nikaya,* and these and other enumerations are continued and much used in the Mahayana. Listed already in the *Majjhima Nikaya* (1.69–72)[37] as well as in the *Mahavastu* (1.159–160)[38] and frequently cited thereafter are the ten powers (*balas*), four grounds of self-confidence (*vaiśaradyas*), and eighteen distinctive attributes (*avenika-dharmas*) of a Buddha.

The ten powers consist in the facts that a Buddha knows causal occasions, the consequences of actions, the elements of the world, the characters of beings, the merits of the conduct of others, the good and bad force of *karma,* the attainments of meditation, the modes of his own former lives, the death and rebirth of all beings, and that his own cankers have been destroyed. The four grounds of self-confidence of a Buddha consist in the knowledge that he has attained perfect enlightenment, has destroyed all the cankers, has correctly indicated the obstacles to the spiritual life, and has taught the way which truly leads to the cessation of ill. It is by virtue of endowment with the ten powers and the four self-confidences that a Buddha "claims the leader's place, roars his lion's roar in assemblies, and sets rolling the Brahma wheel."

TABLE 12.1.
TATHAGATAS, BODHISATTVAS, AND MANUSHI BUDDHAS

Tathagatas
1. Vairocana
2. Akshobhya
3. Ratnasambhava
4. Amitabha
5. Amoghasiddhi

Bodhisattvas
1. Samantabhadra
2. Vajrapani
3. Ratnapani
4. Avalokiteśvara
5. Viśvapani

Manushi Buddhas
1. Krakucchanda
2. Kanakamuni
3. Kaśyapa
4. Śakyamuni
5. Maitreya

By eighteen attributes a Buddha is distinguished from all other beings: he knows the past; he knows the future; he knows the present; his acts are based on knowledge; his speech is based on knowledge; his thought is based on knowledge; his resolution never falters; his energy never slackens; his mindfulness is never relaxed; his concentration always remains the same; his insight is never diminished; his freedom is unchanged; there is no faltering; there is no impetuosity; his mindfulness never fails; his mind is never disturbed; there is no thoughtless indifference; there is no preoccupation with the multiplicity of phenomena. "The knowledge involved in these eighteen special attributes of a Buddha is what is meant by the Buddha eye."

In the Theravada scriptures Śakyamuni Buddha was seen as exercising a compassionate ministry toward his fellow creatures, but it was also remembered that at his death he told his disciples that they would have to work out their own salvation. Furthermore there was at least one Buddhist sect which explicitly argued that a Buddha could not feel compassion because he was free from all passion. This sect was that of the Uttarapathakas (northern districters?), and they appear in the *Kathavatthu* (18.3) as arguing that if there were no passion (*raga*) in the Exalted Buddha, surely there was in him no compassion (*karuna*) either. To this the Theravadin disputant makes rejoinder in these words:

> But this implies that neither did he feel love or sympathetic joy or equanimity. You deny. But could he have these and yet lack pity? Your proposition implies also that he was ruthless. Yet you agree that the Exalted One was pitiful, kindly to the world, compassionate towards the world, and went about to do it good. Nay, did not the Exalted One win to the attainment of universal pity?[39]

In respect of this problem the Mahayana emphatically affirms that not only a *bodhisattva* but also, and in supreme measure, a Buddha is characterized by great compassion (*maha karuna*), universal pity, love, and mercy for all beings. Thus in one passage in the *Saddharmapundarika* (Ch. 7)[40] a *bodhisattva* attains unsurpassable perfect enlightenment (*anuttara-samyak-sambodhi*) after the efforts of many hundreds of millions of years and, at that point, is praised as the refuge, father, and savior of all living beings, and is besought, by the power of his great compassion, to turn the wheel of the law and to deliver all the suffering beings and to cause them to have gladness and joy.

As spiritual beings the Buddhas of Mahayana doctrine are surely superhuman and immortal and, as such, a physical body (*rupakaya*) cannot represent their real nature. Instead, the Mahayana teaches that a Buddha has three bodies (*trikaya*), namely, the *nirmanakaya* (body of transformation), the *sambhogakaya* (body of bliss), and the *dharmakaya* (body of *dharma*).

The idea of the *nirmanakaya* is not like that of the Hindu *avatara*, in which a deity enters into an earthly form, but is rather a continuation of the docetic concept already noted in the *Mahavastu*. In order to do his saving work, it is held, a Buddha projects one or more fictitious bodies and they visit the world in phantom form to preach the truth. So what appears to be the physical presence of a historical Buddha is really an illusion, conjured up by the Buddha as if by a magician.

In contrast with the *nirmanakaya* the *dharmakaya* represents the ultimate reality of a Buddha. Since *dharma* is the law of the universe, and since a Buddha is the embodiment of *dharma*, the *dharmakaya* is an invisible, universal, cosmic body, which encompasses all the elements of the universe. Since in this form the Buddha is the absolute reality of the whole universe, it also follows that all Buddhas are spiritually united in the *dharmakaya*.

As for the *sambhogakaya*, it is a supernatural, radiant, and glorious body, which is the result of the merit acquired by a Buddha through long periods of time. This body is visible only to superhuman beings, in particular to the celestial *bodhisattvas* who gather to hear a Buddha preach. This conception of the preaching of the Buddha in heavenly places and spiritual surroundings is one of the ways in which the Mahayana justifies its introduction of so many new teachings not found in the earlier texts.[41]

It is also held that a Buddha has a Buddha-field (*buddha-kshetra*), in which he lives, and which he guides and develops in spirituality. Such a "field" consists of many universes, with their heavens, earths, and hells, and with the inhabitants of these several levels. Among the innumerable Buddhas and the regions over which they preside, the *Saddharmapundarika* at one point (Ch. 7),[42] for example, locates eight Buddha fields in terms of their directions, and names two Buddhas in each field as follows: in the east Akshobhya (unshakable) and Merukuta (Meru peak); in the southeast Sinhaghosha (lion voice) and Sinhadhvaja (lion form); in the south Akaśapratishthita (sky dwelling) and Nityaparinirvrita (eternal extinction); in the southwest Indradhvaja (Indra form) and Brahmadhvaja (Brahma form); in the west Amitayus (infinite life), usually considered identical with Amitabha (infinite light), and Sarvalokadhatupadravodvegapratyuttirna (saving all worlds from suffering); in the northwest Tamalapatracandanagandhabhijna (yellow flower fragrance supernatural power) and Merukalpa (Meru form); in the north Meghasvara (sound of the clouds) and Meghasvararaja (sound of the clouds king); and in the northeast Sarvalokabhaya (eliminating fear of all worlds) and Śakyamuni (sage of the Śakyas).

TEACHERS AND TEXTS OF THE MAHAYANA

The Mahayana is characterized, Yi Jing said, not only by the worship of the *bodhisattvas* but also by the reading of the Mahayana *sutras*. These *sutras* represent themselves as sayings of the Buddha, and they regularly begin with a statement of the place, whether on earth or in heaven, where the Buddha is said to have delivered the address. As such, the *sutras* are the first and most important part of the Mahayana literature. The second part of the literature is the *śastras,* and these are treatises, under the names of various Mahayana teachers, in the form of commentaries on the *sutras* or in the form of systematic presentations. The third part of the Mahayana literature is the *tantras,* and they in particular represent the Tantrayana or Vajrayana (see below). For the most part the Mahayana literature is in Sanskrit, in Tibetan, in Central Asian languages, and in Chinese. All together it constitutes a very large mass of materials and, because the Mahayana does not constitute one unified sect, there is no specifically delimited canon, as in the Pali Tripitaka of the Theravada.[43]

Vaipulya Sutras

Among the very numerous *sutras* of the Mahayana, nine are considered of special importance and are commonly called the Nine Dharmas (*dharma* here probably an abbreviation of *dharma-paryaya,* religious texts) or the Vaipulya Sutras, meaning "discourses of great extent."

(1) ***Lalitavistara.*** The title of this work means "the detailed narration of the sport (*lalita*)" of a supernatural being, i.e., of the Buddha, and it gives an account of his decision to be born as the son of King Śuddhodana and Queen Maya, and of his life up to the point of his first sermon. In part the account agrees with the oldest Pali records, e.g., the materials in the *Mahavagga* of the Vinayapitaka, but the miraculous element is greatly increased and the viewpoint in the main is that of the Mahayana.

The *Lalitavistara* was composed originally in Sanskrit, was translated into Tibetan, and is also available in part in a Mongolian translation made from the Tibetan.[44] The Mongolian version is called in its own colophon *The Wondrous Twelve Deeds of Buddha.*[45] At the outset, in this Mongolian version, the future Buddha is living in a splendid heavenly palace, and there he is reminded of the resolve he had made in bygone times to relieve the living creatures from the sufferings of being born and becoming old. Then many of his previous existences are recalled briefly, in each of which as a *bodhisattva* he did good deeds. After that the account continues, in much detail, with his life in the palace of Śuddhodana, his great renunciation, and his subsequent experiences up through the temptation by the evil one. As an example of the narrative, when six years had passed and he abandoned the way of extreme hardship, in order to make a robe he found a grave-cloth thrown away in a cemetery.

> After that the *bodhisattva* thought: "What if there were water to wash this now?" Instantly, the gods struck the earth with the palms of their hands and a lake appeared. Then he thought: "I have found water, [but] what if there should be a stone to wash on?" Indra understood his thought and showed [him] a flat stone. When Indra said he would wash it for him, [the *bodhisattva*] did not consent, but washed it by himself in order to explain [to the living beings] that he who has left home should do his own work by himself. [The lake] is until now called "the lake of the palm of the hand."[46]

In this version the evil one is called the vicious and sinful Śimnu (corresponding to Mara in the Sanskrit original), and the hosts of Śimnu are also called Śimnus.

So when the Buddha has repulsed all the attacks of these antagonists, those who have seen in that victory the strength of his truth are moved to say:

> In consequence of truly understanding
> that all that is seen is like a dream and mirage,
> and pitying and thinking with compassion
> of those who are proud of their ego, not understanding
> that [everything] is the same as that (i.e., that
> everything is like a dream or mirage),
> he vanquished alone the multitude of the Śimnus,
> holding no sword or knife in his hands,
> not having surrounded himself with armies from the outside.
> Is this not most admirable (literally, more admirable than admirable)?[47]

(2) **Saddharmapundarika.** The *pundarika* is the white lotus, and the title of this *sutra* is translatable as "the lotus of the true law" or similar renderings, and it is commonly known simply as the Lotus Sutra. In Indian religion generally the lotus is of manifold symbolic significance, and in Buddhism, among other things, it is a metaphor for the All and for the Mind which is behind the All, and is thus appropriate to the teaching of the Buddha as expressing universal meaning. The book was composed and is preserved in Sanskrit, and was also several times translated into Chinese, the best known of these translations being that by an Indo-Iranian missionary named Kumarajiva (circa 350–410 C.E.). The Chinese pilgrim Yi Jing tells us that the *Saddharmapundarika* was the favorite text of his teacher, Hui-hsi, who read it once a day for more than sixty years,[48] and the book remains probably the most important single work of all the Mahayana *sutras*.[49]

As the *Saddharmapundarika* opens (Ch. 1) the Buddha is staying on the Vulture Peak (Gridhrakuta) at Rajagriha, but it is soon evident that this is a spiritual center point of the whole spiritual universe, for with the Buddha are 12,000 monks, all *arhats,* including the well-known Mahakaśyapa, Śariputra, Maudgalyayana, Aniruddha, Ananda, Rahula, and others; 2,000 *śravakas;* the Buddha's own maternal aunt and foster mother Mahaprajapati, and Yaśodhara his wife and the mother of their son Rahula, with their retinues; 80,000 *bodhisattvas,* including Manjuśri, Avalokiteśvara, Maitreya, and others; numerous gods, including Indra, Brahma, and others; many *nagas, kinnaras, gandharvas, asuraess,* and *garudas;* and also King Ajataśatru and his followers. After preaching to this surrounding multitude, the Buddha emits from the tuft of white hair between his eyebrows a ray of light which illuminates 18,000 worlds to the east (the direction he is facing as he sits there) and shines upwards as well to their highest heavens and downwards to their lowest hells. In these regions the six kinds of living beings become visible (inhabitants of hell, animals, ghosts, demigods, human beings, gods), and in all of the worlds *buddhas* are seen teaching vast congregations of disciples. When the *bodhisattva* Maitreya asks the *bodhisattva* Manjuśri why the Buddha has displayed this great wonder, Manjuśri replies that the Buddha will now preach the *Saddharmapundarika,* even as 20,000 Buddhas of the past, all named Candrasuryapradipa (sun and moon light), all performed the same wonder before preaching the same *sutra.*

The Buddha then (Chapter 2) emerges from his state of supreme concentration (*samadhi*) and begins to expound the doctrine of the Mahayana. By the parable (already noted above) of the carts promised to the sons in the burning house he explains that, although there are three "vehicles," two of these are only temporary "expedients," and in reality there is only one, namely, the *buddha*-vehicle—the "great vehicle"—by which all living beings will be able to become *buddhas* in their future lives. By this vehicle, all who hear the Buddha's law and observe its injunctions, and all who express faith in the Buddha—by building a *stupa*, by making an image, or by painting a picture of the Buddha, or by offering flowers or music or a gesture or word or reverence to the *stupa* or the statue or the picture of the Buddha—will attain the enlightenment of the Buddha.

> All in the world who are hearing or have heard the law from the mouth of the Buddhas, and have given alms, followed the moral precepts, and patiently accomplished the whole of their religious duties . . . have all of them reached enlightenment. . . .
> And those who erected *stupas* from marble . . . different sorts of timber . . . bricks, or clay . . . and even the little boys, who in playing erected here and there heaps of sand with the intention of dedicating them as *stupas* to the Buddhas . . . and others who had images of the Buddha made . . . of copper, brass, lead, iron, clay, or plaster . . . and those who made images of the Buddha on painted walls . . . have all of them reached enlightenment.
> Those who offered flowers and those who caused musical instruments to be played—making resound were it but a single musical instrument, or worshiping were it with but a single flower—and those who, when in the presence of a *stupa*, have offered their reverential salutation, be it in a complete form (probably a ceremonial prostration) or by merely joining the hands; who, were it but for a single moment, bent their head or body; and who at *stupas* containing relics have one single time said: "Homage to the Buddha (*namo Buddhaya*)!" albeit they did it with distracted thoughts, all have attained superior enlightenment. . . .
> Never has there been any being who, after hearing the law . . . shall not become Buddha; for this is the fixed vow of every Buddha: "Let me, by accomplishing my course of duty, lead others to enlightenment."[50]

Having heard this exposition, Śariputra is joyous in the knowledge that he is the Buddha's son, and born of the Buddha's mouth, and the Buddha assures him that in the future he will be a Buddha named Padmaprabha (flower light) and will reign over a lovely Buddha world called Viraja (undefiled) (Chapter 3). In subsequent passages the Buddha likewise assures other of his disciples of their future Buddhahood, for example, telling Mahakaśyapa that he will become a Buddha named Raśmiprabhasa (beaming with radiance) in a Buddha world called Prabhasaprapta (radiant virtue) (Chapter 6), and Ananda that he will become a Buddha with a very long name which is descriptive of a great king possessed of the wisdom of mountains and sea, and will reign in a Buddha world called Anavanamitavaijayanti (always raised banner of victory) (Chapter 9).

When (in Chapter 11) a splendid jeweled *stupa* appears in the sky above the Vulture Peak, an ancient Buddha named Prabhutaratna (many jewels) is seen seated within it, and Śakyamuni Buddha takes a place beside him, while innumerable Buddhas (all of them emanations of Śakyamuni Buddha) and *bodhisattvas* come from east and west, from north and south, from zenith and nadir, and the whole company of the Buddha's disciples is also lifted up from the earth into the sky. The Many Jewels Buddha has come, in accordance with his ancient vow, to hear the Lotus Sutra proclaimed by Śakyamuni Buddha, and Śakyamuni Buddha himself declares that the time is near for him to attain *parinirvana*, and that he wishes to entrust the *Saddharmapundarika* to those who will continue to preach it in the world.

The wish of the Buddha to transmit the *sutra* to those who will preserve it after he is gone is answered (in Chapter 12 in the Sanskrit, Chapter 13 in the Chinese) by the vows of many *bodhisattvas, arhats,* and *śravakas* to read, recite, keep, expound, and copy this scripture. At this juncture, however, the Buddha's aunt and foster mother Mahaprajapati (also called Gautami) comes before him with her following of 6,000 nuns, and is obviously anxious because the Buddha has not mentioned her name among those assured of future Buddhahood, but the Buddha tells her that she will in fact in the course of time become a man and a Buddha named Sarvasattvapriyadarśana (seen with joy by all beings), and he also tells Yaśodhara, the mother of his son Rahula, that she too will become a Buddha, with a very long name which connotes the sending out of ten million rays of light. Then Mahaprajapati with her 6,000 nuns, and Yaśodhara with her following of 4,000 nuns, express their joy, and promise to join the *bodhisattvas* and the others in proclaiming the Lotus scripture.

After that (Chapter 13/14), at the request of the *bodhisattva* Mañjuśri, the Buddha prescribes four sets of proper and peaceful methods or practices (*dharmas*), also called four spheres in which to dwell (*sukhaviharas*), by which, even in the evil age to follow the Buddha's own *parinirvana*, the preachers of the Lotus Sutra should be able to do their work without fear. The first is the sphere of approach. In his practice the *bodhisattva* who wishes to expound the *sutra* should be patient and meek, and neither rash nor attached to anything. In his approach to others, he should not be familiar with government officials, nor with hunters or fishermen or any who kill for profit, nor with Ajivikas, *brahmanas,* Nirgranthas, or adherents of the Hinayana. If such come to him, however, he may preach the law to them.

The second sphere is that of a serene mind. The preacher (here called *pandita*, Sanskrit for a learned man, a teacher) is always in a peaceful state. He puts on a clean red robe, washes his feet, rubs his head with ointment, and takes his place on an elevated seat, where he expounds the wonderful law with a pleasant countenance and with a variety of illustrations. He should not point out the faults of others, nor propagate scandal. Whether he knows the *sutra* by heart or has it in a book, he should answer questions not with the teachings of the Hinayana but only with the teachings of the Mahayana. He is always thinking: "How can I and these beings become Buddhas? I will preach this true law, upon which the happiness of all beings depends, for the benefit of the world."[51]

The third sphere is that of thought toward others. The one who wishes to keep, read, and recite the Lotus Sutra in the latter days after the *parinirvana* of the Buddha when the true law is in decay, should not speak ill of any of those who are studying the path of the Buddha, regardless of whether they are monks or nuns (*bhikshus* or *bhikshunis*), or male or female lay devotees (*upasakas* or *upasikas*), and regardless of whether they are seeking *śravakahood, pratyekabuddhahood,* or the way of the *bodhisattva*. The preacher "should never speak a disparaging word of anybody; never engage in a dispute on religious belief; never say to such as are guilty of shortcomings, 'You will not obtain superior knowledge.'"[52]

The fourth sphere is that of charity and compassion. A *bodhisattva* should have goodwill for both laymen and monks, and compassion for all who are not *bodhisattvas*. He should remember that it is their loss if they do not understand the Lotus Sutra, and should resolve that, when he himself attains the highest perfect enlightenment (*anuttara-samyak-sambodhi*), he will lead them to dwell in this law.

As for the Buddha himself, he is pictured in the *Saddharmapundarika* as a father (Chapter 4), a great cloud which pours its rain upon all plants without discrimination (Chapter 5), a physician (Chapter 15/16), and so forth. The images of father and physician are employed, for example, in a parable in which a father who is also a physician finds his sons ill from mistakenly drinking poison, and prescribes for them an appropriate medicine. Some of the sons take the medicine immediately and are cured, but some, their minds unbalanced by the poison, refuse and continue ill. The man thereupon goes away and lets it be thought that he has died. The recalcitrant sons are so shocked that they come to their senses, take the medicine, and get well. Then the man returns and shows himself to them all. In the same manner, the Buddha explains, some beings refuse salvation as long as they think that the Buddha will always be present, so he uses the expedient of saying that he will pass away (in *parinirvana*) in order to instill in them a sense of urgency in the acceptance of his teaching. In fact, however, his extinction is only apparent, and in reality he is eternal, for he became a Buddha countless ages ago, has ever since been teaching living beings in countless worlds, has given himself various names, for example, Dipankara (burning light), and will stay in the world forever.

Among the *bodhisattvas* several are the objects of special praise, e.g., Bhaishajyaraja (medicine king, Chapter 22/23), Gadgadasvara (wonderful voice, Chapter 23/24), Avalokiteśvara (the lord who looks down with compassion, Chapter 24/25), Śubhavyuha (wonderful adornment, Chapter 25/27), and Samantabhadra (all goodness, Chapter 26/28). The best and most widely known is Avalokiteśvara (who becomes Kuan Yin in Chinese, Kwannon in Japanese). Avalokiteśvara is described as taking many forms, both masculine and feminine, in order to save all living beings from misfortunes and sufferings, and it is promised that whoever calls upon Avalokiteśvara in pain or distress will be instantly heard and answered. Indeed it is as meritorious to make offerings to Avalokiteśvara even for a moment, as to make offerings throughout a lifetime to *bodhisattvas* as numerous as the sands of sixty-two million Ganges rivers. In the text, description, salutation, and exhortation follow one another:

> He (Avalokiteśvara) with his powerful knowledge beholds all creatures who are beset with many hundreds of troubles and afflicted by many sorrows, and thereby is a savior in the world....
> O thou whose eyes are clear, whose eyes are kind, distinguished by wisdom and knowledge, whose eyes are full of pity and benevolence; thou so lovely by thy beautiful face and beautiful eyes!...
> Think, O think with tranquil mood of Avalokiteśvara, that pure being; he is a protector, a refuge, a recourse in death, disaster, and calamity.[53]

As for the *Saddharmapundarika* itself, it is the chief of all the *sutras* spoken by the *tathagata*.

> The Lotus of the True Law saves all beings from all fear, delivers them from all pains. It is like a tank for the thirsty, like a fire for those who suffer from cold, like a garment for the naked, like a caravan leader for the merchants, like a mother for her children, like a boat for those who ferry over... like a torch for the dispelling of darkness....[54]

So, in a final commission (Chapter 27 in the Sanskrit, Chapter 22 in the Chinese), Śakyamuni Buddha entrusts the *Saddharmapundarika* to his listeners, saying to the *bodhisattvas*:

> "Into your hands, I transfer and transmit, entrust and deposit this supreme and perfect enlightenment arrived at by me after incalculable ages. Receive it, keep, read, fathom, teach, promulgate, and preach it to all beings.... I am a bountiful giver... follow my example, imitate me in liberally showing this knowledge.... And as to unbelieving persons, rouse them to accept this law."[55]

Then the *bodhisattvas* and the *buddhas* went away, joyful for what they had heard, to their various worlds.

(3) **Prajnaparamita.** The word *paramita* means "perfection," and a *bodhisattva* is commonly described (e.g., *Saddharmapundarika* Chapter 27/25)[56] as attaining six perfections, namely, charity or almsgiving (*danaparamita*), moral conduct or observance of the precepts (*silaparamita*), patience (*kshantiparamita*), energy (*viryaparamita*), meditation (*dhyanaparamita*), and wisdom (*prajnaparamita*), the sixth and last of these being the highest of all. So the texts known collectively as the *Prajnaparamita* are texts on the "perfection of wisdom," and they are considered fundamental in Mahayana Buddhism. Of the texts there are approximately forty, and they are classified in three groups according to length, reckoned in lines (*slokas*, a *sloka* being a unit of thirty-two syllables). The oldest is probably the version of medium length, called *Ashtasahasrika Prajnaparamita* or "The Perfection of Wisdom in Eight Thousand Lines."[57] This, in turn, was probably on the one hand expanded into the large versions which consist of recensions in 10,000, 18,000, 25,000, and 100,000 lines.[58] Also, there are short versions—condensations—in 2,500, 700, 500, 50 lines, and so forth.[59] Two short versions are of special renown, namely, the *Vajracchedika Prajnaparamita,* "The Perfection of Wisdom which Cuts like the Thunderbolt" or the "Diamond Sutra" (since *vajra* may be translated as either thunderbolt or diamond), a work in 300 lines;[60] and the *Hridaya Prajnaparamita* or "Heart of Perfect Wisdom," briefly known as the "Heart Sutra," a work found in a shorter and probably earlier form of fourteen lines, and a longer and probably later form of twenty-five lines.[61] Finally the ultimate concentration of the *Prajnaparamita* is attained in a text which is called "The Perfection of Wisdom in One Letter," in which the Buddha teaches his entire doctrine by simply uttering a single sound. Dwelling at Rajagriha, on the Vulture Peak, with 1,250 monks and innumerable *bodhisattvas,* the Buddha addresses the Venerable Ananda and says: "Ananda, do receive, for the sake of the weal and happiness of all beings, this perfection of wisdom in one letter—A."[62]

In the *Ashta* (short for the title of "The Perfection of Wisdom in Eight Thousand Lines") the Buddha is in the same locale and in the midst of the same company as in the "One Letter" text, and he converses chiefly with three disciples, namely, Subhuti, Sariputra, and Ananda. Subhuti is "the foremost of those who dwell in Peace" (1.6),[63] and the disciple outstanding for the practice of lovingkindness; Sariputra is the disciple preeminent in wisdom; and Ananda is the disciple of long personal devotion to the Buddha, with the most retentive memory for the sayings of the Buddha.

The *Ashta* text (which exists in a shorter verse form and a longer prose form) begins with the question as to how the *bodhisattvas* "go forth into perfect wisdom" (1.3),[64] and contains at a later point (16.321–322) this statement of how a *bodhisattva* should behave and train if he wishes to advance to the full and supreme enlightenment:

> The *bodhisattva* should adopt the same attitude towards all beings, his mind should be even towards all beings, he should not handle others with an uneven mind, but with a mind which is friendly, well-disposed, helpful, free from aversion; avoiding harm and hurt, he should handle others as if they were his mother, father, son, or daughter. As a savior of all beings should a *bodhisattva* behave towards all beings, should he train himself, if he wants to know the full and supreme enlightenment. He should, himself, stand in the abstention from all evil, he should give gifts, guard his morality, perfect himself in patience, exert vigor, enter into the trances, achieve mastery over wisdom. . . . In the same way he should stand in everything from the meditation on the truths to the state when he reaches the certainty that it is as a *bodhisattva* that he will be saved . . . and also others he should instigate to do the same—incite, and encourage them. When he longs eagerly for all that and trains himself in it, then everything will be uncovered to him. . . .[65]

At the same time the central doctrine of the *Prajnaparamita* is that of the "void" (*sunya*) and "voidness" or "emptiness" (*sunyata*).[66] This doctrine affirms that, since all phenomena in the world of becoming (*samsara*) are dependent for their existence upon causes and conditions, they are devoid of independent selfhood, i.e., they are void or empty. But the ultimate source of all phenomena, the Absolute, is not conceivable in terms of attributes or qualities, thus it is also void, or may be said to be voidness itself. Since *nirvana* is likewise transcendent to all the categories of thought, it too is voidness. If then the emptiness of phenomena coincides with the emptiness of *nirvana,* the two are not different, and in reality the universe is not different from the Absolute. Enlightenment, accordingly, does not consist in passing from *samsara* to *nirvana,* i.e., from the universe to the Absolute, as if they were separate realities, but it consists in the realization that they are truly non-different.

To make the point it is declared that even *buddhas* and *bodhisattvas* have no reality. The Buddha asks Subhuti whether, if a clever magician should conjure up a great crowd of people at the crossroads and then make them vanish again, anyone would have been killed by anyone, or murdered, or destroyed, or made to vanish, and Subhuti answers, "No indeed." Then the Buddha goes on: "Even so a *bodhisattva,* a great being, leads countless beings to *nirvana,* and yet there is not any being that has been led to *nirvana,* nor that has led others to it" (1.21). Subhuti, in turn, grasps this thought, and concludes that the *bodhisattva* "should so develop that he does not take his stand on any of these: not on form, feeling, perception, impulses, consciousness; not on eye, ear, nose, tongue, body, mind; not on forms, sounds, smells, tastes." Thus by standing "on emptiness" he will stand "in perfect wisdom" (2.34).[67]

In similar manner the "Diamond Sutra" explains that all conditioned things are in the last analysis unreal (32a):

> As stars, a fault of vision, as a lamp,
> A mock show, dew drops, or a bubble,
> A dream, a lightning flash, or cloud,
> So should one view what is conditioned.[68]

Over against the whole conditioned world, therefore, *sunyata* is the wholly unconditioned, that which is "void" of everything which limits, the "emptiness" which is the Absolute. It is "no-thing-ness" (as *sunyata* is sometimes translated), but it is not naught; it is the fullness which is beyond being and non-being.

But if enlightenment requires the attainment of that perfection of wisdom (*prajna*) which apprehends the real nature of things, it also requires the development of skill in means (*upaya*). The latter term, also translatable as "fitness of action or method," connotes not just expediency and doing what seems obvious or pleasant, but rather the optimum course of doing in a particular case because of knowledge of the actual situation. So the two, *prajna* and *upaya,* are repeatedly linked together (*prajna-upaya, prajnopaya*) in the *Prajnaparamitas,* and on one occasion in the *Ashta,* for example, Sariputra responds to the Buddha's many statements and illustrations related to the subject by saying (16.312):

> As I understand the meaning of the Lord's teaching, although a *bodhisattva* may be joined to a huge equipment of merit, as long as he is not upheld by perfect wisdom and is without skill in means, he lacks the good friend, and his attainment of full enlightenment is in doubt. A *bodhisattva* who wants to win full enlightenment should therefore develop the perfection of wisdom, and become skilled in means.

Farther along, where the *Ashta* devotes a whole chapter (20) to "discussion of skill in means," it is made plain that skill in means is to be equated in particular with the exercise of active compassion (*karuna*). In a simile the Buddha asks if a journeying man would abandon his family if they were beset by inimical forces in a great, wild forest, and Subhuti answers that a heroic man would be aided by such powerful resources, both within and without, as to be able to take his family safely out of the forest and to security. "Just so," says the Buddha, is it "with a *bodhisattva* who is full of pity and concerned with the welfare of all beings, who dwells in friendliness, compassion, sympathetic joy, and evenmindedness, who has been taken hold of by skill in means and perfect wisdom" (20.375).[69]

So, for enlightenment, wisdom (*prajna*) and skill in means (*upaya*) must be combined, and wisdom involves recognition of the emptiness of things (*śunyata*), and skill in means requires active compassion (*karuna*); therefore, emptiness and compassion also belong together.

Finally, in the conclusion of the "Heart Sutra," Prajnaparamita is Wisdom personified as a goddess (*prajna* being grammatically feminine). As such, she communicates "the unsurpassed verse," which is a *mantra* summarizing the whole teaching and expressing the ecstatic joy of at last reaching complete release in the transcendent unconditioned. With accents to indicate its metrical scheme in the Sanskrit, the *mantra* reads (60): *gaté gaté páragaté párasámgate bódhi svahá*, translatable as, "Gone, gone, gone to the other shore, landed at the other shore, enlightenment, all hail!" The last word (*svaha*) is an ejaculation of joy traditionally used in *brahmanical* ritual, and in *tantrism* reserved for *mantras* directed to feminine deities. Visualized as a goddess, Prajnaparamita is often portrayed as possessing four hands, the principal pair in the position of the preaching of the law (*dharmacakra mudra*) and the other two holding a rosary and a book, and it so happens that the earliest such representation so far known is an illustration in a manuscript of "The Perfection of Wisdom in Eight Thousand Lines" dated 1028 C.E. As a goddess Prajnaparamita is also seen as the consort of the Adi-Buddha, and thus the two together represent the combination of wisdom (the feminine) and active compassion (the masculine).[70]

(4) ***Gandavyuha.*** In *Gandavyuha*, a long work,[71] the Buddha is seen holding an assembly at the Jetavana garden in Sravasti, but this is no longer an earthly place but heavenly. The Buddha himself is the Mahavairocana Buddha (great brilliant light), whose radiance shines into the darkest corners of the whole universe. In the company about the Buddha are 500 *bodhisattvas* led by Samantabhadra and Manjuśri, 500 *śravakas* (disciples) including Maudgalyayana, Mahakaśyapa, Revata, Subhuti, Aniruddha, and others, and many worldly lords, but all of these are now spiritual beings, come together from the various quarters of the universe. Under the direction of Manjuśri, as the story unfolds, a young man named Sudhana goes forth in search of enlightenment, and visits one teacher after another, more than fifty in number, until he finally comes to the *bodhisattva* Maitreya. The dwelling of Maitreya is in an incredibly beautiful Tower called the *Vairocana-vyuha-alankara-garbha* (the tower of illumination which holds within itself an array of brilliantly shining ornaments), a Tower which contains innumerable towers within itself. When Maitreya admits Sudhana to these towers, Sudhana perceives within them all the events of the *bodhisattva's* life and how he attained the love (*maitra*) from which he came to be known as Maitreya (loving one).

Maitreya recognizes that Sudhana has experienced the *bodhicittotpada,* which is here the crucial awakening and cherishing of a spiritual aspiration for the attainment of supreme enlightenment, and is thus the initial step in the career of a *bodhisattva*. Accordingly Maitreya commends Sudhana and sends him on to Samantabhadra, through whose instrumentality Sudhana finally reaches his great goal and comes to feel that in love and compassion, in emancipation and mastery over the world, he is in complete identity with Samantabhadra and with all the Buddhas.

In a way somewhat reminiscent of the several realms of existence (*kamaloka, rupaloka, arupaloka*) in the Theravada, the *Gandavyuha* speaks of the *lokadhatu* and the *dharmadhatu*. The *lokadhatu* is the present world system of relativity and particularity; the *dharmadhatu* is the same world, yet it is not the same world because it is the world as seen by an enlightened mind. In the *lokadhatu* there are limitations of all sorts, and each individual reality stands against others; in the *dharmadhatu* there is still a multiplicity of individualities, but at the same time there is an interpenetration of all things, since all are enfolded in one great Reality and therefore form one harmonious whole in an "unobstructed" world. In the latter world light casts no shadow, and all is radiant and wonderful. It is this world which is symbolized by Maitreya's Vairocana Tower, and it is only when Sudhana is far advanced toward enlightenment that he is able to see and enter this tower.

As in other Mahayana literature, the ideal is that of the compassionate *bodhisattva*, and it is the object of the long pilgrimage of Sudhana to find out what constitutes the life of devotion as exemplified by a *bodhisattva*. In this connection there is a strong contrast of the *bodhisattva* with the *śravaka* (the hearer). The *śravaka* may indeed attain enlightenment, but his interest is in an intellectual apprehension of the truth and his goal is to rise above the world of particulars and multiplicities. The *bodhisattva*, however, although having complete knowledge and complete freedom, is characterized by a great compassionate heart (*mahakaruna*) and lives a life of unwearying devotion and self-sacrifice for the sake of the ultimate salvation of all beings. This is the life which Sudhana comes to understand, and upon which he himself embarks.

(5) *Daśabhumiśvara*. Already in the *Mahavastu* there is an enumeration of ten stages *(bhumis)* in the career of a *bodhisattva*, and it is these ten stages *daśabhumis*) which are dealt with in the present work yet more fully. The speaker is the *bodhisattva* Vajragarbha (thunderbolt/diamond embryo), and it is at the invitation of Śakyamuni Buddha that he elucidates the stages.

(6) *Lankavatara* or *Saddharma Lankavatara Sutra*. The title of this work[72] refers to "the revelation of the good religion in Lanka," and at the outset Ravana, the ten-headed king of the *rakshasas*, invites the Buddha to come to Lanka to teach, and the *sutra* is delivered there. The principal questioner, however, is the *bodhisattva* Mahamati, and the discourses of the Buddha are given in response to his interrogations. The principal teaching is a modification and development of the doctrine of emptiness (*śunyavada*), known as the *vijnanavada* or doctrine of consciousness. The objective reality of the external world is still denied, but the subjective reality of the phenomena of consciousness is recognized. While *vijnana* is consciousness in general, the word is also used here in particular for knowledge which deals with the relative aspect of existence. This kind of knowledge is obtained by "discrimination" (*vikalpa*), which sees existence in terms of pairs of opposites, such as birth and death, permanent and impermanent, and so on. But the world seen in this way is our own construction, not the world as it is in its own true nature. In contrast with such *vijnana* as relative knowledge, there is *jnana* (often called *aryajnana*), and it is transcendental knowledge and consists of the intuitions which come with self-realization (*svasiddhanta*).

Thus the Buddha explains to Mahamati that it is their "discriminations," which lead the ignorant and simple-minded to believe in the multitudinousness of external objects, whereas the world is really only something which is seen by the mind, and is like a mirage to which animals run in vain for water, like the city of the *gandharvas* which the unwitting take to be a real city although it is not, or like a wheel of fire made by a revolving firebrand which is not a wheel but only imagined to be one by the ignorant. So Mahamati and all the *bodhisattvas* should discipline themselves in the realization and patient acceptance of the emptiness and non-duality of all things, and thus gain tranquility. What really exists is universal mind (*alayavijnana*), which transcends all individuality and all limits. Fortunately between the individual discriminating mind and the universal mind there is the intuitive mind (*manas*), and the latter is one with universal mind by reason of its participation in transcendental knowledge (*aryajnana*). Transcendental knowledge is not noble wisdom (*aryaprajna*) or ultimate reality itself, but it is an intuitive awareness of it. To reach the state of consciousness in which this inmost truth is directly presented to the mind (*pratyatmaryajnanagocara*) the *bodhisattva* should keep himself away from turmoil, social excitements, and sleepiness, away from the treatises and writings of worldly philosophers, and away from the ritual and ceremonies of professional priestcraft. He should retire by himself to a quiet, secluded place in the forest, where he may reflect within himself without relying on anyone else, and there practice concentrated meditation (*dhyana*), for solitude is the characteristic feature of the inner attainment of self-realization and the realization of noble wisdom. As the fruit of self-realization, the higher stages (*bhumis*) of *bodhisattva* life will be reached, and the higher *samadhis* (levels of bliss arising from a concentrated state of mind) will be experienced, even the highest, which is called *vajravimbopama* (in which even the subtlest forms of ignorance and evil desire—*kleśas*—are destroyed as if by thunderbolt/diamond force). At this point the *bodhisattvas* will be endowed with all the powers and psychic faculties necessary to manifest loving compassion everywhere. As the *Lankavatara Sutra* puts it:

> Before they had attained self-realization of noble wisdom they had been influenced by the self-interests of egoism, but after they attain self-realization they will find themselves reacting spontaneously to the impulses of a great and compassionate heart endowed with skillful and boundless means and sincerely and wholly devoted to the emancipation of all beings.

Making use of these new powers, the *bodhisattva* will assume various transformation bodies (*nirmanakaya*) and personalities for the sake of benefiting others. Finally, passing beyond the tenth and last stage of *bodhisattva*hood, he will himself become a *tathagata,* endowed with all the freedom of the body of truth (*dharmakaya*). Seated on a lotus throne in the *akanishtha* (not the least) heaven (situated at the highest end of the *rupaloka* or world of form), he will be recognized by Buddhas from all the Buddha-lands as one of themselves, and will himself be assigned a Buddha-land that he may possess and perfect it as his own.

On this level there are many Buddhas in many Buddha-lands and in many times, but in the body of truth (*dharmakaya*), i.e., in the ultimate essence of the matter, all the Buddhas of the past, present, and future, are of one sameness (*samata*). Although not quite explicitly stated, it is evidently intended to say that there is really one Buddha, who multiplies himself almost infinitely as he reveals himself in time and space. Just as there are several names for one and the same thing—e.g., both *hasta* and *pani* mean "hand"—so there are innumerable names for the Buddha. Some call him Tathagata (thus come), others Svayambhuva (self-existing), Buddha, Rishi, Brahma, Vishnu, Iśvara, Arishtanemi (the Jaina saint),

Soma (the moon), Rama, Indra, Varuna, and yet others speak of him as e.g., Immortality, Emptiness, Truth, Reality, Dharmadhatu (all ideal realms), Nirvana, Eternity, Jina (conqueror). Even as the moon reflected in water is divided into as many thousands of reflections as there are dipperfuls of water, so is the Buddha in the world. "Those who know me will recognize me everywhere."[73]

(7) **Samadhiraja.** The concentrated meditation (*samadhi*) of the *bodhisattva* is the subject of this work, especially the highest form of meditation called the "king" (*raja*) of meditations. Because the teaching is set forth as a dialogue between the Buddha and a *bodhisattva* named Candrapradipa (moon glow), the work is also known as the *Candrapradipa Sutra*.

(8) **Suvarnaprabhasa.** The title of the work means "splendor of gold." The Sanskrit text was translated into Chinese by Yi Jing in 703 C.E., and his version was in turn translated into Tibetan.[74] As in many other books (e.g., *Saddharmapundarika*), the work opens (Chapter 1) with the Buddha on the Vulture Peak (Gridhrakuta) at Rajagriha, surrounded by almost innumerable *arhats*, *bodhisattvas*, and other beings. In Chapter 2 (in the Chinese version) the *bodhisattva* Ruciraketu asks why the life of the Buddha Śakyamuni is of only eighty years' duration, and it is set forth that in reality the life span of the Buddha is immeasurable. It might be possible to count the drops of water in the sea, but it is not possible to count the years of his life. A *brahmana* named Kaundilya then begs for a relic of the Buddha, even if it be not larger than a grain of mustard. This, a Licchavi prince named Sarvasattvapriyadarśana declares, will be forthcoming only when a series of other impossibilities takes place, when white lotuses grow out of the rushing water of the Ganges, when black crows turn red, when ships sail on the dry land, and so forth. The *brahmana* then perceives that there can be no relic of the Buddha, because the Buddha is not a body of flesh and blood.

This leads (Chapter 3) to an exposition of the doctrine which we have already noted above of the three bodies (*trikaya*) of the Buddha, namely, the utterly immaterial *dharmakaya* (body of truth) which is the cosmic absolute and provides the ground of the other two bodies; the brightly shining *sambhogakaya* (body of bliss) which is assumed for imparting higher truths to advanced *bodhisattvas;* and the illusory *nirmanakaya* (transformation body) in which the Buddha seems to appear in various times and places for the enlightenment of various classes of beings. Inasmuch as the *dharmakaya* encompasses all the beings of the world, even though they do not realize it, every being can and must eventually become one with the Buddha.[75]

In respect of ethics, Chapter 4 is at the heart of the *Suvarnaprabhasa*. This chapter contains long passages in verse in confession of sins, and in expression of love (*maitri*) and compassion (*karuna*) for all beings. In other chapters (beginning in Chapter 6) many protective spells (*dharanis*), mostly consisting of a series of mystic syllables, are introduced, the repetition of which is intended to provide protection for *bodhisattvas* against all enemies, animals, humans, and demons.[76] In Chapter 15 the goddess Sarasvati comes forward to praise the *Suvarnaprabhasa*, and to promise that she will protect and help all those who teach and hear the book. To that end she prescribes the use of thirty-two essences in a magical bath, and divulges the spells to be recited in connection with the bath. So she assures all monks, nuns, laymen, and laywomen (*bhikshus, bhikshunis, upasakas, upasikas*), who hold to the *sutra*, that wherever they are she will guard them and enable them certainly to cross the ocean of *samsara* and attain the highest enlightenment. The great goddess Śri speaks in similar fashion in Chapters 16–17, and so does Dridha, the goddess of the earth, in Chapter 18. Likewise in Chapter 22, the favor of a great number of gods, goddesses, *yakshas, nagas, asuras, gandharvas, kinnaras,* and other spirits is promised. In addition to Sarasvati, Śri, and Dridha, those named individually here include Śakra, Anavatapta, Sagara, Yama, Maheśvara, Vajrapani, Manibhadra, Mucilinda, the mother goddess Hariti, and the *yakshini* Candika. Also (in Chapter 29) the goddess of the *bodhi*-tree comes forward to ask that, after she has unweariedly reverenced the Buddha with the three deeds (of body, speech, and mind), she may speedily pass out of the *samsara* and turn home to the boundary of true reality.

Finally (Chapter 31) all those present praise the Buddha, with special appreciation for his teaching of the *Suvarnaprabhasa*. Those referred to in particular as present at this time are the great *bodhisattvas*, the four kings of heaven, the *devaputras* (sons of the gods) of the Tushita heaven, Brahma Sahampati, Sarthavaha the son of King Mara, King Mara, the *devaputra* Manjuśri, the *bodhisattva* Maitreya, the *sthavira* Mahakaśyapa, and Ananda. All say in effect what Ananda says last of all, namely, that he has accepted the teaching of the *sutra* and will make it known to all those who rejoice in enlightenment. So the whole assembly, numerous as the sands of the Ganges, disperses, to walk faithfully in the doctrine of the "splendor of gold."

(9) *Tathagataguhyaka* or *Guhyasamaja*. The prominence in the *Suvarnaprabhasa* of such items as mystic syllables, and of many female deities, points already in the direction of the Vajrayana or Tantrayana, and the *Guhyasamaja*, the ninth and last of the Vaipulya Sutras, is considered to be itself one of the oldest and most important Buddhist *tantric* texts. It will be cited again below in connection with the Vajrayana/Tantrayana.

Other Sutras. In addition to the Vaipulya Sutras there are many other Mahayana *sutras*. Three of special importance are the following.

(1) *Karandavyuha* or *Avalokiteśvara-gunakarandavyuha*. The full title of this work means "the detailed description of the basket of the qualities of Avalokiteśvara." Much as in the *Saddharmapundarika*, Avalokiteśvara (the "watchful lord," who looks down with infinite pity on all beings) is here described in his many deeds of compassion, intended to bring help and salvation to all sufferers. He descends into hell, where burning heat is changed into pleasant coolness; he visits the hungry ghosts, tortured by hunger and thirst, and refreshes them with food and drink; he converts cannibal witches (*rakshasis*) in Lanka; he preaches in Varanasi to beings born as worms and insects. He is also praised as a cosmic being, out of whose body many gods have proceeded, e.g., the sun and moon from his eyes, Brahman from his shoulders, Sarasvati from some of his teeth. The profound secret to be learned from Avalokiteśvara is "knowledge of the six syllables"—the famous mystic syllables of his *mantra, om mani padme hum,* i.e., "om jewel lotus hum," variously interpreted as "om (here one should inhale), the jewel (male) in the lotus (female), hum (here exhale)," or "om (assent, the cosmic sound), the jewel of the doctrine in the lotus of the world, hum (ratification, amen)"—and the one who knows this profound secret knows release. Even a single recitation of the syllables earns immeasurable merit.

(2) *Sukhavativyuha*. Under this title there are two works of similar import (preserved both in Sanskrit and in Chinese translations), one longer and one

shorter, and they are "detailed descriptions of the land of bliss."[77] Sukhavati, the land of bliss, is the western paradise presided over by Amitabha, the Buddha of infinite light, who is also the Buddha of infinite life in his form of Amitayus, and of infinite compassion in his *bodhisattva* form of Avalokitesvara.

In the longer *Sukhavativyuha* Sakyamuni Buddha is on the Vulture Peak at Rajagriha, in the midst of a large company of *arhats* and *bodhisattvas*. In conversation with Ananda he names eighty-one Buddhas of the past, beginning with Dipankara and coming down to Lokesvararaja as the last in the series. Under the guidance of Lokesvararaja (it is explained) a certain monk named Dharmakara performed the duties of a *bodhisattva* through enormous spans of time and finally, instead of entering *nirvana*, became the *tathagata* of a Buddha-country far distant in the west. In this position he bears the name Amitabha (infinite light) and many other names, all referring to the light, and his Buddha-land is known as Sukhavati (the happy country). In that land are great rivers, fine trees, beautiful flowers, and jewels and treasures of every kind. Light shines everywhere, and there is no mention even of day and night, nor is there any sound of sin, obstacle, misfortune, distress, or pain. Whatever beings direct their thoughts toward Amitabha and enlightenment, and store up good works, will at death see Amitabha and be born in that land of bliss.

In the shorter *Sukhavativyuha* the Buddha is at Sravasti and directs his teaching to Sariputra. The western Buddha-country of Amitayus, as it is called here, is again described as a most beautiful place, and it is explained that it is called by its name Sukhavati, meaning "the happy," because there is there neither bodily nor mental pain for living beings, and the sources of happiness are innumerable. Whoever makes mental prayer for that country will be born there.

(3) ***Amitayurdhyana.*** The work is a "meditation on the Buddha Amitayus." It opens with the historical incident of the imprisonment and starvation of King Bimbisara by his son Ajatasatru, and tells how Queen Vaidehi attempted to smuggle food in to her husband. In her distress the queen was visited by Sakyamuni Buddha, who discoursed to her on the Sukhavati and outlined the proper manner of meditation on Amitayus and on the *bodhisattvas* Avalokitesvara and Mahasthama, by means of which one may be born in that world of highest happiness.[78]

Writers and Sastras

Xuan Zang (629–645 C.E.) names four Buddhist writers as contemporaries of each other, and calls them "the four suns which illumined the world," namely, Asvaghosha, Nagarjuna, Aryadeva, and Kumaralabdha (i.e., Kumaralata).[79] Biographies of the first three were translated into Chinese by Kumarajiva in about 405 C.E.[80] Kumarajiva was born in Kucha of an Indian father and a mother who was a princess of the Kucha royal family. The mother took Kumarajiva to Kashmir for education in Buddhist studies, and he came to China as a famous scholar in 401 C.E., to remain there the rest of his life.

Asvaghosha was a scholar and poet who probably lived not later than the time of Kanishka in the first century C.E. Xuan Zang calls him Asvaghosha *bodhisattva*, describes his wisdom as embracing all subjects, and says that in his career "he had traversed the arguments of the Three Vehicles," by which Xuan Zang probably means the Little (Hinayana), the Middle (Madhyamika), and the Great (Mahayana) Vehicles.[81]

Buddhacarita. The major work of Aśvaghosha is the *Buddhacarita*, a poetic account of the life of the Buddha, preserved partially in Sanskrit and completely in a somewhat divergent Chinese version made by an Indian monk called Charmaraksha, who came to China in 412 and made this translation in about 420 C.E.[82] It was no doubt some Chinese translation or other of this work which was known to Yi Jing (671–695 C.E.), who names the *Buddhacarita* as written by Aśvaghosha, and describes it as widely read or sung throughout India and in the countries of the Southern Sea.[83]

In its entirety the *Buddhacarita* extends from the birth of the Buddha to his *parinirvana*, and concludes with an account of the strife over his relics, the first Council, and the reign of Aśoka. For the most part the viewpoint of the work is that of the Hinayana, but there are points of agreement with points in the Mahayana, and it is possible to think that Aśvaghosha was a member of the Mahasanghika sect,[84] and to consider him as one of the forerunners of the Mahayana and even of the Madhyamika, as the remark of Xuan Zang (just above) may suggest.

Thus, for example, the name Svayambhu occurs in connection with and probably in veiled allusion to the Buddha (*Buddhacarita* 2.51; 10.2, 19),[85] and this name, meaning "self-existent," is a title of the Buddha in the *Ashtasahasrika Prajnaparamita* (9.207)[86] and elsewhere in Mahayana literature. Likewise the human body is described as empty and without a self (*Buddhacarita* 16.28),[87] which is a teaching pointing in the direction of the doctrine of "emptiness" in the *Prajnaparamita*. In one passage (*Buddhacarita* 16.75)[88] the Buddha even says that he has attained the Mahayana, and calls the Mahayana "the instrument of the Law of the perfect Buddha, which is the establisher of the welfare of all beings, set forth by all the Buddhas."

Sutralankara. The *Sutralankara* is extant in a Chinese translation made by Kumarajiva in about 405 C.E., and is attributed in the Chinese sources to Aśvaghosha.[89] The work is a very large collection of tales, both in prose and in verse. Historical characters appear in the stories, e.g., Aśoka (Chapters 16, 27, 30, 55), Kanishka (Chapters 14, 31), Mahakaśyapa (Chapter 56), and others who are unidentified or anonymous, e.g., a king of Lanka (Chapter 4), a mendicant monk (Chapter 23), a magician (Chapter 29). The Buddha himself is exalted and compassionate. When he meets his five former associates at Varanasi, his whole being is so resplendent that they do not recognize him (Chapter 58). When Śariputra and other monks refuse admittance to the order to a man who cannot claim any good deeds in any of his existences, the Buddha, whose heart is full of pity, desires to convert the man, and feels toward him as a mother toward her son. In fact, the Buddha explains, in a previous existence in a moment of terror, when pursued by a tiger, the man had cried out, "Adoration to the Buddha!" and for that the Buddha now declares him worthy of salvation (Chapter 57).

Mahayana-śradhotpada. Aśvaghosha is also credited with the authorship of the *śastra* called *Mahayana-śradhotpada* or the "Awakening of Faith in the Mahayana." This work, however, plainly represents an advanced stage in the development of the Mahayana philosophy, and the attribution to Aśvaghosha may be incorrect, or the person intended may be a second of the same name. The text, presumably written originally in Sanskrit, is available only in Chinese, presumably translations from the original Sanskrit, and the earliest Chinese text is supposed to have been made by a monk from Ujjayini named Paramartha, who came to China by sea in 546 and made this translation in 550 C.E.[90]

At the outset of the work the author explains that when the *tathagata* was in the world, different types of people were able to understand his teaching directly, but later, at least for some persons, the more extensive discourses found in the *sutras* became necessary. On the other hand, some persons found the wordiness of such discourses troublesome, and desired what was comprehensive but at the same time terse, and it is plainly for such as these that the author writes, for his book is clearly intended to give a very concise and logically arranged summary of Mahayana doctrine.

The word *mahayana* is used here, however, in a special sense as a name for the Absolute, which is otherwise also called *tathata*, a word usually translated as "suchness." As the Absolute expresses itself in the temporal order it is known as Mind, and Mind (in this sense) contains within itself both the transcendental and the phenomenal. A sentient being has its existence in the phenomenal order but really belongs to the transcendental order, and this situation and potentiality are stated in terms of the *tathagata-garbha*, translatable as the embryo or matrix of *tathagata*, or the *buddha*-motive, meaning that a person has the intrinsic ability to attain enlightenment, i.e., to come to be in the infinite order. After theoretical exposition along these lines, the book recommends specific practices of charity, observance of precepts, endurance of wrong, perseverance, "cessation" of illusions in quiet mediation, and "clear observation" of the facts that nothing made in all the universe can last long, that the past is like a dream, the present like lightning, and the future will be like a cloud that rises up suddenly.

Kumaralata was a younger contemporary of Asvaghosha, and Xuan Zang, calling him Kumaralabdha, says that he was a native of Takshasila, a person of remarkable intelligence, the composer of many *sastras,* and the founder of the Sautrantika school.[91]

Kumaralata was the author of a work called *Kalpanamanditika* (probably part of a longer title meaning "a series of examples adorned by poetic invention"), fragments of which in Sanskrit have been found in Turpan, with the name of Kumaralata in the colophons. The nature of this work suggests that it was written in imitation of Asvaghosha's *Sutralankara,* and the similarity between the two works is probably the cause of a confusion between Kumaralata and Asvaghosha, in which it has sometimes been held that the *Sutralankara* itself was written by Kumaralata instead of by Asvaghosha.[92]

Within the Mahayana two great traditions came to prevail in the schools known respectively as the Madhyamika and the Yogacara. Of the Madhyamika tradition the recognized founders were Nagarjuna and Aryadeva.

In the *Lankavatara Sutra*, in the probably added section called *Sagathakam* (163–166),[93] Mahamati asks who the bearer of the doctrine will be after the passing of the Buddha, and the Buddha issues a prediction which evidently points to Nagarjuna:

> There will be one who bears the *dharma,* when sometime is past after the *sugata's* entrance into *nirvana*. In Vedali, in the southern part, a *bhikshu* most illustrious and distinguished [will be born]; his name is Nagahvaya, he is the destroyer of the one-sided views based on being and non-being. He will declare my Vehicle, the unsurpassed Mahayana, to the world; attaining the stage of Joy he will go to the Land of Bliss.

In addition to this and some other Sanskrit references, there are details concerning Nagarjuna—not always consistent and often legendary—in Chinese in the record of the travels of Xuan Zang (629–645 C.E.),[94] and in Tibetan in the *History of Buddhism in India and Tibet* by Buston (1290–1363 C.E.), and the *History of Buddhism in India* by Taranatha (completed in 1608 C.E.).[95]

As the story is told by Buston, Nagarjuna (Tibetan name, *Klu sgrub*) was born in a *brahmana* family in South India, but it was predicted that he would only live for seven years. At that age he proceeded to the famous university center at Nalanda where his recitation of the hymns of the *Sama Veda* attracted the attention of the *brahmana* Saraha, who was residing there at that time. Saraha was himself a poet and the author of three works in verse, known as the "King Dohas," "Queen Dohas," and "People Dohas," or collectively the *Three Cycles of Dohas*.[96] As these works show, although he was of *brahmana* background, Saraha was an expositor of Buddhist thought, and in fact his "songs" were ultimately very influential in Tibetan Buddhism. So, as Buston tells us, Saraha saved the life of the young Nagarjuna by consecrating him on the magic circle (i.e., a *mandala*) of Amitayus, and Nagarjuna studied with Saraha the *Guhyasamaja* and other texts, presumably including the works of Saraha himself.

After that, Rahulabhadra, the abbot of Nalanda, ordained Nagarjuna as a monk under the name of Sriman. Later Nagarjuna visited the realm of the *nagas* and received from them the *Satasahasrika Prajnaparamita*, i.e., the *sutra* on "The Perfection of Wisdom in 100,000 Lines." It was on this account that he was called Nagarjuna, i.e., "he who has secured power *(arjuna)* from the *nagas*."

According to the view reflected here, it was the *nagas* who had preserved until this later time the deeper teachings of the Buddha, and Nagarjuna now devoted the rest of his life to promulgating these profound truths. As already noted above, the central doctrine in the *Prajnaparamita* literature is that of *sunyata* or "emptiness," and Nagarjuna systematized the implications of this doctrine in the philosophy known as the Sunyavada and also as the Madhyamika. The latter name means the "middle way" and is thus reminiscent of the "middle path" which Sakyamuni chose between sensualism and asceticism (in his sermon at Isipatana, above page 000), and between opposite extremes in philosophy (in his explanation to Ananda, above page 000).

Nagarjuna's Writings

Mulamadhyamakakarika. This treatise on "the fundamentals of the middle way" is the major work of Nagarjuna which is extant in Sanskrit. It consists of about 450 highly concentrated mnemonic verses (called *karikas*), and is preserved in a Sanskrit commentary by Candrakirti called *Prasannapada* (clear worded), in which the arrangement is in twenty-seven chapters. The text is also incorporated in a commentary by Pingala, the whole of which was translated into Chinese by Kumarajiva in 409 C.E.[97]

The *Karika* (the brief title of the work) begins (Chapter 1) with an analysis of causes and origins (*pratyaya*, relational origination). Here eight negations are maintained, namely, that there is no origination and no extinction, no destruction and no permanence, no identity and no differentiation, no coming into being and no going out of being, and it is declared that existing things can never be found to originate from themselves, from something else, from both, or from no cause whatsoever (Verse 1). This dialectic then provides a basis for further analysis of the concepts of the self (Chapter 15), of *nirvana* (Chapters 16, 25), and so forth, in which the views of both eternalism and annihilationism are shown to be logically untenable. In short, everything is "no-thing," and from this point of view there is no difference, for example, between *nirvana* and *samsara* (25.19–20). If, however—an imaginary opponent objects in Chapter 24—everything is "emptiness" (*śunyata*) and there is no coming into being and no going out of being, then there can be no four noble truths, no *dharma,* no *sangha,* and finally no Buddha. But Nagarjuna answers that it is the "non-emptiness" *(aśunya)* doctrine of his opponent that is self-contradictory for if, in terms of that doctrine, it be affirmed, for example, that suffering exists by its own nature then the destruction of suffering is denied, but if it be affirmed that suffering does not exist then by what kind of path can the destruction of suffering be obtained (Verses 23, 25)? After all, the Buddha taught both relative or worldly truth and also absolute or supreme truth, and only those who know the distinction between the two can understand the profound nature of the Buddha's teaching, and can rightly understand suffering, its origin, its destruction, and the way to enlightenment (Verses 8–10, 40).

A commentary on the *Mulamadhyamakakarika* called the *Akutobhaya* is attributed to Nagarjuna and preserved in Tibetan, but Nagarjuna's actual authorship of the work is doubted. Two other large commentaries, however, are accepted as his, and are preserved in Chinese translations. They are:

Mahaprajnaparamita Śastra. This is a "commentary on the Great Prajnaparamita," and the Chinese translation, known as the *Ta-chih-tu-lun,* was made by Kumarajiva between 402 and 405 C.E.[98]

Dasabhumi-vibhasha Śastra. This commentary is an "exposition of the ten stages of Bodhisattvahood," and the Chinese translation, known as the *Shi-chu-p'i-p'o-sha-lun,* was made by Kumarajiva in 405 C.E.[99]

Of the many other works of Nagarjuna, no doubt the most famous are his two letters to a certain king, as follows:

Suhrllekha. This "letter to a friend" (*lekha,* letter) is preserved in a Tibetan version, which its commentaries say was made by the great Indian scholar Sarvajnadeva in association with the great Tibetan translator *Ka ba dpal brtsegs* (a disciple of Padmasambhava); and in three Chinese translations which were made in 431, 434, and 673 C.E., the last by Yi Jing.[100] Yi Jing made his translation when he first arrived in Tamralipti, and sent it home to China in 692 C.E. He describes the work as composed in verse and as striking in the beauty of the writing, gives a summary of the contents, and says that in India students learn the letter early in the course of instruction, and the most devout make it a special object of study throughout their lives.[101]

The Tibetan commentaries give the name of the king to whom the letter was addressed as *bDe spyod*.[102] Other references make it probable that this was one of the Śatavahana kings of Andhra, perhaps either Gautamiputra Śatakarni (circa 80–104 C.E.) or Śri Yajna Śatakarni (circa 170–199 C.E.). Whoever it was, tradition affirms that the king who was Nagarjuna's friend built for him a monastery in Śriparvata (Bhramaragiri), and that Nagarjuna spent his later days there.[103]

In the Tibetan version the *Suhrllekha* consists of 123 verses. Nagarjuna urges his royal friend to direct sustained attention to six objects, namely, the Buddha, the *dharma,* the *sangha,* charity, ethical conduct, and the supernatural (Verse 4). It is difficult to rise from existence as an animal to the dignity of a human being, but it is at the point of human life that one may proceed on the path to liberation, therefore "remembrance concerning [the care to be taken of] the body is the only way that must be trod" (Verses 54, 59). Nevertheless, everything is impermanent, and the body itself will inevitably reach its end (Verses 56, 68). Therefore one should give up the attachments which bind one in the jail of continued existences (Verse 23), know that of all possessions contentment is the best (Verse 34), and strive by morality, knowledge, and contemplation to attain the *nirvana* which is not subject to age, death, or decay, and is freed from earth, water, fire, wind, sun, and moon (Verse 105).[104]

Ratnavali. The longer designation of this letter is *Rajaparikatha-ratnamala* or "the precious garland of advice for the king." The letter is preserved in part in a Sanskrit fragment,[105] and fully in a Tibetan translation[106] and in a Chinese translation made by Paramartha between 558 and 569 C.E.[107] A commentary on the work was composed by Ajitamitra, and the commentator says that the king to whom the letter is addressed was the same as the recipient of the *Suhrllekha*.

In the Sanskrit text of the *Ratnavali* the virtues of ethical conduct are extolled in much the same way as in the *Suhrllekha*, and it is said that "he who does not transgress the law on account of worldly cravings, hatred, fear, and mental bewilderment must be considered as a man possessed of faith; nobody is a fitter recipient than he for salvation" (Verse 6). Abstention from evil deeds is called for, and their evil consequences if indulged in are explained: "Those who kill any living being shall have a short life in a new existence. . . . Drinking of intoxicating liquors is the cause of mental confusion," and so forth; in short: "From sinfulness every pain and every unhappy destiny are derived; from sinlessness every happy destiny and every pleasure in life are derived" (Verses 8–21).

Philosophically, however, one "cannot maintain either that this world is not or that it is in reality" (Verse 38), and *nirvana* itself is beyond "any notion of existence and non-existence" (Verse 42). Thus the doctrine enunciated can be considered neither nihilism nor realism:

> To say it in a few words, the nihilistic view consists in denying that *karma* brings forth its effect. This view is sinful and causes rebirth in the hells. It is called a wrong view.
>
> To say it in a few words, the realistic view consists in affirming that *karma* brings forth its effect. It is meritorious and causes rebirth in happy conditions of existence. It is called the right view.
>
> But when through the right knowledge one has suppressed any notion of existence or non-existence, one is beyond sin and virtue. Therefore the saints say that this is the salvation from good as well as from bad conditions of existence (Verses 43–45).[108]

Thus for Nagarjuna and the Madhyamika, absolute truth is beyond either negation or affirmation.

Of the "four suns" named by Xuan Zang it remains to mention Aryadeva, also called Deva *bodhisattva*. In close connection with their accounts of Nagarjuna, Xuan Zang, Buston, and Taranatha all tell something of Aryadeva's life, and he figures also in Chinese tradition. According to both Chinese and Tibetan sources, Aryadeva was born as the son of a king of Lanka, but became an ordained Buddhist monk, and went on pilgrimage to the temples and shrines of India. There he met Nagarjuna and became his great disciple. After Nagarjuna passed away, Aryadeva worked for the welfare of living beings by studying and meditating in the lands in the south, then later stayed at Nalanda for a long time. Throughout his career he was very successful in theological debate. It was said that he had given away one of his eyes and, upon one occasion when he had vanquished a heretic, the monks asked, "Who is this one-eyed?" to which Aryadeva replied:

> The Terrific One (Maheśvara, Śiva), though he has three eyes,
> Cannot perceive the Absolute Truth;
> Indra, though endowed with a thousand eyes,
> Is likewise unable to see it.
> But Aryadeva, who has only one eye,
> Has the intuition of the True Essence
> Of all the three Spheres of Existence.[109]

As the outstanding disciple of Nagarjuna, Aryadeva devoted himself to the refutation of contending schools of thought and the systematization of the Madhyamika doctrine, and in the course of this work wrote many books, the *Catuh-Śataka*, the *Akshara-Śatakam*, etc., many of which were translated into Tibetan and Chinese.[110]

Akshara-Śatakam, as an example of Aryadeva's works, is a "treatise in one hundred letters." It was elucidated in a longer commentary, and was translated into Chinese by Bodhiruci between 508 and 535 C.E. As the commentator sets forth the doctrine, there is a discussion, for example, of the *dharmas*. By this time the word *dharma* has many meanings. It can mean ultimate reality, or doctrine, or practice, or event, or condition, or thing, or element. In the present discussion it is evidently used at the outset in the sense of element, but in the last sentence of the quotation below in the sense of doctrine. An opponent declares that *dharmas* are neither born nor destroyed, because they exist eternally. The exponent of the Madhyamika doctrine replies:

> "If it exists previously, no agency is necessary; thus, if the clod of earth is [already] the pot, no potter is necessary; or if the thread is already cloth, no weaver is necessary. Inasmuch as a pot and cloth wait for their being accomplished through able workmen, it is known that in the cause there is no effect. If in the cause there be already the effect, then no future *dharma* exists. If there is no future *dharma*, then there is no birth and destruction. There being no birth and destruction, there is also no good and evil. There being no good and evil, there is also no agency, action, sin, merit, fruit-[and]-retribution. In this way, then, all *dharmas* become non-existent.... All *dharmas* as worldly reality are like a dream, [which is] neither really existent nor non-existent, nor without a cause.... When one examines well a doctrine like this, a feeling of faith and reverence is profoundly originated. The faithful heart seeks for the true *dharma* ... and not taking [either] to non-existence [or] existence, the way to calm extinction is realized."[111]

As just seen, in the Madhyamika school as represented by Nagarjuna and Aryadeva the following of the "middle way" means refusing to think of absolute reality *(śunyata)* in terms of either existence or non-existence. According to the Yogacara school, however, this is an extreme view, and to be rejected. Rather, reality is both existent and non-existent. As in the *Lankavatara Sutra*, the world of phenomena is unreal, but pure consciousness *(vijnanamatra)* is real. Since this consciousness is embraced in the Absolute Mind, the absolute is ultimately attainable by the "yoga practice" *(yogacara)* which this school teaches. So the "middle way" is here in the Yogacara tradition an intermediate position between the pluralism of the Hinayana, which accepts all elements *(dharmas)* as real, and the Madhyamika scepticism, in which all elements are unreal. In the rise of the Yogacara school the major names are those of Asanga and Vasubandhu.[112]

Asanga and Vasubandhu

In the *History of Buddhism in India* by Taranatha (completed in 1608 C.E.) the two teachers just named are described as half-brothers, Asanga the older being the son of a *brahmani* mother and a *kshatriya* father, while Vasubandhu the younger was the son of the same mother and a *brahmana* father.[113] In the record of the visit of Xuan Zang (629–645 C.E.) to Gandhara and its capital Purushapura (Peshawar) "Asanga *bodhisattva*" and "Vasubandhu *bodhisattva*" are named among the "many authors of *śastras*" which "this border-land of India has produced." In Purushapura Xuan Zang saw the house of Vasubandhu in which he prepared the *Abhidharmakośa Śastra,* and later in Ayodhya Xuan Zang saw places where both Asanga and Vasubandhu worked and taught.[114] Yi Jing (671–695 C.E.) also names both Asanga and Vasubandhu, and describes them and others as belonging to the "middle ages" between the "early age" of Nagarjuna, Deva, and Aśvaghosha, and the "recent years" near his own time.[115] It is probable, therefore, that Asanga and Vasubandhu were born toward the end of the fourth century C.E., and it is also probable that at the outset they were members of the Sarvastivada school of the Hinayana which Yi Jing and others say was so strong in North India, but they became adherents of the Mahayana and in particular exponents of the Yogacara doctrine over against the Madhyamika.

Asanga. As Taranatha continues the account, it was upon the advice of his mother that Asanga took up ordination as a Buddhist monk. Devoting himself to study and meditation, he gained a general understanding of the three Pitakas of the Hinayana and of most of the *sutras* of the Mahayana, but found the *Prajnaparamita Sutra* difficult to comprehend because of its verbal repetitions. As a result of special devotions directed to the *bodhisattva* Maitreya, however, Asanga was brought up into the Tushita heaven and there heard the Mahayana doctrine "in its entirety" from the *bodhisattva*. Afterwards, back on earth, he put into written form "the five works of Maitreya," and composed treatises of his own.

In this case it has been supposed by some that Maitreya was an actual earthly teacher of Asanga, whose name was the same as that of the *bodhisattva,* and who was therefore later confused with the future Buddha, and to distinguish between the two the hypothetical earthly teacher is sometimes called Maitreyanatha. On the other hand the more likely explanation may simply be that Asanga really claimed to have been inspired by the *bodhisattva* Maitreya and to have received by revelation the understanding of deeper meanings which had previously eluded him.[116]

Asanga, Taranatha says, was both humble and at the same time extremely firm, and was never satiated with listening to the doctrine nor with preaching the doctrine without consideration of material benefit. As a result of his preaching and that of his disciples, the Mahayana, which had declined, was again spread in all directions and acquired much fame. The latter years of Asanga were spent in Nalanda, where he was regularly successful in doctrinal debate, and at last he passed away in nearby Rajagriha.

According to Tibetan sources "the five works of Maitreya" which Asanga composed are the *Mahayanasutralankara, Madhyantavibhanga, Dharmadharmatavibhanga, Mahayanauttaratantra,* and *Abhisamayalankara.* Other works of Asanga are the *Mahayanasamparigraha* (translated into Chinese by Paramartha in 563 C.E.), and the *Yogacaryabhumi* (on the stages in the *yoga* practice of a *bodhisattva*).[117]

Of the above works, the *Abhisamayalankara,* for example, is preserved in a Sanskrit text and a Tibetan translation.[118] The work is a commentary in the form of a verse summary of the *Pancavimśatisahasrika Prajnaparamita* (The Perfection of Wisdom in 25,000 Lines). The theme is "reunion with the absolute," and the climax of the precisely outlined discussion is a description of the wonderful "*dharma*-body" of "those who have attained a state of purity in every respect."[119]

Vasubandhu. Vasubandhu, younger brother of Asanga, was also ordained as a Buddhist monk, studied thoroughly "the three Śravapitakas" (the *śravaka* was a Hinayana disciple), and then went to Kashmir to study under the teacher Sanghabhadra for an understanding of the "higher doctrine" of the Abhidharma and for learning the views of the eighteen schools. When he returned to Magadha, Vasubandhu read the writings of his brother, but failed to understand the Mahayana and spoke sarcastically of the written works as heavy enough to be an elephant's load, but useless in sense. Afterward, however, he was converted by his brother, and then felt that he had committed a great sin by showing disrespect to the Mahayana, and wanted to cut off his tongue which had uttered the disparaging remarks. Instead, Asanga counseled him to make atonement by preaching the Mahayana doctrine widely and by preparing commentaries on many *sutras*. This Vasubandhu did, composing commentaries on both Hinayana and Mahayana *sutras*, and also writing original works of his own. In fact Vasubandhu was considered to surpass his older brother in the keenness of his intelligence, and it was said that in all the time after the *nirvana* of the Buddha there was none as profoundly knowledgeable as he in the scriptures. For example, he learned the *Satasahasrika Prajnaparamita* (The Perfection of Wisdom in 100,000 Lines) and many other *sutras* word for word, and also their significance, and used to read every day in an hour or two the whole of the *Ashtasahasrika Prajnaparamita* (The Perfection of Wisdom in 8,000 Lines).

After the passing away of Asanga, Vasubandhu served at Nalanda as both a preceptor *(upadhyaya)* and a teacher *(acarya)*, and performed many other activities. He did not visit any non-Buddhist part of the country, nor any distant land, but stayed for the most part in Magadha. In his time the number of monks became greater even than in the time of Asanga. Later he went to Nepal, and vastly increased the number of monks there too.

Of the many works of Vasubandhu, the *Abhidharmakośa* (mentioned by Xuan Zang) is from the Sarvastivadin phase of the life of the author, and is an exposition of the Abhidharma, which is considered the most complete and systematic treatment of the "higher doctrine" ever written, and is accepted as authoritative in both the Hinayana and the Mahayana. The *Trimśika-vijnaptimatratasiddhi* (treatise in thirty stanzas on representation-only) and the *Vimśatika-vijnaptimatratasiddhi* (treatise in twenty stanzas on representation-only) are from the later Mahayana phase of the life of Vasubandhu, and are considered the two classical works on Buddhist idealism, constituting a refutation of belief in the reality of the objective world, and a defense of the Yogacara doctrine of the reality of pure consciousness *(vijnanamatra)*. All three of the just-mentioned works were translated into Chinese by several different scholars, most notably by Xuan Zang.

The *Vimśatika* (as the last of the foregoing works is called for short), for example, begins (in Xuan Zang's Chinese version) with this statement of Vasubandhu's central proposition: "In the Mahayana it is established that the three worlds are representation-only."[120] The Mahayana is here, of course, that of the Yogacara school. The three worlds are the three divisions of the total universe this side of *nirvana*, i.e., the world of desire *(kamadhatu)*, the world of form *(rupadhatu)*, and the world without form *(arupadhatu)*. As for "representation-only," the expression may also be rendered "mere idea," and it corresponds with the other terms already used, such as "thought," "mind," and "consciousness," to express the Yogacara doctrine that all apparently external sense objects constitute only an illusion.

In the body of the work this central doctrine is illustrated by comparisons, for example, with defective eyesight and with dreams, to show that it is only mental concepts which really exist.

> When inner representations arise, seemingly external objects appear; as [persons] having bad eyes see hairs and flies. [But] herein is no particle of truth.
>
> Just as in time of dreaming . . . although there are no outer objects . . . immediate awareness may yet be had, so also must the immediate awareness at other times be understood.[121]

Also in the course of the argument many objections, posed by an imaginary interrogator, are considered and answered. With respect to the analogy of dreams, for example, the questioner points out that the world naturally knows that dream-objects are non-existent, and asks why, if the objects known in waking time are the same, this is not naturally known too? To this the answer is that "before we have awakened we cannot know that what is seen in the dream does not exist," and even so we cannot know the unreality of "the world's falsely discriminated recurrent impressions," which are "confused and fevered as in the midst of a dream," until we attain the true awakening. "[But] if there is a time when we attain that world-transcending knowledge, emancipatory and non-discriminative, then we call it the true awakening."[122] Yet the doctrine of "representation-only" is so profound that only Buddhas can comprehend all of its implications, "because the knowledge of the Buddhas, World-honored Ones, is in all realms and in all kinds without obstacle."[123]

As already noted, the *Madhyantavibhanga* is one of "the five works of Maitreya" composed by Asanga, but the original work of Asanga (in verse form) was later commented on by Vasubandhu, and then in turn the whole was further commented on by Sthiramati (fifth century C.E.), and the entire work including these commentaries of Vasubandhu and Sthiramati is extant in its original Sanskrit.[124]

The title of the work is explained by Buston in this way: "*Anta*—'extremity,' means the extremities of realism and nihilism, or otherwise those of eternalism and materialism. Madhya—'the middle,' is the middle way shunning both these extremities. The treatise, as it gives an analysis *(vibhanga)* of both these points is called *Madhyantavibhanga*."[125]

In the introduction to the work Vasubandhu writes a stanza of salutation:

> I fervently salute (Maitreya),
> That son of the Accomplished Buddha,
> Who has revealed to us this treatise,
> And (Saint Asanga I salute, the teacher)
> Who has explained (to us) its meaning.
> To analyze that meaning now
> I will (myself) attempt an effort.

Sthiramati in turn explains: "It is a rule among educated men to salute their teacher and [to worship] their tutelary deity before beginning a work. Therefore this [our author Vasubandhu] . . . begins his commentary upon the *Discourse on Discrimination between Middle and Extremes* (namely, the extremes of scepticism and of realism) by an expression of devotion to its divine author and to its [first] expositor."

It is plain that Sthiramati does not think of Maitreya as a historical personage on earth, but as a divine *bodhisattva,* and he goes on to say that Maitreya has in fact gone through all the successive stages of a *bodhisattva's* career and is at this point separated from final *nirvana* only by his present and last rebirth in the Tushita heaven. As for Asanga, the first expositor, and Vasubandhu, who studied the text under Asanga's guidance and composed a commentary of his own, Sthiramati describes them as two great men, who were in the highest degree endowed with an analytical understanding, and thus were capable of comprehending the sacred text unmistakably, of retaining its meaning, and of communicating it to others.[126]

Sthiramati further explains the aim of the treatise in the statement:

> This work is undertaken with the aim of establishing the right theory of Absolute Reality, i.e., the theory of the relativity of every element singly and the collective reality of their sum-total. This is done by repudiating a double error, namely, (1) the error that the relativity of every element singly implies the unreality of all the elements collectively (nihilism), and (2) the error that the denial of a substantive soul as an internal controller [of the personality] implies the denial of an Absolute [in the collective totality of the elements of the universe].[127]

In the body of the work an example of the basic text may be seen in the stanza which says:

> We have therefore established this
> That our (consciousness) creates illusion.
> (Reality) is not such (as it appears).
> Nor is it a total blank,
> Because that illusion can be extinguished,
> And this extinction means salvation.

On this Vasubandhu comments:

> Therefore, in the shape in which [the world] appears to us, in that shape it does not really exist. But this does not [mean that in the phenomenal world] there is absolutely nothing real, because this universal illusion [has a real cause] which produces it. . . . Otherwise [without admitting the reality of consciousness itself] there could neither be a real bondage nor a real salvation, and we would bring upon ourselves the blame [of being materialists] who do not recognize the difference between phenomenal impurity and the purity of the Absolute.[128]

Again near the end of the work when Vasubandhu asks how the argument in favor of the existence of an Absolute Reality behind the veil of the phenomenal world is to be determined, the answer is in a stanza of the basic text:

> If there were no phenomenal impurity
> All living beings would be saints,
> But if the pure transcendent Absolute did not exist,
> The effort for salvation would be vain.[129]

VAJRAYANA

As the Hinayana (small vehicle) provided the foundation for the Mahayana (great vehicle), so also the Mahayana became the basis for a yet further development, which may be classified as still falling within the Mahayana, since it uses philosophical concepts of the Mahayana, or since it offers a distinctive system of ritual action to lead the practitioner to salvation. May be classified as a third major form of Buddhism, namely, the Vajrayana (thunderbolt or diamond vehicle), also called the Tantrayana (*tantric* vehicle).[130]

In the Mahayana the Madhyamika school affirmed the doctrine of "emptiness" (*śunyata*), i.e., that no reality attaches to any thing in itself, and the Yogacara school explained that things are neither non-existent (as the Madhyamika doctrine might seem to say) nor existent (in the sense of independent eternality), but are phenomena of consciousness. It may be understood that the religious intent of these theoretical considerations in the Mahayana is to provide the necessary basis in knowledge for proceeding on the path to liberation, for if suffering (*dukkha*), for example, were real in its own nature, it could not change and it could therefore not be eliminated, and if *nirvana* were existent in itself it would not be related to existence in *samsara*, and therefore could not be reached.[131]

The Vajrayana, accordingly, accepts the theoretical basis already provided by the Madhyamika and Yogacara formulations of the Mahayana, and goes on chiefly to elaborate the practical methods by which to come to enlightenment. These methods most characteristically include a whole series of *yogic* practices, e.g., the use of *mudra* (the Sanskrit word means "seal," and is applied to hand gestures, bodily postures, and so forth), of *pranayama* (breath control), of *mantra* (verbal formula), and of *mandala* (symbolic diagram), and the direction of meditation not only toward Buddhas and *bodhisattvas* but also along with them toward many gods and goddesses. In all of these respects there are antecedents or comparable practices in earlier Buddhism and/or in Hinduism, especially in *tantric* Hinduism, but the total configuration in the Vajrayana is distinctive.

Like *tantric* Hinduism, *tantric* Buddhism probably developed chiefly in North India and in the centuries from around 500 c.e. onward. From there it was carried northward and, when all forms of Buddhism were virtually wiped out in India by the Muslim conquest and the revival of Hinduism, it was this *tantric* form of Buddhism that was chiefly preserved and transmitted in Tibet, and is now found also in the mountain regions from Ladakh and Nepal to Sikkim and Bhutan, and in the Indian centers of Tibetan refugees.

Tibetan Buddhism

In the Tibetan form of Buddhism[132] the fully ordained monk is called by the term *dge slong* (pronounced gelong, also gelung), corresponding to the Sanskrit *bhikshu*. The ordinary monk (*grwa pa*, pronounced trapa) is a resident of a monastery; others are married clergy, and there are many adherents who are lay householders. The Sanskrit *guru* (teacher, master, especially of *tantric* practice) is translated in Tibetan as *bla ma* (pronounced lama), and this term describes those who, whether monks are not, are qualified to guide disciples. Such masters as may be recognized (usually in their early childhood) as incarnations of great departed teachers or even of the Buddha, are designated by the term *sprul sku* (pronounced trulku, also tulku). Such an "incarnate" is also usually the central figure in a monastery in which he is in residence. A further title of honor for one of exalted status is *rin po che* (pronounced rimpoche), which means "precious."

As for the term *vajra*, in the Sanskrit this word means both "thunderbolt" and "diamond." In Tibetan it is translated as *rdo rje* (pronounced dorje), where *rdo* means "stone" and *rje* means "ruler," so the *dorje* is here literally the king of stones, i.e., the diamond, and it is the "diamond" connotation which is most prominent in the use of the term. In the sense of "thunderbolt" the *vajra* can mean that which strikes through suddenly and irresistibly, and can provide a picture of the breaking in of the supreme enlightenment, which the Vajrayana believes can indeed happen instantaneously. In the sense of "diamond" the *vajra/dorje* means that which is adamantine, indestructible, and so hard that nothing can stop, mar, or dent it, and it thus provides a synonym for the *śūnyatā*, the substance—which is non-substance—of voidness, and also a symbol for the wisdom which cuts through error and leads to Buddhahood. With this connotation in view the name Vajradhara (Tibetan *rDo rje 'chang*, pronounced Dorje Chhang, "thunderbolt/diamond bearer") is given to *bodhisattvas* and Buddhas, and most especially to the great Buddha from whom all the teachings of Tantra are said to have originated. This great Buddha is also named Vajrasattva (Tibetan *rDo rje sems dpa*, pronounced Dorje Sempa), "adamantine being." In view of its several meanings *vajra/dorje* is also used as a prefix with many other names and words, e.g., a *vajracarya* is a spiritual teacher, the *vajrasana* is the meditation posture, the *rdo rje sku* is the diamond body, the *rdo rje ye shes* is the diamond consciousness, and the *rdo rje theg pa* is the diamond vehicle, i.e., the Vajrayana.

As a symbol and as a ritual instrument the *vajra/dorje* appears in a form probably borrowed originally from the symbol of the Hindu deity Indra and originally signifying a thunderbolt. Made as a scepter the object may appear as a central cylinder from which on either end emerges a stylized lotus blossom, or as having a central nucleus from which on either side three or five rays emerge to join again at the ends. It may also be a *viśvavajra* (double *vajra*) in the form of a Greek cross, with rays radiating from its four ends. Along with the *vajra/dorje* a bell (Sanskrit *ghanta*, Tibetan *dril bu*, pronounced trilpu) is used, and its handle is sometimes like half a *vajra*-scepter so that it is a *vajraghanta*. Together the scepter and the bell stand for skill in means (*upaya*, which is also equated with *karuna*, active compassion) and wisdom (*prajna*, which comprehends *śūnyata*), the inseparable union of which (*prajna-upaya, prajnopaya*) is essential to the attainment of enlightenment. The *vajra/dorje* can also represent the jewel and the *ghanta/trilpu* the lotus in the *mantra, Om Mani Padme Hum*, where the jewel can be the truth in the heart of the doctrine, which is the lotus.

As throughout the entire Buddhist world the *stupa*, known in Tibet as a *chorten*, is a major symbolic monument. The word means literally an "offering holder," and the chorten may hold sacred objects or may serve as a tomb but usually only for a prominent personage. Along with the chorten the religion centers in the monastery (in Tibet a *gompa* or solitary place) and the temple (in Tibet a *lha khang* or god's house), provided innumerable images, tankas, mandalas, and other symbolic objects.

As for writings, the Vajrayana doctrines are set forth most distinctively in the works of a whole series of Indian and Tibetan teachers, and especially in the books called Tantras and Yogas.

TEACHERS, TANTRAS, AND YOGAS OF THE VAJRAYANA

Teachers

According to the already cited *History of Buddhism in India and Tibet* by Buston, the *History of Buddhism in India* by Taranatha, and other Tibetan sources, the Tibetans were converted to Buddhism under their king *Srong btsan sgam po* (pronounced Songtsen Gampo) (r. 629–649 C.E.), while the later king *Khri srong lde brtsan* (pronounced Trhisong Detsen) (755–797) brought to Tibet from India the two famous teachers Śantarakshita and Padmasambhava.[133]

Śantarakshita. Śantarakshita—who is called the *acarya* (teacher) Śantarakshita by Taranatha, and the *acarya bodhisattva* by Buston—was the *upadhyaya* (preceptor) of the university at Nalanda. At the time when Śantarakshita first appears in the account by Buston, he was, on some account, in Nepal, and a minister of King Trhisong Detsen met him there and invited him to come to Tibet. After it was ascertained that he was virtuous and had no untoward thoughts, Śantarakshita was allowed to preach in the king's palace in Tibet, which he did for four months, setting forth basic Buddhist doctrines with an exposition of the ten virtues, the eighteen component parts of the individual, and the chain of twelve causes which account for the misery of earthly existence. The demons of Tibet, it is said in Buston's account, were infuriated by this preaching, and caused many disasters, so the people demanded that the *acarya* go back to Nepal. Later, however, Śantarakshita was invited back again to Tibet, and when he returned this time he suggested to Trhisong Detsen that the king also invite a teacher named Padmasambhava—who was endowed with great power and ability—to come and subdue the demons.

Tattvasangraha. Of many writings which are attributed to Śantarakshita, there is a major example in the very large *Tattvasangraha* which, along with a commentary by the author's disciple Kamalaśila, survives both in its Sanskrit original and in a Tibetan translation.[134] In this work the philosophy of consciousness is expounded along the lines of the Yogacara doctrine, and the views of many other schools and teachers, both Buddhist and also non-Buddhist are refuted.

Padmasambhava. While Śantarakshita stood for the academic and monastic side of Buddhism, Padmasambhava, who was invited to Tibet by King Trhisong Detsen at the suggestion of Śantarakshita, represented its mystical and ritualistic side. His Tibetan name is *Pad ma 'byung gnas* (pronounced Pema Jungnê), and he is the most eminent figure in the spiritual lineage of the oldest order of Tibetan Buddhism, the *rNying ma pa* (pronounced Nyingma-pa) or "old school," as it is called in contrast with the later orders of the "new school" (*gSar ma pa*). Indeed Padmasambhava is so important in Tibetan tradition that all Tibetan Buddhists venerate him as the *Gu ru Rin po che* (pronounced Kuru Rimpochê), the "precious teacher."

The biography of Padmasambhava is given in legendary form in a Tibetan work known as the *Pad ma thang yig* (pronounced Pema Thangyig), meaning the Padma Scroll. Padmasambhava is supposed to have dictated this biography to his Tibetan wife named *Ye shes mtsho rgyal* (pronounced Yeshê Tshogyal), herself regarded as an incarnation of Sarasvati, the goddess of learning, and to have instructed her to hide the book away that it might be rediscovered in a later and more favorable time. This and other texts supposedly similarly hidden by other early teachers of Buddhism in Tibet are called by the term *gter ma* (pronounced terma), meaning "concealed treasure," and the supposedly predestined and inspired persons who later found the long hidden documents and often translated them from some other language into Tibetan are called *gter ston* (pronounced terchen), meaning "discoverer and teacher of concealed treasure." In the case of the *Pema Thangyig,* it was rediscovered more than five centuries after the time of Padmasambhava and recovered from its place in the heart of a doorkeeper figure at a crystal rock cave in Yarlung where Padmasambhava had celebrated a ritual. The finder was a *tantric* named *O rgyan gling pa* (pronounced Urgyan Lingpa) (1323–circa 1360 C.E.), who both here and also at other places discovered many more "concealed treasures."[135]

According to this biography Padmasambhava was born from a lotus (*padma*, pronounced *pema,* hence his name, lotus born) in Lake Dhanakosha in the country of Urgyan (the Tibetan name represents the Indian Uddiyana, probably ancient Swat). The child was raised by a king of that country, named Indrabhuti, who is an actually known author of numerous *tantric* texts, so Swat was evidently a center of *tantric* Buddhism. Later Padmasambhava studied in many places, learned astrology, medicine, and magic, as well as *tantric* doctrine, and practiced *yoga* together with a female companion named Mandarava. To her, when she inquired about his parentage and country, he declared:

> "I have no parents. I am a gift of the Voidness. I am the essentiality of Amitabha and of Avalokiteśvara, born of a lotus in the Dhanakosha Lake; and, being of the same essence as the Adi-Buddha, Vajradhara, and the Buddha of Bodhgaya, I am the Lotus miraculously produced from all these. I will aid all beings. . . . I have collected all perfection doctrines, and I know the past, present, and future in completeness. I will plant the banners of the truth in the ten directions throughout this world. I am the matchless (teacher) of all."[136]

As already noted, Vajradhara, also called Vajrasattva, is the great Buddha from whom the *tantric* teachings originated, and in the present passage he is conceived as closely associated with, or even equivalent to, the primordial Buddha, the Adi-Buddha. As for the Buddha of Bodhgaya, i.e., Śakyamuni, who is of the same essence as Vajradhara and the Adi-Buddha, he is said elsewhere in this same work to have distributed his teachings over four periods: in the first period he taught the four noble truths of the Hinayana; in the second period he preached the Mahayana; in the third period he instructed various orders of spiritual beings; and in the fourth period he taught *tantric* doctrines, but only exoterically, then directed Vajrapani (*vajra* bearer) to teach the esoteric aspects of the Tantras.[137]

In his long life, according to the *Pema Thangyig*, Padmasambhava traveled, taught, and performed miracles in many countries. As for his coming to Tibet, both Buston and the *Pema Thangyig* state that it was Śantarakshita who suggested that he be brought and King Trhisong Detsen (755–797 C.E.) who invited him to come, and both sources also tell how Śantarakshita and Padmasambhava were involved together in the king's attempt to build the monastery of *bSam yas* (pronounced Samyê). When the king's invitation to come to Tibet reached Padmasambhava he was at Bodhgaya. He set out from there on the fifteenth day of the eleventh month according to the Tibetan calendar (which is lunar, and begins the year with the new moon in February), and reached Nepal on the thirtieth day of the same month. He stayed in Nepal for three months and, having subdued many evils, was asked to stay, but said, "I must go; the time has come to subdue the evil spirits of Tibet."

In Tibet Padmasambhava was met at Tod-lung (12 miles [19 km.] from Lhasa) by a royal delegation, and at Zung-khar near the Haopori Pass (7.5 miles [12 km.] from Lhasa) by the king himself, then was taken in procession, to the accompaniment of music and dancing by masked dancers, to Lhasa. Working in Tibet Padmasambhava little by little subdued the gods and goddesses and the evil spirits throughout the land, performed many miracles, and established his reputation as a great exorcist. Up to this point, however, the attempt of Trhisong Detsen to build a monastery at Samye had been thwarted by the demons, because the site had not been properly consecrated. So now the king brought both Padmasambhava and the *acarya bodhisattva* (i.e., Śantarakshita) to Samye, seated them on a gold throne and a silver throne respectively, and made religious offerings. After that, Padmasambhava constrained the gods and the demons to further the work, Śantarakshita made a plan after the model of the famous monastery of Odantapur in

India (the location of which has not been identified), and the construction was completed successfully.

The Samye monastery, founded thus under King Trhisong Detsen (probably about 775 C.E.), was the first in which Tibetans themselves were trained as monks, and it became a great center of Buddhist studies in Tibet, eventually being open to all schools of Tibetan Buddhism. Its full name was "the academy for obtaining the heap of unchanging meditation." Later (between the tenth and fourteenth centuries) other centers of the "old school" were established, and even later the greatest Nyingma monasteries were built, of which the two chief are *rDo rje brag* (pronounced Dorjetrak) founded in 1610, and *sMin grol gling* (pronounced Mintröl-ling) founded in 1676. In succession to Padmasambhava a long line of personages—many considered to be "incarnate" *lamas* and reappearances of Padmasambhava or his disciples—continued the Nyingma tradition. Among these, and prior to Urgyan Lingpa who rediscovered the *Padma Thangyig*, was *Nyang ral Nyi ma 'od zer* (pronounced Nyangrê Nyima Oser) (1136–1203 C.E.) who, like Urgyan Lingpa, was also a discoverer of "concealed treasures" and was himself the founder of the *rDzogs chen mo* (pronounced dzok chhenmo) school, which represents the chief *tantric* tradition of the Nyingma-pa.

Following upon the account of the consecration of the Samye monastery, the *Pema Thangyig* relates further:

> Later on, the Buddhists and Bon-pos in Tibet publicly debated; and, the Bon-pos being defeated, the king expelled most of those who would not embrace Buddhism, to the deserts of the north, to Nepal, Mongolia, and other sparsely populated countries. Buddhism was introduced into all parts of Tibet. The Kangyur and Tengyur and other Mahayana works were translated from the Sanskrit into Tibetan. So also were the exoteric and esoteric Tantras and *mantras*, and treatises on medicine and astrology.[138]

The Bon-pos (*bon po*, pronounced pönpo), mentioned here, are the priests and the adherents of the indigenous pre-Buddhistic religion of Tibet known as Bon, which is probably also the original name of the country, Bod (d and n being often interchanged in Tibetan). This religion is generally described in its early form as a shamanistic animism. The founder is supposed to have been a priest named *gShen rab* (pronounced Shenrap), who came from somewhere in the West, and holds a position in Bon somewhat analogous to that of Padmasambhava in the Nyingma-pa. With the expulsion of most of the Bon-pos by King Trhisong Detsen and the introduction of Buddhism into all parts of the country, as described by the *Pema Thangyig*, Buddhism was recognized as the state religion of Tibet, an event datable in the year 779 C.E. In spite of the rivalry between Bon and Buddhism, there was no doubt some amalgamation between them and in later times Bon itself was reorganized with a doctrinal formulation and a monastic order similar to those of the Buddhists. Also, although the Bon-pos were largely driven out of Central Tibet, there were large numbers of them who continued elsewhere, especially in Eastern Tibet, continuing into the modern period.[139]

The Kangyur and the Tengyur, also mentioned in the immediately preceding quotation from the *Pema Thangyig*, are the two divisions of the complete Tibetan Buddhist scriptures. The *bKa' 'gyur* (pronounced Kangyur, meaning "translation of the word") comprises the Vinaya, Sutras, and Tantras, and the *bsTan 'gyur* (pronounced Tengyur, meaning "translation of treatises") contains commentaries and also works on such subjects as grammar, astrology, and medicine. The same names are also used for the equivalent collection of Bon scriptures. According to

Tibetan tradition, many of these works go back in their Tibetan versions to the time of Padmasambhava and, as in the case of his biography, were hidden away and rediscovered later, and many of the texts were translations from Indian, Central Asian, and Chinese sources, made by specially chosen and appointed persons who were called by the honorary title of *lo tsa ba* (pronounced lotsawa), meaning "translator." Finally the collection and editing of the books to form the canon was done by Buston (1290–1364 C.E.)—whose *History of Buddhism in India and Tibet* we have already cited—and in complete printed form the canon extends to 100 volumes in the Kangyur and 225 volumes in the Tengyur.[140]

After a severe interruption in the history of Buddhism in Tibet through persecution by King Langdarma (838–842 C.E.), it was under the kings *Ye shes 'od* (pronounced Yeshê Ö) and his nephew or grandnephew *Byang chub 'od* (pronounced Changchup Ö), both members of the royal family but living as monks, in the small kingdom of *Gu ge* (pronounced Kukê) in Western Tibet that important work for the renewal of the doctrine was done by Rinchen Sangpo and Atiśa. The king Yeshe O was reportedly unsure of the validity of the Tantras as true expositions of the word of the Buddha, so he chose twenty-one young Tibetan men and sent them to Kashmir to learn Sanskrit and study in the important Buddhist schools which still existed there. Of the twenty-one only two survived to return as scholars, the more famous of the two being *Rin chen bzang po* (pronounced Rinchen Sangpo) (958–1055 C.E.). He came back as an enthusiastic follower of Tantrism, and won renown as a teacher, a translator from the Sanskrit of many Sutras and Tantras and their commentaries, and the builder of many temples (*lha khang*, literally god's house), including that of *mTho gling* (pronounced Tholing), the most famous temple in Kuke. Other men, known by the term *lo tsa ba* (pronounced lotsawa) or "translator," were going to India to study and gather texts, and Changchup O commissioned a delegation headed by *Nag tsho lo tsa ba* (pronounced Naktsho lotsawa) to convey an invitation to the famous Indian scholar Atiśa to come to Tibet.

Atiśa. The life and work of Atiśa (982–1054 C.E.) are known largely from Tibetan sources, especially including the very large work known in full as *The Blue Annals, the Stages of the Appearance of the Doctrine and Preachers in the Land of Tibet*, or in brief simply as the *Blue Annals* (*Deb ther sngon po*, pronounced Tepther Ngönpo), which was composed between 1476 and 1478 C.E. by the Tibetan scholar *'Gos lo tsa ba gZhon nu dpal*, usually known simply as *'Gos lo tsa ba* (pronounced Gos lotsawa) (1392–1481 C.E.).[141] As we learn from these sources, Atiśa was born as the second son of a king in East India, and was given the name Candragarbha. In his early career he was initiated into *tantric* doctrine and given the name Guhya-jnanavajra. While yet a young man he was ordained a monk, and thereupon received the ordination name of Dipankara (the name of a former Buddha) or Dipankara Srijnana. In Tibet, however, he is usually called *Jo bo rje* (pronounced Chowo Jê) Atiśa, meaning the "noble lord" Atiśa, and also *Phul byung*, meaning the "accomplished" or "perfect."

In his educational career Atiśa made a long voyage and studied for twelve years under the teacher Dharmakirti of Suvarnadvipa. Suvarnadvipa is probably the general name for the Malay peninsula and adjacent regions, and Dharmakirti probably taught at Vijayanagara, which is to be identified with Śrivijaya (near Palembang on the island of Sumatra), capital of the state of Śrivijaya, then under the Śailendra kings, who ruled an empire encompassing most of the Malay archipelago and the Malay peninsula. Plainly Śrivijaya was at the time a great center of Buddhist learning.

Back in India, Atiśa distinguished himself in further study and teaching at the Buddhist universities of Somapuri (at modern Paharpur), Odantapuri, and Vikramaśila (the latter two not yet located). Then, under the guidance of his tutelary deity, the goddess Tara, he accepted the invitation to go to Tibet. Leaving in 1040 C.E., he first made a pilgrimage to Bodhgaya and then proceeded to Nepal, where he was received with honor at the Svayambhu shrine (near modern Kathmandu).

From Nepal Atiśa sent a letter back to King Nayapala of Bengal (perhaps on the occasion of the king's formal coronation), which is known as the *Vimala-ratna-lekha-nama*. In it he urged the Buddhist ruler to abide by his vows (for a ruler usually considered as threefold, namely, the vow of an ordinary Buddhist for self-emancipation, the vow of a *bodhisattva* for universal liberation, and the *tantric* or mystic vow), and advised in part:

> Avoiding sleep, folly, and laziness, remain assiduous and ever careful. . . . Behave like [one with] eyes with regard to your own fault but as the blind with regard to the faults of the others. Avoid arrogance and egoism and always meditate on the void *(śunyata)*. . . . Reverence is to be always strengthened. Remember to curb the desires, to remain self-content, and to act in the virtuous way. Give up anger and egoism. Have a humble mind. . . . Do not be garrulous; keep the tongue under control. . . . Look at the objects that attract or repel as but the creations of illusion *(maya)*. . . . Meditate on impermanence and death. . . . Get yourself sprinkled all over first by universal compassion *(karuna)*. . . . Work for removing the sufferings of the living beings. . . . Have the great enlightenment *(mahabodhi)* as the object of all your actions. . . . Make your human life worthwhile, and lead your sight towards *nirvana*.[142]

From Nepal Atiśa went on probably by way of Lake Manasarovara (Tibetan *Ma pham mtsho*, pronounced Mapham Tsho) near Mount Kailasa (Tibetan *Ti se*, pronounced Tisê) to Western Tibet. On the Tibetan border he was welcomed by the representative of the king with a cup of tea prepared in the Tibetan manner and, upon asking the name of the drink, was told that it was *cha* (tea), which was drunk by the Tibetan monks, to which Atiśa replied: "So excellent a beverage as tea must have originated from the moral merits of the monks of Tibet."[143]

Atiśa arrived in Tibet in 1042 C.E., being then in his sixty-first year of life. Rinchen Sangpo was then in his eighty-fifth year, and was accounted the greatest scholar in Tibet, with a specialized knowledge of the Tantras, nevertheless the older man soon acknowledged the superiority of Atiśa. Changchup O also considered himself a disciple of Atiśa, and it was at the special request of the king that Atiśa wrote a work called *Bodhi-patha-pradipa*, or Lamp for the Way of Enlightenment. This is a very compact text of only sixty-six verses (and Atiśa himself later wrote a very large commentary on it called the *Bodhi-marga-pradipa-panjika*), but it is considered Atiśa's major work.

The *Bodhi-patha-pradipa* begins (Verses 1–4) with a threefold classification of personality types *(tri-purusha)*. The person *(purusha)* who is inferior *(adhama)* acts only for worldly pleasures; the mediocre *(madhyama)* person is indifferent to pleasures and opposed to sinful acts, but works for himself alone; the superior *(uttama)* person always wishes to remove all the sufferings of others by his own sufferings. It seems plain that the first of these persons is the one without any concern for the religious ideal; the second is the Hinayanist with the ideal of individual emancipation; the third is the Mahayanist with the ideal of universal liberation.

Of the Mahayana ideal, Atiśa says further (Verses 9–10, 28):

> The first thing to do is to establish empathy *(maitricitta)* with all living beings. . . . Look at all living beings as suffering from miseries and arrive at the firmest determination to work

with the resolution of never turning back for liberating all living beings from the miseries that are born of miseries. . . . Do not be anxious to attain quick enlightenment *(bodhi)* for yourself. Live up to the end [of the *samsara*] for the sake of even a single living being.

The Madhyamika doctrine of the universal void or emptiness (*śunyata*, Tibetan *stong pa nyid*), and the Prajnaparamita requirement of combining wisdom (*prajna*, Tibetan *shes rab,* pronounced sherap) and skill in means (*upaya,* Tibetan *thabs,* pronounced thap), are stated unequivocally (Verses 42, 45, 49, 54):

> The nature of all things *(dharmas),* examined either as unities or as compounds, cannot be determined. Therefore, it is certain that they are void *(śunyata).*
> This world, arising out of delusional thought, is itself delusional.
> One quickly attains enlightenment *(bodhi)* not by mere meditation on the void *(nairatmya)* but by acquiring in oneself the mastery of the *upayas* and by meditation on *prajna.*
> *Prajna* without *upaya* and *upaya* without *prajna* are said to be unfree (literally "tied," i.e., neither one can act by itself). Therefore do not ignore any [of them].

It may be noted that in this quotation *nairatmya* (literally non-selfness," i.e., essencelessness or contentlessness) is used as synonymous with *śunyata,* the two being parallel terms for the "void;" and that "means" are in the plural *(upayas),* presumably to include the first five of the usual six virtues or "perfections" (*paramitas,* Tibetan *phar phyin,* pronounced pharchhin) of the *bodhisattva* path, namely, charity *(dana),* morality *(śila),* forgiveness *(kshanti),* assiduity *(virya),* and meditation *(dhyana),* the sixth *paramita* being *prajna* or wisdom itself. As to the great importance of moral conduct, there is also emphasis upon this in other passages in this same work (even as in the letter of Atiśa to King Nayapala). For example (Verses 26, 30): "Until the attainment of the final enlightenment *(uttama-bodhi),* never allow the mind to be polluted by ill-will, anger, miserliness, and envy. . . . Purify all your actions—physical, oral, and mental—and never indulge in any sinful act."

Finally as to Tantrism, which is explicitly mentioned in the closing part of the *Bodhi-patha-pradipa,* Atiśa says (Verses 59–62) that if one wants to perform the practices *(kriya)* and rites *(carya)* prescribed in the Tantras with the hope of attaining enlightenment quickly, then it should be remembered that these rites can only be performed effectively after one has been properly initiated by a qualified *guru.* "When the *guru,* being fully pleased, confers the initiation that purifies all sins, [the initiate] becomes a fit receptacle for the *siddhis* (a *siddhi* is an "accomplishment," such as, e.g., the remembering of past existences; a *siddha* is an "accomplished one" who has attained to the highest realization)."[144]

Drom. After three years of teaching and writing in Western Tibet, Atiśa was preparing to return to India, but at that point a lay Buddhist of an ancient Tibetan family, named 'Brom ston rGyal ba'i 'byung gnas (pronounced Dromtön Gyelwê Jungnê) and best known simply as Drom (1003–1064 C.E.), became the disciple of Atiśa and persuaded him to stay and come on into Central Tibet. There Atiśa settled at *sNye thang* (pronounced Nethang) only 12 miles (20 km.) from Lhasa, and worked there and at other places in the area including Samye and Lhasa until his death at Nethang in 1054 C.E. Meanwhile Drom was the closest associate of Atiśa and, when Atiśa was about to die, Atiśa asked Drom to continue his work. The conversation of the two at this point is given in the *Blue Annals* as follows:

> The Master said to Drom: "You should build a small monastery, and I shall entrust my teaching to you. Keep it!"

Drom replied: "In general, I am unfit to do it, and in particular, I am only an *upasaka* (lay disciple) unable to perform great works."

The Master replied: "Do the work according to my instructions! I shall bless you. Do not despair!"

So encouraged in spite of his modesty and humility, Drom devoted the ten years that he lived after the death of Atiśa to the work with which he had been charged. He first built a monastery at Nethang and then (in 1057) a shrine at *Rwa sgrengs* (pronounced Reting) (56 miles [90 km.] north of Lhasa). "After that, he never again participated in worldly matters, saying: 'I shall now give up the world,' and only preached the Doctrine." At Reting only a small group of disciples gathered around Drom, not more than sixty "meditative ascetics" residing there permanently, but they formed the nucleus of what became known as the *bKa' gdams pa* (pronounced Kadam-pa) order, with this monastery continuing as the center of the sect. The name of the order, *bKa'*, signifies the words of the Buddha, and *gdams* means teaching; therefore it is all the words of the Buddha which form the Buddhist scriptures to which the name points. In the *Blue Annals* it is explained: "They were called so, because they believed and preached that an individual should practice the entire teaching of the *jina* [the Buddha] (the Sutra and Tantra/Theravada and Mahayana)." Of Drom himself it is said in the *Blue Annals*: "Drom was very learned in both Tantras and Sutras. He kept secret the Vajrayanic doctrine, and did not teach it extensively." In spite of small beginnings the Kadam sect flourished and was eventually reorganized by Tsongkhapa as the Geluk-pa, which became the most influential of all the orders in Tibet. Concluding the account of the Kadam-pa and the spiritual lineage of Drom in the *Blue Annals* it is said: "Drom's labors have been very extensive and lasted for a long period of time."[145]

Drokmi. *'Brog mi* (pronounced Drokmi) (922–1072 c.e.) was a Tibetan scholar who went to Nepal to learn Sanskrit, and on to India where he studied for eight years in the university of Vikramaśila under the teacher Śantipa, known as the Mahasiddha (great accomplished one). Among the *tantric* texts into which Drokmi was there initiated was the *Hevajra Tantra*, on which Śantipa had written a commentary, and which Drokmi himself later translated into Tibetan. In this work and also in the *Guhyasamaja Tantra* (both to be described more fully below) the union of the *tantric* deity Hevajra (Tibetan *Kye rdo rje*, pronounced Kyê Dorje) and his consort Nairatma (*bDag med ma*, pronounced Damema) represents the union of *upaya* and *prajna*, and the climactic meditational teaching set forth is that of the *mahamudra* (Tibetan *phyag rgya chen mo*, pronounced chhakgya chhenmo) or "great seal," a whole complex of *yogic* instruction (to be described more fully below).

In Tibet in 1073 c.e. a disciple of Drokmi named *dKon mchog rgyal po* (pronounced Könchok Gyelpo) (1034–1102 c.e.) founded the monastery of *Sa skya* (pronounced Sakya) on the trade route between Lhasa and the Nepal Valley, and from this place the monastic order known as the *Sa skya pa* (pronounced Sakya-pa) took its name. In this order the *Hevajra Tantra* remained one of the basic texts, and Hevajra was the patron deity of the sect.

Very similar to the Sakya-pa was the *Bu lugs pa* (pronounced Puluk-pa), the order of the "disciples of Buston," founded by the famous Tibetan *lama* and historian, author of the *History of Buddhism in India and Tibet* which we cite so frequently (his full name is *Bu ston Rin chen grub pa* or *Bu ston Rin po che*, pronounced Putön Rinchen Trup-pa or Putön Rimpochê) (1290–1363 c.e.). The sect was also known as the *Zha lu pa* (pronounced Shalu-pa) from the name of the monastery (not far from Xigaze) where Buston did his work.

From a split in the Sakya-pa school arose also the *Jo nan pa* (pronounced Chonang-pa). The founder of the sect was *Shes rab rgyal mtshan* (pronounced Sherap Gyentsen) (1292–1361 C.E.), himself a student of a *pandita* (scholar) from Kashmir named Candranatha (Tibetan *Zla ba mgon po*, pronounced Dawa Gompo). The name of the sect was derived from its head monastery, the *Jo nang* (about 100 miles [160 km.] northwest of Xigaze), which was founded by *Phyogs las rnam rgyal* (pronounced Chhoklê Namgyel) (1306–1386). The school placed its major emphasis on the *Kalacakra Tantra* (to be described below), and its best known *lama* was *Kun dga' snying po* (pronounced Künga Nyingpo), better known as Taranatha (born in 1575 C.E.), author of the *History of Buddhism in India*.

Tilopa and Naropa. Tilopa (988–1069 C.E.) was a famous Indian Buddhist teacher, to whom Naropa came as a pupil, the latter being the subject of a Tibetan biography of the late twelfth century C.E.[146] As related in this work, Naropa (1016–1100 C.E.) was born in Bengal, went at the age of eleven to Kashmir to study, was married for some years, afterward lived and wrote at Pullahari, then joined the university at Nalanda and was there elected abbot, but went off to find his personal *guru* in Tilopa, with whom he stayed for a dozen years.

To his chosen master Naropa demonstrated absolute devotion by subjecting himself, at Tilopa's command, to the severest of sufferings, and, after each, Tilopa healed him and vouchsafed deeper and deeper teachings to him. For example, after Naropa was frozen and eaten by leeches in a deep pool of cold water, Tilopa restored him and gave him instruction "on the mystic heat in which eternal delight and warmth are self-glowing." This involved a disquisition on the psychic structure of the human body, which is conceived much as it is in Hindu Tantrism.

As here explained, the psycho-organism is like a *stupa*, in which there are many psycho-nervous pathways or channels (Sanskrit *nadi*, Tibetan *tsas*), and a number of psycho-nervous focal points or centers (Sanskrit *cakra*, Tibetan *khorlo*, literally "wheels"), in all of which flows the psycho-nervous vital force (Sanskrit *prana*, Tibetan *shugs*). Of the channels, three are the most important: the one in the center (Sanskrit *sushumna-nadi*, Tibetan *uma tsa*) which leads up through the spinal column to the head region; the one on the right (Sanskrit *pingala-nadi*, Tibetan *roma tsa*) which leads up to the right nostril; and the one on the left (Sanskrit *ida-nadi*, Tibetan *kyangma tsa*) which leads up to the left nostril. Of the centers four are mentioned here: the head-center (*sahasrara-cakra*), "the focal point of eternal delight, like a lotus with thirty-two petals;" the throat-center (*vishuddha-cakra*), like a lotus with sixteen petals; the heart-center (*anahata-cakra*), like a lotus with eight petals; and the navel-center (*manipura-cakra*), like a lotus with sixty-four petals.[147]

So by proper posture, breathing, and meditation the inexhaustible store of the vital force in Nature may be drawn upon and used to produce the inner warmth and bliss known as the "mystic heat" (*gtum mo*, pronounced tummo).

In addition to the subject of the mystic heat, other topics on which Naropa received instruction from Tilopa were the illusory body, the dream state, the radiant light, the transference of consciousness, and the after-death state, six topics in all.

Marpa. After the death of Tilopa, Naropa went back to Pullahari in India, and lived and taught there in the Gold Mountain Monastery. At this point a Tibetan *lama* named *Mar pa Chos kyi blo gros* (pronounced Marpa Chhökyi Lodrö) or

Marpa for short (1012–1096 C.E.) enters the picture. Marpa had previously been a pupil of Drokmi, but found the fees required by Drokmi too high, and went off himself to Nepal and then to India. At that point Naropa saw in a vision that Marpa had come to India, and invited him to Pullahari. When Marpa came, Naropa greeted him with the words:

> My son, predicted by my *guru*,
> Worthy Marpa . . .
> It is good that you have come from beyond the snowland
> In order to take over the kingdom of the spirit.

In all, Marpa visited India three times, and stayed with Naropa more than sixteen years. Under Naropa as his *guru*, Marpa was initiated into the *Hevajra Tantra*, and also studied other great *tantric* texts such as the *Guhyasamaja*, "and the essence of all, *mahamudra*." Eventually Marpa returned to Tibet to stay, and passed on the instructions and injunctions he had received, including "the six topics of Naropa," to his own spiritual son Milarepa, and the latter transmitted them to others including Gampopa. Thus Marpa "kindled the lamp of the Buddhist doctrine in the snowland of Tibet."[148]

In Tibet Marpa chose to live the life of an ordinary married householder, with a wife whom he called Nairatma (the consort of Hevajra), and he made it a point to be out plowing his fields when his future disciple Milarepa first came looking for him. Yet Marpa also did a large work as collector and translator of texts—for which he was known as Marpa *lotsawa*—and was also notable for composing a new kind of Tibetan poetry, in which personal feelings and observations were more freely expressed than before, a form of expression in which he was followed by Milarepa. Furthermore Marpa is considered the originator of the *bKa' brgyud pa* (pronounced Kagyü-pa), the order of the "transmitted command," in which *tantric* exercises and the practice of *yoga* were prominent. In this school the immediate successors of Marpa were his disciple Milarepa and Milarepa's disciple Gampopa.

Milarepa. The life and work of *Mi la ras pa* (pronounced Milarepa, meaning the cotton-clad Mila) (1040–1123 C.E.) are known from a biography called the *Mila Khabum* or *Namthar* written by his disciple *Ras chung* (pronounced Re-chung), and from a collection of his own "hundred thousand songs," the *Mila Grubum*, which contains narrative as well as poetry.[149]

Mila was a family name, and at the birth of this son the father was so pleased that he called him Thopaga (delightful to hear), which was afterward deemed singularly appropriate, inasmuch as the son had a fine singing voice. Tragedy struck soon, however, with the early death of his father and the mistreatment and dispossession from her goods of the widowed mother by Mila's wicked uncle and aunt. In revenge, after years of poverty and humiliation, Mila learned magic and wrought destruction and death by his sorcery. But as time went on he was filled with remorse for these evil deeds, and desired to expiate his sins and attain liberation. At the age of thirty-eight he became the disciple of Marpa, who had just returned from one of his trips to India. As Tilopa had treated Naropa harshly, so Marpa imposed many hardships upon Mila. For one thing, Marpa required him to several times build, destroy, and rebuild a nine-story tower (which still stands at Sras). Helped to some extent by the kindness of Marpa's wife, Nairatma, Mila endured every suffering and, after six years, received the initiation he desired. Then for eleven continuous months he meditated alone in a rock cave in the wilderness, and attained a satisfying realization of the truth. In later meditation he saw in a dream that his mother was dead, his sister a beggar, and his former home a ruin. Marpa gave him permission to go back to his home to see if these calamities had indeed come to pass and, knowing that they were parting for the last time, Marpa advised Mila to always remember the illusoriness of the world and therefore to spend most of the rest of his life in solitude and meditation among the mountains and in caves and in places of pilgrimage. At his former home Mila found that what he had seen in a dream was true, and he was impressed afresh with the painful and fleeting character of human existence. He resolved to renounce the world and, obeying Marpa's instruction, spent the rest of his days meditating in caves and wandering on the slopes of the mountains.

In his meditational practice Mila followed the *tantric* methods of both the Nyingma-pa (the *dzok chhenmo*) and the Sakya-pa (the *chhakgya chhenmo* or *mahamudra*), and by his *yogic* exercises gained the inner "mystic heat" *(tummo)*, and was able to live in the coldest weather with only cotton clothing, hence his familiar name, Milarepa, "the cotton-clad Mila." He gained other psychic powers as well, wrought many miracles, and at last attained the supreme enlightenment he sought. As his fame spread, he became widely known as the Great Siddha, and the Tibetan term of reverence and respect for a saint and great teacher, *rJe btsun* (pronounced Jetsün), was applied to him and he was called Jetsun Milarepa (holy Milarepa).

The *Mila Grubum* or "hundred thousand songs" of Milarepa abundantly reflect the wildness of the surroundings in which he spent his life, report his conflicts with demons, contests with the Bon-pos, and dealings with disciples, and express his joy in his own ecstatic experiences. For example, Mount Kailasa (Tibetan Tise) and Lake Manasarovara (Tibetan Mapham Tsho) were holy places of the Bon-pos, but Milarepa overcame the Bon-pos in magic contests, drove them away, and took possession in the name of Buddhism. Then he celebrated his victory in a song in which he describes the mountain, blanketed with snow, as symbolizing the pure, white Buddhist doctrine, and the streams, flowing into the blue lake, as symbolizing deliverance to the realm of the Absolute.[150]

Again Milarepa dwelt happily at the Tiger Cave at Lion Place in the Yolmo *(Yol mo)* Snow Range, rejoiced in the delightful mountain meadows where the rain fell in summer and winter, and the mist and fog rolled up in fall and spring, felt compassion for the helpless cubs of the tigress and when he heard the touching cry of the monkey, and sang of his own previous quest and present joy as a *yogi* with all desirable possessions, always happy wherever he was:

> In fear of death I built a house,
> and my house is the house of the void of truth;
> now I fear not death.
>
> In fear of cold I sought a coat,
> and my coat is the coat of the inner heat;
> now I fear not cold.
>
> In fear of want I sought wealth,
> and my wealth is glorious, unending, sevenfold;
> now I fear not want.
>
> In fear of hunger I sought food,
> and my food is the food of meditation upon truth;
> now I fear not hunger.

> In fear of thirst I sought drink,
> and my drink is the nectar of right knowledge;
> now I fear not thirst.
>
> In fear of weariness I sought a companion,
> and my companion is the everlasting void of bliss;
> now I fear not weariness.
>
> In fear of error I sought a path,
> and my path is the path of transcendent union;
> now I fear not error.
>
> I am a sage who possesses in plenitude
> the manifold treasures of desire
> and wherever I dwell I am happy.[151]

Gampopa. Of the disciples of Milarepa the foremost was *sGam po pa* (pronounced Gampopa) (1079–1153 C.E.). He was born in Eastern Tibet and known from the place of his birth as *Dwags po lha rje* (pronounced Takpo Lha-je), i.e., Lha-je of Takpo Province, but was later called Gampopa as being a reincarnation of King Songtsen Gampo, the first Buddhist ruler of Tibet.

In his youth Gampopa learned medical science from his father, and also the *tantric* teachings of the Nyingma-pa. He married the daughter of a local chieftain, but after his wife, son, and daughter all died of a pestilence, he became a monk. At the age of thirty-two he heard from three beggars of Milarepa, and made a long journey to find him and become his disciple. In thirteen months of study he acquired the master's teachings, and Milarepa gave him the initiation of *vajra-guru* and ordained him as a full-fledged teacher of *tantra*.[152]

Of a number of Tibetan treatises of which Gampopa was the author, one large work is entitled in full, "The Explanation of the Stages on the Mahayanic Path towards Liberation, called a Jewel Ornament of Liberation or the Wish-Fulfilling Gem of the Noble Doctrine," and known more briefly as *The Jewel Ornament of Liberation*.[153] As the long title suggests, this is a manual of instruction intended to lead the student, whether lay or monastic, to grasp the basic principles of Buddhism and go on to the ultimate realization of Buddhahood. As such it is one of many similar works known collectively as "stages on the path" *(lam rim)*.

In an opening invocation Gampopa expresses his indebtedness to both Milarepa and Atiśa, and thus evidently combines in his own work the traditions of both of these preceding teachers and accordingly of both the Kagyu-pa and the Kadam-pa.

The first main paragraph then describes the whole of reality in terms familiar from the Madhyamika philosophy:

> Generally speaking: all entities are subsumed under the duality of *samsara* and *nirvana*. In this statement *samsara* is to be understood in the sense that its ultimate nature is *śunyata;* that its outer aspect is error; and that its intrinsic character is its manifestation as misery. *Nirvana* is also to be understood in the sense that its ultimate nature is *śunyata;* that its outer aspect is the end and disappearance of all error; and that its intrinsic character is liberation from all misery.[154]

On this basis Gampopa proceeds to outline the whole of Buddhism as a way of life. All sentient beings in the three worlds *(kamadhatu, rupadhatu, arupadhatu)* are living in a state of error, but are capable of attaining enlightenment by hard work because in all beings the Buddha-motive *(tathagatagarbha)* is present. Given this fundamental endowment in all beings, it is at the point of life in "the most precious human body"—precious because of the difficulty of obtaining it and precious because of its great usefulness—that there is a unique opportunity to cross, as if in a boat, the ocean of *samsara* and obtain perfect Buddhahood. To do this one needs to find spiritual friends and receive their instructions. With such guidance one may form a desire for perfect enlightenment and learn to practice the six "perfections" of liberality, ethics, patience, strenuousness, meditative concentration, and discriminating awareness born of wisdom. Thus one may ascend the thirteen spiritual levels (two levels of the beginner and the earnest striver, ten levels of the *bodhisattvas,* and finally the thirteenth level of a Buddha), always aspiring for Buddhahood solely in order to destroy the misery of sentient beings and help them to attain happiness.

Another work by Gampopa is called "The Supreme Path, the Rosary of Precious Gems," or more briefly, *The Precious Rosary.* Herein the author hails the inspired *gurus* of the Kagyu-pa line, and puts down in writing a large number of the precepts he has received from them. The precepts are stated compactly, and are organized in arithmetically outlined groups, e.g., "the ten causes of regret," and "the ten things to be done." If one is earnestly in search of enlightenment it is advised to depart from home and kindred and to attach oneself to a *guru* of saintly character (avoiding charlatans), for such a teacher is indispensable, and one esoteric truth which may be learned from him is more valuable then innumerable exoteric doctrines (15.3; 19.2; 24.3). On the Mantrayanic pathway the disciple should practice *yogic* discipline and the threefold *mandala* (dedicated to the spiritual forces or *tantric* deities presiding over body, speech, and mind); as a result of such practices, spiritual powers may be attained capable of transmuting body, speech, and mind, but one should never boast of occult learning nor make public exhibition of *yogic* abilities (7.9; 8.3; 10.10; 15.12). Among errors to be avoided along the way are weakness of faith combined with strength of intellect, which combination is apt to lead to the error of talkativeness; and strength of faith combined with weakness of intellect, which combination is apt to lead to the error of narrow-minded dogmatism (10.1–2). At the same time the one who is sincerely devoted to the religious life, and who thoroughly understands the teachings, enjoys a remarkable freedom, for it is the same whether he refrain from worldly activities or not, the same whether he meet with good fortune or with bad fortune, and the same whether he observe conventional codes of conduct or not (25.1, 8, 9). So there are many joyful realizations upon the way, and above all, "it is great joy to realize that the path to freedom which all the Buddhas have trodden is ever-existent, ever unchanged, and ever open to those who are ready to enter upon it" (28.10).[155]

In the spiritual lineage of the Kagyu-pa, deriving from Marpa, Milarepa, and Gampopa, there came to be no less than a dozen suborders, among which some of the more important are the Drigung-pa, the Druk-pa, and the Karma-pa. The *'Bri gung pa* (pronounced Drigung-pa) takes its name from the *'Bri gung* monastery, which was founded by a student of *'Gro mgon Phag mo gru pa* (pronounced Dromgön Phakmotrupa or just *Phag mo gru pa*) (1110–1170 C.E.), the latter being himself a disciple of Gampopa. The most famous *lama* associated with the monastery was *'Bri gung rin po che* (pronounced Drigung Rimpoche) (1143–1217). In the time of the Mongol overlordship in Tibet the Drigung-pa was a rival to the Sakya-pa for political influence.

The *'Brug pa* (pronounced Druk-pa) suborder was founded by a student of Phakmotrupa named *gLing ras pa Pad ma rdo rje* (pronounced Ling Repa Pema Dorje) (1128–1188 C.E.), and about 1180 his disciple *gTsang pa rgya ras pa* (pronounced Tsangpa Gyarepa) (1161–1211) founded the main monastery of the order at *Rwa lung* (pronounced Ralung) about 30 miles (48 km.) east of Gyangze. At the founding of the monastery it is said that a clap of thunder was heard and was taken for the sound of a thunder dragon in the sky (in Tibetan *'brug* means both thunder and dragon), hence the name of the order. The Druk-pa became prominent in both Ladakh and Bhutan, and the official name of the latter country is derived from the name of the order—Druk Yul, the Land of the Thunder Dragon.

The *Kar ma pa* (Karma-pa) originated with a disciple of Gampopa named *Chos 'dzin dge 'phel Dus gsum mkhyen pa* (pronounced Chhöndzin Gemphel Tüsum Chhenpa), also known as *Kar ma Dus gsum mkhyen pa* (1110–1193 C.E.), and the order took its name from him. As the first of the series of incarnate head *lamas* of the order he is also known as the First *rGyal ba Kar ma pa* (pronounced Gyelwa Karma-pa), *gyelwa* meaning "victor" (the equivalent of Sanskrit *jina*). In 1189 he founded the monastery of *mTshur phu* (pronounced Tshurphu), and this is the head monastery of the sect. In the fourteenth century in the time of the Ming dynasty in China the Karma-pa was especially prominent and influential in Tibet.

It is said that Karma Tusum Chhenpa made a crown or diadem *(cod pan)* for himself out of the hair of a *mkha' 'gro ma* (pronounced khandroma, flier through the air, a class of female deities generally feared, equivalent to Sanskrit *dakini*), and on account of this he was called "black hat" (*zhwa nag,* pronounced shanak). When there was a division of the Karma-pa into two branches, his followers were all known as the "black hats," while the followers of a second series of incarnate *lamas* were from their differently colored headgear known by the designation "red hat" (*zhwa dmar,* pronounced shamar). From this beginning it eventually became the practice, at least among outsiders, to call the members of all the earlier orders of Tibetan Buddhism "red hats," in distinction from the members of the later Geluk-pa, who came to be designated by the term "yellow hat" (*zhwa ser,* pronounced shaser).[156]

Tsongkhapa. *Tsong kha pa bLo gros grags pa* (pronounced Tsongkhapa Lotrö Trakpa) (1357–1419 C.E.) was born in northeastern Tibet, in the district of Amdo in the neighborhood of Lake Koko Nor, came to Central Tibet at the age of seventeen, and studied with many teachers, especially ones of the Kadam-pa and the Sakya-pa orders. By the age of twenty-five he was fully ordained, and began to be known himself as an important teacher and writer. At forty he joined the Kadam-pa monastery at Reting, but a dozen years later (1409 C.E.) founded his own monastery, the *dGa'idan* (pronounced Ganden), northeast of Lhasa, and became the head of his own order. Because of his continuation of the Kadam-pa tradition his order was at first known as the new Kadam-pa *(bKa' gdams pa gsar ma)*, then was called the *dGa' idan pa* from the name of the monastery, and later the *dGe lugs pa* (pronounced Geluk-pa), meaning the "model of virtue," popularly called the order of the "yellow hats" or the "yellow sect." Before the death of Tsongkhapa two of his disciples built the *'Bras spungs* (pronounced Drêpung) and the *Se ra* (Sera) monasteries near Lhasa (in 1416 and 1419 respectively), and later (in 1447) Tsongkhapa's disciple *dGe 'dun grub* (pronounced Gendüntrup, also Geduntruppa) (1391–1475 C.E.) built the *bKra shis lhun po* (pronounced Trashilhunpo) monastery at Xigaze, and these three are the greatest centers of the Geluk-pa. At the main temple in Lhasa (the Jokhang) Tsongkhapa inaugurated an annual New Year ceremony called the Great Vow *(sMon lam chen mo)*, and his own day of death was also commemorated every year in midwinter.

In personal devotion Tsongkhapa was, like Atiśa, a votary of Tara (Tibetan *sGrol ma,* pronounced Drölma, Dolma), the most prominent of all the *tantric* goddesses not only in the Kadam-pa (derived from Atiśa) but also in the Sakya-pa (where her *mantra* is found in the *Hevajra Tantra*) and in the Kagyu-pa (where Gampopa was her devotee), as well as in the Geluk-pa.[157]

In literary work Tsongkhapa wrote several hundred treatises including a commentary on a short work by Atiśa, entitled *Steps to Enlightenment,* which describes the gradual progress of the disciple on the Lower Path (observance of ethics), the Middle Path (understanding of the Four Noble Truths), and the Higher Path (observance of the vow and precepts of a *bodhisattva*), a book which became the basic text of the Geluk-pa order; a survey of the Tantras which Tsongkhapa recommended to his students, entitled *The Great Stage Way to the Occult Sciences;* and a commentary on the teaching of Naropa, known as *The Six Yogas of Naropa.*

It was at a time when, as he says in the colophon of the work, his school was thriving to a great extent but had not yet reached a full-flourishing state, that Tsongkhapa wrote the work of which the full title is, *The Six Yogas of Naropa, with the Successive Instructions leading to the Profound Path—the Book of Threefold Faith.*

After preparatory learning the student of this work begins the essential *tantric* practice with three preliminary exercises called the Vajrasattva Yoga, the Guru Yoga, and the Mandala Offering. The Vajrasattva Yoga is intended for the cleansing of sins. It involves the visualization of the great Buddha Vajrasattva, the "adamantine being" and the source of *tantra.* His body is white, his right hand holds a *vajra/dorje* and his left hand holds a bell, the symbols respectively of *upaya* and *prajna.* He also holds the Mother Buddha, who is called the White Mother of Elegance, and is of beauty beyond description. She holds a curved knife and a human skull, and also a vase filled with nectar and, upon the disciple's supplication, the nectar washes away all filthy matter—which symbolizes the sins.

The Guru Yoga is intended to obtain blessing and grace from the *guru* of the disciple. Here the disciple visualizes in the firmament in front of him a lion-shaped seat of gems with lotus-moon cushions upon it, and his own *guru* sitting thereon. As the disciple offers homage to his *guru* in this way, he should remember that one's own *guru* is even more important than the Great Buddha because it is only through the *guru* that one can be benefited. As for the Mandala Offering, in it a bowl symbolizes the universe, and the bowl is visualized as filled with treasures and offered to the Buddha.

In further study the disciple learns the "six exercises of Naropa," sitting in a lotus posture, breathing alternately through the right and the left nostril, holding the breath as long as possible as if in a vase, etc.

Then the "six yogas" proper are undertaken. These are the six topics which Tilopa communicated to Naropa and he to Marpa, and which in turn Marpa passed on to Milarepa and Milarepa to Gampopa. Here they are listed as the Heat Yoga, Dream Yoga, Illusory Body Yoga, Bardo Yoga, Transformation Yoga, and Light Yoga, and they are elucidated in a commentary of some length.

Of all of these the Heat Yoga is said to be the foundation. In it, for example, the disciple visualizes the psychic nerve-system, and then meditates upon the four words, Ah, Hum, Om, Ham, seen as small and bright as possible at the four focal points of navel, heart, throat, and head, with the aim of kindling and experiencing the rise of the mystic heat *gTum mo* (pronounced tummo).[158]

Khe-trup Je. The chief disciple of Tsongkhapa in *tantric* studies was *mKhas grub dGe legs dpal bzang,* known more briefly as *mKhas grub rje* (pronounced Khêtrup Jê) (1385–1438 C.E.). He is the author of a work called *Fundamentals of the Buddhist Tantras*.[159]

Fundamentals of the Buddhist Tantras. In this work Khe-trup Je surveys the rise of Buddhism, the first three Buddhist councils, and the division into sects, and distinguishes the Hinayana, the Mahayana, and the Mantrayana. In the Mantrayana he divides the Tantras into four divisions. In Tibetan a *tantric* treatise is called *gyud* (pronounced gyüt), which literally means "to weave," corresponding with the understanding of the Sanskrit *tantra* as etymologically meaning "web," and *yoga* is *rnal 'byor* (pronounced naljor). As named by Khe-trup Je the four divisions are (1) Kriya Tantra (Tibetan *bya rgyud*, pronounced cha gyüt), which emphasizes external and internal purification, with ritual acts, offerings, formulas, and so forth; (2) Carya Tantra (*spyod rgyud*, pronounced chod gyüt), which is also for purification, with a balance of external acts and internal meditation; (3) Yoga Tantra (*rnal 'byor rgyud*, pronounced naljor gyüt), which is solely internal, with *yogic* exercises of body and mind; and (4) Anuttarayoga Tantra (*bla na med rgyud*, pronounced lanamê gyüt), which is the highest *tantric* practice of Tibetan Buddhism, stressing the supreme importance of inner activity. In the Anuttarayoga Tantras Khe-trup Je distinguishes between the Father Tantra *(pha rgyud)* and the Mother Tantra *(ma rgyud)*: the Father Tantra deals with skill in means *(upaya)*, i.e., with the active realization of the ideal of compassion, *upaya* being considered as masculine; the Mother Tantra deals with transcendental wisdom *(prajna)*, which is personified as feminine. Of the Mother Tantras Khe-trup Je says that the chief is the *Samvara* (in Tibetan the *'Khor lo bde mchog*, pronounced Khorlo Demchhok, the name of a *tantric* guardian deity); of the Father Tantras the chief is the *Guhyasamaja*.[160]

Tantras

Guhyasamaja. The *Tathagataguhyaka* or *Guhyasamaja Tantra* (in Tibetan the *gSang b'ai 'dus pa*, pronounced Sangwe Düpa) is the "Tantra of secret communion." It has already been mentioned above as one of the Vaipulya Sutras, and as studied by Nagarjuna and by Marpa in India. It is probably the earliest of the Buddhist Tantras, and certainly one of the most important. According to one tradition, an introduction was written to the work by the great Yogacara philosopher Asanga (born toward the end of the fourth century C.E.), and it was said to be the favorite Tantra of Tsongkhapa. It is classified as an Anuttarayoga Tantra, i.e., it is of the highest level of Tibetan Buddhist teaching, and is classified as the foremost of the Father Tantras, i.e., it deals with skill in means *(upaya)* or the active realization of the ideal of compassion. The book is preserved in Sanskrit, and was translated into Tibetan and Chinese.[161]

In the opening chapter the great Buddha reality, here called the lord Bodhicittavajra, is in the midst of an assembly of spiritual beings, and they ask him to reveal to them the *Guhyasamaja*. In response he sits in meditation and, by the power of thought, transforms himself into five cosmic Buddhas, the Tathagatas or Dhyani Buddhas, their five female counterparts, and four gatekeepers. These all are placed in positions which in effect form a *mandala*, a mystic diagram with the first Tathagata and his consort in the center and the other figures distributed in the four directions.

The five Tathagatas correspond to the five cosmic elements (Sanskrit *skandha*, Tibetan *phung po*), which are also the components of a person, and, like those eternal forces, the Buddhas are without beginning or end. Thus the Tathagatas have never passed through the stage of a *bodhisattva* but, as their name indicates, have always been engaged in peaceful meditation. With their consorts, however, they have as their offspring or emanations five principal *bodhisattvas* and yet many more gods and goddesses, who comprise five families *(kulas)*. In this way there is constituted an entire pantheon of *tantric* Buddhism, and it is in the *Guhyasamaja* that this pantheon is for the first time elaborated with the assignment to the several male figures of the corresponding female consorts. As here described and as usually outlined, the major figures of the pantheon, and some of their attributes, are the following (cf. Table 12.1):

In the Dvesha family is the Tathagata Akshobhya (color blue; vehicle elephant; *mudra bhumishparśa*, i.e., earth-touching witness gesture; symbol *vajra*; represents cosmic element of *vijnana*, i.e., consciousness). With him are his consort Mamaki, his principal *bodhisattva* Vajrapani, the gods Heruka and Yamari, and the goddesses Ekajata and Nairatma.

In the Moha family is the Tathagata Vairocana (color white; vehicle dragon; *mudra dharmacakra*, i.e., hands against chest, tips of thumb and forefinger of each hand together, in preaching gesture; symbol discus; represents cosmic element of *rupa*, i.e., form). With him are his consort Locana, his principal *bodhisattva* Samantabhadra, and the goddesses Marici and Vajravarahi.

In the Raga family is the Tathagata Amitabha (color red; vehicle peacock; *mudra samadhi*, i.e., hands on lap, one over the other, palms facing upward, in meditation gesture; symbol lotus; represents cosmic element of *samjna*, i.e., perception). With him are his consort Pandara, his principal *bodhisattva* Avalokiteśvara (Lokeśvara) also known as Padmapani (lotus bearer), and the goddess Kurukulla.

In the Cintamani family is the Tathagata Ratnasambhava (color yellow; vehicle two lions; *mudra varada*, i.e., right hand open, held downward and forward, in gift-bestowing gesture; symbol jewel; represents cosmic element of *vedana*, i.e., sensation). With him are his consort Vajradhatviśvari, his principal *bodhisattva* Ratnapani, the god of wealth Jambhala, and the goddess of plenty Vasudhara.

In the Samaya family is the Tathagata Amoghasiddhi (color green; vehicle *garuda*; *mudra abhaya*, i.e., right hand raised, palm forward, in gesture of reassurance; symbol *viśvavajra*, i.e., double *vajra*; represents cosmic element of *samskara*, i.e., volition). With him are his consort Tara, his principal *bodhisattva* Viśvapani (double *vajra* bearer), and the goddesses Khadiravani Tara and Parnaśavari.

As to the arrangement of the fingers in the cosmic *mandala* in the *Guhyasamaja*, Akshobhya is in the center, Vairocana is in front of him, i.e., in the east (in a drawn figure at the bottom following Indian tradition), Ratnasambhava in the south, Amitabha in the west, and Amoghasiddhi in the north; elsewhere Vairocana is more often in the center, and Akshobhya in the east.[162]

In the opening scene of the *Guhyasamaja*, as described above, the great Buddha essence, who transforms himself into the several Tathagatas, is called the lord Bodhicittavajra, and later in the work much attention is given to the *bodhicitta*, which may be translated as "*bodhi*-mind," "mind for *bodhi*," or "enlightened-mindedness," and can include such related ideas as the wish to attain Buddhahood and the practices aimed toward that end, the aspiration to deliver all sentient beings from suffering, and the intuitive grasp of truth; in other words, in *bodhicitta* are comprised both the compassion of a *bodhisattva* and the wisdom of a Buddha. Using other terms already familiar from the *Prajnaparamita* literature and the Madhyamika doctrine, the *bodhicitta* is constituted of the commingling of *upaya/ karuna* (skillful means/active compassion) and *prajna/śunyata* (wisdom/emptiness), and this union, says the *Guhyasamaja*, is called *advaya* (not two).

It is in expression of this non-duality *(advaya)* of "enlightened-mindedness" *(bodhicitta)* that in the *tantric* pantheon (as also in *tantric* Hinduism) the pairs of male and female figures are often described, and are also so pictured in *tantric* art, as in sexual embrace, known in Tibetan as *yab yum* (father mother). The visualization and worship of the *tantric* deities is then an appropriate way for the devotee to seek to attain the same *bodhicitta* that they symbolize. The ritual for such an evocation of a deity or deities is known by the term *sadhana* (Tibetan *sgrub thabs*), and a *tantric* work named the *Sadhanamala,* for example, contains some 312 *sadhanas,* which were composed by writers from the third to the twelfth centuries C.E., and even cites *mantras* said to have come from Śakyamuni Buddha himself.[163]

It is perhaps because the absolute unity *(advaya)* here envisioned transcends all duality, that the *Guhyasamaja* seems to consider any repression of instincts and emotions as an incorrect way to seek enlightenment, and says (in a way reminiscent of the *Kularnava Tantra* of Hinduism): "No one can succeed in obtaining perfection through processes which are difficult and painful; but one can succeed easily through the satisfaction of all desires."[164]

Of the female deities who appear in the *tantric* pantheon the most prominent of all is Tara (who is also a *tantric* goddess in Hinduism). In the foregoing outline of the pantheon she appears as the consort of the Tathagata Amoghasiddhi, and she is also considered the consort of the bodhisattva Avalokiteśvara.

In the record of Buston concerning King Songtsen Gampo it is stated that the Nepalese princess who became his wife brought with her to Tibet, among other images, a statue of Tara, and this is especially mentioned as being made of sandalwood. According to a Tibetan biography of Atiśa, Tara was the deity to whom he was especially devoted from childhood on. When Atiśa was invited to go to Tibet, and hesitated because of his older age, it was Tara who encouraged him to go, with a prophecy in which she spoke of the benefit he would bring, and of an important disciple whom he would have: "'If [you] go there, your life will be shorter. But you will be very helpful for the doctrine and for many people led by the *upasaka.*' So he agreed (to go to Tibet)."[165]

Because of his devotion to Tara, the work of Atiśa in Tibet did much to promote the cult of this goddess, and in his very extensive literary activity Atiśa translated several Indian texts dealing with the goddess, and also composed several works of his own concerning her. As for the *upasaka* (lay disciple) to whom veiled reference was made in Tara's prophecy, this was Atiśa's chief Tibetan follower, Drom, and the latter built a temple for Tara at Nethang where Atiśa lived.

In Tibet the Sanskrit name Tara is translated as *sGrol ma* (pronounced Drölma, also Dolma), and she is the "savioress" and the embodiment of the highest wisdom *(prajna)*. According to a Geluk-pa tradition, she was born of the tear that fell from the eye of Avalokiteśvara as he looked upon the sorrows of the world. Other originally independent goddesses were recognized as forms of Tara, so that she became known in no less than twenty-one forms all together, of which five are the most prominent, called the White Tara, Green Tara, Yellow Tara, Blue Tara, and Red Tara. Of these it was said that the Nepalese wife of King Songtsen Gampo was an incarnation of the White Tara, and his Chinese wife an incarnation of the Green Tara. Thus in a ritual, said to have been created by Nagarjuna and brought to Tibet by Atiśa, there is visualized, in the center,

> ... the blessed holy noble Tara, her body colored green, bedecked with various precious ornaments, having one face and two hands, with her right in the gift-bestowing gesture fulfilling the wishes of all beings, with her left grasping a full-blown lotus flower, wearing clothes of beautiful silk, adorned upon her crest by the conqueror Amoghasiddhi, sitting in a

posture of royal ease upon a throne of lotus and moon, in the midst of countless Buddhas and bodhisattvas. . . .

and around her on twenty lotus petals are that many more Taras, one (Kurukulla) colored red, who destroys hindering demons and injuries; one (Sitatara) colored white, who defeats disease and evil spirits; and so forth.[166]

Of the male deities in the *tantric* pantheon one of the most prominent is Heruka, who appears in the family associated with the Tathagata Akshobhya, and is often considered to be the wrathful form of Vajrasattva. In his wrathful form Heruka is said to destroy all the wicked demons called by the name of Mara (Tibetan *bdud,* pronounced dü), and to confer Buddhahood on his worshipers.

Heruka is described in this wrathful form in the instructions of a visualization rite preserved in the *Sadhanamala* (p. 473):

> The worshiper should conceive himself as the god (Heruka), who stands on a corpse. . . . He is well clad in human skin and his body is besmeared with ashes. He wields the *vajra* in the right hand and from his left shoulder hangs the *khatvanga* (magic wand) with a flowing banner, like a sacred thread. He carries in his left hand the *kapala* (cup made of a skull), full of blood. His necklace is beautified by a chain of half-a-hundred severed heads. His face is slightly distorted with bare fangs and bloodshot eyes. His brown hair rises upwards and forms into a crown, which bears the effigy of Akshobhya. . . . His head is beautified by five skulls. He bestows Buddhahood and protects the world from the Maras.[167]

Heruka is worshiped not only singly but also in the *yab yum* configuration, and in the latter form he is generally known as Hevajra or Śri Hevajra (Tibetan *Kye rdo rje,* pronounced Kyê Dorje, or *dPal Kye rdo rje,* pronounced Pel Kyê Dorje). As Hevajra he is seen in no less than four different forms, two-armed, four-armed, six-armed, and sixteen-armed, and is in association with many different consorts. In such configurations he is shown, for example, with two arms and one face, and his name is Trailokyakshepa and his *prajna* is Nairatma, or his name is Vajradaka and his consort is Vajravarahi. Again he is shown with four arms and four faces, and his name is Mahamaya and his consort is Vajrayogini, known also as Buddhadakini.

As they stand by themselves all three of these consorts, Nairatma, Vajravarahi, and Vajrayogini are described in similar ways and, like Hevajra, are of fearsome appearance, but are distinguished by their color and their attributes. The name of Nairatma means "no soul," and is thus another name for *śunya,* so this *prajna* of Hevajra is a personification of the "void" of *nirvana.* Her color is blue, because the color of *śunya* is conceived as blue, like the sky. She is described in a visualization rite in the *Sadhanamala* (p. 451):

> The worshiper should conceive himself as Nairatma, who stands . . . in a dancing attitude on the moon over the chest of a corpse. She is blue in color, has brown hair rising upwards, and bears the image of Akshobhya on her crown. Her face looks terrible with bare fangs and protruding tongue, and she carries the *kartri* (a small knife) in the right hand and bears the *kapala* and the *khatvanga* in the left. Her three eyes are red and round, and she is endowed with the five auspicious symbols.[168]

In the case of the three eyes, the third is in the forehead at the junction of the eyebrows, and stands for *bodhic* insight. The five auspicious symbols of a *tantric* goddess are (1) a tiara of human skulls, (2) a necklace of human heads, (3) armlets and wristlets, (4) anklets, and (5) a mirror of *karma,* held in place on the breast by strings of human-bone beads. Otherwise the goddess is normally nude, and to the five symbols there is added on occasion (6) a cemetery-dust ointment rubbed over the whole body, understood to signify renunciation of the world and conquest of the fear of death. Together the six symbols stand for the six perfections necessary for the attaining of Buddhahood.[169]

Vajravarahi is seen as red in color, with three eyes and disheveled hair, holding the *vajra* in the right hand and the *kapala* and the *khatvanga* in the left. She is marked with all six of the auspicious symbols.[170] Vajrayogini is known in three forms, two yellow and one red, and again the appearance and the attributes are much the same as for Nairatma and Vajravarahi. In one of her yellow forms, however, she carries her own head, severed from her shoulders, in her own hand, and the description in the visualization rite of the *Sadhanamala* (pp. 452–453) is especially horrible:

> The worshiper should conceive of himself as Vajrayogini . . . of yellow color, who carries in her left hand her own head severed by herself with her own *kartri* held in her right hand. Her left hand is raised upwards while the right is placed below. She is nude, and her right leg is stretched while the left is bent down. He (the worshiper) should also meditate on the streams of blood issuing from the severed body as falling into the mouths of the two *yoginis* on either side of her.
>
> He (the worshiper) should also conceive the two *yoginis* to the left and right, the green Vajravarnani and the yellow Vajravairocani, both of whom carry the *kartri* in their left and right hands respectively, and the cup made of a skull in the right and left hands respectively. Their left and right legs respectively are stretched forward, while the other legs are bent, and they have disheveled hair. On all sides, between the two *yoginis* and in the firmament there is the awful cremation ground.[171]

Except that the head is intact, the red form of Vajrayogini is no less terrible than that just described. She too is surrounded by the burning grounds, stands upon a corpse as her vehicle *(vahana)*, and carries the *kapala* in her left hand and the *vajra* in the right, while the *khatvanga* hangs from her left shoulder.

Hevajra. The *Heruka* or *Hevajra Tantra* (in Tibetan the *Kye rdo rje,* pronounced Kyê Dorje), already mentioned as of much importance in the life and work of Drokmi and the Sakya-pa, and of Marpa and the Kagyu-pa, is considered an Anuttara Tantra of the Mother class, dealing with transcendent wisdom, and is extant in Sanskrit and Tibetan versions.[172]

As the work opens, the Buddha is found, not on the Vulture's Peak at Rajagriha nor in the Jetavana monastery at Sravasti (as often, for example, in the Theravada literature), nor in heavenly counterparts of these earthly places (as in the *Saddharmapundarika* and the *Gandavyuha*), but in blissful embrace with Vajrayogini, "who is the body, speech, and mind of all the Buddhas," and it is from there that he divulges the esoteric teachings of this Tantra (1.1.1).[173]

As in the Heat Yoga of Naropa, the psycho-nervous channels of the body are described, and here the channel on the left is called Lalana (also Jhunma) and is feminine corresponding with *prajna,* the one on the right is called Rasana (also Roma) and is masculine corresponding with *upaya,* and the one in the center is called Avadhuti (abbreviated Dhuti) and is where *prajna* and *upaya* may meet. The breath, representing the psycho-nervous vital force *(prana),* passes up and down these channels, and the control of the breathing-process *(pranayama),* together with control of the thought-process, brings control over the vital force. The three channels meet at the base of the spinal column, and that is where the goddess Kundalini (the Hindu "serpent power" and the Tibetan *tummo*) sleeps. She is the personification of the divine female power and, when aroused by the proper breath/

thought process, rises like a blazing fire through the central channel, spreads the mystic heat throughout the body, and attains a mystic union in the uppermost region of the head, where the *bodhicitta*—here called the Moon—melts, flows down, and pervades the body with "joy innate" (1.1.13ff.).[174]

The mystic union attained by Kundalini is plainly that of *prajna* with *upaya*, and is also describable as the union of Nairatma with Hevajra. Nairatma is here called *bhagavati* (lady) and *yogini* (female *yogi*). Hevajra is pictured in his form with sixteen arms, eight faces, and four legs. He is black in color, his body is smeared with ashes, he is garlanded with skulls, and wears the five symbolic adornments. Terrible in appearance, he holds Nairatma in loving embrace, and his inner nature is tranquil and full of bliss (2.5.3–12).[175]

The meaning of the various attributes of Hevajra is explained: ". . . his body is black to indicate his sentiments of friendliness; his four legs symbolize the four means of conversion, his eight faces the eight releases, and his sixteen arms are the sixteen voids. The five Buddhas are represented by the symbolic adornments, and he is wrathful for the subduing of the evil-disposed" (2.9.11–12).[176]

The devotee should keep his inner self in union with Nairatma and/or Heruka/Hevajra, and meditate upon them at all times (2.1.207). Identifying himself with *upaya* and with Hevajra, the *yogi* may join himself to his own *yogini* as his *prajna* (as Marpa did, who called his wife Nairatma) (1.6.8–9), for if "by passion the world is bound, by passion too it is released" (2.2.51).[177]

As for the "joy innate," which is associated with the mystic union, it is the fourth of four joys which the *yogi* may hope to experience who accomplishes the *tantric* practice here described. These four joys are "perfect joy" which may be called *samsara*, the "joy of cessation" which is *nirvana*, "plain joy" which is a middle state, and "innate joy" which is free of all three. In "innate joy" there is neither passion nor absence of passion, but a realization of the perfect truth. This truth is to be known intuitively, and is a result of merit and of honoring one's *guru* and the set observances. One should think:

> The whole of existence arises in me,
> In me arises the threefold world,
> By me is this all pervaded,
> Of nought else does this world consist.

Whatever *yogi*, thinking thus, should perform the practice in complete self-control, he will succeed, there is no doubt, even though he be a man of little merit. Eating, drinking, performing ablutions, awake, asleep, it is thus he should think, and so seeking after the "great seal" *(mahamudra)*, he will gain thereby that eternal state (1.8.30–43.)[178]

Kalacakra. Like the *Guhyasamaja* and the *Hevajra Tantras*, the *Kalacakra Tantra* (in Tibetan *Dus kyi 'khor lo*, pronounced Dükyi Khorlo) is also an Anuttarayoga Tantra of the Mother class. While the original work in the form of the so-called Mulatantra (Basic Tantra), supposedly of 12,000 verses, has not been preserved, there are several *Kalacakra* works in the Tibetan Kangyur and Tengyur, as well as commentaries on the *Kalacakra*, and accounts concerning it by Tibetan historians.

According to the Tibetan Buddhist tradition, the Kalacakra (wheel of time) doctrine was first preached by the Buddha at the great *stupa* of Sri Dhanyakataka (in Tibetan *dPal ldan 'Bras spungs*, pronounced Pelden Drepung) in South India near the delta of the Kistna River, either just after his supreme enlightenment or just before his death and final entry into *nirvana*. On this occasion there was present, it is said, a great assembly of gods and sages, and among these was Sucandra, the king of Śambhala, who heard the teaching, took it back with him to Śambhala, wrote it down, and composed commentaries on it.

In the same tradition, Śambhala (Tibetan *bde 'byung,* source of happiness) is a kingdom in the north (perhaps originally a real area, and eventually a mythical realm), hidden within a great ring of snow mountains which keeps out all those who are not worthy to enter. In the center, surrounded by an even higher circle of snow mountains, is Kalapa, the capital of the kingdom, and at its center is a jeweled palace containing the golden throne of the king.

In addition to the many works and commentaries on the *Kalacakra* itself, there are also many related treatises which undertake to describe the road to Śambhala, and these are usually known under the name of *lam yig* or "road description." The most specific indication of location which they provide is the statement that Śambhala is north of the River Sita, a river which there is some reason to identify with the Tarim River in Xinjiang. Naturally the search for the way to Śambhala—whether conceived as a literal outward journey or understood as an inner journey to a hidden kingdom of the mind—has been an important subject among the ascetics and holy men of Tibet.

In Śambhala Sucandra was the first of a line of seven priest-kings, and they were succeeded by a line of twenty-five rulers known as Kulika or Kalki, the last of whom is expected to come yet in the future to establish a new golden age for the world. Under these kings the *Kalacakra* was preserved in Śambhala for more than a thousand years, then was introduced into India and sixty years later brought from India into Tibet. The official introduction of the *Kalacakra* into Tibet is supposed to have been in 1026/1027 C.E., and this is the date from which the Tibetan calendar begins, this calendar with its Sexagenary Cycle being derived from the "wheel of time." According to this date the introduction of the *Kalacakra* into India, sixty years prior to its introduction into Tibet, would have been in 966/967 C.E., and another report to the effect that the "wheel of time" became effective in India in the time of King Mahipala of Bengal (circa 974–1026 C.E.) points to a not too dissimilar date.[179]

In the *Blue Annals* the entire tenth book is devoted to the *Kalacakra* and its dissemination from Śambhala to India and Tibet, and many persons are named (not without inconsistencies in the various traditions) who were involved in the spread of the doctrine, among them perhaps most importantly Tsilupa and Somanatha.

According to one tradition, Tsilupa, also called the senior Kalacakrapada, belonged to the *kshatriya* caste of Madhyadeśa in India, and was born of royal parents.

> He was learned in the five branches of knowledge, and was known to be a manifestation of Arya Manjuśri. He was blessed by the Venerable Tara, whose face he saw clearly. After he had acquired all the "lower perfections" (eight in all), the Venerable One once told him: "In the Northern Śambhala there exist many Tantras and commentaries taught and prophesied by the Buddha. Go in search of them and listen to them!" He then thought of going there. In the opinion of some scholars he had joined a caravan of merchants, and proceeded there. Some said that he was guided there by a phantom monk. Again some said that the Venerable Tara herself helped him. . . . Again some said that when he decided to proceed to Śambhala, and was preparing (for the journey) he visited Śambhala in his vision, and obtained the doctrines from Arya Avalokiteśvara himself. This last statement should be accepted.

According to a variant tradition the same Kalacakrapada was the son of a *yogini,* and she took him with her as a boy to Śambhala. There a monk of beautiful appearance, who was actually a manifestation of Avalokiteśvara, blessed the youth, and he developed the ability to commit to memory a thousand verses of scripture every day. After memorizing the *Kalacakra Tantra* and its commentary, he proceeded to Madhyadeśa, was ordained a monk with the name Tsilupa, wrote the Tantra and commentary in the form of a book, and entrusted the same to disciples.

Somanatha was originally a member of a *brahmana* family in Kashmir, and until the age of ten studied his father's doctrine, having the ability to memorize sixteen verses of scripture after reading them once. Afterward, however, he mastered the Kalacakra doctrine and, intending to spread the system in Tibet, proceeded there. In Tibet, where he spent much time on at least two different journeys, Somanatha was supported by wealthy sponsors who provided him with gold and garments, and he explained the Tantra to various Tibetan scholars and worked with them to provide a translation of the text and the commentary.[180]

In his time Tsongkhapa (1357–1419 C.E.), the founder of the Geluk-pa order, is understood to have made a close study of the *Kalacakra,* and this Tantra has continued to provide one of the most important fundamentals of the "yellow sect" in Tibet. Under the Panchen Lamas the *Kalacakra* was especially venerated and taught in the Trashilhunpo monastery at Xigaze, and the Third (or Sixth) Panchen Lama, Lopsang Pelden Yeshe, was the author in 1775 C.E. of the most widely read guidebook to Śambhala, the *Shambhalai Lamyig* or The Description of the Way to Śambhala. Under the Dalai Lamas there also developed over the past centuries a tradition of giving the Kalacakra Initiation at occasional intervals to large public gatherings, and in 1981 a ceremony was conducted on July 10–21 by the Fourteenth Dalai Lama in Madison, Wisconsin, the first time the Kalacakra Initiation was offered outside Tibet and India. In addition to dealing on a first level with the external world and being the source of the Tibetan calendar and system of astrology, on a second level the *Kalacakra* is concerned with the techniques for controlling the flow of energy in the psychic nervous system, and on a third level with the visualizations of the *tantric* deities, by which the limitations of time may be transcended and *nirvana* experienced even here and now—provided one understands emptiness and devotes one's efforts to the welfare of all beings.[181]

Yogas

Bardo. In the long journey toward enlightenment there are various stages, and these are designated in the *tantric* literature by the term *bar do* (pronounced bardo), which literally means "in-between." Bardo Yoga, it will be remembered, was one of the "six topics" of Naropa, which Naropa's student Marpa transmitted to Milarepa, and Milarepa speaks frequently of various *bardos,* most importantly of the Bardo of Birth and Death, which is the "in-between" state after birth and before death; of the Bardo of Dream and Sleep, which is the state between sleeping (with dreams) and waking; and of the great and momentous Bardo, which is the intermediate state of existence between death and rebirth, in which he further distinguishes three subsidiary *bardos.*[182]

The *bardo* doctrine seems intended to teach, not that these various stages are separate entities, but rather that they are all aspects of one and the same existence.[183] Thus, although in Buddhism a person is described as a constantly changing combination of "aggregates" *(skandhas)* rather than a self *(atman),* it is evident that a continuity of consciousness is presupposed, and Śakyamuni Buddha himself is supposed to have remembered at the time of his enlightenment what took place in many previous incarnations, both animal and human, a capability which is also attributed at least in some degree to some advanced *yogis*.[184]

The Tibetan book on the *bardo* between death and rebirth is the *Bar do thos grol* (pronounced Parto Thötrol, also Bardo Thodol), popularly known as the "Tibetan Book of the Dead." This work is supposed to have been composed by Padmasambhava and written down by his wife Yeshe Tshogyal, along with a *sadhana* describing two *mandalas* of the forty-two peaceful deities and the fifty-eight wrathful deities who figure in the book. Like the similarly composed biography of Padmasambhava, this text too was supposedly hidden at the time and rediscovered later. In this case the discoverer *(terchen)* who brought the book to light was a certain *Kar ma gling pa* (pronounced Karma Lingpa) (fourteenth century C.E.), who was an incarnation of a famous *lotsawa* contemporary with King Trhisong Detsen (eighth century C.E.), and the work was handed down through the Nyingma and Kagyu orders.[185]

In the introduction of the *Bardo Thodol* the work is described as the "great liberation through hearing," an allusion to six types of liberation, namely, through hearing, wearing, seeing, remembering, tasting, and touching. The "hearing" is intended to be that of the dying or deceased person, for whose benefit the book may be read aloud, but it is also intended that the book should be studied in the present lifetime in preparation for the time of death. In fact, what is told in the book is understood to be symbolic of states of consciousness and of mental projections, which may occur at any time but are presumably much heightened in the time of death.

The entire intermediate state between death and rebirth is described as of forty-nine days duration (presumably a symbolic number, seven times seven), and is divided into three subsidiary intervals, as referred to by Milarepa. The first is the Chikhai Bardo. This is "the *bardo* of the moments of death," although it may last for as much as three and one-half or four days. At this point the person is in what is popularly called a "swoon" or a "coma," but is actually set face to face with a luminosity or Clear Light, "wherein all things are like the void and cloudless sky, and the naked, spotless intellect is like unto a transparent vacuum without circumference or center."[186] If adequately prepared by previous *yogic* training, the dying person may be able, in the very moment of death, to accept the Light without fear and become one with it, and thus instantaneously pass on into liberation and into *bodhisattva*hood or Buddhahood.

If this does not happen, the deceased enters the second *bardo*, called the Chönyid Bardo or "the *bardo* of the experiencing of reality."[187] The person is now recovered from the "coma," wonders what has happened, and begins to realize that he is "dead." His body is transformed into a "shining illusory body," which is the ethereal counterpart of the physical body, possessing a psychic nerve system and the principle of consciousness. He can see that his physical body is being disposed of by his relatives and friends, and can hear them weeping and wailing, but when he tries to call to them they cannot hear him. Throughout this period, which is said to be of fourteen days duration, he experiences "karmic illusions," i.e., he hears sounds and sees lights and images which are his own "thought forms," i.e., mental projections. For seven days he sees peaceful deities, Vairocana the central Tathagata embracing his consort the Queen of Vajra Space, and others to the total number of forty-two. Then for seven days more he sees wrathful deities, Heruka and others to the total number of fifty-eight, but these are after all only the former peaceful deities in changed aspect and number. Within this second *bardo*, given faith and the knowledge that all the apparitional appearances are unreal and powerless, the deceased might yet attain liberation but, lacking that, he must enter the third *bardo*.

The third *bardo* is the Sidpa Bardo, "the *bardo* of seeking rebirth," a period usually reckoned at about twenty-two days, or perhaps more, up to the overall total of the forty-ninth day.[188] In this period, if not previously liberated, the deceased begins to desire to be born again in a physical body and thinks, "O what would I not give to possess a body," and wanders about seeking a body. At this point also occurs the judgment, in which the good genius, who personifies the person's good conscience, counts out the person's good deeds with white pebbles, and the evil genius, who personifies the person's bad conscience, counts out the person's evil deeds with black pebbles. The presiding judge is the Lord of Death (Sanskrit *Yama*, Tibetan *gShin rje*, pronounced Shinjê), and he holds the mirror of *karma*, in which every good and evil act is vividly reflected. In this judgment the deceased suffers many punishments, yet in fact these transpire only in the imagination of the deceased, and it is he who is punishing himself in his thoughts as he sees his own self as it really is.

Then the deceased sees six lights which shine upon him from the six worlds of the *samsara*, namely, from the *deva*-world, the *asura*-world, the human-world, the animal-world, the *preta*-world, and the hell-world, in one of which, as determined by his *karma*, he will be reborn. So at last he goes to one of these places, there to begin the next stages in his long journey toward ultimate liberation.

Mahamudra. The *Mahamudra* (in Tibetan the *Phyag rgya chen mo*, pronounced chhakgya chhenmo), the "great seal" or "great symbol," has already been mentioned as studied by Drokmi, Marpa, and Milarepa, and as associated with the supreme experience of the "joy innate" and the "eternal state" in the *Hevajra Tantra*. While the Sanskrit word *mudra* (literally "seal," also understood as "symbol") is used for sacred gestures and postures, it also has the wider meaning of an aid to meditational practice and, in this sense, the *mahamudra* is the highest *yoga* (literally "union") or practice aimed at achieving the union of the individual with the divine source of all, ranking even above the two other main practices of the supreme *yoga (anuttarayoga)*, which are called "arising *yoga*" and "perfecting *yoga*." According to a song of Milarepa the *mahamudra* has four states, the names of which are translatable as one-pointedness, away-from-playwords, one-taste, and non-practice, in the last of which the meditator has reached the ultimate realm and the state of Buddhahood.[189]

In a yet further sense the *mahamudra* is not only the manner in which meditation is practiced and the foregoing four states attained, but the *mahamudra* is itself the ground from which the undertaking arises, the path on which it proceeds if it is to be successful, and the goal to which it finally comes. Thus Saraha, the teacher of Nagarjuna, describes the *mahamudra* as

> Having no shape or color, being all-encompassing,
> Unchanging, and stretching across the whole of time,
> Like celestial space without end or beginning . . .

and goes on to say that *mahamudra* is "instantaneous experience of Buddhahood."[190]

Gampopa virtually repeats the description, and makes a fuller statement as follows:

> Mahamudra has four characteristics: all-encompassing, without color or shape, because it is the actuality of transcending awareness, stretching across the whole of time, and neither coming nor going. When it is present in a man he will not consider *samsara* to be something that

has to be renounced and therefore he will not shun what is said not to be conducive to enlightenment. Neither will he hold *nirvana* to be something restful, and therefore he will not rely on what is said to counter worldliness, and so has neither wishful dreams nor thoughts of despair as to the outcome.[191]

As far as *Mahamudra* texts are concerned, Marpa and several others are said to have produced Tibetan versions from Indian manuscript sources, and a later successor of Marpa in the Kagyu-pa lineage in the sixteenth century wrote a text dealing with this doctrine which is still available. This personage was *Pad ma dkar po* (Padma Karpo, pronounced Pema Karpo, meaning White Lotus) (1526–1592 C.E.), a Tibetan from *Zangs dkar* (pronounced Zanskar, a region of Western Tibet now in Ladakh and Kashmir), who settled in Southern Tibet and is credited with establishing the *'Brug-pa* (pronounced Druk-pa) sub-sect of the Kagyu-pa (founded by *Gling ras pa Pad ma rdo rje*, pronounced Ling Rêpa Pema Dorje, 1128–1188 C.E.) as the dominant order in what is now Bhutan. Padma Karpo wrote a Tibetan history as well as works on many other subjects, and the *Mahamudra* text of which we now speak. In the colophon of this work Padma Karpo says that he wrote it while dwelling in the southern mountains, and at the request of *Gzhan phan Bzang po* (pronounced Zhanphan Zangpo), the king of Zanskar, whose *guru* he was. A further note at the end of the colophon also gives credit to a certain donor who, probably a hundred years after the time of Padma Karpo, contributed one silver coin for the carving of each block-type of the book, which would have been fourteen silver coins in all for the fourteen printing blocks necessary for the printing of the extant text. The title of the work is *The Epitome of the Great Symbol*.[192]

The text is essentially a guide to *yogic* practice, and begins with instructions on assuming the *dorje*-posture (the cross-legged position familiar in images of the Buddha, called in Sanskrit the *padmasana* or lotus posture), and on achieving mental tranquility. Then under the heading of "one-pointedness" procedures of breathing and visualization are outlined, intended to achieve mental concentration. In this connection the author quotes several of his famous predecessors in the teaching of the *mahamudra*.

> The Master of Doctrines (either Gampopa or Tsongkhapa) said:
> "If the mind be left relaxed, it attains tranquility;
> If water be left undisturbed, it attains clearness."
> The Great Lord of Yogis (Milarepa) said:
> "When the mind is left in the primordial, unmodified condition, knowledge dawns;
> When this condition is maintained, comparable in its calmness to the flow of a calm river, knowledge in its completeness is attained."
> The Great Saraha summarized the essence of the teachings in these verses:
> "When bound (or unrelaxed), the mind tries to wander in each of the ten directions;
> When freed, it remains firm and motionless.
> I have come to understand that it is a stubborn thing like a camel."

After that, the further stages of the meditative process are set forth (here called the *yogas* of the uncreated, of transmuting all phenomena and mind into at-one-ment, and of non-meditation). Finally *nirvana* comes into view called, by the accepted rendering of the Sanskrit word in Tibetan, the "nonabiding" *(mignas pahi)* and the "passing beyond sorrow" *(mya ngan las hdas pa)*.

> When the ignorance which was to be overcome has been dispersed, the effort to overcome it ceases, and the path comes to an end and the journey is completed.

> The journeying having ceased, there is no place beyond the ending of the path to explore; and one obtains the supreme boon of the Great Symbol, the state of nonabiding and of passing beyond sorrow (i.e., the state of *nirvana*).[193]

In modern commentary the picture implied in *The Epitome of the Great Symbol* is outlined in the following words:

> The Path through the *Sangsāra* ends upon the realizing of *Nirvāṇa*. There is no *place* beyond *Nirvāṇa* to explore, for *Nirvāṇa* is not a place, but a state of mind. There is, however, according to Mahāyānic Buddhism . . . unending evolutionary progression; so that *Nirvāṇa* is to be regarded as a Spiritual Rest-House on the Highway through Eternity. For the Fully Enlightened Ones, no line of demarcation exists between the *Sangsāra* and *Nirvāṇa*. They live in both states, and for Them neither state is an abiding or fixed state. Were *Nirvāṇa* an abiding state, that is to say, a state of finality . . . no further evolutionary progress would be possible beyond it.
> The Great Ones and the *Bodhisattvas* . . . renounce their right to pass on to a still Higher Evolution and remain within the Cosmos for the good of all sentient beings. It is these *Bodhic* Forces, thus active in the Cosmos, which, little by little, during the ages, modify the harshness of unenlightened Nature; and, by their All-Embracing Love and Compassion, lead mankind, step by step, towards a perfected social order on Earth. We can visualize a time in the infinity of the future when these Forces will have neutralized the sorrowful struggle for existence, will have conquered Evil and transmuted it into Good, will have dissipated Ignorance with the Light of Divine Wisdom, and so transformed the Cosmos that the *Sangsāra* and *Nirvāṇa* really will be in At-one-ment. Then will every living thing have attained the Goal of the Great Symbol. Then will the Journey through the Cosmos be ended for ever; and the Path of the Higher Evolution be entered and lead to a Goal utterly beyond the conception of finite mind.[194]

13

MONUMENTS OF BUDDHISM IN INDIA, PAKISTAN, AND SRI LANKA

INDIA AND PAKISTAN

In Buddhism the center of interest is naturally in the Buddha, but not just in Śakyamuni, the Sage of the Śakyas, who in early life and in many previous existences was a *bodhisattva,* striving toward enlightenment, and who finally attained this goal and was recognized as the Buddha. Additionally, already in the Theravada, the interest is in a whole series of Buddhas past and future, and, in the Mahayana and Vajrayana, in virtually innumerable Buddhas, *bodhisattvas,* and other figures. Within all forms of Buddhism and in all of these figures, the center of interest is ultimately in the supreme and ineffable idea of Buddhahood itself.

Symbols

In his existences as a *bodhisattva,* the future Buddha lived in various earthly forms, both animal and human, and can properly be represented in art in such forms. As the Buddha, however, after he attained enlightenment and especially in death, in his entry into the ultimate *nirvana,* it is no longer proper to represent him in personal form. Rather, symbols can point to his transcendental nature and to the ultimate and inexpressible character of Buddhahood which he forevermore embodies.

Therefore, even as in Jainism where symbols probably precede images of the *tirthankaras,* so also in Buddhism certainly it is symbols of the Buddha rather than human images which are found first. The symbols include the following. An empty space—if it may be called a symbol—stands for the presence of the Buddha. A sort of elongated rectangle (*cankrama,* walking path) is the path on which he went. Footprints show that he is present. So also a throne or other seat signifies his presence. A *bodhi* tree—usually the pipal tree (*aśvattha* or *pippala,* the *Ficus religiosa*)—stands for him and his enlightenment, for it was under such a tree that he attained enlightenment. A disk or wheel, already appropriate to him as a sign of royalty, means in particular the wheel of the doctrine (*dharmacakra*) which he set turning in his first sermon at the Deer Garden. A *stupa* recalls the burial mounds in

420 | An Archaeological History of Religions of Indian Asia

which his earthly remains were placed after his cremation, and stands for his all-pervading presence in those relics; likewise the form of the *stupa* provides a picture of the universe in which the Buddha is the central reality. Such symbols as these are seen on the railings from the Buddhist *stupa* at Bharhut (second century B.C.E.), on the gates of the *stupa* at Sanchi (first century C.E.) (See below Figures 13.17–19), and so forth.

Images

In distinction from the purely symbolical intimations of the Buddha reality in early Buddhist art, the image of the Buddha in human form, which is so universally found in later Buddhism, only comes into view in the first centuries C.E. At this time the empire of the Kushanas held sway from Gandhara (eastern Afghanistan and northwestern Pakistan) to the Ganges-Yamuna valley, with a capital at Purushapura (Peshawar) and a major eastern center at Mathura, and with Kanishka (probably 78–103 C.E.) as its greatest king. It is in Mathura and Gandhara that the earliest Buddha statues are found.

Mathura

In the region of Mathura *yakshas* were already represented in standing stone statues in the third to second centuries B.C.E. (Fig. 8.1), and seated cross-legged *jina* figures were carved on tablets of homage in the first century C.E. (Fig. 10.2). It is in and around Mathura that the greatest number of very early statues of the Buddha have been found; therefore, it is a reasonable supposition that the *yaksha* and *jina* figures provide the antecedents in religious sculpture for the making of the Buddha figure in its standing and seated forms. Such Buddha statues were probably being made by the middle of the first century C.E. and onward.[1]

A seated statue in red sandstone (height 2 feet 3 inches [0.69 m.]), which was found at the village of Katra, near Mathura, and is now in the Archaeological Museum at Mathura, is one of the early Buddha images from the Mathura region (Fig. 13.1).[2] An inscription on three raised rims of the pedestal of the image reads: "Budharakshita's mother Amohasi has erected [this] *bodhisattva* (image) together with her parents in her own convent for the welfare and happiness of all sentient beings."

The paleographical style of the inscription points to the early Kushana period, probably first or early second century C.E. The image is called a *bodhisattva* but possesses the marks of a Buddha, and the tree overhead has the foliage of the pipal tree, so this must be Śakyamuni under the *bodhi* tree, presumably prior to his enlightenment and thus when he was in fact still a *bodhisattva*. Indeed the terms *buddha* and *bodhisattva* appear to be used almost interchangeably in the early inscriptions identifying various images.

In the present sculpture the figure is seated in the cross-legged position (*padmasana*) on a pedestal supported by three lions (*simhasana*), and raises the right hand in the gesture of reassurance (*abhaya mudra*). The garb is a very thin, almost transparent robe which leaves the right shoulder bare. The *urna*, a small circular mark, is between the eyebrows; a line over the forehead gives the impression that the head is shaven; and the protuberance on top of the skull (*ushnisha*) has the spiral shape of a snail shell. The palm of the right hand is marked with a wheel, and the soles of the feet show the signs of the wheel and the three jewels, while the toes are marked with *svastikas*. The halo behind the head has small semicircular

13.1 Seated Bodhisattva/Buddha Image, Gift of Amohasi, from Katra, in the Archaeological Museum, Mathura

indentations around the edge, which may be reminiscent of the many hoods of a serpent. On either side of the main figure is an attendant with flywhisk *(cauri)* in the right hand. Overhead are two flying figures.[3]

Gandhara

The Buddha image was probably also produced in Gandhara at about the same time as in Mathura, i.e., by the middle of the first century C.E. and onward.[4] Gandhara, in the northwest, was especially open to Hellenistic/Roman influence from Alexander the Great onward, and the influence of the Greco/Roman world is recognizable in the styling of the Buddha image in that region.[5] Instead of the almost transparent robe of the early Mathura image (Fig. 13.1), the Buddha here wears a more substantial robe with its folds draped in the Greco-Roman manner, sometimes leaving the right shoulder bare like a Roman toga, sometimes covering both shoulders. Instead of the shaven monk's head of the early Mathura representation, the image here has curly hair, and the hair covers the *ushnisha* in a considerable

13.2 Standing Buddha with Alms Bowl, from Takht-i-Bahi, in the Archaeological Museum, Peshawar

knot, while many of the figures also show Buddhas and *bodhisattvas* with a mustache. The halo behind the head is usually a plain disk, without the small semicircular indentations seen around the edge at Mathura.

Many Buddha and *bodhisattva* images in the Gandhara style are contained in the Archaeological Museum at Peshawar (ancient Purushapura). Of these, many come from Takht-i-Bahi, a site in the center of ancient Gandhara (30 miles [48 km.] northeast of Peshawar). Here on the summit of an isolated hill (650 feet [198 m.] high) are the remains of a Buddhist monastery, with the remains of another at the foot of the hill at Shahr-i-Bahlol. The only actual date available from Takht-i-Bahi is an inscription of the Pahlava king Gondophares in 46 C.E. but most of the Buddhist remains are later than that and date from the third to the fourth century C.E.[6]

In a standing figure from Takht-i-Bahi in the Peshawar Museum the Buddha is shown with his alms bowl in his hand (Fig. 13.2), a representation especially appropriate in this region, inasmuch as the alms bowl of the Buddha was supposed to have been long preserved in Gandhara. In another standing figure from Shahr-i-Bahlol the head of the Buddha is backgrounded by a very large halo (Fig. 13.3); between the eyebrows is a small circular depression, and this is where the *urna* was once represented by a crystal which is now lost.[7] In Gandharan art Śakyamuni is also sometimes portrayed quite exceptionally in great emaciation, representing the extremity of his ascetic practice, and there is an example of this theme in the Taxila Museum (Fig. 13.4).[8]

13.3 Head of Buddha, from Shahr-i-Bahlol, in the Archaeological Museum, Peshawar

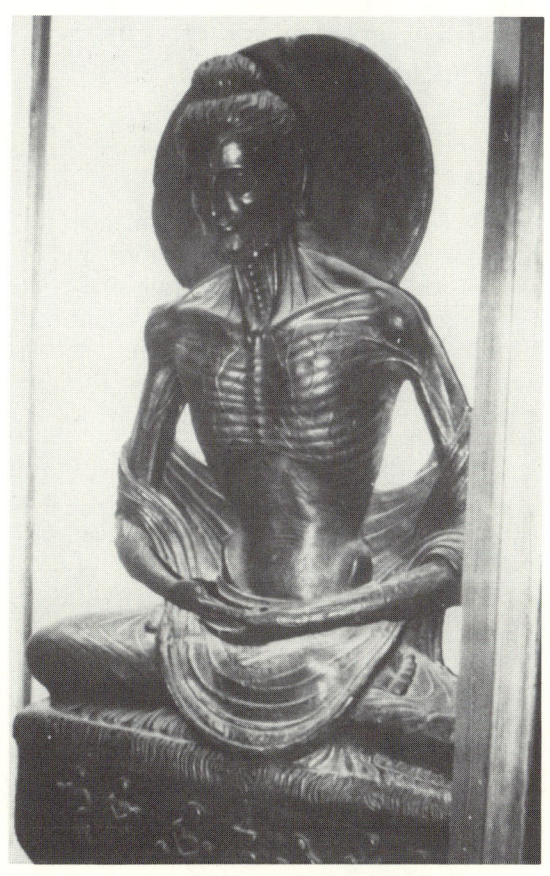

13.4 Śākyamuni in Extreme Emaciation, Replica in the Taxila Museum

Two other figures of importance in Gandharan sculpture are Hariti and Pancika, who are to be seen in a seated group from Shahr-i-Bahlol in the Peshawar Museum. Hariti is the sister of the *yaksha* Satagiri, the protector of Rajagriha, and Pancika her husband is the son of Pancala, the *yaksha* protector of Gandhara. Pancika is also known as a general in the army of Kubera, the lord of the *yakshas,* and Hariti is sometimes called the wife of Kubera. The personal name of Hariti is Abhirati, and the chief story told concerning her explains how she obtained the name Hariti (stealer of children).[9] In this story Hariti appears in a role very similar to that of the *rakshasi* Jara in Hinduism.[10]

As Yi Jing tells the story, in a former birth Hariti was a mother who made a vow to devour all the children at Rajagriha and, in consequence of the wicked vow, was reborn as a *yakshini,* and gave birth to five hundred children. Then she began to eat the children at Rajagriha, which suggests at this point that Hariti is a goddess of disease, probably of smallpox, and is similar to Sitala and Jyeshtha in Hinduism. The people of Rajagriha, accordingly, asked the Buddha for help. He took away Hariti's youngest child, named Priyankara, and it was only after long search that the mother found the child with the Buddha. The Buddha asked her why she grieved so much for only one lost child out of five hundred, when she had no pity on the parents in Rajagriha who had lost their only one or two children on account of her cruel vow. Hariti then repented and agreed to give up eating human flesh, and in return it was promised that in every monastery food would be offered every day to her and her children. So, Yi Jing explains, in the dining hall of every monastery there is an image of Hariti with a babe in her arms and other children around her knee and a daily offering of food is made to the image. Further, if the childless pray to her for children, making such an offering, their wish is fulfilled. So, in the outcome of the story, "the demon mother of the children," as Yi Jing calls her, "is a symbol of the concept of motherhood."[11] Xuan Zang also calls Hariti "the mother of the demons," and mentions a Hariti *stupa* in Gandhara, which was erected by Aśoka.[12]

Gupta Period

Refinement of the Buddha image which, according to the foregoing evidence, originated at Mathura and in Gandhara in the first and second centuries C.E. led to its classical form which was attained in the Gupta period (320–600 C.E.). Outstanding characteristics are now the graceful perfection of the relatively tall and broad-shouldered body, the serenity and compassion of the countenance, and the large ornamental halo. Wherever Buddhism spread, throughout India and far beyond, it was this classical figure which was most influential in the representation of the Buddha.[13]

A standing statue of the Buddha in the Gupta style of about the fifth century C.E. was found in the excavation of the Jamalpur mound at Mathura, and is in the Archaeological Museum at Mathura (Fig. 13.5).[14] The figure, of pink sandstone, is 7 feet 2 inches (2.2 m.) high and 2 feet (0.6 m.) wide across the shoulders. When found it was broken with a fracture above the ankles, and the right hand is missing. The Buddha is clothed with a close-fitting nearly transparent upper garment, worn around both shoulders, and with a lower garment visible above the ankles and held up by a girdle around the waist. The left hand holds the hem of the upper garment; the missing right hand was probably raised in the *abhaya* (no fear) gesture. The hair of the head is tightly curled to the right, and the *ushnisha* is prominent, but there is no *urna.* The nose and elongated ears are slightly damaged. Behind the head is a

13.5 Standing Statue of the Buddha, Gift of the Monk Yaśadinna, from Jamalpur, in the Archaeological Museum, Mathura

13.6 Buddha Head from Camunda Tila, in the Archaeological Museum, Mathura

large (3 foot [.9 m.] in diameter) halo magnificently carved in concentric circles, with flower and leaf patterns. At the feet of the statue are two very small kneeling figures, presumably worshipers or donors. On the front of the base a Sanskrit inscription reads: "This is the pious gift of the Buddhist monk Yaśadinna. Whatsoever merit [there is] in this [gift], let it be for the attainment of supreme knowledge of [his] parents, teachers, and preceptors and of all sentient beings."

A beautiful Gupta style head of the Buddha (fifth century C.E.) in the Archaeological Museum, Mathura, comes from Camunda Tila near Mathura (Fig. 13.6).[15] The hair is arranged in tight curls turned to the right, the *ushnisha* is prominent, the ears are elongated, and the calm countenance exemplifies the Buddhist ideal of peace.

ARCHITECTURAL FORMS

The architectural forms of chief importance in Buddhism are the *stupa*, the *caitya* hall, and the *vihara*.

Stupa

The *stupa* (Pali *thupa*), important also in early Jainism and described above in Chapter 10 in its essential features, is the most characteristic Buddhist architectural structure. In conversation with Ananda, when nearing his own decease, the Buddha remarked that upon the cremation of the body of a world ruler *(cakravartin)* it is customary to erect at the four crossroads a cairn *(thupa)* for the remains, and that the same should be done for a *tathagata,* an Awakened One (*Digha Nikaya* 2.142–143).[16] Such was then, in fact, the disposition of the remains of the Buddha, as several claimants received their respective portions of his relics and put up sacred cairns over them. Such structures, therefore, continued to be used to enshrine Buddhist relics or to mark places and to recall events in Buddhist history. The relics so enshrined may be of three kinds: (1) corporeal relics *(śarira-dhatus)*; (2) relics which were used by the person *(paribhogika-dhatus),* such as clothes, ornaments, or alms bowl; and (3) indicative relics *(uddeśika-dhatus),* such as images.

The shape of the *stupa* also lends itself to interpretation in terms of psycho-cosmic symbolism. The hemisphere, for example, can stand for the vast dome of the sky and thus for the infinite universe; the umbrella on the top can be the tree of life on the summit of Mount Meru. At the same time the *stupa* can be a great person, seated in meditation, crossed legs in the base, body up to the shoulders in the hemisphere, and head in the *harmika*. At the same time there can also be a symbolization of the centers of psychic force *(cakras)* in the human body, and of the ascending development of consciousness from the awareness of material sense objects up through mental realms to the transcendent experience of enlightenment.[17]

Caitya

The word *caitya* (Pali *cetiya*), it has already been observed in Chapter 10, is applied to many kinds of sacred objects, places, trees, buildings (including *stupas*), and so forth, and is thus a general name for a shrine or sanctuary. Many such sanctuaries existed from early times, and the Buddha is recorded as often visiting and living at such shrines, e.g., the Udena shrine *(cetiya)* at Vesali, or the Ananda shrine *(cetiya)* at Bhoganagara (*Digha Nikaya* 2.117–118, 123).[18] Accordingly *caitya* was a familiar term by which Hindus, Jainas, and Buddhists all designated their sanctuaries. In particular, in later Buddhist usage, the term was often a synonym for *stupa,* and then also the name of the hall with a *stupa* inside as the focus of attention, a hall that was in effect a Buddhist chapel or cathedral.

Such *caitya* halls are found in the form of rock-cut sanctuaries, and in these there are often architectural features such as a vaulted roof ornamented with ribs of wood, which show that there were prototypes constructed of wood. The façade of a typical *caitya* has a semicircular or horseshoe-shaped arch over the entrance, with an opening or sun window which admits light to the interior. The interior plan is much like that of a Roman basilica. A long hall is divided by rows of pillars into a broad nave and two side aisles. The hall terminates at the farther end in a rounded apse, within which stands a *stupa,* with room around it for circumambulation, and with the side rows of pillars continuing around the *stupa.* Later a large image of the Buddha may take the place of the *stupa.*

Vihara

As in Jainism so also in Buddhism the monastic nature of the movement called for residences to be used, at least upon occasion (e.g., during the *vassa,* the rainy season retreat), by the monks of the order. The word *vihara* (abiding place) is the name of such a dwelling place; in the older literature it often denotes the private apartment of a single monk; in later times it almost always designates the whole of a building in which several or many monks or nuns reside (*Cullavagga* 2.1.2).[19] Lay persons would often provide such residences for individuals or for the monastic community (*Mahavagga* 3.5).[20] Thus King Milinda, for example, built a *vihara* which was called the Milinda Vihara (*Milinda Panha* 7.7.21).[21] Likewise King Bimbisara built a residence for the Buddhist community, and this was called by the word *pasada,* a term which at least in later times means a building of several stories, each successive story being of smaller area than the one beneath it (*Cullavagga* 6.3.11).[22]

In essential plan the usual *vihara* consists of a single large hall, square or rectangular, with individual cells opening off from it. There may also be an upper story, a verandah, a cloister *(cankama),* a bathhouse *(jantaghara),* and so forth. In addition to mentioning such features of a *vihara,* the *Cullavagga* (5.14.2–3; 6.3.2–3)[23] gives rules, e.g., concerning the use of curtains for privacy, the type of paintings allowed for ornament. As for the paintings, in both the *caityas* and the *viharas,* rock surfaces were prepared by applying a layer of clay mixed with rice-husk and gum, over this a thin layer of lime plaster was added, and then the painted decorations were executed in mineral colors placed on the surface while still semi-wet.

CAVES

Ajanta

The caves of Ajanta are 62 miles (100 km.) north of Aurangabad, and 7 miles (11 km.) northwest of the town of Ajanta. The site is in the Inhyadri hills of the Sahyadri ranges, in the secluded valley of the Waghora River below the Sapta Kunda or Seven Falls (Fig. 13.7). Thirty Buddhist caves are cut in the steep, curving side of the valley, numbered from the lower end of the series. In date they

13.7   Valley of the Ajanta Caves

extend from about 150 B.C.E. to 650 C.E. under the Satavahanas (225 B.C.E. to 225 C.E.), Vakatakas (250–450 C.E.), Guptas (320–500 C.E.), and Calukyas (550–757 C.E.).

Except for a very few that are inaccessible, the caves may be classified as follows. Four caves are *caityas* containing *stupas* (Nos. 9, 10, 19, 26); the others are *viharas*. Six caves are Hinayana, characterized at least in their original form by the absence of the Buddha image (Nos. 8, 9, 10, 12, 13, 30); the rest are Mahayana. Paintings or fragments thereof are still found in many of the caves, the most important paintings being in Caves Nos. 1, 2, 6, 9, 10, 16, 17, and 19.

Dating of the caves is on the basis of inscriptions, architectural features, style of paintings, and so forth. The oldest caves are the Hinayana, the *caityas* Nos. 10 (second century B.C.E.) and 9 (first century B.C.E.), and the *viharas,* extending in date from No. 30 (second century B.C.E.) through No. 8 to Nos. 12 and 13 (first or second century C.E.).[24]

Caityas—Cave No. 10. Chiefly on the basis of an inscription in the cave, Cave No. 10, a Hinayana *caitya,* is considered the oldest of all the Ajanta caves, and is assigned to the first half of the second century B.C.E. The hall, with nave and two side aisles, is 95 feet (29 m.) long, 40 feet (12 m.) wide, and 36 feet (11 m.) high. Thirty-nine octagonal pillars divide the aisles from the nave, and surround the *stupa* at the farther end of the nave. The roof of the nave is vaulted and was once adorned with wooden ribs, the places of which can still be seen, and this and other architectural features reflect the transition from wood to stone. The *stupa* is the largest of these structures at Ajanta. The base is round and surrounded by two stone rings; the dome is hemispherical; the *harmika* on top is rectangular and tall, and is surmounted by three flat stone slabs one above the other, a feature called the *trivarnika* and understood to signify the three refuges, the Buddha, the *dharma,* and the *sangha.*[25]

The paintings in Cave 10 are of two periods. The older paintings, as attested by two inscriptions, are not far in time from the original excavation of the cave, probably late second or early first century B.C.E., and in these there are no figures of the Buddha. Examples are the paintings of a *raja* who is coming with his retinue to pay homage to a *bodhi* tree, and of scenes from the *Shyama Jataka* in which the *bodhisattva* was born as Shyama and lived in the Himalaya with his blind parents, and from the *Shaddanta Jataka* in which the *bodhisattva* was born as a six-tusked white elephant. The later paintings are ascribed to the fifth century C.E. and many of them show the Buddha himself, e.g., a painting on the sixth pillar on the right-hand side of the cave which depicts the Buddha together with a one-eyed monk.[26]

Cave No. 9. Cave No. 9, the other of the Hinayana *caityas,* was probably excavated in the first century B.C.E. The interior plan is similar to that of Cave 10. The dimensions are 44 feet (13.5 m.) long, 23 feet (7 m.) wide, and 23 feet 4 inches (7.1 m.) high. Here also there are paintings of different periods. The oldest, with no figures of the Buddha, probably belong to the first century B.C.E. They include pictures of a group of votaries approaching a *stupa,* and of a *stupa* with many umbrellas on it as emblems of sanctity and dignity. Later paintings (probably fourth or fifth century C.E.) show scenes from the life of the Buddha, and there are also large figures of the Buddha carved along the sides of the cave (probably fifth or sixth century C.E. in date).[27]

Cave No. 19. Cave No. 19 is a Mahayana *caitya* of probably the sixth century C.E. It is approached across a large courtyard, on either side of which was once a chapel. At the entrance to the cave (Fig. 13.8) two small pillars support a decorated porch, above which is the horseshoe-shaped sun window which admits light to the

13.8   Façade of Cave No. 19, Ajanta

interior. On either side of the window are large *yaksha* figures, serving as guardians (*dvarapalas*) of the *caitya*. Elsewhere the entire façade is covered with sculptures. There are many figures of the Buddha in various poses. In one scene he stands, with begging bowl in hand, before his wife Yaśodhara and his son Rahula, both shown in smaller size. Another scene depicts a *naga* king and queen, and there are also a number of *mithuna* figures.

Inside, fifteen round pillars divide the *caitya* into nave and two side aisles. The capitals and the entablature above them are carved with Buddha figures. The ceiling is vaulted and ribbed. The *stupa* is tall and surmounted by three umbrellas and a vase on top of them. On the front of the *stupa* a *torana* frames a standing figure of the Buddha in full relief. On the walls and the ceilings of the aisles are a number of paintings of the Buddha, mostly in seated position, and also geometrical and floral designs.[28]

Cave No. 26. Cave No. 26 is a Mahayana *caitya* of probably the seventh century C.E. The façade is carved with many Buddha figures, and there are two *yakshas* on the sides of the sun window as *dvarapalas*. In the interior on the wall of the left side aisle there is a very large sculpture of the Buddha in his *parinirvana*, reclining on his right side with his head supported by his right hand. Mourners are seated below,, and gods and goddesses are above. In the next panel Ananda, the Buddha's beloved disciple, is seated, weeping. Another scene is that of the temptation of the Buddha, in which he is seated under the *bodhi* tree, with the daughters of Mara attempting to attract his attention from below, and the army of Mara attacking him from either side, all to no avail. On the tall *stupa* there are also many carvings of the Buddha. On the front his large figure is seated in the rather unusual *pralambapada asana,* on a lion throne, with his feet hanging down to rest upon a lotus.[29]

Turning from the *caityas* to the *viharas,* there are important paintings in Caves Nos. 1, 2, 6, 16, and 17, all of which are Mahayana monasteries, dating from the fifth to the seventh centuries C.E.

Viharas—Cave No. 16. Cave No. 16 (fifth century C.E.) has a broad veranda 65 feet [19.5 m.] by 10 feet 8 inches [3.1 m.]), three entrance doors, and a square interior hall (about 66 feet [22 m.] square, 15 feet 3 inches [4.6 m.] high) with twenty pillars. A niche at the back contains a very large Buddha figure, and monks' cells otherwise surround the hall.

The paintings in the cave include scenes from the *jatakas* and from the life of the Buddha. The *Hasti Jataka* scene (in the front corridor) pictures the occasion when the *bodhisattva* was born as an elephant and sacrificed himself in order to provide food for a company of starving wayfarers. The *Maha-Ummagga Jataka* scene (also in the front corridor) depicts an event in which the threatened execution of a supernatural child named Mahosadha was averted by a miracle. Among the scenes in the life of the Buddha, there is the Conversion of Nanda (in the left corridor). Nanda was the half-brother of the Buddha, had just married a beautiful princess, and was to succeed Suddhodana on the throne of Kapilavastu. When the Buddha came back to Kapilavastu, Nanda came out to give him alms, and the Buddha led him away to the monastic life. The paintings show the Buddha at Kapilavastu, where he again meets his wife Yaśodhara and his son Rahula; Nanda being ordained in a monastery; and a dying princess, who is presumably the wife whom Nanda left behind.[30]

Cave No. 17. Cave No. 17 (fifth century C.E.) is of almost the same plan as Cave No. 16, and of dimensions only slightly smaller. An antechamber gives access to the main hall. The cave contains more paintings than any other Ajanta cave, and the paintings are comparatively well preserved.

Above the main entrance leading to the main hall of the cave is a row of seven Manushi Buddhas and Maitreya the future Buddha. Beneath these is a row of *mithuna* couples. In the main hall the largest number of paintings represent scenes from the *jatakas*. These repeat the already noticed *Syama, Shaddanta,* and *Hasti Jatakas,* and also include the *Mahakapi Jataka* (the story of the heroic monkey), the *Hamsa Jataka* (the story of the golden goose), the *Vishvantara Jataka* (the story of the prince devoted to alms giving), the *Sutasoma Jataka* (the story of the king of Indraprastha who endeavored to dissuade Saudasa, king of Varanasi, from cannibalism), the *Sarabha Jataka* (the story of the benevolent stag), the *Matriposaka Jataka* (the story of the white elephant with the blind mother), the *Mahisha Jataka* (the story of the compassionate buffalo and the mischievous monkey), the *Mriga Jataka* (the story of the golden deer), and the *Nigrodhamika Jataka* (the story of the deer who offered its life in place of a doe). There is also an extended rendering of the long *Simhala Avadana* (the story of the seafarers who sailed to the island of Tamradvipa), and of Simhala who alone escaped from the *rakshasis*. Other paintings show events in the life of the Buddha, the subjugation of the wild elephant Nilgiri, and the great miracle at Śravasti in which the Buddha displayed his miraculous powers in the presence of King Prasenajit in order to controvert heretical teachers. At the back of the hall the main shrine contains a massive statue of the Buddha, seated in the attitude of teaching *(dharmacakra mudra)*, and to the left of the entrance to this shrine is a large-scale painting of the Buddha, standing with alms bowl in his right hand, while before him, in small scale, are Yaśodhara and Rahula, his wife and son.[31]

Cave No. 6. Cave No. 6 (fifth to sixth century C.E.) is the only two-storied *vihara* at Ajanta. In the lower story four rows of four pillars each support the ceiling and divide the hall into five aisles, while there are ten monks' cells around the walls, and an antechamber and a shrine with a seated Buddha statue are at the back. In the upper story twelve pillars form a square and support the ceiling, and an antechamber and a shrine with a seated Buddha figure are again at the back.

The walls of both levels were once all covered with paintings. Among surviving paintings in the lower story is the scene of the Temptation of the Buddha. The Buddha is seated cross-legged, with his right hand touching the earth *(bhumishparśa mudra)*, calling upon it to bear witness to his steadfastness. All around him is the fearsome army of Mara. Below the figure of the Buddha is part of the face and hairdress of a lady, probably one of the seven daughters of Mara. In the upper story the paintings include the Great Miracle at Śravasti as in Cave No. 17.[32]

Cave No. 2. Cave No. 2 (later sixth century C.E.) is of essentially the same plan as Cave No. 17 and the upper story of Cave No. 6, with veranda (46 feet 3 inches [14.1 m.] long, 7 feet 9 inches [2.4 m.] wide), main hall (about 48 feet [14.5 m.] square), ten cells, and antechamber and main shrine (13 feet [4.2 m.] long by 11 feet [3.3 m.] wide) with a large seated Buddha statue at the rear. Twelve massive, elaborately carved pillars support the roof. There is also a chapel on either side of the antechamber of the main shrine.

On the wall of the left corridor of the main hall several painted scenes depict the birth of the Buddha. In the chapel at the left side of the antechamber are paintings of votaries bringing offerings, and a sculpture of two seated *yakshas*. In the antechamber a "thousand Buddhas" are painted. In the right side chapel are again paintings of votaries bringing offerings, and a sculpture of Hariti and Pancika, Hariti with a child in her lap and a number of children below. On the wall of the right corridor are depictions of stories, e.g., *Purna Avadana* (the story of the sea voyages of the trader Purna and of the shipwreck of his brother Bhavila), and the *Vidhurapandita Jataka*.[33]

In the story in the *Vidhurapandita Jataka*, Vidhurapandita was the wise minister of Dhananjaya, the king of the Kurus in Indraprastha. Among others, the *naga* king Varuna was greatly impressed by what he heard from Vidhurapandita, but his own wife Queen Vimala feigned illness and said she would die unless the minister's heart were brought to her. Varuna asked his beautiful daughter, Irandati, to seek a husband who could accomplish this, and she successfully attracted a *yaksha* general named Puranaka. Puranaka knew the weakness of King Dhananjaya for the game of dice, and proposed a game in which he would wager a magical precious stone against Vidhurapandita. The king lost the game, and his minister was carried off to the realm of the *nagas*. There Vidhurapandita gave such an eloquent discourse on Law that Varuna and Vimala were so pleased that they allowed him to return safely to the Kuru kingdom.

The depiction of this story on the wall of Cave No. 2 is in several scenes. At the left Puranaka is showing the precious jewel to the king, and proposing the game of dice. To the right Dhanajaya is gambling with Puranaka, and has just thrown the dice on a game board which is prominently placed between them. Again to the right we see the palace of Varuna and Vimala in the *naga* kingdom (Fig. 13.9). In a pillared hall Vidhurapandita is seated on a low stool and, with raised hands, is instructing the *naga* king in the Law of the Buddha. Behind Vidhurapandita, seated on a colorful cushion, is the *yaksha* general Puranaka. King Varuna, also seated on a cushion, and with his status indicated by five serpent-hoods over his head, is listening intently and respectfully, his hands joined in front of his chest. Behind the king, also listening and with their hands folded, are two ladies, probably Queen Vimala and Princess Irandati. On a balcony to the right, two ladies are in conversation; this is probably the queen's private apartment, and she is discussing with Irandati the plan for Irandati's marriage with Puranaka. In a room below the balcony Vidhurapandita is seen again, with a lotus in his hand, in conversation with Vimala. Yet further to the right there is an assembly of *naga* chiefs, evidently in discussion with King Varuna; and a girl in a swing, probably Princess Irandati. Yet another frieze shows horses in a procession, probably depicting the fortunate journey home of Vidhurapandita.

Cave No. 1. Cave No. 1 (beginning of the seventh century) is of plan similar to that of Cave No. 2, with veranda (64 feet [19.5 m.] long, 9 feet 3 inches [2.8 m.] wide), main hall (64 feet [19.5 m.] square), fourteen cells, and antechamber and main shrine (20 feet [6 m.] square) with sculptured Buddha figure at the rear. Here the face of the Buddha, it is said, when illuminated on the right side shows a smile, on the left side sadness, and in front meditation.[34] Twenty pillars support the ceiling of the main hall, and are carved and painted.

The paintings in the main hall of the cave include the following. On the wall of the front corridor to the left of the main entrance is a representation of the *Sibi Jataka* (the story of Prince Sibi, who sacrificed his own flesh to save a pigeon), together with some otherwise unidentified palace scenes. On the wall of the left corridor are scenes from the *Sankhapala Jataka* (the story of a *naga* king named

13.9 Vidhurapandita in the Palace of the Naga King, Cave No. 2, Ajanta

Sankhapala), and from the Buddhist story of the adventures of Prince Kalyanakarin (a story preserved in Sanskrit, Chinese, Tibetan, and Uygur versions).

In the latter story Prince Kalyanakarin (noble doing) sailed with his younger brother Papakarin (evil doing) to the Island of Jewels and obtained a fortune. On the return journey the ship sank and only the two brothers were saved. In the shipwreck Kalyanakarin managed to save his jewels by tying them around his waist, and in order to obtain the riches Papakarin put out his brother's eyes while he was asleep, robbed him, and left him to his fate. Kalyanakarin wandered on as a blind musician and arrived at the royal court in another land. There the daughter of the king fell in love with Kalyanakarin and desired him for her husband. By "the magic power of truth" *(satyakriya)* Kalyanakarin regained his sight and was able to marry the princess, with whom he then returned to ascend the throne in his own kingdom.

Of the scenes illustrating this story in Cave No. 1 the best preserved are, at the right, the sea voyage and the shipwreck and, at the left, the princess speaking with her father in the palace about the marriage, and Kalyanakarin riding out through the palace gate to return to his home kingdom. In the scene in the palace (Fig. 13.10) the king is seated on his throne, wearing a crown, and flanked by two women fan bearers, and the princess, wearing a skirt below her waist, a crown, and some jewelry, is seated on an elaborate chair before him. To the right is the palace gate, beyond which Kalyanakarin is riding away in the successful and happy climax of the story.

On the back wall of the back corridor of the cave, to the left of the antechamber, is the famous painting of the *bodhisattva* Padmapani (lotus bearer), i.e.,

13.10 The King and the Princess in the Story of Kalyanakarin, Cave No. 1, Ajanta

13.12 Couple of Lovers, Cave No. 1, Ajanta   **13.11** Bodhisattva Padmapani, Cave No. 1, Ajanta

Avalokiteśvara, shown with fair skin, a tall crown, and a lotus in his right hand (Fig. 13.11). On his right side is a male figure, perhaps a guardian, and on his left side a female figure, the latter also wearing a tall crown and holding a lotus, presumably the consort of the *bodhisattva*. He, and she too, appear to be looking with compassion upon the world, and various scenes of the world are about them, including monkeys and peacocks and, at the *bodhisattva's* right side above the cell door, a *mithuna* couple (Fig. 13.12).

On the left wall in the antechamber is the Temptation of the Buddha. As in Cave No. 6, he is surrounded by the alluring daughters of Mara and is under attack from the demons of Mara's army but, touching the earth with his right hand *(bhumishparśa mudra),* is calling upon it to bear witness to his steadfastness. On the right wall of the antechamber is the Great Miracle of Śravasti as in Caves Nos. 6 and 17.

On the back wall of the back corridor to the right of the antechamber, balancing the picture of Padmapani on the left side, is another painting of Avalokiteśvara (earlier identified as Vajrapani), here shown with dark skin and a tall crown with a small figure of a deity in the crown. At the right side of the *bodhisattva* is a female figure, holding a lotus flower, and this is presumably his consort. Avalokiteśvara is considered an emanation of the *tathagata* Amitabha (whose figure is usually in Avalokiteśvara's crown), and yet another famous painting in Cave 1, commonly known as the "black princess" (in a palace scene on the back wall of the front corridor to the right of the main entrance), is believed identifiable as Pandara (yellow), the consort of Amitabha.

On the wall of the front corridor to the right of the main entrance of Cave No. 1 is a court scene commonly known as the Persian Embassy. Many of the characters appear to be foreigners from the northwest, and some identify the scene with an embassy which came from the Sassanian king Khusrau II (590–628 C.E.) of Persia to the court of the Chalukya king Pulakeśin II (608–642).[35]

Ellora

At Ellora Caves Nos. 1–12 are Buddhist, and the numerical sequence (counting from the south end of the entire row) corresponds to some extent to the progression of the caves in date and size. Thus Cave No. 1 is the first of the Buddhist excavations (probably fifth century C.E.) and of moderate size (main hall 42 feet [13 m.] square) and Cave No. 12 is one of the latest (probably eighth century) and the very largest (ground floor 116 feet [35 m.] by 42 feet [13 m.], and three stories in height). In function some of the caves are *viharas* (e.g., No. 5), some are *caityas* (e.g., No. 10), and in some cases a *vihara* and a *caitya* are combined in one complex.[36]

Cave No. 5. Cave No. 5 is a very large *vihara,* probably to be dated in the seventh century, and with a main hall measuring about 118 feet (36 m.) by 59 feet (18 m.). Twenty-four massive pillars divide the hall into a central nave and two side aisles, and seventeen cells are cut into the side walls for the residence of monks. Running lengthwise in the central nave are also two rows of raised stone benches, so the cave was probably used as an assembly hall and a place for lectures.

At the back of the hall is the main shrine, and on its back wall is carved the figure of the Buddha, seated in the *pralambapada asana* and the *dharmacakra mudra*. On his right is Avalokiteśvara, holding a stalk of lotus in his left hand and a *cauri* in the right, and wearing a crown of coiled hair *(jatamukuta)* in which is a small figure of Amitabha. On the left of the main Buddha figure is Maitreya, the future Buddha, recognizable by a small *caitya (stupa)* in his crown. He is standing on a lotus, and holds a *cauri* in his right hand, while his left hand rests on the knot of his lower garment.[37]

Cave No. 10. Cave No. 10 is a large *caitya,* probably dating in the latter part of the seventh century. At one time local carpenters believed that the huge image of the Buddha in this cave was a figure of Viśvakarman, the carpenter-architect of the universe, and hence this is still popularly known as the Viśvakarman cave.

There is a large entrance court in front, surrounded by galleries. Steps lead up to the veranda, above which is a railed terrace in front of the main façade of the cave. In the façade are three entrances to the main hall, and over the central door is a large horseshoe-shaped sun window.

The main hall is 85 feet (26 m.) long, 44 feet (13.5 m.) wide, and 43 feet (13 m.) high, and it curves in the shape of an apse at the farther end. Twenty-eight plain, octagonal pillars, 14 feet (4.3 m.) high, divide the hall into a central nave and two flat-roofed side aisles, and also go around the apsidal end of the hall. The vaulted roof of the hall is carved in imitation of wooden ribs.

Many sculptures adorn the walls of various portions of the cave. The *stupa* at the apsidal end of the hall is cylindrical in shape, about 27 feet (8 m.) in height and 15 feet 6 inches (4.7 m.) in diameter, and is covered with sculptures on all sides. In front of the *stupa* is a large mass of rock, almost 17 feet (5 m.) in height, and it is carved in front with a huge figure of the Buddha, almost 11 feet (3.4 m.) in height. The Buddha is seated on a throne in the *pralambapada asana* and the *dharmacakra mudra* (Fig. 13.13, with lamps still in place from worship just completed by the

13.13 Buddha in Cave No. 10, Ellora

13.14 Stupa No. 1 at Sanci, General View from the East

Fourteenth Dalai Lama of Tibet in the year 1959 C.E.). On an arch overhead there is a *bodhi* tree in the center, and on either side there are flying figures carrying garlands and food offerings. On the Buddha's right side is the *bodhisattva* Avalokiteśvara, who holds the stalk of a lotus in his left hand, while his right hand is in the *abhaya* (fear not) gesture and also holds a rosary. On the Buddha's left side is the future Buddha Maitreya, with a small *caitya (stupa)* in his crown. His right hand is broken, his left rests on the knot of his lower garment.

CONSTRUCTIONS

Sanci

A remarkably early, well preserved, and complete assemblage of the main architectural constructions of a major Buddhist center is seen at Sanci in Central India.[38] The present village of this name is about 5 miles (8 km.) from Vidiśa (near modern Bhilsa), which was the home of Aśoka's queen Devi, and the monastery Vedisagiri where Mahinda stayed before departing for Lanka was perhaps at Sanci or surely somewhere nearby. Adjacent to the Sanci village, the Buddhist archaeological site is on the summit of the hill known as Cetiyagiri and in areas immediately to the east, south, and west, and the monuments consist of many *stupas, caityas,* and *viharas*.

Stupa No. 1. Stupa No. 1 or the Great Stupa (Fig. 13.14) is on the central terrace on the summit of the hill, and was almost certainly built in its original form

13.15   Lion Capital of Aśoka Pillar, in the Archaeological Museum, Sanci

by Aśoka (269–232 B.C.E.) as a repository for relics of the Buddha. In its original form the *stupa* was a brick hemisphere, and this is still enclosed within the later stone structure. On the same level and nearby Aśoka also erected a pillar with a lion capital and an inscription. The stump of this pillar with part of the inscription still stands in place beside the South Gate of the *stupa* (below, Fig. 13.20), and the broken capital of the pillar, which was found close by, is in the Sanci Archaeological Museum (Fig. 13.15). This is one of the seven known Aśoka pillars surmounted by sculptured capitals with bull, elephant, or lion symbols, and one of the five with lions. The pillar was originally about 42 feet (13 m.) in height, and the lions on top are 4 feet (1.2 m.) high. The capital has three parts: (1) a bell-shaped lotus with the petals hanging downward; (2) a circular plinth ornamented with pairs of geese; and (3) four lions at the top, standing back to back, looking outward.[39] In the inscription Aśoka says:

> The *sangha* both of monks and of nuns is made united as long as [my] sons and great-grandsons [shall reign, and] as long as the moon and the sun [shall shine].

> The monk or nun who shall break up the *sangha,* must be caused to put on white robes (rather than the normal yellow robes) and to reside in a non-residence (i.e., a residence unfit for members of the *sangha*).
>
> For my desire is that the *sangha* may be united [and] of long duration.[40]

In accordance with the common practice of the enlargement of *stupas* by the addition of one or more enveloping layers of construction (seen elsewhere, e.g., at Sarnath and Nalanda), the original brick *stupa* of Aśoka (third century B.C.E.) was later (probably second century B.C.E.) overlaid with stone and enlarged to its present size, at which time it was also enclosed within a massive, plain, stone railing. In a third phase of development, four great ornamental gateways *(toranas)* were constructed. The style of their sculptures and the paleographical evidence of their inscriptions probably indicate a date for their construction in the middle of the first century B.C.E. or the early part of the first century C.E. On the top architrave of the South Gate an inscription states that this was "the gift of Ananda, the son of Vasishta, in the reign of Śri Śatakarni." This Śatakarni must be one of the several Andhra/Satavahana kings of that name, and it has been held that it was Śri Śatakarni II, with the suggestion that his reign was about the middle of the first century B.C.E. This is later than the date given above (in Ch. 4) for this king, however, and perhaps the Śatakarni involved was another king of the same name. From stylistic considerations it is also judged probable that the order in which the four gates were built and decorated runs from the southern as the earliest to the northern, eastern, and western in that order, but since the name of a certain donor, Balamitra, appears on both the southern and the western gates, i.e., on the earliest and the latest, they must all have been constructed at times not far separated from each other. The relatively early date of the gates is confirmed by the fact that in the sculptural ornamentation the Buddha himself is never shown in person but only represented by symbols (e.g., Figures 13.17–19 below).[41]

With respect to the dimensions of the Great Stupa, the massive stone railing, which encloses a circumambulation path *(pradakshina patha)* around the base of the monument, has an average diameter of about 145 feet (44 m.) and a height of about 11 feet (3.3 m.). The foundation terrace is 121 feet (37 m.) in diameter at its base, and 14 feet (4 m.) in height and, on its top, provides a second circumambulation path 5 feet 6 inches (1.7 m.) wide, also enclosed by a railing. The dome is 105 feet (32 m.) in diameter at its base and 39 feet (12 m.) in height. On top are a reconstructed, enclosed square platform *(harmika)* and a triple umbrella, bringing the total height of the *stupa* with its superstructure to about 82 feet (25 m.). The great ornamental gateways are about 20 feet (6 m.) in the maximum width of their three horizontal architraves, and 33 feet 6 inches (10 m.) in total height to the top of their central ornament.

On the East Gate on the outer side the sculptures of the top architrave show five *stupas* and two *bodhi* trees, each flanked by worshipers. These may be understood to stand for the seven Buddhas, i.e., six Buddhas of previous ages and Śakyamuni himself, all symbolically represented. The middle architrave depicts the Great Departure of the Buddha. The lowest architrave shows the visit of Aśoka to the *bodhi* tree at Bodhgaya. In the rectangular panels on the pillars between the middle and the lowest architrave, at the viewer's right two elephants are sprinkling the goddess Lakshmi with water, probably symbolic of the birth of the Buddha, and at the left the Wheel of the Law on a throne represents the preaching of the Buddha. Under the lowest architrave and on top of the pillars, groups of elephants serve as caryatids. At the right end of the lowest architrave a bracket figure is in the form of a *yakshini* or *vrikshaka* (dryad) holding to a mango tree (Fig. 13.16).[42]

13.16 Vrikshaka Bracket Figure, East Gate, Stupa No. 1, Sanci

On the East Gate on the inner side (Fig. 13.17) the top architrave shows seven sacred trees. The middle architrave pictures wild animals doing homage to the *bodhi* tree in the center, and we see buffalos, lions, a cobra, and so forth, coming from either side. Likewise on the lowest architrave elephants are coming from both sides to do honor to a *stupa* in the center.

Panels of carvings also fill the sides of the pillars of the East Gate. On the front face of the southern pillar the second panel from the bottom (Fig. 13.18) illustrates the miracle in which the Buddha walked on the flooded river Nairanjana in order to convert the *brahmana* ascetic Kaśyapa (Kassapa), an event narrated in the *Mahavagga* (1.20.16).[43] Here we see the flooded river washing the branches of trees in which monkeys have taken refuge, while many waterfowl are about. Kaśyapa, fearing that the water might have carried away the Buddha, has come with two companions, and they are paddling in a small boat on the flood. The Buddha, however, is walking up and down in the midst of the water on a dust-covered spot, and this is represented by the irregular rectangle of his "walking path" *(cankrama)*.

13.17 Inner Side of Architraves, East Gate, Stupa No. 1, Sanci

13.18 Buddha Walking on the Flooded River, Southern Pillar, East Gate, Stupa No. 1, Sanci

On the river bank, at the bottom of the picture, villagers are spectators of the event. Just after the conversion of Kaśyapa, which ensued soon after the river miracle, King Bimbisara came out from Rajagriha to visit the Buddha (*Mahavagga* 1.22.2–3),[44] and this further event is appropriately pictured in the next panel at the bottom of the same pillar, and the Buddha is symbolized here by an empty throne.

On the inside or south face of the northern pillar of the East Gate, the middle panel (Fig. 13.19) pictures the return of the Buddha to his native city of Kapilavastu. In the main part of the scene the king, presumably Śuddhodana, the Buddha's father, is driving out in his chariot to meet the Buddha, while townspeople peer out of upper balconies. At the bottom a sacred tree and people in front of it will probably represent the preaching of the Buddha to his fellow citizens.[45]

On the other gates the architraves and pillars are also covered, as far as they are preserved, with similar sculptures. The South Gate (Fig. 13.20), beside which is the stump of the Aśoka pillar, has lion caryatids. In the modern reconstruction of

13.19 Return of Buddha to Kapilavastu, Northern Pillar, East Gate, Stupa No. 1, Sanci

13.20 South Gate and Stump of the Aśoka Pillar, Stupa No. 1, Sanci

the gate the top and bottom architraves were evidently reversed by mistake, since the more important sculptures on them now face inward toward the *stupa* instead of facing outward. On what is now therefore the back side of the top architrave are three *stupas* and four trees, symbolizing the seven Buddhas. It is on the dome of the central *stupa* that the Śatakarni inscription is found.

The West Gate (Fig. 13.21) has figures of Kubera, the lord of the *yakshas*, as caryatids. The North Gate (Fig. 13.22) is the best preserved of the four *toranas*. It has elephant caryatids and, on top of the uppermost architrave, symbols which combine a wheel and a trident, and the fragment of a large wheel. Also between the architraves are elephants and riders, lions, *vrikshakas*, and so forth (Fig. 13.23).

In the processional path inside the railing of Stupa No. 1, four statues of the Buddha were installed against the terrace wall, facing the four entrances and, of these, the one on the east side is the best preserved (Fig. 13.24). In each case the Buddha is in the attitude of meditation *(dhyana mudra)*, there is an elaborate halo behind the head, an attendant stands on either side, and two *gandharvas* are flying overhead. An inscription of the Gupta Year 131, equivalent to 450/451 C.E., found on an architrave of the East Gate, records endowments for the Buddhist establishments at Sanci and, among other things, provides for the lighting of a lamp day by day "in the place where [the images of] the four Buddhas are seated." This must refer to these very four figures, and thus it is shown that they were probably in place by that date. At least later it was customary to place images of four *tathagatas* (popularly called Dhyani Buddhas) at the base of a *stupa*, facing the cardinal points, Akshobhya on the east, Ratnasambhava on the south, Amitabha on the west, and Amoghasiddhi on the north, so it is likely that these are the four Buddhas represented here, the one on the east (Fig. 12.24) therefore being Akshobhya.[46]

13.21 West Gate, Stupa No. 1, Sanci

13.22 North Gate, Stupa No. 1, Sanci

13.23 Vrikshaka and Lion, North Gate, Stupa No. 1, Sanci

13.24 Seated Buddha, Stupa No. 1, Sanci

Stupa No. 2. Stupa No. 2 at Sanci is situated on an artificial terrace halfway down the hill on its western side. Built of rough stones, this *stupa* is a solid hemisphere, flattened at the top, and surrounded by a massive stone railing. Exclusive of the railing and the processional path, the diameter of the *stupa* is 47 feet (14 m.), and its height to the top of the crowning umbrella is 37 feet (11 m.). The stone railing is adorned with many reliefs, the subjects of which are generally similar to those on the gateways of Stupa No. 1, but there are here no great gateways.

In Stupa No. 1, no actual relics were found, but here in Stupa No. 2 a chamber was found, not in the center of the structure where it would be expected, but 2 feet (0.6 m.) to the west of the center, and 7 feet (2 m.) above the *stupa* terrace, and in the chamber was a stone box containing four small stone caskets, in each of which were some fragments of human bones. These are identified by inscriptions on the box and the caskets as the relics of ten Buddhist saints and teachers, some of whom are known as having taken part in the Third Buddhist Council held under Aśoka, while some others were persons sent on missions to the Himalaya to preach the doctrines determined upon at the Council. Allowing for time for the death of all of these contemporaries of Aśoka and for the collection of the relics, it may be supposed that the date of Stupa No. 2 is in the second century B.C.E.[47]

Stupa No. 3. Stupa No. 3 is situated on the edge of the main terrace about 150 feet (45 m.) northeast of Stupa No. 1, and a modern temple of the Mahabodhi Society stands beyond it. Including the raised terrace the *stupa* is almost 50 feet (15 m.) in diameter, and its height is about 27 feet (8 m.), or about 35 feet (11 m.) including the *harmika* and umbrella. The *stupa* was surrounded by a stone railing, of which only a few fragments remain, and there is one ornamental gateway 17 feet (5 m.) high on the south side. This gate is richly carved with scenes similar to those at Stupa No. 1.

In the center of Stupa No. 3 and on the level of the terrace outside were found two large stone caskets, each with a short inscription on the lid, and these indicated that the boxes contained the relics of Śariputra and Mahamogalana respectively. The casket of Śariputra held a small fragment of bone and seven beads of pearl, garnet, lapis-lazuli, crystal, and amethyst, apparently following the tradition of depositing seven precious stones with holy relics. The casket of Mahamogalana contained only two bits of bone. The Śariputra casket was to the south, the Mahamogalana casket to the north. Śariputra and Moggallana were the most renowned of the early followers of the Buddha, and were often called his right- and left-hand disciples. Facing east, the south is on the right hand and the north is on the left hand, so the respective positions of the two caskets preserved the same positions to the right and the left which the two disciples had occupied in life.

Śariputra and Moggallana came from Rajagriha, and it is probable that their relics were originally deposited there, then brought here at a later date. A date for Stupa No. 3 in the early first century B.C.E. is judged probable, with its gate in the early first century C.E.[48]

Of *stupas* at Sanci there are, in all, many scores, ranging in date and size from the third century B.C.E. to the twelfth century C.E. and from the large Stupa No. 1 down to miniature votive *stupas* no more than 1 foot (0.3 m.) in height. There are also, in ruins, a number of ancient temples and monasteries.

Temple No. 18. Temple No. 18, as it is designated, stands on a raised platform directly opposite the South Gate of Stupa No. 1. This is a structural *caitya* hall of the same essential plan as those found in the caves at Ajanta and Ellora, with pillars marking out the nave and two side aisles, and with a curving apse at the end, the apse enclosed, however, not by pillars as in the caves, but by a solid wall. In the apse was a small *stupa*. The date of the existing pillars and walls is probably in the seventh century C.E. but underneath are three levels of floors which probably represent earlier structures of wood reaching back to the Maurya period, i.e., the period of Aśoka.

Temple No. 17. Temple No. 17 stands near the northeast corner of Temple No. 18. It is a small shrine consisting of a simple flat-roofed chamber with a pillared porch in front. It is attributed to the Gupta age (320–600 C.E.).[49]

Temple No. 45. Temple No. 45 is on the eastern terrace at Sanci. As it stands the structure dates from the tenth or eleventh century C.E. and is one of the latest buildings on the site, but it is a rebuilding of an earlier temple, attributed to the seventh or eighth century, of which some remains are preserved. Seen from the southwest, for example, the lower-level courtyard belongs to the earlier temple; the higher platform with small sculptured panels on its vertical sides, represents the court in front of the central shrine of the later temple. A Buddha image with an oval halo behind the head (a relatively late feature), presently placed against the outside wall of the shrine, bears an inscription on its lotus throne of about the tenth century C.E.[50]

Temple No. 45 is in fact the chapel of Monastery No. 45, and the temple is surrounded by the large courtyard and the cells of that monastery. On the northern and western sides of the court in front of Temple No. 45 there is also another and more elaborate building, and this comprises two monastic courts which are known as Monasteries Nos. 46 and 47. Built after the reconstruction of Temple No. 45, this complex must date in the eleventh century C.E.

In the southern area at Sanci there are also three monasteries, Nos. 36, 37, and 38, and these date from about the seventh century. Again on the western edge of the main terrace there is a relatively late monastery, and in its restored foundations we see the usual rectangular court surrounded by monastic cells (Fig. 13.25).[51]

13.25 Western Monastery, Sanci

Taxila

In the northwest there are very extensive ruins of *stupas* and *viharas* at Taxila.[52] Most of these are in the valleys or on the knolls of the Murree hills to the east of the main urban sites, thus being secluded, yet within easy walking distance of the city. Even where unexcavated, the ruins are readily recognizable for what they are by reason of their distinctive and almost uniform configuration, namely, a circle with a parallelogram beside it, the former marking the site of the *stupa,* the latter the site of the *vihara*. With many smaller edifices around, the whole constituted the *sangharama* (community garden), the collective residence of the *sangha*.

Dharmarajika. Of these establishments at Taxila the most important and probably the oldest is the Dharmarajika, situated at the foot of a small spur of the Murree hills east of the Bhir mound. The word *dharmaraja* (king of *dharma*) was a title of Aśoka and appropriate also to the Buddha, and the name *dharmarajika* was probably applied to *stupas* which Aśoka erected either because they were built by the famous king or because they contained relics of the Buddha—or in many cases probably for both reasons together. From the name, therefore, and from the prominence of the monument, it is likely that the Dharmarajika *stupa* was originally one of the many *stupas* built at so many places by Aśoka, and it is possible that the still existing foundation and lower part of the superstructure are from his time. At any rate, within the first century B.C.E. (a date determined by coins) a series of small *stupas* was erected in a ring around the main *stupa,* and therefore the main Dharmarajika *stupa* itself must have been in existence at the latest by about the middle of that century.

In its existing form the central *stupa* (Fig. 13.26) stands on a raised terrace

approached by four flights of steps at the four cardinal points. The maximum diameter of the terrace is 150 feet (46 m.), the average diameter of the body of the *stupa* is 115 feet (35 m.), and the total height of the ruin is about 45 feet (14 m.).

Among the many other monastic buildings in the Dharmarajika complex, there are a number of small chapels in the area opposite the main *stupa* to the west. In one of these (G5), buried below the original floor, was a vase-like stone casket, in which were an inscribed scroll of silver and a small gold casket containing some minute fragments of bone. The inscription reads:

> In the year 136 of Azes, on the 15th day of the month of Ashadha, on this day relics of the Holy One (Buddha) were enshrined by Urasaka, scion of Imtavhria, a Bactrian, resident of the town of Noacha. By him these relics of the Holy One were enshrined in his own *bodhisattva* chapel at the Dharmarajika *stupa* at Takshaśila, for the bestowal of health upon the great king, king of kings, the son of heaven, the Kushana; in honor of all Buddhas; in honor of the individual Buddhas; in honor of the Arhats; in honor of all sentient beings; in honor of [his] parents; in honor of [his] friends, advisers, kinsmen, and blood-relations; for the bestowal of health upon himself. May this right munificent gift lead to *nirvana*.[53]

Azes, named in the date formula, is probably Azes I, who was probably established in rule at Taxila around 45 B.C.E. and the era which was called by his name at Taxila is probably the same as the Vikrama Era, which began in 57 or 58 B.C.E. Reckoned from 57 B.C.E., the date of the present inscription is equivalent to 79 C.E., and the Kushana king for whom health is wished is presumably Kanishka (probably 78–103 C.E.).

Jaulian. On a hilltop near the village of Jaulian (nearly 1 mile (1.6 km.) southeast of the Sirsukh mound at Taxila) are the extensive and relatively well preserved remains of a Buddhist establishment which was first built not long after the foundation of the Kushana city of Taxila at Sirsukh (circa 80 C.E.), and was extensively reconstructed and renovated in the fourth and fifth centuries C.E.[54]

This entire complex at Jaulian comprises a monastery and by its side two *stupa* courts, an upper court to the south and a lower court to the north. The main *stupa* is in the upper court, with smaller *stupas* around it, and chapels against the walls of the court, facing toward the *stupa*. In the lower and smaller court there are other *stupas* and chapels. The monastery is an open quadrangle, surrounded by cells, together with refectory and other halls.

Much of the main *stupa* has disappeared, including the dome and all but the lowest course of the drum, but the high plinth still stands and bears many Buddha figures in stucco. The smaller *stupas* and the chapels also have very many stucco sculptures, mostly Buddha images, e.g., two seated Buddha figures on a small *stupa* at the foot of the main *stupa* (Fig. 13.27).[55]

Places of Pilgrimage

In Buddhism eight great sanctified spots *(atthamahathanani)* constitute the major places of pilgrimage. These correspond with the Eight Great Events in the life of the Buddha. The first four mark the four stages of his progress in life, and are the four to which he himself pointed his disciples for later visitation in his memory, namely, Lumbini where he was born, Bodhgaya where he attained enlightenment, Isipatana (Sarnath) where he preached his first sermon, and Kuśinagara where he passed away *(parinirvana)*.

13.27 Two Seated Buddhas on Small Stupa, Jaulian Main Stupa Court, Taxila

The second four places are those where extraordinary manifestations or "miracles" transpired, namely, Śravasti, Sankaśya, Rajagriha, and Vaiśali. Śravasti was the site of the Great Magical Feat. Here between the city and the Jetavana monastery King Prasenajit built a large lecture hall and in it the Buddha engaged in disputation with six heretical teachers including Mahavira. The Buddha had instructed his own disciples not to give any public displays of supernatural power but, when his opponents challenged him to a competition in miracles, he (being of course himself exempt from the edict imposed upon his disciples) caused a full-grown mango tree to rise instantaneously to the sky, and then he himself flew into the sky and emitted flames and streams of water from his body.

Sankaśya (probably identifiable with Sankisa or Sankissa in the Farrukhabad district in Uttar Pradesh, where there is still an elephant capital of an Aśoka pillar)[56] was the place where the Buddha made his Descent from the Heaven of the Thirty-three Gods. He went up to that heaven because after her death his mother Maya was reborn there and he desired to teach her the Law. After having preached for three months to Maya and to the gods, he descended on a triple ladder made of precious materials and specially constructed by the gods. He was accompanied on his return by Brahma and Indra, and he came down near Sankaśya where his principal disciples and a crowd of the faithful were waiting for him.

Rajagriha was the locale of the Subduing of Nalagiri. In his attempt to eliminate the Buddha and seize the headship of the order for himself, the Buddha's traitorous cousin and disciple, Devadatta, sent murderers against the Buddha but they only fell at his feet; caused a huge rock to roll down upon him but it only scratched his foot; and then caused the wild elephant Nalagiri to be loosed against him. The Buddha, however, stood his ground with such serenity and manifestation of kindness that the fierce animal suddenly became gentle and peaceful. Vaiśali was the scene of the Monkey's Offering. The remarkable event here remembered was that a monkey filled the Buddha's bowl with honey. In some versions it was monkeys (in the plural) which did this, and the "honey" was perhaps the sweet syrup which is obtained from the incised tops of various palm trees.[57]

Of the eight sacred places which thus comprise the *atthamahathanani*, the Chinese Buddhist pilgrims Fa Xian (399–414 C.E.) and Xuan Zang (629–645 C.E.) visited seven, namely (in the order of Fa Xian's itinerary, in a slightly different order in Xuan Zang's itinerary), Śravasti, Lumbini, Kuśinagara, Vaiśali, Rajagriha, Bodhgaya, and Isipatana, together with certain intermediate and related points.[58] Coming from the northwest, both pilgrims visited first Śravasti, Kapilavastu/Lumbini, and Kuśinagara.

In Śravasti (*She-lo-fa-si-ti* in Chinese), once the capital of the kingdom of Kośala and in the Buddha's day ruled by King Prasenajit, Fa Xian found the inhabitants few and far between, but was at least welcomed at the ancient Jetavana monastery by a crowd of monks who said, "We have never (before) seen men of Han, followers of our system, arrive here." Xuan Zang, however, found even the Jetavana all in ruins, although two pillars erected by Aśoka were still standing, and in a solitary brick building there was still an image of the Buddha. Both pilgrims also saw *stupas* which marked various sacred spots, e.g., the place of the old *vihara* of Mahaprajapati, the maternal aunt and nurse of Śakyamuni, the first woman admitted to the Buddhist order, and the first superior of the first convent.

Kapilavastu (*Kie-pi-lo-fa-su-tu*), the capital of Śuddhodana, the father of the Buddha, was also largely abandoned, and Fa Xian and Xuan Zang both found only a few monks still in residence. The pilgrims were able, however, to observe many ruined *viharas* and many *stupas* in and around the city. At a distance to the east or northeast they came to the Lumbini garden, the actual birthplace of the Buddha, and Xuan Zang mentions several *stupas* at the site, one of which was built by Aśoka, and not far from these a great stone pillar with the figure of a horse on top, erected by Aśoka but afterward broken off in the middle and fallen to the ground.

Kuśinagara (*Kiu-she-na-kie-lo*), where the Buddha died, also had few inhabitants, but Xuan Zang tells of several memorial monuments. At the northeast angle of the city a *stupa* built by Aśoka marked the old house of Cunda, the householder who gave the Buddha his last meal. In a grove of *sala* trees outside the city, a great brick *vihara* with a figure of the Buddha lying as if asleep, and a *stupa* erected by Aśoka, marked the place of the *parinirvana*.

Vaiśali (*Fei-she-li*), visited next by Fa Xian and somewhat later in sequence by Xuan Zang, was also largely abandoned. Inside the city, however, Fa Xian found the *vihara* which the courtesan Ambapali built in honor of the Buddha still standing as it was at first, and outside the city to the south he also visited the garden which the same Ambapali presented to the Buddha for his residence. Both Fa Xian and Xuan Zang observed a number of *stupas* memorializing particular sacred spots. One which both pilgrims mention was the *stupa* marking the place where, when the Buddha was about to attain to his *parinirvana*, as he was leaving the city by the west gate he turned to gaze upon Vaiśali for the last time. Xuan Zang identifies a *stupa* which a king of Vaiśali built to contain his portion of the relics from the cremation of the Buddha. From this *stupa* Aśoka took away nine-tenths of the relics in connection with his program of building reliquaries throughout the land. Nearby was another *stupa* built by Aśoka himself, and beside it a stone pillar about 50–60 feet (15–18 m.) high, with the figure of a lion on the top. To the south of this was a tank, reputedly dug by a band of monkeys for the use of the Buddha, and not far away a *stupa* marking the spot where the monkeys, taking the alms bowl of the Buddha, climbed a tree and gathered honey for him.

From Vaiśali Fa Xian proceeded to Pataliputra and then to Rajagriha, and Xuan Zang was also in both places in due time on his own itinerary. Rajagriha was the earlier capital of Magadha and in the time of the Buddha the capital of Bimbisara and Ajataśatru; Pataliputra was the later capital, founded as a fortress by Ajataśatru, and in the time of Candragupta Maurya and Aśoka a very great city; but in the times of the two Chinese pilgrims both cities were largely in ruins.

At Pataliputra *(Po-t'o-li-tsu)* Fa Xian was impressed by the great stones of the former royal buildings, and was ready to believe that they could not possibly have been the work of mortal hands. Two monasteries were in existence, one Mahayana, one Hinayana, and together they had six or seven hundred monks. Both Fa Xian and Xuan Zang speak of a *stupa* erected by Aśoka as one of the 84,000 such monuments which the emperor built. They also tell of a tall stone pillar on which an inscription recorded a tremendous benefaction bestowed by Aśoka on the Buddhist community: "Asoka gave Jambudvipa to the general body of all the monks, and then redeemed it from them with money. This he did three times."

At Rajagriha *(Ho-lo-shi-ki-li-hi)* Fa Xian and Xuan Zang distinguish Kuśagara as the residence of Bimbisara, and "new" Rajagriha, a few miles away, as built by Ajataśatru. Although there were two small monasteries here, inside the old city all was emptiness and desolation; nevertheless, the pilgrims were able to see many sacred spots. Outside the north gate there was a *stupa* at the place where Devadatta loosed the wild elephant against the Buddha. Not far away was the Bamboo Grove, one of the Buddha's favorite places of residence. To the east was a *stupa* which was built by Ajataśatru to hold his share of the sacred relics after the cremation of the Buddha. Later Aśoka took relics from there, as he did at Vaiśali, and built another *stupa* at the place. Farther away to the northeast was the mountain Gridhrakuta, the Vulture's Peak, a solitary high peak which took its name, it was variously explained, because vultures made their abode there, or because the peak itself was imagined to have the shape of a vulture. "When Tathagata had guided the world for some fifty years," says Xuan Zang, "he dwelt much in this mountain, and delivered the excellent law in its developed form."

On their respective itineraries both Fa Xian and Xuan Zang came to Gaya, which was virtually deserted, and on southward to Bodhgaya, to the place of the sacred tree under which Śakyamuni attained enlightenment and became the Buddha. At this point Fa Xian refers to the monuments which, he says, from the earliest time after the decease of the Buddha marked the places of the four major events of the Buddha's life: "The place of the four great *stupas* have been fixed, and handed down without break, since Buddha attained to *nirvana*. Those four great *stupas* are those at the places where Buddha was born; where he attained to wisdom; where he (began to) move the wheel of his Law; and where he attained to *parinirvana*." This statement makes it probable that there was an already ancient monument at the place of the sacred tree when Fa Xian was there. He also speaks of three monasteries, in all of which monks were residing.

From the site of the *bodhi* tree Fa Xian returned to Pataliputra, then followed the Ganges westward to Varanasi *(Po-lo-na-ssu),* and in the northern outskirts of this city visited the Deer Park (Isipatana), while at an earlier point in his itinerary Xuan Zang was also at Varanasi and Isipatana.

At the Deer Park Fa Xian found two monasteries with resident monks, and saw a number of *stupas* marking the place of the Buddha's first sermon and the places of other particular events which transpired in the vicinity. In contrast with the many relatively deserted pilgrimage places elsewhere visited by the two Chinese pilgrims, Xuan Zang speaks of Varanasi as densely populated. In the city most of the inhabitants were Hindus and Jainas, and there were many *brahmanical* temples, but at the Deer Park there was a vast monastery in which 1,500 monks were studying the doctrines of the Hinayana. Xuan Zang describes the foundation and stairs of the *vihara* as built of stone, and its towers and niches as built of brick. In the niches on all four sides of the building were golden images of the Buddha, and in the middle of the building was a lifesize image in which the Buddha was represented as turning the wheel of the Law. To the southwest was a stone *stupa* built by Aśoka, and in front of it a stone pillar about 70 feet (21 m.) high, presumably erected by Aśoka. Elsewhere in the park were to be seen the pools in which the Buddha used to bathe, wash his robes, and cleanse his alms bowl, while many more *stupas* marked places which figured in events in the Buddha's former lives, e.g., when he was born as the king of the elephants with six tusks.

In connection with his visit to Bodhgaya Xuan Zang tells of various disasters which befell the *bodhi* tree during the reign of Aśoka and again most recently, he says, when the heretical king Śaśanka of Bengal cut it down. It was revived, however, by the good king Purnavarma of Magadha, the last of Aśoka's race, and Xuan Zang describes the sacred tree and the veneration accorded it as follows:

> The *bodhi* tree above the diamond throne is the same as the *pippala* tree. In old days, when Buddha was alive, it was several hundred feet high. Although it has often been injured by cutting, it still is 40–50 feet (12–15 m.) high. Buddha sitting under this tree reached perfect wisdom, and therefore it is called the tree of knowledge (*pu-ti bodhi*). The bark is of a yellowish-white color, the leaves and twigs of a dark green. The leaves wither not either in winter or summer, but they remain shining and glistening all the year round without change. But at every successive *nirvana*-day the leaves wither and fall, and then in a moment revive as before. On this day [of the *nirvana*] the princes of different countries and the religious multitude from different quarters assemble by thousands and ten thousands unbidden, and bathe [the roots] with scented water and perfumed milk; while they raise the sounds of music and scatter flowers and perfumes, and while the light of day is continued by burning torches, they offer their religious gifts.

The diamond throne *(vajrasana)* under the *bodhi* tree was probably a stone slab intended to represent the seat and the adamantine steadfastness of the Buddha as he underwent his final ordeal on the way to enlightenment. Around the *bodhi* tree and the diamond throne there was, according to the description by Xuan Zang, a brick wall about 20 feet (6 m.) in height, with its principal gate opening to the east toward the Nairanjana River (now called the Lilajan or Phalgu). Also to the east of the *bodhi* tree Aśoka built a small *vihara,* and this was later reconstructed on a larger scale so that when Xuan Zang saw it it was a temple 160–170 feet (49–52 m.) high. The four sides of the building were covered with wonderful ornamental work, and the eastern face adjoined a storied pavilion. In a niche on the left of the outside gate was a figure of the future Buddha Maitreya. In a dark inner chamber was a figure of the Buddha in a sitting position, with the right hand hanging down *(bhumisparśa mudra),* calling upon the earth to bear him witness. This image was so beautiful that it was held to have originated by supernatural means. Although this chamber was dark it was lighted by lamps and torches and, in the morning, by sunlight reflected by a great mirror.

Outside the northern gate in the wall around the *bodhi* tree was the Mahabodhi *sangharama,* which was built by a former king of Lanka and provided a guest house for visiting monks from that land. It was also the continuing residence of more than 1,000 monks who were students of the Mahayana. This edifice contained six halls, with towers three stories high, and was protected by a very high wall. Inside there were *stupas* containing relics of the Buddha, and every year on an anniversary occasion these relics were brought out for public exhibition. Not far south of the *bodhi* tree was a lofty *stupa* built by Aśoka, and this and many other monuments in the vicinity marked many spots of particularly sacred significance, at all of which Xuan Zang worshiped.

After eight or nine days of such devotions by Xuan Zang at Bodhgaya, four monks came from the famous Nalanda monastery some 60 miles (97 km.) away, and escorted him back with them, and he stayed at Nalanda for several years of study. The *sangharama* at Nalanda was a vast establishment, surrounded by a wall with only a single gate. In the midst was a great college and eight other halls. Richly adorned towers and fairy-like turrets seemed to soar above the clouds, and from their upper windows one could see the formation of the winds and the clouds. Ten thousand monks were here, all studying the Mahayana, and also the eighteen branches of the Hinayana, the Vedas, grammar, medicine, mathematics, astronomy, and so forth. Daily lectures were held in a hundred classrooms, and the students attended with great punctuality, "not even an inch of shadow on the [sun]dial late." In seven hundred years since the foundation of the establishment there had not been even a single case calling for disciplinary action.

As in the times of Fa Xian and Xuan Zang, so still today the Deer Park and the Bodhi Tree are the climactic and most important of the places of Buddhist pilgrimage in India.

Sarnath. The Deer Park at Isipatana, where the Buddha set the wheel of Buddhist doctrine in motion as he preached his first sermon to his five former ascetical associates, is the modern Sarnath, 4 miles (6 km.) north of Varanasi.[59]

Of the extant monuments at Sarnath the largest and most impressive is the Dhamekh *stupa* (Fig. 13.28), the name of which is perhaps derived from an

13.28 Dhamekh Stupa, Sarnath

original name Dharmacakra *stupa*. If this is the correct derivation of the name it is thereby suggested that the *stupa* was intended to mark the exact spot of the Buddha's first sermon. The *stupa* is a solid cylindrical tower, 93 feet (28 m.) in diameter at the base and 143 feet (44 m.) in total height. The lower part is a circular stone drum which rises to a height of 43 feet (13 m.); the upper part is a cylindrical mass of brickwork. On the exterior of the lower part are eight projecting panels in each of which is a small niche, originally no doubt intended to contain an image. Below the niches is a band of sculptured ornamentation with geometric and floral patterns combined with birds and human figures.[60] This ornamentation appears to be of the Gupta period, and an inscription found in the brickwork is in characters of the sixth or seventh century C.E., which may be the date of the last restoration of the structure. In the interior of the *stupa* the remains of an earlier structure built of bricks of the Maurya period have been found, and the original *stupa* may therefore have been built by Aśoka.

To the east of the Dhamekh *stupa* at a distance of 350 feet (107 m.) is the Dharmarajika *stupa*. The name suggests that this may have been built by Aśoka to enshrine relics of the Buddha at the time when he was redistributing these in so many places. In fact a stone box was found inside the *stupa* which contained a casket with some relics and ashes. At present relatively little remains of the Dharmarajika *stupa* because it was pulled down in 1794 C.E. under the ruler Jagat Singh—whose name is sometimes attached to the ruin. Excavation has shown, however, that the original brick *stupa*—perhaps built by Aśoka—was 44 feet (13 m.) in diameter, and was enlarged in six successive modifications up to the twelfth century C.E.

Near the Dharmarajika *stupa* to the north is a square building measuring about 60 feet (18 m.) on each side, and still standing to a height of 18 feet (5.5 m.). This is built partly of stone and partly of brick, and was apparently intended to support a massive superstructure, probably a temple; hence it is known as the Main Shrine. Carvings on some of the stones suggest a date in the Gupta period.

To the west of the Main Shrine is the stump of an Aśoka pillar, still standing to a height of almost 7 feet (2 m.). The pillar carries an inscription, the text of which is essentially the same as that of the inscription on the Aśoka pillar at Sanci, but preserves some additional instructions concerning the circulation of the edict among the parties concerned.[61] The capital of the pillar was found nearby, and is in the Archaeological Museum at Sarnath. This is a lion capital, like the one at Sanci, with four handsome lions seated back to back. In this case the lions supported a wheel of the Law *(dharmacakra)*, some fragments of which were recovered. On the circular plinth are also four wheels of the Law, each with thirty-two spokes, and between each pair of these is an animal—elephant, bull, horse, and lion.[62]

Many other sculptures brought to light at Sarnath are also in the Sarnath Museum. A very beautiful seated Buddha image of probably the late fifth century is recognized as representing the height of Gupta sculptural art.[63] The hands are in the *dharmacakra mudra*, as if the Buddha were preaching his first sermon; the head is backgrounded by a large halo carved with a lotus-creeper motif; the robe is so diaphanous as to seem almost a part of the body itself; on the front of the throne is the wheel, with figures paying respect to it on either side. Confirmatory of the date suggested for this image are four standing statues of the Buddha of very similar style, all of which were also found at Sarnath and are in the Sarnath Museum. Three bear inscriptions with dates; the fourth was found together with two of the others. The three inscriptions state that these images were commissioned and installed by an otherwise unknown monk named Abhayamitra in order to gain religious merit and to contribute to the attainment of final emancipation not only

13.29 Mahabodhi Temple, Bodhgaya. Photograph from Heinrich Zimmer, *The Art of Indian Asia* (Bollingen Series XXXIX) (Princeton: Princeton University Press, 2 vols., 3d printing with revisions 1968), 2, Pl. 99, by permission of Princeton University Press.

for himself but also for his parents and teachers and for all sentient beings. The first inscription gives a date equivalent to 474 C.E.; the second and third inscriptions give a date equivalent to 477 C.E.[64]

Bodhgaya. The site of the enlightenment of the Buddha under the *bodhi* tree is now known as Bodhgaya, and is 6 miles (10 km.) south of the city of Gaya.[65] At the site the chief features are the *bodhi* or *bo* tree, repeatedly propagated anew, and the great temple called the Mahabodhi, which stands to the east and just in front of the present tree. In its present appearance the Mahabodhi temple (Fig. 13.29) is a tall truncated pyramid with a spire on top and with four lower towers with spires at the four corners. In the four sides of the pyramid are many tiers of niches, one above the other, which presumably once held Buddha figures. The total height of the monument is some 180 feet (55 m.).

As it stands, the Mahabodhi temple represents works of restoration in the nineteenth and twentieth centuries by the Buddhists of Sri Lanka with the financial assistance of the Buddhists of Japan, while important earlier restoration was done by a mission sent by King Kyanzittha (1084–1112 C.E.) of Pagan, Burma. In spite of repairs and alterations, however, the present structure is of approximately the same height as that given by Xuan Zang for the temple which he saw here, and may be essentially the same building which was in existence at that time in the seventh century. Xuan Zang also speaks of an earlier building by Aśoka, and Fa Xian evidently thought that there had been a temple at the place from the earliest time after the decease of the Buddha. A votive plaque of the second century C.E. found at a site called Kumrahar at Patna (Pataliputra) shows what is probably the Mahabodhi temple in much like its present appearance, and therefore the temple was probably in existence in substantially its full present form at that time at the latest, and probably earlier.[66] Architecturally the Mahabodhi temple of Bodhgaya was imitated in the Mahabodhi and certain other temples at Pagan, Burma, and also in several temples at Lamphun and Chiengmai in Thailand. As for the wonderful Buddha image which Xuan Zang saw in the temple at Bodhgaya, it has vanished, but was duplicated in many clay votive tablets and small bronzes that were carried away all over Buddhist Asia.[67]

SITES AND MONUMENTS OF SRI LANKA

Dagoba

In Sri Lanka, as in India and Pakistan, the most important architectural monument of Buddhism is the *stupa* (Pali *thupa*). Here and in other Theravada countries this is usually named a *dagoba* (from *dhatu-garbha*, relic chamber)—in Burma a *pagoda*—and is also often called a *cetiya* (like the Sanskrit *caitya*, with the general meaning of a shrine). The typical Sinhalese *dagoba* is essentially a hemispherical dome rising from three low circular courses, which rest upon a square base, approached by four stairways. The relic chamber is often a relatively large cell inside the dome. On the top of the dome is a square enclosure *(harmika)*, and above this rises a pointed ringed spire *(chatta)*, the equivalent of the Indian umbrella *(chhatra)*.[68]

Of the early Sinhalese monuments, many were damaged or destroyed during the numerous invasions and wars which Lanka suffered; they were also often encroached upon by the jungle, but many were also repaired in later times, especially by King Parakramabahu I (1153–1186 C.E.), and many have been the object of modern works of restoration.[69]

Mihintale

As the place where Aśoka's son Mahinda met King Devanampiyatissa (247–207 B.C.E.) and Buddhism was thus introduced to Lanka, the Missaka mountain east of Anuradhapura, the mountain later named Mihintale after Mahinda is the holiest site of Sinhalese Buddhism.[70]

Maha Seya Dagoba. An ancient stairway of 1,840 shallow stone steps leads up to the summit of the hill, on which stands the Maha Seya Dagoba (Figure 13.30). Built originally in the reign of Devanampiyatissa (circa 243 B.C.E.), this is one of the earliest of the Sinhalese *thupas,* and it was probably reconstructed by Parakramabahu I in the twelfth century.[71]

Kantaka Cetiya. Farther down the hill is the Kantaka Cetiya (Fig. 13.31). It was in the place where the Kantaka Cetiya was later built that Devanampiyatissa

13.30 Maha Seya Dagoba at the Summit of the Mihintale Hill

13.31 Lower Courses of the Kantake Cetiya, Mihintale

made sixty-eight rock cells for Mahinda and the monks associated with him, and there are in fact many rock caves around the Kantaka Cetiya and in them are inscriptions, some of which go back to the third century B.C.E. The name of the builder of the Kantaka Cetiya is not known, but King Lanjatissa (59–50 B.C.E.) is recorded as having made a mantling of stone for this monument, so its original foundation was very probably as early as the second century B.C.E., and there is evidence for a date at least prior to 119 B.C.E.[72]

The *stupa* has a circumference at the base of 425 feet (130 m.) and, even in its ruined state, still stands about 40 feet (12 m.) high. It is constructed with four projecting frontispieces *(vahalakadas)* at the four cardinal points, and these and the panels which flank them are carved with foliage, animals, and human figures. The style of the carvings is archaic, and these are considered to be the earliest identifiable survivals of ancient Sinhalese sculpture, dating at the latest from the first or second century C.E.[73]

Later kings did additional building work at Mihintale, and Parakramabahu I restored more than sixty shrines. The whole area is thus filled with ruins, small monuments, and the caves, cells, and graves of early monks who lived there, and it remains a most important place of hermitage and pilgrimage. From the heights there is a far-reaching view westward to the ruins of Anuradhapura.

Anuradhapura

Anuradhapura, founded in the fourth century B.C.E. and the capital of the Sinhalese kingdom for fifteen centuries, center of the Theravada tradition where the great seat of learning, the Mahavihara, flourished and Buddhaghosa lived, and where famous *thupas* enshrined Buddha relics, is officially a sacred city, set aside to remain an undisturbed historic site, while a new town has been built 1 mile (1.6 km.) to the southeast to be a modern administrative center.

Thuparama Dagoba. The major ruins of the ancient city extend from the vicinity of the Tisawewa (the ancient Tissavapi) tank in the south to the Abhayagiri Dagoba in the north, a distance of somewhat more than 2 miles (3 km.).[74] Nearly in the center of this distance is the Thuparama Dagoba, which was the first *thupa* built in Anuradhapura and in the entire island. Erected in 244 B.C.E. by Devanampiyatissa to enshrine the collarbone relic of the Buddha, the monument was repaired by Parakramabahu I in the twelfth century C.E. and by Parakramabahu II (1236–1271 C.E.) in the thirteenth century, and was reconstructed in 1862 and given its present bell shape with a high spire (Fig. 13.32). The *dagoba* stands on a circular platform 164 feet (50 m.) in diameter, and is surrounded by three concentric circles of monolithic pillars, diminishing in height from the innermost circle. At some stage in the history of the monument these pillars supported a circular roof around the *dagoba,* making a circular relic house known as a *vatadage,* a characteristic Sinhalese architectural feature.[75]

Śri Maha Bodhi. Somewhat more than one-half mile (0.8 km.) south of the Thuparama is the Śri Maha Bodhi or sacred Bo tree, growing from the branch of the original *bodhi* tree brought to Lanka by Mahinda's sister Sanghamitta and planted in the Mahameghavana garden of Devanampiyatissa. The tree is enclosed within a high wall, with a large gateway building, and it towers high above its surroundings.[76]

Isurumuniya Vihara and Vessagiri Vihara. To the southwest from the Bo tree and near the Tissawewa (Tissavapi) tank is the Isurumuniya Buddhist complex,

13.32 Thuparama Dagoba, Anuradhapura

comprising the Isurumuniya Vihara constructed by Devanampiyatissa for Prince Aritttha and his followers, and the Vessagiri Vihara constructed by the king for the *vessa* people. The shrine to which the name Isurumuniya Vihara is presently given is the best preserved part of the whole. It centers around two masses of rock, beside one of which, and abutting on its sheer side, is a pond. Here on both sides of a fissure in the rock are notable relief carvings which are now attributed to the late seventh–early eighth century C.E. One of these seen on the rock face just above the water level, and carved in low relief, shows a great elephant head (Fig. 13.33). The trunk is lifted up and turned back, and the elephant is perhaps in the act of pouring water upon itself. Another is a sculptured panel which was presumably found somewhere in the neighborhood and is now set into the nearby retaining wall; it shows a couple seated on a stone bench in an affectionate pose (Fig. 13.34). The man is evidently a warrior, because the hilt of a sword and a circular shield are seen above his right shoulder. The couple is commonly known as the "Isurumuniya lovers," and it is surmised that the scene may represent an episode in the popular love story of Prince Saliya (Salirajakumara), the son of King Dutthagamani (101–77 B.C.E.), who gave up his right of succession to the throne in order to marry the beautiful Candala maiden, Aśokamala.[77]

Maricavatti Dagoba. Some distance to the west of the Bo tree are the ruins of the Maricavatti Cetiya and the Maricavatti Vihara, which were built by King Dutthagamani. The *cetiya* or *dagoba,* which was intended by the king to enshrine his spear with its Buddha relic, still stands as a massive mound.[78]

Lohapasada. Near the Bo tree to the north is the site of the Lohapasada, the nine-storied "brazen palace," which Dutthagamani built in the Mahameghavana for the monks of the Mahavihara. Of the original building little remains for,

13.33 Elephant Head at the Isurumuniya Rock Temple, Anuradhapura

13.34 Isurumuniya Lovers, Anuradhapura

although it was roofed with copper plates, it was mainly constructed of wood and was razed by fire only a few years later in the reign of Dutthagamani's successor, Saddhatissa (77–59 B.C.E.). Sixteen hundred stone pillars are to be seen at the site, but they are probably to be attributed to a rebuilding by Parakramabahu I rather than to Dutthagamani.[79]

Ruwanweli Dagoba. On the north, about midway between the Bo tree and the Thuparama Dagoba is the Maha Thupa, now known as the Ruwanweli (gold dust) Dagoba, which was begun by Dutthagamani and completed by Saddhatissa. It has undergone complete modern reconstruction, and rises as an enormous dome 254 feet (77 m.) in diameter, upon a platform 475 feet (145 m.) by 473 feet (144 m.) in size, and is surmounted by a high rectangular *harmika* and a lofty spire, the gilded summit of which can be seen from far across the countryside.[80]

Abhayagiri Dagoba. Outside the north wall of the ancient city and on the present Outer Circular Road is the Abhayagiri Dagoba, also known as the Northern Dagoba, together with its *vihara*. This monastic establishment was built by Vattagamani Abhaya (29–17 B.C.E.) on the site where the Jaina monk Giri had mocked him, and it soon became the headquarters of the heretical monks who seceded from the Mahavihara. Today the Abhayagiri Dagoba is an enormous jungle-covered mound, with its rectangular *harmika* and high pinnacle rising above a huge talus of brick and earth fallen from the upper slopes of the dome.[81]

Jetavana Dagoba. The Jetavana Dagoba or Eastern Dagoba, which King Mahasena (334–361 C.E.) built for the heretical monks whom he favored and who were associated with the monks of the Abhayagiri, is located to the east of the Ruwanweli Dagoba, near where the Outer Circular Road begins its northward course. In its original form, this *thupa* was some 400 feet (122 m.) in height and 370 feet (113 m.) in diameter at its base, making it the largest *stupa* in the island and one of the largest anywhere in the Buddhist world. Like the Abhayagiri Dagoba (with which it has often been confused), the Jetavana Dagoba is today a vast mound covered with jungle growth and surmounted by its *harmika* and pinnacle. Part of the pinnacle, however, has long since been lost and as it stands, the total height of the monument has been measured as 231 feet (70 m.). The *thupa* stands on a foundation of brick 26 feet (8 m.) in thickness, a foundation which is itself built on a layer of concrete, while the *dagoba* proper is a solid mass of brick, the total amount of material being enormous. To the west of the *dagoba* are the remains of a vaulted image house, of which the doorposts are monoliths 36 feet (11 m.) in height, including 9 feet (2.7 m.) still buried underground. The fragments of the lotus pedestal found at the site suggest that the main statue in the edifice was a colossus appropriate to the dimensions of the shrine.[82]

Moonstones. Found also in some examples in India and especially characteristic of many Buddhist shrines at Anuradhapura and elsewhere in Sri Lanka is the so-called "moonstone." This is a steppingstone in the form of a semicircular slab of stone carved in concentric circles and placed at the foot of the steps which lead up to the higher platform on which stands a *stupa* or a Buddha image. In a fully elaborated example there is a half-lotus in the center and then, separated by circles of creepers and foliage, a circle of geese *(hamsas)* and a circle of wild quadrupeds following each other in the order, elephant, horse, lion, and humped bull, while an outermost circle of decoration appears to be a circle of flames (Fig. 13.35). In one

13.35 Moonstone at Anuradhapura

of various possible interpretations, the moonstone may be the circle of existence from which the approaching worshiper looks up to the Buddha presence above for deliverance; the outermost circle of flames suggests that the world is aflame with the fires of desire and hatred; the circles of creepers symbolize desire; the four kinds of wild animals stand for the four perils of birth, decay, disease, and death; the geese, with their backs turned to the creepers of desire, stand for discrimination between good and evil; and the lotus represents the ground of existence. A remark in the *Mahavamsa* (31.61) in connection with a *cetiya* and its temple reflects the importance attached to the moonstone: "Nay, but all the jewels in the whole island of Lanka are not of so great worth as the stone slab at the foot of the steps."[83] Here the word for the stone slab is *patika*, which can mean "divider" and, in line with the interpretation above, can suggest that the moonstone divides the phenomenal world from the transcendental world, the latter represented by the sacred shrine. The moonstones are usually dated between the fifth and ninth centuries C.E.[84]

Sigiriya

At Sigiriya, which was the capital of Kassapa (Kaśyapa) I for his eighteen years of reign (478–496 C.E.), the lofty rock rises out of the plain and a gallery winds around the vertical western face and gives access to stairs which reach the Plateau of the Lion on the north side. Here was the body of a lion, made of brick and stucco, appearing as if crouching in its lair with only half of the body emerging from the rock, and with a stairway originating between its forepaws and leading upward. Of this lion figure only the forepaws remain (Fig. 13.36). Above the plateau, the rock ascends steeply to the summit, and grooves in the rock are apparently where an

13.36 Lion's Paw on the Sigiriya Rock

upper pathway was constructed. The summit is nearly three acres in extent, and was filled with brick-walled terraces, gardens, tanks and, on the highest level at the west, the palace and pavilion of the king.

On the western face of the rock the gallery extends for about 500 feet (152 m.), and about 100 feet (30 m.) above it, there is a drip-ledge cut across the rock. Below the drip-ledge and above the gallery, the whole of the rock face was evidently coated with plaster and covered with frescoes.[85] Of the paintings, twenty-two female figures remain in a concavity of the vertical rock face some 42 feet (13 m.) above the floor of the gallery, in which place they were protected from sun and rain to survive to the present. The walls of the gallery are highly polished and inscribed with many graffiti written by visitors during the ninth and tenth centuries C.E., and these refer to five hundred "golden-colored ones" on the rock face, so there is no doubt that there were originally very many figures there.[86]

The figures in the frescoes are painted in colors of red, yellow, green, and blended shades thereof. They are depicted as rising out of clouds, and are arranged sometimes singly, sometimes in pairs. Some are of golden complexion, as mentioned in the graffiti, and some are of darker hue and are called the "lily-colored ones" in the graffiti. Where there is a pair one is fair and the other dark. The fair ones hold flowers or have their hands in a conventional dance pose, while the dark ones bear trays of flowers. All have elaborate coiffures and wear rich jewelry (Figs. 13.37–38).[87]

The Alakamanda of Kubera. As to the intended significance of the frescoes, the statement of the *Culavamsa* (39.5) that the palace of Kassapa on Sigiriya was "like another Alakamanda," and that the king "dwelt there like Kubera," may provide a clue. In Hinduism Kubera, also called Vaiśravana (Pali Vessavana) as the son of the Muni Viśravas, is the lord of wealth and the guardian of the North, and

13.37 Apsara, Fresco on the Sigiriya Rock

13.38 Apsaras, Fresco on the Sigiriya Rock

Alakamanda (or Alaka) is his luxurious city, located on Mount Kailasa, where he rules as king of kings, with Lakshmi as his wife (at least in later texts) and with *yakshas, yakshinis,* and many other divine or semi-divine beings as his attendants.[88] So also in Buddhist texts Alakamanda is "the royal city of the gods," and "the palace of the monarch of Alaka (i.e., Kubera)" is there and is "gay with the dancing of the loveliest heavenly nymphs" *(apsaraess)* (Aśvaghosha, *Buddhacarita* 3.65).[89] Accordingly, in the light of these texts, it would appear that with his palace on top of the rock of Sigiriya, Kassapa intended to simulate the splendid heavenly city of Kubera, and therefore the beautiful figures in the frescoes may be identified as the heavenly nymphs *(apsarases)* of that city, their place in the heights being suggested by the clouds in which they are swathed.

Buddhamitra. An even more detailed explication of this identification is possible on the basis of documents concerning the history of Sigiriya which were compiled by a certain Buddhamitra in the fifteenth century. This personage came to Lanka from Suvarnapura (Palembang) and other centers of trade in the Eastern Islands, was ordained as a monk in the Theravada in which he was known as Anandasthavira, and spent some years as advisor to Parakramabahu IV (1412–1467 C.E.) during the latter part of that king's reign. In that time Buddhamitra made a study of many texts and inscriptions, and wrote historical works which were recorded, by the king's command, in numerous stone inscriptions.[90]

As Buddhamitra tells the story, King Dhatusena (460–478 C.E.), the father of Kassapa, was advised by the abbot of the Mahavihara at Anuradhapura to practice the *daśarajadharma* or ten royal virtues (liberality, good conduct, renunciation, straightforwardness, mildness, asceticism, non-hatred, non-hurting, forbearance, non-animosity) if he desired to acquire the status of a world monarch *(cakravartin),* and the king undertook to do so but found it very difficult in his royal position. At this juncture a *maga brahmana* (i.e., a Magian priest from Persia) heard that Dhatusena was in a state of mental distress and came to help him. The priest said that the kings in Persia in ancient times had also found the *daśarajadharma* extremely difficult to fulfill and, in its place, had observed the ritual of the *parvataraja* and thereby acquired imperial status.

The *parvataraja* ritual, the *maga brahmana* explained, was that of the Mountain King. The word *parvata* being synonymous with *megha* or "cloud," and the rain cloud being the source of all prosperity, it followed that the one who was able to persuade the world that he was himself the Cloud was therewith able to bring the whole world under his subjection. To fulfill the *parvataraja* it was only necessary to administer the kingdom while residing in a palace built on the summit of a rock. As a suitable rock, the *maga brahmana* recommended to Dhatusena the rock of Sigiriya, then known as Akshaśaila and Akshaparvata, which he described as so difficult to ascend that it would be possible to convince people that a person residing in a palace on its summit was one who transcended human status. Accordingly Dhatusena started the project with an architect from the Pallava kingdom and with the *maga brahmana* as the priest in charge *(purohita),* but himself died before the work was much advanced.

After that, Kassapa (478–496 C.E.), Dhatusena's parricide son and successor, resumed the project with a Sinhalese architect who had worked under the architect from the Pallava country, and on a grander scale than before. As a new detail, Kassapa suggested that the palace on the rock should resemble the abode of Kubera, the famed Alakamanda on the top of Mount Kailasa, which should help to persuade the people that he, the king, was himself Kubera. So, when the formidable task was completed, Kassapa and his queen went to Sigiriya and presented themselves before an assembled multitude in the guise of Kubera and Śrī Devī (i.e., Lakshmī), and the people cried: "Hail! the great King Kaśyapa, the lord of Alaka. Hail! Kubera, the consort of the goddess Śrī, and Hail! Śrī Devī, the mistress of the world."[91]

Sihigiri-vitara. In addition to this account of the history, Buddhamitra gives a description of Sigiriya derived from an ancient Sinhalese tract called *Sihigiri-vitara*, which he found in the library of the Maharaja at Suvarnapura and translated into Sanskrit. From the language and other evidence it is surmised that the document was written originally in the time of Agrabodhi II (608–618 C.E.), who is said to have been a direct descendent of Kaśyapa I. In addition to the palace, the pleasure gardens, and so forth, this source describes a large pond which was also on the summit of the rock, which was made by hewing out the rock on one side and building up the other sides with stone slabs and bricks, and in which there were aquatic flowers of various hues throughout the year. Of the pond the text says:

> That pond was called Dharani after the name of the pond located in the city of Alakamanda of Kubera. It is given in the *Atanatiya Sutra* that clouds go about in the directions starting from the pond named Dharani of Kubera, and that other clouds come to it and rain down. It should therefore be accepted that the pond Dharani of Kubera remained full every day. It is said that the pond called Dharani on the summit of Simhagiri also was full every day and that in the dry season water was brought up by means of machinery and the pond was filled.[92]

Concerning the pond in the heavenly Alakamanda, the passage referred to in the *Atanatiya Sutra* reads (*Digha Nikaya* 3.201):

> There too spreads
> The mighty sheet of water, Dharani,
> Whence rain clouds drawing waters pour them forth
> Whence showers rain down.[93]

It seems evident, therefore, that the large pond on the summit of Sigiriya was intended to simulate the heavenly Dharani and, like it, to be, at least figuratively, the source of the clouds and the rain. In this way Kassapa himself, residing on the rock and controlling the pond, was indeed the Mountain King and the Cloud.

The *Sihigiri-vitara* continues with description of other features of Sigiriya, including the lion on the northern side of the rock and the gallery protected by the "mirror wall" on the western face, and then says:

> The face of the rock above the gallery is coated with lime plaster and is white in color. Mount Kailasa is a peak of the Himalayan range. The Himalayan range is covered with snow and is therefore white. The rock of Simhagiri was coated with lime plaster and made to appear white in color, so as to make it accepted that Simhagiri rock was Mount Kailasa.
> On the side of the rock coated with lime plaster above the gallery, there are *apsarases* painted in the form of cloud damsels *(meghalata)* and lightning princesses *(vijjukumari)*.[94]

This therefore provides a specific explanation of the intended character of the figures on the Sigiriya rock and in particular of the fact that they are depicted as half enveloped in the clouds: they are nymphs *(apsarases)* who are personifications of the clouds. In a further detail of interpretation it may be surmised that those of darker hue are the cloud maidens, and those of fairer complexion are the representations of the lightning which flashes forth, golden in color.[95]

Polonnaruwa

Polonnaruwa, also known as Pulatthinagara, was the main capital of Lanka, with various interruptions, for some 400 years, from the ninth to the thirteenth century C.E., and its foremost kings were Vijayabahu I (1059–1114), Parakramabahu I (1153–1186), and Nissanka Malla (1187–1196), with Parakramabahu I being the most famous builder of them all.

The chief remains of the ancient city lie to the east and the north and northeast of the present Parakrama Samudra (Sea of Parakramabahu), a great reservoir which combines three ancient tanks.[96] At the southern approach, alongside the embankment of the Sea of Parakramabahu and outside the south wall of the inner city, is the ruin of a *vihara* locally known as the Potgul-vehera or Library Dagoba (reflecting a tradition that it once contained sacred books), in which, according to an inscription at the site, a hall *(mandapa)* was built by Candravati, the second queen of Parakramabahu I. To the north of the Potgul-vehera, a colossal statue of a man is carved in high relief against the southern face of a great boulder. The figure is 11 feet 2 inches (3.4 m.) in height. The feet are bare; the lower part of the body is draped in material ornamented with flowers and held by a knotted belt; the upper part of the body is bare; the face is of grave appearance; the hair is done up in a high crown *(makuta),* rounded at the top. The hands hold a curved object across the chest, which is variously interpreted as a book or as the inverted yoke of a bullock cart. Taking the object as a book, it is supposed that the figure is that of some famous sage. Taking the object as a yoke, it is recalled that in many ancient texts the word "yoke" *(dhura)* is used in the sense of "burden" and, in particular, the burden assumed or borne by a king in the administration of his kingdom and in the dispensation of justice. In the light of the latter interpretation it is supposed that the statue is that of a great king, and that king probably none other than Parakramabahu I (Fig. 13.39).[97]

13.39 Statue of Parakramabahu I at Polonnaruwa

13.40   Vatadage, Polonnaruwa

Citadel. To the north, in the heart of the walled city, was the royal precinct or citadel, comprising an area of some twenty-five acres, centered around the royal palace.[98] According to the surviving evidence, the palace consisted of a massive brick construction, 150 feet (46 m.) square, with a large hall and a courtyard surrounded on all four sides by galleries, and with a number of upper stories, the uppermost probably of wood. To the east, a covered pathway led from the palace to a pavilion which was the audience hall or council chamber of Parakramabahu I. This building stood on a stone platform of three tiers, surrounded by a frieze of elephants at the base, and ascended by an ornamental stairway guarded by stone lions.

Quadrangle. A quadrangle north of the royal precinct but still within the walls of the ancient city corresponds with the ancient Jetavanarama and contains the ruins of a number of edifices, some of which served in their respective times as Temples of the Tooth. Of these probably the earliest and most important structure is the Vatadage (relic house), which was probably built by Parakramabahu I. This is a *dagoba* which rises upon two circular terraces (Fig. 13.40). A porch on the north side gives entrance to the first terrace; and flights of steps at the four cardinal points, adorned with guardstones, lead up to the upper terrace. Built against the *dagoba* and facing each staircase is a seated Buddha figure. On the upper terrace there are two concentric circles of pillars, the first connected with a carved stone screen, and the second surrounded by a brick wall, evidently making this originally a roofed circular structure. An inscription claims the shrine as a work of Nissanka Malla (1187–1196 C.E.), but the inscription is probably later than the original building.

Other buildings in this area are the Thuparama, an image-house with thick brick walls and a seated Buddha figure of the style of the twelfth century C.E.; a solid pyramidal structure known as the Satmahal *prasada* (edifice in seven stories);

the Nissankalatha Mandapaya, a hall built by Nissanka Malla, with pillars sculptured in the form of lotus stalks with capitals in the form of opening lotus buds; and several shrines of Hindu deities, e.g., the Śiva Devale No. 2 (from the Chola period, eleventh century C.E.), and the Vishnu Devale (the word *devale [deva* and *alaya]* is used to designate the temple of a Hindu god or local deity), which exhibit the coexistence of Hinduism and Buddhism, with the Hindu deities probably considered subservient to the Buddha.

Alahana-parivena. At some distance outside the city wall to the north is the largest of the Polonnaruwa *dagobas,* known as the Rankot Vehera. It is 180 feet (55 m.) in height and 550 feet (168 m.) in circumference at the base, and is surrounded by chapels containing Buddha statues. Farther north are the buildings of the ancient complex known as the Alahana-parivena, in which are the Lankatilaka and the Kiri-vehera. According to an inscription on a guardstone of the building, the Lankatilaka was built by Parakramabahu I (1153–1186 C.E.) and later repaired by Vijayabahu IV (1271–1273).[99] It is a very large image-house, built of brick, 170 feet (52 m.) in length and 66 feet (20 m.) in breadth and, although the roof has collapsed, the walls still stand to a height of 55 feet (17 m.). In the sanctuary, facing the east, is an enormous standing statue of the Buddha, now headless, but estimated to have been originally about 41 feet (12.5 m.) in height. A *tilaka* is the name of an ornament made of colored stuffs and worn on the forehead, so this image-house was the "ornament of the island of Lanka," or popularly the "jewel of Lanka." It is in fact the largest Buddhist temple in Sri Lanka. Just north of the Lankatilaka is the Kiri-vehera, a *dagoba* probably founded by Subhadda, a queen of Parakramabahu I, and still standing in a very good state of preservation (Fig. 13.41).

13.41 Kiri-vehera Polonnaruwa

Monuments of Buddhism in India, Pakistan, and Sri Lanka | 471

13.42 Large Seated Buddha at the Gal Vihara, Polonnaruwa

Uttararama. Yet farther to the north, beyond the Kiri-vehera, is the Uttararama (north monastery), built by Parakramabahu I. The shrine which remains is carved in the face of a long low granite ridge, and is known as the Gal Vihara. It consists of three units which are named in the *Culavamsa* (78.74–75) the Vijjadhara-guha lena (Cave of the Spirit of Knowledge), Nisinna-patima lena (Cave of the Seated Buddha), and Nipanna-patima lena (Cave of the Recumbent Buddha).[100] In the center of the Cave of the Spirit of Knowledge is an excavated grotto, with the ceiling supported by two pillars, and with a seated Buddha (4 feet 7 inches [1.4 m.] in height) at the back. The figure is seated in the posture of meditation *(dhyana mudra)* on a high pedestal and a diamond throne *(vajrasana)*, with a parasol overhead and attendant deities on either side, all sculptured from the solid rock with the figures still connected to the rock. Outside, in a niche at the left (as seen from in front), corresponding with the Cave of the Seated Buddha, is a very large seated Buddha (15 feet [4.5 m.] high), also on a pedestal and in the position of meditation (Fig. 13.42). Outside, at the right, corresponding with the Cave of the Recumbent Buddha, is a colossal reclining figure of the Buddha (46 feet 4 inches [14.1 m.] in length), lying upon his right side with his right hand supporting his head upon a pillow; while at the head of this figure is the colossal figure of a man standing with crossed arms (a figure 22 feet 9 inches [6.9 m.] in height). A figure of the Buddha as recumbent *(nipanna)* could simply signify sleep, but most often indicates the final decease *(parinirvana)* and is probably so to be understood here. The position of the crossed arms exhibited by the standing figure is often found as the expression of a respectful or reverential attitude, and this figure is usually identified as a disciple of the Buddha, probably his specially loved disciple Ananda, attending upon the death of his master. There are examples, however, in which the Buddha is represented with crossed arms, and it can be argued, although with less likelihood, that the present figure, which stands upon a lotus pedestal, is the Buddha himself.[101]

Finally, to the east of the Alahana-parivena and the Gal Vihara, and roughly in a line from south to north are yet more monuments. The Mahathupa of Parakramabahu I, now called the Demalamahasaya or Great Tamil Caitya, although planned in dimensions which would have made it the largest of all the Sinhalese *thupas,* was apparently left unfinished, and what is to be seen now is work of later date, although perhaps built on an older foundation. The Lotus Pond is a stone bath, built by Nissanka Malla, in the shape of a full-blown stylized lotus of eight petals (nearly 25 feet [7.6 m.] in diameter). The Tivanka-pilimage (Tivanka imagehouse) or Northern Temple was built by Parakramabahu I and probably repaired by Parakramabahu II (1236–1271 C.E.) after a period of damage and neglect. This building still stands in relatively massive form, its exterior decorated rather elaborately with pillars and carvings, somewhat in the style of a Hindu temple. Because it features an image of the Buddha standing in the *tribhanga* pose it is called the "house of the standing Buddha in the thrice-bent pose." In the interior there is a giant but now headless statue of the Buddha, and the walls are adorned with a whole series of frescoes. These are executed in the same red, yellow, and green colors as at Sigiriya, but with different style and themes. In the paintings two layers are distinguishable, and may belong respectively to the times of Parakramabahu I and Parakramabahu II. As such they are some of the most extensive and, after Sigiriya, oldest known paintings of Sri Lanka. Among the subjects are many scenes identifiable from the *jatakas,* and also the entreaty of the *devas* to the *bodhisattva* to be born as the Buddha, the dream of Maya, and the descent of the Buddha on the ladder of gold to the city of Sankissa (Sankaśya).[102]

Kandy

The Dalada Maligawa or Temple of the Tooth, final repository of the most sacred relic of Sinhalese Buddhism, is the easternmost structure (east being the most auspicious of directions) in the complex of sacred buildings on the north side of the lake at Kandy, with only a wooded hill behind it. Immediately to the west are four shrines of gods who are subservient to the Buddha, while to the north and south are two monasteries, as well as the former king's palace to the north.

The temple is a rectangular two-storied building, with its main entrance facing the west. On the lower floor there is a Drumming Pavilion, through which priests and worshipers enter and go upstairs. On the upper floor there is a Chanting Pavilion, a Sandalwood Room, and the inner Sanctuary. In the inner Sanctuary the sacred tooth relic is kept behind iron bars (installed by the British Government) and housed in a series of elaborate jeweled caskets dedicated by successive kings. The temple is the center of daily, weekly, and annual celebrations of which the most important is the annual processional festival called Esala Perahera, which falls in August/September and is the largest festival of Buddhist Sri Lanka.[103]

14

MONUMENTS OF HINDUISM AND BUDDHISM IN SOUTHEAST ASIA

In modern usage the term Southeast Asia describes collectively the southeastern portion of mainland Asia, with two peninsulas extending far to the south, namely, the Indochina peninsula (Burma, Thailand, Laos, Kampuchea, Vietnam) and the Malay peninsula (peninsular Malaysia and Singapore); and the long string of islands constituting Indonesia (Sumatra, Java, Bali, and others) and the Philippines.[1]

EXPANSION OF INDIAN INFLUENCE

Early Indian acquaintance with some part or parts of Southeast Asia is well attested. In the *Ramayana* (500–300 B.C.E.) there is reference to Suvarnadvipa and Yavadvipa. The Sanskrit *dvipa* means "land with water on two sides," i.e., a peninsula or an island, while *suvarna* means gold and *yava* barley; thus these names refer to a Peninsula or Island of Gold, and a Peninsula or Island of Barley. In the *Milinda Panha* (circa first century C.E.) the voyages of a wealthy shipowner are described as going on the high seas to a number of places including Suvarnabhumi, and this name means the Land of Gold. In the *jatakas* there are also stories which involve trading voyages between India and Suvarnabhumi, and at Ajanta and elsewhere there are paintings based on these and other texts which depict sailing vessels and no doubt reflect the sea travel of relatively early times.

As to the location of the places just mentioned, equivalent names are found in the *Geography* of Claudius Ptolemy, compiled at Alexandria in about 150 C.E. In this work the Eleventh Map of Asia shows "India beyond the Ganges" (*Asiae Tabula* XI, *India extra Gangem*), and the regions of Southeast Asia are drawn with considerable accuracy, the information presumably having come directly or indirectly through Indian sources. In the area of what is now Lower Burma is the label *Aurea regio,* the Region of Gold, corresponding with the name Suvarnabhumi, the Land of Gold. At the lower end of what is plainly the Malay peninsula the name is *Aurea chersonesus,* the Golden Chersonesus (peninsula), which corresponds with Suvarnadvipa, the Peninsula of Gold. In the sea southeast of the peninsula is an

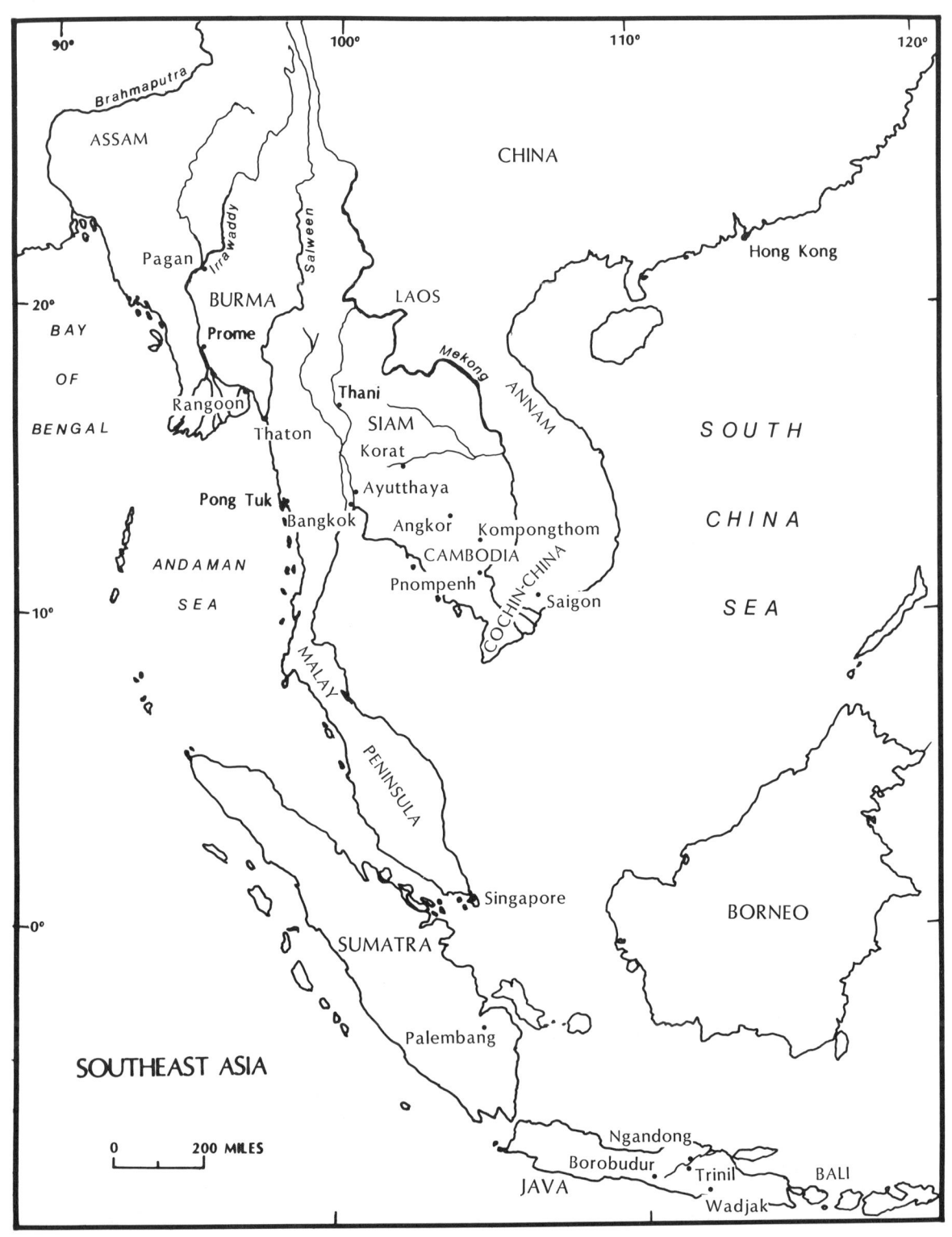

island called Labadius or Barley Island *(Labadij hoc est ordei insula)*, corresponding with Yavadvipa, the Island of Barley, and it is described as producing much gold.[2]

In the times of the Chinese Buddhist pilgrims we also hear of well-traveled sea routes, which had doubtless been long established. Fa Xian (399–414 C.E.) returned from India to China by sea by way of Lanka and Java. Although Xuan Zang (629–645 C.E.) did not choose to do so, it was suggested to him that he take the southern sea route home. Yi Jing (671–695 C.E.) came to India from China by sea, and also returned home the same way, touching ports en route in the Malay peninsula.

Indians were thus quite certainly traveling to various parts of Southeast Asia already in the last centuries B.C.E. and the first centuries C.E., and they quite naturally must have carried with them many elements of Indian culture and, in particular, ideas and practices of Hinduism and Buddhism. That Hindu priests and Buddhist monks soon went on such journeys is also likely. Of the Buddhist mission to Southeast Asia we learn explicitly in the account (*Mahavamsa* 12.6) of the converting of different countries after the Third Buddhist Council under Aśoka (269–232 B.C.E.) when the two *theras* Sona and Uttara were sent to Suvarnabhumi (Suvannabhumi). In the regions to which Hindu and Buddhist missionaries went, there were, of course, long established systems of belief and practice and, even with the acceptance of Hinduism and/or Buddhism, much of this remained as a substratum or was mingled in greater or lesser degree with what was brought in, and the result varied accordingly in various places.[3]

With trade and mission went also naturally the establishment of Indian settlements and colonies, and eventually there arose the kingdoms in Southeast Asia which are describable as Indianized states.[4] Of these and their centers the earliest and most important will appear below.

INDONESIA

In the Indianized states in what is now Indonesia the presence of both Hinduism and Buddhism is well attested, although in varying degrees of strength in various places and times, by the Chinese Buddhist pilgrims. When Fa Xian was in Javadvipa (the island of Java) in the early fifth century C.E. he found that what he called various forms of error or heresies, and *brahmanism,* were flourishing, but that Buddhism was in a very unsatisfactory condition and not really worth speaking of.[5]

Śrivijaya

When Yi Jing came from China in the latter part of the seventh century C.E. he arrived in a Persian ship at a place in the Southern Sea called *Fo-shih* or *Shih-li-fo-shih,* and stayed there for six months to study Sanskrit grammar before going on to India. After this interval he proceeded to India on a ship belonging to the king of *Fo-shih*. Again after his long stay in India he returned to *Fo-shih* and remained for four years to translate Buddhist texts from Sanskrit into Chinese. After a short visit to Kwangchow (Canton) to get helpers he came back once more to *Fo-shih* to do additional writing.

The Chinese name *Shih-li-fo-shih* corresponds to the Sanskrit Śrivijaya and, from Yi Jing and other evidences, it is learned that the city of Śrivijaya was at this time the center of a kingdom which, either then or soon afterward, encompassed much of Sumatra, Malaya, and possibly western Java. As for the city itself, it is almost certainly to be identified with Palembang in southeastern Sumatra. In this location Śrivijaya was in position to command the Strait of Malacca, and was thus favorably situated to develop its own shipping—which Yi Jing utilized in going on to India—and to control other shipping passing through between the East and West. In the eleventh century C.E. the kingdom suffered from attacks by the Chola kingdom of South India, but even so Śrivijaya remained an important sea power until the thirteenth century.[6]

The extended stays in Śrivijaya of Yi Jing also show that this was already an important Buddhist center, and the Chinese pilgrim explicitly describes it as such. He writes:

> In the fortified city of Fo-shih Buddhist priests number more than one thousand, whose minds are bent on learning and good practices. They investigate and study all the subjects that exist just as in Madhyadeśa (the Middle Kingdom in India); the rules and ceremonies are not at all different. If a Chinese priest wishes to go to the West in order to hear (lectures) and read (the original Buddhist texts), he had better stay here one or two years and practice the proper rules and then proceed to Central India.[7]

Yi Jing also says that one of the renowned teachers under whom he studied was residing in *Fo-shih,* namely, Śakyakirti, the author of a Mahayana work called *Hastadandaśastra,* which Yi Jing himself translated into Chinese.[8]

Archaeologically there is confirmation of the Mahayana Buddhist orientation of Śrivijaya to the extent that the sculptures found in the Palembang region, although relatively few and late, are all Buddhist with a predominance of *bodhisattva* images. There is also evidence that the rulers of Śrivijaya fostered Mahayana Buddhism elsewhere in their realm. An inscription bearing a date equivalent to 775 C.E. has been found at Ligor in the northern Malay Peninsula, which praises a great king of Śrivijaya and commemorates his building of a Mahayana Buddhist sanctuary, consisting of a "triad of excellent brick houses, the abode of the Padmapani (i.e., the *bodhisattva* Avalokiteśvara as the lotus bearer), of the Mara-slayer (i.e., Śakyamuni as victor over the prince of evil), and of Vajrapani (i.e., the *bodhisattva* Akshobhya as the thunderbolt bearer).[9]

JAVA

Sanjaya

In the meantime there are also other kingdoms of more localized sway, in particular on the island of Java. The earliest dated record found in Java is an inscription on a stone from temple ruins on the hill of Vukir near the hamlet of Canggal in Central Java (southeast of Borobudur). The date is in the 654th year of the Saka Era, equivalent to 732 C.E. The text is a laudatory poem or royal decree *(praśasti),* and names an illustrious king Sanjaya, the son and successor of a king named Sanna (or Sannaha), recording his erection on this hill of a *linga* (the emblem of Śiva), and expressing extended praises of Śiva, Brahma, and Vishnu. It also describes the great island of Yava as abundantly supplied with grain and rich in gold mines, and says that under the rule of Sanjaya "people can sleep on the roadside without being startled by the thieves or by other fears." A later text credits Sanjaya with conquests in Bali, Sumatra, and Kampuchea, but any such forays abroad were probably at the most of ephemeral significance.[10]

The kingdom over which Sanjaya ruled at this time in Central Java was, therefore, a Hinduized kingdom in which the worship of the main Hindu deities prevailed. On the Dieng plateau well across the island to the north-northwest from Vukir there are some eight relatively small Śiva temples still standing, and these may have belonged to the same kingdom.[11]

Śailendras

Not long after the time of Sanjaya we find the Śailendra dynasty established in Central Java, and it may have been Sanjaya who laid the foundations of their rule. The name Śailendra, by which they are known, means lord or king of the mountain (*śaila*, mountain; *indra*, king), and is probably associated with the early and widespread idea of the residence of the gods on the tops of the mountains. The similar name "mountain lord" *(Giriśa)* is a title of Śiva, and may have some connection here. From their major monuments (to be described below), however, the Śailendras were devoted to Mahayana Buddhism rather than to Hinduism, although it is also probable that for the most part Hinduism and Buddhism coexisted peaceably on Java, with reciprocal tolerance and even syncretism.

The first Javanese record naming the Śailendra dynasty is a stone inscription found at the village of Kalasan (between Yogyakarta and Prambanam, in the plain of Prambanam and the valley of the Opak River, south of the volcanic Mount Merapi), which is dated in the 700th year of the Śaka Era, i.e., in 778 C.E. The text opens with praise of Tara (the Buddhist goddess) and records the foundation of a temple of the goddess by the spiritual preceptors *(gurus)* of the Śailendra king Pancapana Panamkarana, after the preceptors had persuaded the king of the importance of this project. There were also made an image of the goddess, and a dwelling for the monks who knew the Mahayana of the Vinaya. All of this was done in the flourishing kingdom of "the king who is the ornament of the Śailendra dynasty." It is possible that the last phrase does not refer to Panamkarana himself but to a suzerain monarch over him; at any rate, however, Panamkarana is himself called a *maharaja* (great king) and a *rakryan* (a frequently used official title in ancient Java). In addition, the village named Kalasa was bestowed on the congregation of monks, and the text closes with the request of Panamkarana that all future kings should maintain the *vihara* (the temple and the cloister) in a proper way.[12]

Given the respective dates of the Canggal inscription of Sanjaya (732 C.E.) and the Kalasan inscription of Panamkarana (778 C.E.), the beginning of the Śailendra dynasty may be placed around 750 C.E., and the indications are that it endured for somewhat more than a century or, say, to around 860 C.E.[13]

Candi Kalasan. As far as is known, the temple of Tara founded at Kalasa under Panamkarana in 778 C.E. (according to the inscription just cited) was the first Buddhist temple in Java.[14] At the present Kalasan, not far from where the stone inscription of Panamkarana was found, is Candi Kalasan (*candi*, also spelled *tjandi*, is the usual Javanese word for a temple), and the location makes it probable that this is the aforesaid temple of Tara. The present building encloses older constructions, and it is perhaps these which represent the original temple, while the existing structure is perhaps a reconstruction in around the middle of the ninth century C.E.

As it stands, the temple is a massive square building on a high platform, with projecting porches on the four sides. Over the entrances and over niches in the outer walls the most characteristic motif is the *kala-makara* (Fig. 14.1), which is also found elsewhere very extensively in ancient Indonesian art. The *kala* corre-

14.1 Niche and Kala-Makara at Candi Kalasan

sponds with the *kirttimukha* (visage of glory) in Sanskrit, and is a mythical monster head, while the mythical aquatic and/or elephantine animal called the *makara* often appears in the same context or is actually combined with the *kala* in the *kala-makara*. Together they may represent the combination of the celestial/heavenly on the one hand and the earthly/watery on the other. Confirming the celestial character of the *kala*, the top of the head is often shaped like a tree of heaven, and there may be celestial musicians on either side, while above there is a lofty decoration shaped like the top of a temple. The monstrous character of the head, however, emphasizes above all its role as a protective guardian against evil forces, and it is as such that it appears on practically every entrance and image-niche of Javanese temples.[15]

Candi Sari. Candi Sari is near Candi Kalasan, is probably of about the same date, and may have served as the monastery of the Kalasan temple. It is a large rectangular structure on a high platform, and inside it is divided into three halls connected by a corridor. The exterior walls are adorned with many sculptures of semi-divine beings, masculine *nagas* and heavenly musicians, and feminine *kinnaris* and *taras* (the name of the goddess Tara being commonly applied to a number of otherwise unidentified feminine figures) (Fig. 14.2).[16]

14.2 Taras on the Wall of Candi Sari

Candi Sewu. Candi Sewu, not far north of Prambanam, is a large Buddhist temple complex and, from a number of inscribed but undated stones, is thought to belong to the first half of the ninth century C.E. The main temple exhibits a cross-shaped ground plan, and is surrounded by no less than 240 minor temples. There are four entrances to the entire complex at the cardinal points, and each was guarded by a pair of colossal *rakshasas* (ogres), 8 feet 2 inches (2.5 m.) in height.[17]

Candi Plaosan. Candi Plaosan, east of Candi Sewu, is also a very large Buddhist complex, although much of it is in ruins. Two large temples were surrounded by many minor temples and many small *stupas*. The date of the complex is thought to be in the middle of the ninth century C.E., and there is reason to believe that the foundation was due to a princess of the Śailendra Buddhist dynasty who married a king of the Hindu dynasty of Mataram, their cooperation in the project providing an example of the good relations between the adherents of Hinduism and of Buddhism.[18]

Candi Mendut. Candi Mendut, Candi Pawon, and Candi Borobudur are all relatively close together in the plain of Kedu, near the confluence of the Praga and Elo rivers, northwest of Yogyakarta and southwest of Mount Merapi. All three structures probably date to the early ninth century C.E. and may be understood as forming a complex in which Candi Mendut and Candi Pawon are temples or chapels providing an approach to Borobudur. There is reason to think that the nearby confluence of the two local rivers was perceived as corresponding to the coming together of the Ganges and the Yamuna in India, and that there was a conscious intention to make here in Java with these monuments something like a replica of the original holy land of Buddhism in India.

14.3 Candi Mendut

Candi Mendut is at the village of Mendut on the left bank of the Elo River, about 2 miles (3 km.) from Borobudur. It is a square building, oriented to the northwest, standing on a high platform, and rising to two recessed stories ornamented with small *stupas,* above which there probably had been a third story and a small *stupa* on top, making a total height of about 85 feet (26 m.) (Fig. 14.3).

The outer side of the wings of the stairway leading to the entrance of the temple, the outer walls and the walls of the antechamber are all filled with many panels of relief sculptures. A panel on the outer side of the southern wing of the stairway, for example, is identified as an illustration of the *Kacchapa Jataka.* In this story a young man catches the "snake-wind" disease and is told by his parents to go away from home to escape the illness but, after recovering, to come back and dig in the house for buried treasure. The son does as told, recovers treasure, and afterward, carrying oil, clothing, and so forth, goes to the Jetavana monastery at Śravasti to pay homage to the Buddha. The Buddha hears his story, and tells him that in former days when there was danger some people were too attached to their homes to leave them, and died as a result, while others who were willing to go elsewhere saved their lives. In the sculptured panel (Fig. 14.4) the young man is seen three times. At the right he is taking something—presumably some of the treasures—out of a large box in front of a tree. In the center he is holding a pair of circular objects—presumably part of the treasure and possibly a pair of large earrings. At the left he is going on his way—presumably to visit the Buddha—carrying a pole on his right shoulder with a jar on one end and a bundle of clothing on the other.[19]

On the northern and southern walls of the antechamber are the figures in relief of a woman and a man respectively, both of them surrounded by numerous children. The woman in the panel on the north wall is recognizable as Hariti, the *yakshini* who originally devoured children but, after conversion by the Buddha, became a protectress of children and a goddess of fertility. In the panel on the south wall (Fig. 14.5) the man might be Kubera the god of riches, because there are pots

14.4 Kacchapa Jataka Scene on the South Wing of the Stairway, Candi Mendut

14.5 The Yaksha Atavaka and Children on the South Wall of the Antechamber, Candi Mendut

of money at his feet and because he is sometimes considered the husband of Hariti; or Pancika who is most often represented as the husband of Hariti; but is most probably to be identified as the *yaksha* Atavaka, whose history is much like that of Hariti in that, from being a man-eating ogre, he too was converted to Buddhism. In this scene he has large eyes, curly hair, and mustache, and looks at the children around him with kindly gaze. The children are playing freely at the foot of two trees, which some of them are also climbing. At the right one boy is knocking down mango fruits with a stick while another protects his eyes with his hand from the falling fruits. Overhead two doves indicate that there is peace in the land, due to the influence of Buddhism.

In the inner sanctuary of Candi Mendut are three colossal seated statues. In the center is the Buddha, seated as if on a chair with the feet hanging down *(pralambapada asana)* and resting on a double lotus (Fig. 14.6). He wears a very close fitting robe, and there is a pointed halo behind his head. The back of the chair is sculptured with *makaras* and lions standing on elephants. The hands of the Buddha are in the *dharmacakra mudra,* so he is in the first instance Śakyamuni preaching the

14.6 The Buddha in Candi Mendut

Law, yet he is at the same time the expression of ultimate truth and perhaps identifiable with Vairocana, the supreme *tathagata,* the highest visible manifestation of ultimate reality. Four niches in the sides of the room are now empty, but very probably contained statues of the other four *tathagatas.* The central Buddha himself is immediately flanked by two *bodhisattvas,* one on either side. At the Buddha's right (to the left as seen by the viewer), is Avalokiteśvara (watchful lord) Padmapani (lotus bearer), identified by a statuette of Amitabha in his crown and by a lotus, the *bodhisattva* who looks down upon all creatures with great compassion. The figure at the Buddha's left, whose appearance is more severe and whose hand formerly carried the *vajra,* is Vajrapani (thunderbolt bearer), the *bodhisattva* who communicates esoteric Buddhist doctrine. As a threefold group they may also be understood as standing for the three jewels *(triratna),* the Buddha, the *dharma* (Avalokiteśvara), and the *sangha* (Vajrapani).[20]

Candi Pawon. Candi Pawon is across on the right bank of the Elo River near its confluence with the Praga River, a little less than half of the distance on a straight line from Mendut to Borobudur. As restored, Candi Pawon is a small rectangular temple, standing on a platform and rising in recessed stories surmounted by small *stupas.* The inner room is empty, but the exterior walls are decorated with sculptures. The entrance faces to the northwest. On the relatively well-preserved rear wall to the southeast, in the central panel, *kinnaris* (half woman, half bird) are bringing offerings to a celestial tree. Under the tree are vases full of gems, which support the usual explanation of this temple as having been dedicated to Kubera, the god of riches.[21]

Candi Borobudur. It is possible that contemporary information concerning the building of Candi Borobudur is provided by two stone inscriptions found in Central Java. The first of these is dated in the Saka Year 746, i.e., in 824 C.E., and gives the names of a Śailendra king Samaratunga and his daughter Pramodavardhani; the second is dated in the Saka Year 764, i.e., in 842 C.E., and records the dedication of a number of rice fields for the upkeep of a monument of which the only legible part of its name is *sambhara.*[22] Relevant considerations lead to the conclusion that the builder of the monument in question was Samaratunga, that the donor of the lands was his daughter Pramodavardhani, that the full name of the monument was Bhumisamgharabhudhara, meaning "the Mountain of Accumulation of Virtue on the Ten Stages of the Bodhisattva," that the latter part of this name *(bharabhudhara)* was the source of the name Borobudur (Barabudur), and that the monument in question was none other than Candi Borobudur.[23] If this reconstruction is correct, a definite date is provided for the origin of Borobudur; at any rate there seems to be no doubt that Borobudur was built under the Śailendras and in the early part of the ninth century C.E.

Although often called a *stupa,* Candi Borobudur is more accurately described as a terraced pyramid *(prasada)* with a *stupa* on top. In all, there are nine terraces of successively diminishing size: the first six are square, the uppermost three are circular, and the crowning *stupa* is in the center of the topmost circular terrace. On each of the four sides of the monument a staircase goes up through gateways to the open terraces above (Fig. 14.7). The base of the monument is 403 feet (123 m.) square, the present height is 103 feet (31.5 m.) and the original height to the top of the pinnacle, now lost, is supposed to have been about 138 feet (42 m.).[24]

The exterior wall of the original base was filled with panels of relief sculptures but, at a later time, was encased in an additional stone covering, whether intended to strengthen the monument or for some other reason is not known. This made a

14.7 Borobudur, the North Side with Central Staircase

"buried basement," the top of which makes the first terrace and provides a wide processional path *(pradakshina patha)* around the monument. Each of the five square terraces above is walled in by a balustrade, and the space between the balustrade and the body of the monument forms a gallery; thus there are four such galleries extending all around the pyramid, with their inner walls filled with panels of relief sculptures. The topmost balustrade surrounds the topmost square terrace, called the plateau, on which are the uppermost three concentric circular terraces. Each circular terrace bears a ring of small openwork or perforated *stupas,* and each such *stupa* contains a seated Buddha figure. In the center of the highest circular terrace is the large crowning *stupa,* almost 52 feet (16 m.) in diameter. In all, the entire monument contains 504 Buddha statues sculptured in the round, seventy-two of these in the perforated *stupas* on the circular terraces, the others in niches in the walls. The gateways of the staircases are guarded by large *kala* heads; rainspouts in the lower levels are shaped like *makaras* (Fig. 14.8), in the upper levels like *kala* heads (Fig. 14.9).

Buried Basement. On the wall of the "buried basement" of Borobudur there is a series of 158 panels of sculptures. Some of these still bear inscriptions that were apparently instructions to the sculptors as to the scenes which were to be shown, and were intended to be erased after the work was completed. In general the scenes show various good and evil deeds done on earth together with their rewards or punishments in a present or next life on earth, heaven, or hell; i.e., they illustrate the doctrine of *karma.* Furthermore there is a Buddhist work on this subject called the *Karmavibhanga,* which was very widely circulated (with versions found in India, Tibet, Central Asia, and China), and in many cases these scenes have been shown to follow this text so closely that they must actually have been based on it.[25]

Above Panel 0 21 is the word *virupa* (the deformed, ugly one), and this label

14.8 Makara Spout in the Main Wall of the Processional Path, Borobudur

14.9 Kala Spout on the Fourth Terrace, Borobudur

14.10   Relief Panel of the Covered Base, Borobudur

seems to refer to both this panel and the next (Panel O 22), in both of which persons of such appearance are portrayed. The persons in Panel O 22 (Fig. 14.10) are, at the right, a man and woman sitting on a bench, four poorly clad men standing in front of them, and on the ground a young man and a cat; and at the left a man and woman and child sitting on the ground, another family group on a bench, and other individuals standing. Apparently they all do nothing but talk. Presumably the obviously unfortunate condition of these persons is due to their *karma*.

In Panel O 89, evil actions on earth and retribution in future hells are plainly shown. In the right half of this panel, two men are cooking fish and turtles in a large kettle over a fire; then they themselves are seen together with others in a large kettle over a fire in hell. In the left half of the panel a man with a sword is on the point of killing a woman sitting in front of him; then is himself seen with others being dragged into a fiery furnace in hell.[26]

In Panel O 121, in the right half of the panel, a man and woman are on their way to a field of grain, and above as a notation for the sculptor is the word "covetousness" *(abhidhyaya)*. The relevant passage in the *Karmavibhanga* reads: "Covetousness *(abhidhyaya)* is an evil course resulting in the appearance of chaff and tares among the rice, barley, and other standing crops. In consequence of that act one will have to beg one's food from strangers." So the man and woman in the scene are inspecting their corn which has been spoiled by weeds, and they will no doubt soon be reduced to begging for food.

For the left half of the same panel the inscribed word is "violence" *(vyapada)*, and the relevant passage in the *Karmavibhanga* reads: "Violence is an evil course, in consequence whereof the crop becomes void of fruit even when one has sown abundantly. In consequence of this act one grows an unfavorable countenance." Here in the sculptured illustration a man is seated cross-legged together with his wife. The face of the man is disfigured, presumably as the result of some accident, and this must be the "unfavorable countenance" which was the result of his *karma*. In front of the man and woman are two men, each with a hand raised respectfully.

These must be two servants who are reporting to the man the failure of his harvest.²⁷

Above the series of relief scenes on the wall of the covered base just described, was also a frieze of decorative reliefs and, when the lower base was covered, these remained to be seen on the wall beside the processional path which the top of the "buried basement" provided. This frieze consists entirely of representations of beings other than human, i.e., of *rakshasas, nagas, apsarases,* and the like, and the intent of the frieze seems to be to add decoration to the architecture.²⁸ On the balustrades above there are also scattered decorative scenes and individual items as well as the main panels of relief sculptures.

Galleries on the Square Terraces. As already explained, the inner walls of the four galleries on the square terraces are filled with panels of relief sculptures. These walls are describable as the main wall (against the body of the monument) and the balustrade wall. In the First Gallery the main wall is divided into two series of panels, each about 3 feet (1 m.) in height, with the space in between the two series filled with spiral ornament. The upper series of these reliefs gives the life story of Śakyamuni up to his first sermon, and it has been established that the scenes are, for the most part, based upon the account in the *Lalitavistara*.²⁹ The lower series gives scenes from the previous births of the Buddha, and many of the events have been identified in the *jatakas* and *avadanas*. On the balustrade wall there are also *jataka* scenes.³⁰

At the point of the double panel 95 (Fig. 14.11), for example, the upper register (Ia 95) depicts the attempt of the daughters of Mara to distract Śakyamuni from his resolve to attain enlightenment. The text of the *Lalitavistara* (21.89–135) reads:

14.11 Double Relief Panel in the First Gallery, Borobudur, showing above (Ia 95) the Temptation of Śakyamuni by the Daughters of Mara, and below (Ib 95) a scene from the *Bhallatiya Jataka*, with a band of spiral ornament between the upper and lower panels

> Then Mara, the Evil One, spoke to his daughters: "Go now, maidens, to Bodhimanda (the adamantine throne of the great enlightenment, the same as the *vajrasana*) and tempt the *bodhisattva*, if he be subject to passion or free therefrom, if he be wise or foolish, blind or quick sighted, faithful to his resolve, weak or strong." Hearing these words these *apsaras* went to Bodhimanda, where the *bodhisattva* was, and they came before him and displayed the thirty-two kinds of female allurement. . . .
>
> But not with all their ten thousand arts of rousing desire could they tempt the *sugata* (a title of the Buddha, "he who has gone well"). . . . Then the daughters of Mara spoke these verses unto their father: "The female allurements, father, that have been spread before him, that should have bent his heart to passion, not one moment on seeing these was his mind moved; as the king of the mountains he remained firm."

When the Evil One made a last attempt to contradict the Buddha, claiming that the Buddha had no witness to certify his enlightenment and the truth of his teachings, the Buddha touched the earth with his right hand and said: "This earth is my witness. . . . It is unbiased. . . . May it make manifest that I am not lying and may it be my witness against you!" Thereupon the earth goddess emerged, folded her hands in the gesture of reverence *(anjali mudra)* before the Buddha, and declared: "O Supreme Being, it is thus."[31]

In the sculptured scene (Fig. 14.11, upper register) the Buddha is seated in the center in the earth-touching position *(bhumisparśa mudra),* while the daughters of Mara are on either side of him. On the right two are dancing, a man is beating time with a pair of bells, several other women are standing or kneeling, and one woman at the corner has several drums to play on. On the left one of the daughters is seated and making a respectful salutation to the Buddha, while several others are standing behind her with flowers in their hands. Meanwhile the Buddha remains unmoved and, in the left corner of the scene, the failure of the attempt is being reported to Mara, who is seen sitting under a tree, quite dejected.

The lower register (Ib 95) at this same point is one of a long series of scenes (Ib 89–105) based on the *Bhallatiya Jataka* (No. 504).[32] In this former birth story, the Buddha was King Bhallatiya of Varanasi. The king wished to go hunting and went with his dogs toward the Himalaya, first along the Ganges and then up a tributary. This was a beautiful mountain stream, full of fish and tortoises, shaded by trees bearing flowers and fruit, and frequented by birds, bees, and deer. Here the king observed a pair of *kinnaras,* who embraced each other fondly but also wept and wailed. The king left his dogs and weapons behind and went quietly to ask the *kinnaras* the reason for their weeping. The female *kinnari* explained that upon one occasion she was gathering flowers on one bank of the river when a sudden rise in the water separated her from her male companion on the other bank, and it was not until the following morning that the water subsided and they were able to be together again. This event had taken place 697 years before, but the memory of the one night of separation still caused them sorrow, for the separation of loving hearts, however brief, seems to last for ages. The king was much moved by what he heard, lost interest in his hunting, returned to his city, told the story to his courtiers, and thenceforward gave food to the needy and enjoyed his fleeting days.

In the series of reliefs in the First Gallery based upon this *jataka,* in the first panel (Ib 89) we see a wooded landscape with the two *kinnaras* standing on the farther bank of a river, holding their right hands, and King Bhallatiya, hidden from them by the foliage of a tree, listening to them. In the second panel (Ib 90) the *kinnara* couple is still in the same spot, and the king is now sitting on the ground near them, his hands held up in a gesture of respect, and he is hearing them attentively as they tell their story. In the third panel (Ib 91) (Fig. 14.12), which is

14.12 Relief Panel (Ib 91) in the First Gallery, Borobudur, showing a scene from the *Bhallatiya Jataka*

separated by a doorway from the first two panels, the king is seated with two women on a bench under an ornamental canopy. Below is a group of servants represented in small size. In front stands a female servant with a fly whisk. At the left (as seen by the viewer) is a group of seated men in court attire, one with a sword, and the one in front making a gesture of respect. In the background are the king's royal umbrella, his elephant, and two horses. Assuming that this scene belongs in sequence with the two preceding scenes, this must be King Bhallatiya back again in his court and relating his experience to his courtiers.

The scenes which come next are not readily explainable but perhaps in some way still belong to some form of the same *jataka,* for only at Panel Ib 106 is there the plainly recognizable beginning of a new story, namely, that of Maitrakanyaka. In view of the sequence, then, Panel Ib 95 (the lower register in Figure 14.11) may be thought to belong still to the *Bhallatiya Jataka,* although its relevance is not evident. At any rate there is a mass of rock at the left, from which water flows forth across the bottom of the picture. At the right three men are standing, who appear to be servants or guards. At the left a number of children are playing in the water and under the overhanging trees. In the middle are four mothers, and one of these is helping a child up out of the water.[33]

In the Second Gallery the main wall reliefs have been found to be based on the *Gandavyuha,* the work which recounts the visits of the young man Sudhana to more than fifty teachers in his search for enlightenment. Identifiable in the scenes are the *bodhisattva* Mañjuśri who sends Sudhana on his search, and many of those to whom he goes, e.g., the *bhikshus* Meghaśri, Sagaramegha, and Supratishthita; the *bhikshunis* Aśa and Simhavyasambhita; a *brahmana* Siviratra; Gopa and Maya, the wife and mother respectively of the Buddha; Avalokiteśvara; and eight

14.13 Relief Panel (IIa 108) in the Second Gallery, Borobudur, showing Sudhana and a Goddess of Night

Ratridevatas or goddesses of night (Ratri, night, is the sister of Ushas, dawn), who dwell in different localities in Magadha.

In Panel IIa 108 (Fig. 14.13), for example, Sudhana is in the presence of the fourth Ratridevata. The goddess is seated near the center in a small pavilion, with a heavenly figure at each side of the elaborate roof. The goddess has a halo behind her head, and holds a flower in her left hand. There is a tree in the background on each side. The women attendants of the goddess are at the left side (as seen by the viewer). Some are standing, some are sitting, and the first of those standing holds a fan. At the right stands Sudhana with some object in his hand; behind him are six attendants, some with flowers.[34]

Likewise in the main wall reliefs of the Third and Fourth Galleries the same story is continued on the basis of the *Gandavyuha* and also of its later and final chapter, which is the poem called the *Bhadracari*.[35] In the story Sudhana comes at last to Maitreya and Samantabhadra and is helped by them to the final attainment of his goal, and it is these *bodhisattvas* who are the principal characters in these reliefs.

In Panel IVa 54 (Fig. 14.14), for example, we see Samantabhadra together with many Buddhas. In the top row there are seven seated Buddhas. The one in the middle is in the pose of meditation *(dhyana mudra)*, those on either side in the *vitarka, abhaya,* and *dharmacakra mudras* respectively. At either end is a standing Buddha, who is tall enough to relate to both the top row and the bottom row of figures. Of these two standing Buddhas, the one at the viewer's left makes the gesture of reassurance *(abhaya mudra)*; the one at the right may exhibit the *dharmacakra mudra,* although this is difficult to make out with certainty. The central five Buddhas in the top row are separated from each other by trees and, from the trees, flowers and garlands fall down upon the bottom row of figures.

In the bottom row at the left is a Buddha seated in the earth-touching position

14.14 Relief Panel (IVb 54) in the Fourth Gallery, Borobudur, showing Samantabhadra and Many Buddhas

(*bhumisparśa mudra*), and beside him are a tree and, against the base on which the standing Buddha is standing, a water pot. Separated from the seated Buddha by two of his own followers is Samantabhadra, who is seated on a lotus cushion and is making a gesture of respect in the direction of the Buddha. Behind Samantabhadra sits another high personage, who makes a sort of *dharmacakra mudra*, and farther to the right are the followers of this personage.[36]

Buddha Images. In niches in the outer sides of the five balustrades of the square terraces of Borobudur there are five rows of Buddha images, ninety-two in each of the first four rows, and sixty-four in the fifth row, a total of 432 in all. All the figures are represented in the same manner, seated on a lotus cushion with legs crossed and the soles of both feet turned up (*vajrasana*). The garb is the thin monk's garment, worn with the right shoulder bare. The forehead is marked with the *urna*, the head with the *ushnisha*, and the hair is in tight curls twisted to the right. The *mudras*, however, differ. In the first four rows, the Buddhas on the east side exhibit the *bhumisparśa mudra* with the fingers of the right hand pointing downward toward the earth; on the south side there is the *varada mudra* with the palm of the right hand turned up in the gift-bestowing gesture (Fig. 14.15); on the west side the *dhyana mudra* with both hands open in the lap in the attitude of meditation; and on the north the *abhaya mudra* with the right hand raised, palm forward, in the gesture which signifies "fear not." Above in the fifth row all the Buddhas exhibit the same *mudra*, namely, the *vitarka mudra* with the thumb and first finger of the uplifted right hand held together to form a ring in the gesture of discussion or argumentation. From the directions in which they face and from the *mudras*, these Buddhas may probably be identified as the five *tathagatas* or Dhyani Buddhas, in Java called *jinas,* namely, in the first four rows Akshobhya on the east,

14.15 Tathagata (Dhyani Buddha) in Niche, Borobudur

Ratnasambhava on the south, Amitabha on the west, and Amoghasiddhi on the north, and in the top row on all four sides Vairocana, the central *tathagata*.[37]

Stupas on the Circular Terraces. On above in the perforated *stupas* on the three circular terraces, the seventy-two Buddhas within are also seated in the same *vajrasana* as the Buddhas in the niches below, but here they exhibit the *dharmacakra mudra* with both hands against the chest and thumb and forefinger held together in the pose of the preaching of the Law (Fig. 14.16). If the Buddhas below are correctly identified as the five *tathagatas,* the Buddha represented here in these many figures on the three higher circular terraces is presumably a yet higher being, perhaps identifiable as Vajrasattva, considered a form of the Supreme Buddha.[38]

Finally, on the central summit of the monument is the crowning *stupa* (Fig. 14.17). Whether it also originally contained a Buddha image is uncertain. In 1842 an unfinished Buddha statue, seated and exhibiting the *bhumisparśa mudra*, was found near the *stupa* in debris from early exploratory digging, and was later placed at the foot of the monument.[39] If this statue was originally inside the *stupa*, hidden from sight, it could in some way have stood for the highest, invisible Buddha.[40] The *mudra*, however, is the same as that of Akshobhya *(bhumisparśa mudra)*, and it may be that this was a statue originally intended for one of the niches on the east side of the monument, and not satisfactorily completed.[41] In the latter and perhaps more probable case, we may consider that the crowning *stupa* was always intended to be a purely geometrical form and, as such, a symbol of the Ultimate Reality.

Replica of the Cosmos. The entire great monument of Borobudur may therefore be understood as based on the Buddhist view of the cosmos with its three

14.16 Buddha Image in Dismantled Stupa, Borobudur

14.17 Crowning Stupa, Borobudur

major planes or spheres (*loka* or *dhatu*). The base (the "buried basement") with its pictures of earthly existence and the working out of *karma* in the *samsara* represents the *kamadhatu* or sphere of desire; the four galleries above the base contain all the visible reliefs, picturing the way of salvation, and this corresponds with the *rupadhatu* or sphere of form; and the top levels with Buddhas only glimpsed through the openings in the smaller *stupas* and with the crowning *stupa* a pure symbol, suggest the *arupadhatu,* the sphere of formlessness. From the complete invisibility of the Buddha reality symbolized in the crowning *stupa,* to the partially glimpsed Buddhas in the perforated *stupas,* to the fully visible Buddhas in the lower niches, there is a progressive descent of the Buddha reality to come into the realm of earthly need. Likewise, from the pictured realm of unhappy existence in which *karma* holds sentient beings, the pilgrim who climbs the successively higher terraces moves up in a symbolic way to enlightenment and comes out at last to experience a foretaste of release in the pure space above.

Mataram

In the latter half of the ninth century C.E., the power of the Buddhist Śailendras in Central Java was apparently in decline, and we hear of a Śaivite dynasty whose rulers use the title "king of Mataram."

For attestation of the worship of Śiva here at this time we have three inscriptions, found on the Ratubaka plateau a few miles south of the village of Prambanam, and dated in the Śaka Year 778, equivalent to 856 C.E., each of which begins with praise of Śiva and commemorates the erection of a *linga* of Śiva.[42] Yet another inscription, also dated in 778 Śaka (856 C.E.), gives a description in poetry of the building of a great Śiva temple, which was evidently a whole complex of structures. As here described, the "heart" of the foundation, presumably meaning its central temples, had its own wall; at the gateways were two small temple buildings and, apparently outside the wall and presumably enclosed within yet another wall, were many small buildings, all of equal height, to be used as hermitages. The text also mentions "innumerable immovable women," and these were presumably either statues or reliefs, or both. The whole was indeed "a beautiful dwelling for the god," and finally, "after the Śiva sanctuary had been completed in its divine splendor, the [course of the] river was changed so that it rippled along the grounds."[43]

As for the name Mataram—evidently a geographical name for the southern part of Central Java—it occurs for the first time in inscriptions of the reign of a king named Balitung between 899 and 910 C.E. In an inscription of 907 C.E., however, a dynastic list of Mataram kings is given with Sanjaya at its head, so Sanjaya was represented as the first of the line in which the later kings of Mataram were his successors and perhaps descendants.[44] Around 913 C.E. Balitung was succeeded by Daksha, a personage who appears already under Balitung in the role of a high official. A further indication of the relationship of these kings to Sanjaya is seen in the fact that this Daksha introduced an Era of Sanjaya reckoned from 717 C.E., and this era appears in inscriptions of Daksha in 910 (before his accession to rule) and again in 913 C.E.[45]

Candi Lara Jonggrang. The rule of Balitung and Daksha was evidently centered in the vicinity of the present Yogyakarta and Prambanam, and the great Hindu complex commonly itself known as Prambanam from the nearby village has usually been thought to have been founded by one or the other of these two relatively well-known kings, and thus to be datable at the beginning of the tenth century C.E. The description of a great Śiva temple in the above-cited inscription of 856 C.E., however, corresponds in considerable degree with the actual existing structures at Prambanam (central temples enclosed by a wall; two small temples at the gateways; many small buildings between the first wall and a second wall), and this makes it possible to think that this is the temple that is described and that it may therefore be dated at that time just after the middle of the ninth century C.E.

The more specific name of the temple complex is Candi Lara Jonggrang.[46] According to Javanese legend there was a king named Ratubaka whose residence was in the so-called Kraton (*kraton* is the term for a complex of buildings and squares used by Javanese princes as their palaces) of Ratubaka, the ruins of which are on the Ratubaka plateau south of Prambanam. The daughter of this king was Lara Jonggrang (slender maiden) and she, in order to avoid marriage with a youth whom she dared not reject outright, promised to accept him if he could accomplish the presumably impossible task of building a temple with a thousand statues in a single night. When, by magic, he was about to succeed and lacked only the making of one last statue, she deceived him into thinking that the sun was about to rise and mark his failure. When the youth learned of the deception he used his magic power to turn the princess into stone, and thus her figure completed the thousand and is still in the temple which bears her name.

In the Lara Jonggrang complex the main temples were enclosed within three square walls with entrances in the four sides oriented to the cardinal points. The courses of these walls measure on a side respectively 1,280, 728, and 361 feet (390, 222, and 110 m.). In the central courtyard three large temples stand in a row and face to the east. The main temple in the center is dedicated to Śiva, the temple beside it to the north to Vishnu, and the one to the south to Brahma. In front of each temple to the east is a shrine, the one in the center for Nandi, Śiva's bull (whose statue is still in place), and the other two perhaps for minor forms of Śiva. Also within the courtyard are two small temples known as court temples, and they stand beside the north and south gateways in the enclosing wall.

Between the innermost and the second enclosure walls there were no less than 224 minor temples, arranged in four tiers. Between the second and the outermost enclosure walls no structures remain, and such as were once there were perhaps of perishable material. The outermost wall was oriented at an angle to the two inner walls, and may have been related to the course of the adjacent river.

All of the temples, regardless of size, were built on essentially the same plan, with a high square base, a platform supporting a two-story sanctuary, and a tower rising in successive recessed stories, decorated with *stupas,* and with a large *stupa* on the top. The central and largest temple, dedicated to Śiva, stands on a base about 98 feet (30 m.) square, and rises to a height of 154 feet (47 m.) (Fig. 14.18). The two so-called court temples were about 52 feet (16 m.) high, and the 224 minor temples about 46 feet (14 m.) high.

In the Śiva temple the central sanctuary chamber is entered through a small vestibule on the east, and is surrounded by three small cells on the other three sides. In the central chamber is a standing image of Śiva, 10 feet (3 m.) in height (Fig. 14.19). He is shown with four arms. The upper back hands hold two of his attributes, a rosary in his right hand and a fly whisk in his left hand. The right forehand is held in front of his chest, the left holds a round object. There is a skull in his headdress, and a snake provides a caste cord around his body.

In the cell adjoining the central chamber on the north is the image of Durga, the wife of Śiva and the vanquisher of the demon Mahishasura (Fig. 14.20). She is

14.18 Tower of the Śiva Temple, Candi Lara Jonggrang, Prambanam

14.19 Image of Śiva in the Central Chamber of the Śiva Temple, Candi Lara Jonggrang, Prambanam

14.20 Image of Durga in the North Cell of the Śiva Temple, Candi Lara Jonggrang, Prambanam

shown with eight arms, and holds the weapons with which she fought the demon. She stands upon a buffalo, which was the disguise that the demon adopted in the climax of the struggle, and in this moment she has just slain the buffalo and grasps the demon by the hair as he escapes from the buffalo's body. This is the image which is popularly identified as Lara Jonggrang herself.

In the cell adjacent to the central chamber to the west is the image of Ganeśa, son of Śiva and Durga (or Parvati). In the cell to the south is the figure of a *rishi*, and this is probably Agastya. Agastya is known in the Vedas, Epics, and Puranas as a great sage who taught science and literature, and in Java he was worshiped as a divine being and a manifestation of Śiva in the latter's character as a *guru*.[47]

In the decoration of the terrace walls of the Lara Jonggrang temples there is a characteristic combination of elements known as the Prambanam motif. As seen on the Brahma temple, for example, there is a lion in a niche, with a tree of heaven on either side (Fig. 14.21). The ornamentation at the top of the niche is derived from a *kala* head, and there are *makaras* on either side and also at the bottom of the posts. Beside the trees of heaven in this case are monkeys below and birds above. Elsewhere a tree of heaven is flanked by geese, hares, rams, deer, or peacocks.

14.21 Characteristic Prambanam Motif with Lion and Trees of Heaven on the Terrace of the Brahma Temple, Candi Lara Jonggrang, Prambanam

Ramayana Reliefs. On the inside of the balustrade of the Śiva temple and running around the temple clockwise (i.e., in the proper direction of circumambulation) is a series of reliefs with scenes from the story of Rama *(Ramayana),* and this series was probably continued on the temple of Brahma, while the corresponding reliefs found on the temple of Vishnu depict scenes from the youth of Krishna. In the Rama series of the Śiva temple we see, for example, the following:[48]

In Scene Vd (the central stone in Fig. 14.22) a prince, assisted by a kneeling man and in the presence of two princesses, is holding a very heavy bow and shooting an arrow in an upward direction. This is Rama, assisted by Lakshmana, shooting the wonderful bow of Śiva which belonged to King Janaka of Mithila, by which exploit Rama won the hand of Janaka's lovely daughter Sita. Sita is probably the foremost of the two women in the scene, accompanied by a companion. In the preceding scene which extends off to the left (Va–c) Rama is agreeing with King Janaka on the test, and at the right (Ve) there is the figure of one more feminine companion of Sita.

In Scene XXd–e (Fig. 14.23) we see Sita in her abduction in Lanka. She is still dressed as a princess, and is seated and leaning on a cushion, in front of an open house. Beside her and in the house are flowers, and behind her is a curly-haired feminine servant. The occasion is the coming of Hanuman to make a secret visit to her, and Sita is listening intently to him, the arrival of Hanuman being depicted in Scenes XXa–c to the left of the present scene.

In Scene XXIIa–b (Fig. 14.24) Hanuman has returned from Lanka and is reporting on his mission to Rama. The scene is in a forest with trees overhead, and Rama is seated cross-legged and leaning against a cushion in front of a cave. Hanuman holds a small object in his left hand, and this is perhaps a jewel brought as a token from Sita. In a continuation of the scene to the right (XXIIc–d) Lakshmana, Rama's brother, and Sugriva, the king of the monkey people, are also listening to the report.

14.22 Rama shoots the Bow of Śiva and wins the Hand of Sita, Śiva Temple Relief, Candi Lara Jonggrang, Prambanam

14.23 Sita in Lanka, Śiva Temple Relief, Candi Lara Jonggrang, Prambanam

14.24 Hanuman reports to Rama on His Mission in Lanka, Śiva Temple Relief, Candi Lara Jonggrang, Prambanam

14.25 The Monkey Army builds the Bridge to Lanka, Śiva Temple Relief, Candi Lara Jonggrang, Prambanam

14.26 Arrival of Rama, Lakshmana, Sugriva, and the Monkey Army on Lanka, Śiva Temple Relief, Candi Lara Jonggrang, Prambanam

In Scene XXIVb–c (Fig. 14.25) Rama is standing at the left, holding his bow at his right side, Sugriva is beside him, holding his club over his right shoulder, and in front of them are seven of the monkey people, who are carrying large stones and casting them into the sea to build the bridge to Lanka. In the continuation of the scene to the right (XXIVd–e) fish and sea monsters endeavor to obstruct the building of the bridge.

In the further continuation of the scene to the right (XXIVf–h) (Fig. 14.26) we see the arrival of Rama on Lanka. At the left we are still on the edge of the sea, where snakes and a large-beaked bird are seen. Four of the monkey people come next, one especially prominent as he holds a large club and leads a tame mongoose on a leash. Then we see Rama and Lakshmana, both with bows in hand, and Sugriva with a curved sword over his shoulder. In front, three more of the monkey army, armed with clubs and swords, press forward to the fray. This scene is the last of the Ramayana relief series of the Śiva temple. Other pieces found scattered in various places, showing battle and the defeat of Ravana, the many-headed abductor of Sita, probably belonged to the continuation and conclusion of the series on the temple of Brahma.

East Java

In 929 C.E. a king named Sindok (probably the grandson of Daksha) moved his capital to East Java, where his inscriptions, dating from 929 to 948 C.E., are found in the upper Brantas River valley. For the next 500 years East Java was the center of Hindu-Javanese culture on the island.

Those who followed Sindok in rule in East Java were his daughter Queen Śri Iśanatunggavijaya, her son King Makutavamśavardhana, and King Dharmavamśa who was a son or son-in-law of Makutavamśavardhana. Makutavamśavardhana also had a daughter (thus a great-granddaughter of Sindok) who was named Mahendradatta and known too as Gunapriyadharmapatni. Mahendradatta married Udayana (Dharmodayanavarmadeva) the king of Bali, and they ruled on Bali on behalf of Dharmavamśa. The son of Udayana and Mahendradatta was Airlanga, who was born in Bali around 1001 (a date also given as 991) C.E. In his youth Airlanga was invited to come to East Java for betrothal with one of the daughters of Dharmavamśa, and his own name is probably to be understood as meaning "he who crossed the water" (i.e., the strait between Java and Bali).

According to a Javanese inscription a great calamity overwhelmed Java in 1016 (a date also given as 1006) C.E., the hitherto flourishing capital was reduced to ashes, and the great king Dharmavamśa met his end. The nature of the calamity is not clear, but invasion from Śrivijaya and internal revolt may both have been involved. Upon the death of King Dharmavamśa who was both his uncle and his father-in-law, Airlanga, then sixteen years old, fled to the forest and lived for four years among religious hermits on Mount Vanagiri far to the west. In 1019 the loyal followers of Dharmavamśa crowned Airlanga as the successor of Dharmavamśa and, in a series of campaigns, Airlanga recovered the kingdom. Thereafter, Airlanga made his capital at Kahuripan, an unidentified site in East Java, and ruled from 1019 to 1042 C.E. From 1042 on he probably entered the religious life, but still retained power and, before he died in 1049, he divided the kingdom into two parts under his own two sons.[49]

Candi Belahan. A combined sanctuary and bathing place known as Candi Belahan on the eastern slope of Mount Penanggungan is believed to have been constructed as the burial monument of King Airlanga. This is a rectangular basin built of brick, with statues of reddish tufa. On the back wall of the basin are three niches. The central niche once contained a statue of Vishnu on Garuda; the niches on either side still contain statues of Lakshmi and Śri (originally two names for the one goddess of fertility and wealth, here considered as two separate aspects of the one). A large stone slab carries the date of 971 Śaka, i.e., 1049 C.E., and the reference is presumably to that year as the date of the death of Airlanga.

The images are therefore probably to be understood as representations of Airlanga and his two wives in the guise of the divine figures, meaning that Airlanga was regarded as an incarnation of Vishnu, and the wives as incarnations of the consorts of Vishnu. In the case of the two goddesses, the water of the nearby spring was allowed to spout from the breasts of the image in the northern niche, and to flow from a jug and a flower in the hands of the image in the southern niche, thus presumably meaning that the water was thereby filled with auspicious powers. As for the central image of Vishnu/Airlanga in which the god/king is seated on Garuda, it is now in the Municipal Museum, Modjokerto (Fig. 14.27). Here Garuda is shown as a large and ferocious anthropomorphic bird, which is fighting its natural enemies, the snakes, and holding some of them in its claws; thus in this case Garuda may probably be understood as representing the prime minister of the king. The figure of Vishnu/Airlanga himself is shown with four arms. The front hands are in the *dhyana mudra,* the back right hand holds on an extended forefinger a flaming discus *(cakra)* and the back left hand holds a winged conch.[50]

Kadiri

The two states into which, before his death in 1049 C.E., Airlanga divided his kingdom, were Janggala east of the Brantas River, with its capital at Airlanga's

14.27 Portrait Statue of Airlanga as Vishnu on Garuda, from Belahan, in the Municipal Museum, Modjokerto, Java. Photograph from A. J. Bernet Kempers, *Ancient Indonesian Art* (Amsterdam: C.P.J. van der Peet, 1959), Pl. 202, by permission of C.P.J. van der Peet.

former capital of Kahuripan, and Panjalu to the west, with its capital at Daha. The latter was the more important of the two states (actually soon reabsorbing its neighbor), and is better known by the name Kadiri, while its capital, Daha, is the present-day Kediri. The last king of the kingdom of Kadiri was Kritajaya (also known as Śringa), from whom there are inscriptions dated from 1194 to 1205 C.E., and whose reign came to an end in 1222.

Singhasari

At Tumapel in Janggala a man of peasant background named Angrok, who represented himself as a son of Śiva Girindra (Śiva king of the mountain, reminiscent of the title of the Śailendras), assassinated the governor, married the governor's wife Dedes, and proclaimed himself king under the name of Rajasa. He overthrew Kritajaya and incorporated Kadiri in the kingdom of Tumapel, over which he ruled from 1222 to 1227 C.E. His capital was at Kutaraja (in the Malang highlands east of the Brantas River), and this capital was later called Singhasari, the name by which the entire kingdom is usually known. The succeeding kings of Singhasari were Anushapati (1227–1248), Vishnuvardhana (1248–1268), and Kritanagara (1268–1292). Of these kings, Kritanagara in particular accomplished a considerable if in part only temporary expansion of Javanese power, establishing sway as far as the southern part of the Malay Peninsula, and in 1284 bringing back the king of Bali as a captive.

Candi Jago. Upon his decease Vishnuvardhana was deified in the form of Śiva at Waleri (near Blitar, in the curve of the Brantas River) and in the form of Amoghapaśa (a form of the *bodhisattva* Avalokiteśvara, thus showing the continued coexistence of Hindu and Buddhist ideas) at Jajaghu, the modern Jago (southeast of Singhasari). Candi Jago marks the latter site, although it is not certain if the present building is from the time of Vishnuvardhana or later. At any rate the *candi* is in the form of a Buddhist temple, decorated with bas-reliefs illustrating episodes from various Indo-Javanese literary works, including the story of Krishna called the Krishnayana.[51]

Candi Singhasari. When Kritanagara died, he was given more than one burial temple, and these probably include both Candi Singhasari and Candi Jawi. Candi Singhasari is one of several temples at Singhasari and the vicinity.[52] In the central room of Candi Singhasari a *yoni* pedestal was intended to support a *linga* representing Śiva. In surrounding cells were images of the companions of Śiva, Ganeśa (east), Guru Agastya (south), Durga (north), and in niches on either side of the entrance images of two forms of Śiva, namely, Nandiśvara and Mahakala. The statue of Guru Agastya has been restored from fragments and replaced in the southern cell; the other statues are in the National Museum of Ethnology (Rijksmuseum voor Volkenkunde) in Leiden.

A statue of Śiva himself was found in one of the temples in the neighborhood of Singhasari, and is now in the Leiden Museum (Fig. 14.28). The god is portrayed in his terrible form as Bhairava, and an inscription on the backing of the statue gives the name Cakracakra, evidently here the designation of Śiva in this form. He is seated on a dog or jackal, and rests his feet on a base ringed with human skulls. He is naked except for ornaments, most of which are themselves adorned with human heads and skulls. His four hands hold a knife, a trident, a hand-drum, and a skull bowl.[53]

Also found at Singhasari and now in the Leiden Museum is a statue of Prajnaparamita, the Buddhist goddess of transcendent wisdom (Fig. 14.29), and this is thought to have been a portrait statue of Dedesa, the consort of Rajasa, the founder of the dynasty of Singhasari. The two-armed figure is seated, cross-legged, on a lotus throne, with the hands in the position of preaching the Buddhist law (*dharmacakra mudra*). The symbol of the goddess, a book resting on a lotus, is on her left shoulder.[54]

Candi Jawi. Candi Jawi is far north of Singhasari, at the foot of Mount Welirang and facing Mount Penanggungan. It is a temple which combines Hindu and Buddhist characteristics, with a small *stupa* on top and Śaivite statues within. The base of the *candi* is decorated with reliefs, which show musicians blowing double trumpets, a long procession with four persons singled out as of special importance by the parasols carried over their heads, and so forth.[55]

14.28 Statue of Cakracakra (Śiva in the form of Bhairava), from a Temple at Singhasari. Photograph from the Rijksmuseum voor Volkenkunde, Leiden.

14.29 Statue of Prajnaparamita from Singhasari. Photograph from the Rijksmuseum voor Volkenkunde, Leiden.

Majapahit

The kingdom of Singhasari was in turn replaced by the kingdom of Majapahit (in the lower valley of the Brantas River) as the last of the Hindu-Javanese kingdoms. The founder of the kingdom of Majapahit was Raden Vijaya, who reigned under the name of Kritarajasa Jayavardhana (1293–1309 C.E.). He was the great-grandson of Rajasa, the founder of the dynasty of Singhasari, and the four daughters of Kritanagara, the last king of that dynasty, were his wives.

A Śaivite funerary temple was built for Kritarajasa at Simping (the present Sumberjati south of Blitar), and a portrait statue of the king was found there and is in the Museum of Indonesian Culture in Jakarta (Fig. 14.30). The king is shown as a four-armed god, with attributes of both Śiva and Vishnu. The front right hand holds a rosary, a usual attribute of Śiva; the other hands hold attributes usually connected with Vishnu—a conch, a wheel resting horizontally on the index finger of the left back hand and supporting flames, and a club on which the left front hand rests. In the case of the conch supported by the index finger of the back right hand, a living snail is crawling out of the shell, evidently a symbol of the soul being freed from the confines of the material body. Two goddesses are on either side of the king, and may be Lakshmi and Śri as the consorts of Vishnu, and at the same time may represent two queens of Kritarajasa.[56]

Kritarajasa was succeeded by his son Jayanagara (1309–1328 C.E.) but, when the latter died leaving no son to take his place, a regency ensued. The first wife of Kritarajasa was Rajapatni Gayatri, one of the daughters of Kritanagara, and would have been entitled to reign, but had already become a Buddhist nun; therefore, her daughter Tribhuvana became queen regent on behalf of her mother. Tribhuvana married a noble, and their son, Hayam Wuruk, became king at the death of his grandmother in 1350 and reigned (1350–1389) under the name Rajasanagara, while Tribhuvana herself died in 1372.

A general named Gajah Mada was associated with King Jayanagara and continued as general and prime minister (1331–1364 C.E.) during the reign of Tribhuvana and part of the reign of Rajasanagara. Largely due to his efforts, the supremacy of Majapahit was extended throughout most of what is now Indonesia, including Bali, some Śrivijaya territories in Sumatra, and much of the Malay Peninsula.

A portrait statue from Candi Rimbi in the Jakarta Museum (Fig. 14.31) is probably a representation of Tribhuvana in the guise of Parvati. The standing figure is four-armed, and the upper back hands hold a rosary and a fly whisk, usual attributes of Parvati. On either side are lotus plants arising out of vases, probably as symbols of new life arising out of death.[57]

Candi Panataran. Candi Panataran is the largest complex of temples in East Java, and in the main dates from the fourteenth century and the height of the Majapahit period. The site (earlier known as Palah) is north of Blitar on the southwestern slope of Mount Kelut at a height of about 1,500 feet (450 m.) above sea level, and the complex was consecrated to Śiva as the lord of the mountain. In general the layout of Candi Panataran is like that of Balinese temples. There are three courtyards in succession from west to east, and the main temple is at the east nearest the mountain. A very large lintel which probably comes from the main temple bears a date equivalent to 1323 C.E. (in the reign of Jayanagara) and the pedestals of the guardians at the steps of the terrace of the same temple are dated in the equivalent of 1347 C.E. (in the regency period). The so-called "dated temple"

14.30 Portrait Statue of King Kritarajasa of Majapahit, in the Museum of Indonesian Culture, Jakarta. Photograph from A. J. Bernet Kempers, *Ancient Indonesian Art* (Amsterdam: C.P.J. van der Peet, 1959), Pl. 247, by permission of C.P.J. van der Peet.

14.31 Portrait Statue of Queen Regent Tribhuvana of Majapahit, in the Museum of Indonesian Culture, Jakarta. Photograph from A.J. Bernet Kempers, *Ancient Indonesian Art* (Amsterdam: C.P.J. van der Peet, 1959), Pl. 248, by permission of C.P.J. van der Peet.

has a date equivalent to 1369 C.E. over the entrance, and the terrace in front of it bears a date corresponding to 1375 C.E. (both of these dates in the reign of Rajasanagara).

The main temple is decorated with bas-reliefs representing scenes of the *Ramayana* and the *Krishnayana*. The dated terrace has scenes from the Javanese story of two ascetics, the omnivorous Bubukshah and his vegetarian brother Gagang Aking, in the outcome of which the superiority of the "left" path of Bubukshah over the "right" path of Gagang Aking is demonstrated. The "dated temple" is a tall building, its roof decorated with animal figures. Another temple known as the *naga* temple is encircled by enormous snakes.[58]

The long reign of Rajasanagara marked the height of the empire of Majapahit, and decline followed, due both to internal strife and pressure from outside. In particular, Islam gradually penetrated Java, and by around 1520 C.E. the kingdom of Majapahit reached its end. While this meant the substantial end on Java of Indo-Javanese literature and religion, in the meantime and afterward many of the Javanese aristocracy and priesthood, and many artists and artisans, moved to Bali, and much of Indo-Javanese culture and religion was preserved there.[59]

BALI

History

As on Java, so also on Bali, the oldest dated records are *praśasti*, i.e., royal decrees or laudatory poems. The first text, preserved in a later copy, bears a date in the year 804 of the Śaka Era, i.e., 882 C.E. and, like others from within the next one hundred years, is written in Old Balinese.[60] The oldest actual original edict is on a bronze plate which is preserved in the Kehen temple in Bangli, and was written between 833 and 836 of the Śaka Era, i.e., between 911 and 914 C.E.[61] This edict deals with the founding of a Hindu monastery connected with a sanctuary called Hyang Karimama in the territory of a village named Simpat Bunut, probably the present Sidem Bunut near Bangli. The first king's name to be found is that of Kesarivarmadeva (Kesari Warmadewa), who is mentioned in an inscription of 836 Śaka or 914 C.E. (previously read as 839 Śaka/917 C.E.) on a round stone pillar in Belanjong near Sanur on the southern coast of Bali.[62] The immediate successor, apparently, of Kesarivarmadeva was Ugrasena, and he is known from texts extending from 837 to 864 of the Śaka Era, i.e., from 915 to 942 C.E. Then follow, between 955 and 975 C.E., several kings, all of whom, like Kesarivarmadeva, have names ending in -*varmadeva*, evidence pointing to a Varmadeva (Warwadewa) dynasty founded by Kesarivarmadeva, and ruling in Bali in this period.[63]

In these earliest records on Bali it appears that the island was still independent of Java. If the Javanese king Sanjaya did come there in the eighth century C.E. it would seem that he left no lasting influence. In religion the texts indicate that Śaivite Hinduism and Buddhism were both practiced at the same time, and these religions were presumably brought to Bali directly by priests and monks from India. Such teachers appear in some of the records as advisers to the king, and thus it is probable that Hinduism and Buddhism were at the time chiefly influential in court circles. At the same time Old Balinese ideas no doubt persisted, particularly in the villages, and thus it was eventually an amalgam of Indian and Old Balinese elements which emerged in an Indo-Balinese culture.[64]

From 911 to 933 Śaka or 989 to 1011 C.E. the royal inscriptions are in the names of King Udayana (Dharmodayanavarmadeva) and Queen Mahendradatta (Gunapriyadharmapatni), the Balinese/Javanese royal couple whom we have already seen as ruling Bali at this time in association with King Dharmavamśa of East Java. Given these close relationships, Javanese influence was undoubtedly now felt strongly on Bali. In fact the first edict found in Bali that is written in Old Javanese is a text from Buwahan on Lake Batur, issued by King Udayana and his queen and dated in 916 Śaka (994 C.E.), and from this time on the royal decrees continue to be written in Old Javanese.[65]

The disaster which befell Java in 1016 C.E. evidently allowed Bali to at least partially or temporarily regain its independence, but with Airlanga (son of Udayana and Mahendradatta) afterward ruling in Java, it was probably members of his family who held the throne in Bali. Of these the best known is Anak Wungśu (younger son), probably the younger brother of Airlanga, from whom we have inscriptions dating from 971 to 999 Śaka (1049 to 1077 C.E.).[66]

Bali was again subdued by Java, but only briefly, when King Kritanagara (1268–1292 C.E.) of the Singhasari dynasty sent a military expedition to the island and took captive the king of Bali. Independence was regained under the Pejeng dynasty in South Bali. The last king of this dynasty was the legendary Dalem Bedaulu (*beda-ulu*, "he who changed heads," so named because in an accident in his practice of magic he came to have the head of a pig). The center of rule in these times was in what is now the district of Gianyar, where the villages of Pejeng and Bedulu preserve the ancient names.

In 1343 C.E. Bedaulu was confronted and conquered by Gajah Mada, the Javanese minister and general of Majapahit, and thus Bali became a part of the Majapahit empire. Gajah Mada appointed a *brahmana* from Kediri named Arya Kapakisan as king of Bali, with the title of Deva Agung. He and his first two successors made their residence at Samprangan (now Samplangan) near Gianyar and, according to the traditional account of the events, ruled in the period after 1343 and before 1444. Then, sometime around 1450, the next ruler, I Deva Ketut Tegal Besung, moved the capital to Gelgel (somewhat farther east), where this dynasty continued to rule for nearly two centuries. In 1633 the then Deva Agung of Gelgel moved his residence to Klungkung (not far to the north) and there became the Raja of Klungkung, which is still deemed the highest position among the ruling class in Bali, the Satrias.

When, around 1520 C.E., the Majapahit empire reached its end on Java, many more Javanese migrated to Bali, and thus the history of Bali subsequent to that time was in effect a continuation of the history of Majapahit. In fact, until now the majority of the Balinese call themselves Wong Majapahit, or people of Majapahit, while only some hill tribes are Bali Aga or indigenous people of Bali. Since Islam did not cross the strait from Java to Bali, Old Balinese, Indo-Balinese, and Hindu-Javanese elements continued to mingle to form the distinctive culture of the island, which survives until today.[67]

Culture and Religion

Classes. In the social order of Bali the *varnas* of Hinduism persist to the extent that three upper classes (*trivamsa*, Balinese *triwangsa*) are recognized, namely, the priests *(brahmanas)*, the nobility *(kshatriyas, satrias)*, and the warriors *(vaisyas, wesyas)*, while the majority of the population constitute the working class, in caste terminology *śudras*, but preferably known by such designations as *wong kesamen* (the ones of common stock) or *wong jaba* (the ones outside the *triwangsa*).⁶⁸

The modern indigenous name of the religion of Bali is Agama Tirtha, meaning "the religious tradition of the Holy Water," or Agama Hindu-Bali, signifying that this tradition is the Balinese form of Hinduism.⁶⁹

Priests. Within the priestly class more than a half dozen kinds of Balinese priests may be distinguished. Those of highest rank, who officiate on great occasions, are known by the term *padanda*, which is the word for "foot," and reflects the idea of the foot as the symbol of an elevated person. The priests of this status are presently only a few hundred in number. Of these the majority are Śaivite priests *(padanda Śaiva)*, the minority are Buddhist priests *(padanda Bauddha)*, but both claim *brahmanical* descent, and usually consider that Śiva is another name for Buddha and vice versa. The temple or village priest is designated by the term *pamanku*, and these are far more numerous, probably as many as several thousand. The exorcist priest is called by the name *senguhu*, which may derive from the *śankha*, the conch shell which is blown during a ritual of exorcism. These priests may also claim the title of an ancient Indian seer *(rishi)*, and be called *reshi bhujanga* or *reshi Vaishnava* (reflecting association with Vaishnavism as well as Śaivism). The puppeteer of the shadow play *(wayang)* is a *dalang*, and the priestly performer of ritual *wayang* performances is an *amangku dalang*. The priest called *balian* is usually consulted in the home, often about medical problems, and is frequently female as well as male. The priest called *dukuh* was, according to his name, at least formerly even if no longer, a hermit.⁷⁰

Stuti and Stava. The ritual texts of both the Śaiva priest and the Bauddha priest are often collectively called by the name *Veda*, but actual Vedic materials are for the most part limited to a few Vedic *mantras*. More numerous and distinctive Balinese texts are the hymns of praise which are called *stutis* and *stavas*. They were originally written on leaves of the *lontar* palm, and are in Sanskrit and, in part, in so-called (Indonesian) Archipelago Sanskrit. In all, they provide Śaiva, Vaishnava, and Bauddha texts.⁷¹

Among these texts one important type is known as the *digbandha* (tying of the regions), in which the deities are located in the various directions of the sky. The most popular kind of *digbandha* contains the names of nine deities *(nava sana)*, these being the eight *lokapalas* (guardians of the regions), together with Śiva, who occupies the place in the center. When aspects of Śiva are added in the nadir and the zenith, the number is increased to eleven. In a shortened version there is mention only of the four main directions and of Śiva. Together with the names and directions of the deities the texts give many other details concerning them, e.g., the names of their spouses and their attributes. The deities are also described as so many jewels of their respective colors, and they possess Holy Water of the same colors.

On the basis of several not wholly consistent Śaivite texts *(Brahma Vishnu Iśvara devam; Iśvara nama purvanam; Purve Iśvara vajrastra; Purve tu Iśvara-deva)* the outline in Table 14.1 has been prepared.⁷²

In place of the guardians of the regions, one Śaivite *stava (OM Ratna-yuvati devi)* names eight goddesses in the eight directions of the sky, each identified with a color and described as standing on the leaves of the cosmic lotus. This provides the scheme in Table 14.2.⁷³

Again, another Śaivite *stava (Bhutashtakam saha yuktam)* places Ravana, the

TABLE 14.1.
ŚIVA AND THE GUARDIANS OF THE REGIONS

Region	Deity	Color	Spouse	Attribute
1. East	Iśvara	White	Uma	Thunderbolt
2. Southeast	Maheśvara	Reddish-brown	Lakshmi	Incense
3. South	Brahma	Red	Sarasvati	Rod
4. Southwest	Rudra	Orange	Śantani	Mace
5. West	Mahadeva	Yellow	Śaci	Noose
6. Northwest	Śankara	Black	Mahadevi	Hook
7. North	Vishnu	Dark blue	Śri	Club
8. Northeast	Śambhu	Light blue	Uma	Trident
9. Center	Śiva	Nine colors		Lotus
10. Nadir	Sada-Śiva (Eternal Śiva)			Disk
11. Zenith	Parama-Śiva (Supreme Śiva)			Trident

TABLE 14.2.
GODDESSES OF THE REGIONS

Region	Goddess	Color
1. East	Ratna-yuvati devi	White
2. Southeast	Yuvati Mahadevi	White
3. South	Ratna-yauvani devi	Red
4. Southwest	Yauvani Mahadevi	Red
5. West	Ratna Śri Lakshmi devi	Yellow
6. Northwest	Śri Lakshmi Mahadevi	Yellow
7. North	Ratna Śyama Mahadevi	Black
8. Northeast	Ratna Śyama Mahadevi (the names in the north and northeast are identical)	Black

king of the demons, in the center of the cosmic compass, and eight of his manifestations or attendants in the eight directions. Ravana himself is characterized by his sword—Ravana of the Sword—and is described as a great deity with ten heads and a thousand arms, horrible, and bearing all kinds of weapons. With the group of his eight accompanying demons the scheme is as in Table 14.3.[74]

A Buddhist *stuti* (*Suryanandana Isvaram*) assigns to the four directions and the center not only the deities of the Śaivite pantheon but also five great seers and the five *tathagatas* (Dhyani Buddhas) as shown in Table 14.4[75]

Śiva. Among the deities named in the *stutis* and *stavas* it is plain that Śiva is the foremost. Thus the deities who reside in the four quarters are all "fiery energies," and Śiva in the center is "fiery energy . . . (equal to) ten million suns" (*Iśvara purvadeśe ca*);[76] while again Śiva is himself the fivefold fire, namely, as the fires in the four main directions and as Surya in the sky *(OM Śivagni panca-grivam)*.[77] Indeed Śiva is everything. As the great Paśupati (lord of beasts) his attributes (thunderbolt, rod, noose, disk or mace, lotus) are located in the five main directions and are identical with the five great Buddhas (Akshobhya, Ratnasambhava, Amitabha,

TABLE 14.3.
DEMONS OF THE REGIONS

Region	Demon
1. East	Cilipilya
2. Southeast	Phalguna
3. South	Krishna-pingala
4. Southwest	Śulini
5. West	Culukundika
6. Northwest	Candra-krita
7. North	Kikini
8. Northeast	Mata-palita
9. Center	Ravana

TABLE 14.4.
ŚAIVITE AND BUDDHIST FIGURES IN THE REGIONS

Region	Deity	Seer	Buddha
1. East	Iśvara, the gladdening Sun	Kuku	Akshobhya
2. South	Narasimha	Kasturi	Ratnasambhava
3. West	Mahadeva, eternal Quietude	Sukha-yajna	Amitabha
4. North	Vishnu	Keśava	Amoghasiddhi
5. Center	Śiva, the Void	Pingala	Vairocana

Amoghasiddi, Vairocana) (*Paśupati vajrayudhaya*).[78] Śiva is Brahma, Vishnu, and all the gods; he is the multitude of beings, including the sacrificer, the teacher, and the pupil; even the demons belong to his hosts; "the world including movable and immovable beings, beginning with Brahma and ending with a tuft of grass, that all is Siva's body" (*Sivah karta Sivo dhata*).[79] To him prayer is made for forgiveness (*Kshamasva mam Mahadeva*):

> Bestow forgiveness upon me, O great god,
> Thou who art the cause of the good of all creatures;
> deliver me from all evils,
> grant protection, O eternal Śiva.
>
> The sin of the body should be forgiven,
> the sin of my speech should be forgiven;
> the sin of the mind should be forgiven,
> this has been caused by negligence, forgive me.[80]

Sarasvati. Among the goddesses named in the foregoing texts, Sarasvati is of special prominence. She is one of the seven sacred rivers (Ganga, Sarasvati, Sindhu, Vipaśa, Kauśiki, Yamuna, Sarayu, Mahanadi), she is the wife of Brahma, sometimes Brahma's daughter. Beautiful and accomplished, wearing a white garment and loving white flowers, she is the goddess of learning, and it is by her grace that one may undertake the study of poetics, grammar, logic, the Veda, the Puranas, the Tantras, and so forth.[81] In this character she may also sometimes be identified with Prajnaparamita, the goddess of "unsurpassable wisdom."[82]

Pitaras. Along with the gods and goddesses, ancestors are also looked upon as deified and thought of as not greatly different from the celestial deities. In the *stutis* and *stavas* they are called the Fathers *(pitaras)*, and are addressed or referred to in many of the hymns. There are three sorts of ancestors—the Father, the Father's Father, and the Father's Grandfather; and likewise the Mother and the preceding generations in her line. These are "those who have reached their goal." From their exalted position they are able to give love to their descendants, to bless them highly, and to give them wisdom. Brahma, Vishnu, and Śiva exist in the shape of the Ancestors. The Ancestors are to be honored with distinctive counterclockwise circumambulations, with water libations, and with special kinds of food.[83]

Sang hyang Widi. Although the names of many deities are invoked in the *stutis* and *stavas,* and Śiva himself is addressed by many names, these several names are widely regarded as indicating only aspects of one and the same divine being. To designate the ultimate divine reality the term *Sang hyang Widi* is used. The words *sang* and *hyang* connote the more-than-human, the holy, the divine, and the word *widi* (from Sanskrit *vidhi*) means law, rule, order, fate. The *Sang hyang Widi* is therefore a more or less abstract and no more than slightly personal divine order, which is the ultimate ground of all phenomena and is above both the gods and the deified ancestors, although it manifests itself in them all.[84]

Cosmic Order. Under the ultimate divine order of the *Sang hyang Widi,* Balinese thought recognizes in the immediate world both a twofold and a threefold division. Expressive of the twofold division, and reflecting the situation of the island, with the sea round about and the mountains in the interior, the word *kaja* means toward the central mountains and upward, and therefore also the propitious and heavenly (since the mountains are the residences of the gods and the divine ancestors), while the word *kelod* means toward the sea and downward, and therefore also the unfavorable and earthly. For most of the island the direction toward the mountains is also the direction toward the east; therefore, east is the *kaja* direction and west is the *kelod* direction. The same antithesis of *kaja* and *kelod* is also seen in day and night, the waxing moon and the waning moon, light and darkness, life and death, the divine and the demonic, and so forth. Yet *kaja* and *kelod* are complementary, and together form a whole.

The threefold division also reflects the situation of the island, where the main inhabited and cultivated countryside lies between the mountains and the sea. So too the life of human beings is in an intermediate sphere between the extremes, between birth and death, between the gods and the demons.

Living in such an ordered universe and occupying such a place between extremes, it is important for human beings to arrange their lives so that they are in harmony with the cosmic order or at least not contrary to it, and to perform such actions as will establish right relations with the beneficent powers and control, at least as far as possible, the maleficent powers.[85]

Temples. Temple arrangements, for example, are in accordance with the foregoing understanding of proper order. In a Balinese compound the *sanggah,* which is the household temple or group of shrines for ancestors and family gods, lies to the *kaja*-east, while the refuse heap is to the *kelod*-west, and the dwelling is between the two. In a village community *(desa)* there are properly three temples *(puras).* The *pura puseh* (navel temple) is normally in the *kaja*-east of the village and if possible on high ground; it is the place where the deified dead and the deified village founder are venerated. The *pura dalem* (netherworld temple) is normally in the *kelod*-west of the village and if possible on ground lower than the village; this is at the burial ground where the not-yet-deified dead are paid homage. The *pura bale* *agung* (temple of the large hall) is normally in the center of the village; it is the sanctuary where *desa* meetings are usually held.

Beyond the household and village temples there are many others, which are located in places of special sanctity or which serve larger worship groups, e.g., temples of various voluntary associations or state temples of districts or of the entire island. The *pura bukit* is a hill temple, the *pura segara* a sea temple, and the *pura penataran* a regional or state sanctuary. In the last category, Pura Besakih is Bali's chief state temple.

In an ordinary village or larger temple, its limits are usually defined by walls and gates. Of the gates there are two types: the unroofed split gate called *candi bentar* (split *candi*), which is usually the first gate; and the roofed gate called *paduraksa*, which is usually the second gate. Within the walls there are usually three parts or courts, and in these there are various *bales* (*bale*, house, shed, pavilion, hall, tower) and other features. In the forecourt (*jaba*), along with other possible buildings, is the *bale kulkul*, the tower housing the split wooden block which serves as a drum or gong and is beaten to signal temple festivals and meetings, to sound alarms, and so forth. In the central court (*jaba tengah*) the main building is the *bale agung* (great house), which is the large assembly hall for meetings. In the inner court (*jeroan*) are chapels and altars for the gods and ancestors, and sheds where offerings are prepared and arranged. The largest structures are the *merus*, which are multiple-roofed pagodas, named for the cosmic Mount Meru, or Mahameru, the mountain of the gods. In its vertical arrangement the *meru* exhibits a threefold division. The base is usually of stone and rests on a serpent and a tortoise, both of which are animals of the nether world. The middle section is a small wooden chamber, which is the place for the gods when they visit this world. The upper roofs, properly uneven in number, are of sugar palm fiber and represent the various levels of heaven. The *padmasana* (lotus seat) is a large open stone seat or altar, which may also be borne by a turtle and a serpent, and it provides a throne for Śiva/Surya upon the descent of the god to earth. Yet other structures are a *bale pemaruman,* a raised platform from which invoked gods may receive the obeisance of their worshipers and enjoy the sacred music and dance which are offered to them; a *bale piasan,* a small wooden house on an elevated stone platform, with a function similar to that of the *bale pemaruman,* but for only one particular deity or one particular divine couple; and an abode behind the *piasan,* either a *pesimpangan* which is a temporary lodging for a visiting deity, or a *pelinggih* which is a permanent lodging for the permanent god of the temple.[86]

Rites and Rituals. The rites and rituals of Balinese religion, and the festivals with which many of them are associated, are also set within the framework of the understanding of the cosmic order, and are directed both "upward" (*kaja*) and "downward" (*kelod*) according as they are intended to establish contact with the powers of the upper world, or to placate or deter the forces of the nether world. In the former case they are describable as worship, and in the latter as exorcism. The spiritual powers are not usually represented visually, but are believed to come invisibly during the performance of the rituals, and invisibly to partake of offerings which may be presented to them. In the case of food offerings, what is presented to the gods and deified ancestors may be taken back and eaten afterward by the person making the offering, but what is presented to the demons may not be so taken back.

A frequent and important function of a ritual ceremony is also the preparation of Holy Water. After the divine power has been brought down into this water, it may be sprinkled on a living worshiper, or poured on a dead body about to be cremated to give continuation of life and victory over death. It is because of the prominence of this element that Balinese religion is called Agama Tirtha, the religion of Holy Water.

As to the times when they are performed, ceremonies and the festivals to which they may belong take place variously from daily to annually. Two calendars are in use—the Hindu-Balinese calendar of twelve months running from new moon to new moon, and the Javanese-Balinese calendar of thirty seven-day weeks. One important festival *(Nyepi)* is presently celebrated according to the Hindu-Balinese year, while most of the others follow the Javanese-Balinese calendar.[87]

As to the rituals and their texts, there are many, and they are often associated with the distinctive practices of the various kinds of priests, the Śaiva priest *(padanda Śaiva)*, the Buddhist priest *(padanda Bauddha)*, the village or temple priest *(pamanku)*, the exorcist priest *(senguhu, reshi bhujanga)*, and so forth.

Suryasevana. The *Suryasevana* (adoration of the sun) is a devotional rite performed by a Śaiva priest *(padanda Śaiva)* each day in his household temple, and also on other special occasions.[88] As the name indicates, the ritual is directed toward Śiva/Surya (the sun), who is also known as Batara Guru (literally "god teacher" or "god father," as *guru* can have either meaning in Balinese). The central act of the ceremony is the preparation of Holy Water, and the climactic event is the descent of the sun god into the priest and the water.

In the conduct of this ritual, the priest comes to an open square pavilion, and changes his garb to two pieces of freshly washed white cloth. Then he sits down facing the west, washes his feet and hands and rinses his mouth, and after that turns to the east and to the trays on which are his cult objects (flowers, rice, frankincense, lamp, bell, brazier, water vessels). When he has purified himself further with flowers, he cleanses the vessel destined for the Holy Water, and the tripod which supports it, over the brazier with burning incense and the lighted lamp which represents the fire of Śiva. To the accompaniment of *mantras* and *mudras* he pours clean water into the vessel, and invites the eight goddesses of the eight directions (Table 14.2) to sit down on the brim of the vessel. After strengthening his own internal powers by breath control and by uttering many further formulas and invocations, he causes his soul to leave his body, as he believes, and he invites the Śiva-soul (Śivatma) to descend into himself and into the water. In honor of Śiva and of what is now the Holy Water, several litanies follow, and it is declared that the Holy Water is *amrita*, the "immortal" nectar, which gives long life and the preparation of which is victory over death. This is the end of the preparation of the Holy Water and of the worship of the sun, and the priest sprinkles himself with the water and throws some of it to the east for Śiva. If the aim of the ritual is a ceremony of expiation, or the worship of the Śiva *linga*, the relevant procedures for those ends are followed next. Then, with many more ritual acts and formulas, the Śiva-soul, the divine guest, the preparer of the Holy Water, is provided with a dignified return to his celestial abode. Finally the priest praises Surya, the sun, in a long hymn. The ritual over, the priest, no longer the receptacle of the Śiva-soul but again a private person, takes the first sip of the newly prepared Holy Water.

Kusuma Dewa. Once a year (either the twelve-month Hindu-Balinese year, or the 210-day Javanese-Balinese year) a temple celebrates its anniversary with a festival called *odalan*, which is conducted by the temple priest *(pamanku)*. Although there are many local variations in these festivals, a sort of skeleton form is observable which is common to most of them.[89] There are also various texts of the ritual. Some of the best known of these are the *Gaglaran Pamanku* (manual of the temple priest) and the *Kusuma Dewa* (god of flowers), and in these and others the more or less standard words of the ritual can be found.[90]

After various preparations and purifications, the ringing of the priest's bell signals a request to the gods to descend, and the priest addresses the high-exalted deities and says: "Thy servant begs for a favor that all the gods may descend. . . ." Upon their descent, the gods enter invisibly into wooden representations of themselves, and are carried out to a place for bathing, then upon being brought back to the temple are welcomed by a dance of reception. Thereafter the most essential elements of the proceedings are the bringing of offerings *(mebanten)*, including food for the gods and also for the demons who come too, and the sacrament of homage *(mebakti)*, in which the worshipers pay reverence to the gods, and themselves receive Holy Water. In all, the festival lasts for several days and nights and finally, after the gods have been regaled with food and drink, song and instrumental music, dance and dramatic performances,[91] they are invited to take their departure in peace and retire to their own Great Mountain (Gunung Agung).

Purva Bhumi Kamulan. An annual ceremony of purification for the whole island is called *Nyepi* (keeping of silence), and falls at the beginning of the Hindu-Balinese year. At this time the villagers stop their work and stay in their homes, while the *senguhu* or exorcist priests perform their nether-worldly rites at the crossroads, where they call upon the evil spirits to assemble, so that these spirits may be propitiated and persuaded to go on their way without doing harm. A litany which is used for this purpose by the *reshi bhujanga* is called *Purva Bhumi Kamulan*. It amounts to an account of cosmogony and creation, and begins with the coming forth of the exalted goddess Uma from the supreme god, Batara Guru. Further emanations lead to the birth of a great lotus blossom, from which the sun, moon, planets, and stars come forth and the three worlds come to be. In the middle world people evidently become evil, for Batara Guru becomes the fearsome god Kala, and Uma becomes the fearsome goddess Durga, and they together with their minions, who are many demons and fiends, begin to devour humankind. Then Iśvara, Brahma, and Vishnu are created, become respectively a *reshi*, a *brahmana*, and a *bhujanga*, and come down to earth where they undertake to remake humankind. So people are freed from their evil, worship and offerings to the gods are established, Kala and Durga resume their beneficent forms as Guru and Uma, and a covenant is made to the effect that humankind shall no longer be accursed.[92]

Rangda and Barong. In spite of the hopeful conclusion of the *Purva Bhumi Kamulan*, it is still believed that there are many supernatural beings whose activities range from the mischievous to the deadly. There are many demons (*kalas* and *butas*) and they, perhaps most characteristically, follow the gods about and would try to consume first the offerings prepared for the gods, if it were not that offerings were set out for them too. There are also witchlike spirits *(lejaks)*, and they are uncanny, devouring, and deathly.

In the *Purva Bhumi Kamulan*, Kala (originally the form of Śiva as the destroyer of the universe) and Durga (originally a form of Kali, the goddess of terror) are the leaders of the demons and fiends, and it is probably as a manifestation of Durga that we meet Rangda as the consort of Kala and the queen of the witches *(lejaks)*. Rangda is seen as a frightful figure, and she symbolizes all the secret skills of witchcraft and the art of black magic.

The name Rangda literally means "widow" and, in the Balinese text *Calon Arang* and the dramatic performances based on it, she is the witch of that name, Calon Arang, and is identified with Queen Mahendradatta, who was the mother of King Airlanga and the widow of King Udayana. The story is that, contrary to his promise, Udayana took a second wife and Mahendradatta went to the forest and began to practice black magic. When Udayana died and left her a widow, since Airlanga had failed to persuade his father against the second marriage, she used her magic arts to destroy Airlanga's kingdom. A beautiful daughter of Calon Arang named Ratna Mengali was also involved in the happenings, and so too was a priest of Airlanga named Mpu Bharadah, and the latter was finally victorious over the witch. The ashes of Mahendradatta were buried at Buruan, near the present village of Kutri in the district of Gianyar, and a very worn *stela* found there shows Durga Mahishasuramardini dancing on a demon buffalo (or bull), and is thought to be a funeral monument of the sorceress queen.[93]

Over against the realm of black or negative magic, which is personified by the witch Rangda, is the realm of white or positive magic which is capable of counteracting the negative, and here the personification of the positive forces is the Barong, who may have some remote connection with Mpu Bharadah of the *Calon Arang*. The Barong is now seen as a mythical beast, usually as some kind of animal (such as a lion or tiger) and most frequently as a sort of dragon, the dragon form suggesting that Chinese-Buddhist influence may have been involved in the origin of the figure.

The Barong may be considered as the king of the demons *(kalas)* and thus as the only one who can keep them under control, but above all he is the antagonist of Rangda and of her *lejaks*. In every combat the Barong is able to conquer Rangda, but never to kill her, so at least equilibrium is maintained between the negative and the positive forces.[94] Many other figures are also conceived as of such formidable and frightening appearance as to be effective guardians of the good and deterrents of the evil forces.[95]

Cult of the Dead. In the case of *brahmana* priests and some other persons of high position, cremation may be carried out shortly after death, but for most persons the body is buried first and only later, when opportunity and means allow, cremated. The interment is normally in the burial ground which lies to the *kelod*-west of the village, and adjacent to the *pura dalem* or nether-world temple.

Immediately after death souls enter the underworld. The entrance thereto is guarded by Prajapati, a demonic manifestation of the god Brahma, and the whole realm is ruled by Yamaraja, the god of death and the *raja* of hell. Here souls are classified as good or bad, and sinners undergo the severest of punishments. In this time the souls of the dead are potentially dangerous to the living, and rites conducted in the *pura dalem* are intended to restrict and neutralize any malevolent influences and activities, as well as to assist the deceased toward release. At this point they are *piratas* rather than *pitaras* (the former word perhaps a corruption of *preta,* "hungry ghost," "tantalized spirit," later given a formation parallel to *pitara*), i.e., they are souls whose bodies have not yet been purified by cremation.

Only when the cremation is accomplished is the body of the deceased purified and the person free to be reborn among the deified ancestors *(pitaras)* in the heavenly realm. At that point the deified ones (called *batara, deva, devata, sang hyang*) are no longer dependent upon the living, but homage is paid to them in the household temple in order to secure blessings from them.

The cremation ceremony itself normally involves a joyful procession, with musical accompaniment, to the place of the fire. In this procession the body of the deceased is carried in a towerlike structure which is called a *bade* or *wadah* and, at least in more elaborate examples, is much like a *meru*. The lower part of the tower is characterized by a serpent and a tortoise, suggesting the nether world from which the deceased is now being delivered; the middle is a pavilion representing the atmosphere, and is the place for the dead person who no longer belongs to earth but not yet to heaven; and the multiple upper roofs are a replica of the heavens, whither the deceased is bound. After the fire has done its work, the human ashes which remain are carried to river or sea and scattered there, and the cremation ceremony is at an end.

In respect of the ancestors, the chief festival of the year in their honor is called *Galungan*, and at this time offerings are made both at the graveyard to the *piratas* who are still in the underworld (the *kelod* sphere) and also in the household temple to the *pitaras* who are in the heavens (the *kaja* sphere).[96]

Goa Gajah

One of the chief archaeological sites in Bali is at the Goa Gajah or Elephant Cave in the neighborhood of the village of Bedulu, in the area where early Balinese dynasties were centered. This is a rock-hewn cave in the northern bank of the valley of the Petanu River. The narrow entrance is about 7 feet (2 m.) in height; overhead is a fierce *kala*-head, and on either side additional sculptures depict a mountainous country with animals and humans apparently fleeing in fear from the demonic face (Fig. 14.32). An inscription on a side wall of the entrance suggests that the cave was a hermitage of Śaivite monks as early as the beginning of the eleventh century,

14.32 Façade of Goa Gajah, the Elephant Cave near Bedulu Village

14.33 Vidyadharis in the Sanctuary and Watering Place by the Elephant Cave near Bedulu

and other evidence indicates that there was also a Buddhist establishment across on the southern bank of the valley.

Down in the valley in front of the Elephant Cave is a rectangular sanctuary and bathing place, which is much like Candi Belahan in Java and is probably datable to much the same period—at about the middle of the eleventh century C.E. Here, against the back wall of the basin, are six statues of volcanic tufa, and they probably represent *vidyadharis* or heavenly nymphs. Like the goddesses at Belahan, the figures are so made as to provide for pouring forth water into the basin, in this case through large, round waterspouts which they hold in front of themselves (Fig. 14.33).[97]

Klungkung

At Klungkung, which became the Balinese capital in 1633 C.E., the palace was destroyed in war with the Dutch in 1908, but the former law court (Kerta Gosa, hall of justice) and royal pavilion (Bale Kambang, floating pavilion) surrounded by a moat filled with lotus plants are still there. Ceiling paintings still to be seen show scenes of punishment and reward in the afterlife[98] and pictures from the Sutasoma legend. A court poet of the Majapahit period named Mpu Tantular put this legend into a poem known as *Sutasoma* or *Purushada śanta* (the man-eater appeased). Sutasoma, the principal character, was an incarnation of Buddha who gave away his possessions and departed for the Himalaya. On the way he experienced conflicts with powerful demons (Fig. 14.34), and was attacked by a terrifying manifestation of Śiva named Kalarudra, who tried to kill him. The gods, however, endeavored to pacify Kalarudra by reminding him that there is no essential difference between Śiva and Buddha. Although known by different names, Śiva and Buddha are

14.34 Conflict of Sutasoma and the ten-faced demon Daśamukha, Painting in the Royal Pavilion, Klungkung

actually identical, and Kalarudra is urged to meditate on this Śiva-Buddha reality, for in *dharma* there is unity in diversity.[99]

Pura Besakih

Given the residence of the gods on the tops of the mountains, it is appropriate that the chief state temple of Bali is high (3,000 feet [900 m.]) on the southwestern slope of Gunung Agung, the island's highest mountain (9,450 feet [2,880 m.]), and in a location which for most of the island is also in the most favorable *(kaja)* easterly direction. The site was probably sacred even from very early times, prior to the coming of Hinduism and Buddhism, and this is confirmed by the terrace arrangement of the temple, which was probably characteristic of prehistoric sanctuaries.

The foundation of the temple is attributed, in Balinese tradition, to Kesarivarmadeva (circa 917 C.E.), the first ruler of Bali whose name is recorded, and who was the first king of the Varmadeva dynasty. From the fact that until the present century only a Buddhist *padanda* accompanying the ruler as his court priest might enter the temple, it is suggested that this was at the outset a Buddhist sanctuary.

In a lontar palm leaf text called the Royal Charter of the Besakih Temple *(Rajapurana Pura Besakih)* there is a date in the Śaka Year 929 (1007 C.E.), and this falls in the time of King Udayana of the Varmadeva dynasty, Queen Mahendradatta (Gunapriyadharmapatni), and Airlanga, so the temple was presumably associated with some important event of this period.

In the time of I Deva Ketut Tegal Besung, the founder of the Gelgel dynasty (circa 1450 C.E.), we hear that this king was ordained by a *brahmana* from India who first of all consulted with Batara Mahadeva at the temple Wasuki (i.e., Besakih). Batara Mahadeva was the deity of the mountain Gunung Agung, and at least later was also identified with Śiva and Buddha and Surya. Thus at least by this time the temple was associated with Hinduism as well as Buddhism, and I Deva Ketut Tegal Besung was himself regarded as an incarnation of Batara Mahadeva. In the Royal Charter of the Besakih Temple there is an inventory of the temple buildings, including a list of the *merus* dedicated to the deified rulers of Bali, and the first in this list is a *meru* with eleven roofs dedicated to I Deva Ketut Tegal Besung, evidently considered the oldest and most important of them all.

In all, then, Pura Besakih became a Buddhist/Hindu sanctuary and a central place of worship of the royal ancestors, and as such a common cult place for the whole of Bali. In the earthquakes of January/February 1917 in which, according to official statistics, 2,431 temples throughout the island were partially or totally destroyed, Pura Besakih suffered severe damage; and lesser damage was experienced by the temple in the eruption of Gunung Agung in 1963.[100]

At Pura Besakih four small temples line the road which leads up to the main temple complex. The first small temple, on the right or eastern side of the road, is called Bangun Śakti (the awakening of the mystic power) and is dedicated to the world snake, Anantabhoga (infinitely coiled). The next, on the left or western side, is Ulun Kulkul (origin of the belfry), dedicated to Mahadeva and intended for veneration of the spirits manifest in the sound of the bell *(kulkul)* which gives the summons to prayer. The remaining two, on the right, are a temple dedicated to Batari Śri the goddess of fertility, and a temple called Pura Basukian where the world snake is venerated under the name Basuki (Sanskrit Wasuki).

The main temple complex consists of a central sanctuary called Pura Panataran Agung Besakih, which is associated with the entire island; a higher temple to the west called Pura Batu Madeg (temple of the upright stone), which is associated with the district of Bangli; and a higher temple to the east called Pura Dangin Kereteg (temple to the east of the bridge), which is associated with the easternmost district of Karangasem. Together the three temples are understood to symbolize the Hindu trinity, and are marked at important festivals by flags of the appropriate color. The central sanctuary (white flag) stands for Iśvara (i.e., Śiva); the Bangli temple (black flag) for Vishnu (in Bali the water god and god of earthly blessing); and the Karangasem temple (red flag) for Brahma (in Bali the fire god, identical with Agni).

The central sanctuary stands at the top of a stairway of some fifty steps, and is entered through a split gate *(candi bentar)* (Fig. 14.35). In the main courtyard is a great shrine *(sanggar agung)* with three seats for the deities of the trinity; a lotus seat *(padmasana)* for Surya/Śiva; a great hall *(bale agung)* for meetings, and so forth. Beyond the main courtyard a high stone stairway leads to the upper terraces, and here there are various halls, pavilions, altars, and *merus*.[101]

Of the festivals held at Pura Besakih the most important is the *ekadaśa-rudra*, itself the most important of all the festivals held on the entire island. This is theoretically a festival of eleven *(ekadaśa)* days but actually of much longer duration. It is conducted at the start of a new century in the Balinese calendar, or at another time when disasters take place or times are bad enough to seem to require it. The intention of the observance is to propitiate Rudra, the destructive aspect of Śiva, and thus to restore the balance in the world between the forces of good and of evil. An observance in 1963 was not at the turn of the century but at a time which seemed otherwise to call for it. Halfway through the ceremonies an eruption of Gunung Agung killed more than 1,500 people. In 1979 the observance was held from late February to early May to mark the beginning of a new century. The ceremonies included a procession to the sea nineteen miles away to wash the images of the gods, the making of many offerings and the sacrifice of many animals, the

14.35 Stairway and Split Gate leading to the Central Sanctuary at Pura Besakih

setting up of temporary symbolic representations *(sarads)* of the cosmos and its gods, made of wood and rice dough (Fig. 14.36), temple dances, and so forth.[102]

Other observances at Pura Besakih include the festival *panca-bali-krama,* an elaborate offering in which the required sacrificial animals are a buffalo, a tiger, a black monkey, and a cow—the omission of which ceremony could result in the spread of pestilence and misery; and an annual festival called *hayu-hayu.*[103]

Pura Kehen, Bangli

Pura Kehen, to the north of the town of Bangli, is the state temple of the district of Bangli. It is mentioned in an edict as early as 1204 C.E., which gives a list of temple feasts for Bangli and surrounding villages. The temple is a terraced mountain sanctuary, with a steep stairway leading up to a split gate in the enclosure wall. The main *meru* in the inner sanctuary symbolizes the three worlds: the base represents the underworld and is marked by the turtle Bedawang and the two snakes Anatabhoga and Basuki; the enclosed chamber is the middle world where humankind may communicate with Śiva; the eleven roofs in a pagoda-like arrangement stand for the cosmic heavenly upper world (Fig. 14.37). Likewise the lotus throne *(padmasana)* stands on the back of the underworld turtle, held by the two snakes, and it rises in terraces to three seats at the top for Śiva/Surya in the threefold form of Brahma, Vishnu, and Iśvara (Fig. 14.38).[104]

Pura Taman Ayun, Mengwi

The principality of Mengwi was, until 1891, the center of a strong kingdom which originated from the Gelgel dynasty, and the Pura Taman Ayun in the capital city of Mengwi is a state temple in which the royal ancestors continue to be venerated. The temple is protected by a wide moat, which gives the impression that it is a sanctuary lying in the middle of a pond, hence the name *taman,* meaning a

14.36 A Sarad or Symbolic Representation of the Cosmos and Its Gods, at Pura Besakih

14.37 Main Meru in Pura Kehen, Bangli

14.38 Padmasana in Pura Kehen, Bangli

garden with a pond. Guardian figures stand upon the bridge which crosses the moat, and the waters suggest contact with the divine through the celestial nymphs *(vidyadharis)* who bathe there. In the inner courts are additional guardian figures, a royal ancestral altar *(paibon)*, shrines which serve as "sitting places" *(palihggihs)* for visiting deities during temple feasts, pavilions for prayers, offerings, and meetings, and many *merus*.[105]

Sangeh

The temple at Sangeh is set in the midst of a sacred forest known, from its numerous simian inhabitants, as Bukit Sari, the Monkey Forest. The local legend is that Ravana, the demonic ruler of Lanka in the *Ramayana*, could die neither on earth nor in the air, so the monkey god Hanuman planned to suffocate him by pressing him between two halves of the holy mountain Mahameru—a destruction between earth and air. But when Hanuman seized the mountain a part of it fell to the earth in Sangeh, along with a group of his monkey armies. And so the monkeys stayed until now. The temple exhibits a wooden split drum, rows of ancestor shrines, and a lotus seat *(padmasana)* for the god, among other items.

Mas and Ubud

According to legend, Padanda Śakti Bahu Rauh, the first Hindu priest to come to Bali, settled in the area of the present village of Mas, where many *brahmanas* still claim descent from him. In the thirteenth century C.E. a large temple was built here in honor of the ancestors, and is represented by the present Pura Taman Pule. In earlier days the fine arts of wood carving and painting were reserved for royal and religious purposes; in their modern more generalized practice, in which the subject matter is drawn from all of Balinese life as well as from the realm of the gods and mythological heroes, Mas is an important center of wood carving, while the village of Ubud, farther to the north, is a center of painting.[106]

Denpasar

Púri Pemetjutan. In the past the palaces *(puris)* of the rulers of Bali were as abundantly decorated as were the temples *(puras)*, and thus preserved many traditional works of art.[107] Such is the case in the Puri Pemetjutan in the city of Denpasar (in the province of Badung at the south end of the island). The present building was constructed in 1907 in place of the former palace, which was destroyed in the *puputan* or "fight unto death" of the preceding year, in which the *raja* of Badung and his people were killed by the invading Dutch.

Bali Museum. The Bali Museum in Denpasar, built in 1932, combines in its architecture elements of the temple *(pura)*, with a split gate *(candi bentar)* and a roofed gate *(paduraksa)* (Fig. 14.39), and of the palace *(puri)*, with a main building

14.39   Roofed Gate, Bali Museum, Denpasar

14.40 Drummer, Bali Museum, Denpasar

14.41 Vishnu on Garuda, Bali Museum, Denpasar

14.42 Ravana on Wilmana, Bali Museum, Denpasar

with a wide pillared veranda. Among the stone sculptures in the museum is a set of musicians, originally on a wall of the royal palace at Klungkung, and possibly of the sixteenth/seventeenth century in date. One, for example, is a drummer playing on a horizontally held drum (Fig. 14.40). Wood carvings portray Vishnu on Garuda (Fig. 14.41), Ravana on his bird-bearer Wilmana (Fig. 14.42), and others. Dance costumes are those of the good Barong (Fig. 14.43) and of the mistress of the witches, Rangda (Fig. 14.44).

In the Villages

Wedding. For a wedding in the village of Singapadu a *gamelan* orchestra provides music, decorations enhance the surroundings, the principals wait under a canopy, and a white-clad priest rings a bell and chants at his tray of worship materials in the initial phases of the ceremony (Fig. 14.45).

14.43 Barong, Bali Museum, Denpasar

14.44 Rangda, Bali Museum, Denpasar

14.45   Priest conducting Wedding Ceremony in Singapadu

14.46   Cremation Procession at Besan

Cremation. In a cremation at Besan, near Klungkung, the procession moves out, carrying the body of the deceased, to be consumed in the flames that the soul may go above (Fig. 14.46).

Dance. In the Barong dance at the village of Batubukan girl dancers precede the appearances of the Barong and of Rangda (Fig. 14.47).

MALAYSIA

In the Malay Peninsula (which is now Peninsular Malaysia), as elsewhere in Southeast Asia, it may be assumed that early Indian colonies and Indianized states were established in the early centuries C.E.

The first of these states of which we have specific knowledge is described in a Chinese work, the *Liang-shu* or History of the Liang Dynasty (502–556 C.E.). This text calls the kingdom *Lang-ya-hsiu,* which corresponds with the name Langkasuka in later Javanese and Malayan chronicles, and quotes the inhabitants of the country as declaring that their state was founded "more than 400 years ago," i.e., in the early second century C.E. The country is situated in the Southern Sea, and its climate and products are similar to those of Funan. Aloe-wood and camphor are abundant. The men and women wear a cotton sarong, leaving the upper body bare; the king and his nobles also wear shawls, gold girdles, and gold earrings. The capital city is walled, with double gates and towers. When the king goes out he rides upon an elephant, and is shaded with a white parasol. Other references to Langkasuka suggest that it was centered on the east coast of the peninsula, perhaps in the vicinity of modern Patani.[108]

The Buddhist *Milinda Panha,* which refers to the voyages of a wealthy

14.47 Girl Dancers in the Barong-Rangda Dance Drama at Batubukan

shipowner to Suvarnabhumi and other places, begins its list of these places with Vanga, Takkola, and Cina. Vanga is possibly Bengal, and Cina is surely China, so Takkola was apparently between the two. In the *Geography* of Claudius Ptolemy, the first of the place names listed within the Golden Chersonesus is *Takola emporium,* and on Ptolemy's map Takola is located on the northwest coast of the Malay Peninsula (in the approximate location of the modern Trang). Takkola was, therefore, a commercial center and perhaps a small city state or kingdom in Malaya, and in touch with India.[109]

As to Indian influence and presence in these early kingdoms, there is evidence in inscriptions containing Buddhist subject matter, and in Buddhist and Hindu sculptures, found in the states of Kedah and Perak (inland from Penang Island) and elsewhere, and dating probably in the fourth, fifth, and sixth centuries C.E.[110]

As for political domination from outside, as already noted above, Malaya was to a greater or lesser extent and for longer or shorter times included in the dominions of Śrivijaya (seventh century), of Singhasari (thirteenth century), and of Majapahit (fourteenth century). It was a Śrivijayan prince of Palembang named Parameśvara, fleeing from the forces of Majapahit, who established a new kingdom at Malacca about 1400 C.E., and it was he in 1414 who adopted the Muslim religion at his court. Thereafter Islam spread among the people and Malaya, like Sumatra and Java, became predominantly Muslim.[111]

Both Hinduism and Buddhism, however, still persist to some extent in Peninsular Malaysia, as is evidenced, for example, in a Hindu shrine in Batu Cave above Kuala Lumpur, and in a temple of the Reclining Buddha in Penang (Fig. 14.48), while the strong Chinese influence is seen at the Penang Buddhist Association, where the Buddha is flanked by Taoist deities (Fig. 14.49).

14.48 Reclining Buddha in Penang

14.49 Buddha flanked by Taoist Deities, Penang Buddhist Association

KAMPUCHEA

In the ancient inscriptions of Kampuchea (formerly Cambodia) the people are called Kambuja (descendants of Kambu), and the country is called Kambujadeśa (land of the Kambuja) or simply Kambuja. Also used and practically synonymous with Kambuja is the name Khmer, and this term is usually used as the adjective in reference to the Khmer kingdom or Khmer empire.[112]

Funan Period

The earliest kingdom in this area is first attested in Chinese sources, and is there called Funan.[113] This name represents a Chinese transcription of a word the later form of which is *phnom* (mountain), and this name for the kingdom is probably based upon the fact that the king had the title "king of the mountain," the same title used by the Śailendras of Java.

The capital of the kingdom was Vyadhapura (perhaps, the city of the hunter king), called T'e-mu in Chinese. The *History of the Liang Dynasty* (502–556 C.E.) states that the city was 500 *li* (the *li* equals about 1,890 feet [576 m.]) or 125 miles (200 km.) from the sea, which supports a location of the place near the hill Ba Phnom and the village Banam in the delta of the Mekong River southeast of Phnom Penh.

Kaundinya

In the middle of the third century C.E. two Chinese envoys, K'ang T'ai and Chu Ying, visited Funan and wrote an account of the country, of which some portions survive. According to the Chinese report, Funan was originally ruled by a queen named Liu-ye (Willow Leaf). In her time there was a person called Hun-t'ien of Mo-fu, who was a devotee of a *brahmanical* god. Hun-t'ien dreamed that the god gave him a divine bow and directed him to sail on a trading vessel. In the morning he went to the temple of the god and found a bow, then embarked on a sailing vessel which, carried by a change of wind, brought him to Funan. Liu-ye came out to plunder the visiting vessel, but Hun-t'ien shot an arrow which pierced the queen's ship and she, frightened, submitted, and Hun-t'ien became the ruler of the country.[114]

A Sanskrit inscription of the seventh century C.E. from Mi-son in Campa (in modern Vietnam) gives what is evidently a variant version of the same legend. The inscription refers to the foundation of a capital city (later called Bhavapura after the name of the later famous king Bhavavarman I), and says:

> It was there that Kaundinya, the foremost among the *brahmanas*, planted the spear which he had obtained from Drona's son Aśvatthama, the eminent *brahmana*.
>
> There was a daughter of the king of the *nagas*, who founded upon earth the race which bears the name of Soma. Having adopted that state, she lived in a human habitation.
>
> She was taken as wife by the excellent *brahmana* Kaundinya for the sake of accomplishing certain rites. In truth, incomprehensible is the action of destiny in providing conditions leading to future events.
>
> That one (King Bhavavarman) who was born in that pure unbroken line of kings is, even today, the pride of his subjects by reason of his excellent works.[115]

Kaundinya, as the name is given in the Sanskrit inscription, appears to be the same person as the one whose name is rendered as Hun-t'ien in the Chinese record. While Mo-fu, which is named as the original home of Hun-t'ien, is not identifiable, the descriptions of Hun-t'ien as the devotee of a *brahmanical* god, and of Kaundinya as a *brahmana* associated with the son of Drona, a hero of the *Mahabharata*, make it probable that Hun-t'ien/Kaundinya came from India.

From the sequence of later events it is probable that the origin of the kingdom of Funan, to which the foregoing legends evidently refer, is to be dated in about the first century C.E. In the early third century, according to the Chinese sources, a certain Fan Shih-man was king, conquered neighboring states to a distance of five or six thousand *li*, and died when he was about to lead a campaign against Chin-lin (frontier of gold), probably meaning Suvarnabhumi or Suvarnadvipa.[116] In the middle of the third century the Chinese envoy K'ang T'ai describes the people of Funan as agriculturalists, but with walled villages, palaces, and dwellings. They like to engrave ornaments, and many of their eating utensils are of silver. They pay their taxes in gold, silver, pearls, and perfumes. They have books, and depositories of archives, and other things.[117]

In the *History of the Liang Dynasty* we also hear of a Kaundinya who was king in Funan, but he appears to be a second of the same name and datable at about the beginning of the fifth century. He was a *brahmana* of India, who was instructed by a supernatural voice to go and reign in Funan. There the people welcomed him and made him king, and he introduced Indian laws, manners, and customs. Assuming that these are two different persons and that the first Kaundinya already brought the influences of India with him, this coming of a second Kaundinya may be considered to represent a "second Indianization" of Funan.[118]

Kaundinya Jayavarman

Among the elements of Indian culture henceforth noticeable is the use of the honorary Hindu title of *-varman* as a part of the names of kings and also of other persons of high political and religious positions. Thus in the late fifth and early sixth centuries C.E. we find a king with the family name of Kaundinya and the personal name of Jayavarman on the throne. Funan was at its height, and good relations existed with China, to which country both traders and political emissaries went from Funan. An embassy in 503 C.E., for example, carried presents from Jayavarman, including a coral image of Buddha, to the imperial court in China and, in return, an imperial edict was issued which declared:

> The king of Funan Kaundinya Jayavarman lives on the border of the ocean. For generations he and his forefathers have ruled over that distant country of the south and their sincerity [of respectful feelings to the Chinese emperor] is manifested by frequent embassies and presents. It is proper to show some favor in return and to bestow a grand title upon him. Hence [I confer] the title, The General of the pacified south, the king of Funan.[119]

Upon the death of Kaundinya Jayavarman in 514 C.E., his older son Rudravarman born of a concubine, killed the younger son born of the queen, and seized the throne. Like his father, Rudravarman continued to send embassies and gifts to China, and the gifts included, in 519 C.E., a sandalwood image of Buddha and, in 539, a Buddha relic in the form of a long hair.[120] In an inscription at Ta Prohm Rudravarman also makes an invocation to the Buddha.[121]

Rudravarman is the last king of Funan to be mentioned by name in the Chinese texts, and soon afterward Funan was overthrown and absorbed by Chenla.

Chenla Period

Chenla is also a Chinese name, and the oldest text which mentions Chenla is the Chinese *History of the Sui Dynasty* (589–618 C.E.). This source states that Chenla was originally a vassal state of Funan, and describes its capital as near a mountain, which can probably be identified with Vat Ph'u near Bassac in the south of modern Laos.[122] The center of Chenla was therefore in the Middle Mekong valley as compared with Funan in the Lower Mekong valley and delta, and the people were apparently of ethnic stock not far different from the Funanese.

Since the royal houses of Chenla and Funan were probably related, it is not surprising that somewhat the same stories are told about the origin of Chenla as of Funan, in particular representing that the royal dynasty was founded by the marriage of an important personage from India with a local woman, usually represented as a princess of the *naga* people. This association with the serpent people must be at least partly responsible for the long continued prominence of a nine-headed cobra as a royal symbol in Kampuchea.

Thus it is related that a certain Adityavamśa, king of Indraprastha (the capital of Yudishthira in the *Mahabharata*), banished from his kingdom a son with whom he was displeased. The prince arrived in the country of Kok Thlok (the Khmer name of Kambuja, meaning the land of the *thlok* tree), and became king by defeating the local ruler. Then: "One evening the prince met on the seashore a *nagi* of marvelous beauty. He married the *nagi;* and her father, the *nagaraja,* expanded the territory of his son-in-law by drinking off the water which covered the land and changed the name of the country to Kambuja."[123] Here the *naga* king drinking off the water covering the land probably reflects large-scale works of water containment by which land was gained for agriculture.

According to another legend, referred to in a tenth century inscription from Baksei Camkrong, it was Kambu Svayambhuva, an Indian hermit, who married the daughter of a *naga* king, and after whom the kingdom was called Kambuja. Descended from Kambu Svayambhuva were Śrutavarman and his son Śreshthavarman, and they may have been the earliest historical kings of Chenla, presumably in the time when Chenla was still under the suzerainty of Funan.[124]

Bhavavarman I and Jayavarman I

The fusion of Funan and Chenla seems to have been begun by Bhavavarman I, whose name we have heard already along with the name of his city Bhavapura in the seventh century inscription quoted above. He was probably a member of the royal family of Funan, who became king of Chenla through marriage to a princess of this country, and was probably the founder of a new line of kings in Chenla. In turn, according to Chinese sources, there was a conquest of Funan by both of Bhavavarman's immediate successors, namely, Citrasena (who reigned as Mahendravarman) and the latter's son Iśanavarman (whose capital was Iśanapura, named after himself), and the mastery of Funan by Iśanavarman is dated at the beginning of the period Cheng-kuan (627–649 C.E.). In all, the takeover of Funan by Chenla, and the emergence of the resultant new and larger kingdom under the name of Chenla, was probably the work of all three of these kings, and may be dated approximately 550–630 C.E. In the balance of the Chenla period, the most prominent name is that of Jayavarman I, from whom there are inscriptions dating from 657 to 674 C.E.[125]

In contrast with Kaundinya Jayavarman and Rudravarman of Funan, who were evidently Buddhists (sending images of the Buddha to China), the many religious references in Chenla inscriptions from Bhavavarman I to Jayavarman I are mainly to subjects associated with Hinduism, both Śaivism and Vaishnavism. For example, the Phnom Bantay Nan inscription records the erection of a *linga* by King Bhavavarman; the Thma Kre inscription records a similar action by King Citrasena; the Ang Pu inscription refers to King Iśanavarman and records the erection of an image and *linga* of Śiva-Vishnu; and the inscription in the temple of Vat Ph'u contains a hymn to Śiva, a eulogy of King Jayavarman I, and the ordinance of the king in respect to the temple mountain (called *Lingaparvata*), exempting all persons living there from arrest even if found guilty of a crime, prohibiting riding a chariot and using parasol or flywhisk, keeping dogs and fowl within the sacred enclosure, and so forth.[126] Particularly notable is the combined form of Śiva-Vishnu, united in one body and known as Harihara. Hari, a name of Vishnu, means green, greenish-yellow, tawny, which are colors of springtime and growth; Hara, a name of Śiva, means seizer, which suggests taking away; hence the two names combined refer to the creative and destructive forces of the universe which, in the last analysis, are one and the same.[127]

As for Buddhism, one inscription of Jayavarman I (at Vat Prei Var) indeed mentions two *bhikshus*,[128] but otherwise Buddhism seems little in evidence in this time. In fact, Yi Jing, who describes conditions toward the end of the seventh century C.E., says that in the country formerly called Funan, Buddhism once flourished, but now a wicked king has destroyed it and there are no monks, while the adherents of the other religions live intermingled.[129] Buddhism was, however, to become very prominent again in the future, in the Mahayana form at the height of the Angkor period, and in the Theravada form in the last years of the Khmer kingdom.

Angkor Period

In the 8th century C.E. conditions were evidently chaotic and Chenla fell under the sway of the Śailendras of Java, who chose a member of the Chenla royal family, educated him in Java, and sent him back as the new ruler. This was Jayavarman II, who returned to Chenla at the end of the eighth century, reunited the country under his own leadership, and ruled (eventually free from Java) for nearly fifty years (802–850 C.E.).

A long inscription of King Udayadityavarman II (1050–1065 C.E.) in Sanskrit and Khmer at Sdok Kak Thom narrates the history of a priestly family and tells of the various kings served by these priests from Jayavarman II to Suryavarman I (1002–1050), the latter being the immediate predecessor of Udayadityavarman II.[130] Concerning Jayavarman II, we are told in this text that he established himself in several successive capitals, including Hariharalaya and Mahendraparvata, identifiable with sites north of the Tonle Sap (Great Lake) and in the vicinity of the later Angkor, in which region (near modern Siem Reap) his descendants lived continuously into the fifteenth century C.E. Jayavarman II (802–850 C.E.) may be considered, therefore, the founder of the Khmer kingdom of Angkor (802–1431).

The priestly family named in the Sdok Kak Thom inscription is that of a *brahmana*, Śivakaivalya, who was the chief priest *(purohita)* of Jayavarman II. At the point of Jayavarman II's residence in Mahendraparvata, in order that Kambujadeśa might no longer be dependent on Java and might have a universal monarch *(cakravartin)* of its own, another *brahmana* named Hiranyadama, well versed in magical science, came at the king's invitation and performed certain *tantric* rites and the worship of *devaraja*.

> He also initiated Śivakaivalya into these rituals and taught him the sacred books dealing with them. Śivakaivalya, in his turn, taught them to all his relatives, and the king took a vow to employ only the family of Śivakaivalya and none else to celebrate the worship of *devaraja*. Then His Majesty returned to Hariharalaya and reigned there until his death. Sivakaivalya also died during his reign. His Majesty had brought *devaraja* to Hariharalaya, and his successors took the god to various capitals which they founded in the course of time, as he was regarded as the protector of the realm.[131]

From this text and others of the Angkor period it seems that the *devaraja* (divine king) was a designation of the *linga* of Śiva (and of the *tantric* ritual in which it was worshiped), and that this was conceived as a representation of the divine essence of the earthly kingship and a deification of the royal authority, so from Jayavarman II on the Khmer kings partook of the nature of deity. Accordingly the *linga* (or other image of the god) was set up on a natural or artificial mountain as the cult center of the realm. The artificial mountain was usually a terraced pyramidal structure and thus something like Borobudur in Java, which was itself probably built in the early ninth century C.E. and thus exactly in the time of Jayavarman II. In such a form the structure could represent the cosmic Mount Meru, and here it was usually surrounded by a moat corresponding with the ocean that encircles the world. Upon death the king received a posthumous name and entered into identity with the god, and therefore the mountain-temple became also a funerary monument of the deified king. By the time of Jayavarman VII (1181–1201 C.E.), Mahayana Buddhism was in the ascendancy, and therewith the *devaraja* cult was replaced by a comparable *Buddharaja* cult.

After Jayavarman II and down to the fall of Angkor in 1431 C.E., there were as many as thirty-seven more rulers who successively came to power. Of these, the most important were Indravarman I, Yaśovarman I, Rajendravarman II, Suryavarman II, and Jayavarman VII, and they will appear in connection with their sites and monuments in what follows.

The very large enterprises of Jayavarman VII (1811–circa 1218 C.E.) evidently exhausted the country and, after his time, the Khmer kingdom was in decline. There were repeated invasions from Thailand, and in 1431 Angkor was besieged, captured, and sacked by the Thai king Boromoraja II (1424–1448 C.E.). Thereafter the city was abandoned, soon overgrown by the jungle, and only rediscovered and partially restored in the nineteenth and twentieth centuries.

Hariharalaya

The relationship of Indravarman I (877–889 C.E.) to the kings who preceded him is unclear, but at any rate it is known that he continued to reside at Hariharalaya, the chief capital of Jayavarman II. This city, the name of which refers to the conjoint manifestation of Śiva-Vishnu, was at the present-day Roluos, 9 miles (15 km.) southeast of Siem Reap. In the first year of his reign, Indravarman I constructed to the north of the city the first of the huge reservoirs by which the kings of the Angkor period controlled the waters and provided for irrigation of the land. This was called the Indratataka, but is now dry and known as the Lolei Baray.

Indravarman I also began the building of the very large monuments, the ruins of which are still so impressive in the Angkor region. To the south of the Indratataka he erected a funerary temple containing six brick towers *(prasats)*, which were dedicated to statues of his parents, his maternal grandparents, and Jayavarman II and his wife, the latter deified in the forms of Śiva and Devi. The monument was called Parameśvara, which was the posthumous name of Jayavarman II, and it is now known as Preah Ko.[132]

Bakong. In the center of his city Indravarman I built the Bakong, the first major Khmer monument in stone and thus the first of the great mountain-temples still standing in the Angkor region.[133] The structure was dedicated in 881 C.E., and can be seen to be similar enough in plan to Borobudur that it may have been a conscious imitation of the Javanese monument built earlier in the same century. As it stands at Roluos, the base of the pyramid is 220 × 213 feet (67 × 65 m.) in size, rising in five square terraces, 45 feet (14 m.) in height, to a high tower which was rebuilt in the twelfth century. The temple proper is of sandstone; surrounding the base are eight towers built of brick. Enclosing the entire precinct is a moat 262 feet (80 m.) wide. In the topmost tower of the temple was the *linga* of Śiva. A *stela* inscription records the installation of the *linga* and gives its name as Śri Indreśvara, this name combining the name of the god Iśvara (i.e., Śiva) with the name of the king.[134]

Yaśodharapura/Angkor

Yaśovarman I (889–910 C.E.) was the son and successor of Indravarman I. In the middle of the Indratataka, the artificial lake made by his father, Yaśovarman I built four brick towers for the statues of his parents and grandparents, a monument now known as the Lolei. The new king did not stay long, however, in the old capital. The Sdok Kak Thom inscription records that he took the *devaraja* away from Hariharalaya and established it in a new capital city which he founded under the name of Yaśodharapura.

Bakheng. The new city was laid out around the hill Phnom Bakheng, 6 miles (10 km.) northwest of Roluos (Hariharalaya). The summit of the hill provided an elevated place for a mountain-temple, the Bakheng temple, which was built on much the same plan as the Bakong at Hariharalaya. The Śiva *linga* which was enshrined here was called the Yaśodhareśvara.

To the northeast of his new capital Yaśovarman I constructed an immense artificial lake, the Yaśodharatataka, larger even than the Indratataka of his father. This, now dry, is the Eastern Baray at Angkor, and is 4 miles (7 km.) long and 5,900 feet (1,800 m.) wide. On *stelas* at the four corners inscriptions gave the genealogy of the king and extolled his works.[135]

The center of Yaśodharapura was later moved somewhat to the north where the great city of Angkor Thom ultimately arose, while the mountain-temple of Angkor Wat was built to the southeast, and except for short intervals this Angkor area remained the capital of the Khmer kingdom down until the time of the end in the fifteenth century C.E. One such temporary removal was experienced when Yaśovarman I's brother-in-law Jayavarman IV (928–941 C.E.) moved the capital to Koh Ker (about 50 miles [80 km.] northeast of Angkor), where he built some very large buildings. Yaśovarman I's nephew Rajendravarman II (944–968), however, returned to Angkor.

Pre Rup. In the center of the Yaśodharatataka reservoir (the Eastern Baray at Angkor) constructed by Yaśovarman I, Rajendravarman II in 952 C.E. built a temple (the Eastern Mebon) to honor his ancestors (like the Lolei built in the middle of the Indratataka by Yaśovarman I); and in 961 near the south shore of the Yaśodharatataka Rajendravarman II erected the mountain-temple of Pre Rup.

Pre Rup (Fig. 14.50) rises in three large rectangular terraces, the topmost of which has towers at its four corners, and in the center on two small additional terraces there is a tall central tower. Staircases, guarded by lions, ascend at the center of each of the four sides of the temple. A Pre Rup *stela* inscription indicates that a *linga* called Rajendrabhadreśvara was in the central tower, images of Śiva (two in number), Vishnu, and Uma were in the four corner towers, and images of

14.50 Pre Rup at Angkor

14.51   Phimeanakas at Angkor

eight forms of Śiva in additional small chapels.[136] The name of the *linga* in the central tower, to which the temple was dedicated—Rajendrabhadreśvara—combines the names of the king and of Bhadreśvara, who was a national divinity worshiped at Vat Ph'u, the early center of Chenla/Kambuja.

Phimeanakas. Rajendravarman II may also have founded the Phimeanakas, a temple which stands at the intersection point of a north-south line from the center of Phnom Bakheng and an east-west line from the center of the Eastern Baray. This is a relatively small temple pyramid (base 115 × 92 feet [35 × 28 m.]), which rises in three terraces, with axial staircases, guarded by lions, at the sides (Fig. 14.51). The name is derived from *vimana akaśa* or "heavenly palace." A narrow vaulted gallery, which completes the Phimeanakas at the top, was probably added by Suryavarman I (1002–1050 C.E.).

Banteay Srei. Toward the end of the reign of Rajendravarman II (944–968 C.E.) and at the beginning of the reign of his son and successor Jayavarman V (968–1001) a *brahmana* of royal descent named Yajnavaraha occupied an influential position in the government and was responsible for the foundation of the temple now called Banteay Srei (citadel of the women). The site is some 13 miles (21 km.) northeast of Angkor, and was originally known as Iśvarapura. An inscription on a *stela* in the temple records the installation of a *linga* of Śiva called Tribhuvanamaheśvara, and gives the name of Yajnavaraha and the date 889 Śaka (967 C.E.), and the temple work was probably completed by 968 C.E., the last year of the rule of Rajendravarman II and the first year of the reign of Jayavarman V. In the inscription there is also mention of Śri Bhadreśvara (the deity already named at

Pre Rup), and regulations are stated concerning such matters as the feeding of guests at the temple, and the unbroken recitation of the Vedas in the temple. Other temple inscriptions invoke Śiva and also record the installation of images of Sarasvati, Uma, and Vishnu.[137]

The temple, constructed of pink sandstone, is small and all on one level, but very excellently proportioned. The main gateways are at the east and west; the central terrace supports three towers, the central and highest tower (only 32 feet [9.75 mm.] high) dedicated to Śiva; and several subsidiary buildings are in the ensemble including two which are known as "libraries" (a term used for convenience with respect to small side rooms in the Khmer temples, whose actual use is unknown but which may have housed temple accessories, texts, or archives). Guardians of the temple, sculptured in the round, include lion, monkey, and *garuda* figures, and the *garuda* at the east flight of steps of the north tower holds a broken sword in its right hand.

Walls are filled with many relief sculptures of delicate detail. The northern library is decorated with scenes related to Vishnu, the southern library with scenes related to Śiva. Over the door of the southern library, Śiva and Parvati are seated on Mount Kailasa (represented by five superimposed terraces, like a Khmer mountain-temple), which Ravana, the demon king of Lanka, shown with ten heads and twenty arms, is trying in vain to overturn (Fig. 14.52). Ornamenting the walls are also many individual female divinities, known here as *tevodas* (from Sanskrit *devata*), one of them, for example, on the west jamb of the north door of the north tower (Fig. 14.53).[138]

Suryavarman I (1002–1050 C.E.), mentioned above as completing the Phimeanakas, was succeeded by Udayadityavarman II (1050–1065), also mentioned above in connection with the Sdok Kak Thom inscription. To the west of Angkor

14.52 Śiva and Parvati on Mount Kailasa, at Banteay Srei

14.53 Tevoda at Banteay Srei

Udayadityavarman II constructed a huge artificial lake, a reservoir now dry and known as the Western Baray, 5 miles (8 km.) long and 1.4 miles (2.2 km.) wide, even larger therefore than the Eastern Baray of Yaśovarman. In the city just to the south of the Phimeanakas Udayadityavarman II built the Baphuon. This mountain-temple was a very large pyramid of five stories, 393 feet (120 m.) square and 82 feet (25 m.) high, built of laterite, sandstone, and wood, and in the course of time it became very ruined. Just to the north of the Phimeanakas is the Prah Palilay, a sanctuary with a high central tower, built by Jayavarman VI (1085–1107). Surrounded by large trees, it well illustrates the constant encroachment of the jungle.

Banteay Samre. Suryavarman II (1112–1152 c.e.) was a conqueror who led the Khmer armies against Campa, Dai Viet (the future Vietnam), and the Mons of Burma. He was also a great builder if the usual attribution to him is correct of Angkor Wat as well as of a number of smaller temples of similar style, including Banteay Samre.[139]

Banteay Samre (citadel of the Samre, a mountain people living south and east of Angkor) occupies a site about 1,300 feet (400 m.) east of the southeastern corner of the Eastern Baray at Angkor. The temple (Fig. 14.54) is raised on a high platform, surrounded by a terrace adorned with *naga* balustrades, and dominated by a high sandstone tower with four projecting porches and other associated rooms.

Angkor Wat. The two principal groups of monuments to which the name Angkor is most commonly applied are Angkor Wat, the temple, and Angkor Thom, the city.[140] The name Angkor may derive from the Sanskrit *nagara,* meaning capital. The word *wat* (also *vat*) properly designates a monastery, or also a temple, and is generally associated with Buddhism; the word *thom* means great or grand.

14.54 General View of Banteay Samre

Angkor Wat is surrounded by a vast moat, 650 feet (200 m.) wide and about 4,000 × 5,000 feet (1,300 × 1,500 m.) in outside dimensions (Fig. 14.55). The large amount of earth dug out from the moat was piled up in the center to make an elevated place for the temple proper. The main approach is from the west by a long causeway lined on both sides by balustrades in the form of gigantic *nagas* which raise their multiple hoods to guard the way. The fact that the main entrance of the temple faces to the west (the direction of the dead) may be associated with the probable intended function of the monument as the funerary temple of Suryavar-

14.55 View from the Air of Angkor Wat and Its Surrounding Moat

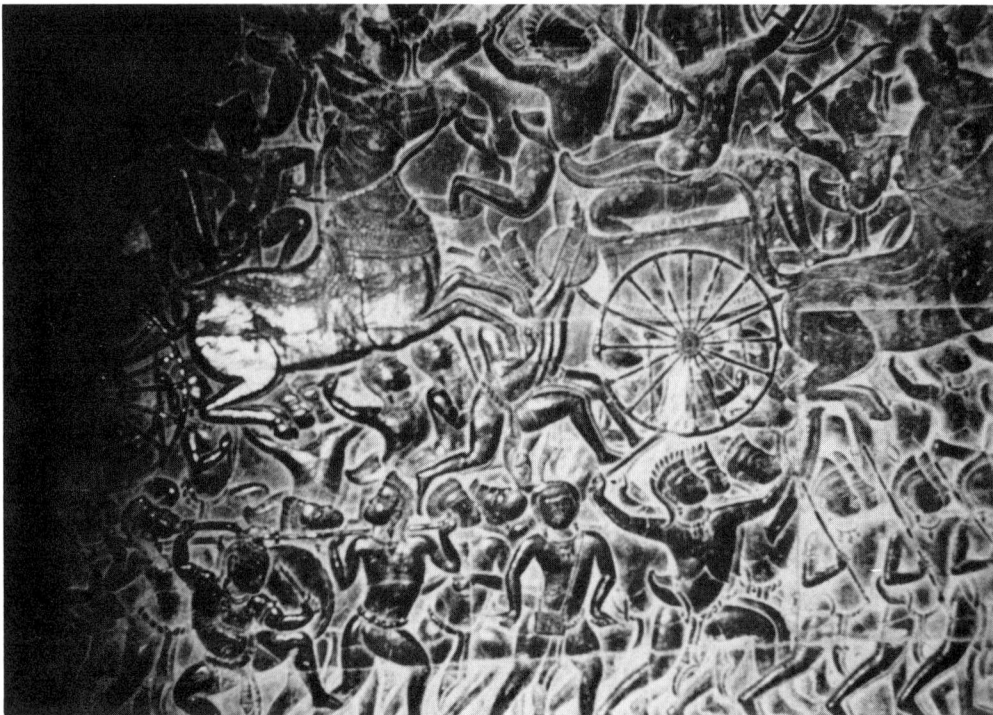

14.56   Battle Scene from the *Mahabharata* at Angkor Wat

man II who, in death, was identified with Vishnu under the posthumous name of Paramavishnuloka. The mountain temple itself rises in three successive terraces to a height of 215 feet (65 m.). Each terrace is reached by stairways, surrounded by a gallery, and marked by corner towers, pavilions, and the like, while the topmost terrace supports a lofty central tower.

The walls of the temple are decorated with many sculptures. The gallery of the first terrace is arranged with pillars on the outside, and the inner walls are covered with panels of bas-reliefs, estimated at some 1,200 square yards in area. On the west wing are battle scenes drawn from the *Mahabharata* (Fig. 14.56) and the *Ramayana;* on the west section of the south wing is the king, presumably Suryavarman II, and an impressive parade of his military forces; in the south section of the east wing is the Churning of the Sea of Milk, with the *asuras* or demons led by Ravana on the left and the gods led by Hanuman on the right (Fig. 14.57), pulling on the serpent Vasuki, etc. Many heavenly maidens *(apsarases, devatas, tevodas)* also adorn the walls, sometimes singly, sometimes in groups (Fig. 14.58). Most characteristically they wear a jeweled headdress with multiple points, and a skirt with flying side panels.

Both the posthumous name of Suryavarman II, Paramavishnuloka, and the scene of the Churning of the Sea of Milk which relates to the Kurma incarnation of Vishnu, suggest the Vaishnavite orientation of Angkor Wat. Under Jayavarman VII (1811–circa 1218 C.E.), however, the monument was converted into a Buddhist shrine, and hence the name Angkor *wat,* using the term for "monastery" usually associated with Buddhism, is appropriate.

In fact the dominance of Buddhism at the royal court appears already with the

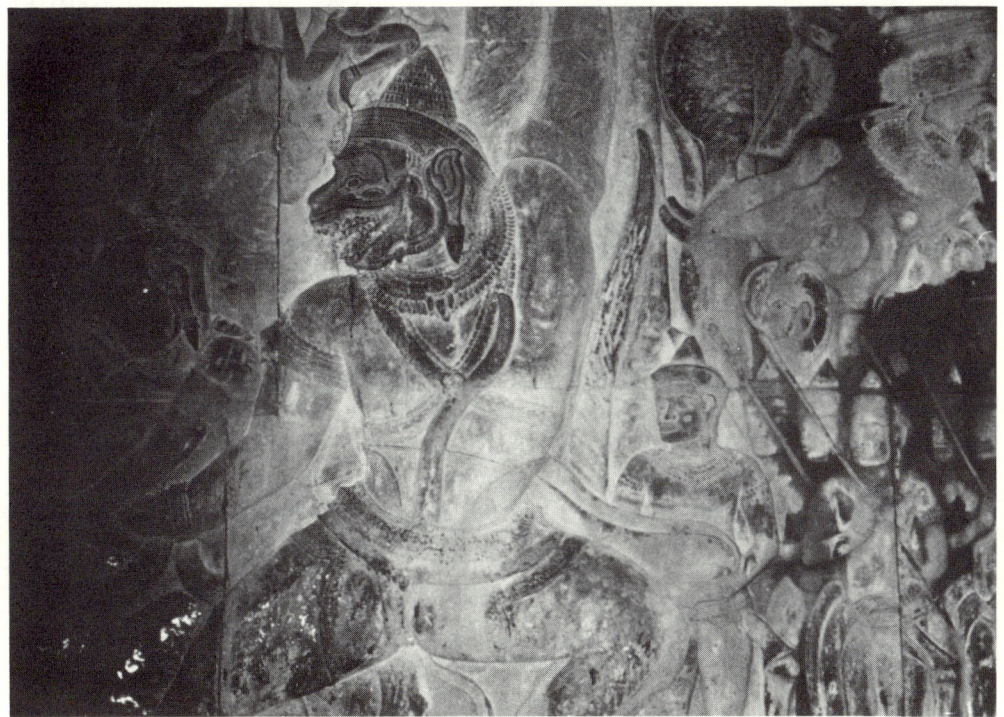
14.57 Team of Asuras in the Scene of the Churning of the Sea of Milk, Angkor Wat

14.58 Apsarases at Angkor Wat

immediate successor of Suryavarman II, who was his cousin Dharanindravarman II. The reign of the latter was apparently brief, but it is at least known that, in contrast with his Hindu predecessors, he was a strong Buddhist and was deified after death in the form of Lokeśvara (Avalokiteśvara) and under the posthumous name of Jayavarmeśvara. A long inscription at Ta Prohm (composed by Suryakumara, a son of Jayavarman VII) says of Dharanindravarman II that he "found his satisfaction in this nectar which is the religion of Śakyamuni," and that "he honored without ceasing the feet of *jina* (i.e., the Buddha)."[141]

After Dharanindravarman II troubled times ensued, but eventually his son, Jayavarman VII, obtained the throne and enjoyed a long reign (1181–circa 1218 C.E.), in which time the country reached the height of its power. In military action, the king put down internal revolts and pushed the limits of the Khmer empire both to the east and the west to their greatest extent. In religion, the same Ta Prohm inscription (cited immediately above) shows that Jayavarman VII, like his father, was an ardent Buddhist. The inscription begins with an invocation to Buddha, *dharma, sangha,* Lokeśvara, and Prajnaparamita, indicating adherence to the Mahayana. Inspired no doubt by Buddhist teachings and by devotion to the compassionate *bodhisattva* Avalokiteśvara (Lokeśvara), Jayavarman VII was concerned for his people and desired their bodily welfare and spiritual salvation. In line with this concern the inscription records the building by the king of 102 hospitals in different parts of the country, and gives a long list of things provided for these institutions. At the end the inscription states the king's desire that these pious works should accrue to the benefit of his mother, Queen Jayarajacudamani, so that she might obtain the state of Buddha. Likewise a long inscription at Preah Khan (composed by Virakumara, a son of Jayavarman VII) records many other pious foundations by Jayavarman VII, and expresses the king's wish that the merit acquired thereby should be for the benefit of his father, Dharanindravarman II.[142]

Angkor Thom. The supreme accomplishment of Jayavarman VII was the building of his new capital, the colossal city of Angkor Thom, Angkor the Great. The site was just to the north of the original Yaśodharapura, between the Eastern Baray and the Western Baray, and the city was laid out as an enormous square, 2 miles (3 km.) on each side, surrounded by a moat and a high wall of laterite stone. At the center of each side, facing the four cardinal points and approached by a long causeway, is an entrance gateway. Each gate, tall enough to permit the passing of canopied elephants, is surmounted by three towers, and these are sculptured with great faces, which make the gateway already a foretaste of the temple in the center of the city. The causeway which leads to the gate is lined with a balustrade on either side in the form of a huge *naga,* pulled by twenty-seven gods (on the left as you enter) and as many demons (on the right) (Fig. 14.59). As in the already described relief at Angkor Wat, the conception is that of the Churning of the Sea of Milk, and here the mountain-temple in the city center represents Mount Meru.

Bayon. As laid out by Jayavarman VII, Angkor Thom enclosed within its limits the already-mentioned Phimeanakas, Baphuon, and Prah Palilay temples, and at the exact city center the king built the Bayon. The Bayon is a great pyramidal mountain-temple of stone, with galleries, pavilions, chapels, and a profusion of towers, more than fifty in number, the central tower rising 150 feet (45 m.) above the ground. The temple is surrounded by an outer gallery 525 × 460 feet (160 × 140 m.) in size, and an inner gallery 262 × 187 feet (80 × 57 m.) in dimension. The galleries are decorated with bas-reliefs showing scenes of land and naval battles, processions of warriors and elephants (Fig. 14.60), festivals, events of daily

14.59 Approach to the South Gate, Angkor Thom

14.60 Food Soldiers and Elephants, Bayon Bas-Relief, Angkor Thom

life, princes and princesses, gods and goddesses. On the towers, facing in the four directions, are carved more than 170 great faces, from 5 feet 10 inches (1.8 m.) to 8 feet 4 inches (2.5 m.) in height, each wearing an elusive smile upon the lips (Fig. 14.61). Given the attested Buddhist orientation of Jayavarman VII, these may be understood as probably representing the *bodhisattva* Avalokiteśvara (Lokeśvara) and, at the same time, as probably suggesting the identification of the king with this divine figure. In the central sanctuary of the temple, instead of the *devaraja* of the earlier Hindu kings, was a large stone statue of the *Buddharaja*. This image, showing the Buddha seated on and sheltered by a nine-headed cobra ("Mucalinda Buddha"), was found in fragments in a pit under the sanctuary and was restored

14.61 Bayon Face, Angkor Thom

and replaced in the temple.¹⁴³ Also on the pillars of the temple are many *devatas (tevodas)* and *apsarases*.

Other temples were also erected by Jayavarman VII in the environs of Angkor Thom—Ta Prohm, Banteay Kedei, Neak Pean, Preah Khan—and elsewhere in his realm, and all were inspired by Buddhism; and almost all built with towers carved with large faces as in the Bayon.¹⁴⁴

BURMA

The indigenous peoples of Burma are for the most part of Mongoloid stock and are generally recognized as representing three main waves of migration: (1) that of the Tibeto-Burman races, including the Burmese and their predecessors or advance contingent the Pyus, who settled in the valley of the Irrawaddy River; (2) that of the Mon-Khmer races, with the Mons settling both in the valley of the Chao Phraya River in Thailand and in the delta and coastal regions of southern Burma; and (3) that of the Thai-Chinese peoples, now the Shans and the Karens.¹⁴⁵

That there were early Indianized states in Burma as elsewhere in Southeast Asia is in itself likely, and is reflected in Burmese traditional history. The chief source for the traditional history is the *Hmannan Yazawindawgyi*, the Glass Palace Chronicle of the Kings of Burma,¹⁴⁶ compiled in 1829 C.E., when King Bagyidaw (1819–1837) appointed a committee of scholars to draw up a history of the happenings in Burma from the earliest times to that date. The name of the work comes from the fact that the scholars met in a chamber of the royal Palace of Glass, as the palace at Ava, then the capital, was called. After consulting existing records and learned monks, and so forth, the committee produced a book in several volumes, and there is no doubt that it recorded as closely as possible what the scholars believed to be historical truth.

Pyus

Tagaung. In the *Hmannan Yazawindawgyi* we are told that the first kingdom in Burma was founded about 850 B.C.E., by an Indian prince named Abhiraja, who marched with an army to Upper Burma, founded the city of Sankissa or Tagaung, and made himself king of the Pyu and Shan people in the surrounding region. The site of Tagaung is on the left bank of the Irrawaddy about 100 miles (161 km.) up the river from the present Mandalay, and is possibly identifiable with the *Tugma metropolis* shown in something like this location on the Eleventh Map of Asia in the *Geography* of Claudius Ptolemy.[147]

After the death of Abhiraja, his kingdom was divided into two parts, with his older son, Kan Rajagyi, ruling over Arakan (Western Burma), and the younger, Kan Rajange, over Tagaung. Counting Abhiraja, Kan Rajange, and their descendants, there were in all thirty-one kings who ruled over Tagaung,[148] the last being Binnakaraja, who was overthrown by invading tribes from China. About this time, when Śakyamuni Buddha was still alive (for the official date of his *nirvana* in 544/543 B.C.E. and the possible date in 501, see above in Chapter 4), another Indian prince, Dhajaraza, who was a member of the Śakiyan family of the Buddha, arrived in Upper Burma, married the widow of Binnakaraja, and founded a new dynasty. This second dynasty, which also had its seat at Tagaung, comprised sixteen kings, and again the last of them was dethroned by invaders.

Śrikshetra. The older son of the last king of Tagaung just mentioned had a miraculous escape and founded a new kingdom, and his son, Duttabaung, established a new capital called Thare Khettara or Śrikshetra (the fortunate field) in the vicinity of modern Prome (Pyè) (from *pyay,* the capital), 150 miles (240 km.) north of Rangoon.

Duttabaung. According to the traditional chronology, Duttabaung (whose name simply means the great king) became king in Year 101 of the Buddhist Era and reigned for seventy years; hence, his dates are 443–375 B.C.E. According to the chronicle, this dynasty endured until Year 638 of the Buddhist Era, i.e., 95 C.E., at which time civil war broke out among the three constituent tribes of the kingdom—the Pyu, Kanran, and Mramma, of whom the Pyus were the chief.

Pyusawti. After the civil war, remnants of the Pyus were supposedly led northward by a legendary king named Pyusawti (168–243 C.E.) where, at a site called Thiripyitsaya and also Arimaddanapura they founded the city which later became known as Pagan.

Śrikshetra itself, however, evidently continued to be a Pyu capital. At the excavated site near Prome (Pyè) some burial urns have been found with inscriptions in the Pyu language and dates: "Suriya Vikrama died in the Year 50; Hari Vikrama died in the Year 57; Siha Vikrama died in the Year 80." According to the Chronicle the Pyus used an era of their own, which was introduced by a *brahmana* astrologer from India, which began in the equivalent of 78 C.E. This must have been the Śaka Era and, assuming that the dates in the inscriptions just cited are in this era, they are equivalent to 128, 135, and 158 C.E. The inscriptions are therefore apparently evidence of a second dynasty which succeeded the first dynasty at Śrikshetra. Finally, in an eleventh century inscription put up by King Kyansittha at a pagoda near Śrikshetra, it is stated that the city fell in the year corresponding to 656 C.E., so the place must have been at last abandoned as a Pyu capital by that time.[149]

Popa Sawrahan. At Pagan there was an early chief named Popa Sawrahan, and he is credited with the introduction of a new era. This new era started in March 638 C.E., is called *kacchapancha* or *culasakaraj,* and is the era which is still in use in Burma and also employed in Thailand.

The name of Popa Sawrahan incorporates the name of Mount Popa, an extinct volcano 4,981 feet (1,518 m.) high, located about 30 miles (50 km.) southeast of Pagan, and suggests his association with the *nats* which were worshiped on that mountain. The *nats* are spirits, and play a prominent part in many forms of Burmese religion. There are *nats* of nature, which are spirits of trees, mountains, and so forth; *nats* of Buddhism, who reside in Indra's heaven and are guardians of the community and the religion; and a category of *nats* who form a group—at first thirty-three, later thirty-six, and finally thirty-seven in number—and are distinguished by legendary historical traits, and reside on Mount Popa which, on that account, is known as the Great Mountain or the Golden Mountain. Two of this last category are the Mahagiri *nats,* a brother and a sister, the Lord of the Great Mountain and the Lady Golden Face, who in human life were personages at the court of the king of Tagaung and were there burned to death, whereby they became spirits. In the course of time these two also became the guardian spirits of Pagan, and every Burmese king's first visit to their mountain, Mount Popa, was considered as important as his coronation, and the date of his "climbing the Golden Mountain" was carefully recorded. It was believed that the Lord of the Great Mountain would make himself visible to the king of Pagan to advise him on matters of state.[150]

Pyinbya. With the final end of Śrikshetra/Prome in 656 C.E., its leading families are supposed to have migrated to Pagan, where there came to be a cluster of nineteen villages. In 847 C.E., under a Pyu ruler named Pyinbya, the immigrants built a protective wall around the entire settlement, and this date and event were considered to mark the official foundation of Pagan.

Mons

Thaton and Pegu. With the final fall of Śrikshetra/Prome and the withdrawal of the Pyus to the north, the leadership of the tribes of Lower Burma passed to the Mons. The chief centers of the Mons were at Thaton and Pegu in the southeastern coastal regions of the land.

According to Mon chronicles, Indian colonists settled in these regions too at an early date. The legend is that two sons of a certain king Tissa, who reigned in the country of Karanaka and the city of Thubinna, came, lived as hermits, and brought up a child born of a dragon on the seashore. This child, when grown up, built the city of Thaton, reigned as its first king under the name of Siharaja, and died in the year in which Śakyamuni Buddha entered *nirvana.* Beginning with Siharaja, fifty-nine kings reigned at Thaton, until the city was taken by Anawrahta about 1044 C.E. In 573 C.E. two sons of the reigning king of Thaton, excluded from the succession to the throne, moved to the northwest and founded the city of Pegu, also called Hamsavati. In all, seventeen kings are listed in the dynasty which ruled at Pegu, the last of whom, also named Tissa, ascended the throne in 761 C.E. for a reign of twenty years. Other settlements of the Mons in Lower Burma were at Dagon (modern Rangoon), Okkala (west of Rangoon near the village of Twante), Syriam (across the Rangoon River to the southeast), and Kosama (modern Bassein). Another name of the Mons was Ramanna, and the Mon territory in Lower Burma was sometimes known as Ramannadeśa. Because of their close connection with India, the Mons were also known as Talaings, meaning people from the Talanga (Telingana) coast of South India.[151]

Introduction of Buddhism

Buddhism must have been introduced into Burma already in the time of the Pyus and the Mons. A Mon tradition relates that the Buddha himself once came to their country but was stoned and driven away by the then savage inhabitants. Another legend relates that two merchants, Tapusa and Bhalluka (Tripusa and Bhallika), went from the Mon kingdom of Okkala to India and visited the Buddha shortly after his enlightenment. The merchants, it is said, gave the Buddha some honey, the first food he received after his enlightenment, and he in turn gave them eight hairs of his head which, upon the return of the merchants, were enshrined by the king Okkalapa in a golden pagoda, identified as the Shwe Dagon (believed to have been built in 585 B.C.E.).[152]

Sona and Uttara. Better attested historically is the mission of Sona and Uttara. It has already been noted above at the beginning of the present chapter that the *Mahavamsa* (12.6) records a mission of these two *theras* to Suvarnabhumi after the Third Buddhist Council under Aśoka (262–239 B.C.E.), and that Suvarnabhumi (Suvannabhumi), the Land of Gold, must correspond with the *Aurea regio* or Region of Gold, shown in the *Geography* of Ptolemy in the area of Lower Burma.

This mission is also recorded on the so-called Kalyani Stones. Under King Dammazedi (1472–1492 C.E.) of Pegu a revival of Buddhism was promoted by the sending of monks to Sri Lanka to receive ordination from the Mahavihara monastery, which clerical standing was transmitted by them upon their return to other monks from all over Burma and also from Thailand. A record of this procedure of ordination was inscribed by the king on ten stones, which are called the Kalyani Stones after the river in Sri Lanka where the visiting monks received their ordination. The account on the Kalyani Stones gives details concerning the earlier history of Buddhism in Sri Lanka and in Burma, and includes this statement about the missions which followed upon the Third Buddhist Council:

> [At the conclusion of this Council] Moggaliputta Tissa *mahathera* reflected that in the future [the religion would be established in neighboring foreign countries and sent such *theras* as Majjhantika *thera* with the injunction: "Do you establish the religion] in those neighboring foreign countries." [Of these *theras* he sent] out lord Mahinda *thera* [to establish the religion in the island of Tambapanni and Sona *thera* and Uttara *thera* to establish the religion in] the Mon country [which was also called Suvannabhumi].[153]

Buddhaghosa. The *Hmannan Yazawindawgyi* claims that the famous scholar Buddhaghosa (who flourished around 430 C.E.) was a native of Thaton, from where he crossed over to a seaport named Bhangiri in the Deccan of India, reached Lanka by ship, and later came back to Thaton and the kingdom of Ramanna, bringing Buddhist scriptures, a visit which provided a great impetus to the religion in that land.[154]

Hmawza. There is also epigraphical and archaeological evidence of the presence of Buddhism in Burma by this time in finds at Hmawza, a village (5 miles [8 km.] south of Prome) which is surrounded to a distance of 10 miles (16 km.) in every direction by the ruins of the ancient capital, Thare Khettara or Śrikshetra. The epigraphs are written on two gold plates, on several fragments of stone, and in a book of twenty leaves of gold. The language is Pali; paleographically, the script is assigned to the fifth and sixth centuries C.E., and in the contents there are formulas of praise of the Buddha, and summaries of and extracts from canonical Pali literature. The affinities of the script are with scripts in South India, and influence from South India is probably represented here, South India being a region in which Theravada Buddhism was flourishing in these centuries, which had close connection with the Buddhaghosa tradition. The archaeological monuments are sculptures in stone and bronze, terracotta votive tablets, and the like, showing Buddhist subjects, and date from about the sixth to the tenth century C.E.[155]

LATER HISTORY

Burmese

When the remnants of the Pyus withdrew from Śrikshetra/Prome to the north, they there mixed with the Burmese, and the Burmese gradually assumed the leadership of the allied tribes, while the city of Pagan, as their capital, soon became the most important place in Burma.[156]

First Burmese Empire. After various struggles for the throne and changes of dynasties, it was the famous king Anawrahta (1044–1077 C.E.) who took the rule and founded the first Burmese dynasty and the kingdom of Pagan, which expanded to encompass practically all of Burma as we know it, and to have tributary regions round about, thus becoming in fact an empire.

The conquests of Anawrahta extended into Arakan in the West, to the mountains in the North, at least to the edge of the Shan states in the East and, most importantly, included the overthrow and absorption of the Mon kingdom of Thaton in the South. The conquest of Thaton was no doubt politically motivated, but was also explained as due to religious interest.

In religion, in addition to the worship of the *nats,* Buddhism was already known at Pagan, apparently in the Mahayana form and represented by teachers whom the Chronicle calls *aris* and portrays as more like shamans and magicians than monks.[157] Under Anawrahta, however, a Mon monk named Shin Arahan, dissatisfied with the acceptance of Hindu ideas in the Buddhism of Thaton, came to Pagan and converted the king to Theravada Buddhism. With Shin Arahan as his religious adviser, Anawrahta undertook to repress the worship of the *nats* and to spread the Theravada throughout his realm. Being told by Shin Arahan that the Mons possessed copies of the Pali Tripitaka, Anawrahta requested these scriptures from Manuha, the king of Thaton. When the request was refused, Anawrahta besieged and captured Thaton (1056 C.E.) and brought back to Pagan the king and

30,000 captives, together with relics and copies of the Tripitaka on thirty-two white elephants.

With respect to the *nats,* finding their cult too deeply entrenched to eradicate, Anawrahta made a compromise by adding Thagyamin—a Hindu-Buddhist king of the gods—to the list of the spirits (making a total of thirty-seven), and making him the head of them all. Also images of the thirty-seven *nats* were set up on a platform at the Shwe Dagon Pagoda to show that they were subservient to the Buddha. As the spirit-king of the Burmese pantheon, Thagyamin is believed to descend to earth at midnight in the first night of the three-day Water Festival in mid-April, preceding the Buddhist New Year *(thingyan).*

Anawrahta also began the construction of very large religious buildings at Pagan, a work which was continued by his successors, giving to him and those who succeeded him the name of the dynasty of the temple builders.

Of the successors of Anawrahta who were also great builders the most important were Kyanzittha (1084–1112 C.E.), Alaungsithu (1112–1167), Narathu (1167–1170), Htilominlo (1210–1234), and Narathihapate (1254–1287). As for Shin Arahan, he continued in his role as religious adviser to the Burmese kings under Kyanzittha and into the reign of Alaungsithu, when he died at the age of eighty-one (about 1115 C.E.).

At the end the kingdom of Pagan was threatened by both the Mongols under Kublai Khan and the Shans, and by internal dissensions as well. In 1277 the Burmese army was defeated by the Mongols in the battle of Ngasaunggyan. In 1287 King Narathihapate's own son Thihathu, the governor of Prome, turned against his father, and the king when surrounded by Thihathu's troops chose to die by eating poisoned food presented to him by his son rather than face certain death in battle. Shortly after the death of the king, the Mongols swept into Pagan, looted and burned the city, and departed with the treasures of the temples and monasteries. For two years the government was in disarray, then Queen Saw, the widow of Narathihapate, and some ministers, chose Kyawsaw, the then sole surviving son of Narathihapate, to be king (1289–1298). He in turn was deposed in 1298, and in 1299 Pagan was again sacked and burned, this time by the Shans. At least two more of the royal line ruled in Pagan as governors, a grandson of Narathihapate named Sawhnit (1298–1325), and his son Uzana (1325–1369), but with them the Pagan dynasty came to an end, and a chaotic period ensued in the history of Burma for the next two and one-half centuries.

Second Burmese Empire. The second Burmese empire was founded by King Tabinshwehti (1531–1550 C.E.) of Toungoo (on the Sittang River, 140 miles [225 km.] north of Rangoon). The capitals of this dynasty were afterward at various sites including Pegu and Ava (6 miles [10 km.] southwest of Mandalay). Tabinshwehti and his brother-in-law and successor, Bayinnaung (1551–1581), began the wars with Thailand which continued intermittently for two centuries. The entire dynasty, known as the Toungoo dynasty, endured until 1752, with Mahadammayaza (1735–1752) as its last king.

Third Burmese Empire. The third and last Burmese empire was founded by King Alaungpaya (1752–1760 C.E.), who made the earlier Mon town of Dagon his capital and renamed it Rangoon (end of strife). Later capitals were at Ava, Amarapura (a suburb of Mandalay), and Mandalay. The most powerful king of the dynasty was Bodawpaya (1782–1819), a son of Alaungpaya who obtained the throne by murdering a usurper. Bodawpaya was succeeded by his grandson,

Bagyidaw (1819–1837), the king who appointed the committee which compiled the *Hmannan Yazawindawgyi*. The last two kings of the empire were Mindon (1853–1878) and Thibaw (1878–1885). It was under King Mindon that the Fifth Great Buddhist Council was convened in Mandalay in 1871. It was Thibaw who surrendered to the British in 1885. It was in modern Burma, under Prime Minister U Nu, that the Sixth Great Buddhist Council met in Rangoon in 1954–1956.

MONUMENTS

The major Buddhist monument in Burma is the *pagoda,* the name derived from the Sinhalese *dagoba* and the Sanskrit *dhatu garbha* (shrine for relics), and it is also commonly called a *zedi* (shrine). Four kinds of *pagodas* are recognized, the *dhatu zedi* which enshrines relics, the *paribhoga zedi* which enshrines implements or garments of the Buddha or of Buddhist saints, the *uddissaka zedi* which enshrines images of the Buddha, and the *dhamma zedi* which enshrines sacred books. Images of the Buddha are generally in four poses, seated in meditation *(dhyana mudra)*, seated at the time of the enlightenment *(bhumisparśa mudra)*, standing with hands raised in the preaching of the Law *(dharmacakra mudra)*, and recumbent, representing the *parinirvana*.

Pagan

Of the archaeological sites in Burma, the greatest is Pagan.[158] The location of the ancient city is 100 miles (160 km.) southwest of Mandalay, on the left bank of the Irrawaddy River, below its confluence with the Chindwin. The area of ancient ruins extends along the river for a length of 15 miles (25 km.) and a width of 2 miles (3 km.). Of a reputed onetime 13,000 temples, the remains of some 5,000 can still be traced. Of these, the main monuments date from the dynasty founded by Anawrahta, the so-called dynasty of the temple builders (1044–1298 C.E.). A general view of the plain at Pagan and of many of the monuments is obtainable from the Thatbyinnyu (Fig. 14.62), the highest of all the temples (210 feet [64 m.]), built by Alaungsithu (1112–1167), fourth king of the Pagan dynasty, and completed by Narathu (1167–1170), the son of Alaungsithu who murdered his father in order to obtain the throne.

Shwezigon Pagoda. The chief monument of Anawrahta (1044–1077) at Pagan is the Shwezigon Pagoda, which was begun in 1059 and was completed after Anawrahta's death by King Kyanzittha (1084–1112) (Fig. 14.63). Three great rectangular terraces form the lower pyramidal part of the monument, with stairways leading up from terrace to terrace in the middle of each side. The four corners of the third terrace are occupied by small *stupas,* and these are models of the great bell-shaped dome which crowns the monument and rises to a height of 197 feet (60 m.). At the base of the monument lions guard the corners, and vases of stone and stylized fig tree standards of iron line the side. In the sides of the terraces glazed brick reliefs with *jataka* scenes are imbedded. In a chapel are golden figures of the Buddha followed by eight of his disciples, Ananda as the first, and all the disciples shown with shaven heads and begging bowls (Fig. 14.64).

Within the precincts of the Shwezigon Pagoda are two stone columns, which are carved with a long inscription of King Kyanzittha. The text begins with a salutation to the Buddha, the *dhamma,* and the *sangha,* and then states that Buddha Śakyamuni himself once upon a time, while dwelling in the Jetavana monastery,

14.62 General View of a Portion of Pagan from the Thatbyinnyu Temple, looking southeast toward the Dhammayangyi Temple (left) and the Shwe Sandaw Pagoda (right)

14.63 Shwezigon Pagoda, Pagan

14.64 Buddha and His Disciples, Shwezigon Pagoda, Pagan

made a prophecy concerning King Kyanzittha. At this time it seems that the future king was a sage named Bisnu, and of him the Buddha prophesies that in his next human incarnation he will become the founder of the city of Śrikshetra, and in a subsequent rebirth king at Pagan (here called Arimaddanapur), after which he will eventually become a Buddha. This prophecy is communicated in the first place to Ananda, then to Gavampati (probably a pre-Buddhist Śaivite divinity, who was a sort of patron saint of the Mons and associated with legendary accounts of the foundation of Thaton), and to Indra, as well as to Bisnu himself. In the course of the prophecy a glowing account is given of the very favorable conditions which will prevail under Kyanzittha as king of Pagan. The king, it is said, will uphold the religion of the Buddha, and will wash away with pure morality, as with water, all sin in deed, word, and thought. With his right hand he will give boiled rice and bread to all the people, and with his left hand will give ornaments and wearing apparel to all. All the people will be like a child that is in its mother's bosom. All who are harsh he will make gentle. Those who are not equal to the rest in body, speech, or spirit, he will make equal. The city of Arimaddanapur, which is the dwelling-place of the king, will gleam with the three precious jewels, which are the Buddha, the Law, and the religious community.[159]

Kubyauk Kyi Pagoda. The Kubyauk Kyi Pagoda is also attributed to Anawrahta, and probably does at least belong to the eleventh century, although its exact date is not known. Wall paintings, attributed to the twelfth century, still adorn its inner halls. In an arrangement of pictures (Fig. 14.65) seen also in other Pagan temples, the Buddha is seen repeatedly in the seated position and earth-touching gesture *(bhumisparśa mudra)* of the time of his attainment of enlighten-

14.65 Wall Paintings in the Kubyauk Kyi Pagoda, Pagan

ment, and a large number of small square panels closely grouped and together covering a large area contain scenes from the *jatakas*.

Ananda Temple. The Ananda Temple was built by King Kyanzittha and dedicated in 1090 C.E. Although Ananda was the name of the Buddha's favorite disciple, the temple was originally named not after him but after the infinite *(ananta)* wisdom of the Buddha. The structure forms a great square 175 feet (53 m.) on a side, with projecting porches on each side so that, in all, it measures nearly 290 feet (88 m.) across each way, and it rises in seven stories and a lofty tower *(śikhara)* to a height of 172 feet (52 m.).

At the rear of each projecting porch there is a tall niche, containing a colossal standing statue of the Buddha (31 feet [9.5 m.] high). Of these, only the south and north figures are original: they are characterized by the hands raised together before the chest in the gesture of preaching *(dharmacakra mudra)* (Fig. 14.66). The statue in the east niche has both hands hanging, an unusual pose for the Buddha; the statue in the west niche has the right hand raised in the gesture of reassurance *(abhaya mudra)*, while the left hand is held out level from the elbow, with the palm upward. Each Buddha stands on a double lotus resting on a large throne which fills the breadth of the recess, and projects at the sides to form thrones for two kneeling figures. These are in each case two chief disciples of the Buddha, except in the west shrine where their places are taken by King Kyanzittha himself, wearing his royal crown and ornaments, and Shin Arahan, his religious adviser, shown with shaven head and no ornaments.[160] In many other smaller niches of the temple are other images of the Buddha, and sculptured reliefs illustrating scenes from his life. On the exterior of the temple are glazed terracotta plaques with the most complete series of

14.66 Colossal Standing Statue of the Buddha in the Ananda Temple, Pagan. Photograph by Arthur S. Merrow, Jr.

scenes from the *jatakas* (considered to number 547) at Pagan, and these are identified by short legends in the Old Mon or Talaing language.[161]

Htilominlo Temple. The Htilominlo Temple was built during the reign of Htilominlo (1210–1234), the eighth king of the Pagan dynasty, who ruled jointly with his four brothers, all sons of the preceding king Narapatisithu (1173–1210), in a council form of government said to have been the origin of the Hlutdaw or supreme council of state, which remained the basis of government in Burma until 1885.

A stone inscription on the west side of the temple deals with the building of the temple, attached monastery, rest house, and library, and with the dedication of slaves and lands for the support of the institution:

> On Friday, the 7th waning Nadaw 585 *sakaraj* (1223 C.E.), the Prime Minister Anandathuya and his wife, being actuated by a desire to free himself and all the inhabitants of this and other universes from the miseries of *samsara* and to attain the bliss of *nirvana*, performed the following good deeds. A piece of land was planted with a number of palm trees and was enclosed with double walls. A domed pagoda was then built and within it was enshrined a relic of Gautama Buddha placed in a receptacle composed of many graduated caskets, the larger enclosing the smaller, and made of many metals and other materials. The innermost was fashioned out of a kernel of the seed of the *tari* palm and the rest were of glass, lacquerware,

gold, silver . . . ivory, copper, and marble successively. The receptacle was placed in a heap of gold and silver flowers, and the outside was painted and secured with brass wire. The top of the lid was of gold. A golden umbrella was placed over all and it was hung with pearls and coral beads. The umbrella was covered with seven layers of cloth and was ornamented with gold-leaf. Besides this there were a golden image weighing 30 *ticals* (a Burmese unit of weight, in which 100 *ticals* equal 3.75 pounds), a silver image weighing 50 *ticals,* and a painted marble image with gold and silver umbrellas over them. The image within the pagoda was lavishly bejeweled and it was surrounded with several small images. The walls within were adorned with paintings illustrating the 550 former births of Gautama Buddha. . . . A masonry library was next built and a complete copy of the Tripitaka was placed therein for the enlightenment of all comers. Then a brick monastery was erected for the residence of an abbot, and several other smaller ones were built outside the first wall close by for the monkhood. Then a well was sunk and a tank was dug and gardens were cultivated all round it. Lastly, a beautiful wall was erected along the boundaries of the monastery land as well as rest houses for pilgrims which might also be used by the people on festive occasions. . . . All these meritorious deeds were performed in order that the religion might last for 5,000 years.

After this the text continues with respect to the arrangements for the support of the temple and its monks, and gives a long list of the names of the slaves dedicated to this purpose.[162]

Mingalazedi Pagoda. The Mingalazedi Pagoda (Fig. 14.67) was built by King Narathihapate (1254–1287), and was the last of the great Pagan temples, being finished in 1274, only a little more than a dozen years before the sack of Pagan in 1287 by Kublai Khan. The monument appears never to have been broken into, and it remains the best preserved of all the Pagan pagodas. In plan much like the Shwezigon, it rises on a pyramidal base of three rectangular terraces, with a

14.67   Mingalazedi Pagoda, Pagan

central stairway on each side. On the corners of the terraces are twelve small and four large *stupas*. In turn the rectangular terraces support the octagonal base of the great bell-shaped dome which crowns the structure.

A stone inscription within the walls of the pagoda describes the building, dedication, and naming of the monument:

> On Sunday, the sixth waxing of Tabaung 603 *sakaraj* (an error of the sculptor in the date, which should be 630 *sakaraj*, i.e., 1268 C.E.), King Narathihapade . . . who is the supreme commander of the vast army of thirty-six million soldiers, and who is the consumer of 300 dishes of curry daily, being desirous of attaining the bliss of *nirvana*, erected a pagoda. Having done so, the king enshrined within it fifty-one gold and silver statuettes of kings, queens, noblemen, and maids of honor, and over these an image of Gautama Buddha in solid silver one cubit high, on Thursday, the full moon of Kason 636 *sakaraj* (1274 C.E.). On that occasion a covered way was erected extending from the palace to the pagoda. Bamboo mats were laid along this. Over these, rush mats were spread, and over these again pieces of cloth twenty cubits each in length were spread; and at each cubit's length of the way banners were placed. During the ceremony the princes, princesses, and nobles threw a large number of pearls among the statuettes, and the pagoda was formally named the Mingalazedi.

A later portion of the inscription is dated in 663 *sakaraj* (1301 C.E.), and was probably inscribed by Sawhnit (1298–1325), the grandson of Narathihapate, who served as a governor in Pagan. It records the dedication of certain paddy-lands to the pagoda.[163]

Mandalay

Replacing the earlier nearby capitals of Ava and Amarapura, Mandalay was founded as the capital of King Mindon (1853–1878) in 1857, and remained the capital of his successor, the last Burmese monarch, King Thibaw (1878–1885).[164]

Mahamuni Pagoda. The Mahamuni Pagoda, also known as the Arakan Pagoda, located toward the south side of Mandalay, was already a shrine before the rise of the city itself. The main Buddha figure is the Mahamuni image, a seated statue of the Buddha, cast in bronze and covered with gold, which was brought back from Arakan by King Bodawpaya in 1785 C.E. According to tradition in Arakan the image was made in the year corresponding to 146 C.E. by a king named Candasurya, and it was considered a national treasure and believed to possess miraculous powers. Along with the Mahamuni image, Bodawpaya brought back from Arakan as other spoils of war bronze figures of warriors, of lions, and of the three-headed elephant of Indra known as Erevan, and these were also kept at the Mahamuni Pagoda. The capital of Bodawpaya was at Amarapura, and the king constructed a brick road from there to the Mahamuni.

Kuthodaw Pagoda. The Kuthodaw Pagoda is located at the foot of Mandalay Hill (954 feet [291 m.] high), which is itself marked by many smaller Buddhist shrines. The Kuthodaw Pagoda was built by King Mindon in 1857 at the same time as the foundation of his capital. It was patterned after the Shwezigon Pagoda at Pagan, and exhibits the same pyramidal terrace and lofty bell-shaped dome (Fig. 14.68). Within the grounds stand the small enclosures which house the 729 marble tablets which are inscribed with the edition of the Buddhist scriptures determined by the Fifth Great Buddhist Council which met in Mandalay during Mindon's reign.

14.68 Kuthodaw Pagoda, Mandalay

Rangoon

Rangoon is a seaport city on the Rangoon (or Hlaing) River, 21 miles (34 km.) from its mouth, the river being the eastern outlet of the Irrawaddy River in the Irrawaddy delta. As already noted, the port was originally called Dagon, and was renamed Rangoon (end of strife) by King Alaungpaya (1752–1760 C.E.), the founder of the Third Burmese Empire, when he made it his capital. The city was the site of the Sixth Great Buddhist Council in 1954–1956.

Shwe Dagon Pagoda. The Shwe Dagon (Golden Dagon) Pagoda stands on Singattura Hill at Rangoon, and is visible from far away. According to tradition, it was built originally in 585 B.C.E. to contain relics of Śakyamuni Buddha. As it exists today, the pagoda stands upon a lofty marble-floored platform (Fig. 14.69), and is surrounded by many smaller *stupas,* shrines, and chapels (Fig. 14.70). The main *stupa* has a circumference at the base of 1,420 feet (433 m.) and rises to a height of 326 feet (99 m.). It is entirely covered with gold leaf, and at the top is enriched with thousands of diamonds and other precious and semi-precious stones. It is one of the most sacred Buddhist shrines in Asia.[165]

Sule Pagoda. The Sule Pagoda, erected by King Alaungpaya as a religious act in connection with the establishment of his capital at Rangoon, is located in the heart of the downtown city and near the harbor, where the Sule Pagoda Wharves are named after it. The spire of the *stupa* is gold plated, and the pagoda's many small shrines and chapels contain golden figures of the Buddha (Fig. 14.71).

14.69 Shwe Dagon Pagoda from Its Main Platform, Rangoon

14.70 Monks at a Small Shrine, Shwe Dagon Pagoda, Rangoon

14.71 Golden Buddha in Side Chapel, Sule Pagoda, Rangoon

14.72 Dome and Spire of the Botataung Pagoda, Rangoon

14.73 Head of Reclining Image of the Buddha, Chauk Htat Kyi Temple, Rangoon

Botataung Pagoda. The Botataung Pagoda is near the Sule Pagoda, and has a great completely gilded dome and spire (Fig. 14.72). It is known for its inner chambers, the walls and ceilings of which are completely covered with mirror glass.

Chauk Htat Kyi Temple. The Chauk Htat Kyi Temple, on the Shwegondine Road in Rangoon, is notable for a very large reclining statue of the Buddha (216 feet [66 m.] long by 58 feet [18 m.] high) (Fig. 14.73). The monastery adjacent takes its name from the image, and is a famous center of Buddhist scholarship.

THAILAND

Dvaravati

In the area of present-day Thailand the earliest kingdom of which we have knowledge is Dvaravati.[166] In the middle of the seventh century C.E. the Chinese Buddhist pilgrim Xuan Zang mentions a kingdom called *To-po-lo-ti,* which is recognized as corresponding with the Sanskrit Dvaravati, and he places it (according to the inquiry he made, since he did not go there in person) beyond the kingdom of Śrikshetra to the southeast, and before the country of Iśanapura still to the east.[167] Since Śrikshetra was at Prome in Burma, and Iśanapura was in Kampuchea, the general location of Dvaravati may reasonably be thought to have been in the basin of the Menam (Chao Phrya) River, i.e., in what is now central and northern Thailand.

Although Dvaravati is called a kingdom by Xuan Zang, it is probably more accurately to be described by the Thai word *muang,* which refers to an earlier form of state in which a group of cities was linked together somewhat loosely by ties of marriage, culture, and the like. That the people of Dvaravati were predominantly Mons is suggested by early Mon inscriptions found at Lamphun (16 miles [25 km.] south of Chiang Mai) and Lopburi (on the Lopburi River 80 miles [129 km.] north of Bangkok),[168] and that their country was a center of Buddhist culture is suggested by many archaeological objects of early Buddhist character (wheels of the Law, images of the Buddha) found at a number of sites including Lopburi and especially Nakhon Pathom (30 miles [48 km.] west of Bangkok).[169] According to local tradition at Nakhon Pathom, this place was visited by the Buddhist missionaries, Sona and Uttara, in the time of Aśoka (third century B.C.E.), and the early character of many of the Buddhist artifacts makes such an early introduction of Buddhism not unlikely.[170]

Sukhothai

In the later history of Thailand, as reconstructed in a number of Thai historical works, most notably in The Royal Autograph Chronicle *(Phraratchaphongsawadan chabap Phraratchahatlekha)*—composed jointly by Kromluang Wongsathiratsanit, a half-brother of King Mongkut (1851–1868 C.E.), by the king himself, and by the king's son, Prince Damrong—three major periods are recognized, represented by Sukhodaya or Sukhothai, Ayudhya or Ayutthaya, and Thonburi/Bangkok.[171]

In the period broadly definable as the eleventh to the thirteenth centuries C.E., the kingdom of Dvaravati came to its end, the Khmers dominated parts of the country with a capital at Lopburi, and the Thai people, also called the Syam (Siamese), came in from the north and established themselves in the middle Menam Valley.[172] At Sukhodaya or Sukhothai (Sanskrit, the dawn *[udaya]* of happiness *[sukha]*) (on the right bank of the Yom River, 225 miles (360 km.) north of Bangkok) the Thai threw off the dominion of the Khmers, and founded a kingdom of their own, with an additional twin capital at nearby Sawankhalok (the place *[loka]* of the community *[sangha]*).

Rama Khamhaeng. The first Thai king of Sukhothai was Phra Ruang, who was crowned as Śri Indraditya (Intaratiya), probably 1238–1275 C.E., and he was followed in turn first by an older son Ban Muang (protector of the kingdom) (1275), and then by a younger son Rama Khamhaeng (Rama the strong) (1275–1317). A long inscription of Rama Khamhaeng, found at Sukhothai and probably composed in 1292 C.E., is the oldest extant inscription in the Thai language and is a chief source of information concerning the kingdom. The text describes the rule of Rama Khamhaeng in these words:

> During the lifetime of Rama Khamhaeng, this city of Sukhothai is prosperous. In the water there is fish, in the fields there is rice; the lord of the country does not levy taxes on his subjects who go along the road together, leading cattle to market, riding horses for sale. Whoever wishes to trade in elephants or in horses, does so; whoever wishes to trade in silver, in gold, does so. If a common man, a noble, or a chief falls ill, dies, or disappears, the house of his ancestors, his clothing, his elephants, his family, his rice granaries, his slaves, the areca and betel plantations of his ancestors are all transmitted to his children. If the common people, the nobles, or the chiefs get into disagreement, the king conducts a thorough inquiry, then settles the matter for his subjects with complete impartiality; he does not connive with the thief and the receiver of stolen goods; if he sees the rice of others, he does not covet it; and if he sees the treasure of others, he is not envious of it. Whoever goes by elephant in search of him and places

his own country under his protection, he gives him aid and assistance; if the stranger has neither elephants, nor horses, nor servants, nor wives, nor silver, nor gold, he gives him some and invites him to regard himself as in his own country. If he captures warriors or enemy soldiers, he neither kills nor beats them. There is a bell suspended in the embrasure of the palace doorway: if an inhabitant of the kingdom has any grievance or any matter that is gnawing at his entrails and tormenting his spirit and he wants to reveal it to the king, it is not difficult; he has only to strike the bell hanging there. Every time King Rama Khamhaeng hears this appeal, he questions the plaintiff about his affair and judges it with complete impartiality.

The text also tells how in the year 1205 (reckoned in the Śaka Era, counted from 78 C.E., equivalent to 1283 C.E.) the king invented the improved kind of characters for the Thai language in which the inscription itself is written; describes the city of Sukhothai with its triple wall and four gates; tells of a monastery named Aranyika to the west of the city; and names a spirit, Phra Khaphung, which resided on a hill to the south of the city and had to be worshiped in order to gain its protection for the city. In spite of this animistic practice, Theravada Buddhism was the prevailing religion, and important ceremonies took place at the Aranyika monastery.

King Rama Khamhaeng, sovereign of this *muang* Sukhothai, as well as the princes and princesses, men as well as women, nobles and chiefs, all without exception, without distinction of rank or sex, devoutly practice the religion of the Buddha and observe the precepts during the period of retreat during the rainy season. At the end of the rainy season, the ceremonies of the *kathin* (presentation of new robes to the monks) take place and last a month.

A postscript to the inscription eulogizes the king:

Rama Khamhaeng is the chief and sovereign of all the Thai. He is the master who instructs all the Thai so that they know in truth the merits and the Law. Among all the men who live in Thai country, one would search in vain for his equal in science and in knowledge, in courage and in endurance, in strength and in energy. He has defeated the throng of his enemies possessing large cities and numerous elephants.

As far as Thai conquests are concerned, the text also gives details showing that at its height under Rama Khamhaeng the kingdom of Sukhothai extended from the present-day Laos in the East to the Andaman Sea in the West, and in the South to the Gulf of Thailand and into the Malay peninsula.[173]

The kings who followed Rama Khamhaeng at Sukhothai were also strong Buddhists. The son and successor of Rama Khamhaeng, Lo Thai (1317–1347 C.E.), his son and successor, Lu Thai (1347–1368), and three more kings after them were apparently all called Tammaraja (*dharmaraja* or *dharmikaraja*), with the signification of "pious king."[174]

A pious work of Lo Thai was to install a replica of the footprint of the Buddha which was on the Sumanakuta mountain in Sri Lanka on a hill similarly called Sumanakutaparvata, probably to be identified with Khau Brah Pada Noy, 2 miles (3 km.) west of Sukhothai, where such a footprint is still venerated. A *stela*, which was probably found on that hill, contains an inscription dated in the year 1281 (1359 C.E.) of a king (probably Lu Thai) who says that he was crowned as Śrisuryavamśa Mahadharmarajadhiraja and that in the year indicated he made a pilgrimage from Sukhothai to pay homage to the sacred footprint, "which his father (probably Lo Thai) had previously placed on the summit of the mountain Sumanakuta."[175]

Lu Thai himself was also learned in the Vedic and Buddhist scriptures, and composed a large work on Buddhist cosmology, the *Traibhumikatha*, which is preserved in an old Thai version known as *Traiphum Phra Ruang* and, in modern versions, is still important in Thailand. In 1357 C.E. Lu Thai sent a mission to Sri Lanka to obtain relics of the Buddha, in 1361 he invited the Patriarch Maha Svami to come from Lanka to reside and teach at Sukhothai, and in the same year he was himself ordained by the Patriarch as a monk, at least for a period of time. In language similar to that descriptive of his grandfather Rama Khamhaeng, an inscription says of Lu Thai that he does not covet the rice or the wealth of others, and that he pardons those who behave wickedly toward him. "The reason why he represses his heart and quells his spirit and does not become angry when it would be proper for him to do so, is that he has the desire to become a Buddha and the desire to lead all creatures beyond the ocean of sorrows of transmigration."[176]

At Sukhothai the kings had as a royal chapel and as the spiritual center of their kingdom a Buddhist temple (Wat Mahathat), which was located within the compound of the royal palace itself, a custom which would be followed later in Ayudhya and in Bangkok.

Ayudhya

In the meantime, even during the reign of Rama Khamhaeng (1275–1317 C.E.), the old kingdom of Lopburi had maintained its independence, and at the same time or soon afterward another state, Suphanburi (40 miles [64 km.] southwest of Lopburi, on the Suphanburi River, variously known as the Nakhon Chaisi and the Thachin), which had been temporarily under the domination of Sukhothai, was again independent. Then in 1351, still during the reign of Lu Thai (1347–1368) of Sukhothai, the new city of Ayutthaya or Ayudhya (45 miles [72 km.] north of Bangkok) was founded, Sukhothai rapidly lost the remnants of its power, and Ayudhya dominated the next period in the history of Thailand.[177]

Among Thai historical works several that are relatively early are especially concerned with Ayudhya. The Luang Prasoet Chronicle of Ayudhya (*Phraratchaphongsawadan Krung Si Ayudhya chabap Luang Prasoet*) is probably the oldest chronicle in the Thai language ever discovered. It was written in 1680 C.E. by a royal astrologer under the orders of King Narai (1656–1688), and was found in 1907 by Luang Prasoet, and hence is called by his name. It deals with events in Ayudhya between *culasakaraj* 686 and 966 (i.e., reckoning from 638 C.E., between 1324 and 1604 C.E.).[178] *The History of the Lesser Battle: On Thai History* (*Culayudhakaravamsa: Ruang phongsawadan Thai*) was written around 1789 by the monk Somdet Phra Wannarat, who was the teacher of the monk-prince Paramanuchitchinorot. The work covers the history of Ayudha up to 1456 C.E. The *Abridged Chronicle (Phraratchaphongsawadan Sangkhep)* was written in 1850 by Paramanuchitchinorot, largely on the basis of the preceding work by his teacher, Somdet Phra Wannarat. As its name suggests, this is a condensed account, but it brings the history of Ayudhya down to *culasakaraj* 1129, i.e., to 1767 C.E., when the city was sacked by the Burmese.[179]

U Thong. In the *Abridged Chronicle* the account of Ayudhya begins with a story concerning the founder of the city.[180] A king (in other sources named Jaya Ciri) was driven from his city by invaders and fled to a deserted principality, the *muang* Paeb, directly across the river from Kamphaengphet (on the Ping River 200 miles [310 km.] northwest of Bangkok), where he built a new capital called Traiyatrunsha (thirty-three [heavens]), and where he was followed by four more monarchs of his dynasty. In that later time a daughter of the king of Traiyatrunsha bore a son, the identity of whose father was unknown. When it was determined by an omen that the father was a man of non-royal blood named Nai Saen Pom, he and the daughter and grandson were sent away in dishonor. The lord Indra, however, recognized the great merit of these three people, and gave Nai Saen Pom a magical drum, through which they had good fortune. By this means a golden cradle was made for the child and, for this reason, his name was U Thong (golden cradle). By the same means, in the year 681 (1319 C.E.), Nai Saen Pom founded a city called Devanagara (city of the gods) and ruled there as King Ciri Jaya Chieng Saen for twenty-five years. Upon the death of his father, U Thong succeeded to the throne and ruled at Devanagara for six years, then desired to build a new capital. A site was found farther to the south, at a place surrounded by water (i.e., on an island), a walled city was constructed, and it was given a compound name which included the name of ancient Dvaravati and the name of Ayodhya, the famous city of Rama. This was Ayudhya (now Ayutthaya), and the *Abridged Chronicle,* the *Luang Prasoet Chronicle,* and the *Royal Autograph Chronicle* all agree in dating the foundation of the city as the capital of U Thong in the year 712 (1350 C.E.).

There are obviously legendary traits in the above account, and there are also divergent versions of the origin of U Thong in other chronicles and in modern reconstructions of his background.[181] The *Abridged Chronicle* provides other information, however, which is presumably accurate. We learn that U Thong began to reign at the age of thirty-seven years and, as king, received the name of Ramadhipati or Ramathibodi. Inasmuch as Phangua, the older brother of U Thong's queen, went to govern Suphanburi, and Rameśvara (or Ramesuan), his own son, went to govern Lopburi, U Thong had family connections with both of those important principalities.[182] In all, U Thong's kingdom included Sukhothai and fifteen other vassal principalities, and he also made a conquest of Kambuja. He built monasteries named Buddhaiyasavarya and Pa Kaeo. He reigned for twenty years, and died in 731 (1369 C.E.) at the age of fifty-six.

Successors of U Thong. When King Ramathibodi I (U Thong) died, his son Rameśvara (or Ramesuan) came down from Lopburi and ascended the throne, but reigned poorly (1369–1370) and in the next year was replaced by Phangua, the brother-in-law of U Thong, who came from Suphanburi and reigned as King Paramarajadhiraja I or Boromoraja I (1370–1388 C.E., following the chronology of the *Luang Prasoet Chronicle* which is generally accepted as correct throughout), while Ramesuan was sent back to govern Lopburi again. When Boromoraja I died, his son Thong Lan, whose age was only fifteen, assumed the scepter of Ayudhya for seven days (1388), but Ramesuan came with an army from Lopburi, took the throne (1388–1395), and ordered the execution of Thong Lan. Ramesuan in turn was succeeded by his son Phra Ram, who reigned as King Ramarajadhiraja (1395–1409), and with him the U Thong dynasty of Ayudhya came to an end, for Indraraja came from Suphanburi, seized Ayudhya, and sent Ramarajadhiraja off to govern a place called Padagucham. King Indraraja I (1409–1424) was a nephew of King Boromoraja I and thus a cousin of Ramesuan and an uncle of Ramarajadhiraja, so the new Suphanburi dynasty of Ayodhya was at least related by marriage to the U Thong dynasty. The Suphanburi dynasty ruled in Ayudhya from 1409 to 1569, i.e., from Indraraja I to the first fall of Ayudhya to the Burmese; then a Sukhothai family returned to power and ruled in Ayudhya until the final sack of the city by the Burmese in 1767.[183]

In political/military affairs the kingdom of Ayudhya was engaged in many wars both within the territory of Thailand and also farther afield, especially with Kampuchea to the east and Burma to the west. The conquest of Kambuja claimed for King Ramathibodi I (U Thong) (1350–1369) has already been noted, and the *Abridged Chronicle* also records the conquest of Angkor by Rameśvara (Ramesuan) during his second reign (1388–1395), and by Paramarajadhiraja II (Boromoraja II) (1424–1448) in 1431, the last event marking the end of the classical period of Khmer civilization.[184]

Boromoraja II was succeeded by his son Rameśvara (or Ramesuan), who reigned as Boromo Trailokanat (or Paramatrailokanatha), and is commonly known as Paramatrailoka or simply Trailok (1448–1488 C.E.). He is one of the most famous of the Thai kings, and was responsible for laws and administrative reforms which prevailed thereafter in Thailand into the nineteenth century. Throughout much of his reign, Paramatrailoka was engaged in intermittent battles with King Tilokaraja (1441–1487) of Lanna Thai (Chiang Mai). In the course of this conflict, in the year 825 (1463 C.E.), as the *Luang Prasoet Chronicle* records, Trailok moved his capital from Ayudhya to Bishnuloka (the realm of Vishnu) or Phitsanulok (210 miles [338 km.] north of Bangkok, and 30 miles [48 km.] southeast of Sukhothai), doubtless in order better to protect his northern frontier. At the same time he left his son (probably Indaraja) to rule at Ayudhya with the title Paramaraja. Finally in the year 836 (1474 C.E.) Trailok was victorious in a battle at Salieng (Chalieng), and in the next year, 838 (1475 C.E.), Tiloka asked for relations of friendship, i.e., a truce. Trailok himself died in the year 850 (1488 C.E.), and his son (probably Indaraja) then reigned at Bishnuloka as Paramaraja III (Boromoraja III) until his own death in 853 (1491 C.E.), after which, under his brother Ramathibodi II (1491–1529), the capital was transferred back to Ayudhya.[185]

As for the wars with Burma, the first Burmese invasion of Thailand was launched by the Burmese king Tabinshwehti (1531–1550) in 1548 and reached its climax with the taking of Ayudhya by King Bayinnaung (1551–1581) in 1569. While Ayudhya was under siege at that time, the Thai king Chakkraphat (1548–1568) died, and his son Mahin (1568–1569) succeeded to the throne, but soon lost the city to the attackers and was himself carried off a prisoner and died of a fever on the way to Burma. Maha Tammaraja I (1569–1590), a pro-Burmese son-in-law of Chakkraphat, then ruled as a vassal of Burma, but in 1584 a famous warrior prince, Naresuan, organized an army of resistance against the Burmese, retook Ayudhya and, upon the death of his father (the vassal king), himself ascended the throne (1590–1605). In a further attack by the Burmese in 1592 King Naresuan distinguished himself yet more by overcoming the Burmese crown prince, Min Chit Swa, in single combat. Although the Burmese were repelled for the time being, they again moved against Ayudhya and laid the city under siege in 1760, only to be driven off again. Finally in the year 1767 and at the end of the second reign of King Boromoraja V (1758–1760, 1762–1767) the Burmese captured, sacked, and almost completely destroyed the city, a destruction in which the bulk of ancient Thai written records and archives also perished.

Religion. In religion the names of Ramathibodi, Rameśvara, Ramarajadhiraja, and Indraraja probably mean that these early Ayudhyan kings were treated as reincarnations of Hindu deities (of Rama, incarnation of Vishnu, and of Indra). Buddhism, however, was also considered very important. The construction of Buddhist monasteries by U Thong has already been noted, and the similar works of Paramatrailoka will be noted immediately below. Trailok was probably also the first Ayudhyan king to follow the example of Sukhothai and have a Buddhist temple as a royal chapel and spiritual center of the kingdom immediately within the precincts of his royal palace.[186]

As he is described in the *Luang Prasoet Chronicle* and the *Abridged Chronicle*, Paramatrailoka or Trailok (1448–1488) was associated with both Hinduism and Buddhism.[187] The king had 500 statues of the Buddha cast, showing his 500 births and, as an inauguration of the statues, plays were performed and large gifts were bestowed not only on Buddhist priests but also on *brahmanas* and hermits. The king also gave over his princely palace to be the Śrī Sarbej monastery, and constructed the Phra Rama monastery on the site on which King Ramadhipati I (U Thong), the founder of the capital, had been cremated (died 1369). Paramatrailoka moved his capital from Ayudhya to Bishnuloka (Phitsanulok) in 1463, and in the next year built a monastery called Culamani, the ruins of which are still visible about 3 miles (5 km.) south of the town. In the next year after that (1465) he was himself ordained in the monastery as a monk, a position in which he remained for eight months, thus emulating King Lu Thai of Sukhothai (1347–1368), who likewise entered the monastic life at least for a time. Also, like Lu Thai, who wrote the *Traiphum* on Buddhist cosmology, Paramatrailoka composed a *jataka* tale known as *Maha chat kham luang* (the royal version of the Maha Jataka).

Probably not long after the victory of Paramatrailoka over Tiloka in 1475, a long Thai poem was composed, called the *Yuan Phai* (in it Tiloka is called the Yuan king, and the title means the defeat of the Yuan), which provides an account of the long struggle of the two kings and eulogizes Paramatrailoka, the author perhaps having been Paramatrailoka's son, Ramathibodi II.[188]

In the long complimentary description of Paramatrailoka with which the poem opens, the king is compared in turn with eleven great gods of Hinduism, namely, Brahma, Vishnu, Śiva, Indra, Yama, Marut, Varuna, Agni, Upendra (a form of Vishnu), the Sun, and the Moon, and is declared to be mixture of all of them. He is also referred to as learned in the three jewels of Buddhism as well as in the Vedas. The *Mahabharata* and the *Ramayana* are also reflected, and Paramatrailoka is said to be as steadfast in battle as Arjuna, as cunning as Krishna, and as expert in archery as Rama. In the climax of the poem there is a vivid account of the final battle between Paramatrailoka and Tiloka, which takes place at Chieng Chün. This place is probably to be identified with the old city of Chalieng, the extensive ruins of which are still to be seen on the right bank of the Yom River, about 35 miles (56 km.) north of Sukhothai. At this site there still stands the tall tower of the Mahadhatu (the temple of the great relic), which was presumably built soon after 1475 by Paramatrailoka to commemorate his victory and to be a symbol of his authority in the region he had recaptured from Tiloka.[189]

Thonburi/Bangkok

Taksin. When Ayudhya was destroyed by the Burmese in 1767 C.E., a general of the Thai forces, himself half Chinese by birth, named Phya Taksin, escaped, established himself at Rayong on the Gulf of Thailand and, from there, ascended the Menam River and captured the city of Thonburi (across the river from the present Bangkok). He proclaimed himself king and, in fifteen years of reign (1767–1782) (recorded in the *Royal Autograph Chronicle*), succeeded in expelling the Burmese and repelling their further attacks, and in reunifying the country under his own rule.

Chakri Dynasty. In succession to Taksin, one of his officers, Chao Phraya Chakri, became king in 1782 as Rama I (1782–1809), and was the founder of the

Chakri dynasty which has ruled Thailand ever since. It was Rama I who moved the capital across the river from Thonburi to Bangkok on the east bank. In Bangkok he built the Grand Palace and within the palace compound (following ancient practice) he built the Royal Chapel, called Wat Phra Keo and popularly known as the Temple of the Emerald Buddha (properly the Temple of the Jade Buddha). On the site of an old temple called Wat Bodharam (temple of the sacred *bodhi* tree) he built Wat Phra Chetuphon (Jetavana), still popularly known as Wat Po or also as the Temple of the Reclining Buddha. The king also composed a Thai version of the *Ramayana,* known as the *Ramakien,* as did also his son and successor, Rama II.[190]

The son who succeeded to the throne upon the death of Rama I was named Phra Buddha Lert-Lah, and he ruled as Rama II (1809–1824). It was during his reign that the tower of Wat Arun was partially constructed, to be completed in the following reign of his son, Rama III.

At the time of his death Rama II had two sons by his chief queen, the eldest being Prince Mongkut, who was then twenty years of age. An older son by a minor queen was judged to be more experienced in affairs of state and was chosen to succeed his father. This was Chetsadabodin or Nang Klao, who ruled as Rama III (1824–1851). In addition to completing the tower of Wat Arun, Rama III built Wat Bovornives.

During the entire period of twenty-seven years of the reign of Rama III, Prince Mongkut lived as a Buddhist monk under the name of Vajiranana and devoted himself to study and contemplation. Upon the death of Rama III, Mongkut came to the throne and ruled as Rama IV (1851–1868) while, at his request, his younger brother, Chuthamani, was given the special position of Second King. In connection with his long experience in the *sangha,* as a reform of the older Thai sect called Maha Nikaya, he established the new sect called Thammayut (*dhammayuti,* adhering to the doctrine), in which rites and practices were brought more nearly into conformity with the teachings and practice of the Buddha.[191]

At the death of King Mongkut in 1868 his son Chulalongkorn was only fifteen years old and, while becoming king in name, spent the next five years in the monastery of Wat Phra Keo, with a regent governing the country, until he himself took up active rule in 1873 and continued until his death in 1910. King Chulalongkorn founded in Bangkok a school which eventually became Chulalongkorn University, a National Library (in which the name of the Vajiranana Library of manuscripts recalls the name borne by King Mongkut when he was in the monastic life), and had a printed edition of the Tripitaka prepared in the Thai language. During his reign the Chakri Palace, the Throne Hall (now the National Assembly Hall), and Wat Benchamaborpit (the Marble Temple) were constructed.

In succession to Chulalongkorn two of his sons and then two of his grandsons occupied the throne: Vajiravudh or Rama VI (1910–1925); Prajadhipok or Rama VII (1925–1934), who established the National Museum, housed in the former palace of the Second King and with Prince Damrong at its head; Ananda Mahidol or Rama VIII (1934–1946), in whose reign the former Siam became officially Thailand (land of the free); and Bhumibol Adulyadej or Rama IX (1946–).

MONUMENTS

In Thailand as in Kampuchea a *wat* (or *vat*) is properly a monastery or, if no monks live there, a chapel, and it is commonly (but somewhat inaccurately) referred to as a temple. Typically a *wat* comprises a whole complex of buildings.

The *bot* houses the main Buddha image, used for the ordination ceremonies of the monks and for their worship and meditation. The *viharn* (from the Indian *vihara*) is the monks' assembly hall, where sacred objects may be kept and the people come to worship. The *chedi* (from Sanskrit *caitya*) is a usually bell-shaped *stupa,* in which there may be a sacred Buddha relic. The *prang* (derived from the *prasat* or corner tower of the Khmer temple) is a sanctuary tower sometimes inelegantly described as shaped like a corncob. The *chofa* is a graceful finial on the roof of a building, which may be derived from the ancient *makara* figure.[192]

Nakhon Pathom

Nakhon Pathom (30 miles [48 km.] west of Bangkok), described above as a capital city in the central region of ancient Dvaravati and supposedly the place where Buddhism was first introduced into the country by Sona and Uttara in the time of Aśoka (third century B.C.E.), is the site of the Phra Pathom Chedi (Fig. 14.74), the largest, highest, and presumably oldest *chedi* in Thailand. It is believed that the original form of the *stupa* in the Dvaravati period was that of a Sinhalese *dagoba,* and that this was later transformed into a Khmer-type tower. The ruins were still standing in the jungle in the nineteenth century when, in 1860, King Mongkut began a reconstruction which was completed during the reign of King Chulalongkorn. Models of the original monuments were placed in the surrounding grounds. In its present form the *chedi* consists of a vast bell-shaped dome, standing on a terraced platform and enclosed by a circular gallery, with four *viharns* grouped around it. The height of the *chedi* is 377 feet (115 m.), which is even 51 feet (15.6 m.) higher than the Shwe Dagon Pagoda in Rangoon. The dome is covered with golden glazed Chinese tiles from the time of King Chulalongkorn. The terrace steps are lined with *naga* heads, and a tall golden Buddha stands within a niche at the entrance to the gallery (Fig. 14.75).[193]

14.74   Approach to Phra Pathom Chedi at Nakhon Pathom

14.75   Golden Buddha in the Phra Pathom Chedi, Nakhon Pathom

Lopburi

Lopburi was an important city already in the kingdom of Dvaravati, and was a center of Khmer rule in Thailand between the eleventh and thirteenth centuries C.E. The two main temples, the ruins of which still stand at Lopburi, are probably works of this Khmer period. Wat Mahathat (*mahadhatu,* temple of the great relic) consists of a number of small edifices around a lofty central sanctuary tower *(prang),* all within a walled enclosure, much as at Angkor. Many Buddha images were found here, and some of these are from the Dvaravati period, so the Khmer temple was probably erected on the site of an earlier temple. Prang Sam Yot (the temple of the three towers) consists, as its name indicates, of a row of three tall *prangs.* Many sandstone images of Khmer type of the Buddha seated on the *naga* were found in this temple. An example of this type of Buddha image from Lopburi, attributed to the thirteenth century C.E., is in the National Museum in Bangkok (Fig. 14.76).[194]

Sukhothai

The site of ancient Sukhothai is adjacent to the modern administrative center of Thani. The Wat Mahathat at Sukhothai is thought to have been founded by King Śri Indraditya, the founder of the Sukhothai kingdom, in the thirteenth century C.E. This temple lay within the compound of the royal palace and served as the royal chapel and spiritual center of the kingdom. The surviving ruins suggest that the entire complex consisted of nearly 190 different structures, with a large *chedi* in the center and to the east of it a huge assembly hall *(viharn),* some 165 feet (50 m.) long. The lower portions of the columns which supported the roof of the

14.76 Buddha on Naga, from Lopburi, in the National Museum, Bangkok

14.77 Buddha Head from Sukhothai, in the National Museum, Bangkok

hall still stand, and there is also an enormous standing Buddha.[195] It was probably on the site of the palace near the temple that the famous inscription of Rama Khamhaeng (quoted above) was found in 1833 by Prince Mongkut, as was also the stone throne which King Vajiravudh (Rama VI) later placed in the Throne Hall at Bangkok, which serves as the coronation stone of Thailand.

Wat Śri Cum, now also known as Wat Sra Śri, is built of brick and stucco and thought to be attributable to the reign of Lu Thai, grandson of Rama Khamhaeng, in the middle of the fourteenth century. The sanctuary of the temple is the best preserved part of the monument. This is a rectangular building with a high, narrow, vaulted entrance, and there is a gigantic seated image of the Buddha within.[196] Inside the thick walls of the sanctuary is a narrow passage which slopes steeply upward to the roof, and fitted into the roof of this corridor are 100 stone slabs on which are engraved *jataka* scenes. In this location the scenes are practically hidden from view, and it is surmised that they were originally set up in Wat Mahathat and only later installed here, perhaps for safety in some time of trouble. The scenes are from the first 100 *jataka* tales in the Pali canon, and the figures are considered Sinhalese in appearance, having perhaps been made with the help of craftsmen from Sri Lanka. These scenes are the earliest evidence of the *jatakas* in Thailand; many other examples are found in mural paintings in many other temples in the land.[197]

The Buddha images of the Sukhothai period were carved from stone, modeled in stucco and, most notably, cast in bronze by the *cire perdue* (lost wax) process, a technique in which the Sukhothai artists excelled, while some were even made in solid gold. In the same period the style of the Buddha representation reached its classical Thai type. As seen in an example from Sukhothai (Fig. 14.77), attributed to the fourteenth to fifteenth century C.E., in the National Museum, Bangkok, the Buddha head exhibits an oval face, elongated earlobes, almond eyes, arched eyebrows, and hair in tight curls, while the *ushnisha* is surmounted by a high finial in the form of a flame. The faint smile on the lips suggests the inner peace which has been attained. The Sukhothai school is also notable for statues of the Buddha pressing his footprint into the ground as a symbol of his presence, and walking, as if proceeding on the many journeys on which he went after his enlightenment.[198]

Ayutthaya

Ayudhya, Thai capital from its foundation in 1351 C.E. until its destruction by the Burmese in 1767, was surrounded by water in the sense that it was built on an island formed by three rivers, the Lopburi River on the north, the Pasak River on the east, and the Menam Chao Phraya River on the west and south. The ruins of the ancient city, now called Ayutthaya, occupy an area of some 40 square miles (64 sq. km.).[199]

Wat Mahathat at Ayutthaya is supposed to have been built by King Ramesuan (1369–1370, 1388–1395) in memory of a vision he saw of the Buddha. The structure was almost totally destroyed in 1767, but its ruins cover a large area.

Wat Rajburana, its ruins still marked by a lofty *prang*, was built by King Boromaraja II (1424–1448) in memory of his two older brothers. Following the death of his father, King Indraraja I (1409–1424), the two brothers had disputed the succession. In mortal combat to decide which should have the throne, they fought each other on elephants on a certain bridge, and both were thrown from their elephants and killed. Thereupon their younger brother became king as Bor-

14.78 Row of Seated Buddhas, Wat Yai Chaya Mongkol, Ayutthaya

14.79 Head of Colossal Reclining Buddha, at Ayutthaya

omoraja II, and Wat Rajaburana was the monument he built in memory of the deceased brothers. The name means "finished by the king."

Wat Yai Chaya Mongkol was built by King Naresuan (1590–1605) following his victory over the Burmese crown prince in 1592. Even in its present state it is still one of the most impressive of the ruins of Ayutthaya, and there are still to be seen the rows of seated stone Buddhas which surrounded the *chedi* on all four sides (Fig. 14.78). On the south side there is a seated Buddha figure against the base of the monument; on the west side there is a large seated Buddha with disciples in front of him; and elsewhere in Ayutthaya are other stone images, for example, a colossal reclining Buddha (Fig. 14.79).

Wat Phra Mongkol Borpit was built by King Ekatosaroth (1605–1620) in memory of King Naresuan, his brother. The modern *viharn* of this name was founded in 1956 by the then Prime Minister Pibul Songgram. It houses a great bronze statue of the Buddha, which is probably attributable to the fifteenth century.

Thonburi/Bangkok

Bangkok (place where olives grow) was once a small fishing village on the east side of the Chao Phrya River, and it was at Thonburi on the west bank that King Taksin (1767–1782) established his capital after the fall of Ayudhya. When Rama I (1782–1809) moved the capital to Bangkok he named the city Krung Thep (city of angels), but it remains best known as Bangkok. With a bridge now across the river between Bangkok and Thonburi, the two cities are for all practical purposes one very large metropolitan area.[200]

In Thonburi an old temple called Wat Chang was restored by Taksin, and it was reconstructed by Rama II (1809–1824) and Rama III (1824–1851), and is best known as Wat Arun (temple of the dawn) (Fig. 14.80). In the center of a

14.80 Wat Arun, Thonburi

square terrace a great tower *(prang)* rises to a height of 243 feet (74 m.), and four smaller towers mark the corners of the terrace. The towers are made of brick covered with stucco, into which are imbedded bits of colored porcelain. In four niches on the four faces of the central tower are figures of Indra seated on Eravan, his three-headed elephant. In similar niches on the sides of the corner towers are figures of the moon god mounted on a white horse. On top of each tower is the trident of Śiva. Other images represent scenes in the life of the Buddha, and the main Buddha image is in the adjacent *bot*, built by King Chulalongkorn (1868–1910). In an annual ceremony *(kathin)* it is customary for the king to come down the river with the royal barges to Wat Arun to present new robes to the monks.

Phra Borom Maha Rajawang. The Phra Borom Maha Rajawang or Grand Palace in Bangkok, begun by King Rama I in 1782 soon after he moved the capital to this site, is a virtual walled town covering an area of more than a square mile (1.6 sq. km.) (Fig. 14.81). Two groups of residences, called the Mahamontien and the Dusit Mahaprasad, are the earliest buildings; the palace called Chakri Mahaprasad was built later by King Chulalongkorn.

Dusit Mahaprasad. The Dusit Mahaprasad was built by Rama I for ceremonial purposes and has been used for the coronation of some kings and for the lying in state of royal remains, ever since the body of Rama I was so received here. The building, perhaps the finest of all the palace structures, has the form of a cross. The four wings are covered with five-tiered roofs, from the center of which rises a tall nine-tiered spire *(prasad)*. The base of the spire is supported by four enormous *garudas; nagas* descend the sloping edges of the roofs; and the upper corners of the roofs are surmounted by *chofa* finials (Fig. 14.82).

14.81 Roofs and Towers of the Grand Palace, Bangkok, seen from the Chao Phraya River

14.82   Roofs and Tower of Dusit Mahaprasad, Grand Palace, Bangkok

Wat Phra Keo. The grounds of the Wat Phra Keo or Temple of the Jade Buddha lie to the north of the Mahamontien complex. Entrances are guarded by demon figures (Fig. 14.83), and guardian lions stand beside the steps which lead up into the *bot*. The *bot*, which serves as the private chapel of the king, contains the Jade Buddha. This, the most sacred image in Thailand, is only 28 inches (70 cm.) in height, and is placed high above on a golden altar. Only the king himself changes the gem-encrusted robes of the image three times a year to correspond with the three seasons, hot, rainy, and cold.

A work known as *The Chronicle of the Emerald Buddha* tells that the image was made originally under miraculous circumstances by Nagasena, the monk who appears in the *Milinda Panha* as a contemporary of King Milinda (circa 161–145 B.C.E.), and relates many travels and vicissitudes of the object.[201] Actually the image is supposed to have been made perhaps toward the end of the thirteenth century C.E., and rediscovered in 1434 when lightning struck an old *chedi* in Chiangrai in the kingdom of Chiang Mai. At this time the gilt stucco with which the image was coated was cracked and revealed gleaming jade. Afterward the image was for many years in Laos, was brought to Thonburi by Taksin in 1778, and was placed here in the royal chapel when the chapel was constructed by Rama I in 1784.

On the walls of the covered gallery which runs around the courtyard of Wat Phra Keo are paintings which represent episodes from the *Ramakien*, the Thai version of the *Ramayana*. The paintings were done originally during the reign of Rama III (1824–1851), restored under Rama IV (Mongkut, 1851–1868) and Rama V (Chulalongkorn, 1868–1910), and again restored under Rama VII (1925–1934).[202]

14.83 Demon guarding an Entrance to Wat Phra Keo, Grand Palace, Bangkok

14.84 Golden Chedi, Wat Phra Keo, Grand Palace, Bangkok

On an upper terrace north of the chapel are other structures belonging to the temple, three in particular from east to west: the Prasad Phra Thepbidorn or Pantheon, begun in 1855 by Rama IV and planned for the Jade Buddha but found to be too small and used instead for statues of the five ancestors of Rama VI (1910–1925); the Mondhop *(mahamandapa),* a square pavilion erected by Rama I on the site of the ancient Library which was destroyed by fire as soon as completed; and the Phra Sri Ratanachetiya, the Golden Chedi, begun in 1855 and completed by Rama V (Chulalongkorn), who adorned it with gold-colored tiles (Fig. 14.84).

Wat Po. Wat Po (*po* standing for the sacred *bodhi* tree) is a very extensive complex, in its entirety the largest temple in Thailand, lying to the south of the Grand Palace. Most of the buildings were constructed by Rama I, but the *viharn* containing the Reclining Buddha was added by Rama III in 1832. The temple buildings are enclosed within a high brick will provided with sixteen gateways (only two now open), and these and other gates within the precincts are guarded by giant figures of demons, Chinese warriors, and the like. The grounds contain the *bot,* a number of *viharns,* and many *chedis* of elegant proportions, with pottery decoration (Fig. 14.85). The *bot* has teak doors carved with scenes from the *Ramakien,* and around its base are marble bas-reliefs brought from the ruins of Ayudhya, which also tell the story of Rama. In the galleries surrounding the *bot* are nearly 400 seated Buddha figures, and on the walls within are murals depicting the life of the Buddha. The *viharn* of the Reclining Buddha is filled for almost its entire length with the colossal image, 148 feet (45 m.) long and 49 feet (15 m.) high. The figure is made of brick, covered with cement, and veneered with gold leaf. The Buddha supports his head with his right hand, and his left arm is stretched out to

14.85 In the Grounds of Wat Po, Bangkok

its full length alongside the body. The feet are remarkable in that all ten toes are of the same length. The soles of the feet are inlaid in mother-of-pearl; the wheel of the law *(dharmacakra)* is in the center, and around it are 108 squares with as many marks of the Buddha.

Wat Traimitr. When Wat Phya Krai was abandoned due to development in downtown Bangkok two Buddha statues were removed from it. One, in bronze, was given to Wat Phai Ngeun Chatinaram in Thonburi; the other, in stucco, was moved to Wat Traimitr, where it was kept for some twenty years in a shed on the temple grounds. In 1953, in the course of preparations for the 1956 celebration of the 2,500th anniversary of the *nirvana* of the Buddha, a new temple hall was completed to house the image. In the process of moving the image to its new home, it fell from the crane which was lifting it. The surface stucco was cracked, and underneath was discovered an image of solid gold, 10 feet (3 m.) high, weighing 5.5 tons. The Buddha is of the Sukhothai style and is no doubt from that period (probably fourteenth century C.E.). From a presumed original home in Sukhothai it was probably taken to the new capital, Ayudhya, and there—probably in the time of the Burmese invasions in the eighteenth century—camouflaged by the stucco covering for protection against the plunderers before it (like many other objects from Ayudhya) was brought at last to Bangkok. There it gives its name to Wat Traimitr as the Temple of the Golden Buddha (Fig. 14.86).

Wat Bovornives. Wat Bovornives (the excellent residence) was built in 1824–1832 in the reign of Rama III (1824–1851). As already noted, Rama III's younger half-brother, Prince Mongkut, spent the twenty-seven years of this reign in the monastic life. The first dozen years were at Wat Rajadhivas and Wat Mahathat (the oldest *wat* in Bangkok, in existence long before Bangkok became the capital), then he came to Wat Bovornives as its first abbot and lived here for more than fourteen years prior to his accession to the throne in 1851 at the age of forty-seven. Many subsequent kings of Thailand have also spent periods of monkhood in Wat Bovornives, including Rama IX (Bhumibol Adulyadej, 1946–) in the tenth year (1956) of his reign.

The *wat* consists of a *bot,* a tall *chedi* (164 feet [50 m.] high), and several *viharns* and other buildings. The main image in the *bot* is a large gilt seated Buddha of the Sukhothai style (Fig. 14.87), which was probably cast either in Sukhothai or Sawankhalok in the middle of the thirteenth century, soon after the Thai had cast off the domination of the Khmers. Referring to this victory, the image is known as the Phra Buddha Jinasiha (lion *jina,* i.e., the victorious Buddha). For many centuries the image was in the Wat Mahathat at Phitsanulok, and then was brought to its present place in 1829 by Rama III. At either side of the image are small standing figures of the two disciples of the Buddha, Mogallana and Śariputra (here called Mokhala and Saributr). In a deep niche behind the Phra Buddha Jinasiha and behind golden curtains is a second, much larger gilt seated Buddha called Luang Po To. This was brought here from an old monastery (Wat Satapan) in Phetburi (62 miles [100 km.] southwest of Bangkok), and was originally meant to be the presiding statue of Wat Bovornives at the time of its foundation (Fig. 14.87).

Wat Benchamaborpit. On the site of an earlier monastery called Wat Sai Thong Rama V (Chulalongkorn) in 1899 constructed Wat Benchamaborpit (the temple of the fifth king), commonly known as the Marble Temple. The *wat* is on the bank of a small waterway *(klong)* and, across a little footbridge, is the pavilion

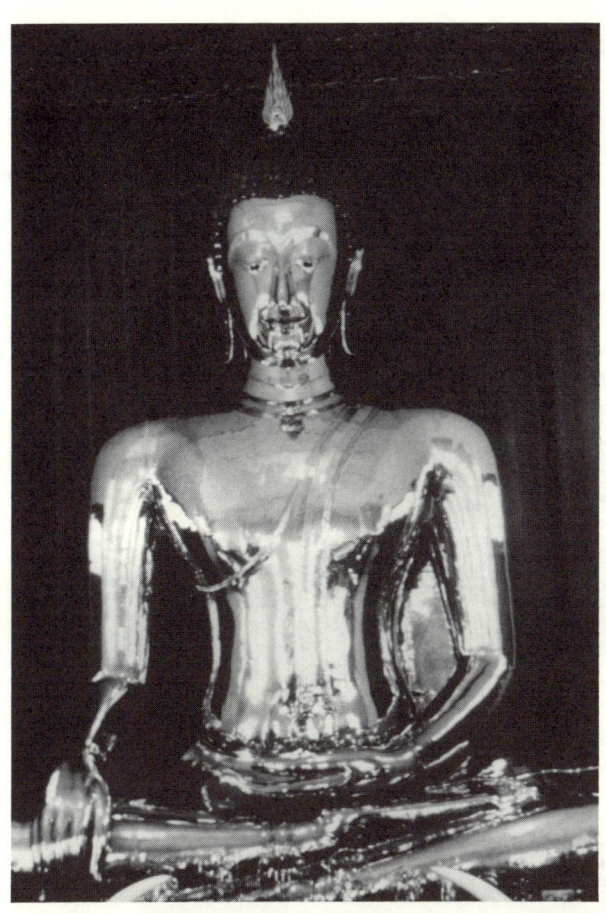

14.86 Buddha of Solid Gold in Wat Traimitr, Bangkok

14.87 Wat Benchamaborpit, Bangkok

14.88 Phra Buddha Jinaraj Replica in Wat Benchamaborpit, Bangkok

which was used by the king when he was a monk at the Wat Phra Keo. The main building is constructed of white Italian marble and roofed with red Chinese tiles (Fig. 14.88). The gables are carved with representations of Vishnu on *garuda* (east), the wheel of the Law (south), the *unalom* or curl of hair on Buddha's forehead (west), and the three-headed elephant of Indra, Eravan (north). The main entrance is to the east, and is guarded by two huge marble lions. In the galleries of the inner courtyard is a very large collection of Buddha images, representing all the types known in Thailand, and also Indian, Burmese, and Japanese examples, either originals or copies.

In the interior hall of the Marble Temple the large gilt seated image of the Buddha (Fig. 14.89) is an exact replica, made and placed here under Rama V (Chulalongkorn), of a Buddha image which is still in the Wat Mahathat at Phitsanulok. The original image is called the Phra Buddha Jinaraj (king *jina,* i.e., the victorious Buddha) and is a companion piece to the Phra Buddha Jinasiha which was brought from Phitsanulok to Wat Bovornives, both of these Buddha images being works of the Sukhothai period, and both reflecting the time when the victorious Thai were freed from the Khmer yoke. The two images, the one brought from Phitsanulok to Wat Bovornives, and the other remaining in Phitsanulok but with its replica here in Wat Benchamaborpit, are in Thailand considered the most beautiful Buddha images known.[203]

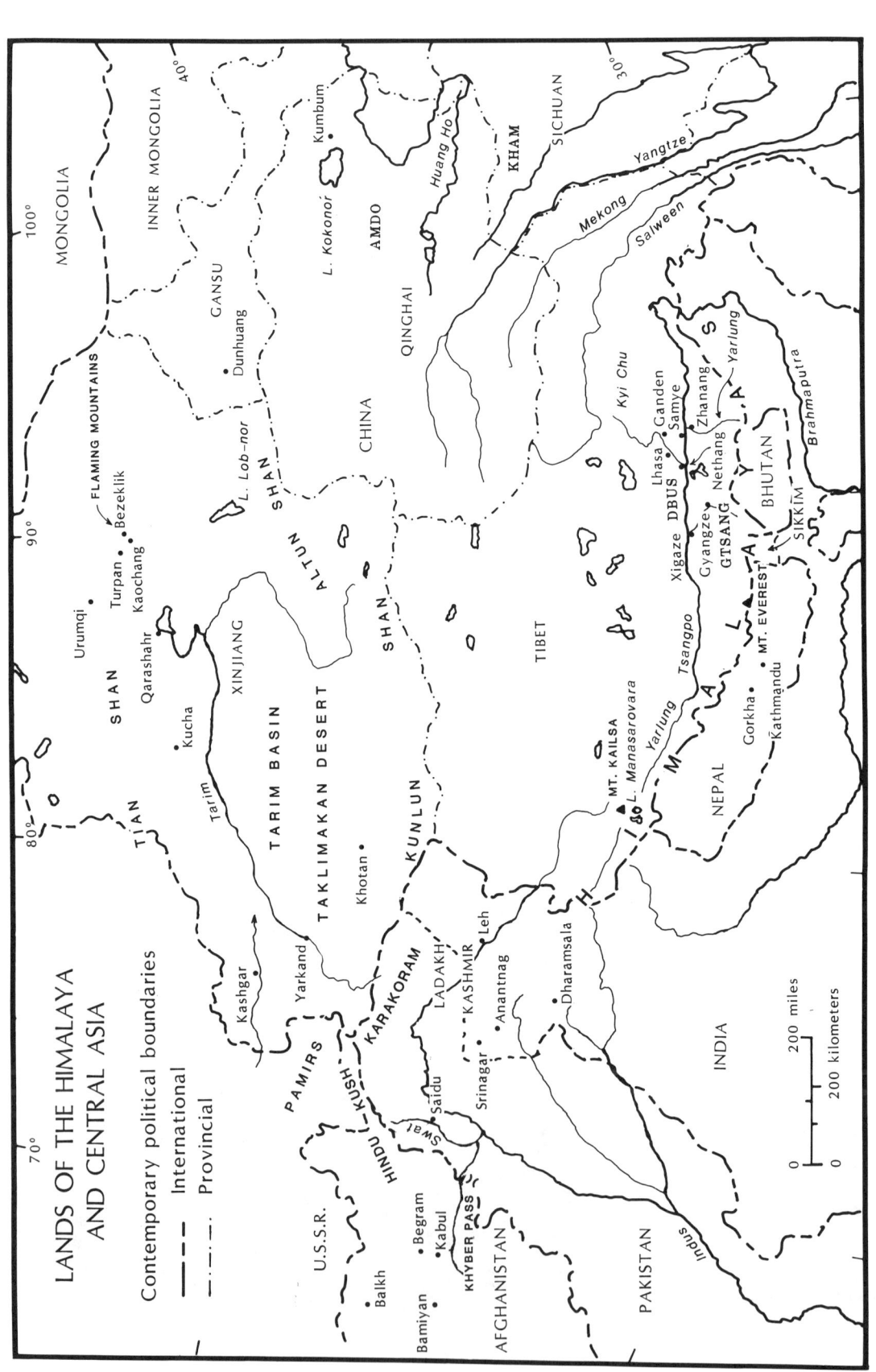

15

MONUMENTS OF HINDUISM AND BUDDHISM BY THE HIGH HIMALAYA AND AT THE GATES OF INNER ASIA

NEPAL

Vaṃśavalis and Svayambhu Purana

The traditional history of Nepal is preserved in the chronicles known as the *vaṃśavalis*. These are genealogical histories of Nepal and are found in both Hindu and Buddhist recensions and in two groups—the earlier compiled in the fourteenth century C.E., the later in the nineteenth century. The later is largely dependent upon the earlier for the ancient history, and all no doubt largely dependent upon oral tradition. An available example of the Buddhist version is found in a manuscript written in the Nepali language (now the official language of Nepal, earlier called Parbatiya, meaning the language of the hill people) with an admixture of Sanskrit and Newari (the old language of the people of the Kathmandu valley), and which sets the history in the framework of the four ages of the world (here called the Satya, Treta, Dvapara, and Kali *yugas*), and extends from the creation of Nepal to events at the beginning of the nineteenth century. In what follows, this work will be cited as the *Vaṃśavali*.[1]

As far as the creation of Nepal is concerned, an account essentially the same as that in the *Vaṃśavali* is also found in the Sanskrit Buddhist literature of Nepal in the *Svayambhu Purana,* a work composed by a poet named Manjuśri, probably in the early part of the tenth century C.E., and copied in the reign of Yakshamalla (died 1480 C.E.).[2]

Satyayuga and Svayambhu. According to the foregoing sources, in the first world age *(Satyayuga)* Svayambhu, the "self-existent" Adibuddha, manifested himself in the form of light on a lotus flower on the waters of Lake Nagrhada (lake of the *nagas*).

Tretayuga and Manjuśri. In the second world age *(Tretayuga)* Manjuśri (known in the Mahayana as one of the greatest *bodhisattvas* and the representative of the wisdom-aspect of the Buddha principle) was living with his two wives,

Varada and Mokshada, on Mount Pancaśirsha (five peaks) in China. When he learned of the manifestation of Svayambhu at Lake Nagrhada, Mañjuśri came to pay homage, but found the god almost inaccessible because of the expanse of waters round about and the aquatic animals in the waters. He then thought of cutting a passage through the mountains to drain the lake. For this purpose he went to the low hills on the southern side, placed his two goddesses on either side, and himself remained in the middle. With his sword (*khadga*, divine weapon) he cut through the mountain, which he called Kotwal, and let the water run out, leaving dry land at the bottom. The dry land is what is now known as the Kathmandu valley, and the cleft in the mountain is Kotwal Gorge, where the Bagmati River passes out of the valley to the south.

As the water escaped, several *nagas* and other animals living in it went out too, but Karkotak, king of the *nagas*, was persuaded to remain, was given a lake to live in, and was given power over all the wealth of the valley. Mañjuśri was now able to approach and worship Svayambhu, whom he saw in the form of Viśvarupa (world shape), the representation of all gods in one, and he also saw in the same form the goddess Guhyeśvari (a colloquial Nepali name for Parvati, the consort of Śiva). At the place of the lotus on which Svayambhu appeared, Mañjuśri made the hill Padma (lotus), which is the same as Svayambhu hill (2 miles [3 km.] west of Kathmandu, 250 feet [76 m.] above the valley, site of the Buddhist shrine, Svayambhunath), and he built a town extending from there to the root of the lotus, a place which was called Guhyeśvari (the site now of a Hindu temple of this name, near Paśupatinath); the name of the whole town was Manjupattan (occupying substantially the area of modern Kathmandu, at the confluence of the Bagmati and Vishnumati rivers).

Other cities and capitals were also founded by the power of Svayambhu and Mañjuśri, and a king of China named Dharmakara (treasure of the law) was anointed king, and he governed the country wisely as his own kingdom. Mañjuśri himself then returned to China, and afterward some of his disciples built a *caitya* near Svayambhu (now a temple on the western peak of Svayambhu hill) in order to worship Mañjuśri in connection with Svayambhu.[3]

In the same second age of the world Brahma, Vishnu, and Śiva also came and took up their abode near Manjupattan in a wood called Mrigasthali (so named because the three deities had appeared in the form of deer; this wood is on the left bank of the Bagmati River, opposite the Paśupati temples), and here Śiva manifested himself in the form of light, even as Svayambhu had done, and in this manifestation was called Paśupati (herdsman, lord of beasts).

Dharmakara, who was made king by Mañjuśri, had no issue and appointed Dharmapala as his successor. In the line of kings which ensued, Sudhanva was on the throne at the time when the second world age *(Tretayuga)* drew toward a close. At this time, being displeased with his palace in Manjupattan, Sudhanva enlarged the capital area by building a new town called Sankasya and a new royal residence on the banks of the river Ikshumati (now the Tukucha, a small tributary of the Bagmati).

Dvaparayuga. Before the reign of Sudhanva was over, the *Tretayuga* ended and the third world age *(Dvaparayuga)* began. Sudhanva himself went off to compete for the hand of Sita, the daughter of Janak, and lost his life, not to return. Thereupon the throne went to his brother, Kusadhvaja, and the descendants of the latter continued to reign for some years until their dynasty became extinct.

In this time, King Prachandadeva of Gaur (capital of the kingdom of Gauda in

Bengal) renounced his throne in favor of his son Śaktideva and came to Svayambhu as a disciple of the *bhikshu* Gunakar, a devotee of Mañjuśri, and himself in due course became a teacher *(acarya)* under the name of Śantikara. Thinking that the fourth world age *(Kaliyuga)* was approaching, and that humankind would become utterly sinful, Śantikara built the *caitya* of Svayambhu, covering the ground where the Svayambhu light shone like a flame. He also built five rooms (said still to exist around the Svayambhu *stupa*), and lived in one of these, absorbed in devout meditation.

Sometime later a descendant of Śaktideva came from Gaur and was accepted as king. Among his successors the most famous was Gunakamadeva, and there were many more kings of this line, but the last died without an heir, and the *rishi* Ne (from whom, according to one explanation, Nepal derives its name) then ruled the country. At this juncture the Kiratas (who will be mentioned again below) made an invasion of the country. Then King Dharmadatta of Kanci (Kancipuram, near Madras) left his city to one of his ten sons, came with the other nine, subdued the Kiratas and took possession of the land. Dharmadatta enlarged Manjupattan/Sankasya again by building a large town called Visalanagara, and he peopled this with the four castes, i.e., with Hindus. He also, with great rites and ceremonies, built the temple of Paśupati, and nearby a *caitya* which he named after himself, the Dharmadatta Caitya.

Due to the activity of a demon named Danasur the valley was again for a time filled with water, and the inhabitants of Manjupattan and Visalanagara had to flee, but the Svayambhu hill was not submerged. When the valley was again habitable, a Chetri *(kshatriya)* named Svayambrata became king, while later kings were Vikramajit and Bhoja. Visalanagara was now destroyed by fire, other calamities ensued, and the third world age drew to a close.[4]

Kaliyuga. In the early part of the fourth and present world age *(Kaliyuga)* the *vamśavalis* tell of a sequence of six dynasties named Gopala, Ahir or Mahishapala, Kirata, Somavamsi, Suryavamsi, and Thakuri.[5]

Gopalas and Ahirs

When the ancient temple of Paśupati had fallen down and the light been buried under the ruins, some cowherds *(gopas)* came into the country and one of them discovered the light but was consumed by it. Then the *muni* Ne came and, having persuaded the people that there would be no Chetri *(kshatriya)* kings in the *Kaliyuga,* installed the son of the cowherd who had been consumed by the light as the first king of the Gopala dynasty. His name was Bhuktamana, and in his reign "Paśupati was discovered," which evidently means that the cowherds were worshipers of Śiva in his form as Paśupati (herdsman). Beginning with Bhuktamana, the Gopalas reigned through eight generations, making their residence near Mata Tirtha, a place sanctified in memory of the deceased mother of one of them.

When the eighth Gopala king died with no heir, the Ahirs or Mahishapalas (buffalo keepers) came and ruled the country through three generations, then were themselves conquered by the Kiratas.

Kiratas

With the Kiratas we begin to move out of legend into history, for the Kiratas are widely mentioned in various works of ancient Sanskrit literature, especially in the Epics (e.g., *Mahabharata* 2.4.23; 3.48.21).[6] They appear as mountain tribes, and are believed to have been of Mongoloid stock, while the modern inhabitants of the Kathmandu valley, the Newars, are believed to be an intermixture of Mongoloid and Aryan strains resulting from the unions between the Kiratas and the Aryans migrating from the plains of India.[7]

According to the *Vamśavali* the Kirata dynasty consisted of a line of twenty-eight kings. The first king was Yalambara, who reigned for thirteen years. His son was Pavi and, in his reign, the astrologers announced that the *Kaliyuga* had entirely overspread the earth, and that humankind was bent on sin. The sixth king was Humati, and in his reign the Pandavas lived in exile in the forest and Arjuna, on his way to the Himalaya, fought with Śiva in the guise of a Kirata mountaineer. The seventh king was Jitadesi, and he went and fought on the side of the Pandavas against the Kauravas, but did not return from the battle.

At this point the *Vamśavali* says that Śakyamuni Buddha came from Kapilavastu and visited the Svayambhu and Manjuśri *caityas,* and also Guhyeśvari, and won some followers, some of whom remained in Nepal and professed his religion. While the home of the Buddha at Kapilavastu was in what is now southern Nepal, this region (the Tarai) was not within the Nepal of ancient and medieval times, and the supposed visit of the Buddha to the Kathmandu valley is not attested to, other than in the Nepali sources, and there certainly must have been a greater interval between the time of the *Mahabharata* war and the time of the Buddha than the *Vamśavali* supposes. According to the Buddhist *Sarvastivadavinaya,* however, a group of *bhikshus* went to Nepal in company with traveling merchants, and Ananda also went there, but was warned by the Buddha about the risks involved in the journey.[8]

In the reign of the fourteenth Kirata king, Sthunko, the *Vamśavali* states that the emperor Aśoka (269–232 B.C.E.) came on a pilgrimage to Nepal, visited the holy places including Svayambhu and Guhyeśvari, and built several *caityas*. Aśoka was accompanied on the pilgrimage by his daughter Carumati, who remained in Nepal, where she married a Chetri *(kshatriya)* named Devapala. The couple settled near the shrine of Paśupati, where they founded and peopled Deva Patan. Becoming aged, they determined to pass the remainder of their lives in religious retirement, and each resolved to build a *bihar (vihara,* in Nepal a large square house built around an open court and containing a shrine) for members of the Buddhist order. The nunnery built by Carumati was first completed, and she died in it after living the life of a *bhikshuni,* but Devapala died in distress because he was not able to complete his monastery before his death.

The pillar inscriptions of Aśoka at Rummindei and Nigalisagar in what is now southern Nepal have been described above (in Chapters 5 and 6); that the emperor was actually also in the Kathmandu valley is affirmed by local tradition and made not improbable by certain archaeological evidence. The capital at the time was Manjupattan, occupying much the same site as modern Kathmandu, and Aśoka, it is said, resolved to commemorate his visit by the foundation of a new city and the erection of monuments. The city, which became Lalitpur or Patan, was placed on some rising ground southeast of Kathmandu. On this site Aśoka built a *stupa* at the center, and four others at the cardinal points on the four sides. In fact four stupas still remain there, hemispherical mounds of plain brick, their form consonant with the antiquity ascribed to them (see below, Fig. 15.13). That the Bodhnath *stupa* east of Kathmandu may also preserve a form representative of the time of Aśoka will be noted below. As for Deva Patan, it is a town west of and adjacent to Paśupatinath, and at Chabahil, a village north of and close to Deva Patan, the convent of Carumati still exists as Carumati Bihar, with the Carumati *stupa* there too.[9]

Somavamśis, Suryavamśis, and Thakuris

Subsequent to the Kirata dynasty the Vamśavali lists in sequence a Somavamśi (lunar) dynasty, a Suryavamśi (solar) dynasty, and a Thakuri dynasty, and gives many items of information concerning various events said to have taken place under various of these rulers.[10]

The first king of the Somavamśi dynasty was Nimisha. The fourth king, Pashupreshadeva, rebuilt the temple of Paśupati, which had become dilapidated, and roofed it with golden plates. The fifth and last king, Bhaskaravarman, caused the rules and ceremonies to be observed and to be engraved on a copper plate, which was placed with the *bhikshus* of Carumati Bihar.

The first king of the Suryavamśi dynasty was Bhumivarman. Under the seventeenth king, Rudradevavarman, the four *caityas* which Aśoka built at Patan were repaired. Under Rudradevavarman's son Vrishadevavarman, Śankaracarya came from India and converted many Buddhists to Hinduism, and Vrishadevavarman's son Śankaradeva was named after Śankara. Dharmadeva, the twentieth king, repaired the Dhanado *caitya* which had been built by King Dharmadatta. Some say that Manadeva, the twenty-first king, built the Bodhnath *stupa* outside Kathmandu on the advice of the goddess Mani Jogini for the expiation of his sin of accidental parricide. Manadeva was followed in succession by Mahadeva, Vasantadevavarman, Udayadevavarman, Manadevavarman, Gunakamadevavarman, and Śivadevavarman. Śivadevavarman, the twenty-seventh king, caused burning ghats for the dead bodies of each caste to be built on the banks of the Bagmati River at Paśupati. He was followed by Narendradevavarman, Bhimadevavarman, Vishnudevavarman, and Vishvadevavarman. Vishvadevavarman, the thirty-first and last king of the dynasty, having no male issue, gave his daughter to Amśuvarman of the Thakuri family, and Amśuvarman became the first king of the Thakuri dynasty.

In the Thakuri line beginning with Amśuvarman the seventh king was Narendradeva and, in both the *Vamśavali* and the *Svayambhu Purana*, he is credited with the institution of a *rathayatra*, i.e., a festival in which the image of a god is drawn along in a huge car or chariot *(ratha)*. The relevant passage in the *Svayambhu Purana* purports to be predictive, and says:

> Later than that, during the reign of Narendradeva, there will be a continuous drought extending over a period of twelve years. Narendradeva will worship the Lokeśvaras by the advice of Bandhudatta. He will bring Lokeśvara from the mount Kapota, and perform the ceremony of drawing the car.[11]

Lokeśvara is the "lord of the world" form of the *bodhisattva* Avalokiteśvara, who is also in Nepal identified with Śiva, and is incarnate in the form of a fish known as Matsyendranath or Machhendranath. In the entire elaborated story Lokeśvara instructs Śiva on how to meditate for enlightenment, and then listens, in the form of the fish, while Śiva tells Parvati about his experience. Later Gorakhnath, a pupil of Machhendranath, wishes to see Machhendranath in this fish incarnation and accomplishes this aim by imprisoning the *nagas* and causing a twelve-year drought in the valley, which leads Machhendranath to appear for the relief of humanity. Concerned about the drought, King Narendradeva consults the wise *acarya* Bandhudatta and he, by his *tantric* power, saves Karkotak, the king of the *nagas,* and they all go together to Lokeśvara and bring Lokeśvara to Patan with the promise that he will be entrusted with the government and that appropriate offerings will be made every year. In the light of this story, Lokeśvara is seen in his Machhendranath incarnation as the god of rain and the god of mercy, and the "ceremony of drawing the car" is the *rathayatra* at Patan in which every year in the month of Baisakh (April/May) the god is installed in a huge car-chariot and taken about the city in a week-long festival, being venerated by both Buddhists and Hindus.

Licchavis

While the *Vamśavali* followed above does not use the name Licchavi, there are inscriptions which contain some of the kings' names just given and indicate that these kings belonged to the Licchavi dynasty. With the inscriptions, which begin in the fifth century C.E.,[12] as do also the earliest dated sculptures,[13] actual historical records are for the first time available, and these and other historical materials make it possible to divide the later ancient and the medieval history of Nepal into three broad periods: Licchavi (circa 300–800 C.E.), Thakuri (800–1200), and Malla (1200–1750).

In the Licchavi period the available inscriptions can be divided into two groups: the first group extends from Manadeva to Sivadeva, and in it dates are given from Year 386 to Year 535; the second group names Amśuvarman and his successors, and in it dates are given from Year 30 to Year 194. Comparisons and correlations with chronological data in Indian, Tibetan, and Chinese sources indicate that the earlier series of dates is stated in terms of the Śaka Era beginning in the equivalent of 78 C.E., and that the later series of dates is stated in terms of a new Nepalese era named for either Amśuvarman or Manadeva and beginning in the equivalent of 576 C.E.; thus, the first series runs from 464 to 613 C.E., and the second series from 606 to 770 C.E.[14]

Manadeva I. The oldest of these inscriptions and the first in a small series relevant to the early history of the Licchavis is on a pillar in the temple of Changu Narayana, a temple of Vishnu, located just beyond Bhadgaon, about 10 miles (16 km.) east of Kathmandu, and said to be the oldest temple in the Kathmandu valley. The text, in Sanskrit, records a donation (perhaps of the pillar itself) to the god of the temple, made by the queen mother Rajyavati, widow of the deceased king Dharmadeva, upon the advice of her son, the king Manadeva, following upon his successful campaigns through which the sovereignty of the kingdom was extended to the east and the west of the Nepal valley.[15] The sequence of kings named in the inscription is Vrishadeva, Śankaradeva, Dharmadeva, and Manadeva, precisely the same as the eighteenth to the twenty-first kings in the Suryavamśi dynasty in the *Vamśavali,* so this Manadeva is the first king of this name and may be designated as Manadeva I. The date of the inscription is in the year 386 and, assuming that the reckoning is in terms of the Śaka Era, the year corresponds with 464 C.E. Other inscriptions of the reign of Manadeva I extend to the Śaka Year 427, i.e., 505 C.E., so he must have ruled for at least forty-one years.[16]

The last inscription in the small series here dealt with, and the inscription which shows that the kings here under consideration belonged to the Licchavi dynasty is found at Paśupatinath and belongs to King Jayadeva II. The inscription is dated in the Year 159, and in terms of the Amśuvarman or Manadeva era the date is equivalent to 735 C.E. The text lists the names of many kings who were the ancestors and predecessors in rule of Jayadeva II. At the point in which we are here interested, the list goes back through Manadeva, Dharmadeva, Śankaradeva, Vrishadeva, and so forth, and on back to the first king of the dynasty, who is named Supushpa. Supushpa is said to have been born at Pushpapura (probably Pataliputra in India), and was himself a descendant of Licchavi—evidently the eponymous hero of the whole family and the source of its collective name as the Licchavi dynasty.[17] The *Paśupati Purāna* mentions that the Licchavis were from Vaiśali,[18] and in the time of the Buddha the Licchavis of Vaiśali were a well-known clan (named above in Chapter 5); therefore, the Licchavis who rule in this period in Nepal were probably descendants of the earlier Licchavis in India.

Concerning the Licchavi kings and the queen named in the Changu Narayana pillar inscription, in that inscription Vrishadeva is described as surrounded by wise, well-disciplined sons as the sun is encircled by dazzling rays; his son Śankaradeva is described as of great renown due to his valor and charity; his son Dharmadeva is described as aspiring to sagacity and excellent in qualities; Dharmadeva's wife Rajyavati is described as like Lakshmi, the wife of Hari (Vishnu), and is pictured as languishing in sorrow after her husband "left to the sojourn of heaven, as he would to a walk in the park," and as thinking to follow him at once in death; and Manadeva, the son of Dharmadeva and Rajyavati, is pictured as turning to his campaigns in the East and West "like a lion shaking his thick mane," and as coming back in victory to give rich gifts to the *brahmanas,* and to call upon his mother to be serene and to make an offering, even as before the death of her husband it had been her pleasure to perform rites in honor of the gods.

In the Śaka Year 387 (465 C.E.), the year after the Changu Narayana inscription, Manadeva I himself set up an inscribed bas-relief of Trivikrama Vishnu (i.e., Vishnu in the three-striding form of the dwarf Vamana) for the sake of Rajyavati, his mother (a monument which was found at the village of Lajanpat east of Kathmandu). Other inscriptions indicate that two of Manadeva's wives, Kshemasundari and Gunavati, set up Śiva *lingas,* and a third wife, Vijayasvamini, installed an image of the goddess Vijaya (victorious, a name of Parvati, the wife of Śiva).[19] If Manadeva I founded the Bodnath *stupa* too, as the *Vamśavali* says,[20] Vaishnavism, Śaivism, and Buddhism must in his time all have been relatively amicably coexistent, as they generally always have been in Nepal. Manadeva I probably also built the palace of Managriha, from which a number of his successors issued their decrees.[21]

From approximately the middle of the sixth to the middle of the seventh century C.E. the inscriptions show that, in addition to the ruling dynasty of the Licchavis, there were powerful Gupta and Thakuri families, members of which from time to time either usurped the throne or exercised rule in fact even if a Licchavi were king in name.

Ganadeva and Bhaumagupta. How the Gupta family here in question was related, if at all, to the Gupta line in India is unclear, but at any rate the family claimed descent from the lunar dynasty, as against the solar dynasty of the Licchavis. Of this Gupta family, a certain Bhaumagupta appears as a high officeholder in the inscriptions of the Licchavi king Ganadeva between the years 482 and 489 (560 and 567 C.E.), but in a later inscription of Jishnugupta, the latter refers to Bhaumagupta as his grandfather and names him among a number of former kings including Manadeva and Ganadeva; thus, Bhaumagupta may have shared rule with Ganadeva or succeeded him in rule.[22]

Śivadeva I and Amśuvarman. Not long afterward, Amśuvarman, who is named in the *Vamśavali* as a Thakuri, seems to have been in a similarly powerful position, and this may be seen first in respect to the sequence of kings, Manadeva, Gunakamadeva, and Śivadeva. There is reason to think that Amśuvarman was already the power behind the throne in 576 C.E., the date from which is reckoned the era which goes by his name. There is reason also to think that he was responsible for the installation at that time of Manadeva II as king, by whose name the same era is also sometimes known. In the same way Amśuvarman may have been responsible for placing in rule Gunakamadeva and Śivadeva I.

At any rate it is certain that under Śivadeva I, Amśuvarman was a very influential and highly regarded official. Inscriptions of Śivadeva I are available which date from the Years 515 to 527 (593 to 605 C.E.), and in these Amśuvarman is called *mahasamanta* and referred to as the one upon whose advice the king sets forth his decrees. An example is an inscribed *stela* found at the village of Khopasi, east of Bhadgaon. The text is issued from Managriha (the palace of the Licchavi kings), and is dated in the Year 520 (598 C.E.). In the text Śivadeva I describes Amśuvarman as a person whose virtues are brilliant, who has dissipated the shadows of ignorance, and who by his own strength has uprooted all enemies.[23]

Then, when the inscriptions of Śivadeva I cease (the last being dated in 527 (605 C.E.), after which Śivadeva I presumably died or was deposed), Amśuvarman begins to issue his own inscriptions, in which he employs his own name or that of his first protegé Manadeva (the era reckoned from 576 C.E.), and from this time on is evidently ruling in his own name.

The first two inscriptions of Amśuvarman are found on *stelas* at a temple in the village of Harigaon (a short distance to the northeast of Kathmandu). Although Amśuvarman mentions the palace of Managriha, which had been the center of rule from the time of Manadeva I, he issues both of the present texts from a palace called Kailasakuta, evidently a new palace and center of rule which he has constructed. The subject matter of the texts deals with donations to gods, temples, and monasteries, and it appears that consideration is given quite equally to the needs of Śaivites, Vaishnavites, and Buddhists. The two texts are dated in the Years 30 and 32 respectively and, in terms of the new era, are equivalent to 606 and 608 C.E. Other inscriptions of Amśuvarman extend to the Year 45 (621 C.E.), so his entire period of official activity may be dated 596–621 C.E.[24]

Confirmation of this time in the history of Nepal for Amśuvarman is also provided by the Chinese Buddhist pilgrim Xuan Zang, who was in India in 629–645 C.E. and near the border of Nepal in about 637, and who mentions Amśuvarman as having been on the throne "lately." Xuan Zang also says that Amśuvarman was distinguished for his learning and had composed a work on the knowledge of "sounds," perhaps meaning etymology. Of the region of *Ni-po-lo* (Nepal) in general, Xuan Zang says that it is situated among the Snowy Mountains, abounds with flowers and fruits, and has a cold climate. The people are described as unlearned but very skilled in the arts. Believers and heretics (i.e., Buddhists and Hindus) are mixed together, with Buddhist monasteries and Hindu *deva* temples close together. The Buddhist priests number about 2,000, and study both the Mahayana and the Hinayana. "The king is a *kshatriya*, and belongs to the family of the Licchavis. His mind is well informed, and he is pure and dignified in character. He has a sincere faith in the law of Buddha."[25]

Before long two more members of the Gupta family appear in the inscriptions in the position of power behind the throne under or with Licchavi kings, namely, Jishnugupta (624–635 C.E.) under Dhruvadeva (624–625) and Bhimarjunadeva (631–641), and Vishnugupta (640–641) under Bhimarjunadeva. As the inscription of Jishnugupta cited above shows, Jishnugupta was a grandson of Bhaumagupta, and Vishnugupta was a son of Jishnugupta.

In Tibet King Songtsen Gampo (b. 617, r. 629–649 C.E.) married a daughter of the king of Nepal, usually identified as Aṁśuvarman, but the marriage was in 632 and the father of the princess must have been one of Aṁśuverman's successors, probably Bhimarjunadeva. In Tibetan the daughter's name was *Khri btsun* (pronounced Trhisün), and she is regarded as having been very influential in the introduction of Buddhism in Tibet, being herself considered an incarnation of the goddess Bhrikuti (one of the manifestations of Tara).[26]

Bhimarjunadeva and Vishnugupta. In an inscription which still stands in Yangal-hiti, an ancient fountain in southern Kathmandu, Bhimarjunadeva and Vishnugupta issued a joint edict dated in the Year 64 (640 C.E.). The text opens with an invocation to Anantaśayana Narayana, and confers upon the citizens of the village of Dakshinakoligrama certain benefits in return for their part in having dragged a huge stone which was suitable for making a *jalaśayana* image of Vishnu. In a similar inscription of Bhimarjunadeva and Vishnugupta of the following year (641 C.E.), found at Sunaguthi south of Kathmandu, the text opens with an invocation to Jalaśayana Narayana, and confers upon the citizens of Bhringaragrama benefits for their work in dragging the stone for a *jalaśayana* image. *Jala* is a Sanskrit word for water, and *śayana* means recumbent, while Narayana (moving on the waters) is the name of Vishnu when he sleeps on the serpent Ananta (endless) or Śesha (remainder) on the cosmic ocean. The image here referred to may therefore be identified with the very large image of Vishnu reclining upon the serpent, known as the Jalaśayana Vishnu and found at Budhanilakantha 8 miles (13 km.) north of Kathmandu (below, Fig. 15.12). Although the two inscriptions relevant to the image are in the names of both Bhimarjunadeva and Vishnugupta, it was probably Vishnugupta who was in particular responsible for the work, for one of the *vaṁśavalis* credits him with the making of such an image, and his own name attests his devotion to Vishnu. As for the origin of the huge stone, it is probable that it was cut and dragged from the southwestern part of the Kathmandu valley or just outside over the rim of the valley.[27]

Further with respect to Vishnugupta, there is a colossal monolithic image of him in the guise of Vishnu, accompanied by his two sons, which is presently mistakenly worshiped as an image of Rama, in the Ramacandra temple at Paśupatinath. For Vishnugupta so to represent himself was an apparently unparalleled action in Nepal, and it has been speculated that it was considered an expression of arrogance and contributed to the overthrow of Vishnugupta and the taking of the throne thereafter by another Licchavi king, Narendradeva.[28]

Narendradeva. The Sunaguthi inscription of the Year 65 (641 C.E.) is the last inscription of Vishnugupta, and Narendradeva may have taken the throne in that year or soon afterward; at any rate, the first inscription of Narendradeva is dated in the Year 69 (645 C.E.). The last of the inscriptions of Narendradeva are dated in the Years 95 and 103 (671 and 679 C.E.), so his reign extended at least to this time. These last inscriptions are issued from Bhadradivasa, which was evidently his royal residence at the time, although all the records of his successors are issued again from the Kailasakuta.[29]

During the reign of Narendradeva a Chinese ambassador named Wong Xuan Ce (Wang Hsüan-tse) visited the court of the king on three different occasions—in 643, 647, and 657 C.E.[30] In his memoirs the ambassador describes the palace of the king as a very large structure, divided into three terraces, with each terrace divided into seven stories, the upper part capable of accommodating 10,000 men. In four pavilions are marvelous sculptures, decorated with stones and pearls. The king himself wears pearls, earrings of gold, pendants of jade, and a belt ornamented with a figure of the Buddha. The houses of the people are constructed of wood, with the walls sculptured and painted. The people are fond of plays and take pleasure in blowing trumpets and beating drums. They understand fairly well calculation of destiny and researches in physical philosophy, and are equally clever in the art of calendar making. They adore five celestial spirits, sculpture their images in stone, and wash the images daily in purifying water. To the south of the town is an isolated mountain, on which temples are so disposed in numerous stories that one would take them for a crown of clouds.[31] That Narendradeva is credited in the *Vaṃśavali* and the *Svayambhu Purana* with the institution of the ceremony of "the drawing of the car" *(rathayatra)* has already been noted.

Jayadeva II. Narendradeva was succeeded by his son, Śivadeva II (685–701 C.E.), and Śivadeva II was succeeded by his son, Jayadeva II. A number of inscriptions of Jayadeva II are extant, but the only one in which a date is preserved is the already-cited inscription at Paśupatinath, with a date in the Year 159 (735 C.E.). The first five verses of this inscription were composed by Jayadeva II himself, and the remainder of the total of nineteen verses were by a court poet named Buddha Kirti. In addition to the genealogy of Manadeva already referred to, the inscription traces the more immediate ancestry of Jayadeva II (Śivadeva, Narendradeva, Udayadeva), and shows that the king's father, Śivadeva II, was married to Vatsadevi, granddaughter of the Gupta king Adityasena of Magadha. The ancestors, it is indicated, were all devotees of Śiva, and the main subject of the text is the record of the offering of a large lotus to Paśupati by the king's mother, Vatsadevi, to gain benefit for her departed husband. Jayadeva II himself is praised as learned and brave, and always concerned for the security and happiness of his kingdom.[32]

From the Licchavis to the Mallas

After Jayadeva II (circa 735 C.E.) there are no more dated records of the Licchavi kings, although the dynasty must have endured yet for some time. It is also thought that there were repeated foreign invasions in the ensuing time. At any rate, a new era known as the Newari Era was inaugurated in 879/880 C.E. by a king named Raghavadeva, and his successors, who are rather arbitrarily called by the dynastic name of Thakuri, ruled until about 1200 C.E., when they were supplanted by the Mallas.[33]

Within these times the name of a king Gunakamadeva occurs again, and this Gunakamadeva is said to have founded the present city of Kathmandu (then called Kantipur) in 723 C.E. The site was at the confluence of the Bagmati and Vishnumati rivers, where Manjupattan was supposedly founded originally by Manjuśri (with Sankasya and Visalanagara in the same area). According to popular belief the name of Kathmandu is derived from the Kastha Mandap (also Maru Satal), a temple in the city which, according to a legend in the *Vaṃśavali,* was built with miraculous help by the Malla king Lakshminarasimhamalla (1619–1641 C.E.) from the wood of a single tree. In fact the name Kashthamandapa, signifying a wooden pavilion, occurs already in a manuscript of the eleventh century C.E., and the temple may be this old and indeed be the source of the name Kathmandu.[34]

Along with Kathmandu the two other main towns in the valley were Patan (3 miles [5 km.] southeast of Kathmandu), earlier called Lalitpur and supposedly founded by Aśoka in the third century B.C.E. and again built by King Viradeva in 299 C.E., and Bhadgaon (9 miles [15 km.] east of Kathmandu), earlier called Bhaktapur (city of devotees), and supposedly founded by King Anandadeva in 899 C.E. In the last years of Thakuri rule the political center tended to shift back and forth between these two towns, Patan and Bhadgaon, while Patan was especially important as a center of Buddhism.

Mallas

Like the Licchavis the Mallas were a well-known people in India already in the time of the Buddha. In the Changu Narayana inscription of Manadeva I in 464 C.E., the triumphs of the king which are commemorated include the conquest of the capital city of the Mallas, and there were no doubt further conflicts between the two regions in the ensuing time.

1200–1480 C.E. About 1200 C.E. a certain Arimalla is found on the throne in the valley of Nepal, and this is considered the beginning of the rule of the Malla dynasty which lasted for more than five and a half centuries, a span of time divisible into two main periods, 1200–1480 and 1480–1768 C.E.[35]

In the thirteenth and fourteenth centuries there were various invasions, including a Muslim raid in 1349 C.E. led by Sultan Samsud-din Ilyas of Bengal, and many refugees from India, fleeing from Muslim pressure there too, also came into the valley. In 1382 C.E. Sthitimalla (or Jayasthitimalla) began a short but influential reign, in which the kingdom was unified and reorganized on the basis of the Hindu caste system. The *Vamśavali* concludes its account of the accomplishment of the king by saying: "Thus Raja Jayasthitimalla divided the people into castes, and made regulations for them. He also made laws about houses and lands, and fostered the Hindu religion in Nepal, thereby making himself famous."[36]

The height of the early Malla period was under Sthitimalla's grandson, Yakshamalla (circa 1428–1480 C.E.). He is remembered for the replacement of Sanskrit by Newari as the court language, for the encouragement of literature, art, and architecture (e.g., the building of the royal palace at Bhadgaon), and for the bringing of *brahmanas* from the south of India to manage the temple of Paśupatinath.[37]

1480–1768 C.E. In spite of the fact that the accomplishments of Sthitimalla and Yakshamalla had fostered greater national consciousness in the Nepal valley, at the end of his reign (1480 C.E.) Yakshamalla divided his kingdom among his heirs. According to the *Vamśavali,* the oldest son of Yakshamalla, Rayamalla, succeeded his father at Bhadgaon; the second son, Ranamalla, became king of Banepa; the third son, Ratnamalla, obtained Kathmandu; and, according to some records, a daughter of Yakshamalla received Patan. Banepa was subsequently absorbed by Bhadgaon, and thus there came to be three independent kingdoms, namely, those of Bhadgaon, Kathmandu, and Patan.[38]

Throughout this later Malla period the three kingdoms were frequently involved in mutual rivalry and strife, but at the same time they developed advanced city civilizations, as characterized by their art and architecture. For the history many inscriptions are available, and these are usually found with dates in the Newari Era (reckoned from 879/880 C.E.).

The most notable kings were Siddhinarasimhamalla in Patan, Pratapamalla in Kathmandu, and Bhupatindramalla in Bhadgaon.

Patan. Siddhinarasimhamalla, king of Patan (Newari Era 740–781, i.e., 1620–1661 C.E.), was the son of Hariharasinha and, upon the death of his father, succeeded to the throne while still a child, with his mother, Lalamatidevi, acting as his guardian and regent. Of his mother the king says in one of his inscriptions that she was faithful, like Sita, to her husband, and was a gracious lady who was the daughter of a king's son. As king, Siddhinarasimha enlarged the royal *durbar* (also *darbar,* audience hall, i.e., palace), occupied himself with the arrangements and administration of the numerous *bihars (viharas)* which existed in his reign, built various temples, and the like. One night he saw Radha-Krishna in a dream in front of the *durbar,* and on that spot he built a beautiful temple and placed the deity (presumably Radha-Krishna together) in it. Another temple was marked by carved wooden images placed around the roof. Siddhinarasimha was also the author of devotional songs, and is credited with starting the Kartik dance drama, a presentation of the *Ramayana* which still takes place in the month of Kartik (October/November). On several occasions the king is said to have entered a hermitage, and he made a pilgrimage to Varanasi and other holy places in India. In his absence he entrusted governmental powers to his son, Srinivasamalla, and eventually renounced the throne in favor of the son and himself went away. According to the *Vamsavali* Siddhinarasimha attained the state of *jivan-mukti* (living release), i.e., salvation while still alive and on earth, and the *brahmanas* composed a verse *(sloka)* in his honor: "Siddhinarasimha, the omniscient, the *jivan-mukta,* the chaste, the favorite of Krishna, the master of *yoga,* the chief of poets, the relinquisher of the world, the son of Harisimha. He who repeats this *sloka* will be absolved from sin."39

Kathmandu. Pratapamalla, king of Kathmandu (1641–1674 C.E.), was the only son and the successor of Lakshminarasimhamalla, his mother being Sarasvatidevi. The king was known for his varied activities in trade, architecture, art, poetry, religion, and culture. The *Vamsavali* states that he invited to his court many scholars from other countries, and learned many things from them. His spiritual guides included the *swami* Jnanananda from the Deccan, the *brahmana* Lambakarna Bhatta from Maharashtra, the *brahmana* Narasimha Thakur from Tirhut (in northern Bihar), as well as a Buddhist *guru* named Jamana, and a Tibetan *lama* named Syamarpa. It was said that Pratapamalla made himself master of all the *sastras* (scriptures), and he was evidently quite respectful of both Saivite/Vaishnavite and Buddhist deities, and gave alms to both *brahmanas* and *bhikshus*. His inscriptions are found at Pasupatinath, Svayambhunath, and many other places, and some contain religious hymns which he himself composed. In some of his inscriptions the language is Parbatiya, the language now called Nepali, the official language of Nepal. He was responsible for many buildings, pillars, and images which are still found in Kathmandu. In the *Vamsavali* special mention is made of the gateway which he built at the royal palace, with its image of Hanuman, the monkey god: "In order to keep away evil spirits, witches, and epidemics, such as smallpox, he made a principal gate to the palace, and set there an image of Hanuman, whence it was called Hanuman Dhoka."

According to the same source, Pratapamalla had four sons, Parthivendramalla, Niripendramalla, Mahipatendramalla, and Cakravartendramalla. A *swami* named Khodhanyasi came to Pasupati and the king appointed him priest of the temple. By the *swami's* advice, the king left the throne for a time to be filled in turn by the four sons, for one year each. Cakravartendramalla, the youngest of these sons and his father's favorite, died within the lifetime of Pratapamalla; upon the death of the king Mahipatendramalla tried unsuccessfully to take the throne; the actual successors were Niripendramalla (1674–1680 C.E.) and Parthivendramalla (1680–1687).[40]

Bhadgaon. Bhupatindramalla, king of Bhadgaon (1696–1722 C.E.), was the son and successor of Jitamitramalla, and came to the throne at the age of twenty-one. In political and military affairs he succeeded in making Bhadgaon the equal of Patan and Kathmandu. As an author he composed devotional poems, hymns in honor of deities, and many dramatic works. The *Vamśavali* tells in particular about his building works both at the royal palace and in the construction of various temples. About his work at the royal palace the chronicle says:

> This *raja* built a *durbar* (audience hall, palace) with fifty-five windows, in one of which he put a small pane of glass, presented to him by a man from the plains of India. This piece of glass was considered so rare and valuable that the *raja* placed it in the window as an object of wonder for the people. To the right and left of the principal door of the *durbar* he erected stone images of Hanuman and Narasimha. He made ninety-nine *choks* (courtyards) in the *durbar*. In the Mula *chok* he placed a golden door, and set up many images of gods; and in other *choks* he made tanks. In one *chok*, which he named Malti Chok, he placed a window of sandalwood.

In an accompanying stone inscription it was provided that the roof of the Malti Chok be repaired annually, the images of Hanuman and Narasimha rubbed with oil on three dates in the year, other worship ceremonies to be performed on specified dates with the *raja* attending in person and assisting at the ceremonies, and certain lands assigned to provide annual income to support these services.

Of the temples which Bhupatindramalla built, two are of special interest. As the *Vamśavali* tells the story, the king built a three-storied temple and placed a Bhairava in it for the protection of the country and the removal of sin and distress from the people, but the Bhairava gave much trouble instead. Those whom the king consulted on the problem advised that if the *tantric* goddess Iśvari, whom Bhairava respected, were placed near him, Bhairava would be appeased. At an auspicious moment, therefore, the king laid the foundation of a second nearby temple. This was a five-storied *(nyatapola)* pagoda, with a flight of stairs, and with images of griffins, lions, elephants, and Jayamalla and Phattamalla (two giant wrestlers) (below, Fig. 15.18).

> This temple is the most beautiful as well as the highest in the whole city. In building it the *raja* set an example to his subjects by himself carrying three bricks, and the people brought together the whole of the materials in five days. When the temple was finished he secretly placed in it a deity of the Tantra *śastra,* who rides on Yama-raja (king of death), whom no one is permitted to see, and who is therefore kept concealed. After this the Bhairava became tranquil.[41]

Gorkha

In the meantime, while the three kingdoms of the Kathmandu valley were engaged in and weakened by quarrels among themselves, an independent kingdom arose at Gorkha, a village outside the valley to the northwest (in the valley of the Gandaki River, between Kathmandu and Pokhara). Dravya Shah became king here in 1559 C.E. and, in his line, Prithvi Narayan Shah ascended the throne in 1742 and in the next year began his incursions into the Kathmandu valley. In 1768 Prithvi Narayan Shah entered Kathmandu, and its ruler, King Jayaprakaśamalla, fled to Patan; a few weeks later Patan was captured and both Jayaprakaśamalla and

Tejanarasimhamalla, king of Patan, fled to Bhadgaon; at Bhadgaon King Ranajitamalla attempted to resist, but the city fell in 1769, and he and the fugitive rulers of Kathmandu and Patan were all taken prisoner. In this manner the whole of the ancient valley was incorporated in the kingdom of Gorkha and became the modern nation of Nepal, the 200th anniversary of which was celebrated in 1969.[42]

MONUMENTS

The Kathmandu valley is occupied by almost innumerable temples, *stupas,* and the like, and, as Xuan Zang remarked, the Buddhist and the Hindu establishments are often "close together" and their adherents "mixed together." The most characteristic temple is erected on a high, stepped, square base and rises in two, three, or even more stories, each with its own widely projecting, sloping roof. The most characteristic *stupa* has a square or circular base, above which rises a hemispherical dome. The dome is surmounted by a square tower (*toran,* corresponding to the Indian *harmika*), and this supports a tapering rectangular or conical spire made up of thirteen squares or rings, standing for as many superimposed worlds or stations along the path to enlightenment. At the very top is a crowning canopy or umbrella. Distinctively, and carrying out the psycho-cosmic symbolism of the *stupa,* on each of the four sides of the *toran* is a pair of huge penetrating eyes which, from whatever angle seen, appear to be looking directly at the viewer.[43]

Svayambhunath

The great *caitya* or *stupa* of Svayambhunath, and the surrounding complex of *caityas,* temples, images, and monasteries, are located on the sacred site (2 miles [3 km.] west of Kathmandu), the supposed antiquity of which, reaching back into the previous ages of the world and visited in the present age by the Buddha and Aśoka, has already been noted. The earliest actual historical record recovered from there is a stone inscription of about 460 C.E., which proves the existence of the main *stupa* at that time.[44] It is also known that the *stupa* and its monastery were destroyed by Sultan Samsud-din of Bengal in 1349 C.E., and were at least partly rebuilt in 1372.[45] The *Svayambhu Purana* considers the *stupa* the most sacred place in the entire world, and thus attests its importance in the time when this work was written (composed in the early tenth century C.E. and copied in the late fifteenth century).

At the Svayambhunath hill (250 feet [76 m.] above the surrounding valley) (Fig. 15.1), some 400 steps, lined by many small stupas, lead up to the summit. On the main *stupa* the usual great, all-seeing eyes look out from the four sides of the *toran,* which also supports on each side a three-cornered plaque on which the five *tathagatas* (Dhyani Buddhas) are represented (Fig. 15.2). The spire above is in conical form, with thirteen superimposed rings. Around the base of the *stupa* is a broad terrace, with altars, chapels, images, and a complete circle of Tibetan prayer wheels to be set in motion by pilgrims as they circumambulate the monument. In the adjacent monastery is a large gilt image of the Buddha (Fig. 15.3), before which the musical services of the monks are conducted (Fig. 15.4).

Bodhnath

The Bodhnath *stupa* is in the plain 3 miles (5 km.) east of Kathmandu. In local tradition, the *stupa* is supposed to have been erected originally by Aśoka, and to house relics of the Manushi Buddha Kaśyapa, the immediate predecessor of

15.1 Svayambhunath Hill, near Kathmandu

15.2 Dome and Tower of the Large Stupa at Svayambhunath

15.3 Gilt Buddha in the Svayambhunath Monastery

15.4 Monks Playing Musical Instruments and Chanting in the Svayambhunath Monastery

15.5   Bodhnath Stupa near Kathmandu

Śakyamuni Buddha.[46] In fact, the hemispherical dome retains the flat shape of a prehistoric tumulus and an archaic *stupa*, and may conceivably represent the form of a *stupa* which Aśoka built previously on the site.[47] The *Vaṃśavali*, however, attributes the building of the monument to Manadeva I in the fifth century C.E.

In its present form, the Bodhnath *stupa* is one of the largest in the world, only slightly smaller than the Shwe Dagon in Rangoon and the *stupa* at Nakhon Pathom in Thailand. The base is octagonal, built in three terraces, and inset with 108 large prayer wheels. The dome is whitewashed; the *toran*, from which the watchful eyes look out, is gilded, as is also the umbrella at the top, and prayer flags are suspended on lines from high on the spire (Fig. 15.5). Particularly in the annual festival of lights in the month of Kartik (October/November), many oil lamps or candles are lighted in niches and on the terraces.

The *stupa* is surrounded by a square of three- and four-story buildings which house monks and their families, pilgrims, artisans, and shopkeepers. Bodhnath is an important center for Tibetan Buddhists, and the Chiniya Lama, who is the abbot of the Bodhnath monastery, is the high priest of the Tibetans in Nepal.[48] In the monastery Tibetan monks, bell and *dorje* (symbolic ritual objects) in hand, chant scriptures (Fig. 15.6), and in 1967 Tenzing Ghelek Rimpoche, a small boy not more than ten years old but recognized as of the highest order of reincarnate *lamas*, was there engaged in study (Fig. 15.7).

Paśupatinath

The Paśupatinath temple, dedicated to Śiva in the form of Paśupati (the herdsman, lord of beasts), is in a small town called Deopatan on the right bank of

15.6 Tibetan Monks in the Bodhnath Monastery

15.7 Tenzing Ghelek Rimpoche in the Bodhnath Monastery

the Bagmati River, 2 miles (3 km.) east of Kathmandu. According to the *Vamśavali*, the temple was founded in the third age of the world *(Dvaparayuga)* by King Dharmadatta, in the fourth and present world age *(Kaliyuga)* was rebuilt and roofed with golden plates by King Pashupreshadeva of the Somavamśi dynasty, and was provided with burning ghats by King Śivadevavarman of the Suryavamśi dynasty. A stone inscription found in the area dates in 533 C.E. and, from that date on, there are many other inscriptions and documents which attest to the history of the temple.[49]

As it stands, the main temple at Pasupatinath has a two-tiered golden roof, and it is surrounded by many other smaller temples, images, and *lingas* of Śiva. In the main temple, entrance into which is restricted to Hindus, the central object is the *linga* of Paśupati, about 3 feet (1 m.) high, with four faces of the deity sculptured on its sides. On the hill opposite—on the other side of the river—is a whole row of small Śiva shrines (Fig. 15.8), each containing *yoni* and *linga* (Fig. 15.9). Below the bridge across the Bagmati, on the right bank of the river, is a row of burning ghats, backed by hostels for the sick and dying, their relatives, and pilgrims to the temples (Fig. 15.10). For some time, affixed to an adjacent wall at the bridge, was the statue of the so-called Paśupatinath Devi (Fig. 15.11), locally known as Lakshmi, a figure attributed to the eighth century C.E., which probably once stood elsewhere in the precincts beside an image of Śiva.[50]

Paśupatinath is considered the most sacred of all the Hindu temples in Nepal. As such it is especially the center of the annual festival in honor of the birthday of Śiva, known as the Śivaratri and held in the month of Falgun (February/March), at which very large numbers of pilgrims are in attendance from different parts of Nepal and India.

15.8 Śiva Shrines at Paśupatinath

15.9 Interior of Śiva Shrine, Paśupatinath

15.10 Burning Ghats and Hostels at Paśupatinath

15.11 Paśupatinath Devi

15.12 Jalaśayana Narayana at Budhanilakantha

Jalaśayana Narayana at Budhanilakantha

The Jalaśayana Narayana image of Vishnu, explained above as made by Vishnugupta in 640 C.E., is at the village of Budhanilakantha, 8 miles (13 km.) north of Kathmandu. The name Budhanilakantha contains the word *budho* (not Buddha) which means old or large. The epithet *nilakantha* (blue throat) which belongs properly to Śiva but is here applied to Vishnu is used here for the monument as well as the village, to designate this as the famous image of its kind, in distinction from a similar but smaller image at a place called Balaju, the Balanilakantha or Little Nilakantha (probably also of the seventh century C.E.). Here the Budhanilakantha image (Fig. 15.12) is a colossal figure (21 feet [6.5 m.] long) of Vishnu lying on entwined coils of the "endless" serpent Ananta, the whole in a spring-fed pool of water that is the cosmic ocean. In his hands the sleeping god holds his usual attributes—the conch, wheel, lotus, and mace.[51]

Patan

In each of the three main ancient cities of the Kathmandu valley, Patan, Kathmandu, and Bhadgaon, the center of the city is the Durbar Square (*durbar, darbar,* audience hall, palace), where normally may be found the main palaces, temples, and other most important works of architecture and sculpture.

As explained above, Patan (ancient Lalitpur) is supposed to have been founded by Aśoka, and four *stupas* of ancient configuration and still named for Aśoka stand on four sides of the city (Fig. 15.13). In the city the palace and temples date mostly from the fifteenth and sixteenth centuries C.E., while King Sid-

15.13 Aśoka Stupa at Patan

dhinarasimhamalla (1620–1661) enlarged the palace and constructed some of the temples. The palace is a three-storied building in red brick, with fine wood carving around the doors, pillars, and windows.[52] The elephant-headed Ganeśa is one of the guardian deities by the main gate, and many other Hindu gods and goddesses appear in other sculptures without and within. Near the palace is the Krishna Mandir, the stone temple built by Siddhinarasimhamalla in 1636 C.E. in consequence of the dream in which he saw Radha-Krishna in front of the *durbar;* it is the center of Krishna's annual birthday celebration held in the month of Bhadra (August/September). Several other temples dedicated to Vishnu and to Śiva are also around the square, and to the south is the Machhendranath Mandir, the huge temple (early fifteenth century) dedicated to Avalokiteśvara (Lokeśvara) in his form as the god of rain and mercy, and the center of his annual chariot festival in the month of Baisakh (April/May).

Kathmandu

In present Kathmandu (ancient Kantipur), believed to have been founded by King Gunakamadeva in 723 C.E., the Durbar Square is the site of the old royal palace, and many other buildings, temples, and the like. From its principal gate the Hanuman Dhoka, which was built by King Pratapamalla (1641–1674) with a huge stone figure of the monkey god to guard it, the palace is called the Hanuman Dhoka Durbar. Near the palace is the temple of the goddess Taleju Bhavani, said to have been founded by Ratnamalla, who received Kathmandu at the division of the kingdom by Yakshamalla (1480), and to have been built in its present form by Mahendramalla (1560–1574), the fourth king of the same dynasty. Bhavani (giver of existence) is a name of Parvati, and Taleju Bhavani was the tutelary deity of the Malla kings and is still considered the guardian deity of the royal family of Nepal. The temple is closed to the people throughout the year except during Dashahara, the festival of new fruits and vegetables in the month of Jestha (May/June). In front of the palace is a tall stone monolith on the lotus capital of which are gilt statues of Pratapamalla and his four sons. In an accompanying inscription the first portion is in Sanskrit and contains verses in honor of the goddess Taleju, and the second portion is in Newari prose and speaks of the sons Niripendramalla and Cakravartendramalla. The date is the Year 784 of the Newari Era, i.e., 1664 C.E..[53]

Not far away is the huge figure of Kalabhairava, the Black Bhairava, the fierce form of Śiva as the lord of destruction (Fig. 15.14). The image, made of black stone on a stone plaque 12 feet (3.6 m.) high, is said to belong to the Licchavi period of perhaps the eighth century C.E., and to have been set up here by Pratapamalla in the seventeenth century. The deity has six hands. Two hands are held in front of his chest; his lower right hand holds the trident of Śiva, of whom he is a manifestation; his upper right hand holds a sword, his upper left hand an unidentified object, and his lower left hand a group of three human heads. Under his feet is the prostrate figure of a man.

Elsewhere in the city is the temple hall called the Kastha Mandap or wooden pavilion (and now the Maru Satal), which may be mentioned as early as the eleventh century, and was restored by Lakshminarasimhamalla in the seventeenth century, supposedly from the timber of a single tree, the temple believed to provide the origin of the name of Kathmandu.

Important also is the Kumari Ghar, the residential building of Kumari Devi, the living goddess. This was built in Buddhist monastery style in the year 1760 C.E. by Jayaprakaśamalla, the last Malla ruler of Kathmandu. Kumari (the maid) is a

15.14   Kalabhairava in Durbar Square, Kathmandu

name of Parvati/Durga, the consort of Śiva and, in her form as Taleju Bhavani, the guardian goddess of the royal family. Once, it is said, the king was playing at dice with the goddess when she became offended and thereafter refused to be seen any more, but later assured the saddened king that she would incarnate from time to time as a daughter of someone in the Śakya clan. A young girl is therefore chosen from the Śakya caste (presently silversmiths and goldsmiths) and serves in her early years in the capacity of this incarnation, living in sequestered quarters as Kumari Devi. Two young boys are also chosen to be her associates, and to represent Ganesha and Bhairava. In an annual ceremony which is a part of the annual festival of Indra *(Indrayatra)* in the month of Bhadra (August/September), starting from Vasantapur Square in front of the temple of the living goddess all three young personages are drawn through the streets in ancient heavy chariots.

Bhadgaon

In Bhadgaon (ancient Bhaktapur), founded by Anandadeva in 899 C.E., the Durbar Square is the site of the royal palace built originally by Yakshamalla (1428–

15.15 Lion and Hanuman at the Lion Gate, Royal Palace, Bhadgaon

1480). The Lion Gate *(singha dhoka),* added in 1686 C.E., is guarded by stone lions and figures of Hanuman the monkey god (Fig. 15.15), and provides the main entrance to the National Art Gallery. In 1697, to commemorate his fifty-fifth birthday, Bhupatindramalla (1696–1722) remodeled the palace with fifty-five carved wooden windows and also, as the *Vaṃśavali* tells, set in a rare pane of glass from India. In 1754 Bhupatindra's son Ranajitamalla, the last Malla king of Bhadgaon, built the Golden Gate *(lu dhoka),* a doorway of brick and embossed copper gilt (Fig. 15.16), in front of which on a high stone column is a gilt statue of his father Bhupatindramalla.[54]

On two adjacent sides of the Tanmadhi Square are the three-storied temple and the five-storied pagoda, both of which are attributed in the *Vaṃśavali* to Bhupatindramalla in the story about the king's successful effort to pacify the Bhairava of the first temple by the secret installation of a *tantric* goddess in the second. According to some evidence, the rectangular three-storied temple was built originally by Jagatjyotimalla (1617–1638), who was also noted for his composition of poetry and drama. The temple is known today as the Bhairav Mandir; beside it stands the huge wagon in which the god is transported through the streets in the Bhairava Festival (Fig. 15.17).[55] The five-storied pagoda-shaped temple, the Nyatapola, built by Bhupatindramalla in 1708, stands on five elevated terraces of brickwork and is surmounted by five tiers of roofs (Fig. 15.18). The stairs which lead up the terraces (Fig. 15.19) are flanked by a pair each of giants (Jayamalla and Phattamalla), elephants, lions, griffins, and many-armed deities (Fig. 15.20), each pair popularly said to be ten times stronger than the pair below it, while the giants at the bottom are ten times stronger than ordinary human beings. At the top of the stairs, in the shrine behind barred doors, unseen, is the tantric goddess, now

15.16 Golden Gate, Royal Palace, Bhadgaon

15.17 Bhairava Temple and Festival Wagon, Bhadgaon

15.18 Nyatapola Temple, Bhadgaon

15.19 Stairs and Pairs of Guardian Figures, Nyatapola Temple, Bhadgaon

15.20 Many-armed Deity, Nyatapola Temple, Bhadgaon

identified as Siddhi Lakshmi Devi, whose presence pacified Bhairava in the other, three-storied temple.

National Museum of Nepal

The National Museum of Nepal is 3 miles (5 km.) west of Kathmandu, at the foot of the Svayambhunath hill, and is especially notable for its collections of *tankas* and bronzes, two art forms most characteristic of Nepal and also of Tibet. In Tibetan a *thang vig* is a written record or scroll, and a scroll painting is a *thang ka* (pronounced tanka), and this name commonly designates a religious painting usually mounted on coarse cotton cloth (occasionally on paper or silk) and used as a temple or processional banner; for example, such a painting of Viśvarupa (having all forms), in the *Rig Veda* a son of Tvashtri and later a form of Vishnu or Krishna (Fig. 15.21). The bronzes as they are commonly called are usually made mainly of copper and preferably produced by the "lost wax" *(cire perdue)* process. Frequently shown, for example, is the goddess Tara (Fig. 15.22), and a divine couple in the *tantric* embrace called in Tibetan *yab yun* (father mother) (Fig. 15.23).[56] Of similar *tantric* significance is also a representation of Agni and his *śakti* (Fig. 15.24). In the same Museum is a limestone plaque, attributed to the ninth century C.E., showing the nativity of the Buddha at Lumbini (Fig. 15.25). The mother, Maya Devi, stands in the "thrice-bent" *(tribhanga)* position and, like a dryad *(vrikshaka)*, supports herself from the branch of a tree overhead, her hands at the same time holding flowers. She wears a diadem, ear ornaments, two necklaces, armlets, waistband, and anklets. The infant child, backgrounded by a large oval nimbus, stands beside her upon a double lotus pedestal. Above, two celestial figures are in the clouds, and are raining down holy water and lotuses.

15.21 Tanka showing Viśvarupa, National Museum of Nepal, Kathmandu

15.22 Bronze Tara, National Museum of Nepal, Kathmandu

15.23 Yab Yum Bronze, National Museum of Nepal, Kathmandu

15.24 Agni and His Śakti, National Museum of Nepal, Kathmandu

15.25 Nativity of the Buddha, National Museum of Nepal, Kathmandu

KASHMIR

Rajatarangini of Kalhana

The *Rajatarangini* or *River of Kings* by Kalhana is the earliest extant history of Kashmir.[57] Kalhana was the son of Campaka, a *brahmana* minister of King Harsha (1089–1101 C.E.) of the Lohara dynasty of Kashmir, and Kalhana wrote his work, dedicated to Śiva, between 1148 and 1150 C.E. The text is in Sanskrit, and is a historical poem of eight cantos, each canto being called a *taranga* or wave. In composing the book Kalhana says that he consulted the works of eleven earlier scholars, among whom he names Suvrata and Kshemendra, the latter an otherwise known author of the period 990–1065 C.E.

As in Nepal, it is said by Kalhana that Kashmir was originally a lake called Satisaras (lake of Sati, or Parvati, wife of Śiva), and was infested by lake demons under a certain Jalodbhava (water born). The ancient *rishi* Kaśyapa caused Jalodbhava to be slain, drained the lake, and founded upon the site the kingdom of Kashmir (named after himself Kaśyapa Mir, later shortened to Kashmir).[58]

Earliest Kings

In this kingdom, according to Kalhana, there were fifty-two kings, whose names have passed into oblivion, prior to a certain Gonanda, the first king to be introduced by name. This king, Gonanda I, took part in the battles of Jarasanda against Krishna and there lost his life. Damodara I, son of Gonanda I, also led an expedition against Krishna, and also perished in the enterprise. The son of Damodara I was Gonanda II (named for his grandfather), still an infant when the *Mahabharata* war took place.[59]

Pandava Dynasty

After the great war, Kalhana speaks of thirty-five kings but says that their names and acts have disappeared, having been submerged in the sea of oblivion. From other sources it is gathered that the kingdom passed at this time into the hands of successors of the Pandavas, the five brothers who are the heroes of the *Mahabharata*. The first of these Pandava kings of Kashmir was Harandeva, the son of Parikshit II, the grandson of Arjuna, who himself first served under Gonanda II, then killed the then aged ruler and usurped the throne. In the reign of Sundarasena, the twenty-second in the line, an earthquake destroyed the capital city, Sandimatnagar, and created what is now Lake Wular over the site (northwest of Srinagar). In popular tradition in present-day Kashmir almost all ancient monuments are ascribed to this period and called *Pandavlari* or buildings of the Pandavas.[60]

Maurya Dynasty

With a further series of kings the *Rajatarangini* brings the history down to Aśoka. Although Kalhana's chronology puts Aśoka long before his correct date in the third century B.C.E., it is presumably the famous Aśoka Maurya who is meant. According to Kalhana, Aśoka founded the city of Śrinagari (the city *[nagara]* of *śri*, i.e., the goddess Lakshmi, also wealth, beauty, and the like), and built many *viharas* and *stupas*. Concerning the city Kalhana says: "Possessing ninety-six *lakhs* (1 *lakh* =

100,000) of dwelling houses resplendent with prosperity, that illustrious king founded the magnificent city of Śrinagari."61

After the death of Aśoka (232 BCE), Kashmir was overrun by foreigners, perhaps Bactrian Greeks, whom the *Rajatarangini* calls barbarians *(mlecchas),* but they were overcome by a king named Jalauka, who established a more substantial government of the country. The chronicle calls Jalauka a son of Aśoka, but this is probably incorrect for such a son is unknown in Indian history and, in contrast with the great Buddhist emperor, Jalauka was a worshiper of Śiva and is supposed to have built the original Śiva temple on the hill now called the Śankaracarya hill or Takht-i-Sulaiman (throne of Solomon) above Dal Lake at Srinagar. The next king, Damodara II, was also a follower of Śiva, thus Śaivite Hinduism was promoted in this time.62

Kushana Dynasty

Afterward, three Kushana kings ruled the land—Kanishka, Huvishka, and Vasudeva, whom the *Rajatarangini* calls Kanishka, Hushka, and Jushka. They founded the three cities of Kanishkapura, Hushkapura, and Jushkapura, the first two of which still exist as the villages of Kanispor and Ushkara, near modern Baramula, west of Srinagar. Under the Kushanas Buddhism flourished again, and it has already been noted (in Chapter 11) that under Kanishka (78–103 C.E.) the Fourth Buddhist Council was held in Kashmir at the Kundalavana *vihara,* probably near Harwan, where Nagarjuna (of probably the same period, and a great teacher of the Mahayana) is also said to have lived and worked.63

Gonanda Dynasty

The sway of Buddhism was soon checked. The next king, Abhimanyu I, founded a town called Abhimanyupura after himself (the modern Bamyun, near Srinagar), and built there a temple of Śiva. Then Gonanda, the founder of the Gonanda dynasty, and his successors, took measures against Buddhism, and Nara, the sixth in the line, burned down thousands of *viharas.*

Again the land was overrun by hordes of Mlecchas (foreigners, now Huns), and in 528 C.E. the Hun leader, Mihirakula, notorious for his gross cruelty, seized the throne. Mihirakula favored the *brahmanas,* and in Śrinagari built a temple of Śiva. Also one of the descendants and successors in this line, named Gopaditya, is said to have built the Jyeshtheśvara temple on the Gopa hill. Jyeshtheśvara is a name under which Śiva was worshiped in Kashmir, so this temple of the sixth century C.E. was probably a replacement of the Śiva temple built originally around 200 B.C.E. by Jalauka, the son of Aśoka, and Gopa hill was probably the name used at that time for the Śankaracarya hill or Takht-i-Sulaiman at Srinagar.

In 580 C.E. another notable king, Pravarasena II (named for his grandfather Pravarasena I), conquered the country. The *Rajatarangini* relates that he desired to found a city after his own name, and did so on a site on the left bank of the Vitasta River, across which he built a bridge of boats. The city was called Pravarasenapura (shortened to Pravarapura), and the site was that of the present city of Srinagar. Under Muslim rule this place was for a time called Kashmir (and locally, Kashir), but eventually it took the name of Srinagar from Aśoka's Śrinagari, the site of which was not far away.

The *Rajatarangini* describes the city as large, attractive, and provided with many well-endowed temples:

Famous with its thirty-six *lakhs* of houses was the city. . . . The high mansions there kissed the sky; by ascending them one could, towards the end of summer, see the world glistening with rain showers, and efflorescent in [the spring month of] Caitra (March/April). Apart from this city, where on earth could one have easily found clean and charming canals from the river in pleasure houses and streets? . . . To each temple of the gods in that city, such treasure had been given by the kings that it would have been possible to buy with it a thousand times the earth draped by the seas.[64]

Xuan Zang, who was in Kashmir early in his travels (629–645 C.E.), mentions both "the old city" (i.e., the Śrīnagarī founded by Aśoka) and "the new city" (i.e., the Pravarapura founded by Pravarasena II), and thus confirms a date for Pravarasena II at least somewhat prior to his own time.[65]

Karkota Dynasty

Xuan Zang's own time in Kashmir, where he stayed for two years (631–633), was under King Durlabhavardhana (627–663). This king was said to be the son of Karkota (also Karkotak), the *naga* who is mentioned in the *Mahabharata* (e.g., 1.31.5; 1.114.60),[66] and figures in the mythology of Nepal as well as of Kashmir, and as of such descent Durlabhavardhana was the founder of the Karkota dynasty. As to Kashmir as he saw it, Xuan Zang says that the country is cold and snowy, and its people are handsome in appearance. Among other things both complimentary and otherwise, he says that the people love learning and are well instructed, and that there are both heretics (i.e., non-Buddhists) and believers (i.e., Buddhists) among them.[67]

Durlabhavardhana was succeeded by his son, Durlabhaka, known also as Pratapaditya II (663–713), and he by three of his own sons in turn, the third of whom was Muktapida, better known as Lalitaditya (715–753), the most famous king of the dynasty and one of the most famous kings of Kashmir. Lalitaditya is credited with very extensive conquests abroad, and with important public works at home, particularly in respect of drainage and irrigation. He built his capital at Parihasapura (now called Paraspur, 14 miles [23 km.] northwest of Srinagar). He was a patron of both Buddhism and Hinduism, and constructed temples dedicated both to the Buddha and to the gods of the Hindu pantheon—Śiva, Vishnu, and others. The largest temple was at Martand (5 miles [8 km.] east of Anantnag) and was dedicated to Surya.[68]

Utpala Dynasty

Avantivarman (855–883 C.E.), son of Utpala, founded the Utpala dynasty and was himself, like Lalitaditya, one of the most famous kings of Kashmir. Under his reign the engineer Suyya did important works of reclamation and flood control, and founded his own city of Suyyapura (the modern village of Sopor) at the point where the Jhelum River leaves the Wular Lake. Avantivarman himself founded the city of Avantipura (18 miles [29 km.] southeast of Srinagar, and still called by the same name). Before his accession to the throne the king had built there a temple dedicated to Vishnu Avantisvamin, and during his rule he built there a temple dedicated to Śiva Avantiśvara.[69]

Lohara Dynasty

Sangramaraja (1003–1028 C.E.) founded the first Lohara dynasty, the line of whose rulers extended from Sangramaraja to Harsha (1089–1101), the king under whom Kalhana's father, Campaka, served as minister. Uccala (1101–1111), who belonged to another line of the Loharas, began the second Lohara dynasty, and it was under Jayasimha (1128–1155) of this line that Kalhana wrote the *Rajatarangini*.[70]

Rule of Islam

References to the Arabs are found already in the reign of Lalitaditya: Muslim captains of troops were employed under Harsha, and under Sahadeva (1301–1310 C.E.) of the second Lohara dynasty. A Muslim saint from Turkestan, named 'Abdur Rahman and popularly known as Bulbul Shah, was the first to preach Islam in Kashmir. In the course of further tangled events a fugitive Buddhist prince from Ladakh, named Rinchana (or perhaps Rinchen, a familiar Tibetan name), seized the throne. He was converted to Islam by Bulbul Shah, took the Islamic name of Sadr-ud-Din, and ruled as the first Muslim king of Kashmir (1320–1323). The minister of Rinchana was Shah Mir, a Muslim adventurer from Swat and, sometime after the death of Rinchana, Shah Mir likewise seized the throne and ruled as Sultan Shamas-ud-Din (1339–1342), becoming the founder of a Sultan dynasty which endured for 222 years. Eventually, in 1586, the independence of Kashmir was lost and the country became a province of the Mughal empire.[71]

MONUMENTS

The pre-Islamic monuments of ancient Kashmir have suffered much from the effects of time and climate, the rivalries of Hindus and Buddhists, and the iconoclasm of Muslim rulers. Among the last, Sikander (1390–1414 C.E.) is especially remembered for his destructive activities, largely conducted in fact by his minister Suhabhatta, a recent convert from Hinduism to Islam, with the Islamic name of Saif-ud-Din. Nevertheless, significant materials remain.[72]

Pandrethan

The city of Śrinagari, founded by Aśoka in the third century B.C.E., is represented by the present village of Pandrethan (about 2 miles [3 km.] southeast of the Śankaracarya hill near the present Srinagar). The name of Pandrethan is a corruption of Puranadhisthana, meaning "old capital." The site is marked by the ruins of level terraces, rubble walls, and mounds of stone debris. The remains of two Buddhist *stupas* and the courtyard of a monastery have been identified. A few fragmentary sculptures have been found, belonging perhaps to the seventh century C.E. or slightly earlier, one object being a life-size statue of a *bodhisattva,* now in the Sri Pratap Singh Museum in Srinagar. Still standing at the site is a small temple (about 17.5 feet [5.3 m.] square) with a pyramidal roof, probably identifiable as a Śiva temple called Rilhaneśvara, which is mentioned in the *Rajatarangini* as built (about 1135 C.E.) by Rilhana, the minister of King Jayasimha.[73]

Harwan

Harwan, probable site of the Fourth Buddhist Council under Kanishka (78–103 C.E.) and residence of Nagarjuna (first century C.E.), is the present name of a small village about 2 miles (3 km.) beyond Shalimar. Excavation has brought to light walls and buildings constructed in an earlier pebble style (with pebbles, abundant in the area, set in mud plaster) and a later rubble style (with smaller stones filling the spaces between larger stones of irregular shape). The buildings include an apsidal temple and a *stupa*. The temple is square in front and circular at the back, and surrounded by a courtyard of molded brick tiles and a pebble wall enclosure. The designs on the tiles show the flora and fauna of the region (e.g., lotus, geese, deer), men and women conversing on a balcony, a lady carrying a flower vase, another playing on a drum, and the like. The individual tiles were originally numbered to show their place in the entire pattern, and the script in which the numerals are written suggests a date circa 300 C.E. The facial characteristics of the people bear resemblance to the features of the inhabitants of Yarkand and Kashgar, coinciding with the time when Kashmir had connections with Central Asia during the supremacy of the Kushanas in the early centuries of the present era. Of the *stupa* there remains its square base, built up in three tiers, but the upper part has disappeared. It and some associated rooms, which might have served as chapels or for residential purposes, are built in the rubble style. Also found in the area were fragments of terra-cotta figures, and a few clay votive tablets bearing in relief miniature *stupas*. Legends on the tablets are in a script ascribed to the fourth century C.E.[74]

Śankaracarya Temple

The Śankaracarya hill rises 1,000 feet (305 m.) above Dal Lake some 2.5 miles (4 km.) southeast of Srinagar, and is crowned by a temple of Śiva. As noted above, the original temple on this site is supposed to have been erected around 200 B.C.E. by Jalauka, the successor of Aśoka, while a later temple on the same site is attributed to Gopaditya of the Gonanda dynasty in the sixth century C.E. In his time the famous Buddhist teacher Padmasambhava (invited to Tibet by King Trhisong Detsen, 755–797 C.E.) is said to have dwelt for a time on this hill, and the famous Hindu teacher Śankaracarya (788–838 C.E.), who came from South India to Kashmir, is also said to have stayed at this temple, and it is his name which still attaches to the hill and the temple, along with the Muslim designation, Takht-i-Sulaiman (throne of Solomon). As for the presently existing temple, it is attributed to the reign of Jahangir (1605–1627 C.E.), although the enclosing wall and plinth are thought to be from the earlier temple. On the terrace is an octagonal raised platform, on which is the temple proper, a square building, with two projections on each side. In the circular interior chamber is the *linga* of Śiva.[75]

Martand Temple

The temple of Martand (5 miles [8 km.] east of Anantnag), attributed in the *Rajatarangini* to Lalitaditya (725–753 C.E.), was dedicated to Surya, the Sun, under the Sun's name Martanda. The site of the temple is on a plateau overlooking an extensive valley. The temple stands in a quadrangular courtyard, measuring 217 × 138 feet (66 × 42 m.), and surrounded by a colonnade of eighty-four fluted pillars. The entrance gateway is in the middle of the western side of the quadrangle, flanked by massive fluted pillars, 17.5 feet (5.3 m.) in height, or 8 feet (2.4 m.) higher than the pillars of the colonnade. The walls of the gateway are ornamented with niches containing standing figures of gods, and rectangular panels sculptured with floral scrolls, geese, human dancers and the like. The temple proper is 27 feet (8 m.) in width at the western or entrance end, 36 feet (11 m.) in width at the eastern end, 59 feet (18 m.) in length, and about 39 feet (12 m.) high, but was probably once surmounted by a pyramidal superstructure making it perhaps 75 feet

(23 m.) in height altogether. The temple has three chambers, the first and second highly decorated, the third and innermost chamber plain and closed on three sides. On the walls of the middle chamber are single figures in relief, two of Surya, two of Lakshmi, one of the river goddess Ganga standing on her vehicle the crocodile, and one of the river goddess Yamuna standing on her vehicle the tortoise.[76]

Avantipur

The two temples built by Avantivarman (855–883 C.E.) at his capital city of Avantipura are extant in massive ruins at the site (18 miles [29 km.] southeast of Srinagar). Of the two, the temple of Avantisvami-Vishnu, which he built first before he occupied the throne, is smaller but more ornate and better preserved. A massive entrance gateway in the middle of the west wall gives access to a large paved courtyard (175 × 149 feet [53 × 45 m.]), surrounded by a wall and a colonnade with fluted columns and sixty-nine cells. Of the temple proper only the base is intact; the sanctuary, which measured 33 feet (10 m.) square, has almost disappeared. In the excavation of the temple various sculptures were brought to light, some of which are in the Srinagar Museum, while others are still to be seen at the site. Most prominent is Vishnu between two of his consorts, Lakshmi and another (Fig. 15.26). A number of storage jars were also found, one of which bears an inscription with the name of Avantivarman.[77]

BUDDHISM IN SWAT

The modern state of Swat, now a part of Pakistan, is in the area anciently known in Sanskrit as Uddiyana. Alexander the Great went into Swat at least as far

15.26 Vishnu and Two Consorts, Relief Sculpture on Pilaster of Gateway Stair, Avantisvami Temple at Avantipur

as Udegram (327 B.C.E.). Buddhism no doubt spread there at least from the time of Aśoka (third century B.C.E.) onward. Fa Xian was in Swat on his pilgrimage (399–414 C.E.), and says that Buddhism was flourishing, with 500 monasteries all belonging to the Hinayana.[78] Xuan Zang (629–645 C.E.) also traversed the country, giving a lengthy account.[79] On both sides of the Suvastu (Swat) river there are, Xuan Zang says, 1,400 old monasteries, but he describes them as, in his time, generally waste and desolate, with very few monks in them, and these engaged in the study of the Mahayana. Some kinds of calamities must have taken place between the fifth and the seventh centuries to result in this general devastation of the monasteries: perhaps it was inroads of Mihirakula in the sixth century; perhaps it was floods or other natural disasters. In the eighth century the famous Padmasambhava was born in Uddiyana and went to Tibet at the invitation of the king, where he is considered the chief founder of the oldest sect of Tibetan Buddhism, the Nyingma-pa. As the birthplace of Padmasambhava, Swat therefore became a holy land in the eyes of the Tibetan Buddhists.

A major excavated Buddhist site in Swat is at Butkara near the town of Mingora, north of Saidu Sharif. The site is in a plain between the Saidu and Jambil rivers, which unite at Mingora and flow on as a single stream into the Swat River. The sacred precinct is in an irregular four-sided enclosure, paved with slabs of stone, and dominated by the ruins of the great *stupa* in the center, around which are many smaller *stupas, viharas,* and columns (Fig. 15.27). The first phase of the construction of the *stupa* is dated in the third century B.C.E. by the finding in the mound of a coin of Candragupta Maurya (322–298 B.C.E.). Further numismatic and other evidence indicate further phases in the history of the *stupa* down to its destruction sometime in the seventh century C.E. At its maximum size, in a fifth

15.27   Ruins of the Butkara Stupa and Surrounding Structures, near Mingora

15.28 Statues of the Buddha at the Butkara Stupa, near Mingora

phase of construction, the *stupa* was circular in plan, with a diameter of 51 feet (15.6 m.). Particularly in its fifth and sixth phases (sixth century C.E.) the *stupa* was adorned with many standing and sitting stucco statues of the Buddha (Fig. 15.28), while hundreds of sculptured slabs and panels of green schist, carved in the style of Gandhara art and depicting the life story of the Buddha, were also found in the excavations.[80]

AFGHANISTAN

Modern Afghanistan occupies an area which was a crossroads of ancient travel between India, China, Central Asia, and the West. Described from a starting point in the West on the Mediterranean Sea, the main route came eastward through Palmyra in Syria and Ecbatana in Iran to Bactria, and from there it either went on east through the Pamirs to Kashgar and around the Taklamakan Desert on the north or south to reach China (the famous Silk Road, traveled from at least the Han dynasty, 206 B.C.E.–220 C.E., onward), or it went south through the Hindu Kush to Kabul, Peshawar, Taxila, and Mathura in India.[81]

The Achaemenid Persians came this way in the sixth century B.C.E., and so too did Alexander the Great in the fourth century. Afterward, Seleucus I Nicator (312–281 B.C.E.) ruled Bactria, but Candragupta Maurya (322–298) held the regions on his side of the Hindu Kush. Then came the nomadic tribes from the North, and from the first century B.C.E. to the fourth century C.E. the Kushanas ruled an empire which, at its height under Kanishka (78–103 C.E.), extended from the Caspian Sea to Mathura in India. Afterward the area was overshadowed by the

Sassanid Persians, invaded by the Ephtalite Huns, ruled by the Occidental Turks, and in the seventh century conquered by the Muslim Arabs.[82]

BUDDHISM ON THE ROUTES TO CENTRAL ASIA

Along the same routes of travel used by caravans and by armies went the missionaries and the pilgrims of Buddhism. Already in the time of Aśoka (third century B.C.E.) the missionaries who went out from the Third Buddhist Council probably reached Afghanistan and Bactria and, at least later, others went on to Central Asia and to China, while Buddhist pilgrims, notably Fa Xian (399–414 C.E.), Xuan Zang (629–645), and Yi Jing (671–695), came back over the same routes.

In the spread of Buddhism on the routes to Central Asia, it was in the first instance the iconography which had developed in Mathura and Gandhara that was carried further. Two main types of the image of the Buddha appear: the figure is standing, with one hand raised, the palm turned outward in the gesture of assurance *(abhaya mudra)*, and the other hand holding the folds of the robe; or the figure is seated cross-legged, with the hands lying one on top of the other in meditation *(dhyana mudra)*, or with one hand reaching downward to call the earth to witness *(bhumisparśa mudra)*. With the increasing importance of the Mahayana there are also images of *bodhisattvas* (at first not clearly differentiated from the Buddha), of various divinities assimilated by Buddhism, of monks and ascetics, and of *mandalas*. As for the great religious centers which arose, they usually coincided with the main trading stations along the way.[83]

Hadda

Proceeding through the Khyber Pass into Afghanistan, the first major Buddhist site is at Hadda, on the plain of the Kabul River about 8 miles (13 km.) south of present-day Jalalabad. Buddhist occupancy of the site is believed to date from at least the reign of Kanishka (78–103 C.E.) onward until destruction, probably experienced from the Huns and Mihirakula in the middle of the fifth and early sixth centuries. Both Fa Xian (399–414 C.E.) and Xuan Zang (629–645) came to Hadda (*Hi-lo* in Chinese). Fa Xian tells especially of a *vihara* and a *stupa* and a skull-bone relic of the Buddha preserved there and honored with many offerings.[84] Xuan Zang tells of this and other relics, and of various *stupas,* but of the surrounding country he says that while the religion of the Buddha is cultivated and the monasteries are many, the monks are few and the *stupas* are desolate and ruined.[85]

In and around Hadda the remains of many monasteries, chapels, and *stupas* have been found, decorated with scenes from the life of the Buddha, statues of the Buddha, of monks, and the like, executed most characteristically in stucco.[86] Particularly impressive are the remains of the *stupas* and chapels of the Tapa Shotor complex, dating probably in the third and fourth centuries C.E.[87] Many of the finds from Hadda are in the Kabul Museum, e.g., a standing Buddha with large crowning *Ushnisha* (Fig. 15.29).[88]

Begram

As described above (in Chapter 6), the Achaemenid capital of Kapiśa and perhaps also the city of Alexander the Great called Alexandria of the Caucasus were in the vicinity of the confluence of the Panjshir and Ghorband rivers in the plain

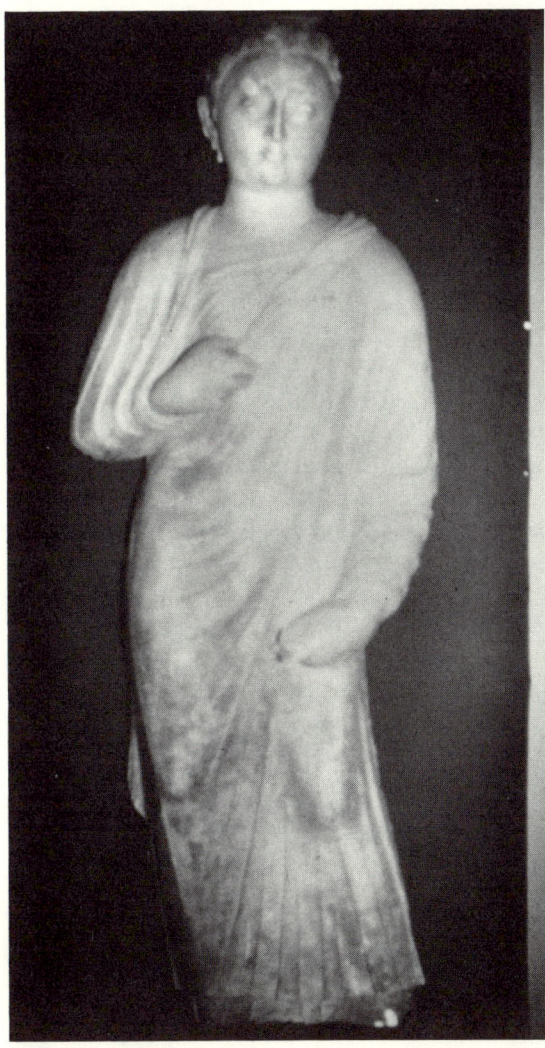

15.29 Buddha from Hadda, in the Kabul Museum

some 28 miles (45 km.) north of Kabul. Here on the west bank of the Panjshir are the present village of Begram and, above it, the citadel of ancient Begram. Excavation indicates occupation in three successive periods and suggests the following identifications: in the first period this was the capital of the Indo-Greek kings of the region and the first rulers of the Kushana dynasty; in the second period, when new palaces and fortifications were constructed, this was the northern capital of Kanishka and his successors, and this period was ended by destruction by fire, perhaps in the time of the Sassanian king Shapur I, who is thought to have sacked Begram between 241 and 250 C.E.; in the third period a new settlement was made on the ruins of the earlier capitals, and this city was probably abandoned at the coming of the Ephtalite Huns in the fifth century.

Xuan Zang came to this region from Bamiyan, coming across what he calls the Black Ridge (now the Koh-i-Baba, a range of the Hindu Kush) and encountering a snowstorm on the way which caused him to miss his road. He describes the country of Kapiśa (*Kia-pi-shi* in Chinese) as bordering on the Black Ridge on three sides and abutting on the Snowy Mountains on the north. While the country produces cereals and many kinds of fruit trees, the climate is cold and windy, and the people wear woolen garments trimmed with fur. When Kanishka held certain evidently high-ranking Chinese hostages (Hwui Li, Xuan Zang's biographer, mentions only one hostage, a son of the emperor of China), he arranged separate residences for them for the several seasons, in India in the cold weather, in Gandhara in the autumn and spring, and in Kapiśa in the summer, so this was evidently his summer capital.

In the country, says Xuan Zang, there are about 100 monasteries and some 6,000 monks, who mostly study the Mahayana. Also, he states, "there are naked ascetics, and others who cover themselves with ashes, and some who make chaplets of bones, which they wear as crowns on their heads" (identifiable respectively as Digambara Jainas; Śaivite Paśupatas who were worshipers of Śiva as "lord of beasts," and who smeared themselves with ashes from cremation grounds; and Kapalikas who were worshipers of Śiva as Kapaleśvara or "skull lord").[89]

The excavation of Begram has brought to light materials which evidently came from the three ends of the great caravan route described above, namely, from the West, Greco-Roman glassware and bronzes, and plaster casts apparently taken from classical originals of a number of different periods (fourth century B.C.E. to second century C.E.); from China, lacquer bowls of the Han period (206 B.C.E.–221 C.E.); and from India, ivory carvings (in the style of the first to third centuries C.E.).

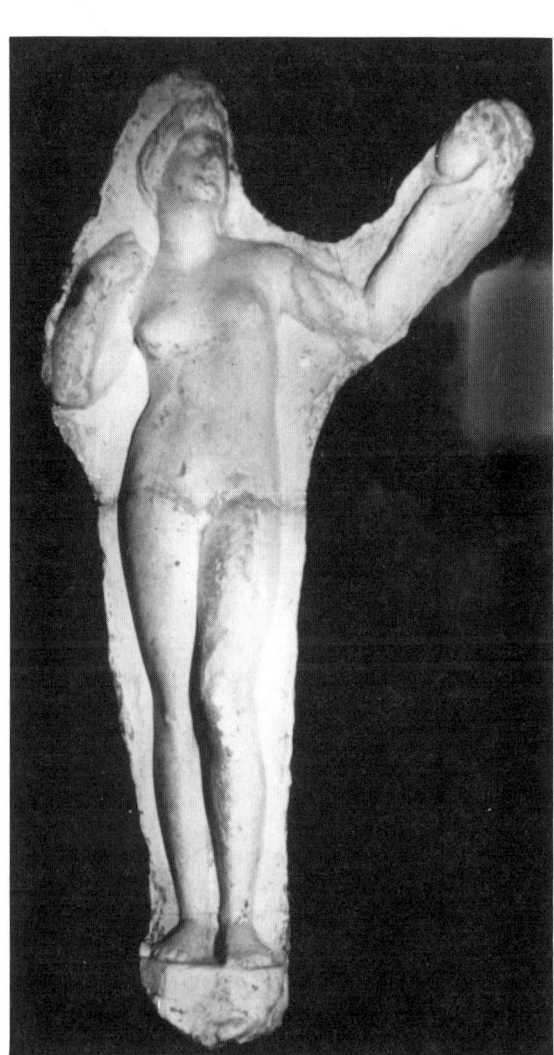

15.30 Aphrodite from Begram, in the Kabul Museum

Monuments of Hinduism and Buddhism in Himalaya and Inner Asia | 627

As seen in the Kabul Museum, the treasures from Begram include the plaster cast of a statue of Aphrodite presenting a fruit (Fig. 15.30); the carved ivory backpiece of a royal throne; an ivory plaque which formed part of the decoration of the royal throne, carved with the figures of two women standing under a gateway *(torana)* like the gateways at Sanci (Fig. 15.31); the ivory statuette of a *yakshi*, like those familiar in many places in India (Fig. 15.32); and the cover of an ivory jewel chest, carved in a manner like that of an engraved drawing, showing in Indian style in each half of the panel two women, one seated, at their toilet (Fig. 15.33).[90]

15.31 Women under a Torana, Ivory Plaque from Begram, in the Kabul Museum

15.32 Ivory Statuette of a Yakshi, from Begram, in the Kabul Museum

15.33 Carved Cover of Ivory Jewel Chest, from Begram in the Kabul Museum

Bamiyan

Coming from Hadda and Begram, the caravan route ascends the canyon of the Ghorband River, climbs over the Shibar Pass (9,800 feet [2,987 m.]), the watershed between the Indus and the Oxus, descends the Balola gorge of the Shibar River until it joins the Bamiyan River, and follows this to a high valley (4,800 feet [2,585 m.]) between the Koh-i-Baba and the Hindu Kush, in which is the famous site of Bamiyan. From here the route continues to Bactria and Central Asia.[91]

Located thus on a major trade route from the Indus to the Oxus, Bamiyan was a great caravan center and became also a great center of Buddhism. The first monasteries were probably established as early as the time of Kanishka (78–103 C.E.), and remained active until the middle of the seventh century, after which, with the coming of Islam, they were gradually abandoned. Within this period of time the great cliff on the north edge of the valley (Fig. 15.34) was honeycombed with monastic cells, chapels, and recesses with Buddha images, while two very large tall alcoves in particular were cut out in which were sculptured two enormous standing Buddha statues.[92]

Xuan Zang tells of coming from Bactria (Balkh, *Po-ho* in Chinese) to Bamiyan (*Fan-yen-na*) and of seeing the two great statues:

> Going 100 *li* (1 *li* equals 1,890 feet [576 m.]) or so south from the kingdom of Po-ho, we arrive at Kie-chi. . . . On the southeast we enter the great Snowy Mountains. These mountains are high and the valleys deep; the precipices and crevasses are very dangerous. The wind and snow keep on without intermission; the ice remains through the full summer; the snowdrifts fall into the valleys and block the roads. The mountain spirits and demons send, in their rage, all sorts of calamities; robbers crossing the path of travelers kill them. Going with difficulty 600 *li* or so, we . . . arrive at the kingdom of Fan-yen-na.

This kingdom of Fan-yen-na or Bamiyan, Xuan Zang goes on to say, is situated in the midst of the Snowy Mountains, where its capital rests against a

15.34 Bamiyan Valley and the Cliff with the Smaller Buddha, with the Snows of the Hindu Kush beyond

precipitous cliff and borders on a valley six or seven *li* in length. The country produces spring wheat and affords pasture for many sheep and horses. The climate is wintry, and the clothes of the people are chiefly made of skin and wool, which are the most suitable for the country. The people are remarkable for their love of religion. There are ten monasteries and about 1,000 monks, who belong to the Hinayana and to the school of the Lokottaravadins.

> To the northeast of the royal city there is a mountain, on the declivity of which is placed a stone figure of Buddha, erect, 140 or 150 feet (43 or 46 m.) high. Its golden hues sparkle on every side, and its precious ornaments dazzle the eyes by their brightness. To the east of this spot . . . there is a standing figure of Śakya Buddha, made of metallic stone, in height 100 feet (30 m.).[93]

The two great Buddha statues described by Xuan Zang still stand at Bamiyan, and examination reveals that the core of each image was cut out of the rock of the cliff, after which the details of the drapery were modeled in stucco over ropes fastened to the image by means of wooden pegs. As Xuan Zang's description intimates, the figures were originally painted and gilded. Also paintings, fragments of which remain, were placed in the alcoves and overhead vaults, while many more paintings adorned many of the other excavations in the cliff, in which there are also other smaller Buddha statues.

Of the two very large Buddha figures, the smaller one to the east is 125 feet (38 m.) in height (Fig. 15.35). The style of the figure is much like that of Gandhara Buddha images of the second century C.E., but on a gigantic scale. In date it may belong to the third century or later. In the vault overhead are fragments of a painting of an astral divinity, and there are also fragments of decoration in the caves adjoining the statue, these caves being linked by interior staircases, which make it possible to climb to the head of the Buddha.

15.35 Smaller Buddha and Adjacent Caves, Bamiyan

The larger Buddha to the west is 174 feet (53 m.) in height (Fig. 15.36), and only when scale is provided by persons standing at its foot (as in Fig. 15.37) is its vastness truly realized. The style of the figure is much like that of Buddha statues of the Gupta period (320–600 C.E.), and it may be dated approximately in the fifth century. Here too the upper part of the alcove still shows painting, and smaller sanctuaries are also carved out around the feet. As for the date of the paintings associated with the two great Buddhas and in the adjacent caves, they are usually assigned to the late fifth to early seventh centuries.[94]

Xuan Zang also tells of a monastery 12 or 13 *li* to the east of the city, at which there was a figure of Buddha lying in a sleeping position, as when he attained *nirvana,* a figure of about 1,000 feet (300 m.) or so in length. If a figure of such dimensions did exist at that time, nothing of it has been found now.

In 1221 C.E. Bamiyan was sacked by Genghis Khan. Both the neighboring fortress of Shahr-i-Zohak (11 miles [18 km.] east of Bamiyan near the confluence of the Bamiyan, Hajjigak, and Qunduz rivers, probably constructed in the sixth and seventh centuries C.E. and renewed in Muslim times) (Fig. 15.38), and also the fortress of Shahr-i-Gholghola (just across the valley from the great cliff at Bamiyan, probably dating from Kushana to Islamic times) (Fig. 15.39), were burned and destroyed.[95] Also the biographer of Genghis Khan reports that the Mongol archers directed their aim against the great Buddha statue, but the arrows fell short of the lofty head. Again in his time the Mughal emperor Aurangzib (1658–1707 C.E.) is said to have bombarded the great Buddha with his cannon. Nevertheless, the colossal images and the associated remains, badly damaged but still standing, attest that Bamiyan was in its time one of the greatest Buddhist establishments of Central Asia.[96]

15.36 Larger Buddha, Bamiyan

15.37 Two Persons standing in front of the Right Foot of the Larger Buddha, Bamiyan

15.38 Looking across the Bamiyan River to Shahr-i-Zohak

15.39 Shahr-i-Gholghola, Bamiyan

XINJIANG

From Central Asia, Buddhism came to China by way of the vast area of mountain and desert most of which is now included in the Xinjiang Uygur Autonomous Region of China. Here, as already described, the famous Silk Road led in its two branches through oases on both the north and the south sides of the Taklamakan Desert (in the Tarim Basin, south of the Tian Shan) and to the Jade Gate at the extremity of the Great Wall of China. Along this route on the way to China are known to have passed such Buddhist missionaries as Shih-kao, a Parthian (148 C.E.); Chu Sho-fu, an Indian (no exact date); and Che Chan a Yueh-chi, i.e., a Scythian (circa 170 C.E.); and along it too went Fa Xian (399–414 C.E.) on his way to India; and Xuan Zang (629–645 C.E.) on his way both to and from India, whose travels have already been narrated (chiefly in Chapter 6), and whose records attest to the existence in their times of flourishing Buddhist communities throughout the region.[97]

Like Buddhism itself, the concept of carving chapels and cells in the rock and adorning these with statues and paintings of the Buddha and of Buddhist subjects came to Xinjiang and China from India. With an artistic heritage derived from Ajanta in India, Gandhara in Pakistan, and Bamiyan in Afghanistan, and here mingled with Persian, Hellenistic-Roman, and Chinese influences, major Buddhist monuments in the form of caves with paintings and sculptures are found near Kucha,[98] near Turpan[99] on the northern branch of the Silk Road in Xinjiang, at Dunhuang[100] in Gansu Province (where the northern and southern branches of the Silk Road meet and also intersect with a north-south route between Mongolia and Tibet), and at many other sites, both farther back in Central Asia and farther on in China.[101]

TURPAN

Kaochang

In the desert some 25 miles (40 km.) southeast of Turpan (formerly Turfan), at the foot of the Flaming Mountains (red in color), are the ruins of the ancient city of Kaochang (Gaochang) (Fig. 15.40). This was the important city on the Silk Road visited by both Fa Xian and Xuan Zang and, in all, the history of the city extended from the first century B.C.E. to the fourteenth century C.E., after which it was abandoned. The ruins show a city pattern much like that of Xian, with an outer city, inner city, and central palace and temple area.

Bezeklik

Above Kaochang, in the heart of the Flaming Mountains, at the site now called Bezeklik, are the Caves of the Thousand Buddhas (Qianfo Dong). These caves, no less than sixty-three in number, are cut into an alluvial terrace in the valley of the Murtuq River (Fig. 15.41). The site thus admirably provides some of the basic requirements for a place of Buddhist retreat, namely, relative seclusion on the one hand, and proximity to water on the other hand. As elsewhere, the caves are adorned with very numerous paintings of Buddhist subjects on the walls and of a "thousand Buddhas" on the vaulted ceilings. From their style the paintings date for the most part in the time of the Sui (581–618 C.E.) and the Tang (618–907) dynasties of China, and even slightly later.[102]

15.40 Ruins of the Ancient City of Kaochang, looking toward the Flaming Mountains

15.41 Caves of the Thousand Buddhas at Bezeklik in the Flaming Mountains

The theme of the "thousand Buddhas" is in line with the Mahayana conception of an infinite number of worlds and a correspondingly infinite number of Buddhas. Prominent among the individual pictures is a series of no less than fifteen so-called *pranidhi* scenes found in the cave identified as Temple No. 9 The word *pranidhi* designates a solemn vow in which, according to the teachings of the Mahayana, a fervent resolve is expressed to become, through many lives of a *bodhisattva's* self-sacrifice and compassion, like the Buddha. It is held that in many past ages various persons met Buddhas and sages who were then on earth and were inspired by the encounter to make this vow and enter upon the "path of fervent resolution" *(pranidhicarya)*, and were given the assurance and prophecy that they would indeed persevere and ultimately attain perfect enlightenment.

As one example, the *pranidhi* scene No. 7 in Temple No. 9 is based on the story of the meeting of the *brahmana* student Sumedha, a very early incarnation of Śakyamuni Buddha, with the Buddha Dipankara, at which time Sumedha made the vow which led him through many births to be at last the historical Buddha.[103]

In other examples in Temple No. 9 the future Buddha is born a number of times as a rich merchant, meets such early Buddhas and sages as the Buddha Śikhin (Scene No. 3), the *rishi* Vasishtha (Scene No. 11), and others, and is inspired to perform acts of great kindness and generosity. In this series it is Scene No. 11 which is shown here (Fig. 15.42). This is a large painting (332 cm. high by 180

15.42 Painting from Bezeklik in the Museum of the Xinjiang Uygur Autonomous Region in Urumqi

cm. wide—or approximately 11 by 6 feet), and is considered to date in the late Tang (618–907 C.E.) or early Sung (960–1280) period. While the style, with the clearly drawn faces, is Chinese, the subject matter and the text at the top, written in the Brahmi script, are Indian. The text reads: "When he saw the arrival of Vasishtha the merchant was glad in his heart [and said], after he had established a park: 'I will build a monastery.'"[104]

The Buddha, shown in large size in the center, is backgrounded by aureole and mandorla, and stands with his feet on two lotuses. He wears a long jeweled necklace, and has a high *ushnisha*. His right hand is held at rest upon a fold of his robe at his breast; his left hand holds scarves *(kata)* which have been received in tribute from the monk kneeling at his side. Surrounding the Buddha there are in all three personages at the right (as seen by the viewer) and two at the left. At the right, the lowest figure is that of an older monk, who is kneeling upon a carpet and holding scarves across his arms. The middle figure is that of a younger monk, and it is he who has already presented his scarves to the Buddha. The top figure at the right is the *bodhisattva* Vajrapani (the *vajra* bearer), shown in the garb of a warrior, holding a flywhisk in his left hand and brandishing the thunderbolt/diamond *(vajra)* scepter in his right hand. As the bearer of the thunderbolt, Vajrapani was originally a name of Indra, the Vedic storm god and king of the gods; in the Hinayana Vajrapani became the faithful assistant and protector of Śakyamuni Buddha; in the Mahayana he is a high *bodhisattva* and the spiritual son of the cosmic Buddha *(tathagata)* Akshobhya; and finally his close association with the *vajra* makes him of special importance in the Vajrayana. In this painting he is presumably present as the Buddha's protector. Balancing Vajrapani at the upper right, and like him no doubt also a faithful companion of the Buddha, is another *bodhisattva* at the lower left. He is richly attired and stands upon a lotus throne, while he salutes the Buddha with his two open hands held together in the *anjali mudra,* the gesture of salutation which in Indian usage normally implies also the word *namaste* as an exclamation of homage meant for deity. Above, the top figure at the left is again that of a young monk, also turned respectfully toward the Buddha. These, the monks, are evidently renewing their vows in the presence of the Buddha, and are receiving from him the assurance of their ultimate success upon the *bodhisattva* way.

TIBET

Historical Events

As noted above (in Chapter 12), we learn from Buston (1290–1363 C.E.) and other Tibetan historians that Buddhism was chiefly introduced into Tibet under King Songtsen Gampo (r. 629-649 C.E.), and under King Trhisong Detsen (755–797) it was made the official religion of the land.[105] These two kings were members—respectively the thirty-third and the thirty-eighth in the entire sequence—of the ancient Yarlung Dynasty, a dynasty which took its name from its original home in the valley of the Yarlung River, a tributary from the south of Tibet's greatest stream, the Yarlung Tsangpo (which continues as the Brahmaputra).

Under Songtsen Gampo, the capital was moved to Lhasa and on the Red Hill the king had his meditation cave and his palace, which he called the Potala. The name of the city means "city of god" *(Lha sa),* and the name Potala derives from the mythical abode in South India of Avalokiteśvara (Chenresik in Tibetan), the patron *bodhisattva* of Tibet.

The king married both a princess from Nepal, named Trhisun (and identified with the goddess Bhrikuti), and a princess from China, named Wencheng, both of whom were already Buddhists. Trhisun brought with her statues of the Tathagata (or Dhyani Buddha) Akshobhyavajra, the future Buddha Maitreya (called Champa in Tibet), and the goddess Tara (called Dolma in Tibet); Wencheng brought a statue of Śakyamuni Buddha said to have been made originally in India. Songtsen Gampo was himself considered incarnations of Avalokiteśvara, and the two princesses were considered an incarnation of Tara, the consort of Avalokiteśvara, Trhisun representing the White Tara, Wencheng the Green Tara (although in some sources these identifications are reversed).[106]

In conjunction with the Nepalese princess, Songtsen Gampo built the first and central temple of Lhasa, known at the outset as the Tsuglakang, and in conjunction with the Chinese princess he built the second and next most important temple, known as the Ramoche. After the death of Songtsen Gampo, Wencheng, who survived him by many years, exchanged the two most famous statues of the two temples, and thus the Akshobhyavajra came to be in the Ramoche and the Śakyamuni Buddha in the Tsuglakang. The Śakyamuni Buddha statue became known as the *Jo bo rimpoche* or Precious Lord Buddha, and accordingly the temple in which it now had the place of honor became the Jokhang or House of the Lord Buddha.

Because there was at the time still no writing in Tibet, Songtsen Gampo sent his minister, Thonmi Sambhota, to India to study the art of writing. Taking the script of Kashmir for a pattern and producing an alphabet of thirty consonants and four vowels, Sambhota formed the Tibetan writing which is still in use, and himself went on to compose works on writing and grammar, and the king studied these earnestly. So Thonmi Sambhota was accounted the first learned man of Tibet, a lamp that expels darkness, while the king was like the sun in the sky. In terms of religious belief, along with Songtsen Gampo as an incarnation of Avalokiteśvara, the *bodhisattva* of compassion, Thonmi Sambhota was considered an incarnation of Manjuśri (Jamyang in Tibetan), the *bodhisattva* of wisdom.

Politically, Songtsen Gampo expanded the borders of his realm and was involved in war with China. It was, in fact, in the resolution of the China conflict that the Chinese princess was sent to become his bride. It may be assumed that the marriage with the Nepalese princess likewise was of political consequence.

In turn, under Songtsen Gampo's grandson Mangsong, the thirty-fifth in the Yarlung succession, the Chinese invaded Lhasa and burned the Potala; in the central temple the *Jo bo* Śakyamuni was so well hidden that the Chinese could not get hold of it, but from the Ramoche they took away the Akshobhyavajra, also known as a *Jo bo*, for a half-day's march.

Between Tibet and China there followed both times of peace and times of war, and again Trhide Tsuktsen, the thirty-seventh Yarlung dynasty king, took a Chinese princess, named Chincheng, as his bride. With Trhisong Detsen (755–797 C.E.), the thirty-eighth king in the same succession, Tibetan power was extended to its farthest point in Asia and, in the year 763, Tibetan armies temporarily occupied even the Chinese capital, Chang'an (modern Xian), an event still recorded in a contemporary Tibetan inscription on the Zhol Doring pillar at the foot of the Potala hill in Lhasa.

From the point of view of the Tibetan histories, however, the most important works of Trhisong Detsen were in his furtherance of Buddhism, and he is regarded as the second (after Songtsen Gampo) great religious king and himself an incarnation of Mañjuśri. Of most significance for the future was the fact that he brought to Tibet the two great Buddhist teachers, Śantarakshita from the University of Nalanda in India, and Padmasambhava the "lotus born" from Uddiyana (now Swat). Under the king, the two built the monastery of Samye (on the north bank of the Yarlung Tsangpo) where, under the instruction of Śantarakshita, Tibetans themselves were for the first time trained as monks. As for Padmasambhava, he remains the greatest figure in the spiritual heritage of the Nyingma-pa, the oldest of the orders of Tibetan Buddhism (popularly known as the Red Hats).

With respect to Buddhism, Ralpacan, the forty-first Yarlung dynasty king, is deemed the third great religious king. In his time, after another successful war against China, peace was made between the two countries, and there is recorded on the Tablet of Unity in front of the Jokhang a contemporary inscription in both Tibetan and Chinese, dated in the equivalent of 821–823 C.E., which avers that Great Tibet and Great China should keep in perpetuity their respective frontiers as then existing, with no enmity and no making of war thereafter.

Langdarma (833–842 C.E.), however, the forty-second and last king in the Yarlung succession, was evidently an adherent of the ancient indigenous Bon religion, and directed such violent persecution against Buddhism that the doctrine was virtually rooted out. Restoration came, nevertheless, notably furthered by the study in India of Rinchen Sangpo and his return to become the Great Translator (of Sanskrit Buddhist texts into Tibetan), and by the coming from India of Atiśa (in Tibet 1042–1054 C.E.), author of the abovementioned (in Chapter 12) *Lamp for the Way of Enlightenment* and many other works.

As also described in Chapter 12, many other teachers arose and Tibetan Buddhism took the form of not a few different orders, of which finally the Geluk-pa, representing the heritage of Atiśa and founded by Tsongkhapa (1357–1419 C.E.), became the most prominent. It was in the Geluk-pa (popularly known as the Yellow Hats) that the office of the Dalai Lama (the lama who is an "ocean [of wisdom]") came to be. The title originated when, in the year 1578, the Geluk-pa head, Sonam Gyatsho (1543–1587), visited the court of the Mongol prince Altan Khan (a descendant of Genghis Khan and an enemy of the Ming Dynasty in China), and the two conferred honors on each other. Afterward the title was carried back retroactively to Genduntrup, disciple of Tsongkhapa, as the First Dalai Lama (1391–1475), and the succession, implying the combined temporal and spiritual headship of Tibet, has been continued ever since in accordance with the theory of reincarnation. It is the Fourteenth Dalai Lama, Tenzin Gyatsho (1935–), who now resides in India in exile.

Sites and Monuments

In the "liberation" of Tibet (in 1950), the Tibetan "uprising" (in 1959), and the incorporation of the land as the Autonomous Region of Xizang in the People's Republic of China (in 1965), and in subsequent dire events including the Chinese "cultural revolution" (1966–1976) and other actions thereafter, more than one million Tibetans perished and 100,000 went into exile, while a reported 6,250 monasteries, the spiritual and cultural centers of the civilization, were demolished and their irreplaceable art and literature largely destroyed or removed from Tibet. In 1979, after twenty years of closure, the Jokhang temple in Lhasa was reopened, and the Potala and a few still-existent monasteries also became accessible to Tibetans and foreign visitors. But again in 1985, 1987, and 1988, movements seeking independence for Tibet were ruthlessly suppressed.[107] Meanwhile in some restoration of some monuments and artifacts, the old and the new are not usually differentiated, so it is difficult to know the age of what is now to be seen.[108]

Supplementary information about the sites and monuments and their treasures as they existed at an earlier time may be found in a work known as *The Temples of Lhasa* by Ngawang Lopsang Gyatsho, the Fifth Dalai Lama (1617–1682 C.E.),[109] *The Geography of Tibet* by Lama Tsenpo (1820),[110] and *Guide to the Holy Places of Central Tibet* by Kyentse (1820–1892).[111]

Yumbulagang. The original home of the Yarlung Dynasty, it has been explained above, was in the valley of the Yarlung River. There, as the Buddhist histories tell the story, the Bon priests recognized a certain Nyatrhi Tsenpo as descended from heaven and made him their king, the first in the long line of forty-two kings of the Yarlung Dynasty, and there Nyatrhi Tsenpo built his palace, called Yumbulagang. In the same place the twenty-eighth king in the succession, named Lhatho Thori, was residing in the upper story when a golden casket fell from the sky, containing Buddhist texts and objects. These Lhatho Thori was unable to understand but learned in a dream that in the fifth generation their meaning would become known—a plain reference to Lhatho Thori's fifth successor, the famous Songtsen Gampo. This is the legend about Lhatho Thori and the Yumbulagang; the added explanation in some of the histories is that it was the Bon who said that the books and objects fell from the sky, whereas they were actually brought by two men named Buddhirakshita and Li Thise, probably early Buddhist missionaries from India and Nepal.

At any rate, a palace still named Yumbulagang still stands upon a precipitous hill overlooking the Yarlung valley (a few miles upstream from the present town of Zhanang), and is reputedly the oldest surviving dwelling in Tibet (Fig. 15.43),

15.43 The Yumbulagang Palace

15.44 Statue of Nyatrhi Tsenpo in the Yumbulagang Palace

while not much farther away, at Chongye, is an ancient royal burial ground with ten tumuli identifiable as the tombs of the kings from Songtsen Gampo (617–650 C.E.) to Trhisong Detsen (755–797) and of certain princes as well.

In the Yumbulagang palace, which in 1985 was being restored and redecorated, the two upper stories are now chapels and in them may be seen images, among others, of Nyatrhi Tsenpo (Fig. 15.44) and of Trhisong Detsen (Fig. 15.45).

Samye. The site of the monastery of Samye, built by Śantarakshita and Padmasambhava in about 775 C.E. under King Trhisong Detsen, is upstream from the Yarlung valley and on the opposite or left bank of the Yarlung Tsangpo, some 35 miles (56 km.) southeast of Lhasa. As described by Kyentse in his *Guide to the Holy Places of Central Tibet* and also as depicted in a Tibetan tanka, executed in colors and gold on cotton and ascribed to the sixteenth-seventeenth century, now in the Albert L. Shelton Collection in The Newark Museum (Fig. 15.46), the entire plan of the monastery amounted to a great mandala or symbolic diagram. The central building symbolized Mount Meru, four chapels on four sides stood for the four main continents, and eight smaller chapels represented the eight minor continents of Buddhist cosmology. In addition there were four large chortens, and

15.45 Statue of Trhisong Detsen in the Yumbulagang Palace

15.46 Tanka depicting the Samye Monastery, Collection of the Newark Museum

15.47 Façade of the Samye Monastery

15.48 Wall Painting of the Buddha in the Samye Monastery

two additional small temples dedicated to the sun and moon. The central building was in three stories, built originally in three different styles, the lower floor Chinese, the second floor Indian, and the top floor Central Asian. Along the path of the pilgrim who visited the various parts of the temple in the search for enlightenment were many images of deities.

As seen in 1985 (Fig. 15.47) the uppermost story of the central temple is completely destroyed, and also most of the surrounding buildings are in ruins, nevertheless Samye is again a place of monastic services and Tibetan pilgrimage. In the two remaining stories of the central building the hall of assembly is intact, and there is a large wall painting of the Buddha (Fig. 15.48) and statues of Padmasambhava (Fig. 15.49), Atiśa (Fig. 15.50), and Atiśa's disciple Drom (Fig. 15.51).[112]

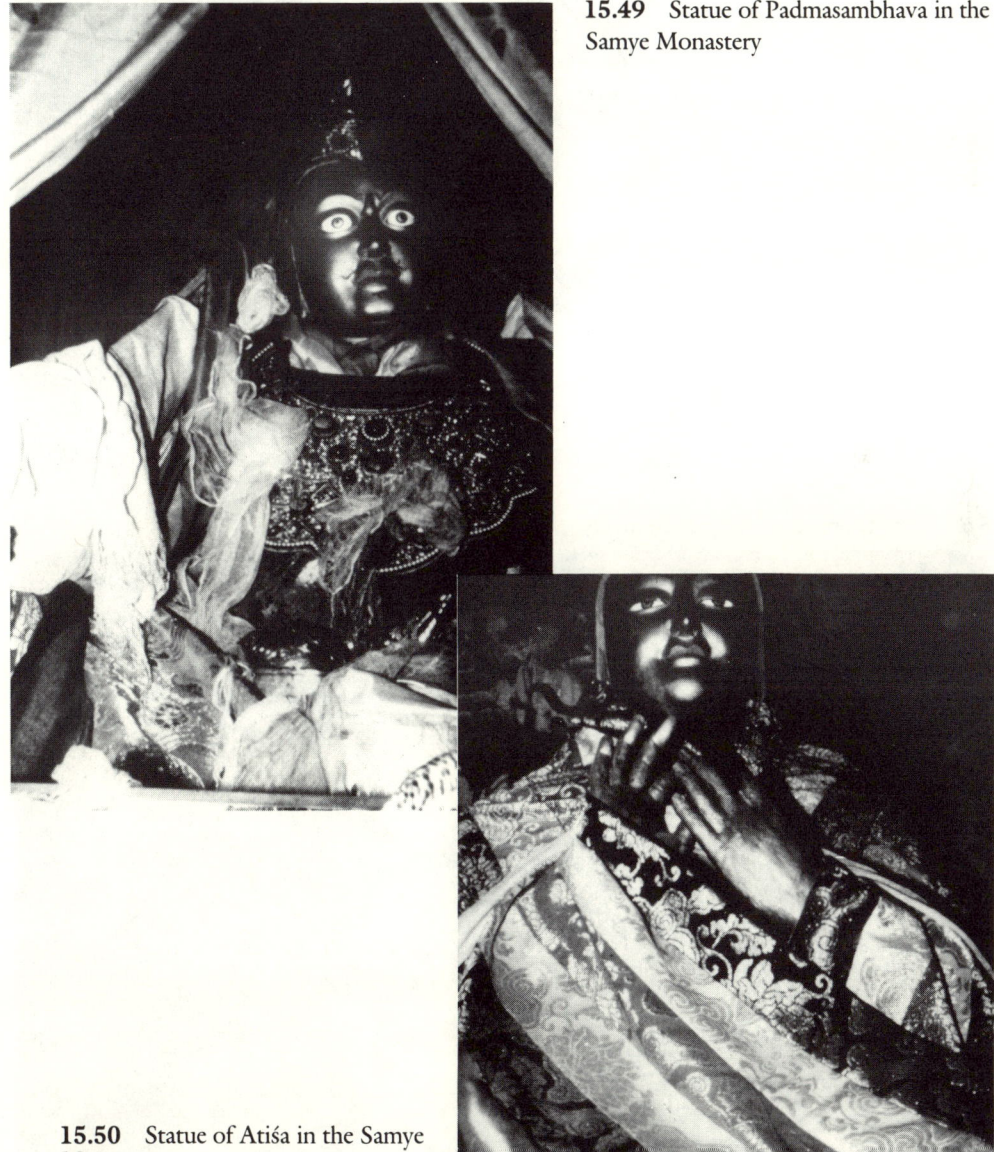

15.49   Statue of Padmasambhava in the Samye Monastery

15.50   Statue of Atiśa in the Samye Monastery

15.51 Statue of Drom in the Samye Monastery

15.52 The Dolma Lhakhang at Nethang

Nethang. Nethang was a main center of the work of Atiśa in Central Tibet and the place where, in 1054 C.E., he died. Approaching death, Atiśa commanded his disciple Drom to build a small monastery, and Tsongkhapa (1357–1419) in his youth studied there. The site of Nethang is on the ancient caravan route and the modern road which follow the Kyi Chu, the River of Lhasa, upstream to Lhasa (at a distance of about 12 miles [19 km.]). The monastery building which remains at Nethang is known as the Dolma Lhakhang or temple of Dolma (Tara), the goddess to whom Atiśa was devoted and at whose bidding he came originally to Tibet (Fig. 15.52). Now being restored, the building contains the memorial chorten of Atiśa (Fig. 15.53).

Potala. The Potala in Lhasa, originally the palace of Songtsen Gampo and his successors, was rebuilt and greatly enlarged by the Fifth Dalai Lama (1617–1682 C.E.) and from then on was the residence of the Dalai Lamas who had previously

15.53 Chorten of Atiśa in the Dolma Lhakhang at Nethang

lived at the Drepung monastery. Built in Tibetan style with stone walls sloping inward as they go up and with windows wider at the bottom than the top, the massive structure rises in the eleven-storied White Palace and the thirteen-storied Red Palace to golden roofs above, and contains a reputed 1,000 rooms (Fig. 15.54). Within, in the vast reception hall the empty throne of the Dalai Lama symbolizes the presence in absence of the country's leader, and is heaped with white scarves *(kata)* in silent tribute (Fig. 15.55). In other halls are the funerary chortens

15.54   The Potala from the Two Glasses Lake in Lhasa

15.55   Empty Throne of the Dalai Lama in the Potala

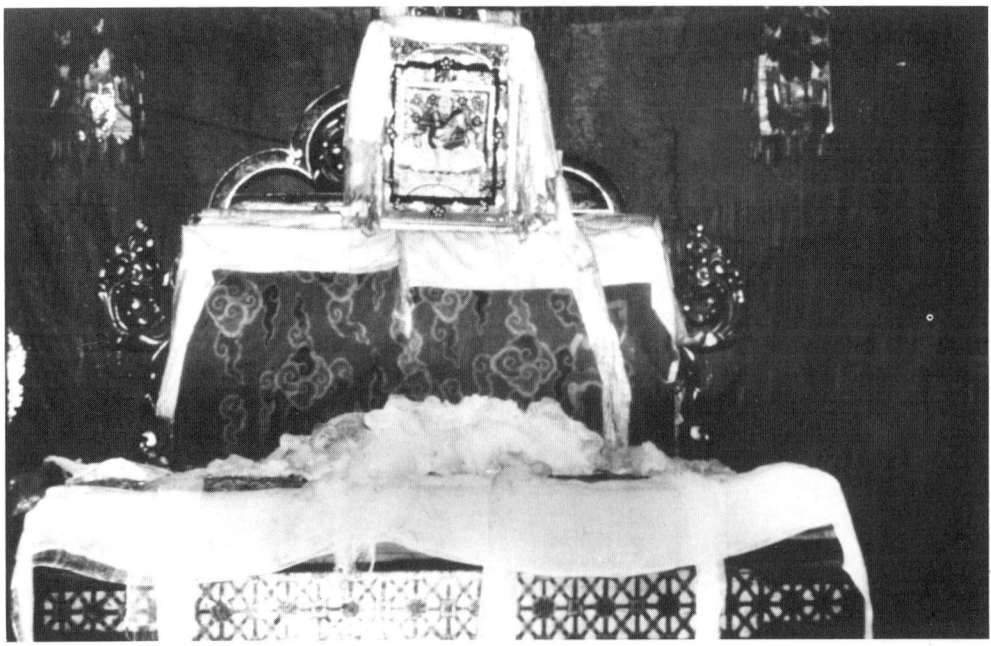

15.56 Chorten of the Fifth Dalai Lama in the Potala

of all the Dalai Lamas from the Fifth to the Thirteenth (1876–1933), with the exception of only the Sixth (1683–1703), who died on his way to Beijing and was denied by the Chinese the burial otherwise befitting his rank. Of the chortens, that of the Fifth Dalai Lama, himself known as the Great, is the greatest of all, and rises through three stories of its hall to a height of 49 feet (14.85 m.) (Fig. 15.56). The chorten of the Thirteenth Dalai Lama was badly damaged in the events of recent times but has been repaired; it rises through three stories to a height of 46 feet (14 m.).

Jokhang. The Jokhang, founded by Songtsen Gampo (r. 629-649 C.E.) in conjunction with his Nepalese wife, is accounted the national "cathedral" of Tibet and, since its reopening in 1979, has been visited constantly by large numbers of pilgrims and worshipers. The approach is now across a new plaza laid out by the Chinese (Fig. 15.57), while the great three-story building itself is still surrounded by the Parkhor ("around the temple") street, which provides a path of circumam-

15.57   The Jokhang seen from the Hospital of Tibetan Medicine

bulation for pilgrims who often measure their length again and again upon the ground as they go. Within, the focal point is provided by the *Jo bo rimpoche* statue, believed to be the very statue brought to Tibet by Songtsen Gampo's Chinese wife, supposed to have been made originally in India and explained as representing Śakyamuni as a twelve-year-old prince (Fig. 15.58).

Ramoche. The Ramoche was founded by Songtsen Gampo in conjunction with his Chinese wife and, along with the Jokhang, is also accounted a national "cathedral" of Tibet. The temple was completely plundered and closed by the Chinese, and the famous Akshobhyavajra statue broken and in part taken off to China, but reportedly has now (1985) been returned, while the building itself is slowly being repaired (Fig. 15.59). The Ramoche was the home monastery of nine hundred monks of the little-known Gyuto order (founded in the fifteenth century by Kunga Dontrub); one hundred escaped to India and have founded a new monastery and tantric university in a remote area in Arunachal Pradesh.[113]

Ganden, Drepung, and Sera. The Ganden monastery was established in 1409 C.E. by Tsongkhapa (1357–1419), the founder of the Geluk-pa, and long preserved the simple quarters in which he lived, and honored his remains in a golden funerary chorten. The site is 25 miles (40 km.) northeast of Lhasa, on a hill 14,000 feet (4,267 m.) in elevation, south of the Kyi Chu. A photograph made in 1959 shows the monastic buildings spread over a large area of the hill; a photograph made in 1980 shows only utter ruins; in 1982 Tibetan volunteers were undertaking rebuilding; in 1983 all were reportedly imprisoned and all monks living there were expelled.[114]

15.58 The *Jo bo* Śakyamuni in the Jokhang

15.59 The Ramoche in Lhasa

15.60   Statue of Tsongkhapa in the Drepung Monastery

The Drepung monastery, at the foot of a mountain 6 miles (10 km.) west of Lhasa, takes its name from Pelden Drepung, the place in South India where the Buddha is supposed to have taught the esoteric doctrine of the Kalacakra Tantra. The monastery was founded in 1416 by a disciple of Tsongkhapa named Jamyang (the Tibetan name of the *bodhisattva* Mañjuśrī). As compared with the ten thousand monks reportedly previously resident at Drepung there are now only a few hundred, but the monastery is open to pilgrims and visitors, and many images and paintings are to be seen. Among these, appropriately, are statues of Tsongkhapa (Fig. 15.60) and of Jamyang, the latter with a small Śakyamuni Buddha behind him (Fig. 15.61). In 1985 the second assembly hall at Drepung provided the backdrop for the filming of an enactment of the engagement of Princess Wenchen and King Songtsen Gampo; thus, the past lived on also to that extent (Fig. 15.62).

The Sera monastery, at the foot of a mountain 3 miles (5 km.) north of Lhasa, was founded in 1419 by a disciple of Tsongkhapa named Chamchen Cho-je. In spite of much destruction and the presence now of comparatively few monks, the first and second assembly halls may be visited. On the porch of the first hall are large wall paintings such as often adorned the vestibules of monasteries when they were intact, namely, paintings of the Four Guardians of the four directions, and of the Wheel of Existence. The Wheel of Existence painting (Fig. 15.63) illustrates the very important Buddhist teaching of the chain of Dependent Origination (described above in Chapter 11). The outer circle symbolizes the twelve links in the chain: a blind woman (ignorance), a potter (deeds forming *karma*), a monkey (restless consciousness), two men in a boat (mind and body), a house with six windows (the six senses), a pair of lovers (contact), an arrow piercing the eye of a man (feeling), a drinker served by a woman (thirst or craving), a man gathering

15.61 Statues of Jamyang and Śakyamuni Buddha in the Drepung Monastery

15.62 Filming an Enactment of the Engagement of Princess Wencheng and King Songtsen Gampo at the Drepung Monastery, Lhasa

15.63 The Wheel of Existence, Wall Painting at the Sera Monastery, Lhasa

fruit (grasping of and clinging to desired objects), a *maithuna* scene of "pairing" (a new process of becoming), a woman giving birth (rebirth in a new existence), and a man carrying a corpse on his back (decay and death). The large segments of the circle portray the six spheres of existence; in the upper half are the relatively happier realms of the gods (in the center), the *asuras* or demigods (at the right), and human beings (at the left); in the lower half are the more wretched realms of the animals (at the left), the *pretas* or hungry spirits (at the right), and those tortured in hells (at the center). The small half-circles show (in the light) figures ascending to higher levels of existence, and (in the dark) figures descending to lower levels of existence. In the center are three fundamental faults: ignorance (the pig), hatred (the snake), and desire (the cock); with the creatures biting each other's tails to show that these evils are inseparably connected. Holding the entire wheel in his grasp is Mara, the Evil One, the ruler of the realm of desire and the personification of death, with five human skulls in his headdress.

Today at Mundgod in South India, where some 4,000 Tibetan refugees are settled in eight villages, a new Drepung monastery has been established and

Drepung, Sera, and Ganden monks in exile are there. Previously in Tibet advanced monastic study for the Geshe ("doctor of philosophy") degree called for separate examinations at Drepung, Sera, and Ganden, as well as a final examination which took place at the Jokhang during the annual New Year's prayer festival, the Monlam Chenmo, inaugurated by Tsongkhapa in 1409. Now the same tradition is maintained at Mundgod, and the Monlam Chenmo brings together a large number of Tibetans.[115] Thus in this case here as well as in other places abroad, the rigorous traditions of Tibetan Buddhism are continued, even if for the time being it is not possible to do so as fully as before in the Land of Snows.

It remains to speak of two lands only mentioned above (in Ch. 12) in which Buddhism of Tibetan origin continues in relative freedom, although even there no longer in isolation untouched by the influences of the outside world, namely, Ladakh and Bhutan (both open to foreign visitors only since 1974).

LADAKH

The watershed of geographical Tibet is at the Maryum La; the country to the west is Ngari or Zhang zhung, i.e., Western Tibet.[116] To the west of the pass are sacred Mount Kailasa and Lake Manasarovara, and nearby are the sources of the Indus and the Sutlej rivers. Along the rivers are the main districts: along the Sutlej are Purang and Guge, which are in political Tibet; farther northwest is Spiti, which is in India; along the Indus is Ladakh, and on the Zanskar a tributary of the Indus is the district of Zanskar, both Ladakh and Zanskar being in Kashmir and belonging to India; farther down the Indus is Baltistan, and it is in Pakistan.

From early time Western Tibet was the home of the indigenous Tibetan religion, Bon, and Mount Kailasa was a holy mountain in Bon as also in Hinduism and Buddhism. Buddhist missionaries may well have come into the region already in the time of the Maurya emperor Aśoka (third century B.C.E.). Under the Kushana king Kanishka (probably 78–103 C.E.) Zanskar probably belonged to his realm, and the Buddhist council held under his auspices probably met at Kundalavana in Kashmir, while at Sani in Zanskar there is a *stupa* which is attributed to his time. After the early influence of Buddhism in its Hinayana and Mahayana form, the Vajrayana began to spread in the eighth century C.E. and on. Kashmir was especially a center of tantric teachings, and the "lotus born" tantric master from Uddiyana (Swat), the widely traveled Padmasambhava, is supposed to have meditated in many caverns in Zanskar and Ladakh and to have overcome many deities and demons of the Bon religion before going on at the invitation of King Trhisong Detsen (755–797) to continue his work in Central Tibet. The oldest order of Tibetan Buddhism, the Nyingma-pa (red hats), looks back to Padmasambhava as the Guru Rimpoche (precious teacher) and most eminent personage in its spiritual lineage; one Nyingma-pa monastery, Trakthok (east of Leh), still exists in Ladakh, its buildings adjacent to the Padmasambhava cave.[117]

The chief source for later history in Western Tibet is the Chronicles of the Kings of Ladakh.[118] We are told that after the assassination (in 842) of Langdarma, the last king of the Yarlung Dynasty and the persecutor of Buddhism, the previously great Tibetan empire fell apart in the hands of his rivalrous descendants. Of these at a time around 930 Nyima Gon (probably a great-grandson of Langdarma) went to Ngari where through marriage to the daughter of the king of Purang he gained that region, then went on to conquer Guge, Zanskar, and Maryul (the later *La dwags*, "high pass land," or Ladakh). Eventually he divided his kingdom among three sons: Pelgyi Gon became king of Maryul; Tashi Gon received Purang and Guge; and Detsan Gon obtained Zanskar, Spiti, and (according to some sources) Guge, the apparent contradiction perhaps explainable by the supposition that he seized Guge upon the death of Tashi Gon.

De Dynasty in Guge

Detsan Gon *(lDe btsan mgon)* thus became the founder of the De *(lDe)* Dynasty in the kingdom of Guge, with its capital at Tsaparang. In the dynasty Detsan Gon's son Yeshe Ö, and the latter's grand-nephew Changchup Ö, lived as royal Buddhist monks and were especially important for the furtherance of Buddhism. Yeshe Ö sent Rinchen Sangpo (958–1055) to Kashmir to study from where he returned to become the great translator and the builder of a reputed 108 temples *(lhakhangs)* in Guge (at Tholing and Tsaparang), Spiti (at Tabo), and Ladakh (Nyarma, south of Leh, now ruined, and possibly Alchi, west of Leh, and others). Through Yeshe Ö and Changchup Ö the great Indian teacher Atiśa came to Tholing (in 1042), from where he went on to work in Central Tibet until his death (at the age of 73, in 1054), and to be honored posthumously in the all-Tibetan Buddhist Council of the Fire-Dragon Year (1076) at the Tabo monastery in Spiti.[119]

First Dynasty of Ladakh (circa 950–circa 1460)

Pelgyi Gon, who received Maryul (Ladakh) from his father, Nyima Gon, became the first king and founder (circa 950) of the First Dynasty of Ladakh, in which many of the kings bore the title of Lhachen (great god).[120] Residence was in Shey (supposedly the most ancient capital of Ladakh, the capital of the earliest kings supposedly descended from the mythical king Gesar) and Sabu near Leh. Early in this time the great Indian *siddha* (accomplished one) Naropa (1016–1100) was associated with the founding of monasteries in Ladakh and Zanskar, and Tibet's most famous poet Milarepa (1040–1123) overcame the Bon deities at Mount Kailasa and took possession of the holy mountain for Buddhism. Both Naropa and Milarepa are significant personages in the spiritual lineage of the Kagyu-pa order of Tibetan Buddhism, in which the Druk-pa suborder was to become very important in both Ladakh and Bhutan. Later the dynastic rule was divided for a time between two brothers, Lhachen Trakbumde (circa 1410–circa 1435) and Trakpabum. The former gave favorable reception to emissaries of Tsongkhapa (1357–1419), the founder of the Geluk-pa (yellow hats), and this led to the establishment of this order in Ladakh; monasteries *(gompas)* of the order are Alchi, Sankar, Tiktse, and others.

Second Dynasty of Ladakh, the Namgyal Dynasty (circa 1460–1842)

A grandson of Trakpabum named Lhachen Bhagan (circa 1460–1485) reunited the kingdom and founded a new dynasty to which he gave the name Namgyal, meaning "great victor."[121] The capital was at Leh, where on Namgyal Peak overlooking the city Tashi Namgyal (circa 1555–circa 1575) built a castle, and just below the castle a temple of the protective deities (Gomkhang). He showed preference for the Drigung-pa suborder of the Kagyu-pa, and Lamayuru and Phyang are now monasteries of this order. The height of the dynasty was under Sengge Namgyal (1616–1642). He was the builder of a new castle, the Leh Khar (Fig. 15.64), on the lower slope of Namgyal Peak immediately above the city.

15.64   The Leh Khar on the Slope of Namgyal Peak in Leh

Rising in nine stories and containing a hundred rooms, but no longer occupied as a palace, there is some similarity to the Potala in Lhasa, but the latter was only begun in 1645 and completed in 1694.

In this time the Druk-pa suborder of the Kagyu-pa became very influential in Ladakh. As noted above (in Chapter 12), the Druk-pa takes its name from its earliest monastery, Druk Ralung (30 miles east of Gyangze), at the founding of which legend says the sound of a thunder dragon was heard in the sky (Tibetan *'brug,* pronounced druk, means both thunder and dragon). The chief Druk-pa missionary to Ladakh was Taktshang Repa (*sTag tshang ras pa,* 1574–1651), whose name was derived from his time spent in meditation in the Tiger's Den cave in Bhutan. After passing through Swat, Kashmir, and Zanskar, he arrived in Ladakh probably in late 1616 and became closely associated with Sengge Namgyal. Of the two it was said: "In the whole world is there a king like Sengge (lion) or a lama like *sTag* (tiger), the priest and the donor, sun and moon, a pair?"

Druk-pa monasteries in Ladakh include Shey and Hemis, the latter founded by and burial place of Taktshang Repa, where ever since the succeeding heads of the monastery have been his reincarnations and bear his name. Also the temple in the Leh Khar is under the administration of the Druk-pa of Hemis.

At Shey the monastery temple was erected in 1633 by Lhachen Deldan Namgyal (1647–circa 1694) in honor of his father Sengge Namgyal. It contains an enormous statue of Śakyamuni Buddha, made of gilded copper. It was the wish of the builder that this should be the largest Buddha figure of its time. The lower part of the figure is seated on a lotus base in the lower story of the building, while the shoulders and head rise into the upper story (Fig. 15.65) to a total height of about 40 feet/12 m. To one side in the upper level is the blue guardian of the Buddhist doctrine, Pelden Lhamo, riding sidewise on her mule-mount (Fig. 15.66).

15.65 Colossal Head of Śakyamuni Buddha in the Monastery Temple at Shey

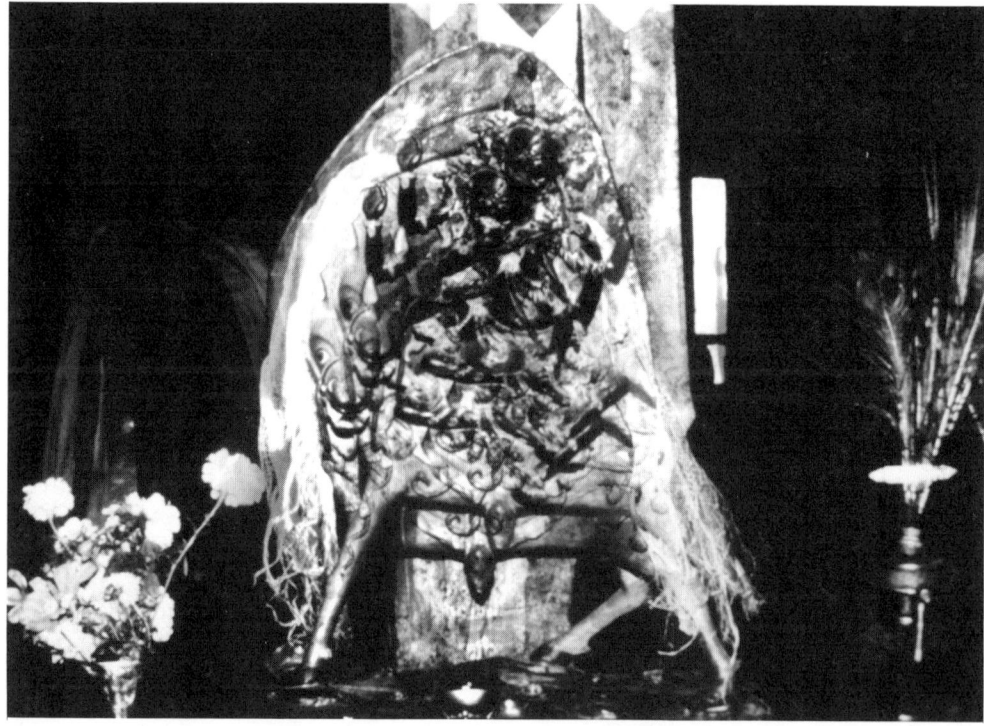

15.66 The Protective Goddess Pelden Lhamo in the Monastery Temple at Shey

15.67 The White Tara in the form of Ushnisha Sitatapatra in the Leh Khar Temple

In the temple of the Leh Khar the central figure is the White Tara (Dolma Karpo) in her form as Ushnisha Sitatapatra, the savioress with a thousand heads and arms and an eye in the palm of each hand expressive of her all-seeing compassion (Fig. 15.67). On either side are smaller figures of Śakyamuni Buddha, and of Padmasambhava seated before shelves of sacred books (Fig. 15.68). At the left wall is the red protective deity Padma Heruka with his consort Padma Dakini (Fig. 15.69), the two together symbolizing in esoteric Buddhism the union of compassion and wisdom.

Finally, after almost a thousand years of independence, Ladakh was invaded in 1834 by Zorowar Singh on behalf of Gulab Singh, ruler of Jammu (and soon of Kashmir too), and in 1842 was incorporated in the dominions of the latter, so Ladakh became a part of Jammu and Kashmir and now belongs to India.[122]

15.68 Padmasambhava and Shelves of Books in the Leh Khar Temple

15.69 The Protective Deity Padma Heruka and Padma Dakini in the Leh Khar Temple

BHUTAN

Bhutan is bounded on the north by Tibet, on the west by Sikkim and the Chumbi Valley of Tibet, and on the east and south by the Indian states of Assam and West Bengal, and extends from tropical lowlands in the south to the heights of the Eastern Himalaya in the north and northwest.[123] The fact that Bhutan is adjacent to but separate from Tibet provides the probable explanation of its name, which is based on the Sanskrit *Bhota ant,* meaning the "end" *(ant)* of Tibet (*Bhota,* Tibetan *Bod,* an ancient name of Tibet). From the same derivation the majority population of Bhutan are called Bhutias, the Indian name for all people of Tibetan descent in these regions.[124] The native name of the country, however, is Druk Yul, the Land of the Thunder Dragon, derived from the Druk-pa or Thunder Dragon order of Tibetan Buddhism, established here as the state religion by the First Shabdrung in the seventeenth century (see below).

The Introduction of Buddhism

The first introduction of Tibetan Buddhism began, however, long before. Already in the seventh century C.E. the country, probably previously under Indian rulers, may have come under the sway of Songtsen Gampo (629–649), known as the first great religious king of Tibet and builder of the Jokhang and Ramoche temples at Lhasa, himself married to a princess from Nepal and to a princess from China as well; legend has it that twelve famous Buddhist temples were erected at that time in Bhutan, among them the Kyichu Lhakhang in the Paro Valley and the Jampa Lhakhang in the Bumthang Valley.[125]

Tradition likewise affirms that at the end of the eighth century Padmasambhava, the Guru Rimpoche, who had already worked in Western and Central Tibet, came to Bhutan. At this time a king of Bumthang named Naguchhi and known as Sindhu Raja (because he had come from India) lost his oldest son, the crown prince, in war with Raja Nabudara in India, and because the deities had seemed to give no help he ordered their temples destroyed, then himself fell desperately ill. At this juncture Padmasambhava was invited to come, and was able to conquer evil spirits and save the king's life and convince him of the efficacy of the Buddhist faith. In gratitude Sindhu Raja restored Jampa Lhakhang, already a hundred years old, and built Kuje Lhakhang. Padmasambhava also proceeded to a high cliff overlooking the Paro Valley (flying there, it is said, on the back of a tiger), meditated in a cave, and overcame more demonic forces; the site is that of the Taktshang or Tiger's Den Monastery, built on the sheer face of the cliff at 10,000 feet elevation, reachable only by a single steep path, and with the main building over the original meditation cave (Figs. 15.70, 15.71). Thus the Nyingmapa order of Tibetan Buddhism, which looks back to Padmasambhava as the chief personage in its spiritual lineage, was introduced to Bhutan, and the Bhutanese consider Padmasambhava an incarnation of the Buddha, a Second Buddha.

The Druk-pa and the Dharma Rajas

It was the Druk-pa suborder of the Kagyu-pa, however, which became predominant. Influential Druk-pa monks at the outset were Padma Karpo (White Lotus, 1527–1592), author of a chronicle of his sect entitled *The Sun which Causes the Lotus of the Teaching to Open,*[126] whose place of retreat was in the southern mountains of Tibet adjacent to the eastern corner of Bhutan; Taktshang Repa

15.70 Taktshang or Tiger's Den Monastery above the Paro Valley

15.71 Tantric Wall Painting in the Taktshang Monastery

(1574–1651) who spent time in meditation at Taktshang prior to his work in Western Tibet; and especially Ngawang Namgyal (1594–1651). The last named was a student of Padma Karpo and his reincarnation, came to Bhutan in 1616, and was recognized by the Bhutanese as their first Dharma Raja (king who rules by law), with the honorary title Shabdrung (at whose feet one submits). Alongside himself as Dharma Raja Ngawang Namgyal appointed a Deb Raja (king who bestows well-being) for secular administration, a dual system which was continued through reincarnation in the case of the Dharma Raja and through election by a Council in the case of the Deb Raja. Ngawang Namgyal also instituted the office of the Je Khenpo as the head of the monastic order, established the division of the country into smaller units, based on *dzongs* (fortress-castles), each with a *penlop* or governor of the district, and himself built the first fortresses, including the Simtokha Dzong at Thimphu and the Rimpong Dzong at Paro.

The Hereditary Monarchy

When the last Dharma Raja died in the early twentieth century and no reincarnation was found, there was rivalry between the *penlops* of Paro and Tongsa, and the Tongsa Penlop, Ugyen Wangchuck, was elected in 1907 by an assembly of the monastic community, government officials, and the people as the first King of Bhutan (1907–1926). This was the beginning of the hereditary monarchy in which he was followed by Jigme Wangchuck (1926–1952), Jigme Dorje Wangchuck (1952–1972), and Jigme Singye Wangchuck (1972–). The title of the king is Druk Gyalpo, Thunder-Dragon King.

Thimphu is the official capital, where the Tashichho Dzong (Fig. 15.72) is

15.72 The Tashicho Dzong in Thimphu

15.73 The Chorten of Jigme Dorje Wangchuck in Thimphu

15.74 The Cosmic Mandala in the Rimpong Dzong in Paro

15.75 Statues of the Buddha and Avalokiteśvara in the Tshongdi Lhakhang in Paro

Bhutan's largest *dzong*, the seat of government, and the home of the central monastic body and the head monk, the Je Khenpo. In Thimphu also is the *chorten (stupa)* of the preceding king, Jigme Dorje Wangchuck (Fig. 15.73), and in it is a wealth of paintings and images representing the several forms of Buddhism.

Paro is the winter capital and the Rimpong Dzong, built by the First Shabdrung, is the center of administration, with the Ugyen Pelri Palace nearby, the residence (in 1987) of the Queen Mother, Her Royal Majesty Ashi Kesang Wangchuck. In the temple in the Rimpong Dzong on the wall beside the entrance there is a large fresco in which an outer fire circle of red surrounds an inner area where intersecting circles of various colors seem to float on clouds of ether and at the center there is a small triple spiral (Fig. 15.74). Presumably embodying ancient tradition, the whole may be understood as a cosmic mandala symbolizing the Buddhist vision of the evolution of energy in the universe.[127] In the Tshongdi Lhakhang in Paro are statues of the Buddha and of the *bodhisattva* Avalokiteśvara in his form with many heads and arms expressive of limitless compassion (Fig. 15.75), the Buddhist virtue which aspires to lead all sentient beings to liberation.

NOTES

1. HARAPPAN CIVILIZATION

1. For the rise of cities see Peter J. Ucko, Ruth Tringham, and G. W. Dimbleby, eds., *Man, Settlement and Urbanism* (London: Duckworth, 1972), with review by Gordon R. Willey in *Antiquity* 47 (1973), pp. 269–279; Dora Jane Hamblin, *The First Cities* (New York: Time-Life Books, 1973). For the Harappan civilization see Gregory L. Possehl, ed., *Harappan Civilization, A Contemporary Perspective* (Warminster, England: Aris and Phillips in cooperation with American Institute of Indian Studies, 1982).

2. For Carbon 14 dates see Walter A. Fairservis, Jr., *The Roots of Ancient India, The Archaeology of Early Indian Civilization* (New York: Macmillan, 1971), pp. 394–397; David and Ruth Whitehouse, *Archaeological Atlas of the World* (San Francisco: W. H. Freeman, 1975), pp. 10, 187, 190; Robert H. Brunswig, "Radiocarbon Dating and the Indus Civilization," in EAW 25 (1975), pp. 111–145.

3. M. Rafique Mughal, "New Evidence of the Early Harappan Culture from Jalilpur, Pakistan," in *Archaeology* 27 (1974), pp. 106–113.

4. F. A. Khan, *Preliminary Report on Koti Diji Excavations, 1957–58* (Karachi: Department of Archaeology, Government of Pakistan, 1960); F. A. Khan, *The Indus Valley and Early Iran* (Karachi: Department of Archaeology and Museums, Ministry of Education, Government of Pakistan, 1964), especially p. 55 for Carbon 14 dates for Kot Diji; and cf. H. D. Sankalia, "Kot Diji and Hissar III," in *Antiquity* 43 (1969), p. 144; and Mughal in *Archaeology* 27 (1974), p. 108 for the corrected dates. See also *Architecture and Art Treasures in Pakistan, Prehistoric, Protohistoric, Buddhist and Hindu Periods* (Karachi: Elite Publishers, 1969), pp. 24–26.

5. Jean-Marie Casal, *Fouilles d'Amri* (Paris: Librairie C. Klincksieck, 2 vols., 1964), especially 1, p. 63 (for the date), and 1, pp. 85, 108; 2, Fig. 63, Pl. XVIII (for the pottery): Jean-Marie Casal, *La civilisation de l'Indus et ses énigmes* (Paris: Librairie Arthème Fayard, 1969), pp. 89–91.

6. George F. Dales, "Harappan Outposts on the Makran Coast," in *Antiquity* 36 (1962), pp. 86–92.

7. For the Mesopotamian seals, see Mortimer Wheeler, *The Indus Civilization* (Supplementary volume of CHI) (Cambridge: University Press, 1960), pp. 91–93. For the Mesopotamian mention of Meluhha and its identification, see ANET p. 268; Mortimer Wheeler, *Early India and Pakistan to Ashoka* (London: Thames and Hudson, rev. ed. 1968), pp. 109f.; A. Parpola, "On the Protohistory of the Indian Languages in the Light of Archaeological, Linguistic and Religious Evidence: An Attempt at Integration," in J. E. van Lohuizen-de Leeuw and J. M. M. Ubaghs, eds., *South Asian Archaeology 1973, Papers from the Second International Conference of the Association for the Promotion of South Asian Archaeology in Western Europe held in the University of Amsterdam* (Leiden: E. J. Brill, 1974), p. 93 n. 3; A. Leo Oppenheim, *Ancient Mesopotamia, Portrait of a Dead Civilization* (Chicago: University of Chicago Press, rev. ed. completed by Erica Reiner, 1977), pp. 63f., 408.

8. Madho Sarup Vats, *Excavations at Harappā, Being an Account of Archaeological Excavations at Harappā carried out between the Years 1920–21 and 1933–34* (Delhi: Manager of Publications, Government of India, 2 vols., 1940); F. A. Khan, *The Glory that was Harappa* (Karachi: Department of Archaeology, Ministry of Education, Government of Pakistan, 1967).

9. John Marshall, ed., *Mohenjo-daro and the Indus Civilization, Being an Official Account of Archaeological Excavations at Mohenjo-daro carried out by the Government of India between the Years 1922 and 1927* (London: Arthur Probsthain, 3 vols., 1931); E. J. H. Mackay, *Further Excavations at Mohenjo-daro, Being an Official Account of Archaeological Excavations at Mohenjo-daro carried out by the Government of India between the Years 1927 and 1931* (Delhi: Manager of Publications, 2 vols., 1937–38); George F. Dales, "New Investigations at Mohenjo-daro," in *Archaeology* 18 (1965), pp. 145–150; Mortimer Wheeler, *Civilizations of the Indus Valley and Beyond* (London: Thames and Hudson, 1966), pp. 14–83; F. A. Khan, *The Glory that was Mohenjodaro* (Karachi: Department of Archaeology, Ministry of Education, Government of Pakistan, 1967); J. E. van Lohuizen-de Leeuw, "Moenjo Daro—A Cause of Common Concern," in *South Asian Archaeology 1973*, pp. 1–11.

10. Ernest J. H. Mackay, *Chanhu-daro Excavations 1935–36* (New Haven: American Oriental Society, 1943), especially pp. 23–25, 103ff., 132ff. for the Jhukar and Jhangar cultures and the date.

11. Robert L. Raikes and R. H. Dyson, Jr., "The Prehistoric Climate of Baluchistan and the Indus Valley," in AMAN 63 (1961), pp. 265–281.

12. Robert L. Raikes, "The End of the Ancient Cities of the Indus," in AMAN 66 (1964), pp. 284–299; Robert L. Raikes, "The Mohenjo-daro Floods," in *Antiquity* 39 (1965), pp. 196–203; Robert L. Raikes, *Water, Weather and Prehistory* (London: John Baker, 1967), pp. 180–183; H. T. Lambrick, "The Indus Flood-plain and the 'Indus' Civilization," in GJ 133 (1967), pp. 483–494.

13. Ernest Mackay, *Early Indus Civilization* (London: Luzac, 2d ed. 1948), pp. 12f. (DK); Marshall, *Mohenjo-daro and the Indus Civilization*, 1, pp. 184–186 (HR), 222f. (VS); Dales in *Archaeology* 18 (1965), p. 147 (HR).

14. Mackay, *Early Indus Civilizations*, p. 13.

15. Marshall, *Mohenjo-daro and the Indus Civilization*, 1, pp. 110–112; R. C. Majumdar, ed., *The History and Culture of the Indian People* (London: George Allen and Unwin), 1, *The Vedic Age* (1951), p. 158 (S. K. Chatterji).

16. P. R. Deshmukh, *The Indus Civilization in the Ṛgveda* (Nagpur: P. N. Banhatti, 1954); Wheeler, *Civilizations of the Indus Valley and Beyond*, pp. 78–83; Wheeler, *Early India and Pakistan to Ashoka*, p. 113; Percival Spear, *India, A Modern History* (Ann Arbor: University of Michigan Press, 1961), p. 31; D. D. Kosambi, *An Introduction to the Study of Indian History* (Bombay: Popular Book Depot, 1956), pp. 67ff.; and *The Culture and Civilization of Ancient India in Historical Outline* (Delhi: Vikas Publications, 1970), pp. 77ff.

17. Chidambara Kulkarni, *Ancient Indian History and Culture* (Bombay: Karnatak Publishing House, rev. ed. 1966), p. 39; Buddha Prakash, *Ṛgveda and the Indus Valley Civilization* (Hoshiarpur: Vishveshvaranand Institute, 1966), p. 51; Majumdar, ed., *The History and Culture of the Indian People*, 1, *The Vedic Age*, p. 194 (A. D. Pusalker).

18. Walter A. Fairservis, Jr., "The Harappan Civilization—New Evidence and More Theory," in AMN No. 2055, Nov. 17, 1961, pp. 18–27.

19. Richard F. S. Starr, *Indus Valley Painted Pottery, A Comparative Study of the Designs on the painted Wares of the Harappa Culture* (Princeton: Princeton University Press, 1941).

20. Asko Parpola, Seppo Koskenniemi, Simo Parpola, and Pentti Aalto, *Decipherment of the Proto-Dravidian Inscriptions of the Indus Civilization* (Copenhagen: Scandinavian Institute of Asian Studies, Special Publication 1, 1969); cf. Gerard Clauson and John Chadwick, "The Indus Script Deciphered?" in *Antiquity* 43 (1969), pp. 200–207, who view the results favorably; and T. Burrow, "Dravidian and the Decipherment of the Indus Script," in *Antiquity* 43 (1969), 274–278, who does not believe that the script has been deciphered. See also George F. Dales, "New Inscriptions from Moenjo-Daro, Pakistan," in *Kramer Anniversary Volume*, ed. Barry L. Eichler (Alter Orient und Altes Testament, 25) (Neukirchen-Vluyn: Neukirchener Verlag, 1976), pp. 111–123.

21. Marshall, *Mohenjo-daro and the Indus Civilization*, 1, pp. 52–56.

22. Ibid., 1, pp. 58–63, Pls. XIII, XIV.

23. Doris Srinivasan, "The So-Called Proto-Śiva Seal from Mohenjo-Daro: An Iconological Assessment," in AAA 29 (1975–76), pp. 47–58.

24. Ralph T. H. Griffith, *The Hymns of the Ṛgveda* (Varanasi: Chowkhamba Sanskrit Series Office, 2 vols., 4th ed. 1963), 1, p. 272; 2, pp. 390f., 537; Deshmukh, *The Indus Civilization in the Ṛgveda*, pp. 42f.; Prakash, *Ṛgveda and the Indus Valley Civilization*, pp. 20–30.

25. Fairservis, *The Roots of Ancient India*, pp. 275f., Nos. 16, 18.

26. Marshall, *Mohenjo-daro and the Indus Civilization*, 1, pp. 49–52, Pl. XII; 3, Pls. XCIV, XCV.

27. Ernest Mackay in Marshall, *Mohenjo-daro and the Indus Civilization*, 1, pp. 356f.; 3, Pl. XCVIII.

2. LITERATURE OF HINDUISM AND THE VEDIC AND EPIC PERIODS

1. ANET p. 316.
2. A. Parpola, "On the Protohistory of the Indian Languages in the Light of Archaeological, Linguistic and Religious Evidence: An Attempt at Integration," in J. E. van Lohuizen-de Leeuw and J. M. M. Ubaghs, eds., *South Asian Archaeology 1973, Papers from the Second International Conference of the Association for the Promotion of South Asian Archaeology in Western Europe held in the University of Amsterdam* (Leiden: E. J. Brill, 1974), p. 94.
3. For the literature of Hinduism see A. Berriedale Keith, *A History of Sanskrit Literature* (Oxford: Clarendon Press, 1928); Maurice Winternitz, *A History of Indian Literature* (Calcutta: University of Calcutta, 3 vols., 1933–59), 1, *Introduction, Veda, National Epics, Puranas, and Tantras*; Krishna Chaitanya, *A New History of Sanskrit Literature* (Bombay: Asia Publishing House, 1962).
4. Jan Gonda, *The Vision of the Vedic Poets* (The Hague: Mouton, 1963); Jeanine Miller, *The Vedas* (London: Rider, 1974); Antonio T. de Nicolás, *Four-Dimensional Man, Meditations through the Ṛg Veda* (Stony Brook, N.Y.: Nicolas Hays Ltd., 1976).
5. T. S. Rukmani, *A Critical Study of the Bhāgavata Purāṇa* (CSS 77) (Varanasi: Chowkhamba Sanskrit Series Office, 1970), pp. 28, 86.
6. A. L. Basham, *The Wonder That Was India* (London: Sidgwick and Jackson, 3d ed., 1967), p. 32; Bridget and Raymond Allchin, *The Birth of Indian Civilization, India and Pakistan before 500 B.C.* (Harmondsworth: Penguin Books, 1968), pp. 154f.
7. Bal Gangadhar Tilak, *The Orion, or Researches into the Antiquity of the Vedas* (Poona City: Tilak Bros., 1893); Chidambara Kulkarni, *Ancient Indian History and Culture* (Bombay: Karnatak Publishing House, 1966), pp. 37f.; Abinas Chandra Das, *Ṛgvedic India* (Delhi: Motilal Banarsidass, 3d ed. 1971), pp. 6ff.; Venkatarama Baghavan in Isma'īl Rāgī al Fārūqī and David E. Sopher, *Historical Atlas of the Religions of the World* (New York: Macmillan, 1974), pp. 73ff., 299ff.; Abinas Chandra Das, *Ṛgvedic Culture* (Varanasi: Bharatiya Publishing House, 1979), pp. v–vi, 37f.
8. Karl Friedrich Geldner, *Der Rig-Veda* (HOS 33–36) (Cambridge: Harvard University Press, 4 vols., 1951–57), 2, p. 335; 3, pp. 255f.; M. Aurel Stein, "On Some River-Names in the Ṛgveda," in *Commemorative Essays presented to Sir Ramkrishna Gopal Bhandarkar* (Poona: Bhandarkar Oriental Research Institute, 1917), pp. 21–28.
9. G. Bühler, *The Laws of Manu* (SBE 25), pp. 32f.
10. Manchar Lal Bhargava, *The Geography of Ṛgvedic India (A Physical Geography of Sapta Saindhava)* (Lucknow: Upper India Publishing House, 1964), pp. 37–127.
11. Das, *Ṛgvedic Culture*, pp. 148–160; Doris Srinivasan, "The Myth of the Paṇis in the Rig Veda," in JAOS 93 (1973), pp. 44–57.
12. Devendrakumar Rajaram Patil, *Cultural History from the Vāyu Purāṇa* (Delhi: Motilal Banarsidass, 1946), pp. 303f.
13. H. H. Wilson, *The Vishṇu Purāṇa* (Calcutta: Punthi Pustak, 3d ed. 1961), p. 139; W. Kirfel, *Die Kosmographie der Inder nach den Quellen dargestellt* (Bonn: Kurt Schroeder, 1920).
14. D. P. Mishra, *Studies in the Proto-History of India* (New Delhi: Orient Longman, 1971), pp. 5–15.
15. Samuel Beal, *Si-yu-ki, Buddhist Records of the Western World, translated from the Chinese of Hiuen Tsiang (A.D. 629)* (TOS) (London: Kegan Paul, Trench, Trübner, 2 vols., 1906), 2, p. 297. This is a reprint of the work as published previously in 1884, and there is also a verbatim reprint in four volumes (with different page numbers) in a new edition, Calcutta: Susil Gupta, 1957–58. Our references are to the work as published in 1906.
16. N. G. Sardesai, "The Land of Seven Rivers," in *Commemorative Essays presented to Sir Ramkrishna Gopal Bhandarkar*, pp. 93–96.
17. Wilson, *The Vishṇu Purāṇa*, pp. 21–24, 209–219; cf. *Mahabharata* 3.18–23, J. A. B. van Buitenen, *The Mahābhārata* (Chicago: University of Chicago Press, 1975ff.), 2, p. 586.
18. Julius Eggeling, *The Śatapatha-Brâhmana* (SBE 12), pp. 216–218; van Buitenen, *The Mahābhārata*, 2, pp. 583–585.
19. Wilson, *The Vishṇu Purāṇa*, pp. 277ff. For the dynastic lists and their historical value see F. E. Pargiter, "Ancient Indian Genealogies—Are They Trustworthy?" in *Commemorative Essays presented to Sir Ramkrishna Gopal Bhandarkar*, pp. 107–113; F. E. Pargiter, *Ancient Indian Historical Tradition* (1922, reprinted Delhi: Motilal Banarsidass, 1962), pp. 144–149, 330f.; R. Morton Smith, "On the Ancient Chronology of India," in JAOS 77 (1957), pp. 116–129, 266–280; 78 (1958), pp. 174–

192; R. Morton Smith, *Dates and Dynasties in Earliest India*, ed., J. L. Shastri (Delhi: Motilal Banarsidass, 1973), pp. 1f., 388–514.

20. M. R. Singh, *Geographical Data in the Early Puranas* (Calcutta: Punthi Pustak, 1972); Sudama Misra, *Janapada State in Ancient India* (Varanasi: Bharatiya Vidyā Prakāśana, 1973).

21. Benjamin Walker, *Hindu World* (London: George Allen and Unwin, 2 vols., 1968), 2, p. 508. The summary is taken mainly from the *Ramayana;* cf. the *Mahabharata* 1.168.14–19 (van Buitenen, *The Mahābhārata*, 1, p. 337). The quotation from the *Hindu World* is made by permission of Benjamin Walker, 84 Church Road, Teddington, Middlesex, TW11 8PY, England.

22. Reprinted from *The Mahābhārata*, translated and edited by J. A. B. van Buitenen, 1973ff., vol. 2, p. 619, by permission of The University of Chicago Press, copyright by The University of Chicago.

23. Romesh C. Dutt, *The Ramayana and the Mahabharata condensed into English Verse*, An Everyman's Library Edition (London: J. M. Dent and Sons; New York: E. P. Dutton and Co., no date), p. 178. Quoted by permission of Elsevier-Dutton Publishing Co., Inc., New York.

24. Wilson, *The Vishṇu Purāṇa*, p. 308.

25. Vasudeva S. Agrawala, *Matsya Purāṇa—A Study* (Varanasi: All-India Kashiraj Trust, 1963), pp. 144f.

26. Wilson, *The Vishṇu Purāṇa*, pp. 348–351.

27. van Buitenen, *The Mahābhārata*, 2, pp. 58–75.

28. Wilson, *The Vishṇu Purāṇa*, pp. 285, 449, 482; *MLBD Newsletter, A Monthly of Indological Bibliography* (Motilal Banarsidass, Delhi), VI, 8, August 1984, p. 8.

29. Agrawala, *Matsya Purāṇa*, pp. 150f.

30. Eggeling, *The Śatapatha-Brâhmana* (SBE 44), p. 399.

31. Geldner, *Der Rig-Veda*, 1, p. 357.

32. Wilson, *The Vishṇu Purāṇa*, p. 364.

33. van Buitenen, *The Mahābhārata*, 2, pp. 302f.

34. Walker, *Hindu World*, 1, pp. 576f.

35. Dutt, *The Ramayana and the Mahabharata condensed into English Verse*, An Everyman's Library Edition, p. 178. Quoted by permission of Elsevier-Dutton Publishing Co., Inc., New York.

3. VEDIC AND UPANISHADIC RELIGION AND PHILOSOPHY

1. For the Rig Veda see F. Max Müller, *Vedic Hymns, 1, Hymns to the Maruts, Rudra, Vâyu, and Vâta* (SBE 32); Hermann Oldenberg, *Vedic Hymns, 2, Hymns to Agni (Mandalas I–V)* (SBE 46); Arthur Anthony Macdonell, *A Vedic Reader* (London: Oxford University Press, 1917); and *Hymns from the Rigveda* (no date); Edward J. Thomas, *Vedic Hymns* (WES), (New York: E. P. Dutton, 1923); Karl Friedrich Geldner, *Der Rig-Veda* (Cambridge: Harvard University Press, 4 vols., 1951–57); Ralph T. H. Griffith, *The Hymns of the Ṛgveda* (CSS 35) (Varanasi: Chowkhamba Sanskrit Series Office, 2 vols., 4th ed. 1963, originally published in 1889); Jean Le Mée, *Hymns from the Rig-Veda* (New York: Alfred A. Knopf, 1975). Our translations generally follow the German of Geldner and also draw upon Max Müller and Thomas. For the topics of this chapter see E. Washburn Hopkins, *Epic Mythology* (EI-AR 3.1.B), (Strassburg: Trübner, 1915); Arthur Berriedale Keith, *The Religion and Philosophy of the Veda and Upanishads* (HOS 31–32), (Cambridge: Harvard University Press, 2 vols., 1925); Alain Daniélou, *Hindu Polytheism* (BS 73), (New York: Pantheon Books, 1964), pp. 63–146; Erich Frauwallner, *History of Indian Philosophy* (Delhi: Motilal Banarsidass, 2 vols., 1973).

2. William Dwight Whitney, *Atharva-Veda-Saṁhitā* (Delhi: Motilal Banarsidass, 2d Indian reprint edition, 2 vols., 1962), 1, p. 393.

3. Julius Eggeling, *The Śatapatha Brâhmana* (5 vols., SBE 12, 26, 41, 43, 44), SBE 44, p. 115.

4. Maurice Bloomfield, *Hymns of the Atharva-Veda* (SBE 42), p. 166.

5. Ibid., p. 204.

6. Ibid., p. 201.

7. *The Matsya Puranam* translated by a Taluqdar of Oudh (Allahabad: Indian Press, 1916), 1, pp. 155–158; Vasudeva S. Agrawala, *Matsya Purāṇa—A Study* (Varanasi: All-India Kashiraj Trust, 1963), pp. 155–169; F. Eden Pargiter, *The Mārkaṇḍeya Purāṇa* (BI), (Calcutta: Asiatic Society, 1904).

8. Ralph R. H. Griffith, *The Hymns of the Sāmaveda* (Varanasi: Chowkhamba Sanskrit Series Office, 4th ed. 1963).

9. Eggeling, *The Śatapatha Brâhmana*, SBE 41, pp. 8, 29; 44, pp. 232f. For *Ephedra intermedia* see Geldner, *Der Rig-Veda*, 3, p. 2; for *Amanita muscaria* see R. Gordon Wasson, *Soma: Divine Mushroom of Immortality* (Harcourt Brace & World, 1968). Against both of these identifica-

tions, and for the difference between the sacred *soma* and the harmful and presumably fermented *sura*, see John Brough, "Soma and *Amanita Muscaria*," in BSOAS 34 (1971), pp. 331–362.

10. W. Norman Brown, "The Creation Myth of the Rig Veda," in JAOS 62 (1942), pp. 85–98; Ajoy Kumar Lahiri, *Vedic Vrtra* (Delhi: Motilal Banarsidass, 1984).

11. For the Upanishads see F. Max Müller, *The Upanishads* (SBE 1, 15); S. Radhakrishnan, *The Principal Upaniṣads* (Hemel Hempstead, England: George Allen & Unwin, 1953); Swami Nikhilananda, *The Upanishads* (New York: Harper, 3 vols., 1949–56); Sri Aurobindo Ghose, *The Upanishads, Texts, Translations and Commentaries* (Sri Aurobindo Birth Centenary Library, 12) (Pondicherry: Sri Aurobindo Ashram, 1972). Our translations are from Max Müller, the present one from SBE 15, p. 245.

12. Hermann Oldenberg, *The Grihya-Sûtras* (SBE 29), p. 256; Ralph T. H. Griffith, *The Texts of the White Yajurveda* (Benares: E. J. Lazarus, 1899).

13. J. Gonda, *Viṣṇuism and Śivaism* (JLCR 9) (University of London: Athlone Press, 1970).

14. Griffith, *The Hymns of the Ṛgveda*, 1, p. 390 n. 10.

15. Gonda, *Viṣṇuism and Śivaism*.

16. Bloomfield, *Hymns of the Atharva-Veda* (SBE 42), pp. 160f.

17. J. A. B. van Buitenen, *The Mahabharata* (1973ff.), 1, p. 148. Reprinted by permission of The University of Chicago Press, copyright by The University of Chicago.

18. H. H. Wilson, *The Vishnu Purāṇa* (Calcutta: Punthi Pustak, 1961), pp. 102f., 313f.; *The Matsya Puranam* translated by a Taluqdar of Oudh, 1, pp. 73–76; Agrawala, *Matsya Purāṇa—A Study*, pp. 128–132; *Ancient Indian Tradition and Mythology,* translated by a Board of Scholars (Delhi: Motilal Banarsidass, 4 vols., *The Śiva-Purāṇa,* 1970), 3, pp. 1307–1312.

19. Radhakrishnan, *The Principal Upaniṣads,* p. 589.

20. van Buitenen, *The Mahābhārata*, 3, p. 408.

21. Eggeling, *The Śatapatha Brâhmana* (SBE 44), p. 62.

22. Bloomfield, *Hymns of the Atharva-Veda* (SBE 42), pp. 9, 33.

23. Eggeling, *The Śatapatha Brâhmana* (SBE 41), p. 281.

24. Whitney, *Atharva-Veda-Saṁhitā*, 2, pp. 695, 705.

25. Eggeling, *The Śatapatha Brâhmana* (SBE 26), p. 11.

26. van Buitenen, *The Mahābhārata*, 2, p. 68.

27. Eggeling, *The Śatapatha Brâhmana* (SBE 12), p. 301.

28. Geldner, *Der Rig-Veda*, 3, pp. 295, 397, 403.

29. Whitney, *Atharva-Veda-Saṁhitā*, 2, pp. 505, 652–655.

30. van Buitenen, *The Mahābhārata*, 1, pp. 68–123.

31. Geldner, *Der Rig-Veda*, 1, p. 236.

32. Ibid., 3, p. 337.

33. Müller, *The Upanishads* (SBE 15), pp. 265, 311.

34. *The Śiva-Purāṇa,* translated by a Board of Scholars (Delhi: Motilal Banarsidass, 4 vols., 1970), 1, pp. 389, 401, n. 295, 301.

35. Eggeling, *The Śatapatha Brâhmana* (SBE 41), p. 378; cf. SBE 44, pp. 12ff.

36. G. Bühler, *The Laws of Manu* (SBE 25), pp. 14, 402.

37. Thomas, *Vedic Hymns*, pp. 121f.

38. Geldner, *Der Rig-Veda*, 3, pp. 347–349.

39. Radhakrishnan, *The Principal Upaniṣads,* p. 449. Quoted by permission of George Allen and Unwin (Publishers) Ltd.

40. Thomas, *Vedic Hymns*, pp. 127f.

41. Eggeling, *The Śatapatha Brâhmana* (SBE 43), pp. 389f.

42. Ibid. (SBE 44), pp. 12ff.

43. Ibid. (SBE 44), pp. 27f.

44. The translations of the Upanishads are from F. Max Müller in SBE 1 and 15, the present one from SBE 15, p. 64.

45. Radhakrishnan, *The Principal Upaniṣads,* p. 695.

46. Ibid., p. 916, cf. pp. 121f.

47. Geldner, *Der Rig-Veda*, 2, p. 235.

48. cf. Franklin Edgerton, "Studies in the Veda," in JAOS 35 (1915), pp. 242–245.

4. CHRONOLOGY OF THE KALI AGE

1. H. H. Wilson, *The Vishnu Purāṇa* (Calcutta: Punthi Pustak, 1961), pp. 481f.

2. Reprinted from *The Mahābhārata*, translated and edited by J. A. B. van Buitenen, 1973ff., vol. 1, pp. 109f., by permission of The University of Chicago Press, copyright by The University of Chicago.

3. D. R. Mankad, *Puranic Chronology* (Vallabhvidyanagar: Gaṅgājaḷā Prakashan, 1951), pp. 1951), pp. 68f.; D. S. Triveda, *Indian Chronology (8231 B.C. to 1963 A.D.)* (Bombay: Bharatiya Vidya Bhavan, 1963), p. 13 and n. 14, 15.

4. *The Indian Astronomical Ephemeris for the Year 1987* (issued under the authority of the Director General of Meteorology, New Delhi, and published by the Controller of Publications, Civil Lines, Delhi-110054), p. 3. For this and other eras in use in India see also L. D. Swamikannu Pillai, *An Indian Ephemeris, A.D. 700 to A.D. 2000* (Madras: Superintendent, Government Press, 8 vols., 1915–22).

5. Wilson, *The Vishṇu Purāṇa*, p. 368.

6. Ibid., pp. 368ff.; Vasudeva S. Agrawala, *Matsya Purāṇa—A Study* (Varanasi: All-India Kashiraj Trust, 1963).

7. For the dynastic lists and their historical value see F. E. Pargiter, *The Purāṇa Text of the Dynasties of the Kali Age* (1913, reprinted Varanasi: Chowkhamba Sanskrit Series Office, CSS 19, 2d ed. 1962); F. E. Pargiter, "Ancient Indian Genealogies—Are They Trustworthy?" in *Commemorative Essays presented to Sir Ramkrishna Gopal Bhandarkar* (Poona: Bhandarkar Oriental Research Institute, 1917), pp. 107–113; F. E. Pargiter, *Ancient Indian Historical Tradition* (1922, reprinted Delhi: Motilal Banarsidass, 1962), pp. 144–149, 330f.; R. Morton Smith, "On the Ancient Chronology of India," in JAOS 77 (1957), pp. 116–129, 266–280; 78 (1958), pp. 174–192; R. Morton Smith, *Dates and Dynasties in Earliest India*, ed. J. L. Shastri (Delhi: Motilal Banarsidass, 1973), pp. 1f., 388–614.

8. T. W. Rhys Davids, *Buddhist India* (New York: G. P. Putnam's Sons, 1903), p. 3 (cf. later Indian editions: Calcutta: Susil Gupta, 1950; Delhi: Motilal Banarsidass, 1971); Sudama Misra, *Janapada State in Ancient India* (Varanasi: Bhāratīya Vidyā Prakāśana, 1973), pp. 52–55. Since different traditions are now involved and the sources are not only in Sanskrit but also in the Prakrit dialects of the oldest Jaina scriptures and the Pali of the earliest Buddhist records, there are differences in names and in the forms of names and terms. For example, in Sanskrit and Pali respectively we have Pataliputra/Pataliputta, Kośala/Kosala, Śravasti/Savatthi, Kauśambi/Kosambi, Ajataśatru/Ajatasattu, Prasenajit/Pasenadi, Udayana/Udena, *śramaṇa/samana*, etc., while the Jainas and Buddhists often call Bimbisara Śreṇika/Seniya, and Ajataśatru Kunika/Kuniya. Under the circumstances, since the Sanskrit is the basic form from which the dialectal forms are ultimately derived, it seems indicated to use the Sanskrit forms for the most part, but to diverge for sufficient reason; for example, reproducing the Prakrit and Pali forms in many references to and direct quotations of Prakrit and Pali sources (cf. F. Max Müller, *The Dhammapada*, SBE 10, 1, pp. liii–lv).

9. Wilson, *The Vishṇu Purāṇa*, pp. 308–310.

10. Ibid., pp. 369–371; Agrawala, *Matsya Purāṇa*, pp. 371f.; Smith, *Dates and Dynasties in Earliest India*, pp. 337–341, 488f., Table X, for the section from Brihadbala to Sumitra II.

11. Wilson, *The Vishṇu Purāṇa*, pp. 365–369; Agrawala, *Matsya Purāṇa*, pp. 150–152; Smith, *Dates and Dynasties in Earliest India*, pp. 321–327, 506, Table XXI, for the section from Abhimanyu to Kshemaka.

12. van Buitenen, *The Mahābhārata*, 1, pp. 130–132.

13. Wilson, *The Vishṇu Purāṇa*, pp. 364f., 371f.; Agrawala, *Matsya Purāṇa*, pp. 373f.; Smith, *Dates and Dynasties in Earliest India*, pp. 304–331, 509f., Table XXIII, for the section from Brihadratha to Ripunjaya.

14. Maurice Bloomfield, *Hymns of the Atharva-Veda* (SBE 42), p. 2.

15. Wilson, *The Vishṇu Purāṇa*, p. 373.

16. Ibid.

17. Agrawala, *Matsya Purāṇa*, p. 374.

18. Ibid., p. 143.

19. Wilson, *The Vishṇu Purāṇa*, p. 372; Agrawala, *Matsya Purāṇa*, p. 374; Smith, *Dates and Dynasties in Earliest India*, pp. 343–349, 512, Table XXVI.

20. Pargiter, *The Purāṇa Text of the Dynasties of the Kali Age*, p. 68.

21. Wilson, *The Vishṇu Purāṇa*, pp. 372f.; Agrawala, *Matsya Purāṇa*, p. 374; Smith, *Dates and Dynasties in Earliest India*, pp. 349–355, 512, Table XXVII.

22. Pargiter, *The Purāṇa Text of the Dynasties of the Kali Age*, p. 69 n. 9.

23. Hemchandra Raychaudhuri, *Political History of Ancient India* (Calcutta: University of Calcutta, 1950), pp. 115–117.

24. CHI 1, pp. 309–311.

25. Wilson, *The Vishṇu Purāṇa*, p. 374; Agrawala, *Matsya Purāṇa*, p. 375; Smith, *Dates and Dynasties in Earliest India*, pp. 359–362, 513, Table XXVII.

26. Pargiter, *The Purāṇa Text of the Dynasties of the Kali Age,* p. 69 n. 17.
27. K. A. Nilakanta Sastri, ed., *Age of the Nandas and Mauryas* (Banaras: Motilal Banarsidass, 1952).
28. Wilson, *The Vishṇu Purāṇa,* p. 389; Agrawala, *Matsya Purāṇa,* p. 378.
29. Wilson, *The Vishṇu Purāṇa,* p. 374; Agrawala, *Matsya Purāṇa,* p. 375; Smith, *Dates and Dynasties in Earliest India,* pp. 362–367, 513, Table XXVII.
30. Wilhelm Geiger, *The Mahāvaṃsa or The Great Chronicle of Ceylon* (1912, reprinted Colombo: Ceylon Government Information Department, 1950), p. 27. For the *Dipavamsa* see Bimala Church Law, *The Chronicle of the Island of Ceylon or the Dipavamsa* (The Ceylon Historical Journal, Vol. VII—July 1957 to April 1958—Nos. 1–4) (Maharagama: Saman Press, 1959).
31. R. Shamasastry, *Kauṭilya's Arthaśāstra* (Mysore: Wesleyan Mission Press, 3d ed. 1929), p. 463.
32. G. P. Malalasekera, *Dictionary of Pali Proper Names* (ITS) (London: John Murray, 2 vols., 1937–38), 2, pp. 673, 972 n. 14.
33. Wilson, *The Vishṇu Purāṇa,* pp. 376f.; Agrawala, *Matsya Purāṇa,* p. 376; Smith, *Dates and Dynasties in Earliest India,* pp. 367–374, 513, Table XXVIII.
34. Wilson, *The Vishṇu Purāṇa,* p. 377; Agrawala, *Matsya Purāṇa,* p. 376; Smith, *Dates and Dynasties in Earliest India,* pp. 374f., 514, Table XXIX.
35. Wilson, *The Vishṇu Purāṇa,* pp. 378f.; Agrawala, *Matsya Purāṇa,* pp. 376f.; Smith, *Dates and Dynasties in Earliest India,* pp. 375–386, 514, Table XXX.
36. Vincent A. Smith, *The Early History of India from 600 B.C. to the Muhammadan Conquest, including the Invasion of Alexander the Great* (Oxford: Clarendon Press, 3d ed. 1914), pp. 215f.; R. C. Majumdar, H. C. Raychaudhuri, and Kalikinkar Datta, *An Advanced History of India* (London: Macmillan, 2d ed. 1950), pp. 115f.; Raychaudhuri, *Political History of Ancient India,* pp. 403–417; K. A. Nilakanta Sastri, *A History of South India from Prehistoric Times to the Fall of Vijayanagar* (London: Oxford University Press, 1955), pp. 88–92; K. Gopalachari, *Early History of the Andhra Country* (MUHS) (Madras: University of Madras, 2d ed. 1976), pp. 31ff. The dates given in our text are those of Sastri and his pupil Gopalachari (between whom there are slight differences).
37. Wilson, *The Vishṇu Purāṇa,* pp. 380ff.; Agrawala, *Matsya Purāṇa,* pp. 377f.
38. Radha Kumud Mookerji, *Chandragupta Maurya and His Times* (Delhi: Motilal Banarsidass, 4th ed. 1966), p. 44.
39. Vincent A. Smith, *Asoka, The Buddhist Emperor of India* (Oxford: Clarendon Press, 2d ed. 1909), pp. 72–74.
40. Geiger, *The Mahāvaṃsa,* p. 28.
41. Amulyachandra Sen, *Asoka's Edicts* (IIS 7) (Calcutta: Institute of Indology, 1956), pp. 24, 102; Mookerji, *Chandragupta Maurya and His Times,* pp. 45f.
42. Geiger, *The Mahāvaṃsa,* p. 136; Radhakumud Mookerji, *Asoka* (Gaekwad Lectures) (London: Macmillan, 1928), p. 45.
43. Sastri, *Age of the Nandas and Mauryas,* p. 246.
44. D. C. Sircar, ed., *The Bhārata War and Puranic Genealogies* (Calcutta: University of Calcutta, 1969), pp. 13 (R. C. Majumdar), 20 (D. C. Sircar), 61 (S. R. Das).
45. Govinda Krishna Pillai, *Vedic History (Set in Chronology)* (Allahabad: Kitabistan, 1959); Govinda Krishna Pillai, *Traditional History of India (A Digest)* (Bombay: Kitab Mahal, 1960); especially *Vedic History,* pp. 15f.; *Traditional History of India,* pp. 5, 301–308, Appendix I, Genealogical Table). For the estimate of twenty years per generation or step see R. Morton Smith, "On the Ancient Chronology of India," in JAOS 78 (1958), p. 191; and Smith, *Dates and Dynasties in Earliest India,* p. 6. Pillai uses an estimate of eighteen years instead of twenty, and thus arrives at slightly different results.
46. Chinmanlal J. Shah, *Jainism in North India 800 B.C.–A.D. 526* (London: Longmans, Green and Co., 1932), p. 28.
47. Raj Bali Pandey, *Vikramāditya of Ujjayinī (The Founder of the Vikrama Era)* (Banaras: Shatadala Prakashana, 1951), p. 38.
48. W. Norman Brown, *The Story of Kālaka, Texts, History, Legends, and Miniature Paintings of the Śvetāmbara Jain Hagiographical Work, The Kālakācāryakathā* (Smithsonian Institution, Freer Gallery of Art, Oriental Studies, 1) (Washington, Baltimore: Lord Baltimore Press, 1933), pp. 78–82, 106.
49. Majumdar, et al., *An Advanced History of India,* pp. 116ff.
50. Brown, *The Story of Kālaka,* p. 80 n. 7 for the "Saka bank," and p. 83 for Balamitra and Bhanumitra.
51. Raychaudhuri, *Political History of Ancient India,* pp. 484–489.
52. Mankad, *Puranic Chronology,* pp. 189, 198.

53. Jyoti Prasad Jain, *The Jaina Sources of the History of Ancient India (100 B.C.–A.D. 900)* (Delhi: Munshi Ram Manohar Lal, 1964), p. 63.
54. Brown, *The Story of Kālaka*, p. 60.
55. Ibid., p. 60 n. 17; Pandey, *Vikramāditya of Ujjayinī*, pp. 77–85.
56. *The Indian Astronomical Ephemeris for the Year 1987*, p. 3. For 58 B.C.E. see Majumdar, et al., *An Advanced History of India*, p. 118; CHI 1, p. 155 n. 1. For the historical origin of the era see Pandey, *Vikramāditya of Ujjayinī*, pp. iii, 2. For the critical view which questions the historicity of Vikramaditya and his connection with the Vikrama era see D. C. Sircar, *Ancient Malwa and the Vikramāditya Tradition* (Delhi: Munshiram Mancharlal, 1969).
57. Majumdar, et al., *An Advanced History of India*, p. 101.
58. Pandey, *Vikramāditya of Ujjayinī*, p. 26.
59. *The Indian Astronomical Ephemeris for the Year 1987*, p. 3.
60. Majumdar, et al., *An Advanced History of India*, pp. 120f.; CHI 1, p. 583.
61. Jain, *The Jaina Sources of the History of Ancient India*, pp. 77–81.
62. Helen M. Johnson, *Triṣaṣṭiśalākāpuruṣacaritra* (GOS 51, 77, 108, 125, 139, 140) (Baroda: Oriental Institute, 6 vols. 1931–37), 6, p. 309.
63. Hermann Jacobi, *Gaina Sutras*, 1 (SBE 22), p. 264.
64. The names of the months in the Indian calendar (and the Gregorian date for the first day of the month at the present time) are: (1) Caitra (Mar. 22, Mar. 21 in a leap year); (2) Vaiśakha (Apr. 21); (3) Jyaistha (May 22); (4) Asadha (June 22); (5) Śravana (July 23); (6) Bhadra (Aug. 23); (7) Aśvina (Sept. 23); (8) Kartika (Oct. 23); (9) Agrahayana (Nov. 22); (10) Pausha (Dec. 22); (11) Magha (Jan. 21); (12) Phalguna (Feb. 20). See *The Indian Astronomical Ephemeris for the Year 1987*, p. 478.
65. Dines Chandra Sircar, *Select Inscriptions bearing on Indian History and Civilization*, 1 (Calcutta: University of Calcutta, 2d ed. 1965), pp. 89f. and n. 3 on p. 90.
66. B. A. Chaugule and N. V. Vaidya, eds., *Pauma-Chariyam (Chapters I–IV) of Vimala-Sūri* (Belgaum: Belgaum Semāchār Press and Mahāvīr Printing Press, 1936), p. vii.
67. Hiralal Jain and A. N. Upadhye, *Mahāvīra, His Times and His Philosophy of Life* (JMG English Series, 2) (New Delhi: Bharatiya Jnanpith, published on the occasion of the celebration of the 2500th Nirvāna of Bhagvān Mahāvīra, 1974).
68. *The Indian Astronomical Ephemeris for the Year 1987*, p. 3.
69. Jacobi, *Gaina Sûtras*, 1 (SBE 22), p. 269.
70. Nagrajji, *The Contemporaneity and the Chronology of Mahāvīra and Buddha*, p. 90; Jain and Upadhye, *Mahāvīra, His Times and His Philosophy of Life*, pp. 17f.; Jyoti Prasad Jain, *The Jaina Sources of the History of Ancient India*, pp. 53f.; Kailash Chand Jain, *Lord Mahāvīra and His Times* (Delhi: Motilal Banarsidass, 1974), pp. 73–88.
71. T. W. and C. A. F. Rhys Davids, *Dialogues of the Buddha* (SBB) (London: Henry Frowde, 3 vols., 1899–1921), 2, p. 167.
72. J. J. Jones, *The Mahāvastu* (SBB) (London: Luzac, 3 vols., 1949–56), 2, p. 196.
73. Rhys Davids, *Dialogues of the Buddha*, 2, p. 107.
74. Law, *The Chronicle of the Island of Ceylon or the Dipavamsa*, p. 170; Geiger, *The Mahāvaṃsa*, pp. 14, 27.
75. Geiger, *The Mahāvaṃsa*, pp. xxiv, xlvi, 27.
76. Ibid., p. 12.
77. Ibid., p. xxviii.
78. P. V. Bapat, ed., *2500 Years of Buddhism* (Delhi: Government of India, Ministry of Information and Broadcasting, Publications Division, first published on the occasion of the 2500th anniversary of the Mahāparinirvāṇa of Buddha, May 1956, reprinted Mar. 1959), p. v.
79. *The Indian Astronomical Ephemeris for the Year 1987*, p. 3.
80. P. Bigandet, *The Life or Legend of Gaudama, the Buddha of the Burmese* (TOS) (London: Kegan Paul, Trench, Trübner, 2 vols., 4th ed. 1911, re-issue 1914).
81. Ibid., 1, p. 13.
82. Ibid., 2, pp. 71–73.
83. Ibid., 2, p. 113.
84. Ibid., 2, p. 133 n. 1.
85. Nagrajji, *The Contemporaneity and the Chronology of Mahāvīra and Buddha*, p. 134.
86. F. L. Woodward and E. M. Hare, *The Book of the Gradual Sayings (Anguttara-Nikāya) or More-Numbered Suttas* (PTS) (London: Luzac, 5 vols., 1951–55), 1, p. 20.
87. Law, *The Chronicle of the Island of Ceylon or the Dipavamsa*, pp. 153, 160.
88. J. Takakusu, "Pali Elements in Chinese Buddhism," in JRAS 1896, pp. 435–437; J. Takakusu, "A Study of Paramartha's Life of Vasu-Bandhu; and the Date of Vasu-Bandhu," in JRAS 1905, p. 51 and n. 2.

89. George N. Roerich, *The Blue Annals* (Delhi: Motilal Banarsidass, 2d ed. 1976), p. 1063.
90. W. Woodville Rockhill, *The Life of the Buddha and the Early History of His Order, derived from Tibetan Works in the Bkah-hgyur and Bstan-hgyur* (London: Kegan Paul, Trench, Trübner, 1884), pp. 17, 32 n. 1.
91. Bhagchandra Jain Bhaskar, *Jainism in Buddhist Literature* (Nagpur: Alok Prakashan, 1972), p. 25.
92. Rhys Davids, *Dialogues of the Buddha*, 1, pp. 74f.; V. Fausböll, *The Sutta-Nipâta* (SBE 10, 2), pp. 85–87.
93. Mrs. Rhys Davids and F. L. Woodward, *The Book of the Kindred Sayings (Saṇyutta-Nikāya) or Grouped Suttas* (PTS) (London: Luzac, 5 vols., 1950–56), 1, pp. 93–95.
94. Rhys Davids, *Dialogues of the Buddha*, 3, p. 111; Robert Chalmers, *Further Dialogues of the Buddha, Translated from the Pali of the Majjhima Nikāya* (SBB) (London: Humphrey Milford, 2 vols., 1926–27), 2, p. 139.
95. Rhys Davids, *Dialogues of the Buddha*, 3, p. 203.
96. Jain, *Mahāvīra, His Times and His Philosophy of Life*, p. 18.
97. E.g., CHI 1, p. 312.
98. Nagrajji, *The Contemporaneity and the Chronology of Mahāvīra and Buddha*, p. 61.
99. Rhys Davids, *Dialogues of the Buddha*, 1, pp. 65–95.
100. Nagrajji, *The Contemporaneity and the Chronology of Mahāvīra and Buddha*, pp. xv, 141, Appendix II.
101. The same objection also applies, and even more strongly, at this point to a figure given in a Tibetan tradition, according to which the death of the Buddha is placed in the fifth year of Ajataśatru. See Rockhill, *The Life of the Buddha and the Early History of His Order*, pp. 91, 233.
102. Fausböll, *The Sutta-Nipâta* (SBE 10, 2), pp. 67–69.
103. T. W. Rhys Davids and Hermann Oldenberg, *Vinaya Texts* (3 vols., SBE 13, 17, 20), 1 (SBE 13), pp. 136–144.
104. Ibid., 3 (SBE 20), pp. 233ff.
105. Mrs. Rhys Davids, *The Book of the Kindred Sayings*, 1, pp. 109f.
106. Jacobi, *Gaina Sûtras*, 1 (SBE 22), p. xiii.
107. Jogendra Chandra Sikdar, *Studies in the Bhagawatīsūtra* (PJIRP 1) (Muzaffarpur: Research Institute of Prakrit, Jainology and Ahimsa, 1964), pp. 433, 490.
108. Jain, *The Jaina Sources of the History of Ancient India*, p. 52.
109. Cf. Nagrajji, *The Contemporaneity and the Chronology of Mahāvīra and Buddha*, pp. 23, 99 for the accession of Ajataśatru in 544.
110. Cf. ibid., pp. 112, 119f. for the *nirvana* of the Buddha in 502. For Buddha *nirvana* dates from 544 to 483 cf. Kailash Chand Jain, *Lord Mahāvīra and His Times*, p. 73 n. 3.

5. GEOGRAPHY, CLANS, KINGDOMS, CITIES

1. M. R. Singh, *Geographical Data in the Early Purāṇas* (Calcutta: Punthi Pustak, 1972).
2. Bimala Churn Law, *India as Described in Early Texts of Buddhism and Jainism* (London: Luzac, 1941).
3. For the geography see Anundoram Borooah, *Ancient Geography of India* (first published 1877, reprinted, Gauhati: Publication Board, Assam, 1971); Bimala Churn Law, *Historical Geography of Ancient India* (Paris: Société Asiatique de Paris, 1954); Isma'īl Rāgī al Fārūqī and David E. Sopher, *Historical Atlas of the Religions of the World* (New York: Macmillan, 1974), p. 163, Map 31; Joseph E. Schwartzberg, *A Historical Atlas of South Asia* (Chicago: University of Chicago Press, 1978). For the cities see Singh, *Geographical Data in the Early Purāṇas*, and also B. N. Puri, *Cities of Ancient India* (Meerut: Meenkashi Prakashan, 1966).
4. T. W. Rhys Davids, *Buddhist India* (published originally in 1903, 1st Indian edition, Calcutta: Susil Gupta, 1950), pp. 12–16.
5. Law, *India as Described in Early Texts of Buddhism and Jainism*, p. 134.
6. Robert Chalmers, *Buddha's Teachings, Being the Sutta-Nipāta or Discourse-Collection* (HOS 37) (Cambridge: Harvard University Press, 1932), p. 101.
7. R. P. Sharma, *Nepal (A Detailed Geographical Account)* (Kathmandu: Pustak-Sansar, 1974), p. 95.
8. Mrs. Rhys Davids, *Psalms of the Early Buddhists*, 2, *Psalms of the Brethren* (PTS) (London: Henry Frowde, 1913), p. 249.
9. T. W. and C. A. F. Rhys Davids, *Buddhist Birth-Stories (Jataka Tales), The Commentarial Introduction entitled Nidāna-Kathā, The Story of the Lineage* (London: G. Routledge and Sons, rev. ed. 1925), pp. 153f.

10. Sharma, *Nepal (A Detailed Geographical Account)*, p. 96.
11. E. Hultzsch, *Inscriptions of Asoka* (CII 1) (Oxford: Clarendon Press, new ed. 1925), pp. xxii–xxiii, 164f.; Amulyachandra Sen, *Asoka's Edicts* (Calcutta: Institute of Indology, 1956), pp. 122f.
12. E. B. Cowell, ed., *The Jātaka, or Stories of the Buddha's Former Births* (PTS) (London: Routledge and K. Paul, 6 vols. in 3, 1973), 5, pp. 219f.
13. Hermann Jacobi, *Gaina Sûtras*, 2 vols. (SBE 22, 45), 1 (SBE 22), pp. 264f.
14. T. W. and C. A. F. Rhys Davids, *Dialogues of the Buddha* (SBB) (London: Henry Frowde, 3 vols., 1899–1921), 2, pp. 78–191. For the description of Kuśavati under King Maha Sudassana see also the *Maha Sudassana Sutta* in T. W. Rhys Davids, *Buddhist Suttas* (SBE 11), pp. 238–289.
15. Sharma, *Nepal (A Detailed Geographical Account)*, p. 74.
16. Cowell, *The Jātaka*, 6, p. 30.
17. Helen M. Johnson, *Triṣaṣṭiśalākāpuruṣacaritra* (GOS 51, 77, 108, 125, 139, 140) (Baroda: Oriental Institute, 6 vols., 1931–37), 1 (GOS 51), pp. 347–349, and see this source for information about all of the *tirthankaras*.
18. Jacobi, *Gaina Sûtras*, 1 (SBE 22), p. 264, and see this passage for enumeration of the other places also where Mahavira spent his rainy seasons.
19. Robert Chalmers, *Further Dialogues of the Buddha, Translated from the Pali of the Majjhima Nikāya* (SBB) (London: Humphrey Milford, 2 vols., 1926–27), 2, p. 39.
20. Jacobi, *Gaina Sûtras*, 1 (SBE 22), pp. 190f.
21. Ibid., 2 (SBE 45), p. 261.
22. F. L. Woodward and E. M. Hare, *The Book of the Gradual Sayings* (Anguttara-Nikāya), *or More-Numbered Suttas* (PTS) (first published 1932–36, reprinted London: Luzac, 5 vols., 1952–55), 2, pp. 200–204; 3, pp. 126f.
23. A poem of Ambapali appears among those of the seventy-three nuns in the *Therigatha* (66), see Mrs. Rhys Davids, *Psalms of the Early Buddhists*, 1, *Psalms of the Sisters* (PTS) (London: Henry Frowde, 1909), pp. 120–125.
24. Rhys Davids, *Dialogues of the Buddha* (SBB), 2, pp. 102–106.
25. For the Second Buddhist Council in Vaiśali see Chapter 11.
26. Mrs. Rhys Davids and F. L. Woodward, *The Book of the Kindred Sayings (Sanyutta-Nikāya), or Grouped Suttas* (PTS) (London: Luzac, 5 vols., 1950–56), 3, p. 1.
27. Eugene Watson Burlingame, *Buddhist Legends translated from the original Pali text of the Dhammapada Commentary* (HOS 28) (Cambridge: Harvard University Press, 1921), p. 247.
28. E. B. Cowell, *Buddhist Mahâyâna Texts*, 1, *The Buddha-Karita of Aśvaghosha* (SBE 49), pp. 123–132.
29. Woodward and Hare, *The Book of the Gradual Sayings*, 1, pp. 170–175.
30. Geiger, *The Mahāvaṃsa*, p. 27.
31. Sudama Misra, *Janapada State in Ancient India* (Varanasi: Bhāratīya Vidyā Prakāśana, 1973).
32. Woodward and Hare, *The Book of the Gradual Sayings*, 1, p. 192; 4, p. 172; Rhys Davids, *Dialogues of the Buddha*, 2, p. 237; Jones, *The Mahāvastu*, 1, p. 29.
33. J. A. B. van Buitenen, *The Mahābhārata* (Chicago: University of Chicago Press, 1973ff.), 2, pp. 790ff.
34. Bimala Churn Law, *Some Jaina Canonical Sūtras* (Bombay: Bombay Branch Royal Asiatic Society, 1949), p. 176.
35. Rhys Davids, *Dialogues of the Buddha*, 1, pp. 144–159.
36. van Buitenen, *The Mahābhārata*, 1, pp. 37, 384.
37. Ibid., 2, pp. 67–75, quoted by permission of The University of Chicago Press, copyright by The University of Chicago.
38. Bimala Churn Law, *Rājagriha in Ancient Literature* (MASI 58) (Delhi: Manager of Publications, 1938).
39. Jones, *The Mahāvastu*, 3, p. 56.
40. Chalmers, *Further Dialogues of the Buddha*, 1, pp. 117f.
41. Rhys Davids and Oldenberg, *Vinaya Texts*, 1 (SBE 13), p. 74.
42. Rhys Davids, *Dialogues of the Buddha*, 2, p. 6.
43. Benimadhab Barua, *Gayā and Buddha-Gayā* (IRIFA 4) (Calcutta: Chuckervertty, Chatterjee, 2 vols., 1931–34).
44. D. C. Sircar, *Studies in the Geography of Ancient and Medieval India* (Delhi: Motilal Banarsidass, 2d ed. 1971), pp. 282–288.
45. V. Fausböll, *The Sutta-Nipâta* (SBE 10, 2), pp. 45f.
46. Jacobi, *Gaina Sûtras*, 2 (SBE 45), pp. 100–107.
47. Law, *Some Jaina Canonical Sūtras*, p. 54.

48. Ibid., pp. 67–73.
49. Rhys Davids, *Dialogues of the Buddha*, 2, p. 123.
50. Ibid., 1, p. 276; 2, p. 87; 3, p. 95.
51. For the First Buddhist Council at Rajagriha see below in Chapter 11.
52. Chalmers, *Further Dialogues of the Buddha*, 2, p. 13. For the Wanderers and the Buddhist criticism of them see also *Majjhima Nikaya* 1.64, 84, 305, 513; 2.30; 3.291; Chalmers, *Further Dialogues of the Buddha*, 1, pp. 42, 59, 219, 363; 2, pp. 16, 321.
53. Rhys Davids and Oldenberg, *Vinaya Texts*, 1 (SBE 13), p. 146. According to the *Mahavastu* (3.60–61; Jones, *The Mahāvastu*, 3, pp. 61f.) Sariputta was converted by Upasena, not by Assaji. For the conversion of Upasena by the Buddha, see the *Buddha-charita* 17.8; Cowell, *Buddhist Mahâyâna Texts*, 1 (SBE 49), p. 192.
54. Rhys Davids, *Dialogues of the Buddha*, 1, pp. 65–76.
55. Chalmers, *Further Dialogues of the Buddha*, 1, pp. 364f.
56. Mrs. Rhys Davids, *The Book of the Kindred Sayings*, 1, p. 90.
57. Chalmers, *Further Dialogues of the Buddha*, 1, pp. 363f.
58. Ibid., 1, pp. 366f.
59. Ibid., 1, p. 369.
60. Ibid., 2, p. 125.
61. Rhys Davids, *Dialogues of the Buddha*, 1, pp. 76–95.
62. T. W. Rhys Davids, *The Questions of King Milinda* (2 vols., SBE 35, 36), 1 (SBE 35), pp. 167f.
63. Rhys Davids, *Dialogues of the Buddha*, 2, pp. 165–169.
64. Rhys Davids, *The Questions of King Milinda*, 1 (SBE 35), p. 8; 2 (SBE 36), pp. 373f.
65. A. L. Basham, *History and Doctrine of the Ājīvikas* (London: Luzac, 1951).
66. Chalmers, *Further Dialogues of the Buddha*, 1, pp. 170f., 371.
67. Rhys Davids, *Dialogues of the Buddha*, 2, pp. 90–95.
68. Geiger, *The Mahāvaṃsa*, p. 19.
69. Rhys Davids, *Dialogues of the Buddha*, 1, p. 68.
70. Law, *Some Jaina Canonical Sūtras*, p. 176.
71. For these later dynasties see below in Chapter 6.
72. J. W. McCrindle, *Ancient India as described by Megasthenês and Arrian* (Calcutta: Chuckervertty, Chatterjee, 1926), pp. 67f.
73. For the Jaina Council at Pataliputra see below in Chapter 9.
74. For the Third Buddhist Council at Pataliputra see below in Chapter 10.
75. Singh, *Geographical Data in the Early Purāṇas*, p. 243.
76. Jones, *The Mahāvastu*, 3, p. 401.
77. van Buitenen, *The Mahābhārata*, 1, pp. 227–237.
78. *Dhammacakkappavattana Sutta*, T. W. Rhys Davids, *Buddhist Suttas* (SBE 11), pp. 146–155; *Mahavagga* 1.6.17–47, Rhys Davids and Oldenberg, *Vinaya Texts*, 1 (SBE 13), pp. 94–102; *Samyutta Nikaya* 5.420f., Mrs. Rhys Davids and Woodward, *The Book of the Kindred Sayings*, 5, pp. 356–365.
79. T. W. Rhys Davids, *Early Buddhism* (Chicago: Open Court Publishing Co., no date), pp. 49f.
80. Mrs. Rhys Davids and Woodward, *The Book of the Kindred Sayings*, 5, pp. 347–349.
81. Ibid., 3, p. 118.
82. Singh, *Geographical Data in the Early Purāṇas*, p. 95.
83. Rhys Davids and Oldenberg, *Vinaya Texts*, 2, pp. 24, 147.
84. Chalmers, *Further Dialogues of the Buddha*, 1, pp. 105f.
85. Rhys Davids and Oldenberg, *Vinaya Texts*, 3, pp. 179–189.
86. Bimala Churn Law, *Śrāvastī in Indian Literature* (MASI 50) (Delhi: Manager of Publications, 1935).
87. Vasudeva S. Agrawala, *Matsya Purāṇa, A Study* (Varanasi: All-India Kashiraj Trust, 1963), pp. 371f.; H. H. Wilson, *The Vishṇu Purāṇa* (Calcutta: Punthi Pustak, 1961), pp. 369–371.
88. Mrs. Rhys Davids, *The Book of the Kindred Sayings*, 1, pp. 93–127.
89. Ibid., 1, pp. 109f.
90. Cowell, *The Jātaka*, 3, pp. 244f.; 5, pp. 48f.
91. Ibid., 3, pp. 13–15; 4, pp. 271f.
92. Ibid., 3, pp. 29f.
93. Rhys Davids, *Dialogues of the Buddha*, 1, p. 244.
94. Rhys Davids and Oldenberg, *Vinaya Texts*, 3 (SBE 20), p. 209.
95. Mrs. Rhys Davids, *The Book of the Kindred Sayings*, 1, p. 122.

96. Mrs. Rhys Davids, *Psalms of the Early Buddhists*, 1, *Psalms of the Sisters*, pp. 19f.
97. Chalmers, *Further Dialogues of the Buddha*, 2, pp. 62–66.
98. For the long relationship of Prasenajit and the Buddha see Mrs. Rhys Davids, "Sage and King in Kosala-Saṁyutta," in *Commemorative Essays presented to Sir Ramakrishna Gopal Bhandarkar* (Poona: Bhandarkar Oriental Research Institute, 1917), pp. 133–138.
99. van Buitenen, *The Mahābhārata*, 1, p. 132.
100. Ibid., 2, pp. 97–106.
101. Woodward, *The Book of the Kindred Sayings*, 5, p. 369; Woodward and Hare, *The Book of the Gradual Sayings*, 3, p. 252.
102. Wilson, *The Vishnu Purāṇa*, pp. 368f.
103. Agrawala, *Matsya Purāṇa, A Study*, pp. 151f.
104. Jones, *The Mahāvastu*, 2, p. 2.
105. Bimala Churn Law, *Kauśāmbī in Ancient Literature* (MASI 60) (Delhi: Manager of Publications, 1939).
106. Rhys Davids and Oldenberg, *Vinaya Texts*, 3 (SBE 20), p. 412.
107. Ibid., 3 (SBE 20), pp. 382–384.
108. Ibid., 2 (SBE 17), p. 312.
109. *Hastinapur, A Jain Pilgrimage* (Delhi: Shri Hastinapur Jain Swetamber Tirth Committee, 1951).
110. Mrs. Rhys Davids, *The Book of the Kindred Sayings*, 2, pp. 64, 75.
111. van Buitenen, *The Mahābhārata*, 1, p. 283.
112. Ibid., 1, pp. 346ff.
113. Ibid., 2, p. 148.
114. Wilson, *The Vishnu Purāṇa*, pp. 76, 308.
115. Woodward and Hare, *The Book of the Gradual Sayings*, 2, p. 66.
116. Ibid., 3, p. 188. For "geni" as translation of *yakkha* see Mrs. Rhys Davids, *The Book of the Kindred Sayings*, 1, p. 262 n. 1.
117. Woodward and Hare, *The Book of the Gradual Sayings*, 1, p. 17.
118. Chalmers, *Further Dialogues of the Buddha*, 2, pp. 43–46.
119. van Buitenen, *The Mahābhārata*, 1, p. 337.
120. Ibid., 2, pp. 83, 401.
121. Agrawala, *Matsya Purāṇa, A Study*, p. 146.
122. Chalmers, *Further Dialogues of the Buddha*, 2, p. 159.
123. Agrawala, *Matsya Purāṇa, A Study*, p. 374.
124. van Buitenen, *The Mahābhārata*, 1, p. 45.
125. Sen, *Asoka's Edicts*, p. 74.
126. Rhys Davids, *The Questions of King Milinda*, 1 (SBE 35), pp. 2f.; I. B. Horner, *Milinda's Questions* (SBB) (London: Luzac, 2 vols., 1963–64), 1, pp. 1–3.
127. Cowell, *The Jātaka*, 1, pp. 126, 137, 148, 173, 203.
128. James Legge, *A Record of Buddhistic Kingdoms, being an Account by the Chinese Monk Fâ-Hien of His Travels in India and Ceylon* (Oxford: Clarendon Press, 1886); H. A. Giles, *The Travels of Fa-hsien (399–414 A.D.), or Record of the Buddhistic Kingdoms* (Cambridge: University Press, 1923); Samuel Beal, *Si-yu-ki, Buddhist Records of the Western World, translated from the Chinese of Hiuen Tsiang (A.D. 629)* (TOS) (London: Kegan Paul, Trench, Trübner, 2 vols., 1906); Samuel Beal, *The Life of Hiuen-Tsiang by the Shaman Hwui Li* (TOS) (London: Kegan Paul, Trench, Trübner, new ed. 1911, re-issue 1914); Jeannette Mirsky, *The Great Chinese Travelers* (New York: Pantheon Books, 1964); René Grousset, *In the Footsteps of the Buddha* (New York: Grossman Publishers, 1971).
129. Beal, *Buddhist Records of the Western World*, 1, pp. xxxiif., 97–109; Legge, *A Record of Buddhistic Kingdoms*, pp. 33f.; Beal, *The Life of Hiuen-Tsiang*, p. 63f.
130. For the Fourth Buddhist Council under Kanishka see Chapter 11.
131. van Buitenen, *The Mahābhārata*, 3, p. 219.
132. B. R. Chatterji, "A Current Tradition among the Kambojs of North India relating to the Khmers of Cambodia," in AA 24 (1961), pp. 253f. For Kambuja/Cambodia/Kampuchea see below in Chapter 14.
133. Beal, *Buddhist Records of the Western World*, 1, p. 163.
134. Sircar, *Geography of Ancient and Medieval India*, pp. 195–200.
135. Rhys Davids, *Dialogues of the Buddha*, 2, p. 161.
136. Ibid., 2, p. 237; Jones, *The Mahāvastu*, 1, p. 29.
137. Rhys Davids, *Dialogues of the Buddha*, 2, pp. 153f.

6. ALEXANDER THE GREAT AND EMPIRES SUBSEQUENT TO HIS COMING

1. Roland G. Kent, *Old Persian Grammar, Texts, Lexicon* (AOS 33) (New Haven: American Oriental Society, 1953), pp. 117, 119, 137f., 183, 199, 214 (DB 16; DNa 23–25).
2. M. Foster Farley, "Alexander in the Punjab," in OR 9,3 (Mar. 1978), pp. 35–48; 9,4 (Apr. 1978), pp. 53ff.
3. Aurel Stein, "Alexander's Campaign on the Indian North-west Frontier," in GJ 70 (1927), pp. 417–440, 515–540; Aurel Stein, *On Alexander's Track to the Indus* (London: Macmillan, 1929); cf. CHI I, Map 3, "The Kābul Valley and the Punjab."
4. Aurel Stein, "The Site of Alexander's Passage of the Hydaspes and the Battle with Poros," in GJ 80 (1932), pp. 31–46.
5. Guy Thompson Griffith, ed., *Alexander the Great, The Main Problems* (New York: Barnes and Noble, 1966); Fritz Schachermeyr, *Alexander in Babylon und die Reichsordnung nach seinem Tode*, Österreichische Akademie der Wissenschaften, philosophisch-historische Klasse, Sitzungsberichte, 268. Band, 3. Abteilung (Wien: Hermann Böhlaus Nachf., 1970); B. C. Sinha, *Studies in Alexander's Campaigns* (Varanasi: Bhartiya Publishing House, 1973).
6. W. W. Tarn, *The Greeks in Bactria and India* (Cambridge: University Press, 2d ed. 1951), pp. 460–462.
7. K. A. Nilakanta Sastri, *The Age of the Nandas and Mauryas* (Banaras: Motilal Banarsidass, 1952); Radha Kumud Mookerji, *Chandragupta Maurya and His Times* (Delhi: M. Banarsidass, 3d ed. 1960).
8. J. W. McCrindle, *Ancient India as described by Megasthenês and Arrian* (Calcutta: Chuckervertty, Chatterjee and Co., 1926); R. C. Majumdar, *The Classical Accounts of India* (Calcutta: K. L. Mukhopadhyay, 1960).
9. Mookerji, *Chandragupta and His Times,* pp. 39–41.
10. R. Narasimhachar, *Epigraphia Caranatica, 2, Inscriptions at Sravana Belgola* (MAS) (Bangalore: Mysore Government Central Press, rev. ed. 1923), Translations, pp. 1, 25 (cf. No. 64 [1163 CE] on p. 16), 116.
11. Wilhelm Geiger, *The Mahāvaṃsa or The Great Chronicle of Ceylon* (Colombo: Ceylon Government Information Department, 1950), p. 75.
12. P. B. Desai, *Jainism in South India and Some Jaina Epigraphs* (JJG 6) (Sholapur: Jaina Saṃskṛti Saṃrakshaka Sangha, 1957), pp. 1–3.
13. Geiger, *The Mahāvaṃsa,* pp. 28f.
14. For Aśoka see Vincent A. Smith, *Asoka, The Buddhist Emperor of India* (Oxford: Clarendon Press, 1909); Radhakumud Mookerji, *Asoka* (Gaekwad Lectures) (London: Macmillan, 1928); Sastri, *The Age of the Nandas and Mauryas,* pp. 202ff.; Sudhakar Chatropadhyaya, *Bimbisāra to Aśoka* (Calcutta: Roy and Chowdhury, 1977); John S. Strong, *The Legend of King Aśoka: A Study and Translation of the Aśokāvadāna* (Princeton: Princeton University Press, 1983). For the inscriptions of Aśoka see E. Hultzsch, *Inscriptions of Asoka* (CII 1) (Oxford: Clarendon Press, new ed. 1925); Amulyachandra Sen, *Asoka's Edicts* (Calcutta: Institute of Indology, 1956).
15. Smith, *Asoka,* pp. 20, 222.
16. Sen, *Asoka's Edicts,* p. 112.
17. Bimala Churn Law, *The Chronicle of the Island of Ceylon or the Dipavamsa,* The Ceylon Historical Journal, Vol. VII, July 1957 to Apr. 1958, Nos. 1–4 (Maharagama: Saman Press, 1959), p. 171; Geiger, *The Mahāvaṃsa,* p. 88.
18. Geiger, *The Mahāvaṃsa,* p. 29.
19. Ibid., p. 27.
20. Sen, *Asoka's Edicts,* pp. 98–104.
21. Law, *The Dipavamsa,* pp. 172–179; Geiger, *The Mahāvaṃsa,* pp. 29, 31f.
22. Mookerji, *Asoka,* p. 18.
23. Sen, *Asoka's Edicts,* p. 84.
24. Samuel Beal, *Si-yu-ki, Buddhist Records of the Western World translated from the Chinese of Hiuen Tsiang (A.D. 629)* (TOS) (London: Kegan Paul, Trench, Trübner, 2 vols., 1906), 1, p. 182 n. 48; 2, pp. 88f.; Samuel Beal, *The Fo-sho-hing-tsan-king, A Life of Buddha by Aśvaghosha Bodhisattva translated from Sanskrit into Chinese by Dharmaraksha, A.D. 420* (SBE 19), pp. xxix, 336.
25. Mookerji, *Asoka,* p. 27.
26. Ibid., p. 8.
27. Geiger, *The Mahāvaṃsa,* p. 33.
28. Ibid., pp. 122f., 136.
29. Ibid., p. 88.

30. Sen, *Asoka's Edicts*, p. 124.
31. Ibid., p. 164.
32. Ibid., p. 60.
33. Ibid., p. 146.
34. Ibid., p. 64.
35. Ibid., p. 94.
36. Ibid., p. 52.
37. Ibid.
38. Ibid., p. 64.
39. Ibid., p. 66.
40. Ibid., p. 162.
41. Law, *The Dipavamsa*, pp. 132, 172 and n. 3; Geiger, *The Mahāvaṃsa*, p. 78.
42. Beal, *Buddhist Records of the Western World*, 1, pp. 139–142.
43. James Legge, *A Record of Buddhistic Kingdoms, being an Account by the Chinese Monk Fâ-Hien of His Travels in India and Ceylon (A.D. 399–414)* (Oxford: Clarendon Press, 1886), p. 31.
44. Sastri, *Age of the Nandas and Mauryas*, pp. 244f.
45. Mookerji, *Asoka*, p. 37 n. 1.
46. Hemchandra Raychaudhuri, *Political History of Ancient India* (Calcutta: University of Calcutta, 1950), pp. 351f.
47. Desai, *Jainism in South India and Some Jaina Epigraphs*, pp. 1–3, 98.
48. Chimanlal J. Shah, *Jainism in North India 800 B.C.–A.D. 526* (London: Longmans, Green, 1932), p. 145.
49. Vincent A. Smith, *The Early History of India from 600 B.C. to the Muhammadan Conquest* (Oxford: Clarendon Press, 3d ed. 1914), pp. 248ff.; Vincent A. Smith, *The Oxford History of India* (Oxford: Clarendon Press, 1919), pp. 127ff.; Raychaudhuri, *Political History of Ancient India*, pp. 527ff.; B. N. Puri, *India under the Kushans* (Bombay: Bharati Vidya Bhavan, 1965); John Rosenfield, *The Dynastic Arts of the Kushans* (CSHA) (Berkeley and Los Angeles: University of California Press, 1967); Alexander C. Soper, "Recent Studies involving the Date of Kaniṣka," in AA 33 (1971), pp. 339–350; 34 (1972), pp. 102–113.
50. Viktor Sarianidi, "The Treasure of the Golden Mound," in *Archaeology* 33, 3, May/Jun. 1980, pp. 31–41.
51. Rosenfield, *The Dynastic Arts of the Kushans*, p. 144, Fig. 2.
52. Ibid., pp. 156f., Fig. 120.
53. Henri Seyrig, "La grande statue parthe de Shami et la sculpture palmyrénienne," in *Syria* 20 (1939), pp. 177–181.
54. Fuad Safar, "Inscriptions of Hatra," in *Sumer* 9 (1953), p. 19, No. 36; pp. 264f., No. 11; André Maricq, "Hatra de Sanatrouq," in *Syria* 32 (1955), pp. 273–286 and Fig. 1.
55. H. H. Wilson, *The Vishṇu Purāṇa* (Calcutta: Punthi Pustak, 1961), p. 385.
56. Beal, *Buddhist Records of the Western World*, 2, pp. 133–135; Geiger, *The Mahāvaṃsa*, p. xxxix.
57. Legge, *A Record of Buddhistic Kingdoms*; H. A. Giles, *The Travels of Fa-hsien (399–414 A.D.), or Record of the Buddhistic Kingdoms* (Cambridge: University Press, 1923).
58. Luce Boulnois, *The Silk Road* (New York: Dutton, 1966); Jan Myrdal, *The Silk Road, A Journey from the High Pamirs and Ili through Sinkiang and Kansu* (New York: Pantheon, 1979); Jack Chen, *The Sinkiang Story* (New York: Macmillan; London: Collier Macmillan, 1977), pp. 85–89; Irene M. Franck and David M. Brownstone, *The Silk Road: A History* (New York: Facts on File, 1986). For the routes of the Chinese Buddhist pilgrims see Albert Hermann, *An Historical Atlas of China*, new ed. by Norton Ginsburg (Chicago: Aldine Publishing Co., 1966), pp. xxiv–xxv, 23, 27, 31.
59. Giles, *The Travels of Fa-hsien*, p. 2.
60. Ibid., pp. 8f., 28, 31ff. On the route of Fa Xian see also Beal, *Buddhist Records of the Western World*, 1, pp. xii–xv.
61. H. B. Sarkar, "The Port of Tamralipti in Fiction and History," in Perala Ratnam, *Studies in Indo-Asian Art and Culture, Commemoration Volume on the 69th Birthday of Acharya Raghu Vira* (SPS 95) (New Delhi: International Academy of Indian Culture, 1972), pp. 219–241.
62. Giles, *The Travels of Fa-hsien*, pp. 30, 36, 41, 45–48, 53.
63. Wilson, *The Vishṇu Purāṇa*, p. 383, and for Mekala see p. 152 n. 18.
64. Raychaudhuri, *Political History of Ancient India*, p. 574.
65. Ibid., pp. 581–613.
66. Beal, *Buddhist Records of the Western World*, 1, pp. 168–172.
67. Raychaudri, *Political History of Ancient India*, p. 596, n. 3.

68. Samuel Beal, *The Life of Hiuen-Tsiang by the Shaman Hwui Li* (London: Kegan Paul, Trench, Trübner, new ed. 1911, re-issue 1914), pp. 110f.
69. Raychaudri, *Political History of Ancient India*, p. 611.
70. E. B. Cowell and F. W. Thomas, *The Harṣa-carita of Bāṇa* (OTF) (London: Royal Asiatic Society, 1897); P. V. Kane, *The Harshacarita of Bāṇabhaṭṭa* (Delhi: Motilal Banarsidass, 2d ed. 1965). For the other best known work of Bana, see C. M. Ridding, *The Kādambarī of Bāṇa* (London: Royal Asiatic Society, 1896).
71. Cowell and Thomas, *The Harṣa-carita of Bāṇa*, p. 44.
72. Ibid., p. 197.
73. Ibid., p. 258.
74. Ibid., pp. 134f.
75. Ibid., p. 244.
76. Ibid., p. 236.
77. Beal, *Buddhist Records of the Western World*, 1, pp. xviii–xix for the route of Xuan Zang; Beal, *The Life of Hiuen-Tsiang by the Shaman Hwui Li*; Jeannette Mirsky, *The Great Chinese Travelers, An Anthology* (New York: Pantheon, 1964), pp. 29–114; René Grousset, *In the Footsteps of the Buddha* (New York: Grossman Publishers, 1971); Sally Wriggins, "A Monk's Journey to the Buddhist Holy Land," in OR 10,10 (Oct. 1979), pp. 54–57.
78. Beal, *The Life of Hiuen-Tsiang by the Shaman Hwui Li*, pp. 12 (Lanzhou), 24–34; Beal, *Buddhist Records of the Western World*, 1, pp. 18 (Qarashahr), 19 (Kucha), 25f. (Tsing Lake), 32 (Samarkand), 43f. (Balkh), 49f. (Bamiyan), 97f. (Gandhara).
79. Beal, *Buddhist Records of the Western World*, 1, pp. 213f.
80. Ibid., 1, p. 207.
81. Beal, *The Life of Hiuen-Tsiang by the Shaman Hwui Li*, pp. 180f.
82. Ibid., pp. 186f.
83. Ibid., pp. 188ff.
84. J. Takakusu, *A Record of the Buddhist Religion as practised in India and the Malay Archipelago (A.D. 671–695)* (Oxford: Clarendon Press, 1896).
85. Ibid., p. 182.
86. Ibid., pp. 65, 154, 177f.
87. Smith, *The Oxford History of India*, pp. 170ff.
88. R. C. Majumdar, H. C. Raychaudhuri, and Kalikinkar Datta, *An Advanced History of India* (London: Macmillan, 2d ed. 1950), pp. 186f., 278f.
89. Legge, *A Record of Buddhistic Kingdoms*, p. 82.
90. Beal, *Records of the Western World*, 2, pp. 42, 91, 118, 121f.
91. S. Dutt, "How India dealt with Buddhism," in IAC 18 (1969), p. 5.
92. Vincent A. Smith, *Akbar, The Great Mughal, 1542–1605* (Oxford: Clarendon Press, 2d ed. 1902, impression of 1927), pp. 162, 166–168.
93. Dutt, "How India dealt with Buddhism," in IAC 18 (1969), pp. 8f.; Isma'īl Rāgī al Fārūqī and David E. Sopher, *Historical Atlas of the Religions of the World* (New York: Macmillan, 1974), p. 86 Map 11, pp. 69 (Venkatarama Raghavan), 103 (Rajendra P. Nanavati), 179 (G. P. Malalasekera).

7. LATER HINDUISM

1. A. C. Bhaktivedanta Swami Prabhupāda, *Bhagavad-gītā As It Is* (New York: Macmillan, 1972), pp. 478, 834. All quotations from the *Bhagavad Gita* are from this translation, and are by permission of The Bhaktivedanta Book Trust, Founder-Acarya: His Divine Grace A. C. Bhaktivedanta Swami Prabhupāda, 3764 Watseka Ave., Los Angeles, CA 90034, Robert Grant, President. For the *Bhagavad Gita* as an integral part of the entire *Mahabharata*, and for a date for the whole work in the 5th or 4th century BCE, see G. A. Feuerstein, *Introduction to the Bhagavad-Gītā, Its Philosophy and Cultural Setting* (London: Rider, 1974), pp. 37f.
2. Bhaktivedanta, *Bhagavad-gītā As It Is*, pp. 317–324.
3. For the latter interpretation see A. L. Herman, *The Bhagavad Gītā* (Springfield, Illinois: Charles C. Thomas, 1973), p. 134 n. 85.
4. R. Shamasastry, *Kauṭilya's Arthaśāstra* (Mysore: Wesleyan Mission Press, 2d ed. 1923).
5. Richard F. Burton, *The Kama Sutra of Vatsyayana* (New York: E. P. Dutton, 1962); S. C. Upadhyaya, *Kama Sutra* (Bombay: D. B. Taraporevala Sons, 1963).
6. G. Bühler, *The Laws of Manu* (SBE 25); Kewal Motwani, *Manu Dharma Śāstra, A Sociological and Historical Study* (Madras: Ganesh and Co., 1958).

7. Pandurang Vaman Kane, *History of Dharmaśāstra (Ancient and Mediaeval Religious and Civil Law)* (Poona: Bhandarkar Oriental Research Institute, 5 vols., 2d ed. 1968).
8. Bhaktivedanta, *Bhagavad-gītā As It Is,* pp. 301, 323.
9. S. Radhakrishnan, *Indian Philosophy* (London: George Allen and Unwin, 2 vols., rev. ed. 1929–31), 1, pp. 277–285; Sarvepalli Radhakrishnan and Charles A. Moore, *A Source Book in Indian Philosophy* (Princeton: Princeton University Press, 1957), pp. 227–249.
10. Arthur Berriedale Keith, *The Sāṁkhya System, A History of the Sāṁkhya Philosophy* (Calcutta: Association Press, 2d ed. 1924); Jajneswar Ghosh, *Sāṁkhya and Modern Thought* (Calcutta: The Book Company, 1930).
11. Charles Johnston, *The Yoga Sutras of Patanjali* (1912, rev. ed. London: Watkins, 1974, 2d impression 1975); James Haughton Woods, *The Yoga-System of Patanjali* (HOS 17) (Cambridge: Harvard University Press, 1914); Surendranath Dasgupta, *Yoga Philosophy in Relation to Other Systems of Indian Thought* (Calcutta: University of Calcutta Press, 1930); J. R. Ballantyne and Govind Sastri Deva, *Yoga-Sutra of Patanjali* (Varanasi: Indological Book House, 2d ed. 1952, reprint 1971); Mircea Eliade, *Patanjali and Yoga* (New York: Funk and Wagnalls, 1969); Harvey Day, *Yoga, Illustrated Dictionary* (London: Kaye and Ward, 1971); M. R. Desai, *The Yoga-Sūtras of Patanjali* (Kolhapur: Prin. Desai Publication Trust, 1972); G. A. Feuerstein, *The Essence of Yoga* (London: Rider, 1974).
12. Nandalal Sinha, *The Vaiśeṣika Sutras of Kaṇâda* (Allahabad: The Panini Office, 2d ed. 1923).
13. Arthur Berriedale Keith, *Indian Logic and Atomism, An Exposition of the Nyāya and Vaiçesika Systems* (Oxford: Clarendon Press, 1921); Ganganatha Jha, *Gautama's Nyāyasūtras, with Vātsyāyana-Bhāṣya* (Poona: Oriental Book Agency, 1939).
14. Arthur Berriedale Keith, *The Karma-Mīmāṁsā* (Calcutta: Association Press, 1921); Mohan Lal Sandal, *The Mimâmsâ Sûtras of Jaimini* (Allahabad: The Panini Office, 1923–25).
15. George Thibaut, *The Vedânta-Sûtras with the Commentary by Śaṅkarâkârya* (SBE 34, 38); Paul Deussen, *The System of the Vedânta according to Bâdarâyana's Brahma-sûtras and Çañkara's Commentary thereon* (Chicago: The Open Court Publishing Co., 1912); Sarvepalli Radhakrishnan, *The Brahma Sūtra, The Philosophy of Spiritual Life* (New York: Harper, 1960); Ernest Wood, *Vedanta Dictionary* (New York: Philosophical Library, 1964).
16. M. K. Venkatarama Iyer, *Advaita Vedānta according to Saṁkara* (London: Asia Publishing House, 1964).
17. Swami Gambhirananda, *Brahma-Sūtra-Bhāṣya of Śrī Śaṅkarācārya* (Calcutta: Advaita Ashrama, 1965), p. 22; V. H. Date *Vedānta Explained, The Śaṁkara's Commentary on Brahma-sutra* (Bombay: Booksellers' Publishing Co., 2 vols., 1954), 1, p. 21.
18. T. M. P. Mahadevan, *The Hymns of Śankara* (Madras: Ganesh and Co., 1970).
19. George Thibaut, *The Vedânta-Sûtras with the Commentary of Râmânuga,* 3 (SBE 48), p. 286.
20. Helmuth von Glasenapp, *Madhva's Philosophie des Vishnu-Glaubens* (Bonn: K. Schroeder Verlag, 1923); Suzanne Siauve, *Les hiérarchies spirituelles selon l'Anuvyākhyāna de Madhva* (Pondicherry: Institut Français d'Indologie, Publications No. 43, 1971).
21. E. Washburn Hopkins, *Epic Mythology* (Grundriss der indo-arischen Philologie und Altertumskunde 3:1, B) (Strassburg: Karl J. Trübner, 1915), pp. 189–231; Alain Daniélou, *Hindu Polytheism* (New York: Pantheon Books [Bollingen Series 73], 1964), pp. 147ff.
22. H. H. Wilson, *The Vishṇu Purāṇa* (Calcutta: Punthi Pustak, 1961), p. 129.
23. Bühler, *The Laws of Manu* (SBE 25), pp. 2–14.
24. Wilson, *The Vishṇu Purāṇa,* pp. 42, 175.
25. J. A. B. van Buitenen, *The Mahābhārata* (1973ff.), 2, p. 608. This quotation and that in n. 27 immediately below are by permission of The University of Chicago Press, copyright by The University of Chicago.
26. Wilson, *The Vishṇu Purāṇa,* pp. 6f.
27. van Buitenen, *The Mahābhārata,* 2, p. 611.
28. Julius Eggeling, *The Śatapatha Brâhmana* (5 vols., SBE 12, 26, 41, 43, 44), SBE 26, p. 426; Pratap Chandra Roy, *The Mahabharata* (Calcutta: Datta Bose, new ed., many vols., no date), 10, pp. 330–351; cf. Swami Chinmayananda, *Thousand Ways to the Transcendental Vishnu Sahasranaama* (Madras: Chinmaya Publication Trust, 2d ed. 1969).
29. F. Max Müller, *The Upanishads* (SBE 15), pp. 244–246; Augustine G. Aranjaniyil, *The Absolute of the Upanishads Personal or Impersonal?* (Bangalore: Dharmaram Publications, 1975), pp. 74ff.
30. *The Śiva-Purāṇa,* translated by a Board of Scholars (Delhi: Motilal Banarsidass, 4 vols., 1970), 3, pp. 1072f.
31. Ibid., 3, pp. 1397–1413.

32. Ibid., 4, p. 2042.
33. Ibid., 3, pp. 1101f.
34. Ibid., 3, pp. 1249, 1252.
35. Ibid., 3, pp. 1253–1258.
36. *Ancient Indian Tradition and Mythology,* translated by a Board of Scholars, 5–6, *The Liṅga-Purāṇa* (Delhi: Motilal Banarsidass, 2 vols., 1973).
37. *Ancient Indian Tradition and Mythology,* translated by a Board of Scholars, 7–9, *The Bhāgavata-Purāṇa* (Delhi: Motilal Banarsidass, 3 vols., 1976), 7, pp. 24–29; A. C. Bhaktivedanta Swami Prabhupāda, *Śrīmad Bhâgavatam* (Los Angeles: Bhaktivedanta Book Trust, 1972ff.), 1:1, pp. 151–173.
38. *The Matsya Puranam,* translated by a Taluqdar of Oudh (SBH) (Allahabad: Indian Press, 2 vols., 1916), 1, pp. 3ff.; Vasudeva S. Agrawala, *Matsya Purāṇa—A Study* (Varanasi: All-India Kashiraj Trust, 1963), pp. 3ff.
39. F. Eden Pargiter, *The Mārkaṇḍeya Purāṇa* (BI) (Calcutta: Asiatic Society, 1904), pp. 348–387.
40. Wilson, *The Vishṇu Purāṇa,* pp. 26–29.
41. Ibid., pp. 105–120.
42. Anand Swarup Gupta, ed., *The Vāmana Purāṇa* (Varanasi: All India Kashiraj Trust, 1968), pp. 131–162, 494–534; Vasudeva S. Agrawala, *Vāmana Purāṇa—A Study (Varanasi: Prithivi Prakashan, 1964), pp. 49–62, 175–182.*
43. van Buitenen, *The Mahābhārata,* 2, pp. 445–447; Wilson, *The Vishṇu Purāṇa,* pp. 320–323.
44. Wilson, *The Vishṇu Purāṇa,* pp. 394–469.
45. Bhaktivedanta, *Bhagavad-gītā As It Is,* pp. 220–228.
46. Wilson, *The Vishṇu Purāṇa,* pp. 479f.
47. *The Matsya Puranam,* translated by a Taluqdar of Oudh, 1, p. 138.
48. Bhaktivedanta, *Śrīmad Bhāgavatam,* 1:1, p. 168.
49. Ibid., 1:1, p. 168.
50. van Buitenen, *The Mahābhārata,* 2, pp. 567–664.
51. Müller, *The Upanishads* (SBE 15), pp. 85f.
52. Bühler, *The Laws of Manu* (SBE 25), pp. 1–14.
53. Wilson, *The Vishnu Purāṇa,* pp. 45–47.
54. Swami Nikhilananda, *The Upanishads* (New York: Harper, 4 vols., 1949–59), 1, pp. 243f.
55. Ernest A. Payne, *The Śāktas* (Calcutta: Y.M.C.A. Publishing House, 1933); John Woodroffe, *Śakti and Śākta* (Madras: Ganesh and Co., 6th ed. 1965).
56. van Buitenen, *The Mahābhārata,* 2, pp. 52, 652.
57. Wilson, *The Vishṇu Purāṇa,* pp. 220, 230 n. 9.
58. Ibid., pp. 52, 65–69.
59. Agrawala, *Vāmana Purāṇa—A Study,* p. 61.
60. Wilson, *The Vishnu Purāṇa,* pp. 26f.
61. Ibid., pp. 52–60; *The Śiva-Purāṇa,* translated by a Board of Scholars, 1, pp. 274ff.; 2, pp. 475ff.
62. *The Śiva-Purāṇa,* translated by a Board of Scholars, 2, p. 500.
63. Kiyoshi Yoroi, *Gaṇeśagītā, A Study, Translation with Notes, and a Condensed Rendering of the Commentary of Nīlakaṇṭha* (The Hague: Mouton, 1968).
64. *The Śiva-Purāṇa,* translated by a Board of Scholars, 2, p. 504.
65. Ibid., 4, p. 1665.
66. Pratapa Chandra Rāy, *The Mahabharata of Krishna-Dwaipayana Vyasa* (Calcutta: Bharata Press, 10 vols., 1889–96), 4, p. 52.
67. Pargiter, *The Mārkaṇḍeya Purāṇa,* pp. 473–481.
68. Ibid., p. 499.
69. *The Śiva-Purāṇa,* translated by a Board of Scholars, 1, p. 426.
70. Rāy, *The Mahabharata,* 3, pp. 11f.
71. *The Matsya Puranam,* translated by a Taluqdar of Oudh, 2, pp. 154–157.
72. Muriel M. Underhill, *The Hindu Religious Year* (Calcutta: Association Press, 1921).
73. Franklin Edgerton, *The Panchatantra Reconstructed* (AOS 2–3) (New Haven: American Oriental Society, 2 vols., 1924), 2, pp. 269–405; Arthur W. Ryder, *The Panchatantra* (Chicago: University of Chicago Press, 1925).
74. Herbert V. Guenther, *Yuganaddha, The Tantric View of Life* (CSS Studies 3) (Banaras: Chowkhamba Sanskrit Series Office, 1952); John Woodroffe, *Introduction to Tantra Śāstra* (Madras: Ganesh and Co., 4th ed. 1963); Chintaharan Chakravarti, *Tantras, Studies on Their Religion and*

Literature (Calcutta: Punthi Pustak, 1963); Agehananda Bharati, *The Tantric Tradition* (London: Rider, 1965); Woodroffe, *Śakti and Śākta;* Ajit Mookerjee and Madhu Khanna, *The Tantric Way* (Boston: New York Graphic Society, 1977).

75. Rai Bahadur Srisa Chandra Vasu, *The Śiva Samhita* (SBH 15, 1) (New York: AMS Press, 1974, reprinted from edition of 1914, Allahabad: Indian Press).

76. Ibid., p. 8.

77. Arthur Avalon, *The Serpent Power, being the Shat-Chakra-Nirūpana and Padukā-Panchaka, Two Works on Tantrik Yoga, translated from the Sanskrit, with Introduction and Commentary* (London: Luzac, 1919), Text pp. 1–163.

78. Ibid., Text p. 144; cf. Gopi Krishna, *Kundalini, The Evolutionary Energy in Man* (New Delhi and Zurich: Ramadhar and Hopman, 1967); Sri Swami Sivananda, *Kundalini Yoga* (Sivanandanagar: Divine Life Society, 6th ed. 1971).

79. Arthur Avalon and M. P. Pandit, *Kulārṇava Tantra* (Madras: Ganesh and Co., 1965), pp. 5, 17f.

80. Ibid., p. 52.

81. Ibid., p. 69.

82. Arthur and Ellen Avalon, *Hymns to the Goddess* (Madras: Ganesh and Co., 2d ed. 1952), pp. 21ff.

83. Ibid., p. 26.

84. Ibid., p. 31.

85. Ibid., pp. 50f.

86. Manmatha Nath Dutt, *A Prose English Translation of Mahanirvana Tantram* (Calcutta: H. C. Dass, 1900).

87. Ibid., pp. 102–104; Avalon, *Hymns to the Goddess,* pp. 40–48.

88. Dutt, *A Prose English Translation of Mahanirvana Tantram,* p. 314.

8. MONUMENTS OF HINDUISM IN INDIA

1. Hermann Oldenberg, *Vedic Hymns,* 2 (SBE 46), p. 236.

2. George Thibaut, *The Vedânta-Sûtras with the Commentary of Râmânuga,* 3 (SBE 48), p. 240; Bharatan Kumarappa, *The Hindu Conception of the Deity as culminating in Rāmānuja* (London: Luzac, 1934), pp. 312f.

3. H. H. Wilson, *The Vishnu Purāṇa* (Calcutta: Punthi Pustak, 1961), pp. 268f.

4. M. R. Desai, *The Yoga-Sūtras of Patanjali* (Kolhapur: Prin. Desai Publication Trust, 1972), p. 130.

5. Giuseppe Tucci, *The Theory and Practice of the Maṇḍala* (London: Rider, 1961).

6. T. S. Rukmani, *A Critical Study of the Bhāgavata Purāna (with Special Reference to Bhakti)* (Varanasi: Chowkhamba Sanskrit Series Office, 1970), p. 250.

7. Ibid., pp. 19, 254; A. C. Bhaktivedanta Swami Prabhupāda, *Śrīmad-Bhāgavatam* (Los Angeles: Bhaktivedanta Book Trust, 1962ff.), 2:1, pp. 76f.

8. For the symbolism and iconography of Hinduism, Jainism, and Buddhism see Willibald Kirfel, *Symbolik des Hinduismus und des Jinismus,* and *Symbolik des Buddhismus* (in Ferdinand Herrmann, ed., Symbolik der Religionen, 4–5) (Stuttgart: Anton Hiersemann, 1959); R. S. Gupte, *Iconography of the Hindus, Buddhists, and Jains* (Bombay: D. B. Taraporevala Sons, 1972). For Hinduism see R. A. Gopinatha Rao, *Elements of Hindu Iconography* (Madras 1914, reprinted New York: Paragon Book Reprint Corp., 2 vols. 4 pts. 1968); Jitendra Nath Banerjea, *Development of Hindu Iconography* (Calcutta: University of Calcutta, 2d ed. 1956); *Symbolik des Hinduismus und des Jainismus,* Tafelband by Volker Moeller (Symbolik der Religionen, 19, 1974), Figs. 1–89; Sheo Bahadur Singh, *Brahmanical Icons in Northern India* (New Delhi: Sagar Publications, 1977).

9. Alain Daniélou, *Hindu Polytheism* (New York: Pantheon Books, Bollingen Series LXXIII, 1964), p. 364.

10. A. C. Bhaktivedanta Swami Prabhupāda, *Bhagavad-gītā As It Is* (New York: Macmillan, 1972), pp. 393, 395.

11. S. Radhakrishnan, *The Brahma Sutra, The Philosophy of Spiritual Life* (London: George Allen and Unwin, 1960), p. 174.

12. George Thibaut, *The Vedânta-Sûtras with the Commentary by Saṅkarâkârya,* 1 (SBE 34), p. 92.

13. J. A. B. van Buitenen, *The Mahābhārata* (Chicago: University of Chicago Press, 1975ff.), 2, pp. 372ff.

14. G. Bühler, *The Laws of Manu* (SBE 25), pp. 135, 149, 153, 269.

15. Hermann Oldenberg, *The Grihya-Sûtras,* 1 (SBE 29), pp. 132, 348, 361.
16. Mulk Raj Anand, *The Hindu View of Art* (Bombay: Asia Publishing House, 1957), p. 71. For the *Brihat-samhita* see Panditabhushana V. Subrahmanya Sastri, *Varahamihira's Brihat Samhita* (Bangalore City: V. B. Soobbiah, 2 vols. 1947), 1, pp. 491–501, 503–518. For the *Manasara* see Prasanna Kumar Acharya, *A Summary of the Mānasāra* (Leiden: E. J. Brill, 1918), pp. 10–28, 49–72; *Architecture of Mānasāra* (Hindu Architecture, 4) (London: Oxford University Press, 1934), pp. 99–372, 516–647; and *Architecture of Mānasāra, Illustrations of Architectural and Sculptural Objects* (Hindu Architecture, 5) (London: Oxford University Press, 1934).
17. van Buitenen, *The Mahābhārata,* 2, pp. 300, 326, 707.
18. Ibid., 2, pp. 379, 390.
19. J. Ph. Vogel, *Archaeological Museum at Mathura* (1910, reprinted Delhi: Indological Book House, 1971), p. 83, C1; Ananda K. Coomaraswamy, *Yakṣas* I and II (Washington: Smithsonian Institution Publications 2926 and 3059, 1928 and 1931); Ananda K. Coomaraswamy, *History of Indian and Indonesian Art* (New York: Dover Publications, 1965, republication of the work first published by Karl W. Hiersemann in 1927), pp. 16f.
20. Moti Chandra, *Stone Sculpture in the Prince of Wales Museum* (Bombay: The Board of Trustees of the Prince of Wales Museum, 1974), Pl. 126; Stella Kramrisch, *The Art of India* (London: Phaidon Press, 1955), Pl. 63. For the Huchchappayya Gudi temple at Aihole see Niharranjan Ray, *The Art and Architecture of Aihole* (Bombay: D. B. Taraporevala Sons, 1967), pp. 27f.
21. Kalpana S. Desai, *Iconography of Viṣṇu* (New Delhi: Abhinav Publications, 1973).
22. Vogel, *Archaeological Museum at Mathura,* pp. 102f., D37; Desai, *Iconography of Viṣṇu,* pp. 58f. For the *makara* see Betty Dashew Robins and Robert F. Bussabarger, "The Makara, A Mythical Monster from India," in *Archaeology* 23 (1970), pp. 38–43; Steven Darian, "The Other Face of the Makara," in AA 38 (1976), pp. 29–34.
23. Chandra, *Stone Sculpture in the Prince of Wales Museum,* Pl. 127; Kramrisch, *The Art of India,* Pl. 62; Desai, *Iconography of Viṣṇu,* pp. 26f.
24. Chandra, *Stone Sculpture in the Prince of Wales Museum,* Pl. 92.
25. Ibid., Pl. 91; Desai, *Iconography of Viṣṇu,* pp. 37–43.
26. Rao, *Elements of Hindu Iconography,* 2:1, pp. 113f., 236–239, 249; Singh, *Brahmanical Icons in Northern India,* p. 23; Ananda K. Comaraswamy, *The Dance of Shiva* (New Delhi: Sagar Publications, rev. ed. 1968), pp. 68f.
27. cf. Rao, *Elements of Hindu Iconography,* 2:1, p. 252 and Pl. LVII; C. Sivaramamurti, *Nataraja in Art, Thought and Literature* (New Delhi: National Museum, 1974).
28. Chandra, *Stone Sculpture in the Prince of Wales Museum,* Pl. 125.
29. Ibid., Pl. 144.
30. Rao, *Elements of Hindu Iconography,* 1:2, p. 360 and Pl. CVIII, Fig. 1.
31. Ibid., 1:2, pp. 373f.
32. C. Sivaramamurti, *Masterpieces of Indian Sculpture in the National Museum* (New Delhi: National Museum, 1971), Pl. Va.
33. Rao, *Elements of Hindu Iconography,* 1:2, pp. 377f.; Gupte, *Iconography of the Hindus, Buddhists, and Jains,* pp. 54f.
34. Chandra, *Stone Sculpture in the Prince of Wales Museum,* Pls. 133, 156.
35. Sivaramamurti, *Masterpieces of Indian Sculpture in the National Museum,* Pl. XXI. For another example of the Vidyadharas see Pl. XII.
36. Surinder Mohan Bhardwaj, *Hindu Places of Pilgrimage in India: A Study in Cultual Geography* (Berkeley: University of California Press, 1973).
37. For Indian temples see Prasanna Kumar Acharya, *A Dictionary of Hindu Architecture* (Hindu Architecture, 1) (London: Oxford University Press, 1927); Stella Kramrisch, *The Hindu Temple* (Calcutta: University of Calcutta Press, 2 vols. 1946); P. R. Srinivasan, "Types of South Indian Vimānas," in AA 21 (1958), pp. 254–258; Louis-Frédéric, *Indian Temples and Sculptures* (London: Thames and Hudson, 1959); Heinrich Zimmer, *The Art of Indian Asia* (Bollingen Series XXXIX) (Princeton: Princeton University Press, 2 vols., 2d ed. 1960, 3d printing with revisions 1968); Krishna Deva, *Temples of North India* (New Delhi: National Book Trust, 1969); K. R. Srinivasan, *Temples of South India* (New Delhi: National Book Trust, 1971); K. V. Soundara Rajan, *Indian Temple Styles* (New Delhi: Munshiram Mancharla, 1972); Rustam J. Mehta, *Masterpieces of Indian Temples* (Bombay: Taraporevala, 1974); S. Padmanabhan, *Temples of South India* (Nagercoil: Kumaran Pathippagam, 1977); Michael W. Meister, *Encyclopaedia of Indian Temple Architecture* (American Institute of Indian Studies) (Philadelphia: University of Pennsylvania Press, 1983ff.).
38. Kramrisch, *The Hindu Temple,* 1, pp. 161–176.
39. Acharya, *A Dictionary of Hindu Architecture,* pp. 299–316.
40. James C. Harle, *Temple Gateways in South India, The Architecture and Iconography of the Cidambaram Gopuras* (Oxford: Bruno Cassirer, 1963).

41. James Fergusson and James Burgess, *The Cave Temples of India* (London: W. H. Allen, 1880; Delhi: Oriental Books Reprint Corp., 1969).
42. For literary descriptions and other examples of the same scene see Rao, *Elements of Hindu Iconography,* 1:1, pp. 128–145.
43. K. R. Srinivasan, *Cave Temples of the Pallavas* (New Delhi: Archaeological Survey of India, 1962); and *Temples of South India,* pp. 46–50; C. Sivaramamurti, *Mahābalipuram* (New Delhi: Director General, Archaeological Survey of India, 1972).
44. James Burgess, *Report on the Elura Cave Temples and the Brahmanical and Jaina Caves in Western India* (ASWI 5) (London: Trübner, 1883), pp. 23–42; Ramesh Shankar Gupte and B. D. Mahajan, *Ajanta, Ellora and Aurangabad Caves* (Bombay: D. B. Taraporevala Sons, 1962), pp. 107ff.
45. Zimmer, *The Art of Indian Asia,* 2, Pl. 203.
46. Burgess, *Report on the Elura Cave Temples . . . ,* Pl. XXXIV, Fig. 1.
47. Zimmer, *The Art of Indian Asia,* 2, Pl. 237.
48. Ibid., 2, Pl. 236.
49. Hirananda Sastri, *A Guide to Elephanta* (Delhi: Manager of Publications, 1934).
50. Acharya, *A Dictionary of Hindu Architecture,* pp. 521f.
51. Srinivasan, *Temples of South India,* pp. 97–105.
52. Ibid., pp. 107f.
53. Zimmer, *The Art of Indian Asia,* 2, Pls. 210–212.
54. Srinivasan, *Temples of South India,* pp. 112f.
55. Mehta, *Masterpieces of Indian Temples,* Pl. 81.
56. Srinivasan, *Temples of South India,* pp. 168, 171.
57. Rustam J. Mehta, *Masterpieces of Indian Sculpture* (Bombay: D. B. Taraporevala Sons, 1968), Pls. 73–75.
58. Srinivasan, *Temples of South India,* p. 157.
59. For similar figures of Mahishamardini at Halebid see Gupte, *Iconography of the Hindus, Buddhists, and Jains,* Pls. 107–108. For all three temples and their sculptors see Rajeshwari Ghose, "Three Hoysala Temples," in OR 12, 10, Oct. 1981, pp. 42–49.
60. Mehta, *Masterpieces of Indian Sculpture,* Pl. 77.
61. Deva, *Temples of North India,* pp. 59f.; O. C. Gangoly, *The Art of the Chandelas* (ISS 1) (Calcutta: Rupa, 1957).
62. Urmila Agarwal, *Khajurāho Sculptures and Their Significance* (Delhi: S. Chand, 1964), p. 9.
63. Kanwar Lal, *Immortal Khajuraho* (Delhi: Asia Press, 1965); and *Apsaras of Khajuraho* (Delhi: Asia Press, 1966).
64. Agarwal, *Khajurāho Sculptures and Their Significance,* pp. 111ff.; Vidya Prakash, *Khajuraho, A Study in the Cultural Conditions of Chandella Society* (Bombay: D. B. Taraporevala Sons, 1967).
65. Y. Krishnan, "The Erotic Sculptures of India," in AA 34 (1972), pp. 331–343.
66. Francis Leeson, *Kama Shilpa* (Bombay: D. B. Taraporevala Sons, 1962); Benjamin Rowland, *The Art and Architecture of India, Buddhist, Hindu, Jain* (Baltimore: Penguin Books, 3d ed. reprinted 1971), p. 174.
67. Kramrisch, *The Hindu Temple,* 2, pp. 346f.
68. Mulk Râj Anand, *Kama Kala, Some Notes on the Philosophical Basis of Hindu Erotic Sculpture* (Geneva: Nagel Publishers, 1960); Alain Daniélou, *l'Erotisme Divinisé* (Paris: Editions Buchet/Chastel, 1962); Kanwar Lal, *The Cult of Desire* (Delhi: Asia Press, 1966); Ajit Mookerjee, *Tantra Art, Its Philosophy and Physics* (New Delhi: Kumar Gallery, 1966); Nik Douglas, *Tantra Yoga* (New Delhi: Munshiram Manoharlal, 1971); Philip Rawson, *The Art of Tantra* (London: Thames and Hudson, 1973); Devangana Desai, *Erotic Sculpture of India* (New Delhi: Tata McGraw-Hill, 1975). For the Kaula cults at Khajuraho in the time of Kirtavarman see Anand, *Kama Kala,* pp. 33, 36.
69. Anand, *Kama Kala,* Pls. XXXI, XXXIII.
70. Douglas, *Tantra Yoga,* Pl. 16 following p. 93.
71. Anand, *Kama Kala,* Pls. VIII, IX; Leeson, *Kama Shilpa,* Pl. 67.
72. Zimmer, *The Art of Indian Asia,* 2 Pl. 318.
73. Leeson, *Kama Shilpa,* Pls. 29, 63; Douglas, *Tantra Yoga,* Pl. 20 following p. 93.

9. LITERATURE AND EARLY HISTORY OF JAINISM

1. Chimanlal J. Shah, *Jainism in North India 800 B.C.–A.D. 526* (London: Longmans, Green and Co., 1932); P. B. Desai, *Jainism in South India and Some Jaina Epigraphs* (JJG 6) (Sholapur: Gulabchand Hirāchānd Doshi, 1957); Walther Schubring, *The Doctrine of the Jainas described after the*

Old Sources (Delhi: Motilal Banarsidass, 1962); Helmuth von Glasenapp, *Der Jainismus, Eine indische Erlösungsreligion* (Hildesheim: Georg Olms, 1964); S. Gopalan, *Outlines of Jainism* (New York: Halsted Press, 1973); Asim Kumar Chatterjee, *A Comprehensive History of Jainism [up to 1000 A.D.]* (Calcutta: Firma KLM Private Limited, 1978).

2. Shah, op. cit., pp. 218–244; Schubring, op. cit., pp. 73–125; von Glasenapp, op. cit., pp. 90–134; Gopalan, op. cit., pp. 28–36; Chatterjee, op. cit., pp. 357–359; Maurice Winternitz, *A History of Indian Literature* (Calcutta: University of Calcutta, 3 vols., 1933–59), 2, *Buddhist Literature and Jaina Literature,* pp. 424–595; Hiralal Rasikdas Kapadia, *A History of the Canonical Literature of the Jainas* (Bombay: Gujarati Printing Press, 1941); Bimala Churn Law, *Some Jaina Canonical Sutras* (Bombay: Royal Asiatic Society, 1949).

3. For the proper names in Prakrit and for detailed references to persons in the canonical texts of the Śvetambara Jainas see Mohanlal Mehta, K. Rishabh Chandra, and Dalsukh Malvania, *Āgamic Index,* 1, *Prakrit Proper Names* (Ahmedabed: L. D. Institute of Indology, 2 parts paged consecutively, 1970–72).

4. Ibid., pp. 100, 846, 270, 435, 854, 281, 743, 515, 350.

5. Winternitz, *A History of Indian Literature,* 2, pp. 430f., 473f.; Kapadia, *A History of the Canonical Literature of the Jainas,* pp. 61–63, 111; von Glasenapp, *Der Jainismus,* pp. 84f.

6. Kapadia, *A History of the Canonical Literature of the Jainas,* pp. 72–75.

7. Hermann Jacobi, *Gaina Sûtras* (2 parts, SBE 22, 45), 1 (SBE 22), p. 1.

8. Ibid., 1 (SBE 22), pp. 189–210.

9. Ibid., 2 (SBE 45), pp. 235, 261.

10. Ibid., 2 (SBE 45), pp. 249, 261 n. 1.

11. Ibid., 2 (SBE 45), pp. 315–319, cf. p. 83 n. 2.

12. Ibid., 2 (SBE 45), pp. 261–268, 271–278.

13. Ibid., 2 (SBE 45), pp. 279–286.

14. Jozef Deleu, *Viyāhapannatti (Bhagavaī), The Fifth Anga of the Jaina Canon* (RGFLW 151) (Brugge: "De Tempel," 1970), pp. 117, 162, 289 (Parśva); 163f. (Jamali); 214–220 (Gośala); K. C. Lalwani, *Sudharma Svāmī's Bhagavatī Sūtra* (Calcutta: Jain Bhawan, 1973ff.), 2 (1974), pp. 228ff. (Parśva).

15. N. A. Gore, *The Uvāsagadasāo, The Seventh Anga of the Jain Canon* (POS 87) (Poona: Oriental Book Agency, 1953), p. 68.

16. Ibid., pp. 118–134.

17. L. D. Barnett, *The Antagada-dasāo and Anuttarovavāiya-dassāo* (OTF New Series, 17) (London: Royal Asiatic Society, 1907), pp. 1–61.

18. Banarsi Das Jain, *Ardha-Māgadhi Reader* (Lahore: University of the Panjab, 1923), pp. 80–93.

19. Schubring, *Die Jainas,* pp. 29f.

20. J. Stevenson, *The Kalpa Sútra and Nava Tatva* (1848, reprint Varanasi: Bharat-Bharati, 1972), pp. 15f., 95f.

21. Jacobi, *Gaina Sûtras,* 2 (SBE 45), pp. 119–129.

22. Desai, *Jainism in South India and Some Jaina Epigraphs,* pp. 152–156, 340; A. Chakravartinayanar, *The Building of the Cosmos or Pañchâstikâyasâra (The Five Cosmic Constituents) by Svami Sri Kundakundacharya* (reprint of vol. 8 of SBJ and in the series BJ, New York: AMS Press, 1974); Uggar Sain, *Niyamsara (The Perfect Law) by Shri Kunda Kunda Āchārya* (reprint of vol. 9 of SBJ and in the series BJ, New York: AMS Press, 1974).

23. J. L. Jaini, *Tattvarthadhigama Sutra (A Treatise on the Essential Principles of Jainism) by Sri Umasvami Acharya* (reprint of vol. 2 of SBJ and in the series BJ, New York: AMS Press, 1974), p. 1.

24. Rai Bahadur J. L. Jaini, *Gommatsara Jiva-Kanda (The Soul) by Shri Nemichandra Siddhanta Chakravarti* (reprint of vol. 5 of SBJ and in the series BJ, New York: AMS Press, 1974).

25. B. A. Chaugule and N. V. Vaidya, *Samarāichch-Kahā (Chapter VI) of Haribhadra-Sūri* (Belgaum: Belgaum Samāchār Press, 1936), p. 64.

26. Helen M. Johnson, *Triṣaṣṭiśalākāpuruṣacaritra* (GOS 51, 77, 108, 125, 139, 140) (Baroda: Oriental Institute, 6 vols., 1931–37).

27. Ibid., 1 (GOS 51), pp. 380ff.; 2 (GOS 77), pp. 105ff.

28. Jacobi, *Gaina Sûtras,* 2 (SBE 45), p. 212.

29. Johnson, *Triṣaṣṭiśalākāpuruṣacaritra,* 1 (GOS 51), p. 401; 2 (GOS 77), p. 127; and 1 (GOS 51), p. 103 n. 140 for the definition of a *rajju;* p. 380 for the universe in the shape of a man.

30. Ibid., 1 (GOS 51), p. 93.

31. Ibid., 1 (GOS 51), pp. 93f., and for the measures of time see p. 29 n. 51, p. 71 n. 97, p. 84 n. 125; Damodar Shastri, "Jain Cosmogony," in Harish Chandra Das, Chillaranjan Das, and Shri Satya Ranjan Pal, eds., *Buddhism and Jainism* (Cuttack: Institute of Oriental and Orissan Studies, 1976), pp. 204–216.

32. Johnson, *Triṣaṣṭiśalākāpuruṣacaritra*, 1 (GOS 51), pp. 100ff., 347–349, et passim; Jagmanderlal Jaini, *Outlines of Jainism* (Cambridge: University Press, 1916), table facing p. 6; Willibald Kirfel, *Symbolik des Hinduismus und des Jinismus* (in Ferdinand Herrmann, ed., Symbolik der Religionen, 4) (Stuttgart: Anton Hiersemann, 1959), pp. 142f.; R. S. Gupte, *Iconography of the Hindus, Buddhists, and Jains* (Bombay: D. B. Taraporevala Sons, 1972), pp. 177f.; B. C. Bhattacharya, *The Jaina Iconography* (Delhi: Motilal Banarsidass, 2d ed. 1974), pp. 26ff.; Jyotindra Jain and Eberhard Fischer, *Jaina Iconography* (IR XIII, 12–13) (Leiden: E. J. Brill, 2 vols., 1978), 1, Pl. XLVII. For detailed references to the twenty-four individual *tirthankaras* see Mehta, Chandra, and Malvania, *Āgamic Index*, 1, *Prakrit Proper Names*. For convenience in consultation of this work the twenty-four *tirthankaras* are here indicated by number together with the relevant pages in the *Āgamic Index:* No. 1, pp. 130f.; No. 2, pp. 25f.; No. 3, p. 742; No. 4, p. 53; No. 5, p. 830; No. 6, p. 416; No. 7, pp. 820f.; No. 8, pp. 248f.; No. 9, p. 469; No. 10, pp. 799f.; No. 11, p. 854; No. 12, pp. 694f.; No. 13, p. 709; No. 14, p. 33; No. 15, p. 398; No. 16, pp. 739f.; No. 17, pp. 185f.; No. 18, pp. 58f.; No. 19, pp. 554f.; No. 20, p. 605; No. 21, p. 310; No. 22, pp. 61f.; No. 23, pp. 452f.; No. 24. pp. 574–584.

33. Jacobi, *Gaina Sûtras*, 1 (SBE 22), pp. 281–285; Johnson, *Triṣaṣṭiśalākāpuruṣacaritra*, 1 (GOS 51), pp. 100ff.; Champat Rai Jain, *Riṣabha Deva, The Founder of Jainism* (Allahabad: Indian Press, 1929).

34. Johnson, *Triṣaṣṭiśalākāpuruṣacaritra*, 1 (GOS 51), p. 155.

35. Ibid., 1 (GOS 51), pp. 324–326; C. H. Tawney, *The Kathákoça* (OTF New Series, 2) (London: Royal Asiatic Society, 1895), pp. 192–195.

36. Jacobi, *Gaina Sûtras*, 1 (SBE 22), pp. 276–279; Johnson, *Triṣaṣṭiśalākāpuruṣacaritra*, 5 (GOS 139), pp. 1–314.

37. Johnson, *Triṣaṣṭiśalākāpuruṣacaritra*, 5 (GOS 139), pp. 37–247.

38. Ibid., 5 (GOS 139), p. 166.

39. Ibid., 5 (GOS 139), pp. 255ff.; Jacobi, *Gaina Sûtras*, 2 (SBE 45), pp. 112–119.

40. Karl Friedrich Geldner, *Der Rig-Veda* (HOS 33–36) (Cambridge: Harvard University Press, 4 vols., 1951–57), 3, p. 369.

41. Jacobi, *Gaina Sûtras*, 1 (SBE 22), pp. 271–275; Johnson, *Triṣaṣṭiśalākāpuruṣacaritra*, 5 (GOS 139), pp. 356–424.

42. Jacobi, *Gaina Sûtras*, 2 (SBE 45), pp. 119–129.

43. Ibid., 1 (SBE 22), pp. 1–213 *(Acarangasutra);* 2 (SBE 45), pp. 235–435 *(Sutrakritangasutra);* 1 (SBE 22), pp. 217–311 *(Kalpasutra);* Johnson, *Triṣaṣṭiśalākāpuruṣacaritra*, 6 (GOS 140); Bimala Churn Law, *Mahavira: His Life and Teachings* (London: Luzac, 1937); Hiralal Jain and A. N. Upadhye, *Mahāvīra, His Times and His Philosophy of Life* (JMG English Series, 2) (New Delhi: Bharatiya Jnanpith, 1974); Kailash Chand Jain, *Lord Mahāvīra and His Times* (Delhi: Motilal Banarsidass, 1974).

44. Johnson, *Triṣaṣṭiśalākāpuruṣacaritra*, 6 (GOS 140), pp. 1ff., 25ff.; Jacobi, *Gaina Sûtras*, 1 (SBE 22), pp. 231–238, 255f.

45. Jacobi, *Gaina Sûtras*, 2 (SBE 45), pp. 74f.

46. T. W. Rhys Davids, *Dialogues of the Buddha* (SBB) (London: Henry Frowde and Humphrey Milford, 3 vols., 1899–1921), 1, pp. 56, 74f.; Bhagchandra Jain Bhaskar, *Jainism in Buddhist Literature* (Nagpur: Alok Prakashan, 1972), pp. 25f.

47. Jacobi, *Gaina Sûtras*, 1 (SBE 22), p. 194.

48. Ibid., pp. 259f.

49. F. L. Woodward and E. M. Hare, *The Book of the Gradual Sayings (Anguttara-Nikāya) or More-Numbered Suttas* (PTS) (London: Luzac, 5 vols., 1951–55), 1, p. 200; Mrs. Rhys Davids and F. L. Woodward, *The Book of the Kindred Sayings (Sanyutta Nikāya) or Grouped Suttas* (PTS) (London: Luzac, 5 vols., 1950–56), 4, p. 280.

50. Jacobi, *Gaina Sûtras*, 1 (SBE 22), pp. 79–87.

51. Jogendra Chandra Sikdar, *Studies in the Bhagawatīsūtra* (PJIRP 1) (Muzaffarpur: Research Institute of Prakrit, Jainology and Ahimsa, 1964), pp. 427–438; Deleu, *Viyāhapannatti (Bhagavaī)*, pp. 214–220.

52. Jacobi, *Gaina Sûtras*, 1 (SBE 22), pp. 201f., 263f. On the Jaina understanding of omniscience see Mohan Lal Mehta, *Jaina Psychology* (Amritsar: Sohanlal Jaindharma Pracharak Samiti, 1955), pp. 109–112; Mohan Lal Mehta, *Jaina Philosophy* (PVS 16) (Varanasi: P. V. Research Institute, 1971), pp. 90f., 148–152.

53. Johnson, *Triṣaṣṭiśalākāpuruṣacaritra*, 6 (GOS 140), pp. 127f.

54. Jacobi, *Gaina Sûtras*, 1 (SBE 22), pp. 202ff.

55. Deleu, *Viyāhapannatti (Bhagavaī)*, p. 117; cf. Sikdar, *Studies in the Bhagawatīsūtra*, p. 466.

56. Jacobi, *Gaina Sûtras*, 2 (SBE 45), pp. 206–232.

57. Ibid., 2 (SBE 45), pp. 196–203.
58. Ibid., 2 (SBE 45), pp. 230f.
59. Lalwani, *Sudharma Svāmī's Bhagavatī Sūtra*, 2, pp. 153f.
60. Jacobi, *Gaina Sûtras*, 2 (SBE 45), p. 29.
61. Deleu, *Viyāhapannatti (Bhagavaī)*, p. 215; Sikdar, *Studies in the Bhagawatīsūtra*, p. 428.
62. Rhys Davids, *Dialogues of the Buddha*, 1, p. 71.
63. Jacobi, *Gaina Sûtras*, 2 (SBE 45), pp. xxvi, xxx.
64. Ibid., 2 (SBE 45), p. 411.
65. V. Fausböll, *The Sutta-Nipâta* (SBE 10, 2), p. 63.
66. Woodward, *The Book of the Gradual Sayings*, 1, p. 265.
67. Johnson, *Triṣaṣṭiśalākāpuruṣacaritra*, 6 (GOS 140), pp. 135f.
68. Jacobi, *Gaina Sûtras*, 1 (SBE 22), p. 267f.
69. von Glasenapp, *Der Jainismus*, pp. 202–205, 425f.; S. Gopalan, *Outlines of Jainism* (New York: Halsted Press, 1973), pp. 159–165, 194f.
70. Jacobi, *Gaina Sûtras*, 1 (SBE 22), pp. 264f.
71. See above in Chapter 4.
72. Jacobi, *Gaina Sûtras*, 1 (SBE 22), p. 266.
73. Margaret Sinclair Stevenson, *The Heart of Jainism* (published in 1915 by Oxford University Press, 1st Indian ed.). New Delhi: Munshiram Mancharlal, 1970), pp. 44, 260f.

10. MONUMENTS OF JAINISM IN INDIA

1. For the iconography of Jainism see Willibald Kirfel, *Symbolik des Hinduismus und des Jinismus* (in Ferdinand Herrmann, ed., Symbolik der Religionen, 4) (Stuttgart: Anton Hiersemann, 1959), pp. 119–156; and Tafelband by Volker Moeller (Symbolik der Religionen, 19, 1974), Figs. 90–121; R. S. Gupte, *Iconography of the Hindus, Buddhists, and Jains* (Bombay: D. B. Taraporevala Sons, 1972), pp. 174–185; B. C. Bhattacharya, *The Jaina Iconography* (Delhi: Motilal Banarsidass, 2d ed. 1974); Jyotindra Jain and Eberhard Fischer, *Jaina Iconography* (IR XIII, 12–13) (Leiden: E. J. Brill, 2 vols., 1978).
2. Helen M. Johnson, *Triṣaṣṭiśalākāpuruṣacaritra* (GOS 51, 77, 108, 125, 139, 140) (Baroda: Oriental Institute, 6 vols., 1931–37), 1 (GOS 51), pp. 183–187.
3. A. Ghosh, ed., *Jaina Art and Architecture, published on the Occasion of the 2500th Nirvana Anniversary of Tirthankara Mahavira* (New Delhi: Bharatiya Jnanpith, 3 vols., 1975), 1, pp. 49–68.
4. Vincent A. Smith, *The Jain Stûpa and Other Antiquities of Mathurâ* (ASI 20) (Allahabad: Government Press, 1901; Varanasi: Indological Book House, 2d ed. 1969), p. 21, Pl. XIV; Ghosh, ed., *Jaina Art and Architecture*, 3, p. 441.
5. Smith, *The Jain Stûpa and Other Antiquities of Mathurâ*, p. 15, Pl. VIII; Bhattacharya, *The Jaina Iconography*, Pl. II.
6. Smith, *The Jain Stûpa and Other Antiquities of Mathurâ*, p. 14, Pl. VII; Ananda K. Coomaraswamy, *History of Indian and Indonesian Art* (New York: Dover Publications, 1965, republication of the work first published by Karl W. Hiersemann in 1927), Fig. 71.
7. Smith, *The Jain Stûpa and Other Antiquities of Mathurâ*, p. 16, Pl. IX; Bhattacharya, *The Jaina Iconography*, Pl. III.
8. Smith, *The Jain Stûpa and Other Antiquities of Mathurâ*, p. 17, Pl. X.
9. Bhattacharya, *The Jaina Iconography*, p. 33.
10. Panditabhushana V. Subrahmanya Sastri, *Varahamihira's Brihat Samhita* (Bangalore City: V. B. Soobbiah, 2 vols., 1947), 1, p. 514.
11. Prasanna Kumar Acharya, *A Summary of the Mānasāra* (Leiden: E. J. Brill, 1918), p. 59; Prasanna Kumar Acharya, *Architecture of Mānasāra* (Hindu Architecture, 4) (London: Oxford University Press, 1934), pp. 562–564.
12. Johnson, *Triṣaṣṭiśalākāpuruṣacaritra*, 1 (GOS 51), pp. 133–137.
13. Ibid., 1 (GOS 51), p. 166.
14. For other *tirthankara* sculptures in the Khajuraho Museum see Ghosh, ed., *Jaina Art and Architecture*, 3, pp. 593f.
15. Johnson, *Triṣaṣṭiśalākāpuruṣacaritra*, 5 (GOS 139), pp. 248f.
16. J. Ph. Vogel, *Archaeological Museum at Mathura* (Varanasi: Indological Book House, 1971), pp. 81f., B77. For *ganadharas* holding *cauris* see Bhattacharya, *The Jaina Iconography*, p. 29.
17. Johnson, *Triṣaṣṭiśalākāpuruṣacaritra*, 5 (GOS 139), p. 381.
18. Ibid., 5 (GOS 139), pp. 391f., 394–397.

19. Ghosh, ed., *Jaina Art and Architecture*, 3, p. 544 and Pl. 321B (wrongly labeled as in the British Museum).
20. Johnson, *Triṣaṣṭiśalākāpuruṣacaritra*, 6 (GOS 140), pp. 34, 91.
21. Moti Chandra, *Stone Sculpture in the Prince of Wales Museum* (Bombay: Trustees of the Prince of Wales Museum of Western India, 1974), Pl. 151; Bhattacharya, *The Jaina Iconography*, p. 61; Ghosh, ed., *Jaina Art and Architecture*, 3, p. 594.
22. For the individual *yakshas* and *yakshinis* and other attendants of the several *tirthankaras* see Gupte, *Iconography of the Hindus, Buddhists, and Jains*, pp. 177–185.
23. Johnson, *Triṣaṣṭiśalākāpuruṣacaritra*, 1 (GOS 51), p. 211.
24. Ibid., 5 (GOS 139), p. 273.
25. Ibid., 5 (GOS 139), p. 403.
26. Chandra, *Stone Sculpture in the Prince of Wales Museum*, Pl. 155.
27. Bhattacharya, *The Jaina Iconography*, pp. 84f., 106f.
28. Johnson, *Triṣaṣṭiśalākāpuruṣacaritra*, 2 (GOS 77), p. 266.
29. Chandra, *Stone Sculpture in the Prince of Wales Museum*, Pl. 153.
30. Gupte, *Iconography of the Hindus, Buddhists, and Jains*, pp. 183–185; Bhattacharya, *The Jaina Iconography*, pp. 108–137; Jain and Fischer, *Jaina Iconography*, 2, pp. 22, 25–29.
31. Johnson, *Triṣaṣṭiśalākāpuruṣacaritra*, 1 (GOS 51), pp. 114ff., 139ff., 149, 163ff., 360ff.; 6 (GOS 140), pp. 25ff., 41f., 351f.
32. Rustam J. Mehta, *Masterpieces of Indian Sculpture* (Bombay: D. B. Taraporevala Sons, 1968), Pl. 78; C. Sivaramamurti, *Masterpieces of Indian Sculpture in the National Museum* (New Delhi: National Museum, 1971), Pl. XXXI.
33. Johnson, *Triṣaṣṭiśalākāpuruṣacaritra*, 6 (GOS 140), p. 26.
34. Ibid., 6 (GOS 140), p. 27.
35. Gupte, *Iconography of the Hindus, Buddhists, and Jains*, pp. 80f., 184.
36. Smith, *The Jain Stûpa and Other Antiquities of Mathurâ*, pp. 1, 8–11, Pls. I–V.
37. Ibid., p. 12, Pl. VI.
38. Ibid., pp. 12f.
39. Ibid., p. 22, Pl. XV.
40. Ibid., p. 19, Pl. XII.
41. Ibid., p. 61, Pl. CIII; Vogel, *Archaeological Museum at Mathura*, pp. 184f., Q2; Jain and Fischer, *Jaina Iconography*, 2, Pl. XIIc.
42. M. R. Kale, *The Mṛichchhakaṭika of Śûdraka* (Bombay: Booksellers' Publishing Co., new ed. 1962). See pp. 19–25 for the date of Śudraka; p. 27 and Act I, p. 39f. for the incident with Radanika. For the identification of the sculptural scene (our Figure 10.11) here accepted as correct see S. P. Gupta, "The Marriage of Gross and Divine," in OR 9, 2, Feb. 1978, p. 40. For other interpretations, here considered incorrect, see Francis Leeson, *Kama Shilpa* (Bombay: D. B. Taraporevala Sons, 1962), Pl. 30; Mehta, *Masterpieces of Indian Sculpture*, Pl. 11.
43. James Burgess, *Report on the Elura Cave Temples and the Brahmanical and Jaina Caves in Western India* (ASWA 5) (London: Trübner, 1883), pp. 43–50; Ramesh Shankar Gupte and B. D. Mahajan, *Ajanta, Ellora and Aurangabad Caves* (Bombay: D. B. Taraporevala Sons, 1962), pp. 218–224.
44. Gupte and Mahajan, *Ajanta, Ellora and Aurangabad Caves*, pp. 222, 271.
45. Heinrich Zimmer, *The Art of Indian Asia* (Bollingen Series XXXIX) (Princeton: Princeton University Press, 2 vols., 2d ed. 1960, 3d printing, with revisions, 1968), 1, pp. 132f., 2, Pls. 242–243.
46. Ghosh, ed., *Jaina Art and Architecture*, 2, pp. 280–83, Pls. 164–165.
47. Ibid., 2, pp. 279f., Pl. 163.
48. Urmila Agarwal, *Khajurāho Sculptures and Their Significance* (Delhi: S. Chand, 1964), p. 110, Fig. 82; Bhattacharya, *The Jaina Iconography*, pp. 82f., 103f.
49. Ghosh, ed., *Jaina Art and Architecture*, 2, pp. 288–292, Pls. 171–172.
50. Ibid., 2, pp. 277, 284–288, Pls. 166–170; 3, p. 444.
51. Mehta, *Masterpieces of Indian Sculpture*, Pl. 57.
52. Leeson, *Kama Shilpa*, Pl. 20.
53. Agarwal, *Khajurāho Sculptures and Their Significance*, pp. 128–164, Fig. 92.
54. Ibid., Fig. 93.
55. Ibid., Fig. 95.
56. Helmuth von Glasenapp, *Heilige Stätten Indiens, Die Wallfahrtsorte der Hindus, Jainas und Buddhisten, Ihre Legenden und Ihr Kulturs* (IKE) (München: Georg Müller, 1928), pp. 124–135; Sarabhai Manilal Nawab, *Jaina Tirthas in India and Their Architecture* (SJKSS 2) (Ahmedabad: Sarabhai M. Nawab, 1944).

57. Ghosh, ed., *Jaina Art and Architecture*, 2, pp. 214f., 219–222, Pls. 129B, 130B.
58. Ibid., 2, pp. 222–224, Pls. 131–132.
59. Ibid., 2, pp. 301f., 305, Pls. 183–188, 190–194; Klaus Fischer, *Caves and Temples of the Jains* (JAP 4) (Aliganj: World Jain Mission, 1956), pp. 13–15.
60. Jain and Fischer, *Jaina Iconography*, 2, p. 42, Pl. XLIIIa. For Śitala as the goddess of smallpox and her relationship to Jyeshtha in South India and to Hariti, see Jitendra Nath Banerjea, "Some Folk Goddesses of Ancient and Mediaeval India," in IHQ 14 (1938), pp. 104–107.
61. Fischer, *Caves and Temples of the Jainas*, p. 15; Ghosh, ed., *Jaina Art and Architecture*, 2, Pl. 201.
62. Jain and Fischer, *Jaina Iconography*, 2, p. 37, Pl. XXIIa.
63. Ghosh, ed., *Jaina Art and Architecture*, 2, Pl. 193.
64. Jain and Fischer, *Jaina Iconography*, 1, Pl. XLIVc.
65. For similar figures at Khajuraho see Devangana Desai, *Erotic Sculptures of India* (New Delhi: Tata McGraw-Hill, 1975), Figs. 66, 123.
66. Nawab, *Jaina Tirthas in India and Their Architecture*, Figs. 143–145.

11. EARLY HISTORY AND LITERATURE OF THERAVADA BUDDHISM

1. T. W. Rhys Davids, *Buddhist Suttas* (SBE 11), p. 112; T. W. and C. A. F. Rhys Davids, *Dialogues of the Buddha* (SBB) (London: Henry Frowde, 3 vols., 1899–1921), 2, p. 171.
2. Maurice Winternitz, *A History of Indian Literature* (Calcutta: University of Calcutta, 3 vols., 1933–59), 2, *Buddhist Literature and Jaina Literature*, pp. 1–423; Bimala Churn Law, *A History of Pāli Literature* (Varanasi: Bhartiya Publishing House, 2 vols., 1974); G. P. Malalasekera, *Dictionary of Pāli Proper Names* (ITS) (London: John Murray, 2 vols., 1937–38).
3. T. W. Rhys Davids and Hermann Oldenberg, *Vinaya Texts* (SBE 13, 17, 20), 2–3, *The Kullavagga*.
4. Bimala Churn Law, *The Chronicle of the Island of Ceylon or the Dipavamsa, A historical poem of the 4th Century A.D.* (The Ceylon Historical Journal, Vol. VII—July 1957 to April 1958—Nos. 1–4) (Maharagama: Saman Press, 1959).
5. Wilhelm Geiger, *Cūlavamsa being the more recent part of the Mahāvamsa* (Colombo: Ceylon Government Information Department, 2 vols., 1953), 1, p. 35.
6. Wilhelm Geiger, *The Mahāvaṃsa or the Great Chronicle of Ceylon* (Colombo: Ceylon Government Information Department, 1950).
7. Geiger, *Cūlavamsa*, 1, pp. 29, 48.
8. Ibid., 2, p. 155.
9. Ibid., 2, p. 263.
10. N. A. Jayawickrama, *The Inception of Discipline and the Vinaya Nidāna, Being a Translation and Edition of the Bāhiranidāna of Buddhaghosa's Samantapāsādikā, the Vinaya Commentary* (SBB) (London: Luzac, 1962).
11. Rhys Davids and Oldenberg, *Vinaya Texts*, 3 (SBE 20), pp. 370–385; Law, *The Dipavamsa*, pp. 152–155, 159f.; Geiger, *The Mahāvaṃsa*, pp. 14–18; Jayawickrama, *The Inception of Discipline*, pp. 3–27. For critical analysis of the records of the first three Councils see H. Kern, *Manual of Indian Buddhism* (EI-AR 3, 8) (Strassburg: Karl J. Trübner, 1896), pp. 101–112; André Bareau, "Les premiers conciles bouddhiques," in AMGBE 60 (1955).
12. Rhys Davids and Oldenberg, *Vinaya Texts*, 2 (SBE 17), pp. 140–142.
13. Rhys Davids, *Dialogues of the Buddha*, 2, p. 184; Rhys Davids and Oldenberg, *Vinaya Texts*, 3 (SBE 20), p. 371.
14. Rhys Davids and Oldenberg, *Vinaya Texts*, 3 (SBE 20), p. 372.
15. Geiger, *The Mahāvaṃsa*, p. 16.
16. F. L. Woodward and E. M. Hare, *The Book of the Gradual Sayings (Anguttara-Nikāya) or More-Numbered Suttas* (PTS) (London: Luzac, 5 vols., 1951–55), 1, pp. 19f.
17. Rhys Davids and Oldenberg, *Vinaya Texts*, 1 (SBE 13), p. xiii; 3 (SBE 20), p. 206.
18. Geiger, *The Mahāvaṃsa*, p. 17.
19. Jayawickrama, *The Inception of Discipline*, p. 11.
20. Rhys Davids and Oldenberg, *Vinaya Texts*, 3 (SBE 20), p. 378.
21. Law, *The Dipavamsa*, p. 160.
22. Geiger, *The Mahāvaṃsa*, p. 18.
23. Rhys Davids and Oldenberg, *Vinaya Texts*, 3 (SBE 20), pp. 386–414; Law, *The Dipavamsa*, pp. 157f., 161f.; Geiger, *The Mahāvaṃsa*, pp. 19–25; Jayawickrama, *The Inception of Discipline*, pp. 27–33.

24. Geiger, *The Mahāvaṃsa*, p. 19.
25. Rhys Davids and Oldenberg, *Vinaya Texts,* 3 (SBE 20), p. 386; cf. 1 (SBE 13), p. xxii; Law, *The Dipavamsa*, pp. 157, 161; Jayawickrama, *The Inception of Discipline*, p. 30.
26. Rhys Davids and Oldenberg, *Vinaya Texts,* 3 (SBE 20), pp. 389f.
27. Rhys Davids, *Buddhist Suttas* (SBE 11), pp. 196–200.
28. Rhys Davids and Oldenberg, *Vinaya Texts,* 3 (SBE 20), pp. 396f.
29. Ibid., p. 407.
30. Ibid., pp. 49–52.
31. Ibid., p. 413.
32. Geiger, *The Mahāvaṃsa*, p. 25; Law, *The Dipavamsa*, p. 162.
33. Law, *The Dipavamsa*, pp. 163f.
34. Geiger, *The Mahāvaṃsa*, pp. 26f.; for the sects see pp. 276–287, and Nalinaksha Dutt, *Buddhist Sects in India* (Delhi: Motilal Banarsidass, 2d ed. 1978).
35. Law, *The Dipavamsa*, pp. 183–185; Geiger, *The Mahāvaṃsa*, pp. 46–50; Jayawickrama, *The Inception of Discipline*, pp. 33–55.
36. Geiger, *The Mahāvaṃsa*, pp. 42–44.
37. Ibid., p. 49.
38. Shwe Zan Aung and Mrs. Rhys Davids, *Points of Controversy or Subjects of Discourse, Being a Translation of the Kathā-Vatthu from the Abhidhamma-Pitaka* (PTS) (London: Luzac, 1960, first published 1915).
39. Geiger, *The Mahāvaṃsa*, p. 49.
40. Law, *The Dipavamsa*, p. 169.
41. Amulyachandra Sen. *Asoka's Edicts* (IIS 7) (Calcutta: Institute of Indology, 1956), p. 130.
42. Ibid., p. 134.
43. Woodward and Hare, *The Book of the Gradual Sayings (Anguttara-Nikāya)*, 4, p. 112.
44. Ibid., 3, pp. 81–87.
45. Geiger, *The Mahāvaṃsa*, p. 82.
46. Samuel Beal, *Si-yu-ki, Buddhist Records of the Western World, translated from the Chinese of Hiuen Tsiang (A.D. 629)* (TOS) (London: Kegan Paul, Trench, Trübner, 2 vols., 1906), 1, pp. 151–156; Samuel Beal, *The Life of Hiuen-Tsiang by the Shaman Hwui Li* (TOS) (London: Kegan Paul, Trench, Trübner, new ed. 1911, re-issue 1914), pp. 71f.
47. Beal, *Buddhist Records of the Western World*, 1, pp. 175f.
48. Kern, *Manual of Indian Buddhism*, pp. 121–127.
49. Law, *The Dipavamsa*, pp. 188ff.; Geiger, *The Mahāvaṃsa*, pp. 51ff.
50. Theja Gunawardhana, *Ravana Dynasty in Sri Lanka Dance-Drama* (Lahore: National Publishing House, Vol. 1, 1977), pp. 2–28; A. Denis N. Fernando, "The Ancient Hydraulic Civilization of Sri Lanka in Relation to its Natural Resources," in *Journal of the Sri Lanka Branch of the Royal Asiatic Society (Colombo)*, N.S. 27 (1982), pp. 4f., 28f.
51. Geiger, *The Mahāvaṃsa*, pp. xxxvi–xxxix; Geiger, *Cūlavamsa*, pp. IX–XV.
52. Geiger, *The Mahāvaṃsa*, p. 58.
53. Sen, *Asoka's Edicts*, pp. 66, 102.
54. Geiger, *The Mahāvaṃsa*, p. 63.
55. Ibid., p. 76.
56. Ibid., pp. 74f.
57. Ibid., pp. 77, 97.
58. Law, *The Dipavamsa*, p. 195.
59. Geiger, *The Mahāvaṃsa*, p. 88.
60. Ibid., p. 78.
61. Ibid., p. 80.
62. Law, *The Dipavamsa*, pp. 198ff.
63. Geiger, *The Mahāvaṃsa*, pp. 88ff.
64. Law, *The Dipavamsa*, pp. 200–202; Geiger, *The Mahāvaṃsa*, pp. 88–90.
65. Law, *The Dipavamsa*, pp. 202–204; Geiger, *The Mahāvaṃsa*, pp. 91–93. For the *Culahatthipadopama Sutta* see Robert Chalmers, *Further Dialogues of the Buddha, Translated from the Pali of the Majjhima Nikāya* (SBB) (London: Humphrey Milford, 2 vols., 1926–27), 1, pp. 125–132; I. B. Horner, *The Collection of the Middle Length Sayings (Majjhima-Nikāya)* (PTS) (London: Luzac, 3 vols., 1954–59), 1, pp. 220–230.
66. Law, *The Dipavamsa*, p. 206; Geiger, *The Mahāvaṃsa*, pp. 95f. For the texts recited by Mahinda see Jean Kennedy and Henry S. Gehman, *The Minor Anthologies of the Pali Canon, 4, Vimāna Vatthu: Stories of the Mansions, and Peta Vatthu: Stories of the Departed* (SBB) (London: Luzac, 1942); C. A. F. Rhys Davids and F. L. Woodward, *The Book of the Kindred Sayings (Saṇyutta-Nikāya) or Grouped Suttas* (PTS) (London: Luzac, 5 vols., 1950–56), 5, pp. 356–365 (56, Sacca Samyutta).

67. Geiger, *The Mahāvaṃsa*, p. 176.
68. For the somewhat similarly named Katthaka Cetiya built by the queen of Udaya I (792–797 C.E.) see the *Culavamsa* 49.23 (Geiger, *Cūlavamsa*, 1, p. 129).
69. Geiger, *The Mahāvaṃsa*, p. 116.
70. Ibid., pp. 122f.
71. Geiger, *Cūlavamsa*, 1, p. 8.
72. Geiger, *The Mahāvaṃsa*, p. 138.
73. Jayawickrama, *The Inception of Discipline*, pp. 90–92.
74. Geiger, *The Mahāvaṃsa*, pp. 122, 133. In the *Mahavamsa* 16.10–11 (Geiger, op. cit., p. 115), Aritṭha is said to have received ordination on an earlier occasion, and either we have two different traditions on the subject, or there were two different men named Aritṭha. For the theory that there were two different men, that they were both ministers and both nephews of Devenampiyatissa, and that they were brothers who had both been given the same name, with the older one distinguished by the prefix Maha (great or elder), as was a common custom, and that it was this Maha-Aritṭha who went twice to Aśoka, was ordained after his second return, and functioned as preacher in the assembly at the Thuparama, see E. W. Adikaram, *Early History of Buddhism in Ceylon* (Colombo: M. D. Gunasena, 1946, 2d impression 1953), pp. 53f. For the respective emphases upon the *vinaya* in Sri Lanka, the *suttas* in Thailand, and the *abhidhamma* in Burma see Heinz Bechert and Richard Gomrich, eds., *The World of Buddhism* (New York: Facts on File Publications, 1984), p. 154 (Bechert).
75. Geiger, *The Mahāvaṃsa*, pp. 146f.
76. Ibid., p. 141.
77. Law, *The Dipavamsa*, p. 194.
78. Geiger, *The Mahāvaṃsa*, p. 143.
79. Ibid., p. 142.
80. Ibid., pp. 143–145.
81. Ibid., p. 164.
82. Ibid., pp. 179–227.
83. V. Fausböll, *The Sutta-Nipâta* (SBE 10, 2), pp. 43f.
84. Geiger, *The Mahāvaṃsa*, p. 224.
85. Ibid., pp. 101–110. For the three visits of Śākyamuni Buddha to Lanka see the *Mahavamsa* 1.19–84 (Geiger, op. cit., pp. 3–9). It was on the third of these visits that the Buddha left his footprint (*Buddhapada* or *Śripada*, illustrious footprint) on the summit of the mountain called Sumanakuta (Samantakuta, Samantagiri, Samanola), the conical peak in the central highlands of Sri Lanka now known as Adam's Peak (7,341 feet [2,238 m.]), a depression in the rock also claimed by the Hindus as the footprint of Śiva, and by the Muslims as that of Adam. See R. Spence Hardy, *A Manual of Buddhism* (London: Partridge and Oakey, 1853), pp. 207–213.
86. N. A. Jayawickrama, *The Chronicle of the Thūpa and the Thūpavaṃsa, Being a Translation and Edition of Vācissarattheta's Thūpavaṃsa* (SBB) (London: Luzac, 1971).
87. Geiger, *The Mahāvaṃsa*, pp. 222f. For Dutthagamani see also Colin de Silva, *The Winds of Sinhala* (Garden City, NY: Doubleday, 1982).
88. Law, *The Dipavamsa*, p. 243; Geiger, *The Mahāvaṃsa*, p. 180.
89. Law, *The Dipavamsa*, p. 246; Geiger, *The Mahāvaṃsa*, pp. 193–197.
90. Law, *A History of Pāli Literature*, 1, p. 12.
91. Geiger, *The Mahāvaṃsa*, pp. 228f.
92. Ibid., pp. 230f.
93. Ibid., p. 232.
94. Adikaram, *Early History of Buddhism in Ceylon*, pp. 74f., 77f.
95. Geiger, *The Mahāvaṃsa*, pp. 236f.
96. Geiger, *Cūlavamsa*, 2, p. 251.
97. Law, *The Dipavamsa*, p. 249.
98. Geiger, *The Mahāvaṃsa*, p. 237.
99. T. W. Rhys Davids, *The Questions of King Milinda* (SBE 35–36).
100. Ibid., 1 (SBE 35), pp. 1f.
101. Ibid., 1 (SBE 35), pp. 28, 34; 2 (SBE 36), p. 244.
102. Ibid., 1 (SBE 35), pp. xxvii–xlii.
103. Robert C. Lester, *Theravada Buddhism in Southeast Asia* (Ann Arbor: University of Michigan Press, 1973), pp. 69, 172 n. 8.
104. Geiger, *The Mahāvaṃsa*, p. 259.
105. Law, *The Dipavamsa*, pp. 260f.
106. Geiger, *The Mahāvaṃsa*, pp. 267ff.
107. Geiger, *Cūlavama*, 2, pp. 103f.

108. Ibid., 1, pp. 1ff.
109. Bimala Churn Law, *The Dāṭhāvaṁsa (A History of the Tooth-relic of the Buddha)* (PSS 7) (Lahore: Moti Lal Banarsi Das, 1925).
110. Geiger, *Cūlavamsa*, 1, p. 7.
111. Ibid., 1, pp. 9–26.
112. James Legge, *A Record of Buddhistic Kingdoms, being an Account by the Chinese monk Fâ-Hien of His Travels in India and Ceylon (A.D. 399–414)* (Oxford: Clarendon Press, 1886), pp. 101–111.
113. Ibid., pp. 34f., 109f.
114. Ibid., pp. 108f.
115. Geiger, *Cūlavamsa*, 1, pp. 22–26; cf. Bimala Charan Law, *The Life and Work of Buddhaghosa* (COS) (Calcutta: Thacker, Spink, 1923).
116. Bhikkhu Ñāṇamoli, *The Path of Purification (Visuddhimagga)* (Colombo: R. Semage, 1956); Pe Maung Tin, *The Path of Purity, Being a Translation of Buddhaghosa's Visuddhimagga* (PTS) (London: Luzac, 3 vols. in 1, 1971); cf. Henry Clarke Warren, *Buddhism in Translations* (HOS 3) (Cambridge: Harvard University Press, 1915); U. Dhammaratana, *Guide through Visuddhimagga* (Varanasi: Maha Bodhi Society, Sarnath, 1964).
117. Mrs. Rhys Davids and F. L. Woodward, *The Book of the Kindred Sayings (Saṇyutta-Nikāya) or Grouped Suttas* (PTS) (London: Luzac, 5 vols., 1922–56), 1, p. 20.
118. Rhys Davids, *Dialogues of the Buddha*, 1, pp. 268–270.
119. Ñāṇamoli, *The Path of Purification*, pp. 2, 836.
120. Pe Maung Tin, *The Path of Purity*, pp. 2, 877.
121. Jayawickrama, *The Inception of Discipline*, pp. 1f.
122. Pe Maung Tin, *The Expositor (Atthasālinī), Buddhaghosa's Commentary on the Dhammasangaṇī, the First Book of the Abhidhamma Piṭaka* (PTS) (London: Luzac, 2 vols., 1920–21, reprinted 1958), 1, p. 3.
123. Geiger, *Cūlavamsa*, 1, pp. 31–38; for the Dhammaruci sect see also *Mahavamsa* 5.13 (Geiger, *The Mahāvaṃsa*, p. 27).
124. Geiger, *Cūlavamsa*, 1, pp. 42f.
125. Ibid., 1, pp. 45–50.
126. Ibid., 1, p. 49.
127. Ibid., 1, pp. 141, 146.
128. Geiger, *The Mahāvaṃsa*, pp. 270f.
129. Geiger, *Cūlavamsa*, 1, p. 85.
130. Ibid., 1, p. 101.
131. Ibid., 1, pp. 186–188.
132. Ibid., 1, p. 144.
133. Ibid., 1, p. 215.
134. Ibid., 1, p. 216.
135. Ibid., 1, p. 230.
136. Ibid., 2, pp. 31–43.
137. Ibid., 2, p. 187.
138. Ibid., 1, p. 232–2, p. 124.
139. Ibid., 2, pp. 64–100.
140. Ibid., 2, pp. 3ff., 116ff.
141. Ibid., 2, pp. 2f., 101ff.
142. Ibid., 2, pp. 18–20.
143. Ibid., 2, p. 117.
144. Ibid., pp. 105–113.
145. Ibid., 2, p. 127.
146. Ibid., 2, p. 111.
147. Ibid., 1, p. 280.
148. Ibid., 2, pp. 113f.
149. Ibid., 2, p. 114.
150. Ibid., 2, pp. 123f.
151. Ibid., 2, pp. 127f.
152. Ibid., 2, pp. 132f.
153. Ibid., 2, pp. 136–142.
154. Ibid., 2, pp. 143ff.
155. Ibid., 2, p. 187.
156. Ibid., 2, pp. 191, 204.

157. Ibid., 2, pp. 203f.
158. Ibid., 2, p. 205.
159. Ibid., 2, pp. 206f.
160. Ibid., 2, p. 215.
161. Ibid., 2, pp. 220, 302.
162. Ibid., 2, p. 228.
163. Ibid., 2, p. 242.
164. Ibid., 2, p. 276.
165. B. Jinananda in P. V. Bapat, ed., *2500 Years of Buddhism* (Delhi: Government of India, Ministry of Information and Broadcasting, Publications Division, 1956, reprinted 1959), pp. 35–55; Lester, *Theravada Buddhism in Southeast Asia*, pp. 69, 78f., 172 n. 8, 174 n. 42, n. 47.
166. Cf. above n. 2.
167. Rhys Davids and Oldenberg, "The Pâtimokkha," in *Vinaya Texts*, 1 (SBE 13), pp. 1–69.
168. I. B. Horner, *The Book of the Discipline (Vinaya-Piṭaka)*, (SBB) (London: Luzac, 6 vols., 1938–66), 1–3.
169. Rhys Davids and Oldenberg, *Vinaya Texts*, 1, pp. 73–355, and vol. 2; Horner, *The Book of the Discipline (Vinaya-Piṭaka)*, 4–5.
170. Horner, *The Book of the Discipline (Vinaya-Piṭaka)*, 6, p. 370.
171. T. W. Rhys Davids, *Dialogues of the Buddha* (SBB) (London: Henry Frowde, 3 vols., 1899–1921).
172. Robert Chalmers, *Further Dialogues of the Buddha, Translated from the Pali of the Majjhima Nikāya* (SBB) (London: Humphrey Milford, 2 vols., 1926–27); I. B. Horner, *The Collection of the Middle Length Sayings (Majjhima-Nikāya)* (PTS) (London: Luzac, 3 vols., 1954–59).
173. Rhys Davids, *Buddhist Suttas* (SBE 11), p. 218.
174. C. A. F. Rhys Davids and F. L. Woodward, *The Book of the Kindred Sayings (Saṃyutta-Nikāya) or Grouped Suttas* (PTS) (London: Luzac, 5 vols., 1950–56).
175. Rhys Davids, *Buddhist Suttas* (SBE 11), pp. 61–63; Rhys Davids, *Dialogues of the Buddha*, 2, pp. 128–130; cf. C. A. F. Rhys Davids, *Buddhist Psychology, An Inquiry into the Analysis and Theory of Mind in Pali Literature* (London: Luzac, 2d ed. 1924); Edward Conze, *Buddhist Meditation* (London: George Allen and Unwin, 1956).
176. Rhys Davids and Woodward, *The Book of the Kindred Sayings (Saṃyutta-Nikāya) or Grouped Suttas*, 5, p. 373, cf. pp. xii–xiii (C. A. F. Rhys Davids).
177. F. L. Woodward and E. M. Hare, *The Book of the Gradual Sayings (Anguttara-Nikāya) or More-Numbered Suttas* (PTS) (London: Luzac, 5 vols., 1951–55).
178. Ibid., 3, p. 61, cf. p. xiv (C. A. F. Rhys Davids). (See immediately below, the *Sattaka Nipata* for seven tendencies, and the *Dasaka Nipata* for ten fetters.)
179. Ibid., 3, pp. 237f., cf. pp. xii–xiii (C. A. F. Rhys Davids); G. P. Malalasekera, "Anattā," in EB 1, pp. 567–576.
180. Ibid., 4, p. 6 (cf. *Digha Nikaya* 3.254, Rhys Davids, *Dialogues of the Buddha*, 3, p. 237).
181. Ibid., 5, p. 13 (cf. *Digha Nikaya* 3.234, Rhys Davids, *Dialogues of the Buddha*, 3, p. 225).
182. Ibid., 5, pp. 84f., 93f., cf. pp. ix–x (C. A. F. Rhys Davids).
183. C. A. F. Rhys Davids, *The Minor Anthologies of the Pali Canon*, I, *Dhammapada: Verses on Dhamma, and Khuddaka-Pāṭha: The Text of the Minor Sayings* (SBB) (London: Oxford University Press, 1931); Bhikkhu Ñāṇamoli, *The Minor Readings (Khuddakapāṭha), The First Book of the Minor Collection (Khuddakanikāya), and The Illustrator of Ultimate Meaning (Paramatthajotikā)*, I, *Commentary on the Minor Readings by Bhadantācariya Buddhaghosa* (PTS) (London: Luzac, 1960).
184. Ñāṇamoli, *The Minor Readings (Khuddakapaṭha), The First Book of the Minor Collection (Khuddakanikāya)*, p. 3.
185. Ibid., p. 10.
186. F. Max Müller, *The Dhammapada, A Collection of Verses* (SBE 10, 1); Rhys Davids, *The Minor Anthologies of the Pali Canon*, I, *Dhammapada: Verses on Dhamma*; Irving Babbitt, *The Dhammapada, Translated from the Pāli with an Essay on Buddha and the Occident* (New York: Oxford University Press, 1936); Somalokatissa Nayaka Thera, *Dhammapada, The Way of Life according to the Buddha* (Colombo: M. D. Gunasena, 1969); Nārada Maha Thera, *The Dhammapada (Text and Translation)* (Calcutta: Maha Bodhi Society of India, 3d ed. 1970); Nārada Thera, *The Dhammapada, Pāli Text and Translation with Stories in Brief and Notes* (Colombo: Colombo Apothecaries Co., 1972); Juan Mascaró, *The Dhammapada, The Path of Perfection* (Harmondsworth: Penguin Books, 1973); *Dhammapada*, Translated into Tibetan from the Pali by dGe-'dun Chos-'phel, Translated into English from the Tibetan by Dharma Publishing Staff (TTS) (Berkeley: Dharma Publishing, 1985).
187. Müller, *The Dhammapada* (SBE 10, 1), pp. 42f.
188. Ibid., p. 53.

189. F. L. Woodward, *The Minor Anthologies of the Pali Canon*, II, *Udāna: Verses of Uplift, and Itivuttaka: As It Was Said* (SBB) (London: Oxford University Press, 1948), pp. 1–114.
190. Ibid., p. 114.
191. Ibid., pp. 115–199.
192. Ibid., p. 130.
193. Ibid., p. 181.
194. Ibid., pp. 188, 191, 193.
195. V. Fausböll, *The Sutta-Nipâta, A Collection of Discourses* (SBE 10, 2); Robert Chalmers, *Buddha's Teachings, Being the Sutta-Nipāta or Discourse-Collection edited in the Original Pali Text with an English Version facing It* (HOS 37) (Cambridge: Harvard University Press, 1932); E. M. Hare, *Woven Cadences of Early Buddhists* (SBB) (London: Oxford University Press, 1944).
196. Hare, *Woven Cadences of Early Buddhists*, p. 23.
197. Ibid., pp. 6ff.
198. Ibid., pp. 32–34.
199. Ibid., pp. 44–46.
200. Ibid., pp. 102ff.
201. Ibid., pp. 61–63.
202. Ibid., pp. 63–65.
203. Ibid., pp. 118ff., 129ff.
204. Ibid., pp. 155–157.
205. Jean W. Kennedy, *The Minor Anthologies of the Pali Canon*, IV, *Vimāna Vatthu: Stories of the Mansions . . .* (SBB) (London: Luzac, 1942), pp. 1–128.
206. Ibid., p. 92, cf. p. viii (C. A. F. Rhys Davids).
207. Henry Snyder Gehman, *The Minor Anthologies of the Pali Canon*, IV, *. . . Peta Vatthu: Stories of the Departed*, pp. 141–250; cf. Bimala Charan Law, *Heaven and Hell in Buddhist Perspective* (Calcutta: Thacker, Spink, 1925); Bimala Church Law, *The Buddhist Conception of Spirits* (London: Luzac, 1936).
208. Gehman, *The Minor Anthologies of the Pali Canon*, IV, *. . . Peta Vatthu: Stories of the Departed*, pp. 176f.
209. C. A. F. Rhys Davids, *Psalms of the Early Buddhists* (PTS) (London: Henry Frowde, 2 vols., 1909–13), 1, *Psalms of the Sisters*, 2, *Psalms of the Brethren*; K. R. Norman, *The Elders' Verses* (PTS) (London: Luzac, 2 vols., 1969–71), 1, *Theragāthā*, 2, *Therīgāthā*; Barbara Stoler Miller, "Ballads of Early Buddhist Nuns translated from the Pāli Therīgāthā," in *Zero* 5, pp. 68–77.
210. Rhys Davids, *Psalms of the Early Buddhists*, 2, pp. 102, 267, 364.
211. Ibid., 2, p. 385.
212. Ibid., 1, p. 53.
213. T. W. and C. A. F. Rhys Davids, *Buddhist Birth-Stories (Jataka Tales), The Commentarial Introduction entitled Nidāna Kathā, The Story of the Lineage* (London: G. Routledge, rev. ed. 1925); E. B.Cowell, ed., *The Jātaka, or Stories of the Buddha's Former Births* (PTS) (London: Routledge and K. Paul, 6 vols. in 3, 1973).
214. I. B. Horner, *The Minor Anthologies of the Pali Canon*, III, *Chronicle of Buddhas (Buddhavamsa), and Basket of Conduct (Cariyāpiṭaka)* (SBB) (London: Routledge and Kegan Paul, 1975).
215. Ibid.
216. C. A. F. Rhys Davids, *A Buddhist Manual of Psychological Ethics of the Fourth Century B.C., Being a Translation Now Made for the First Time from the Original Pali, of the First Book in the Abhidhamma Piṭaka entitled Dhamma-Sangani (Compendium of States or Phenomena)* (OTF) (London: Royal Asiatic Society, 1900); Pe Maung Tin, *The Expositor (Atthasālinī), Buddhaghosa's Commentary on the Dhammasaṅganī, The First Book of the Abhidhamma Piṭaka* (PTS) (London: Luzac, 2 vols., 1920–21, reprinted 1958).
217. Paṭhamakyaw Ashin Thiṭṭila (Seṭṭhila) Aggamahāpaṇḍita, *The Book of Analysis (Vibhaṅga), The Second Book of the Abhidhamma Piṭaka, translated from the Pāli of the Burmese Chaṭṭhasaṅgīti edition* (PTS) (London: Luzac, 1969).
218. U Nārada, *Discourse on Elements, Dhātu-kathā, The Third Book of the Abhidhamma Piṭaka, A Translation with Charts and Explanations* (London: Luzac, 1962).
219. Bimala Charan Law, *Designation of Human Types (Puggala-Paññatti)* (PTS) (London: Oxford University Press, 1924).
220. Shwe Zan Aung and C. A. F. Rhys Davids, *Points of Controversy or Subjects of Discourse, Being a Translation of the Kathā-Vatthu from the Abhidhamma-Piṭaka* (PTS) (London: Luzac, 1960, first published 1915).
221. U Nārada, *Conditional Relations (Paṭṭhāna), Being Vol. I of the Chaṭṭhasaṅgāyana Text of the Seventh Book of the Abhidhamma Piṭaka* (PTS) (London: Luzac, 1969).

222. Bhikkhu Ñāṇamoli, *The Guide (Netti-Ppakaraṇaṁ) according to Kaccāna Thera* (PTS) (London: Luzac, 1962).
223. Chalmers, *Further Dialogues of the Buddha*, 1, p. 77; 2, pp. 264f., 283.
224. Bhikkhu Ñāṇamoli, *The Piṭaka-Disclosure (Peṭakopadesa)* (PTS) (London: Luzac, 1964).
225. T. W. Rhys Davids, *The Questions of King Milinda* (2 vols., SBE 35, 36); I. B. Horner, *Milinda's Questions* (SBB) (London: Luzac, 2 vols., 1963–64); cf. C. A. F. Rhys Davids, *The Milinda-Questions, An Inquiry into Its Place in the History of Buddhism with a Theory as to Its Author* (London: G. Routledge, 1930).
226. Rhys Davids, *The Questions of King Milinda*, 1, pp. 63f.; cf. Winternitz, *A History of Indian Literature*, 2, pp. 179f.; and cf. Horner, *Milinda's Questions*, 1, p. 56 n. 2 for a different translation and interpretation of Nagasena's final statement in the dialogue.
227. Rhys Davids, *Dialogues of the Buddha*, 2, pp. 107f., 173. For the first passage cf. also *Samyutta Nikaya* 5.152–153, Rhys Davids and Woodward, *The Book of the Kindred Sayings (Saṇyutta-Nikāya) or Grouped Suttas*, 5, pp. 132f.
228. Rhys Davids and Oldenberg, *Vinaya Texts*, 1 (SBE 13), p. 115; Bhiksu Sangharakshita, *A Survey of Buddhism* (Bangalore: Indian Institute of World Culture, 2d ed. 1959); Bhikshu Sangharakshita, *The Three Jewels: An Introduction to Modern Buddhism* (Garden City: Anchor Books, 1970).
229. Rhys Davids, *Buddhist Suttas*, pp. 186f.; Rhys Davids, *Dialogues of the Buddha*, 1, p. 316.
230. Rhys Davids, *Dialogues of the Buddha*, 2, p. 173.
231. Rhys Davids and Oldenberg, *Vinaya Texts*, 1 (SBE 13), p. 95.
232. Ibid.
233. Ibid., p. 134.
234. Horner, *The Middle Length Sayings (Majjhima-Nikāya)*, 1, p. 9.
235. Rhys Davids and Woodward, *The Book of the Kindred Sayings (Saṇyutta-Nikāya)*, 2, p. 21; 4, p. 29; Horner, *The Middle Length Sayings (Majjhima-Nikāya)*, 1, pp. 236f.
236. Rhys Davids and Oldenberg, *Vinaya Texts*, 1 (SBE 13), p. 95.
237. Rhys Davids, *The Book of the Kindred Sayings (Saṇyutta-Nikāya)*, 2, pp. 59f.
238. Ibid., 2, pp. ix, 26f.
239. Rhys Davids and Oldenberg, *Vinaya Texts*, 1 (SBE 13), p. 95.
240. Warren, *Buddhism in Translations*, p. 238; cf. Ñāṇamoli, *The Path of Purification*, p. 638; Pe Maung Tin, *The Path of Purity*, p. 663.
241. Rhys Davids, *The Questions of King Milinda*, 1 (SBE 35), p. 111.
242. Ñāṇamoli, *The Path of Purification*, pp. 696, 699.
243. Shwe Zan Aung, *Compendium of Philosophy, Being a Translation now made for the First Time from the Original Pali of the Abhidhammattha-sangaha* (PTS) (London: Luzac, 1956), pp. 137–149; Warren, *Buddhism in Translations*, pp. 289–291.
244. Shwe Zan Aung, *Compendium of Philosophy*, pp. 217f.
245. Ibid., pp. 170–173.
246. Rhys Davids and Oldenberg, *Vinaya Texts*, 1 (SBE 13), pp. 94–97; Chalmers, *Further Dialogues of the Buddha*, 1, p. 117.
247. Woodward, *The Minor Anthologies of the Pali Canon, II, Udāna: Verses of Uplift* . . . (SBB), p. 98; Bechert and Gomrich, eds., *The World of Buddhism*, p. 279 (Bechert).
248. Hare and Woodward, *The Book of the Gradual Sayings (Anguttara-Nikāya)*, 3, pp. 157, 211.
249. Ibid., 3, p. 157; 4, p. 17.
250. Ibid., 1, p. 216.
251. Ibid., 3, p. 123.
252. Rhys Davids and Woodward, *The Book of the Kindred Sayings (Saṇyutta-Nikāya)*, 3, p. 92.
253. Ibid., 4, pp. 108–110, 170.
254. Horner, *The Collection of the Middle Length Sayings (Majjhima-Nikāya)*, 1, p. 217.
255. Rhys Davids and Woodward, *The Book of the Kindred Sayings (Saṇyutta-Nikāya)*, 2, pp. 14, 81; 3, p. 139; 4, p. 90.
256. Ibid., 1, p. 36.
257. Ibid., 1, p. 273.
258. Ibid., 1, p. 226.
259. Horner, *The Collection of the Middle Length Sayings (Majjhima-Nikāya)*, 3, pp. 290–292.
260. Ibid., 2, pp. 278, 353; 3, pp. 58, 174, 322; and see E. J. Thomas, "Nirvāṇa Parinirvāṇa," in *India Antiqua, A Volume of Oriental Studies presented by his friends and pupils to Jean Philippe Vogel* (Leiden: E. J. Brill, 1947), pp. 294f.; Walpola Sri Rahula, *What the Buddha Taught* (Bedford: Gordon Fraser, rev. ed. 1967), pp. 36–44.
261. Shwe Zan Aung, *Compendium of Philosophy*, p. 153.

262. Rhys Davids and Oldenberg, *Vinaya Texts*, 1 (SBE 13), p. 115.
263. Ibid., pp. 191–199.
264. Ibid., p. 203.
265. Ibid., p. 211.
266. Ibid., pp. 1–69.
267. Ibid., 3 (SBE 20), pp. 320–369. For Mahapajapati Gotami see also *Anguttara Nikaya* 4.272–278, Woodward and Hare, *The Book of the Gradual Sayings (Anguttara-Nikāya)*, 4, pp. 181–185. For the status of both monks and nuns in society and culture, see Bechert and Gombrich, eds., *The World of Buddhism;* and for the restriction on ordination of women, see p. 155 (Bechert).
268. Rhys Davids and Oldenberg, *Vinaya Texts*, 1 (SBE 13), pp. 239–297.
269. Ibid., pp. 298–324.
270. Ibid., pp. 325–355.
271. Horner, *The Collection of the Middle Length Sayings (Majjhima-Nikāya)*, 2, pp. 169f.; 3, p. 322.
272. Woodward and Hare, *The Book of the Gradual Sayings (Anguttara-Nikāya)*, 4, p. 149.
273. Pe Maung Tin, *The Path of Purity*, p. 18.
274. Woodward and Hare, *The Book of the Gradual Sayings (Anguttara-Nikāya)*, 4, pp. 170f.
275. Ibid., 3, p. 153.
276. Ibid., 2, pp. 63–66.

12. EARLY HISTORY AND LITERATURE OF MAHAYANA AND VAJRAYANA BUDDHISM

1. Shwe Zan Aung and C. A. F. Rhys Davids, *Points of Controversy or Subjects of Discourse, Being a Translation of the Kathā-Vatthu from the Abhidhamma-Piṭaka* (PTS) (London: Luzac, 1960), p. 351, cf. p. 2 and n. 1, and p. xlvii and n. 1.
2. James Legge, *A Record of Buddhistic Kingdoms, Being an Account by the Chinese Monk Fâ-Hien of His Travels in India and Ceylon (A.D. 399–414)* (Oxford: Clarendon Press, 1886), pp. 14, 16, 41, 78, 98.
3. Samuel Beal, *Si-yu-ki, Buddhist Records of the Western World*, translated from the Chinese of Hiuen Tsiang (A.D. 629) (London: Kegan Paul, Trench, Trübner, 2 vols., 1906), 1, pp. 112, 180, 190, etc.
4. Ibid., 2, pp. 229, 247, 260, 269.
5. Ibid., 1, pp. 18f., 24, 49, etc.
6. Ibid., 1, p. 226.
7. Ibid., 1, p. 230.
8. J. Takakusu, *A Record of the Buddhist Religion as practised in India and the Malay Archipelago (A.D. 671–695) by I-tsing* (Oxford: Clarendon Press, 1896), pp. 7f., 13–15.
9. Legge, *A Record of Buddhistic Kingdoms*, p. 99.
10. Beal, *Buddhist Records of the Western World*, 1, pp. 49, 174, 182, 270, 278.
11. Takakusa, *A Record of the Buddhist Religion*, pp. 9f., 20, 215.
12. Shwe Zan Aung and Rhys Davids, *Points of Controversy*, pp. 64ff., 84ff., 260f., 375–377.
13. Ria Kloppenborg, *The Sūtra on the Foundation of the Buddhist Order (Catuṣpariṣatsūtra)* (NISABA) (Leiden: E. J. Brill, 1973). For texts in Sogdian and Khotanese see D. N. MacKenzie, *The 'Sūtra of the Causes and Effects of Actions' in Sogdian* (LOS 22) (London: Oxford University Press, 1970); R. E. Emmerick, *The Khotanese Śūraṅgamasamādhisūtra* (LOS 23) (London: Oxford University Press, 1970).
14. Wilhelm Geiger, *The Mahāvamsa or The Great Chronicle of Ceylon* (Colombo: Ceylon Government Information Department, 1950), pp. 26f.
15. Beal, *Buddhist Records of the Western World*, 1, pp. 121, 162; 2, p. 287.
16. Shwe Zan Aung and Rhys Davids, *Points of Controversy*, pp. 354f.
17. J. J. Jones, *The Mahāvastu, translated from the Buddhist Sanskrit* (SBB) (London: Luzac, 3 vols., 1949–56).
18. Ibid., 1, p. 3.
19. Ibid., 1, pp. 108–112.
20. Ibid., 1, p. 198.
21. Ibid., 1, pp. 53ff.
22. Ibid., 1, p. 133.
23. Ibid., 2, p. 329.
24. T. W. Rhys Davids and Hermann Oldenberg, *Vinaya Texts*, 1 (SBE 13), p. 112.

25. T. W. Rhys Davids, *The Questions of King Milinda*, 1 (SBE 35), pp. 31, 49.
26. Jeffrey Hopkins, *Meditation on Emptiness* (London: Wisdom Publications, 1983), n. 495, pp. 840–845.
27. I. B. Horner, *The Collection of the Middle Length Sayings (Majjhima-Nikāya)* (PTS) (London: Luzac, 3 vols., 1954–59), 3, pp. 111f., 302.
28. Jones, *The Mahāvastu*, 1, pp. 249f.
29. Har Dayal, *The Bodhisattva Doctrine in Buddhist Sanskrit Literature* (Delhi: Motilal Banarsidass, 1932, reprint 1970), p. 9, and see this book throughout for the *bodhisattva* and *buddha* concepts.
30. Jones, *The Mahāvastu*, 1, p. 50.
31. Ibid., 1, pp. 108, 112; 2, p. 329.
32. H. Kern, *The Saddharma-Pundarîka or The Lotus of the True Law* (SBE 21), pp. 72–81; Senchu Murano, *The Sutra of the Lotus Flower of the Wonderful Law, Translated from Kumārajīva's version of the Saddharmapuṇḍarīka-Sūtra* (Tokyo: Nichiren Shu Headquarters, 1974), pp. 54–59.
33. Kern, op. cit., p. 189; Murano, op. cit., p. 138.
34. See the Indexes in Kern, op. cit., and Murano, op. cit.
35. See the Indexes in Kern, op. cit., and Murano, op. cit.
36. T. W. Rhys Davids, *Buddhism, Being a Sketch of the Life and Teachings of Gautama, the Buddha* (London: Society for Promoting Christian Knowledge, 1890), p. 205; H. Kern, *Manual of Indian Buddhism* (EIAR) (Strassburg: Karl J. Trübner, 1896), p. 64; Willibald Kirfel, *Symbolik des Buddhismus* (in Ferdinand Herrmann, ed., Symbolik der Religionen, 5) (Stuttgart: Anton Hiersemann, 1959), pp. 32, 45f.
37. Horner, *The Collection of the Middle Length Sayings (Majjhima-Nikāya)*, 1, pp. 93–97.
38. Jones, *The Mahāvastu*, 1, pp. 33, 126–128.
39. Shwe Zan Aung and Rhys Davids, *Points of Controversy*, pp. 325f.
40. Kern, *The Saddharma-Pundarîka* (SBE 21), pp. 157–166; Murano, *The Sutra of the Lotus Flower of the Wonderful Law*, pp. 117–123.
41. Edward Conze, *Thirty Years of Buddhist Studies, Selected Essays* (Oxford: Bruno Cassirer, 1967), p. 72; Nalinaksha Dutt, *Mahayana Buddhism* (Calcutta: K. L. Mukhopadhyay, 1973), pp. 158–174.
42. Kern, *The Saddharma-Pundarîka* (SBE 21), pp. 177–179; Murano, *The Sutra of the Lotus Flower of the Wonderful Law*, p. 130.
43. Maurice Winternitz, *A History of Indian Literature* (Calcutta: University of Calcutta, 3 vols., 1933–59), 2, *Buddhist Literature and Jaina Literature*, pp. 1–423.
44. Ph. Ed. Foucaux, *Le Lalita Vistara* (AMG 6, 19) (Paris: Ernest Leroux, 2 vols., 1884, 1892); Maurice Percheron, *The Marvelous Life of the Buddha* (based on the *Lalitavistara* and the Tibetan *Rgya tch'er rol pa*) (New York: St. Martin's Press, 1960); Nicholas Poppe, *The Twelve Deeds of Buddha, A Mongolian Version of the Lalitavistara, Mongolian Text, Notes, and English Translation* (AF 23) (Wiesbaden: Otto Harrassowitz, 1967).
45. Poppe, *The Twelve Deeds of Buddha*, p. 162.
46. Ibid., p. 142.
47. Ibid., p. 162; for Simnu see pp. 140f., etc.
48. Takakusu, *A Record of the Buddhist Religion*, p. 205.
49. Kern, *The Saddharma-Pundarîka* (SBE 21); W. E. Soothill, *The Lotus of the Wonderful Law or The Lotus Gospel, Saddharma Pundarīka Sūtra, Miao-fa Lien Hua Ching* (Oxford: Clarendon Press, 1930); Murano, *The Sutra of the Lotus Flower of the Wonderful Law*; Leon Hurvitz, *Scripture of the Lotus Blossom of the Fine Dharma, Translated from the Chinese of Kumārajīva* (New York: Columbia University Press, 1976).
50. Kern, *The Saddharma-Pundarîka* (SBE 21), pp. 49–53.
51. Ibid., p. 270.
52. Ibid., p. 272.
53. Ibid., pp. 415f.
54. Ibid., p. 388.
55. Ibid., pp. 440f.
56. Ibid., p. 419.
57. Edward Conze, *Aṣṭasāhasrikā Prajñāpāramitā* (BI 284) (Calcutta: Asiatic Society, 1958); Edward Conze, *The Perfection of Wisdom in Eight Thousand Lines and Its Verse Summary* (WS 1) (Bolinas: Four Seasons Foundation, 1973).
58. Edward Conze, *The Large Sutra on Perfect Wisdom with the divisions of the Abhisamayalankara* (London: Luzac, 3 vols., 1961, 1964, 1966; Berkeley: University of California Press, 1975). The translation normally follows the version in 25,000 Lines, but in some passages is

based on the version in 100,000 Lines. For all of these works see Edward Conze, *The Prajñāpāramitā Literature* (IIM 6) ('S-Gravenhage: Mouton, 1960); Edward Conze, *Materials for a Dictionary of the Prajñāpāramitā Literature* (Tokyo: Suzuki Research Foundation, 1967).

59. Edward Conze, *The Short Prajñāpāramitā Texts* (London: Luzac, 1973).
60. F. Max Müller, *The Vagrakkhedikā or Diamond-Cutter* (SBE 49, 2, pp. 111–144; Edward Conze, *Vajracchedikā Prajñāpāramitā* (SOR 13) (Rome: Istituto Italiano per il Medio ed Estremo Oriente, 1957); A. F. Price and Wong Mou-Lam, *The Diamond Sutra and the Sutra of Hui Neng* (CLS) (Berkeley: Shambala, 1969); Hsüan Hua, *A General Explanation of the Vajra Prajñā Pāramitā Sūtra* (San Francisco: Buddhist Text Translation Society, 1974).
61. F. Max Müller, *The Larger Pragñâ-pâramitâ-hridaya-sûtra* and *The Smaller Pragñâ-pâramitâ-hridaya-sûtra* (SBE 49, 2, pp. 147–154); Edward Conze, *Buddhist Wisdom Books containing The Diamond Sutra and The Heart Sutra* (London: George Allen and Unwin, 1958).
62. Conze, *The Short Prajñāpāramitā Texts*, p. 201.
63. Conze, *Aṣṭasāhasrikā Prajñāpāramitā*, p. 2.
64. Ibid., p. 1.
65. Ibid., pp. 119f.
66. Bhikshu Sangharakshita, *A Survey of Buddhism* (Bangalore: Indian Institute of World Culture, 2d ed. 1959), pp. 327f.; Frederick J. Streng, *Emptiness, A Study in Religious Meaning* (Nashville; Abingdon Press, 1967).
67. Conze, *Aṣṭasāhasrikā Prajñāpāramitā*, pp. 8, 16.
68. Conze, *Vajracchedikā Prajñāpāramitā*, p. 92.
69. Conze, *Aṣṭasāhasrikā Prajñāpāramitā*, pp. 116, 145. For the form *prajnopaya* see Conze, *Materials for a Dictionary of the Prajñāpāramitā Literature*, p. 270.
70. Müller, *The Larger Pragñâ-pâramitâ-hridaya-sûtra* and *The Smaller Pragñâ-pâramitâ-hridaya-sûtra* (SBE 49, 2), pp. 149, 154; Conze, *Buddhist Wisdom Books*, pp. 101–107; Dipak Chandra Bhattacharyya, *Tantric Buddhist Iconographic Sources* (New Delhi: Munshiram Manoharlal, 1974), p. 66; Kirfel, *Symbolik des Buddhismus*, pp. 46f.
71. D. T. Suzuki, *On Indian Mahayana Buddhism*, ed. Edward Conze (New York: Harper Torchbooks, 1968), pp. 147–226; Judy Ann Jastram, *Three Chapters from the Gaṇḍavyūha Sūtra: A Critical Edition of the Sanskrit and Tibetan Texts of the Youth Sudhana's Visits to the Bhikṣus Meghaśrī, Sāgaramegha, and Supratiṣṭhita, with English Translation and Commentary* (Thesis in the Library of the University of California at Berkeley).
72. Daisetz Teitaro Suzuki, *Studies in the Lankavatara Sutra, One of the Most Important Texts of Mahayana Buddhism, in which almost all its Principal Tenets are presented, including the Teaching of Zen* (London: George Routledge, 1930); D. T. Suzuki, *The Lankavatara Sutra, A Mahayana Text translated for the First Time from the Original Sanskrit* (London: George Routledge, 1932); Dwight Goddard, *Self-Realization of Noble Wisdom, A Buddhist Scripture, based upon Professor Suzuki's Translation of the Lankavatara-Sutra* (Thetford, Vermont: Dwight Goddard, 1932).
73. Goddard, *Self-Realization of Noble Wisdom*, pp. 24–26, 45f., 55, 68f., 83, 85, 91, 93, 100, 105f., 130f., 134, 139. For the *dharmakaya* in the *Lankavatara* see Suzuki, *Studies in the Lankavatara Sutra*, pp. 316–319, and see pp. 351–354 for the oneness or sameness *(samata)* of the Buddha.
74. Johannes Nobel, *Suvarṇaprabhāsottama-Sūtra, Das Goldglanz-Sūtra, Ein Sanskrittext des Mahāyāna-Buddhismus, I'tsing's chinesische Version und ihre tibetische Übersetzung* (Leiden: Brill, 2 vols., 1958).
75. For the *trikaya* cf. above in the present chapter with the references in n. 41.
76. For the *dharanis* see Dayal, *The Bodhisattva Doctrine in Buddhist Sanskrit Literature*, pp. 267–269.
77. F. Max Müller, *The Larger Sukhâvatî-vyûha*, and *The Smaller Sukhâvatî-vyûha* (SBE 49, 2, pp. 1–107); Nishu Utsuki, *Buddhabhāṣita-Amitāyuḥ-Sūtra (The Smaller Sukhāvati-Vyūha) translated from the Chinese Version of Kumārajīva* (Kyoto: Educational Department of West Hongwanji, 1924).
78. J. Takakusu, *The Amitâyur-dhyâna-Sûtra* (SBE 49, 2, pp. 161–201).
79. Beal, *Buddhist Records of the Western World*, 2, pp. 302f.; cf. Samuel Beal, *The Life of Hiuen-Tsiang by the Shaman Hwui Li* (London: Kegan Paul, Trench, Trübner, 1911), p. 199.
80. Winternitz, *A History of Indian Literature*, 2, pp. 256, 342, 349.
81. Beal, *Buddhist Records of the Western World*, 2, p. 100.
82. E. B. Cowell, *The Buddha-Karita of Asvaghosha* (SBE 49, 1); E. H. Johnston, *The Buddhacarita or, Acts of the Buddha* (New Delhi: Oriental Books Reprint Corporation, 2 vols., 2d ed. 1972, originally published by the University of the Punjab, Lahore, 1936); Samuel Beal, *The Fo-sho-hing-tsan-king, A Life of Buddha by Asvaghosha Bodhisattva, translated from Sanskrit into Chinese by Dharmaraksha, A.D. 420* (SBE 19).
83. Takakusu, *A Record of the Buddhist Religion*, pp. 165f.
84. Johnston, *The Buddhacarita or, Acts of the Buddha*, 1, pp. xxix–xxxi.

85. Ibid., 2, pp. 30, 141, 144.
86. Conze, *Aṣṭasāhasrikā Prajñāpāramitā*, p. 72.
87. Johnston, *The Buddhacarita or, Acts of the Buddha*, 2, p. 177.
88. Cowell, *The Buddha-Karita of Asvaghosha* (SBE 49, 1), pp. 183f.
89. Édouard Huber, *Sûtralâṃkâra, traduit en français sur la version chinoise de Kumârajîva* (Paris: Ernest Leroux, 1908).
90. Timothy Richard, *Ashvagosha, The Awakening of Faith*, ed. Alan Hull Walton (London: Charles Skilton, 1961; text extracted from Timothy Richard, *The New Testament of Higher Buddhism*, T. and T. Clark, 1910); Yoshito S. Hakeda, *The Awakening of Faith attributed to Aśvaghosha* (New York: Columbia University Press, 1967).
91. Beal, *Buddhist Records of the Western World*, 2, p. 302.
92. Winternitz, *A History of Indian Literature*, 2, pp. 267, 624.
93. Suzuki, *The Lankavatara Sutra*, pp. 239f.
94. Beal, *Buddhist Records of the Western World*, 2, pp. 97f.
95. E. Obermiller, *History of Buddhism (Chos-ḥbyung) by Bu-ston*, I, *The Jewelry of Scripture*, II, *The History of Buddhism in India and Tibet* (MKB) (Heidelberg: O. Harrassowitz, 2 vols., 1931–32), 2, pp. 122–130; Lama Chimpa and Alaka Chattopadhyaya, *Taranatha's History of Buddhism in India*, ed. Debiprasad Chattopadhyaya (Simla: Indian Institute of Advanced Study, 1970), pp. 106–119.
96. Herbert V. Guenther, *The Royal Song of Saraha, A Study in the History of Buddhist Thought* (Seattle: University of Washington Press, 1969).
97. Streng, *Emptiness, A Study in Religious Meaning*, pp. 181–220; Kenneth K. Inada, *Nāgārjuna, A Translation of his Mulamadhyamakakārikā with an Introductory Essay* (Tokyo: Hokuseido Press, 1970).
98. Inada, *Nāgārjuna*, p. 191; K. Venkata Ramanan, *Nāgārjuna's Philosophy as presented in the Mahā-Prajñāpāramitā-Śāstra* (Rutland, Vermont: Charles E. Tuttle, for the Harvard-Yenching Institute, 1966).
99. Inada, *Nāgārjuna*, p. 191.
100. Ibid., pp. 187, 190.
101. Takakusu, *A Record of the Buddhist Religion*, pp. 158–162, 166.
102. Heinrich Wenzel, "Nāgārjuna's 'Friendly Epistle,'" in JPTS 13 (1886), pp. 4, 32; Leslie Kawamura, *Golden Zephyr* (TTS) (Emeryville, California: Dharma Publishing, 1975).
103. Ramanan, *Nāgārjuna's Philosophy*, pp. 27f.
104. Wenzel in JPTS 13 (1886), pp. 6ff.
105. Giuseppe Tucci, "The Ratnāvalī of Nāgārjuna," in JRAS 1934, pp. 307–325.
106. Jeffrey Hopkins and Lati Rimpoche with Anne Klein, *The Precious Garland and The Song of the Four Mindfulnesses* (WTS 2) (New York: Harper and Row, 1975), pp. 15–112.
107. Inada, *Nāgārjuna*, p. 191.
108. Tucci in JRAS 1934, pp. 309ff.
109. Obermiller, *History of Buddhism . . . by Bu-ston*, 2, p. 130.
110. Inada, *Nāgārjuna*, pp. 185f., 189.
111. Vasudev Gokhale, *Akṣara-Çatakam, The Hundred Letters, A Madhyamaka Text by Āryadeva after Chinese and Tibetan Materials* (MKB 14) (Heidelberg: O. Harrassowitz, 1930), pp. 10, 14, 16.
112. Sangharakshita, *A Survey of Buddhism*, pp. 390–404.
113. Chattopadhyaya, *Taranatha's History of Buddhism in India*, pp. 155ff.
114. Beal, *Buddhist Records of the Western World*, 1, pp. 98, 105, 225f.
115. Takakusu, *A Record of the Buddhist Religion*, p. 181.
116. Conze, *The Prajñāpāramitā Literature*, pp. 100f.
117. Janice Dean Willis, *On Knowing Reality: the Tattvārtha chapter of Asaṅga's Bodhisattvabhūmi* (New York: Columbia University Press, 1979).
118. Edward Conze, *Abhisamayālaṅkāra* (SOR 6) (Rome: Istituto Italiano per il Medio ed Estremo Oriente, 1954); cf. Edward Conze, *Thirty Years of Buddhist Studies* (Oxford: Bruno Cassirer, 1967), p. 22.
119. Conze, *Abhisamayālaṅkāra*, p. 96.
120. Clarence H. Hamilton, *Wei Shih Er Shih Lun or The Treatise in Twenty Stanzas on Representation-Only by Vasubandhu, Translated from the Chinese Version of Hsüan Tsang, Tripiṭaka Master of the T'ang Dynasty* (AOS 13) (New Haven: American Oriental Society, 1938, reprinted Kraus Reprint Corporation, 1967), p. 19.
121. Ibid., pp. 21, 59.
122. Ibid., p. 63.
123. Ibid., p. 79.
124. Th. Shcherbatskoy, *Madhyānta-Vibhaṅga, Discourse on Discrimination between Middle and Extreme* (SIS 5, reprint BB 30) (Calcutta: Indian Studies Past and Present, 1971).

125. Obermiller, *History of Buddhism . . . by Bu-ston*, 1, p. 54.
126. Shcherbatskoy, *Madhyānta-Vibhaṅga*, pp. 11–15.
127. Ibid., p. 26.
128. Ibid., p. 77.
129. Ibid., p. 211.
130. Sangharakshita, *A Survey of Buddhism*, pp. 407f.; Shashi Bhusan Dasgupta, *An Introduction to Tantric Buddhism* (Calcutta: University of Calcutta, 1950); Geshe Lhundup Sopa and Jeffrey Hopkins, *Practice and Theory of Tibetan Buddhism* (New York: Grove Press, 1976), pp. 67, 122ff.; Detlef Ingo Lauf, *Tibetan Sacred Art, The Heritage of Tantra* (Berkeley & London: Shambhala, 1976); Giuseppe Tucci, *The Religions of Tibet* (Berkeley: University of California Press, 1980); *My Land and My People*, by His Holiness the Dalai Lama of Tibet (New York: Potala Corporation, 1983), pp. 245f. My transcription of the Tibetan language into Roman script follows Tucci, *The Religions of Tibet*; cf. also Turrell Wylie "A Standard System of Tibetan Transcription," in HJAS 22 (1959), pp. 261–267.
131. Streng, *Emptiness, A Study in Religious Meaning*, p. 160.
132. The comparatively brief treatment of Tibetan Buddhism and its monuments in the present book has been written independently but in parallel with the publication of an entire book on Tibet (also including Western Tibet, or Ladakh), namely, Jack Finegan, *Tibet—A Dreamt of Image* (New Delhi: Tibet House, The Cultural Centre of H. H. the Dalai Lama, 1986), and reference is made to that book for additional detail and documentation. To the extent that there is overlap between the material here and in the book published by Tibet House I acknowledge permission from Doboom Tulku, Director of Tibet House, to write concurrently this part of the present book.
133. Obermiller, *History of Buddhism . . . by Bu-ston*, 2, pp. 184–191; Chimpa and Chattopadhyaya, *Taranatha's History of Buddhism in India*, pp. 260, 277.
134. Embar Krishnamacharya, *Tattvasaṅgraha of Śāntarakṣita with the Commentary of Kamalaśīla* (GOS 30–31) (Baroda: Central Library, 1926), and see pp. X–CLVI for the lives of Śantarakshita and Kamalaśila and the contents of the book.
135. W. Y. Evans-Wentz, *The Tibetan Book of the Great Liberation, or the Method of Realizing Nirvāṇa through Knowing the Mind*, preceded by an Epitome of Padma-Sambhava's Biography and followed by Guru Phadampa Sangay's Teachings (London: Oxford University Press, 1954), pp. 105–240, cf. *Maitreya* 2 (1971), pp. 91–98; Keith Dowman, *The Legend of the Great Stupa and The Life Story of the Lotus Born Guru* (Berkeley: Tibetan Nyingma Meditation Center, Dharma Publishing, 1973), pp. 69–107; Kenneth Douglas and Gyendolyn Bays, *The Life and Liberation of Padmasambhava, Padma bKa'i Thang, As Recorded by Yeshe Tsogyal, Rediscovered by Terchen Urgyan Lingpa* (Berkeley: Dharma Publishing, 2 vols., 1978). For the "discoverers of concealed treasure" see Eva M. Dargyay, *The Rise of Esoteric Buddhism in Tibet* (Delhi: Motilal Banarsidass, 1977), and especially for Urgyan Lingpa see No. 7, pp. 123–128.
136. Evans-Wentz, *The Tibetan Book of the Great Liberation*, p. 145.
137. Ibid., pp. 127f.
138. Ibid., p. 188.
139. For the Bon religion see W. W. Rockhill, *Diary of a Journey through Mongolia and Tibet* (Washington: Smithsonian Institution, 1894), pp. 68, 86f.; Robert B. Ekvall, *Religious Observances in Tibet: Patterns and Function* (Chicago: University of Chicago Press, 1964), pp. 14–39; Giuseppe Tucci, *The Religions of Tibet* (Berkeley: University of California Press, 1980), pp. 213–248, and p. 249 for the date of the recognition of Buddhism as the state religion of Tibet.
140. Alaka Chattopadhyaya, *Catalogue of Indian (Buddhist) Texts in Tibetan Translation, Kanjur and Tanjur*, 1, *Texts (Indian Titles) in Tanjur*, 3, *Texts (Indian Titles) in Kanjur* (Calcutta: Indo-Tibetan Stuides, 1972); Richard H. Robinson and Willard L. Johnson, *The Buddhist Religion* (Encino, California: Dickenson, 2d ed. 1977), pp. 239–241; *The Nyingma Edition of the sDe-dge bKa'-'gyur and bsTan-'gyur*, ed. Tarthang Tulku (Berkeley: Dharma Publishing, 1981).
141. George N. Roerich, *The Blue Annals* (Delhi: Motilal Banarsidass, 2d ed. 1976), pp. 244–263; Alaka Chattopadhyaya, *Atīśa and Tibet, Life and Works of Dīpaṃkara Srījñāna in relation to the History and Religion of Tibet, With Tibetan Sources translated under Professor Lama Chimpa* (Calcutta: Indian Studies: Past and Present, 1967).
142. Chattopadhyaya, *Atīśa and Tibet*, pp. 520–524.
143. Ibid., p. 329.
144. Ibid., pp. 525–535; cf. Herbert V. Guenther, *Tibetan Buddhism without Mystification*, revised as *Treasures on the Tibetan Middle Way* (Leiden: Brill, 1966, 1969), pp. 20f., 96 n. 2.
145. Roerich, *The Blue Annals*, pp. 261–265, 327; cf. 385–396. For the whole history of the Kadam-pa see EB 3, pp. 146–152.
146. Herbert V. Guenther, *The Life and Teaching of Nāropa, translated from the original Tibetan with a Philosophical Commentary based on the Oral Transmission* (Oxford: Clarendon Press, 1963).

147. Ibid., pp. 53–61.

148. Ibid., pp. 99–108.

149. W. Y. Evans-Wentz, *Tibet's Great Yogi Milarepa* (London: Oxford University Press, 2d ed. 1951); Lobzang Jivaka, *The Life of Milarepa, Tibet's Great Yogi*, condensed and adapted from the original translation of W. Y. Evans-Wentz (WES) (London: Butler and Tanner, 1962); Humphrey Clarke, *The Message of Milarepa, New Light upon the Tibetan Way, A selection of poems* (WES) (London: John Murray, 1958); Garma C. C. Chang, *The Hundred Thousand Songs of Milarepa* (New York: University Books, 2 vols., 1962); Lobsang P. Lhalungpa, *The Life of Milarepa* (New York: E. P. Dutton, 1977). The *Stories and Songs from the Oral Lineage of Jetsun Milarepa* are being translated by Lama Kunga Rinpoche and Brian Cutillo, see *Virupa* (Kensington, California: Ewam Choden Tibetan Buddhist Center), 3, 3, Fall/Winter 1976, pp. 10–17.

150. Chang, *The Hundred Thousand Songs of Milarepa*, 1, p. 217. For Mount Kailasa (22,028 feet [6,714 m.]), often identified with the cosmic Mount Meru, and Lake Manasarovara (20 miles [32 km.] south of Mount Kailasa) see Swami Pranavananda, *Explorations in Tibet* (Calcutta: University of Calcutta, 1950).

151. Clarke, *The Message of Milarepa*, pp. 15f., quoted by permission of John Murray (Publishers) Ltd.; cf. Chang, *The Hundred Thousand Songs of Milarepa*, 1, pp. 84f.

152. Chang, *The Hundred Thousand Songs of Milarepa*, 2, pp. 463–497.

153. Herbert V. Guenther, "Dvags.po.lha.rje's 'Ornament of Liberation,'" in JAOS 75 (1955), pp. 90–96; Herbert V. Guenther, *The Jewel Ornament of Liberation by Sgam.po.pa* (CLS) (Berkeley: Shambala, 1971).

154. Guenther in JAOS 75 (1955), p. 92.

155. W. Y. Evans-Wentz, *Tibetan Yoga and Secret Doctrines, or Seven Books of Wisdom of the Great Path, according to the Late Lāma Kazi Dawa-Samdup's English Rendering* (London: Oxford University Press, 1935), pp. 67–100.

156. David Snellgrove and Hugh Richardson, *A Cultural History of Tibet* (London: Weidenfeld and Nicolson, 1968), pp. 136f., 181, 273 n. for p. 136.

157. Stephan Beyer, *The Cult of Tārā, Magic and Ritual in Tibet* (Berkeley: University of California Press, 1973), pp. 14f.

158. C. A. Muses, *Esoteric Teachings of the Tibetan Tantra, including Seven Initiation Rituals and the Six Yogas of Nāropā in Tsong-Kha-pa's Commentary*, translated by Chang Chen Chi (Indian Hills, Colorado: Falcon's Wing Press, 1961), pp. 123–282, and for the passages cited see especially pp. 137f., 141, 143, 173ff. For the mystic heat see NT 17, 1 (Jan.–Apr. 1982), pp. 1f.

159. Ferdinand D. Lessing and Alex Wayman, *Mkhas Grub Rje's Fundamentals of the Buddhist Tantras* (IIM 8) (The Hague: Mouton, 1968), see especially pp. 17, 101ff., 261ff.

160. For examples of meditations taken from the practices of the Kriya Tantra and the Anuttarayoga Tantra and from texts of the four main orders of Tibetan Buddhism, the Nyingma-pa, Sakya-pa, Kagyu-pa, and Geluk-pa, see Janice Dean Willis, *The Diamond Light of the Eastern Dawn, A Collection of Tibetan Buddhist Meditations* (New York: Simon and Schuster, 1972), pp. 65–119; cf. Edward Conze, *Buddhist Meditation* (ERCEW 13) (London: George Allen and Unwin, 1956), pp. 133–139.

161. Benoytosh Bhattacharyya, *Guhyasamāja Tantra or Tathāgataguhyaka* (GOS 53) (Baroda: Oriental Institute, 2d ed. 1967), pp. ix–xxxviii.

162. Benoytosh Bhattacharyya, *An Introduction to Buddhist Esoterism* (CSS 46) (Varanasi: Chowkhamba Sanskrit Series Office, 2d ed. 1964), pp. 120–146; Benoytosh Bhattacharyya, *The Indian Buddhist Iconography* (Calcutta: K. L. Mudhopadhyay, rev. ed. 1968), pp. 42–76.

163 Bhattacharyya, *An Introduction to Buddhist Esoterism*, pp. 19, 101–103.

164. Bhattacharyya, *Guhyasamāja Tantra or Tathāgataguhyaka*, p. xi. A further statement of the text (p. xiii) supposes a level on which even fundamental Buddhist commandments are transcended: "You should freely immolate animals, utter any number of falsehoods without ceremony, take things which do not belong to you, and even commit adultery." On these passages in comparison with the *tantric* description of the *śunyata* as *vajra*, i.e., as of an adamantine essence (diamond), and the consequent conclusion that the *tantric* way is still long and difficult, with the ideal of transforming oneself into a "being of diamond," see Mircea Eliade, *Yoga, Immortality and Freedom* (London: Routledge and Kegan Paul; New York: Bollingen Foundation, 1958 [2d ed. Princeton University Press, 1969]), pp. 205f.

165. Sum-pa mKhan-po Ye-śes-dpal-'byor, *dPag-bsam-ljon-bzan*, pp. 184–185, in Chattopadhyaya, *Atīśa and Tibet*, p. 380.

166. Beyer, *The Cult of Tārā, Magic and Ritual in Tibet*, pp. 279, 322, 333–335. For a Kriya Tantra meditation of the White Tara (*sGrol ma dkar po*, pronounced Drölma Karpo) according to a Geluk-pa text see Willis, *The Diamond Light of the Eastern Dawn*, pp. 73–79.

167. Bhattacharyya, *The Indian Buddhist Iconography*, p. 156.

168. Ibid., p. 203.
169. Evans-Wentz, *Tibetan Yoga and Secret Doctrines*, pp. 173f.
170. Bhattacharyya, *The Indian Buddhist Iconography*, p. 218.
171. Ibid., pp. 247f.
172. D. L. Snellgrove, *The Hevajra Tantra* (LOS 6) (London: Oxford University Press, 2 vols., 1959).
173. Ibid., 1, p. 47.
174. Ibid., 1, pp. 27f., 36f., 49f.
175. Ibid., 1, p. 110.
176. Ibid., 1, p. 117.
177. Ibid., 2, pp. 84, 89f., 93.
178. Ibid., 2, pp. 76f.
179. Georges de Roerich, "Studies in the Kālacakra," in JUHRI 2 (1932), pp. 11–22; Helmut Hoffmann, *The Religions of Tibet* (New York: Macmillan, 1961), pp. 124–130.
180. Roerich, *The Blue Annals*, pp. 756f., 762f. (for Tsilupa), 758f. (for Somanatha).
181. Albert Grünwedel, *Der Weg nach Śambhala* (Abhandlungen der Königlich Bayerischen Akademie der Wissenschaften, 29, 3, Munich, 1915); Andrew Tomas, *Shambhala, Oasis of Light* (London: Sphere Books, 1977), pp. 31ff., 68ff.; Edwin Bernbaum, *The Way to Shambhala* (Garden City: Anchor Press/Doubleday, 1980). For the Kalacakra Initiation conducted by the Fourteenth Dalai Lama at Bodhgaya in India see Ernst Haas and Gisela Minke, *Himalayan Pilgrimage* (New York: Viking Press, A Studio Book, 1978), pp. 155ff.; for the Initiation in Madison, Wisconsin, see *Snow Lion* (Kensington, California: Ewam Choden Tibetan Buddhist Center Newsletter), April–June 1981, pp. 8f.
182. Chang, *The Hundred Thousand Songs of Milarepa*, 1, pp. 25, 103, 346, 348; 2, p. 488.
183. Guenther, *The Life and Teaching of Nāropa*, pp. 226, 235, 246.
184. John Blofeld, *The Way of Power, A Practical Guide to the Tantric Mysticism of Tibet* (London: George Allen and Unwin, 1970); also published as *The Tantric Mysticism of Tibet, A Practical Guide* (New York: Dutton, 1970), p. 238.
185. W. Y. Evans-Wentz, *The Tibetan Book of the Dead, or The After-Death Experiences on the Bardo Plane, according to Lāma Kazi Dawa-Samdup's English Rendering* (New York: Oxford University Press, 1960); *The Tibetan Book of the Dead: The Great Liberation through Hearing in the Bardo*, by Guru Rinpoche according to Karma Lingpa. A new translation from the Tibetan with commentary by Francesca Freemantle and Chögyam Trungpa (CLS) (Berkeley: Shambala, 1975); Jung Young Lee, *Death and Beyond in the Eastern Perspective, A Study based on the Bardo Thödol and the I Ching* (New York: Gordon and Breach, 1974). For the "discoverer" Karma Lingpa see Dargyay, *The Rise of Esoteric Buddhism in Tibet,* No. 13, pp. 151–153.
186. Evans-Wentz, *The Tibetan Book of the Dead,* p. 91.
187. Ibid., pp. 101ff.
188. Ibid., pp. 153ff.
189. Chang, *The Hundred Thousand Songs of Milarepa*, 1, pp. 98f.
190. Guenther, *The Life and Teaching of Nāropa*, p. 223.
191. Ibid., pp. 225f.
192. Evans-Wentz, *Tibetan Yoga and Secret Doctrines*, pp. 101–154.
193. Ibid., pp. 130, 149.
194. Ibid., p. 149 and n. 1. Quoted by permission of Oxford University Press.

13. MONUMENTS OF BUDDHISM IN INDIA, PAKISTAN, AND SRI LANKA

1. Ananda K. Coomaraswamy, *History of Indian and Indonesian Art* (New York: Dover Publications, 1965, republication of the work first published by Karl W. Hiersemann in 1927), pp. 56f.; David L. Snellgrove, ed., *The Image of the Buddha* (London and Paris: Serindia Publications/UNESCO, 1978), pp. 48–55.
2. J. Ph. Vogel, *Archaeological Museum at Mathura* (Delhi: Indological Book House, 1971), pp. 47f., A1.
3. Ibid., p. 49, A3, for another seated statue in red sandstone of probably equally early date, found near the site called Jamalpur at Mathura and now in the Mathura Museum.
4. Coomaraswamy, *History of Indian and Indonesian Art*, p. 60.
5. A. Foucher, *L'art gréco-bouddhique du Gandhâra* (PEFEO 5–6) (Paris: Ernest Leroux, 2 vols., 1905–51); Harold Ingholt, *Gandhāran Art in Pakistan* (New York: Pantheon Books, 1957); Madeleine Hallade, *Gandharan Art of North India, and the Graeco-Buddhist Tradition in India, Persia, and Central Asia* (New York: Harry N. Abrams, 1968).

6. Coomaraswamy, *History of Indian and Indonesian Art*, p. 53.
7. Ingholt, *Gandhāran Art in Pakistan*, Figs. 198, 222.
8. Snellgrove, ed., *The Image of the Buddha*, Fig. 68.
9. R. S. Gupte, *Iconography of the Hindus, Buddhists, and Jains* (Bombay: D. B. Taraporevala Sons, 1972), pp. 51, 119.
10. Jitendra Nath Banerjea, "Some Folk Goddesses of Ancient and Mediaeval India," in IHQ 14 (1938), pp. 101–104.
11. J. Takakusu, *A Record of the Buddhist Religion as practised in India and the Malay Archipelago (A.D. 671–695) by I-tsing* (Oxford: Clarendon Press, 1896), pp. 37f.
12. Samuel Beal, *Si-yu-ki, Buddhist Records of the Western World* (London: Kegan Paul, Trench, Trübner, 2 vols., 1906), 1, pp. 110f.
13. Coomaraswamy, *History of Indian and Indonesian Art*, p. 71.
14. Vogel, *Archaeological Museum at Mathura*, pp. 49f., A5.
15. Ibid., p. 65, A70.
16. T. W. and C. A. F. Rhys Davids, *Dialogues of the Buddha* (SBB) (London: Henry Frowde, 3 vols., 1899–1921), 2, pp. 155–157.
17. Lama Anagarika Govinda, *Psycho-cosmic Symbolism of the Buddhist Stupa* (Emeryville, California: Dharma Publishing, 1976).
18. Rhys Davids, *Dialogues of the Buddha*, 2, pp. 124f., 133; Bimala Churn Law, "'Cetiya' in the Buddhist Literature," in Walther Wüst, ed., *Studia Indo-Iranica, Ehrengabe für Wilhelm Geiger* (Leipzig: Otto Harrassowitz, 1931), pp. 42–48; V. R. Ramchandra Dikshitar, "Origin and Early History of Caityas," in IHQ 14 (1938), pp. 440–451.
19. T. W. Rhys Davids and Hermann Oldenberg, *Vinaya Texts* (3 vols., SBE 13, 17, 20), 2 (SBE 17), p. 386 and n. 4.
20. Ibid., 1 (SBE 13), pp. 302–305.
21. T. W. Rhys Davids, *The Questions of King Milinda* (2 vols., SBE 35, 36), 2 (SBE 36), p. 374.
22. Rhys Davids and Oldenberg, *Vinaya Texts*, 3 (SBE 20), pp. 178f. and n. 5.
23. Ibid., 3 (SBE 20), pp. 104f., 172f.
24. Ghulam Yazdani, *Ajanta* (London: Oxford University Press, 4 vols. and 4 portfolios of plates, 1930–55); Madanjeet Singh, *India, Paintings from Ajanta Caves* (UNESCO World Art Series) (New York Graphic Society, 1954); Ramesh Shankar Gupte and B. D. Mahajan, *Ajanta, Ellora and Aurangabad Caves* (Bombay: D. B. Taraporevala Sons, 1962); Hermann Goetz, *Ajanta Portfolio* (New Delhi: National Book Trust, 1964); Madanjeet Singh, *Ajanta, Ajanta Painting of the Sacred and the Secular* (New York: Macmillan, 1965); Walter Spink, *Ajanta to Ellora* (Bombay: Marg Publications for the Center for South and Southeast Asian Studies, University of Michigan, 1967); Debala Mitra, *Ajanta* (New Delhi: Archaeological Survey of India, 6th ed. 1968); Sheila L. Weiner, *Ajaṇṭā, Its Place in Buddhist Art* (Berkeley: University of California Press, 1977). For the dates we give for the caves and their paintings see Gupte and Mahajan, *Ajanta, Ellora and Aurangabad Caves*, p. 46 et passim, and for other opinions on the dating, sometimes agreeing and sometimes differing, see the references in the immediately following notes 25–35.
25. Heinrich Zimmer, *The Art of Indian Asia* (Bollingen Series XXXIX) (Princeton: Princeton University Press, 2 vols., 2d ed. 1960, 3d printing with revisions 1968), 2, Pl. 165.
26. Singh, *Ajanta Painting of the Sacred and the Secular*, pp. 180f., Figs. 3–4, 7–8, 20, Pls. 48, 54.
27. Ibid., p. 179, Figs. 5–6, 19.
28. Zimmer, *The Art of Indian Asia*, 2, Pls. 178–181; Gupte and Mahajan, *Ajanta, Ellora and Aurangabad*, Pls. XLII–XLVI.
29. Zimmer, *The Art of Indian Asia*, 2, Pls. 182–185; Gupte and Mahajan, *Ajanta, Ellora and Aurangabad*, Pl. XLIX.
30. Singh, *Ajanta Painting of the Sacred and the Secular*, p. 182, Figs. 9–10, 13, 21, Pls. 50–53, 62.
31. Zimmer, *The Art of Indian Asia*, 2, Pls. 168–177; Singh, *Ajanta Painting of the Sacred and the Secular*, p. 184, Figs. 1, 11–12, 14, 22, Pls. 3, 5, 8–9, 12–13, 18–19, 22, 30, 49, 55–61, 63–66, 69–73, 75–77.
32. Singh, *Ajanta Painting of the Sacred and the Secular*, p. 177, Figs. 17–18, Pl. 45.
33. Zimmer, *The Art of Indian Asia*, 2, Pls. 153–160; Singh, *Ajanta Painting of the Sacred and the Secular*, Fig. 16, Pls. 4, 31–32, 34–35, 37, 39–44 (note that the paintings are here assigned to the 4th and 5th centuries).
34. Gupte and Mahajan, *Ajanta, Ellora and Aurangabad Caves*, p. 61.
35. Zimmer, *The Art of Indian Asia*, 2, Pls. 146–152; Singh, *Ajanta Painting of the Sacred and the Secular*, Figs. 2, 15, Pls. 6, 14, 16–17, 20–21, 23–28, 33, 36, 47, 68, 78–79 (note that the

paintings are here assigned to the 5th and 6th centuries and possibly—in the case of the "Persian Embassy"—the 7th. For the identification of the paintings of the story of Kalyanakarin (previously thought to represent the *Mahajanaka Jataka*), and for ancient Indian sailing vessels as depicted here and elsewhere, see Dieter Schlingloff, *"Kalyāṇakārin's Adventures: The Identification of an Ajanta Painting,"* in AA 38 (1976), pp. 5–28.

36. James Burgess, *Report on the Elura Cave Temples and the Brahmanical and Jaina Caves in Western India* (ASWI 5) (London: Trübner, 1883), pp. 4–22; Gupte and Mahajan, *Ajanta, Ellora and Aurangabad Caves,* pp. 158–180; Zimmer, *The Art of Indian Asia,* 2, Pls. 187–201.

37. Ramesh Shankar Gupte, *The Iconography of the Buddhist Sculptures (Caves) of Ellora* (Aurangabad: published by Shri M. B. Chitnis, Registrar, Marathwada University, 1964), pp. 69–72.

38. Alexander Cunningham, *The Bhilsa Topes* (London: Smith, Elder, 1854; reprint Varanasi: Indological Book House, 1966) (the word *tope* is an Anglo-Indian corruption of *thupa,* the Prakrit form of *stupa*); James Fergusson, *Tree and Serpent Worship* (London: W. H. Allen, 1868; reprint Delhi: Oriental Publishers, 1971); Frederick Charles Maisey, *Sānchī and Its Remains* (first published in 1892; reprint Delhi: Indological Book House, 1972); John Marshall and Alfred Foucher, *The Monuments of Sāñchī* (London: Probsthain, 3 vols., 1940); S. P. Gupta, "Gateway to Indian Art," in OR 12, 5, May 1981, pp. 47–54.

39. In a comparable and even finer capital at Sarnath the lions evidently supported a wheel above them, but the smooth finish of the top of the Sanci capital shows that that was not the case here.

40. E. Hultzsch, *Inscriptions of Asoka* (CII 1) (Delhi: Indological Book House, new ed. 1969), pp. xxi, 160f.

41. For placing the gates and the reign of Śatakarni II around the middle of the 1st century B.C.E., see Ramaprasad Chanda, *Dates of the Votive Inscriptions on the Stupas at Sanchi* (MASI 1) (Calcutta: Superintendent Government Printing, India, 1919); Marshall and Foucher, *The Monuments of Sāñchī,* 1, pp. 275–277. For the Śatakarni of the South Gate inscription as other than Śatakarni II see K. Gopalachari, *Early History of the Andhra Country* (MUHS 16) (Madras: University of Madras, 2d ed. 1976), p. 32 n. 10.

42. Rustam J. Mehta, *Masterpieces of Indian Sculpture* (Bombay: D. B. Taraporevala Sons, 1968), Pl. 7.

43. Rhys Davids and Oldenberg, *Vinaya Texts,* 1 (SBE 13), pp. 130f.

44. Ibid., 1 (SBE 13), pp. 136f.

45. For the three panels of sculptures see Marshall and Foucher, *The Monuments of Sāñchī,* 1, pp. 204, 211, 217; 2, Pls. 50a, 51b.

46. Ibid., 1, pp. 38f., 250f., 389f. (Inscription No. 834); 2, Pl. 70.

47. Ibid., 1, pp. 79–82, 270; 3, Pls. 71–91, for Stupa No. 2.

48. Ibid., 1, pp. 41–45; 3, Pls. 92–103, for Stupa No. 3.

49. Ibid., 1, pp. 52–57; 3, Pls. 111–114, for Temples 17 and 18.

50. Ibid., 1, pp. 71–75, 252; 3, Pls. 116–120, for Temple 45.

51. Ibid., 1, pp. 68f.; 3, Pls. 121–123, for Monasteries 36–38, 45–47.

52. John Marshall, *Taxila* (Cambridge: University Press, 3 vols., 1951); John Marshall, *A Guide to Taxila* (Cambridge: University Press, 4th ed. 1960).

53. Marshall, *Taxila,* 1, pp. 256f.

54. John Marshall, *Excavations at Taxila, The Stupas and Monasteries at Jauliāñ* (MASI 7) (Calcutta: Superintendent Government Printing, India, 1921).

55. Ibid., p. 12, Pl. XIIIb; Marshall, *Taxila,* 2, pp. 523f.; 3, Pl. 155a.

56. Amulyachandra Sen, *Asoka's Edicts* (IIS 7) (Calcutta: Institute of Indology, 1956), Pl. facing p. 37.

57. For the four "miracles" see A. Foucher, *The Life of the Buddha according to the Ancient Texts and Monuments of India,* abridged translation by Simone Brangier Boas (Middletown, Connecticut: Wesleyan University Press, 1963), pp. 204–218.

58. James Legge, *A Record of Buddhistic Kingdoms, being an Account by the Chinese Monk Fa-Hien of His Travels in India and Ceylon (A.D. 399–414)* (Oxford: Clarendon Press, 1886), pp. 55–99; Beal, *Buddhist Records of the Western World,* 2, pp. 1–136, 149–175; Samuel Beal, *The Life of Hiuen-Tsiang by the Shaman Hwui Li* (London: Kegan Paul, Trench, Trübner, 1914), pp. 92–120; Jeannette Mirsky, *The Great Chinese Travelers* (New York: Pantheon Books, 1964), pp. 73–85; René Grousset, *In the Footsteps of the Buddha* (New York: Grossman Publishers, 1971), pp. 132–165.

59. Daya Ram Sahni, *Guide to the Buddhist Ruins of Sarnath (ASI)* (Simla: Government Central Press, 3d ed. 1923); V. S. Agrawala, *Sārnāth* (Delhi: Manager of Publications, 1956).

60. Helmuth von Glasenapp, *Heilige Stätten Indiens* (IKE) (München: Georg Müller, 1928), Pls. 250–251.

61. Hultzsch, *Inscriptions of Asoka,* pp. 161–164. The same "schism edict" is also found on an Aśoka pillar at Allahabad. See Hultzsch, op. cit., pp. 159f.; Sen, *Asoka's Edicts,* pp. 126–131.

62. Daya Ram Sahni, *Catalogue of the Museum of Archaeology at Sarnath* (Calcutta: Superintendent Government Printing, 1914), Pl. IV.
63. Ibid., Pl. X; Mehta, *Masterpieces of Indian Sculpture*, Pl. 18; Snellgrove, ed., *The Image of the Buddha*, p. 101, Pl. 63.
64. John M. Rosenfield, "On the Dated Carvings of Sārnāth," in AA 26 (1963), pp. 10–26.
65. Benimadhab Barua, *Gayā and Buddha-Gayā* (Calcutta: Chuckervertty Chatterjee, 2 vols., 1931–34), 2 (IRIFA 4).
66. Coomaraswamy, *History of Indian and Indonesian Art*, p. 81; Zimmer, *The Art of Indian Asia*, 1, pp. 244, 352, Text Plate B10b and Pl. 99. For doubt as to the authenticity of the Bodhgaya plaque see Barua, *Gayā and Buddha-Gayā*, 2, pp. 45–47.
67. Philip Rawson, *Indian Asia* (MK) (Oxford: Elsevier-Phaidon, 1977), p. 87.
68. Coomaraswamy, *History of Indian and Indonesian Art*, p. 160.
69. D. T. Devendra, "Seventy Years of Ceylon Archaeology," in AA 22 (1959), pp. 23–40; OR 4, 12, Dec. 1973, pp. 12–25, 77–85.
70. John M. Senaveratna, *Guide to Mihintale* (Colombo: Archaeological Department, 1952).
71. Coomaraswamy, *History of Indian and Indonesian Art*, p. 160.
72. Devendra in AA 22 (1959), p. 30, Fig. 4.
73. S. Paranavitana in Senaveratna, *Guide to Mihintale*, p. 14.
74. W. B. Marcus Fernando, *Ancient City of Anuradhapura*, ed. by C. E. Godakumbura (Colombo: Archaeological Department, 1965). For the plan of ancient Anuradhapura see also Wilhelm Geiger, *The Mahāvaṃsa or the Great Chronicle of Ceylon* (Colombo: Ceylon Government Information Department, 1950), facing p. 137.
75. Coomaraswamy, *History of Indian and Indonesian Art*, p. 160; Fernando, *Ancient City of Anuradhapura*, pp. 11f.
76. N. A. Jayawickrama, *The Chronicle of the Thūpa and the Thūpavaṃsa* (London: Luzac, 1971), Pl. III facing p. 69.
77. Senaret Paranavitana, *Art of the Ancient Sinhalese* (Colombo: Lake House Investments, Publishers, 1971), pp. 15f., Pls. 21–22; J. E. van Lohuizen-de Leeuw, "The Rock-reliefs at Isurumini," in *Acta Orientalia Neerlandica*, ed. P. W. Pestman (Leiden: E. J. Brill, 1971), pp. 113–119.
78. Jayawickrama, *The Chronicle of the Thūpa and the Thūpavaṃsa*, Pl. V facing p. 82.
79. Ibid., Pl. VI facing p. 91.
80. Ibid., Pl. I frontispiece.
81. Fernando, *Ancient City of Anuradhapura*, Pl. XVIII.
82. Ibid., Pl. XIV.
83. Geiger, *The Mahāvaṃsa*, p. 214.
84. C. E. Godakumbura, *Moonstones* (ASCAS 8) (Colombo: Archaeological Department, no date); Dawn R. Rooney, "Sinhalese Moonstones," in OR 12, 4, Apr. 1981, pp. 48–52. For the interpretation above see S. Paranavitana, "The Significance of the Sinhalese 'Moonstones,'" in AA 17 (1954), pp. 197–231. For the "guardstones" also found at the entrance of Sinhalese shrines and other edifices see C. E. Godakumbura, *Guardstones* (ASCAS 7) (Colombo: Archaeological Department, no date); S. Paranavitana, "Śaṁkha and Padma," in AA 18 (1955), pp. 121–127; D. T. Devendra, "The Symbol of the Sinhalese Guardstone," in AA 21 (1958), pp. 259–268.
85. For the composition of the plaster and the paint of the Sigiriya frescoes see R. H. de Silva, "The Technique of Ancient Sinhalese Wall Painting—Sīgiri," in N. A. Jayawickrama, ed., *Paranavitana Felicitation Volume* (Colombo: M. D. Gunasena, 1965), pp. 89–121.
86. For the graffiti see S. Paranavitana, *Sigiri Graffiti* (ASC) (London: Oxford University Press, 2 vols., 1956).
87. W. G. Archer and S. Paranavitana, *Ceylon, Paintings from Temple, Shrine and Rock* (UNESCO World Art Series) (Greenwich, Connecticut: New York Graphic Society, 1957), Pls. I–X.
88. Wilhelm Geiger, *Cūlavamsa being the more recent part of the Mahāvamsa* (Colombo: Ceylon Government Information Department, 2 vols., 1953), 1, pp. 42f.; E. Washburn Hopkins, *Epic Mythology* (EIAR 3.1.B) (Strassburg: Trübner, 1915), pp. 142–149; Walther Wüst, "Ein weiterer irano-skythischer Eigennamen im Ṛgveda," in Walther Wüst, ed., *Studia Indo-Iranica, Ehrengabe für Wilhelm Geiger* (Leipzig: Otto Harrassowitz, 1931), pp. 185–212, especially pp. 207f.; Alain Daniélou, *Hindu Polytheism* (Bollingen Series LXXIII) (New York: Pantheon Books, 1964), pp. 135–137.
89. E. B. Cowell, *The Buddha-Karita of Aśvaghosha* (SBE 49, 1), p. 36; E. H. Johnston, *The Buddhacarita or, Acts of the Buddha* (New Delhi: Oriental Books Reprint Corporation, 2d ed. 1972, originally published by the University of the Punjab, Lahore, 1936), p. 43.
90. Senarat Paranavitana, *The Story of Sigiri* (Colombo: Lake House Investments, Book Publishers, 1972).
91. Ibid., p. 70. The salutation of Kassapa I as lord of Alaka is confirmed by the only

inscription known of his reign, discovered at Timbirivava in the Vilpattu Game Sanctuary, in which he is called Alakapaya, the Old Sinhalese equivalent of Sanskrit Alakapati (i.e., the name of his city with the added word *pati* meaning "lord").

92. Ibid., p. 119.
93. T. W. and C. A. F. Rhys Davids, *Dialogues of the Buddha* (SBB) (London: Oxford University Press, 3 vols., 1899–1921), 3, p. 193.
94. Paranavitana, *The Story of Sigiri*, p. 123.
95. S. Paranavitana, "Sīgiri, the Abode of a God-king," in JCBRAS New Series 1, Centenary Volume (1845–1945), pp. 129–183; S. Paranavitana, "The Significance of the Paintings of Sigiri," in AA 24 (1961), pp. 382–387.
96. *Ancient City of Polonnaruva*, issued by the Archaeological Commissioner (Ceylon: Government Press, 1967), with Maps on pp. 16, 42. For the plan of Polonnaruwa see also MASC 2 (1926), Plan facing p. 3.
97. S. Paranavitana, "The Statue near Potgul-vehera at Polonnaruwa, Ceylon," in AA 15 (1952), pp. 209–217.
98. S. Paranavitana, *The Excavations in the Citadel at Polonnaruva* (MASC 3) (Colombo: Government Press, 1936).
99. A. M. Hocart, "Three Temples at Polonnaruva . . . The Laṅkātilaka," in MASC 2 (1926), pp. 11–15.
100. Geiger, *Cūlavamsa*, 2, p. 111.
101. D. T. Devendra, "An Unusual Hand Position in Ceylon Statuary," in AA 19 (1956), pp. 126–136; L. Prematilleke, "The Identity and Significance of the Standing Figure at the Gal-vihāra, Polonnaruva, Ceylon," in AA 28 (1966), pp. 61–66; C. E. Godakumbura, *Buddha Statues* (ASCAS 6) (Colombo; Archaeological Department, no date), Pls. 3, 13, 15.
102. C. E. Godakumbura, *Murals at Tivanka Pilimage* (ASCAS 4) (Colombo: Archaeological Department, no date); Archer and Paranavitana, *Ceylon, Paintings from Temple, Shrine and Rock* (UNESCO World Art Series), Pls. XVIII–XX.
103. A. M. Hocart, *The Temple of the Tooth in Kandy* (MASC 4) (London: Luzac, 1931); Ananda K. Coomaraswamy, *Mediaeval Sinhalese Art* (New York: Pantheon Books, 2d ed. 1956), pp. 6f., Pl. VIII; H. L. Seneviratne, *Rituals of the Kandyan State* (CSSA) (Cambridge: Cambridge University Press, 1978).

14. MONUMENTS OF HINDUISM AND BUDDHISM IN SOUTHEAST ASIA

1. For the geography and history of Southeast Asia see Kenneth Perry Landon, *Southeast Asia, Crossroad of Religions* (Chicago; University of Chicago Press, 1949); D. G. E. Hall, *Atlas of South-East Asia* (London: Macmillan, 1964); Brian Harrison, *South-East Asia* (London: Macmillan, 3d ed. 1966); D. G. E. Hall, *A History of South-East Asia* (New York: St. Martin's Press, 3d ed. 1968); G. Coedès, *The Indianized States of Southeast Asia*, ed. Walter F. Vella (Honolulu: East-West Center Press, 1968). For the monuments see Louis Frédéric, *The Temples and Sculpture of Southeast Asia* (London: Thames and Hudson, 1965).
2. Edward Luther Stevenson, ed., *Geography of Claudius Ptolemy* (New York Public Library, 1932), pp. 155–157 and *Undecima Asiae tabula;* Paul Wheatley, *The Golden Khersonese* (Kuala Lumpur: University of Malaya Press, 1961).
3. Wilhelm Geiger, *The Mahāvaṃsa or the Great Chronicle of Ceylon* (Colombo: Ceylon Government Information Department, 1950), p. 82; H. G. Quaritch Wales, *Prehistory and Religion in South-East Asia* (London: Bernard Quaritch, 1957).
4. H. G. Quaritch Wales, *Towards Angkor, In the Footsteps of the Indian Invaders* (London: George G. Harrap, 1937); R. C. Mazumdar, *Greater India* (Sain Das Foundation Lectures, 1940) (Bombay: National Information and Publications, 2d ed. 1948); Reginald le May, *The Culture of South-east Asia, The Heritage of India* (Delhi: National Book Trust, 1st Indian ed., 1962); R. C. Majumdar, *Hindu Colonies in the Far East* (Calcutta: K. L. Mukhopadhyay, 2d ed. 1963); Coedès, *The Indianized States of Southeast Asia;* H. G. Quaritch Wales, *The Making of Greater India* (London: Bernard Quaritch, 1974).
5. James Legge, *A Record of Buddhistic Kingdoms, being an Account by the Chinese Monk Fâ-hien of His Travels in India and Ceylon (A.D. 399–414)* (Oxford: Clarendon Press, 1886), p. 113; H. A. Giles, *The Travels of Fa-hsien (399–414 A.D.), or Record of the Buddhistic Kingdoms* (Cambridge: University Press, 1923), p. 78.
6. K. A. Nilakanta Sastri, *History of Sri Vijaya* (Madras: University of Madras, 1949); O. W.

Wolters, "Śrīvijayan Expansion in the Seventh Century," in AA 24 (1961), pp. 417–424; Coedès, *The Indianized States of Southeast Asia*, pp. 81–85.

7. J. Takakusu, *A Record of the Buddhist Religion as practised in India and the Malay Archipelago (A.D. 671–695) by I-tsing* (Oxford: Clarendon Press, 1896), p. xxxiv. Note that in 1896 Fo-shih was rendered as Bhoja.

8. Ibid., p. 184; Sastri, *History of Sri Vijaya*, p. 39.

9. Sastri, *History of Sri Vijaya*, pp. 120f.

10. Himansu Bhusan Sarkar, *Corpus of the Inscriptions of Java (Corpus Inscriptionum Javanicarum) (up to 928 A.D.)* (Calcutta: K. L. Mukhopadhyay, 2 vols., 1971–72), 1, pp. 15–24; Coedès, *The Indianized States of Southeast Asia*, p. 88.

11. Louis Frédéric, *The Temples and Sculpture of Southeast Asia*, Pls. 147–154.

12. Sarkar, *Corpus of the Inscriptions of Java*, 1, pp. 34–40.

13. Sastri, *History of Sri Vijaya*, p. 53.

14. In addition to Louis·Frédéric, *The Temples and Sculpture of Southeast Asia* (cited in full in n. 1 above), and other specific references below, see for the monuments of ancient Java: M. P.-Verneuil, *L'Art à Java, Les temples de la période classique Indo-Javanaise* (Paris: Librarie Nationale d'Art et d'Histoire, 1927), pp. 39–44; A. J. Bernet Kempers, *Ancient Indonesian Art* (Amsterdam: C. P. J. van der Peet, 1959); Claire Holt, *Art in Indonesia, Continuities and Change* (Ithaca: Cornell University Press, 1967); Jan Fontein, R. Soekmono, and Satyawati Suleiman, *Ancient Indonesian Art of the Central and Eastern Javanese Periods* (New York: Asia House Gallery, 1971).

15. Bernet Kempers, *Ancient Indonesian Art*, pp. 32, 49–51, Pls. 99–104.

16. Ibid., Pls. 120–121.

17. Ibid., Pl. 125.

18. Ibid., p. 57.

19. Mary-Ann Lutzker, "Jātaka Tales at Tjandi Mendut," in AA 39 (1977), pp. 5–12, Figs. 2–3.

20. Bernet Kempers, *Ancient Indonesian Art*, Pls. 56–57, 58–61.

21. Ibid., Pls. 65–66.

22. Sarkar, *Corpus of the Inscriptions of Java*, 1, pp. 64–75, 102–111.

23. J. G. de Casparis, *Prasasti Indonesia*, 1 ("Inscripties uit de Çailendra-tijd") (Bandung: A. C. Nix, 1950), pp. 24–50, 79–95, 199–203; W. F. Stutterheim, "Chaṇḍi Barabudur, Name, Form and Meaning," in his *Studies in Indonesian Archaeology* (KITLV), ed. F. D. K. Bosch (The Hague: Martinus Nijhoff, 1956), p. 17 n. 21a (by Bosch); Holt, *Art in Indonesia*, pp. 42, 64f. n. 28.

24. For Borobudur see N. J. Krom and T. Van Erp, *Beschrijving van Barabudur* (AONI 3) ('s-Gravenhage: Martinus Nijhoff, 2 vols. Text, 3 vols. Atlas, 1920–31); N. J. Krom, *Barabudur, Archaeological Description* (The Hague: Martinus Nijhoff, 2 vols., 1927) (see the two preceding works for the standard system of numbering of the Borobudur reliefs); Paul Mus, *Barabudur* (Hanoi: Imprimerie d'Extrême-Orient, 2 vols., 1935); A. J. Bernet Kempers, *Borobudur, Mysteriegebeuren in steen, Verval en restauratie, Oudjavaans volksleven* (Wassenaar: Servire, 1973); A. J. Bernet Kempers, *Ageless Barabudur: Buddhist Mystery in Stone, Decay and Restoration, Mendut and Pawon, Folklife in Ancient Java* (Wassenaar: Servire, 1976); *Borobudur, Kunst en religie in het oude Java* (Amsterdam: Rijksmuseum, 1977); Jacques Dumarçay, *Histoire architecturale du Borobudur* (MAEFEO 12) (Paris: École Française d'Extrême-Orient, 1977).

25. Sylvain Lévi, "The Karmavibhaṅga illustrated in the Sculptures of the Buried Basement of the Barabuḍur," in ABIA 1929, pp. 1–7.

26. Bernet Kempers, *Ancient Indonesian Art*, p. 46, Pl. 70.

27. Lévi in ABIA 1929, Pl. Ia.

28. Cf. Krom and Van Erp, *Beschrijving van Barabudur*, Atlas 1, Serie D.C., Pl. V, 31.

29. N. J. Krom, *De Levensgeschiedenis van den Buddha op Barabuḍur* ('s-Gravenhage: M. Nijhoff, 1926); N. J. Krom, *The Life of Buddha on the Stūpa of Barabudur according to the Lalitavistaratext* (The Hague: M. Nijhoff, 1926).

30. See C. Sivaramamurti, *Le Stupa du Barabudur* (PMGRDAA 8) (Paris: Presses Universitaires de France, 1961) for additional identifications of *jataka* scenes and also for many details of the belongings, activities, and surroundings of many sorts of people depicted in the reliefs.

31. Ph. Ed. Foucaux, *Le Lalita Vistara* (AMG 6, 19) (Paris: Ernest Leroux, 2 vols., 1884, 1892), 1, pp. 273–279; Maurice Percheron, *The Marvelous Life of the Buddha* (New York: St. Martin's Press, 1960), pp. 151f.; Nicholas Poppe, *The Twelve Deeds of Buddha, A Mongolian Version of the Lalitavistara* (AF 23) (Wiesbaden: Otto Harrassowitz, 1967), pp. 157–160; Krom, *Barabuḍur, Archaeological Description*, 1, pp. 203f.

32. E. B. Cowell, *The Jātaka, or Stories of the Buddha's Former Births* (PTS) (London: Routledge and K. Paul, 6 vols. in 3, 1973), 4, pp. 271–275.

33. Krom and Van Erp, *Beschrijving van Barabudur,* Text 1, pp. 224, 272f.
34. Krom, *Barabuḍur, Archaeological Description,* 2, p. 57.
35. J. Fontein, "Bosch and the Barabudur Studies," in *Hiraṇyagarbha, A Series of Articles on the Archaeological Work and Studies of Prof. Dr. F. D. K. Bosch* (The Hague: Mouton, 1964), pp. 64–70.
36. Krom and Van Erp, *Beschrijving van Barabudur,* Text 1, p. 631.
37. Krom, *Barabuḍur, Archaeological Description,* 2, pp. 147–150.
38. Ibid., 2, pp. 153–158.
39. For a photograph of the unfinished statue see Krom and Van Erp, *Beschrijving van Barabudur,* Atlas 2, "Buddha-beelden," Pl. IX.
40. Stutterheim, *Studies in Indonesian Archaeology,* pp. 55–58.
41. Krom, *Barabuḍur, Archaeological Description,* 2, pp. 159–165.
42. J. G. de Casparis, *Prasasti Indonesia,* 2 ("Selected Inscriptions from the 7th to the 9th Century") (Bandung: Masa Baru, 1956), pp. 244–279.
43. Ibid., pp. 280–330 (for the passages quoted see pp. 322–328, verses 14, 15, 17, 25); Sarkar, *Corpus of the Inscriptions of Java,* 1, pp. 128f.
44. Sarkar, *Corpus of the Inscriptions of Java,* 2, p. 75.
45. Coedès, *The Indianized States of Southeast Asia,* p. 127.
46. M. E. Lulius Van Goor, *Prambanam* (Archaeological Service of the Dutch East Indies, 1929); Bernet Kempers, *Ancient Indonesian Art,* Pls. 139–160, 162.
47. Lesya Poerbatjaraka, *Agastya in den Archipel* (Leiden: E. J. Brill, 1926); Piet Zoetmulder in Waldemar Stöhr and Piet Zoetmulder, *Die Religionen Indonesiens* (RM 5, 1) (Stuttgart: W. Kohlhammer, 1965), pp. 250–252.
48. Willem Stutterheim, *Rāma-Legenden und Rāma-Reliefs in Indonesien* (IKE) (München: Georg Müller, 2 vols., 1925). See this work for the numbering of the Lara Jonggrang reliefs.
49. Majumdar, *Hindu Colonies in the Far East,* pp. 46–50; Coedès, *The Indianized States of Southeast Asia,* pp. 127–130, 144–147.
50. Bernet Kempers, *Ancient Indonesian Art,* Pl. 202.
51. Ibid., Pls. 232, 249–257.
52. Jessy Blom, *The Antiquities of Singasari* (Leiden: Burgersdijk and Niermans—Templum Salomonis, 1939).
53. Bernet Kempers, *Ancient Indonesian Art,* Pls. 233–242.
54. Ibid., Pl. 222.
55. Ibid., Pls. 243–246.
56. Ibid., Pl. 247.
57. Ibid., Pl. 248.
58. Ibid., Pls. 271–285.
59. Coedès, *The Indianized States of Southeast Asia,* pp. 158, 179 (Kadiri), 187f., 198–201 (Singhasari), 199–201, 232–242 (Majapahit).
60. Roelof Goris, *Prasasti Bali* ("Inscripties voor Anak Wungçu") (Bandung: Masa Baru, 2 vols., 1954), 1, pp. 6, 53f., No. 001.
61. Ibid., 1, pp. 7, 59–61, No. 005; R. Goris, *Bali, Atlas Kebudajaan* (Government of the Republic of Indonesia, 1953), p. 191, No. 3 05.
62. Goris, *Prasasti Bali,* 1, pp. 9, 64f., No. 103; Goris, *Bali, Atlas Kebudajaan,* p. 190, No. 3 03.
63. Goris, *Prasasti Bali,* 1, pp. 8–11, Bundel 1; Coedès, *The Indianized States of Southeast Asia,* p. 129.
64. Goris, *Bali, Atlas Kebudajaan,* p. 80.
65. Goris, *Prasasti Bali,* 1, pp. 14, 83–86, No. 303; Goris, *Bali, Atlas Kebudajaan,* p. 191, No. 3 06.
66. Goris, *Prasasti Bali,* 1, pp. 17–25, Bundel 4A–4B.
67. Majumdar, *Hindu Colonies in the Far East,* pp. 82–84; Coedès, *The Indianized States of Southeast Asia,* pp. 198f., 234, 239–242. For the Bali Aga see Marcus Brooke, "The First Balinese," in OR 9, 11, Nov. 1978, pp. 20–29.
68. R. Goris, "The Position of the Blacksmiths," in *Bali, Life, Thought, and Ritual* (SSI 5) (The Hague and Bandung: W. van Hoeve, 1960), pp. 293f.
69. In addition to particular references below, for religion in Bali in general see C. Hooykaas, *Āgama Tīrtha, Five Studies in Hindu-Balinese Religion* (VKNAW, AL, NR, 70, 4) (Amsterdam: N. V. Noord-Hollandsche Uitgevers Maatschappij, 1964); Zoetmulder in Stöhr and Zoetmulder, *Die Religionen Indonesiens,* pp. 310–337; C. Hooykaas, *Religion in Bali* (IR 13, 10) (Leiden: E. J. Brill, 1973); J. Gonda, "The Indian religions in pre-Islamic Indonesia and their survival in Bali," in HBO 3.2.1, pp. 1–54, especially pp. 37–54 for Bali.

70. Hooykaas, *Āgama Tīrtha*, pp. 9f.; Hooykaas, *Religion in Bali*, pp. 11–18.
71. T. Goudriaan and C. Hooykaas, *Stuti and Stava (Bauddha, Śaiva and Vaiṣṇava) of Balinese Brahman priests)* (VKNAW, AL, NR, 76) (Amsterdam: North-Holland Publishing Company, 1971).
72. Ibid., pp. 102–104, 234–238, 422f., 423–426, Nos. 157, 363, 703, 706. The names by which the texts are cited are their opening words.
73. Ibid., pp. 354–356, No. 591.
74. Ibid., pp. 88–91, No. 136.
75. Ibid., pp. 509f., No. 854.
76. Ibid., pp. 239f., No. 369.
77. Ibid., pp. 356–358, No. 594.
78. Ibid., pp. 383f., No. 651.
79. Ibid., pp. 450–454, No. 751.
80. Ibid., pp. 258f., No. 417.
81. Ibid., pp. 180f., 484f., 501, Nos. 290.1, 800–803, 839.
82. Hooykaas, *Āgama Tīrtha*, pp. 31f.
83. Goudriaan and Hooykaas, *Stuti and Stava*, pp. 256, 342, 513–515, Nos. 411, 567, 863.
84. J. L. Swellengrebel, "Patterns of the Cosmic Order," in *Bali, Life, Thought, and Ritual*, pp. 52f.
85. Ibid., pp. 36–42.
86. Ibid., pp. 43f., 54f.; see also in *Bali, Life, Thought, and Ritual*, R. Goris, "The Religious Character of the Village Community," pp. 80–90, and "The Temple System," pp. 103–106; and Hooykaas, *Āgama Tīrtha*, pp. 95–106.
87. R. Goris, "Holidays and Holy Days," in *Bali, Life, Thought, and Ritual*, pp. 115ff.
88. C. Hooykaas, *Surya-Sevana, The Way to God of a Balinese Śiva Priest* (VKNAW, AL, NR, 72, 3) (Amsterdam: N. V. Noord-Hollandsche Uitgevers Maatschappij, 1966).
89. Jane Belo, *Bali: Temple Festival* (MAES 22) (Locust Valley, NY: J. J. Augustin, 1953).
90. C. Hooykaas, *A Balinese Temple Festival* (BIIN 15) (The Hague: Martinus Nijhoff, 1977).
91. For Balinese music including the set of instruments *(gamelan)* making up any of various types of percussion orchestras; dance including dance in trance *(sangyang)* and self-stabbing in trance with the dagger *(kris)*; dance with large groups of men singing and moving in rhythm *(kechak)*; martial dance *(baris)*; dance of highly trained young girls as *vidyadharis* or heavenly nymphs; secular dance with high headdress *(janger)*; etc.; and drama including the shadow play using puppets made from hide *(wayang kulit)*, and the play in which human beings are the actors *(wayang wong)*, see Jane Belo, *Trance in Bali* (New York: Columbia University Press, 1960); Jane Belo, ed., *Traditional Balinese Culture* (New York: Columbia University Press, 1970).
92. C. Hooykaas, *Cosmogony and Creation in Balinese Tradition* (BIIN 9) (The Hague: Martinus Nijhoff, 1974), pp. 59–92, "The Litany of the Resi Bhujangga."
93. Hooykaas, *Religion in Bali*, Fig. g2.
94. Jane Belo, *Bali: Rangda and Barong* (MAES 16) (Locust Valley, NY: J. J. Augustin, 1949); Marie-Therese Berthier and John-Thomas Sweeney. *Bali, L'art de la magie* (FMVJ Voyages) (Diffusion Librarie Armand Colin, no date).
95. Hooykaas, *Religion in Bali*, Figs. g1, g4.
96. Paul Wirz, *Der Totenkult auf Bali* (Stuttgart: Strecker and Schröder, 1928); *Bali, Life, Thought, and Ritual*, pp. 41, 43f. (Swellengrebel), 84, 125, 377 n. 11 (Goris).
97. For these and other monuments, objects, and scenes of Bali see Goris, *Bali, Atlas Kebudajaan*; Bernet Kempers, *Ancient Indonesian Art*, Pls. 203, 205–211; Holt, *Art in Indonesia, Continuities and Change*, pp. 168–188; Urs Ramseyer, *The Art and Culture of Bali* (Oxford: Oxford University Press, 1977).
98. Ramseyer, *The Art and Culture of Bali*, Pl. 131.
99. Zoetmulder in Stöhr and Zoetmulder, *Die Religionen Indonesiens*, pp. 269f.; Gonda in HBO 3.2.1, p. 34.
100. R. Goris, "Pura Běsakih through the Centuries," in *Bali, Further Studies in Life, Thought, and Ritual* (SSI 8) (The Hague: W. van Hoeve, 1969), pp. 91–104.
101. R. Goris, "Pura Běsakih, Bali's State Temple," in *Bali, Further Studies in Life, Thought, and Ritual*, pp. 77–88.
102. Peter Miller and Fred and Margaret Eiseman, "Bali Celebrates a Festival of Faith," in NGM 157, 3 (Mar. 1980), pp. 416–427.
103. Goris in *Bali, Further Studies in Life, Thought, and Ritual*, p. 103.
104. Goris, *Bali, Atlas Kebudajaan*, p. 197, No. 4 22.
105. C. J. Grader, "The State Temples of Měngwi," in *Bali, Studies in Life, Thought, and Ritual*, pp. 157–186.

106. For Balinese wood carving and painting see Holt, *Art in Indonesia, Continuities and Change,* pp. 173–187.
107. Ibid., pp. 171f.
108. Wheatley, *The Golden Khersonese,* pp. 253–265.
109. T. W. Rhys Davids, *The Questions of King Milinda* (2 vols., SBE 35, 36), 1, p. xliii; 2, p. 269; Stevenson, *Geography of Claudius Ptolemy,* p. 155 and *Undecima Asiae tabula;* Wheatley, *The Golden Khersonese,* pp. 268–272.
110. Majumdar, *Hindu Colonies in the Far East,* pp. 17–20; R. O. Winstedt and R. J. Wilkinson, *A History of Perak* (MBRAS Reprints, 3) (Kuala Lumpur: The Malaysian Branch of the Royal Asiatic Society, 1974), p. 4; H. G. Quaritch Wales, *The Malay Peninsula in Hindu Times* (London: Bernard Quaritch, 1976), pp. 29–48.
111. Victor Purcell, *Malaysia* (London: Thames and Hudson, 1965), pp. 16–22.
112. Lawrence Palmer Briggs, *The Ancient Khmer Empire* (TAPS 41, 1) (Philadelphia: American Philosophical Society, 1951).
113. Paul Pelliot, "Le Fou-nan," in BEFEO 3 (1903), pp. 248–303.
114. R. C. Majumdar, *Kambuja-deśa, or An Ancient Hindu Colony in Cambodia* (Madras: University of Madras, 1944), pp. 17f.
115. M. L. Finot, "Notes d'épigraphie," in BEFEO 4 (1904), p. 923; Majumdar, *Kambuja-deśa,* p. 18.
116. Majumdar, *Kambuja-deśa,* p. 27.
117. Pelliot in BEFEO 3 (1903), p. 254.
118. Majumdar, *Kambuja-deśa,* p. 31; Coedès, *The Indianized States of Southeast Asia,* pp. 55f.
119. Majumdar, *Kambuja-deśa,* pp. 32f.
120. Ibid., pp. 33f.
121. Mahesh Kumar Sharan, *Studies in Sanskrit Inscriptions of Ancient Cambodia* (New Delhi: Abhinav Publications, 1974), p. 81, No. 3.
122. Majumdar, *Kambuja-deśa,* pp. 46, 48.
123. Ibid., pp. 18f. For possible relationship of the Khmers with the Kambojas of India see B. R. Chatterji, "A Current Tradition among the Kambojs of North India relating to the Khmers of Cambodia," in AA 24 (1961), p. 253.
124. Majumdar, *Kambuja-deśa,* pp. 19, 45.
125. Ibid., pp. 16, 46–49, 57; Coedès, *The Indianized States of Southeast Asia,* pp. 69f.
126. Sharan, *Studies in Sanskrit Inscriptions of Ancient Cambodia,* pp. 82–90, Nos. 5, 9, 12, 26; cf. pp. 230ff.
127. Heinrich Zimmer, *The Art of Indian Asia* (Bollingen Series XXXIX) (Princeton: Princeton University Press, 2 vols., 2d ed. 1960, 3d printing with revisions 1968), 1, pp. 145–149.
128. Sharan, *Studies in Sanskrit Inscriptions of Ancient Cambodia,* p. 87, No. 20.
129. Takakusu, *A Record of the Buddhist Religion as practised in Indian and the Malay Archipelago (A.D. 671–695) by I-tsing,* p. 12.
130. Sharan, *Studies in Sanskrit Inscriptions of Ancient Cambodia,* p. 114, No. 88; pp. 256ff.
131. Majumdar, *Kambuja-deśa,* p. 77.
132. Louis Frédéric, *The Temples and Sculpture of Southeast Asia,* Pls. 293–294.
133. Bernard Groslier and Jacques Arthaud, *Angkor, Art and Civilization* (London: Thames and Hudson, 1957), Pl. 64. See the works cited in these two notes (132, 133) and also in n. 140 for all the main Angkor temples.
134. Sharan, *Studies in Sanskrit Inscriptions of Ancient Cambodia,* pp. 92f., No. 35.
135. Ibid., pp. 95f., Nos. 41–44.
136. Ibid., pp. 104f., No. 68.
137. Ibid., pp. 105f., Nos. 69, 72, 73.
138. Madeleine Giteau, *Khmer Sculpture and the Angkor Civilization* (New York: Harry N. Abrams, 1965), pp. 78–84. See this volume for Khmer sculpture in general.
139. For a question about the otherwise quite universal ascription of Angkor Wat to Suryavarman II see Sharan, *Studies in Sanskrit Inscriptions of Ancient Cambodia,* pp. 298f., citing M. M. Ghosh.
140. *Le temple d'Angkor Vat* (MAEFEO 2) (Paris: G. Van Oest, 3 vols. in 7, 1929–32); Maurice Glaize, *Les monuments du groupe d'Angkor* (Paris: Adrien-Maisonneuve, 3d ed. 1963); Guy Nafilyan, *Angkor Vat, Description graphique du temple* (MAEFEO 4) (Paris: École Française d'Extrême-Orient, 1969); Sima Eliovson, "Angkor," in OR 12, 9, Sept. 1981, pp. 10–25; Wilbur E. Garrett and Peter T. White, "The Temples of Angkor," in NGM 161, 5, May 1982, pp. 548–589.
141. George Coedès, "La stèle de Ta-Prohm," in BEFEO 6 (1906), pp. 44–81, especially p. 72, v. XVII for the passage quoted; Sharan, *Studies in Sanskrit Inscriptions of Ancient Cambodia,* pp. 121f., No. 103.

142. Georges Coedès, "La stèle de Práh Khán d'Aṅkor," in BEFEO 41 (1941), pp. 255–301; Sharan, *Studies in Sanskrit Inscriptions of Ancient Cambodia*, pp. 122f., No. 104.

143. "Chronique," in BEFEO 33 (1933), pp. 1116f. and Pl. XXXV.

144. Glaize, *Les monuments du groupe d'Angkor*, pp. 182–188, 191–194, 212–216, 219–227; Louis Frédéric, *The Temples and Sculpture of Southeast Asia*, Pls. 343–352.

145. For the history of Burma see Arthur P. Phayre, *History of Burma* (TOS) (London: Trübner, 1883); G. E. Harvey, *History of Burma* (London: Longmans, Green, 1925); D. G. E. Hall, *Burma* (London: Hutchinson's University Library, 1960); Maung Htin Aung, *A History of Burma* (New York: Columbia University Press, 1967); F. S. V. Donnison, *Burma* (NMW) (London: Ernest Benn, 1970); Norma Bixler, *Burma, A Profile* (PCP) (New York: Praeger, 1971); Joel M. Maring and Ester G. Maring, *Historical and Cultural Dictionary of Burma* (HCDA 4) (Metuchen, NJ: Scarecrow Press, 1973).

146. G. H. Luce and Pe Maung Tin, *The Glass Palace Chronicle of the Kings of Burma* (Burma Research Society) (London: Oxford University Press, 1923); Maung Htin Aung, *Burmese History before 1287: A Defence of the Chronicles* (Oxford: Asoka Society, 1970).

147. Stevenson, ed., *Geography of Claudius Ptolemy, Asiae Tabula XI, India extra Gangem*.

148. Luce and Pe Maung Tin, *The Glass Palace Chronicle of the Kings of Burma*, pp. 2f. For the lists of the early kings see Phayre, *History of Burma*, pp. 275ff.

149. Maung Htin Aung, *A History of Burma*, pp. 18f.; Maung Htin Aung, *Burmese History before 1287*, pp. 9f.

150. Maung Htin Aung, *Folk Elements in Burmese Buddhism* (London: Oxford University Press, 1962), pp. 61–113; Manuel Sarkisyanz, "Die Religionen Kambodschas, Birmas, Laos, Thailands und Malayas," in András Höfer, et al., *Die Religionen Südostasiens* (RM 23) (Stuttgart: W. Kohlhammer, 1975), pp. 421–432.

151. Phayre, *History of Burma*, pp. 28–31, 288f.; Chas. Duroiselle, *Epigraphia Birmanica* (ASB) 1:2 (Rangoon: Superintendent, Government Printing and Stationery, 1960), pp. 69ff.; Maung Htin Aung, *A History of Burma*, pp. 22–25.

152. R. Spence Hardy, *A Manual of Buddhism* (London: Partridge and Oakey, 1853), pp. 182f.; Phayre, *History of Burma*, pp. 26f.

153. C. O. Blagden, "The Inscriptions of the Kalyāṇīsīmā, Pegu," in *Epigraphia Birmanica* (ASB) 3:2 (Rangoon: Superintendent, Government Printing and Stationery, 1928), p. 185, Text A; Niharranjan Ray, *An Introduction to the Study of Theravāda Buddhism in Burma* (Calcutta: University of Calcutta, 1946), p. 12.

154. Luce and Pe Maung Tin, *The Glass Palace Chronicle of the Kings of Burma*, pp. 46ff.; Ray, *An Introduction to the Study of Theravāda Buddhism in Burma*, pp. 25f.

155. Ibid., pp. 35–46, 57–73.

156. Maung Htin Aung, *A History of Burma*, pp. 30f.; Maung Htin Aung, *Burmese History before 1287*, p. 11.

157. Sarkisyanz in *Die Religionen Süostasiens*, pp. 446f.

158. For the monuments of Pagan see Th. H. Thomann, *Pagan, Ein Jahrtausend buddhistischer Tempelkunst* (Stuttgart and Heilbronn: Walter Seifert, 1923); Gordon H. Luce, *Old Burma-Early Pagán* (AA Supplementum 25) (Locust Valley, NY: J. J. Augustin, published for *Artibus Asiae* and the Institute of Fine Arts, New York University, 3 vols., 1969–70).

159. Duroiselle, *Epigraphia Birmanica* (ASB) 1:2, pp. 90–129.

160. Chas. Duroiselle, *The Ānanda Temple at Pagan* (MASI 56) (Delhi: Manager of Publications, 1937). For the figures of Kyanzittha and Shin Arahan see Pl. VII, 3–4.

161. Chas. Duroiselle, *Epigraphia Birmanica* (ASB) 2:1 (Rangoon: Superintendent, Government Printing, 1961).

162. Tun Nyein, *Inscriptions of Pagan, Pinya and Ava* (Rangoon: Superintendent, Government Printing, 1899), pp. 103f., No. 4.

163. Ibid., pp. 95f., No. 1.

164. Taw Sein Ko, *Archaeological Notes on Mandalay* (Rangoon: Superintendent, Government Printing, 1917); E. C. V. Foucar, *They Reigned in Mandalay* (London: Dennis Dobson, 1946).

165. R. L. Soni, *The Shwe Dagon: The Cultural Lighthouse of Burma* (Mandalay: World Institute of Buddhist Culture, 1954).

166. For the history of Thailand in general see Virginia Thompson, *Thailand: The New Siam* (New York: Macmillan, 1941); Ronald Bishop Smith, *Siam or the History of the Thais from Earliest Times to 1569 A.D.* (Bethesda, Maryland: Decatur Press, 2 vols., 1966–67); Russell F. Moore, *Thailand, Malaysia, Singapore, People, Places, History* (New York: Thai-American Publishers, 1975); Monkol Chang and Tom Chuawiwat, *A Portrait of Thailand* (Bangkok: Tom's Studio, no date). For Dvaravati in particular see Lawrence Palmer Briggs, "Dvāravatī, The Most Ancient Kingdom of

Siam," in JAOS 65 (1945), pp. 98–107; H. G. Quartich Wales, *Dvāravatī: the Earliest Kingdom of Siam (6th to 11th century A.D.)* (London: Quaritch, 1969).

167. Beal, *Buddhist Records of the Western World*, 2, p. 200.

168. Robert Halliday and C. O. Blagden, "Les inscriptions môns du Siam," in BEFEO 30 (1930), pp. 81–105.

169. Reginald le May, *A Concise History of Buddhist Art in Siam* (Rutland, Vermont: Charles E. Tuttle, 2d ed. 1963), pp. 21–28.

170. Charnvit Kasetsiri, *The Rise of Ayudhya, A History of Siam in the Fourteenth and Fifteenth Centuries* (Kuala Lumpur: Oxford University Press, 1976), p. 17.

171. O. Frankfurter, "The Story of the Records of Siamese History—Translation of H. R. H. Prince Damrong's Preface to the History," in JSS 11:2 (1915), pp. 1–20; David R. Wyatt, "Chronicle Traditions in Thai Historiography," in C. D. Cowan and O. W. Wolters, eds., *Southeast Asian History and Historiography, Essays Presented to D. G. E. Hall* (Ithaca: Cornell University Press, 1976), pp. 107–122; Kasetsiri, *The Rise of Ayudhya*, pp. 14, 168.

172. Coedès, *The Indianized States of Southeast Asia*, pp. 140, 190f., 194f.

173. Cornelius B. Bradley, "The Oldest Known Writing in Siamese, The Inscription of Phra Ram Khamhaeng of Sukhothai, 1293 A.D.," in JSS 6:1 (1909), pp. 1–64; G. Coedès, "Notes critiques sur l'inscription de Rāma Khamheng," in JSS 12:1 (1918), pp. 1–27; G. Coedès, *Recueil des inscriptions du Siam* (Bangkok: Bangkok Times Press, 2 vols., 1924–29), 1, *Inscriptions de Sukhodaya*, pp. 37–48, Inscription I; Coedès, *The Indianized States of Southeast Asia*, pp. 204, 207f.

174. Phya Nakhon Phra Ram, "Who Was Dharmarājā I of Sukhothai?" in JSS 28 (1935), pp. 214–220.

175. Coedès, *Recueil des inscriptions du Siam*, 1, pp. 123–129, Inscription VIII.

176. Ibid., 1, p. 107, Inscription V; Coedès, *The Indianized States of Southeast Asia*, p. 221.

177. Kasetsiri, *The Rise of Ayudhya*, pp. 22–25, 51ff.

178. O. Frankfurter, "Events in Ayuddhya from Chulasakaraj 686–966," in JSS 6:3 (1909), pp. 1–21, reprinted in *The Siam Society Fiftieth Anniversary Commemorative Publication, Selected Articles from The Siam Society Journal Volume I, 1904–29* (Bangkok, 1954), pp. 38–64.

179. David K. Wyatt, "The Abridged Royal Chronicle of Ayudhyā of Prince Paramānuchitchinōrot," in JSS 61:1 (1973), pp. 25–50.

180. Ibid., pp. 29–33.

181. Prince Damrong Rājānubhāb, "The Foundation of Ayuthia," in JSS 1 (1904), pp. 7–10; and "Explanatory Remarks in Regard to the Period of Siamese History Antecedent to the Founding of Ayudhyā," in JSS 13:2 (1919), pp. 1–66; both reprinted in *The Siam Society, Selected Articles from The Siam Society Journal*, Vol. III, *Early History and Ayudhya Period* (Bangkok, 1959), pp. 69–74, 97–100, 199–202.

182. Kasetsiri, *The Rise of Ayudhya*, pp. 52f., 89.

183. Ibid., pp. 53, 111, 148, 155.

184. Wyatt in JSS 61:1 (1973), pp. 33–35.

185. Frankfurter in JSS 6:3 (1909), pp. 5–8.

186. Kasetsiri, *The Rise of Ayudhya*, pp. 101, 136f.

187. Frankfurter in JSS 6:3 (1909), pp. 5–8; Wyatt in JSS 61:1 (1973), p. 36.

188. A. B. Griswold and Prasert Na Nagara, "A Fifteenth-Century Siamese Historical Poem," in Cowan and Wolters, eds., *Southeast Asian History and Historiography*, pp. 123–163.

189. Ibid., p. 126, Fig. 2, and pp. 128f.

190. Dhaninivat, "The Ramakien, A Siamese version of the Story of Rama," in *Burma Research Society, Fiftieth Anniversary Publications* No. 1 (Rangoon, 1961), pp. 33–45.

191. O. Frankfurter, "King Mongkut," in JSS 1 (1904), pp. 191–207; Constance M. Wilson, "Toward a Bibliography of the Life and Times of Mongkut, King of Thailand, 1851–1868," in Cowan and Wolters, eds., *Southeast Asian History and Historiography*, pp. 164–189.

192. Silpa Bhirasri, *Thai Buddhist Art (Architecture)* (TCNS 4) (Bangkok: Fine Arts Department, 2d ed. 1961). For attitudes of the Buddha figure in Thailand see O. Frankfurter, "The Attitudes of the Buddha," in JSS 10:2 (1913). For the monuments see Karl Döhring, *Buddhistische Tempelanlagen in Siam* (IKE) (Berlin: Walter de Gruyter, 3 vols., 1920; also Bangkok: Asia Publishing House); J. Y. Claeys, "L'archéologie du Siam," in BEFEO 31 (1931), pp. 361–448; Le May, *A Concise History of Buddhist Art in Siam* (cited above in n. 169).

193. Le May, *A Concise History of Buddhist Art in Siam*, p. 27.

194. Claeys in BEFEO 31 (1931), pp. 398–401. For the National Museum in Bangkok see George Coedès, *Les collections archéologiques du Musée National de Bangkok* (ARAS 12) (Paris: G. van Oest, 1928); "Treasures of the Bangkok Museum," in OR 5, 8, Aug. 1974, pp. 31–37, 67.

195. Le May, *A Concise History of Buddhist Art in Siam*, pp. 120–122.

196. Claeys in BEFEO 31 (1931), pp. 413–420.
197. Elizabeth Wray, Clare Resenfield, Dorothy Bailey, and Joe D. Wray, *Ten Lives of the Buddha, Siamese Temple Paintings and Jataka Tales* (New York: Weatherhill, 1972), and for Wat Śri Cum (Si Chum) see pp. 116f.
198. David L. Snellgrove, ed., *The Image of the Buddha* (Serindia Publications/UNESCO, 1978), pp. 314–317 and Fig. 237.
199. "Graceful Shadows of the Siamese Empire," and "Imperial Ayutthaya," in OR 8, 5, May 1977, pp. 14–23, 68f.
200. For Bangkok see Erik Seidenfaden, *Guide to Bangkok* (Bangkok: Royal State Railway Department of Siam, 1927); Kim Dorwong and Jaivid Rangthon, *A New Guide to Bangkok* (Bangkok: Hatha Dhip, 2d ed. 1950); Martin Hürlimann, *Bangkok* (Zürich: Atlantis Verlag, 1962); Philip Ward, *Bangkok, Portrait of a City* (New York: Oleander Press, 1974).
201. Camille Notton, *The Chronicle of the Emerald Buddha* (Bangkok: Bangkok Times Press, 1932).
202. J. V. Cadiz, "Art of the Thai Ramayana," in OR 6, 10, Oct. 1975, pp. 38–47; Siddhijai Solasachinda and John Laird, "Ramakien Murals in the Wat Phra Kaew," in OR 12, 5, May 1981, pp. 55–58.
203. Le May, *A Concise History of Buddhist Art in Siam*, p. 127.

15. MONUMENTS OF HINDUISM AND BUDDHISM BY THE HIGH HIMALAYA AND AT THE GATES OF INNER ASIA

1. Daniel Wright, ed., *History of Nepal, translated from the Parbatiya by Munshi Shew Shunker Singh and Pandit Shri Gunanand* (Kathmandu: Nepal Antiquated Book Publishers, first published 1877, reprint 1972). For the *vaṃśavalis* and later historical records see Bikrama Jit Hasrat, *History of Nepal as Told by Its Own and Contemporary Chronicles* (Hoshiarpur: V. V. Research Institute, 1970). For the history and culture of Nepal in general see: Sylvain Lévi, *Le Népal, Étude historique d'un royaume hindou* (AMGBE 17–19) (Paris: Ernest Leroux, 3 vols., 1905–08); Percival Landon, *Nepal* (London: Constable, 2 vols., 1928); D. R. Regmi, *Medieval Nepal* (Calcutta: K. L. Mukhopadhyay, 4 vols., 1965–66); D. R. Regmi, *Ancient Nepal* (Calcutta: K. L. Mukhopadhyay, 3d ed. 1969); R. S. Varma, ed., *Cultural Heritage of Nepal* (Allahabad: Kitab Mahal, 1972); Basil C. Hedrick and Anne K. Hedrick, *Historical and Cultural Dictionary of Nepal* (HCDA 2) (Metuchen, NJ: Scarecrow Press, 1972); Pashupati Shumshere J. B. Rana and Kamal P. Malla, ed., *Nepal in Perspective* (Kathmandu: Centre for Economic Development and Administration, 1973); Bal Chandra Sharma, et al., *Nepal, An Introduction to Nepalese Culture* (Kathmandu: Sahayogi Press, 1975); Dhurba K. Deep, *The Nepal Festivals* (Kathmandu: Ratna Pustak Bhandar, 1978); Yagya Raj Satyal, ed., *Nepalese Cultural Heritage* (Kathmandu: H. M. G., Hotel Management and Tourism Training Centre, 1979); Leo E. Rose and John T. Scholz, *Nepal, Profile of a Himalayan Kingdom* (NCA) (Boulder: Westview Press, 1980); Mary Shepherd Slusser, *Nepal Mandala, A Cultural Study of the Kathmandu Valley* (Princeton: Princeton University Press, 2 vols., 1982).
2. Rájendralála Mitra, *The Sanskrit Buddhist Literature of Nepal* (Calcutta: Asiatic Society of Bengal, 1882), pp. 249–259. For the date of the *Svayambhu Purana* see Malla and Rana, *Nepal in Perspective*, p. 4.
3. Wright, *History of Nepal*, pp. 77–79; Mitra, *The Sanskrit Buddhist Literature*, p. 251.
4. Wright, *History of Nepal*, pp. 81–106.
5. Ibid., pp. 107–160.
6. J. A. B. van Buitenen, *The Mahābhārata* (Chicago: University of Chicago Press, 1973ff.), 2, pp. 38, 315.
7. Prayag Raj Sharma in Rana and Malla, *Nepal in Perspective*, pp. 67f.
8. Lévi, *Le Népal*, 3, pp. 181–183.
9. Vincent A. Smith, *Aśoka, The Buddhist Emperor of India* (Oxford: Clarendon Press, 2d ed. 1909), p. 77f.
10. E. Frauwallner, *The Earliest Vinaya and the Beginnings of Buddhist Literature* (IIMEO, SOR 8) (Rome: Is. M. E. O., 1956), pp. 13–22.
11. Mitra, *The Sanskrit Buddhist Literature of Nepal*, p. 258.
12. For a chronological list of inscriptions in the Kathmandu valley from c. 464 to 1475 C.E. see Jagadish Ch. Regmi, *Temples of Kathmandu* (Kathmandu: Culture Centre, 1972), pp. 25–39.
13. Pratapaditya Pal, *The Arts of Nepal* (HBO 7:3:3:2:1–2) (Leiden: E. J. Brill, 2 vols., 1974–78), 1, pp. 4ff.

14. Luciano Petech, "The Chronology of the Early Inscriptions of Nepal," in EAW 12 (1961), pp. 227–232.
15. Lévi, *Le Népal*, 2, pp. 99–103; 3, pp. 1–18, No. I; Regmi, *Ancient Nepal*, pp. 129–139.
16. Regmi, *Ancient Nepal*, pp. 95f., 121.
17. Ibid., pp. 121f.
18. Pal, *The Arts of Nepal*, 1, p. 4 n. 2.
19. Lévi, *Le Népal*, 2, Fig. on p. 101; 3, pp. 19–21, No. II; Regmi, *Ancient Nepal*, pp. 275–277.
20. Wright, *History of Nepal*, pp. 100f. and n. 2 on p. 101; p. 124 n. 2.
21. Lévi, *Le Népal*, 3, p. 9.
22. For these inscriptions of Ganadeva and Jishnugupta and their mention of Bhaumagupta, see Regmi, *Ancient Nepal*, pp. 123, 139f., 142.
23. Lévi, *Le Népal*, 3, pp. 70–81, No. XII; Regmi, *Ancient Nepal*, pp. 149–152, 161f.
24. Lévi, Le Népal, 3, pp. 82–96, Nos. XIII–XIV; Regmi, *Ancient Nepal*, pp. 164–178. For the reconstruction of the dynastic history of the Aṁśuvarman period see Petech in EAW 12 (1961), pp. 230f.
25. Samuel Beal, *Si-yu-ki, Buddhist Records of the Western World, translated from the Chinese of Hiuen Tsiang (A.D. 629)* (TOS) (London: Kegan Paul, Trench, Trübner, 2 vols., 1906), 2, pp. 80f.
26. Slusser, *Nepal Mandala*, 1, p. 33; Stephan Beyer, *The Cult of Tārā, Magic and Ritual in Tibet* (Berkeley: University of California Press, 1973), pp. 5f., 9.
27. Pratapaditya Pal, *Vaiṣṇava Iconology in Nepal* (Calcutta: Asiatic Society, 1970), pp. 77–79; Pal, *The Arts of Nepal*, 1, p. 27 and n. 1; Mary Shepherd Slusser and Gautamavajra Vajrācārya, "Some Nepalese Stone Sculptures: A Reappraisal within their Cultural and Historical Context," in AA 35 (1973), pp. 84–89.
28. Slusser and Vajrācārya in AA 35 (1973), pp. 127–131 and Fig. 19; pp. 269f. and Figs. 1–2.
29. Regmi, *Ancient Nepal*, pp. 189–197, 240.
30. Lévi, *Le Népal*, 2, pp. 164f.
31. K. P. Jayaswal, "Chronology and History of Nepal, 600 B.C. to 880 A.D.," in JBORS 22 (1936), pp. 238–243; Regmi, *Ancient Nepal*, pp. 239, 261, 278, 289, 296.
32. Regmi, *Ancient Nepal*, pp. 198–202, 276.
33. Pal, *The Arts of Nepal*, 1, pp. 7f.
34. Wright, *History of Nepal*, p. 211; Regmi, *Medieval Nepal*, 2, pp. 56–60; Hedrick, *Historical and Cultural Dictionary of Nepal*, p. 78.
35. Surya Bikram Gewali, "Political History," in Rana and Malla, *Nepal in Perspective*, pp. 49ff.
36. Wright, *History of Nepal*, p. 187.
37. Ibid., pp. 188f.
38. Ibid., pp. 189ff., 200ff., 233ff.; Landon, *Nepal*, 1, p. 39.
39. Wright, *History of Nepal*, pp. 233–243; Regmi, *Medieval Nepal*, 2, pp. 268–282.
40. Wright, *History of Nepal*, pp. 212–221; Regmi, *Medieval Nepal*, 2, pp. 64–135.
41. Wright, *History of Nepal*, pp. 193–196; Regmi, *Medieval Nepal*, 2, pp. 235–244.
42. Gewali, "Political History," in Rana and Malla, *Nepal in Perspective*, pp. 52–57; Francis Tuker, *Gorkha, The Story of the Gurkhas of Nepal* (London: Constable, 1957).
43. For a classified list of temples in the Kathmandu valley see Regmi, *Temples of Kathmandu* (cited above in n. 12). In addition to specific references below, for the monuments in general see Stella Kramrisch, *The Art of Nepal* (New York: Asia Society, Harry N. Abrams, 1964); Ernst and Rose Leonore Waldschmidt, *Nepal, Art Treasures from the Himalayas* (London: Elek Books, 1969); P. C. Roy Chaudhury, *Temples and Legends of Nepal* (BBU) (Bombay: Bharatiya Vidya Bhavan, 1972); Amita Rai, "The Art of Nepal," in Varma, ed., *Cultural Heritage of Nepal* (cited above in n. 1), pp. 79–99; Pal, *The Arts of Nepal* (cited above in n. 13); Ulrich Wiesner, *Nepalese Temple Architecture, Its Characteristics and Its Relations to Indian Development* (Leiden: E. J. Brill, 1978). For the iconography of the images see Alice Getty, *The Gods of Northern Buddhism, Their History, Iconography and Progressive Evolution through the Northern Buddhist Countries* (Oxford: Clarendon Press, 2d ed. 1928); Mary Rubel, *The Gods of Nepal, An Introduction to the Deities of Hinduism and Buddhism* (Lalitpur: Viswabandhu Press, 1967); Benoytosh Bhattacharyya, *The Indian Buddhist Iconography* (Calcutta: K. L. Mukhopadhyay, 1968); Pal, *Vaiṣṇava Iconology in Nepal* (cited above in n. 27); K. R. van Kooij, *Religion in Nepal* (IR 13, 15) (Leiden: E. J. Brill, 1978).
44. Regmi, *Temples of Kathmandu*, p. 3.
45. Pal, *The Arts of Nepal*, 1, p. 54.
46. L. Austine Waddell, *The Buddhism of Tibet, or Lamaism* (Cambridge: W. Heffer, 2d ed. 1934, reprinted 1971), pp. 315–317.

47. J. E. van Lohuizen-de Leeuw, "South-east Asian Architecture and the Stūpa of Nandangaṛh," in AA 19 (1956), p. 283.
48. Leung Kui-ting and Sherry Bridson, "A Day at Bodnath Stupa," in OR 9, 11, Nov. 1978, pp. 12–19.
49. Regmi, *Temples of Kathmandu*, p. 1; Wiesner, *Nepalese Temple Architecture*, pp. 1ff.
50. Pal, *The Arts of Nepal*, 1, p. 129, Figs. 216–217.
51. Slusser and Vajrācārya in AA 35 (1973), pp. 87–89, 94, Figs. 1–2.
52. For carved wooden windows in Nepal see Ronald M. Bernier, "Wooden Windows of Nepal, An Illustrated Analysis," in AA 39 (1977), pp. 251–267.
53. Regmi, *Medieval Nepal*, 2, p. 104, No. 11.
54. Ibid., 2, p. 245.
55. Chaudhury, *Temples and Legends of Nepal*, pp. 60–63.
56. Ajit Mookerjee, *Tantra Art, Its Philosophy and Physics* (New Delhi: Kumar Gallery, 1966); Patricia Bahree, "Tantric Art," in OR 5, 2, Feb. 1974, pp. 30–37. For the exhibition in 1975 of both paintings and statues of the Asia House Gallery, New York, in association with the Los Angeles County Museum of Art, see Pratapaditya Pal, *Nepal, Where the Gods Are Young* (New York: The Asia Society in association with John Weatherhill, Inc.).
57. Ranjit Sitaram Pandit, *Rājataraṅgiṇī, The Saga of the Kings of Kaśmīr* (New Delhi: Sahitya Akademi, 1935, reprinted 1968); H. H. Wilson, *The Hindu History of Kashmir* (Calcutta: Susil Gupta, 1960). For the geography of Kashmir see Pandit Anand Koul, *Geography of the Jammu and Kashmir State* (Calcutta: Thacker, Spink, 2d ed. 1925). For the history see G. M. D. Sufi, *Kashīr, Being a History of Kashmīr from the Earliest Times to Our Own* (New Delhi: Light and Life Publishers, 2 vols., 1974); Somnath Dhar, *Jammu and Kashmir* (New Delhi: National Book Trust, 1976).
58. Pandit, *Rājataraṅgiṇī*, p. 10, 1.26–27.
59. Ibid., pp. 13–18, 1.44–82.
60. Sufi, *Kashīr*, 1, pp. 36f.
61. Pandit, *Rājataraṅgiṇī*, p. 20, 1.101–104; Sufi, *Kashīr*, 1, pp. 37f.
62. Pandit, *Rājataraṅgiṇī*, pp. 21ff., 1.108ff.; pp. 26f., 1.153ff.; Sufi, *Kashīr*, 1, pp. 39f.
63. Pandit, *Rājataraṅgiṇī*, pp. 27f., 1.168–171; Sufi, *Kashīr*, 1, pp. 42f. and n. 2 on p. 42.
64. Pandit, *Rājataraṅgiṇī*, pp. 29–32, 1.174–200 (Abhiyamanyu, Gonanda III, Nara); pp. 40–42, 1.289–310 (Mihirakula); p. 45, 1.339–341 (Gopaditya); p. 76, 3.97 (Pravarasena I); pp. 98–100, 3.336–363 (Pravarasena II and his city and bridge); Sufi, *Kashīr*, 1, pp. 29–32, 40–42, 45, 48f.
65. Beal, *Buddhist Records of the Western World*, 1, p. 158.
66. van Buitenen, *The Mahābhārata*, 1, pp. 91, 257.
67. Beal, *Buddhist Records of the Western World*, 1, p. 148.
68. Pandit, *Rājataraṅgiṇī*, pp. 116–151, 4.1–371; Sufi, *Kashīr*, 1, pp. 49–54.
69. Pandit, *Rājataraṅgiṇī*, pp. 182–196, 4.709–5.126; Sufi, *Kashīr*, 1, pp. 55–57.
70. Pandit, *Rājataraṅgiṇī*, pp. 261ff., 7.1ff. (Sangramaraja); pp. 331ff., 7.829ff. (Harsha); pp. 405ff., 8.1ff. (Uccala); pp. 425, 690, 8.239, 3448 (Jayasimha); Sufi, *Kashīr*, 1, pp. 58–65.
71. Sufi, *Kashīr*, pp. 67–69, 75, 118–134, 241ff.
72. For the monuments of Kashmir see Pandit Anand Koul, *Archaeological Remains in Kashmir* (Lahore: Mercantile Press, 1935); Ram Chandra Kak, *Ancient Monuments of Kashmir* (London: The India Society, 1933, reprinted, New Delhi: Sagar Publications, 1971); Dhar, *Jammu and Kashmir* (cited above in n. 57), pp. 152–167, "Archaeological Monuments of Kashmir."
73. Kak, *Ancient Monuments of Kashmir*, pp. 112–116, Pls. XLIV, XLV, LXIII–LXVII; Pandit, *Rājataraṅgiṇī*, p. 601, 8.2409.
74. Kak, *Ancient Monuments of Kashmir*, pp. 105–111, Pls. XV–XLII, LXXVII.
75. Ibid., pp. 73–76, Pls. IV–V; Koul, *Archaeological Remains in Kashmir*, pp. 17–22; A. H. Francke, *Antiquities of Indian Tibet*, 1, *Personal Narrative* (ASI 38) (Calcutta: Superintendent Government Printing, India, 1914), p. 109.
76. Kak, *Ancient Monuments of Kashmir*, pp. 131–135, Pls. LIII, LXXIII; Dhar, *Jammu and Kashmir*, pp. 158–160.
77. Kak, *Ancient Monuments of Kashmir*, pp. 118–125, Pls. XLIII–L, LXVII–LXXII, LXXIV D.
78. James Legge, *A Record of Buddhistic Kingdoms, being an Account by the Chinese Monk Fâ-hien of His Travels in India and Ceylon (A.D. 399–414)* (Oxford: Clarendon Press, 1886), pp. 28f.
79. Beal, *Buddhist Records of the Western World*, 1, pp. 119–135.
80. Domenico Faccenna, *A Guide to the Excavations in Swat (Pakistan) 1956–1962* (Rome: Department of Archaeology of Pakistan and Istituto Italiano per il Medio ed Estremo Oriente, 1964), with Foreword by Giuseppe Tucci, and with Bibliography; F. A. Khan, *Architecture and Art Treasures in Pakistan* (Karachi: Elite Publishers, 1969), p. 89.

81. For maps of the caravan, missionary, and pilgrim routes see H. G. Quaritch Wales, *The Indianization of China and of South-East Asia* (London: Bernard Quaritch, 1967), p. viii, Fig. 1; Madeleine Hallade, *Gandharan Art of North India and the Graeco-Buddhist Tradition in India, Persia, and Central Asia* (New York: Harry N. Abrams, 1968), pp. 246–251, Maps I–IV; Madanjeet Singh, *Himalayan Art* (UNESCO Art Books) (Greenwich: New York Graphic Society, 1968), p. 8. For the Silk Road see Luce Boulnois, *The Silk Road* (New York: Dutton, 1966) Irene M. Franck and David M. Brownstone, *The Silk Road: A History* (New York: Facts on File Publications, 1986).

82. For the history of Afghanistan see Louis Dupree, *Afghanistan* (Princeton: Princeton University Press, 1973). V. A. Romodin, *The History of Afghanistan* (Moscow, 2 vols., 1964–65) is in Russian. For the archaeology see F. R. Allchin and Norman Hammond, *The Archaeology of Afghanistan from the earliest times to the Timurid period* (London: Academic Press, 1978).

83. Simone Gaulier, Robert Jera-Bezard, and Monique Maillard, *Buddhism in Afghanistan and Central Asia* (IR 13.14.1–2) (Leiden: Brill, 2 vols., 1976).

84. Legge, *A Record of Buddhistic Kingdoms*, pp. 36–38.

85. Beal, *Buddhist Records of the Western World*, 1, pp. 91–97.

86. J. Barthoux, *Les fouilles de Haḍḍa* (MDAFA 4) (Paris: G. van Oest, vols. 1–3, 1930–33).

87. Snellgrove, ed., *The Image of the Buddha*, pp. 178–182 and Pls. 132–134.

88. Benjamin Rowland, Jr., *Ancient Art from Afghanistan, Treasures of the Kabul Museum* (New York: Asia Society, 1966), pp. 79–91.

89. Beal, *Buddhist Records of the Western World*, 1, pp. 54–59; Samuel Beal, *The Life of Hiuen-Tsiang by the Shaman Hwui Li* (London: Kegan Paul, Trench, Trübner, 1911), p. 54.

90. R. Ghirshman, *Bégram, Recherches archéologiques et historiques sur les Kouchans* (Cairo: Imprimerie de l'Institut Française d'Archéologie Orientale, 1946); J. Hackin, *Recherches Archéologiques à Begram* (MDAFA 9) (Paris: Les Éditions d'Art et d'Histoire, 1939); Rowland, *Ancient Art from Afghanistan*, pp. 24–64.

91. For the caravan route from Taxila to Bactra see Rowland, *Ancient Art from Afghanistan*, p. 12, Map of Afghanistan. For Balkh see Moh. O. Sidqi, "A Short Historical and Geographical Description of the Cities of Aryana," in *Afghanistan* 27, 3, Dec. 1974, pp. 8–11.

92. J. Hackin, *Nouvelles Recherches Archéologiques à Bāmiyān* (MDAFA 3) (Paris: G. van Oest, 1933).

93. Beal, *Buddhist Records of the Western World*, 1, pp. 48–53.

94. Rowland, *Ancient Art from Afghanistan*, pp. 94–106; S. Sengupta, "India Helps Afghanistan in Preserving Her Heritage," in *Afghanistan* 26, 3, Dec. 1973, pp. 23–34; Dupree, *Afghanistan*, p. 305; Snellgrove, ed., *The Image of the Buddha*, p. 185.

95. Allchin and Hammond, *The Archaeology of Afghanistan*, pp. 278 (D. W. Mac Dowall and M. Taddei), 351 (K. Fischer).

96. Rowland, *Ancient Art from Afghanistan*, pp. 94f.; Nigel Cameron, "The Theater of Heaven," in OR 5, 1, Jan. 1974, pp. 25–30; Francine Tissot, "In Search of Alexander," in OR 7, 2, Feb. 1976, pp. 30–39.

97. Joseph Edkins, *Chinese Buddhism* (TOS) (London: Kegan Paul, Trench, Trübner, preface Peking 1879, 2d ed. no date); Kenneth K. S. Ch'en, *Buddhism in China* (Princeton: Princeton University Press, 1964); Jack Chen, *The Sinkiang Story* (New York: Macmillan; London: Collier Macmillan, 1977), pp. 85–89; *The Tianshan Mountains* (Xinjiang People's Publishing House, 1980).

98. Albert Grünwedel, *Alt-Kutscha, archäologische und religionsgeschichtliche Forschungen en Tempera-Gemälden aus buddhistischen Höhlen der ersten acht Jahrhunderte nach Christi Geburt* (Veröffentlichung der preussischen Turfan-Expeditionen mit Unterstützung des Bässler-Institutes) (Berlin: O. Elsner, 1920).

99. Albert von Le Coq, *Die buddhistische Spätantike in Mittelasien, Ergebnisse der kgl. preussischen Turfan Expeditionen* (Berlin: Dietrich Reimer/Ernst Vohsen, 7 vols., 1922–33).

100. Paul Pelliot, *Les grottes de Touen-Houang, peintures et sculptures bouddhiques des époques des Wei, des T'ang et des Song* (Mission Pelliot en Asie Centrale) (Paris: P. Guethner, 6 vols., 1914–24); Aurel Stein, *The Thousand Buddhas, Ancient Buddhist Paintings from the Cave-Temples of Tun-huang on the Western Frontier of China* (London: Bernard Quaritch, 1921); Irene Vongehr Vincent, *The Sacred Oasis, Caves of the Thousand Buddhas, Tun-Huang* (Chicago: University of Chicago Press, 1953).

101. Gaulier, Jera-Bezard, and Maillard, *Buddhism in Afghanistan and Central Asia;* Annette L. Juliano, "Buddhism in China," in *Archaeology* 33, 3, May/June 1980, pp. 23–30.

102. Albert von Le Coq, *Chotscho, Ergebnisse der Kgl. Preussischen Turfan-Expeditionen* (Berlin: D. Reimer, 1913); Le Coq, *Die buddhistische Spätantike in Mittelasien*, 3, pp. 13f.; Albert Herrmann, *An Historical Atlas of China*, new ed. by Norton Ginsburg (Chicago: Aldine Publishing Co., 1966), p. 39, "The Ruins near Turfan"; Cary Wolinsky in NGM Vol. 165, No. 1, Jan. 1984, pp. 20–21.

103. Henry Clarke Warren, *Buddhism in Translations* (HOS 3) (Cambridge: Harvard University Press, first published 1896, reissued 1953), pp. 5–31.

104. Le Coq, *Chotscho, Ergebnisse der Kgl. Preussischen Turfan-Expeditionen*, Pl. XXVII; Gaulier, Jera-Bezard, and Maillard, *Buddhism in Afghanistan and Central Asia*, 1, Fig. 4.

105. For more detail and documentation on the history, sites, and monuments in Tibet (Xizang) and also in Western Tibet (Ladakh), see Jack Finegan, *Tibet—A Dreamt of Image* (New Delhi: Tibet House, The Cultural Centre of H. H. the Dalai Lama, 1986), cf. above n. 132 in Chapter 12.

106. Stephan Beyer, *The Cult of Tara, Magic and Ritual in Tibet* (Berkeley: University of California Press, 1973), pp. 8f.

107. John F. Avedon, *In Exile from the Land of Snows* (New York: Alfred A. Knopf, 1984); Tenzin Lhundup in NT 20, 1 (Jan.–Apr. 1985), p. 5; United States *Congressional Record*, May 19, 1987 and Oct. 6, 1987; Tinley Nyandak, New York, Feb. 19, 1988, in *Snow Lion* (Ithaca, NY), 3, 1 (Spring 1988), p. 14.

108. Valrae Reynolds in NT 17, 1 (Jan.–Apr. 1982), pp. 3f.

109. Albert Grünwedel, *Die Tempel von Lhasa, Gedicht des ersten Dalailama, für Pilger bestimmt* (Sitzungsberichte der Heidelberger Akademie der Wissenschaften, phil.-hist. Kl., 10:1 [1919], No. 14) (Heidelberg: Carl Winter's Universitätsbuchhandlung, 1919).

110. Turrell V. Wylie, *The Geography of Tibet according to the 'Dzan-gling-rgyas-bshad* (SOR 25) (Rome: Istituto Italiano per il Medio ed Estremo Oriente, 1962).

111. Alfonsa Ferrari, Luciano Petech, and Hugh Richardson, *mK'yen brtse's Guide to the Holy Places of Central Tibet* (SOR 16) (Rome: Istituto Italiano per il Medio ed Estremo Oriente, 1953).

112. Detlef Ingo Lauf, *Tibetan Sacred Art, The Heritage of Tantra* (Berkeley & London: Shambhala, 1976), p. 131.

113. India Trinley in NT 20, 2 (May–Aug. 1985), pp. 4f.

114. Ngawang J. Topgyal in NT 18, 1 (Jan.–Apr. 1983), pp. 6f.; Frances Thargay in NT 20, 2 (May–Aug. 1985), p. 5.

115. Tinley Nyandak in NT 18, 1 (Jan.–Apr. 1983), pp. 8–10.

116. Anneliese and Peter Keilhauer, *Ladakh und Zanskar* (Köln: DuMont Buchverlag, 2d ed. 1982).

117. Ibid., pp. 24f., 373–376.

118. A. H. Francke, *Antiquities of Indian Tibet*, 2, *The Chronicles of Ladakh and Minor Chronicles* (ASI 50) (New Delhi: S. Chand, 1926 reprint 1972); Luciano Petech, *A Study on the Chronicles of Ladakh*, Supplement to IHQ 13 (1937) and 15 (1939); and *The Kingdom of Ladakh c.950–1842 A.D.* (SOR 51) (Rome: Istituto Italiano per il Medio ed Estremo Oriente, 1977).

119. Alaka Chattopadhyaya, *Atīśa and Tibet* (Calcutta: Indian Studies: Past and Present, 1967). For monuments and images in Tsaparang and Tholing in Guge, see Li Gotami Govinda, *Tibet in Pictures*, 2, *Expedition to Western Tibet* (Berkeley: Dharma Publishing, 1979).

120. Petech, *The Kingdom of Ladakh c.950–1842 A.D.*, pp. 14–24.

121. Ibid., pp. 14ff., 171f.

122. Ibid., pp. 138–152.

123. Blanche C. Olschak, with photography by Ursula and Augusto Gansser, *Bhutan, Land of Hidden Treasures* (New York: Stein & Day, 1971); Nagendra Singh, *Bhutan, A Kingdom in the Himalayas* (New Delhi: Thomson Press, [India] Ltd., 1972); Mrs. Nirmala Das, *The Dragon Country, The General History of Bhutan* (Bombay: Orient Longmans, 1974); G. N. Mehra, *Bhutan, Land of the Peaceful Dragon* (New Delhi: Vikas Publishing House, 1974); Guy van Strydonck (photographs), Françoise Pommaret-Imaeda and Yoshiro Imaeda (text), *Bhutan, A Kingdom of the Eastern Himalayas* (Boston: Shambhala, 1985).

124. Windsor Chorlton, *Cloud-Dwellers of the Himalayas, The Bhotia* (Amsterdam: Time-Life Books, 1982).

125. Das, *The Dragon Country, The General History of Bhutan*, pp. 86, 92f.; Mehra, *Bhutan, Land of the Peaceful Dragon*, pp. 78, 82; Olschak, *Bhutan, Land of Hidden Treasures*, p. 27.

126. Lokesh Chandra, *Tibetan Chronicle of Padma-dkar-po'* (SPS 75) (New Delhi: International Academy of Indian Culture, 1968), see the Foreword by E. Gene Smith.

127. Olschak, *Bhutan, Land of Hidden Treasures*, pp. 5f.

INDEX

NOTES: In the interest of consistency, all Asian names are alphabetized beginning with the first letter of the first name.

Page numbers in italics refer to illustrations.

Abhaya, 302–303
Abhayagiri, 314–15, 317, 318; *see also* Dhammarucikas
Abhayagiri Dagoba, 462
Abhayuttara-*vihara,* 314, 315, 316, 318, 324
Abhidhaja Maharattha Guru Bhadanta Revanta, 330
Abhidhamma, 306
Abhidhammapitaka, 292, 342–43
Abhidhammattha-sangaha, 344
Abhimanyu I, 617
Abhiraja, 547
Abridged Chronicle, 565, 566, 567, 568
Abu, Mount, 279–*83*
Abu-l Fazl, 131
Achaemenid Persians, 102–104, 623
Action, path of, 133, 134
Adhisimakrishna, 55, 65
Adinatha, colossal statue of, *268*
Adinatha Temple: at Khajuraho, *270*–71; at Ranakpur, *284*–89
Aditi, 30–31, 32
Adityas, 30, 32
Afghanistan, 623–24
Agama Hindu-Bali, 510
Agama Tirtha, 510
Agamas, 155, 210, 212–20; table listing, 212–13
Ages of the world, 18–19
Agnavi, 34
Agni, 32, 33–34, 36, 259; figure of, 613, *615*
Ahirs, 587
Ahura Mazda, 39
Airlinga, 502, *503,* 509
Ajanta, Buddhist caves at, 427–35, 473
Ajataśatru, 294
Ajita Keśakambalin, 88
Ajivikas, 89, 209, 235, 239

Akbar, 131–32
Akshara-Śatakam, 386
Akshobhvavajra statue, 637, 648
Alahana-parivena, 470
Alakamanda of Kubera, 464–66
Alamgirpus, 1
Alaungpaya, 551, 559
Alaungsithu, 551, 552
Alexander the Great, 63–64, 104–108, 621–22, 623; retreat of, 107
Allakappa, 84
Alms bowl of the Buddha, 318, 323–24, 327–28
Altan Khan, 638
Aluvihara, 315; Second Buddhist Council at, 315–16
Amarapura, 551
Amarddaka, Śiva as, 169
Ambika, 254–55
Amitayurdhyana, 380
Amri, 2, 3
Amśuvarman, 591–93
Ananda, 294–95, 554, 555
Anandadeva, 595
Ananda Temple, 555–*56*
Anarya, 16
Anasya, 16
Anawrahta, 548, 550, 551, 552
Andhras/Śatavahanas, 62–63
Angas, 214
Angas, kingdom of the, 84–85
Angkor, 536–46
Angkor Thom, 537, 540, 544–*46*
Angkor Wat, 537, 540–44
Anguttara Nikaya, 335–36
Animals, divine, 43–46; birds, 44; cattle, 43–44; horses, 43; serpents, 44–46

719

Antariksha, 35
Anula, 304–305
Anuradhapura, 303, 304, 306, 310, 311, 312, 313, 318, 320; Buddhist monuments at, 459–63; capital moved from, 322, 323
Anuruddha, 344–45
Anuttarayoga Tantra, 407
Anyuoqadarasutta, 220
Aornos, 105
Apadana, 342
Aphrodite, *626, 627*
Apsarases, 42
Arahant, 362, 363
Aranyakas, 13, 14
Arbudi, 45
Archaeological Museum at Peshawar, *422, 423,* 424
Archeological Museum at Khajuraho, *248–49, 250–*51
Archeological Museum at Mathura, *163–64,* 166, *167, 263,* 420, *421,* 424, *425, 426*
Archeological Museum at Sanci, *438*
Archeological Museum at Sarnath, 455
Ardha-Magadhi language, 12–13
Arimalla, 595
Arishtanemi, 231–32, 247, 249–51
Artha, 134
Aryadeva, 380, 385–86
Aryan group of languages, 12–13
Aryans, 7, 300–301; deities of Aryan heritage, 31–33
Aryas, 16
Arya Sudharman, 210
Aryavarta, 16
Asanga, 386–87, 407
Asela, 309
Ashi Kesang Wangchuck, 663
Ashtamangalas, 242–43
Aśmakas, kingdom of the, 97
Aśoka, 64, 111–14, 131, 297–98, 438–39, 448, 451–55, 457, 588, 595, 598, 601, 606, 616, 617, 619, 653; Devanampiyatissa and, 303–304, 306, 307; successors of, 115–16
Aśoka pillars, 438–39, 442, *443,* 455, 588
Asparas, 164
Aśrama, 135
Assyrians, 102
Astika systems of philosophy, 136
Asuras, 16, 168
Aśvaghosha, 300, 380, 381–82
Aśvins, 32
Atanativa Sutra, 467
Atavaka, *481,* 482
Atiśa, 396–98, 406, 638, 645; statue of, *643*
Atman, 50
Atthasalini, 320, 344
Aurangzib, 630
Ava, 551
Avalokiteśvara, 637, 663
Avalokiteśvara-gunakarandavyuha, 379
Avantipura, 618; monuments at, 621
Avantis, kingdom of the, 55, 56, 79, 100; Barhadrathas of, 57–58; Pradyotas of, 58–59
Avantisvami-Vishnu Temple, 621
Avantivarman, 618, 621
Avatars, 143–49; of Śiva, 144; of Vishnu, 144–49
Ayagapaptas: images in, 245–46; symbols in, 244–45
Ayodhya, 21–22, 92
Ayudhya, 565–68, 580

Ayutthaya, monuments at, 573–75

Bactria, 624, 628
Badarayana, 138
Badridas Temple at Calcutta, *288,* 289
Bagyidaw, 546, 552
Bahiranidana, 320, 344
Bahubali, 231, 247
Bakheng Temple, 536–37
Bakong, 536
Baladevas, 226, 231
Baladitya, 123, 124
Bali, 508–29; classes in, 509–10; cosmic order, 513; culture and religion of, 509–18; deities of, 510–13; Denpasar, *525–27;* Gao Gajah, *518–19;* history of, 508–509; Klungkung, 519–20; Mas, 525; *pitaras,* 512–13; Pura Besakid, 520–22, *523;* Pura Kehen, Bangli, 522, *523, 524;* Pura Taman Ayun, Mengwi, 522–24; priests in, 510; rites and rituals in, 514–18; Sangeh, 524; *Sang hyang Widi,* 513; *stutis* and *stavas,* 510–11, 512–13; temples in, 513–14; Ubud, 525; village life, 527–29
Bali Museum, *525–27*
Bamiyan, *628–32*
Bana, 124, 125–26, 130
Bangkok, 568, 569; monuments at, 571, *572,* 575–83
Bangli, temple at, 522, *523, 524*
Bangun Śakti, 521
Ban Muang, 563
Banteay Kedei, 546
Banteay Samre, 540, *541*
Banteay Srei, *538–40*
Baphuon, 540
Bardo Thodol, 415
Bardo Yoga, 414–16
Barhadrathas of Magadha and Avanti, 57–58
Barong: and Ranga, 516–17; -Range Dance Drama, *529;* sculpture of, *527*
Batari Śri, 521
Batu Cave, Hindu shrine in, 530
Bayon, 544–46
Begram, *624–28*
Belus, temples at, 187–90
Belur Math Temple at Calcutta, *207*
Bengal, 397
Bezeklik, 633–36
Bhaddakaccana, 302
Bhadgaon, 595, 597, *603–12*
Bhadrabahu, 110, 111, 210, 211
Bhadracari, 490
Bhagavad Gita, 13, 133, 134
Bhaggas clan, 84
Bhairava, Śiva as, 169, *172*
Bhairava Festival, 609
Bhairav Mandir, 609, *610*
Bhakti, 133, 134
Bhallatiya Jataka, scene from, *488–89*
Bhalluka, 549
Bhanucandra Upadhyaya, 131
Bharata, 231
Bhashyas, 221
Bhaskaravarman, 589
Bhavavarman I, 534
Bhimarjunadeva, 592, 593
Bhudevi, 151
Bhuktamana, 587

Bhupatindramalla, 595, 597, 605
Bhutan, 659–63
Bhuvanaikabahu I, 328
Bhuvanaikabahu II, 328
Bimbisara, 361, 427
Bindusara, 64, 111
Birds, identified as deities, 44
Bishnuloka, 568
Bisnu, 554
Blue Annals, 73, 396, 398–99, 413
Bodawpaya, 551, 558
Bodhgava, 101, 449, 451, 452, 454, *456–57*
Bodhi-marga-pradipa-panjika, 397
Bodhi-patha-pradipa, 397, 398, 638
Bodhisattvas, 345, 360, 361, 362–65, 366–67, 419, 624
Bodhi tree, 453, 454, 456, 459
Bodhnath monastery, 601, *602*
Bodhnath *stupa,* 598–*601*
Bombay Museum, images of Hindu gods at, *165, 166, 167, 168, 169,* 170, *171, 172, 174,* 175
Bon religion, 395, 638, 653
Boromaraja II, 567, 573–75
Botataung Pagoda, *561, 562*
Brahma, 150, 151, 586; images of, *165,* 258, 259; *Śaktis* of, 150
Brahmacari, 135
Brahmacarya, 135
Brahman, 13, 16, 46, 50
Brahmanas, 13, 14; knowledge in the, 49–50; philosophy in the, 49–53
Brahmanaspati, 46–47
Brihaspati, 136, 259
Brihat Samhita, 163
Buddha(s), 239, 345–46; images of, 420–26, 430, 431, 435–37, 442, 443, *445,* 447, *450,* 455, 457, 471–72, 482–83; 491–92, *493,* 530–31, 545–56, 552, *554–55, 556,* 558, 559, *561, 562,* 571–73, *574,* 576, 577, 579–80, *581, 582,* 613, *615, 623,* 624, *625,* 629–30, *631,* 633–36, *643,* 650, *652,* 655, *656, 657, 663;* as incarnation of Vishnu, 148; in Mahayana Buddhism, 362, 365–67; numerous Buddhas, 345, 361, 362, 365–67, 635; symbols of, 419–20, 439, *441–*42
Buddha-carita, 300, 381
Buddha chronology, 70–78; Buddha Nirvana Era, 74–77; Burma traditions, 71–72; dates of the life of Buddha, 77–78; Guangzhou tradition, 72–73; Sri Lanka traditions, 70–71; Tibetan traditions, 73
Buddhaghosa, 293, 319–20, 344, 549–50
Buddhamitra, 466–67
Buddhavamsa, 341–42
Buddhirakshita, 639
Buddhist Councils, 293–300, 307–308, 315–16, 318–20, 324–27, 329–30
Buddhism, 209; decline and renewal of, 130–31; Mahayana, *see* Mahayana Buddhism; monuments of, *see* Buddhist monuments; Thervada, *see* Theravada (Hinayana) Buddhism; Vajrayana, *see* Vajrayana Buddhism
Buddhist monuments: by the Himalaya and in Central Asia, 585–*663*; in India, 419–57 *passim;* in Pakistan, 419–57 *passim;* in Southeast Asia, 473–583 *passim;* in Sri Lanka, 457–72
Budha (Mercury), 259
Budha Gupta, 123, 124

Budhanilakantha, monuments at, *605,* 606
Bulbul Shah, 619
Bulis clan, 84
Burma, 307, 362, 546–62; Buddha chronology, 71–72; early history of, 546–50; Hlutdaw (supreme council of state), 556; introduction of Buddhism to, 549–50; later history of, 550–52; the Mons in, 548–59, 550, 563; monuments in, 552–62; the people of, 546; the Pyus, 547–548; version of the Buddhist Councils in, 330; wars with Thailand, 567
Buston, 383, 385, 392, 394, 396, 399–400, 409, 636
Butkara *stupa, 622–23*

Caitya tree, 243
Caityas, Buddhist, 426–27, 428–30, 435, 436
Cakracakra, statue of, 504, *505*
Cakras, 156
Cakravartins, 226, 231
Cakreśvari, 254
Calcutta, temples of, *207*
Calendar: Burmese, 547, 548; Indian, lunar months in, 355; Pyu, 547; Tibetan, 413, 414
Cambodia, *see* Kampuchea
Campa, 85, 90, 100
Camundaraya-basti, 276
Camunda Temple at Mysore City, 196, *197*
Camunda Tila, images of Buddha at, *425,* 426
Canakya/Kautilya, 60–61
Candi Belahan, 520
Candi Borobudur, 479, 483–*94;* Buddha images, 491–*92, 493;* buried basement of, 484–87, 494; galleries on the square terraces, *487–91,* 494; replica of the cosmos, 492–94; *stupas* on the circular terraces, 492, *493*
Candi Jago, 504
Candi Jawi, 504
Candi Lara Jonggrang, 494–501; *Ramayana* reliefs at, 498–*501*
Candi Kalasan, *477–78*
Candi Mendut, 479–83
Candi Panataran, 506–508
Candi Pawon, 479, 483
Candi Plaosan, 479
Candi Sari, 478, *479*
Candi Sewu, 479
Candi Singhasari, 504
Candra, 40, 259
Candradeva, 130
Candragupta-basti, 276
Candragupta Maurya, 63–64, 107, 109–11, 211, 622, 623
Candra Gupta I, 119
Candra Gupta II, 120, 122, 177
Candravati, 468
Cariyapitaka, 342
Carumati Bihar, 588, 589
Carumati convent, 588, 589
Carvaka, 136
Carved temples, *182–86,* 265–67
Carya Tantra, 407
Catal Hüyük, 1
Cattle identified with deities, 43–44
Cave temples, *177–82,* 265–67
Caves, Buddhist and Hindu, 427–37; at Ajanta, 437–35; in Bali, *518–19;* at Bezeklik, 633–36; at Ellora, 435–37; in Malaysia, 530

Caves of the Thousand Buddhas, 633–36
Cedis, kingdom of the, 94
Cennakeśava Temple at Belur, 187–90
Central Asia, 624–63; Bamiyan, 628–32; Begram, 624–28; Bhutan, 659–63; Hadda, 624, 625; Ladakh, 653–58; Tibet, *see* Tibet; Turpan, 633–36; Xinjiang, 633, 638
Ceremonial of the Tooth Relic, 328
Cetis, kingdom of the, 94
Cetiyas, 457–59
Chakri Dynasty, 568–69
Chakri Palace, 569
Chamchen Cho-je, 650
Changchup O, 396, 397, 654
Chanhu-daro, 3, 5–6
Chao Phraya Chakri, 568–69
Chauk Htat Kyi Temple, 562
Che Chan, 633
Cheyasuttas, 219
Chhoklê Namgyel, 400
Chhondzin Gemphel Tüsum Chhepa, 405
Chhota Kailasa, 265–66
China, 120–21, 126, 128, 359, 362, 633, 637; conflicts with Tibet, 637, 638
Chiniya Lama, 601
Chonang-pa order, 400
Chronicle of the Emrald Buddha, 577
Chronicles of the Kings of Ladakh, 653
Chronology: of Hinduism and Vedic and Epic periods, 18–21; Jaina, 225–26; of Kali age, 54–78
Chulalongkorn, 569, 570, 576, 577, 580, 583
Chulalongkorn University, 569
Churning of the Sea Milk, scene of, 542, 543, 544
Chu Sho-fu, 633
Citadel of Polonnaruwa, 469
Cities, 79–101; earliest large, 1
Citragupta Temple at Khajuraho, 204
Clans in ancient India, 79–84
Cola invasion, 323
Cosmography, Jaina, 223–25
Council of Pataliputra, 211
Council of Valabhi, 211–12
Councils in India, Theravada, 292–300; First Council in Rajagriha, 293–95; Second Council in Vaiśali, 295–97; Third Council in Pataliputra, 297–99; Fourth Council in Kashmir, 299–300
Cremation ceremony, Bali, 517–18, 528, 529
Culamani monastery, 568
Culavamsa, 293, 306, 317, 319, 321, 324, 325, 326, 327, 345, 464–66, 471
Cullaniddesa, 341
Cullavagga, 292, 293, 294–95, 296, 427
Cult of the Dead, 517–18
Cunnis, 221
Cyrus II (the Great), 102–103

Dadhikra, 43
Dagobas, 457, 459, 460–62, 469, 470
Dagon, 551, 559
Daksha, 30–31
Dakshinamurti, Śiva as, 168
Dalada Maligawa, 472
Dalai Lamas, 414, 638, 639, 645–47
Dalha, 322
Dammazedi, 549
Damodara I, 616
Damodara II, 617
Darius I (the Great), 103–104

Darśana, 136
Daśabhumiśvara, 376
Daśabhumi-vibhasha Śastra, 384
Daśartha, 115
Dasas, 7, 11
Das Avatara, 181
Dathakondanna, 322
Dawa Gompo, 400
Deb Raja, 661
De Dynasty, 654
Deer Park, 452–54
Deities of Bali, 510–13
Deities of the *Rig Veda,* 16, 17, 30–49; anthropomorphic descriptions, 160; of Aryan heritage, 31–33; as creator, 46–47; divine animals, 43–46; goddesses, 41; of Harappan heritage, 30–31; images of, 162; the many and the one, 46; other superhuman beings, 42; sacrifice of Purusha and the gods collectively, 47–48; of the sphere of aerial space, 35–37; of the sphere of the constellations, 40–41; of the sphere of earth, 33–35; of the sphere of the sky, 37–40; the unnamed and the unknown, 48–49
Demalamahasaya, 472
Denpasar: Bali Museum at, 525–27; palace at, 525
Deopatan, monuments at, 601–604
Detsan Gon, 654
Devadaha, 81
Deva Gupta I, 120
Devanampiyatissa, 303–304, 305, 306, 307, 457–59, 460
Deva Patan, 588
Devaraja cult, 535
Devas, 16
Devi, 150, 172
Devi Jagadambi Temple at Khajuraho, 201, 203
Devotion, path of, 133, 134
Dhajaraza, 547
Dhamekh *stupa,* 454–55
Dhamma, 291, 347–53
Dhammacakkapasada, 317
Dhammapada, 337–38
Dhammarucikas, 319, 322
Dhamma zedi, 552
Dhana Nanda, 107, 109
dharana, 51
Dharanendra, 255
Dharanindravarman II, 544
Dharma, 15, 134, 135
Dharmacakra, 243, 245
Dharmadatta, 587, 603
Dharmakara, 586
Dharma Raja, 661
Dharmarajika, 448–49
Dharmarajika *stupa,* 455
Dhatusena, 320–21, 466
Dhatu zedi, 552
Dhruvadeva, 592
Dhumar Lena, 181
Dhyana, 51–52, 133, 134
Digambara saints, Śantinatha Temple, 268, 269
Digha Nikaya, 331–32
Dikpalas, 257–59
Dikshit, K. N., 3; mounds (DK), 4–5, 6
Dipavamsa, 292–93, 295, 297, 300, 304, 311, 315, 316, 344–45
Dirghagama, 318
Discipline, 53, 133, 134

Doctrine of the universal being in the *Upanishads*, 50–51
Dolma, 406, 409
Dolma Lhakhang, *644, 645*
Dorjetrak monastery, 395
Dravida style of temple architecture, 176, *177*
Dravidian group of languages, 12–13
Dravya Shah, 597
Drepung monastery, 405, *650*, 651; new, 652–53
Drigung-pa suborder, 404, 454
Drigung Rimpoche, 404
Drokmi, 399–400, 416
Drölma, 406, 407
Drom, 398–99, 645; statue of, *644*
Dromgön Phakmotrupa, 404
Druk-pa suborder, 404–405, 417, 655, 659–61
Dukkha, 346–47
Dulva, 73
Durga, 153–54
Durlabhavrdhana, 618
Dusit Mahaprasad, 576, *577*
Duttabaung, 547
Dutthagamani Abhaya, 309–11, 460; Buddhist gatherings under, 311–12
Dvaparayuga, 586–87
Dvaravati, 562–63
Dyaus, 37
Dzak chhenmo school, 396

Eastern Ganges, 79
East Java, 501–502
Egyptian civilization, 1
Ekadaśa-rudra, 521–22
Ekatosaroth, 575
Elara, 309, 310
Elephanta, cave temples at, 181–*82*
Ellora: Buddhist caves at, 435–37; carved temples at, 184–*86;* cave temples at, 181, 265
Ephtalite Huns, 624, 625
Epic period, geographical focus of, 79
Epitome of the Great Symbol, The, 417, 418
Esala Perahera, 472

Fa Xian (Fa Hien), 100, 120–22, 130, 318–19, 323, 358–59, 361, 451, 452, 457, 475, 633; observations outside India, 475, 622, 624
Foreign intervention in India, 102–32
Fundamentals of the Buddhist Tantras, 407

Gaglaran Pamanku, 516
Gahadavala Dynasty, 130
Gaharwar clan, 130
Gairika, 209
Gahah Mada, 509
Galungan, 518
Gal Vihara, *471*
Gampopa, 403–404, 416–417
Gandavyuha, 375–76; scenes based on, 489–*90*
Ganden monastery, 405, 648, 653
Gandhara, images of Buddha from, 421–24
Gandharas, kingdom of the, 98–100
Gandharvas, 42
Ganeśa, 261
Gangadharamurti, Śiva as, 168–69
Ganges River, 79
Gardabhilla, 66
Gatashrama Temple, 166
Gautama Akshapada, 138

Gautama Indrabhuti, 210
Gaya, 86, 122
Gayatri, 38, 150
Geluk-pa order, 405, 406, 414, 638, 648, 654
Gendüntrup, 405
Genghis Khan, 630
Geography, 79; clans and their territories, 80–84; kingdoms, 84–101
Geography (Ptolemy), 473, 530, 547, 549
Geography of Tibet, The, 639
Ghantai Temple, 267
Girivraja, 85
Glass Palace Chronicle of the Kings of Burma, 546–47
Goa Gajah, *518–19*
Goal, the Upanishadic, 52–53
Gomedha, 254–55
Gommateśvara, colossal statue of, 276–*79*
Gomukha, 254
Gonanda Dynasty, 617–18, 620
Gonanda I, 616
Gonanda II, 616
Gopaditya, 617, 620
Gopuras, 177, 184, 185, 187, 196
Gorkha, kingdom of, 597–98
Gopalas, 587
Gośala, 235; similarities and contrasts of Mahavira and, 238–39
Gas lo-tsa-ba, 73
Gaslotsawa, 396
Govinda Candra, 130
Grand Palace at Bangkok, 569, *576, 577, 578*
Great Stage Way to the Occult Sciences, 406
Great Tamil Caitya, 472
Great Vow ceremony, 405
Grihastha, 135
Guangzhou tradition of Buddha chronology, 72–73
Guhyasamaja, 379
Guhyasamaja Tantra, 399, 407–11
Guide to the Holy Places of Central Tibet, 639, 640
Gunakamadeva, 587, 594, 607
Gunung Agung, 520, 521
Gupta Empire, 118–24, 131; Buddha images from Gupta period, 424–26, 455; early imperial Guptas, 119–23; later imperial Guptas, 119, 123–24; latest Guptas, 124
Gupta family in Nepal, 591, 592
Guru, 135
Guttika, 308–309
Gyelwa Karm-pa, 405
Gyuto order, 648

Hadda, 624, *625*
Halebid, temple at, 187–88, 190–*91, 192–94*
Hanuman Dhoka, 607
Hauman Dhoka Durbar, 607
Harappa, 3
Harappan civilization, 1–11, 13; Early, 1–2, 3; end of, 6–7; Mature, 2–6; monument and artifacts of, 7–11, pottery of, 2, 5, 7–8; religion of, 8–11, 30–31; seals of, 8–11, 30
Hargreaves, H., 3; mounds (HR), 4–5
Haribhadra, 222
Hariharalaya, 536
Harishena, 120
Hariti, 424, 432, 480
Harsha, 124–25, 126–28, 130, 131, 618, 619
Harsha, Empire of, 124–29
Harshacarita, 125

Harwan, 619–20
Hastadandasastra, 476
Hastinapura, 79, 96
Hayu-hayu, 522
Hellenization of Northwest India, 107–108
Hemacandra, 115–16, 222–23, 254
Heruka, 410
Hevajra, 399
Hevajra Tantra, 399, 411–12
Hieun Tsang, *see* Xuan Zang
Hinayana Buddhism, *see* Theravada (Hinayana) Buddhism
Hinduism, 131, 132; deities of the *Rig Veda*, *see* Deities of the *Rig Veda*; Later, 133–59; literature of, *see* Literature of Hinduism and Vedic and Epic periods; monuments of, *see* Monuments of Hinduism
Hiravijaya Suri, 131–32
History of Buddhism in India (Tarantha), 383, 386–87, 392
History of Buddhism in India and Tibet (Buston), 383, 392, 396
History of Lesser Battle: On Thai History, 565
History of the Liang Dynasty, 529, 532
History of the Sui Dynasty, 533
Hmannan Yazawindawgyi, 546–47, 549–50, 552
Hmawza, 550
Horses identified with deities, 43
Hoyśaleśvara Temple at Halebid, 187–88, 190–*91*, *192–94*
Htilominlo, 551, 556
Htilominlo Temple, 556–57
Huang (Yellow) River valley, 1
Huchchappayya Gudi temple, 166, 170
Huns, 617, 624, 625
Huyishka, 116
Hvang Karimama, 508
Hwui Li, 626

Ikshvaku, 20–21
Ikshvakus of Kośala, 56
Ila, 21
Images of Buddhism, 420–26; *see also* Buddha(s), images of
Images of the Hindu gods, 160–75; Brahma, *165*, 258, 259; Devi, 172; early literary references, 162–63; Kinds of, 161; Lakshmi, 167, 172, *173*–74, 261; Parvati, *171*, 172, 173; Saravasti, 172, *174*–75, 259–60, 281, *282*; Śiva, 168–*72*, 177, *178*, 199–200, 207; *vidyadharas*, 175; Vishnu, 166–*68*, *169*, 177, *178–79*; *yakshas*, 163–64
Images of Jainism, 245–61; attendants of Tirthankaras, 254–61; *Ayagapatas*, 245–46; characteristics of, 246–47; *jinas* and *tirthankaras*, 245–53; literary references, 247–48
India, 1–417; Alexander the Great and the empire after his coming, 102–32; clans and territories, 80–84; expansion of Indian influence of Southeast Asia, 473–75; Harappan civilization, 1–11; Jainism in, *see* Jainism; Kali age, 54–78; kingdoms in, 84–101; Later Hinduism in, 133–59; literature of Hinduism and the Vedic and Epic periods, 12–29; Mahayana Buddhism in, *see* Mahayana Buddhism; monuments of Buddhism in, 419–57 *passim*; monument of Hinduism in, 160–207; monuments of Jainism in, 242–89;

Theravada Buddhism in, *see* Theravada (Hinayana) Buddhism
Indian calendar, lunar months of the, 355
Indonesia, 475–76; *see also individual islands, e.g.* Bali; Java
Indra, 17, 31, 36, 258–59
Indrabetta, 276–77
Indraprastha, 79
Indraraja I, 566, 571
Indra Sabha, 266–67
Indravarman I, 535, 536
Indus River, 15, 79, 105
Indus Valley, 31; Harappan civilization, 1–11
Iśana, 258, 259
Isipatana, 101, 449, 451
Islam, 530, 619, 628
Isurumuniya Vihara, 460, *461*
I-tsing, *see* Yi Jing

Jagannath Sabha, 267
Jagatyotimalla, 609
Jagdish Temple at Udaipur, *206*
Jahangir, 620
Jaimini, 138
Jaina dates, 65–69
Jainism, 110–11, 15; cosmology and chronology of, 223–26; decline and renewal of, 130–31; derivation of name, 209–10; illustrious persons, 226–41; literature of, *see* Literature of Jainism; monuments of, in India, 242–89; today, 132
Jalaśayana Narayana, *605*, 606
Jalauka, 617, 620
Jalilpur, 2
Jamalpur, images of Buddha from, 424–26
Jambudvipa, 17
Jambukola-*vihara*, caves of, 327
Jampa Lhakhang, 659
Jamyang, statue of, 650, *651*
Jana, 20
Jananthapura, 323
Janapada, 20
Japan, 362
Jasbuvamin, 210
Jatakas, 341, 345, 473, 556, 573
Jaulian, 449
Java, 475; Buddhist and Hindu monuments in, 476–508
Javarśi, 136
Jayachandra, 130
Jayadeva II, 594
Jayaprakaśamalla, 597–98, 607
Jayasimha, 619
Jayavarman I, 534
Jayavarman II, 534, 436
Jayavarman IV, 537
Jayavarman V, 538
Jayavarman VI, 540
Jayavarman VII, 535–36, 542, 544, 545, 546
Jericho, 1
Jetavana Dagoba, 462
Jetavanarama, 326
Jetavana-*vihara*, 316, 324, 451
Jewel Ornament of Liberation, The, 403
Jhang, 1
Jhangar people, 5–6
Je Khenpo, 663
Jhukar people, 5–6
Jigme Dorje Wangchuck, 661, *662*, 663

Jigme Singye Wangchuck, 661
Jigme Wangchuck, 661
Jinas, 209–10, 242; images of, 245–53, 420
Jishnugupta, 592
Jnana, 133
Jokhang Temple, 637, 638, 647–48, 653
Judeirjo-daro, 3
Jyeshtheśvara Temple, 617

Kabul, 15
Kabul Museum, 624, *625, 626–28*
Kabul River, 105
Kacchapa Jataka scene, 480, *481*
Kadam-pa order, 399, 406
Kadiri, 502–503
Kadru, 45
Kagyu-pa order, 406, 417
Kailasanatha temple, 187
Kailasa temple at Ellora, *184–86*
Kaitabha, 168
Kakavannatissa, 309
Kalabhairava: figure of, 607, *608;* Śiva as, 169
Kalacakra Tanra, 400, 412–14
Kalakacaryakatha, 66, 67, 69
Kala-makara, 477–78
Kalamas clan, 84
Kalarimurti, Śiva as, 169
Kalasan, 477
Kalasoka, 295
Kalhana, 616–17, 619
Kali, 152–53, 257, *258*
Kali, Temple of, at Dakshineśvar, 207
Kali age, chronology of the, 54–78; the beginning, 54–55; Buddha chronology, 70–78; Jaina dates, 65–69; Mahabharata war chronology, 64–65; Mahavira chronology, 69–70; Puranic dates, 63–64; Puranic dynastic lists, 55–63
Kalidasa, 26
Kaliyuga, 587, 588
Kalki, 148–49
Kalpas, 19
Kalpa tree, 243
Kalyana Stones, 549
Kalyani, 309
Kama, 134
Kamalaśila, 393
Kamantakamurti, Śiva as, 169
Kama Sutra, 199
Kambojas, kingdom of the, 100
Kampilya, 96
Kampuchea, 531–46; Angkor Period, 534–46; Chenla Period, 533–34; Funan Period, 531–33
Kanauj, 125, 127
Kancipuram, temples of, 187
Kandariya Mahadeva Temple at Khajuraho, *204–205*
Kandy, Buddhist monument at, 472
Kangyur, 395, 396
Kanishka, 69, 116–18, 299–300, 617, 623, 624, 625, 626, 628, 653
Kankali Tila, Mathura, Jaina monuments at, 244–46, 262–64
Kantaka Cetiya, 305, 457–59
Kanvas, 62, 63
Kaochang, 633, *634*
Kao Tsung, 128
Kapilavastu, 80, 122
Karandavyuha, 379
Karkota, 618

Karkota Dynasty, 618
Karma, 133, 134, 349–50
Karma Lingpa, 415
Kamra-pa order, 404, 405
Karma Tusum Chhenpa, 405
Karmavibhanga, 484, 486
Kartik dance drama, 596
Kashmir, 616–*21,* 653; Fourth Buddhist Council in, 299–300; history of, 616–19; monuments in, 619–21
Kaśis, kingdom of the, 90–92
Kassapa, 321, 463–464, 466–67
Kastha Mandap, 607
Kathavatthu, 358, 359–60, 361
Kathmandu, 588, 594, 595, 596–97, 598; mounments at, 607–608
Kaundinya Jayavarman, 532–33
Kauśambi, 94–95, 100
Kautilya/Canakya, 60–61
Kesaputta, 84
Kesarivarmadeva, 520
Keśva Temple at Somnathpur, 187–88, 191–*95, 196*
Ketu, 259
Kevalins, 209, 210–11
Khajuraho, temples at, 196–205, 267–*73, 274–75*
Khajuraho Museum, 268
Khallatanaga, 313
Khandhakas, 331
Khe-trup Je, 406–407
Khuddaka Nikaya, 336–42
Khuddakapatha, 336–37
Kingdoms, 84–101; *see also names of individual kingdoms*
Kinnaras, 42
Kiratas, 587–89
Kiri-vehera, *470*
Kirtti Śri Raja Simha, 329
Kisa Sankicca, 89
Klungkung, 519–*20*
Knowledge: in the Brahmanas, 49–50; path of, 133
Kolita, 361
Koliyas clan, 81
Könchok Gyelpo, 399
Korea, 362
Kośalas, kingdom of, 21, 22, 55, 56, 79, 92–94, 100; Ikshvakus of, 56
Kot Diji, 2, 3
Krishna, 147–48, 231–32; death of, 54
Krishna cave temple, 179, *180*
Krishna Mandir, 607
Krishna I, 184
Krishnayana, scenes from the, 508
Kritajaya, 503
Kritanagara, 509
Kritarajara, portrait statue of, 506, *507*
Kriya Tantra, 407
Kshetrapala, 261
Kubera, 258, 259, 443, 464–66, 480–82
Kublai Khan, 551, 557
Kubyauk Kyi Pagoda, 554–*55*
Kuje Lhakhang, 659
Kulala Kadphises I, 116
Kularnava Tantra, 157–58, 199
Kumara Devi, 119
Kumara Gupta I, 123
Kumara Gupta II, 123
Kumarajiva, 380
Kumaralabdha, 380, 382

Kumari Devi, 607, 608
Kumari Ghar, 607
Kunala, 115
Kundakunda, 221
Kunga Dontrub, 648
Künga Nyingpo, *see* Tarantha
Kurma, 145–46
Kurukshetra, 16
Kurus, kingdom of the, 96
Kushana Dynasty, 617, 620, 623, 625
Kushana Empire, 116–18
Kuśinagara, 81–82, 84, 101, 122, 449, 451
Kusuma Dewa, 515–16
Kuthodaw Pagoda, 558–*59*
Kyansittha, 548, 552, 554, 555
Kyanzittha, 551
Kyentse, 639, 640

Ladakh, 653–*58*
Laity, Buddhist, 356–57
Lake Manasarovara, 397
Lakshmana Temple at Khajuraho, *199, 200–201, 202*
Lakshmi, 41, 151; images of, 167, 172, *173–74*, 261
Lakshminarasimhamalla, 594
Lalitaditya, 618, 619
Lalitavistara, 368–69, 487–88
Lalitpur, 588, 594
Lamayuru, 654
Lama Tsenpo, 639
Lamp for the Way of Enlightenment, 397, 398, 638
Langdarma, 638, 653
Languages: Aryan group, 12–13; Dravidian group, 12–13
Lanjatissa, 313, 459
Lanka, *see* Sri Lanka
Lankatilaka, 470
Lankavatara, 376–78, 382
Later Hinduism, 133–59; four aims, 134–35; four stages, 135–36; six schools, 136–38; three interpreters of Vedanta, 138–40; three paths, 133–34; *trimurti,* 140–59
Laws of Manu, 13, 14, 15; images of gods in, 162
Leh, monuments at, 654, *655,* 657
Leh Khar Temple, 654–*55,* 657
Leiden Museum, 504
Liang-shu, 529, 532
Lhachen Bhagan, 654
Lhachen Deldan Namgyal, 655
Lhachen Trakbumde, 654
Lhasa, 637; monuments in, 645–*47,* 648, *649*
Lhatho Thori, 639
Library Dagoba, 468
Licchavi Dynasty, 590–94
Licchavis clan, 82–83, 84, 119
Linga, Siva as, 168, 177, *178,* 199–200, 207, 476, 504, 535, 536, 539, 603, 620
Ling Rêpa Pema Dorje, 404, 417
Literature of Hinayana Buddhism, 318
Literature of Hinduism and Vedic and Epic periods, 12–29; classes of, 13–14; languages of, 12–13; Lunar dynasty, 24–29; Mount Meru, 17–18; periods of time, 18–21; Solar dynasty, 21–24; Vedic Aryans, 16–17; Vedic geography, 15–16
Literature of Jainism, 210–23; Bhadrabahu and Sthulabhadra, 211; Council of Pataliputra, 211; Council of Valabhi, 211–12; *Kevalins* and *Śrutakevalins,* 210–11; noncanonical writers, 220–23; Śvetambra canon, 212–20
Literature of Mahayana Buddhism, 361–62; 364, 365, 367–90; *Sutras,* 368–80; writers and *Śastras,* 380–90
Literature of Theravada Buddhism, 291–92, 318; canonical texts, 292, 330–43; *dhamma,* 291–92, 346–53; other Pali texts, 434–44; Pali compendia and commentaries, 344–45; *vinaya,* 291–92; *see also* Theravada (Hinayana) Buddhism
Li Thise, 639
Lohala Dynasty, 618–19
Lohapasada, 310, 316, 460–62
Lokapalas, 257–59
Lokeśvara, 589–90
Lokottaravadins, 362
Lopburi, monuments of, 571
Lopsang Pelden Yeshe, 414
Lo Thai, 564
Lothal, 3
Luang Prasoet, 565
Luang Prasoet Chronicle of Ayudhya, 565, 566, 567, 568
Lumbini, 101, 449, 451
Lunar dynasty, 24–29; Paurava line, 24, 26–29; Yadava line, 24–26
Lunar months in the Indian calendar, 355
Luna-vasahi, 281, *283*
Lu Thai, 564–65, 568, 573

Machhendranath Mandir, 607
Madanikai, 164
Madhava Gupta, 124
Madhu, 168
Madhura, *see* Mathura
Madhva, 140
Madhyadeśa, 16, 131
Magadhas, kingdom of the, 55, 56, 64, 79, 85–90, 100; Barhadrathas of, 57–58; Nandas of, 59–61; Śaiśunagas of, 58, 59
Magadhi language, 12
Magga, 348
Magha, 327
Maha-Arittha, 306–307
Mahabalipuram: carved temples at, *181–82*; cave temples at, *177–80*; Shore Temple at, 186–87
Mahabharata, 13, 14, 16, 29, 133, 163, 618; scenes from the, 542
Mahabharata war, 616; chronology of, 64–65
Mahabodhi Temple at Bodhgaya, *456–57*
Maha chat kham luang, 568
Mahajanapadas, 20, 84–101
Mahakassapa, 294, 295, 324–25
Mahamogalana, relics of, 446
Mahamudra, 399, 416–18
Mahamuni Pagoda, 558–59
Mahanama, 317–18, 319, 320, 321
Mahaniddesa, 341
Maha Nikaya sect, 569
Mahanirvana Tantra, 159
Mahaprajnaparamita Śastra, 384
Mahasanghikas, 358, 359, 361–62
Mahasena, 316, 462
Maha Seya Dagoba, 457, *458*
Mahasiva, 308
Maha Svami, Patriarch, 565
Mahathupa, 311–12, 313
Mahavamsa, 70–71, 74, 75–76, 293, 295, 297, 300, 303, 304, 308, 309, 310, 311, 315, 318, 345, 463, 549; author of the, 321
Mahavastu, 361–62, 363, 364

Mahavihara, 305, 314, 315, 322, 324; Third Buddhist Council at the, 318–20; 549;
Mahavira, 79, 209, 210, 212, 233–41, 247; death of, 240–41; Dhatusena and, 320, 321; disciples of, 329–40; Gośala and, 235, 238–39; images of, 252–53; teachings of, 235–38
Mahavira chronology, 69–70
Mahavira Nirvana Era, 69–70
Mahayana Buddhism, 122, 300, 324, 358–90; characteristics of, 362–67, 391; geographic distribution of followers of, 359, 361; literature of, 361–62, 364, 365, 367–90; Mahasanghikas, 358, 359, 361–62; Sarvastivadins, 359–61; split from Theravada Buddhism, 314–15, 316–18, 359; teachers and texts of, 367–90; *see also* Buddhism; Buddhist monuments; Theravada (Hinayana) Buddhism; Vajrayana Buddhism
Mahayana-śradhotpada, 381–83
Mahayuga, 19
Mahendramalla, 607
Maheśamurti, Śiva as, 169
Mahinda, 304–306, 308, 311, 317, 457, 459
Mahinda V, 323
Mahishamardini cave temples, 179, 180
Mahishapala, 587
Mahishmati, 97–98
Maithuna scene, Lakshmana Temple, *202, 203*
Majapahit, 506–508, 509, 530
Majjhima Nikaya, 332–33, 363
Makkhali Gośala, 88, 89
Malaya, 475
Malla Dynasty, 590, 595–97
Malla-linkara-wouttoo, 72
Mallas clan: of Kuśinagara, 81–82, 84; of Pava, 81–82, 84
Malli, 247
Malvan, 1
Manadeva I, 590–91, *592*
Manasara, 163
Mana-stambha, 243, *245*
Mandala, 161, 391
Mandalay, 551; monuments at, *558–59*
Mangala, 259
Manjupattan, 587
Manjuśri, 585–86
Mantra, 13, 51, 161, 162, 391
Manuha, 550
Manushi Buddha Kaśyapa, 598–601
Manvantaras, 19–20
Manus, 20
Maps: of Buddhist India, 290; of the Himalaya and Central Asia, 584; of Hindu India, xxx; of Jaina India, 208; of Southeast Asia, 474
Marble Temple of, *580–83*
Maricavatti Dagoba, 460
Maricavattivihara, 310, 311
Marpa, 400–401, 414, 416, 417
Martand Temple, 618, 620–21
Maruts, 32, 36
Mas, village of, 525
Matanga, 255–56
Matangeśvara Temple of Khajuraho, *199–200*
Mataram kings, 494–501
Matariśvan, 36
Mathura, 96–97; images of Buddha at, *420–21;* Jaina monuments at, 244–*46,* 262–64, *265*
Matsya, 145
Matsyas, kingdom of the, 96
Maurya Dynasty, 63, 64, 109–16, 616–17

Mauryas, 61, 62
Measurement, Jaina unit of, 226
Medieval period, kingdoms of the, 130
Meditation, 51–52, 133, 134, 161–62; in Vajrayana Buddhism, 391, 416, 417–18
Megasthenes, 109
Mengwi, temple at, 522–24
Meru, Mount, 17–18, 223, 514
Merutunga, 65
Mesopotamia, 3
Middle Ganges basin, 79
Mihintale, Buddhist monuments at, 457–59
Mihirakula, 123, 617
Mila Grubum, 401, 402
Mila Khabum, 401
Milarepa, 401–403, 414, 416, 654
Milinda, 427
Milinda Panha, 315, 343–44, 362–63, 427, 473, 529–30
Mimamsa Sutras, 138
Mindon, 552, 558
Mingalazedi Pagoda, *557–58*
Mintröl-ling monastery, 395
Mithila, 22, 83, 84
Mithra, 39
Mitra, 31, 38–39
Moenjo-dara, 3–5, 6–7, 9, 10
Moggaliputta-Tissa, 297–99
Moggallana I, 321–22, 446
Moksha, 134, 135
Monastery Temple at Shey, 655, *656*
Mongkut, 569, 570, 573, 577
Mongols, 551
Monks, ordination of, 353–54
Monlam Chenmo, 653
Mons people, 548–49, 550, 563
Monuments of Buddhism: by the Himalaya and in Central Asia, 585–*663;* in India, 419–57 *passim;* in Pakistan, 419–57 *passim;* in Southeast Asia, 473–583 *passim;* in Sri Lanka, 457–72
Monuments of Hinduism: by the Himalaya and Central Asia, 585–663 *passim;* in India, 160–207; in Southeast Asia, 473–583 *passim*
Monuments of Jainism in India, 242–89; images, 245–61; *stupas,* 261–64; symbols, 242–45; temples, 264–89
Moonstones, 462–63
Moriyas clan, 84
Mount Abu, 279–83
Mount Meru, 17–18, 223, 514
Mount Popa, 548
Mpu Tantular, 519
Mrichchhakatika, 264
Mudra, 391
Muhammad of Ghur, 130
Muktapida, 618
Mulamadhyamakakarika, 383–84
Mulasuttas, 219–20
Muni, 13
Municipal Museum of Modjokerto, 502
Museum of Indonesian Culture, 506, *507*
Museum of the Xinjiang Uygur Autonomous Region, *635*
Muslims, 618, 619, 624
Mutasiva, 303
Mysore City: Nandi Bull above, 195–96, *197;* temple at, 196, *197*

Naga, 258, 259

Nagadipa, 309
Nagara style of temple architecture, 176–77
Nagarangana, 308
Nagarjuna, 300, 380, 382–85, 617
Nagasena, 577
Naigamesha, 261
Nairatma, 410
Nakhon Patham, monuments at, *570–71*
Nakshatras, 40
Naktsho lotsawa, 396
Nalanda, 86, 454
Nalanda monastery, 127, 129, 454
Namgyal Dynasty, 654–55
Namthar, 401
Nanda/Mahapadma, 60
Nandas of Magadha, 59–61
Nanda Vaccha, 89
Nandi: Nandi Bull above Mysore City, 195–96, *197;* Śiva as, 169, 495
Nandikeśvara, Śiva as, 169
Nandisutta, 220
Nandyavarta, 243
Nara, 617
Narai, 565
Narapatisithu, 556
Narasimba, 146
Narasimha Gupta, 123
Narathihapate, 551, 557
Narathu, 551, 552
Narendradeva, 593–94
Naresuan, 575
Naropa, 400, 401, 406, 414, 654
Nastika systems of philosophy, 136
Nataraja, Śiva as, 168, *170–71*
National Art Gallery at Nepal, 609
National Library, Thailand, 569
National Museum at Bangkok, 569, 571, *572,* 573
National Museum at New Delhi, *260,* 264, *265*
National Museum of Ethnology, 504
National Museum of India, 170, *171, 173*
National Museum of Nepal, *613–15*
Nats, 548, 550, 551
Navagrahas, 259
Nayapala, 397, 398
Ne, 587
Neak Pean, 546
Nemi, *see* Neminatha
Nemicandra, 222
Neminatha, 231–32, 247, 249–51
Nepal, 362, 397, *585–615;* history of, 585–98; monuments of, *598–615*
Nethang, *644, 645*
Nettipakarana, 343
Newari Era in Nepal, 594, 595
Newark Museum, 640, *641*
Newars, 588
Ngawang Lopsang Gyatso, 639
Ngawang Namgyal, 661
Nigantha of the Nata clan, 89
Nijjuttis, 220
Nila Tantra, 158–59
Nile valley, 1
Nimisha, 589
Nirganthas, 209, 239
Nirodha, 348
Nirvana, 134, 350–53
Nissankalatha Mandapava, 470
Nissanka Malla, 327, 468, 469, 470, 472

Nrutti, 257, 259
Nuns, reception into the order of, 354–55
Nyagrê Nyima Oser, 395
Nyarbudi, 45
Nyatapola Temple, 609, *611*
Nyatrhi Tsenpo, 637, 639; statue of, *640*
Nyaya Sutras, 138
Nyaya system of philosophy, 138
Nyepi, 515, 516
Nyima Gon, 653
Nyingma-pa sect, 395, 622, 638, 653, 659

Occidental Turks, 624
Ojha, G. H., 69
Okkalapa, 549

Padma Dakini, figure of, 657, *658*
Padma Heruka, figure of, 657, *658*
Padma Karpo, 417, 659, 661
Padmasambhava, 393–96, 415, 620, 622, 638, 640, 653, 659; statue of, *643,* 657, *658*
Padmavati, 255, *256*
Pagan, 547, 550, 551; monuments in, 552–58
Pagodas, 457, *552–55, 557–62*
Painnas, 218
Paintings, Buddhist, 428–29, 430, 431–35, 464, *465,* 467, 472, *520, 554–55,* 577, 612, *613,* 633–36, *643, 660*
Pakistan, monuments of Buddhism in, 419–57 *passim*
Pakudha Kachchayana, 88, 89
Pali language, 212
Pamirs, 18
Panamkarana, 477
Panca-bali-krama, 522
Pancalas, kingdom of the, 96
Panchen Lamas, 414
Pancika, 424, 432
Pandava Dynasty, 616
Pandrethan, 619
Pandukabhaya, 303
Panduvasudeva, 302
Papabhakshana, Śiva as, 169
Parakramabahu I, 324, 325–27, 457, 459, 462, 468, 469, 470, 471, 472; statue of, *468*
Parakramabahu II, 328, 472
Parakramabahu III, 328
Parakramabahu IV, 328, 466
Parakramabahu VI, 328–29
Parakrama Pandya, 327
Paramanuchitchinorot, 565
Paramatrailoka, 567–68
Paramatthajotika, 344
Paramavishnuloka, 542
Parameśvara, 530
Paraśara, 14
Paraśurama, 147
Paravira, 331
Paribhoga zedi, 552
Parikshit II, 65; accession of, 54–55
Paro, monuments at, *662, 663*
Parśva, 232–33, 247, 251–52, 255
Parśvanatha, figure of, *283,* 285–89
Parśvanatha Temple: at Khajuraho, 271–73, *274–75;* at Ranakpur, *288,* 289
Parto Thotrol, 415
Parvati, 152; images of, *171, 172, 173;* Śiva with, 169, *171,* 539

Pasadas, 427
Pashupreshadeva, 589, 603
Paśupatinath Devi, 603, *605*
Paśupatinath Temple, 601–*604*
Paśupati Purana, 591
Pataliputra, 89, 90, 109, 119, 452; Third Buddhist Council in, 297–99, 358
Patan, 588, 589, 590, 594–95, 596, 597–98; monuments at, 605–607
Patanjali, 136–37
Pathiani Kot, 3
Path(s): of Later Buddhism, 133–34; in the Upanishads, 51–52
Paumachariya, 69
Paurava line of the Lunar dynasty, 24, 26–29
Pauravas of Vatsa, 56–57
Pava, 81, 82, 84
Pavarana, 356
Pegu, 549
Pelden Lhamo, 655, *656*
Pelgyi Gon, 653, 654
Pema Thangyig, 393–94, 395
Penang, Reclining Buddha in, *530*
Penang Buddhist Association, 530, *531*
Persians, Achaemenid, 102–104, 623; Sassanid, 624
Peshawar: images of Buddha at, *422, 423*; other Buddhist figures at, 424
Petakopadesa, 343
Petavatthu, 340
Phallic worship, 31
Philip, Macedonian, 108
Philosophy in the *Brahmanas* and *Upanishads*, 49–53
Phimeanakas, 538
Phra Borom Maha Rajawang, *576*
Phra Pathom Chedi, *570–71*
Phra Ruang, 563
Phyang, 654
Pilgrimages: Buddhist sites for, 449–57; Jaina temple cities for, 273–89
Pipphalivana, 84
Pitaras, 512–13
Polonnaruwa: Buddhist monuments at, *468–72*; Fourth Buddhist Council at, 324–27
Popa, Mount, 548
Popa Sawrahan, 548
Poros, 106–107, 108
Potalo, 636–367, 638, 645–*47*
Potana, 97
Potgul-vehera, 468
Pottery: Amrian, 2, 7; Jhukar and Jhangar, 5; Kot Dijian, 2, 7; Mature Harappan, 7–8
Prabhava, 210
Pradyotas of Avanti, 58–59
Prah Palilay, 536
Prajnaparamita, statue of, 504, *505*
Prajnaparamita texts, 316, 373–75
Prakrits, 12–13
Prambanam, Candi Lara Jonggrang at, 494–501
Pramodavardhani, 483
Pranayama, 391
Prang Sam Yot, 571
Prasenajit, 93–94
Pratapaditya II, 618
Pratapamalla, 595, 596, 607
Prativasudevas, 226, 231
Pratyekabuddha, 363
Pravarasenapura, 619–20
Pravarasena II, 617, 618

Preah Khan, 546
Precious Rosary, The, 404
Pre Rup, *537–38*
Prince of Wales Museum, Western India, Bombay, 253, 255, *256*, 257, *258*
Prithivi, 33
Prithyi Narayan Shah, 597
Psycho-nervous channels of the body, 400, 406, 411–12
Ptolemy, Claudius, 473, 530, 547, 549
Pulatthingara, 322–23, 324, 325–27, 328
Puluk-pa order, 399–400
Pura Basukian, 521
Pura Batu Madeg, 521
Pura Besakih, 520–*22, 523*
Pura Dangin Keretog, 521
Pura Kehen, 522, *523, 524*
Purana Kaśyapa, 88, 89
Puranas, 13, 14
Puranic dates, 63
Puranic dynastic lists, 55–63; Andhras/Śatavahanas, 62–63; Barhadrathas of Magadha and Avanti, 57–58; Ikshvakus of Kośala, 56; Kanvas, 62; Mauryas, 61, 62; Nandas of Magadha, 59–61; Pauravas of Vatsa, 56–57; Pradyotas of Avanti, 58–59; Śaiśunagas of Magadha, 58, 59; Śungas, 61–62
Pura Panataran Agung Besakih, 521
Pura Taman Ayun, 522–24
Puri Pemetjutan, 525
Puru Gupta, 123
Purusha, 40, 48; sacrifice of, 47–48
Purushada śanta, 519–20
Purushapura, 100
Purusha-sukta, 47–48
Purva Bhumi Kamulan, 516
Purva Mimamsa system of philosophy, 138
Pushkalavati, 99
Pushyamitra, 64
Puvvas, 213–14
Pyinbya, 548
Pyusawti, 547–48
Pyus of Burma, 547–48

Qutb-ud-din Aibak, 130

Radanika, sculpture of attempted abduction of, 264, 265
Raghavadeva, 594
Rahu, 259
Rajagriha, 85–86, 87, 88, 89, 100, 450, 451, 452; First Buddhist Council in, 293–95
Rajapura, 100
Rajatarangini, 616, 617, 619, 620
Rajendravarman II, 535, 537, 538
Rajyavardhana, 130–31
Rakshasas, 42
Ralpacan, 638
Rimpong Dzong, 661, *662*, 663
Ralung order, 405
Rama, 22–24, 147
Ramagama, 81
Rama Khamhaeng, 563–64, 565, 573
Ramakien, 569, 577
Ramakrishna, 207
Ramannadeśa, 549
Ramanuja, 131, 139–40
Rama I, 568–69, 575, 576, 577, 579

Rama II, 569, 575
Rama III, 569, 575, 577, 580
Rama IV, 569, 570, 573, 577
Rama V, 569, 570, 576, 577, 583
Rama VI, 569
Rama VII, 569, 577
Rama VIII, 569
Rama IX, 569, 580
Ramathibodi, *see* U Thong
Ramayana, 13, 14, 22–24, 473; scenes from the, 508, 542
Ramesuan, 567, 573
Rameśvara, 181
Ramoche, 637, 648, *649*
Ranajitamalla, 598
Ranakpur, Jaina temple at, *284–93*
Rangda: and Barong, 516–17; Barong-, Dance Drama, *529*; sculpture of, *527*
Rangoon, 551, 552; monuments of, 559–62
Rankot Vehera, 470
Rao Bahadur Badridasji Babu, 289
Ratanavali-*cetiya,* 327
Rathas as Mahabalipuram, *183–84*
Rathayatra, 589–90, 594
Ratnapura, Buddhist Council at, 329
Ratnavali, 385
Ravana, 510–11, 539; sculpture of, *526,* 527
Rebirth, 348–49
Re-chung, 401
Reclining Buddhas, *530, 562, 574,* 579–80
Revata, 296
Rig Veda, 7, 11; Aryans in, 16–17; date of composition of, 14; deities of, *see* Deities of the *Rig Veda;* geography, 15–16
Rilhana, 619
Rilhaneśvara, 619
Rinchara, 619
Rinchen Sangpo, 396, 397, 638, 654
Rishabha, 227, 230–31, 247, 248
Rishabhanatha figure at Vimala-vasahi, *280*
Rishis, 13–14, 31
River of Kings, 616, 617, 619
Rivers as sacred, 35
Rohana, 308, 309, 320, 324
Rohini River, 80, 81
Royal Autograph Chronicle, 563, 566, 568
Rudra/Śiva, 11, 36–37, 140, 142–43, 521, 586, 589; *avatars* of, 144; Bali *digbanhas* and, 510, 511; as foremost Bali deity, 511–12; images of, *168–72, 177, 178,* 199–200, 207, 476, 495, 504, *505,* 535, 536, 537–38, 539, *603–604, 607, 608,* 620; *Śaktis* of, 151–54; Śivartri, 603
Rudradevavarman, 589
Rudras, 32–33
Ruwanweli Dagoba, 310–11

Sabbakami, 296
Saddharma Lankavatara Sutra, 376–78, 382
Saddharmapundarika, 364, 365, 367, 369–72
Saddhatissa, 309, 310, 311, 312, 462
Sadr-un-Din, 619
Sahadeva, 619
Śailendra Dynasty in Central Java, 477–94
Śaiśunagas of Magadha, 58, 59
Śaka Era, 68–69
Śakas, 67, 68
Saketa, 92
Śaktideva, 587

Śaktis, 149–50; of Brahma, 150; of Śiva; of Vishnu and his *avatars,* 150–51
Śakyakirti, 476
Sakyamuni Buddha, 79, 487, 547, 636; images of, 422, *423,* 637, 648, *649,* 650, *651,* 655, *656,* 657
Śakyas clan, 80
Sakya-pa monastic order, 399, 406
Salabhanjika, 164
Samadhi, 137
Samadhiraja, 378
Samantapasadika, 293, 295, 297, 320, 344
Samaratunga, 483
Śambhala, 413, 414
Sambhutavijava, 210
Samhita, 13, 155
Samkhya school, 136
Samprati, 115–16
Samudaya, 347–48
Samudra Gupta, 119–20
Samyama, 137
Samye monastery, 394–95, 638, 640–44
Samyuktagama, 318
Samyutta Nikaya, 333–35
Sanci, Buddhist constructions at, 437–47
Sandracottos, 63–64
Sangeh, temple at, 524
Sangramaraja, 618–19
Sandhya, 19
Sandhyansa, 19
Sangha, 353–57
Sanghamitta, 306, 308, 316
Sang Hyang Widi, 513
Sangitivamsa, 329
Sani, 259
Sanjaya, 476–77, 494, 508; of the Belattha clan, 88–89
Śankara, 131, 138–39
Sankaracarya, 620
Śankaracarya Temple, 620
Sankaśya, 450
Sannyasa, 135–36
Sannyasi, 135
Sanskrit, 12, 13
Śantarakskita, 392–93, 394–95, 638, 640
Śantikara, 586–87
Śantinatha Temple, 267–69
Sapta sindhava, 15
Saratha, 416
Sarai Khola, 1
Sarasvasti, 15, 35, 150, 512; images of, 172, *174–75,* 259–60, 281, *282*
Sargon of Akkad, 3
Sariputra, relics of, 446
Sarnath, Buddhist movements at, 454–56
Sarvastivadins, 359–61
Śaśanka, 130–31
Sastras, 13, 14, 384
Satapatha Brahmana, 26, 32, 33, 35, 49–50
Sati, 151–52
Satmahal *prasada,* 469
Satyavati, 14
Sassanid Persians, 624
Satyayuga, 585
Savitar, 38
Savitri, 150
Sayambhava, 210
Seals of Harappan civilization, 8–11, 30

Seleucus I, 109
Seleucus I Nicator, 623
Sena, 308–309
Senaggabodhi shrine, 323
Sena I, 322, 323
Sengge Namgyal, 654, 655
Sera monastery, 405, 650–53
Serpents identified with deities, 44–46
Shah Mir, 619
Shahr-i-Bahlol, Buddha images from, 422, *423*, 424
Shahr-i-Gholghola, fortress of, 630, *632*
Shahr-i-Zohak, fortress of, 630, *632*
Shalu-pa order, 400
Shamas-ud-Din, Sultan, 619
Shambhalai Lamyig, 414
Shanda Gupta, 123
Shang Dynasty, 1
Shans, 551
Shapur I, 625
Shatcakranirupana, 156–57
Shenrap, 395
Sherap Gyentsen, 400
Shey, monuments at, 655, *656*
Shin Arahan, 550, 551, 555
Shih-kao, 633
Shore Temple at Mahabalipuram, 186–87
Shwe Dagon, 549
Shwe Dagon Pagoda, 559, *560*
Shwezigon Pagoda, 552–54
Siddanta, 210, 212–20; table listing, 212–13
Siddhartha, 346
Siddhasena, 221
Siddhayika, 255–56
Siddhinarasimhamalla, 595, 596, 606–607
Siddiqi, A. D., 3; mounds (SD), 3–4
Sigiriya, Buddhist monuments at, 463–67
Sihagiri, 321
Siharaja, 548
Sihigiri-vitara, 467
Sikander, 619
Śikharas: in Hindu temples, 177, 183, 187, 196, 198, 200, 204, 206; in Jaina temples, 267, 270, 272
Silk Road, 121, 623, 635
Silpa-Śastras, 163, 176
Simtokha Dzong, 661
Sindhu Raja, 659
Singhasari, 503–*505*
Singhala, 301
Singhalese race, 301
Singhasari, 530
Sirimeghavanna, 317
Sirivaddhanapura, 329
Sita-ki-Nahani, 181
Śitala, figure of, at Vimala-vasahi, 281, *282*
Śitalanatha, 289
Śiva, *see* Rudra/Śiva
Sivadeva I, 592
Śivadevavarman, 603
Śiva Maheśvara, *182*
Śiva Samhita, 155–57
Six Yogas of Naropa, The, 406
"Slave dynasty," 130
Smriti, 13, 14
Solar Dynasty, 21–24
Soma, 32, 34–35, 40–41
Somavamśi Dynasty, 587, 589, 603
Somdet Phra Wannarat, 565
Somnathpur, temple at, 187–88, 191–*95*, *196*

Sona, 475, 549, 563, 570
Sonam Gyatsho, 638
Songgram, Pibul, 575
Songtsen Gampo, 593, 636–37, 640, 645, 647, 650, *651*, 659
Sotka Koh, 3
Southeast Asia, monuments of Hinduism and Buddhism in, 473–583; Bali, 508–29; Burma, 546–50; expansion of Indian influence, 473–75; Indonesia, 475–76; Java, 476–508; Kampuchea, 531–46; Malaysia, 529–*31;* Thailand, 562–*83*
Śramanas, 209
Śravaka, 363
Śravanabelgola, 275–*79*
Śravasti, 92–94, 100, 122, 450, 451
Śri, *see* Lakshmi
Śrikshetra, 547, 548
Sri Lanka: after Parakramabahu I, 327–30; Buddha chronology, 70–71; Fifth Buddhist Council at Ratnapura, 329; First Buddhist Council at Thuparama, 307–308; foreign invaders of, 308–309, 313, 320, 322, 323, 324, 327, 328; Fourth Buddhist Council at Polonnaruwa, 324–27; kings of, 300–304, 307–30 *passim;* Mahinda, 304–306; Polonnaruwa Period, 322–24; Sanghamitta, 306; Second Buddhist Council at Aluvihara, 315–16; Sihagiri Interval, 320–22; sites and monuments of Buddhism in, 457–72; split between Buddhists in, 314–15, 316–18, 324; Third Buddhist Council at the Mahavihara, 318–20, 549; uniting of, into one kingdom, 310
Śri Maha Bodhi, 459
Srinagar, 617, 619
Srinagar Museum, 621
Śrinagari, 617, 618, 619
Sri Pratap Singh Museum, 619
Śrivatsa, 243, 245, 247
Śrivijaya, 475–76, 530
Śri Vikrama Rajsimha, 329
Śrutakevalins, 210–11
Śruti, 13, 14
State Museum at Lucknow, *244*, 245, *246*
Stavas, 510–11, 512–13
Steps to Enlightenment, 406
Sthitimalla, 595
Sthulabhadra, 210, 211
Stupas, 243, 261–64, 305, 308, 310–11; Buddhist, 419–20, 426, 427, 428, 430, 436, 437–46, 448–49, 451, 452, 453, *454*–55, 459, 479, 480, 483, 484, 492, *493*, 494, 495, 558, 559, 570, 588, 598, *606*, 619, 620, *622*–*23*, 624, *662*, 663; characteristics of, 261–62; remains at Mathura, 262–64; as symbols of Buddha, 419–20
Stutis, 510–11, 512–13
Suhabhatta, 619
Sudhanva, 586
Śudraka, 264
Suhrllekha, 384–85
Sukhavativyuha, 379–80
Sukhothai, 563–65, 566; monuments at, 571–73
Sukra, 259
Suktimati, 94
Sule Pagoda, 559, *561*
Sumatra, 475
Sumerian civilization, 1
Sumsud-din, 598

Sumsumaragiri, 84
Śuṅgas, 61–62
Sun which Causes the Lotus of the Teaching to Open, The, 659
Suphanburi Dynasty, 566
Śurasenas, kingdom of the, 96–97
Surasundari, 164
Suratissa, 308
Surya, 37–38, 259
Suryasevana, 515
Suryavamśi Dynasty, 587, 589, 603
Suryavarman I, 538, 539
Suryavarman II, 535, 541–42, 544
Sutasoma, 519–20
Sutkagen Dor, 1, 3
Sutralankara, 381
Sutras, 13, 14, 368–80; images of the gods in the, 162, 163
Sutta Nipata, 339
Suttapitaka, 292, 331–42
Suttasamgaha, 343
Suttas, 307
Suttavibhanga, 330–31
Suvarnaprabhasa, 378–79
Svastika, 242–43, 247
Svayambhu, 585, 586
Svayambhunath, 598, *599–600*
Svayambhu Purana, 585, 589, 594, 598
Svayambrata, 587
Swat, 621–*23*
Syaha, 34
Symbols of Buddhism, 419–20
Symbols of the Hindu gods, 160–61
Symbols of Jainism, 242–45

Tabinshwehti, 551
Tai Tsung, 126, 128
Takht-i-Bahi, Buddha figures from, *422*
Takshaśila, 99–100
Taksin, Phya, 568, 575, 577
Taktshang, 659, *660*
Taktshang Repa, 655, 659–61
Talaings, 549
Taleju Bhavani, 607
Tambapanni, 301, 302
Tamils, 309, 310, 313, 314, 318, 320
Tanaung, 547
Tang dynasty, 126
Tapusa, 549
Tantras, 13, 14, 154–59; of Later Hinduism, 154–59; of Vajrayana Buddhism, 407–14
Tantrasara, 158
Tantrayana Buddhism, *see* Vajrayana Buddhism
Tapasa, 209
Ta Prohm, 546
Tara, 154, 409, 593, 637, *657;* bronze, 613, *614;* temple of, 477–78
Taranatha, 383, 385, 386, 387, 392, 400
Tashichho Dzong, *661–63*
Tashi Gon, 653–54
Tashi Namgyal, 654
Tathagataquhyaka, 379, 399, 407–11
Tathagata Gupta, 123, 124
Tathagata-oudana, 71–72
Tattvasangraha, 393
Taxila, 100, 105–106, 108; Buddhist monuments in, 448–49, *450*

Taxila Museum, 422, *423*
Taxiles, 105–106, 108
Temple of the Emerald Buddha, 569, 577–79
Temple of the Golden Buddha, 580, *581*
Temple of the Reclining Buddha, 569
Temple of the Tooth, *see* Tooth relic
Temples, Buddhist, at Sanci, 446–47
Temples, Buddhist and Hindu, outside India: in Bali, 513–14, 520–25; in Burma, 555–*57;* in Java, 477–501, 502, 504–508; in Kampuchea, 536–46; in Kashmir, 619, 620, *621;* in Nepal, 601–604, 607, 609, *610–12;* in Thailand, 571–73, 575–83; in Tibet, 638, *644, 645,* 647–48
Temples, Hindu, in India, 176–207; carved, 182–86; cave, 177–*82;* characteristics of, 176–77; later, *206–207;* North India, 196–205; South India, 186–96
Temples, Jaina, in India, 264–89; cave and carved, 265–67; constructed, 267–73, *274–75;* temple cities and places of pilgrimage, 273–89
Temples of Lhasa, The, 639
Tengyur, 395, 396
Tenzing Ghelek Rimpoche, 601, *602*
Tenzin Gyatsho, 638
Tepe Yahya, 1, 3
Thagyamin, 551
Thailand, 307, 362, 562–*83;* history of, 562–69; monuments in, 569–*83;* version of the Buddhist Councils in, 329–30; war with Burma, 567
Thakuri Dynasty, 587, 589, 590, 591, 595
Thammayut sect, 569
Thatbyinnyu Temple, 552, *553*
Thaton, 548–49, 550
Theragatha, 340–41
Theravada (Hinayana) Buddhism, 291–357, 360, 361, 362–63; Four Councils in India, 293–300, 358; geographic distribution of followers of, 359, 362; known as Hinayana Buddhism, 122, 300, 324, 358–59; literature of, *see* Literature of Theravada Buddhism; in Sri Lanka, 300–330; Three Jewels of, 345–57; tradition of, 291–93; *see also* Buddhism; Buddhist monuments, Mahayana Buddhism; Vajrayana Buddhism
Therigatha, 340–41
Thibaw, 552
Thimphu, monuments at, *661–63*
Tholing Temple, 396
Thonburi, 568–69, 575; monuments at, *575–76,* 580
Thonmi Sambhota, 637
Throne Hall, 569, 573
Thulathana, 312
Thuparama, 326, 469; First Buddhist Council at, 306–307
Thuparama Dagoba, 459, *460*
Thupas, 457, 459, 460
Thupavamsa, 311, 345
Tibet, 362, 391, 636–53; Buddha chronology, 73; history of, 636–38; introduction of Buddhism to, 539, 636; sites and monuments of, 638–53; *see also* Vajrayana Buddhism
Tibetan calendar, 413, 414
Tiger's Den Monastery, 659, *660*
Tigris and Euphrates valley, 1
Tikas, 221
Tilopa, 400
Time, *see* Chronology
Tipitaka, 292, 330–43

INDEX | 733

Tirthankaras, 207, 226, 227–41, 242; attendants of, images of, 254–61; images of, 245–53; list of, 228
Tirthas, 275
Tivanka-pilgrimage, 472
Tooth relic, 317, 318, 323–24, 327–29, 469, 472
Toramana, 123
Toungoo Dynasty, 551
Traibhumikatha, 565
Trailok, 567–68
Traiphun Phra Ruang, 565
Trakpabum, 654
Trakthok, 653
Trashilhunpo monastery, 405
Tretayuga, 585–86
Trhisong Detsen, 393, 394, 395, 636, 637–38, 640, 653; statue of, *641*
Tribhuvana, statue of, 506, *507*
Trimurti, 140–43
Triśula, 243, 245
Tsanga Gyarepa, 405
Tshongdi Lhakhang, *663*
Tsongkhapa, 405–406, 407, 414, 638, 645, 648, 650, 653, 654; statue of, *650, 651*
Tshurphu monastery, 405
Tsuglakang, 637
Turpan, 633–36
Tvashtri, 11, 46

Ubud, village of, 525
Uccala, 619
Udaipur, temple at, *206*
Udana, 338
Udayadityavarman II, 539–40
Uddissaka zedi, 552
Ugaigiri, Hindu cave temples at, 177, *178–79*
Ugyen Wangchuck, 661
Ujjayini, 98
Ulun Kulkul, 521
Uma, 41, 152
Umamaheśvaramurti, 168
Umasahitamurti, Śiva at, 169
Umasvati, 221
Units of measurement, Jaina, 226
U Nu, 330, 552
Upali, 294–95
Upanishads, 13, 14; doctrine in the, 50–51; the goal in the, 52–53; the path in the, 51–52; philosophy in the, 49–53; symbols and images of gods in the, 160–61
Upatishya, 361
Upper Ganges basin, 79
Uposatha, 355
Uptala Dynasty, 618
Urgyan Lingpa, 395
Urubilyakaśyapa, 361
Ushas, 38
Ushnisha Sitatapatra, figure of, *657*
U Thong, 565–66, 567, 568
Uttara, 475, 549, 563, 570
Uttara Mimamsa system of philosophy, 138
Uttararama, 471–72
Uttiya, 307–308
Uvangas, 217–18

Vacissara, 311
Vaikuntha Caturmurti, 168
Vaipulya Sutras, 368–79

Vairata, 96
Vaiśali, 83, 84, 450, 451; Second Buddhist Council in, 295–97, 358
Vaiśeshika Sutras, 137
Vaiśeshika system of philosophy, 137–38
Vaitulya Pitaka, 316
Vajii confederation, 82, 84
Vajra, 123, 124
Vajradhara, 392, 394
Vajrapani, 636
Vajravarahi, 410, 411
Vajrayana Buddhism, 390–418, 638, 653; characteristics of, 391–92; geographic distribution of followers of, 391; *tantras*, 407–14; teachers of, 392–407; yogas, 414–18; *see also* Buddhism; Buddhist monuments; Mahayana Buddhism; Theravada (Hinayana) Buddhism
Vajrayogini, 410, 411
Vak, 41
Vamana, 147
Vaṁsa, 20
Vaṁsas, kingdom of the, 94–95, 100
Vaṁśavali, 585, 587, 588, 589, 590, 591, 594, 595, 596, 597, 603, 609
Vanaprasthana, 135
Vanaprasthana, 135
Varadarajaswami temple, 187
Varaha, 146
Varahamihara, 163, 248
Varanasi, 90–91, 100, 361; temple at, 206–207
Vardhamana Jnatriputra, 209, 210
Vardhamana Mahavira, 79, 209, 210, 212, 233–41; death of, 240–41; Dhatusena and, 320, 321; disciples of, 239–40; Gośala and, 235, 238–39; images of, 252–53; teaching of, 235–38
Varuna, 31, 32, 38–39, 257, 259
Vasishtha, 39
Vassa, 355–56
Vastu-Sastras, 176
Vasubandhu, 386–87, 388–90
Vasudeva, 231–32
Vasudevas, 226, 231
Vasudeva I, 116
Vasumitra, 299
Vatadage at Polonnaruwa, *469*
Vats, M. S., 3; mounds (VS), 4–5, 6
Vatsa, kingdom of, 55, 56, 79; Pauravas of, 56–57
Vattagamani Abhaya, 313–15, 462
Vayu, 35–36, 257–58, 259
Vayu Purana, 17
Vedanta, 13; interpreters of, 138–40
Vedanta Sutras, 137
Vedas, 13–14
Vesara style of temple architecture, 176, 177
Vessagiri Vihara, 460
Vedic civilization, 7; geographic focus of, 79
Victoria and Albert Museum, London, 251, *252*
Videha, 22
Viddehas clan, 82–83, 84
Vidyadevis, 259
Vidyadharas, 42; images of, *175*
Vidyadharis, 519
Viharas, Buddhist, 427, 428, 430–36, 469; *see also individual structures*
Vijaya, 300–302
Vijayabahu I, 323, 324, 468
Vijayabahu III, 327–28
Vihayabahu IV, 323, 328, 470

Vijayarajapura, 323
Vijayasena Suri, 131
Vikramabahu, 323
Vikramaditya, 67–68
Vikrama Era, 68
Vimala Dharma Surya, 329
Vima Kadphises II, 116
Vimalasuri, 69
Vimala-vasahi, 280–*81*
Vimanavatthu, 339
Vinata, 45
Vinaya, 291, 307
Vinayapitaka, 292, 317, 320, 330–31
Viradeva, 595
Viravikrama, 329
Visalanagara, 587
Vishnu, 39–40, 140, 141–42, 586; *avatars* of, 144–45; images of, 166–*68, 169,* 177, *178–79, 526,* 593, *605,* 606, *621; Śaktis* of, as his *avatars,* 150–51
Vishnugupta, 592, 593, 606
Visuddhimagga, 319, 344
Viśvakarman, 47
Viśvanath Temple of Varanasi, 206–207
Viśvarupa, 11; *tanka* of, 612, 613
Vivekananda, 207
Voharikatissa, 316
Vriji confederation, 82
Vriksha, 243
Vrikshaka, 164
Vyasa, 14

Wanderers, 87–90
Wat Arun, 569, *575*–76
Wat Benchamaborpit, 569, 580–*83*
Wat Bodharam, 569
Wat Bovornives, 580
Wat Chang, *see* Wat Arun
Wat Mahathat, 571–73
Wat Phra Keo, 569, *577*–79
Wat Phra Mongkol Borpit, 575
Wat Po, 569, *579*–80
Wat Rajburana, 575–75
Wat Sri Cum, 573
Wat Traimitr, 580, *581*
Wat Yai Chaya Mongkol, *574,* 575
Wedding ceremony in Bali, 527, 528

Wheel of Existence painting, 650, *652*
White Tara, *657*
Wong Xuan Ce, 593–94

Xinjiang, 633, 638
Xuan Zang (Hieun Tsang), 18, 100, 113, 120, 123, 124, 125, 126–28, 130–31, 358, 359, 361, 380, 382–83, 385, 386, 388, 424, 451, 453, 454, 457, 475, 562, 592, 598, 624, 625, 626, 633; on Bamiyan, 628–29, 630; on Fourth Buddhist Council in Kashmir, 299, 300; on Kashmir, 618; on Swat, 622

Yadava line of the Lunar dynasty, 24–26
Yakkhas, 300–301
Yakshamalla, 595, 607, 608
Yaksheśvara, 256–57
Yashas, 42, 163–64, 254–57, 420
Yama, 257, 259
Yamuna River, 79
Yantra, 161, 162
Yarlung Dynasty, 636, 637, 638, 639, 653
Yasa, 361
Yasa Kakandakaputta, 296
Yaśobhadra, 210
Yaśodharapura, 536–46
Yaśodhareśvara, 536
Yaśovarman I, 535, 536, 537
Yeshe Ö, 654
Yi Jing (I-tsing), 128–29, 358, 359, 362, 367, 424, 475, 624; observations outside India, 475, 476
Yoga, 52, 133, 134; as school of philosophy, 136–37; Vajrayana yogic positions, 391, 399, 400, 406, 411–12, 417–18
Yoganarayana, 166
Yoga Sutras, 136–37
Yoga Tantra, 407
Yogeśvara Vishnu, 166
Yuan Phai, 568
Yudhisthira, 54, 55
Yugas, 18–19, 54
Yumbulagang Palace, *639–40, 641*

Zanskar, 653, 654
Zedi, 552
Zhanphan Zangpo, 417
Zorowar Singh, 657